LET'S GO
Aust...
Switz...

■ Let's Go writers travel on your budget.

"Guides that penetrate the veneer of the holiday brochures and mine the grit of real life."
—**The Economist**

"The writers seem to have experienced every rooster-packed bus and lunar-surfaced mattress about which they write."
—**The New York Times**

"All the dirt, dirt cheap."
—**People**

■ Great for independent travelers.

"The guides are aimed not only at young budget travelers but at the independent traveler, a sort of streetwise cookbook for traveling alone."
—**The New York Times**

"Flush with candor and irreverence, chock full of budget travel advice."
—**The Des Moines Register**

"An indispensable resource. *Let's Go*'s practical information can be used by every traveler."
—**The Chattanooga Free Press**

■ Let's Go is completely revised each year.

"Only *Let's Go* has the zeal to annually update every title on its list."
—**The Boston Globe**

"Unbeatable: good sight-seeing advice; up-to-date info on restaurants, hotels, and inns; a commitment to money-saving travel; and a wry style that brightens nearly every page."
—**The Washington Post**

■ All the important information you need.

"*Let's Go* authors provide a comedic element while still providing concise information and thorough coverage of the country. Anything you need to know about budget traveling is detailed in this book."
—**The Chicago Sun-Times**

"Value-packed, unbeatable, accurate, and comprehensive."
—**Los Angeles Times**

Let's Go Publications

Let's Go: Alaska & the Pacific Northwest 1999
Let's Go: Australia 1999
Let's Go: Austria & Switzerland 1999
Let's Go: Britain & Ireland 1999
Let's Go: California 1999
Let's Go: Central America 1999
Let's Go: Eastern Europe 1999
Let's Go: Ecuador & the Galápagos Islands 1999
Let's Go: Europe 1999
Let's Go: France 1999
Let's Go: Germany 1999
Let's Go: Greece 1999 **New title!**
Let's Go: India & Nepal 1999
Let's Go: Ireland 1999
Let's Go: Israel & Egypt 1999
Let's Go: Italy 1999
Let's Go: London 1999
Let's Go: Mexico 1999
Let's Go: New York City 1999
Let's Go: New Zealand 1999
Let's Go: Paris 1999
Let's Go: Rome 1999
Let's Go: South Africa 1999 **New title!**
Let's Go: Southeast Asia 1999
Let's Go: Spain & Portugal 1999
Let's Go: Turkey 1999 **New title!**
Let's Go: USA 1999
Let's Go: Washington, D.C. 1999

Let's Go Map Guides

Amsterdam	Madrid
Berlin	New Orleans
Boston	New York City
Chicago	Paris
Florence	Rome
London	San Francisco
Los Angeles	Washington, D.C.

Coming Soon: Prague, Seattle

**Let's Go
Publications**

Let's Go
Austria &
Switzerland
1999

Christina Svendsen
Editor

Justin Rice
Associate Editor

Researcher-Writers:
**Judith Batalion
Daniel Engber
Charles Savage
Sharmila Surianarain**

Macmillan

HELPING LET'S GO

If you want to share your discoveries, suggestions, or corrections, please drop us a line. We read every piece of correspondence, whether a postcard, a 10-page email, or a coconut. Please note that mail received after May 1999 may be too late for the 2000 book, but will be kept for future editions. **Address mail to:**

Let's Go: Austria & Switzerland
67 Mount Auburn Street
Cambridge, MA 02138
USA

Visit Let's Go at **http://www.letsgo.com,** or send email to:

feedback@letsgo.com
Subject: "Let's Go: Austria & Switzerland"

In addition to the invaluable travel advice our readers share with us, many are kind enough to offer their services as researchers or editors. Unfortunately, our charter enables us to employ only currently enrolled Harvard-Radcliffe students.

Published in Great Britain 1999 by Macmillan, an imprint of Macmillan General Books, 25 Eccleston Place, London, SW1W9NF and Basingstoke.

Maps by David Lindroth copyright © 1999, 1998, 1997, 1996, 1995, 1994, 1993, 1992, 1991, 1990, 1989, 1988 by St. Martin's Press, Inc.

Published in the United States of America by St. Martin's Press, Inc.

ISBN: 0 333 74738 0

First edition
10 9 8 7 6 5 4 3 2 1

Let's Go: Austria & Switzerland is written by Let's Go Publications, 67 Mount Auburn Street, Cambridge, MA 02138, USA.

About Let's Go

THIRTY-NINE YEARS OF WISDOM

Back in 1960, a few students at Harvard University banded together to produce a 20-page pamphlet offering a collection of tips on budget travel in Europe. This modest, mimeographed packet, offered as an extra to passengers on student charter flights to Europe, met with instant popularity. The following year, students traveling to Europe researched the first, full-fledged edition of *Let's Go: Europe*, a pocket-sized book featuring honest, irreverent writing and a decidedly youthful outlook on the world. Throughout the 60s, our guides reflected the times; the 1969 guide to America led off by inviting travelers to "dig the scene" at San Francisco's Haight-Ashbury. During the 70s and 80s, we gradually added regional guides and expanded coverage into the Middle East and Central America. With the addition of our in-depth city guides, handy map guides, and extensive coverage of Asia and Australia, the 90s are also proving to be a time of explosive growth for Let's Go, and there's certainly no end in sight. The maiden edition of *Let's Go: South Africa*, our pioneer guide to sub-Saharan Africa, hits the shelves this year, along with the first editions of *Let's Go: Greece* and *Let's Go: Turkey*.

We've seen a lot in 39 years. *Let's Go: Europe* is now the world's bestselling international guide, translated into seven languages. And our new guides bring Let's Go's total number of titles, with their spirit of adventure and their reputation for honesty, accuracy, and editorial integrity, to 44. But some things never change: our guides are still researched, written, and produced entirely by students who know first-hand how to see the world on the cheap.

HOW WE DO IT

Each guide is completely revised and thoroughly updated every year by a well-traveled set of over 200 students. Every winter, we recruit over 160 researchers and 70 editors to write the books anew. After several months of training, researcher-writers hit the road for seven weeks of exploration, from Anchorage to Adelaide, Estonia to El Salvador, Iceland to Indonesia. Hired for their rare combination of budget travel sense, writing ability, stamina, and courage, these adventurous travelers know that train strikes, stolen luggage, food poisoning, and marriage proposals are all part of a day's work. Back at our offices, editors work from spring to fall, massaging copy written on Himalayan bus rides into witty yet informative prose. A student staff of typesetters, cartographers, publicists, and managers keeps our lively team together. In September, the collected efforts of the summer are delivered to our printer, who turns them into books in record time, so that you have the most up-to-date information available for your vacation. Even as you read this, work on next year's editions is well underway.

WHY WE DO IT

We don't think of budget travel as the last recourse of the destitute; we believe that it's the only way to travel. Living cheaply and simply brings you closer to the people and places you've been saving up to visit. Our books will ease your anxieties and answer your questions about the basics—so you can get off the beaten track and explore. Once you learn the ropes, we encourage you to put *Let's Go* down now and then to strike out on your own. You know as well as we that the best discoveries are often those you make yourself. When you find something worth sharing, please drop us a line. We're Let's Go Publications, 67 Mount Auburn St., Cambridge, MA 02138, USA (email: feedback@letsgo.com). For more info, visit our website, http://www.letsgo.com.

HAPPY TRAVELS!

Contents

Maps

How to Use This Book

You have just bought yerself one hell of a dandy little pet and it's here for you to walk. From the most remote Alpine corner to the middle of Vienna, this hunk of paper (which you should feel free to name) will be your friend and confidant. You don't have to feed it; it won't poop on you. But if you understand what goes on in its little paper skull, it will be a better walker and your walks with it will be better.

It begins with something called **Essentials.** That's where you can read about customs (both the kind that will poke fingers in your bags and the kind that will embarrass you when you look like a silly foreigner if you're not careful). It's also where you can find out about getting jobs, traveling solo, finding cheap plane tickets, packing, and other stuff you should figure out before you're there.

Next, it'll tell you something about Austrian history, culture, and food. Mozart, Klimt, Freud, and *Strudel* will be talked about briefly, but with such insight that your head will spin and you might throw up. It's only to help you get your bearings. The little guy will walk you through Austria, the country, the sights, and the museums. The tour will start with cosmopolitan Vienna and its café dreams and move into the surrounding lowlands, lakelands, and Danube river valleys, called Niederösterreich. From there, it'll head toward higher, more mountainous Oberösterreich, followed up by rural Styria and its capital, student-crazed Graz and then Kärnten, which is Catholic and conservative and not footloose at all. From there your yellow friend will talk your ear off about Tyrol or Tirol or whatever the heck you wanna call it, and its cities with casinos. Austria ends with Salzburg, a maze of a city surrounded by lazy lakes and mountains.

Switzerland creeps in after Austria. You can read about its history, culture, and food, about its neutrality and all of the exiles who ended up sitting around smoking cigarettes in its cities. Then it'll plunge you into Geneva, a city of diplomacy, a lake with other cities populating its shores. After that, Valais, quiet and bovine, and then Neuchâtel, dignified and old. You'll be shown Zurich, the seed of dissident and subversive culture, then Bern and its surrounding mountains, and finally Alpine Graubünden with its majestic and very tall rocks.

Switzerland gives way to the massive Liechtenstein, a country of stamps and dental appliance maufacturing, and then to other spaces the guide opens up, gateways if you will. You can be led to the beginning of something outside the guide, to a Prague or a Bratislava or a Munich, or another former bit of the Habsburg empire like Budapest. Your chipper yellow rag will remind you that Austria and Switzerland run up against all kinds of crazy chunks of Eastern European land that you can visit.

Your little dog Toto will always be yapping about things you'll want to do, always letting you in on the word on the street. He will be forthright and honest, but remember that he has his limits, that he can only walk with you, and that the best way to have a great trip is to choose your own adventures.

Austria and Switzerland: Map of Chapter Divisions

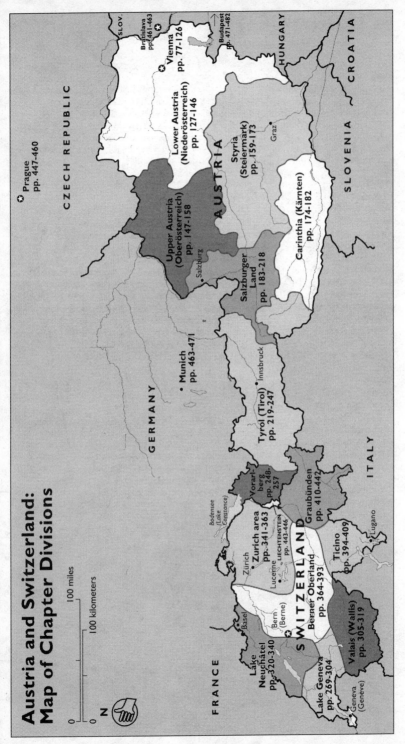

Bodensee (Lake Constance)
Basel
Bern (Berne)
Zürich
Lucerne
Salzburg
Innsbruck
Graz
Lugano

SWITZERLAND
AUSTRIA
FRANCE
GERMANY
CZECH REPUBLIC
SLOV.
HUNGARY
CROATIA
SLOVENIA
ITALY

N

100 miles
100 kilometers
0

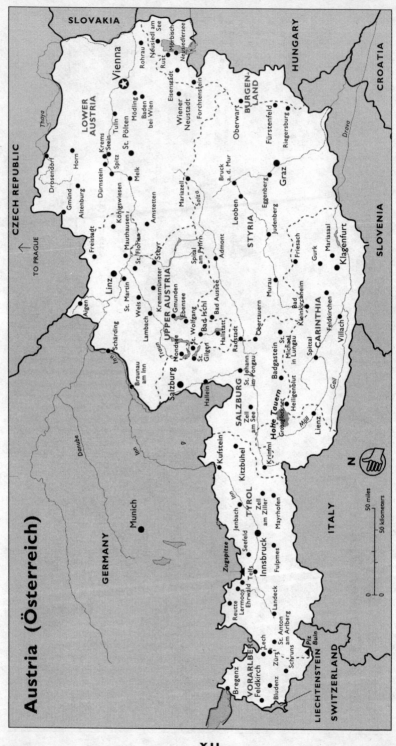

Austria (Österreich)

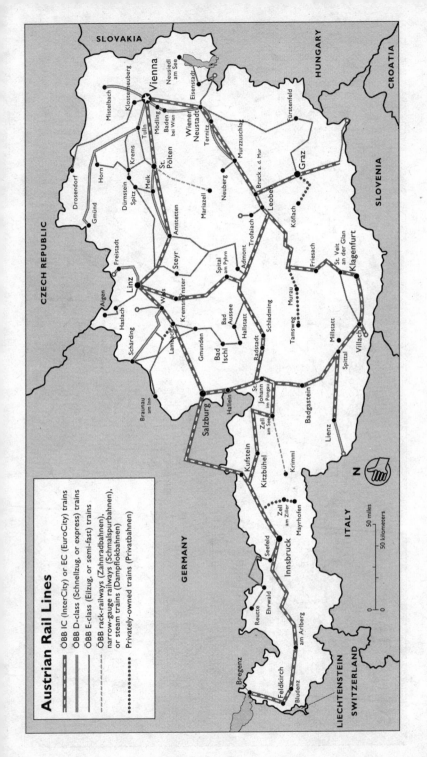

Austrian Rail Lines

ÖBB IC (InterCity) or EC (EuroCity) trains

ÖBB D-class (Schnellzug, or express) trains

ÖBB E-class (Eilzug, or semi-fast) trains

ÖBB rack-railways (Zahnradbahnen),
narrow-gauge railways (Schmalspurbahnen),
or steam trains (Dampflokbahnen)

Privately-owned trains (Privatbahnen)

XIII

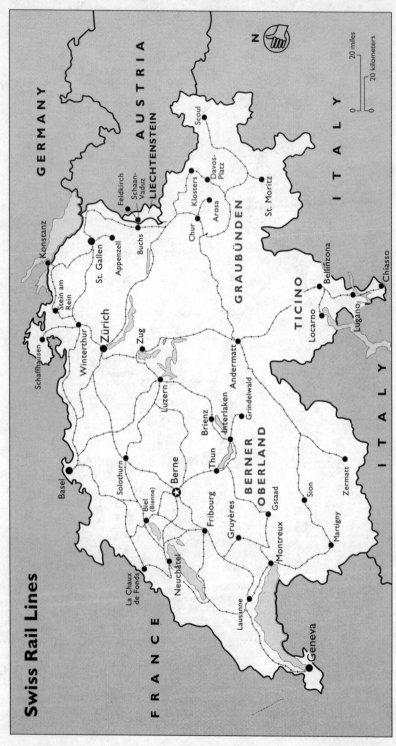

Swiss Rail Lines

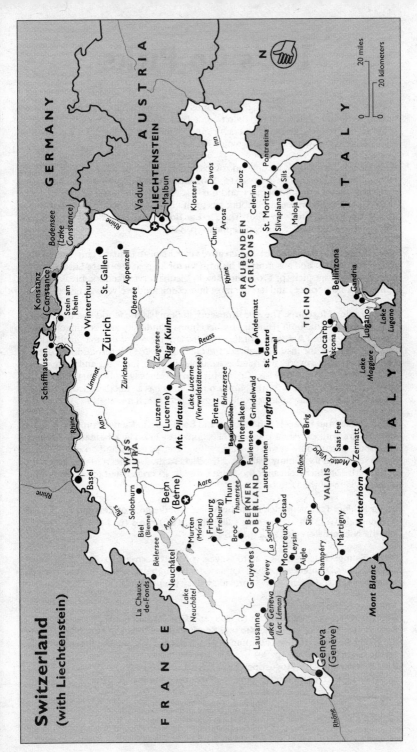

Switzerland
(with Liechtenstein)

Let's Go Picks

These are the places we stayed, the museums we came back to, the spots we'll miss most, the mountains we almost -didn't come back down from. This is not meant as some kind of gospel, but rather as a description of the stuff we liked. Send us mail and tell us what your own list of picks would be.

Best Hostels: Balconies, meditation rooms, and crazy mountain views await at the **Hiking Sheep Guesthouse** in Leysin (p. 296). **Gastehaus Bürgerwehr** in Salzburg has incredible views, friendly owners, and the best *Speckknödeln* we've ever eaten (p. 188). **Haus Bankhammer** in Salzburg has great views, too, and the breakfast was so good it made us cry milk (p. 190). The **Zic-Zac Rock-hotel** in Zurich is our last pick, cuz we're just big suckers for Led Zeppelin (p. 340).

Most Delectable Restaurants: The creative vegetarianism (banana curry rice?), enormous red tongues, and absurdist art by artist Victor Rogy at **Der Rote Lasche** make it our top restaurant pick (p. 176). **Blue Box** in Vienna serves fantastic breakfasts until 5pm (our kind of place) and has the most interesting food we've ever tasted (p. 97).

Most Exciting Museums: The **Kunstmuseum** in Bern has the world's largest Klee collection, along with some paintings by his chums Kandinsky and Feininger (p.363). The **Collection de l'Art Brut** in Lausanne displays the art of the marginalized—the criminally insane, the institutionalized, and children (p. 285). **International Center of Fantastic Art** in Gruyères has mind-expanding demonic, fantastic, and grotesque art (p. 326). The **International Red Cross Museum** in Geneva is sobering yet fascinating (p. 277). The **Kunsthistorisches Museum** in Vienna has a suberb collection of Brueghels, Velazquezes, Egyptian sarcophagi, and much, much more (p. 115).

Killer Castles and Palaces: Schönbrunn and **Belvedere** in Vienna combine gorgeous architecture with excellent painting collections (p. 111). The **Château de Chillon** in Montreux is gruesome yet fascinating, with secret passages and an epic poem by Byron set within its clammy walls (p. 289). Richard the Lion-hearted was imprisoned in the castle of **Dürnstein** after the Third Crusade; its crenellated towers look over a gorgeous view of the Danube (p.147).

Super Hiking: Take your pick from the Alpine wonderlands of **Zermatt** (p. 305) and **Grindelwald** (p. 377), or the river valley beauty of **Krems** (p. 141), **Stein** (p. 143), and the **Niederösterreich** area (p. 128-147).

Prime Skiing: Glaciers allow you to ski year-round at **Zermatt** (p. 305), **Saas Fee** (p. 311), and **Les Diablerets** (p. 296). Otherwise, **Kitzbühel** (p. 231), **St. Anton im Arlberg** (p. 251), and **Lech** (p. 253) provide wintry wonderlands.

The Best of the Rest:
Best Small Villages are **Hallstatt** (p. 208) and **Grindelwald** (p. 377).
Best Water Closets are at the **Klo und So Museum** of toilets in Gmunden (p. 212), the **Hotel Goldener Löwe** bathroom in Mariazell (p. 173), and the **Jugendstil toilets** on the Graben in Vienna (p. 90).
Best Biergarten is the **Augustiner Bräu** in Salzburg (p. 193).
Best Guerilla Artist Colony is Geneva's **Artamis** complex (p. 276).

Essentials

PLANNING YOUR TRIP

Planning makes things better. If you don't know what you're doing when preparing for a trip, if you don't know what you're doing when actually abroad, you'll spend too much time, money, and aggravation fixing things. If you don't anticipate your specific personal needs, you'll be even more miserable. Nasty surprises are always lurking around the corner for the uninformed traveler: this section of the book seeks to prevent problems little and big so you can get the most out of your stay.

When planning which towns to visit, read through the listings. These days, even hostels require reservations, so you can't always do everything last-minute. Just remember: the more you know the more prepared you'll be for fly-by-the-seat-of-your-pants travel.

■ When to Go

Because Austria and Switzerland are a mountain lover's paradise, tourism is a year-round industry. For small towns, especially in western Austria and eastern Switzerland, prices double and sometimes triple during the winter ski months (generally Nov.-Mar.) Travelers should make reservations months in advance. During those same winter ski months, the flatter, eastern half of Austria, the half that includes Vienna and Salzburg, sees significantly fewer tourists. That half is full of summer resorts, and, in the summer, locals in both countries flock to tourist spots *en masse* for school vacations, especially in the last week of June. Although sights and hotels tend to be cheaper in May and June, rowdy and annoying school groups can thwart your plans by booking up even the most rural hostels years in advance. The cities tend to be especially busy then, as families and college students from everywhere whiz through on whirlwind summer vacations. In addition, almost every city has a gala music festival of some type around then (see **Holidays and Festivals,** p. 483). Small Swiss or Austrian ski playgrounds often become desolate ghost towns when the tourists pack up; some completely close down during the inter-seasonal periods (mid-Apr. to late-May and mid-Oct. to late-Nov.). In general, April is a good time to go, since tourists are not pouring from every hotel and museum and activities are still buzzing.

■ Useful Information

NATIONAL TOURIST OFFICES

Austria and Switzerland are old pros at tourism, and any trip to either country begins at home with a visit to the tourist office. These offices can provide copious information for planning your trip, from helping you with a specific itinerary to providing personalized information for travelers with specific concerns.

Austrian National Tourist Offices
Canada: 1010 Ouest rue Sherbourne #1410, **Montreal,** Que. H3A 2R7 (tel. (514) 849-3709; fax 849-9577; email atcmtr@istar.ca); Granville Sq. #1380, 200 Granville St., **Vancouver,** BC V6C 1S4 (tel. (604) 683-8695; fax 662-8528; email atradebc.uniserve.com).
U.S.: 500 Fifth Ave., Suite 800, **New York,** NY 10110 (tel. (212) 944-6880; fax 730-4568; email antonyc@ibm.net).

Swiss National Tourist Offices

Canada: 926 East Mall, **Etobicoke,** Ont. M9B 6K1 (tel. (416) 695-2090; fax 695-2774; sttoronto@switzerlandtourism.com; http://www.switzerlandtourism.com).

United Kingdom: Swiss Centre, Swiss Court, **London** W1V 8EE (tel. (0171) 734 1921; fax 437 4577).

U.S.: 608 Fifth Ave., **New York,** NY 10020 (tel. (212) 757-5944; fax 262-6116)

TRAVEL ORGANIZATIONS

These organizations hunt down cheap airfares, rail passes, and accommodations. Students should inquire about further discounts. Everyone under 26 should.

Council on International Educational Exchange (CIEE), 205 East 42nd St., New York, NY 10017-5706 (tel. (888)-COUNCIL (268-6245); fax (212) 822-2699; http://www.ciee.org). A private, not-for-profit organization, Council administers volunteer, academic, internship, and professional programs around the world, offers identity cards, (including the ISIC and the GO25), and provides a range of publications, including the free and useful *Student Travels.*

Federation of International Youth Travel Organizations (FIYTO), Bredgade 25H, DK-1260 Copenhagen K, Denmark (tel. (45) 33 33 96 00; fax 33 93 96 76; email mailbox@fiyto.org; http://www.fiyto.org). An international organization promoting educational, cultural, and social travel for young people. Member organizations include language schools, educational travel companies, national tourist boards, accommodation centers, and suppliers of travel services to youth and students. FIYTO sponsors the GO25 Card (http://www.go25.org).

International Student Travel Confederation, Herengracht 479, 1017 BS Amsterdam, The Netherlands (tel. (31) 20 421 2800; fax 20 421 2810; http://www.istc.org; email istcinfo@istc.org). The ISTC is a nonprofit confederation of student travel organizations whose focus is to develop, promote, and facilitate travel among young people and students. Member organizations include International Student Surface Travel Association (ISSA), Student Air Travel Association (SATA), IASIS Travel Insurance, the International Association for Educational and Work Exchange Programs (IAEWEP), and the International Student Identity Card Association (ISIC).

USEFUL PUBLICATIONS

Adventurous Traveler Bookstore, P.O. Box 1468, Williston, VT 05495 (tel. (801) 282-3963; fax 677-1821; email books@atbook.com; http://www.AdventurousTraveler.com). Free 40-page catalogue upon request. Specializes in outdoor adventure travel books and maps. There's lots to see at their World Wide Web site.

Blue Guides, published in Britain by A&C Black Limited, 35 Bedford Row, London WC1R 4JH, in the U.S. by W.W. Norton & Co. Inc., 500 Fifth Ave., New York, NY 10110, and in Canada by Penguin Books Canada Ltd., 10 Alcorn Ave., #300, Toronto, Ont. N4V 3B2. Blue Guides provide invaluable and unmatched historical and cultural information as well as sightseeing routes, maps, tourist information, and listings of pricey hotels.

Bon Voyage!, 2069 W. Bullard Ave., Fresno, CA 93711-1200 (tel. (800) 995-9716, outside the US(209) 447-8441; fax 266-6460; email 70754.3511@compuserve.com). Annual mail order catalogue offers a range of products. Books, travel accessories, luggage, electrical converters, maps, and videos. All merchandise may be returned for exchange or refund within 30 days of purchase, and prices are guaranteed (lower advertised prices will be matched and merchandise shipped free).

The College Connection, Inc., 1295 Prospect St. Suite B, La Jolla, CA 92037 (tel. (619) 551-9770; fax 551-9987; email eurailnow@aol.com; http://www.eurailpass.com). *The Passport,* a booklet listing hints about every aspect of traveling and studying abroad, is free to *Let's Go* readers; send requests by email or fax only. The College Rail Connection, one of their divisions, sells railpasses at student discounts.

European Festivals Association, 120B, rue de Lausanne, CH-1202 Geneva, Switzerland (tel. (22) 732 28 03; fax 738 40 12; email aef@vtx.ch). Publishes the free booklet *Festivals,* which lists dates and programs of many major European festivals. To receive the booklet, enclose 5 International Reply Coupons and address request to Dailey-Thorp Travel, Inc., 330 West 58th St, New York, NY 10019-1817.

Forsyth Travel Library, Inc., 1750 East 131st St, P.O. Box 480800, Kansas City, MO 64148 (tel. (800) 367-7984; fax (816) 942-6969; email forsyth@avi.net; http://www.forsyth.com). A mail-order service that stocks a wide range of maps and guides for rail and ferry travel in Europe; also sells rail tickets and passes, and offers reservation services. Sells the *Thomas Cook European Timetable,* a complete guide to European train departures and arrivals (US$28, or $39 with full map of European train routes; postage $4.50 for Priority shipping). Call or write for a free catalogue, or visit their web site.

Hunter Publishing, P.O. Box 7816, Edison, NJ 08818 (tel. (908) 225-1900; fax 417-0482; email hunterpub@emi.net; http://www.hunterpublishing.com). Has an extensive catalogue of travel books, guides, language learning tapes, and quality maps, among them a *Charming Small Hotel Guide* to Switzerland (US$15).

Transitions Abroad, P.O. Box 1300, 18 Hulst Rd., Amherst, MA 01004-1300 (tel. (800) 293-0373; fax 256-0373; email trabroad@aol.com; http://transabroad.com). Invaluable magazine lists publications and resources for overseas study, work, and volunteering (US$25 for 6 issues, single copy $6.25). Also publishes *The Alternative Travel Directory,* a comprehensive guide to living, learning, and working overseas (US$20; postage $4).

Travel Books & Language Center, Inc., 4931 Cordell Ave., Bethesda, MD 20814 (tel. (800) 220-2665; fax (301) 951-8546; email travelbks@aol.com). Over 75,000 items, including books, cassettes, atlases, dictionaries, and specialty travel maps. Offers travel lectures, book signings, newsletter, and free comprehensive catalog upon request.

U.S. Customs Service, P.O. Box 7407, Washington, D.C., 20044 (tel. (202) 927-6724; http://www.customs.ustreas.gov). Publishes books, booklets, leaflets, and flyers on various aspects of customs. *Know Before You Go* tells all about customs requirements; *Pocket Hints* summarizes the most important data.

Wide World Books and Maps, 1911 N. 45th St., Seattle, WA 98103 (tel. (206) 634-3453; fax 634-0558; email travel@speakeasy.org; http://www.ww-books.com). A good selection of travel guides, travel accessories, and hard-to-find maps.

■ Internet Resources

Today, you can make your own airline, hotel, hostel, or car rental reservations on the Internet. **NetTravel: How Travelers Use the Internet,** by Michael Shapiro, is a thorough and informative guide to all aspects of Internet travel planning (US$25).

THE WORLD WIDE WEB

The World Wide Web and Usenet newsgroups are pretty darn useful for booking trips. **Search engines** such as **Lycos** (a2z.lycos.com), **Alta Vista** (www.altavista.digital.com), and **Excite** (www.excite.com) can direct you to relevant pages. **Yahoo!** is slightly more organized; it has travel links at www.yahoo.com/Recreation/Travel. Check out **Let's Go's** web site (www.letsgo.com) and find our newsletter, information about our books, an always-current list of links, and more.

Austrian National Tourist Office (http://www.austria-info.at) has most of what you need to know about Austria: historical and cultural information on cities, train schedules, hiking tips, and links.

Switzerland Tourism (http://www.switzerlandtourism.ch) has all the facts on Switzerland, in a slightly more organized and thorough fashion than its Austrian counterpart. Links cover what the page proper misses.

Microsoft Expedia (http://expedia.msn.com) lists the links you need to make travel plans—compare flight fares, look at maps, make reservations. FareTracker, a free service within Expedia, sends you monthly mails about the cheapest fares to any destination.

The CIA World Factbook (http://www.odci.gov/cia/publications/factbook/index.html) has tons of vital statistics. Check it out for an overview of a country's economy and stuff like that.

Shoestring Travel (http://www.stratpub.com), an alternative to Microsoft's mono-lithic site, is a budget travel e-zine featuring listings of home exchanges and accom-modations information.

Cybercafe Guide (http://www.cyberiacafe.net/cyberia/guide/ccafe.htm) can help you find cybercafes worldwide.

Foreign Language for Travelers (http://www.travlang.com) can help you brush up on your German, French, or Italian. Sorry, no Esperanto.

Just a warning: sometimes it's difficult to distinguish between factual information and marketing. Some sites pose as benign sources of information but are actually tools in a massive marketing machine created and sustained by you know who.

NEWSGROUPS

Another popular source of information are **newsgroups**—forums for discussion of specific topics. One user posts a written question or thought, to which other users read and respond; everyone learns something. In some cases this proliferation has become burdensome; the quality of discussion is often poor, and you have to wade through piles of nonsense to come to useful information.

Usenet can be accessed easily from most Internet gateways. In UNIX systems, type "tin" at the prompt. Most commercial providers offer access to Usenet, and often even have their own version.

There are a number of different hierarchies of newsgroups. For issues related to society and culture, try the "soc" hierarchy (for example, **soc.culture.swiss**). The "rec" (recreation) hierarchy is also good for travelers, with newsgroups such as **rec.travel.air.** The "alt" (alternative) hierarchy houses a number of different types of discussion. "Clari-net" posts AP news wires for many different topics, such as **clari.world.europe.eastern** or **clari.world.europe.alpine.** Since the quality of discussion changes so rapidly, and new groups are always appearing, it's worthwhile to peruse hierarchies to find appropriate topics.

■ Documents and Formalities

It takes a while to get your papers, so you should apply long before you plan to leave. You are relying on slow government agencies to complete transactions. Demand for passports is highest between January and August, and that means backlogs.

It's always a good idea to carry two or more forms of identification, including at least one photo ID. A passport combined with a driver's license or birth certificate works pretty well. In parts of Switzerland (like Geneva) local transportation will cross national borders, so you'll need your passport just to get around. Many establish-ments—most banks for instance—require several IDs before cashing traveler's checks. Never carry all your forms of ID together, however; you risk being left entirely without ID or funds in case of theft or loss. If you plan an extended stay, reg-ister your passport with the nearest embassy or consulate.

ENTRANCE REQUIREMENTS

Citizens of Australia, Canada, Ireland, New Zealand, the U.K., and the U.S. need valid passports to enter both Austria and Switzerland and to get back into their own coun-try. They do not need visas for stays of up to three months in Austria (six months for UK citizens) or Switzerland. Citizens of South Africa need passports, too, and they also need visas to enter Austria. Austria and Switzerland often do not allow entrance if the holder's passport expires in under six months; returning home with an expired passport is illegal, and may result in a fine. If you want to work somewhere, you need permission from the government in charge of the space containing that somewhere.

PASSPORTS

Before you leave, photocopy the page of your passport that contains your photograph, passport number, and other identifying information. Carry one photocopy in a safe place apart from your actual passport, and leave another copy at home. These measures will help prove your citizenship and facilitate the issuing of a new passport if you lose the original document.

If you do lose your passport, notify the local police and the appropriate embassy in Vienna or Bern immediately. To expedite its replacement, you'll need to know all information previously recorded and show identification and proof of citizenship. A replacement may take weeks to process and may be valid only for a limited time. Some consulates can issue new passports within 24 hours with proof of citizenship. Any visas stamped in your old passport will be irretrievably lost. In an emergency, ask for immediate temporary traveling papers that will permit you to go home.

Your passport is a public document belonging to your nation's government. You may have to surrender it to a foreign government official, but if you don't get it back in a reasonable amount of time, inform the nearest mission of your home country.

Australia Citizens must apply for a passport in person at a post office, a passport office, or an Australian diplomatic mission overseas. An appointment may be necessary. Passport offices are located in Adelaide, Brisbane, Canberra City, Darwin, Hobart, Melbourne, Newcastle, Perth, and Sydney. A parent may file an application for a child who is under 18 and unmarried. Adult passports cost AUS$120 (for a 32-page passport) or AUS$180 (64-page), and a child's is AUS$60 (32-page) or AUS$90 (64-page). For more info, call toll-free (in Australia) 13 12 32, or visit http://www.austemb.org.

Canada Application forms in English and French are available at all passport offices, Canadian missions, many travel agencies, and Northern Stores. Citizens may apply in person at any of the 28 regional Passport Offices across Canada. Travel agents can direct applicants to the nearest location. Canadian citizens residing abroad should contact the nearest Canadian embassy or consulate. Children under 16 may be included on a parent's passport. Passports cost CDN$60, plus a CDN$25 consular fee, are valid for 5 years, and are non-renewable. Processing takes approximately 5 business days; allow 3 weeks for mail delivery. For additional info, contact the Canadian Passport Office, Department of Foreign Affairs and International Trade, Ottawa, ON, K1A 0G3 (tel. (613) 994-3500; http://www.dfait-maeci.gc.ca/passport). Travelers may also call (800) 567-6868 (24hr.); in Toronto (416) 973-3251; in Vancouver (604) 775-6250; in Montréal (514) 283-2152. Refer to the booklet *Bon Voyage, But...*, free at any passport office or by calling InfoCentre at (800) 267-8376 (within Canada), or (613) 944-4000 for further help and a list of Canadian embassies and consulates abroad. You may also find entry and background information for various countries by contacting the Consular Affairs Bureau in Ottawa (tel. (800) 267-6788 (24hr.) or (613) 944-6788). There is no charge for re-entering Canada with an expired passport.

Ireland Citizens can apply for a passport by mail to either the Department of Foreign Affairs, Passport Office, Setanta Centre, Molesworth St., Dublin 2 (tel. (01) 671 16 33; fax (01) 671 10 92), or the Passport Office, Irish Life Building, 1A South Mall, Cork (tel. (021) 27 25 25; fax (021) 27 57 70). Obtain an application at a local Garda station or request one from a passport office. The new Passport Express Service, available through post offices, allows citizens to get a passport in 2 weeks for an extra IR£3. Passports cost IR£45 and are valid for 5 years. Citizens under 18 or over 65 can request a 3-year passport that costs IR£10.

New Zealand Application forms for passports are available in New Zealand from travel agents and Department of Internal Affairs Link Centres. Overseas, forms and passport services are provided by New Zealand embassies, high commissions, and consulates. Applications may also be forwarded to the Passport Office, P.O. Box 10526, Wellington, New Zealand. Standard processing time in New Zealand is 10 working days for correct applications. The fees are adult NZ$80, and child under 16 NZ$40. An urgent passport service is also available for an extra NZ$80. Different fees apply at overseas post: 9 posts including London, Sydney, and Los Angeles offer both standard and urgent services for slightly higher prices. Children's names can no longer be endorsed on a parent's passport—they must apply for their own, which are valid for up to 5 years. An adult's passport is valid for up to 10 years. More information is available on the internet at http://www.govt.nz/agency_info/forms.shtml.

South Africa Citizens can apply for a passport at any **Home Affairs Office** or **South African Mission.** Tourist passports, valid for 10 years, cost SAR80. Children under 16 must be issued their own passports, valid for 5 years, which cost SAR60. If a passport is needed in a hurry, an **emergency passport** may be issued for SAR50. An application for a permanent passport must accompany the emergency passport application. Time for the completion of an application is normally 3 months or more from the time of submission. Current passports less than 10 years old (counting from date of issuance) may be **renewed** until December 31, 1999; every citizen whose passport's validity does not extend far beyond this date is urged to renew as soon as possible to avoid the expected glut of applications as 2000 approaches. Politics. Renewal is free, and turnaround time is usually 2 weeks. For further information, contact the nearest Department of Home Affairs Office.

United Kingdom British citizens, British Dependent Territories citizens, British Nationals (overseas), British subjects, and British Overseas citizens may apply for a **full passport,** valid for 10 years (5 years if under 16). Application forms are available at passport offices, main post offices, many travel agents, and branches of Lloyds Bank and Artac World Choice. Apply by mail or in person (for an additional UK£10) to one of the passport offices, located in London, Liverpool, Newport, Peterborough, Glasgow, or Belfast. The fee is UK£31, UK£11 for children under 16. The London office offers same-day, walk-in rush service; arrive early. The formerly available **British Visitor's Passport** has been abolished; every traveler over 16 now needs a 10 yr., standard passport. The U.K. Passport Agency can be reached by phone at (0990) 21 04 10.

United States Citizens may apply for a passport at any federal or state **courthouse** or **post office** authorized to accept passport applications, or at a **U.S. Passport Agency,** located in Boston, Chicago, Honolulu, Houston, Los Angeles, Miami, New Orleans, New York, Philadelphia, San Francisco, Seattle, Stamford, or Washington, D.C. Refer to the "U.S. Government, State Department" section of the telephone directory or the local post office for addresses. Parents must apply in person for children under age 13. You must apply in person if this is your first passport, if you're under age 18, or if your current passport is more than 12 years old or was issued before your 18th birthday. Passports are valid for 10 years (5 years if under 18) and cost US$65 (under 18 US$40). Passports may be **renewed** by mail or in person for US$55. Processing takes 3-4 weeks. **Rush service** is available for a surcharge of US$30 with proof of departure within 10 working days (e.g., an airplane ticket or itinerary), or for travelers leaving in 2-3 weeks who require visas. Given proof of citizenship, a U.S. embassy or consulate abroad can usually issue a new passport. Report a passport lost or stolen in the U.S. in writing to Passport Services, 1425 K St, NW, U.S. Department of State, Washington D.C., 20524 or to the nearest passport agency. For more info, contact the U.S. Passport Information's **24-hour recorded message** (tel. (202) 647-0518). U.S. citizens may receive consular information sheets, travel warnings, and public announcements at any passport agency, U.S. embassy, or consulate, or by sending a self-addressed stamped envelope to: Overseas Citizens Services, Room 4811, Department of State, Washington, D.C. 20520-4818 (tel. (202) 647-5225; fax 647-3000). Additional information (including publications) about documents, formalities, and travel abroad is available through the Bureau of Consular Affairs homepage at http://travel.state.gov, or through the State Department site at http://www.state.gov.

CUSTOMS: GETTING IN

Not to worry, getting in shouldn't be too much of a hassle. Austria and Switzerland prohibit or restrict the importation of firearms, explosives, ammunition, fireworks, booby traps, controlled drugs, most plants, lottery tickets, most animals, and porn. They don't look keenly on items manufactured from protected species, either. To avoid hassles about prescription drugs, ensure that your bottles are clearly marked and carry a copy of the prescription to show the customs officer.

CUSTOMS: GOING HOME

Upon returning home, you must declare all articles you acquired abroad and pay a **duty** on the value of those articles that exceeds the allowance established by your country's customs service.

Australia Citizens may import AUS$400 (under 18 AUS$200) of goods duty-free, in addition to 1.125L alcohol and 250 cigarettes or 250g tobacco. You must be over 18 to import alcohol or tobacco. There is no limit to the amount of cash that may be brought into or taken out of the country, but amounts of AUS$10,000 or more, or the equivalent in foreign currency, must be reported. All foodstuffs and animal products must be declared on arrival. For information, contact the Regional Director, Australian Customs Service, GPO Box 8, Sydney NSW 2001 (tel. (02) 9213 2000; fax 9213 4000; or visit http://www.customs.gov.au).

Canada Citizens remaining abroad for at least 1 week may bring back up to CDN$500 worth of goods duty-free any time. Citizens or residents who travel for a period between 48hr. and 6 days can bring back up to CDN$200. Both exemptions may include tobacco and alcohol. Shipping non-alcohol and tobacco goods home is okay under the CDN$500 exemption as long as you declare them when you arrive. Goods under the CDN$200 exemption, as well as all alcohol and tobacco, must be in your hand or checked luggage. Citizens of legal age (which varies by province) may import in-person up to 200 cigarettes, 50 cigars or cigarillos, 200g loose tobacco, 1.14L wine or alcohol, and 24 355mL cans/bottles of beer; the value of these products is included in the CDN$200 or CDN$500. For more information, write to Canadian Customs, 2265 St. Laurent Blvd., Ottawa, ON, K1G 4K3 (tel. (613) 993-0534), phone the 24-hr. Automated Customs Information Service at (800) 461-9999, or visit Revenue Canada at http://www.revcan.ca.

Ireland Citizens must declare everything in excess of IR£142 (IR£73 per traveler under 15 years of age) obtained outside the EU or duty- and tax-free in the EU above the following allowances: 200 cigarettes, 100 cigarillos, 50 cigars, or 250g tobacco; 1L liquor or 2L wine; 2L still wine; 50g perfume; and 250mL *eau de toilette*. Goods obtained duty and tax paid in another EU country up to a value of IR£460 (IR£115 per traveler under 15) will not be subject to additional customs duties. Travelers under 17 may not import tobacco or alcohol. For more information, contact The Revenue Commissioners, Dublin Castle (tel. (01) 679 2777; fax 671 2021; email taxes@iol.ie; http://www.revenue.ie) or The Collector of Customs and Excise, The Custom House, Dublin 1.

New Zealand Citizens may import up to NZ$700 worth of goods duty-free if they are intended for personal use or gifts. The concession is 200 cigarettes (1 carton) or 250g tobacco or 50 cigars or a combination of all 3 not to exceed 250g. You may also bring in 4.5L of beer or wine and 1.125L of liquor. Only travelers over 17 may import tobacco or alcohol. For more information, contact New Zealand Customs, 50 Anzac Ave., Box 29, Auckland (tel. (09) 377 35 20; fax 309 29 78).

South Africa Citizens may import duty-free: 400 cigarettes, 50 cigars, 250g tobacco, 2L wine, 1L of spirits, 250mL *eau de toilette,* and 50mL perfume, and other consumable items up to a value of SAR500. Goods up to a value of SAR10,000 over and above this duty-free allowance are dutiable at 20%; such goods are also exempted from payment of VAT. Items acquired abroad and sent to the Republic as unaccompanied baggage do not qualify for any allowances. You may not export or import South African bank notes in excess of SAR25,000. For more information, consult the free pamphlet *South African Customs Information,* available in airports or from the Commissioner for Customs and Excise, Private Bag X47, Pretoria 0001 (tel. (12) 314 99 11; fax 328 64 78).

United Kingdom Citizens or visitors arriving in the U.K. from outside the EU must declare goods in excess of the following allowances: 200 cigarettes or 100 cigarillos or 50 cigars or 250g tobacco; still table wine (2L); strong liqueurs over 22% volume (1L), nor fortified or sparkling wine, other liqueurs (2L); perfume (60 cc/mL);

eau de toilette (250 cc/mL); and UK£75 worth of all other goods including gifts and souvenirs. You must be over 17 to import liquor or tobacco. These allowances also apply to duty-free purchases within the EU, except for the last category, other goods, which then has an allowance of UK£145. Goods obtained duty and tax paid for personal use (regulated according to set guide levels) within the EU do not require any further customs duty. More information is available from Her Majesty's Customs and Excise, Custom House, Nettleton Rd, Heathrow Airport, Hounslow, Middlesex TW6 2LA (tel. (0181) 910-3602 or 910-3566; fax 910-3765) and on the web at http://www.open.gov.uk.

United States Citizens may import US$400 worth of accompanying goods duty-free and must pay a 10% tax on the next US$1000. You must declare all purchases, so have sales slips ready. The US$400 personal exemption covers goods purchased for personal or household use (this includes gifts) and cannot include more than 100 cigars, 200 cigarettes (1 carton), and 1L of wine or liquor. You must be over 21 to bring liquor into the U.S. If you mail home personal goods of U.S. origin, you can avoid duty charges by marking the package "American goods returned." For more information, consult the brochure *Know Before You Go,* available from the U.S. Customs Service, Box 7407, Washington D.C. 20044 (tel. (202) 927-6724), or visit the web (http://www.customs.ustreas.gov).

YOUTH, STUDENT, AND TEACHER IDENTIFICATION

The **International Student Identity Card** (ISIC) is the most widely accepted form of student identification. Flashing this card can procure you discounts for sights, theaters, museums, accommodations, meals, trains, ferries, buses, and airplanes. ISIC cards also provide insurance benefits, including US$100 per day of in-hospital sickness for a maximum of 60 days, and US$3000 accident-related medical reimbursement for each accident (see **Insurance,** p.18). In addition, cardholders have access to a toll-free 24hr. ISIC helpline whose multilingual staff can provide assistance in medical, legal, and financial emergencies overseas (tel. (181) 666 9025 from the U.K.; (800) 626-2427 from the U.S. or Canada; elsewhere call the U.S. collect (713) 267-2525 or the UK collect (44) 181 666 9025).

Many student travel agencies around the world issue ISICs, including STA Travel in Australia and New Zealand; Travel CUTS and the web (http://www.isic-canada.org) in Canada; USIT in Ireland and Northern Ireland; SASTS in South Africa; Campus Travel and STA Travel in the U.K.; Council Travel, Let's Go Travel, STA Travel, and via the web (http://www.ciee.org/idcards/index.htm) in the U.S.; and any of the other organizations under the auspices of the International Student Travel Confederation (ISTC). When you apply for the card, request a copy of the *International Student Identity Card Handbook,* which lists available discounts. You can write to Council for a copy. The card is valid from September to December of the following year and costs US$20, CDN$15, or AUS$15. Applicants must be at least 12-year-old degree-seeking students of a secondary or post-secondary school. Because of the proliferation of phony ISICs, many airlines and some other services require other proof of student identity, such as a signed letter from the registrar attesting to your student status and stamped with the school seal or your school ID card. The **International Teacher Identity Card** (ITIC) offers the same insurance coverage, and similar but limited discounts. The fee is US$20, UK£5, or AUS$13. For more information on these cards, consult the organization's website (http://www.istc.org; email isicinfo@istc.org).

Federation of International Youth Travel Organizations (FIYTO) issues a discount card to travelers who are under 26 but not students known as the **GO25 Card.** It's a one-year card offering many of the same benefits as the ISIC, and most organizations that sell the ISIC also sell the GO25 Card. A brochure that lists discounts is free when you purchase the card. To apply, you will need a passport, valid driver's license, or copy of a birth certificate; and a passport-sized photo with your name printed on the

ESSENTIALS

back. The fee is US$20. Information is available on the web at http://www.ciee.org, or by contacting Travel CUTS in Canada, STA Travel in the U.K., Council Travel in the U.S., or FIYTO headquarters in Denmark (see **Travel Organizations,** p.2).

DRIVING PERMITS AND CAR INSURANCE

If you plan to drive a car in Austria, you must have an **International Driving Permit** (IDP) in addition to your driver's license. Most car rental agencies in Switzerland don't require the permit, but it may be a good idea to get one anyway, in case you're in a situation where the police don't speak English.

Your IDP, valid for one year, must be issued in your own country before you depart. You must be 18 years old, and you still gotta carry your regular driver's license. An application usually needs to include one or two photos, a current local license, an additional form of identification, and some money. Australians can obtain an IDP by contacting their local **Royal Automobile Club** (RAC), the **National Royal Motorist Association** (NRMA) if in NSW or the ACT; a permit can be obtained for AUS$15. Applications are available at http://www.rac.com.au, by calling (08) 9421 4271, or fax. (08) 9221 1887. Canadian license holders can obtain an IDP (CDN$10) through any **Canadian Automobile Association** (CAA) branch office in Canada, by writing CAA, 1145 Hunt Club Rd., Ste. 200, K1V 0Y3 Canada. (tel. (613) 247-0117, ext. 2025; fax (613) 247-0118), or on the web at http://www.caa.ca. Citizens of Ireland should drop into the nearest **Automobile Association** (AA) office where an IDP can be picked up for IR£4, or phone (1) 283 3555 (fax (1) 283-3660) for a postal application form. In New Zealand, contact your local **Automobile Association (AA),** or their main office at P.O. Box 5, Auckland (tel. (9) 377 4660; fax (9) 302 2037); procedural information is available at http://www.nzaa.co.nz. IDPs cost NZ$8, plus NZ$2 for return postage if mailed from abroad. In South Africa visit your local **Automobile Association of South Africa** office where IDPs can be picked up or, for more information, phone (11) 799 1000 (fax (11) 799 1010) or write to P.O. Box 596, 2000 Johannesburg. In the U.K. IDPs are UK£4 and you can either visit your local **AA Shop,** call (1256) 49 39 32 (if abroad, fax (44-1256) 46 07 50), or write to AA 5 Star Post Link, Freepost, Copenhagen Ct, 8 New St, Basingstroke RG21 7BA, and order a postal application (allow 2-3 weeks). For further information, call (44) 0990-448-866. Or visit http://www.theaa.co.uk/travel. U.S. license holders can obtain an IDP (US$10) at any **American Automobile Association** (AAA) office or by writing to AAA Florida, Travel Agency Services Department, 1000 AAA Drive (mail stop 28), Heathrow, FL 32746 (tel. (407) 444-4245; fax 444-4247). You do not have to be a member of AAA to receive an IDP.

Austria now requires foreign cars to purchase a special **permit sticker** upon entering the country. The sticker can be purchased at various points near the border, and costs 70AS per week. Failure to buy and display it can result in a 130AS fine.

Most credit cards cover standard **insurance.** If you rent, lease, or borrow a car, you will need a **green card,** or **International Insurance Certificate,** to prove that you have liability insurance. Obtain it through the car rental agency; most include coverage in their prices. If you lease a car, you can obtain a green card from the dealer. Some travel agents offer the card; it may also be available at the border. Verify whether your auto insurance applies abroad; even if it does, you will still need a green card to certify this to foreign officials. If you have a collision abroad, the accident will show up on your domestic records if you report it to your insurance company. Rental agencies may require you to purchase theft insurance in countries that they consider to have a high risk of auto theft. Ask your rental agency about it. Some agencies, for instance, include Switzerland as a high risk country. Don't ask us why.

■ Money

> Prices in *Let's Go* and the exchange rates at the beginning of each country were compiled in the summer of 1998, when *Let's Go* researcher-writers for this edition were in the field. Prices and exchange rates may well change.

Switzerland is expensive; Austria's a bit better. If you stay in hostels and prepare your own food, expect to spend anywhere from US$30-60 per day in Switzerland, US$20-40 in Austria. Transportation, especially through, up, and over mountains, will greatly increase these figures. Plan to keep a larger wad of cash than you do at home, realizing that carrying it around with you, even in a money belt, is risky. Checks from home probably won't be acceptable, though, so you have to find other ways. Inevitably you will have the pleasure of interacting with the innovations of the modern financial world. The innovations of the modern financial world have their shortcomings.

CURRENCY AND EXCHANGE

Currency exchange (*Geldwechsel* in German, *bureau de change* in French, *cambio* in Italian) commissions are scary. If you were to go through every country in Europe and exchange US$100, you would be left with less than a quarter of your original sum at the end. To minimize your losses, convert fairly large sums at one time. Better yet, convert large amounts in small towns, since they usually charge less. Post offices generally offer good exchange rates and charge low commissions. Although it is more expensive to buy Austrian or Swiss currency in other countries, convert enough money to cover the first 24 to 72 hours of your trip before heading out or bring an ATM card and find the machine quickly—you'll be able to zip through the airport and start your vacation without languishing in lines.

The unit of currency in Austria is the **Schilling,** abbreviated as **AS, ÖS,** or, within Austria, simply **S.** Each *Schilling* is subdivided into 100 **Groschen (g).** Coins come in 2, 5, 10, and 50g, and 1, 5, 10, and 20AS denominations. Bills come in 20, 50, 100, 500, 1000, and 5000AS amounts. Exchange rates are standard among banks and exchange counters, while stores, hotels, and restaurants that accept payment in foreign currency apply a slightly lower exchange rate. Every establishment that exchanges currency charges at least 14AS. The primary Swiss monetary unit is the **Swiss Franc (SFr).** A *franc* is divided into 100 *centimes* (called *Rappen* in German Switzerland). Coins are issued in 5, 10, 20, and 50 *centimes* and 1, 2, and 5SFr; bills in 10, 20, 50, 100, 500, and 1000SFr denominations. Currency exchange is easiest (and most convenient) at train stations and post offices, where rates are the same as or very close to bank rates but where commissions are cheaper than bank commissions. American Express services are usually tied to a travel agency. There are AmEx offices in Basel, Bern, Geneva, Lausanne, Lucerne, Lugano, Sion, and Zurich.

TRAVELER'S CHECKS

Traveler's checks are one of the safest and least troublesome means of carrying funds, as they can be refunded if stolen. Traveler's checks are your friend. Several agencies and many banks sell them, usually for face value plus a small percentage commission. (Members of the American Automobile Association and some banks and credit unions can get American Express checks commission-free; see **Driving Permits and Car Insurance,** p.9). **American Express** and **Visa** are the most widely recognized, though other major checks are sold, exchanged, cashed, and refunded almost as easily. In small towns, traveler's checks are less readily accepted than in cities with large tourist industries. Still, there will probably be at least one place in every town where you can exchange them for local currency. If you're ordering checks, do so well in advance, especially if you're requesting large sums.

ESSENTIALS

Each agency provides refunds **if your checks are lost or stolen,** and many provide additional services. (You may need a police report verifying the loss or theft.) Ask about toll-free refund hotlines (in the countries you're visiting), emergency message services, and stolen credit card assistance when you buy your checks.

Expect some red tape and delay if traveler's checks are lost or stolen. For a speedy refund, keep your check receipts separate from your checks and store them in a safe place or with a traveling companion, record check numbers when you cash them, leave a list of check numbers with someone at home, and ask for a list of refund centers when you buy your checks (American Express and Bank of America have over 40,000 centers worldwide). Keep a separate supply of cash or traveler's checks for emergencies. Never countersign your checks until you are ready to cash them, and always bring your passport with you when you plan to use the checks.

American Express: Call (800) 25 19 02 in Australia; in New Zealand (0800) 44 10 68; in the U.K. (0800) 52 13 13; in the U.S. and Canada (800) 221-7282). Elsewhere, call U.S. collect (801) 964-6665. American Express traveler's checks are now available in 10 currencies including Swiss francs (but not Austrian schillings). They're the most widely recognized worldwide and the easiest to replace if lost or stolen. Checks can be purchased for a small fee (1-4%) at American Express Travel Service Offices, banks, and American Automobile Association offices. Cardmembers can also buy checks at American Express Dispensers at Travel Service Offices at airports, or order them by phone (tel. (800) ORDER-TC (673-3782)). American Express offices cash their checks commission-free although they often offer worse rates than banks. You can also buy *Cheques for Two,* as in checks that work for 2 different people. Request the American Express booklet "Traveler's Companion," which lists travel office addresses and stolen check hotlines for each European country. Visit their online travel offices (http://www.aexp.com).

Citicorp: Call (800) 645-6556 in the U.S. and Canada; in Europe, the Middle East, or Africa (44) 171 508 7007; from elsewhere call U.S. collect (813) 623-1709. Sells both Citicorp and Citicorp Visa traveler's checks in U.S., Australian, and Canadian dollars, British pounds, German marks, and other currencies. Commission is 1-2% on check purchases. Citicorp's World Courier Service guarantees hand-delivery of traveler's checks when a refund location isn't convenient. Call 24hr.

Thomas Cook MasterCard: For 24hr. cashing or refund assistance: from the U.S. or Canada call (800) 223-7373; from the U.K. call (0800) 622 101 free or (1733) 318 950 collect; from anywhere else call (44) 1733 318 950 collect. Offers checks in Swiss francs, ECUs, and other currencies. Commission 2% for purchases. Thomas Cook offices will cash checks commission-free; banks will make a commission charge. Thomas Cook MasterCard Traveler's Checks are also available from **Capital Foreign Exchange** (see **Currency and Exchange**) in U.S. or Canadian dollars, Swiss francs, and British pounds.

Visa: Call (800) 227-6811 in the U.S.; in the U.K. (0800) 895 078; from anywhere else in the world call (44) 1733 318 949 and reverse the charges. Any of the above numbers can tell you the location of their nearest office. Any type of Visa traveler's checks can be reported lost at the Visa number.

CREDIT CARDS

Major credit cards, especially **MasterCard** and **Visa,** are widely accepted in both Austria and Switzerland and can be used to extract cash advances from associated banks and teller machines in local currency all over. Credit card companies get the wholesale exchange rate, which is generally 5% better than the retail rate used by banks—and better than other currency exchange establishments, too. However, you will be charged ruinous interest rates if you don't pay off the bill quickly, so be careful. **American Express** cards also work in some ATMs, as well as at AmEx offices and major airports. All such machines require a **Personal Identification Number** (PIN). You must ask your credit card company for a PIN before you leave; without it, you will be unable to withdraw cash with your credit card. MasterCard and Visa have different names elsewhere ("EuroCard" or "Access" for MC, "Carte Bleue" or "Barclay-card" for Visa).

Credit cards are invaluable in an emergency, an unexpected hospital bill or ticket home, the loss of traveler's checks, or anything that may leave you without other resources. Credit cards also offer an array of other services, from insurance to emergency assistance, that depend on the issuer. They're neat, those credit cards.

American Express (tel. (800) 843-2273) has a US$55 annual fee but offers a number of services. AmEx cardholders can cash personal checks at AmEx offices outside the U.S., and Global Assist, a 24hr. hotline with medical and legal assistance in emergencies, is also available (tel. (800) 554-2639 in U.S. and Canada; from abroad call U.S. collect (202) 554-2639). Cardholders can use the American Express Travel Service; benefits include assistance in changing airline, hotel, and car rental reservations, baggage loss and flight insurance, sending mailgrams and international cables, and holding your mail at one of the more than 1700 AmEx offices around the world.

Visa (Telephone Assistance Center (800) 336-8472) and **MasterCard** are issued in cooperation with individual banks and some other organizations; ask the issuer about services that go along with the cards.

CASH CARDS

Cash cards—popularly called ATM (Automated Teller Machine) cards—are widespread in Austria and Switzerland (look for signs reading "Bankomat" with a green and blue "B"). Depending on the system that your bank at home uses, you can probably access your account whenever you need cash. (Keep all receipts–even if an ATM won't give you your cash, it may register a withdrawal on your next statement). Happily, ATMs get the same wholesale exchange rate as credit cards and that's better than you can usually do. Despite the perks, there are problems: there's often a limit on the amount of money you can withdraw per day (usually about US$500, depending on the type of card and account), and computer networks sometimes fail. Memorize your PIN code in numeral form since machines outside the U.S. and Canada often don't have letters on their keys. Also, if your PIN is longer than four digits, ask your bank whether the first four digits will work, or whether you need a new number. Many ATMs are outdoors; be cautious and aware of your surroundings.

The two major international money networks are **Cirrus** (U.S. tel. (800) 4-CIRRUS (424-7787)) and **PLUS** (U.S. tel. (800) 843-7587 for the "Voice Response Unit Locator"; http://www.visa.com). Both of those work at most ATM's in Austria and Switzerland. There will probably be a charge of US$3-5 to withdraw abroad depending on your bank. Carrying one card for each network provides maximum coverage.

GETTING MONEY FROM HOME

If you bring an **American Express** card, you can draw cash from a checking account at any of its major offices and many of its representatives' offices up to US$1000 every 21 days (no service charge, no interest). AmEx also offers Express Cash, with over 100,000 ATMs around the world. Express Cash withdrawals are automatically debited from your checking account or line of credit. Green card holders may withdraw up to US$1000 in a seven day period. There is a 2% transaction fee for each cash withdrawal, with a US$2.50 minimum and $20 maximum. To enroll in Express Cash, call (800) CASH NOW (227-4669). Outside the U.S. call collect (336) 668-5041.

Money can be wired abroad through international money transfer services operated by **Western Union** (tel. (800) 325-6000). The rates for sending cash are generally US$10-11 cheaper than with a credit card, and the money is usually available in the country you're sending it to within an hour.

You can send cash abroad via **Federal Express.** This is illegal and somewhat risky, and you must remain at a legitimate address for a day or two to wait for the money's arrival. However, it is reasonably reliable, free of fees and taxes, and easy.

In emergencies, U.S. citizens can have money sent via the State Department's **Overseas Citizens Service, American Citizens Services,** Consular Affairs, Room

4811, U.S. Department of State, Washington, D.C. 20520 (tel. (202) 647-5225; nights, Sundays, and holidays (202) 647-4000; fax (on demand only) (202) 647-3000; http://travel.state.gov on the web, or email ca@his.com). For a fee of US$15, they will forward money within hours to the nearest consular office. The office serves only Americans in the direst of straits abroad; non-American travelers should contact their embassies for information on wiring cash.

TIPPING AND BARGAINING

No need for **tipping** in **Switzerland**. Gratuities are already automatically factored into prices. **In Austria,** menus will say whether service is included (*Preise inclusiv* or *Bedienung inclusive*); if it is, you really don't have to tip. If it's not, just round up (for a 162AS bill, tip 8AS), which means leaving a tip up to about 10 percent. Austrian restaurants expect you to seat yourself, and servers will not bring the bill until you ask them to do so. Say *"Zahlen bitte"* (TSAHL-en BIT-uh) to settle your accounts. Don't leave tips on the table. Be aware that you may be charged for each piece of bread that you eat during your meal.

■ Safety and Security

Austria and Switzerland are both relatively free of violent crime, but that doesn't mean you can let your guard down. Women travelers see **Specific Concerns, p. 22.**

Emergency Numbers
Austria
Police: tel. 133. **Fire:** tel. 122. **Ambulance:** tel. 144.
Switzerland
Police: tel. 117. **Fire:** tel. 118. **Ambulance:** tel. 144.

PERSONAL SAFETY

Most of this you can figure out: it's a supplement to common sense, a series of suggestions meant to spur you to think about traveling and traveling safely. Safety means not looking like a target. Tourists are vulnerable to crime as they often carry large amounts of cash and lack local street savvy, so looking too much like a tourist is setting yourself up. To avoid unwanted attention, blend in. Walking directly into a café or shop to check a map beats checking it on a street corner. Better yet, look over your map before setting out. Muggings are more often impromptu than planned; nervous, over-the-shoulder glances can be a tip that you have something valuable to protect. When exploring a new city, extra vigilance is wise. Find out about unsafe areas from tourist information or the manager of your hotel or hostel. If you travel alone, be sure that someone at home knows your itinerary and don't tell people that you're traveling alone. Memorize the emergency numbers of the city or area.

When walking at night, stick to busy, well-lit streets and avoid dark alleyways and people with guns and knives. Don't cross through parks, parking lots, or other large, deserted areas. Whenever possible, *Let's Go* warns of unsavory neighborhoods, but you should exercise your own judgment about the safety of your environs. The flow of people reveals a great deal about the safety of an area; look for signs of an active community. If you feel uncomfortable, leave as quickly and directly as you can.

If you are using a **car**, be sure to park your vehicle in a garage or well-traveled area. Wearing a seatbelt is the law in many areas; it's also a good idea. Children under 18kg should ride only in a specially designed carseat, available for a small fee from most car rental agencies. Study route maps before you hit the road; mountain roads might have poor (or nonexistent) shoulders and few gas stations. Twisty Alpine roads may be closed in winter and, when open, require particular caution. Learn the **Alpine honk:** when going blind around an abrupt turn, stop and give the horn a toot before proceeding. Shift your car to low gear, drive slowly, brake occasionally, and *never ever ever* pass anyone, no matter how slow they're going.

Let's Go does not recommend **hitchhiking**, particularly for women; see **Getting There**, p. 29 for more information. **Sleeping in your own car** is one of the most dangerous things you can do. Sleeping out in the open is even more dangerous.

There is no sure-fire set of precautions that will protect you from all of the situations you might encounter when you travel. A good self-defense course will give you more concrete ways to react to different types of aggression, though. **Impact, Prepare, and Model Mugging** can refer you to local self-defense courses in the U.S. (tel. (800) 345-KICK), Vancouver, Canada (tel. (604) 878-3838), and Zurich (tel. 411 261 2423). Workshop and course prices range from US$50-500. Women's and men's courses are offered.

FINANCIAL SECURITY

So maybe Austria and Switzerland aren't exactly full of con artists: there are still people who will steal your money. Be aware of certain classics: sob stories that require money; distractions that allow enough time to snatch your bag. Be careful of little kids with big newspapers. If someone's trying to give you the grift, if you feel like someone's trying to give you the grift, you shouldn't respond or make eye contact. Walk away quickly and keep a solid grip on your belongings. Contact the police if someone is particularly insistent or aggressive.

If your wallet's in your back pocket, be careful. Someone might try and take it. Never count your money in public and carry as little as possible. If you carry a purse, buy a sturdy one with a secure clasp and carry it crosswise on the side away from the street with the clasp against you. Secure packs with small combination padlocks that slip through the two zippers. A **money belt** is the best way to carry cash; you can buy one at most camping supply stores or through the Forsyth Travel Library (see **Useful Publications,** p. 49). A nylon zippered pouch with belt that sits inside the waist of your pants or skirt combines convenience and security. A **neck pouch** is equally safe, though less accessible. Don't keep anything precious in a fanny-pack (even if it's worn on your stomach): your valuables will be highly visible and easy to steal. Actually, just don't wear a fanny-pack.

City crowds and public transportation are favorite places for deft pick-pockets. Rush hour is no excuse for strangers to press up against you. If someone stands uncomfortably close, hold your bags tightly and walk quietly away. Be alert in public telephone booths: make sure no one's watching your calling card number. **Photocopies** of important documents mean you can recover them in case if they're lost or filched. Carry one copy separate from the documents; leave another at home. Keep some money separate for emergencies. Label every piece of luggage both inside and out.

Be particularly careful on **buses** (for example, carry your backpack in front of you where you can see it), don't check baggage on trains, and don't trust anyone to "watch your bag for a second." Thieves thrive on **trains**; professionals wait for tourists to fall asleep and then carry off everything they can. When traveling in pairs, sleep in alternating shifts; when alone, use good judgement in selecting a compartment: never stay in an empty one; use a lock to secure your pack to the luggage rack. Keep important documents and other valuables on your person and try to sleep on top bunks with your luggage above you. Use your bag as a pillow if you can.

Let's Go lists locker availability in hostels and train stations, but you'll need your own padlock. Lockers are useful if you plan on sleeping outdoors or don't want to lug everything with you, but don't store valuables in them. Never leave your belongings unattended. If you feel unsafe, look for places with either a curfew or a night attendant. When possible, keep valuables at home.

If you travel by **car,** try not to leave valuable possessions like radios or luggage or gold bars inside while you're off rambling. Radios are especially tempting. Gold bars, too. If your tape deck or radio is removable, hide it in the trunk or take it with you. If it isn't, conceal it under a lot of junk. Hide baggage in the trunk—although savvy thieves can tell if a car is heavily loaded by the way it sits. So can everyone else.

Travel Assistance International by **Worldwide Assistance Services, Inc.** (http://www.worldwide-assistance.com) provides its members with a 24hr. hotline for travel emergencies and referrals in over 200 countries. Their Per-Trip (starting at US$21) and Frequent Traveler (starting at US$88) plans include medical, travel, and communication services. Call (800) 821-2828 or (202) 828-5894, fax (202) 828-5896, email wassist@aol.com, or write them at 1133 15th St. NW, Ste. 400, Washington, D.C. 20005-2710. The **American Society of Travel Agents** provides extensive informational resources both at their website (http://www.astanet.com) and in their free brochure, *Travel Safety*. Get a copy by sending a request and self-addressed, stamped envelope to them at 1101 King St. Ste. 200, Alexandria, VA 22314.

DRUGS AND ALCOHOL

Police officers, members of the *Polizei* or *Gendarmerie,* typically speak little English and tend to be very businesslike. Treat the police with the utmost respect at all times. Imbibing **alcohol** in Austria and Switzerland is generally trouble-free—beer is more common than soda, and a lunch without wine or beer would be unusual. In Switzerland, you must be 16 to drink legally. Each Austrian province sets a legal minimum drinking age; typically, anyone over 18 can drink whatever he or she wishes, and drinking beer is often legal at younger ages.

Drugs could easily ruin a trip. Every year thousands of travelers are arrested for trafficking or possession of drugs or for simply being in the company of a suspected user. Marijuana, hashish, cocaine, and narcotics are illegal in Austria and Switzerland, and the penalties for illegal possession of drugs, especially for foreigners, range from stern to severe. It is not unknown for a dealer to increase profits by first selling drugs to tourists and then turning them in to the authorities for a reward. Even such reputedly liberal cities as Vienna, Salzburg, and Zurich take an officially dim view of mussed-up tourists. The worst thing you can possibly do is carry drugs across an international border—you could not only end up in prison but also be hounded by a "Drug Trafficker" stamp on your passport for the rest of your life. If you are arrested, all your home country's consulate can do is visit, provide a list of attorneys, and inform family and friends. You are bound by the laws of the foreign country you are traveling in.

Make sure you get a statement and prescription from your doctor if you'll be carrying insulin, syringes, or narcotic medications. Leave all medication in original, labeled containers. What is legal at home may not be legal abroad; check with your doctor or the appropriate foreign consulate to avoid nasty surprises.

■ Health

Common sense is the simplest prescription for good health while you travel: eat well, drink enough, sleep some, don't overexert yourself. Travelers complain most often about their feet and their gut, so take precautionary measures. Drinking lots of fluids can often prevent dehydration and constipation, and wearing sturdy shoes and clean socks can help keep your feet dry and comfortable. To minimize the effects of jet lag, "reset" your body's clock by adopting the time of your destination immediately upon arrival. In a **medical emergency,** call the **emergency number,** 144. That's for both Austria and Switzerland. Many of the first-aid centers and hospitals in major cities that *Let's Go* lists can provide you with medical care from an English-speaking doctor; consulates in major cities should also have a list. In most large towns, a rotating pharmacy is open 24 hours—consult the nearest pharmacy to find out which one is open for the night. *Let's Go* lists hospitals within individual city listings.

BEFORE YOU GO

For minor health problems, bring a compact first-aid kit, including bandages, aspirin, antibiotic cream, a thermometer, a Swiss Army knife with tweezers, a decongestant, tummy medicine, sunscreen, insect repellent, and burn ointment. Always go prepared with any **medication** you may need while away, as well as a copy of the prescription and/or a statement from your doctor. Travelers with chronic medical conditions should consult their physicians before leaving. While **Cortisone** is available over the counter in the U.S., a prescription is required in Switzerland. Be aware that matching prescriptions with foreign equivalents may be hard; bring an extra week's supply. Remember that a *Drogerie* sells only toilet articles like soap and tampons; to purchase any health products (including aspirin, cough drops, contact lens solution, and condoms) or to get prescriptions filled you must go to an *Apotheke*. Austrian and Swiss **pharmacists** often speak English and can suggest proper treatment if you describe your symptoms.

In your passport, write the names of any people you wish to be contacted in case of a medical emergency and a list any allergies or medical conditions you would want doctors to be aware of. For specific up-to-date information about health in the region, you can contact the **United States Centers for Disease Control and Prevention** (based in Atlanta, Georgia), which provides information for travelers around the world and maintains an international fax information service. Call 1-888-232-3299 and select an international travel directory; the requested information will be faxed to you. Similar information is available from the CDC website at http://www.cdc.gov. The **United States State Department** compiles Consular Information Sheets on health, entry requirements, and other issues for all countries of the world. Particularly helpful is the website at http://travel.state.gov. For general health information, contact the **American Red Cross.** The ARC publishes a First-Aid and Safety Handbook (US$5) available for purchase by contacting the American Red Cross, 285 Columbus Ave., Boston, MA 02116-5114 (tel. (800) 564-1234; open M-F 8:30am-4:30pm).

Those with medical conditions (e.g. diabetes, allergies to antibiotics, epilepsy, heart conditions) may want to obtain a **Medic Alert** identification tag (US$35 the first year, $15 annually thereafter), which identifies the disease and gives a 24-hour collect-call information number. Contact Medic Alert at (800) 825-3785, or write to Medic Alert Foundation, 2323 Colorado Ave., Turlock, CA 95382. Diabetics can contact the **American Diabetes Association,** 1660 Duke St., Alexandria, VA 22314 (tel. (800) 232-3472) to receive copies of the article "Travel and Diabetes" and a diabetic ID card, which explains the carrier's diabetic status in 18 languages.

If you are concerned about access to medical support, contact one of these two services: **Global Emergency Medical Services** (GEMS) has this thing called *MedPass* which provides 24-hour international medical assistance and support coordinated through registered nurses who have on-line access to your medical information, your primary physician, and a worldwide network of screened, credentialed English-speaking doctors and hospitals. Subscribers receive a personal medical record that contains vital information in case of emergencies. For more info call (800) 860-1111 (8:30am-5:30pm); fax (770) 475-0058; or write: 2001 Westside Dr., #120, Alpharetta, GA 30201. The **International Association for Medical Assistance to Travelers** (IAMAT) offers a membership ID card, a directory of English-speaking doctors around the world, and detailed charts on immunization requirements. Membership is free, though donations are appreciated and used for further research. Contact chapters in the **U.S.,** 417 Center St., Lewiston, NY 14092 (tel. (716) 754-4883, 8am-4pm/EST); fax (519) 836-3412; email iamat@sentex.net; http://www.sentex.net/~iamat), **Canada,** 40 Regal Rd, Guelph, Ontario, N1K 1B5 (tel. (519) 836-0102) or 1287 St. Clair Avenue West, Toronto, M6E 1B8 (tel. (416) 652-0137; fax (519) 836-3412), or **New Zealand,** P.O. Box 5049, Christchurch 5.

You don't want to purchase unecessary travel coverage, but if your regular insurance policy doesn't cover travel abroad, you may wish to purchase additional coverage. (See **Insurance,** p. 30).

WHILE YOU'RE THERE

Tick-borne encephalitis, a viral infection of the central nervous system, is transmitted during the summer by tick bites and by consumption of unpasteurized dairy products. Austrians often refer to the disease as *Gehirnhautentzündung* (literally, inflammation of the brain; it's similar to meningitis). Be extremely careful when walking through the woods: cover as much skin on your lower body as you can (however unpleasant and unfashionable long pants tucked into high socks may be in the summer, this slight inconvenience is preferable to a hospital stay) and consider using a good tick repellent. Do not attempt to remove ticks by burning them or coating them with nail polish remover or petroleum jelly.

Ticks also carry the infamous **Lyme disease,** a bacterial infection marked by a circular bull's-eye rash of 5cm (2in.) or more that appears around the bite. Other symptoms include fever, headache, and aches and pains. Antibiotics are effective if administered early. Left untreated, Lyme disease can cause problems in joints, the heart, and the nervous system. If you find a tick attached to your skin, grasp the tick's head with tweezers as close to your skin as possible and apply slow, steady traction. If you remove a tick before it has been attached for more than 24 hours, you greatly reduce your risk of infection.

Common sense goes a long way toward preventing **heat exhaustion:** relax in hot weather, drink lots of non-alcoholic fluids, and lie down inside if you feel awful. Continuous heat stress can eventually lead to **heatstroke,** characterized by rising body temperature, severe headache, and cessation of sweating. Wear a hat, sunglasses, and a lightweight longsleeve shirt to avoid heatstroke. Victims must be cooled off with wet towels and taken to a doctor as soon as possible.

Always drink enough liquids to keep your urine clear. Alcoholic beverages are dehydrating, as are coffee, strong tea, and caffeinated sodas. If you'll be sweating a lot, be sure to eat enough salty food to prevent electrolyte depletion, which causes severe headaches. Even **sunburn** is dangerous, as it means risk of skin cancer. It's also painful. If you get sunburned, drink more fluids than usual.

Overexposure to cold brings the risk of **hypothermia.** Warning signs are easy to detect: body temperature drops rapidly, coordination dulls, exhaustion sets in, speech slurs. The afflicted may start to shiver, to feel sleepy, to hallucinate, to suffer amnesia. *Do not let hypothermia victims fall asleep* if they are in the advanced stages—their body temperature will drop more and they may die. To avoid hypothermia, keep dry and stay out of the wind. In wet weather, wool and most synthetics, such as pile, will keep you warm. Most other fabrics (cotton!) will just make you colder. Dress in layers, and watch for **frostbite**—skin that has turned white, waxy, and cold. If you find frostbite do not rub the skin. Drink warm beverages, get dry, and slowly warm the area with dry fabric or steady body contact. Find a doctor.

CONTRACEPTION, AIDS, HIV, STDS

Reliable contraceptive devices may be difficult to find while traveling. Women on the pill should bring enough to allow for possible loss or extended stays. Bring a prescription, since forms of the pill vary a good deal. The availability and quality of condoms and contraceptive jelly vary in Austria and Switzerland—you may want to bring supplies from home. For info contact the **International Planned Parenthood Federation,** European Regional Office, Regent's College Inner Circle, Regent's Park, London NW1 4NS (tel. (0171) 487 7900; fax 487 7950).

Acquired Immune Deficiency Syndrome (AIDS) is a big and growing problem. The easiest mode of HIV transmission is through direct blood to blood contact with an HIV+ person; *never* share intravenous drug, tattooing, or other needles. The most common mode of transmission is sexual intercourse. Health professionals recommend the use of latex condoms; follow the instructions on the packet. Casual contact (including drinking from the same glass or using the same eating utensils as an infected person) does not pose a risk.

For more information on AIDS, call the **U.S. Center for Disease Control's** 24-hour Hotline at (800) 342-2437. In Europe, write to the **World Health Organization,** attn: Global Program on AIDS, Avenue Appia 20, 1211 Geneva 27, Switzerland (tel. (41 22) 791 21 11, fax. (41 22) 791 07 46, for statistical material on AIDS internationally. Or write to the **Bureau of Consular Affairs,** #6831, Department of State, Washington, D.C. 20520. Council's brochure, *Travel Safe: AIDS and International Travel,* is available at all Council Travel offices.

Sexually transmitted diseases (STDs) such as gonorrhea, chlamydia, genital warts, syphilis, and herpes are a lot easier to catch than HIV. Warning signs for STDs include: swelling, sores, bumps, or blisters on sex organs, rectum, or mouth; burning and pain during urination and bowel movements; itching around sex organs; swelling or redness in the throat and flu-like symptoms with fever, chills, and aches. If these symptoms develop, see a doctor immediately. When having sex, condoms may protect you from certain STDs, but oral or even tactile contact can lead to transmission.

■ Insurance

Travel insurance generally covers four basic areas: medical problems, property loss, trip cancellation/interruption, and emergency evacuation. Beware of buying unnecessary travel coverage—your regular insurance policies may well extend to travel-related medical problems and property loss.

Medical insurance (especially university policy medical insurance) often covers costs incurred abroad—check with your provider. Canadians should check with the provincial Ministry of Health or Health Plan Headquarters for details about extent of coverage. The Commonwealth Department of Health and Family Services can provide more information. Your **homeowners' insurance** (or your family's coverage) often covers theft during travel. Homeowners are generally covered against loss of travel documents (passport, plane ticket, railpass, etc.) up to US$500.

ISIC and **ITIC** provide basic insurance benefits, including US$100 per day of in-hospital sickness for a maximum of 60 days, and US$3000 of accident-related medical reimbursement (see **Youth, Student, and Teacher Identification,** p. 8). Most **American Express** cardholders receive automatic car rental (collision and theft, but not liability) insurance and ground travel accident coverage of US$100,000 on flight purchases made with the card. (Customer Service tel. (800) 528-4800).

Remember that insurance companies usually require a copy of the police report or evidence of having paid medical expenses (doctor's statements, receipts) before they will honor a claim and may have time limits on filing for reimbursement. Always carry policy numbers and proof of insurance. Check with each insurance carrier for specific restrictions and policies. Most have 24-hour hotlines.

Council and **STA** offer a range of plans that can supplement your basic insurance coverage, with options covering medical treatment and hospitalization, accidents, baggage loss, and even charter flights missed due to illness.

Access America, 6600 West Broad St., P.O. Box 11188, Richmond, VA 23230 (tel. (800) 284-8300; fax (804) 673-1491). Covers trip cancellation/interruption, on-the-spot hospital admittance costs, emergency medical evacuation, sickness, and baggage loss. 24hr. hotline (call collect (804) 673-1159 or (800) 654-1908).

Avi International, 30 Rue de Mogador, 75009 Paris, France (tel. 33 (0) 144 63 51 86; fax 33 (0) 140 82 90 35). Caters primarily to the international youth traveler, covering emergency travel expenses, medical/accident, dental, liability, and baggage loss. 24hr. hotline.

The Berkely Group/Carefree Travel Insurance, 100 Garden City Plaza, P.O. Box 9366, Garden City, NY 11530-9366 (tel. (800) 323-3149 or (516) 294-0220; fax (516) 294-1095; info@berkely.com; http://www.berkely.com). Offers 2 comprehensive packages including coverage for trip cancellation/interruption/delay, accident and sickness, baggage loss, bag delay, accidental death and dismemberment, and travel supplier insolvency. Trip cancellation/interruption may be purchased separately at a rate of US$5.50 per US$100 of coverage. 24hr. hotline.

Campus Travel, 105/106 St. Aldates, Oxford OX1 IDD (tel. (01865) 25 80 00; fax (01865) 79 23 78). Available to ISIC card holders only. Offers various per trip packages covering medical costs, property loss, trip cancellation/ interruption, personal liability, and extreme activities (i.e. bungee jumping). 24hr. hotline.

Globalcare Travel Insurance, 220 Broadway, Lynnfield, MA 01940 (tel. (800) 821-2488; fax (617) 592-7720; email global@nebc.mv.com; http://www.nebc.mv.com/globalcare.) Complete medical, legal, emergency, and travel-related services. On-the-spot payments and special student programs, including benefits for trip cancellation and interruption. GTI waives pre-existing medical conditions and provides coverage for the bankruptcy or default of cruise lines, airlines, or tour operators. Also included at no extra charge is a Worldwide Collision Damage Provision.

■ Alternatives to Tourism

PERMITS

To study in Switzerland for longer than three months, you need to fill out a residency permit and receive authorization from Swiss authorities. To study in Austria, citizens of non-EU countries must have visas. Because of Austria's EU status, citizens of member countries do not need visas to work or study in Austria. All foreigners, however, must have valid work permits. Most U.S. university programs will arrange permits for students. To work in either country, you must file residency forms from your country of current residence. When you submit your residency application, you must prove that you have been hired and that you have a place to live. While it's possible to go as a tourist and look for work, it's a catch-22: very few companies will hire you without a residency permit; getting a residency permit requires a job.

STUDY

Foreign study programs vary tremendously in expense, academic quality, living conditions, degree of contact with local students, and exposure to culture and luggage. There are soooo many exchange programs for high school students. Also tons for undergrads, which appropriate offices can tell you all about.

American Field Service (AFS), 310 SW 4th Ave., Ste. 630, Portland, OR 97204-2608 (tel. (800) 237-4636; fax (503) 241-1653; email afsinfo@afs.org; http://www.afs.org/usa). Offers summer, semester, and year-long homestay international exchange programs for high school students and graduating high school seniors. They do both Austria and Switzerland. Financial aid available.

American Institute for Foreign Study, College Division, 102 Greenwich Ave., Greenwich, CT 06830 (tel. (800) 727-2437, ext. 6084; http://www.aifs.com). Organizes programs for high school and college study in universities in Austria and other places. Summer, fall, spring, and year-long programs available. Scholarships available. Contact Yesenia Garcia with questions at ygarcia@aifs.com.

Association of Commonwealth Universities, John Foster House, 36 Gordon Square, London WC1H OPF, England (tel. (0171) 387 8572; fax (0170) 387 2655; e-mail info@acu.ac.uk; http://www.acu.ac.uk). Administers scholarship programs such as the Marshall and publishes information about Commonwealth universities.

Central College Abroad, Office of International Education, 812 University, Pella, IA 50219 (tel. (800) 831-3629; fax (515) 628-5375; email studyabroad@central.edu; http://studyabroad.com/central/). Offers semester- and year-long study abroad programs in Austria among other places. US$25 application fee. Scholarships available. Applicants must be at least 18 years old, have completed their freshman year of college, and have a minimum 2.5 GPA.

Childcare International, Ltd., Trafalgar House, Grenville Place, London NW7 3SA (tel. (0181) 959 36 11 or 906 3116; fax 906 3461; email office@childint.demon.co.uk; http://www.childint.demon.co.uk) offers *au pair* positions in Austria and Switzerland. Provides information on qualifications required and local language schools. They prefer a long placement but arrange summer work. Member of the International *Au Pair* Association. UK£80 application fee.

Council sponsors over 40 study abroad programs throughout the world. Contact them for more information (see **Travel Organizations** on p. 2).

Institute of International Education (IIE), 809 United Nations Plaza, New York, NY 10017-3580 (tel. (212) 984-5413; fax 984-5358). For book orders: IIE Books, Institute of International Educations, P.O. Box 371, Annapolis Junction, MD 20701 (tel. (800) 445-0443; fax (301) 953-2838; email iie-boks@iie.org). A nonprofit, international and cultural exchange agency, IIE's library of study abroad resources is open to the public Tu-Th 11am-3:45 pm. Publishes *Academic Year Abroad* (US$43, US$4 postage) and *Vacation Study Abroad* (US$37, US$4 postage).

Peterson's, P.O. Box 2123, Princeton, NJ 08543-2123 (tel. (800) 338-3282; fax (609) 243-9150; http://www.petersons.com). Comprehensive *Study Abroad* guide lists programs all over and provides essential information on the study abroad experience. Available at your local bookstore (US$27) or their toll-free number in the U.S. 20% off the list price when you order online: http://bookstore.petersons/com.

WORKING

There's no better way to submerge yourself in a foreign culture than to become a cog in its economy. It's easy to find a **temporary job,** but it will rarely be glamorous and may not even pay for your plane fare. Officially, you can hold a job in most countries only with a **work permit.** That's pretty much true in Austria and Switzerland. Your employer must obtain this document, usually by demonstrating that you have skills that locals lack—not the easiest of tasks. There are, however, ways to make it easier. Friends in your destination country can help expedite work permits or arrange work-for-accommodations swaps. Be an *au pair;* advertise to teach English. Many permit-less agricultural workers go untroubled by local authorities. European Union citizens can work in any EU country, and if your parents were born in an EU country, you may be able to claim dual citizenship or at least the right to a work permit. (Beware of countries where citizenship obligates you to do military service.) University foreign language departments may have connections to job openings abroad.

Peterson's (see Study Abroad) publishes a **Vacation Work series** with titles that include *Overseas Summer Jobs 1999, Work Your Way Around the World, Teaching English Abroad,* and *The International Directory or Volunteer Work* (US$16.95 each; available in bookstores Peterson's Customer Service, tel. 800-338-3282. 20% off list price if you order through their online bookstore, http://bookstore.petersons.com.)

Volunteer jobs are readily available all over. You may receive room and board in exchange for your labor. You can sometimes avoid the high application fees charged by the organizations that arrange placement by contacting workcamps directly; check with the organizations. Listings in Vacation Work Publications's *International Directory of Voluntary Work* (UK£9; postage UK£2.50) can be helpful.

Accord Cultural Exchange, 750 La Playa, San Francisco, CA 94121 (tel. (415) 386-6203); fax (415) 386-0240; email leftbank@hotmail.com; http://www.cognitext.com/accord), offers Austrian *au pair* jobs to 18-29-year olds. *Au pairs* work 30hr. per week. Light housekeeping and childcare in exchange for room and board plus US$250-400 per month salary. Program fees US$750 for the summer, US$1200 for the academic year. US$40 Application fee.

InterExchange, 161 Sixth Ave., New York, NY 10013 (tel. (212) 924-0446; fax 924-0575; email interex@earthlink.net) provides information on international work, *au pair* programs, and *au pair* positions in Austria and Switzerland.

Office of Overseas Schools, A/OS Room 245, SA-29, Dept. of State, Washington, D.C. 20522-2902 (tel. (703) 875-7800; fax 875-7979; email overseas.shools@dos.us-state.gov; http://state.gov/www/aboutstate/schools/). Keeps a list of schools abroad and agencies arranging placement of Americans abroad.

Surrey Books, 230 E. Ohio St., Chicago, IL 60611 (tel. (800) 326-4430; fax (312) 751-7330; email SurreyBk@aol.com;, http://www.surreybooks.com) publishes *How to Get a Job in Europe: The Insider's Guide* (1995 edition US$18).

Transitions Abroad Publishing, Inc., 18 Hulst Rd., P.O. Box 1300, Amherst, MA 01004-1300 (tel. (800) 293-0373; fax (413) 256-0373; email trabroad@aol.com; http://www.transabroad.com). Publishes a bi-monthly magazine listing all kinds of opportunities and printed resources for those seeking to study, work, or travel abroad. The possibilities are almost endless. They also publish *The Alternative Travel Directory,* a truly exhaustive listing of info for the "active international traveler," and *Work Abroad,* a comprehensive guide to finding a job overseas. For subscriptions (U.S. US$20 for 6 issues, Canada US$30, other countries US$42), contact them at Transitions Abroad, P.O. Box 1300, Amherst, MA 01003-1400.

Vacation Work Publications, 9 Park End St., Oxford OX1 1HJ, UK (tel. (01865) 24 19 78; fax 79 08 85; http://www.vacationwork.co.uk). Publishes a wide variety of guides and directories with job listings and info for the working traveler. Opportunities for summer or full-time work in numerous countries. Write for catalogue.

World Trade Academy Press, 50 E. 42nd St., #509, New York, NY 10017-5480 (tel. (212) 697-4999). Publishes *Looking for Employment in Foreign Countries* (US$16.50), which gives information on federal, commercial, and volunteer jobs abroad and advice on resumes and interviews. Check the library for *The Directory of American Firms Operating in Foreign Countries* (1996; US$200).

■ Specific Concerns

WOMEN TRAVELERS

Women travelers will likely feel safer in Austria and Switzerland than in other parts of Europe (like Budapest or Prague)—violent crime is generally rare. Socially defined gender roles are much more clearly demarcated in Austria and Switzerland than in the U.S. or Canada, although women's incomes are catching up with men's. Austria's feminist community thrives in Salzburg and Vienna, where a number of establishments cater to liberated clientele. Unlike some parts of southern Europe, catcalls and whistling are not acceptable behavior in Austria and Switzerland. In German-speaking areas, tell jerks to leave you alone by saying *"Lasse mich in Ruhe"* (lass mish in roo-uh). In French-speaking regions, *"Laissez-moi tranquille"* (lay-say mwa trrah-keel) is a useful phrase. In Italian Switzerland try, *"Vai via!"* (viy vee-uh.)

Women exploring on their own inevitably face additional safety concerns, but it's not hard to be adventurous without taking undue risks. Trust your instinct when choosing a place to stay: if you'd feel better somewhere else, move on. You might consider staying in hostels that offer single rooms that lock from the inside or in religious organizations that offer rooms for women only. Stick to centrally located accommodations and avoid solitary late-night treks. When traveling, always carry extra money for a phone call, bus, or taxi. Hitching is never safe for lone women.

Don't hesitate to seek out a police officer or a passerby if you are being harassed. *Let's Go* lists emergency numbers (including rape crisis lines) in the Practical Information listings of most cities. Memorize the emergency numbers in the countries you visit. A Model Mugging course will prepare you for a potential mugging and also raise your level of awareness and your confidence (see **Safety and Security,** p. 13).

Directory of Women's Media is available from the National Council for Research on Women, 11 Hanover Sq., 20th Fl., New York, NY 10005 (tel. (212) 785-7335; fax 785-7350). The publication lists women's publishers, bookstores, theaters, and news organizations (mail orders US$30).

A Journey of One's Own: Uncommon Advice for the Independent Woman Traveler, by Thalia Zepatos, (US$17). Interesting and full of good advice, with a bibliography of books and resources. **Adventures in Good Company: The Complete Guide to Women's Tours and Outdoor Trips,** on group travel by the same author, costs US$17. These books are available in bookstores across North America or can be ordered directly from the publisher. (US$2 shipping for the 1st book, 50¢ for each additional order). Available from The Eighth Mountain Press, 624 Southeast 29th Ave., Portland, OR 97214 (tel. (503) 233-3936; fax 233-0774; email soapston@teleport.com).

Women's Travel in Your Pocket, Ferrari Guides, P.O. Box 37887, Phoenix, AZ 85069 (tel. (602) 863-2408; ferrari@q-net.com; http://www.q-net.com), an annual guide for women (especially lesbians) traveling worldwide. Hotels, nightlife, dining, shopping, organizations, group tours, cruises, outdoor adventure, and lesbian events (US$14, plus shipping).

More Women Travel: Adventures, Advice & Experience, by Miranda Davies and Natania Jansz (Penguin, US$16.95). Essays by women travelers plus a decent bibliography and resource index. From Rough Guides, 345 Hudson St. 14th fl., New York, NY 10014 (tel. (212) 366 2348; fax 414 3395; email rough@panix.com; http://www.roughguides.com/women).

Active Women Vacation Guide, by Evelyn Kay (US$17.95; shipping free for *Let's Go* readers). Includes listings of 1000 trips worldwide offered by travel companies for active women and true stories of women's traveling adventures. Blue Panda Publications, 3031 Fifth St., Boulder, CO 80304 (tel. (303) 449-8474; fax 449-7525).

OLDER TRAVELERS

Austria and Switzerland have among the highest mean life spans in the world. It's a place full of hearty well-aged kids. Seniors often qualify for hotel and restaurant discounts as well as discounted admission to many tourist attractions. If you don't see a senior citizen price listed, ask and ye may receive. In **Switzerland,** women over 62 and men over 65 qualify as seniors, and women over 60 and men over 65 make the cut for senior status in **Austria.** A **Seniorenausweiß** (senior identification card) entitles holders to a 50% discount on all Austrian federal trains, Postbuses, and Bundes-Buses, and the card works as an ID for discounted museum admissions. The card costs about 350AS, requires a passport photo and proof of age, and is valid for one calendar year. It is available in Austria at railroad stations and major post offices. Both National Tourist Offices offer guides for senior citizens. Many discounts require proof of status; prepare to be carded. There are also agencies for senior group travel. **Elder-Treks** (597 Markham St., Toronto, ON, Canada, M6G 2L7 (tel. (800) 741-7956 or (416) 588-5000, fax 588-9839, email passages@inforamp.net; http://www.elder-treks.com) and **Walking the World** (P.O. Box 1186, Fort Collins, CO 80522 (tel. (970) 498-0500; fax 498-9100; email walktworld@aol.com), have trips in Europe.

Elderhostel, 75 Federal St., 3rd Fl., Boston, MA 02110-1941 (tel. (617) 426-7788; email Cadyg@elderhostel.org; http://www.elderhostel.org). For those 55 or over (spouse of any age). Programs at colleges, universities, and other learning centers in over 70 countries on a variety of subjects lasting 1-4 weeks.

The Globe Piquot Press, P.O. Box 833, Old Saybrook, CT 06475-0833 (tel. (800) 243-0495; fax (800) 820-2329; email: info@globe-piquot.com; http://www.globe-piquot.com). Publishes *Europe the European Way: A Traveler's Guide to Living Affordably in the World's Great Cities* (US$14) with hints for budget-conscious seniors considering long stays or retirement abroad.

National Council of Senior Citizens, 8403 Colesville Rd., Silver Spring, MD 20910-31200 (tel. (301) 578-8800; fax 578-8999). Memberships cost US$13 per year, US$33 for 3 years, or US$175 for a lifetime. Individuals or couples can receive hotel and auto rental discounts, a senior citizen newspaper, and use of a discount travel agency.

Pilot Books, 127 Sterling Ave., P.O. Box 2102, Greenport, NY 11944 (tel. (516) 477-1094 or (800) 79PILOT (797-4568); fax (516) 477-0978; email feedback@pilotbooks.com; http://www.pilotbooks.com). Publishes a large number of helpful guides including *Doctor's Guide to Protecting Your Health Before, During, and After International Travel* (US$10, postage US$2) and *Have Grandchildren, Will Travel* (US $10, postage US$2).

No Problem! Worldwise Tips for Mature Adventurers, by Janice Kenyon. Advice and info on insurance, finances, security, health, packing. US$16 from Orca Book Publishers, P.O. Box 468, Custer, WA 98240-0468.

A Senior's Guide to Healthy Travel, by Donald L. Sullivan (US$15; can be found at http://www.amazon.com). What it says, man.

Unbelievably Good Deals and Great Adventures That You Absolutely Can't Get Unless You're Over 50, by Joan Rattner Heilman. After you finish reading the title page, check inside for some great tips on senior discounts. US$10 from Contemporary Books, or on-line at http://www.amazon.com.

BISEXUAL, GAY, AND LESBIAN TRAVELERS

Austria and Switzerland are less tolerant of homosexuals than some other nations; this intolerance is especially pronounced in conservative western Austria. Few establishments will turn away homosexual couples, but public displays of affection are cultural taboo and could attract unfriendly attention in some rural areas. Very unfriendly. Places like Geneva, Zurich, and Vienna have just about every variety of homosexual organization and establishment, from biker and Christian groups to bars and barber shops, but these services can be difficult to find; tourist offices sometimes have info, otherwise check the local listings. The German word for gay is *schwule;* for lesbian, *lesben* (LES-ben) or *lesbische* (LEZ-bisch-uh). Bisexual is *bisexual* or simply *bi* (bee). In French, *homosexuelle* can be used for both men and women, but the preferred terms are *gai* (GEH) and *lesbienne* (les-bee-YENN).

The age of consent in **Austria** is 14. **Homosexuelle Initiative** (HOSI) is a nationwide organization with offices in most cities which provides information on gay and lesbian establishments, resources, and supports and publishes warnings about aggressively intolerant areas and establishments. HOSI Wien, II, Novarag. 40, Vienna (tel. 216 66 04), publishes Austria's leading gay and lesbian magazine, the *Lambda-Nachrichten,* quarterly. A number of smaller and alternative organizations operate throughout the country. **Switzerland** does not officially recognize gay couples (even though homosexual prostitution has been legal since 1992 and is now on par with heterosexual prostitution). The age of consent in Switzerland is 16. There are several gay working groups in the larger cities, such as **Homosexuelle Arbeitsgruppe. Dialogai,** headquartered in Geneva, av. Wendt 57; mailing address: Case Postale 27, CH-1211, Geneva 7 (tel. (022) 340 00 00; fax 340 03 98), formed a partnership with **l'Aide Suisse contre le Sida** (ASS), an organization that works against AIDS. Several gay publications are available in centers and bookshops; *Dialogai Info* provides information on French Switzerland, articles, interviews, and more. For information about organizations, centers, and other resources in specific cities, consult the city's **Practical Information** section; for information on bars and nightclubs, see the individual **Sights and Entertainment** sections. Listed below are more general contact organizations and publishers.

Damron Travel Guides, P.O. Box 422458, San Francisco, CA 94142-2458 (tel. (415) 255-0404 or (800) 462-6654; fax (415) 703-9049 or 703-8308; email damronco@damron.com; http://www.damron.com). Publishers of the *Damron Address Book* (US$15), which lists bars, restaurants, guest houses, and services catering to gay men. The *Damron Road Atlas* (US$16) contains color maps of 70 major cities and resorts along with listings of bars and accommodations. *The Women's Traveller* (US$13) lists over 7500 bars, restaurants, accommodations, bookstores, and services catering to lesbians. *Damron's Accommodations* lists gay and lesbian hotels around the world (US$19). Mail order is available for an extra US$5 shipping.

Ferrari Guides, P.O. Box 37887, Phoenix, AZ 85069 (tel. (602) 863-2408; fax 439-3952; email ferrari@q-net.com; http://www.q-net.com). Gay and lesbian travel guides: *Ferrari Guides' Gay Travel A to Z* (US$16), *Ferrari Guides' Men's Travel in Your Pocket* (US$16), *Ferrari Guides' Women's Travel in Your Pocket* (US$14), *Ferrari Guides' Inn Places* (US$16). Available in bookstores or by mail order (postage/handling US$5 for the 1st item, US$1 for each additional item mailed within the U.S. In Canada, 1st item $10. Overseas, call or write for shipping cost.)

Gayellow Pages, P.O. Box 533, Village Station, New York, NY 10014 (tel. (212) 674-0120; fax 420-1126; email gayellow@banet.net; http://gayellowpages.com). An annually updated listing of accommodations, resorts, hotlines, gay community centers, and other items of interest to the gay traveler.

Giovanni's Room, 345 S. 12th St., Philadelphia, PA 19107 (tel. (215) 923-2960; fax 923-0813; email giophilp@netaxs.com). An international feminist, lesbian, and gay bookstore with mail-order service that carries the publications listed here; they accept email orders.

International Gay and Lesbian Travel Association, 4331 N. Federal Hwy., Ste. 304, Fort Lauderdale, FL 33308 (tel. (954) 776-2626 or (800) 448-8550; fax (954) 776-3303; email IGLTA@aol.com; http://www.iglta.org). An organization of over 1350 companies serving gay and lesbian travelers worldwide. Call for lists of travel agents, accommodations, and events.

International Lesbian and Gay Association (ILGA), 81 rue Marché-au-Charbon, B-1000 Bruxelles, Belgium (tel./fax 32-2-502-24 71; email ilga@ilga.org; http://www.ilga.org). Not a travel service. Provides political information, such as homosexuality laws of individual countries.

Spartacus International Gay Guides, (US$32.95), published by Bruno Gmunder, Verlag GMBH, Leuschnerdamm 31, 10999 Berlin, Germany (tel. (49) 030 615 0030; fax (49) 030 615 9007; email bgvtravel@aol.com). Lists bars, restaurants, hotels, and bookstores around the world catering to gays. Also lists hotlines for gays in various countries and homosexuality laws for each country. Available in bookstores and in the U.S. by mail from Lambda Rising, 1625 Connecticut Ave. NW, Washington D.C., 20009-1013 (tel. (202) 462-6969).

DISABLED TRAVELERS

Austria and Switzerland are relatively accessible to travelers with disabilities (*Behinderung*). Tourist offices can usually offer info about which sights, services, etc. are accessible. Disabled visitors to **Austria** may want to contact the **Vienna Tourist Board,** Obere Augartenstr. 40, A-1025 Vienna (tel. (1) 211 14; fax 216 84 92), which offers booklets on accessible Vienna hotels and a general guide to the city for the disabled. The Austrian National Tourist Office in New York and Vienna offers many pages of listings for wheelchair-accessible sights, museums, and lodgings in Vienna—ask for the booklet *Wien für Gäste mit Handicaps (Vienna for Guests with Handicaps).* With three days notice, the Austrian railways will provide a wheelchair for the train. The international wheelchair icon or a large letter "B" indicates access. In **Switzerland,** disabled travelers can contact **Mobility International Schweiz,** Hard 4, CH-8408 Winterthur (tel. (052) 222 68 25; fax 222 68 38). Most Swiss buildings and restrooms have ramps. The Swiss Federal Railways have adapted most of their train cars for wheelchair access, and InterCity and long-distance express trains have wheelchair compartments. The Swiss National Tourist Office publishes a fact sheet detailing *Travel Tips for the Disabled.*

Cities, especially Vienna, Zurich, and Geneva, publish mounds of information for handicapped visitors. *Let's Go* attempts to indicate which youth hostels have full or partial wheelchair access. All Hilton, InterContinental, and Marriott hotels have wheelchair access, but these accommodations aren't cheap.

Those with disabilities should inform airlines and hotels of their disabilities when making arrangements for travel; some time may be needed to prepare special accommodations. Hotels and hostels have become more accessible to disabled persons, and many attractions are trying to make exploring the outdoors more feasible. Call ahead to restaurants, hotels, parks, and other facilities to find out about the existence of ramps, the widths of doors, the dimensions of elevators, etc.

Guide dog owners should inquire as to the specific quarantine policies of each destination country. At the very least, they will need to provide a certificate of immunization against rabies. Hertz, Avis, and National car rental agencies have hand-controlled vehicles at some locations.

There are also a number of more general books helpful to travelers with disabilities. The following organizations provide info or publications that might be of assistance:

The Diabetic Traveler, P.O. Box 8223 RW, Stamford, CT (tel. (203) 327-5832). A short quarterly offering advice on flying, eating abroad, and visiting extreme climates. A subscription ($18.95) includes a list of organizations worldwide.

Directions Unlimited, 720 N. Bedford Rd., Bedford Hills, NY 10507 (tel. (800) 533-5343; in NY (914) 241-1700; fax (914) 241-0243). Specializes in arranging individual and group vacations, tours, and cruises for the physically disabled. Group tours for blind travelers.

Flying Wheels Travel Service, 143 W. Bridge St., Owatonne, MN 55060 (tel. (800) 535-6790; fax 451-1685). Arranges trips for groups and individuals in wheelchairs or with other sorts of limited mobility.

Graphic Language Press, P.O. Box 270, Cardiff by the Sea, CA 92007 (tel. (760) 944-9594; email niteowl@cts.com; Contact person: A. Mackin). Publishes *Wheelchair Through Europe,* a guide covering accessible hotels, transportation, sightseeing and resources for disabled travelers in many European cities. Available for $12.95 (includes S&H) check payable to Graphic Language Press.

Mobility International USA (MIUSA), P.O. Box 10767, Eugene, OR 97440 (tel. (541) 343-1284 voice and TDD; fax 343-6812; email info@miusa.org; http://www.miusa.org). Sells the 3rd Edition of *A World of Options: A Guide to International Educational Exchange, Community Service, and Travel for Persons with Disabilities* (individuals US$35; organizations US$45).

Moss Rehab Hospital Travel Information Service, (tel. (215) 456-9600, TDD (215) 456-9602). A telephone information resource center on international travel accessibility and other travel-related concerns for those with disabilities.

Twin Peaks Press, P.O. Box 129, Vancouver, WA 98666-0129 (tel. (360) 694-2462; fax (360) 696-3210; email 73743.2634@compuserve.com; http://netm.com/mall/infoprod/twinpeak/helen.htm). Publishers of *Travel for the Disabled,* which provides travel tips, lists of accessible tourist attractions, and advice on other resources for disabled travelers (US$20). Also publishes *Directory of Travel Agencies for the Disabled* (US$20), *Wheelchair Vagabond* (US$15), and *Directory of Accessible Van Rentals* (US$10). Postage US$4 for 1st book, US$2 for each additional book.

MINORITY TRAVELERS

It is difficult to generalize and say that either Switzerland or Austria discriminates against any minorities, but minority travelers will undoubtedly encounter odd stares in smaller villages. The majority of travelers may never really notice anything, but will merely feel a prickly vibe from annoying once-overs. In Switzerland, a growing population of foreign workers (Turks, for example) has received an especially bad image in these recessionary times; minority travelers may feel some of this resentment. The French Swiss maintain that intolerance is particularly prevalent in German Switzerland. Austria is overwhelmingly ethnically and racially homogeneous, which might make some travelers feel uncomfortable. Actual run-ins, however, are rare—Austrians and Swiss tend to be much too mild-mannered to hurl crude insults or provoke physical violence. *Let's Go* asks that its researchers exclude from the guides establishments that discriminate. If in your travels, you encounter discriminatory treatment, you should firmly but calmly state your disapproval and leave it at that. Please mail a letter to *Let's Go* if the establishment is listed in the guide so that we can investigate the matter next year (see **Helping Let's Go** in the very front of this guide).

TRAVELERS WITH CHILDREN

Family vacations are recipes for disaster—unless you slow your pace and plan ahead. When deciding where to stay, remember the special needs of young children; if you pick a *Pension,* call ahead and make sure it's child-friendly. If you rent a car, make sure the rental company provides a car seat for younger children. Consider using a papoose on walking trips. Be sure that your child carries some sort of ID in case of emergency and arrange a meeting spot in case of separation when sight-seeing.

Restaurants often have children's menus and discounts. Virtually all museums and tourist attractions also have a children's rate. Children under two generally fly for 10% of the adult airfare on international flights (this does not necessarily include a seat). International fares are usually discounted 25% for children from two to 11.

Some of the following publications offer tips for adults traveling with children or distractions for the kids themselves. You can also contact the publishers to see if they have other related publications that you might find useful.

Backpacking with Babies and Small Children, (US$9.95). Published by Wilderness Press, 2440 Bancroft Way, Berkeley, CA 94704 (tel. (800) 443-7227 or (510) 843-8080; fax 548-1355; email wpress@ix.netcom.com; http://wildernesspress.com). The third edition scheduled for release in August 1998.

Take Your Kids to Europe, by Cynthia W. Harriman (US$16.95, shipping US$3.95). A budget travel guide for families. Published by Globe-Pequot Press, 6 Business Park Rd., Old Saybrook, CT 06475 (tel. (800) 285-4078; fax (860) 395-1418).

How to Take Great Trips with Your Kids, by Sanford and Jane Portnoy (US$9.95, shipping and handling US$3). Advice on how to plan trips geared toward the age of your children. The Harvard Common Press, 535 Albany St., Boston, MA. 02118 (tel. (888) 657-3755; fax 695-9794).

DIETARY CONCERNS

The growing health- and environmentally-conscious movements in Austria and Switzerland mean more options for vegetable-eaters. Vegans will have trouble outside of large cities such as Vienna, Zurich, and Geneva, but non-vegan vegetarians can find all sorts of traditional, traditionally meatless Austrian and Swiss food throughout both countries. Try *Steinpilze* (mushroom steaks), *Spaetzle* (a kind of noodle made with potatoes), some varieties of *Knödeln* (dumplings), many classic soups like *Fritatten-suppe* (soup with thin pancake strips in it), *Rösti, raclette,* or (obviously) fondue. Hiking areas are good places to look for specifically vegetarian restaurants. If you're looking for kosher, the Swiss National Tourist Office distributes the pamphlet *The Jewish City Guide of Switzerland* (published by Spectrumpress International, Spectrum-House, Tanegg., 8055 Zurich), which lists synagogues, rabbis, butchers, kosher hotels and restaurants, and other useful information and phone numbers for kosher and Jewish travelers. They also publish a fact sheet listing hotels and restaurants that serve vegetarian, organically grown, or whole food. The Austrian National Tourist Office offers similar publications.

The International Vegetarian Travel Guide, (UK£2) was last published in 1991. Order back copies from the Vegetarian Society of the UK (VSUK), Parkdale, Dunham Rd., Altringham, Cheshire WA14 4QG (tel. (0161) 928 0793; fax (0161) 926 9182; email veg@minxnet.co.uk; http://www.vegsoc.org). VSUK publishes other titles, including *The European Vegetarian Guide to Hotels and Restaurants.* Call or send a self-addressed, stamped envelope for a listing.

The Jewish Travel Guide lists synagogues, kosher restaurants, and Jewish institutions in over 80 countries. Available from Vallentine Mitchell Publishers, Newbury House 890-900, Eastern Ave., Newbury Park, Ilford, Essex, U.K. IG2 7HH (tel. (0181) 599 88 66; fax 599 09 84). It is available in the U.S. ($15 plus $3.00 shipping) from Sepher-Hermon Press, 1265 46th St., Brooklyn, NY 11219 (tel./fax (718) 972-9010; contact person Samuel Gross).

TRAVELING ALONE

There are many benefits to traveling alone, among them greater independence. Without distraction, you can write a great travel log, in the grand tradition of Mark Twain, John Steinbeck, and Hunter S. Thompson. That "travel log" thing has been done, though. As a lone traveler, you have greater opportunity to interact with the residents of the region you're visiting.

On the other hand, a solo traveler is a more vulnerable target for harassment and the distractions that accompany street theft. Lone travelers need to be organized and look confident at all times. Maintain contact with someone who knows your itinerary. A number of organizations supply information for solo travelers.

American International Homestays, P.O. Box 1754, Nederland, CO 80466 (tel. (303) 642-3088 or (800) 876-2048). Lodgings with English-speaking host families all over the world.

Connecting: Solo Traveler Network, P.O. Box 29088, 1996 W. Broadway, Vancouver, BC V6J 5C2, Canada (tel. (604) 737-7791 or (800) 557-1757; http://www.travel-wise.com/solo). Bi-monthly newsletter features member reports, going solo tips, single-friendly tips and travel companion ads. Annual directory lists holiday suppliers that avoid single supplement charges. Advice and lodging exchanges facilitated between members. Membership US$25.

A Foxy Old Woman's Guide to Traveling Alone, by Jay Ben-Lesser. Available in bookstores and from Crossing Press in Freedom, CA (tel. (800) 777-1048). Encompasses practically every specific concern, offering anecdotes and tips for anyone interested in solitary adventure US$11.

Roadrunner Hostelling Treks, 6762 A Centinela Ave., Culver City, CA 90230 (tel. (617) 984-1556 or (800) 873-5872). Inexpensive guided trips (maximum 13 travelers). Hostelling International accommodations.

Traveling Solo: Advice and Ideas for More Than 250 Great Vacations, by Eleanor Berman. Published by Globe-Pequot Press, 6 Business Park Rd., Old Saybrook, CT 06475 (tel. (800) 285-4078; fax (860) 395-1418). Vacation ideas and how to translate them into the perfect solo vacation. Chapters for women traveling alone, single parents, and older travelers. US$17.

■ Packing

The more stuff you have, the more stuff you have to lose. The larger your pack, the more cumbersome it is to carry and store safely. Before you leave, pack your bag, strap it on, and imagine yourself walking uphill for the next three hours. At the slightest sign of heaviness, unpack something. A good general rule is to lay out only what you absolutely need, then take half the clothes and twice the money.

LUGGAGE

If you plan to cover most of your itinerary by foot, a sturdy **backpack** is unbeatable. Unbeatable. A **suitcase** or **trunk** is harder to carry, which means less mobility. Hard-sided luggage is more durable but also heavier. Soft-sided luggage should have a PVC frame, a strong lining to resist bad weather and rough handling, and triple-stitched seams. If you are not backpacking, a lightweight **duffel bag** packed inside your luggage will be useful for storing dirty clothes, although a plastic bag does just as well. A smaller bag like a **daypack, rucksack,** or **courier bag** in addition to your pack or suitcase allows you to leave your big bag behind while sight-seeing and also works as an airplane carry-on. Guard your money, passport, railpass, and other important articles in a **moneybelt** or **neck pouch,** available at any good camping store, and keep it with you at all times. The moneybelt should tuck inside the waist of your clothes.

CLOTHING AND FOOTWEAR

When choosing your travel wardrobe, aim for versatility and comfort. No matter what time of year you are visiting Austria and Switzerland, be prepared for cold weather and shifting mountain climates. Black is a popular color because it doesn't show dirt, so you can just keep wearing it...and wearing it...for a while. In winter, bring warm clothing: pile or wool, hat and mittens, wind-proof layers. Summer in these countries brings rain. Appropriate **rain gear** includes a waterproof jacket and a backpack cover. Gore-Tex® is a miracle fabric that's both waterproof and breathable; it's all but mandatory if you plan on hiking. Avoid cotton as outerwear, especially if you'll be outdoors a great deal. (Many hikers swear that "cotton is death.") Even casual hikers should bring water-proof **hiking boots;** pavement-pounding city-types should wear well-cushioned **sneakers.** Break in your shoes before you leave. A double pair of socks—light silk or polypropylene inside and thick wool outside—will cushion feet, keep them dry, and help prevent blisters. Bring a pair of flip-flops for protection against the foliage and fungi that inhabit some hostel showers.

MISCELLANEOUS

Note that some items may not always be readily available or affordable on the road: razors, condoms, tampons, and contact lens solution. A **first-aid kit** (see **Health,** p. 16) can prove invaluable. Most **youth hostels** in Austria and Switzerland provide **sleepsacks.** Even if they don't, don't pay the linen charge—make the thing yourself. Fold a full-size sheet in half the long way and then sew it closed along the open long side and one of the short sides. You can also tape it shut with duck tape. *Let's Go* attempts to provide information on **laundromats** in the **Practical Information** for each city, but it may be easiest to use a sink. In Austria and Switzerland, electricity is 220 volts AC, enough to fry any 110V North American appliance. Visit a hardware store for an adapter (which changes the shape of the plug) and a converter (which changes the voltage). Get both or a two-in-one adapter-converter. Machines that heat-disinfect **contact lenses** will require a small converter (about US$20); consider switching temporarily to a chemical disinfection system. Contact lens supplies are sometimes rare or expensive in Austria and Switzerland. Bring enough saline and cleaner for your entire vacation. Bring a backup pair of glasses.

Film is expensive just about everywhere. Bring rolls from home and develop them at home. If you're not a serious photographer, you might want to consider bringing a **disposable camera** or two rather than an expensive permanent one.

Other useful items include: umbrella, resealable plastic bags (for damp clothes, soap, food, and pens), alarm clock, waterproof matches, sun hat, needle and thread, safety pins, sunglasses, tape player with headphones, pocketknife, notebook and pens, plastic water bottle, compass, string (makeshift clothesline and lashing material, necessary in hostage crisis), towel, padlock, whistle, toilet paper, flashlight, cold-water soap, earplugs, robot, insect repellant, electrical tape (for patching tears), clothespins, maps and phrasebooks, tweezers, garbage bags, and sunscreen.

Packing Light, the Austrian Way

Back in the summer of 1870, when the air was clean and all snow came from clouds, Austrian climbing legend Hermann von Barth took to the hills of the Karwendel Range in the Tirol and climbed no fewer than 88 peaks, 12 of which were first-ever ascents. His luggage: a drinking cup, binoculars, smelling salts, a lighter, a paintbrush to paint his name on each peak, and a bottle of poison in case he fell and wasn't able to rescue himself. He never fell.

GETTING THERE

The first challenge in European budget travel is getting there. Zurich is Switzerland's primary travel hub, but it's often cheaper to fly into Paris and take the TGV to your destination. Vienna is the cheapest destination in Austria, but it may be cheaper to fly into Munich and take a train to your destination. Traveling with an "open return" ticket can be pricier than fixing a return date and paying to change it. If you show up at the airport before your date of departure, the airline just might rewrite your ticket, even if it is supposedly precluded by company restrictions. Avoid one-way tickets— the flight to Europe may be economical, but the return fares can be outrageous.

■ By Plane

The price you pay for airfare varies widely depending on whom you purchase your ticket from and how flexible your travel plans are. Understanding the airline industry's byzantine pricing system is the best way of finding a cheap fare. Very generally, courier fares (if you can deal with restrictions) are the cheapest, followed by tickets bought from consolidators and stand-by seating. Last-minute specials, airfare wars, and charter flights can often beat these fares, however. Always get quotes from different sources; an hour or two of research can save you hundreds of dollars. Call every toll-free number and don't be afraid to ask about discounts, as it's unlikely they'll be volunteered. Knowledgeable **travel agents,** particularly those specializing in the region, can provide excellent guidance. Travel agents may not want to spend time finding the cheapest fares (for which they receive the lowest commissions), but if you travel often you should definitely find an agent who will cater to you and your needs and track down deals in exchange for your frequent business.

Students and others under 26 should never need to pay full price for a ticket. Seniors can also get great deals; many airlines offer senior traveler clubs or airline passes with few restrictions and discounts for their companions as well. Sunday newspapers often have travel sections that list bargain fares from the local airport. Outsmart airline reps with the phone-book-sized *Official Airline Guide* (check your local library; at US$359 per year, the tome costs as much as some flights), a monthly guide listing nearly every scheduled flight in the world and toll-free phone numbers for all the airlines that allow you to call in reservations directly. More accessible is Michael McColl's *The Worldwide Guide to Cheap Airfare* (US$15).

There's a wealth of travel information to be found on the Internet. The **Air Traveler's Handbook** (http://www.cs.cmu.edu/afs/cs.cmu.edu/user/mkant/Public/Travel/airfare.html) is excellent. **TravelHUB** (http://www.travelhub.com) provides a directory of travel agents that includes a searchable database of fares from over 500 consolidators (see **Ticket Consolidators**, below). Edward Hasbrouck maintains a **Consolidators FAQ** (http://www.travel-library.com/air-travel/consolidators.html) that provides great background on finding cheap international flights. Groups such as the **Air Courier Association** (http://www.aircourier.org) offer information about traveling as a courier and provide up-to-date listings of last minute opportunities. **Travelocity** (http://www.travelocity.com) operates a searchable, on-line database of published airfares that allows you to make reservations.

COMMERCIAL AIRLINES

The airlines' published airfares should be just the beginning of your search. Even if you pay an airline's lowest published fare, you may waste hundreds of dollars. For the adventurous or the bargain-hungry, there are other, perhaps more inconvenient or time-consuming options.

The commercial airlines' lowest regular offer is the **Advance Purchase Excursion Fare** (APEX); specials advertised in newspapers may be cheaper, but have more restrictions and fewer available seats. APEX fares provide you with confirmed reservations and allow "open-jaw" tickets (landing in and returning from different cities). Generally, reservations must be made seven to 21 days in advance, with seven- to 14-day minimum and up to 90-day maximum stay limits, and hefty cancellation and change penalties (fees rise in summer). Book APEX fares early during peak season; by May you will have a hard time getting the departure date you want.

BUDGET TRAVEL AGENCIES

Students and people under 26 ("youth") with proper ID qualify for enticing reduced airfares. These are rarely available from airlines or travel agents, but instead from student travel agencies that negotiate special reduced-rate bulk purchase with the airlines, then resell them. Return-date change fees also tend to be low (around US$35 per segment through Council or Let's Go Travel). Most flights are on major airlines, though in peak season some agencies may sell seats on less reliable chartered aircraft. Student travel agencies can also help non-students and people over 26, but probably won't be able to get them the same low fares.

Campus Travel, 52 Grosvenor Gardens, London SW1W 0AG (http://www.campus-travel.co.uk). 46 branches in the U.K. Student and youth fares on plane, train, boat, and bus travel. Skytrekker, flexible airline tickets. Discount and ID cards for students and youths, travel insurance for students and those under 35, and maps and guides. Puts out travel suggestion booklets. Phone booking service: in Europe call (0171) 730 34 02; in North America (0171) 730 21 01; worldwide (0171) 730 81 11; in Manchester (0161) 273 17 21; in Scotland (0131) 668 33 03.

Council Travel (http://www.ciee.org/travel/index.htm), the travel division of Council, is a full-service travel agency specializing in youth and budget travel. They offer discount airfares on scheduled airlines, railpasses, hosteling cards, low-cost accommodations, guidebooks, budget tours, travel gear, and international student (ISIC), youth (GO25), and teacher (ITIC) IDs. U.S. offices include: Emory Village, 1561 N. Decatur Rd., **Atlanta,** GA 30307 (tel. (404) 377-9997); 2000 Guadalupe, **Austin,** TX 78705 (tel. (512) 472-4931); 273 Newbury St., **Boston,** MA 02116 (tel. (617) 266-1926); 1138 13th St., **Boulder,** CO 80302 (tel. (303) 447-8101); 1153 N. Dearborn, **Chicago,** IL 60610 (tel. (312) 951-0585); 10904 Lindbrook Dr., **Los Angeles,** CA 90024 (tel. (310) 208-3551); 1501 University Ave. SE #300, **Minneapolis,** MN 55414 (tel. (612) 379-2323); 205 E. 42nd St., **New York,** NY 10017 (tel. (212) 822-2700); 953 Garnet Ave., **San Diego,** CA 92109 (tel. (619) 270-6401); 530 Bush St., **San Francisco,** CA 94108 (tel. (415) 421-3473); 1314 NE 43rd St. #210, **Seattle,** WA 98105 (tel. (206) 632-2448); 3300 M St. NW, **Washington, D.C.** 20007 (tel. (202) 337-6464). **For U.S. cities not listed,** call 800-2-COUNCIL (226-8624). Also 28A Poland St. (Oxford Circus), **London,** W1V 3DB (tel. (0171) 287 3337), **Paris** (tel. (146) 55 55 65), and **Munich** (tel. (089) 39 50 22).

Educational Travel Centre (ETC), 438 North Frances St., Madison, WI 53703 (tel. (800) 747-5551; fax (608) 256-2042; email edtrav@execpc.com; http://www.edtrav.com). Flight information, HI-AYH cards, Eurail, and regional rail passes. Write for their free pamphlet *Taking Off.* Student and budget airfares.

Students Flights Inc., 5010 East Shea Blvd., #A104, **Scottsdale, AZ** 85254 (tel. (800) 255-8000 or (602) 951-1177; fax 951-1216; email jost@isecard.com; http://isecard.com). Also sells Eurail and Europasses and international student exchange identity cards.

Council Charter, 205 E. 42nd St., New York, NY 10017 (tel. (212) 661-0311; fax 972-0194). A combination of cheap charter and scheduled airfares from U.S. gateways to most major European destinations. One-way fares and open jaws available.

CTS Travel, 220 Kensington High St., W8 (tel. (0171) 937 33 66 for travel in Europe, tel. 937 33 88 for travel world-wide; fax 937 90 27). Tube: High St. Kensington. Also at 44 Goodge St., W1. Tube: Goodge St. Specializes in student/youth travel and discount flights.

Eurolines, 52 Grosvenor Gardens, Victoria, London SW1W 0AU (main office tel. (0158) 240 45 11, or tel. (0171) 730 82 35 in London). Specializes in coach travel throughout Western and Eastern Europe.

Let's Go Travel, Harvard Student Agencies, 17 Holyoke St., Cambridge, MA 02138 (tel. (617) 495-9649; fax 495-7956; email travel@hsa.net; http://hsa.net/travel). Railpasses, HI-AYH memberships, ISICs, ITICs, FIYTO cards, guidebooks (including every *Let's Go* at a substantial discount), maps, bargain flights, and a complete line of budget travel gear. All items available by mail; call or write for a catalogue (or see the catalogue in center of this publication).

Rail Europe Inc., 226 Westchester Ave., White Plains, NY 10604 (tel. (800) 438-7245; fax 432-1329; http://www.raileurope.com). Sells all Eurail products and passes, national railpasses, and point-to-point tickets. Up-to-date information on all rail travel in Europe.

STA Travel, 6560 Scottsdale Rd. #F100, Scottsdale, AZ 85253 (tel. (800) 777-0112 nationwide; fax (602) 922-0793; http://sta-travel.com). A student and youth travel organization with over 150 offices worldwide offering discount airfares for young travelers, railpasses, accommodations, tours, insurance, and ISICs. 16 offices in the U.S. including: 297 Newbury Street, **Boston,** MA 02115 (tel. (617) 266-6014); 429 S. Dearborn St., **Chicago,** IL 60605 (tel. (312) 786-9050); 7202 Melrose Ave., **Los Angeles,** CA 90046 (tel. (213) 934-8722); 10 Downing St., Ste. G, **New York,** NY 10003 (tel. (212) 627-3111); 4341 University Way NE, **Seattle,** WA 98105 (tel. (206) 633-5000); 2401 Pennsylvania Ave., **Washington, D.C.** 20037 (tel. (202) 887-0912); 51 Grant Ave., **San Francisco,** CA 94108 (tel. (415) 391-8407); **Miami,** FL 33133 (tel. (305) 461-3444). In the U.K., 6 Wrights Ln., **London** W8 6TA (tel. (0171) 938 47 11 for North American travel). In New Zealand, 10 High St., **Auck-**

land (tel. (09) 309 97 23). In Australia, 222 Faraday St., **Melbourne** VIC 3050 (tel. (03) 349 69 11).

Travel CUTS (Canadian Universities Travel Services Limited), 187 College St., Toronto, ON M5T 1P7 (tel. (416) 979-2406; fax 979-8167; email mail@travelcuts). Canada's national student travel bureau and equivalent of Council, with 40 offices across Canada. Also in the U.K., 295-A Regent St., **London** W1R 7YA (tel. (0171) 637 31 61). Discounted domestic and international airfares open to all; special student fares to all destinations with valid ISIC. Issues ISIC, FIYTO, GO25, and HI hostel cards, as well as railpasses. Offers free *Student Traveller* magazine, as well as information on the Student Work Abroad Program (SWAP).

Usit Youth and Student Travel, 19-21 Aston Quay, O'Connell Bridge, Dublin 2 (tel. (01) 677-8117; fax 679-8833). In the U.S.: New York Student Center, 895 Amsterdam Ave., New York, NY, 10025 (tel. (212) 663-5435; email usitny@aol.com). Additional offices in Cork, Galway, Limerick, Waterford, Maynooth, Coleraine, Derry, Athlone, Jordanstown, Belfast, and Greece. Specializes in youth and student travel. Offers low-cost tickets and flexible travel arrangements all over the world. Supplies ISIC and FIYTO-GO 25 cards in Ireland only.

TICKET CONSOLIDATORS

Most airlines in the world are heavily regulated, which means that their published fares may be significantly more expensive than the market price available from a **ticket consolidator.** Ticket consolidators resell unsold tickets on commercial and charter airlines at unpublished fares; a 30-40% price reduction is not uncommon. Consolidator tickets provide the greatest discounts over published fares when you are traveling on short notice, on a high-priced trip, to an off-beat destination, or in the peak season when published fares are jacked way up. There are rarely age constraints or stay limitations, but unlike tickets bought through an airline, you won't be able to use your tickets on another flight if you miss yours and you will have to go back to the consolidator rather than the airline to get a refund. Keep in mind that these tickets are often for coach seats on connecting (not direct) flights on foreign airlines, and that frequent-flyer miles may not be credited. Decide what you can and can't live with before shopping.

Not all consolidators deal with the general public; many only sell tickets through travel agents. **Bucket shops** are retail agencies that specialize in getting cheap tickets. Although ticket prices are marked up slightly, bucket shops generally have access to a larger market than would be available to the public and can get tickets from wholesale consolidators. Generally, a dealer **specializing** in travel to the country of your destination will provide more options and cheaper tickets. The **Association of Special Fares Agents** (ASFA) maintains a database of specialized dealers for particular regions (http://www.ntsltd.com/asfa). Look for bucket shops' tiny ads in the travel section of weekend papers; in the U.S., the Sunday *New York Times* is a good source; in Australia, use the *Sydney Times.* Kelly Monaghan's *Consolidators: Air Travel's Bargain Basement* is invaluable for more information, as it lists consolidators by location and destination (US$8 plus $3.50 shipping) from the Intrepid Traveler, P.O. Box 438, New York, NY 10034 (email info@intrepidtraveler.com).

Be a smart shopper; check out the competition. Among the many reputable and trustworthy companies are, unfortunately, some shady wheeler-dealers. Contact the local Better Business Bureau to find out how long the company has been in business and its track record. Although not necessary, it is preferable to deal with consolidators close to home so you can visit in person if necessary. Ask to receive your tickets as quickly as possible so you have time to fix any problems. Get the company's policy in writing: insist on a **receipt** that gives full details about the tickets, refunds, and restrictions, and record who you talked to and when. It may be worth paying with a credit card (despite the 2-5% fee) so you can stop payment if you never receive your tickets. Beware the "bait and switch" gag: shyster firms will advertise a super-low fare and then tell a caller that it has been sold. Although this is a viable excuse, if they can't offer you a price near the advertised fare on *any* date, it is a scam to lure in customers—report them to the Better Business Bureau. Also ask about accommodations and car rental discounts; some consolidators are doin' that too.

Regional specialists are better. The following agents provide general services. For destinations **worldwide,** try **Airfare Busters,** (in Washington, D.C. (tel. (202) 776-0478), Boca Raton, FL (tel. (561) 994-9590), and Houston, TX (tel. (800) 232-8783); **Pennsylvania Travel,** Paoli, PA (tel. (800) 331-0947); **Cheap Tickets,** in Los Angeles, CA, San Francisco, CA, Honolulu, HI, Seattle, WA, and New York, NY, (tel. (800) 377-1000); **Interworld** (tel. (305) 443-4929; fax 443-0351); and **Travac** (tel. (800) 872-8800; fax (212) 714-9063; email mail@travac.com; http://www.travac.com). **NOW Voyager,** 74 Varick St. #307, New York, NY 10013 (tel. (212) 431-1616; fax (212) 334-5243; email info@nowvoyagertravel.com; http://www.nowvoyagertravel.com) acts as a consolidator and books discounted international flights, mostly from New York as well as courier flights (see **Courier Companies and Freighters,** below) for an annual fee of US$50. For a processing fee, depending on the number of travelers and the itinerary, **Travel Avenue,** Chicago, IL (tel. (800) 333-3335; fax (312) 876-1254; http://www.travelavenue.com) will search for the lowest international airfare available, including consolidated prices, and will even give you a 5% rebate on fares over US$350. To **Europe,** try **Rebel,** Valencia, CA (tel. (800) 227-3235; fax (805) 294-0981; email travel@rebeltours.com; http://www.rebeltours.com) or Orlando, FL (tel. (800) 732-3588).

COURIER COMPANIES

Those who travel light should consider flying internationally as a **courier,** where ridiculously low fares often come at the price of heavy restrictions. The company hiring you will use your checked luggage space for freight; you're usually only allowed to bring carry-ons. You are responsible for the safe delivery of the baggage claim slips (given to you by a courier company representative) to the representative waiting for you when you arrive—don't screw up or you will be blacklisted as a courier. You will probably never see the cargo you are transporting—the company handles it all—and airport officials know that couriers are not responsible for the baggage checked for them. Restrictions to watch for: you must be over 21 (18 in some cases), have a valid passport, and procure your own visa (if necessary); most flights are round-trip only with short fixed-length stays (usually one week); only single tickets are issued (but a companion may be able to get a next-day flight); and most flights out of the US are from New York. Keep in mind that last-minute deals for all courier flights can get you significantly cheaper or even free flights. Becoming a member of the **Air Courier Association** (tel. (800) 282-1202; http://www.aircourier.org) is a good way to start; they give you a listing of all reputable courier brokers and the flights they are offering, along with a hefty courier manual and a bi-monthly newsletter of updated opportunities ($30 one-time fee plus $28 annual dues). For an annual fee of $45, the **International Association of Air Travel Couriers,** 8 South J St., P.O. Box 1349, Lake Worth, Florida 33460 (tel. (561) 582-8320; email iaatc@courier.org; http://www.courier.org) informs travelers (via computer, fax, and mailings) of courier opportunities worldwide. **NOW Voyager,** 74 Varick St. #307, New York, NY 10013 (tel. (212) 431-1616; fax 334-5243; email info@nowvoyagertravel.com; http://www.nowvoyagertravel.com), acts as an agent for many courier flights worldwide primarily from New York and offers special last-minute deals to such cities as London, Paris, Rome, and Frankfurt for as little as US$200 round-trip plus a US$50 registration fee. (They also act as a consolidator; see **Ticket Consolidators,** above.) Another agent to try is Halbart Express, 147-05 176th St., Jamaica, NY 11434 (tel. (718) 656-5000; fax 917-0708; offices in Chicago, Los Angeles, and London).

You can also go directly through courier companies in New York, or check your bookstore, library, or on-line at http://www.amazon.com for handbooks such as *Air Courier Bargains* (US$15 plus $3.50 shipping from the Intrepid Traveler, tel. (212) 569-1081; email info@intrepidtraveler.com; http://intrepidtraveler.com). *The Courier Air Travel Handbook* (US$10 plus $3.50 shipping) explains how to travel as an air courier and contains names, phone numbers, and contact points of courier companies. It can be ordered directly from Bookmasters, Inc., P.O. Box 2039, Mansfield, OH 44905 (tel. (800) 507-2665).

STAND-BY FLIGHTS

Airhitch, 2641 Broadway, 3rd Floor, New York, NY 10025 (tel. (800) 326-2009 or (212) 864-2000; fax 864-5489) and Los Angeles, CA (tel. (310) 726-5000), will add a certain thrill to the prospects of when you will leave and where exactly you will end up. Complete flexibility in the dates and cities of arrival and departure is necessary. Flights to Europe cost US$159 each way when departing from the Northeast, $239 from the West Coast or Northwest, $209 from the Midwest, and $189 from the Southeast. Travel within Europe is also possible, with rates ranging from $79-139. The snag is that you buy not a ticket, but the promise that you will get to a destination near where you're intending to go within a window of time (usually 5 days) from a location in a region you've specified. You call in before your date-range to hear all of your flight options for the next seven days and your probability of boarding. You then decide which flights you want to try to make and present a voucher at the airport that grants you the right to board a flight on a space-available basis. This procedure must be followed again for the return trip. Be aware that you may only receive a monetary refund if all available flights that departed within your date-range from the specified region are full, but future travel credit is always available. There are several offices in Europe, so you can wait to register for your return; the main one is in Paris (tel. (1) 47 00 16 30).

AirTech.Com, 588 Broadway #204, New York, NY 10012 (tel. (212) 219-7000; fax 219-0066; email fly@airtech.com; http://www.airtech.com) offers a very similar service. Their travel window is one to four days. Rates to and from Europe (continually updated; call and verify) are: Northeast US$169; West Coast US$229; Midwest/Southeast US$199. Upon registration and payment, AirTech.Com sends you a FlightPass with a contact date falling soon before your travel window when you are to call them for flight instructions. Note that the service is one-way—you must go through the same procedure to return—and that no refunds are granted unless the company fails to get you a seat before your travel window expires. AirTech.Com also arranges courier flights and regular confirmed-reserved flights at discount rates.

Be sure to read all the fine print in your agreements with either company—a call to The Better Business Bureau of New York City may be worthwhile. Be warned that it is difficult to receive refunds, and that clients' vouchers will not be honored when an airline fails to receive payment in time.

■ By Boat

If you really have travel time to spare, **Ford's Travel Guides,** 19448 Londelius St., Northridge, CA 91324 (tel. (818) 701-7414; fax 701-7415) lists **freighter companies** that will take passengers worldwide. Ask for their *Freighter Travel Guide and Waterways of the World* (US$16, plus $2.50 postage if mailed outside the US).

ONCE THERE

■ Tourist Information and Town Layouts

The **Swiss National Tourist Office** and the **Austrian National Tourist Office** both publish a wealth of information about tours and vacations; every single town has a tourist office. To simplify things, all offices are marked by a standard green "i" sign (blue in Switzerland). *Let's Go* lists tourist offices in the Practical Information section of each city. The staff may or may not speak English—the skill is not a requirement in smaller towns, and we'll try and let you know whether they do or don't. Tourist offices are good for free maps. In Swiss cities, look for the excellent **Union Bank of Switzerland maps,** which have very detailed streets and sites.

One thing to keep in mind is that the Austrian and Swiss creative palette for small-town names is pretty meager. Many towns, even within the same state or province, have the same names (Gmünd or Stein, for instance). Most Austrian and Swiss train stations have luggage storage, currency exchange, and bike rentals (at a discount if you have a train ticket for that day or a valid railpass). The **post office** is often next door to the train station, even in larger cities. Most towns are small enough that all sights are within walking distance. Public transportation is usually pretty good, too. Buy local public transport tickets from *Tabak* stands, which sell them for reduced rates. Most ticket validation is based on the honor system, and many tourists interpret that as a free ride. Though certainly a tempting budget option, **Schwarzfahren** (black riding, i.e., riding without a ticket) can result in big anti-budget fines, and playing "dumb tourist" probably won't work. Watch out for the man.

■ Getting Around

BY TRAIN

European trains retain the charm and romance that their North American counterparts lost generations ago. Second-class travel is pleasant, and compartments, which seat from two to six, are excellent places to meet fellow itinerants of all ages and nationalities. Trains are also a good place to be a spy. Train trips tend to be short since both Austria and Switzerland are relatively small. Get your stuff together a few stops early since trains pause only two to three minutes before zipping off. For longer trips, make sure that you are on the correct car, as trains sometimes split at crossroads. Towns in parentheses on schedules require a train switch at the town listed immediately before the parenthesis. "Salzburg-Attnang-Puchheim-(Bad Ischl-Hallstatt)" means that in order to get to Bad Ischl or Hallstatt, you have to disembark at Puchheim and pick up a different train. You might want to ask if your route requires a change of trains, as the schedules are sometimes about as decipherable as dolphins.

Trains are in no way theft-proof; lock the door of your compartment when you nap and keep your valuables on your person at all times. Non-smokers probably won't be comfortable in smoking compartments, which tend to be very, very smoky. For overnight travel, a tight, open bunk called a *couchette* is an affordable luxury (about US$20; reserve at the station at least several days in advance).

The **Österreichische Bundesbahn** (ÖBB), Austria's federal railroad, is one of Europe's most thorough and efficient. The ÖBB prints the yearly *Fahrpläne Kursbuch Bahn-Inland*, a compilation of all rail, ferry, and cable-car transportation schedules in Austria. The massive compendium is available at any large train station, along with its companion tomes, the *Kursbuch Bahn-Ausland* for international trains, and the *Internationales Schlafwagenkursbuch* for sleeping cars.

Getting around Switzerland is also a snap. Federal **(SBB, CFF)** and private railways connect most towns and villages, with trains running in each direction on an hourly basis. **Schnellzüge** (express trains) speed between metropoli, while **Regionalzüge** chug into podunk cowtowns. The national telephone number for rail information is 157 22 22 and has English-speaking operators.

Be aware that sometimes only private train lines go to remote tourist spots, and therefore Eurail and Swisspasses might not be valid. Yellow signs announce departure times *(Ausfahrt, départ, partenze)* and platforms *(Gleis, quai, binario)*. White signs are for arrivals *(Ankunft, arrivé, arrivo)*. On major Austrian lines, make reservations at least a few hours in advance.

International Passes

Buying a railpass is both a popular and sensible option under many circumstances. Ideally conceived, a railpass allows you to jump on any train in Europe, go wherever you want whenever you want, and change your plans at will. With your railpass you will receive a timetable for major routes and a map with details on possible ferry, steamer, bus, car rental, hotel, and **Eurostar** (the high speed train linking London and Paris or Brussels) discounts. In practice, it's not so simple. You still have to stand in line to pay for supplements, seat reservations, and couchette reservations, and you have to have your pass validated when you first use it. Railpasses don't always pay off. For ballpark estimates, consult the **DERTravel** or **RailEurope** railpass brochure for prices of point-to-point tickets. If you're under age 26, BIJ tickets are probably a viable option (see **Rail tickets,** p. 39).

A **Eurailpass** remains perhaps the best option for non-EU travelers who plan to cover long distances. Eurailpasses are valid in most of Western Europe (not Britain, though). Eurailpasses and Europasses are designed by the EU itself, and are purchasable only by non-Europeans almost exclusively from non-European distributors. These passes must be sold at uniform prices determined by the EU, so no one travel agent is better than another as far as the pass itself is concerned. However, some agents tack on a $10 handling fee or offer perks with your purchase, so shop around.

The first class Eurailpass rarely pays off; it is offered for 15 days (US$538), 21 days (US$698), one month (US$864), two months (US$1224), or three months (US$1512). Those traveling in a group of two to five might prefer the **Eurail Saverpass,** which allows unlimited first-class travel for 15 days (US$458 per person), 21 days (US$594), one month (US$734), two months (US$1040), or three months (US$1286). Travelers ages 12-25 can buy a **Eurail Youthpass,** good for 15 days (US$376), 21 days (US $489), one month (US$605), two months (US$857), or three months (US $1059) of second-class travel. The two-month pass is most economical. **Eurail Flexipasses** allow limited first-class travel within a two-month period: 10 days (US$634), 15 days (US$836). These prices drop to $540 and $710, respectively, when traveling in a group of two to five. **Youth Flexipasses,** for those under 26 who wish to travel second-class, are available for US$444 or US$585, respectively. Children 4-11 pay half price, and children under 4 travel free.

The **Europass** combines France, Germany, Italy, Spain, and Switzerland in one plan. With a Europass you can travel in any of these five countries from five to fifteen days within a window of two months. First-class adult prices begin at US$326 and increase incrementally by US$42 for each extra day of travel. With purchase of a first-class ticket you can buy an identical ticket for your traveling partner for 40% off. Second-class youth tickets begin at US$216 and increase incrementally by $29 for each extra day of travel. Children between the ages of 4-11 travel for half the price of a first-class ticket. You can add associate countries (Austria/Hungary, Belgium/Luxembourg/Netherlands, Greece Plus (Greece and ADN/HML ferry between Italy and Greece), and Portugal) for a fee: $60 for one associated country; $90 for two; $110 for three, and $120 for all four. The Europass introduces planning complications; you must plan your routes so that they only make use of countries you've "purchased." They're serious about this: if you cut through a country you haven't purchased, you will be fined.

You should plan your itinerary before buying a Europass. It will save you money if your travels are confined to between three and five adjacent Western European countries, or if you know that you want to go only to large cities. Europasses are not appropriate if you like to take lots of side trips—you'll waste rail days. If you're tempted to add lots of rail days and associate countries, consider the Eurailpass.

It is best to buy your Eurail or Europass before leaving. Otherwise, once you are in Europe, you will probably have to use a credit card to buy over the phone from a railpass agent in a non-EU country (one on the North American east coast will be closest), who can send the pass to you by express mail. Contact Council Travel, Travel CUTS, Let's Go Travel (see **Budget Travel Agencies,** p. 27), or almost any travel agent handling European travel. Eurailpasses are not refundable once validated; if your pass is completely unused and unvalidated and you have the original purchase documents, you can get an 85% refund from the place of purchase. You can only get a replacement for a lost pass if you've purchased insurance on it under the Pass Protection Plan (US$10). All Eurailpasses can be purchased from a travel agent, or from **Rail Europe Group,** 500 Mamaroneck Ave., Harrison, NY 10528 (tel. (800) 438-7245; fax (800) 432-1329 in the U.S.; and tel. (800) 361-7245; fax (905) 602-4198 in Canada; http://www.raileurope.com), which also sells point-to-point tickets. They offer special rates for groups of 10 or more traveling together. **DER Travel Services,** 9501 W. Devon Ave. Suite #301, Rosemont IL 60018 (tel. (800) 782-2424; fax (800) 282-7474; http://www.dertravel.com) also deals in rail passes and point-to-point tickets.

For EU citizens, there are **InterRail Passes,** for which six months' residence in Europe makes you eligible. There are 8 InterRail zones: A (Rep. of Ireland, Great Britain Passenger Railway, N. Ireland), B (Norway, Sweden, and Finland), C (Germany, Austria, Denmark, and Switzerland), D (Croatia, Czech Rep., Hungary, Poland, and Slovakia), E (France, Belgium, Netherlands, and Luxembourg), F (Spain, Portugal, and Morocco), G (Italy, Greece, Slovenia, Turkey, and the ADN/HML ferries between Italy and Greece), and H (Bulgaria, Romania, Yugoslavia, and Macedonia). You can buy a pass good for 22 days in one zone (under 26 UK£159, over 26 £229), or one month in two (£209, £279), three (£229, £309), or all 8 (£259, £349) zones. For information and ticket sales in Europe contact **Student Travel Center,** 1st Fl. 24 Rupert St., London, W1V7FN (tel. (0171) 437 01 21, 437 63 70, 437 81 01, or 434 13 06; fax 734 38 36; http://student-travel-centre.com). Tickets are also available from travel agents or main train stations throughout Europe.

Austria

Children under six travel free in Austria. Fares are 50% off for children ages six to 14. The **Austrian Rail Pass** is valid for four days of travel within a 10-day period on all rails, including Wolfgangsee ferries and private lines (2nd class US$111, 1st class US$165). **Austrian Rail Pass Junior,** for travelers under 15, provides the same discounts as its parent, but for less (2nd class US$64, 1st class US$95). The card itself has no photo, so you must carry a valid ID in case of inspections. Keep in mind that the Rail Pass Junior is cheaper than many round-trip fares, so it may be an economical option even for short stays. The pass also entitles its holders to a 50% discount on bicycle rental in over 160 railway stations as well as the steamers of Erste Donau Dampfschiffahrts Gesellschaft (EDDG) operating between Passau, Linz and Vienna. The pass is sold in the U.S. by Rail Europe. **Bundesnetzkarte** are valid for unlimited travel through Austria, also including Wolfgangsee ferries and private lines. The cards getcha half-price tickets for Bodensee and Danube ferries, and there's no surcharge on EC and SC first-class trains. (1 month of 2nd class 3800AS, 1st class 5700AS. Picture necessary.) The passes are sold only in Austria.

Switzerland

In Switzerland, children under 16 can travel free when accompanied by an adult with the **Swiss Family Card** (20SFr, no expiration date), which is not connected with the Swiss Family Robinson gift package. A **Swisspass** grants unlimited free travel on government-operated trains, ferries, buses, and private railways, and a 25-50% discount on many mountain railways and cable cars. Second-class prices are as follows: a four-day pass costs US$176; eight-day US$220; 15-day US$256; one month US$350 (ages 6-16 half-price, free if traveling with parents and the Swiss Family Card). The pass is sold abroad through Rail Europe or any major U.S. travel agency. Depending on exchange rates, it may be cheaper to buy the pass at train stations in Switzerland. The pass also has a very strict no-replacement policy. A **Swiss Flexipass** (US$176) is valid for any three days of second-class travel within 15 days. Unless you're planning to speed through Switzerland, the pass may not pay for itself. **Regional Passes** are available in major tourist offices for holders of Eurailpasses (50-175SFr). The **Swiss Card,** sold only abroad, works as a one-month Half-Fare Card and provides one free round-trip from an airport or border station (US$96). Travelers who plan on driving might consider the **Swiss Rail 'n 'Drive Pass.** It works like a Swiss Flexipass but adds three days of car rental with unlimited mileage and unlimited travel on some of the private railways, such as the Glacier Express near Zermatt and the Panoramic Express. If you're traveling with three or four people, only two will have to buy the pass and the others need only buy the Swiss Flexipass. The pass includes car rental with manual transmission only, and rates vary depending on the car category you choose (2nd class runs US$325-415).

Rail Tickets

You can **purchase tickets** at every train station, at Bahn-Total service stations, at the occasional automat, or from the conductor for a small surcharge. You can pay by check. Over 130 stations accept the major credit cards as well as American Express Traveler's Cheques and Eurocheques.

For travelers under 26, **BIJ** tickets (Billets Internationals de Jeunesse) are a great alternative to railpasses. Available for international trips within Europe, they knock 20-40% off regular fares. Tickets are good for 60 days after purchase and allow a number of stopovers along the normal direct route of the train journey. Issued for a specific international route between two points, they must be used in the direction and order of the designated route (side- or back-tracking must be done at your expense) and must be bought in Europe. Tickets are available from European travel agents, at Wasteels or Eurotrain offices (usually in or near train stations), or directly at the ticket counter in some nations. Contact Wasteels in Victoria Station, adjacent to Platform 2, London SW1V 1JT (tel. (0171) 834 70 66; fax 630 76 28).

British and Irish citizens **over the age of 60** can buy their national senior pass and receive a 30% discount on first- and second-class travel in Austria and Switzerland. Restrictions on travel time may apply.

Useful Resources

The ultimate reference for planning rail trips is the **Thomas Cook European Timetable** (US$28; US$39 which includes a map of Europe with all train and ferry routes; postage US$5). This timetable, updated monthly, covers all major and most minor train routes in Europe. In North America, order it from **Forsyth Travel Library** (see p. 3). In Europe find it at any **Thomas Cook Money Exchange Center;** in the rest of the world call 044 1733 503 571 or write Thomas Cook Publishing, P.O. Box 227, Thorpe Wood, Peterborough, PE3 6PU, UK. Also available from Forsyth Travel library or in bookstores is **Traveling Europe's Trains** (US$15) by Jay Brunhouse, with maps and sightseeing suggestions. Available in most bookstores or from **Houghton Mifflin Co.,** 222 Berkeley St., Boston, MA 02116 (tel. (800) 225-3362; fax (800) 634-7568; http://www.hmco.com) is the annual **Eurail Guide to Train Travel in the New Europe** (US$15), giving timetables, instructions, and prices for international train trips, day trips, and excursions in Europe. **Hunter Publishing,** P.O. Box 7816, Edison, NJ 08818 (tel. (800) 255-0343; fax (732) 417-1744; http://www.hunterpublishing.com), offers a number of rail atlases and travel guides. The huge online bookstore at **http://www.amazon.com** also sells and ships most of the above titles.

BY BUS

Trains cost a pretty penny. Fortunately, Austria and Switzerland have a fair range of bus services. **Eurolines,** 4 Cardiff Rd., Luton LU1 1PP (tel. (01582) 40 45 11; fax (01582) 40 06 94); in London, 52 Grosvenor Gardens, Victoria (tel.(0171) 730 82 35); email welcome@eurolines.uk.com; http://www.eurolines.co.uk), is Europe's largest operator of Europe-wide coach services. A Eurolines Pass offers unlimited 30-day (under 26 and over 60 UK£159; 26-60 UK £199) or 60-day (under 26 and over 60, UK£199, 26-60 UK£249) travel between 30 major tourist destinations. Eurolines also offers **Euro Explorers,** seven complete travel loops throughout Europe with set fares and itineraries. **Eurobus UK Ltd.,** Coldborough House, Market Street, Bracknell, Berkshire RG121JA (tel.(01344) 30 03 01; fax (01344) 86 07 80; email info@eurobus.uk.com; http://www.eurobus.uk.com), offers cheap bus trips in 25 major cities in 10 major European countries for those between ages 18 and 38. The buses, with English speaking guides and drivers, stop door-to-door at one hostel or budget hotel per city, and let you hop on and off. Tickets are sold by zone; any one zone costs US$195, any two zones cost US$299, all three zones US$319. Included with purchase of all three zones or added for a nominal fee with other tickets is **London Link,** a London/Paris return ticket. Travelers under 26 are eligible for discounts on all tickets. For purchase in the United States contact Commonwealth Express (tel. (800) EUROBUS); in Canada contact Travel CUTS (see **Budget Travel Agencies,** p. 39).

Austria

The efficient Austrian system consists mainly of orange **BundesBuses** that generally complement the train system, serving mountain areas inaccessible by train rather than duplicating long-distance, intercity routes already covered by rail. Bus stations are usually adjacent to the train station. They cost about the same as trains, but no rail-passes are valid. Always purchase round-trip tickets if you plan to return to your starting point. Buy tickets at a ticket office at the station or from the driver. For buses in heavily touristed areas during high season (such as the Großglockner Straße in summer), you should probably make reservations. All public buses are non-smoking.

Anyone can buy discounted tickets, valid for one week, for any particular route. A **Mehrfahrtenkarten** gives you six tickets for the price of five. A **Seniorenausweiß** for women over 60 and men over 65 entitles senior citizens to half-price bus and train fares for a year (350AS). **Children under six** ride free as long as they're on a lap. **Children ages 6-15** and **large pets** (other than seeing-eye dogs) ride for half-price within Austria. Trips can be interrupted under certain conditions, depending on your ticket—be sure to ask. Small, regional bus schedules are available for free at most post offices. For more **bus information,** call (0222) 711 01 within Austria (outside Austria dial (1) instead of (0222)).

Switzerland

PTT **postal buses,** a barrage of banana-colored, three-brake-system coaches delivered to you expressly by the Swiss government, connect rural villages and towns, picking up the slack where trains fail to go. Swisspasses are valid on many buses, Eurailpasses are not. Even with the Swisspass, you might have to pay a bit extra (5-10SFr) if you're riding one of the direct, faster buses. In cities, public buses transport commuters and shoppers alike to outlying areas. Buy tickets in advance at automatic machines, found at most bus stops. The system works on an honor code and inspections are infrequent, but expect to be hit for 30-50SFr if you're caught riding without a valid ticket. *Tageskarte,* valid for 24 hours of free travel, run 2-7.50SFr, but Swiss cities are so small that you might as well travel by foot.

BY AIRPLANE

What d'ya want a plane for? Austria and Switzerland are train and bus countries. Many youth discounts can make airfare comparable to train tickets for longer distances (Geneva to Prague, for instance), but even these discounts can't touch railpass deals. Flying across Europe on regularly scheduled flights can devour your budget. **Alitalia** (tel. (800) 223-5730; http://www.alitalia.it) sells "Europlus": in conjunction with a transatlantic flight on Alitalia, for US\$299 you may purchase a package of three flight coupons good for anywhere Alitalia flies within Europe; unlimited additional tickets cost \$100. To non-Europe residents, **Lufthansa** (http://www.lufthansa.com) offers "Discover Europe," a package of three flight coupons that vary in cost, depending on country of origin. For US residents, the tickets cost US\$125-200 each depending on season and destination; up to six additional tickets are US\$105-175 each (tel. (800) 399-LUFT (5838); fax (800) 522-2329).

US citizens can also purchase **Eurair** passes (US\$90 each, airport taxes not included, reservations recommended) to travel between 50 European cities (information tel. (888) 387-2479; fax (512) 404 1291; http://www.eurair.com). The **Air Travel Advisory Bureau** in London (tel. (0171) 636 50 00; http://www.atab.co.uk), can also point the way to discount flights. In addition, many European airlines offer visitor ticket packages, which give intercontinental passengers discounts on flights within Europe (as well as on accommodations and car rentals) after arrival. Check with a travel agent for details.

BY CAR AND VAN

Yes, there really is no speed limit on the Autobahn. Cars offer speed, freedom, access to the countryside, and an escape from the town-to-town mentality of trains. Unfortunately, they also insulate you from the *esprit de corps* of rail traveling, if you haven't done that kind of thing before. Although a single traveler won't save by renting a car, four usually will. If you can't decide between train and car travel, you may benefit from a combination of the two; Rail Europe and other railpass vendors offer rail-and-drive packages for both individual countries and all of Europe. Travel agents may offer other options. Fly-and-drive packages are often available from travel agents or airline/rental agency partnerships.

To rent a car in **Austria,** you must be over 21 (older in some cases) and must carry an International Driver's Permit and a valid driver's license that you have had for at least one year (see **Driving Permits and Car Insurance,** p. 10). Most Austrian companies restrict travel into Hungary, the Czech Republic, Poland, and maybe Slovakia. Rental taxes are high (21%). In **Switzerland,** the minimum rental age varies by company but is rarely below 21. You must possess a valid driver's license that you have had for at least one year (foreign licenses are valid). Rates for all cars rented in Switzerland include an obligatory 40SFr annual **road toll,** called a *vignette*.

You can **rent** a car from a U.S.-based firm (Alamo, Avis, Budget, or Hertz) with European offices, from a European-based company with local representatives (Europcar), or from a tour operator (Auto Europe, Europe By Car, Kemwel Holiday Autos, and Rob Liddiard Travel), which will arrange a rental for you from a European company at its own rates. Multinationals offer greater flexibility, but tour operators often strike better deals. Rentals vary by company, season, and pick-up point. Expect to pay US$80-400 per week, plus tax (5-25%), for a teensy car. Reserve well before leaving for Europe and pay in advance if at all possible. It is always significantly less expensive to reserve a car from the U.S. than from Europe. Always check if prices quoted include tax and collision insurance; some credit card companies will cover this automatically. Ask about discounts and check the terms of insurance, particularly the size of the deductible. Ask your airline about special fly-and-drive packages; you may get up to a week of free or discounted rental.

Try **Alamo** (tel. (800) 522-9696; http://www.goalamo.com); **Auto Europe,** 39 Commercial St., P.O. Box 7006, Portland, ME 04101 (tel. (800) 223-5555; fax (800) 235-6321; email webmaster@autoeurope.com; http://www.autoeurope.com); **Avis Rent a Car** (tel. (800) 331-1084; http://www.avis.com), with locations throughout western and eastern Europe; **Budget Rent a Car** (tel. (800) 472-3325; http://www.budgetrentacar.com); **Europe by Car,** 1 Rockefeller Plaza, New York, NY 10020 (tel. (800) 223-1516 or (212) 581-3040; in California (800) 252-9401; fax (212) 246-1458; http://www.europebycar.com); **Hertz Rent a Car** (tel. (800) 654-3001; http://www.hertz.com), throughout Europe; **Kemwel Holiday Autos** (tel. (800) 678-0678; email kha@kemwel.com; http://www.kemwel.com); **Payless Car Rental** (tel. (800) 729-5377) in the U.K.; or **Rob Liddiard Travel** (tel. (800) 272-3299 or (818) 980-9133; email liddiard@jps.net);

For longer than 17 days, **leasing** can be cheaper than renting; it is often the only option for those ages 18-21. The cheapest leases are agreements to buy the car and then sell it back to the manufacturer at a prearranged price. As far as you're concerned, though, it's a lease and doesn't entail enormous financial transactions. Leases generally include insurance coverage and are not taxed. The most affordable ones usually originate in Belgium, France, or Germany. Expect to pay at least US$1200 for 60 days. Contact **Auto Europe, Europe by Car, Kemwel Holiday Autos,** or **Rob Liddiard Travel.** You will need to make arrangements in advance.

If you're brave and know what you're doing, **buying** a used car or van in Europe and selling it just before you leave can provide the cheapest wheels for longer trips. Check with consulates for import-export laws concerning used vehicles, registration, and safety and emission standards. Camper-vans and motor homes give the advantages of a car without the hassle and expense of finding lodgings. Most of these vehicles are diesel-powered and deliver roughly 36-45km per gallon of diesel fuel, which is cheaper than gas. David Shore and Patty Campbell's **Europe by Van and Motorhome** (US$14; postage US$3, overseas US$6) guides you through the entire process of renting, leasing, buying, and selling vehicles in Britain and on the Continent, including buy-back options, registration, insurance, and dealer listings. To order, write, call, or email Shore/Campbell Publications, 1842 Santa Margarita Dr., Fallbrook, CA 92028 (tel./fax (800) 659-5222 or (760) 723-6184; email shorecam@aol.com; http://members.aol.com/europevan).

Eric Bredesen's **Moto-Europa** (US$16; shipping US$5), available from Seren Publishing, 2935 Saint Anne Dr., Dubuque, IA 52001 (tel. (800) 387-6728; fax (319) 583-7853), is a thorough guide to all these options and includes itinerary suggestions, a motorists' phrasebook, and chapters on leasing and buying vehicles. More general info is available from the **American Automobile Association** (AAA), Travel Agency Services Dept., 1000 AAA Dr., Heathrow, FL 32746 (tel. (800) 222-4357, (407) 444-4300, or (407) 894-3333; http://www.aaa.com). For regional numbers of the **Canadian Automobile Association** (CAA), call (800) 222-4357 or go to their website (http://www.caa.ca).

On the Road

Austrian and Swiss highways are excellent. With armies of mechanized road crews ready to remove snow at moment's notice, roads at altitudes of up to 1500m generally remain open throughout winter. (Mountain driving does present special challenges, however; see **Personal Safety,** p. 14.) The **speed limit** is 50km per hour (31mph) within cities unless otherwise indicated; outside towns, the limit is 130km per hour (81mph) on highways and 100km per hour (62mph) on all other roads. Driving under the influence of alcohol is a serious offense—fines begin at 700SFr (5000AS) and rise rapidly from there. Violators may also lose their licenses. The legal blood-alcohol limit is *very low.*

Many small Austrian and Swiss towns forbid cars to enter; some forbid only visitors' cars, require special permits, or restrict driving hours. Parking poses further problems: it's unavailable or restricted in some small cities, and while parking garages exist in larger cities, you'll have to battle the tourist hordes for a spot. Blue lines on the sidewalks mark short-term parking areas; purchase tickets for these spots from the machine nearby. **Gasoline stations** are self-service and open around the clock. To use them, first insert money into the pump. U.S. gasoline credit cards (or regular credit cards) are accepted only at American gas stations, including Exxon, Mobil, Shell, and Texaco. Consult local tourist offices for further information on driving.

EU citizens driving in Austria and Switzerland don't need any special documentation—registration and license will suffice. All cars must carry a first-aid kit and a red emergency triangle. All passengers in both countries must wear seatbelts, and children under 12 may not sit in the front passenger seat unless a child's seatbelt or a special seat is installed. Emergency phones are located along all major highways. The **Austrian Automobile, Motorcycle, and Touring Club** (ÖAMTC; tel. (1) 71 19 97, in emergencies 120) provides an English-language service and sells a set of eight detailed road maps, far superior to the tourist office's map. (Open daily 6am-8pm.) The **Swiss Touring Club,** rue Pierre-Fatio 9, CH-1211 Geneva 3 (tel. (022) 737 12 12) operates road patrols that assist motorists in need; call 140 for help.

BY BICYCLE

Today, biking is one of the key elements of the classic budget Eurovoyage. With the proliferation of mountain bikes, you can do some serious natural sight-seeing. Remember that touring involves pedaling both yourself and whatever you store in the **panniers** (bags that strap to your bike). Take some reasonably challenging daylong rides at home to prepare yourself before you leave, and have your bike tuned up by a reputable shop. Wear visible clothing, drink plenty of water (even if you're not thirsty), and use the international signals for turns. Know how to fix a modern derailleur-equipped mount and change a tire, and practice on your own bike. A few simple tools and a good bike manual will be invaluable. For info about touring routes, consult national tourist offices or any of the numerous books available. The **Touring Club Suisse,** Cyclo Tourisme, chemin Riantbosson 11-13, CH-1217 Meyrin (tel. (022) 785 12 22; fax 785 12 62), will send you information, maps, brochures, route descriptions, and mileage charts. May, June, and September are prime biking months. **The Mountaineers Books,** 1001 S.W. Klickitat Way #201, Seattle, WA 98134 (tel. (800) 553-4453 or (206) 223-6303; fax 223-6306; email mbooks@mountaineers.org; http://www.mountaineers.org) offers several nation-specific tour books. Send for a free catalogue. **Michelin road maps** are clear and detailed.

If you are nervous about striking out on your own, **Blue Marble Travel** (in Canada tel. (519) 624-2494; fax 624-4760; email blumarbl@mgl.ca; in Paris tel. (01) 42 36 02 34; fax (01) 42 21 14 77; email blumarbl@club-internet.fr; in U.S. tel. (800) 258-8689 or (973) 326-9533; fax 326-8939; email blumarbl@gti.net; http://www.blumarbl.com) offers bike tours designed for adults aged 20 to 50. Pedal with or without your 10 to 15 companions through the Alps. Full-time grad students may get discounts, and "stand-by" fares may be obtained through the Paris office. **CBT Tours** offers one- to seven-week biking, mountain biking, and hiking tours, priced around US$95 per day, including all lodging and breakfasts, one-third of all dinners, complete van support, airport transfers, three staff, and extensive route notes and maps each day. Tours run May through August, with departures every seven to 10 days. In 1999, CBT will visit Switzerland among other places. Contact CBT Tours, 415 W. Fullerton, #1003, Chicago, IL 60614 (tel. (800) 736-BIKE (2453) or (773) 404-1710; fax (773) 404-1833; email adventure@cbttours.com; http://www.cbttours.com).

Many airlines will count your bike as your second free piece of luggage, although a few charge. The additional or automatic fee runs about US$60-110 each way. Bikes must be packed in a cardboard box with the pedals and front wheel detached; airlines sell bike boxes at the airport (US$10). Most ferries let you take your bike for free or a nominal fee. You can always ship your bike on trains, though the cost varies from small to substantial.

Riding a bike with a frame pack strapped on it or your back is about as safe as pedaling blindfolded over a sheet of ice; panniers are essential. The first thing to buy, however, is a **bike helmet** (about US$25-50). U-shaped **Citadel** or **Kryptonite locks** are expensive (starting at US$30), but the companies insure their locks against theft of your bike for one to two years. **Bike Nashbar,** 4111 Simon Rd., Youngstown, OH 44512 (tel. (800) 627-4227; fax (800) 456-1223; http://www.nashbar.com), has excellent prices and cheerfully beats advertised competitors' offers by US$.05. They ship anywhere in the U.S. or Canada.

Renting a bike beats bringing your own if your touring will be confined to one or two regions. *Let's Go* lists bike rental shops for most larger cities and towns. Some youth hostels rent bicycles for low prices. In Switzerland, train stations rent bikes and often allow you to drop them off elsewhere, and Austrian train stations generally reduce rental rates for travelers holding train tickets or valid Eurailpasses. Some stations also rent racing, mountain, and tandem bikes. Reservations are recommended, and you should bring photo ID.

BY MOPED AND MOTORCYCLE

Motorized bikes have long spiced up European roads with their flashy colors and perpetual buzz. They don't use much gas, can be put on trains and ferries, and are a good compromise between the high cost of car travel and the limited range of bicycles. However, they're uncomfortable for long distances, dangerous in the rain, and unpredictable on rough roads. Always wear a helmet; never ride with a backpack. If you've never been on a moped before, a twisting Alpine road isn't the place to start. Motorcycles are more expensive and normally require a license, but are better for long distances. **Bosenberg Motorcycle Excursions,** Mainzer Str. 54, 55545 Bad Kreuznach, Germany (tel. (011) 49 671 673 12; fax (011) 49 671 671 53; email Bosenberg@compuserve.com; http://www.bosenberg.com) arranges tours in the Alps, Austria, France, Italy, and Switzerland; they also rent motorcycles from April to October.

Before renting, ask if the quoted prices include tax and insurance or you may be hit with an unexpected fee. Avoid handing your passport over as a deposit; if you have an accident or mechanical failure, you may not get it back until you cover all repairs. Pay ahead of time.

BY THUMB

Hitching means entrusting your life to a random person who happens to stop beside you on the road and risking theft, assault, and sexual harassment. In spite of these risks, there are things to be gained—you can meet locals and get where you're going.

Men and women traveling in groups and men traveling alone might consider hitching (called *"Autostop"*) beyond the range of bus or train routes. If you're a woman traveling alone, don't hitch. It's just too dangerous. A man and a woman are a safer combination, two men will have a harder time, and three will go nowhere. Avoid getting in the back of a two-door car, and never let go of your backpack. Don't get into a car that you can't exit again in a hurry. If you ever feel threatened, insist on getting out. Acting as if you are going to open the car door or vomit on the upholstery will usually get a driver to stop. Nocturnal hitching is particularly risky.

As for the actual process itself, where one stands is vital. Experienced hitchers pick a spot (well lit, if at night) outside of built-up areas, where drivers can stop, have time to look over potential passengers as they approach, and return to the road without causing an accident. Hitching (or even standing) on super-highways is usually illegal: one may only thumb at rest stops or at the entrance ramps to highways. In the **Practical Information** section of many cities, *Let's Go* lists the tram or bus lines that take travelers to strategic points for hitching out. Success will depend on appearance. Most Europeans signal with an open hand rather than a thumb; many write their destination on a sign in large, bold letters. Drivers prefer hitchers who are neat and wholesome—no one stops for anyone wearing sunglasses or carrying weapons, so leave your international terrorist costume at home.

Most Western European countries offer a ride service (listed in the Practical Information for major cities), a cross between hitchhiking and the ride boards common at many universities, which pairs drivers with riders; the fee varies according to destination. Riders and drivers can enter their names on the internet through the **Taxistop** website (http://www/taxistop.be). Not all of these organizations screen drivers and riders; ask in advance.

BY FOOT

Much of Europe's grandest scenery is accessible only by foot. *Let's Go* describes many daytrips for those who want to hoof it, but native inhabitants (northern Europeans are obsessive hikers), hostel proprietors, and fellow travelers are the best source of information. See **Camping, Hiking, and the Outdoors** for extensive listings and information. **Walking Europe from Top to Bottom** by S. Margolis and G. Harmon details one of Europe's most popular trails (US$11); check your local bookstore.

■ Accommodations

Like most things Austrian and Swiss, accommodations in these countries are usually clean, orderly, and expensive. Wherever you stay, be sure to ask for a **guest card.** Normally, the "card" is merely a copy of your receipt for the night's lodging, sometimes available only after staying three nights or more. Guest cards generally grant discounts to local sports facilities, hiking excursions, town museums, and public transportation. In Austria, the 10AS tax that most accommodations slap on bills fund these discounts—take advantage of them to get your money's worth.

Let's Go is not an exhaustive guide to budget accommodations. Most local tourist offices distribute extensive listings (the *Gastgeberverzeichnis*), and many will reserve a room for a small fee. National tourist offices (and **Travel Organizations, p. 3**) will also supply more complete lists of campsites and hotels. Be aware that *Privatzimmer* and *Pensionen* may close their doors without notice; it's best to call ahead.

Are You Ready to Choose Exciting Moments?

For Example: The lovely olympic city of Innsbruck within the heart of the European Alps. We offer the budget accomodation for skiing and sightseeing. It's young, it's trendy, it's open to the world. It's THE solution for groups, families and individuals. It's one out of more than hundred modern youth hostels in Austria. Be ready to choose: pure nature, crystal-clear lakes, historic cities, thrilling adventures in the heart of Europe.

ÖSTERREICHISCHES
JUGENDHERBERGSWERK

Austria is ready for you!

For more information contact the Austrian Youth Hostelling Association: call ++431-533 18 33, email: oejhw@oejhw.or.at, www.oejhw.or.at/oejhw/

HOSTELS

Hostels (*Jugendherbergen* in German, *Auberges de Jeunesse* in French, *Ostelli* in Italian) are the hubs of the gigantic backpacker subculture that rumbles through Europe every summer, providing innumerable opportunities to meet travelers from all over the world. Hostels are generally dorm-style accommodations, often in single-sex large rooms with bunk beds, although some hostels do offer private rooms for families and couples. They sometimes have kitchens and utensils for your use, bike or moped rentals, storage areas, and laundry facilities. There can be drawbacks: some hostels close during certain daytime "lock-out" hours, have a curfew, don't accept reservations, impose a maximum stay, or, less frequently, require that you do chores. Fees range from US$5 to $25 per night. Check out the **Internet Guide to Hostelling** (http://www.hostels.com), which provides a directory of hostels from around the world in addition to oodles of information about hosteling and backpacking worldwide. **Eurotrip** (http://www.eurotrip.com/accommodation/accommodation.html) has information and reviews on budget hostels and several international hostel associations. The Backpackers Guide offers sometimes haphazard information and links to hostels and national directories around the world.

For their various services and lower rates at member hostels, hosteling associations, especially **Hostelling International (HI),** can definitely be worth joining. HI hostels, over 4500 of them, are scattered worldwide and many accept reservations via the International Booking Network (IBN) for a nominal fee. Reservations can be made from any other IBN hostel or via phone. From within the U.S. call (202) 783-6161; outside call your respective national hosteling organization or check http://www.hiayh.org/ushostel/reserva/ibn3.htm for international IBN booking numbers. HI's umbrella organization's web page lists the web addresses and phone numbers of all national associations and can be a great place to begin researching hostelling in a specific region (http://www.iyhf.org). Although you can join HI on the road, it's much easier to do so at home. Here are some of the national associations:

An Óige (Irish Youth Hostel Association), 61 Mountjoy St., Dublin 7 (tel. (353) 1 830-4555; fax 1 830-5808; email anoige@iol.ie; http://www.irelandyha.org). 1-year membership IR£7.50, under 18 IR£4, family IR£7.50 for each adult with children under 16 free.

Australian Youth Hostels Association (AYHA), Level 3, 10 Mallett St., Camperdown NSW 2050 (tel. (02) 9565 1699; fax 9565 1325; email YHA@yha.org.au; http://www.yha.org.au). Memberships AUS$44, renewal AUS$27; under 18 AUS$13.

Hostelling International-American Youth Hostels (HI-AYH), 733 15th St. NW, Suite 840, Washington, D.C. 20005 (tel. (202) 783-6161, ext. 136; fax 783-6171; email hiayhserv@hiayh.org; http://www.hiayh.org). Maintains 35 offices in the U.S. Memberships can be purchased at many travel agencies (see p. 30) or the national office in Washington, D.C. 1-year membership US$25, under 18 US$10, over 54 US$15, family cards US$35.

Hostelling International-Canada (HI-C), 400-205 Catherine St., Ottawa, ON K2P 1C3, (tel. (613) 237-7884; fax 237-7868; email info@hostellingintl.ca; http://www.hostellingintl.ca). IBN booking centers in Edmonton, Montreal, Ottawa, and Vancouver. Membership packages: 1-yr, under 18 CDN$12; 1-year, over 18 CDN$25; 2-year, over 18 CDN$35; lifetime CDN$175.

Scottish Youth Hostels Association (SYHA), 7 Glebe Crescent, Stirling FK8 2JA (tel. (01786) 89 14 00; fax 89 13 33; email syha@syha.org.uk; http://www.syha.org.uk). Membership UK£6, under 18 UK£2.50.

Youth Hostels Association of England and Wales (YHA), Trevelyan House, 8 St. Stephen's Hill, St. Albans, Hertfordshire AL1 2DY, England (tel. (01727) 85 52 15; fax 84 41 26; email yhacustomerservices@compuserve.com; http://www.yha.org.uk). Enrollment fees are: adults UK£10; under 18 UK£5; UK£20 for each parent with children under 18 enrolled free; UK£10 for 1 parent with children under 18 enrolled free; UK£140 for lifetime membership.

Hostelling International Northern Ireland (HINI), 22-32 Donegall Rd., Belfast BT12 5JN, Northern Ireland (tel. (01232) 32 47 33 or 31 54 35; fax 43 96 99; email info@hini.org.uk; http://www.hini.org.uk). Prices range from UK£8-12. Membership packages: 1-year, UK£7, under 18 UK£3, family UK£14 for up to 6 children; lifetime UK£50.

Youth Hostels Association of New Zealand (YHANZ), P.O. Box 436, 173 Cashel St., Christchurch 1 (tel. (643) 379 9970; fax 365 44 76; email info@yha.org.nz; http://www.yha.org.nz). Annual membership fee NZ$24.

Hostelling International South Africa, P.O. Box 4402, Cape Town 8000 (tel. (021) 24 25 11; fax 24 41 19; email info@hisa.org.za; http://www.hisa.org.za). Membership SAR50, group SAR120, family SAR100, lifetime SAR250.

DORMS

Many **colleges and universities** open their residence halls to travelers when school is not in session—some do so even during term-time. These dorms are often close to student areas—good sources for information on things to do, places to stay, and possible rides out of town—and are usually very clean. No one policy covers all these institutions. Getting a room may be difficult, but rates tend to be low, and many offer free local calls. *Let's Go* lists colleges that rent dorm rooms among the accommodations for appropriate cities. The **Campus Lodging Guide (18th Ed.)** details 609 university and college accommodation options around the world, in addition to more general accommodation information (available in bookstores or via B&J Publications/ Campus Travel Service, P.O. Box 5486, Fullerton, CA 96635-0468, tel. 714-525-6683). College dorms are popular with many travelers, especially those looking for long-term lodging, so reserve ahead.

HOTELS

Hotels are expensive in Austria (singles 200-350AS; doubles 400-800AS) and ridiculously exorbitant in Switzerland (50-75SFr; 80-150SFr). Switzerland has set the international standard for hotels; even one-, two- and three-star accommodations may be much nicer than their counterparts in other countries. The cheapest hotel-style accommodations have **Gasthof** or **Gästehaus** ("inn") in the name; **Hotel-Garni** also means cheap. Continental breakfast *(Frühstuck)* is almost always included.

PRIVATE ROOMS AND PENSIONS

Renting a **private room** *(Privatzimmer)* in a family home is an inexpensive and friendly way to house yourself. Such rooms generally include a sink with hot and cold running water and use of a toilet and shower. Many places rent private rooms only for longer stays, or they may levy a surcharge (10-20%) for stays of less than three nights. *Privatzimmern* start at 25-60SFr per person in Switzerland. In Austria, rooms range from 150-200AS a night. Slightly more expensive, pensions *(Pensionen)* are similar to the American and British notion of a bed and breakfast and to the private rooms described above. Generally, finding rooms for only one person might be difficult, especially for one-night stays. Most places have room with double beds *(Doppelzimmer);* if the rooms have two beds, single travelers will have to pay more. You may have a private bathroom; you'll almost never have to share with more than four or five people. Continental breakfast is *de rigeur;* in classier places, meat, cheese, and an egg will grace your plate and palate. Since pensions are people's homes, be sure to treat them kindly. These popular lodgings fill quickly; reserve ahead.

HOME EXCHANGE AND RENTALS

Home exchange offers the traveler the opportunity to live like a native in various types of homes (houses, apartments, condominiums, villas, even castles in some cases), and to cut down dramatically on accommodation fees—usually only an administration fee is paid to the matching service. Once you join or contact one of the exchange services listed below, it is then up to you to decide with whom you would like to exchange homes. Most companies have pictures of members' homes and information about the owners (some will even ask for your photo!). A great site listing many exchange companies can be found at http://www.aitec.edu.au/~bwechner/Documents/Travel/Lists/HomeExchangeClubs.html. In order to assist you with exchanging your home with another person or family that suits your living habits, most of the companies offer some sort of personalized matching services, connecting compatible families and travelers. Home rentals, as opposed to exchanges, are much more expensive, and most likely not an option for the budget traveler. However, they can be cheaper than comparably-serviced hotels, and thus may be suitable for business travelers. Both home exchanges and rentals are ideal for families with children, or travelers with special dietary needs, as you often get access to your own kitchen, maid service, TV, and telephones.

Intervac U.S., International & USA Home Exchange, P.O. Box 590504, San Francisco, CA 94159 (tel. 415-435-3497; fax 435-7440; email IntervacUS@aol.com; http://www.intervac.com). Part of a worldwide home-exchange network. Catalogues list over 10,000 homes in 30 countries worldwide. Members contact each other directly. You must pay for each catalogue you receive and for listing your home in a catalogue.

fair tours, Postbox 615, CH-9001 St. Gallen, Switzerland (email fairtours@gn.apc.org; http://www.gn.apc.org/fairtours) is a home exchange program that specializes in offering "personal" service—they take pride in matching home-owners with suitable exchange partners and in providing multiingual service for French, Italian and German speakers. After paying a small administrative fee (US$40), you then pay an introduction fee (US$130-$180, depending on your destination) after you have confirmed an exchange

arrangement. Contact them via mail or email to receive an application form (which entails a personal cover letter, pictures of yourself and your home, some general tourist info on the city you live in, and the administration fee). fair tours services home-owners in Austria and Switzerland.

■ Camping, Hiking, and the Outdoors

With over 1200 campgrounds in Switzerland and more than 400 in Austria, **camping** is a popular option. In Switzerland, prices average 6-9SFr per person, 4-10SFr per tent—a joy to behold in such an expensive country. In Austria, prices run 50-70AS per person and 25-60AS per tent (plus 8-9.50AS tax if you're over 15), seldom making camping substantially cheaper than hosteling. You must obtain permission from land-owners to camp on private property. Don't hold your breath—the traditionally conservative Austrians and Swiss are often very protective of their privates. Most sites are open in the summer only, but some 80 sites are specifically set aside for winter camping. Camping along roads and in public areas is forbidden.

USEFUL PUBLICATIONS

A variety of publishing companies offer hiking guidebooks to meet the educational needs of novice or expert. For information about camping, hiking, and biking, write or call the publishers listed below to receive a free catalogue.

Automobile Association, AA Publishing. Orders and enquiries to TBS Frating Distribution Centre, Colchester, Essex, CO7 7DW, U.K. (tel. (01206) 25 56 78; fax 25 59 16; http://www.theaa.co.uk). Publishes a wide range of maps, atlases, and travel guides, including *Camping and Caravanning: Europe* (UK£8).

The Caravan Club, East Grinstead House, East Grinstead, West Sussex, RH19 1UA, U.K. (tel. (01342) 32 69 44; fax 41 02 58; http://www.caravanclub.co.uk). Produces one of the most detailed English-language guides to campsites in Europe.

Family Campers and RVers/National Campers and Hikers Association, Inc., 4804 Transit Rd., Bldg. #2, Depew, NY 14043 (tel./fax (716) 668-6242). Membership fee (US$25) includes their publication *Camping Today*. For US$35, you can also get the International Camping Carnet, which is required by some European campgrounds, but can usually be bought on the spot.

Stanfords Ltd., 12-14 Long Acre, London, WC2E 9LP, U.K. (tel. (0171) 836 2260; fax (0171) 379 4776). Supplies maps, especially of Europe and the British Isles.

The Mountaineers Books, 1001 SW Klickitat Way, #201, Seattle, WA 98134 (tel. (800) 553-4453 or (206) 223-6303; fax 223-6306; email mbooks@mountaineers.org; http://www.mountaineers.org). Many titles on hiking (the *100 Hikes* series), biking, mountaineering, natural history, and conservation.

CAMPING AND HIKING EQUIPMENT

Purchase **equipment** before you leave. This way you'll know exactly what you have and how much it weighs. Spend some time examining catalogues and talking to knowledgeable salespeople. Whether buying or renting, finding sturdy, light, and inexpensive equipment is a must.

Sleeping bags: Most good **sleeping bags** are rated by "season," or the lowest outdoor temperature at which they will keep you warm ("summer" means 0-5°C, "three-season" usually means -20°C, and "four-season" or "winter" often means below -40°C, rarely necessary). Sleeping bags are made either of down (warmer and lighter, more expensive and miserable when wet) or of synthetic material (heavier, more durable, and warmer when wet). Prices vary, but might range from US$65-100 for a summer synthetic to US$250-550 for a good down winter bag.

Sleeping bag pads, including foam pads (from US$15) and air mattresses (US$25-50) cushion your back and neck and insulate you from the ground. Another good alternative is the **Therm-A-Rest,** which is part foam and part air-mattress and inflates to full padding when you unroll it.

Tents: The best **tents** are free-standing, with their own frames and suspension systems; they set up quickly and require no staking (except in high winds). Tents are also classified by season, which should be taken into account to avoid baking in a winter tent in the middle of the summer. Low profile dome tents are the best all-around. When pitched their internal space is almost entirely usable, which means less unnecessary bulk. Tent sizes can be somewhat misleading: two people *can* fit in a two-person tent, but will find life more pleasant in a 4-person. If you're traveling by car, go for the bigger tent; if you're hiking, stick with a smaller one, no more than 1.5-2kg. Good 2-person tents start at US$150, 4-person tents at US$400. You can sometimes find last year's model for half the price. Be sure to seal the seams of your tent with waterproofer, and make sure it has a rain fly.

Backpacks: If you intend to do a lot of hiking, you should have a **frame backpack. Internal-frame packs** mold better to your back, keep a lower center of gravity, and can flex adequately to allow you to hike difficult trails that require a lot of maneuvering. **External-frame packs** are more comfortable for long hikes over even terrain since they keep weight higher and more evenly distributed. Whichever you choose, make sure your pack has a strong, padded hip belt, which transfers the weight from the shoulders to the legs. Any serious backpacking requires a pack of at least 4000 cubic inches. Allow an additional 500 cubic inches for your sleeping bag in internal-frame packs. Sturdy backpacks cost anywhere from US$125-500. This is one area where it doesn't pay to economize—cheaper packs may be less comfortable, and the straps are more likely to fray or rip. Before you buy any pack, try it on and imagine carrying it, full, up a friggin' mountain.

Boots: Be sure to wear hiking boots with good **ankle support** that are appropriate for the terrain you are hiking. Your boots should fit snugly and comfortably over 1 or 2 wool socks and a thin liner sock. Be sure that the boots are broken in—a bad blister will ruin your hiking for days.

Other necessities: Rain gear should come in 2 pieces, a top and pants, rather than a poncho. **Synthetics,** like polypropylene tops, socks, and long underwear, along with a pile jacket, will keep you warm even when wet. Plastic **canteens** or water bottles keep water cooler than metal ones do, and are virtually shatter- and leak-proof. Large, collapsible **water sacks** will significantly improve your lot in primitive campgrounds and weigh practically nothing when empty, though they can get bulky. Bring **water-purification tablets** for when you can't boil water. Though most campgrounds provide campfire sites, you may want to bring a small **metal grate** or **grill** of your own. For those places that forbid fires or the gathering of firewood (this includes virtually every organized campground in Europe), you'll need a **camp stove.** The classic Coleman starts at about US$30. In Europe, consider the "GAZ" butane/propane stove. Its little blue cylinders can be purchased anywhere on the continent—just don't try to take them onto a plane. Campers heading to Europe should also look into buying an **International Camping Carnet.** Similar to a hostel membership card, it's required at a few campgrounds and provides discounts at others (available in North America from the **Family Campers and RVers Association,** and in the U.K. from **The Caravan Club**—see **Useful Publications,** above). A **first-aid kit, Swiss Army knife, insect repellent, calamine lotion,** and **waterproof matches** or a **lighter** are essential camping items. Other items include: a **battery-operated lantern,** a **plastic groundcloth,** a **nylon tarp,** a **waterproof backpack cover** (although you can also store your belongings in plastic bags inside your backpack), and a **"stuff sack"** or plastic bag to keep your sleeping bag dry.

The mail-order firms listed below offer lower prices than those you'll find in many stores, but shop around locally first in order to determine what items actually look like and weigh. Many of these firms have on-line shopping available from the web. Keep in mind that camping equipment is generally more expensive in Australia, New Zealand, and the U.K. than in North America.

Campmor, P.O. Box 700, Saddle River, NJ 07458-0700 (tel. (888) CAMPMOR (888-226-7667), outside the U.S. (201) 825-8300; email customer-service@campmor.com; http://www.campmor.com). A wide selection of name brand equipment at low prices. 1-year guarantee for unused or defective merchandise.

Discount Camping, 880 Main North Rd., Pooraka, South Australia 5095, Australia (tel. (08) 8262 3399; fax 8260 6240; http://www.austdiscount.com.au/camping). Specializes in tents, but carries other equipment and spare parts.

L.L. Bean, Freeport, ME 04033-0001 (tel. (800) 441-5713 in Canada or the U.S., (0800) 962 954 in the U.K., (207) 552-6878 elsewhere; fax (207) 552-4080; http://www.llbean.com). This monolithic equipment and outdoor clothing supplier offers high quality and loads of information. Call or write for their free catalogue. Guaranteed 100% satisfaction on everything; if it doesn't meet your expectations, they'll replace or refund it. The Freeport store is open 24 hr., 365 days.

Mountain Designs, P.O. Box 1472, Fortitude Valley, Queensland 4006, Australia (tel. (07) 3252 8894; fax (07) 3252 4569). A leading Australian manufacturer and mail order retailer of camping and climbing gear.

Mountain Safety Research Inc., P.O. Box 24547, Seattle, WA 98124 (tel. (800) 877-9677; email info@msrcorp.com; http://www.msrcorp.com). Stores in North America, South America, Europe, the Middle East, Asia, South Africa, and Australia. High quality maintenance kits, emergency kits, stoves, water filters, and climbing gear.

CAMPERS AND RVS

Many North American campers harbor a suspicion that traveling with a **camper** or **recreational vehicle** (RV) is not "real camping." The stigma's not as strong in Europe, where RV camping, or "caravanning," is both popular and common.

European RVs are smaller and more economical than the 40-foot Winnebagos of the American road. Renting an RV will always be more expensive than tenting or hosteling, but the costs compare favorably with the price of renting a car and staying in hotels, and the convenience of bringing along your own bedroom, bathroom, and kitchen makes it an attractive option for some, especially older travelers and families with small children.

It is not difficult to arrange an RV rental from overseas, although you will want to begin gathering information several months before your departure. Rates vary widely by region, season (July and August are the most expensive months), and type of RV. It always pays to contact several different companies to compare vehicles and prices. **Avis** (tel. (800) 331-1084) and **Hertz** (tel. (800) 654-3001) are U.S. firms that can arrange RV rentals overseas; **Auto Europe** (tel. (800) 223-5555) and **National Car Rentals** (tel. (800) 227-3876, (800) 227–7368 in Canada) are European firms with branches in North America.

Camping Your Way through Europe by Carol Mickelsen (Affordable Press, US$15) and *Exploring Europe by RV* by Dennis and Tina Jaffe (Globe Pequot, also US$15) are both good resources for planning this type of trip.

ENVIRONMENTALLY RESPONSIBLE TOURISM

While protecting yourself from the elements, take a moment to also consider protecting the wilderness from you. At the very least, a responsible traveler practices **"minimum impact camping"** techniques. Leave no trace of your presence when you leave a site. Don't cut vegetation or clear new campsites. A campstove is the safer (and more efficient) way to cook, but if you must, make small fires using only dead branches or brush. Make sure your campsite is at least 40m from water supplies or bodies of water. If there are no toilet facilities, bury human waste (but not paper) at least 10cm deep and above the high-water line 40m or more from any water supplies and campsites. Always pack your trash in a plastic bag and carry it with you until you reach the next trash can.

Responsible tourism means more than picking up your litter, however. Growing numbers of "ecotourists" are asking hard questions of resort owners and tour operators about how their policies affect local ecologies and local economies. Some try to give something back to the regions they enjoy by volunteering for environmental organizations at home or abroad. Above all, responsible tourism means being aware of your impact on the places you visit and taking responsibility for your own actions.

ORGANIZED ADVENTURE

Organized adventure tours offer another way of exploring the wild. Activities include hiking, biking, skiing, canoeing, kayaking, rafting, climbing, and archaeological digs, and go *everywhere*. Begin by consulting tourism bureaus, which can suggest parks, trails, and outfitters as well as answer more general questions. Another good source for organized adventure options is the stores and organizations specializing in camping and outdoor equipment listed earlier. Usually the people at REI, EMS, or Sierra can inform you of a range of trips. They also often offer training programs for people who want to have an independent trip. The **Specialty Travel Index,** 305 San Anselmo Ave., Ste. 313, San Anselmo, CA 94960 (tel. (800) 442-4922 or (415) 459-4900; fax 459-4974; email spectrav@ix.netcom.com; http://www.specialtytravel.com) is a directory listing hundreds of tour operators worldwide.

HIKING

Austria and Switzerland are renowned for their hiking, with paths ranging from simple hikes in the foothills of the Swiss Jura to ice-axe-wielding expeditions through the glaciers of the Berner Oberland. Free **hiking** maps are available from even the most rinky-dink of tourist offices. Hiking trails are marked by signs indicating the time to nearby destinations, which may not bear any relation to your own expertise and endurance. ("Std." is short for *Stunden,* or hours.) Paths marked *"Für Geübte"* require special mountain-climbing equipment and are for experienced climbers only. For lengthy hikes, consider taking a detailed map of the region you will be hiking. The best maps are the **Freytag-Berndt** maps (around US$10), available in bookstores all over Austria and Switzerland and from **Pacific Travellers Supply,** 12 W. Anapamu St., Santa Barbara, CA 93101 (tel. (805) 963-4438). Check these books out, too:

100 Hikes in the Alps. Details various trails in Austria and Switzerland (US$15). Write to The Mountaineers Books, 1001 Klickitat Way, Ste. 201, Seattle, WA 98134 (tel. (800) 553-4453; fax 223-6306).

Walking Austria's Alps, by Jonathan Hurdle. The Mountaineers Books (US$11).

Walking Switzerland the Swiss Way, by Marcia and Philip Lieberman. The "Swiss Way" refers to hiking hut-to-hut. The Mountaineers Books (US$13).

Downhill Walking in Switzerland, (US$12). Old World Travel Books, Inc., P.O. Box 700863, Tulsa, OK 74170 (tel. (918) 493-2642).

Swiss-Bernese Oberland, by Philip and Loretta Alspach. (US$17, handling US$2.50). Intercon Publishing, P.O. Box 18500-L, Irvine, CA 92623 (tel. (714) 955-2344; fax 833-3156).

Walking Easy in the Austrian Alps and **Walking Easy in the Swiss Alps,** by Chet and Carolee Lipton (US$11). Gateway Books, 2023 Clemens Rd., Oakland, CA 94602 (tel. (510) 530-0299, orders only (800) 669-0773; fax 530-0497).

Austria

A membership in the **Österreichischer Alpenverein** gives an in-depth experience with the Tirolean Alps. The group offers a series of **huts** across the Tirol and throughout Austria, all located a day's hike from each other. This hut-to-hut option is provided to members at half-price and a place in any of the huts is always assured. Third-party insurance, accident provision, travel discounts, and a wealth of maps and mountain information are also included with membership. For information, contact Österreichischer Alpenverein, Willhelm-Greil-Str. 15, A-6010 Innsbruck (tel. 58 78 28; fax 58 88 42). Membership (US$55, students under 25 US$40; one-time fee US$10) also includes use of some of the huts that the **Deutscher Alpenverein** (German Alpine Club) operates, all of which have beds. Sleeping in one of Austria's refuges is safer for the environment and generally safer for you—when you leave, you are expected to list your next destination in the hut book, thus alerting search-and-rescue teams if a problem should occur. Prices for an overnight stay without membership in the Alpenverein are 50-150AS, and no reservations are necessary.

The Austrian National Tourist Office publishes the pamphlet *Hiking and Backpacking in Austria*, with a complete list of Freytag-Berndt maps and additional tips. The **Touristenverein "Die Naturfreunde,"** Viktoriag. 6, A-1150 Vienna (tel. (01) 892 35 34), also operates a network of cottages in rural and mountain areas.

Switzerland

"A pocket knife with a corkscrew, a leathern drinking cup, a spirit flask, stout gloves, and a piece of green crepe or coloured spectacles to protect the eyes from the glare of the snow, should not be forgotten," wrote Karl Baedeker in his 1907 guide to Switzerland. The Swiss National Tourist Office still suggests ski glasses to avoid **snow blindness,** but somehow the spirit flask has dropped out of the picture.

It's a good place for walkin': 9000km of **hiking trails** lace the country; yellow signs give directions and traveling times to nearby destinations. Bands of white-red-white mark trails; if there are no markings, you're on an "unofficial" trail, which is not always a problem—most trails are well maintained. Blue-white-blue markings indicate that the trail requires special equipment, either for difficult rock climbs or glacier climbing. Lowland **meandering** at its best awaits in the Engadin valley near St. Moritz; for steeper climbs, head to Zermatt or Interlaken. **Swiss Alpine Club (SAC) huts** are modest and extremely practical for those interested in trekking in higher, more remote areas of the Alps. Bunk rooms sleep 10 to 20 weary hikers side by side, with blankets (no electricity or running water) provided. SAC huts are open to all, but SAC members get discounts. The average rate for one night's stay without food is 30SFr, members 20-25SFr. Membership costs 126SFr, but as a bonus you'll receive the titillating publication *Die Alpen*. Contact the SAC, Sektion Zermatt, Haus Dolomite, CH-3920 Zermatt, Switzerland (tel. (028) 67 26 10).

SKIING

Western **Austria** is one of the world's best skiing regions. The areas around Innsbruck and Kitzbühel in the Tirol are saturated with lifts and runs. Skiers swoosh year-round down some glaciers, including the Stubaital near Innsbruck and the Dachstein in the Salzkammergut. High-season normally runs from mid-December to mid-January and from February to March. Local tourist offices provide information on regional skiing and can point you to budget travel agencies that offer ski packages.

Contrary to popular belief, **skiing in Switzerland** is often less expensive than in the U.S. if you avoid the pricey resorts. Ski passes (valid for transportation to, from, and on lifts) run 30-50SFr per day and 100-300SFr per week. A week of lift tickets, equipment rental, lessons, lodging, and *demi-pension* (half-pension—breakfast plus one other meal, usually dinner) averages 475SFr. Summer skiing is no longer as prevalent as it once was, but it's still available in Zermatt, Saas Fee, Les Diablerets, and on the Diavolezza in Pontresina.

With peaks between 3000 and 30,000m, the Alpine vertical drop is ample—1000 to 2000m at all major resorts. For mountain country, winter **weather** in the Austrian Alps is moderate, thanks to lower elevation and distance from the ocean. Daytime temperatures in the coldest months (Jan. and Feb.) measure around -7°C (20°F). Humidity is low, so snow on the ground stays powdery longer.

■ Keeping in Touch

MAIL

Austria and Switzerland maintain rapid, efficient postal systems. Letters take one to three days within Switzerland and one to two days within Austria. Airmail to North America takes four to five days from either country. Mark all letters and packages *"Mit Flugpost"* or *"Par Avion."* In all cases, include the *postal code* if you know it; those of Swiss cities begin with "CH," Austrian with "A".

Mail can be sent internationally through *Poste Restante* (the international phrase for General Delivery) to any city or town; it's well worth using, generally without any surcharges, and much more reliable than you might think. Mark the envelope "HOLD" and address it, for example, "Erik <u>REDBEARD,</u> Poste Restante, City, Country." The last name should be capitalized and underlined. The mail will go to a special desk in the central post office, unless you specify a post office by street address or postal code. As a rule, it is best to use the largest post office in the area; sometimes, mail will be sent there regardless of what you write on the envelope. When possible, it is usually safer and quicker to send mail express or registered.

It helps (though is not imperative) to use the appropriate translation of Poste Restante (*Postlagernde Briefe* in German). When picking up your mail, bring a form of photo ID, preferably passport. If the clerks insist that there is nothing for you, have them check under your first name as well. In some countries, you may have to pay a minimal fee per item received. *Let's Go* lists post offices in the **Practical Information** section for each city and most towns.

Aerogrammes, printed sheets that fold into envelopes and travel via airmail, are available at post offices. It helps to mark "airmail" in the appropriate language if possible (*par avion* in French, *mit Luftpost* in German), though *par avion* is universally understood. Most post offices will charge exorbitant fees or simply refuse to send Aerogrammes with enclosures. Airmail from Europe and the U.S. averages one to two weeks. Allow two weeks from Australia and New Zealand; most of Africa takes upwards of two weeks. Much depends on the national post office that handles the mail before it leaves the country.

If regular airmail is too slow, there are a few faster, more expensive, options. **Federal Express** (U.S. tel. for international operator (800) 247-4747) can get a letter from New York to Paris in two days for a whopping US$28.50, or from New York to Jerusalem for $32.50 (not that those figures are relevant for your vacation in Austria or Switzerland, but you get the point); rates from non-U.S. locations are prohibitively expensive (Paris to New York, for example, costs upwards of US$60). By U.S. Express Mail, the same letter would arrive in two to three days and would cost US$21, although rates vary according to country.

Surface mail is the cheapest and slowest way to send mail. It takes one to three months to cross the Atlantic and two to four to cross the Pacific—appropriate for sending large quantities of items you won't need to see for a while. It is vital, therefore, to distinguish your airmail from surface mail by explicitly labeling "airmail" in the appropriate language. When ordering materials from abroad, always include one or two International Reply Coupons (IRCs), which provide postage to cover delivery. IRCs should be available from your local post office as well as abroad (US$1.05).

American Express travel offices throughout the world will act as a mail service for cardholders if you contact them in advance. Under this free **"Client Letter Service,"** they will hold mail for no more than 30 days, forward upon request, and accept telegrams. Just like *Poste Restante,* the last name of the person to whom the mail is addressed should be capitalized and underlined. Some offices will offer these services to non-cardholders (especially those who have purchased AmEx Travellers' Cheques), but you must call ahead to make sure. *Let's Go* lists AmEx office locations for most large cities. A complete list is available free from AmEx (tel. (800) 528-4800) in the booklet Traveler's Companion or on-line at http://www.americanexpress.com; connect from there to worldwide sites.

TELEPHONES

You can place **international calls** from most telephones. To call direct, dial the international access code followed by the country code (see **Appendix**), the city code (see the city's **Essentials** listings), and the local number. Country codes and city codes may sometimes be listed with a zero in front (e.g., 033), but after dialing the international access code, drop successive zeros (with an access code of 011, e.g., 011 33). Often, you must wait for a tone after the international access code. Wherever possible, use a calling card (see **calling cards** below) for international phone calls, as it tends to be less expensive than national phone services.

You can also usually make direct international calls from **pay phones,** but you may need to drop your coins as quickly as your words. In some countries, pay phones are card-operated; some even accept major credit cards. Be wary of more expensive, private pay phones; look for pay phones in public areas, especially train stations. One should avoid the insidious in-room hotel phone call. Although incredibly convenient, these calls invariably include a sky-high surcharge (as much as US$10 in some establishments). It's cheaper to just find a pay phone in the lobby.

English-speaking operators are available for both local and international assistance. In most countries, these operators will place collect calls for you. American operators can be reached by dialing the MCI or AT&T access number specific for the country from which you are calling. These operators will place **collect calls** for you as well as placing calls with your AT&T or MCI **calling card.** For more information, call **AT&T** about its **USADirect** and **World Connect** services (tel. (888) 288-4685; from abroad call (810) 262-6644 collect), **Sprint** (tel. (800) 877-4646; from abroad, call (913) 624-5335 collect), or **MCI WorldPhone** and **World Reach** (tel. (800) 444-4141; from abroad dial the country's MCI access number). In **Canada,** contact Bell Canada **Canada Direct** (tel. (800) 565 4708); in the **U.K.,** British Telecom **BT Direct** (tel. (800) 34 51 44); in **Ireland,** Telecom Éireann **Ireland Direct** (tel. (800) 25 02 50); in Australia, Telstra **Australia Direct** (tel. 13 22 00); in **New Zealand, Telecom New Zealand** (tel. 123); and in **South Africa, Telkom South Africa** (tel. 09 03). A **calling card** is probably your best and cheapest bet; the calls (plus a small surcharge) are billed either collect or to the calling card. MCI's WorldPhone also provides access to MCI's **Traveler's Assist,** which gives legal and medical advice, exchange rate information, and translation services. Many other long distance carriers and phone companies provide such travel information; contact your phone service provider.

Depending on the service you have previously set up, it may be cheaper to find a pay phone and deposit just enough money to be able to say "Call me" and give your digits. Phone rates tend to be highest in the morning, lower in the evening, and lowest on Sunday and late at night. Remember **time differences** when you call.

OTHER COMMUNICATION

Domestic and international **telegrams** offer an option slower than phone but faster than post. Fill out a form at any post or telephone office; cables arrive to all international locations in one or two days. Telegrams can be quite expensive; **Western Union** (tel. (800) 325-6000) adds a surcharge to the per-word rate depending on the country. You may wish to consider **faxes** for cheaper, more immediate communication. Major cities have bureaus where you can pay to send and receive faxes.

Between May 2 and Octoberfest, **EurAide,** P.O. Box 2375, Naperville, IL 60567 (tel. (630) 420-2343; fax (630) 420-2369; http://www.cube.net/kmu/euraide.html), offers **Overseas Access,** a service useful to travelers without a set itinerary. The cost is US$15 per week or US$40 per month plus a US$15 registration fee. To reach you, people call, fax, or use the internet to leave a message; you receive it by calling Munich whenever you wish (cheaper than calling overseas). You may also leave messages for callers to pick up by phone.

The wave of the future, **electronic mail (email)** is an attractive option, and increasingly easy to access worldwide. With a minimum of computer knowledge and a little planning, you can beam messages anywhere and instantly for no per-message charge. **Traveltales.com** (http://traveltales.com) gives free, web-based email for travelers and maintains a list of over 500 cybercafés throughout the world as well as providing travel links and a travelers' chat room. Other free email providers include **Hotmail** (http://www.hotmail.com), and **USANET** (http://www.usa.net). Many of these are funded by advertising and may require subscribers to fill out a questionnaire. Search through http://www.cyberiacafe.net/cyberia/guide/ccafe.htm to find a list of **cybercafés** around the world. Contact http://www.nsrc.org for a host of connections to sites supplying further internet information on any country. If you're already hooked up to the Infobahn at home, you should be able to find access numbers for your destination country.

Internal Calls: Switzerland

Local calls cost 60 centimes. Phones take 10, 20, and 50 centime and 1 and 5SFr coins. Phones do not return change—press the red button to make additional calls before the money runs out. City codes are three digits long, numbers themselves six or seven. You can buy **phone cards (Taxcards)** at any post office, change bureau, or kissed. In all areas, dial 111 for **information** (including directory assistance, train schedules, and other minutiae) and 114 for an **English-speaking international operator.** The **Anglo-phone** number is 157 50 14. It provides information ranging from weather reports to English-speaking doctor referrals (1.40SFr per minute). Call collect by dialing 1151.

Internal Calls: Austria

Wertkarten (telephone cards), available in post offices, train stations, and at *Tabak Trafik,* come in 50AS and 100AS denominations sold for 48AS and 95AS, respectively. To use a coin-operated pay phone, deposit 1AS and keep feeding the thing every time you hear a beep. Phones that take cards are found even in remote villages—they announce themselves with blue stickers on the telephone booth. Green stickers mean that a phone accepts incoming calls. All others simply accept coins. When calling from a **post office,** take a number, run up a tab while talking, and pay the cashier when you're done. **Long distance** charges vary—drop in 5AS or so to start. The display next to the receiver indicates how much money has been deposited and shows the deductions made during the course of the call. Even when calling collect or using a phone card, you must pay for the local cost of the call. On weekdays between 6pm and 8am and from 1pm Saturday to 8pm Monday, all phone calls within the country are one-third cheaper. This rate does not apply to international calls.

AUSTRIA

US$1= 12.56 Schillings (AS)	10AS = US$0.80
CDN$1= 8.26AS	10AS = CDN$1.21
UK£1= 20.41AS	10AS = UK£0.49
IR£1= 17.67AS	10AS = IR£0.57
AUS$1= 7.50AS	10AS = AUS$1.33
NZ$1= 6.33AS	10AS = NZ$1.58
SAR1= 2.00AS	10AS = SAR3.00
1SFr = 8.44AS	10AS = 1.19SFr
1 DM = 7.03AS	10AS = DM1.42
1kč = 0.39AS	10AS = 25.71kč
1Ft = 0.06AS	10AS = 176.77Ft

Country Code: 43
International Dialing Prefix: 900 from Vienna, 00 from elsewhere

At 32,276 square miles, Austria is not the largest country in the world and not the smallest either (see Liechtenstein, p. 443). Austria comprises nine semi-autonomous provinces, or *Bundesländer*. Counterclockwise from the northeast they are: Vienna (Wien), Lower Austria (Niederösterreich), Upper Austria (Oberösterreich), Salzburg, Tyrol (Tirol), Vorarlberg, Carinthia (Kärnten), Styria (Steiermark), and Burgenland. Austria as a country has only existed since the dismantling of the Habsburg Empire by the Treaty of Versailles in 1918, and is in many ways a haphazard conglomeration of German-speaking provinces that each have more deep-rooted regional identities. The Tyrolers are fervently Tyrolean; the province nearly seceded from Austria after WWI to stay united with Südtirol when the Allies ceded it to Italy. The Styrians are also extremely micro-patriotic (possibly because no one else can understand their dialect). Austria's population of 7.8 million is 99 percent German-speaking, but that statistic belies the presence of significant ethnic minorities. Many of the country's inhabitants were once on the other side of what is in many cases an arbitrary line. The Burgenlanders, for example, have a strong Hungarian heritage, and the Slovenes of southern Carinthia and the Croats in Burgenland form their own distinct minorities. Eighty percent of the Austrian population is Roman Catholic; a further 4.9% is Protestant, most ascribing to the Augsburg Confession.

For all its political transformations, Austria maintains an overpowering physical beauty. Onion-domed churches set against snow-capped Alpine peaks, lush meadows blanketed with edelweiss, pristine mountain lakes, dark cool forests, and mighty castles towering over the majestic Danube—there's a lot to see in Austria. In the eastern portion of the European Alps, more than half of the country is covered by mountains. Western Austria is almost entirely taken over by them, rising to the Großglockner, the highest peak in Austria at 3797m (12,457 ft.). The mountains generate year-round tourism: Alpine sports dominate the winter scene, while lakeside frolicking draws visitors in the warmer months. The Danube, Europe's longest river, has been central to Austrian industry and aristocracy since the country's beginning: both the Babenburgs and the Habsburgs set up residences on its shores. Vienna, once the imperial headquarters and now the country's capital, stands on the river's banks. Its mainly Baroque and modern urban landscape houses artistic treasures, historical landmarks, and an increasingly dynamic and cosmopolitan population. To cap off all the scenery, forests and meadows cover two thirds of the total area of Austria.

▓ History and Politics

For centuries, Austria was the locus of a Germanic empire that stretched throughout Europe. When nationalist sentiments first took root in the 19th century, they were

Germanic nationalist sentiments. But the region has always also consisted of an ethnic mix of Magyars, Slovenes, Flemings, Slavs, and Italians, and each group has always
had different ideas about what comprises Austria. Diversity made it difficult for any
sort of unified and unifying identity to form, and the push and pull of various forces in
the region meant constant changing hands of authority. Austria moved through gov-
ernments like some people go through clothes: from centuries of imperial rule to the
Austrian Republic to Hitler's mad barbarism to the 20th century's sedate and san-
guine Second Republic. Since the Second World War, however, Austria has cultivated
a new identity—internationally neutral, democratic, Western-oriented, and a recently
admitted member of the European Union. The Second Republic has fashioned a progressive social democratic welfare state as stable as any other in the hemisphere.

EARLY YEARS (10,000 BCE-800 CE)

Though humans have lived in Austria since Paleolithic times (80,000-10,000 BCE), little evidence of the early inhabitants remains. Around 5000 BCE, hunter-gatherers
began to settle the highlands, where they farmed their food, raised stock animals,
mined salt in the salt mines, and periodically froze in the Alpine passes. Archaeologists discovered one of these unfortunate creatures in 1991 (CE, that is), his body preserved in the glacial ice of the Ötztal Alps.

Around 400BCE, the **Celts** took control of the salt mines and established the kingdom of **Noricum,** which developed a relatively affluent economy as far as those early
economies go based on a far-ranging salt and iron trade. The **Romans** to the south
appreciated the trade-link but conquered their Austrian neighbors anyway in 30-
15BCE to secure the Danube frontier against marauding **Germans.** During the two-
century *Pax Romana,* Noricum thrived and things turned urban, giving rise to cities
like **Vindobona** (Vienna), **Juvavum** (Salzburg), **Aguntum** (Lienz), and **Brigantium**
(Bregenz). **Marcus Aurelius** wrote his famous Meditations and then died in Vindobona, starting a long tradition of Viennese immigré (and emigré) artists. Roman roads
along the Danube and through the Alps facilitated the movement of legions, traders,
and missionaries (both pagan and Christian) through the region. Germanic raids
finally forced Romans to abandon the province in the 5th century.

Over the next three centuries, Huns, Ostrogoths, and Lombards occasionally
romped through the Austrian territories, but none established any lasting settlement.
Three primary groups did occupy the region: the **Alemanni** in the south, the **Slavs** in
the southwest, and the **Bavarians** in the north. Modern placenames ending in -*itz*
indicate Slavic origins, while -*heim* and -*ing(en)* reveal Germanic settlement. The few
Celts left in the highlands retained both Celtic place
names and Christianity, something that the lowland settlers did not adopt until Irish missionaries arrived in the
early 7th century deadset to convert the world. The
dukes of Bavaria further converted the population in an
attempt to bring a semblance of law and order to the area
and to create a power-base free of Frankish influence.
The missionaries' successes created an archbishopric of
Salzburg in 798. The city remained Austria's ecclesiastical capital well into the modern era.

> *Marcus Aurelius wrote his Meditations and then died in Vindobona, starting a long tradition of Viennese immigré (and emigré) artists.*

Charlemagne, crowned Holy Roman Emperor, claimed what is now Austria as a
border province, setting it up as a buffer zone between his empire and the Bavarians'
ever-expanding rule. The name *Österreich* means "Eastern Empire," referring to the
easternmost lands that Charlemagne conquered.

THE HOUSE OF BABENBERG

There was an invasion by the Asian **Magyars**, that ended with their defeat at Lechfeld
in 955 at the hand of **Otto I**, the first magnate elected in Germany to continue the
Holy Roman Empire. To buttress the Empire against attack, Otto installed **Leopold of
Babenberg** as ruler of Austrian territories in 976. The Babenbergs ruled *Ostarrichi*

(eastern Austria) from 976 to 1246. They stabilized frontiers (in other words, strengthened military presence at the edges of the empire), extending their protectorate north of the Danube and east and south into Magyar (later Hungarian) lands. The Babenbergs' monasteries and abbeys played an important role in the recolonization of the depopulated country, as **German-speaking settlers** cleared the land for farming. Although the Babenbergs supported the pope against Henry IV during the **Investiture Conflict,** they were otherwise very loyal to the Holy Roman Emperors, including **Leopold III** (1095-1136), later Austria's patron saint.

The Babenberg economy benefited from east-bound traffic during the Crusades. The family secured a large part of the ransom that England paid to rescue **Richard the Lionheart,** detained in Dürnstein by **Leopold V** on his way home from the Third Crusade, money that was used by Leopold to fortify the towns of Wiener Neustadt and Vienna. In that same year, 1192, Leopold V obtained the Duchy of **Styria** (today part of southeast Austria) through a contract of inheritance. In the first half of the 13th century, cultural life at the court of the Babenbergs came to full bloom. **Minnesingers** (minstrels) wrote epic ballads (including the **Nibelungenlied**) and **Romanesque architecture** came to a late fruition.

THE RISE OF THE HABSBURGS

The last Babenburg, **Friedrich II** ("the Quarrelsome") was confronted with an angry emperor to the west, rebellious nobles to the north, and nervous Hungarians (threatened by Mongol invasion) to the east. The Hungarians were the first to get to him, and he died childless at their hands in 1246, leaving things fragmented and unruly. Bohemian King **Ottokar II** stepped in, married Friedrich's sister, restored order, reconquered Styria, and added the Duchy of **Carinthia** to his holdings.

While Ottokar was taking control, a new emperor emerged in the Holy Roman Empire after the 19-year *Interregnum,* a Swiss guy named **Rudolf of Habsburg.** Rudolph immediately demanded the Slavic Ottokar's allegiance. When Ottokar refused, Rudolf attacked with the support of Austrian nobles and defeated Ottokar at Marchfeld in 1278. In 1282, Rudolf granted his own two sons the Duchies of *Ostarrichi* and Styria, thus laying the foundations for Habsburg dynastic rule in the region. The Habsburgs would retain power in Austria almost continuously until 1918, through 19 Habsburg emperors and one (glorious) empress.

At the inception of Habsburg rule, the family's dominance was far from secure. Due to the lack of primogeniture (full inheritance by the first son), the Habsburg territory was divided among every son, and this division was a constant source of instability. People were always revolting: even the Swiss, once the most loyal Habsburg supporters, proved unruly. During the late Middle Ages, the Habsburgs expanded their holdings and defended their inflating borders. Rudolf the Founder's short rule (1358-1365) was marked by the acquisition of the Earldom of **Tirol** along with various social and cultural improvements, such as the founding of the **University of Vienna** and renovations of St. Stephen's Cathedral. When Rudolf felt he and his family had been snubbed by the Luxembourg Emperor Karl IV, he forged several documents, later called the **Privilegium maius,** to prove his dynasty's higher rank and importance. Rudolf's descendant, Emperor **Friedrich III,** a shrewd politician, affirmed the claims made in these documents. He then strategically arranged the marriage of his son, **Maximilian I,** to the heiress of the powerful Burgundian kingdom, giving the Habsburgs control over the Low Countries. In 1493, Maximilian became the first Habsburg to claim the title of Holy Roman Emperor without papal coronation, giving the Habsburgs hereditary rights to the imperial throne. Through prudent marital alliances, he ensured the accession of lands far and wide and laid the foundations for the territory that came under Habsburg rule during the pinnacle of the empire. Maximilian's son Philip was joined in one of these shrewd marriages to the daughter of Spain's royal duo, Ferdinand and Isabella, putting his progeny in the running for rule of the **Kingdom of Spain.** And indeed, Max's son, Karl V, inherited a vast empire—Austria, the Netherlands, Aragon and its Italian and Mediterranean possessions, Castile, and the Spanish Americas—and was elected Holy Roman Emperor in 1519, gaining dominion over Germany. The Habsburg Empire was really, really big.

Under Karl V and through advantageous marital alliances, the Habsburgs came the closest to their prophetic motto **"A.E.I.O.U.,"** allegedly meaning *"Alles Erdreich ist Österreich untertan"* (All the world is subject to Austria). A more accurate motto might have been a popular couplet written by the shrewd organizer of this whole affair, Maximilian, that stated: *"Bella gerant alii, tu felix Austria nube."* (Let other nations go to war; you, lucky Austria, marry—an early riff on "Make love, not war").

THE HABSBURG EMPIRE

Despite the massive territory, beneath the imperial veneer, there were anxieties among the Habsburgs. The **Ottoman Empire,** which had been creeping into Central Europe since the 14th century, began to threaten the region more and more in the 1500s and 1600s. After the conquest of Constantinople, the Turks consistently undertook expeditions farther west, becoming a permanent threat. In 1529, Turkish armies got all the way to the gates of Vienna before they were beaten back.

Meanwhile, social unrest, fomented by the **Reformation,** further threatened stability. Burghers and nobles were drawn to Protestantism because it affirmed rationality; peasants found it attractive because it freed them from onerous tithes to the Church. And while social hierarchies kept the two groups from forming a united front, the peasant rebellion that the Reformation sparked was nonetheless upsetting to the ruling class, who were forced to hire mercenaries to deal with the problem. The mercenaries brutally crushed the rebels in the **Peasants' Wars** of 1525-6. While several leaders tolerant of Protestantism discouraged the bloodshed, the Protestant Bohemians felt increasing annoyance at the Habsburgs, and generally felt increasingly impinged upon by the whole two religions in one region thing. Those feelings came to a head when the emperor **Matthias** (1612-1619) sent two Catholic emissaries to talk things over. The Bohemians took matters into their own hands, throwing the emissaries out the window in the **defenstration of Prague** (1618) and then overthrowing Matthias. His successor, Archduke Ferdinand II (1619-1637), was not so easy to handle. His early victories over Protestant forces during the **Thirty Years War** (1618-1648) won the Habsburgs control of Bohemia and led to the forcible conversion of most of the peasants back to Catholicism. The conflict lasted quite a while (30 years even), and by the time the **Peace of Westphalia** rolled around in 1648, the Habsburg dream of consolidating the German states seemed unrealizable.

By 1683, the Ottoman Turks sat on Vienna's doorstep once again, setting up siege tents in the hills around the city fortifications. Austria's ensuing military response, which was highly effective, was largely the handiwork of Polish king Jan Sobieski and **Prince Eugene of Savoy.** Not content to rest at home, Prince Eugene pressed his forces into Turkish lands and captured Hungary, Transylvania, and Croatia. Victory over the Turks generated an era of celebration; to honor Austrian prowess, magnificent buildings were constructed and wounded castles, churches, and monasteries were finally repaired. Opera flourished. This patriotic exuberance, tempered by a deep religious conviction, was the trademark of the Austrian **Baroque.** After Eugene of Savoy rescued Vienna from this second Turkish siege, **Leopold I** gave him control of the army. Eugene then led the happy Habsburg troops to victory over the French in the **War of Spanish Succession,** which lasted from 1701 to 1714, in which **Louis XIV** fought to defend his newly inherited Spanish empire, passed to him by **Charles II,** ruler of Spain. When the war ended with the **Treaty of Utrecht** in 1713, France kept Spain and the Habsburgs gained Belgium, Sardinia, and parts of Italy. By 1718, the Habsburg emperors had direct control of Bohemia, Moravia, Silesia, Hungary, Croatia, Transylvania, Belgium, Lombardy, Naples, Sicily, and, of course, Austria.

> By 1683, the Ottoman Turks sat on Vienna's doorstep once again, setting up siege tents in the hills around the city fortifications.

Over the next 20 years, the empire atrophied. By the 1730s the empire was extremely decentralized and poorly run: nobles maintained power over small regions and over the large serf population; the minuscule middle class and the guilds of artisans were hindered by Austria's location very far away from any trade route. Though a benevolent and loyal man, Emperor **Karl VI** wasn't really wise to the techniques necessary to run an empire. He wasn't a shrewd diplomat; he couldn't fight wars. One thing he did do, however, was get the **Pragmatic Sanction** of 1713 passed, a sanction in which most of the powers in Europe agreed to recognize succession of the Habsburgs through the female line. Awfully pragmatic given the fact that he didn't have a son, rather a daughter, **Maria Theresa,** who, because of the sanction, became empress in 1740. Maria Theresa married Franz Stephan of Lorraine in 1736, who, though elected Emperor of the Holy Roman Empire in 1745, was overshadowed throughout his life by his wife's personality and intelligence.

Meanwhile, King of Prussia **Friedrich the Great** was beginning to build a powerful German state through military conquest. In one of his many successful campaigns, he snatched Silesia (now southwest Poland), one of the Habsburg's most prosperous provinces; Maria Theresa spent the rest of her life unsuccessfully maneuvering to reclaim it. Silesia wasn't the only loss: in the **Wars of Austrian Succession,** which lasted from 1740 to 1748, Maria Theresa maintained her rule with help from the Hungarians at the cost of the Italian lands of Lombardy. In the ensuing diplomacy, the Empress' wily foreign minister, **Count Kaunitz,** realized the potential of burying hatchets and forging an alliance with France. The marriage of Maria Theresa's daughter Marie Antoinette to the future Louis XVI was one outcome of his scheming, and his scheming was part of what came to be known as the **Diplomatic Revolution** of 1756. But Kaunitz's new alliance was not as successful as he planned, and the stalemate that resulted from the **Seven Years War** (1756-1763) underscored Austria's waning influence and the rise of Prussia as a great power. Maria Theresa and her son **Josef II** passed a series of reforms hoping to stimulate the economy, including attempts to improve tax collection, increase settlements, encourage religious freedom, aid industry, lower the numbers of economically wasteful convents and monasteries, and decrease feudal burdens. A new state system transformed the agglomeration of lands that had hitherto been only loosely connected into a tightly administered central state. The empire, and Vienna in particular, became a center of culture and commerce. **Christoph Willibald Gluck, Josef Haydn,** and **Wolfgang Amadeus Mozart** composed their main works in the Theresian court of imperial Vienna. When Josef took over after Maria Theresa's death in 1780, Austria's movement toward a centralized and "rational" government accelerated. In 1781 Josef issued the **Toleration Patent,** granting numerous Protestant sects religious freedom, and liberated the serfs everywhere except Hungary (unlucky Hungarians had to wait a while). Though Josef initially encouraged public political consciousness and expression, his centralized bureaucracy relied on the Ministry of Police, which he used to censor the media and repress political dissidents.

THE END OF THE HOLY ROMAN EMPIRE

The doctrines behind the **French Revolution** gained ground in 18th-century Austria and represented a serious threat to Austrian absolutism. **Emperor Franz II,** grandson of Maria Theresa and nephew of the newly headless French Queen Marie Antoinette, joined the coalition against revolutionary France. The French Revolutionary National Assembly declared war on Austria in 1792, a war that continued through France's Second Revolution and that showcased the military genius of young commander General **Napoleon Bonaparte.** The defeat of the Austrians in Northern Italy and the ensuing **Treaty of Campo Formio** in 1797, in which Austria recognized French possession of Belgium and parts of Italy, became the first in a long series of his victories. As you know, he was short. The treaty's reorganization of Germany heralded the final demise of the Holy Roman Empire. Facing the inevitable, Franz II renounced his claim to the now-defunct Holy Roman crown in 1804 and proclaimed himself Franz I, Emperor of Austria—"Screw that! I'm Emperor of Austria now!" Only at this point was an Austrian empire as such founded. At the Congress of Vienna in 1815, which redrew the map of Europe after Napoleon's defeat, Austrian Chancellor of State Clemens **Wenzel Lothar Metternich,** "the Coachman of Europe," restored the old order while masterfully orchestrating the re-consolidation of Austrian power. Metternich preached the gospel of "legitimacy" and stability—in other words, the perpetuation of conservative government—to achieve a European balance of power. His machinations ushered in a long peace, during which commerce and industry flourished.

1848 AND THE REIGN OF FRANZ JOSEF

The first half of the 19th century was marked by immense technological progress. Things turned industrial and urban. There was rapid population growth. Social classes were born. The French philosophy of middle-class revolution reached Austria in the spring of 1848. Working together, students and workers built barricades, took control of the imperial palace, and demanded a constitution and freedom of the press. Metternich was so stunned he fled to England. A constituent assembly abolished feudalism in all non-Hungarian lands (unlucky Hungarians). Ethnic rivalries and political differences divided the revolutionary forces, however, and the Habsburgs were able to suppress the revolution in October of 1848. That year also marked the brutal suppression of a Hungarian rebellion (unlucky Hungarians), the forced abdication of the weakened emperor **Ferdinand I,** and the coronation of **Kaiser Franz-Josef I,** whose reign (1848-1916) stands as one of the longest of any monarch in history. The new leader created a highly centralized state.

Losses to France and Italy were overshadowed by **Otto von Bismarck's** victory over the Austrian armies in 1866, which dislodged Austria from its leadership position among Germanic peoples and established Prussia in its place. Franz-Josef assented to what passed as a constitutional monarchy, but *The French philosophy* he remained firmly in control; the Austrian state became *of middle-class revolu-* more centralized and autocratic than it was before. Under *tion reached Austria in* the terms of the **Ausgleich** (compromise) of 1867, a dual monarchy was established. **Hungary** gained theoretically *the spring of 1848.* equal status as a kingdom alongside Austria. In theory, Communism works, too. In reality, German speakers still dominated the so-called **Austro-Hungarian Empire.** This construction was additionally flawed in its lack of concern for the countless other nationalities represented in the dual empire; Czechs, Poles, Slovenes, and Croats remained essentially powerless. By 1907 the Austrian Kingdom had ceded basic civil rights to the population and accepted universal male suffrage.

Along with liberalism and socialism, a new movement began to take hold in Austria during this period. **Pan-Germanism,** the desire to abandon the eastern empire and unite with the German *Reich,* flourished under the leadership of **Georg von Schönerer,** whose doctrines were to have a profound influence on Adolf Hitler. By the turn of the century, Vienna was in political turmoil; the anti-Semitic **Christian Socialists,** under **Karl Lueger,** were on the rise. *Ruhe und Ordnung* (peace and order) was the *Kaiser's* motto, but his policies amounted to trying to stop the irreversible tide of modernity. (He was known to eschew even indoor plumbing.)

The long period of peace that lasted until World War I was safeguarded by a complicated system of European **alliances** in which minor disputes could easily escalate into a conflict involving dozens of nations. In 1879 Austria-Hungary joined the German Empire, which, with the addition of Italy in 1882, formed the **Triple Alliance,** balancing the **Triple Entente** of France, Britain, and Russia (and later, the U.S.—hey, that's quadruple). Meanwhile, burgeoning nationalist sentiments, especially among the Serbia-inspired South Slavs, led to severe divisions within the multinational Austro-Hungarian Empire. Everything was complicated by working-class tension.

WORLD WAR I AND THE FIRST REPUBLIC

Brimming with ethnic tension and locked into the rigid system of alliances, the Austro-Hungarian Empire was a disaster waiting to happen. The spark that set off the explosion was the assassination of Franz Ferdinand, the heir to the imperial throne, by a Serbian nationalist named Gavrilo Prinzip on behalf of his terrorist organization The Black Hand on June 28, 1914. Austria's declaration of war against Serbia set off a chain reaction that pulled most of Europe into the conflict: Russia ran to support Serbia, Germany to support Austria, and France to support its Entente partner, Russia. The technologically and organizationally backward Austrian army performed with spectacular ineptitude on the battlefield and was defeated every time it faced serious competition. Only the subordination of the Austrian forces to German command saved the empire from collapse.

Franz Josef died in 1916, leaving the throne to his grandnephew **Karl I,** who tried to extricate Austria from the war empire intact. The Entente powers, recognizing that the Habsburg goose was already cooked, rebuffed Karl's advances and proclaimed a goal of self-determination for the Habsburg nationalities. On November 11, 1918, a week after signing an armistice with the Entente, Karl abdicated, bringing the 640-year-old dynasty to a close.

Worry over the country's economic viability following World War I caused revolution in the streets of Vienna and brought about the proclamation of the **Republic of Deutsch-Österreich** (German Austria), a constituent component of the Greater German Republic. The Entente was, however, leery of a powerful pan-German nation and forbade the merger. The new **Austrian republic,** or the **First Republic,** consisted of the German-speaking lands of the former Habsburg empire minus those granted to Italy, Czechoslovakia, and Hungary—or, in the famous words of French Premier Georges Clemençeau, "what's left over." The old empire had sprawled over 676,615 sq. km and encompassed some 51.4 million people. After WWI, the new republic covered only 83,850 sq. km and 6.4 million inhabitants. Everyone felt bad.

The new Austria experienced an unhappy **inter-war period.** The break-up of the empire undermined economic life as former markets became independent sovereign states and closed their borders to Austrian goods. Vienna's population was on the verge of famine. By the mid-1920s, however, the Austrian government had stabilized the currency and established economic relations with neighboring states. As in Germany, **Communists** attempted to revolt, but the Social Democrats suppressed the rebellion without relying on the right. Durn Commies. Political divisions were sharp, especially between "Red Vienna" and the staunchly Catholic provinces; Social Democrats (Reds) and Christian Socialists (Blacks) really hated each other in an overboard way. The parties set up paramilitary organizations, and political violence became a fact of life. On this shaky democratic foundation, the authoritarian **Engelbert Dollfuss** created a government in 1932 on a one-vote majority in the National Assembly.

THE ANSCHLUß

The minority **Austrian Nazis** had been agitating for unification with Germany since Hitler took power. Their demands became more menacing after his stunning success facing down the Western powers. Four months after the establishment of the authoritarian Federal State of Austria, Nazi sympathizers attempted a coup in which they murdered Dollfuss. Dollfuss's successor, **Kurt Schuschnigg,** put down the insurgents but faced a stepped-up campaign headed by Hitler's agents. Schuschnigg sought to maintain Austria's sovereignty by allying with Italy and Hungary (Hungary? after all that?). In 1938, however, Hitler met with Schuschnigg in Berchtesgaden and threatened to invade Austria if Nazi **Arthur Seyss-Inquart** was not named Interior Minister. With the Austrian police under their control, the Nazis brought Austria to near chaos. On March 9, 1938, hoping to stave off a Nazi invasion, Schuschnigg called a referendum on unity with Germany. One day before the thing was to take place, Nazi troops crossed the frontier, completing the *Anchluß* (annexation). Hitler, a born Austrian himself and a failed artist repeatedly rejected by Viennese art schools, quickly moved in to give a mass rally in Heldenplatz. Although Josef Goebbels' propaganda wildly exaggerated the enthusiasm of Austrians for Hitler (as did a phony referendum in April, in which 99% of Austrians approved of the *Anschluß*), Austria wasn't merely a prostrate victim. There was acceptance. When German troops marched into Vienna on March 14, thousands of Austrians turned out to cheer them on. The German Nazi **Racial Purity Laws** were subsequently extended to Austria, a disaster for Austrian Jews. Many managed to emigrate, but few were allowed to flee after March 1938. Those left in Austria perished later in Nazi extermination camps. Today, less than 0.05% of Austria's population is Jewish.

THE SECOND REPUBLIC

After the German defeat in WWII, a coalition of Christian Socialists and Social Democrats declared a Republic with **Karl Renner** as president. The Allies didn't impose reparation payments on Austria, but they did occupy the country and withhold recognition of sovereignty for the decade following the war. Pretty embarrassing. The country was divided into four occupation zones: Britain, France, and the U.S. held the west; the Soviets held the east. Vienna was split into four zones, divided between the four tensely allied powers. (The British got the Schönbrunn Palace and built airstrips on its lawn). When Stalin assented to free elections, the Soviet-occupied zone voted overwhelmingly to rejoin western compatriots in a united, democratic Austrian nation. The 1945 Austrian **Declaration of Independence** proclaimed the existence of an Austrian nation that, unlike the First Republic, claimed no fraternity with Greater Germany. Under the **Constitution Act** and the **State Treaty** of 1955, signed in Vienna's Belvedere Palace, Austria declared its absolute neutrality.

CURRENT GOVERNMENT

The foundation for the Second Republic rests upon the federal constitution of 1920 and its 1929 amendment. The constitution provides for a bicameral parliament, consisting of a popularly elected lower house, or **Nationalrat,** headed by a **Chancellor;** and an upper house, or **Bundesrat,** whose delegates are appointed by the provincial parliaments. The constitution also created the office of **Federal President,** a largely ceremonial (the president lacks executive power in peacetime) post.

Politics in the Second Republic have since been dominated by the **Socialist Party of Austria** (*Sozialistische Partei Österreichs*—**SPÖ**), renamed the **Social Democratic Party of Austria** (*Österreichische Sozialdemokratische Partei*, same abbreviation) in 1991. The party has often been compelled to govern in coalition with the second-largest party, the **People's Party of Austria** (*Österreichische Volkspartei*—**ÖVP**), the descendant of the Christian Socialists. In 1989, the fascist League of Independents tallied a surprising 10% of the vote. The League later renamed itself the **Freedom Party** (*Freiheitliche Partei Österreichs*—**FPÖ**), and still fields successful candidates to Parliament. On a brighter note, the **Green Party** has been showing well in the polls, and they recently fielded a woman candidate, Dr. Madeleine Petrovic, for chancellor. When the Social Democratic party candidate won instead, she became head of the Green Party and parliament speaker for the Greens.

While bitter struggle and confrontation characterized prewar politics, postwar politics have mainly seen cooperation, accommodation, and consensus. (Sounds like propaganda.) Under the SPÖ's stewardship, Austria built up one of the world's most successful **industrial economies**—Austria's unemployment and inflation rates are enviably low, even as Austrians enjoy the security of a generous, comprehensive **welfare state.** Austria joined the **European Union (EU)** in 1995, despite having a better economy, stricter ecological laws, and better welfare provisions than most of the other member states. Since then, it has prospered as a member and will be one of the first countries to adopt the **ecu**, or **euro** in German. Beginning January 1, 1999, prices will be listed in both *Schillings* and euros, and by the year 2002 all hard currency will be completely converted to euros.

Disturbingly, the Freedom Movement, under the leadership of xenophobic far-rightist **Jörg Haider,** continued to do well among younger voters, especially as anxiety about immigration from war-troubled Eastern Europe grew. On a more visible political level, Austrians elected former Secretary-General of the United Nations **Kurt Waldheim** to the largely ceremonial Austrian presidency in 1986 despite his having served as an officer in a Nazi-era German Army unit that allegedly committed heinous war crimes. As an international pariah, barred from making state visits to some places and forbidden to enter the U.S., Waldheim was a serious embarrassment for Austria.

RECENT YEARS

In January 1997, **Viktor Klima** succeeded Franz Vranitzky as Chancellor, and **Thomas Klestil** was re-elected as President in 1998. Austria's application to the EU was accepted in early 1995, and soon after the Austrian Schilling joined the European **Exchange Rate Mechanism**. Now, after being shut out for a while from the forthcoming **European Monetary Union** (EMU), Austria has become a firm member and will make the official transition to the **ecu** on January 1, 1999. It will also take over the presidency of the EU for a six-month term that extends into 1999. The government hopes to maintain economic stability by streamlining subsidies, cutting welfare benefits and public expenditures, and beginning a larger privatization program. Participation in **NATO** has kindled much discussion, with Foreign Minister Wolfgang Schüssel advocating a more limited neutrality, and recent popular referenda have addressed issues of gender equality and genetically altered food. Austrian political figures are also becoming more active in arbitrating conflicts in neighboring Eastern Europe.

■ Music

Austrian music occupies a central position in the Western Classical music tradition. The historical embryo for this phenomenon is the unique constellation of composers who created **Viennese Classics.** These Austrian greats, including Haydn, Mozart, Schubert, and Beethoven, invented "Classical music" as we know it today. The rules they made up govern and constrain Western music still. There are challenges, however; there are attempts to call those rules into question. And in many ways, the origin of those challenges is also Austria, birthplace of the modern, home to luminaries like Gustav Mahler and Arnold Schönberg. Austria is where Western Classical music is done and undone.

THE CLASSICAL ERA

Toward the end of the 18th century, Vienna became a place where people sat around and furiously wrote music. They hung out in salons, made fun of each other, listened to themselves play music they wrote or music their friends wrote. The whole thing fed on itself: the more music was written, the more people wanted to write music. The word "flourished" might be appropriate.

Christoph Willibald Gluck

Gluck arrived in Vienna at age 22 and quickly became an integral figure in the music scene. He composed many of his best-known operas in Vienna, including "Alceste" and early versions of "Orfeo," while at the same time acting as *Kapellmeister* for the court of Empress Maria Theresa. A staunch opponent of Italian opera factions, Gluck defended the use of German in song and revived German operas by such illustrious contemporaries as Carl von Weber and Wolfgang Amadeus Mozart. Gluck was a steadfast admirer of Mozart's ability, and on one occasion invited Wolfgang and wife to lunch at his country house after a piano concert by the younger man. Through his friendships with much younger composers and his own pioneering approach to music, Gluck had immense importance for later Romantic composers.

Franz Josef Haydn

Haydn is the first master musician wholly identified with Viennese Classicism. Born into the family of a poor wheelwright in Rohrau (Lower Austria) in 1732, Haydn began his career as a chorister in the cathedral of St. Stephen in Vienna before working for the princes of Eszterházy (see **Eisenstadt,** p. 132). He quickly became the conductor of the court orchestra and one of the most celebrated composers in Europe.

Haydn created a variety of new musical forms that led to the shaping of the sonata and the symphony, structures that dominated musical doctrines throughout the 19th century. Fifty-two piano sonatas, 24 piano and organ concertos, 104 symphonies, and 83 string quartets provide rich and abundant proof of his pioneering productivity. Some of his most famous work, including "The Creation" and "The Seasons," were first performed in the old Palais Schwarzenberg in Vienna (currently Neuer Markt 8, I). In his last years, Haydn began composing the superb masses; some call them his finest work. He even churned out the imperial anthem, *Gott erhalte Franz den Kaiser,* in order to rouse patriotic feeling during the Napoleonic wars. After WWI, when the new Austrian republic abandoned its anthem, Germany adopted *Gott erhalte.* You may know it as *Deutschland über Alles.*

Wolfgang Amadeus Mozart

Mozart's work may be the peak of Viennese Classicism. The study and interpretation of the compositions spanning the 35 years of his tragically short life have busied most great musicians (and most great hacks) ever since. Mozart was born in Salzburg in 1756 to a father who quickly realized (and exploited) his son's musical genius. He was playing violin and piano by age four and composing simple pieces by five, all before formally learning the art of composition. When he was six, his father took him and his similarly talented sister Nannerl on their first concert tour of Europe, where they played the piano for the royal courts of Munich and Pressburg and the imperial court of Vienna. At 13, Mozart became *Konzertmeister* of the Salzburg court, but soon learned to dislike the town's narrow bourgeois atmosphere. In 1781 he finally broke free of Salzburg, provoking the Archbishop to literally give him the boot due to persistent "insubordination." Mozart reached the musical capital of Vienna at age 25 and immediately began composing some of his most mature and interesting work.

During his Viennese period, the twenty-something Wunderkind produced his first mature concerti, his best-known Italian operas, *Don Giovanni* and *La Nozze di Figaro (The Marriage of Figaro),* and the beloved and shamefully overwhistled string showpiece, *Eine kleine Nachtmusik.* He also ran up huge debts. Not very fiscally responsible, that Mozart.

Mozart wrote with unprecedented speed, creating 626 works of all forms and sizes during the 35 years of his short life, always jotting down music without preliminary sketches or revisions. In his final years he moved into a more Germanic style, creating works with reserved dramatic impact like *Die Zauberflöte* (The Magic Flute)—a *Singspiel* (comic opera) very different from the flamboyant *opera buffa* of his early years. Mozart's overwhelming emotional power found full expression in the (unfinished) *Requiem,* which he continued composing until the last hours before his death, fulfilling his bitter aside to favorite student Franz Süssmayr: "You see, I *have* been writing this Requiem for myself." Although speculations concerning Mozart's death have been rife, most historians agree that, rather than being poisoned by Salieri, Mozart simply died of kidney failure. His remains were interred in an unmarked grave of the St. Marx cemetery outside what was then Vienna's city walls, in a pauper's funeral. Only a few decades after his death, Mozart was recognized once more as a classical master, a musician who in Tchaikovsky's words was "the culmination of all beauty in music...He alone can make me tremble at the awareness of the approach of what we call the Ideal."

Ludwig van Beethoven

Beethoven is considered the most remarkable representative of the new genre of artists working after Mozart. Born into a family of Flemish musicians in Bonn in 1770, he lived in Vienna all his adult life, and died there, too.

Beethoven created a furor as a formal innovator in a music scene steeped in tradition. His gifts were manifest in his 32 piano sonatas, string quartets, overtures, and concertos, but shone most intensely in his nine epoch-shattering symphonies. The cultural impact of his *Ninth Symphony* is enormous. Among its innovations was the introduction of a human voice to the symphonic form—the chorus sings the text to Friedrich Schiller's *Ode to Joy*. Beethoven's *Fidelio,* which premiered May 23, 1814 at the Kärntnertortheater in Vienna after two failures in 1805 and 1806, is regarded as one of the greatest German operas.

Cut off at an early age by increasing deafness, the composer could maintain contact with the world only through a series of conversational notebooks, which provide an extremely thorough, though one-sided, record of his conversations (including that famous emotional outpouring the Heiligenstadt Testament, written in Vienna's 19th district). Beethoven is somewhere between Viennese Classicism and the Romantic movement; his lasting influence facilitated major shifts in the way things were.

Johannes Brahms

Brahms is yet another composer who was born outside the civilized realms of the Austro-Hungarian Empire in Hamburg but came young to cultural powerhouse Vienna. From his home near the Karlskirche, Brahms composed his Hungarian Dances, piano concertos, and numerous symphonies which were first performed by Hans Richter and the Vienna Philharmonic. Brahms is commonly regarded as a classicist in music who used his position in the famous Viennese Musikverein and status as a major composer to stand opposed to the Romanticism and musical experiments of his arch-rival, Wagner. In the process, Brahms became the grand old man of the Viennese music scene. Despite rigorously formalist tendencies in art, Brahms assimilated into Viennese culture and its genius for the lighter things in life. When a well-wisher approached him in the opera house and asked the great composer for a momento of their meeting, he chivalrously penned the opening bars of the Blue Danube Waltz on her fan and wrote underneath: "Unfortunately not by your Johannes Brahms."

THE ROMANTIC ERA

Franz Schubert

Schubert was born in the Viennese suburb of Lichtenthal in 1797. He began his career as a chorister in the royal imperial Hofkapelle and later made his living teaching music. Mainly self-taught, he composed (almost) the *Unfinished Symphony* and the *Symphony in C Major,* now considered masterpieces but virtually unknown during his lifetime. His lyrical genius found a more popular outlet in a series of Lieder, poems set to music; works by Goethe, Schiller, and Heine were his favorites. Through his compositions, the *Lied* became a serious work in the tradition of Viennese Classicism.

> **Mainly self-taught, he composed (almost) the Unfinished Symphony *and the* Symphony in C Major, *now considered masterpieces.***

Schubert's refreshingly new form was ideally suited to a new type of social and artistic activity—musical evenings. Originally meetings of Schubert and talented friends, the **Schubertiade** or musical soirée became a widely popular and is still practiced today in Vorarlberg and Vienna. The great song cycles made famous during these musical evenings—*Die schöne Müllerin* and the quietly despairing *Winterreise*—frame Schubert's greatest and most mature creative period. This burst of creativity was cut short by his early death in 1828 at the age of 32. Despite the brevity of

Schubert's career, his genius for pure melody was a catalyst for later musical innovations by (among others) Schumann, the Strausses, and Gustav Mahler.

Anton Bruckner

Anton Bruckner is a composer of ample, measured symphonies whose symmetric and almost architectonic movements build to a massively orchestrated culmination. Born and bred in the Danube valley, Bruckner sang as a choirboy and became organist at the monastery of St. Florian before moving to Vienna in 1868 at the age 44 to write his most renowned compositions, including the Third, Fourth, and Seventh Symphonies. A late bloomer, Bruckner obsessively admired Wagner and took the young Mahler as his protege at the Vienna Conservatorium, often treating the younger man to beer after one of his lectures. Bruckner was derided as a bumpkin during his life, but posthumously recognized as a virtuoso organist and one of the greatest symphonic masters of the 19th century.

The Strauss Family

Beginning with Johann Strauss the Elder (1804-1849), the Strauss dynasty whirled the heels of Vienna for much of the 19th century. Johann senior composed mostly waltzes and showy pieces, including the famous *Radetzkymarsch,* played every New Year by the Vienna Philharmonic. Largely responsible for the "Viennese Waltz," Johann Strauss the Younger (1825-1899) shined in his youth as a brilliant violinist and savvy cultural entrepreneur. The waltz first caught on in the Congress of Vienna in 1815, offering a new exhilaration that broke free from older, more stiffly formal dances. The quick step allowed for more intimate physical contact as partners whirled about the room, arm in arm, constantly on the verge of falling down or getting intoxicatingly dizzy. Richard Wagner, of all people, noted admiringly on a visit to the city that Viennese waltzing was "more potent than alcohol." Sensing the trend, Johann became its master, eventually writing the *Blue Danube* and *Tales from the Vienna Woods,* two of the most recognized waltzes of all time, thereby earning the title, the "King of the Waltz." You think maybe he came up with that title himself? In his spare time he managed to knock off some pretty popular operas as well; *Die Fledermaus* is his most celebrated. His brothers, Josef (1827-1870) and Eduard (1835-1916) also worked as conductors and composers.

Hugo Wolf

Hugo Wolf's lack of name recognition in the English-speaking world is due mainly to the fact that his chosen form, the *Lied,* is not an established genre in the average concert repertoire. Wolf perfected the *Lied* as a dramatic symphonic miniature, in which music and words are indissolubly linked. He frequently set poems by Goethe, Eichendorff, and Mayreder to music, creating such masterful collections as the *Mörike Lieder* (1888) and the *Italienisches Liederbuch* (1890). A key figure in the development of Austrian classical music, Wolf's *Lieder* rank among some of the loveliest and most evocative music ever composed in Vienna.

Gustav Mahler

A direct precursor to the Second Viennese experiments of Arnold Schönberg, Gustav Mahler's music works within a fractured Romantic idiom, often incorporating fragments and deliberately inconclusive segments which read like nostalgic remnants of a once certain and orderly world. During his lifetime Mahler was mainly known as a conductor—he famously reformed and revolutionized the opera houses of Prague, Vienna, and New York, although his most interesting work took place at the Viennese *Staatsoper.* After his death, conductors like Bruno Walter began adding such gorgeous and neglected music as the Third, Fourth, and Ninth Symphonies and *Das Lied von der Erde* to permanent repertoires. Mahler allowed himself new freedoms in composition, employing unusual instrumentation and startling harmonic juxtapositions. His Eighth Symphony, often called *Symphony of Thousand,* requires an orchestra and two full choruses. Mahler's music hides formalist experimentation beneath a deeply moving emotional beauty. His works form an integral part of the *fin de siècle* Viennese avant-garde.

THE MODERN ERA

Arnold Schönberg

While Mahler destabilized the traditional forms of composition, Schönberg broke away from traditional tonality altogether. Originally a devotee of Richard Wagner, he was a contemporary of such thinkers as Hofmannsthal and Klimt. Schönberg rejected tonal keys in favor of what is generally called atonality but which Schönberg himself preferred to think of as pantonality, or the disappearance of any dominant tone. The guy wrote a lot of books, a lot of music theory. His system of whole tones uses all 12 notes before any is repeated. His music, no longer confined to linear relationships of centered sounds, becomes an unlimited medium of abstractions based on a 12-tone scale that is symmetrically rearranged in a kind of serialism. Some of his most famous works are *Pierre Lunaire* and the string piece *Verklärte Nacht.* Strangely, the 12-tone system became a fad around the same time psychoanalysis did. Schönberg moved to Hollywood after the rise of Nazism.

Anton von Webern

Webern was raised an aristocrat. His mother taught him piano. He later studied under Schönberg, and ended up adopting and expanding on the 12-tone system. His music is incredibly sparse, a sharp contrast to the lush, opulent, often overwritten music of his contemporaries. His music is also concerned with reinterpretation of traditional forms: he wrote *Lieder* and was obsessed with words and poetry in relation to music. His highly formal style was at once the height of tradition and its reversal, its overturning. Webern drifted into obscurity and depression as the Nazis took over. He was killed by US troops in Salzburg: he was running away from the war with his wife (also his cousin) and children. The shooting was an accident.

Alban Berg

Born bourgeois, a student of Schönberg, a friend of Loos and Kokoschka, Berg was always a little out there. He was a perfectionist and didn't compose in many works because he was obsessed with ideal expression. His music started a riot in March 1913 when both the audience and performers, upset with his disruption of all recognizable structure or melody, got violent. Berg wrote using the 12-tone system, but also using complex chromaticism—technically within the traditional tonal system but obscuring it. His work achieved a strange effect through combination: it employed classical styles and motifs but always set with and against atonality. Like Schönberg and Webern, he suffered under the Nazis as a producer of "degenerate art" and died young after a short illness in 1935.

Falco!

Somewhere between the 12-tone system of Schönberg and the sweeping harmonics of Brahms, Falco bursts into Austrian musical history. Attempting to reconcile an artistic quest for the self with the nationalistic and naturalistic intellectual bent of the era, his rockin' *Amadeus* permeated the subconscious of radio listeners across the globe in the 80s. The song took as its subject Wolfgang Amadeus Mozart, and attempted, in the infamous "historical breakdown," to reconcile the classical past with the rock 'n' roll present. History goes something like: Mozart, then Falco, nothing in between. Sadly, Falco died in a car crash in the Dominican Republic in February 1998 while allegedly planning a comeback. For a nostalgic reexamination of Falco's happy bubblegum talent, seek out **The Remix Collection,** a compendium of his greatest hits. David Bowie is slated to play Falco in an upcoming film about the singer's life. Always crashing in the same car?

MUSICAL INSTITUTIONS

Opera

From 17th-century Italian beginnings, opera quickly grew into one of the most popular forms of music. Grand and emotional, overbearing at times, it fits right into the Baroque period. In Austria, under the patronage of the emperors, a strong operatic tradition developed that included such famous 18th-century works as Mozart's *Le nozze di Figaro* and *Cosi fan tutte* and **Johann Joseph Fux's** *Costanza e fortezza*. **Emperor Josef II** promoted Germanic opera as a national counterpart to the Italian stuff, resulting in Mozart's *Die Entführung aus dem Serail* (The Abduction from the Seraglio) and *Die Zauberflöte* (The Magic Flute).

In 1869, the **Vienna Court Opera,** today's State Opera *(Staatsoper)*, was opened by Emperor Franz Josef. It was designed as an alternate performance space to the famous **Theater an der Wien,** which hosted among other things the first performance of *The Magic Flute*. The State Opera soon managed to take over the serious opera scene, hosting the newest Wagner to an occasionally turbulent audience. Mahler became Director of the Opera in 1897, transforming the *Staatsoper* from a place of elegant, palatable entertainment into a serious music place. In 1919, composer **Richard Strauss** and director Franz Schalk took control. Since then, the Vienna *Staatsoper* has become one of the three great opera houses of the world, along with Milan's *La Scala* and the New York Metropolitan Opera. Despite heavy damage during WWII and the difficulties of the post-war years, artistic standards remain in full force. The opera house, constructed by August Siccard von Siccardsburg and Eduard van der Nüll, is one of the most magnificent edifices on the Ringstraße, and holds special sentimental value for the Viennese. When reconstructing the bombed-out center of the city after the Second World War, the opera was the first public building to be reconstructed, outranking even St. Stephen's cathedral. It reopened on November 5, 1955, with a phenomenal production of Beethoven's *Fidelio*.

The Musikverein

Operated by the *Gesellschaft der Musikfreunde* (Society of Music Lovers) since its founding in 1812, the *Musikverein* is Austria's—perhaps the world's—premier concert hall. Danish architect Theophil Hansen constructed the building in 1867, creating a concert hall of unparalleled acoustic perfection. The building is now a National Trust, and the Vienna Philharmonic shares its stage with the world's finest orchestras. The *Musikverein*'s program is essentially conservative, although it occasionally includes contemporary classical music. It leaves experimental and ultra-modern programs to its sister institution across the river Wien, the **Konzerthaus.**

The Vienna Boys' Choir

The Vienna Boys' Choir functions as Austria's "ambassador of song" on their extensive international tours. Dressed in sailor suits, they export prepubescent musicality to the entire world. Emperor Maximilian I founded the group in 1498, and the list of illustrious names associated with the choir is astounding: Franz Schubert was a chorister, Wolfgang Amadeus Mozart was appointed court composer, and Anton Bruckner held the post of organist and music teacher. Today, the choir provides a forum where Mozart, Hadyn, Schubert, and Bruckner, not to mention Beethoven's gorgeous Mass in C Op 86, can be heard as they were originally meant to be performed—sung liturgically by the clear sweet voices of a boy's choir. Besides going on world tour, members of the *Sängerknaben* are always on hand to perform mass in the Hofburg chapel at 9:25am Sunday mornings (open to all; Sept. 15-June 30).

■ Art and Architecture

Landlocked in the middle of Europe and rolling with cash, the Habsburgs married into power and bought into art. In keeping with the cosmopolitan nature of their empire and outlook, the imperial family pursued a cultural policy that decidedly favored foreign artists over their own native sons and daughters. With the intense popularity of Baroque design for 17th- and 18th-century palaces, however, Austro-Hungarians began to develop a distinct, graceful architectural style that still dominates the old centers of former Habsburg towns across Central and Eastern Europe. Around the turn of the 20th century, Austrian artists finally got fed up with traditionalism and foreign decadence and decided to stir up the coals a bit. See **Vienna Sights** (p. 100) for more discussion of art and architecture.

THE BAROQUE

Emphasizing grandiosity, Baroque architecture looks like Imperialism: its gaudiness stems from the desire to inspire awe and opulence, the desire to be rich and to look it. With fluidly ornate forms orchestrated into a succession of grand entrances, dreamy vistas, and overwrought, cupid-covered facades, the Baroque invokes what was then the most popular art form in Europe, music. The turbulent swell of Haydn or Beethoven is incarnated in stone and mortar. Austria's preeminent Baroque architects were Johann Bernhard Fischer von Erlach, Lukas von Hildebrandt, and Johann Prandtauer. **Fischer von Erlach,** born in Graz to a sculptor father, drew up the plans for Vienna's Schönbrunn and Hofburg. His best works, however, were ecclesiastical in nature, including the **Trinity** and **Collegienkirche** in Salzburg and the ornate **Karlskirche** in Vienna. **Prandtauer** was a fave of the Church. His yellow **Benedictine abbey** at **Melk** perches on rocky cliffs over the Danube. **Hildebrandt** shaped Austria's profane side. After battering the Turks, Prince Eugene of Savoy got him to revamp his newest acquisition, the Belvedere palace. Hildebrandt's penchant for theatricality shows up in the palace's succession of pavilions and grand views of Vienna; stone sphinxes dotting his enormous ornamental gardens make a silent allusion to Eugene's victory over the Ottomans.

THE RINGSTRAßE

Austria's 19th-century conservative modernism is showcased by the **Ringstraße,** the broad circular boulevard that demarcates Vienna and that was authorized in 1857 by Emperor Franz Josef to replace fortified medieval walls. Although the Ringstraße was the pet project of Viennese bourgeois liberals, the street has distinctly authoritarian roots. During the Revolution of 1848, rebels barricaded themselves inside the old city wall. After quashing the rebellion, unnerved generals of the Habsburg military insisted the wall be razed and the grand boulevard built in its place. The leafy, tree-lined *straße* was built exceptionally wide not merely for beauty's sake, but also with the covert intention of preventing barricades and giving the imperial army ready access to subversive behavior in any part of the city. Emperor Franz Josef lined the boulevard with centers of bourgeois constitution and culture: a *Universität,* a *Rathaus,* a *Parlament,* and a *Burgtheater.* Architects designed each building in a different historical style deemed symbolic of its function. The neo-gothic *Rathaus* celebrates the civic strength of the *Bürgermeister* and their medieval town halls; the early baroque style of the *Burgtheater* recalls the 17th-century golden era of the theatrical arts, while the stately Renaissance design of the university highlights the cult of rationalism and science. This historicist taste was identified with Vienna and came to be known as the **Ringstraße Style .**

BIEDERMEIER

Between Napoleon and the foundation of the republic, Austria witnessed the development of a huge dissatisfied middle class. Since political expression or social critique was virtually impossible during this era, artistic expression was funneled into a narrow channel of naturalistic and applied art centered around the family circle and domestic ideals. Genre, landscape, and portrait painting dominated. The Biedermeier is mostly remembered as a furniture style today, but it was also an art movement with a small amount of crossover into literature. Its characteristics are a predilection for symmetries, exquisite technique, naturalism, and harmonious detail.

JUGENDSTIL (A.K.A. ART NOUVEAU)

As the odometer rolled into the first years of the 20th century, revolt among Vienna's artistic community became the norm. In 1897, the "young" artists split from the "old," as proponents of *Jugendstil* modernism took issue with the Viennese Academy's rigid conservatism and traditional symbolism. The idea was to leave behind prevailing artistic conventions and formulate a new way of seeing the world.

Gustav Klimt and his followers founded the **Secession** movement. They aimed to provide the nascent Viennese avant-garde with an independent forum in which to show their work and to encourage contact with foreign artists. In their revolt against the calcified artistic climate of the old-guard Künstlerhaus, Secessionists sought to create space and appreciation for symbolist, naturalist, impressionist, and other new artistic styles. Their trademark style was Art Nouveau. Josef Maria Olbrich's **Secession building** was a reaction to the self-aggrandizing kitsch of the Ringstraße. The composer Richard Wagner's idealization of the *Gesamtkunstwerk* (total work of art) was an important subtext of Secessionist aesthetic ambitions. Their 14th exhibition was their crowning glory, an attempted synthesis of all major artistic media, featuring **Max Klinger's** Beethoven statue, Klimt's allegorical tribute to the composer, Josef Hoffmann's interior, and Mahler's music.

Klimt's cult of art for art's sake culminated in the flowing Art Nouveau; then the fever broke. Ornamentation was firmly streamlined, and a new ethic of function over form gripped Vienna's artistic elite. Vienna's guru of architectural modernism became **Otto Wagner,** who cured the city of its "artistic hangover." His Steinhof church and Postal Savings Bank enclose fluid *Jugendstil* interiors within stark, delineated structures. Wagner frequently collaborated with his student **Josef Maria Olbrich,** notably on the Majolicahaus (on the Linke Wienzeile, VII) and the Karlsplatz Stadtbahn. Wagner's admirer **Josef Hoffmann** founded the **Wiener Werkstätte** in 1903, drawing on Ruskin's English art and crafts movement and Vienna's new brand of streamlined simplicity. The *Werkstätte* appropriated objects from daily life and reinterpreted them, using basic geometry and pricey materials (marble, silk, gold). The school's influence would resonate in the **Bauhaus** of Weimar Germany.

Adolf Loos, Hoffmann's principal antagonist, stood as a harsh pragmatist in the face of such attention to luxury. Loos once said, "Ornamentation is criminal," setting himself against the Baroque grandeur that Imperial Vienna supported. Thanks to this opposition, few examples of his work reside in his native city, though he remains one of Vienna's most important architects. His indictment of the Ringstraße, entitled *Potemkin City,* affiliated him with the early Secessionist movement, but his notorious **Goldman and Salatsch building** (1909-1911) in the Michaelerpl. went a step beyond their aesthetic toward a more starkly functional architecture.

> *Loos once said "Ornamentation is criminal."*

EXPRESSIONISM

Oskar Kokoschka and **Egon Schiele** would revolt against "art *qua* art," seeking to present the frailty, neuroses, and sexual energy formerly concealed behind the Secession's aesthetic surface. **Kokoschka** is often considered (though never by himself) the founder of Viennese **Expressionism.** Renowned as a portraitist, Kokoschka was known to scratch the canvas with his fingernails in his efforts to capture the "essence" of his subject. Kokoschka's work is profoundly humanist and unafraid to be emotionally and psychologically involved with its subject. **Schiele,** like the young Kokoschka, paints with a feverish intensity in line and color. His paintings often depict tortured figures seemingly destroyed by their own bodies or by debilitating sexuality, and a lot of his work is self-portraiture. His figures are twisted and gnarled and incredibly erotic. **František Kupka** studied at the Vienna academies at the same time as Kokoschka and Schiele, but soon left for France to study Pointilism, developing a strongly musical expressionism in his style. Kupka became one of the early pioneers of abstract art.

URBAN SOCIALISM

In the 1920s and early 1930s, the **Social Democratic** administration permanently altered Vienna's cityscape. The city built thousands of apartments in large **municipal projects,** their style reflecting the newfound assertiveness of the workers' movement. The most outstanding project of the era is the **Karl Marx complex** (Heiligenstädter Str. 82-92, XIX). The huge structure, completed in 1930 from plans by Karl Ehn, extends over a kilometer and consists of 1600 apartments clustered around several courtyards. The Austrian Socialist party fought a pitched battle with rightist rioters in this apartment complex just before the outbreak of World War II. Another impressive socialist edifice is the Art Nouveau public baths of **Amalienbad** (X, Reumannpl. 9).

Friedensreich Hundertwasser (translation: Peaceful Hundredwaters; given name: Friedrich Stowasser) began with big brush strokes and bright colored canvas and moved on into more plastic material. A builder of buildings, he designed Kunst Haus Wien and the Hundertwasser House which attempt to make architecture organic, to bring life back to the "desert" that the city had become. He has a bizarre, childish, dark fairy-tale aesthetic.

Architect **Hans Hollein** learned his craft in Las Vegas and the University of Berkeley; his structures recall the sprawling abandon of his training ground while maintaining the Secessionists' attention to craftsmanship and elegant detail. His exemplary contribution to Viennese **postmodern** architecture is the **Haas House** (I, Stock-im-Eisen-Pl.), completed in 1990. Controversy has surrounded the building ever since sketches were published in the mid-80s, mainly because it stands opposite Vienna's landmark, St. Stephen's Cathedral. Over the past 20 years, Vienna's architects have focused their attention on designing interiors for boutiques and bistros. Examples of these designs are the **Restaurant Salzamt** (I, Ruprechtspl. 1) and **Kleines Café** (III, Franziskanerpl. 3), both by **Hermann Czech.**

■ Literature

THE EARLY YEARS

A collection of poetry dating from around 1150 and preserved in the abbey of Vorau in Styria marks the earliest known Austrian literature. Apart from sacred poetry, a courtly and knightly style developed in the 12th and 13th centuries that culminated in the works of minstrel **Walther von der Vogelweide.** The **Nibelungenlied,** which dates from around 1200, is one of the most impressive heroic epics preserved from this era. It's also the basis for Richard Wagner's operatic *Ring* series.

Emperor Maximilian I (1459-1519), with the unlikely moniker "The Last Knight," provided special support for theater and the dramatic arts during his reign. Splendid operas and pageants frequently involved the whole of the imperial court and led to a flurry of popular religious drama that has survived in the form of rural **passion plays.**

THE CLASSICAL WRITERS

Born in Vienna in 1801, **Johann Nestroy** grew up in the intrigue-laden court of the Austro-Hungarian capital and wrote biting comedies and satires lampooning social follies. Although his name is not readily recognized by Anglophones, Nestroy is one of the canonical figures of German drama, famous for such plays as *"Der Talisman"* and *"Liebesgeschichten und Heiratssachen,"* as well as the *"Tannhäuser"* on which Wagner based his famous opera. Karl Kraus was one of his great fans; across the ocean Thornton Wilder busily adapted Nestroy's *"The Match-maker"* into what eventually became the hit American musical *"Hello Dolly."*

Often known as Austria's greatest novelist and short storyteller, **Adalbert Stifter** wrote during roughly the same time period as Nestroy but concerned himself much more with classical *Bildungsroman* themes and strongly metaphysical descriptions of nature. Stifter was a poetic realist who falls into the same school as Fontane. His short stories, such as *Der Condor* (1840), *Die Mappe meine Urgroßvaters* (1841), and *Der Nachsommer* (1857), form part of the classical canon of German literature.

A German classicist with a more exuberantly lyrical style, **Franz Grillparzer** penned plays about the conflict between a life of thought and a life of action. Although his work often looks back to the great classical achievements of writers such as Goethe and Schiller, it chronicles the disillusionment of idealism as it encounters painful compromise with reality. Grillparzer spent his life as a clerk in the Austrian bureaucratic system and wrote some of his most critically acclaimed plays, such as *The Waves of the Sea and Love* (1831) in his spare time. Most of Grillparzer's fame came posthumously, when interest grew in his published work and the beautifully composed autobiography *Der arme Spielmann* was discovered among his papers.

FIN DE SIÈCLE

Around 1890, Austrian literature rapidly transformed in the heat of the "merry apocalypse" atmosphere that permeated society at the turn of the century. The literature dating from this second heyday of Austrian culture is legendary. **Sigmund Freud** diagnosed the crisis, **Karl Kraus** implacably unmasked it, **Arthur Schnitzler** dramatized it, **Hugo von Hofmannsthal** ventured a cautious eulogy, and **Georg Trakl** commented on the collapse in feverish verse. It was a crazy time and a crazy place.

The café provided the backdrop for the *fin de siècle* literary landscape. Like many popular institutions of its time, the relaxed elegance of the Viennese café was part fantasy, part imaginative camouflage of an ugly and best ignored reality. Vienna faced severe shortages of both housing and firewood, and the café was the only place where many people could relax in relative comfort and warmth. Some even had their mail addressed to them at their habitual cafe. At the Café Griensteidl, **Hermann Bahr**—lyric poet, critic, and one-time director of the *Burgtheater*—loosely presided over a pioneer group known as **Jung Wien** (Young Vienna). Featuring Hofmannsthal, Altenberg, and Schnitzler Jung Wien rejected the **Naturalism** of Emile Zola in favor of a psychological realism that aimed to capture the subtlest nuances of the Viennese atmosphere. Hofmannsthal walked a tightrope between Impressionism and verbal decadence, creating such exquisite pieces of drama as *Yesterday* (1891) and *Everyman* (1911) while at the same time collaborating with Richard Strauss to write librettos for, among other things, *Der Rosenkavalier*. Altenberg, "discovered" while putting furious pen to paper in the Café Central by Bahr, remained philosophically at odds with the rest of the avant-garde. His first work, *Wie ich es sehe* (As I See It), explores the act of seeing and its place in an Impressionist documentary of moments. Schnitzler, playwright and colleague of Freud, was the first German to write stream-of-consciousness prose. He skewered Viennese aristocratic decadence in dramas and essays, exposing the moral bankruptcy of their code of honor in such works as *Leutnant Gustl* (translated as None but the Brave). He also shocked contemporaries by portraying the complexities of erotic relationships in many of his plays, including his famous *Merry-Go-Round* (1897). **Stefan Zweig,** another member of the group and author of *Die Welt von Gestern* (Yesterday's World), established himself with brilliant analyses of Freud. Zweig was especially noted for his historical biographies, as well as his skilled psychological fiction.

> *Vienna faced severe shortages of both housing and firewood, and the café was the only place where many people could relax in relative comfort and warmth.*

The renegade cultural critics of Jung Wien found an acerbic opponent in **Karl Kraus.** Upon the destruction of Café Griensteidl, Kraus published a critical periodical, *Die Fackel* (The Torch), that attacked the literary Impressionism of Bahr and his ilk and plunged Bahr into literary obscurity. Kraus' journalistic desire for pure, clear language and his demand for truth and simplicity contrasted with the dilettantish escapism he saw in Bahr's work. Kraus, though a Jew, remained virulently anti-Zionist throughout his life and launched scathing attacks on Zionism's modern founder, **Theodor Herzl,** a frequent contributor to the *Neue Freie Presse* and habitué of Café

Landtmann. Kraus allied himself closely with Adolf Loos; both were among the most controversial figures in Vienna.

The collapse of the Austro-Hungarian monarchy marked a major turning point in the intellectual and literary life of Austria. Novelists **Robert Musil** and **Joseph Roth** concerned themselves with the consequences of the empire's breakdown. Roth's novels, *Radetzkymarsch* and *Die Kapuzinergruft*, portray a romanticized portrait of the former empire. Musil invented the term *Parallelaktion* (parallel action) to describe his symbolic use of the moribund monarchy. His writing is fiercely subversive and anti-hierarchical, and shows the potential for narrative to be used as a tool of resistance. He is most famous for his unfinished work in three volumes *Der Mann Ohne Eigenschaften* (*The Man Without Qualities*). Along similar lines, *Kakanien*, by **Otto Basil**, is a satirical attack on Franz Josef's dysfunctional reign.

THE 20TH CENTURY

By the First World War, the cult of despair had replaced the cult of art. **Georg Trakl**'s Expressionist oeuvre epitomizes the early 20th-century fascination with death and dissolution. "All roads empty into black putrefaction" is his most frequently quoted line, and his *Helian* remains one of the most important Germanic lyrical works. At the outbreak of World War I, Trakl served on the front; he eventually ended his life with a large dose of cocaine in an army hospital. The comical plays by **Fritz von Herzmanovsky-Orlando,** including *Der Gaulschreck im Rosennetz* (The Horse Scarer in the Rose Net), also popular at the time, are also pretty bleak.

Few of Austria's literary titans lived outside Vienna. A notable exception, **Franz Kafka** resided in Prague, in the Habsburg protectorate of Bohemia although he regularly traveled to visit Vienna and drank coffee at the Herrenhof cafe. *The Metamorphosis*, a bizarre and disorienting tale, confronts the idea of **"All roads empty into** one day waking up and *really* not feeling oneself. Unless you usually feel like a giant cockroach, which Kafka might **black putrefaction."** have. In *The Trial,* Kafka pries into the dehumanizing power of the bureaucratized modern world. After World War II, Kafka's oppressive parables of a cold world became the models for a new generation of writers. Prague also housed such greats as **Franz Werfel** *(The Forty Days of Musa Dagh)* and **Rainer Maria Rilke.** Although Rilke also wrote important novels and essays, he is most famous for the lyric poetry cycles the *Duino Elegies* and *Sonnets to Orpheus*. Rilke pushed his language to such extremes of subtlety, purity, and nuance that he came close to creating his own language within the poems.

These artistic movements owe their fascination with the unconscious to the new science of psychoanalysis and its founder, **Sigmund Freud.** Freud has been accused of extracting too readily from the Viennese paradigm, and his intellectual opponents have charged that Freud's theories of repression (LUST) apply only to bourgeois Vienna (PATRICIDE). Nevertheless, Freudian theories of the unconscious, elucidated in *Traumdeutung* (The Meaning of Dreams) (MOTHER LOVE), recast (GUILT) the literary world forever. Freud, a Jew, fled (AGGRESSION) Vienna in 1938. His house is currently on display, with the historic couch wrapped (PHALLIC SYMBOL) in plastic.

Today words still flow, affected and informed and liberated by the long-standing literary tradition. **Jelinek** wrote *Lust,* an explicit novel, critically feminist, written by a woman, which shook and shocked Catholic church-goers with its audacity. A swift kick in the balls. **Thomas Bernhard** wrote *Holzfällen* (Woodcutters) and *Wittgenstein's Nephew.* His relationship with his homeland was a strange one, and his work is in many ways a cogent and mature critique of Austrian society. Things are still happening; people are still upset enough to write.

■ Food and Drink

With a few notable exceptions, Austrian cuisine is foreign in origin: *Gulasch* is Hungarian, dumplings are Bohemian. Even the archetypal Austrian dish, *Wiener Schnitzel,* probably originated in Milan. Immigrants continue to influence Austrian cooking,

---

Sacher Scandal

Austria takes its desserts very seriously. *Linzer Torte* is extremely important to the Linzers, and the whole country has a love affair with *Apfel Strudel*. But things work a little differently in Vienna. *Sacher Torte* ranks with *Linzer Torte* as one of the country's most famous cakes, but it is not clear who can lay claim to this celebrated dessert. Franz Sacher claims to have concocted the confection for Prince von Metternich, but Café Demel doesn't agree—its proprietors claim to hold the original recipe. Demel sued the Hotel Sacher, and the suit has resulted in bankruptcy, the sale of Demel to a corporation, and the suicide of Sacher's general manager. It's probably safest to stick to *Strudel*.

---

and Turkish dishes like *Dönerkebab* are on their way to becoming an integral part of Austrian cuisine. Most of Austria's culinary invention appears on the dessert cart. *Tortes* commonly contain *Erdbeeren* (strawberries) and *Himbeeren* (raspberries). Don't miss *Marillen Palatschinken*, a crepe with apricot jam, or *Kaiserschmarr'n*, the *Kaiser's* favorite (pancake bits with a plum compote). Austrians adore sweet dessert *Knödeln* (dumplings), and the archetypal street-stand dessert is the *Krapfen*, a hole-less doughnut usually filled with jam. The pinnacle of Austrian baking, however, are the twin delights of *Sacher Torte* (a rich chocolate cake layered with marmalade) and *Linzer Torte* (raspberry jam in a rich pie crust).

Loaded with fat, salt, and cholesterol, traditional Austrian cuisine is a cardiologist's nightmare. Staples include *Schweinefleisch* (pork), *Kalbsfleisch* (veal), *Wurst* (sausage), *Ei* (egg), *Käse* (cheese), *Brot* (bread), and *Kartoffeln* (potatoes). Austria's most renowned dish, *Wiener Schnitzel*, is a meat cutlet (usually veal or pork) fried in butter with bread crumbs. Although *Schnitzel* is Austria's most famous, its most scrumptious meat dish is *Tafelspitz*, beautifully cooked boiled beef. Soups are also an Austrian speciality; try *Gulaschsuppe* (gulasch soup) and *Frittatensuppe* (pancake strips in a delicious broth). Recently, vegetarianism has become more and more popular in Vienna, and even meaty dishes are showing the influence of a lighter, vegetable-reliant style. Vegetarians should look for *Spätzle* (a potato-based noodle often served with cheese and wine sauces), *Steinpilze* (enormous delicious mushrooms native to the area), or anything with the word "Vegi" in it.

Of course, you've got to have something to wash all that down. The most famous Austrian wine is probably *Gumpoldskirchen* from Lower Austria, the largest wine-producing province. *Klosterneuburger*, produced in the eponymous district near Vienna, is both reasonably priced and dry. Austrian beers are outstanding. *Ottakringer* and *Gold Fassl* flow from Vienna breweries; *Stiegl Bier* and *Augustiner Bräu* from Salzburg; *Zipfer Bier* from upper Austria; and *Gösser Bier* from Styria. Austria imports a great deal of Budweiser beer a.k.a. *Budvar*—the original Bohemian variety, not the chintzy American imitation.

In mid-afternoon, Austrians flock to *Café-Konditoreien* (café-confectioners) to nurse the national sweet tooth with *Kaffee und Kuchen* (coffee and cake). Try a *Mélange*, the classic Viennese coffee with frothed cream and a hint of cinnamon, or nibble on the heavenly *Mohr im Hemd*, a chocolate sponge cake topped with hot whipped chocolate. Anything with the word *Mohn* (poppyseed) is nearly always a happy choice.

Supermarket connoisseurs should have a blast with Austrian staples: yogurt (rich, creamy, almost dessert-like); the cult favorite Nutella (a chocolate-hazelnut spread); *Almdudler* (a lemonade-like soft drink); *Semmeln* (very cheap, very fresh rolls); the original *Müsli* (trail mix of the gods); and Milka (the purple cow) chocolate.

Vienna (Wien)

It was not without reason that home-grown satirist Karl Kraus once dubbed Vienna—birthplace of psychoanalysis, atonal music, functionalist architecture, Zionism, and Nazism—a "laboratory for world destruction." Vienna's heyday carried the seeds of its own decay, and did so in such a blatant way that café-goers analyzed the phenomenon-in-process desultorily over coffee. *Fin de siècle* Vienna had a cultural importance that rivaled Paris, thanks to its enormous school of musicians (Mozart, Beethoven, Schubert, Strauss, Brahms) and imperial wealth and taste in imported Baroque art, architecture, and decor. At the height of its artistic ferment, during the smoky and caffeine-permeated days of the great café culture, the Viennese were already self-mockingly referring to their city as the "merry apocalypse."

That nervous atmosphere of rebellion, disruption, and disintegration was the reaction of a civilization staring down its own dissolution, a dissolution made inevitable by an antiquated political system, a pathetically inadequate army, and a patchwork empire in an age when empires were toppling to nationalism and guerrilla independence movements. The smooth veneer of waltz music, whipped cream, and *Gemütlichkeit* covered a darker reality whose symptoms were Sigmund Freud, Kafka, Georg Trakl, and the beautiful, deathly, fragmenting music of Gustav Mahler. The talent of Vienna was to invent a culture of fantasy, good humor, and elegance to mask facts that seemed better ignored. Vienna's schizophrenia was perhaps one of bad faith, but at the same time it was almost naively quixotic. Its forced direction of attention on what was beautiful, even what was dark and madly beautiful, was responsible for the city's desperate and febrile artistic activity.

Streets filled with Baroque curlicues and flora, stucco onion-domed churches, sinuous art nouveau facades, and cafés with pooling light and worn, nicotine-stained velvet sofas. Vienna has a certain air of living absent-mindedly in the past, but that mood is rapidly fading as the city picks up speed with the second half of the 20th-century. Postmodern architecture and ecological fantasies by Friedensreich Hundertwasser share space with Biedermeier apartment buildings. One street graffiti artist has even taken to painting Andy Warhol's Velvet Underground banana on random walls and surfaces in all 23 of Vienna's districts.

Post-war diplomatic debates positioned Vienna in a threshold position between East and West. Now that the Cold War is over and the Iron Curtain has mostly crumbled, Vienna has been trying to renew business connections in the former Communist bloc and reestablish itself as the political, cultural, and economic gateway to Eastern Europe. The city has also made concerted efforts to broaden its international status by attempting to match Geneva as a European center for the United Nations.

Despite notions of a Vienna filled exclusively with white, Catholic conservatives, its population's social, cultural, and ethnic diversity is remarkable and immediately recognizable in the devotion to activist causes such as women's rights, gay rights, and environmentalism. From July to December 1998, Austria held the European Union's (E.U.) presidency. Vienna threw a "celebration between E and U" festival, referring not only to Vienna's role as a truly central-European city easily accessible to the former Communist Bloc, but also to the city's fusion of "E" (a term for classical, traditional music) and "U" (popular and modern). Vienna is once more reconnecting with its turn-of-the-century identity as a place where experimentalism thrives, where rules of genre, style, and even structure are made and unmade in everything from music to contemporary film and art.

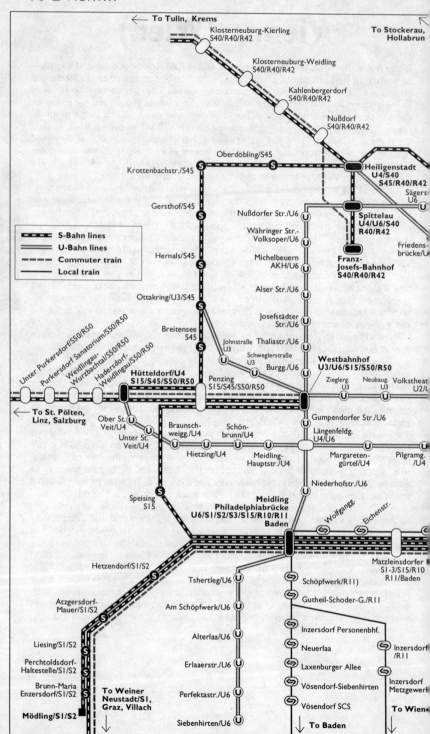

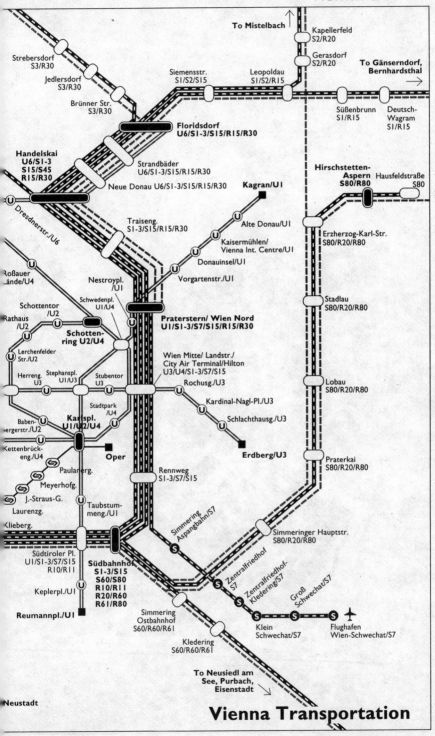

Vienna Transportation

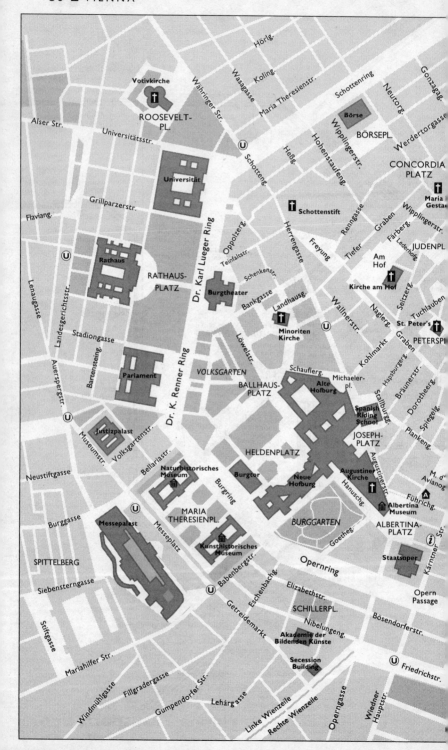

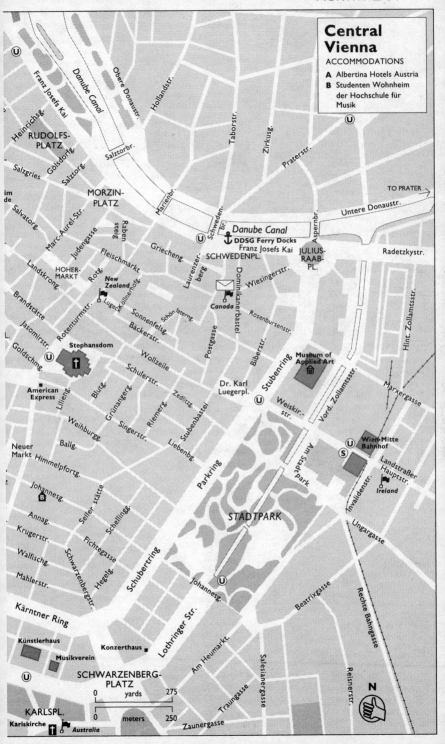

Central Vienna

ACCOMMODATIONS

A Albertina Hotels Austria
B Studenten Wohnheim der Hochschule für Musik

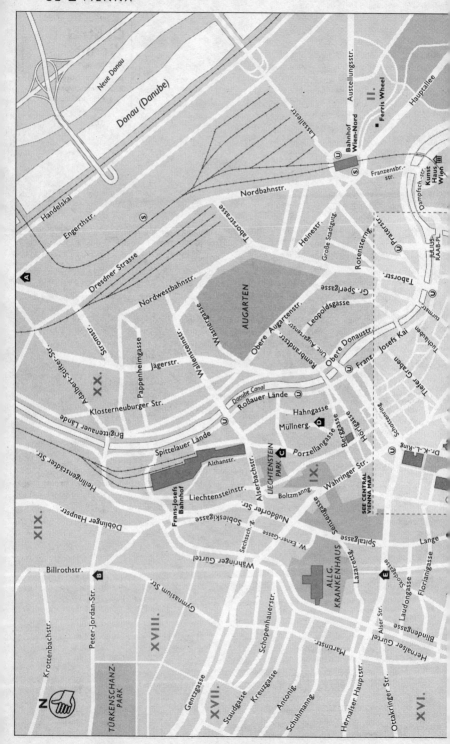

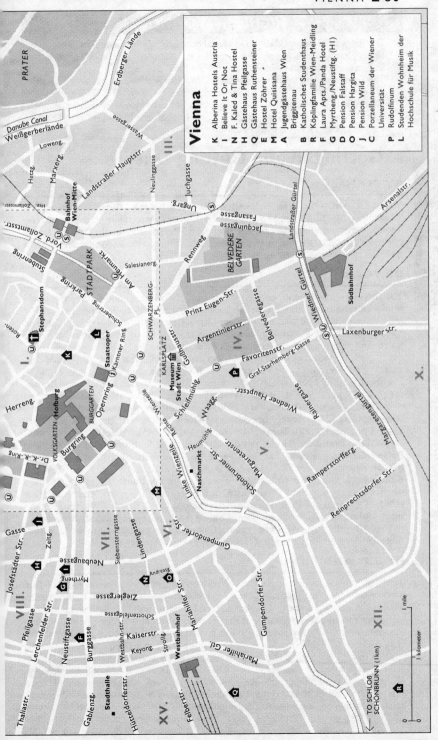

Vienna

- K Alberina Hostels Austria
- I Believe It Or Not
- N F. Kaled & Tina Hostel
- H Gästehaus Pfeilgasse
- Q Gästehaus Ruthensteiner
- E Hostel Zöhrer
- M Hotel Quisisana
- A Jugendgästehaus Wien
-    Briggitenau
- B Katholisches Studenthaus
- R Köplingfamilie Wien-Meidling
- F Laura Apts./Panda Hotel
- G Myrtheng./Neustiftg. (HI)
- D Pension Falstaff
- O Pension Hargita
- J Pension Wild
- C Porzellaneum der Wiener
-    Universität
- P Rudolfinum
- L Studenden Wohnheim der
-    Hochschule für Musik

🖑 *HIGHLIGHTS OF VIENNA*

- The Ringstraße circles Vienna's medieval first district and contains many famous sights such as the *Parlament,* the *Rathaus,* the *Staatsoper,* and the *Volksgarten.*
- St. Stephen's cathedral *(Stephansdom)* is the heart of Vienna.
- The *Kunsthistorisches Museum, Kunsthaus, Museum Moderner Kunst,* and *Secession* are some of Vienna's most popular art museums.
- The *Hofburg* is the imperial Habsburg palace and offers tours of state rooms.
- The Vienna Woods and the vineyards and wine gardens *(Heurigen)* in the outlying suburbs of Vienna are also popular destinations.

■ Getting In and Getting Out

BY PLANE

Vienna's airport is the **Wien-Schwechat Flughafen,** home of **Austrian Airlines** (tel. 17 89; open M-F 8am-7pm, Sa-Su 8am-5pm). There is a daily flight to and from **New York** and frequent flights to **London, Rome,** and **Berlin,** among other places. Travelers under 25 qualify for discounts if tickets are bought two weeks in advance. Student travelers ages 25 and 26 also qualify.

BY TRAIN

The three main train stations—Westbahnhof, Südbahnhof, and Franz-Josefs Bahnhof—all send trains in different directions and serve various European cities. For train information, call 17 17 (24hr.) or check times at http://www.bahn.at. The **Westbahnhof,** XV, Mariahilferstr. 132, runs trains west to destinations including **Salzburg** (3hr., every hr., 410AS), **Linz** (2hr., every hr., 270AS), **Innsbruck** (6hr., every 2hr., 660AS), **Bregenz** (8hr., 5 per day, 820AS), **Zurich** (9hr., 3 per day, 1160AS), **Amsterdam** (14hr., 1 per day, 2258AS), **Paris** (14hr., 2 per day, 2198AS), **Hamburg** (9½hr., 2 per day, 2100AS), **Munich** (4½hr., 5 per day, 740AS), and **Budapest** (3-4hr., 9 per day, 374AS). The Westbahnhof train **information counter** is open daily 7:30am-8:40pm. The second station, **Südbahnhof,** X, Wiedner Gürtel 1a, sends trains to **Graz** (2¾hr., every hr., 310AS), **Villach** (5hr., every hr., 470AS), **Prague** (5hr., 3 per day, 524AS), **Rome** (14hr., 2 per day, 1230AS), **Venice** (8hr., 5 per day, 760AS), and **Bratislava** (1hr., 4 per day, 100AS), along with trains to other cities in **Poland, Germany, Russia, Turkey, Greece,** and **Spain.** The Südbahnhof train **information counter** is open daily 6:30am-9:20pm. The third major station, **Franz-Josefs Bahnhof,** IX, Althamstr. 10, handles mostly commuter trains. There are also two smaller stations: **Bahnhof Wien Mitte,** in the center of town, and **Bahnhof Wien Nord,** by the Prater on the north side of the Danube Canal. Bahnhof Wien Nord is the main S-Bahn and U-Bahn link for trains heading north, but most Bundesbahn trains go through the other stations. Some regional trains (Krems, for example) also leave from **Spittelau,** located on the U-4 and U-6 subway lines.

BY BUS AND BOAT

Travel by bus is seldom cheaper than travel by train; compare prices before you buy a ticket. **City Bus Terminals** stand at Wien Mitte/Landstr., Hüttelsdorf, Heiligenstadt, Floridsdorf, Kagran, Erdberg, and Reumannpl. Domestic Bundesbuses run from these stations to local and international destinations. (Ticket counter open M-F 6am-5:50pm, Sa-Su 6am-3:50pm.) Many international bus lines also have agencies in the stations, each with different hours. For bus information, call 711 01 (7am-7pm).

For a more exotic trip to or from Vienna, try a **ferry.** The famous **Donaudampfschiffahrtsgesellschaft Donaureisen** (DDSG), I, Friedrichstr. 7 (tel. 588 800; fax 588 80 440; email ddsg.blue.danube@telecom.at; http://www.ddsg_blue_danube), organizes several cruises up and down the Danube, ranging from 84AS to 1032AS. Supersleek **hydrofoils** to **Budapest** run April to October (750AS, round-trip 1100AS), with special rates and reduced service in early April and from mid-September to October. Boats dock at the Reichsbrücke on the New Danube (U-1: "Vorgartenstr."). You can buy tickets at the tourist offices; reservations are necessary.

BY CAR

Traveling to Vienna by car is fairly simple; the capital city lies on numerous *Autobahn* routes. From the **west,** take A1, which begins or ends in Vienna. From the **south,** take A2, A21, or A3 (the latter two intersect A2, which runs directly into the city). From the **east,** take A4. From the **north,** take A22, which runs along the Danube. There are also a number of smaller (as in really small smaller) highways that access Vienna, including Routes 7 and 8 from the north and Route 10 from the south.

Ride-sharing is another option. **Mitfahrzentrale Wien,** VIII, Daung. 1a (tel. 408 22 10), off Laudong., pairs drivers and riders. From Schottentor, take tram #43: "Skodag." and walk down Skodag. to Damag. Call first to see which rides are available. (Open M-F 8am-noon and 2-7pm, Sa-Su 1-3pm.) A ride to **Salzburg** is 210AS, to **Prague** 450AS. Two days advance reservation is recommended. **Hitchhikers** headed for Salzburg have been seen taking U-4: "Hütteldorf"; the highway leading to the *Autobahn* is 10km farther. Hitchers traveling south are spotted riding tram #67 to the last stop and waiting at the traffic circle near Laaerberg.

■ Getting Around

FROM THE AIRPORT AND TRAIN STATIONS

The **airport** is a good distance from the city center (18km), but it's serviced by public transportation. The simplest way to get to and from the airport is the **Vienna Airport Lines Shuttle Bus** (70AS). Buses leave the airport for the City Air Terminal (at the Hilton across Landstr. and Hauptstr. from "Wien Mitte") every 20 minutes from 6am to 11pm and every 30 minutes from 11pm to 6am. Buses leave from the airport for Südbahnhof and Westbahnhof every 30 minutes from 8:10am to 7:10pm and on into the night with less frequent service. Similarly, buses travel to the airport from the city stations. A cheaper option is to take the U- and S-Bahns. U-3 and U-4 both reach "Wien Mitte/Landstraße" where you can catch the S-7 "Flughafen/Wolfsthal" which stops at the airport (on the hour; 34AS; Eurailpass not valid). There is also a daily 30 minute train service between Wien Nord or Wien Mitte and the airport (every 30 min; 34AS).

The heart of the city, Stefansplatz, is an easy ride from the **Westbahnhof** on the orange U-3 line (dir: Erdberg). From the **Südbahnhof,** take tram D (dir: Nußdorf) to "Opera/Karlspl." From **Franz-Josefs Bahnhof,** take tram D (dir: Südbahnhof).

WITHIN THE CITY

Public transportation in Vienna is extensive and dependable. The **subway** (U-Bahn), **tram** (Straßenbahn), **elevated train** (S-Bahn), and **bus** operate under one ticket system. A single fare is 20AS if purchased from a machine that lives on a bus, 17AS if purchased in advance from a machine that lives in a station, ticket office, or tobacco shop *(Tabak).* This ticket permits you to travel anywhere in the city and switch from bus to U-Bahn to tram to S-Bahn, as long as your travel is uninterrupted. This bit's tricky. To validate a ticket, punch it in the machine **immediately** upon entering the first vehicle of your journey. This action records the time and date of your trip, and you should not stamp the ticket again when you switch trains. A ticket stamped twice or not stamped at all is invalid, and plain clothes inspectors may fine you 500AS plus the ticket price for "black riding" *(Schwarzfahren).*

Other ticket options are a **24-hour pass** (50AS), a **three-day "rover" ticket** (130AS), a **seven-day pass** (142AS; valid from M 9am to the following M 9am), or an **eight-day pass** (265AS; valid any 8 days, not necessarily consecutive; valid also for several people). The three-day **Vienna Card** (180AS) offers substantial discounts at many museums, sights, and events, and is especially useful for non-students.

If you are traveling with a child over five years old, a bicycle, or a dog, you must buy a half-price ticket (9AS) for your companion. Children under five always ride free, and, on Sundays and school holidays, anyone under 15 rides free, something you may need to prove with a photo ID. (The schedule in the pocket map available at the tourist offices lists official holidays.) While you may take bicycles on all underground trains, the U-6 line limits bikes to the middle car, marked with a bicycle symbol.

All regular trams and subway cars fail to run between 12:30am and 5am. **Night buses** run all night, about once every 30 minutes along most tram, subway, and major bus routes. In major hubs like Schottentor, some of the buses leave from slightly different areas than their daytime counterparts. "N" signs with yellow cat eyes designate night bus stops (25AS; day transport passes not valid). A complete night bus schedule is available at bus info counters in U-Bahn stations.

The **public transportation information line** (tel. 587 31 86) gives public transportation directions to any point in the city. (Open M-F 6:30am-6:30pm, Sa-Su 8:30am-4pm.) **Information stands** in many stations also provide detailed instructions, with helpful pictures to ensure you don't unwittingly end up in the wrong place. The friendly staff can explain how to purchase tickets and can provide an indispensable, free pocket map of the U-Bahn and S-Bahn systems. A comprehensive map of Vienna's public transportation is 15AS. Stands in the U-Bahn at Karlspl., Stephanspl., and the Westbahnhof are the most likely to have information not in German. (Stands open M-F 6:30am-6:30pm, Sa-Su and holidays 8:30am-4pm.) Other stands are at Praterstern, Philadelphiabrücke, Landstr., Florisdorf, Spittelau, and Volkstheater. (Open M-F 6:30am-6:30pm.) The website http://www.wiennet.at/efa will calculate the shortest route between two points (known in Euclidean geometry as a "line").

■ Orientation

Vienna's layout reflects its history. The city is divided into 23 **districts** *(Bezirke)*. The oldest area, the first district, is the *innere Stadt,* the city center, and the rest of the districts radiate out from it like the rings of a large tree. The *innere Stadt* is bounded by the **Ringstraße,** once the site of the old city fortifications, now a massive automobile artery, on three sides. It's defined by Josefs Kai and the Danube Canal on the fourth. The Ringstraße (or Ring), identified as a single entity, really consists of many different segments: Opernring, Kärntner Ring, Dr.-Karl-Lueger-Ring, etc. This fragmentation occurs because of the confusing tendency of Austrian streets to change names after a few blocks. Many of Vienna's major attractions are in the first district and around the Ringstraße, including the **Kunsthistorisches Museum,** the **Rathaus,** and the **Burggarten.** At the intersection of the **Opernring, Kärntner Ring,** and **Kärntner Straße** stands the **Staatsoper** (Opera House). The main **tourist office** and the **Karlsplatz** U-Bahn stop, a hub of the public transportation system, are nearby. Districts two through nine spread out from the city center following the clockwise, one-way traffic of the Ring. The remaining districts expand from yet another ring, the **Gürtel** ("belt"). Like the Ring, this major two-way thoroughfare has numerous components, including Margaretengürtel, Währinger Gürtel, Neubaugürtel, etc. Each of the districts has both a neighborhood and numerical title: II, **Leopoldstadt;** III, **Landstraße;** IV, **Wieden;** V, **Margareten;** VI, **Mariahilf;** VII, **Neubau;** VIII, **Josefstadt;** IX, **Alsergrund;** X, **Favoriten;** XI, **Simmering;** XII, **Meidling;** XIII, **Hietzing;** XIV, **Penzing;** XV, **Rudolfsheim Fünfhaus;** XVI, **Ottakring;** XVII, **Hernals;** XVIII, **Währing;** XIX, **Döbling;** XX, **Brigittenau;** XXI, **Floridsdorf;** XXII, **Donaustadt;** XXIII, **Liesing.** Street signs indicate the district number in Roman or Arabic numerals, and postal codes correspond to the district number: 1010 for the first district, 1020 for the second, 1110 for the eleventh, usw. *Let's Go* includes district numbers after most establishments.

> Vienna is a metropolis with crime like any other; use common sense, especially after dark. Be careful in Karlsplatz, home to many pushers and junkies, and avoid areas in the 5th, 10th, and 14th districts, as well as the rather scuzzy Landstraßer Hauptstr., after dark. Vienna's skin trade operates in some sections of the Gürtel; **Prater Park** is also questionable at night. Bad things happen.

■ Practical Information

TOURIST OFFICES

Main Tourist Office: I, Kärntnerstr. 38, behind the Opera House. A small office trying to serve hordes of people. If possible, try calling Wiener Tourismusverband (see below) first. This office has an assortment of brochures, including a free, comprehensive city map (which unfortunately lacks a much needed index). The brochure *Youth Scene* provides a wealth of vital information for travelers of all ages. The restaurant and club sections are particularly useful. Books 300-400AS rooms for a 40AS fee plus a one-night deposit. Open 9am-7pm.

Branch offices at the following locations offer similar services. **Westbahnhof:** Open Apr.-Oct. 7am-10pm, Nov.-Mar. 7am-9pm **Airport:** Open 8:30am-9pm. **Highway exit "Wien Auhof,"** off A1. Open Easter Week to Oct. 8am-10pm, Nov. 9am-7pm, Dec.-Mar. 10am-6pm. **Highway exit "Zentrum,"** off A2, XI, Trierstr. 149. Open July-Sept. 8am-10pm; Easter Week to June and Oct. 9am-7pm. **North Danube Island:** Open May-Sept. 10am-7pm. **Vienna International Center:** Tu and F 9am-2pm, Th noon-5pm

Wiener Tourismusverband: II, Obere Augartenstr. 40 (tel. 211 140; fax 216 84 92). No walk-in hours, but the knowledgeable staff responds to telephone inquiries and sends faxes and brochures. Open M-F 8am-4pm.

Jugend-Info Wien (Vienna Youth Information Service), Bellaria-Passage (tel. 17 99; email jugendinfo.vie@blackbox.ping.at), in the underground passage at the Bellaria intersection. Enter at the "Dr.-Karl-Renner-Ring/Bellaria" stop (trams #1, 2, 46, 49, D, or J) or at the "Volkstheater" U-Bahn station. Hip staff has information on cultural events, housing, and employment opportunities and sells discount youth concert and theater tickets. Get the indispensable *Jugend in Wien* brochure here. Open M-Sa noon-7pm

Budget Travel: Österreichisches Verkehrsbüro (Austrian National Travel Office), I, Operng. 3-5 (tel. 588 62 38), opposite the Opera House. Though not intended exclusively for budget travelers, the office sells BIJ tickets. Open M-F 9am-6pm, Sa 9am-noon.

EMBASSIES AND CONSULATES

Most embassies and consulates are located in the same building, listed under *"Botschaften"* or *"Konsulate"* in the phone book. Contact consulates for assistance with visas and passports and in emergencies.

Australia, IV, Mattiellistr. 2-4 (tel. 512 85 80), behind Karlskirche. Open M-Th 8:30am-1pm and 2-5:30pm, F 8:30am-1:15pm.

Canada, I, Laurenzerburg 2, 3rd fl. (tel. 531 38, ext. 3000). Open M-F 8:30am-12:30pm and 1:30-3:30pm. Leave a message in an emergency.

Ireland, III, Hilton Center, Landstraßer Hauptstr. 21, 6th fl. (tel. 715 42 47; fax 713 60 04). Open M-F 9:30-11:30am and 2-4pm.

New Zealand, XIX, Springsiedleg. 28 (tel. 318 85 05; fax 318 67 17). No regular office hours; call in advance. If there is no answer, contact the consulate in Bonn at 0049 228 228 070.

South Africa, XIX, Sandg. 33 (tel. 320 64 93). M-F 8:30am-noon.

U.K., III, Jauresg. 10 (tel. 716 13 53 38), near Schloß Belvedere. Open M-F 9:15am-noon.

U.S. Embassy, IX, Boltzmanng. 16, off Währingerstr. and **Consulate** at I, Gartenbaupromenade 2 (tel. 313 39 for both), off Parkring. Phone hours M-F 8:30am-noon and 1-5pm. Open M-F 8:30am-noon. Some services for American citizens are open at different or variable times; call ahead.

TRANSPORTATION SERVICES

Ökista, IX, Türkenstr. 8 (tel. 40 14 80) specializes in student travel. Open M-F 9am-7:30pm.

Taxis: (tel. 313 00, 401 00, 601 60, 814 00, or 910 11). Stands at Westbahnhof, Südbahnhof, and Karlspl. in the city center. Accredited taxis have yellow and black signs on the roof. Rates generally 27AS plus 14AS per km. 26AS surcharge for taxis called by radiophone; 27AS surcharge Sundays, holidays, and nights (11pm-6am); 13AS surcharge for luggage over 20kg, 26AS for over 50kg.

Car Rental: Avis, I, Opernring 3-5 (tel. 587 62 41). Open M-F 7am-6pm, Sa 8am-2pm, Su 8am-1pm. **Hertz,** (tel. 700 72 661), at the airport. Open M-F 7:15am-11pm, Sa 8am-8pm, Su 8am-11pm.

Auto Repairs: If your car needs fixing, call **ÖAMTC** (tel. 120) or **ARBÖ** (tel. 123).

Parking: In the 1st district, parking is allowed for 1½hr., M-F 9am-7pm. Buy a voucher (6AS per 30min.) at a *Tabak* and display it, with the time, on the dashboard. It's easiest to park cars outside the *Ring* and walk into the city center. Garages line the Ringstr., including 2 by the Opera House, 1 at Franz-Josef Kai, and 1 at the Marek-Garage at Messepalast. In districts VI through IX, parking is permitted M-F 9am-8pm for 2hr. **Parking cards** (50AS) enable all-day parking there.

Bike Rental: At Wien Nord and the Westbahnhof. 150AS per day, 90AS with a train ticket from the day of arrival. Elsewhere in the city, including Donauinsel, rentals average 50AS per hr. **Pedal Power,** II, Ausstellungsstr. 3 (tel. 729 72 34; fax 729 72 35; http://www.pedalpower.co.at/) rents bikes for 60AS per hr., 200AS per half day, 365AS for 24hr. with delivery. Open May-Oct. 8am-8pm. Pick up *Vienna By Bike* at the tourist office for details on the bicycle scene.

Luggage Storage: Lockers (40AS per 24hr.) at all train stations. Adequate for sizable backpacks. **Luggage watch** 30AS. Open 4am-1:15am.

Lost Property: Fundbüro, IX, Wasag. 22 (tel. 313 44 92 11 or 92 17). For items lost on public transportation, call 790 94 35 00. Open M-F 8am-3pm. For items lost on trains, call 580 03 29 96 (Westbahnhof) or 580 03 56 56 (Südbahnhof).

FINANCIAL SERVICES

Currency Exchange: Banks and **airport exchanges** use the same official rates. Minimum commission 65AS for traveler's checks, 10AS for cash. Most are open M-W and F 8am-12:30pm and 1:30-3pm, Th 8am-12:30pm and 1:30-5:30pm. **ATMs** are everywhere, offering excellent rates, and nearly all accept Cirrus, Eurocard, MC, and Visa. **Train station** exchanges offer long hours and a 50AS charge for changing up to US$700 of traveler's checks. The 24hr. exchange at the **main post office** has excellent rates and a 80AS fee to change up to $1100 in traveler's checks. **24hr. bill exchange** machines with horrid rates dot the *innere Stadt.* The **casino** (open late on weekends) has slightly better rates.

American Express: I, Kärntnerstr. 21-23, P.O. Box 28, A-1015 (tel. 515 40), down the street from Stephanspl. Cashes AmEx and Thomas Cook (3% commission) checks, holds mail for 4 weeks for AmEx customers, and, for everyone, sells theater, concert, and other tickets. Open M-F 9am-5:30pm, Sa 9am-noon.

LOCAL SERVICES

Bookstores: Shakespeare & Company, I, Sterng. 2 (tel. 535 50 53; fax 535 50 53 16; email bookseller@shakespeare.co.at; http://www.ping.at/members/shbook). Eclectic and intelligent. Great English magazine selection. Occasional readings and signings. Open M-F 9am-7pm, Sa 9am-5pm. **Frauenzimmer,** Langeg. 11 (tel. 406 86 78; fax 407 16 20). Women's bookstore with some English language books and travel literature. Open M-F 10am-6:30pm, Sa 10am-1pm (10am-5pm the first Saturday of each month). The **British Bookshop,** I, Weihburgg. 24 (tel. 512 19 45; fax 512 10 26) has an extensive collection of books, many of them British; many travel-oriented books, too. Open M-F 9am-6:30pm, Sa 10am-5pm. **Big Ben's Bookstore,** IX, Serviteg. 4a (tel. 319 64 120; fax 31 96 41 23) sells English books along with a bigger selection of ESL books, meaning books in English for people whose mother tongue isn't English. Open M-F 9am-6:30pm, Sa 9:30-12:30am.

Bisexual, Gay, and Lesbian Organizations: The bisexual, gay, and lesbian community in Vienna, though small, is more integrated than in other cities; acts of hate are directed at property, not people, and are few and far between. The lovely **Rosa Lila Villa,** VI, Linke Wienzeile 102 (tel. 586 81 50), is a favored resource and social center for Viennese homosexuals and visitors to the city. Friendly staff provides counseling, information, a library, and nightclub listings (see **Nightlife,** p. 121).

Open M-F 5-8pm. **Homosexuelle Initiative Wien (HOSI),** II, Novarag. 40 (tel. 216 66 04; fax 585 41 59). Lesbian group and phone network Wednesdays at 7pm. Youth group Thursdays at 8pm. Prints a political newspaper, "Lambda Nachrichten." Open Su 6-8pm (includes phone counseling), Th 7-9pm (for youth). Café open Su 5-10pm. **Lesbischwul und Transgender Referat** (tel. 588 01 58 90; email efisher@mail.zserve.tuwien.ac.at). Gay student counseling group. Open F 4-6pm. There's also a monthly Viennese magazine for gays called **Connect.**

Laundromat: Schnell und Sauber, VII, Westbahnhofstr. 60 (tel. 524 64 60); U-6: "Burgg. Stadthalle." Wash 60AS for 6kg. Detergent included. Spin-dry 10AS. Open 24hr. **Münzwäscherei Karlberger & Co.,** III, Schlachthausg. 19 (tel. 798 81 91). Wash 90AS per 7kg, dry 10AS. Soap 10AS. Open M-F 7:30am-6:30pm. Many hostels offer laundry facilities (50-70AS).

Public Showers and Toilets: At Westbahnhof, in Friseursalon Navratil downstairs from subway passage. Well-maintained. 30min. shower 48AS, with soap and towel 60AS (10AS extra for either on Sunday). Showers are also available at **Amalienbad,** X, Reumanpl. 23, **Jörgerbad,** XVII, Jörgerstr. 42-44, and at the airport. Toilets in all underground stations (1-5AS), as well as a special *Jugendstil* toilet in Kärtnerstr.

Snow reports: Vienna, Lower Austria, and Styria (tel. 15 83); Salzburg, Upper Austria, and Carinthia (tel. 15 84); Tirol and the Voralberg (tel. 15 85).

EMERGENCIES

Emergencies: Police, tel. 133. **Ambulance,** tel. 144. **Fire,** tel. 122. Alert your consulate of any emergencies or legal problems.

Poison Control: tel. 406 43 43. Open 24hr.

Medical Assistance: Allgemeines Krankenhaus, IX, Währinger Gürtel 18-20 (tel. 404 00). **Emergency care** 141. **24hr. pharmacy** 15 50. A consulate can provide a list of English-speaking physicians.

Crisis Hotlines: All hotlines can find English speakers.

House for Threatened and Battered Women: tel. 545 48 00 or 202 55 00. 24hr. emergency hotline.

Rape Crisis Hotline: tel. 523 22 22. Open M 10am-6pm, Tu 2-6pm, W 10am-2pm, Th 5-9pm. **24hr. immediate help:** tel. 717 19.

Psychological Counseling Hotline: tel. 310 87 80. Open M-F 8pm-8am, Sa-Su 24hr.

English-language "Befrienders" Suicide Hotline: tel. 713 33 74. Open M-F 9:30am-1pm and 6:30-10pm, Sa-Su 6:30-10pm. They have message machines.

COMMUNICATIONS

Internet Access: National Library, I, Neue Burg 1 (tel. 53 41 00), in Heldenpl. at the Hofburg, provides free access at numerous terminals and long waits in long lines. Open M-Sa 10am-4pm, Su 10am-1pm. **Libro,** XXII, Donauzentrum (tel. 202 52 55). Free access at 6 terminals. Open Su-F 7am-7pm, Sa 9am-5pm. **Public Netbase,** VII, Museumsquartier, Museumpl. I (tel. 522 18 34). Free 2-7pm. **Jugend-Info des Bundesministeriums,** Franz-Josefs-Kai 51 (tel. 533 70 30). Free access at 2 PC's. M-F 11am-6pm.

English Language Radio: Blue Danube radio, 103.8FM. Mixes classical, oldies, and mainstream music with news updates every 30min. until 7pm in English, French and German, including the BBC World Service. "What's on in Vienna" airs at 1pm.

Post Offices: Hauptpostamt, I, Fleischmarkt 19. Vast structure containing exchange windows, phones, faxes, and mail services. Open 24hr. Address *Poste Restante* to "MAAS, Oedipa; Postlagernde Briefe; Hauptpostamt; Fleischmarkt 19; A-1010 Wien." Branches throughout the city and at the train stations; look for the yellow signs with the (un)muted trumpet logo. Feel the rich chocolaty goodness.

Postal Codes: In the 1st district A-1010, in the 2nd A-1020, in the 3rd A-1030, and so on, to the 23rd A-1230.

Telephone Code: 0222 from within Austria, 1 from outside the country.

VIENNA

■ Accommodations and Camping

One of the few unpleasant aspects of Vienna is the hunt for cheap rooms during peak season (June-Sept.). Don't leave your shelter to the vagaries of chance; write or call for reservations at least five days in advance. Otherwise, plan on calling from the train station between 6 and 9am during the summer to put your name down for a reservation. If your choice is full, ask to be put on a waiting list, or ask for suggestions—don't waste time tramping around. A list of budget accommodations in Vienna is available at almost every tourist office. Those unable to find a hostel bed should consider a *Pension.* One-star establishments are generally adequate and are most common in the seventh, eighth, and ninth districts. Singles start around 350AS, doubles around 500AS. The summer crunch for budget rooms is slightly alleviated in July, when university dorms are converted into makeshift hostels. Bear in mind that these "dorms" are singles and doubles, not dormitories, and are priced accordingly.

If you're looking for a place to stay for a longer period of time, try **Odyssee Reisen und Mitwohnzentrale,** VIII, Laudong. 7 (tel. 402 60 61). They find apartments for 225-350AS per person per night. A week runs about 1200AS, and a month starts at 2000AS. They charge 20% commission on each month's rent (120% limit). Bring your passport to register. (Open M-F 10am-2pm and 3-6pm.) Otherwise, visit either *Österreichische Hochschülerschaft* at Rooseveltpl. 5 or the bulletin boards on the first floor of the NIG building on Universitätstr. near the *Votivkirche.*

HOSTELS AND DORMITORIES

Myrthengasse (HI), VII, Myntheng. 7 and **Neustiftgasse (HI),** VII, Neustiftg. 85 (for reservations at either: tel. 523 63 16 or 523 94 29; fax 523 58 49; email oejhv-wien-jgh-neustift@oejhv.or.at). The hostels, under the same management, are around the corner from each other. From Westbahnhof, U-6 (dir: Heiligenstadt): "Burgg./Stadthalle" then bus #48A (dir: Ring): "Neubaug." Walk back on Burgg. 1 block and take the first right on Myntheng. (15min.). From Südbahnhof, bus #13A (dir: Skodag./Alerstr.): "Kellermanng." Walk 2 blocks to your left on Neustiftg. and turn left on Myntheng. This simple and Swedish-modern hostel is only a 20min. walk from the *Innenstadt.* From Jan. 1-Mar.14 and Nov. 1-Dec. 23 4- to 6-bed dorms with shower 165AS; 2-bed dorms 195AS. All other times 4- to 6-bed dorms with shower 180AS; 2-bed dorms with shower 210AS. Non-member surcharge 40AS. Breakfast and sheets included. Lockers and keys provided. Lunch or dinner 65AS. **Laundry** 50AS. Reception at Myntheng. 7am-11:30pm. Curfew 1am. Lockout 9am-2pm. Reservations recommended; accepted only by fax or email.

Believe It Or Not, VII, Myntheng. 10, apt. #14 (tel. 526 46 58), across the street from the Myntheng. hostel. Ring the bell. Funky and extremely social, the place offers 2 bedrooms, bunks rising to spacious ceilings, and a working kitchen. Comes complete with a gonzo caretaker who, after helping you plan your itinerary for the day, kicks you out 10:30am-noon to clean. Her personal crash-course on Vienna is a must. 160AS; Nov.-Easter 110AS. Reception 8am until early afternoon—call if in doubt. Reservations recommended.

Gästehaus Ruthensteiner (HI), XV, Robert-Hamerlingg. 24 (tel. 893 42 02; fax 893 27 96). 10min. from the Westbahnhof and about 15min. ride from the city center. Exit Westbahnhof at the main entrance (on Äußere Mariahilferstr., beyond the Gürtel), turn right and head to Mariahilferstr. Turn right again and continue until Haidmahnsg. Take a left and first right on Robert-Hammerlingg., and continue to the middle of the 2nd block. Spotless rooms and a beautiful sun-filled oasis of ivy for a courtyard, complete with a barbecue and oversized chess set. Summer dorm 125AS; 10-bed dorms 145AS; 3- to 5-bed dorms 169AS; singles 245AS; doubles 470AS. Breakfast 25AS. Showers and sheets (except for 10-bed rooms) included. Snack bar open all day. Lockers and kitchen available. **Bike rental** 89AS per day. Email-checking costs 20AS; for 30min. on the web, 50AS. Reception 24hr. Flexible 4-night max. stay. Phone reservations recommended, but empathetic hostel owners promise to hold open beds for more spontaneous travelers.

Hostel Zöhrer, VIII, Skodag. 26 (tel. 406 07 30; fax 408 04 09), about 10min. from the city center. From Westbahnhof, U-6 (dir: Heiligenstadt): "Alserstr." then street-car #43 (dir: Schottentor): "Skodag." From Südbahnhof, bus #13A: "Alserstr./Skodag." Crowded but comfortable and well located. Furnished **kitchen.** 42 beds. 5- to 8-bed dorms with showers 170AS; 2-bed dorms 230AS. Breakfast (7:30-9:30am), lockers, and sheets included. **Laundry** 60AS. Front door/locker key deposit 100AS, with ID deposit 50AS. Reception 7:30am-10pm. Check-out 9am. Lockout 11am-2pm. No curfew. Visa.

Turmherberge Don Bosco, III, Lechnerstr. 12 (tel. 713 14 94), near the "Kardinal-Nagl-Pl." U-Bahn. The cheapest beds in town are here in a barren former bell tower, which gets hot in summer. 75AS for hostel members. Curfew 11:45pm. Open Mar.-Nov.

Hostel Panda, VII, Kaiserstr. 77, 3rd Fl. (tel. 524 78 88). From Westbahnhof, tram #5: "Burgg." From Sudbahnhof, tram #18: "Westbahnhof," then tram #5: "Burgg." Fun and eclectic in an old-fashioned, semi-*Jugendstil* Austrian apartment building. 18 mattresses packed into a pleasant co-ed dorm with huge ceilings. Dorms 160AS; Nov.-Easter 110AS. 50AS surcharge for 1-night stays. Kitchen and TV. Bring lock for lockers. No curfew.

Schloßherberge am Wilhelminenberg (HI), XVI, Savoyenstr. 2 (tel. 485 85 03, ext. 700; fax 485 85 03, ext. 702; email SHB@wigast.com). U-6: "Thaliastr." then tram #46 (dir: Joachimsthalerpl.): "Maroltingerg." From Schottentor, tram #44: "Wilhelminenstr." then bus #146B or #46B: "Schloß Wilhelminenberg." The bus will pull up to the palace and you will think *Let's Go* is pulling your leg. Accommodations are actually to the left of the palace and—though not quite as opulent—are still comfortable. Near the Vienna woods, the hostel has a fantastically great view of the city. 164 impeccable 4-bed dorms with bathrooms 220AS. Keycard 25AS. Sheets included. **Laundry** 65AS. Group discounts. Reception 7am-11pm. Lockout 9am-2pm. Curfew 11pm. Reserve by phone, fax, or letter at least 2 days in advance.

Kolpingfamilie Wien-Meidling (HI), XIII, Bendlg. 10-12 (tel. 813 54 87; fax 812 21 30). U-4 or U-6: "Niederhofstr." Head right on Niederhofstr. and take the 4th right onto Bendlg. This well-lit, modern hostel has 200 beds and stores valuables at the reception. Kind of boring, but then you didn't come to sit in the youth hostel, did you? 8- and 10-bed dorms 120AS; 4- and 6- bed dorms 180AS. Breakfast 45AS. Sheets included. Showers in all rooms, baths in some. Non-members add 40AS. Flexible reception times, but always open 6am-midnight. Check-out 9am. Lockout midnight-4am. Curfew midnight.

Jugendgästehaus Wien Brigittenau (HI), XX, Friedrich-Engels-Pl. 24 (tel. 332 82 940 or 330 05 98; fax 330 83 79; email oejhv-wien-jgh-brigiltneu@oejhv.or.at), 25min. from city center. U-1 or U-4: "Schwedenpl." then tram N: "Floridsdorfer-brücke/Friedrich-Engels-Pl." or take U-6: "Handelskai" and bus #5a or 11a to tram stop. Either way, follow the signs. It's the large green building behind the tram stop across the street and to the left of the tracks. Very distant from the center of the city. Roomy, with exceptional facilities for the disabled. 5-night max. stay. 24-bed dorms 145AS; 4-bed dorms 180AS; 2-bed dorms with bath 210AS. Breakfast, lockers, and sheets included. Lunch and dinner 65AS. Non-members pay 40AS extra. Reduction of 10-15AS Jan. 1-Mar. 31 and Nov. 1-Dec. 23. Reception 24hr. Lockout 9am-1pm. Reservations by fax or phone.

Jugendgästehaus Hütteldorf-Hacking (HI), XIII, Schloßbergg. 8 (tel. 877 15 01; fax 877 02 632; email JGH@wigast.com). From Karlspl., U-4: "Hütteldorf," then take the Hadikg. exit, cross the footbridge, and follow signs to the hostel (10min.). Weary backpackers take bus #53B from the side of the footbridge opposite the station to the hostel. From Westbahnhof, S-50: "Hütteldorf." 35min. from the city center, this secluded hostel with sprawling sunny green grounds sits in one of Vienna's most affluent districts and has great views of northwest Vienna. Often packed with high school groups. 271 beds in 2-, 4-, 6-, and 8-bed rooms, one room with 22-beds; some doubles with showers. 170AS (200AS for a more exciting and filling "American Breakfast.") Add 30AS for rooms with showers or for one of the few singles. Keycard 25AS. Laundry 70AS. Free luggage storage. Lunch and dinner 65-72AS. Reception 7am-11:45pm. Lockout 9:30am-3:30pm. Curfew 11:45pm. Bring a lock for lockers. Reservations by phone or fax. MC, Visa.

UNIVERSITY DORMITORIES

From July through September, the following university dorms become hotels, usually with singles, doubles, and a few triples and quads. These rooms don't have much in the way of character, but showers and sheets are standard, and their cleanliness and relatively low cost suffice for most budget travelers, particularly for longer stays.

Porzellaneum der Wiener Universität, IX, Porzellang. 30 (tel. 31 77 28 20; fax 31 77 28 30). From Südbahnhof, tram D (dir: Nußdorf): "Fürsteng." From Westbahnhof, tram #5: "Franz-Josefs Bahnhof" then tram D (dir: Südbahnhof): "Fürsteng." Flag display at entryway is worthy of the U.N. 10min. from the Ring. Singles 190AS; doubles 380AS. Sheets included. Reception 24hr. Reservations recommended.

Rudolfinum, IV, Mayerhofg. 3 (tel. 505 53 84; fax 505 53 85 450). U-1: "Taubstummeng." Rock 'n' Roll and MTV, a vacation like your college days. More intense guests watch CNN. Large rooms in a well-managed facility. Great location. Singles 270AS; doubles 480AS; triples 600AS; quads 800AS. Breakfast included. **Laundry** facilities. **Kitchen** available if you make arrangements.

Gästehaus Pfeilgasse, VIII, Pfeilg. 6 (tel. 401 74; fax 401 76 20; email acahot@academia-hotels.co.at). U-2: "Lerchenfelderstr." Right on Lerchenfelderstr., right on Lange Gasse, and left on Pfeilg. The homesick will be reminded not of home but of their freshman dorm (except with clean sheets and no *Reservoir Dogs* posters). Singles 270AS; doubles 480AS; triples 600AS; quads 800AS. Breakfast included. Reception 24hr. Reservations recommended. Credit cards accepted.

Katholisches Studentenhaus, XIX, Peter-Jordanstr. 29 (tel./fax 347 47 312). From Westbahnhof, U-6 (dir: Heiligenstadt): "Nußdorferstr." then bus #35A or tram #38: "Hardtg." and turn left. From Südbahnhof, tram D: "Schottentor" then tram #38: "Hardtg." Laid-back atmosphere in the leafy 19th district. Singles 250AS; doubles 400AS. Showers and sheets included. Reception closes at 10pm. Call ahead.

Studentenwohnheim der Hochschule für Musik, I, Johannesg. 8 (tel. 514 84 48; fax 514 84 49). Walk 3 blocks down Kärnterstr. away from the Stephansdom and turn left onto Johannesg. Fabulous location. Scrumptious, inexpensive meals. Singles 420AS, with bath 490AS; doubles 760AS, with bath 980AS; triples 810AS; quads 1000AS; quints 1250AS. Breakfast and showers included. Reduction for groups larger than 20. Apartment also available (includes 2 double rooms, bathroom, kitchen, living room): 350AS per person, 500AS per person using room alone, 1200 AS for entire apartment. Reception 24hr.

Albertina Hotels Austria, I, Fürichg. 10 (tel. 512 24 66; fax 572 19 68), also commandeers dorms during the summer months, including **Albertina Auersperg,** VIII, Auerspergstr. 9 (tel. 406 25 40). Modern rooms practically on the Ring, right behind the opera house, and a hop, skip, and jump from U-2: "Lerchenfelderstr." up Alserstr. 2010AS per person per month. Minimum stay 2 weeks. Reception M-Th 7:30am-2pm, F 7:30am-noon. Reservations by fax.

HOTELS AND PENSIONS

Check the hostels section for good singles deals as well. The prices are higher here, but you pay for convenient reception hours, no curfews, and no lockouts.

Hotel Quisisana, VI, Windmühlg. 6 (tel. 587 71 55; fax 587 71 56 33). U-2: "Babenbergerstr.," turn right on Mariahilferstr., go 3 blocks, and bear left on Windmühlg. An old-fashioned *Jugendstil* hotel run by a charming older couple. It's difficult to feel uncomfortable here. Singles 330-350AS, with shower 400AS; doubles 500-540AS, 660AS. Breakfast 40AS. 5% discount for students.

Lauria Apartments (also see Hostel Panda), VII, Kaiserstr. 77, 3rd Floor (tel. 522 25 55). From Westbahnhof, tram #5: "Burgg." From Sudbahnhof, tram #18: "Westbahnhof" then tram #5: "Burgg." Modern apartments offering rooms and dorm beds. Apartments have fully equipped and ultra-social kitchens, and are close to the center of the city and to Westbahnhof. Dorms 160AS; singles 480AS; doubles 530AS; 700AS; triples 700AS, 800AS; quads 850AS, 940AS with shower. The dorm beds might be the best deal: clean, cheap, modern, access to **kitchen.** Reduced rates for apartments in buildings under construction. Sheets and TV included. Two night min. for reservations. Credit cards accepted except for dorm-beds.

Pension Hargita, VII, Andreasg. (tel. 526 19 28; fax 526 04 92). U-3: "Zieglerg." then head down Mariahilferstr. to Andreasg. The sun shines brightly through the windows on the carved wood of this comfortable *Pension*. Prime location. Singles 400AS, with shower 450AS; doubles 600AS, 700AS, with bath 800AS. Breakfast 40AS. Reception 8am-10pm.

Pension Wild, VIII, Langeg. 10 (tel. 406 51 74; fax 402 21 68). U-3: "Volkstheater" then U-2: "Lerchenfelderstr." and take the 1st right. From Südbahnhof, bus #13A (dir: Alserstr./Skodag.): "Piaristeng." Turn left onto Lerchenfelderstr. and left again onto Langeg. 44 modest, clean beds. 15min. walk from the city center. Singles 450-540AS; doubles 590-890AS; triples 860-1250AS. Breakfast and shower included. **Kitchen** access. Reception 7am-10pm. Reservations by fax recommended.

Pension Kraml, VI, Brauerg. 5 (tel. 587 85 88; fax 586 75 73). U-3: "Zierierg." exit onto Otto-Bauerg. Take your 1st left, then your 1st right. From Südbahnhof, take bus #13A to Esterhazyg. and walk up Brauerg. Situated near the *Innenstadt* and the Naschmarkt. Large rooms and a lounge with (cable) TV. 38 beds. Singles 310AS; doubles 620AS, with shower 700AS, with bath 820AS; triples 810AS, with shower 870AS. Apartment with bath 1020-1400AS for 3-5 people. Breakfast included.

Pension Falstaff, IX, Müllnerg. 5 (tel. 317 91 27; fax 317 91 864). U-4: "Roßauer Lände." Cross Roßauer Lände, head down Grünentorg., and take the 3rd left onto Müllnerg. This small *Pension* is much quieter than its namesake, with a campy, linoleum flavor. Singles 390AS, with shower 500AS; doubles 650AS, 750AS, with bath 850AS. Extra bed 220AS. Breakfast included. Reduced rates for longer stays and 15% discounts Dec.-Mar. Reception 7:30am-9pm. Reservations by phone or fax. Credit cards accepted.

Pension Reimer, IV, Kircheng. 18 (tel. 523 61 62; fax 524 37 82), is centrally located and has huge rooms adorned with some funky orange decor. Singles 490AS; doubles 700AS, with bath 800-840AS. Breakfast included. Reduced rates in winter. Credit cards accepted.

Pension Amon, VII, Daung. 1 (tel. and fax 405 01 94). Tram #5 from Westbahnhof or #13 from Südbahnhof to Alserstr. and Skodag. Walk down Skodag. and turn left onto Daung. Pleasant rooms in a colorful and warmly cluttered pension. Singles with shower 400AS; doubles with shower 700AS. Reception 24hr. **Kitchen.** Reservations by fax or phone. Credit cards accepted.

F. Kaled and Tina, VII, Lindeng. 42 (tel. 523 90 13; fax 526 25 13). U-3: "Zieder g." Follow Zieder g. 2 blocks to Lindeng.; the hotel is on the right. Lovely private rooms with cable TV (CNN!). Singles 400AS, with bath 450AS; doubles 550AS, 650AS; triples 800AS. Breakfast 75AS. 2-night minimum stay. Reservations by phone or fax.

CAMPING

Wien-West, Hüttelbergstr. 80 (tel. 914 23 14; fax 911 35 94). U-4: "Hütteldorf" then bus #14B or 152 (dir: Campingpl.): "Wien West." The most convenient campground, about 8km from the city center. Crowded but grassy and pleasant. Prices vary according to season, generally range between 67-73AS per person, children 38AS, tent 37-42AS, camper 62-69AS. In July and Aug. 2 person and 4 person cabins available for 250AS and 400-440AS. **Laundry** machines, grocery stores, handicapped access, and cooking facilities. Reception 7:30am-9:30pm. Closed Feb.

Aktiv Camping Neue Donau, XXII, Am Kleehäufel 119 (tel./fax 202 40 10). U-1: "Kaisermühlen" then bus 91a "Kleehäufel." 4km from the city center and adjacent to Neue Donau beaches. July-Aug. 73AS, children 38AS, camper 69AS, tent 42AS, electricity 40AS. May, June, and Sept. 67AS, children 38AS, camper 62AS, tent 37AS, electricity 40AS. Showers included. Laundry, supermarket, kitchen. Handicapped access. Open May to mid-Sept.

Campingplatz Schloß Laxenburg (tel. 02236/713 33; fax 02236/71 33 44), at Münchendorfer Str., Laxenburg. 15km from Vienna, but extremely popular and beautifully situated near the Gumpoldskirchen vineyards. Facilities include a restaurant, boat rental, heated pool, and supermarket. 69AS, children 36AS; caravans 65AS; tents 40AS. Open Apr.-Oct.

■ Food and Coffee

"Here the people think only of sensual gratifications."
—Washington Irving, 1822

In a world full of uncertainty, the Viennese believe that the least you can do is face things with a full stomach. Food is not mere fuel for the body; it is an aesthetic, even philosophical experience that begins when you wish someone *"Mahlzeit"* (enjoy). Food and drink are in endless harmony here, and the city consumes both in great quantities. Cafés, *Beisln* (pubs), and *Heurigen* (wine gardens) all maintain their own particular balances between consumption and entertainment.

Viennese culinary offerings reflect the crazy patchwork empire of the Habsburgs. *Serbische Bohnensuppe* (Serbian bean soup) and *Ungarische Gulaschsuppe* (Hungarian spicy beef stew) exemplify Eastern European influences. *Knödeln*, bread dumplings found in most side dishes, come from the former Czechoslovakia. Even the famed *Wiener Schnitzel* (fried and breaded veal cutlets) probably first appeared in Milan. Boiled beef *(Tafelspitz)* is one of the few original national treasures. Vienna is renowned for sublime desserts and chocolates—unbelievably rich, and priced for patrons who are likewise blessed. Most residents, however, maintain that the sumptuous treats are worth every *Groschen*. Unless you buy your sin wholesale at a local bakery, *Sacher Torte, Imperial Torte*, and even *Apfel Strudel* can cost up to 50AS.

Vienna's restaurants are as varied as its cuisine. *Gästehäuser* and *Beisln* serve inexpensive meals that stick to your ribs and are best washed down with much beer. *Würstelstände*, found on almost every corner, provide a quick, cheap lunch (a sausage runs 25AS or so). The restaurants near **Kärntnerstraße** are generally expensive—a better bet is the neighborhood north of the university and near the Votivkirche (U-2: "Schottentor"), where **Universitätsstraße** and **Währingerstraße** meet. Cafes with cheap meals also line **Florianig** in the eighth district. The area radiating from the **Rechte** and **Linke Wienzeile** near Naschmarkt (U-4: "Kettenbrückeg.") houses a range of cheap restaurants, and the **Naschmarkt** itself contains open-air stands where you can purchase aromatic delicacies (bread and a variety of ethnic food) to sample while shopping at Vienna's premier flea market. Come before 11am and walk to the far end of the square to find the cheapest prices from local farmers. (Open M-F 7am-6pm, Sa 7am-1pm.) Most of the nearby 7th district **(Neubau)** is funky and pleasant. Almost all year long, **Rathausplatz** hosts inexpensive food stands tied into whatever the current festival happens to be. At Christmastime, **Christkindlmarkt** offers hot food and spiked punch amid vendors of Christmas charms, ornaments, and candles. From the end of June through July, the **Festwochen** celebration brings international foodstuffs to the stands behind the seats of the various films. (Stands open 11am-11pm.) The open-air **Brunnenmarkt** (U-6: "Josefstädterstr." then walk up Veronikag. 1 block and turn right) is extremely colorful and, as it's in a traditional workers' district, tends to be cheap. The **Wienerwald** chain has branches for chicken-lovers in most districts (Annag. 3, Freyung 6, Bellariarstr. 12, and Schotteng; open 7am-midnight). Bakeries, or *Bäckereien*, permeate the city and sell all sorts of fresh, delicious, and affordable baked goods.

As always, supermarkets provide building blocks for cheap, solid meals. Supermarkets in more affluent and touristed neighborhoods are more expensive. The lowest prices can be found on the shelves of **Billa, Hofer,** and **Sparmarkt.** Slightly less common chains are **Ledi, Mondo, Renner,** and **Zielpunkt.** Travelers can buy kosher groceries at the **Kosher Supermarket,** Hollandstr. 10 (tel. 216 96 75). Be warned that most places close Saturday afternoons and all of Sunday (on the first Sa of every month, most shops close at 5 or 6pm.) In general, restaurants stop serving after 11pm. To join the legions of Viennese conquering the summer heat, seek out the **Italeis** or **Tichy** ice cream vendors or visit the delicious **Gelateria Hoher Markt,** I, Hoher Markt, just off Rotenturmstr. Expatriate Italians flock here to sample all 23 mouthwatering ice cream flavors. (Open daily Mar.-Oct. 9am-11pm.)

RESTAURANTS

The Innere Stadt

Trzesniewski, I, Dorotheerg. 1 (tel. 512 32 91; fax 513 95 65), 3 blocks down the Graben from the Stephansdom. A famous stand-up restaurant, this unpronounceable establishment has been serving petite open-faced sandwiches for over 80 years. Favorite toppings include salmon, onion, paprika, and egg. This was Franz Kafka's favorite place to eat. 19 varieties of spreads on bread. 10AS per *Brötchen*— you'll want 3-4 of them for a solid lunch. Open M-F 9am-7pm, Sa 9am-1pm. **Branches** at VI, Mariahiferstr. 95 (tel. 596 4291); III, Hauptstr. 97 (tel. 712 99 64) in Galleria.

Levante, I, Wallnerstr. 2 (tel. 533 23 26; fax 535 54 85). Walk down the Graben away from the Stephansdom, bear left on Kohlmarkt, and turn right on Wallnerstr. This Greek-Turkish restaurant features street-side dining and heaps of affordable dishes, including vegetarian delights. Entrees 80-150AS. **Branches** at I, Wollzeile 19 (off Rotenturm, U-3 or U-1: "Stephanspl."); Mariahilferstr. 88a; and VIII, Josefstädterstr. 14 (U-2: "Rathaus"). All open 11am-11pm.

Brezelg'wölb, I, Lederhof 9 (tel./fax 533 88 11). Near Am Hof. Excellent hearty cuisine even the Viennese call *"Altwiener"* (old Viennese). Cobblestones and classical music enhance the atmosphere of this old-fashioned *Backstube*. Don't leave without glancing at the rare piece of the intact medieval city wall in the courtyard—the rest was torn down to build the Ringstraße. Reservations recommended in the evening. Open daily 11am-1am, hot food until midnight.

Bizi Pizza, I, Rotenturmstr. 4 (tel. 513 37 05), on the corner of Stephanspl. Good food and a great deal in the heart of the city. An institution among the young and cashless, Bizi boasts a fresh salad bar (small 35AS, large 60AS) and pizza (60-75AS, slices 28AS). Open daily 11am-11:30pm. **Branches** with the same hours at Franz-Josefs-Kai (tel. 535 79 13), and X, Favoritenstr. 105 (tel. 600 50 10).

La Crêperie, I, Grünangerg. 10 (tel. 512 56 87), off Singerstr. near Stephanspl. A very enthusiastic decorator gave the interior a sweetly kitschy patchwork of Versailles and Louis XIV: Baroque wallpaper with metallic tassels alternate with indoor sculpted bushes and a bar disguised as a rustic, paint-peeled gazebo. Scrumptious crepes, both sweet and savory, for 40-250AS. Open 11:30am-midnight.

Café Ball, I, Ballg. 5 (tel. 313 17 54), near Stephanspl. off Weihburgg. On a narrow cobblestone lane, the black and white stone floor, dark wood, and brass bar create an elegant, Bohemian atmosphere. Falafel 45AS, *Menüs* 95-145AS. Open M-Th 10:30am-midnight, F-Sa 10:30am-2pm, Su 6pm-midnight.

Maschu Maschu, I, Rabensteig 8 (tel. 533 29 04). This hole-in-the-wall joint serves excellent, filling, and super-cheap Israeli falafel (38AS), sometimes outdoors in summer. Opens later and later to be open in symbiotic conjunction with Bermuda Triangle bars. Open M 11am-midnight, Tu 11am-1am, W 11am-2am, Th 11am-3am, F-Su 11am-4am.

Margaritaville, I, Bartensteing. 3 (tel. 405 47 86). Serves interesting Mexican food, most notably the *Fajita Lupita*. *Fajitas* aren't the only things sizzling as the night wears on. Tiny outdoor garden. Entrees 90-250AS. Open M-Sa 6pm-2am (heated food until 1am), Su 6pm-midnight.

Rosenberger Markt, I, Mayscderg. 2 (tel. 512 34 58), behind Sacher Hotel. This large and chaotic subterranean buffet offers a gargantuan selection of decent food at reasonable prices. Food stations include salad, fruit salad, waffle, antipasto, potato, and pasta bars. You pay by the size of your plate—pile high. Salads 29-64AS, waffles 55AS, vegetable dishes 24-64AS. Open 10:30am-11pm.

Inigo, I, Bäckerstr. 18 (tel. 512 74 51). Across from Vienna's pretty stucco Jesuit church and founded by a Jesuit priest, this restaurant is part of a socio-economic reintegration program. It provides transit employment, training, and social work for 17 people who are long-term unemployed or have no job qualifications. Menu includes eclectic international dishes, many whole wheat and vegetarian options, and a salad bar. Entrees 60-90AS, salad 22-58AS. Casual mixed crowd. Open M-Sa 8:30am-11pm, Su 10am-2pm.

Koh-i-noor, I, Marc Aurel-Str. 8 (tel. 533 00 80), on a small street near the Bermuda Triangle. Indian restaurant with a huge selection of delectable curry, tandoori, and vegetarian dishes. Superb quality and large portions account for a slightly elevated price. This is a place for a treat-yourself evening. Entrees 80-200AS. M-F lunch buffet 98AS. There is a cover charge. Open 11:30am-2:30pm and 6-11pm.

Outside the Ring

⊛**Tunnel,** VIII, Florianig. 39 (tel. 42 34 65). U-2: "Rathaus," then with your back to the *Rathaus* head right on Landesgerichtstr. and left on Florianig. Pronounced "Toonehl." Dark and smoky with funky paintings, thick, heavy tables, and the occasional divan. The Tunnel is an extremely popular place prized for its dilapidated hipness, live nightly music, and affordable food. Daily lunch *Menüs* 45AS. Italian, Austrian, and Middle Eastern dishes, with many vegetarian options (45-125AS). Some of the cheapest beer in Vienna (0.50L *Gösser* 27AS), good pizza (55-85AS), and a breakfast menu (35AS) until 11:30am. Open 10am-2am.

⊛**Blue Box,** VII, Richterg. 8 (tel. 523 26 82). U-3: "Neubaug." then turn onto Neubaug. and take your 1st right onto Richterg. Although the interior looks more like a nightclub than a restaurant—a jaundiced orange chandelier, blue leather couches, and not much light—the emphasis is on the food. Dishes are fresh, flamboyant, and above all, original. They often center around themes, whether regional (Russia, Louisiana, Tuscany) or general (sailors' fare, "color lessons," picnics, garlic). DJs pick music to match the meals. A great place to come for a late (or really late) breakfast (until 5pm). Choose from Viennese, French, rustic, or vegetarian. Open Tu-Th and Su 10am-2am, F-Sa 10am-4am, M 6pm-2am.

⊛**Café Willendorf,** VI, Linke Wienzeile 102 (tel. 587 17 89), in Vienna's gay and lesbian center, the Rosa Lila Villa. A café, bar, and restaurant with a leafy outdoor terrace and excellent, creative vegetarian fare. Mixed crowd and a warm community atmosphere. Open 7pm-2am; meals until midnight.

Fischerbräu, XIX, Billrothstr. 17 (tel. 319 62 64). U-6: "Nußdorfer Str." then up Währinger Gürtel, left on Döblinger Hauptstr., and left on Billrothstr. Popular spot for young locals. The leafy courtyard and jazz music make this restaurant an ideal spot to consume home-brewed beer (large 40AS) and delicious food. The veal sausage (60AS) and the chicken salad (87AS) are excellent. Open M-Sa 4pm-1am, Su 11am-1am. Jazz brunch Su noon-3pm.

Amerlingbeisl, VII, Stiftg. 8 (tel. 526 16 60). U-2: "Babenberger" or U-3: "Neubaug." Halfway between the stops on Mariahilferstr., turn onto Stiftg. After a couple of blocks you'll hit a cluster of outdoor restaurants. Walk past the first to reach Amerlingbeisl, a bamboo courtyard roofed with grape vines. Eat vegetarian food in this green little unofficial alternative community center while listening to sprays of water falling on leaves. Occasional live music. Entrees 80-110AS, late breakfast 55-90AS. Open daily 9am-2am (hot food served until 1am).

Lecker, III, Ungarg. 57, on the #O tram line. This Taiwanese vegetarian restaurant offers you tofu, seitan, and soy-delights artfully disguised as beef, chicken, and fishies. Open 11:30am-2:30pm and 5:30-11:45pm.

Restaurant am Radetzkyplatz, III, Radetzkypl. 1 (tel. 712 57 50). An old, mellowed, Austrian pub. At least 150 years of beer (0.50L 30AS) and food (60-160AS) have given the place worn bar railings and faded green walls. Sit outside under the striped awning and enjoy some of the cheapest food and drink in Vienna. Robust servings and veggie options. Open 8am-11pm.

⊛**Elsäßer Bistro,** IX, Währingerstr. 30 (tel. 319 76 89). U-2: "Schottentor." Within the palace now housing the French Cultural Institute—walk in the garden and follow your nose. Wonderful food that even the French cultural attachés to Vienna call authentic. Lots of beautiful French wines. Most dishes hover at or below 120AS. Open M-F 11am-3pm and 6-11pm. Kitchen closes 1hr. earlier.

Nells, XVII, Alseggerstr. 26 (tel. 479 13 77). U-2: "Schottentor" then tram #40: "Alseggerstr." The garden tables, warm wooden interior, and original interpretations of traditional Viennese food draw a hip twentysomething crowd. Lots of different beers and *Heuriger* wines. Open M-Sa 4pm-2am, Su 11am-2am.

Stomach, IX, Seeg. 26 (tel. 310 20 99). Tram D: "Fürsteng." then walk down Porzellang. to Seeg. and turn right. 1st-class Austrian cooking with a Styrian kick; lots of vegetarian food (100-210AS). Eat your beautifully cooked food inside next to the tile ovens and warm dark wood furnishings or outside in a lovely inner courtyard. Twentysomething crowd. Open W-Sa 4pm-midnight, Su 10am-10pm.

Hatam, IX, Währingerstr. 64 (tel. 310 94 50). Tram #38, 40, or 41: "Spitalg." Persian food at good prices. Try their unbeatable *gorme sabse* (spiced eggplant dish with rice) or grab a *Döner* to go (40-60AS). Entrees 75-165AS. Open daily 11am-11pm.

Schnitzelwirt Schmidt, VII, Neubaug. 52 (tel. 523 37 71). U-2 or U-3: "Volkstheater," then bus #49: "Neubaug." Every kind of *Schnitzel* (60-110AS) imaginable. It's not gourmet *Schnitzel,* but the pieces of meat are guaranteed to be so big they go over the edge of the plate. Open M-Sa 11am-11pm.

University Mensa, IX, Universitätsstr. 7, on the 7th floor of the university building, between U-2: "Rathaus" and "Schottentor." Visitors can ride the old-fashioned elevator (no doors and it never stops; you have to jump in and out) to the 6th floor and take the stairs up. Typical university meals 40-60AS. Open M-F 8am-6pm. Other inexpensive student cafeterias serve their constituencies at:

Music Academy, I, Johannesg. 8 (tel. 512 94 70). Open M-F 7:30am-3pm. Food served 11am-2pm; in July and Aug. and weekends 7:30-10am.

Academy of Applied Art, I, Oskar-Kokoschka-Pl. 2 (tel. 718 66 95). Open M-Th 9am-6pm, F 9am-3pm.

Academy of Fine Arts, I, Schillerpl. 3 (tel. 58 81 61 38). Open M-F 9am-5pm. Closed June to early Sept.

Afro-Asiatisches Institut, IX, Türkenstr. 3, near U-Bahn station Schottentor. Multi-ethnic cafeteria. Open M-F 11:30am-2pm.

Vienna Technical University, IV, Wiedner Hauptstr. 8-10 (tel. 586 65 02). Open M-F 11am-2pm.

Catholic University Student's Community, I, Ebendorferstr. 8 (tel. 408 35 87 39). *Menü* 33-40AS. Open M-F 11am-2pm.

Economics University, IX, Aug. 2-6 (tel. 310 57 18). Open M-F 8am-7pm, holidays only until 3pm.

COFFEEHOUSES AND KONDITOREIEN

"Who's going to start a revolution? Herr Trotsky from Café Central?"
—Austrian general quoted on the eve of the Russian Revolution

There is a steadfast rule for the Vienna coffeehouse—the drink matters, but the atmosphere *really* matters. The 19th-century coffeehouse was a haven for artists, writers, and thinkers who flocked to soft, brooding interiors to flee badly heated, telephoneless apartments. In the coffeehouses, they surrounded themselves with dark wood and dusty velvet, ordered a cup of coffee, and stayed long into the night composing operettas, writing books, and cutting into each other's work. The bourgeoisie followed suit, and the coffeehouse became the living room of the city. At its tables gathered the intellectual world of Vienna and, in many cases, Europe. A grand coffeehouse culture arose. Peter Altenberg, "the café writer," scribbled lines, Kokoschka grumbled alone, and exiles Vladimir Lenin and Leon Trotsky played chess. Here Theodor Herzl made plans for a Zionist Israel, and here Kafka came from Prague to visit the Herrenhof. Karl Kraus and a circle of minor writers baited Hugo von Hofmannsthal and Arthur Schnitzler. The original literary café, right on the cusp of the "merry apocalypse" *fin de siècle* culture, was Café Griensteidl. After its 1897 zenith faded, the torch passed first to Café Central and then to Café Herrenhof. Cafés still exist under all these names, but only Café Central looks like it used to. Adolf Loos, prophet of 20th-century Minimalist architecture, designed the interior of the Museum Café in smooth, spacious lines. Coffeehouses now rest partway in the past. The best places resist massive overhauls, succumbing to a noble, comfortable decrepitude.

Viennese coffee is distinct, not quite as strong as an espresso, but with more kick than your average Dripmaster. The quintessential Viennese coffee is the *Melange,* made with foamed cream or thick milk. Otherwise, you can order a *Kleiner* (small) or *Grosser* (large), *Brauner* (brown, with a little milk) or *Schwarzer* (black—enough said). Whipped cream is known as *Schlag* (short for *Schlagobers*); if you don't like it, say *"ohne Schlag, bitte."* A Viennese favorite is *Mokka mit Sclagrahm,* a mocha coffee with whipped cream. A *Mazagron* is iced and laced with rum. Be traditional and order an *Einspänner* (coffee and a glass filled with whipped cream), or wow everyone in the café by drinking a *Kaisermélange*—a regular *Melange* with the yolk of an egg mixed in. Opulent pastries complete the picture. *Apfel Strudel,* cheesecakes, tortes, *Buchteln* (warm cake with jam in the middle—diabolical), *Palatschinken, Krapfen,* and *Mohr im Hemd* have all helped place Vienna on the culinary map.

Most cafés also serve hot food. Don't order food and coffee together (excepting pastries), unless you want to be really gauche. Coffee may seem expensive (30-40AS) if you only consider the drink you're buying, but when you realize that you're actually paying to linger for hours and read newspapers, the price suddenly seems much more reasonable. The most serious dictate of coffeehouse etiquette is the requirement to linger. The waiter (often outfitted with black bow tie and always committed to his work) will serve you as soon as you sit down, and then leave you to sip, brood, and read. He's known as *Herr Ober* (a slangy honorific) in Austria, not as a *Kellner.* Daily newspapers and magazines, many in English, are neatly racked for patrons. When you are ready to leave, signal to the waiter by asking to pay: *"Zahlen bitte!"*

The *Konditoreien* are no less traditional, but they focus their attention onto delectables rather than coffee. These pastries are something of a national institution—Switzerland may have its gold reserves, but Austria could back its currency with its world-renowned *Sacher Torte.* If you want to see a menu, ask for a *Karte.*

The Innere Stadt

⊛**Café Hawelka,** I, Dorotheerg. 6 (tel. 512 82 30), 3 blocks down Graben from the Stephansdom. Dusty wallpaper, dark wood, and red-striped velvet sofas that haven't been reupholstered in years—the Hawelka is shabby and glorious. Josephine and Leopold Hawelka put this legendary café on the map when they opened it in 1937—Leopold received an award from the Austrian government and Josephine a visit from Falco (see the picture on the wall). *Buchteln* (served fresh from the oven at 10pm) 35AS. Coffee 30-50AS. Open M and W-Sa 8am-2am, Su 4pm-2am.

⊛**Café Museum,** I, Friedrichstr. 6 (tel. 56 52 01), near the Opera. Head away from the *Innere Stadt* to the corner of Operng. and Friedrichstr. Built in 1899 by Adolf Loos, with striking curves, red leather, and lots of space. Simple and elegant, this café once attracted a crowd of cabaret artists, painters, and famous musicians including Lehár, Berg, Musil, Roth, Kokoschka, and Schiele. Known in the day as "Café Nihilism," the place lost much of its importance (and a number of its clientele) after the bloody 1918 revolution. This comfortable meeting place now attracts a mixed bag of artists, lawyers, students, and chess players. Open 8am-midnight.

⊛**Café Alt Wien,** I, Bäckerg. 9 (tel. 512 52 22) is a bohemian, nicotine-stained place on a street behind the Stephansdom amid ancient restaurants and cobblestones. Smoky red sofas and layers of avant-garde posters lend atmosphere. At night the buzz allows comfortable conversation. Open M-Th 10am-2am, F-Su 10am-4am.

Kleines Café, I, Franziskanerpl. 3. Turn off Kärtnerstr. onto Weihburg. and follow it to the Franziskanerkirche. Whimsical mix of the traditional and the funky, designed by architect Hermann Czech. Brown leather and wood, a low-vaulted ceiling, art exhibits, and nightclub posters coexist harmoniously. The salads here are minor works of art. Yes, it's *klein.* Open M-Sa 10am-2am, Su 1pm-2am.

Café Central, I (tel. 533 37 63), at the corner of Herreng. and Strauchg. inside Palais Ferstel. Café Central has unfortunately been mainly given up to the tourists because it has become too famous. Theodor Herzl, Sigmund Freud, satirist Karl Kraus, and Vladimir Ilych Ulianov (better known by his pen name, Lenin) all hung out here, as well as Leon Trotsky, who played chess. Alfred Polgar published an essay titled *Theorie de Café Central,* where he wrote: "It is a place for people who know how to abandon and be abandoned for the sake of their fate, but do not have the nerve to live up to this fate. It is a true asylum for people who have to kill time so as not to be killed by it...a first-aid station for the confused...all their lives in search of themselves and all their lives in flight from themselves..." Oh, they serve coffee, too. Elegant tables in a beautiful arcade court. Open M-Sa 9am-8pm. Live piano music 4-7pm.

Taster's Choice

Legend dates Vienna's love affair with coffee back to the second Turkish invasion of 1683. Two months into the siege, Vienna was on the verge of falling to the Turks, until a Polish-born citizen named Kolschitzky volunteered his services. A dashing adventurer who had spent time within the Sultan's territories, Kolschitzky used his knowledge of Turkish language and customs to slip through the enemy camp and deliver a vital message to Vienna's relief forces, led by the Duke of Lorraine. The Duke then engaged the Turks in a bitter battle that sent them fleeing, leaving most of their camp behind. Kolschitzky claimed as his only compensation the many sacks of greenish beans left by the routed armies of the Sultan. The grateful city readily granted this reward, and Kolschitzky opened the first Viennese coffeehouse, Zur Blauen Flasche, became a huge success, and died a wealthy, revered, and caffeinated man.

Demel, I, Kohlmarkt 14 (tel. 535 17 17), 5min. from the Stephansdom down Graben. The most luxurious Viennese *Konditorei,* Demel's was confectioner to the imperial court until the empire dissolved. Chocolate is made fresh every morning. A fantasy of mirrored rooms and cream walls topped by a display case of legendary desserts. Waitresses in convent-black serve the divine confections (40-50AS). Don't miss the *crème-du-jour.* Open 10am-6pm.

Cafe Opera Zum Peter, I, Riemberg. 9 (tel. 512 89 81). A low-key crowd lingers among hodgepodge walls plastered with autographed photos, posters, and pictures of opera performers and performances. Open M-F 8am-2am, Sa 5pm-2am.

Bräunerhof, I, Stallburgg. 2 (tel. 512 38 93). This delightfully shabby cafe's location—on a small alley near the Hofburg—has left it virtually untouched by tourists. Hosts many readings and piano concerts. You can order bread, *Käse* and *Schinken,* or Austrian salad from a menu lined with Peter Altenberg prose. Open M-F 7:30am-8:30pm, Sa 7:30am-6pm, Su 10am-6pm.

Café Prückel, I, Stubenring 24 (tel. 512 61 15). Spacious, with high ceilings. A 50s renovation added lime-green upholstery, now faded, and time has conferred a noble slouch. Hosts numerous readings and performances. Patronized by art students from the MAK (Museum of Applied Arts), which is down the street. Open 9am-10pm. Kitchen open noon-8pm.

Hotel Sacher, I, Philharmonikerstr. 4 (tel. 512 14 87), around the corner from the main tourist information office. This historic sight has served the world-famous **Sachertorte** (50AS) in red velvet opulence for years. During the reign of Franz Josef, elites invited to the Hofburg would make late reservations at the Sacher—the emperor ate quickly, Elisabeth was always dieting, and as nobody dared eat after the imperial family had finished, all the guests left hungry and had a real dinner later at Hotel Sacher. Exceedingly opulent; most of the clientele is bedecked and bejeweled. Open 7am-11:30pm.

Hotel Imperial, I, Kärnter Ring 16 (tel. 50 11 03 63; fax 50 11 03 55). This ostentatious chandeliered cafe, with a lovely flower-hung courtyard, serves its own insignia-stamped, marzipan-filled *Imperial Torte* (50AS), which some prefer to the rival *Sachertorte.* Karl Kraus became a regular here after deciding Café Central was too noisy, and brought the likes of Hugo von Hofmannsthal, Rainer Maria Rilke, Peter Altenberg, and Franz Werfel with him. Freud occasionally came here and was not above having an informal psychoanalytic consultation at his table. Trotsky played chess here, too. Wagner and Mahler dropped by. Open 7am-11:30pm.

Waldland, I, Peterspl. 11 (tel. 533 41 56). This tiny *Konditorei* bakes everything imaginable topped with poppyseed and honey. Decadent *Mohn* cookies, cakes, rolls, pastries...Open M-F 9am-6pm, Sa 9am-1pm.

Cafe MAK, I, Stubeuring 3-5 (tel. 714 01 21), in the MAK museum. See **Bars,** p. 122.

Outside the Ring

⊕**Café Sperl,** VI, Gumpendorferstr. 11 (tel. 586 41 58), 15min. from the Westbahnhof. Built in 1880, Sperl is one of Vienna's oldest and most beautiful cafes. Although some of the original trappings were removed during renovations, the *fin de siècle* atmosphere remains. Franz Lehár was a regular here; he composed operettas at a table by the entrance. Also the former home for Vienna's *Hagenbund,* an Art Nouveau coterie excluded from the Secession. Coffee 30-50AS; cake 30AS. Open M-Sa 7am-11pm, Su 3-11pm; July-Aug. closed Su.

Café Drechsler, VI, Linke Wienzeile 22 (tel. 587 85 80), near Karlspl. Head down Operng. and continue on Linke Wienzeile. *The* place to be the morning after the night before. Early birds and night owls roost here over pungent cups of *Mokka.* Great lunch menu—try the *Spinatz.* Open M-F 4am-8pm, Sa 4am-6pm.

Café Savoy, VI, Linke Wienzeile 36. Scruffy *fin de siècle* café with dark wood and decrepit gold trim. A large gay and lesbian crowd moves in to make it a lively nightspot on weekends. Open Tu-F 5pm-2am, Sa 9am-6pm and 9pm-2am.

Cafe Nil, VII, Siebensterng. 39 (tel. 526 61 65). Drink, eat, and play *bakshish* in this serene and low-key incense-scented Middle Eastern cafe. Tasty dishes are all pork-free and many are vegetarian (54-105AS). Open M-Th 10am-midnight, F-Sa 10am-1am, Su 10am-midnight. Breakfast until noon, Sa until 3pm.

Kunsthaus Wien Cafe, III, Untere Weißgerberstr. 13 (tel. 712 04 97). In a courtyard in the middle of the melodic, undulating, and draped-in-an-overgrown-garden Kunsthaus, this café serves typical drinks in a Hundertwasserian atmosphere. Open 10am-midnight.

Cafe Rüdigerhof, V, Hamburgerstr. 20 (tel. 586 31 38). Lodged in a 1902 building designed by Otto Wagner students, this Jugendstil cafe is adorned with floral patterns, leather couches, and a large outside garden. Lots of soups (30AS), omelettes, and meat and fish dishes (30-100AS). Open daily noon-10:30pm, garden open for drinks until midnight.

Café Stein, IX, Währingerstr. 6 (tel. 319 72 41; fax 31 97 24 12), near Schottentor. Chrome seats outside to see and be seen, and clustered tables indoors in the smoky red-brown and metallic interior. Intimate and lively, it slides into night as "Stein's Diner," when DJs appear. Billiards and **internet access** (65AS per 30min. 5-11pm; reserve your slot in advance). Breakfast until 8pm. Open M-Sa 7am-1am, Su 9am-1am. **Stein's Diner** in the basement open M-Sa 7pm-2am.

Alte Backstube, VIII, Langeg. 34 (tel. 406 11 01). Around the corner from Theater in der Josefstadt, this popular after-theater café/restaurant functioned as a bakery from 1701—when its extant sandstone relief of the Holy Trinity was crafted—until 1963. The café serves Austrian dishes, coffees and pastries, but more interestingly, it serves as a **museum of bakery art.** On display are the original baking ovens, 300-year-old bakers' equipment, articles, photos, and all sorts of baked-goods devotionalia. Open Sept. to mid-July Tu-Sa 10am-midnight, Su 4pm-midnight.

Das Frauencafé, VIII, Lange Gasse 11, near the U-6 U-Bahn station Lerchenfelderstr. Small, friendly, and very much left of center, this is Vienna's sole permanent women's café. Open M-Sa 8pm-1am.

■ Sights

Viennese streets are by turns scuzzy, startling, *gemütlich,* and grandiose. The best way to get to know the city streets is simply to get lost in them. To do that in a more organized manner, grab the brochure *Vienna from A to Z. (With Vienna Card discount 50AS; available at the tourist office.)* Vienna's array can boggle the mind; the tourist office's free *Museums* brochure lists all opening hours and admission prices. Individual museum tickets usually cost 20-80AS, discounted with the **Vienna Card.** (The Vienna Card discounts are only a good deal if you're not a student or senior citizen.) Whatever you do, don't miss the **Hofburg,** the **Schloß Schönbrunn,** the **Kunsthistorisches Museum,** the **Schloß Belvedere,** or any of the buildings along the **Ringstraße.** The range of available **tours** is equally overwhelming—walking tours, ship tours, bike tours and tram tours, bus tours, tours in a cup, tours over easy. The tourist office provides a brochure "Walks in Vienna," which lists all 57 theme tours. Tours are 130AS; some require admission fees to sites. Call the tourist office in advance to verify that they're operating on schedule. All are worthwhile, but "Vienna in the Footsteps of the Third Man," which takes you into the sewers and the graffiti-covered catacomb world of the Wien River's underground canals, is one of the best. (Bring your own flashlight). Tours on turn-of-the-century "old-timer" **trams** (tel. 790 94 40 26) run May to October. *(1½hr. 200AS. Departs from Karlspl. near the Otto Wagner Pavilion Sa-Su 9:30, 11:30am, and 1:30pm.)* The legendary drivers of **Fiakers,** or horse-drawn carriages, are happy to taxi you wherever your heart desires, but be sure to agree on the price before you set out. **Cycling tours** occur every day; contact **Vienna-Bike,** IX, Wasag. (tel. 319 12 58), for bike rental (60AS) or a two- to three-hour tour. *(280AS.)* Early booking is advised. **Bus tours** operate through various companies such as **Vienna Sight-seeing Tours,** III, Stelzhamerg. 4/11 (tel. 712 46 83) and **Cityrama,** I, Börgeg. 1 (tel. 534 13). Tours start at 200AS. On the other hand, one of the best tours is simply a ride around the Ring on a #1 or #2 tram—buy a ticket, ride around the old city's boulevards, and gawk to your heart's content.

THE INNERE STADT

The **First District** (*die Innere Stadt* or "inner city"), Vienna's social and geographical epicenter, is enclosed on three sides by the massive **Ringstraße** and on the northern end by the **Danube Canal.** With the mark of master architects on everything from palaces and theaters to tenements and toilet bowls, the *Innere Stadt* is a gallery of the history of aesthetics, from *Jugendstil* to Baroque.

From Staatsoper to Stephansplatz

The **Staatsoper** (State Opera House) holds special space in the hearts of the Viennese. It had first priority in the massive construction of the Ringstraße (see p. 106), and was completed in 1869. Due to a mistake laying the foundation, however, the builders had to cut a full story from the building's height. When Franz Josef saw the building, he agreed with the general consensus that it was "a little low." The two architects wanted so badly to impress that the lukewarm reactions drove one to suicide and caused the other to die two months later "of a broken heart." The emperor was so shocked that for the rest of his life, whenever he was presented with something he responded, *"Es ist sehr schön, es hat mich sehr erfreut"* (It's very beautiful, I enjoyed it very much). Opinions about the opera house changed over the years, and Vienna's collective heart broke when Allied bombing destroyed the building in 1945. Vienna meticulously restored the exterior and re-opened the building in 1955. The list of its former directors is formidable, including Gustav Mahler, Richard Strauss, and Lorin Maazel. If you can't make it to a performance, at least **tour** the gold, crystal, and red velvet interior. *(Tours July-Aug. 10, 11am, 1, 2, and 3pm; Sept.-Oct. and May-June 1, 2, and 3pm; Nov.-Apr. 2 and 3pm. 40AS, students 25AS.)* Seeing an opera is cheaper, though—ground-floor standing room tickets with an excellent view are only 20AS, and standing room anywhere else costs 15AS.

Just across from the Opera lies another reminder of silk hats and white gloves—the flag-bedecked **Hotel Sacher.** This legendary institution once run by the formidable, cigar-smoking Anna Sacher served magnificent dinners over which the elite discussed affairs of state. The hotel's *separées* provided discreet locations where the elite conducted affairs of another sort. Behind the Sacher in Albertinapl., Alfred Hrdlicka's painful 1988 sculpture **Monument Gegen Krieg und Faschismus** (Memorial Against War and Fascism) commemorates the suffering caused by World War II. The twisted figures are a reminder of the horror of the Nazi period and of the shameful events after the *Anschluß*.

From Albertinapl., Tegetthoffstr. leads to the spectacular **Neuer Markt.** In the middle stands the George Raphael Donner's **Donnerbrunnen,** a graceful Danube figure surrounded by four gods representing her tributaries. The 17th-century pale orange **Kapuzinerkirche** stands modestly in one corner of the square. *(Open 9:30am-4pm. 30AS, children 20AS.)* Inside, its **Imperial Vault** *(Gruft)*, a series of huge subterranean rooms filled with coffins, includes the remains (minus heart and entrails) of all the Habsburg rulers since 1633. Empress Maria Theresa rests next to beloved hubby Franz Stephan of Lorraine in an ornate Rococo sepulcher surrounded by cherubim and a dome. Maria Theresa was crushed by the death of her husband and visited his tomb frequently. When she got old, the Empress had an elevator built. On her last trip, the elevator stalled three times, prompting the empress to exclaim that the dead did not want her to leave. She was entombed a week later.

Just a quick step down Donnerg. lies **Kärntner Straße,** a grand boulevard lined with costly cafés and boutiques. Street musicians play everything from Peruvian folk to Neil Diamond ballads. Heading left brings wanderers back to Vienna's heart. You can see the **Stephansdom** reflected in the glass and aluminum of the **Haas Haus.** The view is even better inside the *Haus,* which has a café on the top floor. The *Haus,* considered something of an eyesore by most Viennese (much to the dismay of postmodern architect Hans Hollein), opened in 1990.

Stephansplatz to Michaelerplatz

From Stephanspl., walk down Rotenturmstr., cross Fleischmarkt to Rabensteig, and turn left onto Seitenstettneg. to reach Ruprechtspl., home to a slew of street cafés and the Romanesque **Ruprechtskirche,** the oldest church in Vienna. The **Danube Canal** demarcates the area north of the square and the northern boundary of the *Innere Stadt.* Walk back down Ruprechtsstiege onto Seitenstetteng. to find the **Synagogue,** Seitenstetteng. 2-4. This building, one of over 94 temples maintained by Vienna's 180,000 Jews until 1938, escaped Nazi destruction only because it stood on a residential block; the Nazis destroyed most of Vienna's other synagogues on November 9-10, 1938, during **Kristallnacht.** The event received the terrible beautiful title because the glass shards littering the streets the next day glittered like crystal. Sixty-odd years later, an armed guard patrols the synagogue.

Back at the top of Seitenstetteng. runs **Judengasse** ("Lane of the Jew"), a remnant of Vienna's old Jewish ghetto. *Biedermeier* apartments line the streets. **Hoher Markt** is down the street; this square stands on the site of the Roman encampment **Vindobona** and served as the town's center during the Middle Ages. The oldest square in town, it was once both market and execution site. The square's most remarkable piece of architecture is the corporate-sponsored *Jugendstil* **Ankeruhr clock.** Built in 1911, the mechanical timepiece has **12 historical figures** that rotate past the old Viennese coat of arms, accompanied by music of their period. *(One figure per hr. At noon, all the figures appear in succession.)* The figures depict the city's history from the era of Roman encampment up to Joseph Haydn's stint in the Boys' Choir.

Wipplingerstraße heads west (right) from Hoher Markt past the impressive Baroque facade of the **Bohemian Court Chancellery,** now the seat of Austria's Constitutional Court. The **Altes Rathaus,** Friedrich-Schmidt-Pl. (tel. 34 36 77 90), stands directly across the street. *(Open M-Th 9am-5pm. Tours M, W, and F 1pm.)* Occupied from 1316 until 1885, when the government moved to the Ringstr., the building is behind. another Donner fountain depicting the legend of Andromeda and Perseus. It holds frequent temporary exhibitions on the bottom floor. **Judenplatz,** on the opposite side of the Chancellery, contains a statue of Jewish playwright Ephraim Lessing. Originally erected in 1935, the statue was torn down by Nazis and only returned in 1982. There is also an outdoor exhibit and viewable excavations of a synagogue built in 1294.

A quick right off of Wipplingstr. down Stoss im Himmel brings you to **Maria am Gestade,** a gem of a Gothic church with an extraordinarily graceful spire of delicately carved stone. On the other side of Judenpl., Drahtg. opens into the grand courtyard **Am Hof.** *(Open Sa-Su 11am-1pm.)* The Babenbergs used this square as the ducal seat when they moved the palace in 1155 from atop **Leopoldsberg** (in the Wienerwald) to the present site. The medieval jousting square now houses the **Church of the Nine Chairs of Angels** (built 1386-1662). Pope Pius VI gave the papal blessing here at the request of Baron von Hirsch on Easter in 1782, and Emperor Franz II proclaimed his abdication as Holy Roman Emperor in 1806 from the terrace. Am Hof was in use long before the Babenbergs, as evidenced by the **Roman ruins.** In the middle of the square stands the **Mariensäule,** erected to fulfill a vow sworn by Emperor Ferdinand III when the Swedes threatened Vienna during the Thirty Years War.

From Am Hof, a jaunt down Schulg. to Steindlg. and Milchg. leads to Peterspl., home of the **Peterskirche.** Charlemagne founded the first version in the 8th century.

Town architects just couldn't resist tinkering with the structure throughout the ages. The present Baroque ornamentation was completed in 1733, with Rottmayer on fresco duty. Head out Jungferng. to the **Graben,** one of Vienna's main drags. Its landscape shows the debris of Baroque, *Jugendstil,* and postmodern trends. One of the most interesting (and interactive) sights is the underground *Jugendstil* public toilet complex, designed by Adolf Loos. The **Pestsaüle** (Plague Column) in the square's center was built in 1693 in gratitude for the passing of the Black Death. According to the inscription, the monument is "a reminder of the divine chastisement of plagues richly deserved by this city." The Viennese had ways of dealing with guilt complexes (and phallic symbols) long before Freud.

At the western end of the Graben, away from the Stephansdom, Kohlmarkt leads off to the left past **Demel Café**—though few people can pass up Demel's—and the **Looshaus** (1910). Shocked by its lack of decorative elements, disgruntled contemporaries branded it "the house without eyebrows." The bottom two floors stand behind green marble, and the top four floors are of pale green stucco with (gasp!) no facade decoration. Franz Josef was reportedly so disgusted with the atrocity built outside his bedroom window that he refused to use the Hofburg gate facing it. The Looshaus sits on **Michaelerplatz,** named for the **Michaelerkirche** on its eastern flank. Leopold "the Glorious" of Babenberg purportedly founded the church in gratitude for his safe return from the Crusades. The church's Romanesque foundation dates back to the early 13th century, but construction continued until 1792 (note the Baroque embellishment over the doorway). In the middle of Michaelerpl. lie the **excavated foundations** of Roman Vienna—the Roman military camp called Vindobona where Marcus Aurelius penned *Meditations.*

Ecclesiastical Vienna: The Stephansdom

Vienna's most treasured symbol, the **Stephansdom** (known affectionately as *"Der Steffl"*), fascinates viewers with its Gothic intensity and smoothly tapered **South Tower.** *(Tours of the cathedral in English M-Sa at 10:30am and 3pm; Su and holidays 3pm; 30AS. Spectacular evening tour July-Sept. Sa 7pm; 100AS.)* The **North Tower** was originally intended to be equally high and graceful, but construction ceased after a spooky tragedy (see **Making Pacts with the Devil: Not Good,** above). Take the elevator up the North Tower (open Apr.-Sept. 9am-6pm; Oct.-Mar. 8am-5pm; elevator ride 50AS) for a view of the Viennese sprawl, or climb the 343 steps of the South Tower for a 360-degree view, as well as a close-up view of the gargoyles. *(Open 9am-5:30pm; 25AS).* Nazi artillery almost leveled the entire place, and much had to be rebuilt. A series of photographs inside chronicles the painstaking process. The exterior boasts some remarkable sculpture; it deserves a lap before you enter the building. The oldest sections, the Romanesque **Riesentor** (Giant Gate) and **Heidentürme** (Towers of the Heathens), were built during the reign of King Ottokar II when Vienna was a Bohemian protectorate. Habsburg Duke Rudolf IV later ordered a complete Gothic retooling and thus earned the sobriquet "the Founder." Inside, some of the important pieces include the Albertine Choir built in the early 14th century and the Gothic

---

Making Pacts with the Devil: Not Good

Years ago, during the construction of the North Tower of the Stephansdom, a young builder named Hans Puchsbaum wished to marry his master's daughter. The master, rather jealous of Hans's skill, agreed on one condition: Hans had to finish the entire North Tower on his own within a year. Faced with this impossible task, Hans despaired until a stranger offered to help him. The good Samaritan required only that Hans abstain from saying the name of God or any other holy name. Hans agreed, and the tower grew by leaps and bounds. One day during construction the young mason spotted his love in the midst of his labor, and, wishing to call attention to his progress, he called out her name: "Maria." With this invocation of the Blessed Virgin, the scaffolding collapsed, and Hans plummeted 500ft. to his death. Rumors of a satanic pact spread, and work on the tower ceased, leaving it in its present condition.

organ loft by **Anton Pilgram,** so delicate that Pilgram's contemporaries warned him that it would never bear the organ's weight. Pilgram replied that he would hold it up himself and carved a self-portrait at the bottom, bearing the entire burden on his back. The high altar piece of the **Stoning of St. Stephen** is just as stunning. Downstairs in the **Catacombs,** thousands of plague-victim skeletons line the walls. Look for the lovely **Gruft** (vault), which stores all of the Habsburg innards. *(Tours M-Sa 10, 11, 11:30am, 2, 2:30, 3:30, 4, and 4:30pm, Su and holidays 2, 2:30, 3:30, 4, and 4:30pm. 50AS.)* Everyone wanted a piece of the rulers—the Stephansdom got the entrails, the Augustinerkirche got the hearts, and the **Kapuzinergruft** got the leftovers. The **bell** of the Stephansdom is the world's heaviest free-ringing bell (the whole bell and not just the clapper moves)—it is hardly ever rung because the repeated stress of vibrations might crack the church foundations.

Imperial Vienna: The Hofburg

The sprawling **Hofburg** is a chronicle of the vicissitudes of the Habsburg family. *(Enter at Michaelerpl. 1; Imperial apartments open 9am-4:30pm.)* Its construction began in 1279, and hodge podge additions and renovations continued virtually until the end of the family's reign in 1918, when the structure had become a mini-city. Today, the complex houses the Austrian President's offices and the performance halls of the Lipizzaner stallions and the Vienna Boys' Choir.

A stroll along the perimeter is the best way to start. From Michaelerpl. and facing the palace, go left to find the **Stallburg** (Palace Stables) right inside the passage, home to the Royal Lipizzaner stallions of the **Spanische Reitschule** (Spanish Riding School; tel. 533 90 32; fax 53 50 186). This renowned equine breed is a relic of the Habsburg marriage to Spanish royalty. The **Reitschule performances** are always sold out; you must reserve tickets six months in advance. *(Apr.-June and Sept. Su 10:45am, W 7pm; Mar. Su 10:45am; 1½hr. Write to: Spanische Reitschule, Hofburg, A-1010 Wien. If you reserve through a travel agency, expect at least a 22% surcharge. Reservations only; no money accepted by mail. Tickets 250-900AS, standing room 200AS.)* Watching the horses train is much cheaper. *(Mid-Feb. to June and Nov. to mid-Dec. Tu-F 10am-noon; Feb. M-Sa 10am-noon, except when the horses tour. Tickets sold at the door at Josefspl., Gate 2, from about 8:30am. Call first. 100AS, children 30AS. No reservations.)* You can also learn about the Lipizzaner's history and training since the 16th century at the **Lipizzaner Museum,** I, Reitschulg. 2 (tel. 526 41 84 30; fax 526 41 86). *(Open daily 9am-6pm. 50AS, students 35AS.)*

Keep walking around the Hofburg, away from the Michaelerkirche, to hit the Baroque **Josefsplatz.** The modest Josef II would no doubt be appalled at his statue's bare-chested Roman garb, but the sculptor probably couldn't bring himself to depict the decrepit hat and patched-up frock coat the emperor favored. The **Augustinerkirche** also sits on this square. Eighteenth-century renovation (and some Napoleonic flourishes) have altered the interior of this 14th-century Gothic church. The church is the proud possessor of the **hearts of the Habsburgs,** stored in the crypt. Augustinerstr. leads right past the **Albertina,** the palatial wing once inhabited by Maria Christina (Maria Theresa's favorite daughter) and her hubby Albert. The Albertina now contains a film museum and the celebrated **Collection of Graphic Arts** (tel. 534 83), with old political cartoons and drawings by the likes of Dürer, Michelangelo, da Vinci, Raphael, Cezanne, and Schiele. *(Open Tu-F 10am-4pm, Sa 10am-6pm.)*

Upon rounding the tip of the Albertina, cut around the monument to Erzherzog Albrecht and stroll through the exquisite **Burggarten** (Imperial Palace Gardens). The sloping green grass and odd billiard ball bushes are a favorite place for university students to fall asleep with an open book in the sun. At one end of the Burggarten is an enormous greenhouse of tropical plants that also houses the **Schmetterlinghaus** (Butterfly House), an enclosure where soft-winged beauties fly free in the tropical environment. The opposite end of the garden opens onto the Ring and then the main entrance into the Hofburg, just a few meters to the right. Enter through the enormous stone gate into the sweeping **Heldenplatz** (Heroes' Square). During the Second World War, the entire square was planted with potatoes to feed the starving populace. The equestrian statues (both done by Anton Fernkorn) depict two of Austria's

Sisi, the Austrian Sensation

One hundred years ago in Switzerland, an anarchist killed the Empress of Austria. Today, Austria remembers Empress Elisabeth (better known everywhere as Sisi) not for her untimely death, her accomplishments, or even her life—the country has instead immortalized her beauty. When she married Franz Josef in 1854, the 16-year-old Bavarian princess was widely considered to be the most gorgeous woman in the world. Love, however, did not flourish—even in the hundreds of rooms of the Hofburg and Schönbrunn palaces, the imperial couple could not get far enough away from each other. Franz Josef built the Hermes Villa in the Vienna Woods for his wife's private residence. There, she unhappily wrote (in translation): "Love is not for me. Wine is not for me. The first makes me ill. The second makes me sick." In other poems, she complained about her duties as Empress, disparaged her husband, and labeled her children bristle-haired pigs. Austrians never got over their love affair with Sisi's good looks. Over a century later, this melancholy, inconsequential, tight-lipped, beautiful woman is plastered on postcards and in guide books all over Austria. As recently as 1996, three separate "Elisabeth" plays and musicals were running in Vienna. She inspired a famous movie trilogy and even a Barbie doll. On April 4, 1998, a triple exhibit entitled, appropriately, "Elisabeth—Beauty for Eternity" opened at the Imperial Palace, at Schönbrunn, and at the Hermes Villa. The exhibit will run until February 16, 1999, as a monument to the power of an unhappy woman's face.

greatest military commanders. Archduke Karl's charger rears triumphantly on its hind legs with no other support, a feat of sculpting never again duplicated. The poor Fernkorn went insane, supposedly due to his inability to recreate the effect. To the right is the **Neue Hofburg** (New Palace), built between 1881 and 1913. The double-headed golden eagle crowning the roof symbolizes the double empire of Austria-Hungary. Planned in 1869, the Neue Hofburg's design called for a twin across the Heldenplatz, and both buildings were to be connected to the Kunsthistorisches and Naturhistorisches Museums by arches spanning the Ringstraße. World War I put an end to the Empire and its grand designs. Today, the Neue Hofburg houses branches of the **Kuntshistorisches Museum,** including an extensive weapons collection and an assortment of antique instruments. Among the harps and violins are Beethoven's harpsichord and Mozart's piano with a double keyboard. The **Ephesus Museum** contains the massive findings of an Austrian excavation of Roman ruins in Turkey, and the Völkerkunde Museum houses artifacts from non-European places collected by Austro-Hungarian colonists in 18th- and 19th-century expeditions (see **Art Museums,** p. 113). Also within the Neue Hofburg is the **Nationalbibliothek** (National Library; tel. 53 41 03 97), which boasts an outstanding collection of papyrus, scriptures, and musical manuscripts. *(Open Jan.-Feb. M-Sa 10am-2pm; Mar. to mid-May and Nov.-Dec. M-Sa 10am-noon, mid-May to Oct. M-Sa 10am-4pm, Su 10am-1pm. 40AS.)* The library's **Prunksaal** (Gala Hall) is an awesome display of High Baroque. The Hofburg continues an association with the Austrian government; the building attached to the Neue Hofburg is the **Reichskanzleitrakt** (State Chancellery Wing), most notable for the labors of Hercules, a group of buff statues said to have inspired the 11-year-old Arnold Schwarzenegger, then on his first visit to Vienna, to pump up.

The arched stone passageway at the rear of Heldenpl. leads into the courtyard called **In der Burg,** surrounded by the wings of the **Alte Hofburg** (Old Palace). In the center is a monument to Emperor Franz II. Turn left under the arch of red and black stones crowned by a black eagle on a gilded shield to arrive at the **Schweizerhof** (Swiss Courtyard), named for the mercenaries who formed the Emperor's guard. This section is the oldest part of the Hofburg. Although the building's architecture is now mostly Renaissance, some pieces remain of the medieval fortress so necessary for the upwardly mobile aristocratic dynasty—the Habsburg stronghold was frequently under attack, twice by the Viennese themselves. On the right side of the courtyard stands the **Schatzkammer** (treasury), which contains such wonders as the crowns of the Holy Roman and Austrian Empires and the imperial christening robes. The **Holy Lance** is reportedly the one that pierced Christ's side during the Crucifixion. Looking at the lance, a young Hitler was purportedly inspired to return to Germany and found the Nazi party. Don't get any ideas. Just ahead is the Gothic **Burgkapelle** where the **Wiener Sängerknabenchor** (Vienna Boys' Choir) performs (see **Music,** p. 116).

Back at In der Burg, turn right to find yourself under the intricately carved ceiling of the **Michaeler Küppel.** The solid wood door on the right leads to the **Schauräume,** the former private rooms of Emperor Franz Josef and Empress Elisabeth. Amid all the Baroque trappings, the two most personal items seem painfully out of place: Emperor Franz Josef's military field bed and Empress Elisabeth's personal wooden gym bear mute testimony to lonely lives. Franz Josef's rooms are unelectrified—he didn't approve of most of the advances of the Industrial Age, although Sisi did manage to convince him to install running water for her bathtub. The door on the left opens to reveal the **Hofsilber und Tafelkammer,** a display of outrageously ornate cutlery that once adorned the imperial dinner table.

Monumental Vienna: The Ringstraße

The leafy **Ringstraße** defines the boundaries of the inner city. In 1857, Emperor Franz Josef commissioned this 57m wide and 4km long boulevard to replace the city fortifications that separated Vienna's medieval center from suburban districts. The military, still uneasy in the wake of the revolution attempted nine years earlier, demanded that the first district be surrounded by fortifications; the erupting bureaucratic bourgeoisie, however, argued for the removal of all formal barriers and for open space within the city. Imperial designers struck a compromise: the walls would be razed to make way for the Ringstraße, a peace-loving, tree-studded spread of boulevard and, at the same time, a sweeping circle designed for the efficient transport of troops. This massive architectural commitment attracted participants from all over Europe. Urban planners put together a grand scheme of monuments dedicated to staples of Western culture: scholarship, theater, politics, and art. The collected Historicist result became known as the **Ringstraße Style.** Freud used to walk the circuit of the Ring every day during his lunch break. It took him a brisk two hours.

The Hofburg, the nexus of Vienna's imperial glory, extends from the right side of the Burgring. On the left is **Maria-Theresien-Platz,** flanked by two of the monumental foci of culture: the **Kunsthistorisches Museum** (Museum of Art History) and the **Naturhistorisches Museum** (Museum of Natural History). When construction was complete, the builders stepped back and gasped in horror, realizing that they had put Apollo, patron deity of art, atop the Naturhistorisches Museum, and Athena, goddess of science, atop the Kunsthistorisches Museum. Tour guides claim that each muse is situated intentionally to *look upon* the appropriate museum (see **Art Museums,** p. 113). A large statue immortalizes the throned Empress Maria Theresa, surrounded by her key statesmen and advisers, in the center of the square. The statue purportedly faces the Ring so that the Empress may extend her hand to the people. She holds a copy of the Pragmatic Sanction granting women the right to succeed to the throne.

As you continue clockwise around the Ring, the zonking rose display of the **Volksgarten** on your right (see **Gardens and Parks,** p. 111) is across from the **Parlament** building. *(Tours mid-Sept. to mid-July M-F at 11am and 3pm; mid-July to mid-Sept. M-F 9, 10, 11am, 1, 2, and 3pm; Easter holidays 11am and 3pm.)* This gilded lily of Neoclassical archi-

---

Starch or No Starch? Starch, Please

The Habsburgs habitually strolled around Vienna with a full retinue of bodyguards. These casual jaunts were supposedly incognito—the emperor *demanded* that his subjects pretend to not recognize the imperial family. On one of these constitutionals in 1853, a Hungarian insurrectionist leapt from nearby bushes and attempted to stab the emperor. Franz Josef's collar was so heavily starched, however, that the knife drew no blue blood, and the crew of bodyguards dispatched the would-be assailant before he could strike again. Saved by starch but nevertheless afraid, Franz Joseph began the building of Ringstraße.

tecture, built from 1873 to 1883, is the first of four principal structures designed to fulfill the program of bourgeois cultural symbolism. Now the seat of the Austrian National and Federal Councils, it was once the meeting place for elected representatives to the Austro-Hungarian Empire. Its Historicist style was intended to evoke the great democracies of ancient Greece.

Just up the Dr.-Karl-Renner-Ring is the **Rathaus,** another masterpiece of historical symbolism. The neo-Gothic town hall with its fluted arches and red geraniums in the windows are meant to recall the Flemish burghers, who pioneered the idea of town halls and civic government in Europe. The Viennese, emerging from imperial constraints through the strength of the growing bureaucratic middle class, sought to imbue their city hall with the same sense of budding freedom and prosperity. There are art exhibits inside, and the city holds outdoor festivals in the front.

The Baroque and Rococo flourishes of the **Burgtheater,** across the *Rathauspark* and the Ring, contain the roaring spirit of the theatrical arts. *(Tours July-Aug. M, W, and F 1, 2, and 3pm; Sept.-June on request. 40AS.)* Inside, frescoes by Gustav Klimt, his brother, and his partner Matsch depict the interaction between drama and history through the ages. Klimt used contemporary faces as models for the audience members; notables of the day sent him baskets of fruit and tasteful presents in hopes of being covertly included in one of the murals.

Immediately to the north, on Karl-Lueger-Ring, is the **Universität Wien,** founded in 1365. The university was the originating cell for the failed 1848 uprising and so received the most care; above all, the symbolism had to be *safe*. The planners sought to dispel all of the ghosts of dissatisfaction and revolt in the building's design, taking as their model the cradle of state-sponsored liberal learning—Renaissance Italy. Inside the university is a tranquil courtyard with busts of famous departed professors in the archways. Any Austrian who passes their final high school examinations can attend university free of charge.

The surrounding side streets (in an area called **Schottentor**) have a happy assortment of university-bred cafés, bookstores, and bars. To the north, across Universitätsstr., the twin spires of the **Votivkirche** come into view. This neo-Gothic wonder and home of a number of expatriate religious communities is surrounded by rose gardens. Frequent classical music concerts afford opportunities to see the chapel's interior; look for posters announcing the dates throughout the year. Franz Josef's brother Maximilian commissioned the church as a gesture of gratitude after the *Kaiser* survived an assassination attempt in 1853 (see **Starch or No Starch?** above).

OUTSIDE THE RING

Operng. cuts through Opernring, leading to the Ringstraße nemesis, the **Secession Building** (tel. 587 53 07). The cream walls, restrained decoration, and gilded dome (giving the building its jolly nickname, the "Golden Cabbage") are meant to clash with the Historicist Ringstraße. Cacophony was exactly the point. Otto Wagner's pupil Josef Olbrich built this *fin de siècle* Viennese monument to accommodate artists who scorned historical style and broke with the rigid, state-sponsored Künstlerhaus. Note the inscription above the door: *"Der Zeit, ihre Kunst; der Kunst, ihre Freiheit"* (To the age, its art; to art, its freedom). The Secession exhibits of 1898-1903, which attracted cutting-edge European artists, were led by Gustav Klimt. His painting, *Nuda Veritas* (Naked Truth), became the icon of a new aesthetic ideal. Wilde's *Salomé* and paintings by Gauguin, Vuillard, van Gogh, and others created an island of modernity amid an ocean of Habsburgs and Historicism. The exhibition hall remains firmly dedicated to the displaying the cutting-edge (see **Art Museums,** p. 113). Those ensnared by the flowing tendrils of *Jugendstil* can find plenty of other turn-of-the-century works in Vienna—ask the tourist office for the *Art Nouveau in Vienna* pamphlet, which contains photos and addresses in town.

Painting the Town Red

Concerned that the Secession building was losing its iconoclastic status and rapidly being absorbed into the mainstream of Viennese bourgeoisdom, an anonymous group of fans of the Secession sneaked over to the building one night and painted the entire thing a bright clay red, in honor of its 100th anniversary. It is still red. Controversy over the propriety of this guerrilla installation rages, however, so get over there before they sandblast it or something.

The **Künstlerhaus,** Karlspl. 5, from which the Secession seceded, is just to the east, down Friedrichstr. This exhibition hall, attacked for its stodgy taste by Klimt and company, continues to display worthwhile stuff. Next door the acoustically miraculous **Musikverein** houses the **Vienna Philharmonic Orchestra** (see **Music,** p. 116). The **Karlskirche** lies on the other side of Friedrichstr., across the gardens of Karlspl. Completed in 1793, this wacky church was to fulfil a vow Emperor Karl VI made during a plague epidemic in 1713. In a curious amalgam of architectural styles, Byzantine wings flank minaret-like Roman columns, and a Baroque dome towers atop a classical portico. This blending continues in front of the church, with a reflecting pool and modern sculpture designed by 20th-century sculptor **Henry Moore.**

Modern Architecture: Wagner and his Disciples

Otto Wagner, even more than big name Adolf Loos, is the architect responsible for Vienna's *Jugendstil* face. He built the massive **Karlsplatz Stadtbahn Pavilion.** This enclosure is one of many produced for the city's rail system when the system was redesigned at the turn of the century. All of the U-6 stations between Längenfeldg. and Heiligenstadt are other examples of Wagner's work. His attention to the most minute detail on station buildings, bridges, and even lampposts gave the city's public transportation an elegant coherence. Wagner's two arcades in Karlspl. are still in use: one functions as an entrance to the U-Bahn station, the other as a café. Wagner diehards should also visit the acclaimed **Majolicahaus,** at Linke Wienzeile 40, a collaborative effort by Wagner and Olbrich. Olbrich's *Jugendstil* ornamentation complements Wagner's penchant for geometric simplicity. The wrought-iron spiral staircase is by Josef Hoffmann, founder of the **Wiener Werkstätte,** a communal arts-and-crafts workshop and key factor in the momentum of *Jugendstil.* The Majolicahaus' golden neighbor, the palm-leafy **Goldammer** building, is another Wagnerian mecca. In order to see the finest examples of Wagner's work and *Jugendstil* architecture, however, one must journey outside the city center.

Wagner's **Kirche am Steinhof,** XIV, Baumgartner Höhe 1 (tel. 91 06 02 00 31; U-2 or 3: "Volkstheater" then bus #48A), stares down from high on a hill in northwest Vienna. *(Open M-F 8am-3pm, Sa 3-4pm. Free. Guided tours (German only) for 40AS.)* The church combines streamlined symmetry and Wagner's signature functionalism with a strangely Byzantine influence. Hospital-like white walls give way to shockingly bright, spangly gold mosaics of holy figures. The church has, at 27 seconds, the longest reverberation in the world. Koloman Moser, vanguard member of the Secession, designed the stained-glass windows, while *Jugendstil* sculptor Lukasch fashioned the statues of Leopold and Severin poised upon each of the building's twin towers. The widely spaced pews are functional; they give nurses easy access to any disruptive worshipers, a reminder that Steinhof still serves as a lunatic asylum.

Postsparkasse (Post Office Savings Bank) is just inside the Ring at George-Coch-Pl. 2. *(Open M-W and F 8am-3pm, Th 8am-5:30pm.)* A bulwark of modernist architecture, the building raises formerly concealed elements of the building, like the thousands of symmetrically placed metallic bolts on the rear wall, to a position of exaggerated significance. This building was Wagner's greatest triumph of function over form; don't miss—you can't miss—the heating ducts. The distinctly Art Nouveau interior is open during banking hours free of charge.

Modern Architecture: Hundertwasser and Public Housing

After constructing massively opulent palaces and public edifices before the war, post-WWI Vienna turned its architectural enthusiasm to the socialist (and desperately necessary) task of building public housing. The Austrian Social Democratic Republic set about building "palaces for the people." Whatever your political opinions, the sheer scale of these apartment complexes impresses. The most famous and probably the wackiest is the **Karl-Marx-Hof,** XIX, Heiligenstadterstr. 82-92 (U-4 or 6: "Heiligenstadt"). This single building stretches out for a full kilometer and encompasses over 1600 cookie-cutter orange-and-pink apartments, with common space and interior courtyards to garnish the urban-commune atmosphere. Some might call this the shabby Florida hotel look on steroids, except for the quirky cornice statues and the geraniums. The Social Democrats used this structure as their stronghold during the civil war of 1934, until army artillery shelled the place and broke down the resistance.

Breaking with the ideology of *"Rot Wien"* (Red Vienna, the socialist republic from 1918 until the *Anschluß*) that resulted in housing complexes like Karl-Marx-Hof, Fantastic Realist and environmental activist **Friedensreich Hundertwasser** (translation: Peace-filled Hundredwaters; given name: Friedrich Stowasser) designed **Hundertwasser Haus,** III, a 50-apartment building at the corner of Löweng. and Kegelg. Completed in 1985, the building goes for both artistic and political statements. The trees and grass in the undulating balconies were to bring life back to the "desert" that the city had become; trees sticking out of windows, oblique tile columns, and free-form color patterns all contribute to the eccentricity of this blunt rejection of architectural orthodoxy. Hundertwasser created what he called a "Window Bill of Rights," which guaranteed everyone living within a building he designed the ability to decorate the area around their window for as long a space as their arm could reach. Architectural politics aside, this place is fun, bordering on the nutsy—Hundertwasser's design team must have included droves of finger-painting toddlers. Viennese nickname it the "Bowling Pin House."

Kunst Haus Wien, another Hundertwasser project, is just three blocks away at Untere Weißgerberstr. 13. The house is a museum devoted to the architect's graphic art (see **Art Museums,** p. 113) on the lower floors and controversial contemporary artists above (Mapplethorpe and Annie Lennox have both been exhibited here). There is a (somewhat scammy) café built along the lines of a Hundertwasser blueprint nearby. Hundertwasser fanatics may also want to check out the **Müllbrennerei** (garbage incinerator), behind the "Spittelau" U-Bahn station. This huge jack-in-the-box of a trash dump has a high smokestack topped by a golden disco ball. There is also a ferry designed by him that cruises the Danube under the auspices of the DDSG.

Palatial Vienna: Schwarzenberg, Belvedere, and Schönbrunn

The elongated **Schwarzenbergplatz** is a quick jaunt from Karlspl. along Friedrichstr., which becomes Lothringerstr. During the Nazi era, the city renamed the square "Hitlerplatz." Other evidence of unsavory military history dots the square. At the far end, a patch of landscaped greenery surrounds a fountain and a statue of soldiers inscribed with quotes from Stalin, left to the city as a "gift" from Russia. The Viennese have attempted to destroy the monstrosity three times, but the product of sturdy Soviet engineering refuses to be demolished. Vienna's disgust with their Soviet occupiers is further evident in their nickname for an anonymous Soviet soldier's grave: "Tomb of the Unknown Plunderer." Behind the fountain is Hildebrandt's **Schwarzenberg Palace.** The 1697 building is now a swank hotel. Rumor has it that daughters of the super-rich travel here annually to meet young Austrian noblemen at the annual grand debutante ball.

While grand, the palace is but a warm-up for the striking **Schloß Belvedere,** IV, whose landscaped gardens begin just behind the Schwarzenberg. (tram #D: "Schwarzenberg"). The Belvedere was once the summer residence of Prince Eugene of Savoy, Austria's greatest military hero. His distinguished career began when he routed the Ottomans in the late 17th century. Though publicly lionized, his appearance was most unpopular at Court—Eugene was a short, ugly, impetuous man. The

VIENNA

Belvedere summer palace (originally only the **Untere** (Lower) **Belvedere**), ostensibly a gift from the emperor in recognition of Eugene's military prowess, was more likely intended to get Eugene out of the imperial hair. Eugene's military exploits, however, had left him with a larger bank account than his Habsburg neighbors (a fact that certainly didn't improve their relationship), and he decided to improve upon his new home. The result is the **Obere** (Upper) **Belvedere,** a masterpiece of the great Baroque architect Hildebrandt, designed not as a residence but as a place to throw parties with bacchanalian excess. The building has one of the best views of Vienna. This bit of bombastic architectural symbolism did not sit well with the Habsburgs. Eugene's *pièce de resistance* was a rooftop facsimile of an Ottoman tent, which called undue attention to Eugene's martial glory. After Eugene's death, the Habsburgs snatched up the building (he never married or had children), and Archduke Franz Ferdinand lived there until his 1914 assassination. The grounds of the Belvedere, stretching from the Schwarzenberg Palace to the Südbahnhof, now contain three spectacular sphinx-filled gardens (see **Gardens and Parks,** p. 111) and an equal number of eclectic museums (see **Art Museums,** p. 113).

In truth, the Habsburgs need not have fretted over being outshown by Prince Eugene; **Schloß Schönbrunn,** XIII (U-4: "Schönbrunn"), the imperial summer residence, makes Belvedere appear waifish. *(Apartments open daily Apr.-Oct. 8:30am-5pm; Nov.-Mar. 8:30am-4:30pm. 100AS. Headphone tour 90AS, students 80AS. More worthwhile grand tour 120AS, students 105AS. English tour 145AS, students 130AS.)* The original plans for the palace were intended to make Versailles look like a gilded outhouse. The cost, however, was so prohibitive that construction on the original main building never even began. Building finally commenced in 1695, but Maria Theresa's 1743 expansion created the most obvious architectural embellishments. Its cheery yellow color has been named *"Maria Theresien gelb"* after her.

The view of the palace's Baroque symmetry from the main gate impresses, but this image is only a preparation for the spectacle that stretches out behind. An encyclopedic orchestration of various elements, including a **palm house,** a **zoo,** a massive stone **fountain of Neptune,** and bogus **Roman ruins,** sits among geometric flower beds and handsomely coiffed shrubbery. The trees have been selectively pruned to create the effect of a vaulted arch of leaves. Walk past the **flower sculptures** to reach Schönbrunn's labyrinths, rose gardens, and nature preserves. *(Park open 6am-dusk. Free.)* The compendium is crowned by the **Gloriette,** an ornamental temple serenely perched upon a hill with a beautiful view of the park and much of Vienna. If you're feeling indulgent, drink a somewhat pricey *Melange* in the temple's new café and survey your prospects. Tours of some of the palace's 1500 rooms reveal the elaborate taste of Maria Theresa's era. The frescoes lining the **Great Gallery** once looked upon the giddy Congress of Vienna, which loved a good party after a long day of divvying up the continent. The six-year-old Mozart played in the **Hall of Mirrors** and gave the Empress a famous kiss on the cheek there. The **Million Gulden Room** wins the prize for excess: Indian miniatures cover the chamber's walls. In summer, concerts and festivals abound in the Hof.

Built to amuse Maria Theresa's husband in 1752, the **Schönbrunn Zoo** *(Tiergarten)* is the world's oldest menagerie. *(Zoo open daily May-Sept. 9am-6:30pm; Feb. and Oct. 9am-5pm; Nov.-Jan. 9am-4:30pm; Mar. and Oct. 9am-5:30pm; Apr. 9am-6pm. 95AS, students 45AS.)* The style is allegedly Baroque, but the conditions used to border on the Gothic. The zookeepers have been remedying the situation, and now the place is much greener, larger, and more humane.

Former Vienna: The Zentralfriedhof

The Viennese like to describe the **Zentralfriedhof** (Central Cemetery), XI, Simmeringer Hauptstr. 234, as half the size of Geneva but twice as lively. *(Open May-Aug. 7am-7pm; Mar.-Apr. and Sept.-Oct. 7am-6pm; Nov.-Feb. 8am-5pm.)* The phrase is meant not only to poke fun at Vienna's rival but also to illustrate Vienna's healthy attitude toward death. In the capital city, the phrase "a beautiful corpse" is a common way of describing a dignified funeral, and the event of one's death is treated as, well, an event. Death doesn't get any better than at the Zentralfriedhof. The tombs in this massive park (2 sq. km with its own bus service) memorialize the truly great along with the ones who want to be so considered. The cemetery is the place to pay respects to your favorite Viennese decomposer: the second gate **(Tor II)** leads to Beethoven, Wolf, Strauss, Schönberg, Moser, and an honorary monument to Mozart. Amadeus' true resting place is an unmarked paupers' grave in the **Cemetery of St. Mark,** III, Leberstr. 6-8. St. Mark's deserves a visit not just for sheltering Mozart's dust, but also for its Biedermeier tombstones and the wild inundation of lilac blossoms that flower everywhere in sight for two weeks in spring. Zentralfriedhof's Gate T or I leads to the **Jewish Cemetery** and Arthur Schnitzler's burial plot. The state of the Jewish Cemetery mirrors the fate of Vienna's Jewish population—many of the headstones are cracked, broken, lying prone, or neglected because the families of most of the dead are no longer in Austria. Various structures throughout this portion of the burial grounds memorialize the millions slaughtered in Nazi death camps. To reach the cemetery, take streetcar #71 from "Schwarzenbergpl." To the east of the *Zentralfriedhof* is the beautifully melancholy **Friedhof der Namenlosen,** where the nameless corpses of people fished out of the Danube are buried. Take bus #6A to get here.

GARDENS AND PARKS

Gardens, parks, and forests are common Viennese attractions, brightening the urban landscape with scattered patches of green. The Habsburgs opened and maintained the city's primary public gardens throughout the last four centuries; the areas only recently become public property. Especially noteworthy are the **Volksgarten** (Vienna's first public park) and the gardens of **Schloß Schönbrunn, Palais Belvedere,** and the **Augarten.** During food shortages after WWII, the city distributed plots of land in sections of the 14th, 16th, and 19th districts to citizens to let them grow their own vegetables. These community *Gärten* still exist, full of roses, garden gnomes, and little huts for urban gardeners.

The **Augarten,** Obere Augartenstr., is the oldest extant Baroque garden in Austria; Kaiser Josef II commissioned the garden in the 17th-century for Vienna's citizens. Children play soccer between flowers and various athletic facilities (including a swimming pool and tennis courts) that opened in 1940. Standing in the Augarten is the **Vienna China Factory,** founded in 1718, and the **Augarten Palace,** home to the Vienna Boys' Choir. The daunting concrete tower is the **Flakturm,** constructed as Nazi anti-aircraft defense during WWII. This structure and similar creations in parks around the city were so sturdily constructed that an attempted demolition failed (the walls of reinforced concrete are up to 5m thick). To reach the park, take streetcar N: "Obere Augartenstr." and walk to the left down Taborstr.

By the Danube

The **Danube** provides a number of recreational possibilities northeast of the city. The recurrent floods became problematic once settlers moved outside the city walls, so the Viennese stretch of the Danube was diverted into canals (and the sewer-like structures filmed in "The Third Man") from 1870 to 1875 and again from 1972 to 1987. This generated recreational areas, like new tributaries (including the **Alte Donau** and the **Donaukanal**) and the **Donauinsel,** a thin slab of island stretching for kilometers. *(Open May-Sept. M-F 9am-8pm, Sa-Su 8am-8pm. Beach admission is roughly 50AS.)* The Donauinsel is devoted to bike paths, swimming areas, barbecue plots, boats, and summer restaurants. Several bathing areas line the northern shore of the island, along the Alte Donau. Take U-1 (dir: Kagran): "Donauinsel" or "Alte Donau." You can experience one of the most **spectacular views** of Vienna from the Donaupark: take the elevator up to the revolving restaurant in the **Donauturm** (Danube Tower), near the UN complex (U-1: "Kaisermühlen/Vienna International Center"). Also of note is the **Donauinsel Fest,** which brings stages for jazz and rock in late June. Previous performers have included Erasure, Joe Cocker, and Sheryl Crow (see **Festivals,** p. 118).

The **Prater,** extending southeast from the Wien Nord Bahnhof, is an old-school amusement park. *(Open May-Sept. 9am-midnight; Oct.-Nov. 3 10am-10pm; Nov. 4-Dec. 1*

10am-6pm. 50AS. Ride lasts 20min.) The park functioned as a private game reserve for the Imperial Family until 1766 and as the site of the World Expo in 1873. Squeezed into a riverside woodland between the Donaukanal and the river proper, it boasts ponds, meadows, and stretches of lovely virgin woods. The area near U1: "Praterstern" is the actual amusement park, offering various rides, arcades, restaurants, and casinos. Entry to the complex is free, but each attraction charges admission (generally 40AS). Rides range from garish thrill machines and wonderfully campy spookhouse rides to the stately wooden 65m **Riesenrad** (Giant Ferris Wheel). The wheel, which provides one of the prettiest views of Vienna, is best known for its cameo role in Orson Welles' *The Third Man.* Locals cherish this wheel of fortune, and when it was destroyed in World War II, the city promptly built an exact replica, which has been turning since 1947. Beloved by children during the day, the Prater becomes less wholesome after sundown, thanks to the many girlie and peep shows.

The Danube Canal branches into the tiny **Wien River** near the Ring; this sliver extends to the southwest, past the *innere Stadt* and Schloß Schönbrunn. First, however, the Wien, replete with ducks and lilies, bisects the **Stadtpark** (City Park; U-4: "Stadtpark"), off the Park Ring. Built in 1862, this area was the first municipal park outside the former city walls. The sculpted vegetation provides a soothing counterpoint to the central bus station and nearby Bahnhof Wien-Mitte. One of Vienna's most photogenic monuments, the gilded **Johann-Strauss-Denkmal,** sits there.

Hot to Trot

White, royal, dancing, and one of the biggest tourist attractions in Vienna? No, it is not the Royal Ballet's performance of *Swan Lake.* In Vienna, these three traits classify horses—more specifically, the Lipizzaner stallions of the *Spanische Reitschule* (Spanish Riding School). The Royal Stables, some of the best original Renaissance buildings in Vienna, were built as a residence for the Archduke Maximilian in the mid-16th century and were later converted to the stables of the royal stud. The choice of Lipizzaner horses, known for snowy-white coats and immense physical strength and grace, descend from a "celebration" equine breed ordered by the Austrian Emperor in Lipizza, near Trieste, upon the Habsburg's annexation of the Spanish realms in the late 16th century. Breeders mixed Arab and Berber genes, and once the stud line had been established, the Lipizzaners were imported to Austria proper to dance in the spotlight of the Renaissance heyday of *haute école* horsemanship. Despite their fame, the Lipizzaners have held on tenuously to their survival over the centuries. The horses ran from the French in the Napoleonic wars, and they barely survived the poverty that ensued after World War I and the breakup of the Empire. During World War II, they escaped destruction in a safe haven in Czechoslovakia. In 1945, U.S. General Patton flagrantly violated his own orders to stay put by leading a madcap Eastern push to prevent the plundering Russians, who confiscated just about everything in their path, from reaching the four-legged treasures first. In the early 1980s, an epidemic of virus in the stud killed upwards of thirty of the brood mares, and today, stud farmers worry that the decreasing number of Lipizzaners may lead to health problems resulting from inbreeding. Recently, UN peace keepers ran across starving Lipizzaners near Banja Luca in Bosnia, prompting the Lipizzaner Society to start a successful fund-raiser to save the beasts from an ugly death. The horses seem doomed to an edgy existence.

Along the Ring

Stroll clockwise around the Ring to reach the **Burggarten** (Gardens of the Imperial Palace), a well-kept park with monuments to such Austrian notables as Emperor Franz Josef and Emperor Franz I. The **Babenberger Passage** leads from the Ring to the bubble-gum **Mozart Memorial** (1896), which features Amadeus on a pedestal surrounded by instrument-toting cherubim. In front of the statue is a lawn with a treble clef crafted of red flowers. Reserved for the imperial family and members of the court until 1918, the Burggarten is now a favorite for young lovers and lamentably hyperactive dogs. Walk behind the Hofburg to the area near the vaulted greenhouse/café to find students sunbathing in this prime hangout for the twentysomething set.

Heldenplatz, farther up the Ring, abuts the **Volksgarten,** once the site of the Bastion Palace destroyed by Napoleon's order. Be sure to seek out the **"Temple of Theseus,"** the monument to Austrian playwright Franz Grillparzer. The Volksgarten's monument to Empress Elisabeth was designed by Hans Bitterlich. The throned empress casts a stony glance upon Friedrich Ohmann's goldfish pond. The most striking feature, though, is the **Rose Garden,** populated by thousands of different species.

West of the 13th *Bezirk* is the **Lainzer Tiergarten** (Lainz Game Preserve). Once an exclusive hunting preserve for the royals, this enclosed space has been a nature park and reserve since 1941. Along with paths, restaurants, and spectacular vistas, the park encloses the **Hermes Villa.** *(Open Tu-Su and holidays 10am-6pm, Oct.-Mar. 9am-4:30pm. 70AS, students 35AS.)* This erstwhile retreat for Empress Elisabeth houses exhibitions by the Historical Museum of Vienna. Take U-4 (dir: Hütteldorf): "Hietzing," change to streetcar #60: "Hermesstr.," then take bus #60B: "Lainzer Tor."

The **Türkenschanz Park,** in the 18th *Bezirk,* attracts a plethora of leashed dachshunds bristling at the peacocks. The long-haired garden is famous for its arabesqued Turkish fountain and lovely pools. In summer, feed ducks or gaze in Monet-like rapture at the water lilies. In winter, come for sledding or ice-skating. Enter the park anywhere along Gregor-Mendel-Str., Hasenauerstr., or Max-Emmanuelstr.

The **Pötzleindorfer Park,** at the end of tram line #41 (dir: Pötzleindorfer Höhe) from Schottentor, overlaps the lower end of the Vienna Woods. Wild deer roam through overgrown Alpine meadows and woodland.

Far to the north and west of Vienna sprawls the illustrious **Wienerwald,** made famous by Strauss's catchy waltz, "Tales of a Vienna Woods." The woods extend up to the slopes of the first foothills of the Alps. Take U-4: "Heiligenstadt" then bus #38A: "Kahlenberg" (nicknamed "the Granny-mover" for the number of old folk in linen gloves and *Dirndl*s it carries up the leafy hills.) **Kahlenberg** is the highest point of the rolling *Wienerwald,* and affords spectacular views of Vienna, the Danube, and even distant Alps. The Turks besieged Vienna in 1683 from here, and Polish king Jan Sobieski celebrated his liberation of the city from Saracen infidels in the small **Church of St. Joseph.** *(Open May-Oct. Sa noon-6pm, Su and holidays 9am-6pm.)* Just off the central square of Kahlenberg stands the trusty *Stefania Warte* tower; catch the views from part of the river valley's old fortifications. The area around Kahlenberg, Cobenzl, and Leopoldstadt is criss-crossed with hiking paths *(Wanderwege)* marked by colored bars painted on tree trunks. Kahlenberg and its country cemetery is within easy walking distance of the wine-growing districts of **Nußdorf** and **Grinzing.** You can follow in the Pope's footsteps and hike over to the **Leopoldskirche,** a renowned pilgrimage site. It's 20 minutes away from Kahlenberg on **Leopoldsberg,** site of a Babenberg fortress destroyed by the Turks in 1529. Leopoldsberg is named for St. Leopold III of the royal Babenberg family, and offers crazy views of the surrounding city and river valleys. **Klosterneuburg,** a decadently Baroque monastery town founded by Leopold, (see p. 125) is only a 90-minute hike from Leopoldsberg.

▓ Museums

Vienna owes its vast selection of masterpieces to the acquisitive Habsburgs as well as Vienna's own crop of unique art schools and world-class artists (see p. 70 for the complete story). Though painting and architecture may dominate, Vienna's treasures are as diverse as the former imperial Habsburg possessions. An exhaustive list is impossible to include here. Check the *Museums* brochure at the tourist office for other listings or simply stumble into more museums as you wander the streets.

ART MUSEUMS

◉**Kunsthistorisches Museum** (Museum of Fine Arts; tel. 525 240), across from the Burgring and Heldenpl. on Maria Theresa's right. The world's 4th-largest art collection and one of the best. Vast amounts of 15th to 18th century Venetian and Flemish paintings. The works by Brueghel are unrivaled, and the museum possesses entire rooms of Rembrandt, Rubens, Titian, Holbein, and Velazquez. Ancient and classical art, including an Egyptian burial chamber, are also well represented. The lobby is pre-Secession Klimt—a mural depicting artistic progress from the classical era to the 19th century—painted in the Historicist style he would later attack. Open Tu-Su 10am-6pm. Picture gallery also open Th until 9pm. During the summer, Easter, and Christmas, informative English guided tours are offered at 11am and 3pm (30AS). 100AS, students and seniors 70AS. Another **branch** of the museum resides in the Neue Burg (Hofburg) and contains the fabulous **Ephesus Museum** housing an ancient Greek temple and statues transported from the Ephesus, the **Arms and Armor Collection** (the 2nd-largest collection in the world), and **Ancient Musical Instruments Collections**. Same hours as picture gallery. 30AS, students and seniors 15AS.

Austrian Gallery, III, Prinz-Eugen-Str. 27 (tel. 795 570), in the Belvedere Palace behind Schwarzenbergpl. The collection is split into 2 parts. The **Upper Belvedere** (built in 1721-22 by Hildebrandt) houses Austrian Art of the 19th and 20th centuries. Most of the famous Secessionist works reside here. Especially well represented are Schiele, Kokoschka, and Klimt, whose gilded masterpiece, *The Kiss*, has enthralled visitors for nearly a century. As you wander among the works, pause to take in views of the city from the upper floors. Use the same ticket to enter the **Lower Belvedere,** where the **Baroque Museum** has an extensive collection of sculptures by Donner, Maulbertsch, and Messerschmidt and David's famous portrayal of Napoleon. The **Museum of Medieval Austrian Art** is also here. Romanesque and Gothic sculptures and altarpieces by *Süddentisch* masters abound. Both Belvederes open Tu-Su 10am-5pm. Admission until 4:30pm. English guided tours at 2:30pm. 60AS, students 30AS.

Akademie der Bildende Kunst (Academy of Fine Arts), I, Schillerpl. 3 (tel. 588 16 225), near Karlpl. Designed in 1876 by Hansen of *Parlament, Musikverein,* and *Börse* fame. The collection, almost hidden in a quiet gallery surrounded by studios and classrooms, houses Hieronymus Bosch's *Last Judgment* and works by a score of Dutch painters, including Rubens. Open Tu-Su 10am-4pm. 50AS, students 20AS.

Secession Building, I, Friedrichstr. 12 (tel. 587 53 07), on the western side of Karlspl. Originally built to house artwork that didn't conform to the *Kunsthaus*'s standards, the Secession building gave the break-out prophets of modern art space to hang their work. Klimt, Kokoschka, and the "barbarian" Gauguin were featured early on in the building that the Viennese nicknamed "The Golden Cabbage." Rather than canonize early *Jugendstil* pioneers, the museum continually seeks to exhibit that which is new and fresh. Substantial contemporary works are exhibited here, whereas most major Secessionist works are housed in the Belvedere. Klimt's *Beethoven Frieze* is the exception—this 30m-long work is his visual interpretation of Beethoven's *Ninth Symphony.* Open Tu and Th-Su 10am-6pm, W 10am-8pm. 90AS, students 60AS.

Museum Moderner Kunst (Museum of Modern Art; tel. 317 69 00; fax 317 69 01; email museum@MMKSLW.or.at; http://www.MMKSLW.or.at/). Split between 2 locations. The 1st is in the **Liechtenstein Palace,** IX, Fürsteng. 1. Tram D (dir: Nußdorf): "Fürsteng." The *Schloß,* surrounded by a manicured garden, boasts a collection of 20th-century masters including Magritte, Motherwell, Picasso, Miró, Kandinsky, Pollock, Warhol, and Klee. The 2nd location is at the **20er Haus** (tel. 799 69 00), III, Arsenalstr. 1, opposite the Südbahnhof. Its large, open *Bauhaus* interior provides the perfect setting for the substantial collection of ground-breaking 60s and 70s work—Keith Arnnat and Larry Poons among them—alongside contemporary artists. It sits in a large sculpture garden stocked with pieces by Giacometti, Moore, and others. Open Tu-Su 10am-6pm. 45AS, students 25AS for each exhibit; 60AS, children 30AS for both exhibits. Wheelchair accessible.

Museum für Völkerkunde, I, (tel. 534 300), in Heldenpl. The Habsburg agents brought back a surprisingly good collection of African and South American art. Visit Benin bronzes, West African Dan heads, and Montezuma's feathered headdress. The museum also displays art and artifacts from North America, the Middle East, and the Far East. Open Apr.-Dec. Su-M and W-Sa 10am-4pm; Jan.-Mar. Su-M and W-Sa 10am-6pm. Tours Su 11am.

Österreichisches Museum für Angewandte Kunst (aka the MAK; Austrian Museum of Applied Art), I, Stubenring 5 (tel. 711 360). U-3: "Stubentor." The oldest museum of applied arts in Europe. Each room, designed by a different artist, displays an international collection of furniture, textiles, and relics. Collection includes Oriental carpets, Art Deco goblets, Biedermeier coffee-pots, Renaissance linens, a Baroque palace room, a 20th-century fire table, and the designs and archives of the Wiener Werkstätte arts and crafts workshop. The basement displays study collections of jewelry, textiles, and divans from the 17th-century to the present. Open Tu-W and F-Su 10am-6pm, Th 10am-9pm. 90AS, students 45AS.

Kunst Haus Wien, III, Untere Weißgerberstr. 13 (tel. 712 04 91). U-1 or 4: "Schwedenpl." then bus N: "Radetzkypl." Built by Hundertwasser, the museum displays many of his paintings, graphic drawings, architectural models, and environmental machines (the "plant water purification plant," for instance). The building itself is one of Hundertwasser's greatest achievements, and the floor bends and swells, creating (in Hundertwasser's words) "a melody for the feet." In addition to the Hundertwasser exhibit, the crazily pastiched Kunst Haus houses exhibits of the work of contemporary artists from around the world. Open 10am-7pm. 90AS, students 50AS for each exhibit; 150AS, students 110AS for both exhibits.

Kunsthalle Wien, IV, Treitlstr. 2 (tel. 521 890), in Karlspl. Intriguing international exhibits of contemporary painting, sculpture, photography, film, music, and more. Open daily 10am-3pm, Th 10am-10pm. Adults 80AS, students 60AS.

Künstlerhaus, Karlspl. 5 (tel. 587 96 63). Temporary exhibits, usually contemporary and non-European art. The theater hosts numerous film festivals. Open M-W and F-Su 10am-6pm, Th 10am-9pm. 90AS, students 60AS.

Palais Surreal, Josefspl. 5 (tel. 512 25 49). The Baroque former palace of the Pallavicini family now houses a small but renowned collection of Surrealist sculptures by Dalí, including a delicious wobbly work called "Space Elephant" and bizarrely ethereal sculptures done in glass. Open 10am-6pm. 90AS, students and elderly 50AS.

OTHER COLLECTIONS

Historisches Museum der Stadt Wien (Historical Museum of the City of Vienna), IV, Karlspl. 5 (tel. 505 87 47), to the left of the Karlskirche. A collection of historical artifacts and paintings document the city's evolution from the Roman encampment through the Turkish siege of Vienna (note copies of the Koran, scimitars, and siege maps left behind by defeated troops) and the subsequent 640 years of Habsburg rule. Memorial rooms to Loos and Grillparzer, plus temporary exhibitions on all things Viennese. Open Tu-Su 9am-6pm. Free on Fridays 9am-noon. 50AS, students 20AS, seniors 25AS.

Sigmund Freud Haus, IX, Bergg. 19 (tel. 319 15 96; http://freud.tø.or.at), near the Votivkirche. U-2: "Schottentor," then walk up Wahringerstr. to Berggasse. This meager museum (no cigars) was Freud's home from 1891 until the *Anschluß*. Almost all of Freud's original belongings moved with him out of the country, including the leather divan. Lots of photos and documents, including the young Freud's report cards and circumcision certificate. Open July-Sept. 9am-6pm; Oct.-June 9am-4pm. 60AS, students 40AS.

Naturhistorisches Museum (Natural History Museum; tel. 52 17 70), across from the Kunsthistorisches Museum. Displays the usual animalia and decidedly unusual giant South American beetles and dinosaur skeletons. Two of its star attractions are man-made: a spectacular floral bouquet comprised of gemstones and the fascinating Stone-Age beauty *Venus of Willendorf.* Open W-M 9am-6pm, admission until 5:30pm; in winter, 1st floor only 9am-3pm. 30AS, students 15AS.

Bestattungsmuseum (Undertaker's Museum), IV, Goldeg. 19 (tel. 501 95 227). The Viennese take their funerals seriously, giving rise to a morbidly fascinating exhibit that is, in its own way, as typically Viennese as *Heurigen* (wine taverns) and waltzes. Contains coffins with alarms (should the body decide to rejoin the living) and Josef II's proposed reusable coffin. Open M-F noon-3pm by prior arrangement only.

Jewish Museum, I, Dorotheerg. 11 (tel. 535 04 31). This museum focuses on the history and contributions of Austria's Jewish community. The permanent display tells Viennese Jewish history through holographs. Temporary exhibits focus on prominent Jewish figures and contemporary Jewish art. Open daily 10am-8pm. Adults 70AS, students 40AS.

■ Entertainment

MUSIC

> The State Opera and the Philharmonic Orchestra are closed in July and August. The Vienna Boys' Choir is on tour in August. The Lipizzaner Stallions do not dance in July and August. Many an unsuspecting tourist has carefully planned a trip, only to be disappointed by these most inconvenient facts of Viennese life.

Vienna is a city of music. Mozart, Beethoven, and Haydn created their greatest master-pieces in Vienna, as part of the First Viennese School. A century later, Schönberg, Webern, and Berg teamed up to form the Second Viennese School. Every Austrian child must learn to play an instrument during schooling, and the **Konservatorium** and **Hochschule** are world-renowned conservatories. All year, Vienna presents per-formances ranging from the above-average to the sublime, with much surprisingly accessible to the budget traveler.

"Too many notes, dear Mozart," observed Josef II after the premiere of *Abduction from the Seraglio.* "Only as many as are necessary, Your Majesty," was the genius's reply. The Habsburgs may be forgiven this critical slip, for they have provided invalu-able support of opera: the **Staatsoper** remains one of the top five companies in the world and performs about 300 times from September through June. **Standing-room tickets** provide a glimpse of world-class opera for a pittance. *(Balcony 20AS, orchestra 30AS. Formal dress not necessary, but no shorts.)* Those with the desire (and the stamina) to say "been there" should start lining up on the western side of the Opera (by Operng.) half an hour before curtain (2-3hr. in tourist season) in order to get tickets for the center—the side views are rather limited. Find a space on the rail and tie a scarf around it to reserve your spot if you wish to grab a coffee or *Wurst.* Students feeling lucky should try the box office a half-hour before curtain; unclaimed tickets go for 50AS (ISIC *not* valid—bring a university ID). Advance tickets range from 100 to 850AS and go on sale a week before the performance at the **Bundestheaterkasse,** I, Hanuschg. 3 (tel. 514 44 29 60; http://oebthv.gv.at), next to the opera along the Burg-garten. *(Open M-F 8am-6pm, Sa-Su 9am-noon. ISIC not valid for student discounts, university ID required.)* Get there at 6-7am of the first day for a good seat; some Viennese camp over-night for major performances. Bundestheaterkasse also sells tickets for the three other public theaters: the **Volksoper, Burgtheater,** and **Akademietheater.** The Volksoper shows operas and operettas in German, sometimes translated; the other two venues feature classic dramas in German. Discount tickets go on sale a half-hour before curtain at the individual box offices (50-400AS).

The world-famous, top-notch **Wiener Philharmoniker** (Vienna Philharmonic Orchestra) included Gustav Mahler among its directors; a bust in his honor stands in the concert hall. Regular performances take place in the **Musikverein,** I, Dumbastr. (yes, dumbass, for real) 3 (tel. 505 81 90), on the northeast side of Karlspl. *(Box office open Sept.-June M-F 9am-7:30pm, Sa 9am-5pm. Write Gesellschaft der Musikfreunde, Bösen-dorferstr. 12, A-1010 Wien for more information.)* The Philharmoniker also play every Staatsoper production. Tickets to Philharmoniker concerts are mostly on a subscrip-tion basis, with few tickets at the Musikverein box office. Call ahead for availability. Vienna's second fiddle, the **Vienna Symphony Orchestra,** is frequently on tour but plays some concerts at the Konzerthaus, III, Lothingerstr. 20 (tel. 712 12 11).

The 500-year-old **Wiener Sängerknabenchor** (Vienna Boys' Choir) is another famous and beloved attraction. The pre-pubescent prodigies perform Sundays at 9:15am (mid-Sept. to June) in the **Burgkapelle** (Royal Chapel), the oldest section of the Hofburg. Reserve tickets (60-310AS) at least two months in advance; write to Hof-musikkapelle, Hofburg, A-1010 Wien, but do not enclose money. Pick up tickets at the Burgkapelle on the Friday before mass from 11am to noon or on the Sunday of the mass by 9am. Unreserved seats go on sale from 5pm on the preceding Friday, maximum two per person. Standing room is free, but arrive before 8am to make it into the *Burgkapelle.* The lads also perform every Friday at 3:30pm at the Konzer-thaus in May, June, September, and October. For tickets (390-430AS), contact Reise-büro Mondial, Faulmanng. 4, A-1040 Wien (tel. 588 04 141; fax 587 12 68). Or have gorgeous—and free—musical experiences at the **Sunday High Masses** at 10 or 11am in the major churches (Augustinerkirche, Michaelerkirche, Stephansdom).

Grassroots Demonstration

A vocal group of women concerned over women's status in Austrian society have joined forces to form the U.F.F. *(Unabhängiges Frauen Forum).* This non-radi-cal, non-separatist women's group, comprised of an equal number of journalists, single mothers living in poverty, and middle-class women, formed in response to recent budget cuts they found especially detrimental to women. The U.F.F. devel-oped a manifesto that focuses on economic equality between women and men. Their demands, relayed through media, demonstrations, and sit-ins, include: salary increases in badly paid jobs almost exclusively held by women, an end to glass ceilings, all-day, all-year child care facilities throughout the country, and the right to part-time work for both men and women with children with the right to return to full-time. The U.F.F. received such support that a national plebiscite was held—the *Frauenvolkbegehrens.* The U.F.F.'s mandate received enough votes to force discussion of the issue in Parliament. Their demands were debated by the Aus-trian government, which consisted of 20% female members and a conservative Minister of Women's Affairs. However, to the deep dissatisfaction of the U.F.F. and many Austrians, only the most minor reforms on the list were actually imple-mented. The U.F.F., now with branches in Salzburg, Tirol, and Vorarlberg, and a platform that has evolved to include issues of violence and discrimination, contin-ues to lobby, and holds demonstrations in Stephanspl. on the first Saturday of each month. The U.F.F. is currently considering forming an independent political party. You can check their web page for updates at http://www.uff.at.

THEATER AND CINEMA

In the past few years, Vienna has made a name for itself as a city of musicals, with pro-ductions of such Broadway and West End favorites as *Phantom of the Opera* and *Les Misérables,* or the long-running home-grown favorite *Elisabeth,* a creative interpreta-tion of the late empress's life. The **Theater an der Wien,** VI, Linke Wienzeile 6 (tel. 588 30), once produced musicals of a different sort, hosting in its 18th-century edifice the premieres of Beethoven's *Fidelio* and Mozart's *Die Zauberflöte* (The Magic Flute). The nobility found that Mozart had crossed the line of good taste by compos-ing an opera in German (such an *ugly* language), so they blocked the scheduled pre-miere at the Staatsoper. The masterpiece was finally performed here, thrilling the regular citizens, who could finally understand the plot. For the sake of tradition, the Staatsoper still occasionally sends productions of Mozart opera to be performed here.

 Vienna's English Theatre, VIII, Josefsg. 12 (tel. 402 12 60), presents English-lan-guage drama. (Box office open M-F 10am-6pm, Sa-Su 10am-4pm. Tickets 150-420AS, student rush 100AS.) The **International Theater,** IX, Porzellang. 8 (tel. 319 62 72; tickets 260-280AS, under 26 140AS), is another English-language venue. **WUK,** IX, Währingerstr. 59 (tel. 401 21 10), is a workshop and cultural center that puts on dance, concerts, and readings. **Films** in English usually play at **Burg Kino,** I, Opern-ring 19 (tel. 587 84 06; last show usually around 8:30pm, Sa around 11pm); **Top Kino,** VI, Rahlgassel 1 (tel. 587 55 57; open 3pm-10:30pm), at the intersection of Gumpendorferstr.; and **Haydnkino** (last show usually around 9:30pm), on Mariahil-ferstr. near U-3: "Neubaug." As the language becomes fashionable, more theaters show movies in English or with subtitles—look in the newspaper for films with OF, OV, EOV, or OmU after the title. **Votivkino,** Währingerstr. 12 (tel. 317 35 71), near Bergg. and Schottentor, is an art-house popular with the university crowd and shows all films with German subtitles. **Artis Kino, Filmcasino,** and **Stöberkino** also show subtitled art and foreign films. **Künstlerhauskino,** I, Karlspl. 5 (tel. 505 43 28), hosts art house film festivals. Be warned—you pay for the row you sit in. On Monday, all seats are discounted to 70AS. In summer, there is an **open-air cinema** in the Augarten park (all shows at 9:30pm; 70AS). From Schottenring, take tram #31: "Gaußpl." While Vienna hosts a full-sized film festival in August (see **Festivals**), the rest of the year the Austrian **Filmmuseum,** Augustinerstr. 1 (tel. 53 37 05 40), shows a rotating program of classic and avant-garde films.

FESTIVALS

Vienna hosts an array of important annual festivals, mostly musical. Look for the tourist office's monthly calendar for dozens of concerts and performances. The **Vienna Festival** (mid-May to mid-June) has a diverse program of exhibitions, plays, and concerts. (For info, contact tel. 58 92 20; fax 589 22 49; email festwochen@festwochen.at; http://www.festwochen.or.at/wf.) Of particular interest are the celebrated orchestras and conductors joining the party. The Staatsoper and Volkstheater host the annual **Jazzfest Wien** during the first weeks of July, featuring many famous acts. For information, contact Jazzfest Wien (tel. 503 56 47; http://jazz.at.) While other big guns take summer siesta, Vienna has held the **Klangbogen** every summer since 1952, featuring excellent concerts across Vienna, including **Wiener Kammeroper** (Chamber Opera) performances of Mozart's operas in an open-air theater set among the ruins of Schönbrunner Schloßpark. Pick up a brochure at the tourist office. From the end of July to the beginning of August, the **Im-Puls Dance Festival** (tel. 523 55 58; http://impuls-tanz.wien.at) attracts some of the world's great dance troupes and offers seminars to enthusiasts. Some of Vienna's best parties are thrown by the parties (political, that is). The Social Democrats host a late-June **Danube Island Festival,** which drew over two million politically active booty-shakers in 1997, and the Communist Party holds a **Volkstimme Festival** in mid-August. Both cater to impressionable youngsters with free rock, jazz, and folk concerts. In mid-October, the annual city-wide film festival, the **Viennale,** kicks off. In past years, the program has featured over 150 movies from 25 countries. One final free treat not to be missed is the **nightly film festival** in July and August, in the Rathauspl. at dusk. Taped operas, ballets, operettas, and concerts enrapture the diverse audience.

HEURIGEN (WINE GARDENS)

Created by imperial edict in the early 18th-century, *Heurigen* are one of Vienna's most beloved institutions. Citizens have collectively met, discussed, and celebrated

---

The Regenbogenparade

At the beginning of every July, Austrians and their neighbors gather for an afternoon and evening in Vienna to celebrate gay pride at the Rainbow Parade. The parade—much more colorful than a regular rainbow—consists of over 40 floats sponsored by social, political, and commercial organizations from Vienna and around Austria, as well as the Czech Republic and Slovakia (everyone from Dykes on Bikes and the Rosa Lila Villa to Jewish Homosexuals and AIDS awareness organizations take part). The effervescent parade parties its way along the Ringstrasse and ends in Karlspl. for a jam-packed evening celebration continued later in bars throughout the city. Besides the Rainbow Parade, the Viennese gay community hosts the annual "Life Ball," which raises money for people with AIDS and HIV, the only charity event held in Vienna's town hall. The gay community is fairly well integrated in relatively safe and non-violent Vienna. The gay movement began here in the 1970s. Despite a strongly Catholic population, homosexuality has been legal since 1972, and in 1982, the municipal government funded the founding of Rosa Lila Villa Gay-Lesbian-Bisexual Center. However, Austria is the only country in the European Union that decrees a different age of consent for gay men. Although straight and lesbian couples can have sex at 16, in gay male couples, both men must be over 18. Every year about 50 men are charged for non-consensual sex and 20 go to jail.

life in these pastoral settings for generations, with no signs of letting up. To this day, the *Heurigen,* marked by a hanging branch of evergreen at the door, continue to sell their young wine and rustic snacks.

The wine called *Heuriger* is young wine from the most recent harvest and has typically been grown and pressed by the *Heuriger* owner himself. Good *Heuriger* is generally white (*Grüner Veltliner* or *Riesling* are best), fruity, and full of body. *Heuriger* is ordered by the *Achtel* or (more commonly) the *Viertel* (eighth or quarter liter respectively). In local parlance, one doesn't drink the wine, one "bites" it, mixing it with air inside the mouth to better taste its youth and freshness. *G'spritzer* (wine and soda water) is a popular drink, and patrons frequently order a bottle of wine and water to mix themselves.

Half of the pleasure of visiting a *Heuriger,* however, comes not from the wine but from the atmosphere. The worn picnic benches and old shade trees provide an ideal spot to contemplate, converse, or listen to *Schrammelmusik,* sentimental, wine-lubricated folk songs played by grungy elderly musicians who inhabit the *Heuriger.* Drunken patrons often take the matter into their own hands and begin to belt out verses praising the *Bäckchen* (cheeks) of girls in the Wachau. A *Heuriger* generally serves simple buffets (grilled chicken, salads, pickles) that make for enjoyable and inexpensive meals. Those looking for some traditional fare should order *Brattfett* or **Liptauer,** a spicy paprika soft cheese for your bread.

At the end of the summer, *Sturm* (sweet, cloudy, unpasteurized wine) is available at the *Heuriger.* At the end of August or the beginning of September in **Neustift am Walde,** now part of Vienna's 19th district, the *Neustifter Kirtag mit Winzerumzug* rampages through the wine gardens: local vintners march in a mile-long procession through town, carrying a large crown adorned with gilt nuts. After the **Feast of the Martins** on November 11, the wine from last year's crop becomes "old wine," no longer proper to serve in the *Heuriger.* The Viennese do their best to spare it this fate by consuming the beverage in Herculean quantities before the time's up. Grab a liter of wine to help the locals in their monumental task.

Heurigen cluster together in the northern, western, and southern Viennese suburbs, where the grapes grow. They are each open for only a couple of months during the year—stroll along the street and look for the evergreen branches. The most famous region, **Grinzing,** produces strong wine, perhaps to distract the touristy clientele from the high prices. *Heurigen* in Grinzing (incidentally Beethoven's favorite district) are unfortunately well known to tour bus operators. Better atmosphere and prices are all over the hills of **Sievering, Neustift am Walde, Stammersdorf,** and **Neuwaldegg.** Authentic, charming, and jolly *Heurigen* abound on Hochstr. in **Perchtoldsdorf.** To reach Perchtoldsdorf, take U-Bahn #4: "Hietzing" and tram #6: "Rodaun." Walk down Ketzerg. until Hochstr. and continue for a few minutes to reach the *Heurigen* area. True *Heuriger* devotees should make the trip to **Gumpoldskirchen,** a celebrated vineyard village with decent bus and train connections to Vienna (S-Bahn from Südbahnhof) and Mödling, and on the S-bahn line from the Südbahnhof. Most vineyard taverns are open 4pm to midnight. *Heuriger* costs about 25AS per *Viertel.*

⊛Heuriger Josef Lier, XIX, Wildgrubeng. 44 (tel. 320 23 19). Tram #38 from Schottentor to the end of the line. Walk up the Grinzigersteig to the Heiligenstädter Friedhof (cemetery), and follow the road uphill to the left (5min. from the cemetery). Set right into the vineyards, this *Ur-Heuriger* recalls the times before electric-powered grape presses and mass commercialism. The place boasts clambering roses and a panoramic view of Vienna from the natural beauty of the Vienna Woods. Only one white and one red wine here—Josef Lier's own, from the vineyards you're sitting in. The dishes are equally *Alt-Wiener* and equally excellent—boiled eggs, pickles, *Liptauer,* and *Wurst. G'spritzer* 18AS. Quarter liter 24AS. Open W-F from 3pm, Sa-Su from noon.

Buschenschank Heinrich Niersche, XIX, Strehlg. 21 (tel. 440 21 46). U-1: "Währingerstr./Volksoper" then tram #40: "Pötzleing." or bus #41A: "Pötzleindorfer Höhe." Walk uphill one block and turn right on Strehlg. On a small side-street hidden from

> ### Thicker than blood
>
> The Viennese connection to wine is a strong one, so strong that the stuff played a vital role in the Habsburg's rise to power. In 1273 Ottokar II of Bohemia, Rudolf of Habsburg's one rival to the throne of the Holy Roman Empire, holed himself up in Vienna, where he enjoyed strong support. Rudolf marched to the town walls and told the Viennese in no uncertain terms that if Ottokar did not go, the surrounding vineyards would. The Viennese got their priorities straight. The *Heurigen* also owe their existence to another Habsburg. In 1784 Josef II, the man who gave Vienna the Edict of Tolerance and the reusable coffin, promulgated another enlightened edict allowing wine growers to sell their most recent vintage, as well as food and fruit juices. Farmers soon sold their crops, pork, and poultry out of the rooms where customers used to sample their wines. Those rooms evolved into the buffets that now serve the patrons.

tourists, the beautiful garden overlooks the fields of Grinzing—an oasis of green grass, cheerful voices, and relaxation. *Weiße G'spritzer* (white wine with soda water) 18AS. Open Su-M and W-Sa 3pm-midnight.

Zum Krottenbach'l, XIX, Krottenbachstr. 148 (tel. 440 12 40). U-6: "Nußdorferstr." then bus #35A (dir: Salmannsdorf): "Kleingartenverein/Hackenberg." With a terraced garden on the fertile slopes of Untersievering, the *Heuriger* offers a lush perch for savoring the fruit of the vine. An underground spring flows through the terraces, gurgling into fountains and running past tables in the rustic tavern with thick wooden beams. Hot and cold buffet. Open daily 3pm-midnight.

Weingut Helm, XXI, Stammersdorferstr. 121 (tel. 292 12 44). Tram #31 to the last stop, turn right by the *Würstelstand,* then turn left. The family who owns and staffs this establishment keeps it low-key and friendly. Their garden and wooden tables are shaded by enormous old trees. Open Tu-Sa 3pm-midnight.

Franz Mayer am Pfarrplatz Beethovenhaus, XIX, Pfarrpl. 2 (tel. 37 12 87). U-4: "Heiligenstadt" then bus #38A: "Fernsprechamt/Heiligenstadt." Walk up the hill and head right onto Nestelbachg. Beethoven used to stay in the *Heuriger* when it offered guest quarters. Festive and cool patios. Somewhat pricey. Open M-F 4pm-midnight, Su and holidays 11am-midnight. Live music 7pm-midnight.

Weingut Heuriger Reinprecht, XIX, Cobenzlg. 22 (tel. 32 01 47 10). U-4: "Heiligenstadt" then bus #38A: "Grinzing." This *Heuriger* is a fairy-tale stereotype—picnic tables as far as the eye can see under an ivy-laden trellis, with *Schrammel* musicians strolling from table to table. One of the more touristed establishments, but don't be surprised to hear whole tables of nostalgic Austrians break into song on their own. Quite a bottle opener collection near the entryway. *Viertel* 30AS. Open Mar.-Nov. daily 3:30pm-midnight.

WINTER IN VIENNA

The Viennese don't let those long winter nights go to waste. Christmas festivities begin in December with *Krampus* parties. *Krampus* (Black Peter) is a hairy devil that accompanies St. Nicholas on his rounds and gives bad children coal and sticks. On December 5th, people in Krampus suits lurk everywhere from nightclubs to supermarkets, rattling their chains and chasing passersby. Small children nibble marzipan *Krampus* effigies, giving the holiday a perverse Halloween-like feel.

As the weather gets sharper, huts of professional *Maroni-* (chestnut) roasters and *Bratkartoffeln-* (potato pancake) toasters pop up everywhere. Cider, punch, red noses, and *Glühwein* (a hot, spicy mulled wine) become ubiquitous on sidewalks. **Christmas markets** *(Christkindlmärkte)* open around the city. The somewhat tacky **Rathausplatz Christkindlmarkt** is probably the best known of the yule marketplaces, offering, among other things, excellent *Lebkuchen* (a spicy, very strong gingerbread-like cake), *Langos* (a Hungarian round bread soaked in hot oil, garlic, and onions), and beeswax candles. (Open 9am-8pm.) **Schloß Schönbrunn's** *Weihnachtsmarkt* offers old-fashioned Christmas decorations. (Open M-F noon-7pm, Sa-Su 10am-7pm.) Visit the happy **Spittelberg** market, where artists and university kids hawk off-beat creations. (Open M-F 2-8pm, Sa-Su and holidays 10am-8pm.) The **Trachten-markt** shop in Schotteng. near Schottentor offers atmospheric Christmas shopping. Most theaters, opera houses, and concert halls have Christmas programs (see **Music,** p. 116 or **Theater and Cinema,** p. 117). The city also turns the Rathauspl. into an enormous outdoor skating rink in January and February.

Before Christmas festivities have even died down, the Viennese gear up for New Year's Day. The emotional highpoint of the New Year's season is the **Neujahrs-konzert** (New Year's concert) by the Viennese Philharmonic, broadcast worldwide. The refrain of the *Radetzkymarsch* by Strauss signals that the new year has truly begun. New Year's also brings a famously flashy **Imperial Ball** in the Hofburg (for tickets, contact Kongresszentrum Hofburg, A-1014 Wien; tel. 587 36 66, ext. 23; fax 535 64 26). For those lacking seven-digit incomes, the City of Vienna organizes a huge chain of Silvester parties in the Inner City. Follow the **Silvesterpfad,** marked by lights hung over the street, to hit outdoor karaoke, street waltzing, firecrackers, and hundreds of people drinking champagne in the streets. At midnight, the giant bell of St. Stephen's rings across the country, its sound broadcast by public radio stations.

New Year's is barely over before **Fasching** (Carnival season) arrives in February and spins the city into a bubbly daze of bedlam. These are the weeks of the Viennese waltzing balls. The most famous is the **Wiener Opernball** (Viennese Opera Ball), which draws Princess Stephanies and Donald Trumps the world over (last year Princess Fergie was the date of one Austrian businessman). Tickets must be reserved years in advance (international celebrities, contact Opernball-Büro, A-1010 Wien, Goetheg. 1; tel. 514 44 26 06). You don't have to sit out if you can't make the Opernball—there's something for everyone. Even the kindergarteners in public pre-schools have *Fasching Krapfen* parties, and McDonald's puts up carnival crepe banners. For a free *Fasching* celebration, come to the **carnival parade** that winds its way around the Ring, raucously stopping traffic the day before Lent.

▓ Nightlife

You can find a lively place to drink in Vienna at any hour of the day, but certain areas contain a high bar to cobblestone ratio, making a night of bacchanalian wandering deliriously easy. The most interesting local evening spots are Vienna's *Heurigen* or wine taverns. Otherwise, the traditional standby of loud, crowd-loving, and smoky types is the **Bermuda Dreieck** (Triangle), named after its regulars who, listing to port like overstuffed Spanish treasure galleons, lose their wind and their way and slowly sink. If your vision isn't foggy yet, walk down **Rotenturmstrasse** from St. Stephen's cathedral and around the areas bounded by the Jewish synagogue and Ruprecht's church, or arrive via the "Schwedenpl." U-Bahn stop. Another good zone to wander in search of nightlife in the inner city is smooth dark **Bäckerstraße** and its cellar bars. Slightly outside of the Ring, the university area (8th and 9th districts) and the streets off Burgg. and Stiftg. in the 7th district have tables in outdoor courtyards and loud, hip bars. They can be a good place to seek refuge when the summer crowd in the Bermuda Triangle feels too pubescent or touristy.

Vienna's groovy, kinetic club scene rages every night of the week, later than most bars. DJs spin wax until 4 or even 6am, and some clubs will keep it going after hours until 11am the next morning. A fact of Viennese nightlife: it starts late. If you arrive at some place at 11pm, it will be a scene from your high school dance. As usual, the best nights are Friday and Saturday, beginning around 1am or so. Cover charges are reasonable, and the theme nights are varied and frenetic enough to please anyone. While techno still rears its digitalized head, house, jungle, and trip-hop have a strong following as well. Pick up a copy of the indispensable **Falter** (28AS) if you're planning to hit the nighttime streets—besides some excellent articles in German, it prints listings of everything from opera to obscure live rock and punk concerts across the city, and will list places that have sprung up too recently for *Let's Go* to review. (Vienna's club turnover is too rapid to keep up with in a guide updated only once a year.) Also, be sure to grab a schedule for the **night-bus** system, which runs across Vienna all night after the regular public transportation shuts down at midnight.

BARS

The term "bar" has a loose definition in Vienna. Many restaurants (see **Restaurants,** p. 95) live a Dr. Jekyll-Mr. Hyde dual existence as a place both to eat and to party.

The Innere Stadt

Benjamin, I, Salzgries 11-13 (tel. 533 33 49). Just outside of the Triangle area. Go down the steps from Ruprecht's church, left onto Josefs Kai, and left again on Salzgries. Dark and groovy. Persian rugs hang on the walls; candles shine from wine bottles covered with wax. Filled with old, eclectic furniture. Can get rowdy on weekends, but the place designates a separate area for the more mellow types. Student crowd and great beer—*Budvar* (37AS) and *Kapsreiter* (43AS). Open Su-Th 7pm-2am, F-Sa 7pm-4am.

Santo Spirito, I, Kampfg. 7 (tel. 512 99 98). From Stephanspl., walk down Singerstr. and turn left onto Kampfg. (5min.). This bar will change your idea of classical music forever. The stereo here pumps out Rachmaninoff's second piano concerto while excited patrons co-conduct. Little busts on the wall pay homage to famous baton-wavers. Heats up in the winter, when the volume soars behind closed doors. Owner vacations in July, otherwise open from 6pm until people leave.

Jazzland, I, Franz-Josefs-Kai 29 (tel. 533 25 75). U-1 or U-4: "Schwedenpl." Serious jazz of all styles and regions, extending to folk and blues—check the schedule first. Excellent live music filters through the soothing brick environs. The bar is packed with older jazz fans. 50AS cover. Open Tu-Sa 7pm-2am. Music 9pm-1am.

Café MAK, I, Stubenring 3-5 (tel. 714 01 21), in the museum. Tram #1 or 2: "Stubenring." Light, bright, white, and very tight at night. The bar feels like another display case in the museum, but the people are stunning and the furniture is *Bauhaus* one step funkier. Peak through glass walls into the museum, or dine outside among the sunflowers. Hops with a rowdy university students after 10pm. Open Tu-Su 10am-2am (hot food until midnight).

Zwölf Apostellenkeller, I, Sonnenfelsg. 3 (tel. 512 67 77), behind the Stephansdom. To reach this underground tavern, walk into the archway, take a right, go down the long staircase, and discover grottos that date back to 1561. One of the best *Weinkeller* (wine cellars) in Vienna and a definite must for catacomb fans. Beer 37AS. *Viertel* of wine from 25AS. Open Aug.-June 4:30pm-midnight.

Esterházykeller, I, Haarhof 1 (tel. 533 34 82), off Naglerg. One of Vienna's least expensive *Weinkeller*. Relaxed cellar bar, popular with local twenty- and thirtysomethings. Try the Burgenlander *Grüner Veltliner* wine (26AS). Open in summer M-F 11am-11pm; in winter M-F 11am-11pm and Sa-Su 4-11pm.

Kaktus, I, Seitenstetteng. 5 (tel. 533 19 38), in the heart of the triangle. Packed with the bombed and the beautiful. Candles and atmospheric slouch. Open Su-Th 6pm-2am, F-Sa 6pm-4am.

Stadtheuriger Specht, I, Bäckerstr. 12 (tel. 512 26 37). One of Bäckerstr.'s cool subterranean grottos. Excellent beer bar. Also a restaurant with lots of Styrian specialties. Live music Th-Su. Open M-Sa 5pm-2am, Su 11:30am-10pm.

Club Berlin, I, Gonzag. 12 (tel. 533 04 79). Muscular men and black-clad women wind their way around the partitions in this former wine cellar—a simultaneously intimate and expansive atmosphere. Open Su-Tu 6pm-2am, F-Sa 6pm-4am.

Krah Krah, I, Rabensteig 8 (tel. 533 81 93). From Stephanspl., head down Rotenturmstr. and continue straight and slightly to your left on Rabensteig. Consummate "Triangle" spot. Long bar serves 50 kinds of beer on tap. Popular outdoor seating until 10pm. Open Su-W 11am-2am, Th-Sa 11am-3am.

Outside the Ring

◉**Alsergrunder Kulturpark,** IX, Alserstr. 4 (tel. 407 82 14). On the old grounds of a turn-of-the-18th-century hospital, Kulturpark is not one bar but many. A favorite outdoor hangout for the Viennese who flock to the beautifully landscaped grounds for the beer garden, *Heurigen,* champagne bar—the list goes on. All sorts of people and all sorts of nightlife—just about anything you might want for a happening night out. Open Apr.-Oct. daily 4pm-2am. Call about the frequent concerts.

Miles Smiles, VIII, Langeg. 51 (tel. 405 95 17). U-2: "Lerchenfelderstr." Head down Lerchenfelderstr. and take the 1st right. Cool as "Sketches of Spain." The music is post-1955 jazz. Open Su-Th 8pm-2am, F-Sa 8pm-4am.

Chelsea, VIII, (tel. 407 93 09), Lerchenfeldergürtel under the U-Bahn between Thaliastr. and Josefstadterstr. The best place in Vienna for underground music. Live bands from across Europe play here (except in summertime). Cover generally runs between 50-200AS. Open daily 4pm-4am.

Berg das Café, IX, Bergg. 8 (tel. 319 57 20). A super-swank gay café/bar by night and casual hang-out by day, this place is always crowded. It recently merged with nearby gay and lesbian bookstore **Das Löwenherz,** so you can browse during the day while you drink your *Melange.* Plenty of English titles. Open 10am-1am.

Das Möbel, VII, Burgg. 10 (tel. 524 94 97). Founded by the *Forum Für Wohnkultur,* this high-ceilinged, metal-barred cafe functions as a showcase for furniture designers. At night, the metal couches, car seat chairs, Swiss-army-tables, and other pieces —which rotate every 6 weeks if not bought—are in full use by a hip crowd. (Open M-F noon-midnight, Sa-Su breakfast buffet 10am).

Kunsthalle Café, IV, Treitlstr. 2 (tel. 586 98 64). Inside the bright yellow contemporary art museum, as well as outside on its large rocky terrace, this café-by-day is filled nightly with students and the bright sounds of funk-jazz-blues shows (open 10am-3am or whenever the last person leaves).

Flieger, IV, Schleifmühlg. 19 (tel. 586 73 09). One of Vienna's 1st new wave bars, Flieger still flies high and is usually crowded and lively. The Katu drink, made with cactus juice, is rumored to be "mind-moving." You can also tipple more tame drinks and imagine moving in the silver airplane that hangs from the ceiling. Open M-Th 6pm-2am, F-Su 6pm-4am.

Europa, VII, Zollerg. 8 (tel. 526 33 83). Buy a drink, scope the scene, and just vogue. Surrounded by concert posters and funky light fixtures, the hip twentysomething crowd hangs out late *en route* to further intoxication. Open 9am-4am.

Plutzer Bräu, VII, Stiftg. 6 (tel. 526 12 15). U-3: "Neubaug." Follow signs for Stiftg., on the right-hand side. Spacious, popular brewhouse makes beer hounds out of even the stuffiest non-believers. Pleasant outdoor seating.

Eagle Bar, VI, Blümelg. 1 (tel. 587 26 61). A bar for gay men. Diverse but young clientele derived from the leather and/or denim set. Good beer. Open 9pm-4am.

Nightshift, VI, Corneliusg. 8 (tel. 586 23 37). This place caters to gay men, preferably in black leather. Lots of bare chests cruise by. Su-Th 10pm-4am, F-Sa 10pm-5am.

DISCOS AND DANCE CLUBS

U-4, XII, Schönbrunnerstr. 222 (tel. 85 83 18). U-4: "Meidling Hauptstr." Formerly *the* disco in Vienna and still crowded. A behemoth with all the trappings, including 2 separate dance areas, a dancer's cage, and slide shows. 5 floors and rotating theme nights (including Italian music Mondays!) please a varied clientele. Thursdays are always Gay Heaven Night. Cover 50-100AS. Open daily 11pm-5am.

Volksgarten, I, Burgring/Heldenpl. (tel. 63 05 18). Nestled on the edge of the Volksgarten Park near the Hofburg. Zip up that leisure suit and strap on your platform soles. Definite 70s vibe. Comfy red couches provide the perfect spot for wallflowers to mellow. In good weather, the place rolls back the roof so clubbers can pulse under the stars. Monday "Vibrazone" kicks out the funk and groove while the Sunday morning breakfast club (6am-2pm) is the place to prolong the buzz of Saturday's uproarious "Kinky Disco." Cover 70-100AS. Open Th-Su 10pm-5am.

Why Not, I, Tiefer Graben 22 (tel. 535 11 58). A relaxed gay and lesbian bar/disco. Neon interior holds a sweaty dance crowd on weekends. Open F-Sa 10pm-4am, Su 9pm-2am. Women-only 1 Thursday per month.

B.A.C.H., XVI, Bachg. 21 (tel. 450 18 58). Lots of live funky concerts and theater acts as well as straight-up dancing in this subterranean nightclub. Definitely left of center. Open M-Th 8pm-2am, F-Sa 8pm-4am.

Flex Halle, I, Donaulände/Augartenbrücke (tel. 533 75 29), near the Schottenring U-Bahn station, is a small, dark, on-the-water club with neon lights and a slummy feel. Lots of good dancing here. Open 10pm-whenever.

■ Daytrips from Vienna

For other possible daytrips, see **Eisenstadt** (p. 132), **Melk,** and **Krems** (p. 130).

■ Mödling

"Poor I am, and miserable," Beethoven wrote before his arrival in Mödling. Seeking physical and psychological rehabilitation, he schlepped all this way for that *je ne sais quoi* only a mineral spring could offer. He wrote *Missa Solemnis* within Mödling's embrace, and his spirits thoroughly improved. About 20 minutes from Vienna by S-Bahn (Eurailpass valid), industrial-suburban Mödling has completely lost the charm that drew the likes of Schubert, Wagner, Strauss, Hugo Wolf, Schönberg, and Gustav Klimt here. Nevertheless, Mödling is worth the trip, if only to use it as a hub for reaching nearby Heiligenkreuz, Mayerling, and Hinterbrühl.

For more info and *Privatzimmer* lists, head to Mödling's **tourist office** (*Gästedienst),* Elisabethstr. 2 (tel. (02236) 267 27), next to the *Rathaus.* From the train station, walk up the hill and left down Hauptstr. all the way to the end at the *Rathaus.* (Open M-F 8am-noon and 1-4pm.) Trains and *Schnellbahn* leave from Vienna's Südbahnhof and arrive in Mödling all day long (30AS), and a bus leaves every hour from Südtiroler-Pl. in Vienna.

■ Heiligenkreuz

Heiligenkreuz is a pink-cheeked surprise, an uncannily harmonious Cistercian monastery that seems to have grown whole from the grassy hills in this remote spot of Austrian countryside. Buses from Mödling (dir: Hinterbrühl) will drop you off in what appears to be the middle of a pasture or some local farmer's vineyard, but follow the shady salmon-tinted pilgrimage shrines along the hillside and you'll reach this 700-year-old monastic retreat. Founded by Leopold V, the man who imprisoned Richard the Lionhearted for ransom, the church was originally intended as a "school of love" and a reformation of the pre-existing Benedictine order. Life at Heiligenkreuz has never been particularly austere, however—visit the *Weinkeller* where the monks still press their own grapes, or simply stand in the Zen-like quiet of their blooming central courtyard to experience the serene continuity of centuries. The vaulted chapel houses magnificent stained-glass windows, still intact despite repeated medieval missives from stern church elders threatening to put the abbot, prior, and cellarers on a fast of bread and water every sixth day until they were removed. Visitors can enter the abbey itself only by taking a tour. (Open 9am-6pm. 45AS, children 25AS.)

■ Mayerling and Hinterbrühl

The #365 bus that goes to Heiligenkreuz halts one stop later at **Mayerling,** the hunting lodge where heir to the throne Archduke Rudolf committed either murder or a double suicide. He and his secret lover Maria Vetsera, who was a lower ranking aristocrat not allowed to marry into the imperial family, were both found shot through the head in the bedroom of the hunting lodge. There was no suicide note. In its time, this was the biggest scandal of the continent, and the tragedy of Franz Josef's and Elizabeth's lives. It was also a tragic event for Austria as a nation—Rudolf was rumored to be a liberal and intellectual who had a much better idea than his old-fashioned father of how to deal with modern, turn-of-the-century political realities.

Hinterbrühl, the first stop on the #365 bus line (34AS), is the site of the largest underground lake in Europe. This former mineral mine was flooded in 1912, but the Nazis drained it and assembled the fuselage of the first jet fighter in the grotto. Tours of the lake are available.

■ Klosterneuburg

Easily accessible via buses from Heiligenstadt (every 10min., 17AS), the **monastery** Klosterneuburg was founded by Leopold III in 1114. (Museum open May-Nov. 15 Sa-Su and holidays 10am-5pm.) The church contains the renowned high Gothic master-piece, the Verduner Altar. In 1730, Karl IV moved into Klosterneuburg and began a **palace** that was to match the scale of the monastery, which was to symbolize the importance of the *Kaiserreich* (Emperor's kingdom) to the *Gottesreich* (God's king-dom). Only two of the nine projected domes were completed, but it's still damn impressive. The library is worth a visit, with over 200,000 ancient tomes. Call the abbey (tel. (02243) 62 10) early to arrange a tour.

Klosterneuburg has a **Jugendherberge,** Hüttersteig 8 (tel. (02243) 83 501), an easy commute to Vienna. The hostel offers 50 beds at 145AS each in drab rooms often overrun by schoolgroups. Its small luxuries include a pretty flower garden and **laun-dry.** (Sheets 30AS. Discounts available for the under-19 set. Open May 1 to Sept. 1.)

■ Carnuntum

The Romans strategically conquered the Alps, Dolomites, and Danube river valleys by 15 BCE, using the river route to transport soldiers, slaves, and trade through the empire. Of their many outposts, which included Vindobona (Vienna), Iuavum (Salzburg), and Brigantium (Bregenz), Carnuntum was by far the largest and most impressive until conquered by the Germanic Alemanni tribe in the 3rd century CE. Archaeological digs have uncovered houses, public baths, canals, and a temple to the goddess Diana all dating from the first to 3rd centuries CE. Most are on display in the **Archäologischer Park Carnuntum,** Hauptstr. 465 (tel. (02163) 337 70; fax 337 75; email info@carnuntum.co.at; http://www.carnuntum.co.at). You can sign up to tour the place or to take part in the digging. (Open Apr.-Nov. M-F 9am-5pm, Sa-Su 9am-6pm. 45AS, students 35AS; guided tours 35AS.)

Twenty kilometers of bike paths lead from the train station through the Heidentor ruins (from 300 BCE), an amphitheater, an ancient military camp, and (in nearby Bad Deutsch-Altenburg) the **Archäologisches Museum Carnuntinum.** The largest Roman museum in Austria, it holds jewelry, coins, weapons, *u.s.w.* (Open Jan. 15-Dec. 15 Tu-Su 10am-5pm. 60AS, students 40AS; guided tours 35 AS. Combo museum/park ticket 85AS, students 60AS.) Carnuntum hosts annual Roman festivals including the **Roman Athletic Competition** in April, the **Art Carnuntum** fest from July to August with open-air cinema, theater, and concerts (tel. (02163) 34 00 for information; email pb@artcarnuntum.co.at), and a **Roman Christmas market** in December.

Carnuntum is easily reached by **S-bahn** S7 from Wien Mitte or Wien Nord (1hr., every 30min., 68AS). The park is a heavily signed 10-minute walk from the station, and you'll pass a little **tourist office booth** on the way to the park on Hauptstr. By **car** from Vienna, drive along highway A4, exit at Fischamend, and follow road B9 to Petronell-Carnuntum.

■ Stift Altenburg

Stift Altenburg can be reached by bus from Vienna directly (7am) or with a change in Horn (5 per day, 155AS). A pleasant option is to walk along the picturesque 6km path from Horn to the Stift (follow green signs). **Open** *May-Nov. Tu-Su 9am-noon and 1-5pm. To see the crypt and library, you must take a guided* **tour** *10:30am, 2, and 4pm. 60AS, students 30AS. Guided tours of the art exhibit 9:30am, 1, and 3pm. 60AS, students 30AS. Combination ticket for both tours 100AS, students 50AS. For more info contact the Stift (tel. (02982) 34 51 21; fax 34 51 13; email stift.altenburg@wvnet.at). For concert tickets, call (02982) 530 80, in winter (011) 586 19 00.)*

This Benedictine abbey, initially founded in 1144 by Countess Hildburg von Poigen-Rebgau in memory of her deceased husband, swells with Baroque paintings and sculpture. The abbey was frequently attacked by ravenous Hussites and Swedes, and most of what is visible now dates from after the disastrous sacking of the monastery by Swedish soldiers in 1645. Altenburg was subsequently rebuilt under the architect and pupil of Prandtauer, Joseph Munggenast, who replaced most of the Gothic cloister, although remnants of it have been excavated and are visible today. Stift Altenburg is famous not only for its magnificent church buildings, but also for the **library** housed within the abbey, conceived in the Baroque mind as a temple to human wisdom, in playful symmetry with the neighboring temple to Divine Wisdom. Much of the art in the church and library, as well as the ceremonial staircase and intriguing **crypt,** was done by **Paul Troger.** His sculptures, paintings, and frescoes depict Biblical scenes along with benevolent mythological divinities. The abbey underwent extensive restoration after being badly damaged in both world wars. It hosts annual art exhibits and summer concerts given by the **Stift Altenburger Music Akademie.**

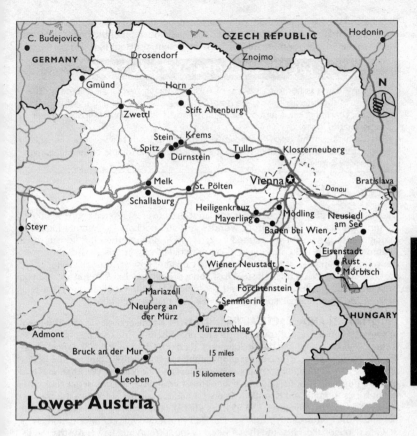

Lower Austria

Lower Austria (Niederösterreich)

Though it bears little resemblance to the foreign stereotype of Austria, the province of **Niederösterreich** is the key to understanding Austrians' image of themselves. Forget *The Sound of Music*—rolling, forested hills replace jagged Alpine peaks, and wildflowers stand in for hillside edelweiss. The region gets its name not from its position at the bottom of the state but because it sits at the lower end of the Danube. Rugged castle ruins are remnants of defensive bastions against invading Turkish forces. Often billed as "the province on Vienna's doorstep" (warning: class A daytrips ahead), Niederösterreich accounts for a quarter of the nation's land mass—and 60% of its wine. Local specialties include *Wienerwald* cream strudel, a sinful mixture of flaky crust, curds, raisins, and lemon peel (it tastes *far* better than it sounds).

The **Wachau** region of Lower Austria, between the northwestern foothills of the Bohemian Forest and the southeast Dunkelsteiner Wald, is a magnificent river valley invoked nostalgically in tons and tons of Austrian drinking songs. You can savor celebrated Wachau wines at the wine cellar of any local vintner. Off the tourist track, the **Waldviertel** region is a vast expanse of mountains and trees stretching between the

Danube and the Czech Republic. Enjoy the forest, but beware—dangerous ticks here carry a virus that results in *Gehirnentzündung* (inflammation of the brain), a disease similar to meningitis (for more information, see **Essentials: Health,** p. 16).

🍯 HIGHLIGHTS OF LOWER AUSTRIA

- Lower Austria is home to several of Austria's beach towns, all located on the shores of the Neusiedlersee. Neusiedl am See is the tackiest and most popular, Rust is charming, rural, and home to many storks, and Mörbisch hosts summertime floating operas.
- Melk's big beautiful yellow Benedictine abbey dates from 1089.
- Eisenstadt is home to Hadyn and to the sumptuous apartments of the Hungarian Esterházy family.

■ St. Pölten

Like an againg opera star undergoing the latest makeover, St. Pölten (pop. 50,000) is attempting to cover up scars from World War II and pockmarks from her industrial heritage. Bishop von Passau granted a charter to St. Pölten, then the Roman town Aelium Cetium, in 1159, making St. Pölten the oldest city in Austria. It is, however, the youngest capital—St. Pölten became the capital of Lower Austria in 1986. There are fault lines between the industrial past and a present-day bid for tourism, and you can find a little patch of marketing and consumerism in the pinkly restored Baroque *Altstadt* and loads of small summer music festivals that happen here.

ORIENTATION AND PRACTICAL INFORMATION Kremsergasse divides the town in two. As you leave the train station and cross Bahnhofpl., Kremserg. is at ten o'clock. Follow it until you hit the Riemerpl. then turn right to reach St. Pölten's center, the **Rathausplatz.** The **train station** rumbles at Bahnhofpl., abutting the pedestrian zone and sending direct trains to **Hütteldorf** and the **Vienna Westbahnhof** two or three times every hour. Right in front of the train station, the **bus** depot runs infrequent buses to **Melk** and **Krems.** A free schedule is available at the bus information booth. The **tourist office** (tel. 353 354; fax 28 19), is in the Rathauspassage, the tunnel under the cotton-candy *Rathaus.* The staff provides oodles of information about St. Pölten, regional events, and the wonders of the surrounding Lower Austrian lands. They'll also give you a room list, lead you on a one-hour **tour** of the inner city (call up to a week in advance), and distribute a **free cassette tour** in several languages. (Open M-F 8am-6pm; May-Oct. M-F 8am-6pm, Sa 9:30am-5pm, Su and holidays 10am-5pm.) They won't make room reservations; look next door on the wall of the Reisebüro for a free reservations phone. The best place to **exchange money** is the **Postsparkasse Österreichischer Bank** (PSK), Rathausg. 2 (tel. 545 71; fax 545 75), across the street from the tourist office. **Lockers** are available 24 hours a day (30AS). You can **rent bikes** (tel. 528 60) at the train station (150AS, with train ticket 90AS; open daily 5:45am-10pm). The main **post office,** Bahnhofpl. 1a, is right by the station. (Open M-F 7am-8pm, Sa 8am-1pm.) The **postal code** is A-3100. The **telephone code** is 02742.

ACCOMMODATIONS AND FOOD St. Pölten works well as a day trip. Quoth the tourist brochure, "Because you're in St. Pölten, not in New York. And that's the way it should be." Since the town lost its only youth hostel a few years ago, you might consider staying in the hostels in **Krems** (tel. (02732) 834 52; see p. 140), **Melk** (tel. (02752) 26 81; see p. 143), or **Vienna** (see p. 90). The tourist office maintains a list of *Privatzimmer,* most of which are outside the city limits.

St. Pölten's local specialties include oysters, fried black pudding, and savory Wachau wine. **B&B (Bier & Brötchen),** Schreing. 7 (tel. 20 72), has soup and sandwiches, good beer, and outside seating. (Open M-F 10:30am-11pm, Sa 9:30am-2pm.) A comfortable Viennese café with newspapers and lingering guests, **Café Melange,** Kremserg. 11 (tel. 23 93), on the second floor, tends to draw a younger crowd. (Open M-F 7:30am-6:30pm, Sa 7:30am-5pm.) **Café Punschkrapfel,** Domg. 8 (tel. 63

83), is named for its specialty—a small, chocolate, pink-icinged rum cake. Other offerings include fruit frappes (34AS) and a salad buffet (35AS), which taste best in the popular outdoor seating area. (Open M-F 7am-7pm, Sa 7am-1pm.) Cheap and healthy fixins await at the St. Pölten **Julius Meinl** supermarket, Kremserg. 21. (Open M-F 7:30am-6pm, Sa 7:30am-12:30pm.)

SIGHTS AND ENTERTAINMENT St. Pölten's architecture suffered heavy damages during WWII. The city fixed the broken Baroques because it loves "culture." As the tourist brochure explains, "St. Pölten for cultural connoisseurs, St. Pölten for lovers of culture, St. Pölten for those eager for culture, St. Pölten for cultural gourmets, St. Pölten for cultural individualists, St. Pölten for culture freaks and friends and all those who would like to be so." Who is it that wants to be a culture freak but can't?

The **Rathausplatz** at St. Pölten's core was erected in the 13th century, though recent archaeological excavations reveal that a Roman settlement sprouted there in the first millennium. The building at Rathauspl. 2 earned the name **Schubert Haus** due to Franz's frequent visits to the owners, Baron von Münk and family. A neo-Grecian Schubert (bare-chested, no less) conducts above the window at the portal's axis. The **Institut der Englischer Fräulein** (Institute of Mary Ward), Linzer Str. 9-11, was founded in 1706 for the instruction of girls from noble families. The exciting facade sports Corinthian columns along with pink stucco and vaguely religious life-sized reliefs. Follow Linzerg. to Dr. Karl-Renner-Promenade to see the only Art Nouveau synagogue in Lower Austria (and beyond?). Joseph Maria Olbrich designed several other Art Nouveau (a.k.a. *Jugendstil*) buildings in St Pölten's *Altstadt*.

St. Pölten's **Wiener Straße** has been a thoroughfare since the Romans rolled through. After 1100, the street became the central axis of the bourgeois-trader settlement established by the Bishop of Passau. At the corner of Wienerstr. and Kremserg. stands the oldest pharmacy in St. Pölten, the **Hassack-Apotheke,** happily curing headaches and hemorrhoids since 1595. Dig the shutters. **Herrenplatz** has witnessed the haggling of St. Pölten's daily market for centuries. A narrow alley just after Wienerstr. 31 leads to **Domplatz,** retaining its charm despite new-found parking-lot status. The remains of the Roman settlement of Aelium were discovered here when some clumsy sewer installers tripped over Roman hypocausts (ancient floor heating systems). Be sure to stop by the actual **Dom** (cathedral) to see its pleasant salmon tones and gilded Baroque encrustations, added by Prandtauer when he transformed the original Roman basilica.

St. Pölten maintains a few good museums. The encyclopedic **Stadt Museum,** Prandtauerstr. 2, near the *Rathaus,* has special exhibits on cultural and historical themes It also houses a very thorough permanent collection describing St. Pölten from pre-Roman times to the present, and containing artifacts ranging from transplanted church pews to 18th-century cloth samples. *(Open 9am-5pm. 50AS, students 20AS.)* Part of the exhibit is located in **Schloß Pottenbrunn** outside of St. Pölten. Buses run from the train station to the palace every hour.

The town supports two **theaters. "Die Bühne im Hof,"** Linzerstr. 18 (tel. 352 291; fax 522 94), has mostly modern theater and dance performances. The tourist office offers a program detailing the productions. Prices range from 70 to 350AS, depending on what's showing (students and seniors 50% off). **Landeshauptstadt Theater,** Rathauspl. 11 (tel. 352 02 619), stages traditional opera and ballet. Tickets run 160 to 290AS, but the box office sells 150AS standing room tickets on the evenings of performances. Seasonal festivities include the **St. Pöltner Festwoche,** which brings all kinds of events to local theaters and museums at the end of May. From the end of September to early October, the **Sacred Music Festival** features free concerts in various churches. The **Donaufestival** from June to early July celebrates dance, theater, and music in the Festspielhaus. *(For information, call 23 56; for tickets call 21 22.)*

For fun with money, check out the **flea market** that comes to the Einkaufszentrum Traisenpark (just outside town) from 8am to 3pm every Sunday, featuring crafts, toys, art, antiques, books, and furniture. The tourist brochure deserves the last word here: "Shopping makes you happy. Especially in St. Pölten."

LOWER AUSTRIA

■ Baden bei Wien

Baden is the favorite weekend spot for Viennese trying to get away from it all. All day, every day, jets of water with a natural temperature of 36°C (96°F) spring from the ground. Since the age of Roman rule, bathers have flocked to the spa for the therapeutic effects of its sulfur springs. The Holy Roman Emperors used Baden as a summer retreat, and the honor became official in 1803 when Emperor Franz I moved the summer court here. The Emperor gave Baden an imperial reputation, and many big names have relaxed at its baths: Mozart, Schubert, Strauss, Beethoven, and, of course, Falco. Under imperial patronage in the 19th century, Biedermeier culture flourished. City notables generated magnificent specimens of architecture and art and encouraged the burgeoning science of horticulture. As a tribute to the Emperor's presence, Baden created a rosarium extending from the center of town to the *Wienerwald* (90,000 sq. m) containing over 20,000 roses. In one step, you can leave behind the carefully tended roses and enter the enormous, trail-laced tract of woodland. In another, you can wine, dine, and gamble in the town's recently cultivated crop of upscale restaurants, shops, and casino. Baden's prices are the snakes slithering through this paradise. Resist temptation and make Baden a daytrip from Vienna, only 27km away.

ORIENTATION AND PRACTICAL INFORMATION The easiest way to get to Baden is by the **Badener Bahn,** a tram that runs every 15 minutes from Vienna's Opera House in the Karlspl. (70min., 5am-10:30pm, 51AS) and Baden's Josefpl. **Trains** travel frequently between Vienna's Südbahnhof (4:40am-11:15pm, 51AS) and the Josefpl. (4:16am-11:43pm). **Buses** run at longer intervals between the Opera (40min., 7:10am-3:15am, 58AS) and Josefpl. (6:51am-2:21am). **By car** from the west, take the West Autobahn to "Alland-Baden-Mödling (Bundesstr. 20)." From Vienna, take the Süd Autobahn and exit at "Baden."

Baden's **tourist office,** Brusattipl. 3 (tel. 868 00; fax 441 47), is accessible from the Josefpl. bus and tram stop. Walk toward the fountain, keep right, and follow Erzherzog-Rainer-Ring to the second left (Grüner Markt). The tourist office awaits at the end of the cul-de-sac. The patient staff speaks English and will provide English brochures on request. In the summer, they offer free **tours** of the *Altstadt* (M at 2pm and Th at 10am, 1½hr.) and the wine region (W 3pm, 2hr.), as well as **wine tastings** (Th 4-7pm or by appointment) and free guided **hiking** or **biking** tours. (Open May-Oct. M-Sa 9am-12:30pm and 2-6pm, Su 9am-12:30pm.) The train station offers **bike rental** (50AS) and **luggage storage** (20AS). **Public toilets** are at Grüner Markt, the Rosarium, and the train station. The **postal code** is A-2500. The **telephone code** is 02252.

ACCOMMODATIONS AND FOOD If you want to spend the night in Baden despite admonishments from the budget fairy, ask at the tourist office for options. One good bet is **Pension Steinkellner,** Am Hang 1 (tel. 862 26), which offers decent rooms at reasonable prices. It's a bit of a walk from the center of town, but the friendly proprietors will pick you up if you need a short ride. Doubles with shower run 320AS.

Food in Baden is plentiful but, once again, not cheap. **Café Damals,** Rathausg. 3 (tel. 426 86), in a cool, ivy-hung courtyard facing the Hauptpl., is a relaxing place to lunch and linger, despite replays of happy-camper American Top 40 tunes circa 1983. Try a delicate salad for 40AS. (Open M-F 9:30am-11pm, Sa 9:30am-5pm, Su 11am-5pm.) **Zum Vogelhändler,** Vöslauerstr. 48 (tel. 852 25), is a pub where Baden youth flock to imbibe the local wine and snack on small, hot dishes. The specialty, *Nockerl,* is available in many varieties (including vegetarian) for 60-87AS. (Open 6pm-2am. Live music some nights.) If you're looking for a little history with your *Tafelspitz,* visit the **Gasthaus zum Reichsapfel,** Spielg. 2, the oldest guesthouse in Baden. Follow Antong. one block from Theaterpl.; the restaurant is on the corner. Since the 13th century, Gasthaus zum Reichsapfel has served as a tavern for hungry wayfarers. Those less interested in the history may still be entertained by the chess, checkers, and huge collection of *Hagar the Horrible* comic books and *Mad* magazines—in

German, of course. (Open Su-M and W-Sa 11am-2pm and 5-11pm.) **Sektbar Schluck-specht,** Josefpl. 3, is where Baden "nightlife" happens. Go for snacks (38-120AS), drinks, and the saloon-like decor. (Open M-Th 10:30am-2am, F 10:30am-4am, Sa 9:30am-4am, Su 4pm-2am.) For a meal on the run, **Billa,** Wasserg. 14, lies on the way from the train station to the *Fußgängerzone.* (Open M-Th 7:30am-6:30pm, F 7:30am-8pm, Sa 7am-5pm.) A fresh **farmer's market** beckons at Grüner Markt. (Open M-F 8am-6pm, Sa 8am-1pm.)

SIGHTS AND ENTERTAINMENT The baths were the biggest attraction in the days of Mozart and Beethoven (and Augustus), and they are still the siren call for guests today. Although they smell like sulfur (i.e., bad), they're warm, relaxing, and good for you. The largest one, the **Strandbad,** Helenenstr. 19-21, lets you simmer in the hot sulfur thermal pool and cool off in normal chlorinated pools. *(Open M-F 67AS, Sa-Su 79AS; after 1pm, 57AS and 67AS. Swimming pool only, 25AS.)* Kids will get hysterical over the huge water slide and pool—questionably Roman, but definitely fun. From May until September 28, visit the smaller (but just as toasty) pool at Marchetstr. 13, behind the *Kurdirektion. (49AS.)* The **Kurdirektion** itself, Brusattipl. 4 (tel. 445 31), is the center of all curative spa treatments, housing an indoor thermal pool mainly for patients but open to visitors. *(72AS.)* The spa has underwater massage therapy (295AS), sulfur mud baths (305AS), and regular or "sport" massages (310AS). In the summer of 1999, a new gigantic spa complex called the *Römertherme Baden* will open.

Centered around Hauptpl., Baden's lovely *Fußgängerzone* features the **Dreifaltigkeitsäule** (Trinity Column), erected in 1718 to thank God for keeping the plague from Baden, as well as the local **Rathaus** and Franz Josef I's summer home at #17. The **Beethovenhaus,** where the composer spent his summers from 1804 to 1825, stands at Rathausg. 10. Beethoven banged out part of *Missa Solemnis* and much of his *Ninth Symphony* here. The reverent museum features such relics as the composer's death mask and locks of hair. *(Open Tu-F 4-6pm, Sa-Su and holidays 9-11am and 4-6pm.)*

North of Hauptpl. via Maria-Theresa-G. lies the glory of Baden, the **Kurpark.** Set into the southeast edge of the Wienerwald, this carefully landscaped, shady garden is studded with statues including a stony Mozart and Beethoven who watch as you wander through their domain. The park became an important frolic zone in Europe when the Congress of Vienna met in the early 19th century. Bigshot European political figures could escort the Imperial Court here, and after Sunday mass throngs of townsfolk would gather to watch the dignitaries strut through the park. The delightful **Theresiengarten** was laid out in 1792, when the *Kurpark* was still called "Theresienbad," and the **flower clock** in the middle of the *Kurpark* grass began ticking in 1929. If you're feeling lucky, visit the park's **Casino.** *(Opens daily at 3pm. Must be 19 or older. Semi-formal dress required. Free entrance.)* The **Emperor Franz-Josef Museum,** Hochstr. 51 (tel. 411 00), perches atop the Badener Berg at the end of the park (follow signs through the *Sommerarena* along Zöllner and Suckfüllweg) and holds exhibitions of folk art, weapons, religious pieces, and photography. *(Open Apr.-Oct. Tu-Su 1-7pm; Nov.-Mar. Tu-Su 11am-5pm.)* A **Doll and Toy Museum,** Erzherzog-Rainer-Ring 23 (tel. 410 20), displays over 300 dolls from different countries, including a 12mm Tyrolean doll from the early 1800s. *(Open Tu-F 4-6pm, Sa-Su and holidays 9-11am and 4-6pm.)* The collection's other little people include teddy bears, Japanese ceremonial dolls, and marionettes from Prague.

Baden's **Beethoven Festival** takes place from mid-September to early October, featuring performances by famous Austrian artists and film screenings at the Stadttheater. For tickets, contact Kulturamt der Stadtgemeinde Baden, Hauptpl. 1, A-2500 Baden (tel. 868 00 231; fax 868 00 210). From late June to mid-September, the **Sommerarena** in the *Kurpark* offers a magnificent, open-air setting for performances of classic Viennese operettas, including works by Fall and Lehár. *(50-500AS, standing room 30AS.)* For tickets, call 485 47, write to Stadttheater Baden Kartenbüro, Theaterpl. 7, A-2500 Baden, or stop by the box office in the Stadttheater on Kaiser-Franz-Ring-Str. *(Open Tu-Sa 10am-noon and 5-6pm, Su and holidays 10am-noon.)* Last-minute tickets go on sale at the door 30 minutes before the concert.

LOWER AUSTRIA

In the blooming days of June, Baden holds the **Badener Rosentage,** a multi-week celebration of local roses at the height of the season. The wide range of activities are generally free. Many take place in the Rosarium in the **Doblhoffpark,** where you can also rent boats and float around on a shady pond. *(Open 9am-7pm. 40AS for 30min., 70AS for 1hr.)* World-class **horse racing** also occurs near the Casino from May to September. Call 887 73 or 886 97 for details. In September, Baden hosts **Grape Cure Week,** a Bacchanalian gathering of stands from local wineries in Hauptpl. selling fresh grapes and grape juice. The theory behind the event is that periodically one needs to irrigate one's system, and the best way to do so is by gobbling grapes (1kg of grapes per day). Some take the medicinal philosophy to heart, but for most, it's an excuse to party. For details, stop by one of the *Buschenschanken. (Stands open daily 8am-6pm. First 500 guests get free grape juice.)* Baden rules state that the *Lokalen,* or pubs, can only open for two weeks at a time—the rotating schedule is available at the tourist office. Pine branches hanging outside a shop's doors mean it's open.

BURGENLAND

South and southeast of Vienna, from the easternmost portion of the Wienerwald to northwest Burgenland, lies a region of rolling hills and dense woodlands. The Leitha River runs along the Burgenland border north of Wiesen to Wiener Neustadt and to nations east, while the peaks of the Rosaliengebirge glower at the borderlands near Hungary. The Burgenland has a very Hungarian-influenced cuisine, and you may run across pockets of strangely accented Hungarian speakers in the more rural parts of the province. Burgenland vineyards produce world-famous wines and vine-hung taverns (often with Gypsy musicians) serving the fruits of their labor.

▪ Eisenstadt

Where I wish to live and die.

—Josef Haydn

Haydn, *Heurigen,* and Huns are three Hs that pushed Eisenstadt into cultural significance. **Josef Haydn** composed the melodies that inspired Mozart here, and his wish to live and die in Eisenstadt was happily met by his patrons, the **Esterházys,** powerful Hungarian landholders claiming descent from Attila the Hun. To this day one of the wealthiest families in Europe, they were instrumental in helping the Habsburgs maintain their power. They first lived in Eisenstadt when it was part of Hungary and decided to keep their palace even when borders changed. Today they own many of the region's famed vineyards, whose divine *Heurige* (new wine, or a place selling new wine) is often compared to wine produced in Bordeaux.

ORIENTATION AND PRACTICAL INFORMATION Only 50km from Vienna, Eisenstadt is centered around Hauptstraße, a big chunk of the city's *Fußgängerzone.* From the train station, follow Bahnstr. (which becomes St. Martinstr. and Fanny Eißlerg.) to the middle of this central area (20min.). From the bus stop, walk along Dompl. toward the church and turn right onto Martinstr. (10min.). At Hauptstr., the Schloß Esterházy is on your left at the end of the street, and the **tourist office** (tel. 673 90; fax 673 91; email tue.info@bnet.at) is sheltered in the right wing of the Schloß Esterházy. The wonderful, English-speaking staff has information on accommodations, musical events, tours, and *Heurigen* in Eisenstadt and throughout the region. For countryside immersion, ask for *Beim Bauern Zu Gast,* which lists winegrowers renting rooms in their houses. The office organizes several **guided tours** of the city, including one focusing on Josef Haydn, one on the "Trail of the Esterházy Princes," and one on Judaism in the Burgenland. The tours last up to 2½ hours and cost 600AS for as many as 50 people. Tailor-made tours are available with advance notice. (Open May-Oct. M-Sa 9am-5pm, Su 9am-1pm.)

Trains leave for Eisenstadt from **Wien Meidling** in Vienna (1hr., 2-3 per hr., 69AS) with a possible switch at Wulkaprodersdorf. Another option is to take the S-bahn from Vienna Südbahnof (1½hr., every hr., 85AS) and switch trains in Neusiedl am See. You may find it more convenient to take a **bus** from Wien Mitte directly to Eisenstadt (1½hr., every hr. 6am-8:45pm, 70AS). Buses also run from Eisenstadt to **Rust, Mörbisch,** and **Wiener Neustadt.** The **bus station** (tel. 23 50) is on Dompl. next to the cathedral. To get to Eisenstadt by **car,** take Bundestr. 16 or Autobahn A2 or A3 south from Vienna. From Wiener Neustadt, take Bundestr. 153 or Autobahn S4 east. There is an underground parking garage (25AS per hr.) just outside the Esterházy Palace in the *Zentrum.* The train station (tel. 626 37) **rents bikes** (150AS per day, 120AS per half-day; with train ticket 90AS, 70AS; mountain bikes 150-200AS; reservations advised). **Luggage lockers** are also available (30AS). **Exchange currency** at the post office or at **Creditanstalt Bankverein** on the corner of St. Martin and Dompl. (Open M-Th 8am-1pm and 2-4pm, F 8am-3pm.) Public **bathrooms** are at Dompl., the Esterházy Palace, and the parking lot behind Colmanpl. near the tourist office. The **post office** (tel. 622 71), on the corner of Pfarrg. and Semmelweise near the other end of Hauptstr., has package services and the best rates for traveler's checks. (Open M-F 7am-6pm, Sa 7am-1pm.) The **postal code** is A-7000. The **telephone code** is 02682.

ACCOMMODATIONS AND FOOD Consider Eisenstadt as a daytrip—with no youth hostel in the vicinity, *Privatzimmer* are the only budget option. Most are on the outer city limits and rent only during July and August. The youth hostels in **Vienna** (see p. 90), **Neusiedl am See** (see p. 136), and **Wiener Neustadt** are cheaper and only an hour away. During July and August, migrant hordes descend and reservations are a must. At **Wirtshaus zum Eder,** Hauptstr. 25 (tel. 626 45), in Hauptpl., you can engage in deep conversation over wine in an airy courtyard with oil paintings and pristine, white awnings. (Singles 440-590AS; doubles 590AS; triples 790AS. Breakfast included.) Although a bit of a steep climb from the town center, **Das Sportliche Haus,** Hotterweg 67 (tel. 623 26), offers super-clean rooms right in the middle of hilly terraced vineyards. The *Haus* specializes in accommodating soccer players, but welcomes all travelers who knock on its doors. To reach it, follow Bankg. from Hauptstr. and turn left when you hit Hotterweg. (Doubles 630AS. Breakfast, gym, and sports facilities included.)

Gasthaus Kiss, Neusiedlerstr. 34 (tel. 611 82), cooks up huge servings of hearty Austrian food in a snug inn. (Open M-F 8am-midnight, Sa 9am-1pm.) Borrowing its name from the famed Viennese haunt, **Café Central,** Hauptstr. 40 (tel. 75 22 34), is a pleasant, unassuming little café in a shady, tree-filled courtyard off the main street. A mainly student crowd consumes offerings like hot milk and rum (31AS) and filling tuna salads (42AS). Near the palace and across from the hospital, **Stüberl zum "alten Gewölbe,"** Esterházystr. 21 (tel. 738 13), features a daily *Menü* of homemade soup, entree, and dessert for 58AS. Sit down at a rustic pine table and quench your thirst with fresh-pressed carrot or apple juice for 15AS. (Open M-F 6:30am-6pm.) Or grab some big, cheap *Schnitzelsemmel*s (a mere 29AS) and other sandwiches at **Fischhandlung Gulusetti** (tel. 624 37), in the middle of Joseph Stanislaus Albechg. off the Hauptpl. The many **Heurigen** offer modest, generally affordable meals with their wines. Eisenstadt also has a few grocery stores: **Spar Markt,** Esterházystr. 38 and Bahnstr. 16-18 (both open M-F 7am-12:30pm and 2:30-6pm, Sa 7am-noon), and **Julius Meinl,** Hauptstr. 13 (open M-F 8am-6pm, Sa 7:30am-noon).

SIGHTS AND ENTERTAINMENT Built on the footings of the Kanizsai family's 14th-century fortress, the castle-turned-palace now known as **Schloß Esterházy** acquired its cheerful hue when the Hungarian Esterházy family showed allegiance to the great Austrian Empress in the 18th century by painting the building *Maria Theresien gelb* (Maria Theresian yellow). *(Tours Easter-Oct. daily every hr. 9am-4:30pm; Oct.-Easter M-F 40min. 50AS, students and seniors 30AS.)* More recently, the fabulously wealthy Esterházys, who still own the building, leased the family home to the Austrian provincial government, allowing the bureaucrats to occupy 40% of the castle while the family retrenched itself into the remaining 60%. When it bought its portion for 125,000AS, the government apparently overlooked the Esterházys's clause that made it responsible for renovation and maintenance costs. Rumor has it the government has spent more than 40 million *Schillings* on the upkeep of the Red Salon's silk tapestry alone. In the magnificent **Haydnsaal** (Haydn Hall), the hard-working composer conducted the court orchestra almost every night from 1761 to 1790. Classical musicians consider Haydnsaal an acoustic mecca. When the government took over the room, they removed the marble floor and replaced it with a wooden one. Now the room is so acoustically perfect that seats for concerts in the room are not numbered—supposedly every seat provides the same magnificent sound. Guest artists are invited to sing, but more often than not Haydn fills the hall. During tours of the *Schloß*, tourists are encouraged to lift their voices in song in order to test out the hall's sound properties. Even when the music stops, the room is an aristocratic symphony of red velvet, gold, monumental oil paintings, and woodwork.

Extending the town's Haydn obsession, **Haydnmatinees** (tel. 633 84 15; fax 633 84 20), from May to October feature four fine fellows, bewigged and bejeweled in Baroque costumes of imperial splendor, playing a half-hour of impeccable Haydn. *(Tu and F 11am in the palace. 80AS.)* The palace also hosts **Haydnkonzerte.** *(July-Aug. Th at 8pm; May-June and Sept.-Oct. Sa at 7:30pm. 160-320AS.)* True Haydn enthusiasts can wait for The Big One: the **International Haydntage,** featuring loads of concerts, operas, and large free video screenings of the best of past festival concerts outdoors near the *Schloß*. The festival runs from September 10 to 20. *(Tickets 200-1400AS.)* For more information and reserved tickets, contact festival officials (tel. 618 66; fax 618 05; email office@hadynfestival.at).

The *Kapellmeister* had a short commute to the concert hall each day: he lived just around the corner. His modest residence is now the **Haydn-Haus,** Haydng. 21 (tel. 626 52), exhibiting original manuscripts and other memorabilia. *(Open Easter-Oct. daily 9am-noon and 1-5pm. Guided tours by appointment. 20AS, students 10AS. Combination ticket for Haydn-Haus and Landesmuseum 40AS, students 20AS.)* After composing in Eisenstadt, Haydn now decomposes here. The *maestro* lies buried in the **Bergkirche** (tel. 626 38), placed there in 1932 after phrenologists removed his head to search for signs of musical genius on the skull's surface. Displayed at the Vienna Music Museum for years, the head was reunited with its body in 1954. Entrance to the Bergkirche includes admission to the **Kalvarienberg,** a pilgrimage annex housing the 14 Stations of the Cross. *(Open Easter-Oct. daily 9am-noon and 1-5pm. 25AS, students 10AS.)* The fixed, passionate expressions on the hand-carved Biblical figures' faces give this extended shrine a freakishly disturbing impact. It's worth it braving the statues in order to reach the church's rooftop stations, where you find a great view of surrounding Burgenland. Stand in the central nave and try to distinguish the real Doric columns from the *trompe l'oeil* paintings.

The **Jüdisches Museum,** Unterbergstr. 6 (tel. 651 45; email info@oejudmus.or.at; http://www.oejudmus.or.at/oejudmus), presents a history of Jewish life in Eisenstadt and the Burgenland region. *(Open May-Oct. T-Su 10am-5pm. 50AS; students 40AS.)* The Esterházys were known for their hospitality toward Jews, who played a major part in their rise to power. By settling Jews in Eisenstadt, they circumvented the law preventing Christians from lending money with interest. The museum's display is organized according to Jewish holidays and contains religious items dating from the 17th cen-

---

Eisenstadt's Jewish Community

The history of Jews in Eisenstadt is an extraordinary tale of growth and tragic downfall. As early as 1675, Prince Paul Esterházy was moved by the plight of the persecuted Jews and decided to shelter them as "Schutzjuden" (protected Jews) on his estates. From 1732 on, the Jewish quarter of Eisenstadt formed the prosperous independent community of "Unterberg-Eisenstadt," which remained unique in Europe until 1938. In that year, the Jews of the Burgenland were among the first to be affected by the deportation orders of the Nazis. Today, only two Jewish families remain in Eisenstadt.

tury. Once the home of an important community figure, the building still contains his original private synagogue space with a beautiful ark in the style of Empress Josephine as well as Gothic and Oriental murals from the early 1800s. Around the corner on Wertheimer-Str., near the hospital, is a small **Jewish cemetery** with headstones dating back several decades.

For a more frivolous afternoon, stop by the **Burgenländische Feuerwehrmuseum,** Leithabergstr. 41 (tel. 621 05). *(Open M-Th 8am-noon and 1-4pm, F 9am-1pm. 10AS, students 5AS.)* Austria's first fire-fighting museum displays tasseled fire-buggies—crossbreeds between a steam engine and a circus wagon. Also on hand are spectacular fire helmets worthy of Greek heroes.

Of course, leaving Eisenstadt without wine is like leaving Vienna without the *Sachertorte.* In early July the **Winzerkirtag Kleinhöflein** floods Hauptpl. with kegs, flasks, and bottles as local wineries attempt to sell their goods. Mid-August brings the **Festival of 1000 Wines,** when wineries from all over Burgenland crowd the palace's Orangerie with their Dionysian delicacies. If you like music with your wine, visit in June when the outdoor **Eisen Stadt Fest** provides all kinds of sounds, from *Schrammelmusik* to rock. At any other time of the year, fresh wine is available straight from the source in the wineries themselves. Most are small and aren't allowed to open for more than three weeks per year to sell their wine. Fear not—the wineries stagger their opening times so that wine is always available. To find out which *Buschenschank,* or *Schenkhaus,* is open, ask the tourist office for the schedule or look in the local newspaper. Most of the *Buschenschanken* are clustered in Kleinhöfler Hauptstr. For a little variety, friends of Haydn can also hit the **Lizst Fest** in late May. *(Get ticketed for 200-400AS.)*

NEUSIEDLER SEE

Covering 320 sq. km, the Neusiedler See is a vestige of the water that once blanketed the entire Pannenian Plain. With no outlets or inlets save underground springs, this steppe lake is only 2m at its deepest, receding periodically to expose thousands of square meters of dry land. Indeed, in the mid-19th century, the lake dried up entirely. Warm and salty, the lake is a haven for birds and humans alike. More than 250 species of waterfowl dwell in the thickets formed by its reeds, and every summer thousands of sun-hungry vacationers flock to its resorts for swimming, sailing, fishing, and cycling. **Cruises** on the Neusiedler See allow you to travel between Rust, Illmitz, and Mörbisch with your bike for about 60AS one-way and 100AS round-trip. **Gangl** (tel. (02175) 21 58 or 27 94) runs boats every hour from Illmitz to Mörbisch (May-Sept. 9am-6pm). In Mörbisch, **Schiffahrt Weiss** (tel. (02685) 83 24) cruises to Illmitz (every 30 min., May-Sept. 8:30am-9pm). For more information about the lake region, contact the Neusiedler See Regionalbüro at Hauptpl. 1, A-7100 Neusiedl am See (tel. (02167) 87 17; fax (02167) 26 37; email info@neusiedl-tourism.or.at; http://www.neusiedl-tourism.or.at/info-ns/).

■ Neusiedl am See

Less than an hour from Vienna by express train, Neusiedl am See is the gateway to the Neusiedler region. The principal attraction is the lake, not the town, so consider Neusiedl a day at the beach. There are two **train stations** in Neusiedl. The **Hauptbahnhof** is 15 minutes by foot from the town center. (Information and ticket window open 5am-9pm. Eisenstadt round-trip 17AS; Vienna one-way 68AS, round-trip 98AS.) To get to town, take a right on Bahnstr. and follow the road right onto Eisenstädterstr. (which becomes Obere Hauptstr.) and into Hauptpl. The other train station, **Neusiedl Bad,** is centrally located on Seestr., right at the end of Untere Hauptstr. The adjacent **bus station,** Seestr. 15a (tel. 24 06), offers a **Fahrradbus** (#1813) that carries bikers and bikes to and from Mörbisch, Neusiedl, and Illmitz. There's frequent service to Vienna (85AS) and Bruck an der Leitha (34AS).

The **tourist office** (tel. 22 29; fax 26 37), in the *Rathaus* on Hauptpl., distributes pamphlets, helps with accommodations, and offers advice on boat and bike rentals. (Open July-Aug. M-F 8am-7pm, Sa 10am-noon and 2-6pm, Su 4-7pm; May-June and Sept. M-F 8am-4:30pm; Oct.-Apr. M-Th 8am-noon and 1-4:30pm, F 8am-1pm.) **Raffeis-bank,** Untere Hauptstr. 3 (tel. 25 64), has the best rates for your ducats. (Open M-F 8am-12:30pm and 1:30-4pm.) Given the town layout, it may make your day easier to **rent a bike** at Seestr.-Schilfweg 3, by Pension "La Paloma." (1st day 200AS, additional days 100AS, 40AS per hr.) Or try the train station, which rents for 70AS per half-day and 90AS per day with train ticket, otherwise for 120AS and 150AS. **Store luggage** at the train station (30AS). Dial 133 in case of **emergency.** The **post office** is on the corner of Untere Hauptstr. and Lisztg. (Open M-F 8am-noon and 2-6pm, Sa 8-10am.) The **postal code** is A-7100, and the **telephone code** is 02167.

Heavy tourist activity, partly generated by Neusiedl's proximity to Vienna, makes finding accommodations tough. To reach the newly renovated **Jugendherberge Neusiedl am See (HI),** Herbergg. 1 (tel./fax 22 52), find Wienerstr. then take a left onto Goldbergg. The hostel is on the corner at Herbergg. It's an uphill walk, but don't get discouraged—renovations have equipped the hostel with a sauna and winter greenhouse in which to unlace your steaming boots and stretch toes. The hostel sports 86 beds in 20 quads and three doubles. There are showers in every room, but the bathrooms are in the hall. (161AS, under 19 145AS. Breakfast included. Sheets 15AS. Key deposit 100AS. Reception 8am-2pm and 5-8pm. Open Mar.-Oct. Reservations recommended.) **Gasthof zur Traube,** Hauptpl. 9 (tel. 24 23), has a cordial staff and pretty pink rooms with bath. (Singles 410AS; doubles 650AS. Breakfast included.) **Rathausstüberl** (tel. 28 83; fax 28 83 07), around the corner from the *Rathaus* on Kircheng., has a lovely shaded courtyard, great wine, and plenty of fresh fish and vegetarian dishes. (Entrees 70-150AS. Open Mar.-Dec. daily 10am-midnight.) Rathausstüberl doubles as a sunny *Pension.* (225-375AS per person with breakfast buffet. Reservations recommended.) On your way to the beach grab a picnic at the **Billa** grocery store on Seestr. (Open M-Th 7:30am-6:30pm, F 7:30am-8pm, Sa 7am-5pm.) **Rauchkuchl,** Obere Hauptstr. 57 (tel. 25 85), offers *Blaufränker* red wine or other homemade specialties as well as the opportunity to hear friendly Neusiedl's *mundart* dialect. (Open Tu-Sa 5-11pm.)

You're here, you've got your bathing suit and towel, now where's the **beach?** Head to the end of Seestr. (1km), or catch the bus from the *Hauptbahnhof* or Hauptpl. (every hr. until 6pm). The beach is a bit rocky, but pleasant (25AS, children 20AS). The **Segelschule Neusiedl am See** (tel. 34 00 44) at the docks on the far right will get you on the water on a sailboat (1hr. 140-340AS, half- or full-day 345-1730AS), dinghy (3- to 4-person boat 140AS per hr.), or standard surfboard (300AS for the weekend; open daily 8:30am-6pm). Close by on Seestr., find **motorboats** (140-200AS per hr.), **paddleboats** (80AS per hr.), and **rowboats** (40AS per hr.) at **Bootsvermietung Leban.** Neusiedl hosts a **Stadtfest** in August, bringing mostly modern music to town.

■ Rust

During the summer, tourists inundate the tiny wine capital of Austria to partake of the fruit of the vine. Ever since 1524, when the Emperor granted the wine-growers of Rust the exclusive right to mark the letter "R" on wine barrels, Rust has been synonymous with good—nay, really good—wine. The town is particularly known for sweet dessert wines, called *Ausbruch* (literally "break out"). They come from grapes allowed to dry toward raisinhood and sweeten up before the farmer "breaks out" the center and presses the juice. The quantity of dessicated grapes needed for a bottle is astounding, and consequently, so is the price. Income from the wine enabled the town to purchase its independence from Kaiser Leopold I in 1861. The price? 60,000 gold guilders and 36,000 liters of priceless *Ausbruch.* Wine isn't Rust's only attraction, however. The unspoiled town center with medieval houses and nesting storks and Rust's location on the Neusiedlersee make this town one of the most addictively beautiful places of the Austrian countryside.

ORIENTATION AND PRACTICAL INFORMATION Rust is 15km east of Eisenstadt on the Neusiedler See. By **car** from Vienna, take Autobahn A3 to Eisenstadt and then from Eisenstadt take Bundesstr. 52 straight into Rust. **Buses** run between Eisenstadt and Rust several times per day (34AS), and between Rust and Vienna (Wien Mitte/Landstr.) four times a day (120AS). Rust does not have a train station. The **bus station** is located just behind the post office at Franz-Josef-Pl. 14. To reach the *Fußgänger-zone* (whose *Fußgänger* status is sometimes disrupted by the gentle roar of tractors rumbling down village streets), leave the post office and turn left. You will almost immediately come to the intersection of Oggauerstr. and Conradpl. Take a left onto Conradpl. and go to a triangular plaza. There's the *Rathaus*. Inside, the **tourist office** (tel. 45 02 or 65 74; fax 502 10) hands out maps, plans bicycle tours, and gives information on wine tastings, the beach, and *Privatzimmer*. It also offers tours of its own on Rust's history, culture, wine, and storks. (Open M-F 9am-noon and 2-6pm, Sa 9am-noon, Su 10am-noon; Oct.-Apr. M-F 9am-noon and 1-4pm.) The hyper-bionic display board outside the tourist office shows all the best accomodations; green lights indicate vacancies and a convenient phone allows you free calls to hotels. The **Raiffeisen-kasse Rust,** Rathauspl. 5 (tel. 607 05), is the best place to **exchange money.** (Open M-F 8am-noon and 1:30-4pm.) The Raiffeisenkasse has a 24-hour **ATM. Reisebüro Bla-guss** in the *Rathaus* and **Ruster Freizeitcenter** (tel. 595) by the beach are open late and provide emergency currency exchange. Call **taxis** at 218 or 65 76. The **post office** exchanges money but not traveler's checks. (Open M-F 8am-noon and 2-6pm.) The **postal code** is A-7071, and the **telephone code** is 02685.

> Rust's phone system is being overhauled and numbers will be in flux during 1999.

ACCOMMODATIONS AND FOOD Rust has a new **youth hostel** at Conradpl. 1 (tel. 591; fax 59 14) on the beachfront near tennis courts and bike paths. Dorms range from 150-180AS per night. Reservations at plentiful *Privatzimmern* are strongly recommended during festival times. Some will not accept telephone reservations for a one-night stay, but most won't turn you away at the door if there's a free room. Be warned: prices rise in the high season. From April through October, there's always room for tent-dwellers at **Ruster Freizeitcenter** (tel. 595), which offers showers, washing machines, a game room, a playground, and a grocery store. (Reception 7:30am-10pm. 44-55AS, children 16-27AS; tent 38-44AS. Showers included.) The grounds are only five minutes from the beach, to which guests receive free entrance.

For the truly hungry, **Zum Alten Haus** (tel. 230), on the corner of Raiffenstr. and Franz Josefpl., serves up Superman portions of *Schnitzel* and salad for only 80AS. (Open Tu-Su 9am-10pm.) Since they're not selling wine to Kaiser Leopold anymore, the local vineyards have opted to open the ubiquitous restaurants called *Buschen-schanken*, offering cheap snacks and superb wine. To avoid a restaurant tax, *Buschenschanken* stay open six months per year; the calendar of openings is available at the tourist office. **Peter Schandl,** Hauptstr. 20 (tel. 265), lets guests luxuriate at elegant outdoor tables while eating their beautiful salads and drinking heavenly wine. The restaurant is a bit on the expensive end (wine from 16AS; 70AS for the classic *Ausbruch*), but it's a wonderful experience. (Open M and W-F 4pm-midnight, Sa-Su 11am-midnight.) Hung with corn-cobs, **Alte Schmiede** (tel. 467), Seezeile 24, has a courtyard roofed with grape vines and a rustic stone-and-wood interior. Listen to (often live) gypsy music while feasting on traditional Austrian food with a Hungarian twist or on a variety of vegetarian dishes. **A & O Markt Dreyseitel** (tel. 238) on Wein-bergg. between Mitterg. and Schubertg. sells the raw materials for a meal. (Open M-F 7am-noon and 3-6pm.)

SIGHTS AND ENTERTAINMENT Rust's *Altstadt* is one of the three in Austria to be named a "model city" by the Europa-Rat committee in Strasbourg (the others are Salzburg and Krems). The award praises Rust's architectural and natural preservation. Rust's dusty stucco lanes are quiet and slow, lined with shady elms whose name, *Szil*, is the root for the place-name Rust and the Hungarian version of the town's name.

Rust's **Fischerkirche,** around the corner from the tourist office, was built between the 12th and 16th centuries and is the oldest church in Burgenland. *(Open May-Sept. M-Sa 10am-noon and 2:30-6pm, Su 11am-noon and 2-4pm. Tours by appointment. Call Frau Kummer at 550. 10AS, students 5AS.)* In the 13th century, the church gained buildings when Queen Mary of Hungary, attempting to escape the Mongols, stranded herself on the Neusiedl See and was saved by a fisherman. Grateful Mary donated the *Nikolausbeneficium* and the *Marienkapelle,* a chapel within the church holding lovely 15th century sculptures of Madonna. Because Rust is such a small village, the Romanesque and Gothic sections have survived untouched by the ravages of Baroque remodeling. Beautiful medieval frescoes contrast with a crude brick floor. Rust also houses the only **Weinakademie** (tel. 64 51 or 453; fax 64 31) in Austria. *(Open for wine tastings F-Su 2-6pm. 60-80AS for 5-10 tastes.)* The institution offers courses in everything from wine cultivation to basic bartending and legal points. They also hold wine tours and tastings. The offices are at Hauptstr. 31. Many vintners *(Weinbauern)* offer wine tastings and tours of their cellars and vineyards: **Rudolf Beilschmidt,** Weinbergg. 1 (tel. 326) has tours May through September on Fridays at 5pm. **Weingut Marienhof,** Weinbergg. 16 (tel. 251), also offers vineyard tours and tastings every Tuesday from April through September at 6pm for 60AS.

Just Storky

Since 1910, Rust's storks have been attracted to the high chimneys of the Bürger houses, and at one point in 1960 nearly 40 pairs were nesting in the old city. Soon, however, locals noticed a decline and began to voice their concern over the dwindling number of these endangered birds. In 1987, Rust and the World Wildlife Federation initiated a special joint program to protect and reestablish the birds. The storks eat mainly frogs, fish, snakes, and beetles—critters found among Neusiedler See's reedy marshes. When the reeds grew too tall, the storks had difficulty finding food. The city of Rust therefore borrowed cattle from another part of Austria and plunked them down in the marshes to act as natural lawnmowers. Blue placards mark the houses with chimneys that the storks habitually return to nest in.

Sun bunnies can lounge and splash on the south shore of the **Neusiedler See.** There is a **public beach** (tel. 591) complete with showers, lockers, restrooms, phones, water slide, and snack bar (30AS per person, after 4pm 70AS). Though the murky waters of the lake daunt some swimmers, the water is actually of drinking quality. The muddy color comes from the shallow, easily disturbed clay bottom (the deepest section is 2m). For wimps who remain unconvinced, the beach also has a chlorine pool. Be sure to keep the entrance card—you'll need it to exit the park again. To reach the beach, walk down Hauptstr., take a left onto Am Seekanal, then a right onto Seepromenade, which cuts through all of the marsh lands (about 7km) surrounding the perimeter of the lake. These marsh reeds (sometimes almost 2m high) create a bug-infested beach inconvenient for bathing anywhere other than at the designated areas. **Storks,** however, thrive on this vegetation—see if you can spot their chimney-nests, which are considered good luck. The storks come to Rust at the end of March, and from the end of May you can see the (stork) babies in the nests. The chicks stay home for two months before flying away and beginning their adult lives. The storks have also hatched a second post office, the **Storks' Post Office,** A-7073 Rust, at the *Rathaus.* Its stork postmark provides funds to support the birds.

If lounging at the beach strikes you as too inactive, try **renting a boat** from **Family Gmeiner** (tel. 493 or (62683) 55 38), next to the beach on the water's edge. **Sailboats** are 60AS per hour or 270AS for five hours. **Paddleboats** are 70AS per hour and 310AS for five hours. **Electric boats** are 110AS per hour and 330AS for five hours. The same company runs **Schiffsrundfahrten** (boat tours) that can transport you to Illmitz on the opposite shore. *(Boats leave Rust Apr.-Oct. Th-Su and holidays at 10am and 4pm and return from Illmitz at 11am and 5pm.)* Besides swimming, boating, and bird-watching, tourists flock to the Neusiedler See area to **bike.** The lake area is criss-crossed with bicycle routes, many along the lake shore or winding in and out of the little towns of both Austria and Hungary. The route is about 170km long, but those out for less intense biking can do a section and then take the bus back, or take the Illwitz boat to the opposite shore and then bicycle back.

■ Near Rust: Mörbisch

The tiny village of Mörbisch lies 5km along the Neusiedler See to the south, the last settlement on the western shore of the lake before the Hungarian border. **Buses** from Eisenstadt to Mörbisch leave every two hours (38AS). Many buses also go through the Rust-Mörbisch stretch (18AS) on their way to other places. A walk or bike from Rust along the 6km country lane to Mörbisch is extremely pleasant (about 1½hr. by foot) and provides a fantastic foray into the countryside. Small vineyard tractors and the worn-out country bikes of the vineyard wives weave past on the road. Notice the *Hütterhütte* (stone huts) where young men would spend weeks in solitude, guarding grapes from human and birdian trespassers. The village is centered around Hauptstr., where the **tourist office** lies at #23 (tel. (02685) 88 56; fax 843 09). Pick up very helpful brochures on Mörbisch and the surrounding Burgenland, as well as a list of accommodations. (Open 9am-noon and 1-6pm; Nov.-Feb. M-Th 9am-3pm.) The town has its own beach, which includes a floating theater that hosts an operetta festival each summer—the **Mörbisch Seefestspiele.** The operetta slated for 1999 is *Eine Nacht in Venedig* (A Night in Venice) by Strauss. Performances float atop the lake most Thursdays and every Friday, Saturday, and Sunday from mid-July to the end of August. Tickets are 200AS to 800AS. **Blaguss Reisen** (tel. (01) 50 18 00) in Vienna arranges a shuttle bus to Mörbisch at 6pm from Wiener Hauptstr. 15 in Vienna. It returns after the fat lady has sung (round-trip 180AS).

There are many *Pensionen* and *Privatzimmer* in Mörbisch, but for a sunny room and cheerful surroundings less than five minutes from downtown, stay at **Winzerhof Schindler,** Kinog. 9 (tel./fax 83 18). Taste their homegrown wine and grape juice on a seaside terrace. (300-350AS per person. 15AS surcharge for 1-night stays. Breakfast included. Open Apr.-Nov.)

Mörbisch is truly a wine town, and never is this more evident than during the **Weinfesttage** just before the opening of the *Seefestspiele*—the main street becomes one large *Heurige* and thousands flock to the little town from Vienna. During the **Weinblutenfest** in mid-June, visitors can ride a horse-drawn carriage from one vineyard to the other, stopping at each to sample the wine (100AS per person).

THE DANUBE (DONAU)

The "Blue Danube" may largely be the invention of Johann Strauss's imagination, but this mighty, muddy-green river still merits a look. The Danube was once Europe's most important trade conduit, and the *Nibelungenlied* sagas made famous by Wagner took place along its shores. You can glide between its banks on a ferry or pedal furiously along its shores on a bike—either way, you'll experience the exhilarating, fluid beauty of Austria's most famous river.

The legendary **Erste Donau Dampfschiffahrts-Gesellschaft** (DDSG—creators of the longest known German word in existence, *Donaudampfschifffahrtgesellschaftkapitänswitwe,* which translates as "the widow of a captain working for the Danube Steamship Company") runs ships every day from May to late October. The firm operates an office in **Vienna,** II, Friedrichstr. 7 (tel. 58 88 00; fax 58 88 04 40; email ddsg.blue.danube@telecom.at; http://www.ddsg-blue-danube.at). Elsewhere, tickets are available at most tourist offices. The **ferries** run from Vienna to **Krems, Melk, Dürnstein, Tulln,** and the **Wachau valley** (many options available, most run 120-440AS). **Hydrofoils** will take you to **Bratislava** (1¾hr., 230AS, round-trip 350AS) or **Budapest** (5-6hr., 750AS, round-trip 1100AS). Eurailpasses win a 20% discount on travel within Austria, and families may travel for half-price (min. one parent and one child ages 6-15; under 6 travel free with a parent). Contact the DDSG or local tourist offices for special ship/bus and ship/train ticket combinations. Specialty tours include the "Nibelungen," which goes through the areas described in the ancient saga, a summer solstice cruise *(Sonnendfahrt),* which steams by the Midsummer's Night bonfires in the Wachau valley, and a *Heurigen* Ride with a live *Liederabend* trio. Other exciting options include the hearty "Pork at its Best" cruise, as well as a trip past Hundertwasser's most famous monuments on a boat designed by the Austrian eco-architect himself.

Cyclists should take advantage of the **Lower Danube Cycle Track,** a velocipede's Valhalla. This riverside bike trail between Vienna and Passau links most Danube villages, and offers captivating views of crumbling castles, latticed vineyards, and medieval towns. Area tourist offices carry the route map and bike rental information—you can **rent bikes** at the Melk, Spitz, and Krems train stations. Bike transport is free.

Between Krems and Melk along the Vienna-Grein bike route, numerous ruined castles testify to Austria's quite dignified historical pedigree. One of the most dramatic fortresses is the 13th-century **Burg Aggstein-Gastein,** which commands the Danube. The castle was formerly inhabited by Scheck von Wald, a robber-baron known to fearful sailors as **Schreckenwalder** (terrible forest man). The lord was wont to impede the passage of ships with ropes stretched across the Danube and then demand tribute from his ensnared victims.

■ Krems and Stein

Located in the Danube valley at the head of the Wachau region, a region known particularly for its rich wine heritage, Krems and Stein are surrounded by lush, green hills filled with terraced vineyards. Historically, Krems and Stein shared a mayor to coordinate trade and military strategy on the critical Danube trading route, and through the years the two towns have grown into each other's territories. Much of the region's wealth came from the tolls on this riverbend's Danube traders—no wonder the Kremser Penny was the first coin minted by the Habsburgs.

Stein, the medieval half of this duo, seems still to live in the first millennium—its crooked, narrow, cobblestone passages twist and wind back on themselves. A few steps to the east, the stuccoed walls of **Krems** have a frivolously pastel charm, channeling wanderers to a modern, shop-filled *Fußgängerzone* (when medieval Stein's your neighbor, Baroque *is* modern).

In the same valley, vineyards give rise to 120 different wines and, in years past, were the stomping-ground of French wine legend **Hans Moser.** Moser developed the now-standard **"raised vine" technique,** raising the poor things from whence they had lain, technologically impaired, for centuries. Head for **Kellergasse,** the high street in Stein that lies next to those hills of plenty, where *Heurigen* offer the fruit of these vines as well as great views of the **Stift Göttweig** (abbey) across the Danube.

ORIENTATION AND PRACTICAL INFORMATION Most visitors arrive on bicycles, but the **train station** is a five-minute walk from Krems's *Fußgängerzone.* Stein is west of Krems. Exit out the front door of the *Bahnhof,* cross Ringstr., and continue straight on Dinstlstr., which leads to the *Fußgängerzone.* The station has **lockers** for 30AS, **luggage storage,** and **bike rental** (tel. 825 36 44; 150AS per day, 120AS per half-day; with train ticket 120AS, 70AS). Regional trains connect Krems to **Vienna** (Spittelau station; 139AS) through Tulln. Travelers to other big cities must change trains in St. Pölten. Right in front of the station is a **bus depot,** with routes to Melk and St Pölten. Krems lies along the popular **DDSG ferry** route from **Passau** through **Linz** and **Melk** to **Vienna** (for information, see p. 139). The ferry station is on the riverbank close to Stein and the ÖAMTC campground, near the intersection of Donaulände and Dr.-Karl-Dorreck-Str. To reach Krems from the landing, walk down Donaulände until it becomes Ringstr. and then take a left onto Utzstr. To reach Stein, follow Dr.-Karl-Dorreck-Str. and then take a left onto Steiner Landstr.

The **tourist office** is housed in the Kloster Und at Undstr. 6 (tel. 826 76; fax 700 11; http://www.krems.gv.at). From the train station, take a left on Ringstr. and continue

(10min.) to Martin-Schmidt-Str. Turn right and follow the street to the end; the office is across the street and to the right. The excellent staff has amassed tons of information on accommodations, sports, and entertainment, as well as the indispensable *Heurigen Kalendar,* which lists the opening times of regional wine taverns. Guided walking tours in several languages leave for Krems or Stein (1½hr., 600AS per group or 20AS per person if more than 20 people show up). They also book hotel reservations. (Open Easter-Oct. M-F 9am-6pm, Sa-Su 10am-noon and 1-6pm.) **ATMs** dot the shopping streets, but the **post office** also offers **currency exchange** (tel. 826 06) and is right off Ringstr. on Brandströmstr. (Open M-F 8am-noon and 2-6pm, Sa 8-11am.) You can **rent bikes** at the Donau Campground (half-day 40AS, full-day 60AS) and the train station (90AS per day, with ticket 40AS). **Public toilets** are at the tourist office and in Stadtpark. The town **postal code** is A-3500. The **telephone code** is 02732.

ACCOMMODATIONS AND FOOD

No matter where you stay, ask your hosts for a **guest card** that grants a number of discounts. The **Jugendherberge Radfahrer (HI),** Ringstr. 77 (tel. 834 52; for advance bookings, call the central office in Vienna at 586 41 45 or fax at 586 41 453), is a clean hostel accommodating 52 in comfortable four- and six-bed rooms. (Members only. Dorms 180AS. 20AS surcharge on stays less than 3 nights. Tax, breakfast, bicycle storage, and sheets included. Lockers 10AS. Reception 7-9:30am and 5-8pm. Open Apr.-Oct.) Karl and Ingred Hietzgern's **Baroque Burgerhaus,** Untere Landstr. 53 (tel./fax 761 84 or 740 36), lies in the *Altstadt* of Krems. The building was three small houses in the Middle Ages, joined with one facade in the Baroque period. The Hietzgerns have filled the house with *Jugendstil* furniture and hand-painted wood and will happily tell you about anything and everything Krems. (2- and 3-bed dorms with shower 270-295AS; 25AS surcharge for 1 night stays; open July-Aug.) Although slightly more expensive, Krem's centrally located **Gasthof Zur Alte Post,** Obere Landstr. 32 (tel. 822 76; fax 843 96), can host you comfortably amid its old doll collection, dark velvet couches, terry-cloth curtains, and garden café. (Singles 320-340AS, with shower 480AS; doubles 620-820AS. Breakfast included.) *Privatzimmer* abound on Steiner Landstr. **ÖAMTC Donau Camping,** Wiedeng. 7 (tel. 844 55), sits between a grassy Danube riverbank and the highway. (50AS per person plus 10.50AS tax, children 35AS; tents 30-60AS (bring your own); cars 40AS. Reception 7:30-10am and 4:30-7pm. Showers included. Electrical hookup 25AS. Facilities for disabled guests. English spoken. Open Easter to mid-Oct.)

The area around the pedestrian zone overflows with restaurants and streetside cafés. **Schwarze Kuchl,** Untere Landstr. 8 (tel. 831 28), offers a salad buffet (small 38AS, large 48AS), assorted goulashes (20-30AS), and bread. (Open M-F 8am-7pm, Sa 8am-1pm, 1st Sa of the month until 5pm.) Right next door is the famous **Café-Konditorei Hagmann** (tel. 83 167; http://www.hagmann.co.at/konditorei), known throughout Krems for its outstanding pastries and chocolates. Try the *Marillenstrudel* (28AS), but beware—you may find yourself returning for breakfast, lunch, and dinner. Grab a *Wachauer Kugel* (ball of chocolate and nougat) for the road. (Open M-F 7am-7pm, Sa 7am-1pm, 1st Sa of the month until 6pm.) At **Haus Resch,** Kellerg. 40 (tel. 826 36), you can tipple the strong wines (only 18AS for a quarter liter!) right in the vineyard. To round off your decadence, share the cheese platter with a friend (48AS). **Haus Hamböck,** Kellerg. 31 (tel. 845 68), in Stein, has a charming leafy terrace with a view of the town's spires and a restaurant bedecked with old *Faß* (kegs), presses, and other vineyard tools. The jolly proprietor gives free tours of the cellar, with a free tasting. (Wine 22AS a glass, snacks 30-50AS. Open daily 3pm 'til people leave.) The cheapest eats in town are available at the **Julius Meinl** supermarket, in front of the train station or on the corner of Gaheisstr. and Obere Landstr. (Open M-F 7:30am-6:30pm, Sa 7:30am-5pm.)

SIGHTS AND ENTERTAINMENT

In Stein, almost every building is on **Steiner Landstraße,** a stunningly preserved vestige of the Middle Ages. Don't stop here, however—climb the hills. Above Krems and Stein, the lovely terraced vineyards, with the vines photosynthesizing in neat little rows, tempt travelers to seek a bottle of wine and a patch of grass in the sun. The **Heurigen** (wine cellars) are not to be missed.

Plan carefully, however—the cellars can stay open only three weeks every two months from April to October. Better-safe-than-sorry types pick up a schedule from the tourist office; press-your-luck gamblers just stroll down Kellerg. in Stein and hope to happen upon on an open cellar. If you don't have time for *Heurigen,* stop by the city-owned **Weingut Stadt Krems,** Stadtgraben 11 (tel. 80 14 40; fax 80 14 42), on the edge of the pedestrian zone. *(Open for tours M-F 8am-noon and 1-4pm, Sa 8am-noon.)* This winery lacks the attached restaurant, but it does offer free tours of the cellar and bottling center. The free tastings that follow the tour usually seduce one or two visitors into buying a bottle of wine, which runs 40-100AS. Those who can still walk straight should lurch down to the historic abbey cellar of **Kloster Und,** Undstr. 6 (tel. 730 73; fax 832 23 78), by the tourist office. *(Open June 10-Aug.)* The cellar has all of Austria's regional wines—for 140AS, you get a basket of bread, mineral water to cleanse the palate, and two hours to weave through the selection of more than 100 wines, from the noble Riesling of Wachau to the nutty Neuburger of Burgenland. Bring a sweater—dry white wines complain if not kept at 10 to 11 degrees Celsius.

Built in the Dominekanerkloster, the excellent **Weinstadt Museum,** Kornermarkt 14 (tel. 80 14 41), features a curious combination of paintings by the world-renowned Baroque artist Marten Johann Schmidt and, in the cloister cellars, archaeological treasures from the Paleolithic Era through the Middle Ages. *(Open Mar.-Nov. M-Sa 1-6pm, Su 9am-6pm. 30AS.)* Most charming are the many exhibits about the history, practice, and religious symbolism of viticulture.

Krems's *Fußgängerzone,* the center of mercantile activity, runs down Obere and Untere Landstr. The entrance to the pedestrian area is marked by the **Steiner Tor,** one of four medieval city gates flanked by two Gothic towers. Various market places line Obere Landstr. The first is Dominikanerpl., which houses the **Dominikaner Kirche,** now the Weinstadt Museum. Farther down the pedestrian zone is **Pfarrkirche Platz,** home of the Renaissance **Rathaus** and the **Pfarrkirche** with its piece-meal Romanesque, Gothic, and Baroque architecture. While there, walk up the hill to the **Piaristen-Kirche,** where newly renovated, life-sized statues depict Jesus' crucifixion. Finally, at the end of the pedestrian zone is the **Simandlbrunnen,** a fountain depicting a husband kneeling in front of his domineering wife, begging for the house keys so he can stay out late with the boys.

The Wyse Women of Krems

The Burgenland is packed not only with yellow remnants of the Habsburg days, but also a few memento mori from prehistoric times. Krems rates as one of the top paleontology centers in Austria, and its researchers have recently unearthed the remains of a 32,000-year-old hunting community settled in the Danube bend near a place now named Galgenberg. Among the usual shards of bone and clay animal figurines, archaeologists excavated eight pieces of slate that, when fitted together, form a well-endowed female statuette. Fanny von Galgenberg, named for the famous dancer Fanny Elßler, is Austria's oldest known work of art and the world's only known female sculpture from the Aurignae Period. Barely three inches tall and half an inch thick, the figure is engraved with sketches and positioned in a pose that classifies her as part of the archetypal prehistoric Venus figures, like her much younger sister symbol of fertility, the "Venus of Willendorf," who was found between Krems and Melk. Even younger, but still quite old, is the Simandl fountain in Krems's *Fußgängerzone.* The fountain's statue depicts a pleading man kneeling before his robust, stern wife. In Renaissance Krems, the women held such influence over their men that they closed down the Simandl brotherhood, a small town fraternity of carousing and late-night debauchery.

Culturally, the double city enjoys a number of theater and music events, as well as other rotating exhibits. The **Kunsthalle Krems,** Steiner Landstr. 8 (tel. 826 69; fax 826 69 16), has recently opened a new building on the corner of Steiner Landstr. and Dr.-Karl-Dorreck-Str., near Stein. *(Open Th-Su 10am-6pm. 40-90AS, discounts for students and seniors.)* The large exhibition hall always has a large cultural or historical exhibit, usually on interesting postmodern or non-European art. The **Motorrad-Museum Krems-Egelsee**, idling at Ziegelofeng. 1 (tel. 41 30 13), will keep the moto-maniac in you entranced for an afternoon. *(Open daily 9am-5pm. 40AS, students 20AS.)* The museum features an extraordinary collection of exhibits on the history of motorcycles and motor technology. Each year the one-day **Donaufestival** brings open-air music and dancing at the end of June and kicks off a summer of cultural activities that includes theater, circus, symposia, *Lieder*, folk music, and even flamenco. From July 15 to August 15, Krems hosts a **Musikfest**, featuring a number of organ, piano, and quartet concerts that take place in the Kunsthalle and various churches. Tickets are available at the Kulturamt, Körnermarkt 4 (tel. 80 15 60), and Österreichticket (tel. (01) 536 01). Throughout the year, many **churches** have sacred music and organ concerts, which resonate beautifully within Gothic vaults and are usually free.

▓ Melk

The enormous yellow mass of Melk's monastery floats over dark blue Danube waters and stucco houses of the village below in one of the most surreal vistas you'll find in Austria. Melk's eerie monastery was constructed atop the cliffs on March 24, 1089, when Austrian Margrave Leopold II turned over the land to Benedictine Abbot Sigibod, begetting the Benedictine Monastery and, subsequently, the village of Melk. The monastery was a renowned ecclesiastical force in the medieval world, famed for its monumental library and learned monks (who incidentally merited several admiring references in Umberto Eco's novel *The Name of the Rose*). Today, the site is known more for its gorgeous scenery; over 400,000 folks visit Melk each year as a daytrip from Vienna or a stop on the Passau-Vienna cycling route. Nevertheless, Melk remains a living monastery, home to 25 monks who toil away, praying, brewing drinks, and teaching Austrian youth at the highly scholastic monastery school. Below the abbey, life putters along by the Renaissance houses in narrow pedestrian zones, cobblestone streets, old towers, and remnants of the medieval city wall.

ORIENTATION AND PRACTICAL INFORMATION **Trains** link Melk to Vienna's Westbahnhof (1½hr., 145AS) although you will have to switch trains in St. Pölten first. **Bike rental** (150AS for full day, 120AS for half-day; with rail ticket 90AS, 70AS), **currency exchange,** and **luggage storage** (30AS) are all available at the station. Just outside the station's main entrance is the **bus depot.** Bus #1451 chugs from Melk to Krems (80AS) and #1538 from Melk to St. Pölten (46AS). Melk lies on the **DDSG ferry** route between Vienna and Passau (from Vienna 530AS; from Krems 238AS; for more information, see p. 139).

Melk's **tourist office** (tel. 523 07 32 or 23 07 33; fax 523 07 37), on the corner of Babenbergerstr. and Abbe-Stadler-G. next to the Rathauspl., has maps and pamphlets on the town's history and athletic activities in the Wachau region. The office has large **lockers** (10AS) and bike racks. It also makes room reservations for free. From the train station, walk down Bahnhofstr. and then straight on Bahng. Turn right at Rathauspl. and cross it, staying to the right side until you hit Abbe-Stadler-G. (Open July-Aug. daily 9am-7pm; Sept.-Oct. and Apr.-June M-F 9am-noon and 2-6pm, Sa 10am-2pm.) The **post office** is at Bahnhofstr. 3. (Open M-F 8am-noon and 2-6pm, Sa 8-10am.) The **postal code** is A-3390. The **telephone code** is 02752.

ACCOMMODATIONS AND FOOD The recently renovated **Jugendherberge,** Abt-Karl-Str. 42 (tel. 526 81; fax 542 57), is about a 10-minute walk from the train station (turn right as you exit and follow the green signs). The friendly hostel offers 104 beds with picnicky checkered sheets in quads with private showers and hall toilets. In summer, guests can eat outside in an ivy-hung yard or make use of the ping-pong tables, volleyball net, and soccer area. (Dorms 174.50AS; under 19 140AS. Tax 10.50AS. Breakfast and bicycle storage included. Reception 8-10am and 5-9pm. Open Apr.-Oct.) *Privatzimmer* are another option—the tourist office has a list. **Camping Kolomaniau** (tel. 532 91) overlooks the Danube next to the ferry landing. To get

LOWER AUSTRIA

LOWER AUSTRIA

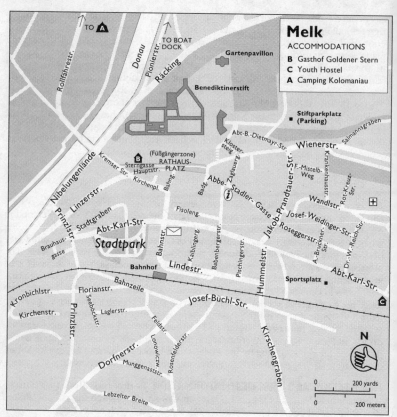

there, follow Kremserstr. to the Danube, cross the bridge, and keep right along Roll-fährestr. (35AS, children 20AS; tents 35AS; cars 25AS. Tax 10.50AS. Showers 15AS. Reception 8am-midnight.) **Gasthof Goldener Stern,** Sterng. 17 (tel. 522 14; fax 522 14 44), has respectable rooms and hearty Austrian fare at its downstairs restaurant. Try a vegetable *Pfannegerichte,* brought to the table in the pan—a full month's sup-ply of vitamins and cheese for only 85AS. (Singles 320AS; doubles 520AS. Discounts on stays over 2 days. Breakfast included. Reception 7am-midnight. Fax reservations.)

Restaurants abound on Rathauspl., but look elsewhere for the less tourist-oriented

---

Clemens and Friedrich: Holier than Wood?

In the fourth century, the bodies of early Christian martyrs persecuted by the Romans would be hidden in the catacombs, their graves marked by urns of blood. When people found urns of blood by a tomb (as with Clemens and Friedrich, the two housed in the side altar of Melk's abbey church), they knew they'd found a saint. By the 18th century, a major relic cult was flourishing, helped by the stipulation that a church could not be consecrated without a saint's remains. Traffic in relics of every conceivable body part raged. Not that Melk needed skeletons: the Melker Kreuz contains something that suffices quite nicely—a highly polished, thumbnail-sized piece of wood believed to be from the Holy Cross itself.

---

joints. A five-minute walk west through Hauptpl. brings you to **Restaurant zum "Alten Brauhof,"** Linzerstr. 25 (tel. 522 96), with charming outdoor seating that

If you're stuck for cash on your travels, don't panic. Millions of people trust Western Union to transfer money in minutes to 153 countries and over 45,000 locations worldwide. Our record of safety and reliability is second to none. So when you need money in a hurry, call Western Union.

WESTERN UNION | MONEY TRANSFER®

The fastest way to send money worldwide.®

MCI Spoken Here

Here

Worldwide Calling Made Simple

For more information or to apply for a Card call: **1-800-955-0925**

Outside the U.S., call MCI collect (reverse charge) at: **1-916-567-5151**

International Calling As Easy As Possible.

Calling Card

123 456 7890 1234
J.D. SMITH

WorldPhone

The MCI Card with WorldPhone Service is designed specifically to keep you in touch with the people that matter the most to you.

The MCI Card with WorldPhone Service....

- Provides access to the US and other countries worldwide.
- Gives you customer service 24 hours a day
- Connects you to operators who speak your language
- Provides you with MCI's low rates and no sign-up fees

For more information or to apply for a Card call:
1-800-955-0925

Outside the U.S., call MCI collect (reverse charge) at:
1-916-567-5151

Pick Up the Phone, Pick Up the Miles.

You earn frequent flyer miles when you travel internationally, why not when you call internationally? Callers can earn frequent flyer miles if they sign up with one of MCI's airline partners:

- American Airlines
- Continental Airlines
- Delta Airlines
- Hawaiian Airlines
- Midwest Express Airlines
- Northwest Airlines
- Southwest Airlines
- United Airlines
- USAirways

And, it's simple to call home.

1. Dial the WorldPhone toll-free access number of the country you're calling from (listed inside).

2. Follow the voice instructions in your language of choice or hold for a WorldPhone operator.
   - Enter or give the operator your MCI Card number or call collect.

3. Enter or give the WorldPhone operator your home number.

4. Share your adventures with your family!

Your MCI Worldphone Access Numbers

COUNTRY	WORLDPHONE TOLL-FREE ACCESS #
# Singapore	8000-112-112
# Slovak Republic (CC)	00421-00112
# Slovenia	080-8808
# South Africa (CC)	0800-99-0011
# Spain (CC)	900-99-0014
# Sri Lanka (Outside of Colombo, dial 01 first)	440100
# St. Lucia ÷	1-800-888-8000
# St. Vincent	1-800-888-8000
# Sweden (CC) ♦	020-795-922
# Switzerland (CC) ♦	0800-89-0222
# Syria	0800
# Taiwan (CC) ♦	0080-13-4567
# Thailand ★	001-999-1-2001
# Trinidad & Tobago ÷	1-800-888-8000
# Turkey (CC) ♦	00-8001-1177
# Turks and Caicos ÷	1-800-888-8000
# Ukraine (CC) ÷	8▼10-013
# United Arab Emirates ♦	800-111
# United Kingdom (CC) To call using BT ■	0800-89-0222
To call using C&W ■	0500-89-0222
# United States (CC)	1-800-888-8000
# Uruguay	000-412
# U.S. Virgin Islands (CC)	1-800-888-8000
# Vatican City (CC)	172-1022
# Venezuela (CC) ♦ ÷	800-1114-0
Vietnam ●	1201-1022
Yemen	008-00-102

#	Automation available from most locations.
(CC)	Country-to-country calling available to/from most international locations.
◆	Limited availability.
÷	Wait for second dial tone.
▶	When calling from public phones, use phones marked LADATEL.
■	International communications carrier.
★	Not available from public pay phones.
●	Public phones may require deposit of coin or phone card for dial tone.
▲	Local service fee in U.S. currency required to complete call.
♦	Regulation does not permit Intra-Japan calls.
÷	Available from most major cities

MCI

The MCI Card with WorldPhone Service... The easy way to call when traveling worldwide.

MCI · Calling Card
123 456 7890 1234
J.D. SMITH
WorldPhone

For more information or to apply for a Card call:
1-800-955-0925

Outside the U.S., call MCI collect (reverse charge) at:
1-916-567-5151

Please cut out and save this reference guide for convenient U.S. and worldwide calling with the MCI Card with WorldPhone Service.

COUNTRY	WORLDPHONE TOLL-FREE ACCESS #
American Samoa	633-2MCI (633-2624)
#Antigua (available from public card phones only)	1-800-888-8000
#Argentina (CC)	0800-5-1002
#Aruba ÷	800-888-8
#Australia (CC) ◆ To call using OPTUS ■	1-800-551-1111
To call using TELSTRA ■	1-800-881-100
#Austria (CC) ◆	022-903-012
#Bahamas	1-800-888-8000
#Bahrain	800-002
#Barbados	1-800-888-8000
#Belarus (CC) From Brest, Vitebsk, Grodno, Minsk	8-800-103
From Gomel and Mogilev	8-10-800-103
#Belgium (CC) ◆	0800-10012
#Belize From Hotels	815
From Payphones	557
#Bermuda ÷	1-800-888-8000
#Bolivia (CC) ◆	0-800-2222
#Brazil (CC)	000-8012
#British Virgin Islands ÷	1-800-888-8000
#Brunei	800-011
#Bulgaria	00800-0001
#Canada (CC)	1-800-888-8000
#Cayman Islands	1-800-888-8000
#Chile (CC) To call using CTC ■	800-207-300
To call using ENTEL ■	800-360-180
#China ◆	108-17
For a Mandarin-speaking Operator	108-12
#Colombia (CC)	980-16-0001
Collect Access in Spanish	980-16-1000
#Costa Rica ◆	0800-012-2222
#Cote D'Ivoire	1001
#Croatia (CC) ★	0800-22-0112
#Cyprus ◆	080-90000
#Czech Republic (CC) ◆	00-42-000112
#Denmark (CC) ◆	8001-0022
#Dominica	1-800-888-8000
#Dominican Republic	1-800-888-8000
Collect Access	1121
Collect Access in Spanish	1-800-888-8000
#Ecuador (CC) ÷	999-170
#Egypt (CC) ÷ (Outside of Cairo, dial 02 first)	355-5770
El Salvador	800-1767

COUNTRY	WORLDPHONE TOLL-FREE ACCESS #
#Federated States of Micronesia	624
#Fiji	004-890-1002
#Finland (CC) ◆	08001-102-80
#France (CC) ◆	0800-99-0019
#French Antilles (CC) ◆ (Includes Martinique, Guadeloupe)	0800-99-0019
#French Guiana (CC)	0-800-99-0011
#Gabon	00-005
#Gambia ◆	00-1-199
#Germany (CC) ◆	0-800-888-8000
#Greece (CC) ◆	00-800-1211
#Grenada ÷	1-800-888-8000
#Guam (CC)	1-800-888-8000
#Guatemala (CC) ◆	99-99-189
#Guyana	177
#Haiti ÷	193
Collect Access in French/Creole	190
#Honduras ÷	8000-122
#Hong Kong (CC)	800-96-1121
#Hungary (CC) ◆	00▼800-01411
#Iceland (CC) ÷	800-9002
#India (CC) ◆	000-127
Collect Access	000-126
#Indonesia (CC) ◆	001-801-11
#Iran ÷	(SPECIAL PHONES ONLY)
#Ireland (CC)	1-800-55-1001
#Israel (CC)	1-800-940-2727
#Italy (CC) ◆	172-1022
#Jamaica ÷	1-800-888-8000
Collect Access	873
#Japan (CC) ◆ To call using KDD ■ (from Special Hotels only)	00539-121▼
(from public phones)	*2
Collect Access	
To call using IDC ■	0066-55-121
To call using ITJ ■	0044-11-121
#Jordan	18-800-001
#Kazakhstan (CC)	8-800-131-4321
#Kenya ◆	080011
#Korea (CC) To call using KT ■	009-14
To call using DACOM ■	00309-12
To call using ONSE ■	00369-14
Phone Booths÷ Press red button, 03, then *	
Military Bases	550-2255
#Kuwait	800-MCI (800-624)

COUNTRY	WORLDPHONE TOLL-FREE ACCESS #
#Lebanon (CC) Collect Access	600-MCI (600-624)
#Liechtenstein (CC) ◆	0800-89-0222
#Luxembourg (CC)	0800-0112
#Macedonia (CC)	99800-4266
#Malaysia (CC) ◆	1-800-80-0012
#Malta	0800-89-0120
#Marshall Islands	1-800-888-8000
#Mexico (CC) Avantel	01-800-021-8000
Telmex ▲	001-800-674-7000
Collect Access in Spanish	01-800-021-1000
#Monaco (CC) ◆	800-90-019
#Montserrat	1-800-888-8000
#Morocco	00-211-0012
#Netherlands (CC) ◆	0800-022-91-22
#Netherlands Antilles (CC) ÷	001-800-888-8000
#New Zealand (CC) ◆	000-912
#Nicaragua (CC) (Outside of Managua, dial 02 first)	166
From any public payphone	*2
#Norway (CC) ◆	800-19912
#Pakistan	00-800-12-001
#Panama	108
#Papua New Guinea (CC)	2810-108
#Paraguay ÷	05-07-19140
#Peru	0-800-500-10
#Philippines (CC) ◆ To call using PLDT ■	105-14
To call using PHILCOM ■	1026-14
Collect Access via PLDT in Filipino	1237-77
Collect Access via ICC in Filipino	1105-15
#Poland (CC) ÷	00-800-111-21-22
#Portugal (CC) ÷	05-017-1234
#Puerto Rico (CC)	1-800-888-8000
#Qatar ◆	0800-012-77
#Romania (CC) ÷	01-800-1800
#Russia (CC) ◆ ÷ To call using ROSTELCOM ■	747-3322
(For Russian speaking operator)	747-3320
To call using SOVINTEL ■	960-2222
#Saipan (CC) ÷	950-1022
#San Marino (CC) ◆	172-1022
#Saudi Arabia (CC) ÷	1-800-11

FOLD

almost looks out on the Danube. Try the buttery *Schnitzel* with fries or rice (90AS) or veg out at the salad bar (48AS). Black lacquered wood and oh-so-chic decor greet you at **Il Palio,** Wienerstr. 3 (tel. 547 32), but you'll be there to drink beer and taste some gorgeous ice cream. (Open daily 9am-midnight.) At night, the streets may seem empty, but **"Nostalgiebers I" Alt Melk,** Wienerstr. 25 (tel. 44 58), certainly won't be. Step into the intimate warmth of deep red velvet curtains, cream-colored walls, and old black-and-white photo portraits and enjoy a *cabernet sauvignon* (28AS) or a milkshake with the genial, mixed-age crowd. (Live music 1st and 3rd Th of the month. Open Su-Th 4pm-2am, F-Sa 4pm-4am.) During the day, **SPAR Markt,** Rathauspl. 9, has bread to spread, pears to share, apples to grapple, oranges to…well, um…never mind. (Open M and W-F 7am-6pm, Sa 7am-noon.)

SIGHTS AND ENTERTAINMENT
To visit Melk is to visit the **Benediktinerstift** (Benedictine abbey), which commands fantastic views of the city and the surrounding Danube countryside. *(Abbey open daily Apr. and Oct. 9am-5pm; May-Sept. 9am-6pm. Last entry 1hr. before closing. Guided tours Nov.-Mar. at 11am, 2pm, and by arrangement in English. 55AS, students 30AS, tour 15AS. Call 231 22 32 for more information.)* The "profane" wing is open to the damn public and includes the friggin' imperial chambers where such *%#!*@! notables as Emperor Karl VI, Pope Pius VI, and Napoleon took shelter. You won't find "Napoleon wuz here" scribbled anywhere, but (if you read German) the great and informative exhibits more than compensate. Stroll through the cool, marble halls and gaze at the Habsburg portraits lining the wall: in an act of political deference, royal consort Franz I points to his wife, the reigning Maria Theresa. The stunning **abbey library** is brimming with sacred and secular texts that were painstakingly hand-copied by monks. The two highest shelves in the gallery are fake—in typical Baroque fashion, the monks sketched book spines onto the wood to make the collection appear even more formidable. The **church** itself, maintained by 25 monks, is a Baroque masterpiece. Maria Theresa donated the two skeletons that adorn the side altars—unknown refugees from the catacombs of Rome, lounging in full costume. The centerpiece of the monastery is probably the **Melker Kreuz** (Melk Cross)—gold, jewels, the works, all circa 1363. Stolen twice, the Cross always exposed its thief and returned home to Melk through supernatural movement, perhaps inspiring the monastery's aggressive slogan *"Non coronabitur nisi legitime certaverit"* (Without a legitimate battle, there is no victory). The monks keep up with the times, curating temporary exhibits of contemporary art and even commissioning modernist artist Peter Bischof to create new murals over weather-ruined frescoes in the interior of the main courtyard.

Five kilometers out of town is **Schloß Schallaburg** (tel. (02754) 63 17), one of the most magnificent Renaissance castles in central Europe. *(Open May-Sept. M-F 9am-5pm, Sa-Su 9am-6pm. 60AS, students 20AS.)* The castle's architecture is reason enough to visit: Romanesque, Gothic, Renaissance, and Mannerist influences converge in the terra cotta arcades of the main courtyard. The floor is composed of a 1600-piece **mosaic** depicting mythological figures and gods. The place doubles as the **International Exhibition Center of Lower Austria** (tel. 63 17), a center that goes out of its way to bring foreign cultures to life. Buses leave Melk's train station every day at 10:30am and 3:10pm and leave the castle 15 minutes later. *(10min., 30AS.)* Or you can hike up to the complex; ask the tourist office for a map from Melk to the palace.

Hikers can enjoy the network of trails surrounding Melk that wind through tiny villages, farmland, and wooded groves. The tourist office provides a great map, which lists area sights and hiking paths, and handouts on the 10km Leo Böck trail, 6km Seniorenweg, and 15km Schallaburggrundweg. **Cyclists** might enjoy a tour along the Danube toward Willendorf on the former canal-towing path. The 30,000-year-old **Venus of Willendorf,** an 11cm voluptuous stone figure and one of the world's most famous fertility symbols, was discovered there in 1908. She is now on display in Vienna. A more sedate option, **ferries** travel to the other side of the Danube to **Arnsdorf,** where the local *jause* (an Austrian version of British high tea), here called *Hauerganse* (vintner's special), will load enough carbos to send you through the

LOWER AUSTRIA

vineyards and apricot orchards back to Melk. The ferry returns past the **Heiratswald** (Marriage Woods). Romantic Melk awards a young sapling tree to couples who marry in Melk, which the happy couple plants and tends for the rest of their lives.

The **Sommerspiele Melk** (Melk Summer Festival) comes to town in early July. An open-air stage in front of the monastery's pavilion provides the perfect setting for creative staging and world-class theater. *(Performances mid-July to mid-Aug. F-Sa 8:30pm. For more information, call 523 07 or fax 523 07 27.)* Tickets (from 105AS) are available at the Melk city hall, theater ticket offices, travel agencies throughout Austria, and the box office next to the monastery after 7:15pm, before performances.

■ Dürnstein

A bend or two down the Danube from Krems, planted among deep green vineyards, Dürnstein is a hilltop medieval village with a mythic charm attracting tourists and artists alike. The ruined **castle** at the highest point of the town once imprisoned **Richard the Lionhearted,** captured on his way back from the Third Crusade in 1192. Apparently the English king had quarreled fiercely with Leopold V, Duke of Austria, while in the Holy Land. When his ship was wrecked en route to England, Richard was forced to cross this enemy land disguised as a peasant. Unfortunately, Leopold's men recognized him despite the costume and locked him up until they received a large ransom from England (giving **Robin Hood** time to flourish under evil Prince John).

Although Richard's capture was the last big splash onto history pages for the Kuenninger dynasty, they continued to prosper on their home turf, building an enormous Baroque abbey called the **Augustiner Chorherrenstift** (tel. 375; fax 432) to show the Joneses. It was originally commissioned by the daughter of the penultimate heir of the family line in 1372 and dedicated to the Virgin Mary, but Joseph II dissolved it at the same time as he dismantled most of Austria's ecclesiastical institutions and introduced the re-useable coffin. You'll find adrenalin-inducing views from its somewhat grandiose blue and white steeple. (Open Apr.-Oct. 9am-6pm. 25AS, with tour 40AS, tour for students 35AS.)

Trains connect Dürnstein to **Krems** (every hr., 6am-8pm, 25AS) and **Vienna's Franz Josef Bahnhof** (periodic, 145AS). To reach town from the train station, descend the hill, turn right, and pass through the underground walkway (5min.). **Boats** dock at the DDSG ferry station on the Donaupromenade, a riverside road with beaches and bike paths. To reach downtown from the landing docks, turn right on Donaupromenade and left on Anzugg. which intersects with Hauptstr. The **tourist office** (tel. 200) is located in a shack in a parking lot down the hill and to the right of the train station. The office and the local *Rathaus* (on Hauptstr.) provide lists of *Privatzimmern* (from 180AS) and open *Heurigen*. (Tourist office open M and W-F noon-7pm, Sa 11am-7pm.) The **telephone** code is 02711.

The nearest youth hostel is in Krems. Dürnstein makes an equally good daytrip from Vienna. You can stay in the geranium-bedecked **Pension Altes Rathaus** (tel./fax 252) on Hauptstr. 26 behind the *Rathaus*. It's clean, pretty, and balconied. (Doubles 600-660AS. Breakfast included.)

Upper Austria
(Oberösterreich)

Upper Austria (Oberösterreich)

Oberösterreich (Upper Austria) derives its name not from its northern position but from the flow of the Danube in Austria; sister province Niederösterreich (Lower Austria) is where the river flows down into Hungary. The province comprises three distinct regions: the **Mühlviertel** in the north, the **Innviertel** to the west of Linz in the Danube valley, and the **Pyhrn-Eisenwurz** in the south. The provincial capital is **Linz,** a major center of iron, steel, and chemical production, and home to many modern Danube port installations. The area has been Austria's second most productive source of oil and natural gas since World War II, and several large-scale hydroelectric power stations have been built along the Danube and its tributary, the Enns. Despite all this, development still can't obscure the natural beauty of the Danube river valley.

While the mountains here are less rugged, the relatively flat terrain makes for wonderful **bicycling tours.** Well-paved paths, suitable for cyclers of any age and ability, wind their way through the entire province.

> ### ✍ HIGHLIGHTS OF UPPER AUSTRIA
>
> ■ Linz is a small regional capital with an excellent Ars Electronica museum and huge Bruckner and street performer festivals every summer.
> ■ St. Florian abbey and Kremsmmünster are both lovely Baroque abbeys in the rolling hills of Upper Austria. Kremsmünster is especially noteworthy for its *Fischkalter,* or arcaded pools.
> ■ Freistadt is a tiny, beautifully preserved medieval town with an excellent communal brewery open for tours.

■ Linz an der Donau

The third largest city in the country and one-time home to Kepler, Mozart, Beethoven, Bruckner, and Hitler, Linz sits on the banks of the blue(ish) Danube and magisterially rules over the industrial sector of Austria. Sandwiched between Vienna to the east and Salzburg to the west, Linz suffers from the typical middle-child syndrome—not as cosmopolitan as Vienna yet not as small-town-charming as Salzburg, it makes a lot of effort to stand out from the pack. Although Linz's outskirts may not be particularly scenic, the wealth from the factories and smoke stacks has been used to modernize and gentrify the central city, which is now replete with expensive shops, modern art galleries, and electronic bus stops. Linz's citizens are unusually friendly (unburdened by the tourist overload of Vienna and Salzburg), and its annual festivals—the classy Brucknerfest and the bedlam nuttiness of the Pflasterspektakel (street performer's fair)—draw artists and crowds from all over the world.

GETTING TO LINZ

Midway between Salzburg and Vienna on the line between Prague and Graz, Linz is a transportation hub for both Austria and Eastern Europe. Frequent **trains** connect to major Austrian and European cities. (Train station info open M-F 8am-6pm, Sa 8am-2pm.) All **buses** come and go from the **Hauptbahnhof,** where schedules are available. (Bus ticket window open M-F 7am-5:50pm, Sa 7am-1:20pm.) **Motorists** can arrive on the main West Autobahn (A1 or E16).

ORIENTATION AND PRACTICAL INFORMATION

Linz sprawls across the **Danube,** which curves west to east through the city. Most of the *Altstadt* sights crowd along the southern bank, near **Nibelungenbrücke.** This pedestrian area includes the huge **Hauptplatz,** just south of the bridge, and extends down **Landstraße,** which ends near the train station.

Trains: Hauptbahnhof, Bahnhofpl. (tel. 17 17). To: **Vienna** (2hr., every 30min., 270AS); **Salzburg** (1½hr., every 30min., 200AS); **Innsbruck** (3½hr., every 2hr., 490AS); **Munich** (3hr., every 1-2hr., 504AS); and **Prague** (4hr., 4 per day, 362AS).

Ferries: Wurm & Köck floats between **Passau** (tel. (0851) 92 92 92; fax 355 18) and **Linz** (tel. (0732) 78 36 07; fax 783 60 79). 5-7hr., depending on current. 242AS, round-trip 284AS. Boats dock in Linz at the **Donau Schiffstation,** on the south side of the river, and stop at a number of Austrian and Bavarian towns along the way. Discounts for seniors and children under 15. Ferries run late Apr. to Oct.

Public Transportation: Linz's public transport system runs to all corners of the city. 2 trams (#1 and 3) start near the *Hauptbahnhof* and run north through the city along Landstr. and Hauptpl. and across Nibelungenbrücke. Several buses crisscross Linz as well. Nearly all vehicles pass through **Blumauerplatz,** down the block and to the right from the train station. The hub closer to the city center is **Taubenmarkt,** south of Hauptpl. on Landstr. A ticket for 4 stops or less ("Mini") costs 9AS; more than 4 ("Midi") 18AS; and a day ticket ("Maxi") 36AS. Buy tickets from any machine at all bus or streetcar stops and stamp them before boarding; those caught *Schwarzfahren* (riding without a ticket) fork over 400AS. The tourist office sells a 48AS ticket covering all transportation to and from the **Pöstlingberg.**

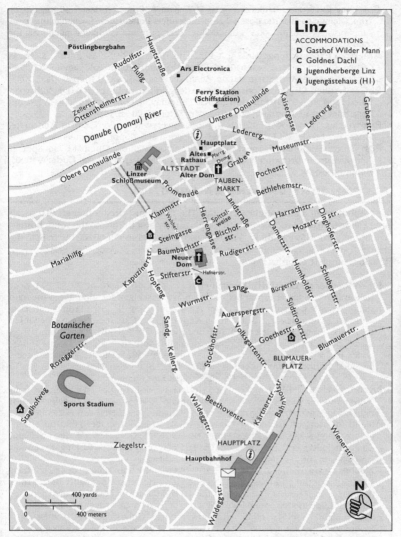

Taxis: At the *Hauptbahnhof,* Blumauerpl., and Hauptpl., or call 69 69 or 17 18.
Parking: Free parking at **Urfahrmarkt.**
Bike Rental: At the train station. 80AS per day, with train ticket 50AS. **Oberösterreich Touristic Zentrale,** Kapuzinerstr. 3 (tel. 311 49 67), 15AS per hr., 80AS per
day, 120AS for 2 days, 250AS for 5 days, 200AS per weekend.
Automobile Service: ARBÖ, Hatenstr. 6 (tel. 123), or **ÖAMTC,** Wankmüllerhofstr.
58 (tel. 120).
Tourist Office: Hauptpl. 1 (tel. 70 70 17 77; fax 77 28 73; email info.linz@upperaus-
tria.or.at; http://tourist.linz.at), in the *Altes Rathaus.* The multilingual staff helps
find rooms at no charge. Pick up *A Walk Through the Old Quarter* for a summary
of the *Altstadt's* main attractions. The tourist office sells the **Linz City Ticket**
(299AS) which provides discounts at various sights around the city. Open May-
Sept. M-F 8am-7pm, Sa 9am-7pm, Su 10am-7pm; Oct.-Apr. M-F 8am-6pm, Sa 9am-
6pm, Su 10am-6pm. There is a tourist info brochure counter in the train station.

Currency Exchange: Banks are open M-W 8am-4:30pm, Th 8am-5:30pm, F 8am-2pm. Change cash at the **post office,** which offers better rates. Exchange open M-F 7am-5pm, Sa 8am-1pm. 60AS commission. 24hr. currency exchange machine at the train station.

American Express: Bürgerstr. 14, A-4021 Linz (tel. 66 82 95). All traveler's checks cashed, but no currency exchanged. Open M-F 9am-5:30pm, Sat. 9am-noon.

Luggage Storage: At the train station, 30AS. Lockers 20-30AS. At tourist office, 10AS.

Bi-Gay-Lesbian Organizations: Homosexuelle Initiative Linz (HOSI), Schubertstr. 36 (tel. 60 98 98). Discussion tables Thursday at 8pm at Gasthaus Agathon, Kapuzinerstr. 46. **Frauenbüro,** Klosterstr. 7 (tel. 77 20 18 50).

Pharmacies: Downtown Linz has *Apotheke* everywhere. Try **Central Apotheke,** Mozartstr. 1 (tel. 77 17 83). Open M-F 8am-noon and 2-6pm, Sa 8am-noon.

Post Office: Bahnhofpl. 11, next to the train and bus stations. Open M-F 7am-8pm, Sa 7:30am-4pm. Information open M-F 8am-5pm, Sa 8am-4pm. **Postal Code:** A-4020.

Telephone Code: 0732.

ACCOMMODATIONS AND CAMPING

Linz suffers from a lack of cheap rooms. The city is just urban enough that locals aren't allowed to rent rooms privately, so it's usually best to stick to the youth hostels. You should probably call ahead. You may also want to consider taking the train to the nearby town of Steyr (45min., every hr., change trains in St. Valentin). See **Steyr,** p. 154, for complete information.

Jugendherberge Linz (HI), Kapuzinerstr. 14 (tel. 78 27 20 or 77 87 77), near Hauptpl., offers the cheapest beds in town in an excellent location. From the train station, tram #3: "Taubenmarkt" then cross Landstr., walk down Promenade, continue on Klammstr., and turn left on Kapuzinerstr. Cats roam the picnic-tabled courtyard. 36 beds in pleasant 4- to 6-bed rooms. The friendly young proprietress speaks perfect English with an American-English-Australian accent. Dorms 160AS, under 19 130AS. Nonmembers add 40AS. Breakfast 30AS. Private showers. Sheets included. **Laundry** 45AS. Reception 8-10am and 5-8pm or so. No curfew; the key to your free locker opens the front door. Reservations recommended.

Jugendgästehaus (HI), Stanglhofweg 3 (tel. 66 44 34; fax 60 21 64). From the train station, bus #27 (dir: Schiffswerft): "Froschberg." Walk straight on Ziegeleistr., turn right on Roseggerstr., and continue on to Stanglhofweg. Bland exterior conceals a bland interior. Clean and spacious with lots of closet space. Plentiful school groups. Singles 335AS; doubles 235AS; triples 165AS. Guest tax 8AS. Breakfast and sheets included. Private showers and hall toilets. Tennis courts. Parking. Reception 7:30am-4pm and 6-11pm. Curfew 11pm. Call ahead.

Goldenes Dachl, Hafnerstr. 27 (tel. 77 58 97). From the train station, bus #21: "Auerspergpl." Continue in the same direction along Herrenstr. for half a block, then turn left onto Wurmstr. Hafnerstr. is the 1st right. Narrow corridors and staircases allow for large modern rooms. Run by a motherly woman with an eye for comfort. Singles 260AS; doubles 460AS, with shower 490AS. Only 15 beds—call ahead.

Gasthof Wilder Mann, Goethestr. 14 (tel. 65 60 78). From the station, go down Bahnhofstr., turn left on Landestr. at Blumauerpl., then turn right on Goethestr. (7min. total). 2min. from Blumauerpl., the main transportation hub. Large, homey rooms, with embroidered drapes and more embroidery on the chairs and sofas. Restaurant downstairs. Singles 300AS, with shower 370AS; doubles 520AS, with shower 620AS. Breakfast 50AS. Reception 8am-9pm.

Camping Pleschinger See (tel. 24 78 70). Tram #1 or 3: Rudolfstr. and bus #22: "Pleschinger See." On the Linz-Vienna biking path on Pleschinger Lake. You can take tram #1 or 3: "Pleschinger See" and continue on foot, but you'll still have a long way to go. 45AS. Tents only. Open May to late Sept.

FOOD

Duck into the alleyway restaurants off Hauptpl. and Landstr. to avoid ridiculously inflated menu prices. Linz's namesake dessert, the **Linzer Torte,** is unique for its deceptively dry ingredients—very little flour and absolutely no cream. The secret is in the red-currant jam filling, which slowly seeps through and moisturizes the dry, crumbly crust. Not all *Linzer Torten* are the same; the best *Torten* sit out for at least two days after baking for maximum jam saturation.

🅦**Café Traxlmeyer,** Promenadestr. 16. Giant orange awnings shade the garden tables of this Viennese-style café. For 50AS you can nibble on rolls and jam, sip coffee from your own little pot, flip through newspapers, and watch people play chess until the afternoon. *Torten* 24AS. Open M-Sa 8am-10pm.

🅦**Gelbes Krokodil,** Dametzstr. 30 (tel. 78 40 90), in the Moviemento Theater. Varying nightly menu includes large selection of soups (30AS), elegant salads (60-80AS), and savory vegetarian entrees (80-90AS). Open 5-11pm. Theater shows diverse international contemporary and classic films. The summer special is a double feature and a drink, all for only 120AS.

Mangolds, Hauptpl. 3 (tel. 78 56 88). Vegetarian Valhalla. This cafeteria-style restaurant in screaming primary colors offers only the fresh stuff. Nearly all the vegetables and eggs are 100% organic. Extravagant salad bar and freshly squeezed fruit and vegetable drinks. Pay by weight—100g for 14AS, 60AS per plate. Open M-F 11am-8pm, Sa 11am-5pm.

Levante, Hauptpl. 13 (tel. 79 34 30). Crowded outdoor seating in the Hauptpl. Real Turkish and Greek food at real prices. Open daily 11:30am-11:30pm.

Gasthaus Goldenes Schiff, Ottensheimerstr. 74 (tel. 23 98 79). On the scenic banks of the Danube. From Hauptpl., cross the bridge, turn left, go around the *Neues Rathaus*, and walk upstream along the river for 7min. Local fisherman pound on wooden tables and drink beer in the *Gastgarten* while eating their 100AS dinners. Open W-Su 9am-10pm.

Pizzeria D'Alfredo and **Shalimar,** Bethlehemstr. 38 (tel. 77 80 55). In 1 room, enjoy Greek and Italian specialties under a fish-filled net and plant-hung ceiling. Huge selection of large pizzas (65-110AS), pasta dishes (80-95AS), and salads (40-80AS). If you're longing for more Eastern fare and tunes, move to the next room and taste a variety of Pakistani and Indian dishes, many of which are vegetarian (80-110AS). Open 11:30am-2:30pm and 5:30-11:30pm.

Jindrak Konditorei, Herrenstr. 22, though other branches dot Linz. Rumored to serve the best *Linzer Torte* (19.50AS) in Linz. Other mouth-watering sweets and sandwiches line up behind the counters. Open M-Sa 8am-6pm.

Markets

Julius Meinl, Landstr. 50. Open M-F 7:30am-6:30pm, Sa 7:30am-5pm.

SPAR Market, Steing. at Walterg., near the hostels. Open M-F 7:30am-1pm.

SIGHTS AND ENTERTAINMENT

Start your exploration of Linz at **Hauptplatz,** which hugs the Danube's south bank. The city constructed the enormous plaza in the 14th and 15th centuries when it gained new wealth from the taxation of all the salt and iron passing through the town. The focus of the square is the marble **trinity column,** commemorating the city's escape from the horrors of war, famine, the plague, and the 18th century. An octagonal tower and an astronomical clock crown the Baroque **Altes Rathaus.** To date, only two people have ever addressed the public from the its balcony: Adolf Hitler and Pope John Paul II. Free-spirited star-gazer Johannes Kepler (the fellow who formulated the elliptical geometry of planetary orbit) wrote his major work, *Harmonices Mundi,* while living around the corner at Rathausg. 5. In 1745, Linz's first print shop opened here. The building now houses Onkel Dagobert's Dart Kneipe (Uncle Dagobert's Dart Den)—a few beers may inspire you to rethink the geometrical harmonies of the dartboard. On nearby Domg. stands Linz's twin-towered **Alter Dom** (Old Cathedral). *(Open daily 8am-noon and 3-6:30pm.)* The 19th-century symphonic composer Anton Bruckner played here during his stint as church organist. To the south, the neo-Gothic **Neuer Dom** (New Cathedral) impresses visitors with the 19th-century hubris necessary to create this Godzilla-scale edifice (the largest in Austria). For sheer olfactory ecstasy, visit the **Botanischer Garten's** world-famous cactus and orchid collections at Rogeggerstr. 20 (tel. 70 70 18 72). *(Open daily May-Aug.*

7:30am-7:30pm; Sept. and Apr. 8am-7pm; Oct. and Mar. 8am-6pm; Nov.-Feb. 8am-5pm. 10AS, under 18 free.) The hill where the garden is now located was saved from housing developments only by grace of the fact that it is hollow—it was the site of an exploded ammunitions plant during World War II.

Cross Nibelungenbrücke to reach the left bank of the Danube. This area, known as **Urfahr,** was a separate city until Linz swallowed it up in the early decades of the 20th century. It boasts some of the oldest buildings in the city and a captivating view of Linz from the apex of the **Pöstlingberg** (537m). To reach the base of the summit, take tram #3: "Bergbahnhof Urfahr." From there, either hike 0.5km up Hagenstr. (off Rudolphstr., which is off Hauptstr. near the bridge) or hop aboard the **Pöstlingbergbahn** (tel. 78 01 75 45), a trolley car that ascends the summit in a scenic 20 minutes. *(Every 20min., M-Sa 5:20am-8pm, Su 11:40am-8pm. 25AS, round-trip 40AS, children half-price.)* The twin-towered **Pöstlingbergkirche** (Parish Church), the city symbol, stands guard over the city from the hill's crest. Indulge any nascent romanticism by taking the **Grottenbahn** into the dippily fairy-tale caves of Pöstlingberg. *(Open May-Sept. M-F 9am-6pm, Sa-Su 10am-5pm; Apr. and Oct.-Nov. daily 10am-5pm. 50AS, under 15 25AS.)*

Linz is equipped with many intriguing museums. The **Neue Galerie,** Blütenstr. 15 (tel. 23 93 36 00), on the second floor of the Lentia 2000 shopping center across the river, boasts one of Austria's best modern and contemporary art collections. *(Open June-Sept. M-W and F 10am-6pm, Th 10am-10pm, Sa 10am-1pm; Oct.-May M-W and F-Su 10am-6pm, Th 10am-10pm. 60AS, students 30AS.)* Works by Klimt, Kokoschka, Lieberman, and others line the walls. The **Ars Electronica,** Hauptstr. 2 (tel. 727 20; fax 727 22; email info@aec.at; http://www.aec.at), just over the bridge from Hauptpl., bills itself as the "museum of the future." *(Open W-Su 10am-6pm. 80AS, students and seniors 40AS.)* It's a bird, it's a plane, it's *you* strapped to the ceiling in a full-body flight simulator that sends you soaring over Upper Austria. After this not-so-natural high, head downstairs to the **CAVE,** an amazing exciting extreme interactive 3-D room. The museum cafe offers **email access** for visitors. The **Linzer Schloßmuseum,** Tummelpl. 10 (tel. 77 44 19), presents the city's history as well as temporary exhibits. *(Open Tu-F 9am-5pm, Sa-Su 10am-4pm. 50AS, students 30AS. English brochure available.)*

From mid-September to mid-October, the month-long **Brucknerfest** brings a rush of concerts and homages to native son Anton Bruckner at the **Brucknerhaus** concert hall, an acoustically perfect venue. *(220-1100AS, standing room 40-50AS.)* Contact Brucknerhauskasse, Untere Donaulände 7, A-4010 Linz (tel. 77 52 30; fax 761 22 01; http://www.brucknerhaus.linz.at) for tickets. The opening concerts (the end of the 2nd week in Sept.), billed as *Klangwolken* (sound-clouds), include spectacular outdoor lasers, a children's show, and a classical evening with Bruckner's Seventh Symphony broadcast live into the surrounding Donaupark to 50,000 fans. During the third weekend of July, the city hosts **Pflasterspektakel,** a free, three-day, international street performers' festival. Every few steps down Landstr. and Hauptpl., different performers from as far away as New Zealand perform Houdini acts, fire-eating, outdoor theater, bongo concerts, punk rock, and other such feats before the young, funky, social crowd from neighboring cities in Austria, Switzerland, and Germany.

Linzer nightlife is sleepy but does have a pulse. Prod it awake at the **Bermuda Dreieck** (Bermuda Triangle), behind the west side of Hauptpl. (head down Hofg. or just follow the crowds of decked-out pub crawlers). Frequented by *Linzers* as well as tourists, this area has the highest bar- and nightclub-to-square-meter ratio in the city. In Hauptpl. itself, try **Alte Welt Weinkeller,** Hauptpl. 4, a popular hangout for a mixed crowd. *(Open M-Sa 5pm-2am. Food served 6-11pm.)* Soak up wine and spirits in this arcaded, Renaissance-era "wine and culture cellar." **17er Keller,** Hauptpl. 17 (duck through the archway and enter the steel door on your right), will serve you an apple-juice-and-cinnamon tequila while you listen to a mix of jazz, funk, blues, and rock. *(Open M-Sa 7pm-2am, Su 7pm-1am.)* The hopping **C+C Café,** Bethlehemstr. 30 (tel. 77 08 62), managed by a grandmotherly hostess who may be the nicest *Linzerin* in all Linz, draws a sophisticated, mainly gay and lesbian crowd. *(Open M-Sa 6pm to whenever people go home.)* Linzers also flock to the other side of the Danube for after-hours entertainment. The candle-lit **Cafe Ex-Blatt,** Waitherstr. 15 (tel. 77 93 19), is covered in old Austrian advertisements and movie posters and attracts a hip retro crowd. *(Open M-F 10pm-2am, Sa-Su 6pm-1am).* Grab a bench at **Fischergartl,** Flußg. 3 (tel. 71 01 23), the beer garden on the left as you cross the bridge. *(Open M-Th 11:30am-2pm and 5pm-1am, F-Sa 6pm-1am.)* Many busy night spots line Landstr.—look between shops for entrances to courtyard *Biergartens.* **Josef,** Landstr. 49 (tel. 77 31 65), is tree-filled and huge and has multiple patios and lots of beer.

■ Near Linz

■ Mauthausen

About half an hour down the Danube from Linz stand the terrible remains of a Nazi concentration camp (*Konzentrationslager,* abbreviated KZ). Unlike other camps in south Germany and Austria, Mauthausen remains very much intact. Built by Dachau prisoners in 1938, Mauthausen was the central camp for all of Austria and administered 49 subcamps throughout the country. The barracks housed 200,000 prisoners, mainly Russian and Polish POWs, along with Austrian homosexuals and political criminals, Italian POWs, Jews from Hungary and the Netherlands, Gypsies, and Communists. Mauthausen was infamous for its **Todessteige** (Staircase of Death), which led to the stone quarry where inmates were forced to work until exhaustion. The steep, even steps currently in place were added for tourists' safety—when the inmates worked here, there was nothing but a stony drop dotted with boulders and jagged rocks. As the prisoners climbed up or down the path, the guards often shoved the last in line so that the entire group fell down the slope, often along with the stones they were carrying on their shoulders. The inner part of the camp is now a museum (tel. (07238) 22 69). Also accessible are the barracks, roll-call grounds, cremation ovens, and torture rooms. A free brochure or audio-tape tour (in English) walks you though the central part of the camp. There is also a museum displaying the history of the camp, a permanent exhibit on Austrians in the camp, and video documentaries in various languages. (Open Apr.-Sept. 8am-6pm; Oct. to mid-Dec. and Feb.-Mar. 8am-4pm. Last entrance 1hr. before closing. 25AS, students and seniors 10AS.) To reach the camp from **Linz,** take a **train** to Mauthausen (transfer at St. Valentin). A special **Oberösterreichischer Verkehrsverbund day pass** (102AS) pays for the round-trip train ticket from Linz plus all city transportation in Linz and Mauthausen. Beware—the Mauthausen train station is 6km away from the camp, and a bus stops 2km from the camp only twice a day during the week and not at all on weekends. A better option is to **store your pack** (30AS) at the Mauthausen **train station** (tel. (67238) 22 07) and rent a **bicycle** (70AS with train ticket). You'll walk past pastureland, fields of mown hay, and orchards—an eerie prologue—before reaching the bleak walls of the camp. Pick up a map from the train station. If traveling **by car,** exit Autobahn A1 (Vienna-Linz) at Enns.

■ St. Florian's Abbey

Seventeen kilometers from Linz lies the abbey of St. Florian, Austria's oldest Augustinian monastery. According to legend, the martyr Florian was bound to a millstone and thrown in the Enns river. Although Florian perished, his stone miraculously floated (ouch—the irony) and serves as the abbey's cornerstone. The complex owes much of its fame to composer Anton Bruckner, who began his career here first as choirboy, then as teacher, and finally as a virtuoso organist and composer. His body is interred beneath the organ, allowing him to vibrate in perpetuity to the sound of his dearly-beloved pipes. The abbey (tel. (07224) 89 02 10; fax 89 02 60) contains the **Altdorfer Gallery,** filled with altarpieces by 15th-century artist Albrecht Altdorfer of Regensburg, an Old Master of the Danube school. The 14 **Kaiserzimmer** (imperial rooms), built in case of an imperial visit, virtually rumble with Baroque splendor. Inside the spectacular, recently renovated church (the only part of the abbey accessible without a tour) sits the enormous aforementioned **Bruckner Organ.** Twenty-minute concerts on the monster instrument occur May to October Sunday to Friday at 2:30pm (30AS, students 25AS). Tours of the abbey minus the *Kaiserzimmer* leave daily. (Abbey open Apr.-Oct. 60AS, children 20AS. Tours 10, 11am, and 2, 3, and 4pm). To reach the abbey from Linz, take the bus: "St. Florian Stift." It will drop you off at "Kotzmannstr." (30min., 24AS) in downtown St. Florian or "Lagerhaus." Both are a 15-minute walk from the abbey. The **tourist office,** Marktpl. 3 (tel./fax (07224) 56 90), provides info about the abbey and accommodations listings (open M-F 9am-1pm).

■ Kremsmünster

The fabulous **Kremsmünster Abbey** (tel. (07583) 527 52 16; fax 527 52 90), 32km south of Linz, belongs to Austria's oldest order and dates from AD 777 (an auspicious year for an abbey). Some 75 monks still call the abbey home, and it administers parish churches as far-flung as Brazil. The abbey owns most of the land in the area, including 3800 hectares of woods and a wine-producing vineyard (the monks' wine is sold at the ticket office). Their Borgesian **library,** which has two rows of books on every shelf and hidden doors in the bookcases, is Austria's third largest and boasts many medieval tomes. Visitors are not allowed to handle the books, but guides will take out any volume and page through it for you on request. The **Kaisersaal,** built in case of an imperial visit, is a rich Baroque gallery with marble columns and cartoonish ceiling frescoes that make the rooms seem much higher than they actually are. The abbey's **Kunstsammlung** (art collection) tour covers the library, the *Kaisersaal,* several art galleries, and the **Schatzkammer** (treasury), which shelters a beautifully engraved golden chalice dating from the time of Charlemagne. The monks' collection of minerals and semi-exotic animal specimens is on display in the seven-story **Sternwarte.** Also open to visitors is the **Fischkalter,** five fantastic fish fens for feeding fasting friars' friends fresh flounder. Actually, the Fischkalter is a series of arcaded pools set with pagan and pastoral statues (including Falstaff look-alikes) spouting water. Wooden stag heads stuck with real antlers adorn the room—see if you can find the two with radishes in their mouths. (Open 9am-noon and 1-6pm. Central chapel free. Fischkalter 10AS—entrance through the ticket office. Kunstsammlung tours Apr.-Oct. at 10, 11am, 2, 3, and 4pm; Nov.-Mar. at 11am and 2pm. 1hr. 55AS, students 30AS. Sternwarte tour May-Oct. 10am, 2, and 4pm. 1½hr. 60AS, students 30AS. Both tours include the Fischkalter.)

The town of Kremsmünster itself boasts twisty medieval streets and daunting, steep stairway paths overgrown with moss and wildflowers. Kremsmünster also claims to be the home of **Europe's first high-rise,** constructed in 1748-1758 as a research center for the natural sciences. Fresh fruit sprouts up at the **open-air market** in Marktpl. Fridays from 1 to 6pm. **Café Schlair** (tel. (07583) 77 72), on Hauptstr. kitty-corner from the tourist office, serves pastries and fresh fruit drinks for 25-40AS. (Open M-Tu and Th 8am-7pm, W 8am-noon, F 8am-8pm, Sa-Su 8am-6:30pm.) If you decide to stay the night, try the **Bauernhof Gossenhub,** Schürzendorf 1 (tel. (07583) 77 52), a lovely farmhouse with clean, simple rooms for 200AS (40AS surcharge for stays of less than 3 days). To get there, climb Gosenhuberstr. until the cow pasture, then turn left at the "Föhrenleiten" sign.

Trains go to Kremsmünster from **Linz** (45min., every hr., 128AS). From the station, follow Bahnhofstr. as it curves left, then right, then left again, and continue on to Marktpl. The path to the abbey starts at the **tourist office,** Rathauspl. 1 (tel. (07583) 72 12; open Tu-F 9am-noon and 3-6pm).

■ Steyr

Steyr is famous as a jewel of medieval city planning. Much of the city looks as it has for the past 500 years, with winding, narrow cobbled alleyways, carved arches, and high stone walls. Two mountain rivers, the **Steyr** and the **Enns,** intersect in the middle of the town, dicing Steyr into three parts. Steyr's comely surface hides the city's industrial identity. The city is well known for its iron trade and holds a unique position in the annals of modern technology—in 1884, Steyr was the first town in Europe to use electric street lighting. Who would have guessed?

The **Stadtplatz,** packed with 15th-century buildings, is the *Altstadt*'s focal point. The 16th-century **Leopoldibrunnen** (Leopold fountain), with its ornamental, wrought-iron spigots and bright flowers, vies with the Rococo *Rathaus* across the square for the title of ornamental heavyweight champion. Gotthard Hayberger, Steyr's famous mayor, architect, and Renaissance man-about-town, designed the town hall. The former **Dominican Church** (Marienkirche), also crammed into Stadtpl., was born a Gothic building but grew a Baroque facade in the early 17th century. Most of Steyr's beautiful residences have been transformed into banks or shops with modern interiors hidden behind ornate facades. The major exception is the **Innerberger Stadel,** Grünmarkt 26. Now the local **Heimatmuseum,** it contains a plethora of puppets, an extensive stuffed bird collection, and the three Cs of medieval weaponry: crossbows, cannons, and cutlery. Cutlery? (Open Apr.-Oct. Tu-Su 10am-4pm. Free.) Berggasse, one of the numerous narrow lanes typical of Steyr, leads from Stadtpl. up to the pink **Lamberg Schloß,** where the **Schloß Galerie** showcases temporary exhibits. (Open Tu-Su 10am-noon and 2-5pm. 25AS, students and children free.) If you're not in the museum mood, wander in the palace's green courtyards.

Trains connect Steyr to **Linz** (45min., every hr. until 9:30pm, 69AS, round-trip 138AS). To reach the city center from the station, exit the station right and turn left on Bahnofstr. After crossing the river, turn left immediately down Engeg., which leads to Stadtpl. The **tourist office,** Stadtpl. 27 (tel. 532 29; fax 532 29 15; email steyr-info@ris.at; http://www.upper.austria/at/regionen/steyr), in the *Rathaus,* offers **guided tours** (May-Oct. Sa 2pm) and **headset tours** (anytime the office is open). Both are 45AS. (Open Jan.-Nov. M-F 8:30am-6pm, Sa 9am-5pm, Su 10am-4pm; Dec. M-F 8:30am-6pm, Sa 9am-4pm, Su 10am-3pm.) Steyr hosts a **Musik Festival** from mid-August to mid-September featuring international classical, jazz, and folk.

■ Admont

The tiny town of Admont, the gateway to the Gesäuse Alpine region, lies just over the Styrian border on the Enns River. Benedictine monks first built an abbey here in the 11th century, and, although fire has repeatedly ravaged the complex, the stubborn friars have refused to let the church go up in smoke. The current **Benediktinerstift** (Benedictine abbey) was completed in 1776. Its domed ceiling, supported by thick brick walls, saved the library from one of those fires in 1865; the abbey was the sole unharmed building. The frescoed **library,** the largest monastery collection in the world, contains over 150,000 volumes. Joseph Stemmel statues dominate the central gallery. There are representations of death, heaven, hell, and the seven deadly sins (intemperance has a bottle and bloated sausages). There are also devils (one of which looks a lot like the abbey treasurer of Stemmel's time), angels, poets, philosophers, and historians. It's pretty overwhelming. Hidden stairways lead to the upper balconies—the guides happily direct wayward wanderers. The same building holds the **Schatzkammermuseum** (tel. 23 12), which contains Admont artifacts, and the **natural history museum,** full of bottled snakes and insects. (Library and museums open May-Sept. 10am-1pm and 2-5pm; Apr. and Oct. 10am-1pm and 2-4pm; Nov.-Mar. by appointment. Combined admission 60AS, students 30AS. English info sheets 5AS.)

The other reason to come to Admont is—honestly—the youth hostel, **Schloß Röthelstein** (tel. 24 32; fax 27 95 83), reputedly the most beautiful in Europe. Housed in a restored 330-year-old castle, the hostel presides over the town and boasts winter ice skating, a sauna (costs extra), a tennis court, a soccer field, even a small track. Indoors, a huge stone hall draped with ivy, chandeliers, and two floors of arches serves as the main dining area, and an exquisite *Rittersaal* (knights' hall) functions as a concert venue. The rooms contain bay windows, brass fixtures, wood furniture, private telephones, and elegant lamps. The only challenge is getting here—yes, it *is* that lone castle sitting very high on the very big hill. From the train station, turn left down Bahnofstr. and left again at the post office. Cross the tracks and continue straight down that road for 25 minutes (don't turn right at the "Fußweg" sign pointing to the castle, unless you feel mountain-goatish), past the lumberyard. Turn right at the

"Schloßherberge Röthelstein" sign and follow the paved road as it curves up and up. **Taxis** (tel. 28 01 or 23 23) from the station run about 80AS. (2-bed dorms 280AS; nonmembers add 40AS. Breakfast 20AS, hearty meals 50AS. Open Jan.-Oct. Parking. Reception 7am-midnight.) If the trek is too intimidating, try a *Privatzimmer.* Several line Paradiesstr. along the route to the hostel and generally run about 180-250AS. Closer to the town center, **Frühstückspension Mafalda,** Bachpromenade 75 (tel. 21 88), awaits. At the post office, turn left and cross over the rail tracks, then make the next two rights and cross over the tracks again. Mafalda is right under the tracks—a fact all too evident come sleepy-time. (Singles 240AS; doubles 420AS. Hall showers and breakfast included. 40AS surcharge for 1-night stays.) The **ADEG supermarket** is on the way to the tourist office. (Open M-F 7:30am-noon and 3-6pm, Sa 7:30-noon.)

Trains run to **Selzthal,** the regional hub (every 1-2hr., 34AS). Get to Selzthal from Linz (2hr., 168AS; see **Linz,** p. 147) or via Bruck an der Mur (1¼hr., every 2hr.) **Buses** to Linz depart from the front of the post office and market place. The Admont **tourist office** (*Fremdenverkehrsbüro;* tel. 21 64; fax 36 48) tracks down rooms for free. To get there from the train station, turn left down Bahnhofstr. and take the second right at the conspicuous post office; the tourist office is five minutes away on the left. (Open M-F 8am-noon and 2-6pm, Sa 9am-noon; Sept.-May M8am-noon, Tu-F 8am-noon and 2-5pm.) The **postal code** is A-8911. Admont's **telephone code** is 03613.

THE MÜHLVIERTEL

Far north of Linz, the Mühlviertel offers shaded woodland paths, quiet farmy fields, and pastures populated only by the occasional cow. It is becoming an increasingly popular hiking area for Austrians. This region was once the stomping grounds of pagan Celts. When the Christians stormed in during the Middle Ages and decided to civilize, they decorated the terrain with churches constructed out of the supposedly Celt-proof local granite. This same granite filters the famed mineral-rich waters of the region, which are considered curative in homeopathic circles.

Although the Mühlviertel is considered part of industrial Austria, it's more of an arts and crafts place. Along the popular old **Mühlviertel Weberstraße** (Fabric Trail), analogous on a country-lane scale to the Middle Eastern Silk Road, various textile-oriented towns display their unique methods of linen preparation. Other vacation trails include the **Gotische Straße,** which winds past multitudes of High Gothic architectural wonders, and the **Museum Straße,** which boasts more **Freilichtmuseums** (open-air museums) than you can shake a loom at. Shake that loom. These museum villages typically recreate the 15th- and 16th-century peasant lifestyle of a functional hamlet. Poppies are also a big selling point, with products ranging from poppy-seed oil and lubricants to mouth-watering poppyseed strudels and poppyseed-and-honey-filled tarts bringing the valley fame. Iron from Steiermark (Styria) flowed through the Mühlviertel on its way to Bohemia along the **Pferdeisenbahn,** an ancient trade route once traversed by horse-drawn caravans that is now a hiking fave. All through this pastoral countryside, *Bauernhöfe* (farm houses) open their doors to world-weary vacationers in search of a little rural R&R. For nifty tourist brochures about trails, *Bauernhöfe,* and the general area, contact the **Mühlviertel Tourist Office,** Blütenstr. 8, A-4040 Linz, Postfach 57 (tel. (0732) 23 50 20 or 23 81 55).

■ Freistadt

Due to its strategic location on the *Pferdeeisenbahn* between Babenberg and Habsburg lands, **Freistadt** was a stronghold of the medieval salt and iron trade and remains the main city in industrial Mühlviertel. Unlike most industrial cities, however, Freistadt basks in fresh air and lush, verdant crop fields; coming up from Linz, you'll be surprised by the sudden shift from brick walls to rolling pastures. In 1985, Freistadt received the International Europa Nostra Prize for the finest restoration of a medieval *Altstadt.* Visitors can journey around its well-preserved inner and outer wall fortifications, scan the horizon from its watch tower, feast inside its castle, and swim in the surrounding moat. Come sit in one of the many *Gastgärten* perched on the city's inner wall overlooking the moat and enjoy the locally brewed **Freistädter Bier.** Many liken Freistadt to Germany's Rothenburg, another town seemingly untouched for the past, oh, five or six centuries.

ORIENTATION AND PRACTICAL INFORMATION Freistadt, at the juncture of the Jaunitz and Feldiast Rivers, is easily accessible from **Linz. Buses** are the most convenient option, leaving from Linz's main train station every two hours (round-trip 78AS) and arriving at Böhmertor in Freistadt, which lies just outside the old city walls, a two-minute walk to Hauptpl. **Trains** from Linz run every two hours until 10pm (round-trip 78AS) and arrive at the *Hauptbahnhof,* 3km outside of town. You can catch the city **shuttle bus** from the back of the station to Hauptpl. (10AS). The shuttle only runs weekdays, leaving the train station twice daily at 8 and 11am. To hoof it to the city center, turn right, walk down the street (it will merge with Leonfeldnerstr.), turn left on Bahnhofstr. (which becomes Brauhausstr.), and follow it until the end at Promenade/Linzerstr. The main gate to the town, the Linzertor, will be visible (30min.); **Hauptplatz** lies within. **Taxis** (tel. 723 54) to the old town cost 70-100AS. The tiny **tourist office,** Hauptpl. 14 (tel./fax 757 00), has a free reservations service and provides info about the surrounding Mühlviertel villages. (Open May-Sept. M-F 9am-9pm, Sa 9am-1pm; Oct.-Apr. M-F 9am-noon and 2-5pm.) **Store luggage** (30AS) and **rent bikes** (150AS, with train ticket or railpass 90AS) at the station. The **post office,** Promenade 11 at St. Peterstr., **exchanges** only hard cash. (Open M-F 8am-noon and 2-5:30pm, Sa 8-10:30am.) The **postal code** is A-4240. The **telephone code** is 07942.

ACCOMMODATIONS AND FOOD Freistadt has a few reasonably priced accommodations. To get to the **Jugendherberge (HI),** Schlosshof 3 (tel. 743 65), from the tourist office, walk around the corner to the red building next to Café Lubinger. The hostel is fairly empty and the owner doesn't have reception hours, so you should call to let them know you're coming. Hand-painted stripes, silly cartoons, and homemade paintings decorate the walls, and the rooms are very comfortable and clean. The accommodating proprietor, Margarete Howel, will wait from 6 to 8pm to give you a key; if no one is there or you don't arrive in time, call her at home at 32 68. (Dorms 70AS, non-members 90AS. Hall showers and toilets. Breakfast 30AS. Sheets 30AS. **Kitchen** facilities in the youth center below.) For a perfectly positioned place, pick **Pension Pirklbauer,** Höllg. 2/4 (tel. 724 40), in the *Altstadt* right next to the Linzertor. All rooms have bath, phone, and TV. If you ask in advance, you can have breakfast in the *Gästegarten* overlooking the old moat. (Singles 230AS; doubles 400AS. Breakfast included.)

There are a variety of cheap eats at cozy *Gästehäuser;* prowl around for different offerings. Enjoy a *tête-à-tête* at **Café Vis à Vis,** Salzg. 13 (tel. 742 93). It offers such local fare as *Mühlviertel Bauernsalat mit Suppe* (farmer's salad with soup; 60AS) and *Freistädter* beer in a garden crowded with young people. Midday *Menüs* run 63-90AS. (Open M-F 9:30am-2am, Sa 5pm-1am.) **Foxi's Schloßtaverne,** Hauptpl. 11 (tel. 39 30), right next to the tourist information center, caters to an older but no less raucous crowd. Weekday *Menüs* (70-90AS) offer soup, a main course, and a side order. The Greek salad (75AS) is humongous, and pizza is available for sit-in and take-out. They, too, serve *Freistädter* beer. (Open daily 11am-1am, kitchen open until 11pm.) The best ice cream in all of Mühlviertel (what an honor) awaits at **Café Lubiner,** Hauptpl. 10 (soft-serve 12AS, scoops of the hard stuff 7AS each). Pastries (25AS) and a great breakfast selection round out the menu. (Open Su-M and W-F 8am-7pm, Sa 8am-6pm.) The most convenient grocery store is **Uni Markt,** Pragerstr. 2, at Froschau behind the Böhmertor side of the *Innere Stadt.* The market is a one-stop bargain shop for six varieties of *Freistädter* beer. (Open M-F 8am-7pm, Sa 7:30am-12:30pm.)

SIGHTS AND ENTERTAINMENT The tower of Freistadt's remarkable 14th-century castle, the **Bergfried** (50m from the hostel), houses the **Mühlviertler Heimathaus**

UPPER AUSTRIA

Hooked on Pfonics

Ach, German—the musical language. A few German sounds are particularly charming to non-native speakers, such as the happy "pf" combination, found at the beginning of many German words and pronounced with two distinct consonants: "p-f." Try these few sentences to practice sounding like a native: *"Ein pfan in der Pfalz freßt einen pfirsichen Pfarrkuchen. Ein Pflaume-farber Pferrd fahrt pfeilschnell durch eine Pforte und freßt den Pfau. Das Pferd ein Pflanzenfresser war, aber er hat gedacht, der Pfau ein Pflanze oder vielleicht eine Pfingrose war."* (Translation: "A peacock at the imperial palace ate a peach pancake. Quick as an arrow a plum-colored horse burst through a gate and ate the peacock. The horse was an herbivore, but he mistook the peacock for a plant, perhaps a peony.")

(tel. 722 74). *(By tour only May-Oct. Tu-Sa 10am and 2pm, Su 10am; Nov.-Apr. Tu-F 2pm. 10AS).* This regional museum displays traditional tools, clothing, and period piece stuff. Descend through an archway down Ölberggasse's cobbled, shoulder-width twistings and its lovely hidden garden, or walk around the old moat that circumscribes the old city, now a stretch of gardens and mossy duck ponds. Numerous **hiking trails** branch out to amazing Mühlviertel destinations; consider hiking out of town and catching a bus back. Freistadt lies on the Mühlviertel **Museumstrasse,** a path linking many of the region's museums, and on the **Pferdeisenbahnwanderweg,** a 237km hiking trail along the former medieval trade route (see **Hooked on Pfonics,** above). A mildly strenuous one-hour hike zigzags up Kreuzweg to **St. Peter's Church.** A large map on the Promenade illustrates other local hiking paths, but there are no organized tours. Stop by **Wolfsgruber Bookstore,** Pfarrg. 16 (tel. 7305 61), for help planning an excursion. (Open M-F 7:30am-noon and 2:30-6pm, Sa 7:30am-noon.) The tourist office provides hiking maps (10-35AS), free bus schedules, and biking maps (25AS).

Freistadt's pride and joy is the **Freistädter Brauerei,** a community-owned brewery. Don't be surprised to see "I only drink Freistadt beer" stickers plastered on the steering wheels of most of the area's buses. It doesn't mean drunk driving, they're just really proud. In the 13th century, Freistadt granted every male citizen the right to brew and sell his own beer. Production soared. Herzog Rudolph IV, realizing the potential of the whole thing, revoked the right to establish a **beer monopoly** in 1363, and, as he grew rich, people grew angry. Popular outrage led eventually to a compromise: in 1737 when the city dissolved all small breweries and established a commonly held community brewery, still in operation outside the town walls at Promenade 7 (tel. 757 77). Unfortunately, the brewery is no longer open to the public. Each July and August, Freistadt holds a two-month festival of food and international music, the **Wirthausmusi,** with daily events scattered throughout town. Multicultural meets medieval—or just another excuse to drink *Freistädter* beer? You make the call.

Styria (Steiermark)

Styria is one of Austria's most stubbornly individualistic regions, cultivating a dialect that few outsiders can parse, a rich and gamey local cooking style, and a gruff sense of humor. Outside of Graz, the province is heavily forested and boasts an excellent local wine-making tradition. Rich deposits of iron ore made it very exciting to many over the centuries, rendering Styria one of Europe's first centers of primitive industry. The region also cashes in on the gold and precious stones of Graz, its burgeoning provincial capital. It is home to numerous pilgrimage shrines, a strong rural economy, and (among other things) the stud farm for Austria's breed of Lipizzaner horses.

🐎 HIGHLIGHTS OF STYRIA

- Graz has a vibrant student population and a healthy smattering of museums, including the strangely fascinating Old Arsenal.
- The cosmological hunting lodge Schloss Eggenberg has game preserves and Baroque encrustations.
- Mariazell is an international pilgrimage sight and an absolutely stupendous little alpine village. It is also home to some of the best *Lebkuchen* bakeries around.

THE MURTAL

Eons ago, before the mining of iron ore and manganese became *de rigueur* in south Austria, the **Mur River** in central and southern Styria carved a valley among the Gleinalpen to the west, Seetaler Alpen to the south, and Seckauer and Niedere Tauern to the north. Long, upland, pastured ridges flank the valley. Half of the region is covered by forests, and another quarter by grasslands and vineyards.

The Mur begins in the Salzburger Land and eventually joins the Drau in the former Yugoslavia. Low, rolling hills (2000m high at most) make the region golden for cyclists and hikers. Sprinkled among the ups and downs are small towns, old fortresses, and farms, surrounded by the vineyards that produce some of Austria's finest wines. Even cosmopolitan Graz remains connected to the land: a half hour's walk can take one out of the city and deep into hill and dale. The mostly rural countryside retains the charm of an earlier age, and the industry depends upon the mineral resources buried within the rounded mountains. The old commercial iron trade route, the **Steirische Eisenstraße** (Styrian Iron Road), winds through valleys and waterfalls from Leoben to Styria's pride and joy, the Erzberg (Iron Mountain), and on through the Enns Valley. The Murtal represents yesterday's Austria.

■ Leoben

Cloistered in the heartland of Austria's "Iron Belt," Leoben (pop. 35,000) lies between a ring of mountains and the Mur River. Although 1000-year-old Leoben is the largest city in Styria next to Graz, it still maintains a pastoral, rustic atmosphere. At the southernmost point on the *Steirische Eisenstraße,* Leoben is the proud home of a rather competitive **Mining University,** as well as seven other research institutions. Happily, the world of heavy labor and industry doesn't mar the natural beauty of Leoben. Three-quarters of the town's area is woodland, crowned by the idyllic city park "Am Glacis," visited by, among other notables, **Emperor Napoleon Bonaparte.** Its floral splendors have several times won Leoben the title of "most beautiful town in Styria" in the **Provincial Flower Competition,** and nearly all residents boast kaleidoscopic backyard gardens brimming with tiger lilies and marigolds that would make Martha Stewart jealous. Leoben makes a nice change of pace from the more hectic, bustling, tourist-oriented sites in Austria. You have the time to enjoy the local specialties, including mushroom goulash, **"Shepherd's Spit,"** and the excellent (and cheap) local **Gösser beer.**

ORIENTATION AND PRACTICAL INFORMATION The Mur River surrounds the town; from the train station, you must cross it to reach the heart of Leoben. **Franz-Josef-Strasse** (the main town artery) and **Peter-Tunner-Strasse** run parallel for the length of the town, leading to Hauptpl. and beyond. Leoben is just minutes from Autobahn A9, which runs south to Graz and northwest to Steyr and Linz.

The **train information counter** (tel. 425 45) at the station can help decipher the snarl of rail lines (open M-F 8am-6pm). Several major routes pour into the transit hub at **Bruck an der Mur** (15min., every 20min., 38AS). Direct trains run to **Graz** (every 2hr., 114AS), **Vienna** (every 2hr., 260AS), **Salzburg** (370AS), and **Klagenfurt** (every 2hr., 240AS). The train station also has **lockers** (20AS) and **luggage storage** (30AS; open 6:30am-9pm). The main **bus station** is a 10-minute walk from the train station at the corner of Franz-Josef-Str. and Parkstr. Buses run from Leoben to the rest of Styria (Graz: 100AS). Pick up bus schedules from the train station.

Leoben's **tourist office,** Hauptpl. 12 (tel. 440 18; fax 482 18), will help you plan your visit to the Murtal and cheerfully dispense a hotel list and a complimentary map. (Open M-Th 7am-noon and 1:30-5pm, F 7am-1pm.) Walk straight out of the train station, cross the river, and take your second right onto Franz-Josef-Str. Follow the road past the bus terminal to the main square. The tourist office is on the right. A new underground **parking garage** is under Hauptpl.; the old one stands on Kärtnerstr. (5AS per 30min.). **Taxi stands** are at Hauptpl. and the train station. Mail a postcard at the Otto Wagner-esque **post office** at Erzherzog-Johann-Str. 17. (Open M-F 8am-7pm, Sa 8-10am.) The **postal code** is A-8700. The **telephone code** is 03842.

ACCOMMODATIONS AND FOOD Leoben has few—make that no—budget accommodations and only nine establishments total. During the summer, the **Schulverein der Berg-und-Hüttenschule Leoben** dorm, Max-Tendlerstr. 3 (tel. 448 88; fax 44 88 83), rents 80 beds as a bed and breakfast. From the train station walk straight and cross the river. Turn right on Stadtkai until Peter Tunner Str., and follow Peter Tunner Str. until Max-Tendlerstr. Turn right and walk to the end. (10min.) Rooms are large, plain, and dorm-like. (207AS for 2-bed dorms; 910AS per week. Bath on floor. Ouch.) Otherwise, the closest thing to a good deal is **Hotel Altman,** Südbahnstr. 32 (tel. 422 16), with 22 beds and a small bowling alley in a convenient, albeit busy, location. The three-lane bowling alley tends to fill with locals joyfully and copiously partaking in the beverage that has been linked to the sport since the time of Adam. You know what that is. To reach the hotel, walk out of the train station and immediately turn left on Südbahnhofstr. Walk alongside the rail tracks for 10 minutes; the hotel is on the right. Private TV sets, showers, and hardwood floors help make Altman more luxurious than most hotels in this price range. (Singles 330AS; doubles 550AS. Breakfast included. Other meals 55-155AS. Bowling alley open Tu-Su 10am-midnight; 10AS for 10min. English spoken. Free parking. MC, Visa.) Cheaper hostels await in neighboring towns from May to September, like the **Jugendherberge (HI)** in Bruck an der Mur, Theodor-Körner-Str. 37 (tel. (03862) 534 65; fax 560 89), 16km to the east, with 50 beds in quads and larger dorms.

Fans of Italian or typical Austrian cooking will have no trouble in Leoben. **Gasthof Familie Hölzl,** Homanng. 8 (tel. 421 07), across from the Stadttheater, seems caught between two worlds, with Italian flags on the walls and *Wiener Schnitzel* on the menu. Pasta (60-76AS), salads drenched in olive oil (42-54AS), and fish (95-98AS) also appear. (Open M-F 8am-8pm, Sa 8am-2pm.) Kirchgasse is home to a number of cheap restaurants. Another alternative is **La Pizza,** Langg. 1 (tel. 453 47), which has larges for two (59-94AS) but nowhere to sit—take out a pie to enjoy by the river. (Open M-F 11am-2pm and 5-10pm, Sa-Su 11am-10pm.) Or get some edibles at the **markets** along Franz-Josef-Str. or at **Billa,** Langg. 5. (Open M-Th 7:30am-6:30pm, F 7:30am-8pm, Sa 7am-1pm.) A **farmer's market** sets up in Kirchpl. (Tu and F 7am-1pm.)

SIGHTS AND ENTERTAINMENT Most of Leoben's attractions cluster around **Hauptplatz,** 10 minutes from the train station (cross the bridge and bear right onto Franz-Josef-Str.). Sights are designated by a square with a bizarre imprint of an ostrich eating iron horseshoes, one held daintily between its toes and the other protruding from its beak. This city symbol alludes to Leoben's dependence on the iron trade—in the Middle Ages, ostriches were thought capable of eating and digesting iron. That's a goose, you say? Alright, smarty, think of this: when it was designed, no one knew what an ostrich looked like.

Most of the buildings on Hauptpl. are former homes of the **Hammerherren** (Hammer men). The most ornate of the bunch is the 1680 **Hacklhaus,** bearing a dozen statues on its pink facade. Justice holds a sword and a balance, Hope brandishes an anchor, and Wisdom views the world through the mirror in his hand. Now that's wise. Standing guard at the entrance to Hauptpl. are the **Denkmäler und Monumente** (memorial statues and monuments), beautifully crafted works erected to ward off the fires and plague that devastated much of Styria in the early 18th century. Look for St. Florian the fire-proof and St. Rosalia the plague-resistant. Just outside Hauptpl. is the **Pfarrkirche Franz Xavier,** a rust-colored church with twin towers built from 1660 to 1665 by the Jesuits. The simple facade belies an elaborate interior and a high altar bedecked with remarkable Solomonic columns. An ever-vigilant fungus, the **Schwammerlturm** (Mushroom Tower) guards the bridge over the Mur.

Leoben is full of meticulously manicured gardens. Stroll through the **Stadtpark "Am Glacis"** one block past Hauptpl. There, you can visit the **Friedensgedenkstätte** (Peace Memorial), which commemorates the 1791 treaty with Napoleon. *(Open May-Sept. daily 9am-1pm and 2-5pm. Free.)* The small museum showcases an exhibit detailing the political and military events surrounding the treaty—see the very feather pen that Napoleon used to inscribe his signature.

A scenic 30-minute walk along the Mur rewards you with the chance to inspect the **Gösser brewery** (tel. 20 90 58 02). Examine antique brewing machinery, wander around inside the **Göss Abbey** (the oldest abbey in Styria), and swill down a free stein of fresh brew. You can only tour if you arrange ahead of time (the **free beer** is worth it). The **Stadttheater,** Homanng. 224 (tel. 406 23 02), is the oldest functioning theater in all of Austria. *(Box office open M-Sa 9:30am-12:30pm and Th-F 4pm-6:30pm. Theater on vacation June-Sept.)* The city fills the summer void with the **Leobener Kultursommer,** a program of theater, classical and pop concerts, literary readings, and treasure hunts. Pick up a free program from the tourist office.

■ Graz

Despite its size (second in Austria only to Vienna) and its dignified medieval and Baroque past, Graz remains surprisingly undertouristed, even during the exciting festival season in late July and August. The city's energy comes largely from the 45,000 students studying at the famous Karl-Franzens-Universität, founded in 1585 and once home to Johannes Kepler. The thriving arts community has adapted comfortably to the eclectic architecture and bustling plazas of the city center. Concerts and performances are held in churches, arcades, and squares throughout the beautiful *Altstadt.* The university even features the only jazz department in all of Europe.

Since Charlemagne claimed this strategic crossroads for his empire, Graz (now 60km from the Slovenian and Hungarian borders) has witnessed over a thousand years of European-Asian hostility. The ruins of the fortress perched upon the **Schloßberg** commemorate the turmoil—the stronghold withstood battering at the hands of the Ottoman Turks, Napoleon's armies (three times), and most recently the Soviet Union during WWII. Down below, the city and its red-tiled roofs, extensive parks, and large-scale museums show no evidence of the centuries of conflict. In fact, the city is as healthy as ever—healthy enough to produce the likes of hometown hero **Arnold Schwarzenegger,** who was reared in Graz before he left his family and ath-

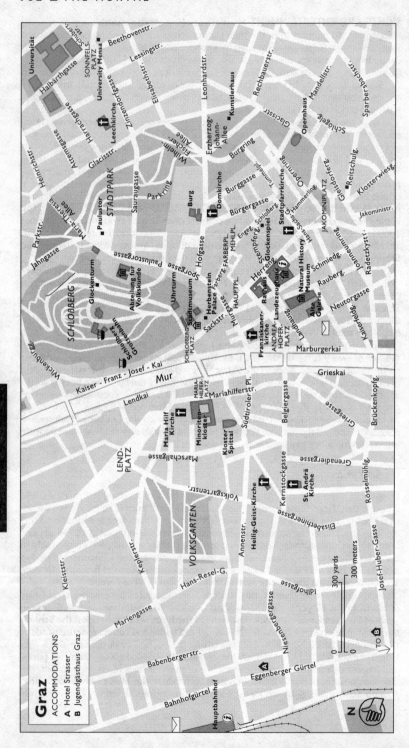

STYRIA

Graz
ACCOMMODATIONS
A Hotel Strasser
B Jugendgästhaus Graz

TO B →

letic trainer (who still live here) to become Conan, the Terminator, and, in the biggest leap of Hollywood imagination, pregnant. The small pond where Arnold proposed to Maria Shriver is now a pilgrimage site for determined fans, despite the bemused protestations of tourist officials that it's "nothing special."

GETTING TO AND FROM GRAZ

Flights arrive at the **Flughafen Graz,** Flughafenstr. 51, 9km from the city center (Bus #631 from the *Hauptbahnhof:* 30min., 6 per day, 5:10am-6:15pm, 20AS). All transcontinental flights are routed through Vienna. **Trains** depart from the **Hauptbahnhof,** on Europapl., west of the city center. (The *Ostbahnhof* on Conrad-von-Hötzendorf-Str. is mainly a freight station; don't get off here unless you came in a crate.) The **Graz-Köflach Bus** (GKB) departs from Griespl. for West Styria. For the remainder of Austria, the **BundesBus** departs from Europapl. 6 (next to the train station) and from Andreas-Hofer-Pl.

ORIENTATION AND PRACTICAL INFORMATION

Graz lies on both banks of the Mur River in the southeast corner of Austria, on the northern edge of the Graz plain. The city serves as a gateway to Slovenia (50km south) and Hungary (70km east). Fully two-thirds of Graz's five square km consist of beautiful parklands, earning it pithy nicknames like "Garden City" and "Green City." **Hauptplatz,** on the corner of Murg. and Sackstr., directly in front of the *Rathaus,* forms the social and commercial center of the city. **Jakominiplatz,** near the *Eisernes Tor* and five minutes from Hauptpl., is the hub of the city's bus and streetcar system. **Herrengasse,** a pedestrian street lined with cafes, boutiques, and ice cream shops, which runs from the Hauptpl. to Jakominipl., forms the heart of the *Fußgängerzone.* The **Universität** is tucked away in the northeast part of Graz, near the posh residential district of St. Leonhard. The **Hauptbahnhof** lies on the other side of the river, a short ride from Hauptpl. on tram #1, 3, or 6. To get to the city center by foot from the train station, follow Annenstr. up and over Hauptbrücke (15min.).

If you're staying in Graz for at least three days and are eligible for student or senior discounts, you might consider purchasing a **Graz Card** from the tourist office (180AS). It entitles you to three days of free bus and tram travel, 10 to 60% reductions on most museums, and 5 to 10% off at some shops and restaurants. The **Graz Card Light** offers the same discounts without the free transportation (69AS).

Transportation

Flights: Flughafen Graz (tel. 29 02). Shuttles (20AS) leave the airport to Graz 6 times per day, with the last bus at 6:45pm. They also stop at Hotel Daniel, Hotel Weitzer, and Griespl. before arriving at the airport 30min. later. The information office at the airport is open 6am-8pm.

Trains: Hauptbahnhof, Europapl. (tel. 78 48, info 17 17; lines open 7am-9pm). To: **Salzburg** (4¼hr., 10 per day, 1st train 6:22am, last train 10pm, 410AS), **Linz** (3¾hr., 7 per day, 1st train 6:22am, last train 6:22pm, 350AS), **Innsbruck** (6¼hr., 8 per day, 1st train 6:22am, last train 10pm, 560AS), **Vienna** (3¾hr., 7 per day, 1st train 6:22am, last train 6:22pm, 350AS), **Zurich** (10hr., 2 per day, 1st train 8:22am, last train 10pm, 1026AS), and **Munich** (6¼hr., 8 per day, 1st train 6:22am, last train 6:22pm, 714AS).

Buses: Graz-Köflach Bus (GKB), Köflneherg. 35-41 (tel. 59 87), is open M-F 8am-5pm. The BundesBus office, Andreas-Hofer-Pl. 17, is open M-F 6am-6:30pm. **Branch** at the *Hauptbahnhof* open M-F 9am-noon.

Public Transportation: For information on all buses, trams, and trains call 82 06. Open M-F 8am-5pm. Purchase single tickets (20AS) and 24hr. tickets (40AS) from the driver, booklets of 10 tickets (150AS) or week-tickets (92AS) from any *Tabak.* Tickets are valid for all trams, buses, and the **cable car** that ascends to the Schloßberg. Children half-price. The penalty for "black-riding" (without a ticket) is 500AS. Most tram lines run until 11pm, most bus lines until 9pm. Check the schedules posted at every *Haltestelle* for details.

Taxi: Funktaxi, Griespl. 28 (tel. 983). **City-Funk,** Glockenspielpl. 6 (tel. 878). We want da noise, we want da funk!

Car Rental: Avis, at the airport and Schlögelg. 10 (tel. 81 29 20; fax 84 11 78). **Budget,** Europapl. 12 (tel. 71 69 66; fax 72 20 74), and at the airport (tel. 29 02, ext. 342). **Hertz,** Andreas-Hofer-Pl. 1 (tel. 82 50 07; fax 81 02 88). **Europcar,** at the airport (tel. 29 67 57; fax 24 25 47).

Automobile Clubs: ÖAMTC, Giradig. (tel. 50 42 61) and **ARBÖ,** Kappellenstr. 45 (tel. 271 60 00).

Bike Rental: At the train station. 150-200AS per day, 90-160AS with Eurailpass or valid ticket. Open M-F 6:30am-6pm, Sa 6:30am-4pm, Su 7am-3:30pm.

Tourist and Financial Services

Tourist Office: Main office, Herreng. 16 (tel. 807 50; fax 807 55 55; email info@graztourismus.at; http://www.graztourismus.at). Cordial staff gives away detailed city maps and sells a walking guide of the city (10AS). Room reservations 30AS in person, free if you call in advance. The office leads **tours** of the *Altstadt* in English and German that start out front (2½hr., June-Sept. 2:30pm; Oct.-May Sa only; 75AS). Open in summer M-F 9am-7pm, Sa 9am-6pm, Su and holidays 10am-3pm; in winter M-F 9am-6pm, Sa 9am-3pm, Su and holidays 10am-3pm. **Branch,** Europapl. 6 (tel. 91 68 37), at the *Hauptbahnhof.* Open M-Sa 9am-1pm and 2-6pm.

Consulates: South Africa, Villefortg. 13 (tel. 322 548). **U.K.,** Schmiedg. 10 (tel. 82 61 05).

Currency Exchange: Best rates at the main **post office** (open M-F 7am-11pm, Sa 7am-2pm, Su 8am-2pm). Most banks open M-F 8am-noon and 2-4pm. At the train station, extensive hours (M 5am-10pm, Tu-Su 5:45pm-10pm).

Local Services

Luggage Storage: At the station. 30AS per day. Open daily 6am-midnight. Lockers 30-50AS.

English-Language Bookstores: English Bookshop, Tummelpl. 7 (tel. 82 62 66; fax 81 23 96; email english.books@aon.net; http://members.aon.net/english.books), sells virtually everything and in English. Hardcovers are sometimes cheaper than paperbacks, but then you have to carry them. Open M-F 9am-6pm, Sa 9am-noon.

Bi-Gay-Lesbian Organizations: Rosarote Panther/Schwul-lesbische Arbeitsgemeinschaft Steiermark, Postfach 34 (tel. 47 11 19). **Frauenberatungstelle** (Women's Information Center), Marienpl. 5/2 (tel. 71 60 22).

Laundromat: Putzeri Rupp, Jakominstr. 34 (tel. 82 11 83), has do-it-yourself (5kg load 65AS) and professional handling. Open M-F 8am-5pm, Sa 8am-noon.

AIDS Hotline: Steirische AIDS-Hilfe, Schmiedg. 38 (tel. 81 50 50). Drop-in´hours W 11am-1pm, Tu and Th 6:30am-7:30pm, F 4-7pm.

Pharmacy: Bärenapotheker, Herreng. 11 (tel. 83 02 67), opposite the tourist office. Open M-F 8am-12:30pm and 2:30-6pm, Sa 8am-noon. AmEx, MC, Visa.

Emergency and Communication

Hospital: Krankenhaus der Elisabethinen, Elisabethinerg. 14 (tel. 90 63).

Emergencies: Police, tel. 133. **Ambulance,** tel. 144.

Police Office: Europapl. 7 (tel. 888 27 75), outside of the main train station. From 8pm-5am, enter from train platform 1.

Post Office: Main office, Neutorg. 46. Open M-F 9am-11pm, Sa 8am-2pm, Su 8am-noon. A **branch office,** Europapl. 10, is next to the main train station. Open 24hr. **Postal code:** A-8010; branch office A-8020.

Internet Access: Café Zentral, Andreas-Hoger-Pl. 9 (tel. 83 24 68). Well, you're not here for the bar. 60AS for 1hr. minimum, divided among as many visits as you want. Open M-Sa 6:30-10pm. The **hostel** also has internet access.

Telephone Code: 0316.

ACCOMMODATIONS

Sniffing out a cheap bed in Graz may require a bit of detective work, as most budget hotels, guest houses, and pensions run 300-450AS per person, and many are located in the boondocks. Luckily, the web of local transport provides a reliable and easy commute to and from the city center. Ask the tourist office about *Privatzimmern* (most 150-300AS per night), especially in the tourist-bloated summer months.

Hotel Strasser, Eggenberger Gürtel 11 (tel. 71 39 77; fax 71 68 56; email hotel.strasser@noten.com), 5min. from the train station. Exit the station, cross the street, and head right on Bahnhofgürtel; the hotel is on the left, across from the Midas station. Big, breezy rooms with big windows and attractive rugs. Top-rate restaurant downstairs serves the best budget cocoa you'll get on your entire trip. Singles 340AS, with shower 440AS; doubles 560AS, 660AS; triples 840AS; quads 1000AS. Breakfast included. Free parking.

Hotel Zur Stadt Feldbach, Conrad-von-Hötzendorf-Str. 58 (tel. 82 94 68; fax 84 73 71), 20min. south of Jakominipl. From Hauptpl. or Jakominipl., take tram #4 (dir: Liebnau) or 5 (dir: Puntigam): "Jakominigürtel." The hotel is on the corner to the right. A central staircase with a sky-blue wrought-iron balustrade curves up to lino-leum-floored bedrooms with patterned blankets and shower stalls. Singles 350AS; doubles 500AS, with shower 650AS; triples with shower 800AS. Breakfast 50AS. 24hr. reception on the 2nd floor.

Jugendgästehaus Graz (HI), Idlhofg. 74 (tel. 71 48 76; fax 71 48 76 88), 15min. from the train station. Exit the station and cross the street, head right on Eggen-berger Gürtel, take a left at Josef-Huber-G. (after the car dealership), then take the 1st right at Idlhofg. The hostel is hidden behind a parking lot on your right. Buses #31, 32, and 33 run here from Jakominipl. (last bus around midnight). Institutional dorm rooms off halls bedecked with student art. 4-bed dorms 200AS; singles 300AS; doubles 500AS. Non-members add 40AS. Small breakfast included (all-you-can-eat 45AS). Lunch 65AS. Sheets 20AS. **Laundry** 40AS, soap 5AS. **Internet access** 15AS for 30min. Reception 7am-11pm. No real curfew; security guard opens the doors every 30min. from 10pm-2am. Key available (300AS deposit).

Camping Central, Martinhofstr. 3 (tel./fax 28 18 31). Bus #31 (dir: Webling.) to the last stop (20min.), continue down main street, turn right onto Weiberfelerweg after McDonalds, then make the 1st right onto Martinhofstr. (15min. from the bus stop). A clean campground with an enormous swimming pool (free) and miniature golf (25AS, children 20AS). 60AS, children 30AS; tent 100AS; camper 125AS; guest tax 5AS; laundry 70AS; showers included. Reception 8am-10pm. Open Apr.-Oct.

FOOD

Graz's 45,000 students sustain a bonanza of cheap eateries. Inexpensive meals await at Hauptpl. and Lendpl., off Keplerstr. and Lendkai, where concession stands sell *Wurst,* ice cream, beer, and other fast food until about 8pm. There are markets along Rösselmühlgasse, an extension of Josef-Huber-G., and on Jakoministr. directly off Jakominipl. Low-priced student hangouts line Zinzendorfg. near the university. Note that most salads come dressed in the local dark pumpkin-seed oil.

Restaurants

University Mensa, Sonnenfelspl. 1 (tel. 32 33 62), just east of the Stadtpark at the intersection of Zinzendorfg. and Leechg. Bus #39: "Uni./Mensa." The best deal in town in a brand-new building with a tree growing among the tables. Simple and satisfying *Menüs,* vegetarian *(Vollwert)* or with meat, for 47-53AS. Large à la carte selection includes diverse salads (16AS) and pizza (25AS). 29AS gets a breakfast of two rolls, butter, jam, and coffee or tea. Blue tickets, distributed only to university students, shave 8AS off the price of a meal. Open M-F 8:30am-2:30pm.

Kebap Haus, Jakoministr. 16 (tel. 81 10 06), just south of Jakominipl. A superior Turkish restaurant with inexpensive sandwiches on homemade pitas (38-52AS) and delicious Mediterranean pizzas (72-89AS). Try the *Etli Pidde,* a fresh pizza with lamb, tomatoes, garlic, peppers, and oregano. Lunch specials include soup, entree, and dessert (80-86AS). High-quality falafel (76AS). Open M-Sa 11am-midnight.

Gastwirtschaft Wartburgasse, Halbärthg. 4 (tel. 38 87 50). Trendy posters and loud music make this indoor/outdoor café/bar Graz's premier student hangout. Well-made standard dishes make up for the wait. Lunch specials 50-70AS. Pasta, vegetar-ian, and meat dishes 42-120AS. Open 9am-2am.

Calafati, Lissag. 2 (tel. 91 68 89), a 3min. walk from the hostel away from the train station. Lunch combos (main course, soup or spring roll, dessert 42-75AS) make this slightly out-of-the-way Chinese restaurant quite a bargain. Several vegetarian and take-out options 65-89AS. Lunch special 11:30am-3pm; dinner 5:30-11:30pm.

Interspar Restaurant, Lazarett-Gürtel 55, at the supermarket in the City Park mall. Nice salad bar and an extensive warm buffet. *Schwammergulasch mit Knödel* (69AS) and attractive fruit tarts (17AS) among many options. Open M-F 7am-7:30pm, Sa 8am-5pm.

Markets

There are **outdoor markets** at Kaiser-Josef-Pl. and Lendpl., where vendors hawk their fruits and vegetables amid a happy splash of colors. (Open M-Sa 8am-1pm.) Other markets line Hauptpl. and Jakominipl. (Open M-F 7am-6pm, Sa 7am-12:30pm.)

Merkar, Europapl., left as you leave the *Bahnhof*. Free parking in underground garage for customers. Open M-Th 8am-7pm, F 7:30am-7:30pm, Sa 7am-5pm.

Interspar, Lazarett-Gürtel 55 (tel. 71 04 36), in the enormous City Park shopping mall. Open M-F 9am-7:30pm, Sa 8am-5pm. Also next door to the *Mensa*. Open M-F 8am-1pm and 4-6:30pm, Sa 7:30am-12:30pm.

SIGHTS

"Tastes, architecture, and slaps in the face are all different," goes one old Styrian proverb, and Graz proves it. The first two, at least. Classical arches, domes, and red-tiled roofs fold into a twisting maze of cobblestone streets, while the stark modern buildings of Technical University a few blocks away show the influence of Graz's well-known School of Architecture. An entertaining and systematic way to explore diverse Graz is through the tourist office's guide, *Old Town Walk* (10AS). The tourist office in the **Landhaus,** still the seat of the provincial government, is a sight in itself. The building was remodeled by architect Domenico dell'Allio in 1557 in masterful Lombard style. Through the arch to the right is a glorious arcaded stone courtyard, overflowing with geraniums in summer, and the site of the annual *Classics in the City* festival (see **Entertainment,** below).

On the other side of the tourist office is the strangely fascinating **Landeszeughaus** (Provincial Arsenal), Herreng. 16 (tel. 877 36 39 or 877 27 78), built from 1642 to 1644 by Anton Solar. *(Open Apr.-Oct. M-F 9am-5pm, Sa-Su 9am-1pm. Tours 11am and 3pm, call ahead for English ones. Admission with a Joanneum ticket (see below). Free English info sheet.)* The first floor details the history of the arsenal and the Muslim Ottoman aggression in a series of excellent placards and displays, with English translations. In 1749, when the Turkish threat dissipated, the armory was marked for dismantling, but an eloquent protest by the Styrian nobles convinced Empress Maria Theresa to preserve the arsenal as a symbolic gesture. The building, with its massive collection of arms and armor intact, served as a firehouse until 1882, when it first opened as a museum. Today, the eerie four-story collection includes enough scintillating spears, muskets, and armor to outfit 28,000 burly mercenaries. The full experience is one of extravagant spectacle, with thousands of metal barrels and blades spread out (from the ceiling and walls) in abstract geometrical patterns. Windows from the poorly lit halls look out over the *Landhaus* arcade. Leave at least two hours to learn the history and peruse the collection.

The arsenal is just a tiny part of the collection of the **Landesmuseum Joanneum,** the oldest public museum in Austria. The assembled holdings are so vast and eclectic that officials have been forced to categorize the legacy and to house portions in separate museums scattered throughout the city. One ticket, purchased at any of the locations, is valid for all. *(60AS, 40AS for students and seniors.)* The **Neue Galerie,** Sackstr. 16 (tel. 82 91 55; fax 81 54 01; email neue-galerie-graz@sime.com; http://www.sime.com/neue_galerie), in the gorgeous Palais Herberstein at the foot of the Schloßberg, showcases off-beat, avant-garde contemporary works and a collection of 19th- and 20th-century paintings. *(Open Tu-Su 10am-5pm.)* The **Alte Galerie,** Neutarg.

45 (tel. 80 17 47 70), presents a mid-sized collection of Medieval and Baroque art, mostly by Styrian artists. *(Open Tu-Su 10am-5pm. Tours Su at 11am. English descriptions available.)* Notable holdings include **Lucas Cranach's** *Judgment of Paris* and Jan Brueghel's copy of his father's gruesome *Triumph of Death.* The Alte Galerie shares space with the **Kunstgewerbe** (tel. 8017 4780), an exhibition space for late 19th- and 20th-century art and design. (Hours vary by exhibition.) The **Natural History Museum,** Rauberg. 10, (tel. 30 17 47 60, -50, -40, or -30), encompasses geology, paleontology, mineralogy, zoology, and other -ologies. *(Open M-F 9am-4pm, Sa-Su 9am-noon.)* The museum boasts a specimen of the largest beetle in the world and a truly splendid collection of minerals and semi-precious stones. Ask in the Geology gallery to leave the museum through the secret coal mine.

Across Herreng. from the Landzeughaus is the lemon yellow **Stadtpfarrkirche,** originally the Abbey Church of the Dominicans in the 16th century. Done up in late Gothic style, the church suffered severe damage in WWII air raids. When Salzburger artist Albert Birkle designed new stained-glass windows for the church in 1953, one made worldwide news: the left panel behind the high altar portrays the scourging of Christ, silently watched over by two figures bearing a marked resemblance to Hitler and Mussolini. The church holds **organ concerts** early July to early September on Thursdays at 8pm. *(70AS, students 40AS.)*

North of Herreng. and Hauptpl., the wooded **Schloßberg** pokes up 123m. *(Tours in German or English Apr.-Oct. Tu-Su 10am-4pm on the hour; 30AS, students and children 15AS; meet at the Glockenturm.)* The castle after which the hill is named stood from 1125 until its destruction at the hands of Napoleon in 1809. With the castle almost completely gone, the Schloßberg remains a beautiful city park. From Schloßbergpl., visitors can climb the zigzagging stone steps of the **Schloßbergsteig,** built by Russian prisoners during WWII and traditionally known as the *Russensteig* (Russian steps) or the *Kriegsteig* (war steps). The path continues through the terraced **Herberstein Gardens** to the top of the hill. Napoleon never managed to defeat the Schloßberg fortress until *after* he conquered the rest of Austria—he then razed the fortress in an infantile rage. The town, however, managed to rescue the bell and clock towers by paying the little Emperor a sizeable ransom. The **Glockenturm** (bell tower), built in 1588, is one of the few castle structures still standing. *(Tower open 9am-5pm, except during guided tours; 15AS, students and children 10AS.)* Its enormous bell ("Liesl") draws a crowd with its 101 clangings daily at 7am, noon, and 7pm. The nearby **Uhrturm** (clocktower) dates from 1265. A guided tour of the Schloßberg includes viewing the Uhrturm clockworks of 1712. The **Garnisonsmuseum** shows a modest hilltop collection of military uniforms and feathered helmets. *(Open Tu-Su 10am-5pm. 20AS, students and children 10AS. Combo ticket including Schloßberg tour 40AS, 20AS.)*

From Schloßbergpl., the **Schloßberg Passage** penetrates the *Berg.* *(Open daily 8am-8pm; free.)* A network of tunnels were blasted into the hill during WWII to serve as an enormous bomb shelter for up to 50,000 civilians. Visitors may walk through the cool, dark main passage and peer down spooky side tunnels. The **Grazer Schloßberg Grottenbahn** travels for 30 minutes through the mountain past an array of illuminated scenes from fairy tales, history, and literature, including stuffed dummy Gulliver restrained by dozens of dusty Lilliputian Ken dolls. *(Open daily 9am-6pm; tickets up to 35AS.)*

Next door to the Neue Galerie at the western foot of the Schloßberg is the **Stadtmuseum,** Sackstr. 18 (tel. 82 25 80). *(Open Tu 10am-9pm, W-Sa 10am-6pm, Su 10am-1pm; 50AS. students and children 30AS.)* On the third floor, a series of 19th-century drawings of the city are presented alongside modern photographs and a large-scale model circa 1800. Down the hill on the eastern side near the Uhrturm and through the Paulustor arch is the lovely **Stadtpark.** Separating the old city from the university quarter, the carefully tended gardens provide a large island of calm right in the heart of the city, attracting walkers, sun-bathers, and frisbee players. Damn frisbee players. Graz acquired the ornate central fountain, which has eight figures holding huge spitting fish, at the 1873 Vienna World's Fair. Paris snatched up the two complementary side pieces, now in Pl. de la Concorde. The **Künstlerhaus,** a museum nestled in the Stadtpark, showcases eclectically themed exhibitions ranging from Tibetan artifacts to Secessionist paintings by Klimt and others. *(Open M-Sa 9am-6pm, Su 9am-noon. Prices vary with exhibitions.)* The 13th-century Gothic **Leechkirche,** Zinzendorfg. 5, between the Stadtpark and the university, is the city's oldest structure.

South of the fish fountain, the Stadtpark blends into the **Burggarten,** a bit of carefully pruned greenery complementing what remains of Emperor Friedrich III's 15th-century **Burg.** *(Garden open 7:30am-7pm.)* The cryptic wall inscription "A.E.I.O.U." remains a mystery, varyingly interpreted as *"Austria Est Imperare Orbi Universo," "Austria Erit In Orbe Ultima,"* or *"Alles Erdreich Ist Österreich Untertan."* A vague desire for Austria to **rule the universe** can be intuited. Or a love of vowels. Friedrich's son, Maximilian I, enlarged the building and in 1499 commissioned the unique Gothic double spiral staircase, predating Watson and Crick by almost 500 years. He also inserted the **Burgtor** (Castle Gate) into the city wall.

Stroll through the Burg's courtyard and out through the giant gate to find Hofg. and the **Dom** (cathedral). In 1174, Friedrich III had the existing Romanesque chapel redone to transform the three-bayed cathedral into late-Gothic style, but the simple exterior hides the interior's wacky Baroque embellishments. In 1485, the church mounted a picture of the "Scourges of God" on the south side of the building to remind Christians of the most palpable trinity of the time: the Black Death, Ottoman invasions, and the locusts—a combination that had wiped out 80% of the population five years earlier. The huge fresco of Christ over the lintel inside the church bears the features of Emperor Friedrich III—worshippers believed that if they caught a glimpse of his eyes, they would pass without harm.

Next door, on Burgg., is the solemn 17th-century Habsburg **Mausoleum,** one of the finest examples of Austrian Mannerism. *(Open M-Sa 10am-12:30pm and 2-4pm. 10AS, children 5AS.)* The domed tomb holds the remains of Ferdinand II in the damp underground chamber. Somewhat cryptic English placards are pasted to the cool, stone walls. Master architect Johann Bernard Fischer von Erlach (responsible for, among other things, much of Vienna's Ringstraße) designed the beautiful frescoes upstairs. The **Opernhaus** (opera house), at Opernring and Burgg., was built in under two years by Viennese theater architects Fellner and Helmer. The Graz **Glockenspiel,** located just off Engeg. in Glockenspielpl., opens its wooden doors every day at 11am, 3, and 6pm to reveal life-size wooden figures spinning to a slightly out-of-tune folk song. The black and gold ball underneath turns to show the phases of the moon.

ENTERTAINMENT

There's entertainment in Graz to suit even the most curmudgeonly vacationer. Students can check the **student administration office** of the university, which has billboards papered with concert notices, student activity flyers, and carpool advertisements for all of Austria. For professional music and dance performances, Graz's remarkable neo-Baroque **Opernhaus** (opera house), at Opernring and Burgg. (tel. 80 08), sells standing-room tickets at the door an hour before curtain call. The yearly program includes operas and ballets of worldwide repute; for many young hopefuls, Graz is considered a stepping stone to an international career. One big show comes each July while the regular companies are on vacation—1996 and 1997 brought the Bolshoi Ballet and 1998 the Kirov. Tickets cost a pretty penny (360-1490AS), but standing-room slots start at 100AS, and phenomenal student rush tickets cost 150AS. The **Schauspielhaus,** a theater at Freiheitspl. off Hofg. (tel. 80 05), also sells bargain seats just before showtime. All tickets and performance schedules are available at the **Theaterkasse,** Kaiser-Josef-Pl. 10 (tel. 80 00; fax 800 85 65; open M-F 8am-6:30pm, Sa 8am-1pm), and the **Zentralkartenbüro,** Herreng. 7 (tel. 83 02 55).

In late September and October, the **Steierischer Herbst** (Styrian Autumn) festival celebrates avant-garde art with a month of films, performances, art installations, and parties. Contact the director of the festival, Sackstr. 17 (tel. 823 00 70; fax 83 57 88; email stherbst@ping.at; http://www.ping.at/members/stherbst), for details. Since 1985, the city has hosted its own summer festival, **Styriarte,** as well. Mostly classical concerts are held daily from late June to early July in the gardens of the Schloß Eggenberg, the large halls of Graz Convention Center, and the squares of the old city. The renowned Graz conductor, Nikolaus Harnoncourt, sets the tone. Tickets available at Palais Attems, Sackstr. 17; tel. 82 50 00; email styriarte@mail.styria.co.at; http://www.styriarte.com. *(Open M-F 8:30am-12:30pm and 2-6pm, Sa 9am-1pm;)* The award-winning movie theater **Rechbauerkino,** Rechbauerstr. 6 (tel. 83 05 08), occasionally screens undubbed arthouse films in English (85AS, children 70AS). The **Royal Kino,** Conrad-von-Hötzendorfstr. 10, a few blocks south of Jakominipl., shows only new releases in English, without subtitles (70AS before 6:45pm, 85AS after). In summer, the **Classics in the City Festival** shows films of great opera performances in the *Landhaus* courtyard next to the tourist office (July-Aug. daily at 8:30pm; free). Every summer the **American Institute of Musical Studies** transfers to Graz. Vocal and instrumental students perform constantly on the streets and in concert halls—ask for a schedule of works ranging from Broadway to Schönberg at the tourist office. From July to mid-August, organ concerts are held every Thursday at the Stadtpfarrkirche and every Sunday at the *Dom* (8pm; 70AS, students 40AS). July and August also bring **Jazz-Sommer Graz** (tel. 60 53 11), a festival of free concerts by international jazz legends like Art Farmer, Toots Thielemans, and Tommy Flanagan (Th-Sa, 8:30pm at Maria Hilferpl.). Also be sure to pick up the cultural magazine *Graz Derzeit,* free at the tourist office, for a daily, mind-boggling list of events with details on prices and locations (http://www.iic.wifi.at/graz/veranstaltungen/derzeit).

NIGHTLIFE

The hub of after-hours activity in Graz can be found in the **"Bermuda Triangle,"** an area of the old city behind Hauptpl. and bordered by Mehlpl., Färberg., and Prokopiag., and Puerto Rico. The Triangle's dozens of beer gardens and bars are packed with people all night, every night; sitting in an outdoor café is *de rigueur,* at least until 11pm, when local ordinance requires that festivities move indoors. Most of the university students prefer to down their beers in the pubs lining Zinzendorfg. and Halbärthg. on the other side of the Stadtpark.

Kulturhauskeller, Elisabethstr. 30 (tel. 38 10 58), underneath the Kulturhaus. Young crowd and cool locale dictate the loud, sometimes overwhelming dance-pop music in this bar. The partying doesn't really get started until 11pm on weekends. Tall glass of *Weißbier* 34AS. No shorts or military duds. 19 or over. Obligatory coat check and security fee 20AS. Open Tu-Sa 10pm-3:30am.

Café Harrach, Harrachg. 26 (tel. 32 26 71). A bustling hangout with a grad student feel. A half-liter of *Gösser* goes for 29AS, but almost everyone's throwing back white wine spritzers (26AS). Open M-F 5pm-midnight, Sa-Su 7pm-midnight.

Tom's Bierklinik, Färberg. 1 (tel. 84 51 74), has the largest stock of international beers in Austria. Go ahead and try prescriptions from Hawaii, Trinidad, or India (all 75AS), or just get a local fix with a glass of *Murauer Pils* (32AS). Walk-in hours daily 8pm-4am. No appointment necessary.

Triangel, Burgg. 15 (tel. 82 23 74), underneath the Kommod bar/restaurant. Vaulted brick ceilings, mirrored arches, and a low-key, well-dressed clientele of trendy 20-somethings. Open 8pm-4am. Occasional bands, no cover.

■ Near Graz: Schloß Eggenberg

To the west of Graz, the grandiose **Schloß Eggenberg,** Eggenberger Allee 90 (tel. 58 32 64), stands in contrast with the shabby suburban neighborhood that surrounds it. Built under the auspices of the Imperial Prince Ulrich of Eggenberg, this five-towered palace now holds an extensive coin museum, an exhibition of artifacts from antiquity, and a prehistoric museum (featuring the fascinating 7th-century BCE **Kultwagen** from **Streltweg**), all under the auspices of the Landesmuseum Joanneum. The guided tour of the elegant **Prunkräume**—filled with 17th-century frescoes, towering tile ovens, and ornate chandeliers—reveals the convoluted cosmological design of the palace. Three-hundred sixty-five windows look out from 24 state rooms with 60 panes of glass, 52 something-elses, and 12 whatchumacallits. (Tours in German and

English; 1 per hr., 10am-noon and 2-4pm. 20AS, plus entrance to the museums. Without the tour, the museums are 80AS; children and students 60AS. Antiquities and coin collection open Tu-Su 9am-noon and 12:30-5pm; prehistoric museum open Tu-Su 9am-1pm and 1:30-5pm.) Royal blue peacocks wander freely among the trees and grasses of the game preserve surrounding the palace. (Free with castle entrance; 2AS for gardens only; open daily 8am-7pm.) Take tram #1 (dir: Eggenberg): "Schloß Eggenberg" (5am-midnight). Classical concerts are given in the **Planetensaal** (Planet Hall; tel. 82 50 00) in the palace. (Aug.-Sept. Mondays at 8pm. Tickets from 130AS.)

■ Riegersburg

The hillside town of Riegersburg has known little peace since its founding in the 9th century BCE—Roman domination and Hungarian invasions periodically forced the citizens to seek solace and safety in the broad fortress at the top of the extinct volcano. Baroness Katharina Elisabeth Freifrau von Galler completed the castle in a flurry of construction, making it one of the largest and most impregnable strongholds in Austria—108 rooms surrounded by 3km of walls with five gates and two trenches. The fearsome castle withstood the 1664 Ottoman onslaught, with Riegersburg and the surrounding villages driving back the Turks in the great Battle of Mogersdorf. Surrounded by rolling hills and lush vineyards, the castle now finds itself continually besieged by weekend tourists bent on looting the souvenir shop.

ORIENTATION AND PRACTICAL INFORMATION If you've got a **car,** Riegersburg makes an excellent day trip from Graz. Take A-2 and exit at Ilz. Otherwise, poor train-bus connections necessitate precise planning. Ride the **bus** directly from **Graz** (Andreas-Hofer-Pl.; 2hr., M-Sa 12:35pm, M-F 5:30pm, Su 10:45am, 100AS), or take the **train** from Graz to **Feldbach** (1hr., every hr., 6:18am-10:43pm, 100AS) and switch to the bus into Riegersburg (M-F 7 per day, Sa-Su 0-2 per day, 20min., 20AS). Buses from Riegersburg to Graz generally leave at ungodly hours (2hr., M-Sa 5:40 and 6:05am, Su 5:35pm). Still, a 100AS ticket purchased on the bus back to Feldbach (7 per day, M-F 6:50am-5:50pm) is valid for train connections back to Graz (every hr., 4:20am-8:22pm). Riegersburg serves as a fine stopover on route from Graz into **Hungary:** a one-way ticket from Feldbach to border town **Szentgottard** costs 60AS (30min., 6 per day). If necessary, you can always call a **taxi** (tel. (03152) 25 35) to take you back to Feldbach (170-210AS). Otherwise, the **tourist office** (tel. 86 70), just up the street toward the castle from the bus stops, can help you find a room. (Open M-Sa 11am-6pm, Su 10am-6pm.) **Currency exchange** is at the **post office,** Riegersburg 26 (open M-F 8am-noon and 2-6pm, Sa 8am-noon; exchange until 5pm) or at **Raiffeisen Bank,** across the street at Riegersburgstr. 30. (Open M-Th 8am-noon and 2-4:30pm, F 8am-noon and 2-5pm.) The town **postal code** is A-8333. The **telephone code** is 03153.

ACCOMMODATIONS AND FOOD The **Jugendherberge im Cillitor (HI),** Riegersburg 3 (tel. 82 17; fax 821 74; email oejhu-stmk@oejhv.or.at), is on the path up to the castle and is actually incorporated into the fortress walls. Walk toward the castle, and up the very steep stone path. The hostel entrance is in the archway you pass through as you veer left. Fourteen-bed dorms have arrow-slits from which to fight off advancing school groups. (Dorms 135AS. Non-members add 30AS. Breakfast included; other meals 55-65AS. Sheets 30AS. Hall showers and toilets. Curfew 10pm. Open May-Oct.) At the bottom of Riegersburg's hill is **Lasslhof** (tel. 82 01 or 82 02), a yellow hotel with a popular bar/restaurant. A truly ghastly art collection fills the halls between the two-, three-, and four-bedded rooms. (Doubles 360AS, 480AS with private shower; triples 540AS, 720AS; quads 720AS, 960AS. Breakfast included. Reception 8am-10pm.) At the restaurant downstairs, wolf down *Wiener Schnitzel* with potatoes and salad (77AS), or snack on the *Frankfurter mit Gulaschsaft* (38AS). Castle hikers stock up on groceries at **SPAR Market,** across from the start of the stone path. (Open M-F 7am-noon and 2:45-6:15pm, Sa 7am-12:30pm.)

SIGHTS AND ENTERTAINMENT Riegersburg relies heavily on the revenue from tourists who gawk at the well-preserved remains of the huge **medieval fortress** (tel. 83 46), the town's only man-made attraction. But like the foreign invaders of the past, sightseers must also tackle the treacherously steep, stone-paved path leading up to the castle. Bring sturdy shoes and bottled water, lest you share the fate of many a young 17th-century Turk. The path itself is arguably the best part of the castle: sweeping views of the surrounding farms and villages reward visitors at every turn, and benches, vineyards, stone arches, and monuments provide good excuses to catch your breath. Ask a local to point out the prince and princess's current residence—note the swimming pool instead of a moat. You might circle the castle and climb up the *Eiselstieg* (donkey stairs) instead. Legend claims that this back entrance was built in the 17th century when two feuding brothers owned the place—one closed off the way to the top. Actually, the stairs were laid in the 15th century as a food transportation route before the two quarrelsome brothers were even a glint in their aristocratic father's eye. On your way up, look for an inconspicuous crescent moon carved into the stone wall to mark the highest point reached by invading Turks. The castle itself houses several banal but well-maintained exhibits and museums. The **Burgmuseum** showcases 16 of the castle's 108 rooms, packed with art and self-congratulatory historical notes on the Liechtenstein family (yes, like the country), who own this and other Austrian castles. *(Open Apr.-Oct. daily 9am-5pm. 1hr. tours in German on the hr. 10AS. Self-guided English tour available. Admission to each museum 85AS, students and soldiers 50AS; combination ticket for both 120AS, 80AS.)* The **Weiße Saal** (White Hall), with its wedding-cake ceiling flourishes and crystal chandeliers, lacks only couples in decolleté gowns waltzing around the floor. The **Witches' Room** contains an eerie collection of portraits of alleged witches (including Katharina "Green Thumb" Pardauff, executed in 1675 for causing flowers to bloom in the middle of winter) and a real iron maiden. There's also Prince Friedrich's (the current owner of the castle) gallery of derivative amateur photography. The **Hexenmuseum** (Witch Museum) spreads over 12 more rooms, with an exhibit on the most expansive witch trial in Styrian history (held between 1673 and 1675). Filled with torture devices, funeral pyres, and other ghastly exhibits, the museum investigates, with some historical rigor, the abrupt accusation that 95 women and men had caused hail and thunderstorms.

You can best appreciate the castle's beauty from the surrounding network of gravel **paths** and stone staircases. Take a good look at the elaborate iron pattern covering the well in the castle's second courtyard—it's said that any woman who can spot a horseshoe within the complex design will find her knight in shining armor within a year. In the shadow of the castle chirps the rather meager **Greifvogelwarte Riegersburg,** showcasing caged birds of prey. *(Open Apr.-Oct. 60AS, students 30AS. Shows with trainers dressed in castle finery M-Sa 11am and 3pm, Su 11am and 2 and 4pm.)* At one of the many *Buschenschank* on the hills surrounding the castle, try the Schilcher wine, a rosé grown from hearty native grapes. After a long, hot day of castle conquering and hiking, you might want to plunge into the **Seebad Riegersburg,** a small swimming lake created by nature and nurture together. *(30AS, under 16 15AS.)*

■ Mariazell

The local Benedictine superior's motto for Mariazell is *"Gnadenzentrum Europas"* (Europe's Center of Mercy). While this moniker may be something of an exaggeration, time spent here does feel blessed. Tilting precariously on the side of the Alps, the little town is both unabashed resort and important pilgrimage site. It's also beautiful. The faithful come here to pay homage to a miraculous Madonna made of linden wood, once owned by the traveling monk who founded the town by establishing a shrine to the Virgin here in 1157 (see **Mary, Mary, Quite Contrary,** p. 173). Travelers not so spiritually inclined come to Mariazell to ski in the Bürgeralpe or bake by the waters of the Erlausee.

ORIENTATION AND PRACTICAL INFORMATION Mariazell is accessible by a zippy little mountain train called the **Mariazellerbahn** (2½hr., 7 per day, 135AS). The **train station,** Erlaufseestr. 19 (tel. 22 30), **rents bikes** (90AS per day) and **stores luggage** (30AS per day; open daily in summer 5am-7:10pm; in winter 5am-6:30pm). **Buses** leave Mariazell for **Bruck an der Mur** (5:45am-6:10pm, 94AS), **Graz** (5:45am-3:30pm), and **Vienna** (3hr., 5:25am-4:10pm, 170AS). The **bus station** is directly behind the post office near Hauptpl. (Open M-F 8am-noon and 2-4pm, Sa 8-11am. Information desk open M-F 9:30-11:30am and 2:30-4:30pm, Sa-Su 9:40-10:10am and 3:15-3:55pm.) To reach Mariazell **by car** from **Vienna,** take Autobahn A-1 west to St. Pölten, and exit onto Rte. 20 south (1hr.). From **Graz,** take Rte. S-35 north to Bruck an der Mur then Rte. S-6 to Rte. 20 north.

The **tourist office,** Hauptpl. 13 (tel. 23 66; fax 39 45), has information on skiing, boating, fishing, hiking, buses, trains, and accommodations. They make free room reservations. From the train station, turn right on St. Sebastian and walk till the fork, then left up the hill to Wienerstr. Follow it to Hauptpl.; the office is straight ahead. (Open May-Sept. M-Sa 9am-12:30pm and 2-5:30pm, Sa 9am-noon and 2-4pm, Su 10am-noon; Oct.-Apr. M-F 9am-noon and 2-5pm, Sa 9am-noon.) For **currency exchange** or a 24-hour **ATM,** stop by **Sparkasse,** Grazerstr. 6 (tel. 23 03), just behind the post office. (Open M-F 8am-noon and 2-4pm, Sa 8-11am.) In medical **emergencies,** call the St. Sebastian Hospital, Spitalg. 4 (tel. 22 22). Head to **Zur Gaudenmutter,** Hauptpl. 4 (tel. 21 02), for pharmaceutical needs. (Open M-F 8am-noon and 2-6pm, Sa 8am-noon, Su 9am-noon.) The **post office** is upstairs. (Open M-F 8am-noon and 2-6pm, Sat. 8-10am.) The **postal code** is A-8630. The **telephone code** is 03882.

ACCOMMODATIONS AND FOOD Mariazell's **Jugendherberge (HI),** Fischer-von-Erlach-Weg 2 (tel. 26 69; fax 26 69 88), closes in the winter of 1998, to be reopened near the train station for the summer of 1999. Call ahead to find out opening dates and new prices. Enjoy the comforts of home at **Haus Wechselberger,** Bilderiweg 8 (tel. 23 15). The Wechselberger family rents out a few rooms in their house, complete with antique beds with high, ornate head- and footboards. Several rooms have balconies and views of the surrounding hills. (180AS; 10AS surcharge in winter. Breakfast and (hall) showers included.) Though crowded, **Camping Erlaufsee** (tel. 21 48 or 21 16), behind Hotel Herrenhaus near the west dock, is in a beautiful spot just by the lake on Erlaufseestr. It's equipped with showers, toilets, a refrigerator, and an activity room. (50AS, children under 15 25AS; tents 40AS. Open May to mid-Sept.) For a quiet stay on the mountainside, try the lovely **Alpenhaus Ganser,** Brünnerweg 4 (tel. 46 85). On the way to town from the train station, turn left from Wienerstr. at the tennis courts. Around the bend, stairs built into the mountain provide a shortcut. Uphill and indoors you'll find homemade furniture, hand-carved wood, and fantastic views. Other amenities include a parking garage and sleds in the winter that you can ride directly to the cable car. A ski trail leads straight to the front door. (180AS per person. Breakfast and showers included. 2-night min. stay.)

Cheap food and occasional live music can be found at **Stüberl Goldener Stiefel** (tel. 27 31) at the corner of Wiender Neustädtstr. and Dr.-Karl-Lueger-Str. (Pizza 45-80AS. Open daily 8:30am-midnight.) For some history with your supper, stop by the **Wirsthaus Brauerei,** Wiener Str. 5 (tel. 25 23). Made with a warmer fermentation process than industrial lagers, the unfiltered *Altbier* is best when fresh (27AS). Grab a handful of sweet malt or a homemade pretzel (17AS) to accompany the beer. The restaurant proudly displays four generations of family portraits and a photo of Kaiser Franz Josef's 1910 visit to Mariazell. (Open M-W 10am-11pm, F-Sa 10am-midnight, Su 10am-7pm.) There is a **Julius Meinl** supermarket on Wienerstr. (open M-F 5am-6pm, Sa 8am-5pm), and many wonderful *Lebkuchen* stands operate outside the town church. Specializing in bee products, **Hotel Goldener Löwe,** Hauptpl. 1a, across from the church, lets you sit on the terrace overlooking Hauptpl. while sipping homemade mead (drink of the gods). The hotel also lets the craft-happy try candle-making (Sa and Su 3pm) or gingerbread baking (by appointment; 35AS, plus a fee for materials). But the real reason to visit is the **first-floor bathroom**—as you enter, the

STYRIA

Mary, Mary, Quite Contrary

In 1157, Magnus the Good Monk set out on a mission in the mountains. Ever prepared, he brought a servant, a horse, and his precious hand-carved statue of the Holy Mary. One night, unfortunate Magnus and his companion encountered a robber who, seeing how fiercely Magnus defended the statue, drew his dagger and demanded that Magnus hand it over. Magnus rose and held the statue at arm's length in front of him. The mesmerized robber dropped his dagger and muttered "Maria," giving the monk and his companion time to flee. They set up camp a safe distance away and went to bed. Shortly after midnight, Magnus heard a woman's voice pleading with him to wake up. The monk opened his eyes to a shimmering vision of Mary, insisting that he take the statue and run. The monk woke his companion, and they took off into the night. Turns out a pack of robbers was in hot pursuit. Thanks to Mary, the two had a head start, and they were getting away just fine until they came to a huge, impassable sheer cliff. Without hesitation, Magnus held the statue aloft and said a heartfelt prayer. With a great rumble and creak, a passage opened in the stone, just wide enough for the two travelers. They walked into a lush green valley, where slightly bewildered lumberjacks said something like, "Make yourselves at home." At Magnus's request the locals built a little wooded chapel, or "Zell," for the miraculous Mary statue. That gives you "Maria in der Zell," and then "Mariazell."

pissoir lights up by itself. A waterfall runs on the wall, and a map of constellations in the stall helps you ponder your fate. Each stall is also equipped with a 15-minute hourglass. Says a vendor across the street: "I have been to Paris; I have been in the grand hotels of New York City. But never have I seen such a bathroom."

SIGHTS AND ENTERTAINMENT This pilgrimage town—Mariazell means "Mary's chapel"—has received hundreds of thousands of devout Christians over the centuries, all journeying to visit the **Madonna** within the **Basilika** (tel. 25 95), with its black spires visible from any point in town. *(Open daily 6am-7pm. Free guided tours by appointment through the Superiorat, Kardinal-Tisserant-Pl. 1.)* Crowds speaking German, Czech, Hungarian, and in tongues file into the incense-loaded church. The miraculous Madonna rests on the **Gnadenaltar** (Mercy Altar) smack dab in the middle. Empress Maria Theresa, who had her first holy communion in Mariazell, donated the silver and gold grille that encloses the Gnadenaltar. The church's amazing **Schatzkammer** (treasure chamber) contains gifts from scores of former pilgrims. *(Open Tu-Sa 10am-3pm, Su 11am-3pm. 40AS, students 20AS.)*

With a range of activities, Mariazell caters to throngs of bronzed, ultra-healthy (rhymes with wealthy...) outdoor types. Located just under the Bürgeralpe and a short jaunt from the Gemeindealpe, the area is ideal for **skiing.** A **cable car** at Wienerstr. 28 (tel. 25 55) zips to the top of the Bürgeralpe. *(Every 20min. July-Aug. 8:30am-5:30pm; Apr.-June and Oct.-Nov. 9am-5pm; Sept. 8:30am-5pm. Ascent 60AS, descent 40AS, round-trip 90AS; with guest card or student ID 55AS, 40AS, 75AS.)* Ski lifts and trails line the top. *(One-day pass 260AS, 2-day 470AS.)* For ski information on the Bürgeralpe, Gemeindealpe, Gußwerk, Tribein, and Köcken-Sattel Mountains (no lifts), call the Mariazell tourist office. In the summer, you can hike until you shout on Mariazell's **hiking trails.**

All of Mariazell's water sports revolve around the **Erlaufsee,** a wondrous Alpine oasis 6km outside city limits. Bunches of lakeside beaches allow for some of the best sunbathing in central Austria. **Buses** (tel. 21 66) run from Mariazell to the lake at 9:10am, 1:10, 3, and 3:15pm (20AS). **Steam train engines** (tel. 30 14), proclaimed by the tourist office to be "the oldest in the world," also whiz 'round the lake. *(July-Sept. weekends and holidays. 50AS, round-trip 80AS.)* Once at the water's edge, try renting an **electric boat** (100AS for 30min.) or a **paddle** or **row boat** (70AS for 30min.) from **Restaurant Herrenhaus** (tel. 22 50). Those interested in **scuba diving** in the Erlaufsee can contact **Harry's Tauchschule,** Traismauer 5 (tel. (02783) 77 47).

STYRIA

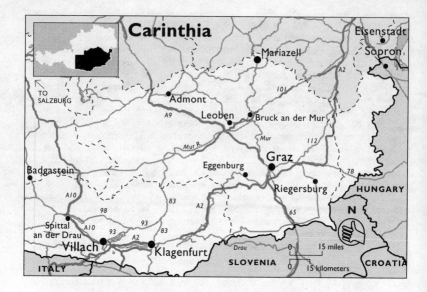

Carinthia (Kärnten)

Austria's harshest peaks guard the Italian and Slovenian borders in the southern regions of **Carinthia** (Kärnten) and **East Tirol** (Osttirol). Italian architecture, a sunny climate, and a laid-back atmosphere give Carinthia a Mediterranean feel not unlike Switzerland's Ticino region. The palpable warmth of the local population, however, can be deceiving. Four percent of the state's inhabitants are ethnic Slovenes (Austria's only significant national minority), and the xenophobic Carinthian Homeland Movement makes no secret of its desire to assimilate or evict them. In the "Town-Sign War" of the 1970s, for example, the Slovenes lobbied for bilingual street signs (in both German and Slovene); the Austrian majority soundly and meanly defeated the measure. Waves of migration from the former Yugoslavia have only exacerbated the situation. Carinthia is one of the most rural parts of Austria, and also the most conservative—Catholicism is a powerful force in people's lives, as a stream of rebellious (and highly acclaimed) contemporary novels by Austrian women like Elrike Jelinek and Lilian Faschinger have made abundantly clear.

If you'll be in Carinthia for an extended period, consider investing in a **Kärnten Card,** good for up to three weeks of unlimited local transportation, free admission to most area sights and museums, and discounts on many cable cars, boat cruises, toll roads, stores, and restaurants. The card is a great deal at 365AS (ages 6-14 150AS) and is available at area tourist offices.

🖐 HIGHLIGHTS OF CARINTHIA

- Klagenfurt was once home to a 16th-century provincial diet, a mythical monster called the *Lindwurm,* and Robert Musil.
- Near Klagenfurt is the legendarily warm and seductive Wörthersee, home base to many an escapist vacationer as well as one Austrian soap opera.
- Villach is a beautiful little town in its own right, and also forms one end of the great mountain-pass road, the Großglockner Straße, which goes along gut-wrenching hairpins above the treeline to some of the highest points in the Alps.

■ Klagenfurt

At the crossroads of north-south and east-west trade routes, Klagenfurt (pop. 90,000) has burgeoned into a major summertime destination. Playfully dubbed "the Austrian Riviera," the easygoing, southernmost provincial capital of Austria attracts thousands of work-weary Austrians who unwind in its beachfront suburbs. Klagenfurt's Wörthersee is the warmest alpine lake in Europe and serves as Europe's largest skating arena in winter. Only 60km north of Italy, this Carinthian capital leads a lifestyle like its southern counterparts; locals enjoy casual strolls around a palette of outdoor cafés, Italian Renaissance courtyards, and tree-lined avenues framed by Alpine peaks.

GETTING TO KLAGENFURT

Planes arrive at the **Klagenfurt-Wörthersee Airport** (tel. 41 50 00). Flights from Vienna are budget-hostile (every 3hr., round-trip 4080AS; ask travel agents about weekend and youth discounts). To get to the airport from the train station, take bus #40, 41, or 42: "Heiligenpl." then switch to bus #45: "Flughafen." **Trains** chug to the **Hauptbahnhof** at the intersection of Südbahngürtel and Bahnhofstr. To reach the town center from the station, follow Bahnhofstr. to Paradieserstr and turn left. Neuerpl. is two blocks down on the right. The **Ostbahnhof,** at the intersection of Meißtalerstr. and Rudolfsbahngürtel, is for shipping only. **Buses** depart across the street from the main train station. **By car,** Klagenfurt lies on Autobahn A2 from the west, Rte. 91 from the south, Rte. 70 from the east, and Rte. 83 from the north. From **Vienna** or **Graz,** take Autobahn A2 south to Rte. 70 west.

ORIENTATION AND PRACTICAL INFORMATION

Alterplatz, Neuerplatz, and **Heiligengeistplatz,** the town's bus centers, comprise the three-ring circus of the city's center. They lie within the **Ring,** the inner district of Klagenfurt, which bustles with social and commercial activity. St. Veiter Ring, Völkermarkter Ring, Viktringer Ring, and Villacher Ring border this area. Streets within the Ring generally run in a north-south/east-west grid. The **Lendkanal,** a narrow waterway, and **Villacherstr.** go from the city's center 3km to the Wörthersee.

Trains: Hauptbahnhof (tel. 17 17). To: **Lienz** (1¾hr., 2 per day, 200AS), **Salzburg** (3 hr., 9 per day, 226AS), the **Vienna Südbahnhof** (4¼hr., 12 per day, 430AS), and **Villach** (30min., 68AS). Make other connections in Salzburg or Vienna. Open 24hr.

Buses: BundesBuses reach most destinations in Carinthia. To: **Villach** (74AS), **Pörtschach** (44AS), **St. Veit** (44AS), **Friesach** (96AS), and **Graz** (201AS). Ticket window open M-F 7-11am and 11:30am-3pm. Phone Info line (tel. 50 08 30 or 543 40) open M-F 7am-4:30pm. For info on weekends call 06 60 51 88.

Public Transportation: Klagenfurt boasts a punctual and comprehensive bus system. The tourist office can provide a *Fahrplan* (bus schedule). The central bus station is at Heiligengeistpl. Single-fare rides 22AS. Buy individual tickets or a 24hr. pass (40AS) from the driver. *Tabak* kiosks sell cut-rate blocks of tickets. Illegal riders risk a 400AS fine.

Car Rental: Hertz, Villacherstr. 4 (tel. 561 47). **Avis,** Villacherstr. 1c (tel. 559 38).

Bike Rental: At the *Hauptbahnhof.* 150AS, with that day's train ticket 90AS. **Impulse** (tel. 51 63 10) has 9 stations all over town—including the tourist office, across from the train station, and the campground—that rent bikes for 30AS for 1hr., 50AS for 3hr., 90AS for 1 day (students 50AS), 300AS for 1 week. The tourist office distributes the pamphlet *Radwandern,* detailing local bike paths.

Tourist Office: Gäste Information (tel. 53 72 23; fax 53 72 95; email klagenfurt-info@w-see.or.at; http://www.w-see.or.at/Klagenfurt) is on the 1st floor of the *Rathaus* in Neuerpl. From the station, go down Bahnhofstr. and left on Paradieserg., which opens into Neuerpl. The well-staffed, English-speaking office supplies colorful brochures and helps find rooms for free. Daily tours of the *Altstadt* July-Aug. 10am (call 2 weeks in advance to arrange a tour in English). Open May-Sept. M-F 8am-8pm, Sa-Su 10am-5pm; Oct.-Apr. M-F 8am-5pm. The **Jugend Info**

youth information office, Fleischbankg. 4 (tel. 17 99), focuses on academic, social and legal issues and has a helpful and knowledgeable staff that can recommend entertainment and restaurants as well. Open M-Th 7:30am-4pm, F 7am-1pm.

Currency Exchange: Best rates in town are at the main post office (exchange machine 24hr.) and its train station branch.

Luggage Storage: At the train station. 30AS per piece. Lockers 20AS. Open M-Sa 6:30am-10:30pm, Su 7am-10:30pm.

Bi-Gay-Lesbian Organizations: Gay Hot-Line Klagenfurt, Postfach 193 (tel. 50 46 90). Hotline open W 7-9pm. **Bella Donna Frauenzentrum** (Women's Center), Villacherring 21/2 (tel. 51 12 48). Open M-F 9am-1pm.

Pharmacy: Pharmacies abound. **Landschafts-Apotheke,** Alterpl. 32, and **Obir-Apotheke,** Baumbachpl. 21, provide two distinguished options. Check local newspaper to find out which are open each night and on weekends.

Hospital: Klagenfurt Krankenhaus, St.-Veiter-Str. 47 (tel. 538).

Emergencies: Ambulance, tel. 144. **Medical Assistance,** tel. 141. **Police,** tel. 133 or 53 33.

Post Office: Main post office, Pernhartg. 7, off Neverpl. (tel. 556 55). Open M-F 7:30am-8pm, Sa 7:30am-1pm. **Train station branch,** Bahnhofpl. 5. (tel. 58 10). Open 24hr. **Postal Code:** A-9020.

Telephone Code: 0463.

ACCOMMODATIONS AND CAMPING

Though the summer heat dries up the pool of available rooms, Klagenfurt does find ways to compensate: two student dorms convert to youth hostels during July and August. The tourist office helps sniff out rooms for free and distributes the helpful *Hotel Information* (with a city map) and *You are Welcome* pamphlets, in English, and the German *Ferienwohnunger, Ferienhäuser, Privatequartiere,* which list private rooms. If you're staying in a hotel or *Pension,* ask for the **Gästepaß** (guest card), which entitles you to a free city guide and discounts at specified cafés, museums, and other area attractions.

Jugendherberge Klagenfurt, Neckheimg. 6 (tel. 23 00 20; fax 23 00 20 20), at Universitätstr., is close to the university, a 20min. walk from the Wörthersee, and a 30min. walk from the center of the city. From the train station, bus #40, 41, or 42: "Heiligengeistpl." then bus #10 or 11: "Neckheimg." from stand 2. This immaculate hostel, seemingly designed for the Jetsons, features a bubblegum-pink and baby-blue color scheme and assorted foliage. Most rooms are quads with bunks and bath. 190AS, non-members 230AS. For singles add 100AS; doubles add 50AS. Breakfast (7-8am) and sheets included. Dinner 80AS. Key deposit 200AS, a passport, or a student ID. Reception 7-9am and 5-10pm. Curfew 10pm. Reservations recommended.

Jugendgästehaus Kolping, Enzenbergstr. 26 (tel. 569 65; fax 569 65 32). From the station, head down Bahnhofstr. and right at Viktringer Ring, left at Völkermarkter Ring, right at Feldmarschall-Conrad-Pl. (which becomes Völkermarkterstr.), right on Enzenbergstr. (20min.). The friendly family Kolping provides simple, large rooms decorated by a single cross. 2- or 3-bed dorms with shower 160AS, non-students 200AS, under 18 180AS. Singles 200AS, non-members 240AS. Surcharge for 1-night stay 20AS. Breakfast included. 24hr. reception. Open early July to early Sept.

Pension Klepp, Platzg. 4 (tel. 322 78). Klepp is a 10min. walk from both the station and the city center. From the station, follow Bahnhofstr., take the 3rd right onto Viktringer Ring, then the 2nd right onto Platzg. Comfortable rooms with large windows. Singles 250AS; doubles 415AS; triples 600AS. Hall showers and toilets.

Jugendheim Mladinski Dom, Mikschallee 4 (tel. 356 51; fax 356 51 11). Follow the directions to Jugendgästehaus Kolping, but instead of turning down Enzenbergstr., continue down Völkermarkterstr. and right on Mikschallee (25min.). Another option is to take bus #40, 41, or 42: "Heiligergeistpl." then bus #70 or 71 (dir: Eben-tal): "Windischkaserne" from stand 13, and continue in the same direction (bus runs M-Sa until 6:50pm). Mladinski Dom serves as a dorm during the school year and converts into a pleasant bed-and-breakfast from early July to early Sept. Singles

255AS; doubles 410AS; triples 435AS. Children under 12 130AS, under 6 90AS. Discount after 3 nights 20AS. Breakfast 25AS. Private baths. Gym and Parking available. Reception M-F 6am-midnight, Sa-Su 24hr. Curfew 10pm; key available.

Klagenfurt-Wörthersee Camping-Strandbad (tel. 211 69; fax 211 69 93), at the Metnitzstrand off Universitätsstr. From the train station, bus #40, 41, or 42: "Heiligengeistpl." then bus #12: "Strandbad Klagenfurter See." Turn left immediately upon disembarking and walk for 2min. The crowded campsite will be to the left, on the edge of the Wörthersee. On-site grocery store, miniature golf, and beach. Mid-June to Mid-Aug. 80AS per person, ages 3-14 40AS; large site 100AS; small site 20AS. May to mid-June and late Aug. to Sept. 50AS, ages 3-14 25AS. 12AS tax for persons over 18. Showers and beach entry included. Open May-Sept.

FOOD

You don't have to walk far or look hard to find a cheap place to eat in Klagenfurt, especially in Neuerpl. and Kardinalpl. and along Burgg. The tourist office prints *Sonntagsbraten,* a pamphlet listing the addresses and operating hours of cafés, restaurants, clubs, and bars.

⊛**Rote Lasche** (Red Tongue), Villacherstr. 21, on the corner of Villacherstr. and Villacher Ring. File under: "Eatery of the Absurd." This ultracool, vegetarian-specialty restaurant was inspired and decorated by Klagenfurter absurdist artist Victor Rogy. It's like a diner upholstered tip-to-tail with his artwork, from the 4m red rubber tongue that greets you at the door and lends its name to the restaurant to the racks of postcards displaying some of his tamer stuff. The impeccably tuxedoed waiters help complete the overload by delivering what could be the most delicious vegetarian dishes in Austria. Banana curry rice 75AS; peppers stuffed with potato purée 88AS. Open M-F 11am-midnight, Sa 11am-3pm.

Café Musil, 10 Oktoberstr. 14, is the city's most famous cookie, cake, and coffee connection. Open 7am-7:30pm. A fairly dressy, larger bistro version awaits at Oktoberstr. 14, open until 10pm.

Zuckerbäckerei-Café-Konditorei-Imbiße D. Todor, Feldmarschall-Conrad-Pl. 6 (tel. 51 18 35). Now *that's* a mouthful. This everything-in-one café is a quick and cheap haven for any meal. Chow down on *Salatschüssel* (a salad concoction; 35-50AS) and *Schinken-Käse Toast* (ham and cheese on toast; 30AS) in the sun-drenched, ivy-enclosed *Gastgarten* out back. Also serves ice cream (7AS), candy, and fresh baked goods (12-28AS). Open M-F 7am-8pm, Sa 7am-1pm.

Rathausstüberl, Pfarrpl. 35 (tel. 579 47), on a hidden cobblestone street right by the *Pfarrkirche.* Freshly prepared Carinthian specialties at attractively low prices. *Käsenudel mit grünem Salat* (cheese and potato dumplings with green salad) and other daily specials 75AS. Italian entrees 65-78AS. People-watch on the outdoor terrace on balmy summer evenings. English menus available. Open M-F 8:30am-midnight, Sa 8:30am-2pm and 7pm-2am.

Seerestaurant-Strandbad, Strandbad Klagenfurt See (tel. 26 13 96). Large salad buffet, snacks, and, from 4:30pm in summer, scrumptious fish, flesh, or fowl grilled before your eyes. Try the *Grillhendl* (grilled chicken; 59AS) and enjoy the open air. Open 8am-midnight.

La Crêperie, 8 Mai Str. 19 (tel. 503598). This small, jazzy restaurant serves small, jazzy crepes (20-45AS). Open M-F 10:30am-9:30pm, Sa 10:30am-6pm.

Markets

Every Thursday and Saturday from 8am to noon, the compact **Benediktinerplatz** on the lower west side of the *Altstadt* welcomes a barrage of rickety, wooden stands showcasing fresh fruits and vegetables.

SPAR Markt, Hermang. just off Heiligengeistpl. Open M-F 8am-6:30pm, Sa 8am-1pm. Another on Bahnhofstr. with a small, cheap restaurant inside. After 3pm, breads and sweets in the *Konditorei* are half-price. Open M-F 7:30am-6:30pm, Sa 7:30am-5pm. There is also a **SPAR** on Villacherstr. 5min. from the youth hostel.

SIGHTS AND ENTERTAINMENT

The tourist office has a pamphlet, *A Walk Round Klagenfurt's Old Town*, as well as several **free guided tours** leaving from the front of the *Rathaus*. *(July-Aug. M-Sa 10am; usually in German.)* Still, it's probably easiest and most fun to explore the *Altstadt* on your own. Buildings in this part of town display a strange amalgam of architectural styles: Biedermeier, Italian Renaissance, Mannerist, Baroque, and *Jugendstil* facades all attempt to upstage each other. At the edge of Alterpl. stands the 16th-century **Landhaus**, originally an arsenal and later the seat of the provincial diet. *(Open Apr.-Sept. M-F 9am-noon and 12:30-5pm. 10AS, students 5AS.)* The symmetrical towers, staircases, and flanking projections create an elegant courtyard sprinkled with the banana umbrellas of numerous outdoor cafés. The flourishes of the interior truly deserve accolades—665 brilliant coats of arms blanket the walls. Artist Johann Ferdinand Fromiller took nearly 20 years to complete these pieces. Don't let the ceiling's "rounded" edges fool you—the room is perfectly rectangular.

A stroll through Kramerg., one of the oldest streets in Klagenfurt, leads directly to **Neuerplatz.** Here, merry-go-rounds for the young, cafés for the caffeine-addicted, and soapboxes for the cantankerous are all readily available amid a torrent of motion and activity. Standing proudly over the eastern end, a (rather large) statue of (rather large) Maria Theresa glares regally at the skateboarders launching themselves off her (rather large) pedestal. Confounding the indignity, a 60-ton half-lizard/half-serpent copper creature with an overbite spits water in her direction. This fountain depicts the **Lindwurm,** Klagenfurt's heraldic beast. This virgin-consuming monster once terrorized the Wörthersee area and prevented settlers from draining the marshes. Enter Hercules, monster-slayer, and all-around *Übermensch,* who quickly dispatched the beast—somewhat unsportingly lodging a barbed hook in the throat of a sacrificial cow—and saved the village. Today, the Lindwurm still terrorizes Klagenfurt, albeit more subtly—Puff the Magic Dragon-esque stuffed animals turn up *everywhere.*

One of Klagenfurt's largest museums was Franz Josef's favorite, the **Landesmuseum,** Museumg. 2 (tel. 53 63 05 52). *(Open Tu-Sa 9am-4pm, Su 10am-1pm. 30AS, children 15AS.)* The museum houses the *Lindwurmschädel,* the fossilized rhinoceros skull discovered in 1335 that, three centuries later, inspired the Lindwurm statue at Neuerpl. Other pieces include 18th-century musical instruments, a giant Großglockner Strasse relief map, and ancient Celtic and Roman artifacts. The Medusas at the corners of the miraculously intact 3rd-century Dionysus mosaics could take on a Lindwurm any day. The **Kärntner Landesgalerie,** Burgg. 8 (tel. 53 63 05 42), two blocks east of Neuerpl., is home to an eccentric collection of 19th- and 20th-century artwork, with a focus on Carinthian Expressionism and well-endowed papier-mâché turkeys. *(Open M-F 9am-6pm, Sa-Su 10am-noon. 20AS, students 5AS.)* The **Robert Musil Museum,** Bahnhofstr. 50 (tel. 501 429), honors the work of its namesake, perhaps Austria's most famous modern writer, with an archive of his writings. *(Open M-F 10am-noon and 2-4pm, Sa 10am-2pm. 40AS, students 20AS.)*

Two blocks south of Neuerpl. off Karfreitstr. is Klagenfurt's **Domplatz** and **Kathedrale.** Rebuilt after Allied bombing in 1944, the modern exterior and surrounding square render the church almost indistinguishable from the surroundings. The cathedral's interior, however, is awash in high arches, crystal chandeliers, pink and white floral stucco, and a brilliant gold altar. Other ecclesiastical paraphernalia are on display in the tiny **Diözesanmuseum** (tel. 57 70 84), next door at Lidmanskyg. 10, including the oldest extant stained-glass window in all Austria—a humble, 800-year-old sliver portraying Mary Magdalene. *(Open mid-June to mid-Sept. 10am-noon and 3-5pm; mid-Sept. to mid-Oct. and May to early June 10am-noon. 30AS, students 15AS, children 15AS.)*

Klagenfurt and its suburbs are home to no fewer than 23 castles and mansions; the tourist office's English brochure *From Castle to Castle* suggests a path to view them all and gives details on architecture and operating hours. Another tourist office brochure, the German *Museumswandern,* gives addresses and opening hours for the city's 15 museums and 22 art galleries.

Homesick or eager to see more of the world? Don't miss Klagenfurt's most shameless concession to tourist kitsch, the **Minimundus** park, Villacherstr. 241 (tel. 21 94), minutes from the Wörther See. *(Open July-Aug. Su-Tu and Th-F 9am-7pm, W and Sa 9am-9pm; May-June and Sept. 9am-6pm; Apr. and Oct. 9am-5pm. 90AS, children 6-15 30AS, seniors 75AS, groups of 10 or more 60AS per person. Extensive and necessary English guidebooks 30AS.)* Artists have created intricately detailed models of over 170 world-famous buildings and sights—all on a 1:25 scale. You'll be on eye level with the Parthenon, Big Ben, the Taj Mahal, and many more. For a taste of home, depending on where home is, check out the Sydney Opera House, a Maori Communal House, Buckingham Palace, or the Statue of Liberty. So this is what Godzilla feels like. At night, an outstanding lighting system illuminates the models. From the train station, take bus #40, 41, or 42: "Heiligengeistpl." then switch to bus #10, 11, 20, 21, or 22 (dir: Strandbad): "Minimundus." All profits go to the Austrian "Save the Child" society, a fact you can use to soothe your stinging wallet.

Next door to Minimundus is **Happ's Reptilien Zoo** (tel. 23425). *(Open May-Sept. 8am-6pm; Oct.-Apr. 9am-5pm. 75AS, students 65AS, children 35AS.)* To prevent the persecution of the Lindwurm's descendents, the zoo presents varied exhibits on snakes' environments and histories. Evidently Herr Happ has a rather loose definition of "reptile"—along with the puff adders, tortoises, and iguanas, the reptile zoo features spiders, scorpions, rabbits, guinea pigs, and Wörther See fish. The accident-prone should avoid Saturday's weekly piranha and crocodile feeding. The **planetarium** (tel. 217 00), behind the zoo, screens frequently. *(Daily; Oct.-Apr. Sa-Su only. 85AS, under 18 45AS.)* Elton John croons beneath the German narration—you'll never view the stars in quite the same way again.

To maximize your entertainment *Schilling*, read the tourist office's *Veranstaltung-Kalender* (calendar of events), available in English. In June, Klagenfurt hosts the **Bachmann Literature Competition** and a comedy festival. The tourist office distributes brochures listing concerts, gallery shows, museum exhibits, and plays, including cabaret performances in the **Theater im Landhauskeller** (tel. 59 04 46). *(120AS, students 80AS; performances in German.)* Tickets are available through **Reisebüro Springer** (tel. 387 00 55). The **Stadttheater**, built in 1910, is Klagenfurt's main venue for major operas and plays. For tickets, call the tourist office or the box office (tel. 55 26 60). *(40-520AS; students and seniors half-price; open mid-Sept. to mid-June Tu-Sa 9am-noon and 4-6pm.)* The best of Klagenfurt's nightlife rages in the pubs of **Pfarrplatz** as well as **Herrengasse** and **Theatergasse Sansibar**, Theaterg. 7, is a sushi bar with live South American music. *(Open M-F 5pm-2am, Sa 6pm-2am.)* **Kamot** is a candle-lit cellar with live jazz. *(Open Tu-Su 8pm-2am.)* **Absolut**, St. Vieterstr.3 (tel. 59 99 99) is a gay bar/cafe with outdoor seating on wicker couches. *(Open M-F 9am-4am, Sa-Su 7pm-4am.)* In summer, the **Disco Bus** leaves every 30 minutes between 10pm and 1am from Neuerpl. and brings party-goers to **Fabrik** discoteque on the Wörther See (30AS). Va va voom.

On humid spring and summer days, crowds bask in the sun and loll in the clear water of the nearby **Wörther See.** This water sport haven is Carinthia's warmest, largest, and most popular lake. The two closest beaches to Klagenfurt are the **Strandbad Klagenfurt See** and the **Strandbad Maiernigg.** *(Both open 8am-8pm. 35AS, children 15AS; after 3pm 20AS, children 7AS. Family card with 1 adult and up to 5 children 50AS, with 2 adults 80AS. Locker key deposit 50AS.)* The former is crowded but near the hostel and easily accessible by public transportation. From the train station, take bus #40, 41, or 42: "Heiligengeistpl." then bus #10, 11, or 12: "Strandbad Klagenfurter See." To enjoy the water without getting wet, rent a **rowboat** (30min., 24AS), **paddle boat** (42AS), or **electric boat** (66AS). Strandbad Maiernigg is far from the noise and fuss of its busier counterpart, but you'll need a car or a bicycle to get there. From downtown, ride along Villacherstr. until it intersects Wörther See Süduferstr., and then follow signs to "Wörther See Süd." **Stadtwerke Klagenfurt Wörthersee-und-Lendkanal-Schiffahrt** (tel. 211 55; fax 211 55 15) offers scenic cruises on the lake and short rides down the canal. The two-hour **cruise** goes as far as **Velden,** on the opposite shore, and allows stops at designated docks along the way. *(Round-trip 190AS, advance purchase 170AS.)* The Stadtwerke Klagenfurt information center in Heiligengeistpl. sells advance tickets. A *Radwandern* brochure, free at the tourist office, suggests numerous bike tours such as one that runs through a circuit of castles and churches.

CARINTHIA

■ Near Klagenfurt: Gurk

North of Klagenfurt, the minuscule town of Gurk, located in a remote valley and bisected by the Gurk River, is centered around a resplendent **Romanesque cathedral.** After the deeply religious Carinthian Countess Hemma (canonized as St. Emma in 1938) lost her husband and son in the early half of the 11th century, she devoted her life to building churches, including the famous one at Admont, and this one dedicated to the Virgin Mary. Hemma's tomb at the small Gurk church became a site for centuries of pilgrims. Her chapel was swallowed by a magnificent cathedral built under the prince-bishop Roman I, councillor to Frederick Barbarossa.

The onion-domed cathedral is one of the most important Romanesque churches in northern Europe, featuring Gothic stained-glass windows, excellent carved panels describing the life of St. Emma, and a **crypt** dating from 1140 supported by a forest-like crowd of 100 marble leaf-carved pillars in a dim half-light. St. Emma's sarcophagus rests in a central place on three carved heads. Her original chapel has been incorporated into a gallery within the cathedral that preserves the highly important series of **Romanesque murals** of Solomon's throne, the Transfiguration of Christ, and the Garden of Eden. Some later additions also deserve mention, including an impressive early Baroque high altar consisting of 72 full gilded figures, including Mary, the apostles, the evangelists, the great teachers of the Western church, numerous saints and emperors, and holy women, as well as 82 gilded angels' heads. Architect Georg Donner added a Baroque pulpit in 1740. The cemetery surrounding the cathedral also impresses with its 1392 **Gothic death lamp** and more recent war memorial. The cathedral is open from 8am to 7pm. (Free.) A worthwhile English guidebook (45AS) with detailed information about the history, art, and architecture of the church is available outside the entrance. There are guided tours of the *Bischofskapelle* at 10am and 2pm (25min., 50AS) and of the entire structure at 10:30am and 2:30pm (1hr., 40AS). For info, call (04266) 823 60.

To get to Gurk, take a **bus** from Klagenfurt (1½hr., 4 per day, 94AS one-way, but a bus day pass is 120AS and more worthwhile). Tourist stands outside the cathedral have information about local *Privatzimmern* and Gurk's **Kulturstätte der Heimat** Museum (tel. (04266) 81 25).

■ Near Klagenfurt: Maria Saal

The church at Maria Saal, located atop a rocky hill 8km north of Klagenfurt, dates from the 8th century, when it was called "Sancta Maria in Solio." It's the oldest in Carinthia. In fact, a settlement has existed here since 1000 BCE, and it continues to be an important pilgrimage site. The church's brooding Gothic exterior contains reliefs and inscriptions from the Roman era as well as a heap of medieval tombstones. A fortress wall encircles the compound; it was erected as protection from any Turkish invasions. The church's twin towers are made from local volcanic rock, and its 6600kg bell was fabricated out of 11 Turkish cannonballs. For more info, call (04223) 22 14.

The church also houses the **Land Schaftsmuseum Schloß Trautenfels** (tel. (03682) 251 30), which displays temporary art exhibits and a collection of Carinthian furniture dating from the 17th century (open Easter-Oct. 9am-5pm; 60AS, students 40AS). Signs from the church point to the **Kärntner Freilichtmuseum** (tel. (04223) 21 82) a small village of Carinthian farmhouses. (Open May-Oct. Tu-Su 10am-6pm; 60AS, students 30AS.) Numerous **buses** and **trains** (every hr.) leaving Klagenfurt stop in Maria Saal daily, including the bus to Gurk.

THE DRAUTAL

With its moderate climate and proximity to southern Europe, central Carinthia's **Drautal** (Drau Valley) evokes locales decidedly un-Teutonic. The region offers skiing and water sports in high- and lowlands carved by the **Drau,** between the Höhe

Tauern and the Villacher Alps. At a mere 2000m (a baby-step above the timberline), the mountains are favored not just with lumber and the white stuff but also with valuable minerals: iron ore, lead, tungsten, zinc, and manganese. Between and below the peaks are numerous lakes, streams, and curative warm-water springs.

Although the Drautal contains the transportation hub of **Villach** and an electronic components industry at its core, a variety of lakeside resorts fill out the region. These resorts include Millstätter See, the Ossiacher See, and the baths of smaller towns like the Broßer-Mühldorger See near Gmünd and the Faaker See near Villach. Fitness buffs can enjoy hiking, water sports, and mountain biking. When the frost arrives, ice-skaters make loops on the lakes while skiers swoosh down the nearby slopes.

■ Villach

Awe-inspiring mountain backdrops and an intriguing, multicultural atmosphere make Villach (pop. 55,000) a more interesting transportation hub than most. Just north of the border between Austria, Italy, and Slovenia, Villach has a split personality; even the street musicians betray the influence of neighbors with their lilting, traditional Slavic, German, and Italian tunes. The **Villach Kirchtag** celebrates these three heritages simultaneously with food, song, and dance (see below). Although Carinthia formally declared allegiance to Austria in 1920, a Slavic influence is still apparent even in the street names of the central district.

ORIENTATION AND PRACTICAL INFORMATION Villach sprawls on both sides of the Drau River. Bahnhofstr. leads from the train station and over a 9th-century bridge to the economic and social heart of Villach, **Hauptplatz.** Narrow cobblestone paths weave through this central area, revealing hidden restaurants and cafés on every new corner. Two sweeping arcs of stores flank Hauptpl., closed off at one end by a towering church and by the Drau at another.

Trains go to **Vienna Südbahnhof** (5hr., 12 per day, 1:21am-6:12pm, 470AS), **Innsbruck** (4½hr., 10 per day, 1:37am-10:55pm, 410AS), **Klagenfurt** (25min., 43 per day, 1:31am-11pm, 68AS), **Salzburg** (2¾hr., 9 per day, 1:37am-8pm, 270AS), and **Graz** (3½hr., 13 per day, 1:31am-8:12pm, 370AS). A **free city bus** travels a circuit every 20 minutes (M-F 8:40am-6:20pm, Sa 8:40am-12:20pm). **Ferries** cruise the Drau, departing from the dock beneath the north end of the main bridge (1½hr.; 10, 11:50am, 2:30, and 4:15pm; 110AS, ages 6-15 55AS). A **taxi** stand is located at the *Bahnhof*, or call 288 88 or 233 33. **Hertz,** inside the **Springer Reisebüro** at Hans-Gasser-Pl. 1 (tel. 269 70), rents cars. (Open M-F 8am-noon and 2-5pm.) You can **rent bikes** at the **train station** (150-200AS per day, with train ticket or Eurailpass 90-160AS) or at **Das Radl,** Italienstr. 22b (tel. 269 54), in the alley next to the large pink building (120-140AS per day). Villach's **tourist office,** Rathauspl. (tel. 24 44 40; fax 244 44 17), gives advice on attractions and skiing and helps find accommodations for free. From the train station, walk out to Bahnhofstr. over the bridge and through Hauptpl. to Rathauspl. (at the far end and on the left; open M-F 8am-12:30pm and 1:30-6pm, Sa 9am-noon). The **regional tourist office** in St. Ruprecht (tel. 420 00; fax 427 77) offers up-to-date ski information. There are **ATMs** throughout the city, including locations on Hauptpl. and in the *Hauptbahnhof*. The station also has 24-hour electronic **lockers** fit for a cyber-king (20-40AS), as well as a **luggage check** (tel. 20 20 31 61; open 6:30am-8:30pm; 30AS). The local **hospital** is at Nikolaig. 43 (tel. 20 80). Dial 203 30 to reach the **police** headquarters at Tralteng. 34. Full **internet access** is available at **Cafeteria Nikolai,** Nikolaig. 16, for 60AS per hour. (Open M-F 7:30am-2am, Sa 9am-2pm and 6pm-2am, Su 6pm-2am). The mailman cometh to the main **post office** (tel. 255 10), at 8 Mai-Plotz 2, and **exchanges** his **currency.** (Open daily 8am-noon and 2-5pm.) The **postal code** is A-9500. The **telephone code** is 04242.

ACCOMMODATIONS AND FOOD Budget accommodations accessible by foot in Villach are rare. You might consider spending the night in nearby Klagenfurt (20min. by train; see above). Travelers with cars should check out the tourist office's Pension list, which details many outlying bargains accessible only by car. The most reasonably priced establishment in town is **Jugendgästehaus Villach (HI),** Dinzlweg 34 (tel. 563

68). From the train station (20-30min.), walk up Bahnhofstr. and go over the bridge and through Hauptpl. Turn right on Postg., walk through Hans-Gasser-Pl., which merges into Tirolerstr., and bear right at St. Martinstr. Dinzlweg is the first street on the left. The hostel is tucked away past all of the tennis courts. This cheerful facility, plastered with neon yellow and orange à la 1976, houses 150 in spacious five-bed dorms, each with its own shower. (Dorms 170AS. Breakfast and sheets included. Lunch or dinner 80AS each. **Bike rental** 120AS per day. Keys available with passport or ID deposit. Reception 7-10am and 5-10pm. Curfew 10pm.)

There's plenty of affordable food in Villach. **Lederergasse** overflows with small, cheap eateries, while **Hauptplatz** and the sprawling **Kaiser-Josef-Platz** seat swankier Raybanned patrons. **Pizzeria Trieste,** Weißbriachg. 14 (tel. 25 00 58), bakes its great-smelling pies for 65-120AS. (Open 10am-11pm.) Overlooking the Drau at Nikolaipl. 2, **Konditerei Bernhold** (tel. 254 42) tempts with warm pastries (12-29AS), devilish ice cream concoctions, and a river view worthy of a slowly sipped cappuccino (29AS). (Open M-F 7:30am-8pm, Sa 8am-8pm, Su 9:30am-8pm.) Picnic supplies wait at the **SPAR Markts,** in Hans-Grasser-Pl. and at 10 Oktoberstr. 6 (open M-F 7:30am-6:30pm) or at the **farmer's market** in Burgpl. on Wednesday and Saturday mornings.

SIGHTS AND ENTERTAINMENT   Any tour of Villach traverses the bustling **Hauptplatz,** the 800-year-old commercial heart of the city. The southern end of the square lives in the mighty Gothic shadow of the **St. Jakob-Kirche,** one of Villach's 12 lovely churches. *(Open July-Aug. M-Th and Sa 10am-6pm, F 10am-9pm, Su noon-6pm; June-Sept. M-Sa 10am-6pm; Oct. and May M-Sa 10am-4pm. 20AS, students and children 10AS.)* Slightly raised on a stone terrace, this 12th-century church was converted during the Reformation in 1526 and thereby became Austria's first Protestant chapel. Today, one Counter-Reformation later, the Catholic high altar's gilt Baroque canopy dazzles the most jaded eyes and almost obscures the Gothic crucifix suspended just in front (**free organ concerts** June-Aug. Th at 8pm). An ascent up the tallest steeple in Carinthia (94m), the church's **Stadtpfarrturm** (tel. 20 54 75), provides your daily exercise and a view of Villach and its environs.

Villach's **Stadtmuseum,** Widmanng. 38 (tel. 20 53 49), founded in 1873, exhibits archaeological and mineral displays from six millennia, clocks, hats, 18th-century portraits, and the original gold-on-black Villach coat of arms from 1240. *(Open May-Oct. daily 10am-4:30pm; Nov.-Apr. M-F 10am-6pm, Sa 10am-noon and 2-5pm. 30AS, students 20AS, children under 15 free.)* The 90kg, soldered statue of Eisner Leonhard, patron saint of prisoners, formerly stood in St. Leonhardskirche. A local tradition required that anyone who wanted to marry must first be able to carry the statue around the church. Many honeymoons were ruined by hernias.

Five minutes from the congested streets of Hauptpl. is the small **Schillerpark,** home of the Relief von Kärnten, an enormous topographic model of Carinthia. *(Open May-Oct. M-Sa 10am-4:30pm. 20AS, students 10AS, under 15 free.)* The park has made molehills out of mountains—all the better to see them, my dear. Walk up Hauptpl. until it turns into 10 Oktoberstr. and turn left on Peraustr. The park is one block in on your right. Two blocks farther down Peraustr. looms the Baroque **Heilig-Kreuz-Kirche,** the dual-towered pink edifice visible from the city bridge. On the other side of the Drau, the **Villacher Fahrzeugmuseum** (tel. 255 30 or 224 40; fax 255 30 78) is parked at Draupromenade 12. *(Open M-Sa 10am-noon and 2-4pm; mid-June to mid-Sept. M-Sa 9am-5pm, Su 10am-5pm; 50AS, ages 6-14 25AS.)* Hundreds of antique automobiles present a rubber-burning ride into the history of transportation.

Less crowded than the Wörther See, the small but no less beautiful **Faaker See** lies at the foot of a mountain between Villach and its suburb **Maria Gail.** In 1998, little Faakersee hosted a continent-wide reunion of Harley Davidson bikers. The sleek peaks around Villach make for excellent **skiing,** with a plethora of resorts to woo the winter traveler. A one-day regional lift ticket valid for four areas costs 300AS (children 180AS) with other combinations available. In summertime, the **Villach Kirchtag** (church day), held since 1225 on the first Saturday of August, helps the town to celebrate its "birthday" with raucous revelry. *(Entrance to the Altstadt 80AS, 60AS with advance tickets.)*

Salzburger Land

Salzburger Land was united in the 1st century under emperor Claudius and the Roman Empire, but it wasn't until the 8th- century that the province became known for "white gold"—salt, not cocaine. Salzburg's name comes from the German word for salt, *Salz*, while Hallstatt, an important salt-mining locale for the past 3000 or so years, derives its name from the Celtic translation, *Hall*. Salt brought tremendous wealth to the region, which remained an autonomous and internationally important bishopric until 1815 when that crazy Congress of Vienna up and gave it to Austria. Not long after this political defeat, much of Salzburger Land's churchy artifacts and art were whisked away to Munich and Vienna, leaving only the Baroque architecture and gilded churches of the province capital, Salzburg. Although tourism displaced the salt trade long ago, figures of St. Barbara, the patron saint of miners, linger everywhere. The dramatic natural scenery and shatteringly blue lakes of the Salzkammergut, which stretch across the provincial boundaries of Salzburg, Styria, and Upper Austria, make for one of Austria's favorite vacation spots.

"Brrr," he whimpered softly...

If you're planning a trip to Upper Austria in late spring or early summer, think about some warm clothes. The region receives two blasts of unseasonably cold weather in mid-May and mid-June. Three saints whose holy days fall during the first cold front are known as the *Eisheiligen*, or "ice-saints." They are Pankratius (May 12th), Bonifatius (May 14th), and Sophie (May 15th). A little later, the *Schaffskälte* ("sheep's cold") hits, shortly after the poor animals have been taken up the mountain to higher ground. Only after the June chill ends is the wool shaved off their frisky pink bodies.

When the Salzburger Land lets down its hair, it unleashes some very stylish locks. Besides the world-famous music festival in Salzburg, regarded as one of the premier events of the classical music world (see p.218), many smaller local festivals pop up all summer. For example, every three years on the last Sunday in July, an historic **Pirates' Battle** is held on the Salzach River at **Oberndorf.** According to the ritual plot, the brigands attack and rob a saltboat and then fire on the town of **Laufen,** on the

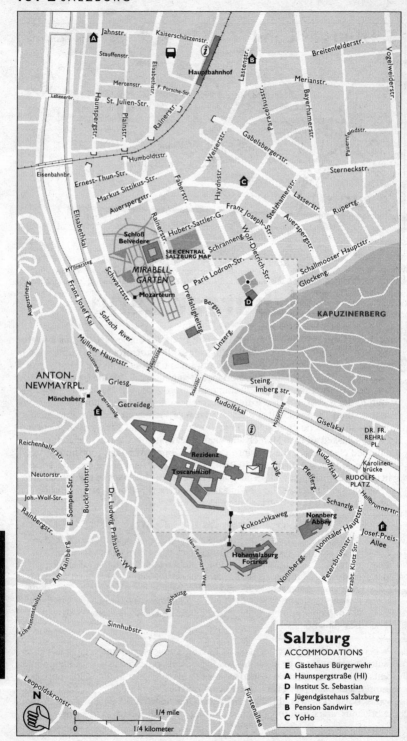

Salzburg

ACCOMMODATIONS

E Gästehaus Bürgerwehr
A Haunspergstraße (HI)
D Institut St. Sebastian
F Jügendgästehaus Salzburg
B Pension Sandwirt
C YoHo

N

0 _____ 1/4 mile
0 _____ 1/4 kilometer

opposite (Bavarian) side of the river. Eventually, the defeated pirates try to escape. They are arrested and condemned to death, but in the typical Salzkammergut spirit their sentence is quickly modified to "death by drowning in beer," which signifies the beginning of a lavish feast.

🖑 HIGHLIGHTS OF SALZBURGER LAND

- Salzburg itself is home to Mozart's birthplace, a largely intact and highly scenic medieval castle (complete with torture museum), and the setting for much of the too-sweet musical *The Sound of Music*.
- Hallstatt is one of the most beautiful laketowns in the world, and has an oddly fascinating pair of prehistoric and 18th-century burial sites.
- Crescent-shaped Mondsee is the region's warmest lake and one of the area's most pleasing little stucco towns.

SALZBURG

For the city of Salzburg (pop. 150,000), the three most important factors for real estate values are Mozart, Mozart, and Mozart. *The Sound of Music* is a close fourth. Wedged between three foliage-covered peaks and dotted with church spires, medieval turrets, and resplendent palaces, Salzburg nevertheless considers its forte not the spectacular sights but rather its relationship with the music of favorite son Wolfgang Amadeus Mozart. For the past century the city's adulation reaches a deafening roar every summer during the **Salzburger Festspiele** (summer music festival), when financially endowed admirers from the world round come to pay their respects. The *Festspiele* is a five-week event featuring hundreds of operas, concerts, plays, and open-air performances. Salzburg's main contribution to 20th-century music falls into the catchy tunes category, with the occasional yodel—*The Sound of Music*'s trilling von Trapp family made the city famous all over again.

Crowds wander the streets of Salzburg year-round, thanks more to the one-two combination of "Wolfie" and Julie Andrews than Salzburg's (incidentally gorgeous) castle and Baroque palaces. Never mind that both Mozart and the von Trapps eventually left, finding Salzburg a bit too stifling (the former fled from the oppressive bourgeois atmosphere and his over-managerial father, the latter from the tone-deaf Nazis)—this Little City That Could couldn't keep away its onslaught of visitors even if it wanted to.

■ Getting to and from Salzburg

The cheapest way to reach Salzburg by plane is to fly into **Munich** and take the train from there. Salzburg does, however, have its own airport—the **Flughafen Salzburg** (tel. 858 00), 4km west of the city center. Several airlines jet each day between such major European cities as **Paris, Amsterdam, Vienna,** and **Innsbruck.** Bus #77 (dir: *Bahnhof* from the airport, Walserfeld from the train station) connects the train station and the airport (15min., every 15-30min. 5:32am-11pm). A taxi from the airport to the train station should cost roughly 150AS.

Trains run to Salzburg from all over and connect directly to many major international and domestic cities. There are two train stations: the **Hauptbahnhof** on Südtirolerpl. is the first depot for trains coming from Vienna; the Rangier *Bahnhof* is the first stop when coming from Innsbruck but serves mainly as a cargo station, so don't get off there. A new **regional bus depot** is under construction. In the meantime, buses leave from behind the construction site, across from the train station. Bundes-Buses chug throughout the Salzkammergut region.

Motorists coming from Vienna can exit at any of the numerous Salzburg-West exits on Autobahn A1. Among these, the Flughafen exit is near the airport, the Salzburg Nord exit is near Itzling and Kasern, and the Salzburg Süd exit lies south of the city

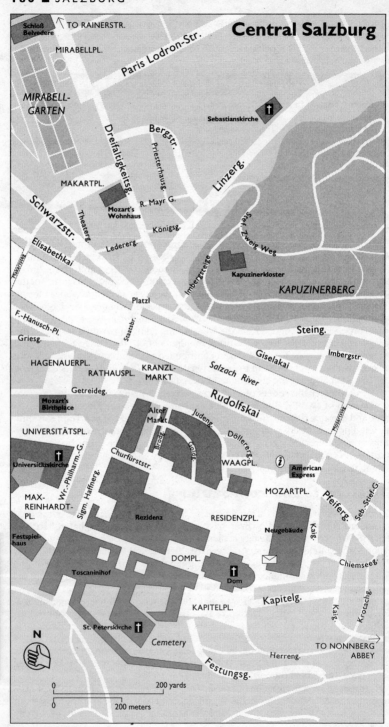

Central Salzburg

Schloß Belvedere

TO RAINERSTR.

MIRABELLPL.

Paris Lodron-Str.

MIRABELL-GARTEN

Bergstr.

Sebastianskirche

Priesterhausg.

Dreifaltigkeitsg.

Linzerg.

MAKARTPL.

Schwarzstr.

Theaterg.

Mozart's Wohnhaus

R. Mayr G.

Königsg.

St. Zweig Weg

Elisabethkai

Ledererg.

Imbergsteige

Kapuzinerkloster

KAPUZINERBERG

Platzl

Saatstr.

Steing.

F.-Hanusch-Pl.

Giselakai

Imbergstr.

Griesg.

HAGENAUERPL.

RATHAUSPL.

KRANZL-MARKT

Salzach River

Getreideg.

Rudolfskai

Mozart's Birthplace

Alter Markt

Judeng.

UNIVERSITÄTSPL.

Churfürstr.

Brodg.

Goldg.

Döllererg.

WAAGPL.

Universitätskirche

Wr.-Philharm.-G.

American Express

MOZARTPL.

MAX-REINHARDT-PL.

Sigm. Haffnerg.

Rezidenz

RESIDENZPL.

Pfeiferg.

Seb. Stief-G.

Neugebäude

Festspielhaus

DOMPL.

Kaig.

Chiemseeg.

Toscaninihof

Dom

Kapitelg.

Kaig.

Krotachg.

KAPITELPL.

N

St. Peterskirche

Cemetery

TO NONNBERG ABBEY

Festungsg.

Herreng.

0 ——— 200 yards

0 ——— 200 meters

SALZBURGER LAND

near Schloß Hellbrunn and Untersberg. Rte. A8 and E52 lead from the west into Rosenheim and then branch off to Munich and Innsbruck. Autoroute A10 heads north from Hallein to Salzburg. To reach the Salzkammergut area and the scenic road that leads to the top of Gaisberg, take Grazer Bundesstr. (Rte. 158) from Gnigl behind Kapuzinerberg. Since public transportation is efficient within the city limits, consider the **"Park and Ride"** parking lots—park for free when you get off the highway and take the bus into town. The most convenient lot is **Alpensiedlung Süd** on Alpenstr. (exit: Salzburg Süd), but a bigger lot is open in July and August at the **Salzburger Ausstellungszentrum** (exit: Salzburg-Mitte).

■ Orientation and Practical Information

Salzburg, the capital of the province of the same name, lies at Austria's midpoint, right at the navel, 470m above sea level. Three wooded hills surround the town which hugs the banks of the **Salzach River** a few kilometers from the German border. The *Hauptbahnhof* is on the northern edge of downtown, and buses connect it to downtown proper: #1, 5, 6, 51, and 55. The river divides downtown Salzburg. On the west bank is the *Altstadt,* crouching below the **Mönchsberg** (Monk's Mountain); on the east bank is the *Neustadt,* centered around **Mirabellplatz.** From the bus, disembark at "Mirabellpl." or "Mozartsteg." to access the city sights. By foot, Mirabellpl. is 10 to 15 minutes from the train station and left down Rainerstr.

TRANSPORTATION

Trains: Hauptbahnhof, (tel. 17 17 for information) in Südtirolerpl. To: **Innsbruck** (2hr., every hr., 12:30am-10:36pm, 350AS); **Graz** (4½hr., every hr., 3am-7:21pm, 410AS); **Vienna** (3½hr., every 30min., 1:15am-9:32pm, 410AS); **Munich** (2hr., every 30min., 4am-10pm, 260AS); **Zurich** (6hr., 6 per day, 12:39am-4:30pm, 615AS); **Budapest** (6½hr., 10 per day, 1:16am-8pm, 525AS); **Prague** (7hr., 4 per day, 544AS, connect in Linz); and **Venice** (6hr., 6 per day, last connection at 10:36pm, 520AS). For reservations call 17 00, M-F 7am-6:15pm, Sa 8am-1pm. Regular ticket office open 24hr.

Buses: Bus depot (tel. 0660/51 88). BundesBuses zip all over. To: **Mondsee** (1hr., every hr., 6:40am-7:20pm, 60AS); **St. Wolfgang** (1½hr., every hr., 6:40am-8:10pm, 90AS); and **Bad Ischl** (1½hr., every hr., 6:40am-7:15pm, 100AS). For schedule information, call 167.

Public Transportation: Information at the **Lokalbahnhof** (tel. 87 21 45), next to the train station. An extensive network of 18 buses cuts through the city, with central hubs at Hanusch-Pl. by Makartsteg, Äußerer Stein by Mozartsteg., Mirabellpl., and the *Bahnhof.* Tickets are cheapest from *Tabaks* (day pass 40AS, week 105AS). You can also purchase packs of 5 single-ride tickets from vending machines at bus stops for 75AS. You must punch your ticket when you board in order to validate it or suffer a fine of 500AS. Buses usually make their last run from downtown to outer destinations at 10:30-11:30pm, earlier for less-frequented routes. Check the schedule posted at stops.

Parking: Consider the "Park and Ride" option (see p. 185). If you must park within the city, try **Altstadt-Garage** inside the Mönchsberg (open 24hr.); **Mirabell-Garage** in Mirabellpl., (open 7am-midnight; 28AS per hr.); or **Parkgarage Linzergasse** at Glockeng. off Linzerg., (open 7am-10pm; 20AS per hr. or 160AS for a full day). Other lots are at the airport, Hellbrunn, and Akademiestr. (15AS per hr.). Blue lines on the sidewalk indicate that parking is available; buy a ticket for the space from one of the nearby automated machines.

Taxis: (tel. 81 11 or 17 16). Stands at Hanuschpl., Residenzpl., Makartpl., and the train station. **BusTaxi** fills in when the public buses stop running at night. Pick it up at the stop at Hanuschpl. or Theaterg. and tell the driver where you need to go. Every 30min. nightly 11:30pm-1:30am. 35AS for any distance within the city limits.

Car Rental: Avis, Ferdinand-Porsche-Str. 7 (tel. 87 72 78; fax 88 02 35), and **Budget,** Innsbrucker Bundesstr. 95 (tel. 85 50 38; fax 85 49 87), are in the airport. All offices offer insurance and unlimited mileage.

Bike Rental: Climb every mountain and ford every stream with a bicycle from the train station counter #3 (tel. 88 87 31 63). 150AS per day, 90AS with that day's train ticket, half-day 70AS, 1 week 670AS. Bike paths wind all through the city.

Hitchhiking: Hitchers headed to Innsbruck, Munich, or Italy (except Venice), take bus #77 to the German border. Thumbers bound for Vienna or Venice take bus #29 (dir: Forellenwegsiedlung) until the *Autobahn* entrance at "Schmiedlingerstr." or bus #15 (dir: Bergheim) to the *Autobahn* entrance at "Grüner Wald."

TOURIST AND FINANCIAL SERVICES

Tourist Office, Mozartpl. 5 (tel. 84 75 68 or 88 98 73 30; fax 88 98 73 42; email tourist@salzburginfo.or.at; http://www.salzburginfo.or.at), in the *Altstadt*. From the train station, bus #5, 6, 51, or 55: "Mozartsteg." then curve around the building into Mozartpl. On foot, make a left on Rainerstr., go to the end, cross Staatsbrücke, then continue along the river's west bank upstream to Mozartsteg. (20min.). The office has free hotel maps (exactly the same as the 10AS city map). Reservation service 30AS, for 3 or more people 60AS, plus a 7.2% deposit deductible from the 1st night's stay. The overworked staff will tell you which hostels have available rooms. The office is your source for the Salzburg Card (see p. 195). Open July-Aug. 9am-8pm; Sept.-June 9am-6pm. There are other **branches** at the **train station** platform #2a (tel. 88 98 73 40; open M-Sa 8:45am-8pm); and the **Alpensiedlung Süd "Park and Ride"** lot (tel. 88 98 73 60).

Budget Travel: ÖKISTA, Wolf-Dietrich-Str. 31 (tel. 88 32 52; fax 88 32 52 20; email info@oekista.co.at; http://www.oekista.co.at/oekista), near the International Youth Hotel. Open M-F 9am-5:30pm. **Albatross Travel Service,** Bergstr. 22 (tel. 881 67 10; fax 88 16 79), serves your travel needs in English and German. Open M-F 8:15am-6pm.

Consulates: South Africa, Buchenweg 14 (tel./fax 62 20 35). Open M-F 8am-1pm and 2-5pm. **U.K.,** Alter Markt 4 (tel. 84 81 33; fax 84 55 63). Open M-F 9am-noon. **U.S. Consulate Agency,** Alter Markt 1/3 (tel. 84 87 76; fax 84 97 77), in the *Altstadt*. Open M, W, and F 9am-noon.

Currency Exchange: Banks offer better rates for cash than AmEx offices but often charge higher commissions. Banking hours are M-F 8am-12:30pm and 2-4:30pm. **Rieger Bank** at Alter Markt and Getriedeg. has extended currency exchange hours. July-Aug. M-F 9am-7:30pm, Sa 9am-6pm, Su 10am-5pm; Sept.-June M-F 9am-6pm, Sa 9am-3pm, Su 10am-5pm. The train station's currency exchange is open 7am-9pm. **Panorama Tours** offers cash currency exchange at bank rates with no commission; available only to guests taking their tour (see **Sights,** p. 195).

American Express: Mozartpl. 5, A-5020 (tel. 80 80; fax 808 01 78). The office provides all banking services and charges no commission on AmEx checks. Better rates than banks for cash and other checks. Holds mail for check- or card-holders, books sightseeing tours, and reserves music festival tickets. Open M-F 9am-5:30pm, Sa 9am-noon.

LOCAL SERVICES

Luggage Storage: At the train station. Large lockers 30AS for 2 calendar days. Small lockers 20AS. Luggage check 30AS per piece per calendar day. Open 6am-10pm.

English-Language Bookstores: American Discount, in a passage in Alter Markt 1 (tel. 75 75 41). Tiny store bursting with American teamwear, bestsellers, and magazines, as well as an international selection of pornography; *Love Between the Cheeks* only 38AS. To help you plan your next trip, pick up a *Let's Go* at **Buchhandlung Motzko Reise,** Rainerstr. 24 (tel. 88 33 11), near the train station. English-language books at their main store across the street at Elisabethstr. 1. Both open M-F 9am-6pm, Sa 9am-5pm.

Bi-Gay-Lesbian Organizations: Frauenkulturzentrum (Women's/Lesbians' Center), Elisabethstr. 11 (tel./fax 87 16 39). Office and hotlines open M 10am-12:30pm. Runs a **Woman's Café** on the 1st and 3rd Friday of every month, from 8pm to midnight. **Homosexual Initiative of Salzburg** (HOSI), Müllner Hauptstr. 11 (tel. 43 59 27), hosts regular workshops and meetings, including a **Café-bar** open Fridays at 9pm and Saturdays at 8pm.

Laundromat: Norge Exquisit Textil Reinigung, Paris-Lodronstr. 16 (tel. 87 63 81), on the corner of Wolf-Dietrich-Str. Self-serve wash and dry 82AS, soap 28AS. (You may not use your own soap.) Open M-F 7:30am-4pm, Sa 8-10am. Full-serve 185AS. Open M-F 7:30am-6pm, Sa 8am-noon. **Westinghaus,** Kaiserschützenstr. 10 (tel. 87 33 90), across from the train station. Self-serve 135AS. Open in the summer M-F 7:30am-7pm, Sa 7:30am-1pm. Winter hours M-F 8am-6pm, Sa 8am-noon.

Public Toilets: In the *Altstadt* under the archway between Kapitelpl. and Dompl. (7AS). Cheaper ones in the Festungsbahn lobby (3AS) and at the fish market in Hanuschpl. (2AS.). McDonald's sparkling free toilets are popular with tourists, including those who "forgot" to purchase their fries on the way out.

EMERGENCY AND COMMUNICATIONS

Emergencies: Police, tel. 133. Headquarters at Alpenstr. 90 (tel. 63 83). **Ambulance,** tel. 144. **Fire,** tel. 122.

Rape Hotline: tel. 88 11 00.

AIDS Hotline: AIDS-Hilfe Salzburg, Gabelsburgerstr. 20 (tel. 88 14 88).

Pharmacies: Elisabeth-Apotheke, Elisabethstr. 1 (tel. 87 14 84), a few blocks left of the train station. **Alte f.e. Hofapotheke,** Alter Markt 6 (tel. 84 36 23), is the oldest pharmacy in Salzburg. Pharmacies in the city center are open M-F 8am-6pm, Sa 8am-noon; outside the center M-F 8am-12:30pm and 2:30-6pm, Sa 8am-noon. There are always 3 pharmacies available for emergencies; check the list on the door of any closed pharmacy.

Medical Assistance: When the dog bites, when the bee stings, when you're feeling sad, call the **Hospital,** Dr. Franz-Rebirl-Pl. 5 (tel. 658 00).

Post Office: At the *Hauptbahnhof* (tel. 889 70). Mail your brown paper packages tied up with string at the main office next to the train station. The office has self-serve photocopiers and currency exchange. Address *Poste Restante* to Post-lagernde Briefe, Bahnhofspostamt, A-5020 Salzburg. Open 6am-11pm. Exchange open M-Th 6am-5pm, F 6am-6pm. **Branch** at Residenzpl. 9 (tel. 84 41 21). Open M-F 7am-7pm, Sa 8-10am. **Postal Code:** A-5020.

Email: Cybercafé, Gstätteng. 29 (tel. 84 26 16 22); offers internet access for 70AS per hr. Open M-F 2-11pm, F-Su 2pm-1am.

Telephone Code: 0662.

■ Accommodations and Camping

Salzburg has no shortage of hostels—but, then again, the city has no shortage of tourists either. Real estate in Salzburg is even more expensive than in Vienna. Most affordable accommodations are on the outskirts of town, easily accessible by local transportation. Ask for the tourist office's list of private rooms (separate from the hotel map) or the *Hotel Plan* for information on hostels. The tourist office charges 30AS plus a 7.2% fee to make reservations. From mid-May to mid-September, hostels fill by mid-afternoon—call ahead. During the festival, show up with reservations or before noon. Hotels fill months in advance, and most youth hostels and *Gästehäuser* are full days before.

HOSTELS AND DORMITORIES

⊛**Gästehaus Bürgerwehr,** Mönchsberg 19c (tel. 84 17 29), towers over the old town from the top of the Mönchsberg. The easy way: bus #1 (dir: Maxglan): "Mönchsberg-gaufzug" then down the street a few steps and through the stone arch on the left to the Mönchsberglift (elevator). The elevator takes you to the top of the mountain (runs 9am-11pm, round-trip 27AS). At its summit, turn right, climb the steps, and follow signs for "Gästehaus Naturfreundehaus." Or try the hard way: bus #1 (dir: Maxglan): "Karajanpl." then continue straight ahead, across the street, and along the front of the Festspielhaus. Go through the arch on the right, up the 332 stairs in the corner, bearing right on the top paths up to the red-umbrella-bedecked hostel. Get a princely view on a pauper's budget at the most scenic hostel in Salzburg. Genial proprietors also run the terrific restaurant downstairs. Only holds 28 in 2- to 6-bed rooms; reservations are recommended. Dorms 120AS. Delicious fresh-baked breakfast (on the terrace with a magnificent view of Salzburg) 30AS. Showers 10AS per 4min. Sheets 20AS. Reception 8am-9pm. Curfew 1am—start hustling up those stairs at quarter till. Open May to mid-Oct.

International Youth Hotel (YoHo), Paracelsusstr. 9 (tel. 87 96 49 or 834 60; fax 87 88 10), off Franz-Josef-Str. Exit the train station to the left and turn left onto Gabels-bergerstr. through the tunnel. Take the 2nd right onto Paracelsusstr. (7min.). A rol-licking pitstop for homesick Americans and Canadians—you may even forget you're in a German-speaking country. Filled with beer-sipping postcard writers in the afternoon and a frat-party atmosphere in the evening. Despite the raucous inhabitants, the hostel is remarkably clean and well run, while double doors keep the dorms quiet. *The Sound of Music* screened daily at 1:30pm. 24hr. CNN in the bar (beer 25AS). Dorms 140AS; doubles 360AS; quads 640AS. Breakfast 30-55AS. Dinner entrees 30-75AS. Showers 10AS per 6min. Lockers 10AS. Stylish sleepsacks require 30AS deposit. The new YoHo membership card grants holders discounts at some of Salzburg's attractions. Reception 8am-noon. "Curfew" 1am (not very strict); theoretical quiet time starts at 10pm.

Institut St. Sebastian, Linzerg. 41 (tel. 87 13 86; fax 87 13 86 85). From the station, turn left on Rainerstr., go past Mirabellpl., turn left onto Bergstr., and turn left at the end onto Linzerg. The hostel is through the arch on the left just before the church. This privately owned hostel-like accommodation, built right on the St. Sebastian church grounds, is clean and modern with wooden furniture and match-ing wood crosses on the walls. Located smack-dab in the middle of the historic *Neustadt,* the institute is a women-only university dorm but accepts travelers of either gender in summer. The cemetery of the St. Sebastian church, which abuts the dormitory, makes for a very quiet neighborhood. Rooftop terrace and piano practice room. Only 90 beds, so reservations are strongly recommended. Dorms only Oct.-June. Dorms 180AS; hotel-like singles 340AS, with shower 390AS; dou-bles 520AS, 680AS; triples 900AS. Free lockers. Dorm sheets 30AS. **Kitchen** facili-ties available, including refrigerators with little lockable cupboards. **Laundry** 40AS. 24hr. reception, but call ahead. No curfew.

Eduard-Heinrich-Haus (HI), Eduard-Heinrich-Str. 2 (tel. 62 59 76; fax 62 79 80). It's a bit *fa* (a long, long way to run), *so* (a needle pulling thread) take bus #51 (dir: Salzburg Süd): "Polizeidirektion." Cross the street, continue down Billrothstr., and turn left on the Robert-Stolz-Promenade footpath. Walk 200m and take the 1st right; the hostel is the large building up the driveway on the left. Enormous 6- to 7-bed rooms with lockers to match. Significantly more beds July-Aug. Dorms 166AS, non-members add 40AS. Showers and breakfast (7-9am) included: Reception 7-9am and 5-11pm. Lockout 9am-5pm. Summer curfew midnight, winter 11pm; key with 300AS deposit.

Haunspergstraße (HI), Haunspergstr. 27 (tel. 87 50 30; fax 88 34 77), just minutes from the train station. Walk straight out Kaiserschützenstr. (past the Forum depart-ment store), which becomes Jahnstr. Take the 3rd left onto Haunspergstr. A stu-dent dorm that becomes a hostel in summer. Houses 125 in spacious 2- to 4-bed rooms. Dorms 166AS. Non-members add 40AS 1st night. Breakfast, shower, and sheets included. **Laundry** 80AS. Reception 7am-2pm and 5pm-midnight, but the hostel fills by late afternoon. Curfew 11pm. Open July-Aug.

Jugendgästehaus Salzburg (HI), Josef-Preis-Allee 18 (tel. 842 67 00; fax 84 11 01), southeast of the *Altstadt.* Bus #5, 51, or 55: "Justizgebäude," or walk from the tour-ist office southeast (with traffic) along the river, bear right onto Hellbrunnerstr., turn right onto Nonntaler Hauptstr., then take the 1st left. Rule-oriented hostel with a Las Vegas lobby. School groups make frequent use of the on-site video game room, café, and disco. Boys lodged in the red sector of the hostel, girls in blue. Dorms 164AS; doubles with shower 528AS; quads with shower 856AS. Non-mem-bers add 40AS 1st night. Breakfast, shower, and sheets included. Lunch or dinner 68AS. **Kitchen** available. **Bike rental** 90AS. Handicapped access. Twitchy recep-tion hours: M-F 7-9am, 11-11:30am, noon-1pm, 3:30-5:30pm, 6-9:30pm, and 10pm-midnight, Sa-Su 7-9am, 11-11:30am, noon-1pm, 4:30-7:30pm, and 10pm-midnight. Curfew midnight. Reservations recommended.

Aigen (HI), Aignerstr. 34 (tel. 62 32 48; fax 232 48 13). From the station, bus #5: "Mozartsteg." then bus #49 (dir: Josef-Käut-Str.): "Finanzamt," and walk 5min. farther. It's the yellow, estate-like building on your right. Large, sporty hostel with a nearby basketball net. Huge, bare 6-bed rooms with linoleum floors. TV, weight machines, and ping-pong table downstairs. Accommodates 135 in rooms with 2-6 beds. Dorms 166AS, non-members add 40AS. Breakfast, showers, lockers, and sheets included. Reception 7-9am and 5pm-midnight. Curfew midnight.

HOTELS AND PENSIONS

Pensionen in the center of the city can be quite expensive. Better quality and lower prices await on the outskirts. Public transportation puts these establishments within minutes of downtown Salzburg. Rooms on **Kasern Berg** are officially out of Salzburg, which means the tourist office can't officially recommend them, but the charming hosts and bargain prices make these pensions little-known steals. All northbound regional trains run to Kasern Berg (generally 4min., every 30min. 6:17am-11:17pm, 17AS, Eurailpass valid). Get off at the first stop, "Salzburg-Maria Plain," and take the only road uphill. All the Kasern Berg pensions are along this road. If you call in advance, many proprietors will pick you up at the Kasern station. Or, from Mirabellpl., take bus #15 (dir: Bergheim): "Kasern" then turn up Söllheimerstr. and hike up the mountain (15min.). By car, exit Autobahn A1 on "Salzburg Nord." The Kasern Berg pensions Haus Lindner, Haus Christine, Haus Seigmann, and Germana Kapella work together to find rooms for guests. Another option is camping, a possibility even for domestic souls who have never spent a night under the stars. Some of Salzburg's campsites have beds in pre-assembled tents. Be wary of proprietors who accost you at the station, as they are sometimes up to no good.

Haus Bankhammer, Mooshammerstr. 77 (tel./fax 83 00 67). A grand farmhouse on the plains in southern Salzburg. Hotel-quality doubles with bath include a scrumptious breakfast of homemade strawberry-rhubarb jam and fresh milk from the family dairy. Helga speaks English fluently and will do small quantities of laundry for guests. Rooms 440-500AS year-round.

Haus Lindner/Christine, Panoramaweg 3/5 (tel. 45 67 73). Frau Lindner's house is on a gravel road set 15m back from the main Kasern Berg street. Spacious rooms have hardwood floors and the occasional balcony. The *Haus* is run by 2 amiable sisters who offer a sausage-and-eggs breakfast (included) on their enclosed patio. Families with children are welcome—there's even a playground around back. Gorgeous views from mountaintop. Doubles 320-400AS; triples 480-600AS; quads 640-800AS. Reservations recommended.

Haus Rosemarie Seigmann, Kasern Berg 66 (tel. 45 00 01). English-speaking Rosemarie welcomes guests to rooms with hand-painted cupboards, flowered curtains, and stuffed animals. Listen to birds singing from the stone terrace overlooking the Alps. Bright rooms with fluffy comforters. Doubles 340-400AS; triples 510-600AS. Breakfast included. 1-night stays welcome.

Germana Kapeller, Kasern Berg 64 (tel. 45 66 71), below Haus Lindner. English-speaking hostess oversees enchantingly traditional rooms and screens *The Sound of Music* upon group demand (guests only). Doubles 340-400AS; triples 510-600AS. Showers and complete pastoral breakfast included. Call ahead.

Haus Moser, Turnebuhel 1 (tel. 45 66 76), above Haus Rosemarie Seigmann; climb up the hidden secret stairs on the right side of Kasern Berg road across from #64. A mountainside, dark-timbered home with spacious rooms filled with fur rugs and deer heads. Singles 170-200AS; doubles 340-400AS; triples 510-600AS; quads 700-800AS. "Welcome drink," all-you-can-eat breakfast, and shower included.

Haus Ballwein, Moostr. 69 (tel./fax 82 40 29). Bus #1: "Hanuschpl." then bus #60 and ask the driver to stop at Gsengerweg (guh-zang-ehr-veg). Enormous, spotless rooms decorated with pastels and beautiful new furniture. The country farmhouse has wonderful farmland for hiking and offers a relaxing rural reprieve from the bustle of city tourism. Breakfast includes eggs from the *Pension*'s own chickens. 200AS per person, with shower 240AS. Rooms with shower in the newly built house with gorgeous pastoral views 270AS. Breakfast included.

Haus Elisabeth, Rauchenbichlerstr. 18 (tel./fax 45 07 03). Bus #51: "Itzling-Pflanzmann" (last stop) then walk up Rauchenbichlerstr. over the footbridge and continue right along the gravel path. Plush rooms with TVs, balconies, and sweeping views of the city. Hostess stuffs her guests with a huge breakfast of corn flakes, yogurt, bread, and jam. Singles with shower 300-330AS; doubles 500-550AS; one 4-person suite with kitchen 1000AS.

Haus Kernstock, Karolingerstr. 29 (tel. 82 74 69; fax 82 74 69). Bus #77 (dir: Flughafen): "Karolingerstr." and follow signs for the street number as the road twists (25min. from rail station). Large, pleasant bedrooms far away from the bustling *Altstadt,* but near the airport, a warehouse, and 2 bus lines. Friendly hostess screens *The Sound of Music* and has 2 bikes to lend. Singles 170AS; doubles 340-360AS; triples 510-750AS; quads 880-1000AS. All-you-can-eat breakfast included. **Laundry** 80AS. MC, Visa.

Pension Sandwirt, Lastenstr. 6a (tel./fax 87 43 51). Exit the station from the platform #13 staircase, turn right on the footbridge, turn right at the bottom onto Lastenstr., and go behind the building with the post sign (3min.). Rooms are filled with aging furniture and chipped mirrors, but luckily it is very close to the train station and offers **free laundry.** Singles 300AS; doubles 440AS, with shower 550AS; triples 660AS. Breakfast included.

CAMPING

Camping Stadtblick, Rauchenbichlerstr. 21 (tel. 45 06 52; fax 45 80 18), next to Haus Elisabeth and run by Elisabeth's brother. By car, take exit "Salzburg-Nord" off A1. Behind a copse of trees with a sweeping view of the city. On-site store. 65AS, *Let's Go*-toting students 60AS; tent 15AS; bed in a tent 80AS; car 25AS. 4-person mobile home with refrigerator and stovetop, 100AS per person. **Laundry** 70AS. Open March 20-Oct. 31.

Camping Nord-Sam, Samstr. 22-A (tel. 66 04 94). Bus #33 (dir: Obergnigl): "Langmoosweg." Shady, flower-bedecked campground with a small swimming pool to boot. May to mid-June and Sept. 50AS; mid-June to Aug. 79AS. **Laundry** 75AS.

■ Food

Blessed with fantastic beer gardens and countless pastry-shop patios, Salzburg is a great place to eat outdoors. The local specialty is *Salzburger Nockerl,* a large soufflé of egg-whites, sugar, and raspberry filling baked into three mounds that represent the three hills of Salzburg. Another regional favorite is *Knoblauchsuppe* (garlic soup), a rich cream soup loaded with croutons and pungent garlic—a potent weapon, use it wisely against those pesky bunkmates. During the first two weeks of September, local cafés dispense *Stürm,* a delicious, cloudy cider (reminiscent, aptly enough, of a storm) that hasn't quite finished fermenting.

There are more of the world-famous **Mozartkugeln** (chocolate "Mozart balls") lining café windows than notes in all of Mozart's works combined. A Salzburg confectioner invented the treats in 1890, but mass production inevitably took over. Although the mass-produced *Kugeln* wrapped in gold and red are technically *echt* (authentic), try to sniff out the rarer, handmade ones wrapped in blue and silver, which are impossible to find outside of Salzburg. Reasonably priced samples are sold individually at the **Holzmayr** confectioners in the *Alter Markt* (5AS each, 7AS for the real, handmade McCoy). Confectioners make the *Kugeln* by covering a hazelnut-marzipan with nougat and then dipping it in chocolate; the blue and silver variety have more marzipan than the mass-produced ones.

Bars, restaurants, and cafés in Salzburg are difficult to classify because, more often than not, they become each of those things at different times during the day. A *beisl,* for example, serves coffee in the morning, tea in the afternoon, and beer in the evenings. Flexibility is warranted.

⊛**Restaurant Zur Bürgerwehr-Einkehr,** Mönchsberg 19c (tel. 84 17 29). Follow the directions to the Bürgerwehr. The mom-and-pop owners of the Bürgerwehr (see **Hostels and Dormitories,** p. 189) operate this restaurant at the top of the Mönchsberg. On sunny days, escape the tourist throng below as you recline beneath the terrace's red umbrellas and enjoy the best views in town. This restaurant has one of the most reasonably priced (and tastiest) *Menüs* around. Extraordinary *Gammerknödel* (bacon-filled dumplings with sauerkraut) for just 65AS. Mmmm, these are a few of our favorite things. Open May-Oct. 10am-8:30pm.

Zum Fidelen Affen, Priesterhausg. 8 (tel. 87 73 61), off Linzerg. Phenomenal food in a dark-wood pub, pleasantly crowded with locals and tourists, but no apes. Sorry. Drinks 30AS. Full meal of salad and main course 87-110AS. Try the spinach *Spätzle* (doughy dumpling noodles, 88AS) or the beef with onion gravy (89AS). English menu available. Open M-Sa 5pm-midnight.

Vegy, Schwarzstr. 21 (tel. 87 57 46). Relaxing vegetarian restaurant feels like an eat-in kitchen. Finally, a place that understands that vegetarian food doesn't have to mean cheese. Dozens of filling options to choose from, including a daily *Menü* with soup, coffee, and dessert for 87AS. Open M-F 10:30am-6pm.

Der Wilde Mann, Getreideg. 20 (tel. 84 17 87), in the passage. Huge portions of *Wiener Schnitzel,* potatoes, and *Stiegl Bier* for the wild man (or woman) in all of us. Sit in carved wooden chairs for a traditional Austrian meal, cooked in a lovely tiled oven. Entrees run 75-145AS and are worth every *Groschen*. Pleasantly less touristed than nearby bistros; crowded by locals at lunch. Open M-Sa 11am-9pm.

University Mensa (tel. 844 96 09), across from Sigmund Haffnerg. 16 and through the iron fence. A good deal for penny-pinchers. 2 hot entrees, 1 for carnivores (49AS) and 1 for veggie-eaters (37AS). Desserts and drinks not included. Valid student ID required (ISICs accepted). Open M-Th 9am-4pm, F 9am-3pm. Get there early—ravenous students sometimes deplete the food supply.

Fischmarkt, at Hanuschpl. in the *Altstadt*. Mammoth trees poke through the roof of this Danish seafood restaurant. A local fave. Very casual and very packed—the crowds may force you to eat outside. Fish sandwiches 50AS; glasses of beer 21AS. The restaurant also sells fresh seafood and seafood salad by the kg. Open M-F 8:30am-6:30pm, Sa 8:30am-1pm.

Trześniewski, Getreideg. 9 (tel. 84 07 69), behind the chocolate counter and butcher shop. Dubiously enough, Kafka's favorite hangout in Vienna now has a new franchise on the ground floor of Mozart's *Geburtshaus* (birthplace). While indulging in their wonderful open-faced sandwiches, you can ponder who would roll over in his grave first. Sandwiches only 9AS, but you'll probably need about 4 to make a good lunch. Open M-F 8:30am-6pm, Sa 8:30am-1pm.

Pizza Casanova, Linzerg. 23 (tel. 87 50 31). Don't be put off by the burlesque joint with the same name next door—Pizza Casanova knows that the way to a man's heart is through his stomach. Large pies 66-105AS. Healthy selection of veggie and whole-grain pizza. Open 11am-3pm and 6-11pm.

Shakespeare, Hubert Sattlerg. 3 (tel. 87 91 06), off Mirabellpl. Culturally schizophrenic: wonton soup, Greek salad, *Wiener Schnitzel,* and just about anything else 23-88AS. Doubles as a bar(d) with understated chic and hopping **live music,** from tango to *chansons*. Behind the bar is the **Electric Café,** a trip-hop and techno lounge. Restaurant open M-F 11:30am-2:30am, Sa-Su 10am-2am, but the Chinese cook takes Sundays off. MC, Visa.

CAFÉS

Café im Kunstlerhaus, Hellbrunnerstr. 3 (tel 84 56 01). Low-key café popular with students, artists, and their fans. Wide variety of drinks—treat yourself to a café amaretto or a shot of tequila. Local bands play Tuesday and Thursday nights. Saturday is lesbian night. Open M-F 11am-11pm.

Café Tomaselli, Alter Markt 9 (tel. 84 44 88). A favorite haunt for wealthier Salzburger clientele since 1705. In 1820, Mozart's widow and her second husband came here to write the dead man's bio. Today anyone can sit in its wood-paneled rooms with antique portraits, or find a chair on the balcony overlooking the *Alter Markt*. Coffee (27-37AS) and a mobile dessert counter. Open M-Sa 7am-9pm, Su 8am-9pm.

Café Bazar, Schwarzstr. 3 (tel 87 42 78). Affordable drinks and small meals in a tree-lined garden along the banks of the Salzach. Yogurt with raspberry juice 38AS. Come here for your Turkish coffee fix (37AS). Open mid-July to Aug. M 10am-6pm, Tu-Sa 7:30am-11pm; Sept. to mid-July M-Sa 9:30am-11pm.

Café Fürst, Brodg. 13 (tel. 84 37 59). Faces off with the equally haughty Café Toma-selli across *Alter Markt.* Specializes in the original *Mozartkugeln* (10AS a pop—savor slowly). Vast selection of candies, chocolates, pastries, *torte,* strudels, and cakes. Grab one of the sunny tables outside if you can. Branch in Mirabellpl. Open daily in summer 8am-9pm; in winter 8am-8pm.

Kaffeehäferl, Getreideg. 25 (tel. 84 32 49), in the passage across from McDonald's. Unpretentious courtyard café provides a needed respite from the tourist rush of G-street. The neighboring flower shop adds to the olfactory pleasure. Quiche Lor-raine 45AS; strawberry milkshake 35AS. Open M-Sa 9am-7pm, Su noon-7pm.

Salad and Friends, Linzer Bundesstr. 44 (tel. 651 51 54), bus #27 (dir: Obergnigl): to "Sterneckstr." This little *Beisl* is a cafeteria-style, vegetable-friendly restaurant, with an ample salad bar (all-you-can-eat 55AS), pasta with 4 kinds of sauce (49AS), and veggie burgers (35AS). Open M-Sa 11am-10pm.

MARKETS

In most cases, markets are open weekdays 8am to 6pm, Saturday 8am to noon. Salzburg has many supermarkets on the Mirabellpl. side of the river but very few in the *Altstadt.* **SPAR** is widespread, and the giant **EuroSpar** sprawls next to the train station bus terminal. **Open-air markets** occur at Universitätpl. (M-F 6am-7pm, Sa 6am-1pm) and Mirabellpl. down into Hubert-Sattlerg. (Th 5am-1pm). If you're in town on Saturday morning, you can pick up your organic tomatoes and sausage lard at Max Rheinhardtpl. in the *Altstadt.*

BEER GARDENS AND BARS

Munich may be the beer capital of the world, but a good deal of it flows south to Aus-tria's beer gardens *(Biergärten)*. Beyond Mozart and *The Sound of Music,* beer gar-dens are an essential part of Salzburg's charm and an absolute must-visit for travelers. Many of the gardens also serve moderately priced meals, but like everything else in Salzburg, they tend to close early. These lager oases cluster in the center of the city by the Salzach River. Nightclubs in the *Altstadt* (especially along Gstätteng. and near Chi-emseeg.) generally attract younger types and tourists. For a less juvenile atmosphere, hit the other side of the river—especially along Giselakai and Steing.

Augustiner Bräu, Augustinerg. 4 (tel. 43 12 46). From the *Altstadt,* pick up the foot-path at Hanuschpl. and follow it alongside the river, walking with the current. Go left up the flight of stairs past the Riverside Café, cross Müllner Hauptstr., and walk uphill. Augustinerg. is the 1st left. The brewery, inside the Kloster with the big tower, is a Salzburg legend. The great beer brewed by the Müllner Kloster is poured into massive *Steins* from even more massive wooden kegs. The outdoor garden provides room for 1300, and the indoor salons seat an additional 1200, cre-ating a rambunctious stadium atmosphere. Different halls attract different crowds, from hard-core drunk Austrians shouting German drinking songs to the American collegiate scene. Bratwurst stands for the hungry. 1 Liter 56AS (be nice and tip the tap-*meister* 4AS), half-liter 28AS. Open M-F 3-11pm, Sa-Su 2:30-11pm.

Sternbräu, Getreideg. 34 (tel. 84 21 40), in the *Altstadt*—duck into any number of passages at the end of Getreideg. Formerly a brewery, now just a place to drink and eat a lot. 2 beer gardens, a shady arcade, traditional mural-covered interiors. Aus-trian entrees 85-145AS, beer 37AS. Open 9am-midnight.

2 Stein, Giselakai 9 (tel. 88 02 01). Possibly the funkiest bar in town. Previously a gay bar, 2 Stein is now a fave for a mixed clientele of all genders and orientations. Zebra print barstools, inflatable animals, and occasional transvestite performances. Open 5pm-4am.

Pub Passage, Rudolfskai 22-26, under the Radisson Hotel by the Mozartsteg bridge. A shopping promenade for youthful bar-hopping. All these bars are located in the corridors of the "mall" and are open until 2-4am. Though remarkably similar, each bar has its own "unique" gimmick: **Tom's Bierklinik** brags beers from all over the world; **The Black Lemon** offers Latino night every Wednesday; **Bräu zum From-men Hell** burns with 80s music; and **Hell** sells itself as a TV sports bar.

Vis à Vis, Rudolfskai 24 (tel. 84 16 10). A swish lounge cut in the shape of an arched stone tunnel with plush, paisley armchairs, smoking-room couches, and spindly dark-wood coatracks. A mixed crowd parties late into the sparkly night. Open Su-Th 8pm-4am, F-Sa 8pm-5am. **Shamrock,** Rudolfskai 24 (tel. 480 12 90). Up the block from the Pub Passage, this sprawling Irish pub has a friendly tucked-in-shirt atmosphere and plenty of room for beer-guzzling groups to mingle. Open M 3pm-2am, Tu-W 3pm-3am, Th-Sa 3pm-4am, Su 2pm-2am.

Disco Seven, Gstätteng. 7 (tel. 84 41 81). Fun-loving bar with billiard tables and a dance floor upstairs. Drinks half-price Wednesday; on Saturday midnight-1am drinks are 20AS; Friday is "ladies' night" (choke). Get a free drink if you show them a *Let's Go*. Open daily till 4am.

Frauen Café, Sittikusstr. 17 (tel. 87 16 39). A relaxed lesbian hangout where women convene to drink and chat. Open W-Sa 8pm-midnight.

Schwarze Katze, Fruhdiele, Auerspergstr. 45 (tel 87 54 05). For those who miraculously found a late-night scene in Salzburg and/or got locked out of their hostels, the Black Cat magnanimously opens its doors. Dark, low-key atmosphere guaranteed not to grate on early morning nerves. Open Tu-Sa 4am-noon.

■ Sights

The tourist office sells a **Salzburg Card,** which grants admission to most museums and sights and access to all public transportation. *(24hr. card 200AS, 48hr. 270AS, 72hr. 360AS; children ages 7-15 half-price.)* The card is a good deal only if you plan to cram a great deal of sight-seeing into a short period of time.

THE ALTSTADT

Salzburg sprang up under the protective watch of the **Hohensalzburg** castle and fortress (tel. 84 24 30; fax 84 24 30 20), which towers atop the imposing Mönchsberg. *(Open July-Sept. 8am-7pm; Nov.-Mar. 9am-5pm; Apr.-June 9am-6pm. 25AS, children 15AS. 1hr. castle tours in English and German. July-Aug. 9:30am-5:30pm, Apr.-June and Sept.-Oct. 9:30am-5pm, Nov.-Mar. 10am-4:30pm. Combo ticket including castle tour, museum, and fortress 70AS, children 35AS.)* Built between 1077 and 1681 by the ruling archbishops, the structure is now the largest completely preserved castle in Europe. To view the splendid rooms inside, visitors must take one of the castle's tours, which wind through torture chambers, formidable Gothic state rooms, the fortress organ (nick-named the "Bull of Salzburg" for its off-key snorting), and an impregnable watchtower that affords an unmatched view of the city. They'll also show you the archbishop's medieval indoor toilet—a technological marvel of its day. The **Rainer Museum** (see p. 199) inside the fortress displays medieval instruments of torture. To reach the castle, walk up the hill or take the overpriced **Festungsbahn** (cable car; tel. 84 26 82) from Festungsg. *(Every 10min. 9am-9pm; Oct.-Apr. 9am-5pm; ascent 59AS, children 32AS; round-trip 69AS, 37AS.)* Since the ride terminates inside the fortress walls, cable-car tickets include entrance. The many footpaths atop the Mönchsberg give a bird's-eye view of the city; hikers meander down the leafy trails to the *Altstadt* below or descend via the **Mönchsberglift** (elevator) built into the mountain at Gstätteng. 13, near Café Winkler. *(Elevator operates daily 9am-11pm. 16AS, round-trip 27AS.)*

Bovine Befuddlement

Salzburg's clever archbishop once saved the city's pride, the **Hohensalzburg** fortress, from imminent destruction. During the **Peasant Wars** (see **The Habsburg Empire,** p. 60), the peasants surrounded the fortress in an attempt to starve the archbishop out. When the archbishop had only one cow left, he painted the remaining beast with different spots on both sides and paraded him back and forth along the castle wall in distinct view of the peasants below. Since the peasants, as the saying goes, were simple-minded folk, they believed that the archbishop had a great reserve of food and promptly canceled their embargo.

At the bottom of the Festungsbahn is **Kapitelplatz,** home of a giant chess grid, a fountain depicting Poseidon wielding his scepter, and a bunch of tradespeople bartering their wares. If you stand at the chess board and face the mountain, you'll see the entrance to **St. Peter's Monastery** at the back right corner through the cemetery. The lovely cemetery, **Petersfriedhof,** is one of the most peaceful places in Salzburg—possibly because guided tours are barred entry. *(Open Apr.-Sept. 6:30am-7pm; Oct.-Mar. 6:30am-6pm.)* The tiny courtyard is filled with delicate flowerbed graves, some dating back to the 1600s. Though a popular subject for romantic painters, this secluded spot is best known as the site where Liesl's Nazi boyfriend Rolf blew the whistle on the von Trapp family in *The Sound of Music.* Near the far end of the cemetery, against the mountains, is the entrance to the **Katakomben** (catacombs; tel. 844 57 80), a relatively bare set of cave-like rooms where Christians allegedly worshipped in secret as early as 250 CE. *(Open in summer Tu-Th 10:30am-4pm, F-Su 10:30am-5pm; in winter W-Su 10:30am-3:30pm. 12AS, students 8AS.)* Past the arch near the catacombs stands **Stiftskirche St. Peter.** *(Open daily 9am-12:15pm and 2:30-6:30pm.)* The church began as a Romanesque basilica and still boasts a marble portal from 1244. In the 18th century, the building was remodeled in the Rococo style, with green and pink moldings curling delicately across the graceful ceiling and gilded cherubim blowing golden trumpets. The church has the look and feel of a Fabergé egg turned inside-out. The steeple tower and clock are also new(er) additions. The courtyard on the other side of the gate facing St. Peter's entrance leads to the monastery at **Toscaninihof.** One wall of the complex is part of the Felsenreitenschule, formerly the Rock Riding School for the archbishops' horses and now the **Festspielhaus** (Opera House), which houses many of the events of the Festspiele. **Tours** of the opera house are given every day for 70AS, children 40AS. *(June-Sept. daily at 9:30am, 2pm, and 3:30pm; Oct.-Dec. and Apr.-May at 2pm.)*

The distinctive dome of the **Universitätskirche** (University Church) stands watch over Universitätspl. near the Festspielhaus and daily farmer's market. Generally considered Fischer von Erlach's masterpiece, this massive chapel is one of the largest Baroque chapels on the continent. Sculpted clouds coat the nave, with pudgy cherubim (lit by pale natural light from the dome) splattered all over the immense apse of the church.

From Universitätspl., several passages lead through tiny courtyards filled with geraniums and creeping ivy and eventually give way to the stampede of **Getreidegasse.** This labyrinth of winding pathways and 17th- and 18th-century facades is one of the best-preserved (and touristed) streets in Salzburg. Many of Getreidegasse's shops have wrought-iron signs dating from the Middle Ages when the illiterate needed pictorial aids to understand which store sold what. Or so they claim. Some suspect a few of these signs are modern tourist revivals…golden arches, for example, don't objectively suggest hamburgers. Maybe Pavlov could explain.

Wolfgang Amadeus Mozart was unleashed upon the world from the imaginatively dubbed **Mozart's Geburtshaus** (birthplace), on the second floor of Getreideg. 9 (tel. 84 43 13; fax 84 06 93), one of Salzburg's most touristed attractions. *(Open July-Aug. 9am-6:30pm; Sept.-June 9am-5:30pm. In summer show up before 11am to beat the crowds. 70AS, students and seniors 55AS, children 20AS.)* The long red and white flag suspended from the roof serves as a beacon for music pilgrims worldwide. Although he eventually settled in Vienna, his birthplace holds the most impressive collection of the child genius' belongings: his first viola and violin, a pair of keyboardish instruments, and a lock of hair purportedly from his noggin. A set of skillful dioramas chronicle previous *Festspiele* productions of Mozart's operas.

The **Neugebäude,** opposite the AmEx office, supports both the city government's bureaucracy and a 35-bell **Glockenspiel.** Every day at 7am, 11am, and 6pm, the delightful, slightly off-key carillon rings out a Mozart tune (specified on a notice posted on the corner of the *Residenz*), and the tremendous pipe organ atop the Hohensalzburg fortress bellows a response.

Long before the Mozart era, Archbishop Wolf Dietrich dominated the town's cultural patronage. The clergyman's image still inspires masterful music at the annual Salzburger Festspiele, when opera comes to the courtyard of the archbishop's magnificent **Residenz** (tel. 80 42 26 90), opposite the Glockenspiel. The ecclesiastical elite of Salzburger Land have resided here, in the heart of the *Altstadt*, for the last 700 years. **Tours** lead through crazy Baroque staterooms (*Prunkräume*) and an astonishing three-dimensional ceiling fresco by Rottmayr. *(Tours in German and English May-Oct., Dec. 40min.; every 30min.; 10am-4:30pm; Jan.-Apr. M-F every hr. 10am-4:30pm; 70AS, students and seniors 55AS.)* The *Residenz* also houses a gallery (see p. 200).

Dead-center in Residenzpl. is an immense and very hard-to-miss 15m fountain—the largest Baroque fountain in the world—which features amphibious horses charging through the water (note the webbed hooves). Appropriately, **fiakers** (horse-drawn carriages) congregate around the fountain, which explains the barnyard odor. *(Carriage rides 380AS for 25min.)* The immense Baroque **Dom** (cathedral) forms the third wall of Residenzpl. Wolf Dietrich's successor, Markus Sittikus, commissioned the cathedral from Italian architect Santino Solari in 1628. Inside, the ceilings are resplendent with cartoonish paintings and ornate carvings. Taken together, these resemble a peculiar sort of architectural comic book. The three dates above the archways list the years of the cathedral's renovations. The statue in front of Dompl. depicts the Virgin Mary. Around her swarm four lead figures representing Wisdom, Faith, the Church, and (buh?) the Devil. Mozart was christened here in 1756 and later worked at the cathedral as *Konzertmeister* and court organist.

THE NEUSTADT

Staatsbrücke, the only bridge from the *Altstadt* over the Salzach open to motorized traffic, leads into the new city along **Linzergasse,** a medieval-esque shopping street much in the style of Getreideg. From under the stone arch on the right side of Linzerg. 14, a tiny stone staircase rises up the Kapuzinerberg. At its crest stands the simple **Kapuzinerkloster** (Capuchin Monastery) that Wolf Dietrich built in the late 16th century. Stages of the cross are represented by rubbery mannequins locked behind iron gates. Farther along Linzerg. at quiet little #41 is the 18th-century **Sebastianskirche.** *(Open Apr.-Oct. 9am-7pm, Nov.-Mar. 9am-4pm.)* Its graveyard contains the gaudy mausoleum of Wolf Dietrich and the tombs of Mozart's wife Constanze and father Leopold.

At 17, Mozart moved across the river to Makartpl. From Linzerg. take Dreifaltigkeitg., which leads to **Mozarts Wohnhaus,** Makartpl. 8 (tel. 313; fax 84 06 93), the composer's residence from 1773 to 1780. The house suffered major damage in World War II air raids, but subsequent renovations allowed the building to reopen on the composer's 240th birthday, January 27, 1996 with expanded displays about Mozart and his family. He was not alive to celebrate. Visitors with true Mozart mania should head down the street to Salzburg's conservatory for young musicians, the **Mozarteum,** Schwartzstr. 26-28, for the enormous **Mozart Archives.** Inside the grounds stands a tiny wooden shack transplanted from Vienna, the **Zauberflötenhäuschen,** where Wolfgang Amadeus allegedly composed *The Magic Flute* in just five months. The Mozarteum was originally constructed for the Salzburg Academy of Music and the Performing Arts, but now holds regular performances in the concert hall (see **Entertainment,** p. 200).

What about Joe?

Legend has it that the robes of the Kapuzinerkloster's resident monks inspired the world's first cup of cappuccino. A café proprietor with an overactive imagination observed the pious gents on a noonday stroll and *voilà*—the world witnessed the birth of a drink with the rich coffee color of the monk's robes topped by white froth hoods. According to this theory, Italy's cappuccino is no more than a rip-off of the much older *Kapuziner,* still ordered in Austrian cafés today.

Mirabellplatz holds the marvelous **Schloß Mirabell.** *(Open M-F 7am-4pm.)* The supposedly vowed-to-celibacy Archbishop Wolf Dietrich built this rosy-hued wonder in 1606 for his mistress Salome Alt and their 10 children, christening it "Altenau" in her honor. When successor Markus Sittikus imprisoned Wolf Dietrich for arson, he seized the palace for himself and changed its name. The castle is now the seat of the city government, and some of the mayor's gorgeous offices are open for public viewing. The castle hosts classical concerts in the evening; some fans swear that the *Marmorsaal* (Marble Hall) is in the running for best concert hall in Europe. Next to the palace sits the delicately manicured **Mirabellgarten,** which includes extravagant rose beds and labyrinths of groomed shrubs. Students from the nearby Mozarteum often perform here, and Maria and her over-worked children made this one of their stops in *The Sound of Music* for a rousing rendition of "Do-Re-Mi." Slightly more adorable than the von Trapp children are the vertically challenged statues in the **Dwarf Garden,** a favorite Mirabellgarten play area for Salzburg toddlers. The statues' grotesque marble faces were modeled after Wolf Dietrich's court jesters.

THE SOUND OF MUSIC

In 1964, Julie Andrews, Christopher Plummer, and a gaggle of 20th-Century Fox crewmembers arrived in Salzburg to film *The Sound of Music*, based on the true story of the von Trapp family. Salzburg has never been the same. The city voraciously encourages the increased tourism due to the film's popularity (although interestingly enough Salzburgers themselves have never liked the film, and some flat out hate it). Salzburg now hosts three official companies that run **Sound of Music Tours**. These companies are remarkably similar; the best choice is often the one that stops closest to your accommodation—many hostels and pensions work exclusively with one of the firms and offer discounts to guests. **Salzburg Sightseeing Tours** (tel. 88 16 16; fax 87 87 76) and **Panorama Tours** (tel. 87 40 29; fax 87 16 18; email panorama@alpin.or.at) operate rival kiosks on Mirabellpl. *(350AS, with Let's Go or student ID 315AS. Tours leave from Mirabellpl. daily 9:30am and 2pm.)* The renegade **Bob's Special Tours,** Kaig. 19 (tel. 84 95 11; fax 84 95 12), has no high-profile kiosk, but they do have a minibus. *(330AS; tours daily in summer 9am and 2pm; in winter 10am.)* The smaller vehicle enables them to tour more of the *Altstadt*, a location that the big tour buses can't reach. All three companies offer free pick-up from your hotel, and all tours last four hours. The tours are generally worth the money only if you're a big *Sound of Music* fan or if you have a short time in Salzburg and want an overview of the area—the tours venture into the Salzkammergut lake region as well.

If you have time, however, consider renting a bike and doing the tour on your own. The film's writers and producers took a great deal of artistic license with the von Trapps' story—many of the events were fabricated for Tinseltown. Though Maria was a nun-apprentice in the film, in reality she merely taught at **Nonnberg Abbey,** high above the city near the Festung. In this abbey, the crew filmed the nuns singing "How Do You Solve A Problem Like Maria?" and parts of the wedding scene. To reach the abbey, walk out of Kapitelpl. along Kapitelg. and turn right onto Kaig., where stairs lead up to the nunnery. The darling little gazebo where Liesl and Rolf unleashed their youthful passion is on the grounds of **Schloß Hellbrunn** (see **Near Salzburg,** p. 202). The gazebo is disappointingly small but photogenic (no worries), and the walk back from Hellbrunn to Salzburg's *Altstadt* is lovely on summer afternoons. From the Hellbrun parking lot, head down Hellbrunner Allee. You'll pass the yellow castle used for the exterior of the von Trapp home (Maria sang "I Have Confidence" in front of the long yellow wall). The house is now a dorm for music students at the Mozarteum. Continue along Hellbrunner Allee until it turns into Freisaalweg. At the end of Freisaalweg, turn right on Akadamiestr., which ends at Alpenstr. and the river. The river footpath leads all the way back to Mozartsteg. and Staatsbrücke (1hr.). The back of the von Trapp house (where Maria and the children fell into the water after romping around the city all day) was filmed at the **Schloß Leopoldskron** behind the Mönchsberg, now a center for academic studies. Take bus #55: "Pensionistenheim Nonntal" and turn left on Sunnhubstr., then left again up Leopoldskroner Allee to the castle.

There are several film locations within the *Altstadt*. The von Trapp family hid behind the headstones of the **Petersfriedhof,** the cemetery where Rolf blew the whistle. At the **Festspielhaus** (Opera House), the family sang their final performance while all the Nazis swayed to the melodious "Edelweiss." The opera house is closed to the public, but the stairs leading up to the right sometimes provide a glimpse of the stage—the opera occasionally leaves the top of the house open. The **Mirabellgarten** by Mirabellpl. was a favorite haunt of Maria and the children while they made their forbidden daytrips. Several statues and fountains should look familiar.

The von Trapps were actually married in the church at Nonnberg Abbey, but Hollywood filmed the scene in **Mondsee** instead (see p. 206). The sightseeing tours allow guests to waddle around Mondsee for 45 minutes, but the town is really worth a whole daytrip for its beautiful lake and pastry shops. **Buses** leave the Salzburg train station from the main bus depot *(45min., every hr., 57AS).* The hills that are alive with the sound of music, inspiring Maria's rapturous twirling in the opening scene, are along the Salzburg-St. Gilgen route near Fusch, but any of the hills in the Salzkammergut region could fit the bill. For your own re-creational and recreational purposes, try the Untersberg, just south of Salzburg (see **Near Salzburg,** p. 202).

As if all this wasn't enough, the Stieglkeller hosts a **Sound of Music Live Dinner Show** (tel. 83 20 29; fax 83 20 29 13). *(May-Oct. 8:30pm. 400AS. Dinner at 7:30pm plus the show 560AS. 30% student discount, children under 13 free.)* Performers sing your favorite film songs while servers ply you with soup, *Schnitzel* with noodles, and crisp apple strudel.

■ Museums

Salzburg's small, specialized museums often get lost in the shadow of the *Festung, The Sound of Music,* and the *Festspiele.* The keywords in that sentence are "small" and "specialized." There are also small and specialized private galleries on Sigmund-Haffnerg. that provide budget art viewing.

Rainer Museum, inside the fortress. Medieval relics, including torture devices. Open 9am-5pm. Entrance only with entrance to the castle. 35AS, children 20AS.

Museum Carolino Augusteum, Museumpl. 1 (tel. 84 31 45; fax 84 11 34 10). Named after Emperor Franz I's widow, Caroline Augusta. The lower floors house Roman and Celtic artifacts, including excellent mosaics and burial remains, preserved compliments of the region's salt. Gothic and Baroque art on the upper floors. Open W-Su 9am-5pm, Tu 9am-8pm. 40AS, students 15AS.

Dom Museum (tel. 84 41 89; fax 84 04 42). Inside the cathedral's main entrance. Houses an unusual collection called the **Kunst- und Wunderkammer** (Art and Miracles chamber) that includes conch shells, mineral formations, and a 2ft. whale's tooth. The archbishop accumulated all of these curiosities in his spare time to impress distinguished visitors. Open mid-May to mid-Oct. M-Sa 10am-5pm; Su 1pm-6pm. 70AS, students and ages 16-18 25AS, ages 6-15 10AS.

Domgrabungsmuseum (tel. 84 52 95), entrance on Residenzpl. Displays excavations of the Roman ruins under the cathedral. You'll feel like an archaeologist clambering around in a dig. Open May-Oct. W-Su 9am-5pm. 20AS, students 10AS.

Stiegl Brauwelt, Brauhausstr. 1 (tel. 838 73 80; http://www.stiegl.co.at). Bus #1: "Brauhaus" and walk up the street to the giant yellow building. The *Brauwelt* (Brew World) is Salzburg's own beer museum, attached to the Stiegl brewery just minutes from downtown. 3 floors showcase beer-making, the history of brewing, and modern beer culture—including "30 Ways to Open a Beer Bottle," a photo essay featuring Stiegl employees, and the wonder of the *Brauwelt,* a 2-story beer-bottle pyramid constructed of 300 Austrian beers. Hop on down to the final hands-on exhibit—the tour concludes with 2 complimentary glasses of Stiegl beer, a beer *Brezel* (pretzel), and a souvenir beer glass. Open W-Su 10am-5pm, last entrance 4pm. 75AS, students 50AS, children 40AS.

Rupertinum Gallery, Wiener Philharmonikerg. 9 (tel. 80 42 23 36; fax 80 42 25 42), across from the Festspielhaus. Temporary exhibits of modern painting, sculpture, and photography are housed in an graceful building remodeled by Hundertwasser.

Open mid-July to Sept. Su-Tu and Th-Sa 9am-5pm, W 10am-9pm; Oct. to mid-July Tu-Su 10am-5pm, W 10am-9pm. 40AS, students 20AS, under 16 free.

Haus der Natur (Museum of Natural History), Museumpl. 5 (tel. 84 26 53; fax 84 79 05), across from the Carolino Augusteum. An enormous natural history museum with an eclectic collection—from live alligators to fossils to gems. Get up close and personal (through the glass, of course) with over a dozen giant snakes. Open 9am-5pm. 55AS, students 30AS.

Residenz Gallery, Residenzpl. 1 (tel. 80 42). Not really known for its permanent collection, the gallery has rotating exhibits of 16th- to 19th-century art. Open Apr.-Sept. 10am-5pm; Oct.-Mar. Su-Tu and Th-Sa 10am-5pm. 45AS, students 34AS.

Spielzeug Museum (Toy Museum), Bürgerspitalg. 2 (tel. 84 75 60), near the Festspielhaus. 3 floors of puppets, wooden toys, dolls, and electric trains. Nifty pre-Lego castle blocks from 1921. Puppet show Tu-W 3pm. Open Tu-Su 9am-5pm. 30AS, students 10AS.

Baroque Museum (tel. 87 74 32; fax 80 72 20 85), in the Mirabellgarten's Orangerie. Elaborate tribute to the ornate aesthetic of 17th- and 18th-century Europe. Open Tu-Sa 9am-noon and 2-5pm, Su 9am-noon. 40AS, students and seniors 20AS, ages 6-14 free.

■ Music and Entertainment

Max Reinhardt, Richard Strauss, and Hugo von Hofmannsthal founded the renowned **Salzburger Festspiele** (Festivals) in 1920. Every year since, Salzburg has become a musical mecca from late July to the beginning of September. A few weeks before the festival, visitors strolling along Getreideg. often bump into world-class stars taking a break from rehearsal. On the eve of the festival's opening, over 100 dancers don regional costumes, accessorize with torches, and perform a *Fackeltanz* (torch-dance) on Residenzpl. During the festivities themselves, operas, plays, films, concerts, and tourists overrun every available public space. Information and tickets for Festspiele events are available through the **Festspiele Kartenbüro** (ticket office) and **Tageskasse** (daily box office) in Karajanpl., against the mountain and next to the tunnel. (Ticket office open M-F 9:30am-noon and 3-5pm. Box office open M-Sa 9:30am-5pm.) The festival prints a complete program of events that lists all crucial concert locations and dates one year in advance. The booklet is available at any tourist office (10AS). Music fans snap up the best seats months in advance. To order tickets, contact **Kartenbüro der Salzburger Festspiele,** Postfach 140, A-5010 Salzburg (tel. 84 45 01; fax 804 57 60; email info@salzb-fest.co.at; http://www.salzb-fest.co.at/salzb-fest), no later than the beginning of January. After the early January deadline, the office publishes a list of remaining seats, which generally include some cheap tickets to the operas (around 300AS), concerts (around 100AS), and plays (around 100AS), as well as some standing room places (50-100AS). These tickets, however, are often gobbled up quickly by subscribers or student groups, leaving very expensive tickets (upwards of 1000AS) and seats at avant-garde modern-music concerts (often as little as 200AS). Middle-man ticket distributors sell marked-up cheap tickets, a legal form of scalping—try American Express or Panorama Tours. Those 26 or younger can try for cheap subscription tickets (2-4 tickets for 200-300AS each) by writing about eight months in advance to Direktion der Salzburger Festspiele, attn: Carl-Philip von Maldeghem, Hofstallg. 1, A-5020 Salzburg.

The powers that be have discontinued hawking last-minute tickets for dress rehearsals to the general public—nowadays, you've got to know somebody to get your hands on one of these tickets ("Oh, sure, Placido and I go *way* back!"). Those without the foresight to be hit by an international opera star while walking across the street should take advantage of the **Fest zur Eröffungsfest** (Opening Day Festival), when concerts, shows, and films are either very cheap or free. Folksingers perform in the evenings, and dancers perform the traditional *Fackeltanz* around the horse fountain, literally kicking off the festivities. Tickets for all these events are available on a first-come, first-served basis during the festival's opening week at the box office in the Großes Festspielhaus on Hofstallg. The only other event visitors can always attend without advance tickets is **Jedermann.** The city stages Hugo von Hofmannsthal's modern morality play every year on a stage in front of the cathedral. At the end, people placed in strategic locations throughout the city cry out the eerie word "Jedermann," which then echoes all over town. Shouting contests determine which locals win the opportunity to be one of the ghostly criers. Standing-room places for shows are available at the Festspielhaus or a ticketing agency (60AS).

Even when the *Festspiele* are not in full force, many other concerts and events glimmer around the city. The popular **Mozarteum** (Music School) performs a number of concerts on a rotating schedule, available at the tourist office. The school often dedicates one cycle of concerts to students and reduces the ticket price to 80AS. For tickets to any of the Mozarteum concerts, contact Kartenbüro Mozarteum, Postfach 156, Theaterg. 2, A-5024 Salzburg (tel. 87 31 54; fax 87 29 96). (Open M-Th 9am-2pm, F 9am-4pm). For a bit more money but a lot more kitsch, check out the evening **Mozart Serenaden** (Mozart's Serenades) in the Gothic Hall on Getreideg. (daily 8:30pm in summer, otherwise 7:30pm. 380AS.) Musicians in traditional garb (knickers, powdered hair, etc.) perform Mozart favorites; an intermission buffet is included. For information and tickets, contact Konzertdirektion Nerat, A-5020 Salzburg, Lieferinger Hauptstr. 136 (tel. 43 68 70; fax 43 69 70).

For a particularly enchanting (and expensive) evening, attend a **Festungskonzert** (Fortress Concert) in the fortress's ornate *Fürstenzimmer* (Prince's chamber) and *Goldener Saal* (Golden Hall). Concerts occur year-round and include dinner at the fortress restaurant. Tickets are 590AS. For more information, contact Festungskonzerte, Anton-Adlgasserweg 22, A-5020 Salzburg (tel. 82 58 58; fax 82 58 59. http://alpin.or.at/festungskonzerte). (Open daily 9am-9pm.) A less tourist-oriented concert activity is the year-round **Salzburger Schloßkonzerte** in Schloß Mirabell or the Residenz. Mozart is still the most-performed composer, but he doesn't hold a monopoly. Tickets for the matinees are 300AS, students 150AS. In July and August, **outdoor opera** occasionally rings out from the historical hedge-theater of Mirabellgarten (330AS, students 190AS). Tickets for both series are available from the box office in Schloß Mirabell (tel. 84 85 86; fax 84 47 47). (Open M-F 9am-5:30pm.)

The **Dom** also has a large concert program. The church's organ has four separate pipe sections, creating a dramatic "surround sound" effect during its Thursday and Friday concerts at 11:15am. Tickets are available at the door (100AS, students 70AS, children free). The church has periodic evening concerts. Check the door for upcoming programs (280AS, students 180AS, standing room 100AS, children free). Other churches throughout Salzburg perform wonderful music during services and post information on other concerts, particularly near Easter and Christmas.

From May through August **outdoor performances,** including concerts, folk-singing, and dancing, dot the Mirabellgarten. The tourist office has a few leaflets on scheduled events, but an evening stroll through the park might prove just as enlightening. Listen to the word on the street. Mozartpl. and Kapitelpl. are also popular stops for talented street musicians and touring school bands, and the well-postered Aicher Passage next to Mirabellpl. is a great source of information for other upcoming musical events.

At the **Salzburger Marionettentheater** (tel. 87 24 06; fax 88 21 41), handmade marionettes perform to recorded *Festspiele* opera. The theater is small in order to accommodate the diminutive size of the actors. For more information, contact Marionettentheater, Schwarzstr. 24, A-5020 Salzburg. (Box office open on performance days M-Sa 9am-1pm and 2hr. before curtain. 250-400AS, students 200AS. AmEx, MC, Visa.) Track down English-language **movies** with the film program in the **Das Kino** newspaper. Cinemas rotate a few films each month and often offer films in English with German subtitles.

Win enough money to pay off your concert ticket loans at **Casino Salzburg** (tel. 85 46 20), located in Klessheim Palace. Slot machines, blackjack tables, and much more await you. Ask at the tourist office about the free shuttle service from the city center. Open from 3pm onwards.

■ Near Salzburg: Lustschloß Hellbrunn and Untersberg

Just south of Salzburg lies the unforgettable **Lustschloß Hellbrunn** (tel. 820 00 30; fax 82 03 72 31), a one-time pleasure dome for Wolf Dietrich's nephew, the Archbishop Markus Sittikus. The sprawling estate includes fish ponds, trimmed hedge gardens, the "I Am Sixteen, Going On Seventeen" gazebo, and tree-lined footpaths through open grassy fields. The neighboring **Wasserspiele** (water fountains) are perennial favorites—Archbishop Markus amused himself with elaborate water-powered figurines and a booby-trapped table that could spout water on his drunken guests. Prepare yourself for an afternoon of wet surprises. (Open July-Aug. 9am-10pm; May-June and Sept. 9am-5:30pm; Apr. and Oct. 9am-4:30pm. Obligatory castle tour 30AS, students 20AS. Obligatory Wasserspiele tour 70AS, 35AS. Tours of both 90AS, 45AS.) The **Steintheater** on the palace grounds is the oldest natural theater north of the Alps. On the hill above the manicured grounds sits the tiny hunting lodge **Monatsschlößchen** (Little Month-Castle), so named because someone bet the archbishop that he couldn't build a castle in a month. As one of the archbishop's many weaknesses was gambling, he accepted the challenge and began spending the church's money on architects, engineers, and laborers who toiled around the clock. He won. The castle now houses the **Folklore and Local History Museum** (tel. 82 03 72 21), with three floors of surprising exhibits, including animals made out of bread, a papier-mâché-and-glitter diorama of St. George slaying the dragon, and several *Salzburger Schönperchten*—bizarre 2m hats worn in a traditional Austrian ceremony intended to scare away the demons of winter. Open mid-Apr. to mid-Oct. 9am-5pm. 20AS, students 10AS. Near the castle lies the very large **Hellbrunn Zoo** (tel. 82 01 76; fax 820 17 66). The zoo is full of exotic animals and home to a gross-out masterpiece—the *Hansratte*—a domestic kitchen scene infested with slithery rats. Open 8:30am-4pm; extended summer hours. 80AS, students 60AS. To reach Hellbrun, take bus #55 (dir: Anif): "Hellbrunn" from the train station, Mirabellpl., or Mozartsteg., or bike 40 minutes down beautiful, tree-lined Hellbrunner Allee.

Bus #55: "Untersberg" runs south to the luscious **Untersberg peak,** where Charlemagne supposedly rests deep beneath the ground and prepares to return and reign over Europe once again. There are dozens of splendiferous hikes through Alpine meadows soaked with color, blue mountains in the distance. The Eishöhle (ice caves, despite what you might be thinking) are only a 90-minute climb away from the peak. A **cable car** (tel. (06246) 87 12 17 or 724 77) glides over Salzburg to the summit. (July-Sept. Su-Tu and Th-Sa 8:30am-5:30pm, W 8:30am-8pm; Mar.-June and Oct. 9am-5pm; Dec.-Feb. 10am-4pm. Ascent 130AS, descent 110AS, round-trip 215AS; children 75AS, 55AS, 105AS.)

THE SALZKAMMERGUT

During early summer, tourists in the know, bands of Austrian school children, and passels of the elderly move east from Salzburg up into the smooth lakes and wrinkled mountains of the Salzkammergut. They stop at the Alpine resort towns that speckle the countryside, taking in the almost-too-perfect views of rolling hills and dark, furry evergreens. Like everything else in the area, the region takes its name from the salt mines that, in their glory days, underwrote Salzburg's architectural treasures. Salzkammergut translates literally as "Salt Treasure Land," a reference to the times when salt was commonly considered white gold. The region is remarkably accessible, with 2000km of footpaths, 12 cable cars and chairlifts, and dozens of hostels. Winter brings mounds of feathered snow to the valleys and downhill skiers to the slopes.

Within the region, there is a dense network of **buses.** Most routes run four to 12 times per day, and since the mountainous area is barren of rail tracks, buses are the most efficient and reliable method of travel into and through the lake region. Dial 167 from Salzburg for complete schedule information.

Hitchers from Salzburg allegedly take bus #29 to Gnigl and come into the Salzkammergut at Bad Ischl. The lake district is one of the rare, refreshing Austrian regions in which hitchhikers can make good time. Two-wheeled transport is much more entertaining, but only with a good **bike**—some mountain passes top 1000m. Pedaling the narrow, winding roads on the lake banks is far less strenuous and equally scenic. Reasonably priced **ferries** serve each of the larger lakes, with railpass discounts on the **Wolfgangsee** line and the private **Attersee** and **Traunsee** lines.

Hostels abound, but you can often find far superior rooms in private homes and *Pensionen* at just-above-hostel prices. *"Zimmer Frei"* signs peek out from virtually every house. **Campgrounds** dot the region, but many are trailer-oriented. Away from large towns, many travelers camp discreetly almost anywhere, generally without hitting trouble. Hikers can capitalize on dozens of **cable cars** in the area to gain altitude before setting out on their own, and almost every community has a local trail map available. At higher elevations there are **Alpine huts**—check carefully at the tourist office for their opening hours. These huts are on trails for experienced hikers and are difficult to reach. Contact the **Österreichischer Alpenverein** (Austrian Alpine Club; tel. 512 594 47), for info and rental. Their central office is in Innsbruck, but locally experienced volunteers staff regional branches.

Every February brings **Carnival,** called *Fasnacht* in Western Austria and *Fasching* everywhere else. Carnival commences with the January ball season. In the countrified areas, traditional processions of masked figures are the season headliners, featuring *Schiache* (ugly evil masks). All this celebration requires months of preparation, with only men allowed. At the **Ausseer Fasching,** the carnival at Bad Aussee, *Trommelweiber* (men impersonating women in white nighties and night-caps while beating drums) march through town. The Carnival near Ebensee culminates in the **Fetzenfasching** (carnival of rags): the people sing in falsetto, imitate spooky voices, and wave old umbrellas.

On January 5, the **running of the figures with special caps** *(Glöcklerlaufen)* takes place after dark in the Salzkammergut. These *Glöckler* derive their name from the custom of knocking at the door (*glocken* means "to knock") and not from the bells attached to their belts (*Glocke* means "bell"). These caps, reminiscent of stained-glass windows, have an electric light inside; several are on display at the **Monats-Schlößchen** at Hallbrunn (just South of Salzburg). In return for their Happy New Year wish, runners are rewarded with a special doughnut, the *Glöcklerkrapfen.* Although the satisfaction of legions of stained-glass-hat fetishists seems enough, the masked figures also get money and refreshments from the citizenry, which indicates a little about their origin—a long, long time ago, seasonal workers needed such handouts to survive.

On the Sunday after November 25, about 30 bird-catcher clubs in the Salzkammergut region organize a **bird exhibition.** The birds squawk away the winter in people's living rooms and are then released. A **Christmas passion play** is performed every fourth year (next in 2002) at Bad Ischl.

Visitors to the region can purchase a **Salzkammergut Card** from any local tourist office. Introduced last year to replace the town specific guest cards, the Salzkammergut Card, (65AS) gives 25% discounts on 82 local sites and attractions.

▓ Bad Ischl

For centuries, Bad Ischl (population 15,000) was a salt-mining town, until a certain Dr. Franz Wirer arrived in 1821 to study the curative properties of the heated brine baths. Pleased with his findings, he began to prescribe brine bath vacations in Bad Ischl for his patients as early as 1822. Real fame descended on the resort only when the brine's healing powers kept the Habsburgs from sputtering into extinction. Archduke Francis Charles and Archduchess Sophia journeyed to Bad Ischl seeking a cure for their state of childlessness. The magical, mystical, almost fairy-tale results were three sons, the so-called **Salt Princes.** When the first Salt Prince, Franz Joseph I, ascended the throne in 1848, he proceeded to make Bad Ischl his annual summer residence, vacationing here for 40 years. Bad Ischl quickly became an imperial city, attracting noblemen, rich merchants, and well-known composers like Brahms, Bruckner, and Lehár. It's one of the few towns in the region not on a lake, but it attracts a geriatric brigade of brine-loving pilgrims alongside a spate of younger tourists. In June of 1998, even the Dalai Lama visited town.

ORIENTATION AND PRACTICAL INFORMATION Bad Ischl lies at the junction of the **Traun** and **Ischl** rivers, which form a horseshoe around the city. The Ischl runs from the Wolfgangsee to the Traun on the way to the Danube. Bad Ischl is within splashing distance of eight Salzkammergut oases: the Hallstättersee, Gosausee, Wolfgangsee, Mondsee, Attersee, Traunsee, Grundlsee, and the Altausee.

By car, Bad Ischl lies on Rte. 158 and 145. From **Vienna,** take the A-1 West to Rte. 145 at the town of Regau. From **Innsbruck** or **Munich,** take the A-1 East past Salzburg and exit onto Rte. 158 near Thalgau. From **Salzburg** proper, the best way is to take Rte. 158 straight through the beautiful towns of St. Gilgen and Fuschl. One **train** comes through the station, running from **Attnang-Puchheim** in the north (84AS) through **Hallstatt** (36AS) and **Bad Aussee** (66AS). Indirect trains go to **Vienna** (390AS), **Linz** (301AS), and **Zell am See** (147AS). **Buses** leave from Salzburg to Bad Ischl every hour or so (1½ hr., 6:40am-7:15pm, 100AS), making stops in Fuschl and St. Gilgen.

The **train station** (tel. 244 070) has **bike rental** (summer only; mountain bikes 160AS per day, 920 AS per week; discount with train ticket) at the **luggage storage** window (open daily 8am-6pm; 30AS per piece per day; ring for service). Smaller **lockers** (20AS) are around the corner. Bad Ischl's **bus station** (tel. 231 13) is right next to the train station. The **tourist office** (tel. 27 75 70 or 23 52 00; fax 277 57 77) is straight out of the train station and two minutes down the road, across from the large, pillared **Kaiser Therme** building at Bahnhofstr. 1. The office has extensive lists of *Pensionen* and *Privatzimmer,* and will gladly help find a room. A free basic English brochure is available. (Open June-Sept. M-F 8am-6pm, Sa 9am-4pm, Su 9-11:30am; Oct.-May M-F 8am-6pm, Sa 9am-4pm, Su 9-11:30am.) The mustard-colored **post office** is two minutes farther down Bahnhofstr., on the corner of Auböckpl. (Open June-Sept. M-F 8am-8pm, Sa 9am-noon; Oct.-May M-F 8am-7pm, Sa 9-11am; phone, fax, and **currency exchange** available.) The **postal code** is A-4820. The **telephone code** is 06132.

ACCOMMODATIONS AND FOOD Every guest who stays the night must register with his or her individual hotel or pension and pay a *Kurtax,* a tax levied by the local government. (June to mid-Sept. 15-20AS per person per night depending on proximity to the city center; Oct.-May 12-13AS.) In return, the local **guest card** gives moderate discounts on museums, mountain cable cars, and other treats. Bad Ischl's **Jugendgästehaus (HI),** Am Rechenstag 5 (tel. 265 77; fax 265 77 75), is minutes from the *Kaiser's* summer residence. From the tourist office, walk left on Bahnhofstr., turn right on Kaiser-Franz-Josef-Str., keep going until you see the *Jugendgästehaus* sign to the left across from the gas station. The hostel offers many clean but non-descript one- to five-bed rooms off long corridors. Since it often fills with school groups, call in advance. (Dorms 155AS plus *Kurtax.* Sheets, showers, and breakfast included. Reception 8-9am and 5-7pm. Quiet hour 10pm; keys available.) If the hostel is full, try **Haus Stadt Prag,** Eglmoosg. 9 (tel. 236 16), where the rooms are beautiful and spacious with gorgeous balconies. From the train station, walk left on Bahnhofstr., turn right on Kaiser-Franz-Josef-Str., and left on Kreuzpl. Follow until it becomes Salzburgerstr., and bear left again on Stiegeng. at the *Goldschmied* sign. Continue along Stiegeng. and go up the steps—Haus Stadt Prag is the pink building on your right. (Singles 250AS, with bath 320AS; doubles 500AS, 600AS; 20AS extra for room with charming balcony. Breakfast included.)

Restaurants are tucked into every possible niche along Schulg. and the other streets of the pedestrian zone. When Bad Ischlers make a run for the border, they head to the very American-friendly **Amigos Tex-Mex Restaurant,** Auböckpl. 9 (tel.

213 17), across from the Konsum market. This restaurant's slogan (in English), "Warm beer, lousy food, shitty service," doesn't deter a thick crowd of tourists who tumble in for the *quesadillas* (60-82AS). Burgers run 68AS, salads 45-95AS. Nearly all entrees are under 100AS. (Open M and W-F 11:30am-2pm and 5:30-11:30pm, Sa-Su 5-10:30pm; take-out available.) Almost as famous as the *Kaiser* himself is the **Konditorei Zauner,** Pfarrg. 7 (tel. 235 22). Established in 1832, this crowded eatery has an international reputation among old money for heavenly sweets and *tortes.* Franz Josef was a fan. Zauner also operates a riverside restaurant-café on the **Esplanade.** Seat yourself and nosh on extravagant desserts (up to 90AS) or gourmet sandwiches (26-42AS). The **Konsum grocery store** is conveniently located at Auböckpl. 12. (Open M-Th 8am-6pm, F 8am-6:30pm, Sa 8am-12:30pm.) There is an **open air market** all day every Friday in Salinenpl.

SIGHTS Other than the baths, Bad Ischl's main attraction is what the Habsburgs left behind. Walking tours leave **Trinhalle** at 10am on Sunday mornings and Thursdays at 4pm in summer (free with guest card). In 1854, Austria's last emperor, Franz Josef, received the **Kaiservilla** (tel. 232 41) as a wedding present. *(Open May to mid-Oct. 9-11:45am and 1-4:45pm. 95AS, 90AS with guest card, students 50AS.)* The emperor made it his summer getaway palace and crammed it with expensive hunter kitsch. Inside, a vast collection of mounted chamois horns looks like the world's most decadent collection of coathooks. Amidst the dazzling animal remains are many interesting relics of Franz Josef's reign, including the desk where in 1914 he signed the declaration of war against Serbia that led to WWI. Entrance is available only through a guided tour in German, with English text available. Buy tickets for the tour when you enter the **Kaiserpark** (off of Franz-Josef-Str.; parking 30AS, students 20AS). Also located in the lush Kaiserpark is the attractive, ivy-covered **Marmorschlößl** (tel. 244 22) and the **Photo Museum** inside. *(Open Apr.-Oct. 9:30am-5pm. 15AS, 12AS with guest card, students 10AS.)* Entrance to the Photo Museum requires a pair of fluffy slippers (provided at the front desk) to protect the exquisite wood floors. A collection of Habsburg family photos complements temporary exhibitions.

In the center of town, the **Stadtpfarrkirche** (city parish church) houses the magnificent **Kaiserjubiläumsorgel** (Emperor's Jubilee Organ). Played by the likes of organ virtuoso and composer Anton Bruckner, the organ is one of the best in the world. Compact discs of performances are available for 230AS.

A tour through Bad Ischl's **Salzbergwerke** salt mines (tel. 239 48 31) lets you see salt mining from the inside, as in from the inside. *(Open July-Aug. 10am-4:45pm, May 1-June and Sept. 1-20 9am-3:45pm. 135AS, with guest card 120AS, children 65AS.)* The mines are outside the city in Perneck and are best reached by car via Grazerstr. to Pernechstr. City bus #8096 also travels to Perneck and leaves from the *Bahnhof* two to five times daily (16AS, day pass 25AS). The last bus from Perneck is at 4:15pm.

ENTERTAINMENT Whether or not the **salt baths** really contain curative powers, something must be said for the town's relaxed atmosphere. The bath facilities are mostly in the **Kaiser Therme,** a resort across from the tourist office on Bahnhofstr. 1 (tel. 233 24; fax 233 24 44; email Verwaltung@Kaisertherme.com; http://www.salz-kammergut.at/badischl/Kaisertherme). Splash around in the heated salt baths with whirlpool (open M-Sa 9am-9pm, Su 1:30-9pm, last entrance 8pm. 3hr. for 105AS, students 108AS, children 56AS). Or, consider relaxing in the spacious **sauna** (open Tu-Su 1:30-9pm, Th women only, Tu men only. 3hr. including pool entrance 145 AS, children 77AS). Confront your inner effete with a **full-body massage** (274AS for 25min.). Mud baths, acupuncture, and other more exotic experiences generally require a doctor's prescription (see your doctor).

For the low-down around town, pick up the brochure *Bad Ischl Events* from the tourist office. A free outdoor **Kurkonzert** takes place every day except Tuesday at the Kurpark along Wienerstr. (Summer only, 10am and 4pm). The exact program of pieces performed by the 20-piece *Kurorchestra* is posted weekly on kiosks, in the hotels, and at the *Kurhaus* itself. It also makes appearances as the word on the street.

Every year in mid-August, the **Bad Ischler Stadtfest** brings a weekend of music—classical, pop, jazz, boogie-woogie, oom-pah-pah, usw. Just before the Stadtfest on August 15th, the Bad Ischlers celebrate Franz Josef's birthday with live music on the Esplanade. From July 5th until August 29th, the **Bad Ischl Operetten Festspiele** celebrates the musical talent of operetta composer **Franz Lehár,** who lived in Bad Ischl for 30 years and created *The Merry Widow, Gypsy Love,* and *The Land of Smiles.* Tickets are available from Büro der Operettengemeinde Bad Ischl, Wiesengerstr. 7, A-4820 Bad Ischl (tel. 238 39; fax 238 39 39; open M-Sa 9am-noon and 2-5pm; 200-500AS). After June 30, purchase tickets from the Bad Ischl Kurhaus (tel. 237 66; fax 233 84; open M-F 9am-noon and 3-6pm). The **Lehár Villa,** Franz's house, is a place to visit. (Open May-Sept. daily 9am-noon and 2-5pm. Obligatory tour 55AS, with guest card 45AS; students and children 25AS.) From April to October, a **flea market** comes to the Esplanade on the first Saturday of the month. Fun.

Hiking paths around the town are shown on a 66AS map available at the tourist office. A good place for hiking is around the summit of nearby Mt. Katrin (1544m). Get to the **Katrinseilbahn** (cable car; 100AS) by taking a city bus from the train station (last bus 5pm) or by walking for 15 minutes. **Bikers** can get a small 35AS trail map as well as a 98AS trail map which details the entire region. In winter, there's skiing. Besides an excellent network of **cross-country skiing** trails (free maps at the tourist office), Bad Ischl offers all sorts of Yuletide festivities, including a **Christkindlmarkt** (Christmas market), Advent caroling in the *Kurhaus,* tours of elaborate **Weihnachtskrippen** (nativity scenes) in the area, and horse-drawn sleigh rides *(Pferdeschliffen)* through the snow.

■ Mondsee

The Salzkammergut's warmest lake, the **Mondsee** (Moon Lake), gets its romantic name from its crescent shape. Misty mountains lend the lake breath-taking views, and even the air tastes exhilarating. All forms of water activity are raised to a higher level in this stunning locale, taking on almost spiritual connotations. The town of Mondsee (pop. 2000) lies at the Northern tip of the crescent lake, adding some of its own small charm to the scene.

ORIENTATION AND PRACTICAL INFORMATION The town has no train station but is accessible by **bus** from Salzburg. (50min., 1 per hr., 6:40am-7:20pm, 60AS.) Buses also run three times a day from Mondsee to **St. Gilgen** on the Wolfgangsee (20min., 29AS). To get to the town of Mondsee by car, take Autobahn A-1, or, for a more scenic drive, take Rte. 158 from Salzburg to St. Gilgen and then Rte. 154 along the edges of the lake to downtown Mondsee.

The **tourist office** *(Tourismusverband),* Dr.-Franz-Müllerstr. 3 (tel. 22 70; fax 44 70; email robert.hanh@ris.telecom.at), is a five-minute walk from the bus station, half-way between the church and the lake. From the bus stop, head up the road past the post office, turn right on Rainerstr., and continue to the end. Turn right again, and the office is on the left. The English-speaking staff gladly gives out every brochure they have and finds accommodations. The free sightseeing pamphlet suggests three solid tours: the shortest (1-2hr.) covers just the town highlights; the longest (6-7hr.) requires a car. (Open mid-June to Aug. M-F 8am-6pm, Sa-Su 9-11am; Sept.-June M-F 8am-noon and 1-5pm.) The **post office,** on Franz-Kreuzbergerstr. to the left and across the street from the bus station, is the most convenient place for **currency exchange.** (Open M-F 8am-noon and 2-6pm, in summer also open Sa 8-10am. Exchange closes at 5pm.) There are **ATMs** at the Volksbank by the tourist office and at the Raffeisenbank on Rainerstr. **Public restrooms** are under the *Rathaus* in Mark-tpl. The **postal code** is A-5310. The **telephone code** is 06232.

ACCOMMODATIONS AND FOOD Mondsee is brimming with *Pensionen, Privatzimmer,* and hotels. The **Jugendgästehaus (HI),** Krankenhausstr. 9 (tel. 24 18; fax 24 18 75), offers doubles and quads with private showers, as well as one 10-bed dorm.

From the bus station, walk up Kreuzbergerstr. toward the post office, turn right on Rainerstr., walk uphill, then go left on Steinbachstr. At the first intersection, go left 10 meters and then right up narrow little Krankenhausstr. Follow the signs to the hostel; it's hidden off a driveway to the left and uphill. The main entrance is below the brown balcony. The color scheme is straight out of the 70s, and the bunk beds tucked into every nook make for a cozy stay. But it's clean. It's normally filled with groups; call ahead. (Dorms 140AS; doubles 340-440AS; quads 560-680AS. Breakfast included; lunch and dinner available in the restaurant below. Non-members pay extra. Reception 8am-1pm and 5-10pm. Curfew 10pm; key available.)

Pizzeria Nudelini, Marktpl. 5 (tel. 41 93), upstairs in the blue building just down from the church, spins inexpensive but delicious Italian-style pizza (68AS for a large cheese) and provides a terrific salad bar (small 34AS, large 54AS). (Open Su-W noon-2pm and 5:30-11pm, F-Sa 5:30-11pm.) For delicious coffee and cake (and at better prices than the glowing cafés in front of the church), head to **Café Übleis,** Badg. 6 (tel. 24 33), right by the tourist office. They specialize in homemade *Mozartkugeln* and yummy ice cream. (Open July-Aug. 9am-11pm; Sept.-June 9am-9pm.) **China Restaurant,** Rainerstr. 13 (tel. 44 68), has a great lunch deal that includes soup and an entree for 62 to 69AS. (Open daily 11:30am-2:30pm and 6-11pm. MC, Visa.) **SPAR Markt** is on Steinbachstr. just past the main square on the way up to the hostel. (Open M-F 7:30am-6:30pm, Sa 7:30am-1pm.) A **farmer's market** comes to town during the summer in Karlsgarten, nearby to the church. (Open Sa 8-11:30am).

SIGHTS AND ENTERTAINMENT

Mondsee is the closest lake resort to Salzburg and one of the least touristed, despite occasional air-conditioned tour buses which rumble in and out the town to see the local **Pfarrkirche,** site of the wedding scene in *The Sound of Music*. The church connects to the authentic remains of a Benedictine monastery dating from 748 that now peek out of plaster reconstruction in the **Museum Mondsee.** *(Open May-Sept. Tu-Su 9am-6pm; first 2 weeks of Oct. Tu-Su 9am-5pm, last 2 weeks Sa-Su 9am-5pm. 30AS, seniors 25AS, students 15AS.)* The museum holds an assortment of churchy odds and ends, of interest mainly for dedicated historians of Mondsee. The open-air **Freilichtmuseum,** on Hilfbergstr. (behind the church and uphill to the right), features a giant, 500-year-old smokehouse, dairy, and farmhouse all in one. *(Open May-Sept. Tu-Su 9am-6pm; Oct.1-14 Tu-Su 9am-5pm; Apr. and Oct. 15-31 Sa-Su and holidays 9am-6pm. Same prices as Museum Mondsee.)* A ticket gives free rein to wander all around playing with myriad antique farm tools and utensils.

Time in Mondsee means time at the **lake.** In summer, the waters buzz with activity; in winter, the lake cold and frozen, everyone seems to hibernate. **Alpenseebad,** the public beach (tel. 22 91), is fine for swimming, but jumping in at undesignated areas along the shore is forbidden by the lake's wildlife conservation laws. *(Open in fair weather May-Sept. daily 8:30am-7pm. 30AS, children 12AS; after 1:30pm 18AS, 6AS.)* To go out a a little farther, rent a **boat** from **Peter Hemetsberger** (tel. 24 60) on the shore by the playground, down the street from the tourist office. *(Rowboats 75-90AS per hr., paddleboats 100AS, electric boats 130-150AS.)* Hemetsberger also offers *Seerundfahrten,* boat rides around the lake. *(40min. ride 63AS, 60min. 90AS, 90min. 120AS; children half-price.)* Water skiing, with **Wasserschizentrum** (tel. (06 64) 43 23 103), costs 110AS per circuit, and 2-person rafting costs 120AS per circuit. The Wasserskiclub puts on a **Wasserschischau** (read: clowns on skis) at Mondsee-Kaipromenade. *(June and Sept. Sa 7pm; July-Aug. Tu 7pm and F 9pm. 25AS.)*

Mondsee holds the **Musiktage,** an annual classical music festival in early September. Contact the tourist office well in advance for more information. Every year **Hugo von Hofmannsthal's** 1922 morality play, **Jedermann,** is performed (in German) at the open-air **Freilichtbühne** theater every Saturday from mid-July to August. *(Tickets 120-160AS. Advance tickets are available at the Salzburger Sparkasse in Marktpl. and at the tourist office but aren't required.)*

SALZBURGER LAND

■ St. Wolfgang

In 976, Wolfgang of Regensburg hurled his axe into the valley of the Abersee. He established a new church where the axe landed, a church that lasted until 1429. To protect his church, Wolfgang invoked a spring from the earth and battled the devil on a rocky outcropping. The remains of their struggle are still visible just North of town. Once its founder had been canonized for his miraculous feats, the church on the Abersee (now the Wolfgangsee) became the object of mass pilgrimage. St. Wolfgang still draws thousands of devotees on foot and many more tourists by car and bus. The **Pilgrimage Church** boasts a gorgeous view of the Wolfgangsee as well as the famous Michael Pacher altar. The nearby **Schafberg** provides hiking and skiing to complement the resort activity on the lake.

ORIENTATION AND PRACTICAL INFORMATION St. Wolfgang rests lazily on the shore of the Wolfgangsee, across the water from St. Gilgen. St. Wolfgang has no train station, but **buses** run every hour to **Bad Ischl** (35min., 5:17am-8:10pm, 45AS) and **Salzburg** (1½ hr., last bus 8:10pm mid-July to mid-Sept., 6:20pm otherwise, 90AS; change at Strobl). A breezy option is the Wolfgangsee **ferry** (tel. 223 20), which runs to nearby **St. Gilgen** (40min., 52AS) and **Strobe** (20min., 38AS) and between St. Wolfgang's two ferry landings at St. Wolfgang Markt and the Schafbergbahnhof. (Runs May-Oct. 8:15am-6:15pm. Day and week passes also available. Children half-price. Eurailpasses valid.) To get to St. Wolfgang from **Vienna** by **car**, take A1 West to Mondsee and then head south through St. Lorenz and Scharfling and on to St. Wolfgang. From **Salzburg,** take Rte. 158 east through Hof, Fuschl, and St. Gilgen.

St. Wolfgang is itself a minor miracle of civic planning, existing almost entirely without street names. A tunnel cuts around the downtown area, with the **bus stop** just outside its Western entrance. The **tourist office,** Pilgerstr. 28 (tel. 22 39; fax 22 39 81; email info@stwolfgang.gu.at; http://www.salzkammergut.at/wolfgangsee), is a block or so away from the bus stop. (Open summer 8am-noon and 1-6pm; winter 8am-noon and 2-5pm.) Look for a pea-green building on the left, labeled *Marktgemeindeamt*. The **Wolfgangsee Info** pamphlet has addresses and prices for a vast selection of summer and winter activities. An **information kiosk** is farther down the main stretch, by Hotel Peter. **ATMs** are adjacent to the tourist office and in the wall of the **Sparkasse** in Marktpl. **Public bathrooms** are located at the bus stop and behind the tourist office. Reliable **currency exchange** rates are available at the **post office** (tel. 22 01), around the corner and down the block from the bus stop. (Open M-F 8am-noon and 2-6pm, Sa 8-11am. Exchange open M-F 8am-5pm.) The **postal code** is A-5360. The **telephone code** is 06138.

ACCOMMODATIONS AND FOOD Almost 2000 tourists troop through St. Wolfgang every sunny summer day. The tourist office's brochure features a cannonical list of hotels, *Pensionen,* and private rooms. St. Wolfgang has no youth hostel, but **Haus am See,** Michael-Pacher-Str. 98 (tel. 22 24), offers 50 beds in a rambling old house right on the lake at hostel prices. From the tourist office, simply continue down the main road away from the post office (7min.) until you reach the east entrance of the tunnel. The happy Herr Brosch's *Haus* is just beyond, on the right. Look for a *Zimmer frei* banner. The bathrooms are not as gorgeous as the view, but the swimmable-shore access more than compensates. Herr Brosch will even let guests borrow his paddleboat and rowboat. (Singles 150-280AS; doubles 360-550AS; 2-room quads 800-1000AS. Prices depend on balcony and view. Hall showers. Breakfast included. Parking available. Open May-Oct.) The best deal might be Haus Am See's renovated **boathouse,** with 10 beds in singles and doubles starting at 150AS. The rooms are primitive, but the balcony is literally over the lake and the boathouse has a large, well-kept grass area for sunning and picnicking. Also check out **Gästehaus Raudaschl,** Deschbühel 41 (tel. 25 61), on the way to the major hiking paths. From the tourist office, continue down the main road, and turn left at Hotel Peter. Climb up the small hill, and it's on the left (5min.). This smaller *Pension* offers a private balcony in each of seven well-furnished rooms. Antlers and country knick-knacks cover the walls and tables. (Singles 210AS, with shower 250AS; doubles 380-420AS. Breakfast included. Open May-Oct.) You can set up your tent at **Appesbach,** Au 99 (tel. 22 06). (Tents 120AS; one-time charge of 120AS; 75AS per night, children 45AS). **Camping Berau,** Schwarzenbach 16 (tel. 25 43) rents tents for 60AS (one-time charge of 128AS; 73AS per night, children 50AS).

Most of St. Wolfgang's restaurants and *Imbiße* price their wares very competitively. Try any of the snack shacks lining the main road, where almost nothing is above 45AS. *Konditoreien* also serve up a local specialty—*Schafbergkugeln* (about 23AS), named after the mountain. A variant of the *Mozartkugel*, the *Schafbergkugel* is a tennis-ball-sized hunk of milk chocolate filled with cream, spongecake, nuts, and marzipan. Pick one up at **Bäckerei Gandl,** Im Stöckl 84 (tel. 22 94; open daily 7am-7pm). **Cafe Dilara,** Markt 34 (tel. 31 57), up the street from the church, serves relatively inexpensive pizzas (from 71AS) and salads (45-85AS). **Hauer's Imbißstube** (tel. 25 74), a self-service restaurant, lies near the kiosk on the main road and serves up Austrian standards for under 90AS. (Open daily 9am-6pm.) Across from the tourist office, the **ADEG** market sells fruits of all kinds and standard groceries. (Open M-Tu and Th-F 7am-noon and 2-6pm, Sa 7am-1pm.)

SIGHTS AND ENTERTAINMENT For St. Wolfgang's top attraction, follow the throngs to the **Wallfahrtskirche** (Pilgrimage Church) in the center of town. **Michael Pacher's altarpiece** is the magnificent focal point of the church's interior. Completed by Pacher in 1480, the altarpiece has two pairs of altar wings—originally, the inner shrine was revealed only on Easter and Christmas. Fully closed, the altar displays scenes of a humble pilgrim's life. When the outer wings are opened, eight scenes in the life of Christ are revealed. The final pair of wings displays the Coronation of Mary, with Christ blessing his mother. The **Schwanthaler Altar,** in the middle of the church behind wrought-iron gates, is also somewhat interesting. Installed in 1676, the frenetic, high-Baroque altar was originally made to replace Pacher's "obsolete" one, but the sculptor Thomas Schwanthaler bravely persuaded the abbot to leave Pacher's masterpiece alone. Together the two altars almost overwhelm the church— try not to miss the smaller treasures, like Schwanthaler's **Rosenkranzaltar** (Rose Garland Altar) in the Maria Chapel.

St. Wolfgang's other big sight is the **Schafbergbahn** (tel. 22 320), a romantic steam engine that laboriously ascends to the 1732m summit of Schafberg. *(Train runs May-Oct., 1 per hr., 7:15am-6:40pm. Round-trip tickets discounted at 7:15 and 8:10am. Children half-price.)* The railway was built in 1892, and in 1964 Hollywood found it charming enough to deserve a cameo in *The Sound of Music*, with the children waving from the windows. From the top, dozens of trails wind down the mountain, leading the way to such nearby towns as St. Gilgen, Ried, and Falkenstein. Train tickets for the 40-minute ride run as steep as the mountain (ascent 140AS, half-way 110AS, round-trip 250AS; Eurailpasses valid). If you must pay full price, you might as well take advantage of the special deal offered by the **Berghotel Schafbergspitze** (tel. 22 32 18), a lovely mountain inn peeking over the Schafberg's steepest face. For 500AS per person, you get a round-trip ticket on the railway, a night's lodging, and breakfast. Reserve in advance.

Nature-lovers glow with big smiles around here—the **lake** provides plenty of water-sport activities. If you like swimming, you can go off the deep end at **Strand-bad Ried** (tel. 25 87; 40AS, children 20AS). Water skiing is available through **Stadler** (tel. (0663) 917 97 53; 120AS per round) on the Seepromenade. Daredevils can try the water-ski jump. Rent **boats** at the beach on Robert-Stolz-Str. across from the tennis courts or in town at the landing near Marktpl. *(Motor boats 30min. 90AS, 1hr. 150AS. Pedal boats 90AS. Row boats 55AS. Open in the summer daily 8am-7pm.)*

Hiking the mountains at the lake's edge is another possibility. All trails are marked clearly and described in detail in the English *Info* brochure, available free at the tourist office. The tourist office also sponsors guides. Hiking maps cost 10AS (small) and

65AS (big). More adventurous activities include **hot-air ballooning** (tel. 30 27; fax 302 74; 4000AS per half-day) and **paragliding** from Schafberg (tel. 22 32).

St. Wolfgang's 20th century claim to fame revolves around local composer Ralph Benatzky's romantic-comic-pastoral operetta "White Horse Inn" (a.k.a. *Am Weißen Rössl*), which became world famous in 1930. A production of the operetta is put on every Friday in May, June, and September at 7:30 pm. Purchase tickets (220-360AS) through the *Singspielbüro* (tel. 22 39).

■ Hallstatt

Teetering on the banks of the **Hallstätter See** in a valley surrounded on all sides by the sheer rocky cliffs of the Dachstein mountains, Hallstatt is easily the most beautiful lakeside village in the Salzkammergut. It was declared a UNESCO World Cultural Heritage site in 1997. Many travelers with limited time prefer Hallstatt to the staler charms of Salzburg. The tiny village of 1100 inhabitants seems to defy gravity, with medieval buildings clinging to the face of a stony slope. Over four millennia ago, a highly advanced Celtic culture thrived in Hallstatt, but they didn't come for the view—Hallstatt was a world-famous settlement back when Rome was still a village, thanks to its "white gold." The salt also helped to guarantee the preservation of Hallstatt's archaeological remains, so extensive that the pre-historical era in Celtic studies (800-400 BCE) is dubbed the "Hallstatt period." Rich in sites and isolated high in the mountains, Hallstatt merits more than a day-trip; stay the night in a room overlooking the shatteringly clear blue lake or stop over instead in nearby Obertrauen.

ORIENTATION AND PRACTICAL INFORMATION   Hallstatt is tucked away on the Hallstätter See, a pristine emerald oasis at the southern tip of the Salzkammergut. From Salzburg, the **bus** is the cheapest option at 130AS, but it requires layovers in both Bad Ischl and Gosaumühle. The **bus stop** is at the edge of downtown on Seestr, fielding frequent buses to nearby **Obertrauen** (10 min., 22AS). Hallstatt's **train station** lies on the opposite bank of the lake from downtown and has no staffed office. All trains come from Attnang-Puchheim in the north or Stanach-Irnding in the south. Trains run to **Attnang-Puchheim** (116AS), **Bad Ischl** (36AS), and **Salzburg** via Attnang-Puchheim (210 AS). After every train, there is a **ferry** across to town that waits for all train passengers (last ferry 6:45pm, 23AS). If you do happen to arrive later, stay on the train to the next stop (Obertraun) and take a taxi (170AS) or walk (5km) to downtown Hallstatt. After a brief, spectacular trip across the lake, the ferry terminates at Landungspl.; it leaves again half an hour before the train departs. If **driving** from Salzburg or the Salzkammergut towns, take Rte. 158 to Bad Ischl and then Rte. 145 toward Bad Aussee. After Bad Goisern, it's approximately 5km to the narrow road leading along the Hallstätter See into Hallstatt. Automobile access to Hallstatt is severely limited. Ample day **parking** lots are available by the tunnels leading into town (free for those staying in town).

The **tourist office** *(Tourismusbüro),* in the Kultur- und Kongresshaus at Seestr. 169 (tel. 82 08; fax 83 52), offers free maps and finds vacancies among the plentiful, cheap rooms for free. (Open July-Aug. M-F 8:30am-6pm, Sa 10am-6pm, Su 10am-2pm; Sept.-June M-F 9am-noon and 2-5pm.) There is an **ATM** next to the post office. **Public bathrooms** are adjacent to the Heimatmuseum. The **post office**, Seestr. 160, below the tourist office, offers the best **currency exchange** rates. (Open M-Tu and Th-F 8am-noon and 2-6pm, Sa 8-10am. Exchange open until 5pm.) The **telephone code** is 06134. The **telephone code** is 06134.

ACCOMMODATIONS AND FOOD   *Privatzimmer* at just-above-hostel prices speckle the town, and the tourist office will help you locate one for free. Wherever you end up laying your head for the night, don't forget to ask for Hallstatt's free **guest card,** which offers local discounts. **Gästehaus Zur Mühle,** Kirchenweg 36 (tel. 83 18), is a quasi-hostel close to the city center with pleasant three- to 18-bed dorm rooms and lots of English-speaking backpackers. From the tourist office, walk a few steps up the hill as if heading toward the Heimatmuseum, and swing right at the end of the *Platz*. The hostel is through the little tunnel on the left, by the cascading water-fall. (Dorms 110AS. Showers and lockers included with deposit of 200AS. Sheets 35AS. Breakfast 40AS. Lunch and dinner available at the restaurant downstairs. Recep-tion 8am-2pm and 4-10pm.) The largest youth hostel is **Landesjugendherbergswerk**, Salzbergstr. 50 (tel. 82 79; fax 87 63), just outside the center of town in a quiet valley area. (Open May-Sept. Dorms 100AS. Groups only July-Aug.) **Frühstückspension Sarstein**, Gosaumühlstr. 83 (tel. 82 17), offers the prettiest accommodations in town, luring visitors with homey rooms, painted cupboards, wonderful vistas of the lake and village, and a beachside lawn for sunning and swimming. Diving from your bal-cony, though tempting, is forbidden. We would never suggest such a thing. From the tourist office, head toward the ferry dock and continue along the road nearest the lake (7-8min.) past the Pfarrkircher steps. (Dorms 190-210AS, with bath 250-300AS. Hall showers 10AS for 10min. Breakfast included.) Frau Sarstein's sister **Franziska Zimmerman** (tel. 83 09) lives up the block toward town on the other side of the street at #69 and offers similar (but fewer) accommodations. (Dorms 190-200AS. Showers 10AS. Breakfast included. Call ahead.) **Frühstückspension Seethaler**, Dr.-F.-Mortonweg 22 (tel. 84 21), sits on the hill near the tourist office. Head uphill, bear left, and follow the signs. Many rooms have linoleum floors and balconies with lake views. The breakfast room is adorned with innumerable antlers and furs, many of them hunted down over the years by the friendly proprietor himself. (Dorms 195-215AS, with bath 280AS, with kitchen 380AS.) **Camping Klausner-Höll**, Lahnstr. 6 (tel. 83 22), is three blocks past the bus stop on Seestr., one street from the public beach. (45AS plus 10AS tax, children under 14 25AS plus 5AS; tents 40AS; cars 30AS. Breakfast 100AS. Showers included. Laundry 60AS. Open mid-Apr. to mid-Oct. Check-out noon; gate closed daily noon-2:30pm and 10pm-7am.)

Many of the guesthouses in Hallstatt have restaurants downstairs. **Gästehaus zum Weißen Lamm** (tel. 83 11), across from the Heimatmuseum, serves large portions of good food. (Open daily 10am-noon and 5-10pm.) Head downstairs for the "mountain man's cellar" with a vigorous mining motif. Here you'll find two daily *Menü*s (90 and 120AS) for lunch and dinner, each one including soup, entree, and dessert. **Gäste-haus zur Mühle**, below the hostel, offers pizza (68-94AS) and pasta (72-88AS) along with a wide range of salads (from 34AS). Three kinds of *canneloni* (one vegetarian) are 88AS each. (Open daily 10am-2pm and 4-10pm.) The recently opened **Amigos Tex-Mex Take-Away Restaurant**, Seestr. 156 (tel. 83 54), near the main bus stop at the edge of town, is a pit-stop for the guacamole-starved. Tuck away or take away tasty Tex-Mex treats like chicken *quesadillas* (70AS) and veggie cheeseburgers (42AS). Close your eyes, sip your margarita, and the Hallstättersee *may* start to resem-ble the Gulf of Mexico (if you have a *very* active imagination and *very* many margari-tas). It's also Hallstatt's only late-night scene for the under-25 crowd. (Open daily 10am-2am.) To spend less, try **Imbiß Karl Forstinger** (tel. 61 35 or 82 19) on Seestr. near the bus station. Hot dogs and bratwurst are greasily abundant for 35AS along with a number of cheap regional specialties. (Open daily May-Oct. 10am-6pm.) There's a **Konsum Market** right by the main bus stop at the edge of town. (Open M-F 7:30am-12:30pm and 3-6:30pm, Sa 7:30am-12:30pm and 2-5pm.)

SIGHTS AND ENTERTAINMENT Hallstatt packs some heavy punches for tourists, despite its lean frame. The tourist office sells a 30AS English cultural guide, but you don't really need it—exploring the narrow, crooked streets is entertainment in itself. St. Michael's Chapel at the **Pfarrkirche** offers a fascinating if macabre anthro-pological twist on the more famous prehistorical burial scene in Hallstatt. *(Open May-Sept. daily 10am-5pm. In winter, call the Catholic church (tel. 82 79) for an appointment. 10AS.)* Next to the chapel is the parish charnel house, filled with remains of villagers dating from the 16th-century onwards. Bones from the surrounding cemeteries are transferred here after 10 to 20 years because the graveyard is too small to accom-modate all those who wish to rest there. (They're buried vertically as it is.) Each neatly placed skull is decorated with a wreath of flowers (for females) or ivy (for males) and inscribed with the name of the deceased and the date of death. The skulls are then packed in pyramids resting on a shelf which is supported by their neatly stacked femurs, tibiae, and fibulae.

In the mid-19th century, Hallstatt was the site of an immense, incredibly well-preserved Iron Age archaeological find: a plethora of artifacts, a pauper's grave, and the well-maintained crypts of the ruling class—all circa 1000-500 BCE. The **Prähistorisches Museum** (tel. 82 08; fax 82 80), across from the tourist office, exhibits some of these finds, as well as lovely coiled copper jewelry from the tombs and artifacts from the famous excavation site on Hallstatt's *Salzberg* (salt mountain) that give scientific proof of prehistoric salt-mining activity. *(Open May-Sept. daily 10am-6pm. 50AS, students 25AS.)* Extensive salt-trading brought bronze ornaments from Northern Italy and amber from the east coast to this remote valley. The price of admission also covers entrance to the **Heimatmuseum,** around the corner, with exhibits on the artifacts of daily living, such as clothes, kitchenware, and mining tools. *(Open May-Sept. daily 10am-6pm.)* It also maps the work of Dr. Franz Morton, who studied the evolution of local fauna.

The 2500-year-old **Salzbergwerke** (tel. 82 51 46) are the oldest saltworks in the world, though these days tourists have replaced miners in the tunnels. *(Open June to mid-Sept. 9:30am-4:30pm; Apr.-May and mid-Sept. to Oct. 9:30am-3pm. 135AS, with guest card 120AS, students 60AS, children under six 35AS.)* The guided tours (1½hr., in English and German) include a tumble down a mining slide on a burlap sack which leads to an eerie lake deep inside the mountain. To reach the salt mines, wander up the steep path near the Pfarrkirche to the top (1hr.) or take the **Salzbergbahn** at the southern edge of town (follow the black signs with the yellow eyes to the bottom of the train station). *(June to mid-Sept. 9am-6pm; Apr.-May and mid-Sept. to Oct. 9am-4:30pm. Last train runs 30min. before the last tour. 60AS, round-trip 97AS, children 60AS.)* If walking from the tourist office, head away from the ferry dock along the lake, and turn right at the large bus circle.

Hallstatt offers some of the most spectacular day hikes in the Salzkammergut, many through forests where drops of water cling to the pine needles year-round thanks to a climate very close to that of a temperate rainforest. The tourist office offers a 70AS English Dachstein hiking guide, detailing 38 hikes in the area, as well as a 35AS mountain bike trail map. Beyond the Salzbergwerk is the **Echental,** a valley carved out millennia ago by glaciers and now blazed with trails leading deep into the valley. Hardy (or foolhardy) hikers can attempt the **Gangsteig,** a slippery, nefarious, primitive stairway carved onto the side of the cliff that makes up the valley's right wall—for experienced hikers only. Those without the gumption or experience to delve so deep into the forest can visit the **Waldbachstub waterfall** or the **Glacier Gardens** in the valley. These beautiful hills, nooks, and crannies are the scars left in the glacier's wake. The melting glacier water ("glacier-milk") was filled with so much sand and silt and rushed past at such a high velocity that it had the same effect as a sand-blaster, permanently scouring the rocks. To reach the Echental, head toward the Salzbergwerk and continue on either Malerweg or Echenweg; about 20 minutes later, a sign will post the area's layout. Gangstieg is about one hour up on the right, and the glacier gardens are about 40 minutes up on the left side, right before the mountain tunnel. Up above the town lies the 700-year old **Rudolfsturm** (Rudolph's tower). Perched on a mountain 855m above the village, the lonely tower guards the entrance to the Salzburg Valley. Hikers can earn a special pin by visiting various points on the map and getting their guide stamped. For **Wild Water Canoeing,** try Gasthof Seewint (tel. 82 46).

For a view of the mountains from below rather than above, try a scenic boat trip around the lake (*Schiffrundfarten;* tel. 82 28), departing from either ferry landing. *(May to late Sept. 10:30am-4:45pm. 50min. ride 80AS.)* **Boat rental** costs 120AS per hour for an electric boat, 95AS for a paddle boat, and 75AS for a row boat. Winter visitors can take advantage of Hallstatt's free **ski bus** (tel. (7612) 646 13), which runs to the Krippenstein and Dachstein-West Ski areas, leaving Hallstatt several times a day; the last bus goes back at 4:05pm. The tourist office can provide a map for area skiing.

■ Near Hallstatt: Obertraun

At the end of the lake in Obertraun, the prodigious (and innocently kitschy) **Dachstein Ice Caves** (tel. 362) testify to the geological hyperactivity that forged the region's natural beauty. (Open May to mid-Oct. 9am-5pm. Admission to either Giant Ice Cave or Mammoth Cave 90AS, children 45AS; combined "Gargantuan Experience" 130AS, 65AS.) To reach the caves from Hallstatt, catch the bus (22AS) at the stop near the lake,' six minutes from the tourist office in the direction away from the ferry dock. Obertraun is also accessible by boat or train, but the bus runs most frequently and drops you right at the **Dachstein cable car** station. Ride the cable car up 1350m to "Schönbergalm." (Open 9am-5pm. Round-trip 168AS, children 105AS.) The **tourist office** stands in the Gemeindeamt, Obertraun 180 (tel. 351; open M-F 8am-noon and 2-6pm; in summer also Sa 9am-noon). Obertraun's bright yellow **Jugendherberge (HI),** Winkl 26 (tel. 360), is a refuge for summer hikers and winter skiers, as well as dozens of school children on class trips. Rooms are clean and institutional. (Dorms 130AS, under 19 90AS. Breakfast included. Reception daily 8-9am and 5-7:30pm. 10pm curfew.) The **telephone code** is 06131.

■ Gmunden

Gmunden, a lovely Salzkammergut resort town on the **Traunsee,** is the birthplace of Thomas Bernhard and the favorite watering-hole of many Biedermeier artists. Along with sunny lake-side beaches and splendorous mountains, the town is renowned for its ceramics. **Trains** run frequently to Gmunden's train station (tel. 17 17) from **Salzburg** and **Linz** (every hr., 114AS); switch first in **Attnang-Pucheim.** To reach the town center from the station, either turn left upon exiting and follow Bahnhofstr. down the hill, or else hop on the tram in front of the station (16AS). From the tram's Franz-Josef Platz terminal, continue one block and turn left to reach the **tourist office**, at Am Graben 2 (tel. 643 05). **Cruises** (tel. 652 15) around the Traunsee are available on an old paddle steamer, and leave from the dock near Rathauspl. daily from May to October. The **telephone code** is 07612.

The tourist office provides a list of *Privatzimmern* (190-300AS) and will call to find out if rooms are available. (Open M-F 8am-6pm, Sa-Su 10am-noon and 4-8pm). A free accommodation phone is outside the office. **Ebensee,** 15km from Gmunden, has a youth hostel. A **farmer's market** sells fresh produce Friday afternoons 2km north of town off Ohlsdorferstr. between Puhrzaunstr. and Stelzerweg. There is a **SPAR** supermarket on the Esplanade. Restaurants are generally incredibly expensive.

You can follow the lake-side, tree-lined Esplanade from the town center to the Habsburg **Villa Toscana,** where the St. Germain peace treaty was ratified in 1920, and to the **Schloß Ort** (tel. 744 19), a picturesque Habsburger island castle now housing wine kellers. (Tours Th and Su 2:30pm; 40AS.) The royal Johannes Nepomuk Salvator bought the castle, married an actress, changed his name to Johannes Ort, and never returned from a trip to the Falklands. The Esplanade also leads to the **Standesamt** ceramics museum (tel. 771 03; open M-F 8am-noon, M and Th also 2-4pm, Sa 8-11am). Gmunden has been a ceramic producing town since the 15th century. Enjoy the ceramic chimes on the Renaissance town hall, Austria's only ceramic fountain in Rinnholzpl., and the showroom of **Gmunder Keramik,** on Keramikstr. off Bahnhofstr. (Open M-F 9am-6pm, Sa 9am-1pm.) Call ahead to arrange a tour (tel. 654 41).

The most exciting display of ceramics can be seen at the **Klo and So Museum für Historische Sanitärobjekte,** which is basically a collection of 19th- and 20th-century toilets. (Museum is in Pepöckhaus, Trang. 4 (tel. 79 42 42). Open May-Oct. Tu-Sa 10am-noon and 2-5pm, Su 10am-noon. 20AS.) The eccentric exhibit, partially outdoors and entirely authentic, includes the early 19th-century chameleon chair with a removable seat, Biedermeier wooden boxes, gilded *Jugenstil* toilets adorned with floral and faunal engravings, a fin-de-siècle circular bench draped in red robes and tassels, international specimens including short, blue stoned Japanese urinals, a selection of potties, and ceramic flushers galore. The pièce-de-résistance is the Habsburg room where you can see Franz-Josef's bedroom john and Sisi's ornate bidet. There isn't info about the toilets in English, but you can ponder how one used the pot resting on the elaborate 1m metal structure, or the box covered in knives.

Admission to the Klo and So also includes entrance to the **Volkskunde-Ausstellung,** an exhibit of regional folklore. (Open June-Oct. Tu-Sa 10am-noon and 2-5pm, Su 10am-noon.) Across the street is the **Kammerhofmuseum.** Housed in the original area's salt mines administration building, it focuses on salt mining, local art and artists, and Brahms. That makes sense. On display are Brahms's *Bösendorfer,* slippers, and toothbrush, as well as photos donated by his close friend and Gmundenite, Dr. Miller Zu Aichholz. (Open May-Oct. Tu-Sa 10am-noon and 2-5pm, Su 10am-noon. 20AS.)

Festwochen Gmunden, an outdoor concert series, takes place from mid-August to early September. (Tickets 40-450AS. Info tel. 706 30.) From June to August, outdoor concerts are held on the Esplanade or on boats. Get info at the tourist office.

■ Zell am See

Surrounded by a ring of snow-capped mountains that collapse into a broad, pale turquoise lake, Zell am See (TSELL am ZAY) functions as a year-round resort spot for mountain-happy Northern and Eastern European tourists. Zell am See's horizon is dominated by 30 "three-thousanders," that is, 30 peaks over 3000m tall, part of the Hohe Tauern National Park, making it a fine base for hiking expeditions and Alpine day-trips. Buses and trains leave frequently for the Krimmler Wasserfälle and Kaiser-Franz-Josef Höhe on the breathtaking Großglockner Str. For *Wanderlust*-filled tourists, the Alpine terrain around Zell offers hiking and skiing challenges, while the cool blue lake calls to those who desire summer rest and relaxation. The center of town has bars and dance clubs to accommodate necessary ski-trip debauchery.

GETTING TO ZELL AM SEE

The **train station** is at the intersection of Bahnhofstr. and Salzmannstr. on the waterfront. There are direct connections to most major Austrian cities. **BundesBuses** travel to nearby cities, to Krimml, and along the Großglockner Straße.Zell am See lies at the intersection of Rte. 311 from the north and Rte. 168 from the west. It's also accessible by Rte. 107 from the south, which runs into Rte. 311 north. From Salzburg, take Rte. 21 south to 312 south; at Lofer, switch to 311 south to Zell.

ORIENTATION AND PRACTICAL INFORMATION

Zell am See's relative proximity to the German border makes it a prime destination for international tourists. The town's accessibility to Salzburg and Innsbruck and its magnificent mountain slopes make it popular among Austrians, too. Go to the right and up the hill from the train station to reach the *Fußgängerzone.*

Trains: The **train station** (tel. 73 21 43 57) is at the intersection of Bahnhofstr. and Salzmannstr. To: **Salzburg** (1¾hr., 24 per day, 1:36am-9:24pm, 140AS), **Innsbruck** (2hr., 8 per day, 5:06am-10:42pm, 240AS), **Vienna** (5¼hr., 5per day, 1:36am-4:19pm, 520AS), and **Kitzbühel** (45min., every hr., 8:42am-10:42pm, 100AS). Ticket office open M 5am-8pm, Tu-Sa 6am-8pm, Su 7am-8:50pm.

Buses: BundesBus station on Postpl., behind the post office and facing Gartenstr. Buy tickets from the driver.

Taxis: At the train station, or call 731 71, 733 59, or 575 51.

Car Rental: ARAC Inter-Auto, Schmittenstr. 2 (tel. 744 52).

Auto Repairs: ÖAMTC (Austrian Automobile and Touring Club), Loferer Bundesstr. (tel. 741 32). In case of a breakdown, dial 120.

Parking: 24hr. parking garage at the Kurcenter sport center past the post office.

Bike Rental: At the train station. 150AS per day, with ticket 90AS. Mountain bike 160AS, 120AS.

Tourist Office: Brucker Bundesstr. 1 (tel. 770; fax 720 34; email zell@gdd.at; http://zell.gold.at), within walking distance of the train station. From the station, take a right and follow the green "i" sign by the stairs on the left. A nifty computer prints information in German or English on accommodations, events, and services (printer open 8am-midnight). The staff can't make reservations, but they will ferret out vacancies and bury you under brochures. Open July to mid-Sept. and mid-Dec. to Mar. M-F 8am-6pm, Sa 8am-noon and 4-6pm, Su 10am-noon; Apr.-June and Sept. to mid-Dec. M-F 8am-noon and 2-6pm, Sa 9am-noon.

Currency Exchange: At banks or the post office. **ATMs** at almost every bank.

Luggage Storage: At the train station. 30AS per piece, open M-Sa 6am-8:30pm. 24hr. electronic lockers with accommodations for both bags and skis 40AS.

Mountain Rescue: Bergrettung Zell am See (tel. 140).

Police: Bruckner Bundesstr. (tel. 737 01).

Post Office: Postpl. 4 (tel. 737 91). Open early July to mid-Sept. and late Dec. to Mar. M-F 7:30am-6:30pm, Sa 8-10am; mid-Sept. to late Dec. and Apr. to early July M-F 7:30am-6:30pm, Sa 7:30-10am. Currency exchange closes at 5pm. **Postal Code:** A-5700. **Telephone Code:** 06542.

ACCOMMODATIONS AND CAMPING

Zell am See has more than its share of four-star hotels (and prices), but it has not forgotten the budget traveler. Many affordable accommodations roll out the red carpet for the cost conscious. Ask for a **guest card,** which provides numerous discounts on activities throughout the city.

Haus der Jugend (HI), Seespitzstr. 13 (tel. 571 85; fax 57 18 54). Exit the back of the train station, turn right, and walk along the well-lit footpath beside the lake; at the end of the footpath, take a left onto Seespitzstr. (15min.). A clean, new hostel on the lakefront. Large rooms with bath and lakeside terraces. Other goodies include a TV room with VCR, a pinball machine, and a snack shop in the reception area. Screaming school groups sometimes descend, so reserve ahead. 106 beds divided into doubles, quads, and 6-bed rooms. Only socks allowed upstairs, so leave your kicks in the sweet sweet smelling "Shoe-Room" by the Reception. Dorms 165AS 1st night, then 140AS. Breakfast included. Lunch and dinner each 65AS. 10AS deposit for lockers in some rooms. Key deposit 300AS. Reception 7-9am and 4-10pm. Check-out 9am. Lockout noon-4pm. Curfew 10pm. Open Dec.-Oct.

Pensione Sinilill (Andi's Inn), Thumersbacherstr. 65 (tel. 735 23). BundesBus (dir: Thumersbach Ort):"Krankenhaus" (19AS, last bus 7:14pm). Turn left upon exiting, walk about 200m, and look for a Zimmer Frei sign on the left side of the street. If you call ahead, Andi will pick you up. On the north shore of the lake, with simple 70s furniture and easy-going, hippie flavor. Andi's swimming trophies and stories, Joy's culinary and karaoke prowess, and the friendliest hound this side of the Großglockner make for an eminently homey atmosphere. 160AS per person. Camping in the front yard 50AS. Hall shower. Huge breakfast 40AS.

Camping Seecamp, Thumersbacherstr. 34 (tel. 21 1; fax 21 15 15), in Zell am See/ Prielau, just down the road from Pension Sinilill. Situated on the lakefront, it offers phones, a restaurant, a café with terrace, and even a small shopping market. 87AS per person, ages 2-15 45AS; tents 50AS; cars 30AS; trailers 100AS. Guest tax 9AS for adults. Showers included. Reception 7am-noon and 2-10pm. Check-out 11am. AmEx, MC, Visa.

FOOD

Here in the Pinzgau region, food is prepared to sustain the strenuous labors of hearty farmers. Try the *Brezensuppe* (a clear soup with cheese cubes) as an appetizer and then *Pinzgauer Käsnocken* (homemade noodles and cheese, topped with fried onions and chives). Top it all off with *Lebkuchen Parfait* (spice cake parfait). *Blattlkrapfen* (deep-fried stuffed pancakes) and *Germnudeln* (noodles served with poppy seeds, butter, and sugar) are also yummy. Happy tummy times.

Ristorante Pizzeria Giuseppe, Kirchg. (tel. 723 73), in the *Fußgängerzone*. From the station walk past the church and continue straight. Plenty of vegetarian options. English menu. Pasta dishes 78-115AS; pizza 50-125AS; salads 55-89AS. Open Tu-Su 11:30am-11pm. AmEx, DC, MC, Visa.

Fischrestaurant "Moby Dick," Kreuzg. 16 (tel. 733 20). The great white hope—with fries. Staggering double fishburger with potatoes and salad for only 85AS. Single fishburger 25AS. A few entrees feature fish straight from the lake. Most dishes 85-160AS. English menu available. Open M-F 9am-6pm, Sa 8am-1pm.

Crazy Daisy Restaurant, Bruckner Bundesstr. 10-12 (tel. 725 16 58). Mexican and American food very popular with young, English-speaking types. Hamburgers 95AS; burritos 120AS; salads 40-60AS; "breath-killer garlic bread" 30AS. Children's portions available. Open daily 7pm-midnight.

Schloß Kammer, Maishofer 22 (tel. 782 02), in the nearby village of Maishofer. Bike up the road past a hospital to a superb restaurant run by the local mayor. Vaulted ceilings, an authentic *Kochelofen* (tiled clay oven), and a large selection of regional dishes. *Fleischknocken* 95AS, *Kaiserschmarr'n* (pancakes with plum compote; serves 2) 75AS. Open daily 10am-10pm.

Markets

SPAR Markt, Brucker Bundesstr. 4. Open M-F 8am-6:30pm, Sa 7:30am-1pm.

Billa Markt, on Schulstr. near the Mozartstr. intersection. Open M-W 8am-7pm, Th 7:30am-7pm, F 7:30am-7:30pm, Sa 7:30am-5pm.

SIGHTS AND ENTERTAINMENT

Zell's buildings are clustered in the valley of the broad, beautiful, blue **Zeller See.** Stroll around the lake on the well-kempt path or get your feet wet at one of the beaches. There's **Strandbad Zell am See,** near the center of town (walk toward the lake down Franz-Josef-Str.), complete with platform diving and a waterslide; **Strandbad Seespitz,** by the Haus der Jugend; and **Thumersbacher Strandbad** on the eastern shore. *(All open late May to early Sept. daily 9am-7pm; 30-60AS, generally half-price after 5pm and free after 6pm.)* **Boat tours** around the lake depart from and return to the Zell Esplanade, off Salzmannstr. along the river. *(40min., 8 per day 10am-5:30pm, 80AS, ages 6-14 40AS.)* **One-way trips** across the lake leave every half-hour. *(May to mid-Oct. 9am-6:45pm, 22AS, round-trip 38AS.)* Purchase tickets on the boat. From the lake, the land rises swiftly into verdant peaks crowned with snow. You can conquer these local mountains on one of the town's five **cable-cars.** The BundesBus (dir: Schmittenhöhebahn/Sonnenalmbahn Talstation) goes to the **Schmittenhöhebahn,** about 2km north of town on Schmittenstr. *(Mid-July to late-Oct. daily every half-hour from 8:30am-5pm. Ascent 180AS, children 90AS; round-trip 230AS, with guest card 205AS, children 115AS.)* The **Sonnenalmbahn,** which travels half the height, is adjacent to the Schmittenhöhebahn. *(Early June to early Oct. daily 9am-5pm. Ascent 95AS for each lift, with guest card 85AS, children 50AS; round-trip 125AS, 110AS, 65AS.)* It connects to the **Sonnkogelbahn,** which rises to 1834m. The **Zeller Bergbahn** (780-1335m) is right in the center of town at the intersection of Schmittenstr. and Gartenstr. *(Mid-June to late Sept. daily 9am-5pm. Ascent 105AS, with guest card 95AS, children 55AS. Round-trip 140AS, 125AS, 70AS.)*

The Zell area provides many opportunities to work those expensive hiking boots. The Schmittenhöhe lift provides five brochures (with English translations) detailing **hikes** ranging from leisurely strolls to hot-blooded cliff-hangers. In the former category, the Erlebnisweg Höhenpromenade connects the top stations of the Schmittenhöhe and Sonnkogel lifts. Seventeen displays on history, nature, and ecology along the way exercise your mind. The brochure *Three Panorama Trips of the Schmittenhöhe,* available at any cable-car station, suggests other light hikes. **Free guided hikes** leave from the lower stations. *(July-Oct. M-F, with a variety of themes including botanical hikes, forest walks, and children's hikes.)* Contact the **Schmittenhöhebahn Aktiengesellschaft** (tel. 78 90) or the lower station for details. For longer hikes, grab a *Wanderplan* or consider the *Pinzgauer Spaziergang,* a long, leisurely 10-hour hike. The trail begins at the upper terminal of the Schmittenhöhebahn and is marked as "Alpenvereinsweg" #19 or 719. A brochure is available. For **rafting** (350-680AS), **canyoning** (550-790AS), **paragliding** (600-700AS), **climbing** (490AS), or **mountain bike** information, contact **Adventure Service,** Steinerg. 9 (tel. 735 25; fax 742 80).

No visit to Zell would be complete without a glimpse of the toilet Franz Josef used when he visited the Schmittenhöhe. This artifact and four floors of equally eclectic exhibits (the largest pike ever caught in the lake, old gingerbread-making utensils, and hundreds of minerals) join the erstwhile royal throne in the entertaining **Heimat-museum** (tel. (06582) 727 59) within the *Vogtturm* (tower), Kreuzg. 2. *(Open mid-Sept. to mid-June M-Tu and Th-F 10am-noon and 2-5pm, W, Sa, and Su 2-4pm; 20AS, ages 6-18 10AS. English guide available.)* The tower itself is more than 1000 years old, and its walls have cracked from the vibrations caused by cannon fire through the roof hatches. The cannons were fired not at enemies of old but at oncoming thunder-storms, a practice believed to disperse the clouds, a process that continued until the science of meteorology reached Zell sometime in the mid-19th century.

Winter turns Zell am See into an Alpine ski resort. The new **Zell/Kaprun Ski Pass** covers both Zell am See and nearby Kaprun; a free bus runs between the two every 15 minutes from Dec. 20 to Apr. 13. *(2 days 710-780AS, students 640-700AS, children 435-470AS.)* One-day passes available for Zell's Schmittenhöhe lift run. *(370-410AS, children 220-240AS.)* For a report in German on ski conditions in the Schmittenhöhe area call 736 94; for the Kitzsteinhorn-Kaprun area call (06547) 84 44. The **Kitzsteinhorn** mountain (3203m) and its glacier in Kaprun offer **year-round skiing.** Get there as early as possible to avoid skiing in slush. A day pass for the mountain costs 255AS, children 140AS. Skis, boots, and poles run 255AS per day and snowboards 180AS per day; all are available at **Intersport Bruendl** (tel. (06547) 862 13 60; email office@bruendl.co.at; http://www.bruendl.co.at) on the glacier. *(Open 8am-4:30pm.)*

NIGHTLIFE

If all the mountain exercise isn't enough, cut some serious rug at Zell's clubs. Those who want to get really hammered check out the local bar game **Nageln**, in which drinkers compete to see who can drive a nail into a tree stump first—with the sharp end of a hammer. Somehow, you end up drunk.

Bierstad'l, Kircheng. 1 (tel. 470 90). 33 different brews in stock; you'll be on the floor by number 9. Creamy, dark Hirtl for 33AS. Open 8:30pm-4am.

Crazy Daisy's Bar, Brucker Bundesstr. 10-12 (tel. 725 16 59). A pleasant (touristy) joint featuring their own wacky, irreverent t-shirts and the ever-popular aforemen-tioned hammer-in-stump game. Open in summer 8pm-1am; in winter 4pm-1am. 2-for-1 happy hour in summer 8-10pm; in winter 4-6pm.

Wunderbar, Esplanade 4-6 (tel. 23 88; fax 238 83 05), at the Grand Hotel. On the top floor of a classy waterfront hotel with glass walls and crazy views. A romantic spot for young professionals and resort-happy tourists. Open 7am-2am.

Pinzgauer Diele, Kircheng. 3 (tel. 21 64). 2 bars and a small dance area guaranteed to get you moving. Move. A mostly under-25 crowd. Mixed drinks 50-95AS, beer 60-75AS. Cover 85AS. Open Su-M and W-Sa 10pm-3am.

■ Near Zell am See: Krimml

From the small mountain town of Krimml, over 700,000 visitors per year pow up the sloping path to extraordinary **Wasserfälle**—a set of three roaring cascades totalling over 400m in height. These grandest falls in Europe are pleasantly secluded amidst the spindly pines and mountain grasses of the Höhe Tauern National Park and the path that runs just alongside them (built in 1900-1 by ÖAU) allows for dozens of unusually intimate and pulse-quickening views.

Krimml is accessible by bus and train. **Buses** are most convenient, since they drop you at the start of the path to the falls (bus stop: Maustelle Ort). Direct lines run from **Zell am See** (1½hr., 10 per day, 6:02am-9:22pm, 100AS) and **Zell am Ziller** (1hr., 3 per day, 9:21am-1:26pm, 58AS). **Trains** come only from the east, through **Zell am See** (9 per day, 1½hr., 190AS round-trip, railpasses valid). The train station (tel. 7214) is 3km from the waterfall—either cross the street to catch the bus (19AS) to the falls, take a **taxi** (7281 or 7356, 50AS) or hike on the foot path. Don't forget a raincoat and camera bag; the mist is very wet. Entrance to the falls costs 15AS (children 5AS) between 8am and 6pm; at all other times entrance is free. The lowest and most spectacular cascade is visible a few meters past the entrance booth and to the left, and the highest point is 1 hour of arduous hiking up.

The ÖAU Information Booth, next to the ticket booth, offers a variety of English pamphlets and sells a number of German guides to the flowers, mushrooms, and rocks of the Höhe Tauern (50-180AS). Open May to Oct. A-Sa 11am-4pm (tel.7212; fax 72124). With a minimum of 10 people, the office offers free guided tours of the falls in English (call in advance). Munchies are available at the myriad **food stands** on the path, but prices are inflated. Stock up at the **Nah und Frisch** market down the main road in Krimml (Open M-F 7:30am-noon and 3-6pm, Sa 7:30am-noon) and picnic at one of the many scenic benches overlooking the falls.

The town of Krimml provides a base for multiple waterfall trips and other hikes in summer, and significant skiing in winter. The **tourist office** (tel. 7550; email Krimml.info@aon.at; http://www.salzburg.com/krimml-tourismus; open M-F 9am-noon and 2:30-5:30pm, Sa 8-10am) is two minutes from the "Krimml Ort" bus stop, just down the hill and next to the **post office** (tel. 7201, open M-F 8am-noon and 2-5pm). Good **currency exchange** rates are at the post office, but there is a 24-hr. **ATM** at the bank across the street from the church. **Bike rental** and cheap food can be had at **ADEG**, in front of the church (open M-F 7:30am-noon and 3-6pm, Sa 7:30am-noon; city and mountain bikes 200AS per day). **Ski and boot rental** at **Sport Lechmayer**, right next to ADEG (tel. 7247; open M-F 8am-noon and 2:30-6pm, Sa 8am-noon; full rental 175-275AS per day, 935-1490AS per week; DC, MC, Visa). Large double-rooms with waterfall views are only 380AS at **Bauernhof Mühleg**, Krimml 24 (tel. 7338). Follow the main road past the church (5 min.); the brown farmhouse is on the right, with flowers on every terrace. Skipasses are 200AS for a full day, and 1745 per week. Youth get 15% off, children 35%. The **postal code** is A-5743. The **telephone code** is 06564.

Central Tyrol

Tyrol (Tirol)

Tyrol's Alps overwhelm with their superhuman scale and beauty; the sight of mountaintop rock and *névé* (partially compacted granular snow) is unforgettable. Jagged contours in the Kaisergebirge above St. Johann and Kufstein in the northwest fade slightly to the rounded shapes of the Kitzbühel Alps to the south, but the peaks rise again above the beautiful blue-green **Zeller See** at Zell am See. Mountainous crags create two of the most spectacular natural wonders in all of Europe; if you're within hours of Central Tyrol, take a detour to the **Krimmler Wasserfälle** or the **Großglockner Straße** in the **Hohe Tauern National Park**.

🏔 HIGHLIGHTS OF TYROL

- Innsbruck, home to several past Winter Olympics and a stupendous skiing industry, also holds some gorgeous medieval buildings and a provincial Habsburg palace.
- The dizzying Großglockner Straße crosses the Hohe Tauern park, a range of mountains with 246 glaciers, and goes through a mountain pass on Austria's highest mountain, the Großglockner. Hiking opportunities abound.
- Italianate Lienz's crumbly castle fortress and mountain chalets provide one of the few opportunities in Austria to explore the hiking and skiing possibilities of the jagged Dolomite mountain chain.

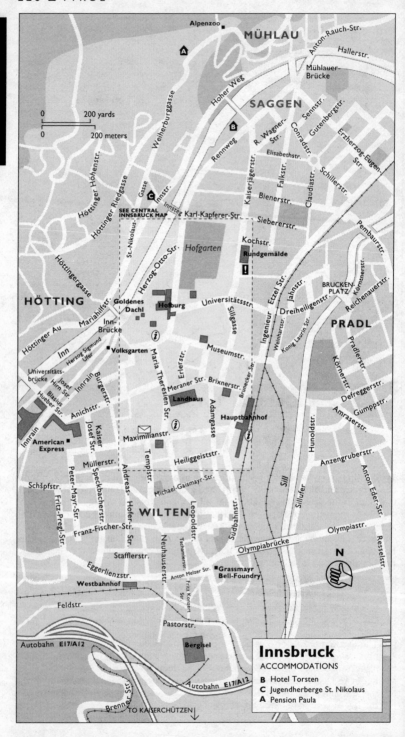

Innsbruck

ACCOMMODATIONS

B Hotel Torsten
C Jugendherberge St. Nikolaus
A Pension Paula

East Tirol is the geopolitical oddity of the region, technically a semi-autonomous, wholly owned subsidiary of the province of Tyrol. The two provinces, however, share no common border. During World War I, Italy signed the secret Treaty of London and was awarded part of Austria—the South Tyrol—as booty in exchange for switching sides to join England, France, and Russia. *Südtirol* is now a completely bilingual Italo-German province, leaving the Austrian province awkwardly divided by an Italian sliver. Although East Tyrol resembles its mother province culturally and topographically, Easterners retain a powerful independent streak.

▓ Innsbruck

In 1964 and 1976 the Winter Olympics were held in Innsbruck, bringing international renown to the beautiful mountain city. The landscape is far more immediate here than in nearby Salzburg. Massive, snow-capped peaks seem to advance down quaint, cobblestoned streets at every turn. The tiny *Altstadt* is peppered with intricate facades and Baroque remnants of the Habsburg stronghold that emerged here under Emperor Maximilian I. The close coincidence of majestic mountaintops and imperial artifacts makes Innsbruck one of Austria's most touristed cities, although the unpretentious university district near the center of town and several quiet, gorgeous mountain suburbs can leave visitors with the impression of a city relatively untarnished by its ski-resort status.

■ Getting to Innsbruck

Flights arrive and depart from **Flughafen Innsbruck,** Fürstenweg 180 (tel. 225 25). The airport is 4km from town. Bus F shuttles to and from the main train station every 15 minutes (21AS). **Austrian Airlines** and **Swissair,** Furstenweg 176 (tel. 17 89), have offices in Innsbruck. (See **Essentials: Getting There,** p. 29.) **Trains** arrive at the **Hauptbahnhof** on Südtirolerpl., on bus lines A, D, E, F, J, K, R, S, and #3; **Westbahnhof** and **Bahnhof Hötting** are cargo stops. **Cars** from the east or west take Autobahn A12. From Vienna take A1 west to Salzburg then A8 west to A12. From the south, take A13 north to A12 west. From Germany and the north, take A95 to Rte. 2 east.

■ Orientation and Practical Information

Most of Innsbruck lies on the eastern bank of the **Inn River. Maria-Theresien-Straße,** the main thoroughfare, runs north to south and south to north. The street is open only to taxis, buses, and trams. Tourists and open-air cafés crowd its flanks. To reach the *Altstadt* from the main train station, take tram #3 or 6 or bus A, F, or K: "Maria-Theresien-Str.," or turn right and walk to Museumstr. then left and walk for about 10 minutes. Small maps of the city are available at the train station information booth, the *Jugendwarteraum,* or any tourist office. Continue down Museumstr. and toward the river (curving left onto Burggraben, across Maria-Theresien-Str., and onto Marktgraben) to reach the **University district,** near Innrain. The university itself is to the left down Innrain. Most sights are clustered between the **Innbrücke** and the **Hofgarten,** a relatively short walk from the train station.

TRANSPORTATION

Trains: Hauptbahnhof, Südtirolerpl. (tel. 17 17). Open 7:30am-7:30pm. To: **Salzburg** (2hr., 10 per day, 4:39am-11:33pm, 350AS); **Vienna** (5¼hr., 10 per day, 4:39am-11:33pm, 660AS); **Zurich** (4hr., 4 per day, 2:38am-2:39pm, 568AS); **Munich** (2hr., 37 per day, 4:39am-9:30pm, 394AS); and **Berlin** (10hr., 37 per day, 4:37am-9:30pm, 1688AS).

Buses: BundesBuses (tel. 58 51 55) leave from the station on Sterzingerstr., next to the *Hauptbahnhof* and left of the main entrance. For information, call 35 11 93.

Public Transportation: The main bus station is in front of the main entrance to the train station. You can purchase single-ride, 1-zone tickets (21AS), 1-day tickets (33AS), 4-ride tickets (60AS), and week-long bus passes (115AS) from any driver or

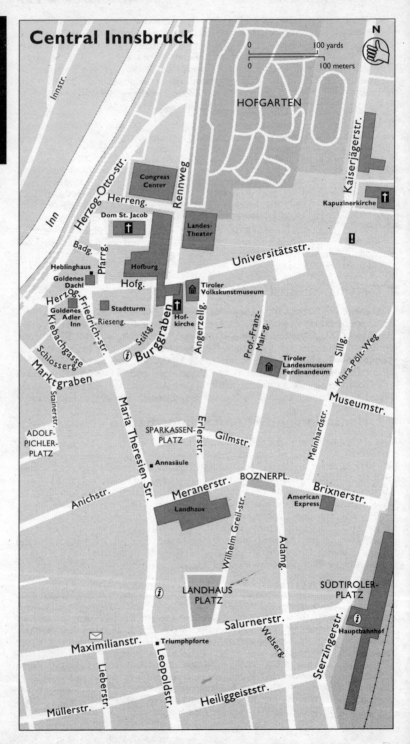

Tabak. Punch your ticket when you board the bus or pay a 400AS fine. Most buses stop running 10:30-11:30pm; check each line for specifics. A free *Nachtbus* runs on Friday and Saturday nights, heading east from Marktpl. at 1 and 2am, and heading west from Maria-Theresien-Str. at 1:30 and 2:30am.

Taxis: Innsbruck Funktaxi (tel. 53 11, 17 18, or 335 00). About 120AS from the airport to the *Altstadt,* dig?

Car Rental: Avis, Salurnerstr. 15 (tel. 57 17 54). **Budget,** Leopoldstr. 54 (tel. 58 84 68; fax 58 45 80).

Auto Repairs: ARBÖ (tel. 123). **ÖAMTC** (tel. 120).

Hitchhiking: Hitchers usually take bus K: "Geyrstr." and go to the Shell gas station by the DEZ store off Geyrstr. Tricks of the trade trade hands.

Bike Rental: At the train station (tel. 503 53 95). Open Apr. to early Nov. 150-200AS per day, with Eurailpass or that day's train ticket 90-160AS. **Sport Neuner,** Salurnerstr. 5 (tel. 56 15 01), near the station, rents mountain bikes. 200AS per day.

TOURIST AND FINANCIAL SERVICES

Although Innsbruck's myriad tourist offices offer comparable services, the city-run office on the third floor at Burggraben 3 will probably give the most straightforward information. All offices hawk the **Innsbruck Card,** a veritable monkey's paw of sightseeing giving free access to dozens of local attractions and all public transportation for 24, 48, or 72 hours (230AS, 300AS, 370AS; children 115AS, 150AS, 185AS). A two-hour **bus tour,** including the *Altstadt* and a visit to the ski jump, leaves from the train station. (Summer noon and 2pm; winter noon. 160AS, children 70AS.)

Innsbruck Information Office, Burggraben 3 (tel. 598 50; fax 598 07; email info@innsbruck.tub.co.at; http://discover.com/innsbruck/), on the 3rd floor. Official and not-for-profit, with tons of brochures and a helpful staff. Open M-F 8am-6pm, Sa 8am-noon. It's in the same building as **Innsbruck-Information,** Burggraben 3 (tel. 53 56; fax 53 56 14), on the edge of the *Altstadt* just off the end of Museumstr. Huge and high-tech with hundreds of brochures. A private, profit-maximizing consortium of local hotels oversees the offices, so arrange tours and concert tickets but don't expect to reserve budget accommodations. Exchange closes 20min. before office. Open M-Sa 8am-7pm, Su and holidays 9am-6pm. **Branches** at the train station and major motor exits. **Jugendwarteraum** (tel. 58 63 62), in the *Hauptbahnhof* near the lockers. Gives directions, suggests hostels, and hands out free maps and skiing information. English spoken. Open M-F 11am-7pm, Sa 10am-1pm. Closed July to mid-Sept.

Österreichischer Alpenverein, Wilhelm-Greil-Str. 15 (tel. 595 47; fax 57 55 28). The Austrian Alpine Club's main office. Provides mountains of hiking information and discounts on Alpine huts and hiking insurance. Members only. Membership 530AS, ages 18-25 and over 60 390AS, under 18 180AS. Open M-F 9am-1pm and 2-5pm.

Budget Travel: Tiroler Landesreisebüro (tel. 598 85) on Wilhelm-Greil-Str. at Boznerpl. Open M-F 9am-6pm. AmEx, MC, Visa.

Currency Exchange: Innsbruck Information tourist office, on Burggraben. Open M-Sa 8am-6:40pm, Su 9am-5:40pm. **Banks** are open M-F 8am-noon and 2:30-4pm.

American Express: Brixnerstr. 3, A-6020 Innsbruck (tel. 58 24 91; fax 57 33 85). From the station, take a right then the 1st left. Holds mail. No commission on its checks; small fee for cash. Open M-F 9am-5:30pm, Sa 9am-noon.

Consulate: U.K., Matthias-Schmidtstr. 12 (tel. 58 83 20). Open M-F 9am-noon.

LOCAL SERVICES

Luggage Storage: Luggage watch for 30AS at the train station. Open July-Aug. 6:30am-midnight; Sept.-June 6:30am-10:30pm.

Bookstores: Wagner'she, Museumstr. 4 (tel. 59 50 50; fax 595 05 38). Open M-F 9am-6pm, Sa 9am-5pm. **Buchhandlung Tirolia,** Maria-Theresien-Str. 15 (tel. 596 11; fax 58 20 50). Travel literature. Open M-F 9am-6pm, Sa 9am-5pm.

Library: Innsbruck Universität Bibliothek, Innrain 50, where it crosses Blasius-Heuber-Str. Take bus O, R, or F: "Klinik." Copy machine 1AS per page. Open July-Aug. M-F 8am-8pm, Sa 8am-noon; Sept.-June M-F 8am-10pm, Sa 8am-6pm.

Bi-Gay-Lesbian Organizations: Homosexuelle Initiative Tirol, Innrain 100, A-6020 Innsbruck (tel. 56 24 03). **Frauenzentrum Innsbruck** (Women's Center), Liebeneggstr. 15, A-6020 Innsbruck (tel. 58 08 39) runs a women's-only café for lesbians and straights 3 times per week, as well as discotheques and poetry readings. Call for schedules and information.

Laundromat: Bubble Point, Andreas-Hofer-Str. 37 (tel. 336 97 28). It really tries, but it's just a laundromat (with a pinball machine and a lot of graphics). 5.5kg washer 45AS, 7kg 55AS, 5min. in the dryer 5AS.

Public Showers: At the train station, near the rest rooms. 30AS.

Mountain Guide Information Office: tel. 532 01 75. Open M-F 9am-noon.

Weather Report: tel. (04501) 99 15 56 08. **Snow report:** tel. (04501) 99 00 00 11.

Ski Rental: Skischule Innsbruck, Leopoldstr. 4 (tel. 58 17 42). Skis, boots, poles, and insurance 270AS.

EMERGENCY AND COMMUNICATIONS

Emergencies: Police, tel. 133. Headquarters at Kaiserjägerstr. 8 (tel. 590 00). **Ambulance,** tel. 144 or 142. **Fire,** tel. 122. **Mountain Rescue,** tel. 140.

Medical Assistance: University Hospital, Anichstr. 35 (tel. 50 40).

Post Office: Maximilianstr. 2 (tel. 500), down from the Triumphpforte and straight ahead from the station. Open 24hr. Address *Poste Restante:* Postlagernde Briefe, Hauptpostamt, Maximilianstr. 2, A-6020 Innsbruck. **Branch** next to the station (tel. 500 74 09). Open M-F 7am-8pm, Sa 8am-6pm. **Postal Code:** A-6020.

Telephone Code: 0512.

■ Accommodations and Camping

Although 9000 beds are available in Innsbruck and suburban Igls, inexpensive accommodations are scarce in June when only two hostels are open. The opening of student dorms to backpackers in July and August alleviates the crush. Book in advance if possible. Visitors should join **Club Innsbruck** by registering at any Innsbruck accommodation. Membership gives discounts on museums, skiing, ski buses (Dec. 21-Apr. 5), bike tours, and the club's fine hiking program (June-Sept.).

Hostel Torsten Arneus-Schwedenhaus (HI), Rennweg 17b (tel. 58 58 14; fax 585 81 44; email youth.hostel@idk.netwing.at; http://www.goli.org/youth-hostel). From the station, bus C: "Handelsakademie," continue to the end and straight across Rennweg to the river. Or walk right from the station, left on Museumstr., right at the end of the street onto Burggraben, and follow it under the arch and onto Rennweg (20min.). This 95-bed hostel offers a convenient location and a front-yard view of the Inn River. On summer weekdays, you can store your luggage at the front desk any time. 3- to 4-bed dorms 120AS. Private shower included. Breakfast 7-8:30am (45AS). Dinner 65AS. Sheets 20AS. Reception 7-10am and 5-10:30pm. Lockout 9am-5pm. Curfew 10:30pm; keys on request. Open July-Aug. Reservations recommended, honored until 7pm.

Jugendherberge Innsbruck (HI), Reichenauer Str. 147 (tel. 34 61 79 or 34 61 80; fax 34 61 79 12; email yhibk@tirol.com). Bus R: "König-Laurin Str." then bus O: "Jugendherberge." With tinted octagonal windows and sliding doors, this 178-bed hostel resembles a high-powered corporation. 3 large lounges with hot plates, TV, and a small library. Large turquoise lockers in the rooms offset flowered quilts the Partridge family left behind. Quiet time from 10pm. 6-bed dorms 146AS 1st night, then 116AS; 4-bed dorms 176AS, 146AS. Showers and sheets included. July-Aug. singles and doubles in an adjacent building with private showers and no lockout 350AS, 500AS. Non-members add 40AS. Breakfast 7-8:30am; dinner 6-8pm. **Laundry** 45AS, but you must notify the desk by 5pm if you intend to do some washing. Reception 7am-12:30pm and 5-10pm. Lockout 10am-5pm. Curfew 11pm; key available. Open July 15-Aug. 31. Phone reservations honored until 5pm.

Youth Hostel St. Niklaus (HI), Innstr. 95 (tel. 28 65 15; fax 28 65 15 14; email yhniklaus@tirol.com; http://tirol.com/yhniklaus). From the train station bus K: "Schmelzerg." and cross the street. A happening bar/restaurant/hostel with wooden bunkbeds and a sleepover-camp feel. Dorms 160AS 1st night, then 145AS; singles 245AS; doubles 390AS; triples 555AS; quads 700AS. Breakfast included.

7min. showers 10AS. **Internet access** 10AS per 10min., but no telnet. Reception 8-10am and 5-8am. Lockout 10am-5pm. Curfew 11pm; key available.

Haus Wolf, Dorfstr. 48 (tel. 54 86 73), in Mutters. Stubaitalbahn tram: "Birchfeld" then walk down Dorfstr. in the same direction. (The Stubaitalbahn stop is on the 3rd traffic island in front of the train station's main entrance. 25AS, week-long ticket 94AS. Last train 10:30pm. Buy tickets from driver.) An appealingly nutty and very social atmosphere prevails here on the mountainside. Large rooms and a thorough breakfast await you after a splendid 30min. tram ride out of Innsbruck. Singles 190AS; doubles 380AS; triples 570AS. Breakfast and shower included.

Haus Kaltenberger, Schulg. 15 (tel. 54 85 76), near Haus Wolf. Take the Stubaitalbahn: "Mutters," then walk towards the church, turn right on Dorfstr., and take the 1st left. Well-kept rooms with attractive balconies and gorgeous mountain views. Doubles 360-400AS. Breakfast and shower included.

Technikerhaus, Fischnalerstr. 26 (tel. 28 21 10; fax 28 21 10 17). Bus R: "Unterbergerstr./Technikerhaus." Or walk from the train station onto Salurnerstr. Take the 1st right onto Maria-Theresien-Str. then left onto Anichstr. Cross the bridge on Blasius-Hueber-Str., left on Fürstenweg, left on Fischnalerstr. Though far from the station, this student housing complex is near the university district and the *Altstadt*. Restaurant and 2 TV rooms. Breakfast room straight from a Disney animator's sketchbook. Singles 220AS, with student ID 185AS; doubles 420AS, 370AS; triples 600AS, 555AS. Breakfast and showers included. Reception 24hr. Open mid-July to Aug. Reservations recommended.

Pension Paula, Weiherburgg. 15 (tel./fax 29 22 62). Bus K: "St. Nikolaus" then walk uphill. Satisfied guests frequently return to this inn-like home downhill from the Alpenzoo. Views of the river and city center in bare rooms with solid furniture. Singles 320AS, with shower 420AS; doubles 540AS, 620AS, with bath 640AS. Breakfast included. Reservations recommended.

Internationales Studentenhaus, Recheng. 7 (tel. 50 15 92 or 59 47 70; fax 501 15). Bus O, R, or F: "Klinik" on Innrain then turn right on Recheng.; or bus C: "Studentenheim." To walk from the station, go straight out onto Salurnerstr., right on Maria-Theresien-Str., left on Anichstr., left on Innrain. Pass the main university complex and turn right on Recheng. A 60s era, 560-bed dormitory reminiscent of the cover of a Beck album. Parking available a short distance away on Innrain. Singles 260AS, with shower 350AS; with student ID 210AS, 300AS. Doubles 440AS, with shower 600AS. All-you-can-eat American buffet breakfast 70AS. **Laundry** facilities. Reception 24hr., but call in advance. Open July-Aug.

Camping Innsbruck Kranebitten, Kranebitter Allee 214 (tel. 28 41 80; http://www.cda.at/tourismus/campibk.html). Bus LK: "Klammstr." (20min.), or bus F, R, or O: "Klinik" and switch to the LK. Walk downhill, then right, and follow the road. Pleasant grounds with lots of space and a sizable playground for the kiddos. 60AS, children under 15 45AS; tents 40AS; cars 40AS. Tax 6AS. Showers included. **Laundry** available (50AS). Reception 8am-noon. If reception is closed, find a site and check in the next morning.

■ Food

Most tourists first glimpse cosmopolitan Innsbruck from the glamour of Maria-Theresien-Str. Gawking at the overpriced delis and *Konditoreien* won't fill your stomach, so escape the *Altstadt* and its profiteers by crossing the river to Innstr. in the university district where you'll uncover ethnic restaurants, *Schnitzel Stuben*, and grocers.

Philippine Vegetarische Küche, Müllerstr. 9 (tel. 58 91 57), at Lieberstr. near the post office. A vegetarian rest stop on a highway of meat, this whimsically decorated restaurant serves some of the best food in carnivorous Innsbruck. Everything is tasty and expertly prepared, from carrot-orange soup (44AS) to potato cannelloni with smoked tofu (112AS). Daily specials. Less expensive smaller portions available. *Menü* with soup and entree 75AS. Open M-Sa 10am-11pm. DC, MC, Visa.

Gasthof Weißes Lamm, Mariahilfstr. 12 (tel. 28 31 56). Home-style, Tirolean restaurant popular with the locals. Window tables with lavender tablecloths offer a pleasant view of the river. 100AS can go a long way with the heaping portions and special *Menüs* (soup, entree, and salad 80-115AS). Other entrees 100-200AS. Open M-W and F-Su 11:30am-2pm and 6-10pm.

Salute Pizzeria, Innrain 35 (tel. 58 58 18). Popular student hangout near the university with fake grapes and a neon-lit Edward Hopper painting. Pizza 35-100AS; pasta 55-90AS. Open 11am-midnight.

Churrasco la Mamma, Innrain 2 (tel. 58 63 98). Shady outdoor seating next to the river—watch the moon rise, and fall in love over a plate of spaghetti. Pasta 78-112AS. Brick-oven pizza 68-118AS. Open 9am-midnight. DC, MC, Visa.

Al Dente, Meranestr. 7 (tel. 58 49 47). Snug, candle-lit place with lots of those hand-colored photographs of little children in adult's clothing kissing each other on the lips. After finishing your entree (82-142AS), try the delicious *tiramisú* (46AS). Plenty of vegetarian options. English menu. Open M-Sa 7am-11pm, Su and holidays 11am-11pm. AmEx, DC, MC, Visa.

Crocodiles, Maria-Theresien-Str. 49 (tel. 58 88 56). Tiny restaurant on the right of Intersport Okay serving 33 different brick-oven pizzas, including 8 vegetarian options. English menus and a "croco-crew" of waiters available to help you decide. Large pizzas 55-85AS. Open M-F 10:30am-10pm, Sa 11am-3pm.

Rosenkavalier, Südtirolerpl. 5 (tel. 58 20 24), by the train station. 4 dining rooms serve fine *Wiener Schnitzel* for cheap. Popular with locals and mid-morning drunks. *Tiroler Gröstl* 78AS, spaghetti with meat sauce 74AS. Open M-F 7am-10:30pm, Sa-Su 7am-8:30pm.

University Mensa, Herzog-Siegmund-Ufer 15 (tel. 58 43 75), on the 2nd floor of the university at Blasius-Hueber-Str. near the bridge. Student cafeteria open to the public. Soup and entree 30-54AS. Open M-Th 11am-2pm, F 11am-1:30pm.

MARKETS

M-Preis Supermarket has the lowest prices around. Branches on the corner of Reichenauerstr. and Andechstr.; on Maximilianstr. by the arch; at Innrain 15; and on the corner of Salurnerstr. and Sterzingerstr. Open M-Th 7:30am-6:30pm, F 7:30am-7:30pm, Sa 7:30am-5pm.

Indoor Farmer's Market, in the Markthalle near the river at Innrain and Marktgraben. Food, flowers, and other stuff. Open M-F 7am-6:30pm, Sa 7am-1pm.

Farmer's Markets on Thursdays from 9am-1pm at Franziskanerpl., on Fridays from 9:30am-3pm at Sparkassenpl., on Saturdays from 8-11:30am at Viktor-Franz-Hess-Str. and 8am-noon at St. Nikolaus-Brunnenpl.

■ Sights

The centerpiece of the *Altstadt,* **Goldenes Dachl** (Little Golden Roof) on Herzog Friedrichstr., is a shiny, shingled balcony built to commemorate the marriage of the Habsburg couple Maximilian I and Bianca. They were great-great-great-great-great-great grandparents of Maria Theresa. Beneath the 2657 shimmery gold squares, Maximilian and his wife kept watch over a crew of jousters and dancers in the square below. (Unfortunately, the balcony may be obscured by scaffolding for a restoration scheduled to be completed in October 1998.) Inside the building, the **Maximilianeum Museum** commemorates Innsbruck's favorite nosy emperor. *(Open May-Sept. 10am-6pm; Oct.-Apr. Tu-Su 10am-12:30pm and 2-5pm. 50AS, students 20AS, seniors 40AS, family pass 120AS.)* Nifty headphones provide multilingual commentary on the small room of exhibits, sometimes with exciting background music. Maximilian's suit of armor is explicated over a track of **hot beats.** Many splendid old buildings surround the Goldenes Dachl. To the left, the flush salmon facade of the 15th-century **Helbling-haus** is blanketed with a pale green, 18th-century Baroque floral stucco. A modest climb up the graffiti-lined staircase of the 15th-century **Stadtturm** (city tower), across from Helbinghaus, yields a modest view of the city, perhaps worth exactly the modest cost of admission. *(Open daily July-Aug. 10am-6pm; Sept.-Oct. and Apr.-June 10am-5pm; Nov.-Mar. 10am-4pm. 22AS, students and children 11AS.)* The 15th-century **Goldener Adler Inn** (Golden Eagle Inn) is a few buildings to the left. Goethe, Heine, Sartre, Mozart, Wagner, Camus, and even Maximilian I ate, drank, and made merry here. A block behind the Goldenes Dachl rise the twin towers of the **Dom St. Jakob** (remodeled 1717-1724). *(Open daily Apr.-Sept. 8am-7:30pm; Oct.-Mar. 8am-6:30pm. Free.)* Inside there's a *trompe l'oeil* ceiling by C. D. Asam depicting the life of St. James and an overdone altar framing Lukas Cranach's painting *Intercession of the Virgin*. A 1944 air raid destroyed much of the church, but renovations have restored its pink.

The grand *Hofburg* (Imperial Palace), *Hofkirche* (Imperial Church), and *Hofgarten* (Imperial Garden) converge at the intersection of Rennweg and Hofg., forming an unstoppable imperial axis. Built between the 16th and 18th centuries, the **Hofburg** brims with Habsburgness. *(Open daily 9am-5pm. Last entrance 4:30pm. 55AS, students 35AS, children 10AS. German tours at 10am and 3pm. English guidebook 25AS.)* Imposing furniture and large portraits fill more than 20 excessively decorated rooms. Highlights include a set of fine mesh reliquaries, the dubious "Chinese Room," and a portrait of Maria's youngest daughter, Marie Antoinette (with head). Around the corner, the cavernous **Gothic Cellar,** a kitchen in Maximilian's time, holds temporary exhibits. The **Hofkirche** holds an intricate sarcophagus decorated with alabaster scenes from Maximilian I's life and the *Schwarze Mander,* 28 larger-than-life bronze statues that line the nave. *(Open daily July-Aug. 9am-5:30pm; Sept.-June 9am-5pm. 20AS, students 14AS, children 10AS.)* Dürer designed the statues of King Arthur, Theodoric the Ostrogoth, and Count Albrecht of Habsburg. All for an empty coffin: Maxi was buried outside Vienna because the monument didn't meet his specifications when he died. The elegant Silver Chapel does hold the corpse of Archduke Ferdinand II amidst wallpaper with faded cherubim resembling hard-boiled eggs. A 50AS combination ticket will admit you to the **Tiroler Volkskunstmuseum** (Tirolean Handicrafts Museum) in the same building. *(Open July-Aug. M-Tu and Th-Sa 9am-5:30pm, W 9am-9pm; Sept.-June M-Sa 9am-5pm, Su 9am-noon. Museum alone 40AS, students 25AS, children 15AS.)* Built between 1553 and 1563 as the "New Abbey," the building was converted into a school in 1785 and a museum in 1929. The exhaustive collection of odd implements, peasant costumes, and period rooms provides a dusty introduction to Tirolean culture. Learn how medieval Tiroleans worked, dressed, fell asleep, moved dirt, and carried things. The **Hofgarten** across the street is a beautifully groomed, shaded picnic spot, complete with ponds, flowers, and a concert pavilion.

The **Tiroler Landesmuseum Ferdinandeum,** Museumstr. 15 (tel. 594 89), some blocks from the *Hauptbahnhof,* showcases the history of Tirolean art, from medieval altars to modern abstractions. *(Open May-Sept. M-W and F-Su 10am-5pm, Th 10am-5pm and 7-9pm; Oct.-Apr. Tu-Sa 10am-noon and 2-5pm, Su 10am-1pm. 50AS, students 30AS.)* A small collection of non-local art includes a Schiele, a Klimt, and a pint-sized Rembrandt. The **Zeughaus extension** (across town) collects arms (as in weapons).

Near the Schwedenhaus youth hostel, across the covered bridge, signs point to the **Alpenzoo** (tel. 29 23 23), the highest-altitude zoo in Europe, way up there with every vertebrate species indigenous to the Alps. *(Open daily summer 9am-6pm; in winter 9am-5pm. 70AS, students and children 35AS.)* When you've had your fill of high-altitude baby ibex, descend the network of scenic trails that weave across the hillside. Tram #1 or 4 or bus C, D, or E: "Hungerbergbahn" drops you at the summit's cable car.

In town, Baroque **Maria-Theresien-Straße** gives a clear view of the snow-capped *Nordkette* mountains. At the beginning of the street stands the **Triumphpforte** (Triumphal Arch) built in 1765 to commemorate the betrothal of Emperor Leopold II. Down the street, the **Annasäule** (Anna Column), erected between 1704 and 1706 by the provincial legislature, commemorates the Tiroleans' victory after a bloody and unsuccessful Bavarian invasion during the War of Spanish Succession.

Farther from the city center, the **Grassmayr Bell-Foundry** at Leopoldstr. 53 (tel. 594 16 37) has been crafting bells for 14 generations of Grassmayrs. Learn how bells are made at the **Bell Museum,** then watch the casting itself. *(Open M-F 9am-6pm, Sa 9am-noon. Castings take place every Friday at 1, 2, and 4pm. Entrance 40AS, children 25AS.)* The Rococo **Basilika Wilten** and the Baroque **Stiftskirche Wilten** are just down the street. There are plenty of weapons at area museums, from the **Kaiserschützen** to the **Bergisel,** and, nearby, farther away from town on tram #1 or 6: "Bergisel," there's the **Olympische Skischanze** (Olympic Ski Jump). At the bottom of the hill, a graveyard takes care of all the unfortunate Olympic failures. Spanning the Sil River on the *Brennerautobahn* (motorway) is Europe's tallest bridge, the 1699m **Europabrücke.**

Elsewhere outside the city, Archduke Ferdinand of Tirol left a stash of 16th-century armor and artwork (including pieces by Velazquez and Titian) at **Schloß Ambras.**

(Open Su-M and W-Sa 10am-5pm. 60AS, children and students 30AS; with tour 85AS, 55AS.) The medieval castle was a royal hunting lodge, but Ferdinand transformed it into one of the most beautiful Renaissance castles and gardens in Austria. A detailed portrait gallery depicts European dynasties from the 14th to the 19th centuries. The collection also includes armor displays and a 16th-century bathroom. To reach the palace at Schloßstr. 20, take tram #6 (dir: Igls): "Schloß Ambras," and follow the signs, or hop on the shuttle bus that leaves hourly from Maria-Theresien-Str in the months from Apr.-Oct. Walk only if you have a hiking map, as the trail is poorly marked.

Also outside the city but well worth seeing is the **Swarovski Kristallwelten,** a multimedia crystal theme-park with a veneer of New Age hokeyness and modern art pretension. *(Open daily 9am-6pm. 75AS, students 65AS, children free.)* Above the underground entrance, the fabulous **Giant,** a mossy face on the side of a hill, spits water and peers through glowing eyes. Inside, purple walls, moving sculptures, and a stele by Keith Haring are augmented by unusual smells and a heavily synthesized soundtrack. The creator of the Kristallwelten, André Heller, has filled it with homages to fellow Viennese artist Gustav Klimt. Creative interpretations of High Modernism greatly enhance the experience. To get there, take bus #4125 from the *Busbahnhof* to Waltens *(35min., every 30min., 7:45am-8:22pm, 82AS round-trip.)*

■ Innsbruck Outdoors

A **Club Innsbruck** membership (see **Accommodations,** p. 224) lets you in on one of the best deals in all Austria. The club's excellent mountain **hiking** program provides guides, transportation, and equipment (including boots) absolutely free to hikers of all ages. Participants assemble in front of the Congress Center (June-Sept. daily at 8:30am), board a 9am bus, and return from the mountain ranges by 5pm. The hike isn't strenuous, the views are phenomenal, and the guides are qualified and friendly. Free night-time lantern hikes leave every Tuesday at 7:45pm for Gasthof Heiligwasser, just above Igls; enjoy an Alpine hut party once there. The **Peterskofelbahn** in Igls takes hikers up beautiful trails to the **Alpine Garden,** the highest botanical garden in Europe. *(Open daily 9am-4:30pm, round-trip 180AS, kids 90AS; one-way 110AS, kids 55AS. Garden open June-Sept. 9:30am-4pm; free; guided tours Friday 2 and 3pm for 20AS).* If you wish to attack the Alps alone, pick up a free guidebook at any of the tourist offices.

The Club Innsbruck membership also significantly simplifies winter **ski** excursions; just hop the complimentary club ski shuttle (schedules at the tourist office) to any suburban cable car (Dec. 21-Apr. 5). Membership provides discounts on ski passes. **Innsbruck Gletscher Ski Pass** (available at all cable cars and at Innsbruck-Information offices) is a comprehensive ticket valid for all 53 lifts in the region. *(3 days 1260AS, 6 days 2270AS; with Club Innsbruck card 1040AS, 1880AS.)* The tourist office also **rents equipment** on the mountain. *(Alpine approximately 270AS per day; cross-country 160AS; bobsled 300AS per person per ride.)* The summer bus to **Stubaier Gletscherbahn** (for glacier skiing) leaves at 7:20 and 8:30am. Take the earlier bus—summer snow is often slushy by noon. In winter, buses also leave at 9:45, 11am, and 5pm. *(1½hr., last bus back at 4:30pm, round-trip 150AS.)* One day of winter glacier skiing costs 420AS; summer passes cost 330AS after 8am, 275AS after 11am, and 170AS after 1pm. You can rent skis for about 270AS at the glacier. Innsbruck-Information and its train station branch offer the most reliable daily glacier ski packages: in summer 660AS, including bus, lift, and rental; in winter 540AS.

For a one-minute thrill, summer and winter **bobsled** rides are available at the Olympic bobsled run in Igls (tel. 33 83 80; fax 33 83 89), 5km from Innsbruck. Summer rides, however, are akin to spruced-up *Cool Runnings* carts with wheels. Professionals pilot the four-person sleds. Reservations (tel./fax (512) 39 44 66) are necessary. *(Summer Th-Sa 4:30-6pm; winter Tu at 10am, and Th from 7pm on; 360AS.)* For a calmer ride, try the **Hafelekar Cable Car.** *(Daily; 264AS with Club Innsbruck card.)*

■ Entertainment

At a corner of the *Hofgarten,* the **Congress Center** and **Tiroler Landestheater** (tel. 52 07 44) host a number of festivals and concert series in Innsbruck. In August, the **Festival of Early Music** features concerts by some of the world's leading soloists on period instruments at the Schloß Ambras, Congress Center, and *Hofkirche.* (For tickets, call 53 56 21 or fax 53 56 43.) The Landestheater also presents top-notch plays, operas, and dance most nights of the year. (Concerts 85-590AS, standing room 50AS; plays 70-500AS, standing room 40AS; rush tickets 90AS, available 30min. before the show to anyone under 21 and students under 27.)

The **Tiroler Symphony Orchestra of Innsbruck** (tel. 58 00 23) plays in the Congress Center, across from the *Landestheater,* between October and May (tickets 280-440AS; 30% discount for children and students). **Chamber music concerts** cost 160 to 260AS; the same discounts apply. The Spanish mall at Schloß Ambras holds **classical music concerts** most Tuesday nights in summer (140-600AS, 30% discount for students and children). Late June and mid-July bring the **International Dance Summer** to the Congress Center. Renowned dancers from Paris, New York, and Moscow perform in a full range of styles. (Modern dance 315-650AS, classical 540-1000AS; no student or rush tickets.) The **Volksgarten,** near Marktpl., has an open-air theater which presents free jazz, blues, and world music concerts from June to mid-July. The annual **Christmas market** (Nov. 22-Dec. 23) brings chestnuts and caroling.

■ Nightlife

Most visitors collapse into bed after a full day of Alpine adventure, but there is enough action to keep party-goers from pillows. Nightlife revolves around students, making the **university quarter** a mecca for late-night revelry. The **Viaduktbogen,** a cluster of bars and music joints along Ingenieur Etzel Str., is also a good bet.

Krah Vogel, Anichstr. 12 (tel. 58 01 49), off Maria-Theresien-Str. Amber walls and sleek black railings line this packed place. Dozens of couples flirt at the angled bar with fake hanging sunflowers. Big screen TV, outdoor tables, and a garden. Ice cream 38-56AS; beer 29-37AS. Open M-Sa 9:30am-1am, Su 4pm-1am.

Hofgarten Café (tel. 58 88 71), inside the *Hofgarten* park. Follow Burggrabenstr. around under the archway and past Universitätstr., enter the park after passing the Landestheater through the small gateway, and follow the path—you'll hear the crowd. A slightly upscale scene under a white tent with a constellation of Christmas-tree lights. Note: the park closes at 10pm—use the back entrance to get to the café. Snack food 50-100AS, beer 28-48AS, wine spritzers 31AS. Open summer 10am-2am, winter M-Sa 5pm-1am, Su 10am-6pm.

Treibhaus, Angerzellg. 8 (tel. 58 68 74), in an alley to the right of China Restaurant. Innsbruck's favorite alternateen hangout. A well-lit watering hole with colorful plastic squiggles hanging from the ceiling and a brightly illuminated tent outside. Jazz-oriented. Food 50-95AS. Open M-F 9am-1am, Sa-Su 10am-1am.

Die Alte Piccolo Bar, Selerg. 2 (tel. 58 21 63). Apparently the only gay bar in Innsbruck, located in the center of the *Altstadt.* Open Su-Th and Th-Sa 10pm-4am.

Jimmy's, Wilhelm-Greilstr. 17 (tel. 57 04 73), by Landhauspl. The front end of an old-fashioned yellow Opel sticks out of the bar. *Happy Days* meets Hard Rock; they elope and head for the Tirol. Packs in students with Italian, Mexican, and American food. The "Go to Hell" pasta is a fave. Burgers 76-104AS. Open M-F 11am-1am, Sa-Su 7pm-1am. AmEx, MC, Visa.

■ Near Innsbruck: Stams

When you're going for Baroque, you might as well go all out and head for **Stift Stams,** a magnificent monastery 34 km west of Innsbruck. Founded by the Tirolean Duke Meinhard II in 1273, the cloisters were completely restyled in the 18th century. The 26 Cistercian monks who reside there allow several guided tours per day through the ornate and majestic **Basilika** and the heavily frescoed **Fürstensaal.** The

> ### Three Men Plus Baby
>
> During the first week of the new year on Three Kings' Day, troupes of devout Austrian school children go door to door singing the story of Casper, Melchior, and Balthasar in exchange for charity. Donors receive a chalk inscription on their doors worth a year of good luck. The inscriptions read "wx—C+M+B—yz" where w, x, y, and z stand for the digits of that given year in order. So good luck for 1999 is 19—C+M+B—99. Write that on some doors!

basilica, restored for its 700th anniversary in 1974, features the Baroque masterwork of local artist Andrä Thamasch. Twelve of his gilded wooden statues line the walls of the **crypt** where Meinhard and his wife, among many others, are buried. A little farther down the nave, Thamasch's modest *Madonna* hangs on the wall—its strikingly asymmetrical composition makes it unique in its genre. Thamasch died while making it, leaving an empty space for St. John. At the far end of the church, the 14km. **tree of life** towers over the altar. Designed by Bartholomäus Steinle in 1613, the tree features 84 golden figures suspended against a blue plaster background added for structural support in the early 1700s. The **Rose Screen** was completed in 1716, and is comprised of almost 100 flower bulbs, each carved laboriously from a single piece of iron. Entrance to the cloisters is only permitted with the tour. (Oct.-Apr. at 9, 10, 11am, 2, 3, and 4pm; in May also at 5pm; June and Sept. also at 1 and 5pm.)

■ Seefeld in Tirol

With the '64 and '76 Olympiads padding its resume, ritzy Seefeld in Tirol lays a serious claim to winter-sports-mecca status. Innsbruck twice used Seefeld's terrain for nordic skiing events (although disappointing snowfall in '64 required an appalling 20,000 metric tons of imported snow). Skiing is the cash cow here, but lush meadows and breathtaking Alpine scenery invite travelers in all seasons. Haflinger mountain horses pulling Tirolean wagons on narrow cobblestone streets take visitors on the grand tour, past every spa and sports complex around (1hr. tour 400AS). Biannual festivals liven up the *Fußgängerzone* with giant ice sculptures in the winter and grand fireworks in July.

ORIENTATION AND PRACTICAL INFORMATION The **Hohe Munde, Wetterstein,** and **Karwendel** mountain ranges surround Seefeld 1180m above sea level. The **Wildsee,** a short walk south of the *Fußgängerzone,* provides swimming and a gorgeous promenade. **Innsbruck,** 26km away, runs 17 trains to Seefeld each day (40min., 6:32am-9:05pm, last return train from Seefeld at 8:12pm, 48AS). **Buses** leave from in front of the train station. To get to the *Fußgängerzone* and the center of town, head down Bahnhofstr. and you're good to go. Seefeld's main square, Dorfpl., will appear on your left at the first major intersection. Bahnhofstr. becomes Klosterstr. beyond Dorfpl., and the cross-street (the other main arm of the *Fußgängerzone*) is Münchenstr. to the right of the plaza and Innsbruckstr. to the left.

Seefeld's **tourist office,** Klosterstr. 43 (tel. 23 13; fax 33 55; email info@seefeld.tirol.at; http://tiscover.com/seefeld), is in the know. From the station, walk up Bahnhofstr. and past Dorfpl. (Open in summer and winter high seasons M-Sa 8:30am-6:30pm; mid-Sept. to mid-Dec. and Mar. to mid-June M-Sa 8:30am-12:15pm and 3-6pm.) You can **exchange money** at banks (open M-F 8am-12:30pm and 2-4pm) and at the post office until 5pm. **ATMs** are at every bank and across from the train station at the Sparkasse. You can find **taxis** in front of the train station or by calling 26 30, 22 21, or 27 00. You can **store luggage** (30AS) and **rent bikes** (90-160AS with train ticket, otherwise 150-200AS per day) at the station. If all the station bikes are rented, try **Sport Sailer** (tel. 25 30) in Dorfpl. A mountain bike costs 220AS for a full day, 350AS for the weekend. (Open during the high seasons M-F 9am-12:30pm and 2:30-6:30pm; off-season M-F 9am-noon and 3-6pm; in Aug. also 8-10pm; in Dec. also Sa 3-6pm.) The **Tip-Top Laundromat,** Andreas-Hofer-Str. 292 (tel. 20 44), is behind and to the right of the station. Leave a load to be wash-and-dried for 150AS. (Open M-F 8am-12:30pm and 2:30-6:30pm, Sa 9am-noon.) For a **snow report,** call 27 90. The **post office,** Klosterstr. 367 (tel. 28 28; fax 38 73) is right down the road from the tourist office. (Open M-F 8am-noon and 2-6pm; Dec. 16-Apr. 15 and July-Sept. also open Sa 9am-noon.) The **postal code** is A-6100, and the **telephone code** is 05212.

ACCOMMODATIONS AND FOOD Seefeld boasts seven five-star hotels (that's *thirty-five* stars!), but no hostel. This proliferation of constellations means the price of a hotel bed runs 540 to 4260AS depending on the season. *Pensionen* or *Privatzimmer* are the best budget option. Prices for these rooms average 220AS to 320AS per night in the summer; slap on about 50AS more in winter. Make reservations well in advance particularly if you're traveling alone, since singles are few and far between. The tourist office has a list of all accommodations; call ahead and the staff will help you find a room. Wherever you stay, inquire about a **guest card** *(Kurkarte)* for 10-20% discounts off skiing, swimming, concerts, and local attractions.

Several *Pensionen* cluster along Kirchwaldstr. To get there, walk from the Dorfpl. down Klosterstr. past the sports center, then clamber up the narrow, uphill road (Kirchwaldstr.). One of the best guest houses here is **Haus Felseneck,** Kirchwaldstr. 309 (tel. 25 40), the third house on the right. Each luxurious room has a balcony, TV, lace lampshades, bathroom, and a view you'll wish you could write a quick message on the back of, stamp, and send home. The friendly owners like to practice their English. (In summer singles 260AS; doubles 520AS; 4-person apartment with kitchen 750AS. Winter singles 360AS; doubles 740AS. Breakfast and shower included.) **Haus Carinthia,** Hocheggstr. 432 (tel. 29 55), is only a few minutes walk from the train station. Exit on the left, turn left onto Reitherspitzstr., left again on Milserstr., and then right onto Hocheggstr. Antlers still hang on the wall in tidy Tirolean rooms. (Summer singles 190AS, with bath 250AS; doubles 380AS, 500AS. Winter singles 290AS, 340AS; doubles 580AS, 680AS. Breakfast and shower included. Call ahead.) **Bozherhof,** Hocheggstr. 355 (tel. 29 41), offers guests the use of a kitchen, free parking, and enough breakfast to hold you until dinner. (Singles 250AS, with bath 260AS; doubles 500AS, 520AS. Winter, singles 300AS, 330AS; doubles 600, 660AS. Breakfast and shower included.)

Finding cheap food in Seefeld is tough. The entire *Fußgängerzone* is stocked with rows of pricey restaurants, outdoor cafés, and bars. **Luigi and Lois,** Innsbruckstr. 12 (tel. 22 58 67), operates on a goofy gimmick—Italian fare on the Luigi side and Tirolean fare *chez* Lois. The food is decent and the decor entertaining. Luigi's pasta costs 89-125AS; Lois' *Gröstl* is 98AS. (Kitchen open 10:30am-11pm, bar open 'til 1am. AmEx, MC, Visa.) Locals recommend *Wiener Schnitzel al fresco* at the **Tiroler Weinstube,** Dorfpl. 130 (tel. 22 08), next to the tourist office. Most dishes are 80-155AS, and daily menus including soup, salad, entree, and dessert cost 150-200AS. Some vegetarian offerings. (Open 9am-midnight. MC, Visa.) The **Albrecht Hat's supermarket,** Innsbruckstr. 24 (tel. 22 29), is located across from Sport Sailer just off Dorfpl. (Open M-Th 8:30am-6:30pm, F 8am-7:30pm, Sa 8am-6pm.)

Knee-Deep in Church

In 1384, Oswald Milser put Seefeld on the map. Although dutifully attending Easter Mass like a good li'l knight, Oswald fancied himself better than the masses. Rejecting the small host usually given to laypeople, he demanded the consecrated wafer reserved for the clergy, and the timid priest complied. When Oswald took the host in his mouth, he suddenly began to sink into the ground, deeper and deeper, until the priest pulled the now blood-red wafer from his mouth. Hailed as an acute example of the proverb "pride goeth before a fall," the miracle turned Seefeld into a pilgrimage site. The devout come to see the 0.5m hole in the ground (now covered by a protective grate) and the deep hand-print on the altar where the sinking Oswald tried to support himself. The Miraculous Host has also been preserved, in a monstrance made for it over 500 years ago.

SKIING, SIGHTS, AND ENTERTAINMENT The tourist office prints *Seefeld A-Z*, an unbelievably detailed listing of summer and winter activities. The extreme **Olympia Sport Center** (tel. 32 20; fax 32 28 83) is a popular attraction year-round, featuring an **indoor pool** with decorative boulders and greenhouse windows and a massive **sauna** complex, ready to stupify tired hikers and skiiers with heat. *(Pool open summer and winter 9:30am-10pm; fall and spring 1-10pm. 88AS with guest card, children 44AS. Sauna open daily 2-10pm. Sauna and pool 160AS with guest card, children 120AS.)* The Center screens **movies** nightly during the high seasons. *(80AS.)*

Summer in Seefeld brings a multitude of outdoor activities. The tourist office and the **Tirol Alpine School** run an excellent summer **hiking** program of four- to six-hour hikes that wind among local sky-scraping peaks, including the **Pleisenspitze** (2569m) and the **Gehrenspitze** (2367m). *(Hikes leave Tu-F at 8am mid-June to mid-September. Register by 5pm the day before the hike. 250AS with guest card.)* The **Kneipp Hiking Society** invites visitors to join its free weekly three- to five-hour outings, which depart from the train station Thursdays at 12:30pm. The **Bergbahn Rosshütte** (tel. (05242) 241 60) offers "four hours of mountain adventure", with its "Cable Car Experience." For 155AS (with guest card), participants ride a tram, a cable car, and the *Jochbahn* railway to heights of 2000m, followed by jaunts on several short trails. The **Strandbad Wildsee** (tel. 33 87) is open for swimming from 9:30am to 7pm. *(June-Sept. only. 30AS.)*

If not overwhelmed by Seefeld's immense sporting machinery, the Renaissance jock can plunge into the full program of cultural events around town. For the summer, the tourist office prints a pamphlet of events and a children's program that include nature adventure days, music, sports, and farm animals. When the day is done, gussy up and head to the **Tirolean Evenings** on Tuesday at Ferienhotel (behind the tourist office) or Thursday at Hotel Tirol (Müacherstr. 140; June-Sept. 9pm; 200AS). The Parish Church holds year-round **chamber music concerts** Fridays at 8:30pm, and free summertime **brass band concerts** occur in the Music Pavilion on Mondays at 8:30pm. During high seasons, the rustic **Bauerntheater** performs regional plays in regional dialect every week at the Olympic Center on Wednesday evenings. On the first Sunday in August, the **Blumencorso** sweeps through town, a parade of flower-bedecked floats, cars, and bicycles.

Seefeld offers two money-saving ski passes to the flocks of winter tourists. The **Seefelder Card** is valid for Seefeld, Reith, Mösern, and Neuleutasch. *(1-day pass 350AS, ages 5-15 210AS, ages 16-17 315AS.)* The **Happy Ski Pass** is valid for skiing at (take a deep breath) Seefeld, Reith, Mösern, Neuleutasch, Mittenwald, Garmisch-Zugspitze, Ehrwald, Lermoos, Biberwier, Bichlbach, Berwang, and Heiterwang. This pass is available for three to 20 days and requires a photograph. Three days of happy skiing cost 990AS, ages 5-15 620AS, ages 16-17 910AS. Smile. Twelve different **sports equipment rental shops** lease alpine and cross-country skis, snowboards, and toboggans at standardized rates. Downhill skis with poles and boots cost 100-200AS, children 80-130AS; boots 50-80AS; snowboard 200-300AS. A **ski bus** is free with the Seefeld guest card, and runs every 20 minutes daily from 9am to 4:40pm between the town center and the Rosshütte and Gschwandtkopf ski areas. For those who prefer their skiing on the level, choose from the 100km of *langlaufen* (cross-country skiing) trails. The tourist office has a trail map. *Seefeld A-Z* and the tourist office's winter calendar of events cover other winter activities, from skating to tobogganing to snow hiking.

THE LECHTALER ALPS

The Lechtaler Alps, a region of 3000m peaks and lake-speckled valleys, hugs the German border in northwestern Tirol. Friendly to mountain beasts and mythical dwarves—but not to rear-wheel-drive cars—the alpine terrain is four-fifths uninhabitable. As a result, guest beds are concentrated in large resort areas, and cheap lodgings are few and far between. Portions of the Lechtal do offer alternative accommodations; the Innsbruck branch of the **Tirol Information Service,** Adamg. 3-7, A-6020 Innsbruck (tel. 56 18 82), prints *Urlaub am Bauernhof* ("Vacation on the Farm").

The best time to visit the Lechtal is when the mountains are your only companions; consider a trip in the off-season, April to June or October to November. Carry your passport at all times, since you may jump over a border or two in the course of travel. The **Inn River,** the primary waterway of the valley, runs southwest to northeast from the Swiss frontier at Finstermünz to the German border by Kufstein. Cutting a swath of land through Innsbruck, Imst, and Landeck before heading to Switzerland, the Inn has served as a pivotal transport route for two millennia. Parallel to and north of the Inn, the **Lech River** has eroded its own wide valley. Between the lowlands of the Inn and Lech, the mountains are virtually people-free.

The Lechtaler Alps offer some of the best skiing in Austria and the world. For a 24-hour **weather report,** call (0512) 15 66. Swimming, skiing, hiking—all of this hearty cardiovascular activity will make you hungry. Try the *Tiroler Speckknödel* (bacon-fat dumplings), served either *zu Wasser* (in broth) or *zu Lande* (dry, with salad or sauerkraut); or try *Gröstl* (meat and potato hash with a fried egg dropped on top).

▓ Ehrwald

Of his hometown Ehrwald, poet Ludwig Ganghofer once said to God, "If You love me, please let me live here forever." His request went unheeded: he died abroad in 1920 and was buried near Munich. But some divine power has certainly smiled on the city. Other than a few damaged buildings, the World Wars spared the hamlet, and to date nothing has blemished Ehrwald's prized attraction, the majestic **Zugspitze** (2962m, Germany's highest). Of course, what could? It's a big mountain that lies along the German-Austrian border and brings 400,000 tourists a year. Many also flock like lemmings to the peak's substantial German resort **Garmisch-Partenkirchen.** Plucky Ehrwald responds, "Ehrwald—on the *sunny* side of the Zugspitze." While no meteorologist has confirmed this oddity, Ehrwald *is* more pleasant than its German counterpart in many ways: it's quieter, it boasts a faster cable car (the Tiroler Zugspitzbahn), and it's cheaper (rooms run 50-100AS less). Compare for yourself; trains cross between the countries nine times per day.

ORIENTATION AND PRACTICAL INFORMATION Ehrwald lies in a cul-de-sac of the Austrian Alpine railroad: all trains to and from major cities must pass through Garmisch-Partenkirchen in Germany, where Ehrwald-bound travelers must switch onto a two-car train. **Trains** go to **Garmisch-Partenkirchen** (25min., 5:55am-7:58pm, 37AS), **Innsbruck** (2hr., 5:55am-6:58pm, 118AS), **Munich** (2hr., 5:55am-7:58pm, 255AS), and **Salzburg** (4hr., 6:55am-6:58pm, 430AS). Ehrwald has few street signs. To reach the town center from the train station, bear left and cross the tracks onto Bahnhofstr., which then meets Hauptstr. After about 20 minutes, Hauptstr. veers left and uphill as it becomes Kirchpl. Autobahn A12 follows the Inn from Innsbruck to Mötz, the old market town. Bundesstr. 314 runs north from Mötz to Ehrwald, close to Germany and Garmisch-Partenkirchen. Bundesstr. 198 runs along the Loesach river. For a **taxi,** call 22 68 or 23 25. **Rent bikes** at **Zweirad Zirknitzer,** Zugspitzstr. 16 (tel. 32 19), across the tracks and up the hill. (70AS per half-day, 90AS per day. Mountain bikes 50AS per hr., 100-150AS per half-day, 200AS per day, 350AS per weekend. Lower rates for children's bikes.) The **tourist office,** Kirchpl. 1 (tel. 23 95; fax 33 14; email ehrwald@zugspitze.tirol.at; http://www.tiscover.com/ehrwald), lies a few steps beyond the church. The staff is eager to help with brochures. (Open M-F 8:30am-noon and 1:30-6pm; mid-June to Sept. and mid-Dec. to Feb. also open Sa.) **Currency exchange** is available at banks (open M-F 8am-noon and 2-4:30pm) and the post office. There is a 24-hour **ATM** at BTV, Kirchpl. 21a. The little Ehrwald **train station** (tel. 22 01 34) offers **luggage storage** (30AS; open M-Sa 6am-9pm, Su 7am-9pm). The **post office,** Hauptstr. 5 (tel. 33 66; fax 31 40), is on the right about 100m before the town center as you walk from the train station. (Open M-F 8am-noon and 2-5:30pm.) Ehrwald's **postal code** is A-6632, and its **telephone code** is 05673.

ACCOMMODATIONS AND FOOD Ehrwald is filled with kinda cheap guest houses. The tourist office has a complete listing of prices and locations. Wherever you stay, be sure to pick up a **guest card** for tourist discounts. **Gästehaus Konrad,** Kirweg 10 (tel. 27 71), is only a few minutes down Hauptstr. from the station toward the town center. After you pass the post office and SPAR market, take the first right onto Kirweg. Konrad is on your right, down a private driveway. Each room has a painted Alpine scene. Step out onto the balcony for the real thing: a phenomenal view of green fields, small villages, and mountains in every direction. You may never want to go back into that room. (Singles with shower 220-250AS, doubles 440-500AS. Breakfast included.) Camping is available—if you're willing to walk about 25 minutes uphill—at **Camping Dr. Lauth** (tel. 26 66; fax 266 64). Head left out of the train station and immediately turn left up the hill. Take the right-hand fork past Zweirad Zirknitzer and continue uphill (ignore the "Leaving Ehrwald" sign). As the road curves left at the Thörleweg intersection, the well-marked campground soon appears on the right. (Open 2pm-midnight. Phones, restaurant, and **laundry** on-site. 70AS per person; tent and car 70AS; tax 10.50AS.) The town center is filled with cafés and restaurants serving Tirolean specialties as well as pizza and *gelato*. The **Metzgerei Restaurant,** Hauptstr. 15 (tel. 23 41), serves a large variety of tradition in its friendly dining room, including several vegetarian entrees. The *Tiroler Knödel,* two balls of starch laced with succulent ham and served scalding hot over sauerkraut, are a bargain at 54AS. (Open 11:30am-8:30pm, limited menu from 2-5pm.) If you're planning a picnic on the summit of the Zugspitze, try the local **SPAR supermarket,** Hauptstr. 1 (tel. 27 40), next to the post office. (Open M-Th 8am-7pm, F 8am-7:30pm, Sa 7:30am-1pm; July to mid-Sept. and mid-Dec. to Mar. extended Sa hours 7:30am-6pm.)

SIGHTS AND ENTERTAINMENT The **Tiroler Zugspitzbahn** (tel. 23 09) is Ehrwald's leading tourist attraction and greatest engineering feat to date. This cable car climbs 2950m to the summit of the Zugspitze in a hold-your-breath (for some, hold-your-lunch) seven minutes and 12 seconds. It burns, dude. The outdoor platforms of the crowded restaurant (open mid-May to mid-Oct.) at the ride's end have what some deem the most breathtaking view on the continent: on a clear day, visibility extends from Salzburg to Stuttgart. Be sure to bring a sweater, since snow may still be on the ground. (Open late May to late Oct. and late Nov. to mid-Apr. daily 8:40am-4:40pm. Round-trip 410AS with guest card, ages 16-17 290AS, children 250AS.) The **Ehrwalder Almbahn** (tel. 24 68) doesn't climb quite so high ("only" 1510m), but the prices aren't so high either. (May-Oct. 9am-4:30pm; Dec.-Apr. 9am-4pm. 120AS with guest card, children 65AS.) To reach either cable car, hop on a Summerrund bus at the town green, across from the train station, or at any of the orange "H" signs scattered throughout town. (Schedules are at the stops. The cable cars are at either end of the line; 10AS.) In summer the Ehrwald tourist office organizes free **mountain bike tours** every Friday, leaving from the office at 8:30am, as well as daily guided mountain hikes. Registration for both is open until Thursday at 5pm at the tourist office. The tourist office also provides information on hiking, fishing, swimming, billiards, boats, skating, climbing, paragliding, horseback riding, squash, tennis, kayaking, and rafting in Ehrwald and neighboring areas. Visitors can **swim** outdoors at **Hotel Spielmann,** Wetterstr. 4 (tel. 22 25), or indoors at the **Familienbad Ehrwald,** Hauptstr. 21 (tel. 27 18), a short distance before the town center (look for the Sport Center sign).

For winter guests Ehrwald offers the happy **Happy Ski Pass.** The cheerful little card gives access to 128 lifts, 244km of alpine ski runs, 100km of cross-country trails, and several other winter time sports arenas. (For more information and prices, see **Seefeld,** p. 230.) You can rent **skis** at **Intersport Leitner,** in the main square at Kirchpl. 13 (tel./fax 23 71). (230-360AS per day for downhill skis or snowboards, 190AS for cross-country skis. Open M-Th 8:30am-noon and 2:30-6pm.)

■ Kitzbühel

When Franz Reischer arrived in Kitzbühel in 1892, his 2m snowshoes and wild ideas about sliding down mountains stirred up a fair amount of skepticism. Two years later the first ski-championship was held in town, and everyone wanted a piece of the big-shoe action. The six peaks surrounding Kitzbühel were named the "Ski-Circus," and life was never the same again. Now the annual international Hahnenkamm race (see p. 237) boasts the toughest course in the world, attracting amateurs, professionals, and spectators alike. Even so, Kitzbühel hasn't expanded much geographically—the town still makes do with only two traffic lights.

GETTING TO KITZBÜHEL

Several rail lines converge on Kitzbühel. The routes from Munich and Innsbruck funnel through Wörgl and into town before running on to Zell am See. Kitzbühel has two **train stations.** From Salzburg, you arrive first at the **Hauptbahnhof;** from Innsbruck or Wörgl, at the **Hahnenkamm Bahnhof. Buses** stop next to both train stations. Kitzbühel lies on Rte. 161 north/south and the east terminus of Rte. 170. By **car** from Salzburg, take Rte. 21 south to 312 west; at St. Johann in Tirol, switch to 161 south, which leads straight to Kitzbühel. From Innsbruck, take Autobahn A12 east to Wörgl and switch to either Rte. 312 or Rte. 170.

ORIENTATION AND PRACTICAL INFORMATION

Kitzbühel sits pretty on the hilly banks of the Kitzbüheler Ache River. Nearby, the warm, mud-bearing Schwarzsee proffers luscious, curative waters. The town is in the shade of a number of impressive peaks, including the Kitzbüheler Horn (1996m) and the Steinbergkogel (1971m). The center of town *(Fußgängerzone)* hosts tons of cafés and benches where the paparazzi lie in wait for strolling celebrities. To reach the *Fußgängerzone* from the main train station, head straight out the front door down Bahnhofstr. and turn left at the main road. At the traffic light, turn right and follow the road uphill. The city center is a maze of twisting streets; if you get confused, look for the *Zentrum* (center) signs to point you back to the middle.

Trains: Hauptbahnhof (tel. 64 05 53 85) and **Hahnenkamm Bahnhof.** To: **Innsbruck** (1hr., 12 per day, 5:12am-11:30pm, 134AS); **Salzburg** (2½hr., 17 per day, 12:39am-8:23pm, 240AS); **Vienna** (6hr., 13 per day, 12:39am-8:23pm, 580AS); and **Zell am See** (45 min., 14 per day, 12:39am-8:23pm, 100AS).

Taxis: In front of the *Hauptbahnhof,* or call 661 53, 69 69, or 661 28.

Car Rental: Hertz, Josef-Pirchlstr. 24 (tel. 48 00; fax 721 44), at the traffic light on the way into town from the main station. Open M-F 8am-noon and 2-6pm, Sa 9am-noon. 20% discount with valid guest card. AmEx, MC, Visa.

Bike Rental: At the main train station. 150AS per day, with train ticket for that day 90AS. Mountain bikes 200AS, 160AS.

Parking: There are 4 lots in Kitzbühel: **Griesgasse, Pfarrau, Hahnenkamm,** and **Kitzbühlerhorn.** The latter 2 are next to the 2 major ski lifts. In winter a free park-and-ride service operates between the 2 and 2. Free parking at the Fleckalmbahn for the cable car (open 8am-6pm). Winter parking at Hahnekamm is 40AS per day.

Tourist Office: Hinterstadt 18 (tel. 62 15 50 or 622 72; fax 623 07), near the *Rathaus* in the *Fußgängerzone.* Free room reservation service; after hours, try the free telephone at the **electronic accommodations board** (operates daily 6am-10pm). Maps and English brochures are also available at the board. A small **bank** in the office exchanges money during the high season. Free 1hr. **city tours** in English start at the office in summer daily at 8:45am. From mid-July to mid-Aug. there's a cultural tour Friday at 9:15am. Open July-Sept. and mid-Dec. to late Apr. M-F 8:30am-6:30pm, Sa 8:30am-noon and 4-6pm, Su 10am-noon and 4-6pm; Oct. to mid-Dec. and late Apr. to June M-F 8:30am-12:30pm and 2:30-6pm.

Budget Travel: Reisebüro Eurotours, Rathauspl. 5 (tel. 713 04; fax 71 30 44). Provides discounts on package tours and makes local room reservations for free.

Exchanges currency at so-so rates. Open M-F 8:30am-noon and 3-6:30pm, Sa 8:30am-noon and 4:30-6:30pm, Su 9am-1pm.

Currency Exchange: All banks, travel agencies, and the post office. The post office and most banks have **ATMs** outside.

Luggage Storage: At both stations. Open 5am-12:30pm. 30AS.

Laundromat: Kleider-Fix, Wegscheidg. 3 (tel. 35 20). Wash and dry 180AS; wash only 150AS. Open M-Th 7am-6pm, F 7am-5pm, Sa 9-11am.

Emergencies: Police, tel. 133. **Fire,** tel. 122. **Red Cross Ambulance Service,** Wagnerstr. 18 (tel. 40 11). **Medical,** tel. 144. **Auto Repair,** tel. 123.

Ski Conditions: tel. 181 (German) or 182 (English).

Post Office: Josef-Pirchlstr. 11 (tel. 627 12; fax 715 58), between the stoplight and the *Fußgängerzone*. Bus schedules, fax, and a self-serve copier inside. Open M-F 8am-noon and 2-6pm, Sa 8-11am. **Currency exchange** open M-F 8am-noon and 4-5pm. **Postal Code:** A-6370.

Telephone Code: 05356.

ACCOMMODATIONS AND CAMPING

Kitzbühel has almost as many guest beds (7445) as inhabitants (8000), but the only youth hostel is far from town and restricted to groups. Pricey hotels with fancy pastel facades dominate the town center. Austrians claim that in Kitzbühel, you pay German prices for German comfort (read: twice the price, half the comfort). Rooms during the summer generally run 200 to 300AS per person; expect to shell out an extra 100AS during the winter. The Hahnenkamm Ski Competition in January creates a bed shortage so great that many residents vacate their homes and rent to visitors. During the year, cheaper lodging is also available a short bus ride away in nearby **Kirchberg.** Wherever you stay, be sure to ask for your **guest card** upon registration—it entitles you to discounts on all sorts of local attractions.

Hotel Kaiser, Bahnhofstr. 2 (tel. 647 08 or 647 09), 2min. down the street from the main station. The native English-speaking owner and staff, all former backpackers, are happy to greet road-weary travelers. Terrace and an inexpensive bar. Rates are generally 200AS per person, although there may be winter surcharges. Popular with groups. Sometimes closes during summer and off-season months like Oct. and early Dec., so be sure to call ahead first. Nov.-Dec. brings a special deal for backpackers looking for work in the area: 120AS per person for a 4-bed dorm, plus free career advice from those who've done it before. **Laundry** facilities 75AS (wash and dry). Parking available. AmEx, DC, MC, Visa.

Pension Hörl, Josef-Pirchlstr. 60 (tel. 631 44). From the main station, take a left after Hotel Kaiser; Pension Hörl will be on the left. Quiet and unassuming with old motel-style furnishings and drab balconies. Reasonable rates. If they don't have a free bed, they'll try to put you up at their nearby **Gästehaus Hörl** (Bahnhofstr. 8). 180-220AS per person, with private shower 190-260AS. Add 40AS in winter. Breakfast included. English spoken.

Pension Neuhaus "Motorbike," Franz-Reischstr. 23 (tel. 622 00). Facing the tourist office, walk through the archway to the left and follow Franz-Reischstr. to the right (look for Wienerwald). The *Pension* is on the left, near the chairlift. Its name is not capriciously chosen—the English-speaking proprietors here really like motorcycles. Sporting chic Kawasakis, if that can indeed be said, the chopper crowd is more hubris than Harley. Rooms house up to 6 people. 200-300AS per person. Winter 300-400AS. Prices vary depending on length of stay. Breakfast included.

Camping Schwarzsee, Reitherstr. 24 (tel. 628 06; fax 644 79 30). Train: "Schwarzsee" (1 stop past "Hahnenkamm" coming from the main train station) and walk toward the lake. If you're up for the walk, turn right at the tourist office and pass under the archway. Bear right at the Wienerwald up Franz-Reischstr., which becomes Schwarzseestr. and leads to the lake, or follow the signs from Franz-Reichstr. to the Waldweg zum See (forest path to the lake). 88AS, ages 2-12 67AS, under 2 free; guest tax 6AS; tents 95AS; caravans 185-195AS; dogs 40AS. Aug. 16-June 80AS per person, all other prices the same.

FOOD

Although many of Kitzbühel's restaurants prepare gourmet delights at astronomical prices, cheaper places pepper the area surrounding the *Fußgängerzone*.

Huberbräu-Stüberl, Vorderstadt 18 (tel. 656 77). Located smack in the center of town, Huberbräu offers high-quality traditional cuisine at comparably low prices. A local hangout. Besides their *Wiener Schnitzel* (98AS) and pizza margherita (65AS), check out the incredibly filling *prix fixe* menu—soup, entree, potato, and dessert for 85AS. Open 9am-midnight.

Café-Restaurant Prima, Bichlstr. 22 (tel. 638 85), on the 2nd floor. Inexpensive meals on a sunny patio or inside at coffeeshop booths. This self-serve eatery chain has a wide selection of food, including spaghetti (60AS), and *Wiener Schnitzel* with soup, salad, and dessert (85AS). Open 9am-10pm.

La Fonda, Hinterstadt 13 (tel. 736 73). An eclectic eatery deep in the heart of Kitzbühel, down the road from the tourist office. Serves cheap, snack-style meals like hamburgers, nachos, spare ribs, curry, and tsatsiki. The Tirol-Mex tacos don't taste quite like the ones they make in Texas, but you can afford to try them anyway—nothing on the menu is over 80AS. Open noon-midnight.

Markets

SPAR Markt, Bichlstr. 22 (tel. 74 88), on the corner of Ehrenbachg. and Bichlstr. Open M-F 8am-6:30pm, Sa 7:30am-1pm.

Billa Markt, Hammerschmiedstr. 3 (tel. 642 54), next to Hotel Hummer. Open M-W 8am-7pm, Th 7:30am-7pm, F 7:30am-7:30pm, Sa 7:30am-5pm.

SKIING, SIGHTS, AND ENTERTAINMENT

Few visitors to Kitzbühel remain at ground level for long. The Kitzbühel **ski area,** jovially dubbed the "Ski Circus," is one of the best in the world. Site of the first ski championships in 1894, the range challenges skiers and hikers with an ever-ascending network of lifts, runs, and trails. These very mountains honed the childhood skills of Olympic great Toni Sailer. Since 1931, Kitzbühel has hosted the **Hahnenkamm Ski Competition,** part of the annual World Cup. The competition turns the town into a rollicking seven-day party. Entry tickets are available at the gate.

Amateurs can also partake of Kitzbühel's skiing. The best deal is the new **Kitzbüheler Alpen SkiPass,** which gives access to 260 lifts in 22 villages. *(1990AS, children 995AS; good for any 6 days of the ski season.)* A one-day ski pass *(385-410AS, children 205AS)* grants you free passage on 64 lifts and on shuttle buses that connect them. Lift ticket prices drop after the first day. You can purchase passes at any of the lifts or at the *Kurhaus* **Aquarena.** *(Pool, sauna, solarium; open May-Oct. 9:30am-8pm; 80AS, 70AS with guest card, children 50AS, 45AS.)* You can **rent skis** at the Hahnenkamm lift or from virtually any sports shop in the area. Try **Kitzsport Schlechter,** Jochbergerstr. 7 (tel. 22 04 11). *(Open M-F 8:30am-noon and 2:30-6pm, Sa 8:30am-12:30pm.)* Downhill equipment rental runs 170-500AS per day; lessons cost 500AS, snowboards 180AS to 350AS. Ask at the tourist office about prefab **ski packages:** one week of lodging, ski passes, and instruction (available right before Christmas and after Easter). The rock-bottom rate for a week-long package without instruction is 3900AS.

For summer visitors, an extensive network of 70 **hiking trails** snakes up the mountains surrounding Kitzbühel. The tourist office provides maps with suggestions in English, but some of the best views are from the Kampenweg and Hochetzkogel trails. Most are accessible by Bichalm bus which leaves from the Hahnenkamm parking lot. *(Every hr. 8am-5:10pm; 26AS, with guest card 20AS.)* You can also take the Hahnenkammbahn. *(8am-5:30pm, 160AS up or round-trip, with guest card 140AS, children 80AS.)* You might also consider climbing up (about 2hr. of varying terrain). At the top are two cafeteria-style restaurants and the free **Bergbahn Museum Hahnenkamm.** Historical information on the cable car pales in comparison to video clips of past Hahnenkamm races and a ski-simulator (10AS). Assume the tuck position, look through the viewer, and experience three minutes of a breathtaking virtual run down the

Hahnenkamm. The **Kitzbüheler Hornbahn lift** ascends to the **Alpenblumengarten,** where more than 120 different types of flowers blossom each spring. *(Open late-May to mid-Oct.; cable car 80AS per section; gondola 120AS, with guest card 105AS, children 80AS.)* The smaller **Gaisberg, Resterhöhe,** and **Streiteck** lifts run in the summer. A three-day **summer holiday pass** is valid for unlimited use of all cable cars, free Bichalm bus service, and Aquarena pool entrance. *(390AS, children 195AS.)* Guest card holders can take advantage of the tourist office's *wunderbar* **mountain-hiking program.** *(Mid-May to mid-Oct. M-F at 8:45am from the tourist office; call ahead for weekend hikes (min. 5 people). Free, but you pay for any cable car rides.)* Daily hikes led by Pepi, Klaus, and Madeleine (3-5hr.) cover over 100 routes and come in two flavors: easy and moderate. Former Olympic ski champion Ernst Hinterseer (tel. 629 20) leads hikes down the Streif downhill course by request. **Mountain bike trails** abound; rent a bike from **Stanger Radsport,** Josef-Pirchlstr. 42 (tel. 25 49), for 250AS per day. *(Open M-F 8am-noon and 1-6pm, Sa 9am-noon.)* A booklet detailing bike paths through the Kitzbüheler and other Alps is available at the tourist office (54AS). The tourist office also leads free guided cycle tours. *(June-Sept. M, W, and Sa at 9:30am; call a day in advance.)*

Way down below, the **Schwarzsee** (Black Lake), 2.5km northwest of Kitzbühel, is famed for its healing mud packs. *(Open 7am-8pm. 45AS, with guest card 40AS, children 12AS; discounts after 1pm; more discounts after 5pm. Electric boats 80AS for 30min., 150AS for 1hr.; rowboats 45AS, 85AS.)* Float in the deep blue water and gaze at the snow-capped mountains high above. (Same directions as to Camping Schwarzsee.)

Kitzbühel's stark and somber church steeples dominate the town's diminutive skyline. The **Pfarrkirche** and the **Liebfrauenkirche** (Church of Our Lady) lie in an ivy-enclosed courtyard surrounded by an old-fashioned cemetery. Between the churches stands the **Ölberg Chapel,** dating from 1450 with frescoes from the late 1500s. The town built its **fountain** in the *Hinterstadt* to mark its 700th anniversary in 1971. The local **Heimatmuseum,** Hinterstadt 34, stocks its wares in Kitzbühel's oldest house, which dates from the 12th century. *(Open M-Sa 9am-noon. 30AS, with guest card 25AS, children 5AS.)* Rustic and rusty tools from days of yore are displayed, including prehistoric European mining equipment and the first metal bobsled.

Eclecticism reigns at the *gratis* **music concerts** during July and August; you might find anything from folk harpists to Sousa bands. *(Every Friday at 8:30pm, weather permitting, in the center of town.)* Check for signs around town, or call the tourist office for the day's performers. **Casino Kitzbühel** is near the tourist office. *(Open daily July-Sept. 7pm-late. Monday is ladies' night: free glass of champagne; Tuesday is men's night: free glass of beer. No cover. 18 or older. Semi-formal.)* Go on, raise the stakes—you've got to finance that lift ticket for tomorrow. God is on your side. At the end of July, the **Austrian Open** Men's Tennis Championships come to town, frequently drawing such athletes as Austrian Thomas Muster and Goran Ivanesevic to the Kitzbühel Tennis Club (tel. 633 25; fax 661 25; email ticket-tennis@kitzbuehel.netwing.at; http://www.atp-turnier-kitzbuehel.com). Nearby, the 18-hole Golfclub Kitzbühel Schwarzsee offers a 30% discount with guest card. From mid-September until June trips to the driving range are 100AS.

■ Near Kitzbühel: Kirchberg

Only 6km from the center of Kitzbühel, the village of Kirchberg provides easy, bike-able access to all of the skiing attractions with less hassle and cheaper accommodations. Wide streets and small buildings are surrounded by open fields and matchstick trees. The babbling, walled Aschauer Ache (brook) runs through the middle of town. To get to Kirchberg, take the **bus** from any stop in Kitzbühel (20min., 6:20am-6:20pm, 25AS). The **train** runs almost every hour as well (10min., 8:24am-11:30pm). Find hiking maps (80AS) at the **tourist office,** Hauptstr. 8 (tel. 23 09 or 26 88; fax 37 32; open M-F 8:30am-6pm, Sa 8:30am-noon). **Bike rental** is at **Sport Rieser,** Landstr. 12 (tel. 26 78; fax 26 78 11; open M-F 8am-noon and 3-6pm, Sa 8am-noon; 130AS per day) or at the **train station** (150AS, 120AS with a train ticket). Skiers and hikers can ride the **Gaisberglift** (open 8:30am-5pm; 60AS, children 30AS) or the **Fleckalmbahn** (open 8:30am-5pm; 160AS, children 80AS). Tennis, minigolf, bowling, and horseback riding are also available. A **24-hour accommodations board** includes a free courtesy phone for making reservations. A **currency exchange** sits behind the tourist office at the **post office** (tel. 22 66; open M-F 8am-noon and 2-6pm). **Taxis** wait for you at tel. 27 11, 33 33, and 25 52. **Public toilets** are also behind the tourist office. The **postal code** is 6365. The **telephone code** is 05357.

Cheap accommodations can be found along Reitherstr. and Reitherg. (turn left down Hauptstr. from the tourist office and left again at the 1st intersection). **Haus Schipflinger,** Reitherg. 86 (tel. 31 80), offers first-rate doubles with breakfast (bath in hall) for 360AS in summer and 400AS in winter. **Haus Holzastner,** Reitherg. 64 (tel. 29 78) offers modest rooms at better prices. 300AS in summer, 360AS in winter. Breakfast and (hall) shower included.

THE ZILLERTAL ALPS

The Zillertal (Ziller River Valley) Alps are a popular destination for Austrians seeking a weekend escape from camera-toting international tourists. Transportation in the region is simple and convenient, thanks to the **Zillertalbahn** (better known by its nickname, the **Z-bahn**), an efficient network of private buses and trains connecting all the villages (tel. (052) 24 46 06; railpasses not valid). The starting point is **Jenbach,** and the route's southern terminus is **Mayrhofen** (round-trip 118AS). You can reach Jenbach from **Innsbruck** (30min., 60AS, Eurailpass valid). The Z-bahn has two types of trains, the **Dampfzug** and the **Triebwagen.** The Dampfzug is an old, red steam train targeted at tourists; it costs twice as much and moves half as fast. The Triebwagen and the Z-bahn Autobus have the same rates, and one or the other leaves daily every hour from 6am to 8pm.

In the Zillertal, skiing reigns supreme. If you plan to ski in the area for more than three days, the most economical choice is the **Zillertal Super Skipass** (tel. 716 50), available at any valley lift station and valid on all of the area's 151 lifts (4 days 1210AS, 7 days 1860AS, 10 days 2450AS, discounts for children). The cost of the lift ticket includes unlimited use of the Z-bahn transportation network. The Zillertal Alps also have some of the best **hiking** in western Austria—the region claims more footpaths than roads and more Alpine guides than police officers. The popular four-out-of-six-day **Z-Hiking Ticket** is valid on all lift stations in the Zillertal, including Zell am Ziller, Fügen, Mayrhofen, Gerlos, and Hintertux (360AS, children ride free with the purchase of 2 regular tickets; 590AS for unlimited local transportation as well). Procure passes at any lift or at the railway stations in Zell am Ziller and Mayrhofen. When strolling around the mountain paths, be especially careful where you place your feet—don't dislodge any stones into the **Wetter See** (Weather Lake), under the shadow of Mount Gerlos. According to local lore, anyone who throws a rock into its waters will be pummeled by torrential thunderstorms, hail, and winds.

■Zell am Ziller

Twenty kilometers south of Jenbach and deep in the Ziller valley rests the quiet resort town of Zell am Ziller. Z.a.Z.'s brief commercial zone along the river soon gives way to fields of tall grass and clusters of chocolate-shuttered Alpine houses. Founded by monks in the second half of the 8th century, Zell soon fell to materialism in the 1600s when it became a flourishing gold-mining town. It has mostly backed away from this commercial orientation over the past few centuries, however, and the beautiful and unassuming locale now stands out as one of the least egregious ski-towns in Austria. Local festivals like the *Gauderfest* and the autumn *Almatrieb* offset flashier, more modern growths like the popular high tech ski slopes and the recently established Paragliding World Championships.

ORIENTATION AND PRACTICAL INFORMATION Zell stands at the south end of the Zillertal, between Jenbach and Mayrhofen. Those traveling by train should get off at Jenbach and switch to the **Zillertalbahn** (Z-bahn) train or bus (tel. 22 11; Jenbach to Zell am Ziller 49AS; see **The Zillertal Alps** above for more information), which leaves from the front of the train station. Z-bahn trains and buses leave every hour for Jenbach or Mayrhofen. Railpasses are not valid in this region. For a **taxi**, call 26 25, 23 45, or 22 55. **Bike rental** is either at the train station (150AS per day) or at **SB-Markt Hofer,** Gerlosstr. 30 (tel. 22 20), across from the campground. (Mountain bikes 170AS per day; open M-F 7am-noon and 2:30-6:15pm.) The center of Zell am Ziller is **Dorfplatz,** which can easily be reached by walking straight out of the train station down Bahnhofstr. Dorfpl. intersects with Zell's main drag, Gerlosstr., toward the river and Unterdorfstr. near the railroad tracks. The town **tourist office** is at Dorfpl. 8a (tel. 22 81; fax 22 81 80; email tourist.info.zell@netway.at; http://www.tiscover.com/zell). From the rail station, head right along Bahnhofstr., and right at the end. The office is on your left, just before the tracks. Pick up a town map, skiing information, and a Frühstückspension list if you want to track down a room on your own, although the staff will make reservations for free. (Open May-Nov. M-F 8:30am-12:30pm and 2:30-6pm, Sa 9am-noon and 4-6pm; Dec.-Apr. M-F 8am-noon and 2-6pm, Sa 9am-noon and 4-6pm.) **Christophorus Reisen,** Bahnhofstr. 2 (tel. 25 20), handles all **budget travel** concerns. Banks offer the best rates for **currency exchange** (open M-F 8am-noon and 2-5pm), and most have 24-hour **ATMs. Luggage storage** (30AS) is at the train station. In an **emergency,** call 22 12; for an **ambulance,** call 23 45. The **post office** (tel. 23 33) is at Unterdorf 2. (Open M-F 8am-noon and 2-6pm; in summer also Sa 9-11am.) The **postal code** is A-6280. The **telephone code** is 05282.

ACCOMMODATIONS AND FOOD Zell am Ziller has no shortage of lodgings. To reach **Haus Huditz,** Karl-Platzer-Weg 1 (tel. 22 28), cross the rail tracks by the tourist office and continue onto Gerlosstr.; bear left onto Gauderg. (at the Mode Journal building) and look for Karl-Platzer-Weg on the left (10min.). The owner provides beverages, conversation *(auf Deutsch),* cable TV (with CNN) downstairs, and luscious down comforters. Most rooms have balconies with mountain views. (Singles 200AS 1st night, then 180AS; winter 210AS, 180AS. Doubles 380AS, 340AS; winter 390AS, 350AS. Breakfast and shower included. Reception 8am-noon and 1-10pm.) **Camping Hofer,** Gerlosstr. 33 (tel. 22 48; fax 224 88), offers a space for your tent only a block or so from the town center. **Laundry** (70AS), showers, barbecues, free bike tours, weekly hikes, and even a house band (the inimitable **Hans & Didi**) round out the offerings. There's a grocery across the street. (Summer high-season 55AS per person; winter high-season 60AS. Off-season 50-55AS. 60-80AS per campsite. Guest tax 12AS.)

When you stop for a bite to eat, savor some local specialties. **Gasthof Kirchenwirt,** Dorfpl. 18 (tel. 22 80), serves up *Zillertaler Kasrahmspätzln,* doughy noodles cooked with onions and garnished with cheese, for 80AS. (Open 8am-midnight.) A traditional summer dish is the *Scheiterhaufen,* a monstrous mixture of rolls, apples, eggs, milk, lemon, cinnamon, sugar, butter, and raisins, drizzled with rum. *Zillertaler Krapfen* are sweet, heavy doughnuts, available in every bakery. All sorts of red meat outlets flank **Dorfplatz.** The cheapest place around is **SB Restaurant Zeller Stuben,** Unterdorf 12 (tel. 22 71), which serves big, buffet-style portions (*Knödeln mit Sauerkraut* 50AS, *Gulaschsuppe* 35AS). The less casual restaurant upstairs features five daily *Menüs* including soup, entree, and dessert for 90-170AS. (Children's and vegetarian menus available. Open 11am-9pm.) Cap off dinner with a decadent visit to **Café-Konditorei Gredler,** Unterdorf 10 (tel. 24 89), where 1995 Confectioner of the Year Tobias Gredler whips up gorgeous desserts for patrons to enjoy on the riverside patio (hazelnut creamcake 34AS, intricate sundaes 50-100AS; open 10am-11pm). The local **SPAR Markt** is close to the tourist office, across from the brewery on Roherstr. (Open M-F 7:30am-12:30pm and 2-6:30pm, Sa 7:30am-12:30pm and 2-5pm.)

SKIING AND ENTERTAINMENT Zeller **skiing** comes in two packages: **day passes** for shorter visits, valid on the Kreuzjoch-Rosenalm and Gerlosstein-Sonnalm slopes (1 day 350AS, children 210AS; 2 days 650AS, 390AS; 3 days 915AS, 550AS); and **Super Skipasses** for longer visits (see **The Zillertal Alps,** p. 239). Single tickets are available for non-skiers who tag along to watch. Obtain passes at the bottom of the **Kreuzjoch**

(tel. 716 50), **Gerlosstein** (tel. 22 75), or **Ramsberg** (tel. 27 20) cable cars. The lifts are all open from 8:30am to 5pm. **Rent skis** at any of Zell's sporting goods stores. Try **Pendl Sport,** Gerlosstr. 3 (tel. 22 87; open M-F 8am-noon and 2:30-6:30pm, Sa 8am-noon and 3-6pm, Su 9-11am and 4-6pm; MC, Visa). **Summer skiing** is possible at the **Hintertux Glacier,** 15km south of Zell am Ziller and accessible by Z-bahn and BundesBus (tel. (05287) 85 06 for lift tickets; 1-day lift tickets 390AS, youth 330AS, children 260AS).

Register in any town hotel or Pension to get a **guest card,** which snags you a free **hike** led by the tourist office (June-Sept.; register one day in advance at the office). Two of the three ski lifts in Zell's vicinity offer **Alpine hiking:** the **Kreuzjochbahn** (tel. 716 50; open 8:40am-12:15pm and 1-5:10pm; round-trip 150AS, to mid-station 100AS) and the **Gerlossteinbahn** (tel. 22 75; open 8:30am-12:20pm and 1-5pm; round-trip 100AS). The **Paragliding World Championships** glide into Zell during the last week of June, when many a modern-day Icarus fills the skies. You can try too— tandem flights cost 700-1500AS for five to 25-minute rides. The term "take-out" will develop a whole new meaning when you trust your life to the gliding guides at **Pizza-Air,** Zelbergeben 4 (tel. 228 90; fax 228 94; book your flight at Gerlosstr. 7).

For a glimpse of Zell am Ziller's history, take a tour of the nearby **gold mine** (tel. 230 10; fax 230 14; 2hr. tours leave daily on the hr. 9am-4pm; 130AS, children 65AS; reserve in advance for English tours). The eclectic journey begins at a petting zoo and adjacent cheese factory before proceeding on a scenic 45-minute hike down to the mine entrance. For liquid gold, visit the town on the first weekend in May for the **Gauderfest,** when the whole town gets sauced in a three-day celebration of cold, frothy beverages. The name is not derived from the German word *"Gaudi"* (fun) but from the farmer's estate that owns the local private brewery. The Bräumeister's vats, Tirol's oldest, concoct the beloved and rather potent Gauderbock for the occasion. The festival even has its own jingle: *"Gauderwürst und G'selchts mit Kraut,/ hei, wia taut dösmunden,/ und 10 Halbe Bockbier drauf,/ mehr braucht's nit zum G'sundsein!"* ("Gauder sausage and smoked pork with sauerkraut, / Hey, how good it tastes,/ and 10 pints of beer to go with it,/ what more could you need for your health!") The rhyme is in near-incomprehensible dialect, but fear not—pronunciation deteriorates as the festivities wear on, so by midnight you'll blend in perfectly. The festival's highlight is the **Ranggeln,** traditional wrestling for the title of "Hogmoar." There are also animal fights (attended by a veterinary surgeon) and customary activities like the **Grasausläuten** (ringing bells in order to wake the grass up and make it grow). Revelry continues into the night with Tirolean folk singing and dancing. By June, at least half of the residents are sober enough to court the tourist trade.

THE HOHE TAUERN NATIONAL PARK

The enormous **Hohe Tauern range** is part of the Austrian Central Alps, comprising parts of Carinthia, Salzburg, and Tirol. This range, spanning about 10 towns across the south of Austria, boasts 246 glaciers and 304 mountains over 3000m. Expanses of ice, mountain pasture land with Alpine heaths of grass, and forested bulwarks partition the Ice-Age valleys. The heart of this Alpine landscape remains largely unspoiled, a fact that prompted conservationists to lobby for the creation of a **national park.** In Salzburg and Carinthia, between 1958 and 1964, large tracts of mountain land were declared preserves, and on October 21, 1971, the provincial government leaders of Carinthia, Salzburg, and Tirol signed an agreement at Heiligenblut to "conserve for present and future generations the Hohe Tauern as a particularly impressive and varied region of the Austrian Alps." Thus designated, the Hohe Tauern National Park became the largest national park in all of Europe, officially enclosing 29 towns and 60,000 residents. The *Glocknergruppe,* in the heart of the park, boasts the highest of the Hohe Tauern peaks (at 3797m). A number of lakes crowd together amid the Glocknergruppe, including the Weißsee, the Tauernmoos See, and the Stausee. The spectacular **Gloßglockner Straße** runs north to south through this region, and the **Krimmler Wasserfälle** is in the far west.

The Hohe Tauern peaks are accessible by **car, bus,** and, in certain parts, **train.** Schnellstr. 167 runs north to south, intersecting Schnellstr. 168, which runs west to Krimml. If you drive, make sure your brakes work, as there are blind spots. Don't muck around in the car or you could die. Concentrate. Shift to low gear, drive slowly, brake occasionally, and never, ever pass anyone. The federal **BundesBus** travels the main arteries flowing through the Hohe Tauern. Bus #3230 (162AS) runs from **Böckstein** to **Badgastein** roughly once an hour, and bus #4094 (58AS) runs from **Zell am Ziller** to **Krimml** five times a day. Buses also run from **Zell am See** to Krimml (10 per day, 100AS). A rail line from Zell am See terminates at Krimml; **trains** run nine times per day in each direction (190AS round-trip). Another line runs south from **Salzburg** through Badgastein to **Spittal an der Drau,** with trains approximately every two hours. For general information about the park, contact Nationalparkverwaltung Hohe Tauern, 5741 Neukirchen Nr. 306, Austria (tel. (06565) 655 80; fax 65 58 18).

■ Großglockner Straße

Each day more than 3000 visitors pack up their cars for a full-day sail among the Austrian Alps along the breath-taking **Großglockner Straße,** one of the most beautiful highways in the world. Skirting the country's loftiest mountains, Bundesstr. 107 (its less catchy moniker) winds for 50km amid silent Alpine valleys, meadows of edelweiss, tumbling waterfalls, and a staggering glacier. The slow, steady climb is choked with rubber-neckers and over-ambitious cyclists soaking up the stupifying views. Many of the high-mountains-sweeping-panorama-hairpin-turn-sports-car commercials (you thought German words were long) are filmed here. Switzerland and France used the Großglockner as a model when engineering their own mountain highways. Consider the Austrian work ethic that made them possible: in only five years (1930-35), during a global economic crisis, over 3000 workers constructed the mother-Bahn.

The trip up to Kaiser-Franz-Josefs-Höhe (the midway point of the Großglockner Straße) and Edelweißspitze (the highest point) takes you from the flora and fauna of Austria into Arctic-like environments (never exceeding 50°F even during the hottest summers). Although tours generally run from **Zell am See** or **Lienz** to the park, the highway is officially only the 6.4km stretch from **Bruck an der Großglockner** to **Heiligenblut.** Coming from Zell am See, you'll pass the **Alpine Nature Exhibit** (2300m) on the way up to Kaiser-Franz-Josefs-Höhe. The small museum features well-designed nature exhibits, a 25-minute movie (in German), and frightening photos of hikers who forgot to wear sunblock. If you take the bus up here in the summer, you'll have half an hour to roam through the exhibits before the bus leaves for Kaiser-Franz-Josefs-Höhe. (Open 9am-5pm. Free. English headphones 20AS.) Once you reach Kaiser-Franz-Josefs-Höhe, you can gaze on Austria's highest peak, the **Großglockner** (3797m), and ride the **Gletscherbahn funicular** (tel. (04824) 25 02 or 22 88) to Austria's longest glacier, the **Pasterze.** (Funicular runs mid-May to Oct. every hr. 9:30am-5pm. Round-trip 98AS, children 50AS. Glacier also accessible via cable car from Heiligenblut.) The **Gamsgrube Nature Trail** is a spectacular path (1½hr.) along the glacier, leading to the roaring, pouring **Wasserfallwinkel** (2548m). Beware of the rare alpine **quicksand** that exists in places in the park. No joke.

The Großglockner Straße snakes through the **Hohe Tauern National Park.** The park was created to safeguard indigenous flora and fauna, including the stone pine, ibex, grouse, and the ubiquitous marmot. Hiking, biking, or cross-country skiing around the Großglockner Straße or the **Old Großglockner Straße** (a defunct but eminently scenic road that curls up to Kaiser-Franz-Josef-Höhe) can be splendid, but a number of important safety issues and park regulations must be considered. Many regions pose special problems; some are strictly off-limits. Contact the **Regional Großglockner Association** (tel. (04824) 20 01 21; fax 20 01 43; email heiligenblut@netway.at; http://www.permedia.co.at/glockner) in Heiligenblut or the **Carinthian Park Center** (tel. (04825) 61 61) in little Dollach, 10km from Heiligenblut. (Offices open M-F 9am-5pm.) You can also hire a **guide** for hiking, rock and ice climbing, or ski touring (tel. (04824) 27 00; fax 270 04; daily 9am-6pm; prices vary—for Großglockner, 3100AS per day for 1 person, 3900AS for 2 people, 4500AS for 3, 5200AS for 4). The friendly **information office** at Kaiser-Franz-Josef-Höhe (tel.

(04824) 27 27 sells English maps and guides to the area (119AS; open 10am-4pm). For info on sleeping in the regional Alpine huts from mid-June to September, check out **Edelweißhütte's** roadside information kiosk, by the Edelweißspitze.

TRANSPORT ON THE GROßGLOCKNER

Total transport time on the Großglockner (with scenic rest stops in between) is five hours. Many visitors find that they're much happier dividing these five hours over several days: that's how good looking this stretch of road is. If you only have one day, resist the urge to disembark at any of the cutesy villages along the way; buses come so infrequently that you'll be stuck in Nöwheresdorf for hours. Your time is better spent at the magnificent Kaiser-Franz-Josefs-Höhe. Try to choose a clear day for your excursion—you don't wanna pay the entrance fee when viewing conditions are poor.

Many visitors traverse the Großglockner Straße in a **tour bus** or **rental car,** neither of which is recommended for those with light pocketbooks or weak stomachs. The hairpin curves along the narrow roads are dizzying, and driving through the mountains incurs a hefty 350AS toll (390AS pass includes a return-trip within 30 days; motorbikes 230AS). Parking and pull-off areas are strategically situated at numerous lookout points along the road. The warmer weather from June to September creates the best driving conditions; be aware that the park forbids traffic from 10pm to 5am. Snowfalls, sometimes dumping up to 18m of heavy snow on the road, force the Großglockner to close entirely from October to April. For info on the road's condition (in German) call the information office (tel. (04824) 26 06), or the Heiligenblut (tel. (04824) 22 12) or Ferleiten toll booths (tel. (06546) 517).

Wise budget travelers choose **BundesBus.** Cashing in on the incredible demand for a cheap means of traveling the Großglockner Straße, the federally owned postal bus offers daily return trips from Zell am See or Lienz to Kaiser-Franz-Josefs-Höhe in the summer. The trips are sometimes accompanied by a pleasant narration, compliments of the bus driver. Watch in disbelief (and horror) as the driver dispenses educational facts about the Hohe Tauern (in German) and delivers mail along the road, all the while nonchalantly navigating the harrowing loops and hairpins. From the **north,** bus #3064 leaves for Kaiser-Franz-Josefs-Höhe from **Zell am See's** main bus station behind the post office, swinging by the stop directly across from the train station (2hr.; June 11-Oct. 11 at 9:50am; also July 11-Sept.13 M-Sa at 8:50am and 12:15pm; including additional toll fees, 145AS). From the **south,** the odyssey begins in **Lienz** (1½hrs.; June 21-Sept. 26, M-Sa at 8:20am and 11:25am; July 12-Sept.12 also daily at 10am; 120AS, including all fees). Return trips run from Kaiser-Franz-Josefs-Höhe to Zell am See at run 11:45am, 3pm, and 4pm; to Lienz at 10:28am, 2:45, and 4pm.

Travel to and from Lienz is cheaper with the new 24-hour **Verkehrs Verbund Kärnten** card (80AS), which provides for unlimited **train** travel in one region of Carinthia and discounts on buses. This card will save you a bundle on the Großglockner, although you still have to pay the entrance fee. Get the red and yellow card at the Lienz train station (drivers can only give you the regular rate). Look out for discounts on travel to the valley village of Heiligenblut, a great base for exploring the Hohe Tauern. The ride from Heiligenblut to Franz-Josefs-Höhe is on the Lienz line (47AS).

The most convenient and inexpensive accommodations can be found in Heiligenblut. The **Jugendherberge,** Hof 36 (tel./fax 22 59), is down the street from the bus station and past the tourist office. Turn right at the skateboarding park, and then loop around again to the right before the swimming pool (5min.). It offers plain, institutional rooms and clean toilets. (Dorm bed with breakfast 160AS. Reception May-Sept. 7-11am and 5-9pm. Curfew 10pm, key available.) **Pension Lärchenheim,** Winki 79 (tel. 22 49) is almost as cheap. Across the street from the bus station, head down the sloping street that bends to the right. The pension is set back from the street on the right-hand side. You'll find wood-paneled rooms with sloping ceilings, just a few minutes' walk from a supermarket and bakery. (1st night 190AS, then 180AS.) **Möllfluß-CAMPING,** Pockhorn 25 (tel. 21 29), is down the hill from the youth hostel. Inexpensive, deep-valley sites have showers and restaurant on the premises. (Open June-Sept. and late Dec. to late Apr. Adults 60AS, children 35AS; guest tax 9AS.) **Bike and ski rental** are available at **Intersport Pichler,** across from the tourist office (open M-Sa

9am-6pm, Su 10am-4pm; bikes 220AS per day; ski package 180AS per day). **Ski passes** are 335AS per day, 200AS for children; one week 1850AS, 925AS.

For anyone planning a lengthy stay in the area, BundesBus also offers a **National Park Ticket,** good for 10 days of unlimited travel between Lienz, Heiligenblut, Hochtor, and other stops in the region and reduced fares on cable cars and other sights. The bus to the **Krimmler Wasserfälle** (see p. 217), the **Gletscherbahn** in Kaprun, and the **Schmittenhöhebahnen** in Zell am See (see p. 217) are all fair game (mid-June to mid-Oct.; 590AS, children 295AS). For further details, check the brochure *Der BundesBus ist WanderFreundlich* (available at the bus stations in Lienz and Zell am See and the tourist offices in Lienz and Heiligenblut), which contains a schedule of bus departure times, destinations, maps, hiking paths, and other general information.

■ Lienz

Bordered on the south by the jagged Dolomites (the badass human-tornado-looking mountain range shared with Italy and Slovenia, know what I'm sayin'?) and cut off from the rest of Tirol by the Alps, Lienz is distinctive for its hybrid Mediterranean personality. Although the Alpine vista and the pink 'n' yellow, low-slung houses betray an Austrian heritage, the dusty cobblestone roads, hazy summer heat, and authentic pizzerias suggest Northern Italy (just a 3hr. bike ride away). Even the weather cooperates—the valley around Lienz registers about 2000 sunshine hours per year. Nevertheless, the warm, palm tree-and-cactus atmosphere of the summer months give way to a vigorous ski-season in January and February as eager visitors hit the snowy Hohe Tauern slopes to the north.

GETTING TO LIENZ

Lienz lies at the conjunction of several highways: Rte. 108 from the northwest, 106 and 107 from the northeast, 100 from the west, and E66 from the east. **Trains** arrive at the **Hauptbahnhof,** at Bahnhofpl., and connect directly to points all over Austria and indirectly to points elsewhere. **Buses** leave from the station in front of the *Hauptbahnhof* for destinations all over the region and throughout Austria. (Ticket window (tel. 670 67) open M-F 7:45-10am and 4-6:30pm, Sa 7:45-10am.) By **car** from Salzburg, take Autobahn A-10 south to 311, and just before Zell am See switch to 107 south to Lienz. From Innsbruck, take Autobahn A-12 east to 169 south. At Zell am Ziller, switch to 165 east, and at Mittersill take 108 south to Lienz. The more direct route from Innsbruck passes through Italy.

> Lienz is distinct from Linz, an industrial city in northeast Austria. Lienz is pronounced "LEE-ints"; Linz is known as Linz an der Donau. Make the distinction before boarding any trains.

ORIENTATION AND PRACTICAL INFORMATION

Though somewhat isolated geographically, Lienz is the unofficial capital of **East Tirol** (Osttirol). The city is about three hours by train from Innsbruck or Salzburg but just 40km from the Italian border. The **Isel River,** which feeds into the Drau, splits the town. From the train station, the centrally located Hauptpl. is across Tirolerstr. and to the left through Bozenerpl.

Transportation: Trains leave from the **Hauptbahnhof,** Bahnhofpl. (tel. 660 60; information booth open M-F 9am-4:50pm; ticket window open M-Sa 6:20am-6:35pm, Su 8:15am-6:35pm). To: **Klagenfurt** (2¼hr., 16 per day, 5:20am-10:17pm, 176AS), **Innsbruck** (3hr., 4 per day, 5:28am-6:38pm, 154AS), and the **Vienna Südbahnhof** (6½hr., 10 per day, 6:30am-5:57pm, 580AS). **Buses** leave from just beside the train station in the direction of **Arnbach** (1hr., 18 per day) and **Kitzbühel** (2hr., 3 per day). Bus information booth open a scanty M-F 7:45-8:15am and 5-6:20pm. From July 7 to Aug. 23, a **free Stadtbus** circles the city, making 14 stops, before returning to the train station parking lot. (1 per hr.; 8am-7pm.)
Taxi: tel. 638 63.
Parking: Free parking at Tirolerstr.; at Europapl., 3hr. for 15AS

Automobile Association: ÖAMTC, Tirolerstr. 19a (tel. 633 22).
Car Rental: Pontiller Autohaus, Kärtnerstr. 70 (tel. 627 05).
Bike Rental: At the train station. 150AS per day, with train ticket or Eurailpass 90AS. Mountain bike 200AS, 160AS.
Tourist Office: Tourismusverband, Europapl. 1 (tel. 652 65; fax 652 652; email lienz@netway.at; http://www.tiscover.com/lienz). From the station, turn left onto Tirolerstr. and right onto Europapl. Courteous staff showers you with brochures (mostly in English) including a list of private accommodations. A 24hr. electronic accommodations board is outside. Free **city tours** leave the office M and F at 10am (in German; groups may arrange English tours in advance). National park tours are offered in summer several times per week from neighboring towns (40AS, children free; call the **Igelsberg-Stronach Information Center,** tel. 641 17).
Currency Exchange: Best rates are in the **post office.** Exchange desk open M-F 8am-noon and 2-5pm. Also at the train station and banks. Try **Lienzer Sparkasse,** Johannespl. 6. Open M-F 8am-noon and 2-4pm.
Luggage Storage: At the train station. 30AS per piece per day. Small lockers 20AS, ski lockers 40AS.
English-Language Books: Two shelves of bestsellers on the 2nd floor of **Tyrolia Lienz,** Roseng. 3, open M-F 8am-noon and 2-6pm, Su 8am-noon.
Hospital: Emanuel-von-Hibler-Str. 5 (tel. 606).
Emergencies: Police, Hauptpl. 5 (tel. 631 55; fax 616 57). **Fire,** tel. 122. **Mountain Rescue,** tel. 140. **Ambulance,** tel. 144 (also for **water rescue**).
Post Office: Boznerpl. 1 (tel. 66 88 80), on the corner of Hauptpl. across from the train station. Open M-F 7:30am-7pm, Sa 8-11am. **Postal Code:** A-9900.
Internet Access: Free (!) web access at the post office and at Raffeisenbank in the Hauptpl.
Telephone Code: 04852.

ACCOMMODATIONS AND CAMPING

Although the Lienz Youth Hostel closed in 1993, the town still offers affordable accommodations, most just beyond Hauptpl. and the town center. Most *Pensionen* and *Privatzimmern* have rooms that cost between 250 and 300AS per person.

Bauernhof in the Siechenhaus, Kartnerstr. 39 (tel. 621 88). From the station, turn right onto Tirolerstr., walk across the Isel, take the 1st left, and then an immediate right. Walk 1 block to Kartnerstr. and turn left. The hotel, with its 17th-century frescoes of Lazarus, is on the right. A working farmhouse that served as a home for the sick in the Middle Ages, it has thick, dark wooden beams and painted doors. Doubles 320AS in summer, 400AS for fewer than 3 nights; in winter 360AS, 400AS.
Egger, Alleestr. 33 (tel. 720 98). From the station, Stadtbus: "Hochsteinbahn" and walk 2 blocks, or walk through Hauptpl., left on Andrä Krazg. to Roseng., and right at the ice cream shop onto tree-lined Alleestr. (30min.) Large, high-ceilinged rooms with new wooden furniture in an old-fashioned square building. Doubles 320AS, 340AS for stays under 3 nights. Showers and big breakfast included.
Camping Falken, Eichholz 7 (tel. 640 22; fax 640 226), across the Drau River near the foot of the Dolomites. From the station, turn left onto Tirolerstr. and left at the ÖAMTC garage, then pass through the tunnel and over the Drau. Follow the road as it curves past the soccer and track facilities, then head left down the small paved footpath through the field. Plenty of sites surrounded by wide fields and mountains. Ping-pong table, soccer field, and a mini-playground. 45-60AS, depending on the season, children 30-45AS; site 60-80AS; guest tax for adults 8AS per night; electricity 30AS. Showers (7am-10pm only), **laundry** facilities, and a small store. Gate closed 1-3pm and 10pm-7am. Reception 8-10am and 4-8pm. Reservations strongly recommended July-Aug. Open July-Aug. and mid-Dec. to Mar.

FOOD

Calorie-laden delis, bakeries, butcher stores, and cafés lie in wait in **Hauptplatz** and along **Schweizergasse.**
Imbiße Köstl, Kreuzg. 4 (tel. 620 12). Mother-daughter dynamic duo prepares the cheapest eats in town (19-54AS) in this diner-style restaurant/bakery. Chow down

on the *Wienerschnitzel* (49AS), curry *Würstl* (32AS), or pastries (8-17AS). Pizza lunch special (54AS) from 11am-2pm. Eat-in or take-out. Open M-Th 7:30am-8pm, F 7:30am-10pm, Sa 7:30am-12:30pm.

Pizzeria-Spaghetteria "Da Franco," Ägidius Peggerstr. (tel. 650 51). Head through Hauptpl. to Johannespl., turn left at Zwergerg., and continue down the small alley. Captained by Franco, a native Italian who decided to try to make it big up north. Terrific potato *gnocchi* and garlicky, fresh tomato sauce. Pizza and pasta 65-115AS; salad 40-110AS. Open in summer 11:30am-2:30pm and 6pm-midnight; in winter 11:30am-2pm and 5pm-midnight. AmEx, MC, Visa.

China Restaurant Szechuan, Beda-Weberg. 13 (tel. 651 22). Cross the bridge adjoining Neuerpl., bear right in the gardens, and turn left onto Marcherstr. The restaurant is on the left. Tasty entrees (75-100AS) and a 55AS lunch special with soup or spring roll (15 entree choices) reward those willing to cross the Isel. Open 11:30am-2:30pm and 5:30-11:30pm.

Markets

ADEG Aktiv Markt, Südtirolerpl; next to the tall pink Hotel Traube; and in Hauptpl. Open M-F 8am-6:15pm, Sa 8am-12:30pm.

Bauernmarkt (farmer's market), Marktpl. Local produce. Sa 9am-noon.

SIGHTS AND ENTERTAINMENT

Above Lienz, the **Schloß Bruck** is home to the **East Tyrolean Regional Museum,** as well as several interesting frescoes and tapestries, but will be closed for all of 1999 in preparation for a huge exhibition of Tyrolean culture planned for the year 2000.

The **Hochsteinbahnen** chairlift, which runs from the base station near the castle at the intersection of Iseltaler-Str. and Schloßg., rises 1500m in two segments up to the Alpine wonderland of **Sternalm.** *(Segment 1 open daily 9am-noon and 1-5pm; segment 2 open 9:15am-12:15pm and 1:15-4:45pm; runs July-Sept.; round-trip for both 140AS, children 70AS; segment 1 only 100AS, 50AS.)* At the top, the unforgiving Dolomites to the south and the gently rounded Hohe Tauern to the north appear in spectacular confrontation. A "Fairy Tale Hike" (1½hr.) leads past limestone peaks to part of the Großglockner Strasse (details at the tourist office or chairlift station). Also at the summit of the chairlift is the **Moosalm Children's Zoo,** with a menagerie of rabbits, goats, and ducks available for your petting pleasure. *(Open 10am-5:30pm. Free.)* The **Dolomiten-Wanderbus** delivers nature lovers to another challenging hiking base, the **Lienzer Dolomitenhütte** (1620m). *(Buses leave from the left side of the train station mid-June to late Sept. 8am, 1:10, and 4:30pm. 75AS, round-trip 120AS.)* Over 40 trails of varying difficulty spiral off from this Alpine hut. Seventeen other huts dot the area—for more mountain hiking information, contact Lienz's chapter of the **Österreichischer Alpenverein,** Franz-von-Defreggerstr. 11 (tel. 721 05). *(Open F 8:30-11:30am and 3-6pm.)*

A 5km hike from Lienz leads to the **Tristacher See,** a sparkling blue lake at the base of the Rauchkofel mountain (tel. 638 20; 40AS, children 20AS; open June-Sept.). Couch potatoes can enjoy the lake by riding the free **Bäder- und Freizeitbus** (Bath- and Leisure-Bus) from the *Dolomitenstadion* across the Drau to "Parkhotel Tristachersee." *(Runs in July and Aug.; every hr. from 9:23am-5:46pm.)*

Lienz serves as an excellent base to attack the **ski** trails comprising the **Lienzer Dolomiten Complex.** *(One-day ski pass 320AS, seniors and youths 270AS, under 15 160AS. Half-day tickets 230AS, 185AS, 115AS. Off-season: one-day 275AS, 220AS, 145AS. Half-day 250AS, 210AS, 125AS.)* The **Skischule Lienzer Dolomiten** (tel. 656 90; fax 710 80) at the Zettersfeld lift offers hour-long private lessons at 450AS for one person, 150AS for each additional person. Four-hour lessons cost 440AS. Private snowboard lessons are also available (450AS per hour). **Hans Moser und Sohn** (tel. 691 80), at the apex of the Zettersfeld lift, supply **ski or snowboard rental.** A complete set of downhill equipment, here or elsewhere, runs 210AS per day, children 110AS; a snowboard with boots costs 300AS, 210AS.

During the second weekend of August, the sounds of alcohol-induced merriment reverberate across the pastel facades of Lienz's town buildings in celebration of the

Stadtfest. *(Admission to town center 50AS.)* The summer months also welcome the reaffirmation of Tirolean culture and heritage in a series of **Platzkonzerte.** Watch men dust off their old *Lederhosen* and perform the **acclaimed shoe-slapping dance.** *(Free; July-Aug. W and Sa at 8pm; June-Sept. Su at 8pm.)* On January 24th, 1999, the world's greatest male cross-country skiers will gather in Lienz to compete in the annual 65km **Dolomitenlauf.** *(Entrance fee 450AS before Dec. 15, 500AS afterwards; for 25km race 300AS, 350AS.)* All year, disco-lovers get stoked at hotspot **Stadtkeller-disco,** Tirolerstr. 30, near Europapl. *(Two bars and a large dance floor open 9pm-3am; cover 40AS.)* Across from the Pizzeria Da Franco in the Gastogarden, live jazz and the occasional pianist entertain a youngish crowd at **Türml Nightcafe** *(open Tu-Su 5pm-2am.)* The young and the counter-cultural might venture to **Cafe Wha,** Schweizerg. 3. Wha? You heard me! Body-pierced crowd rocks and rolls way past the midnight hour, smoking and playing pool. *(Beer 24-35AS; wine 21-25AS. Open Tu-Su 6pm-1am.)*

■ Kufstein

In a region dotted with ski-burrows, the town of Kufstein provides a freckle of historical appeal as well as the gorgeous hiking squiggles and slanting slopes typical of its Alpine neighbors. The swirling green Inn river winds past cobblestone streets, framing the western side of the center of town. Kufstein is upscale but sincere.

Free hiking, biking, and skiing maps are available at the **tourist office,** Unterer Stadtpl. 8 (tel. 622 07; fax 614 55; open M-F 8:30am-12:30pm and 2-5pm, Sa 9am-noon), just across the river from the **train station.** (Ticket office open M 5:25am-8pm, Tu-Sa 5:35am-8pm, Su 7:30am-8:30pm. Regular trains to Innsbruck: 45min., 127AS.) The tourist office gives out a complete list of accommodations and restaurants. **Bike rental** can be found at the train station for 150AS, or 90AS with ticket. **Taxis** idle their engines at the train station (call 17 15). **Currency exchange** at the **post office,** Oberer Stadtpl. 5 (tel. 625 51; open M-F 7am-7pm, Sa 8-11am). **ATMs** lie next to **Spar Market** in Unterer Stadtpl. and in the **Sparkasse** in Oberer Stadtpl. There's a **Hospital** at Krankenhausg. 8 (tel. 696 60) and a **police station** at Salurnerstr. 1 (tel. 60 24 01). The **telephone code** is 05372. The **postal code** is 6332.

Nights are cheap at Haus Reheis, Hugo-Petler-Str. 1 (tel. 683 22). 340AS for simple, cozy doubles without bath; call ahead. Otherwise, try Camping Kufstein, Salurnerstr. 36 (tel. 622 29 55; fax 63 68 94). Shady spots along the river will cost you a mere 47AS, 30AS for children; cars 38AS, guest tax 6AS. Reception 7:30-9am and 6-8pm.

The town's highlight is the 13th-century **Festung** (fortress), which raises its crenellated fist high above the river Inn. Climb to the fortress grounds via a medieval *Gangsteig* (covered staircase) designed by Balthasar Laumianello, or take the elevator (tel. 622 95; open Apr.-Oct. daily 9am-5pm; one-way 20AS, students 15AS; round-trip 30AS, 20AS). Once you're within the walls of the *Festung,* you have free reign to wander about the quiet grassy knolls and stone ramparts. Poorly lit archways beckon everywhere, making you feel like a spelunker. The drafty, drippy *Rockpassage* cuts from one side of the fortress to the other and was used as a refuge during both World Wars. At the top of the fortress is the **Heimatmuseum,** (tel. 60 23 50; fax 710 60) featuring a motley crew of pre-historic and early modern artifacts, as well as a room of sacred art with crushed red velvet wallpaper and a pickled two-headed chicken. (Open daily 9am-5pm; guided tours Apr.-Oct. Combined entrance to fortress and museum 100AS, students 50AS.) The *Festung* also houses the *Heldenorgel* (Heroes' Organ), the world's largest open-air organ, with 4307 pipes. The organ is played for all to hear every day at noon and, during the summer season, again at 6pm. To reach some non-man-made heights, take the **Wilder Kaiser Chairlift** high into the mountains. (Open M-F 8:30am-4:30pm, Sa-Su 8am-4:30pm. Round-trip 130AS; children 55AS, ascent only 100AS, 40AS.)

Vorarlberg

Perched on the intersection of three nations, the residents of the **Vorarlberg** (1004 sq. mi.; pop. 322,551), Austria's westernmost province, speak like the Swiss, eat like the Germans, and deem their land a world unto itself. From the tranquil Bodensee in the west, the country juts increasingly upward with each easterly move; at the boundary with Tirol, the Arlberg Alps form an obstacle passable only through the 10km Arlberg Tunnel. The mountainous terrain that characterizes Western Austria isn't hospitable to agriculture or manufacturing (except chocolate), so tourism is by far the leading industry. In fact, Tirol earns more foreign currency from tourism than any other province. The skiing in the region is perhaps the best in the world—we only say "perhaps" because we don't want to offend the Swiss.

Here, at the crossroads of four nations, carry your passport at all times; foreign borders are never more than two hours away, and a little daytrip may become an international excursion. The area's dialect, Allemannian, combines accents from Swiss-German and German Swabia. **Feldkirch,** on the Ill River, lies just off Liechtenstein's border. **Bregenz,** on the banks of the Bodensee (Lake Constance), would be German but for half a dozen kilometers. Snow conditions are dependably *wunderbar* from December to April, with trails as high as 2600m. Glaciers provide summer skiing in many areas. Over 1610km of marked hiking paths ranging in altitude from 400 to 3350m crisscross Vorarlberg, and mountain railways carry hikers to the summit quickly and conveniently. Alpine associations maintain 39 huts that provide hikers with accommodations and refreshments from May to October; opening times depend on the altitude, so contact the local tourist offices. Vorarlberg's 161km network of cycling paths ranges from leisurely rolls through the Bodensee and Rhine

👆 HIGHLIGHTS OF VORARLBERG

- Bregenz's medieval *Altstadt* is an excellent base for exploring the warm waters of Lake Constance.
- Feldkirch is the former seat of the Prince of Liechtenstein, and it's still a good base for traveling into the tiny principality. In its own right, Feldkirch has cobbly medieval towers and frescoed town buildings dating from the same period.

plain to challenging climbs in the Alps. The 125km Bodensee circuit circumnavigates the lake. Cycling maps are available at bookstores and tourist offices. For more info on the region, contact the **Vorarlberg Information Office** in Bregenz (tel. (05574) 42 52 50; fax 42 52 55; http://vorarlberg-tourism.at). Travel in the Vorarlberg region is made easier with the **Network Vorarlberg Ticket,** valid on all public transportation (150AS per day, 280AS per week.)

▓ Feldkirch

On the banks of the Ill river just minutes from the borders with Switzerland and Liechtenstein lies Feldkirch, a small international city dating from the 13th century. The small cobblestoned city center, dotted with sagging medieval towers and crumbling ramparts, is still lively. Students from a nearby *Hauptschule* flood the *Fußgängerzone* during midday break and in the evening. Specialty groceries and *Kebap* restaurants are evidence of the city's Turkish community. The young atmosphere, interesting medieval buildings, and the annual Schubert festival make Feldkirch a decent stopover on anyone's itinerary. Decent.

ORIENTATION AND PRACTICAL INFORMATION Feldkirch is easily accessible by train from major Austrian cities: **Bregenz** (40min., 5:29am-11:59pm, 58AS); **Innsbruck** (2hr., 5:26am-10:10pm, 240AS); and **Salzburg** (4hr., 5:26am-10:10pm, 520AS). **Swiss PTT buses** travel from the train station to Buchs and Sargans in Switzerland, with connections to Liechtenstein (for bus info, call 739 74; open M-Th 8am-12:30pm and 2-4:30pm, F 8am-noon). **City buses** *(Stadtbusse)* connect Feldkirch's various subdivisions (13AS, day pass 25AS). Hop in a **taxi** outside the station, or call 17 15 or 17 12. Eleven generations of city planners have left their marks on Feldkirch, confounding any navigator. Free maps are available outside the **tourist office,** Herreng. 12 (tel. 734 67; fax 798 67; email tourismus@wtg.feldkirch.com). Walk from the train station to the end of the road, turn left, and cross the pedestrian underpass at the first major intersection. Head toward the *Zentrum* and into the *Bezirkhauptmannschaft* building. The office is about 50m ahead on the right. The office helps with reservations and hands out historic walking-tour maps and info about cultural events. (Open M-F 9am-6pm, Sa 9am-noon.) **Currency exchange,** an **ATM,** **bike rental** (150AS, with train ticket 90AS), and **lockers** (20-30AS) are available at the train station. Feldkirch's **post office** is on Bahnhofstr. across from the station. (Open M-F 7am-7pm, Sa 7am-noon.) The **postal code** is A-6800. The **telephone code** is 05522.

ACCOMMODATIONS AND FOOD Feldkirch's youth hostel, **Jugendherberge "Altes Siechenhaus,"** Reichstr. 111 (tel. 731 81; fax 793 99), might be the highlight of your visit. Buses #2 and 60: "Jugendherberge" run to the hostel from the station (5min.). You can also walk straight out of the station to the end of the road, then right on Bahnhofstr. (which becomes Reichstr.), then go 15 to 20 minutes. Buses to and from the city center run twice per hour until 2pm and once an hour until 11pm (M-Sa). The hostel is an ancient white brick and wood building on the right of the street next to a small stone church. This 600-year-old structure served as an infirmary during the Black Plague and several other epidemics. Later it was a poor house and then a grammar school after a 1697 fire. Thick wooden beams and vaulted ceilings give you that uniquely medieval hosteling sensation. (Dorms 134AS. Key 14AS plus 200AS deposit. Breakfast 30AS. **Laundry** 40AS. Linen 20AS. Candy, soft drinks, wine, and beer sold at the desk. Wheelchair accessible. Oct.-Apr. heating 25AS. Reception M-Sa 7:30am-10pm, Su 7:30-10am and 5-10pm.) Take bus #1 or 3: "Burgweg" for **Gasthof Löwen** (tel. 728 68; fax 378 57), in Tosters-Feldkirch. From the stop, walk a half-block toward the tall pink and white building on Egelseestr. The hotel offers spartan rooms in a quiet neighborhood. (Singles 350AS; doubles 660AS. All come with TV and private bath. Breakfast included.)

Restaurants and snack bars are everywhere in the *Fußgängerzone.* **Pizzeria-Trattoria La Taverna,** Vorstadtstr. 18 (tel. 792 93), offers a small vegetarian menu and affordable pizza (60-110AS) and pasta (70-90AS). (Open 11:30am-2pm and 5pm-midnight.) For a quick meal, head to vegetarian-friendly **König Kebap,** Kreuzg. 9 (tel. 380 42), down the street from the tourist office. (Veggie *Kebap* 30AS. Open M-Sa 9am-11pm, Su 11am-11pm.) The restaurant inside the huge iron doors of the **Schattenburg Castle** serves enormous portions of *Wiener Schnitzel* (135AS) and *Apfelstrudel* (35AS), as well as their specialty *Jägertöpfle,* smoked ham with noodles and cream (135AS). (Open Tu-Su 10am-midnight.) And, of course, for cultural enlightenment, there's **Hooters,** Schloßgraben 13 (tel. 72 07 00), where ample burgers run 65-80AS. (Open 1pm-1am.) In the center of the *Altstadt,* find picnic supplies at **Interspar Markt,** under Hervis Sport Mode at the top of Johanniterg. off Marktpl. (Open M-F 9am-7:30pm, Sa 8am-5pm.) Its smaller cousin, **Spar Markt,** is across from the hostel, one minute toward the city center. (Open M-F 7am-noon and 2:30-6pm, Sa 7am-12:30pm.) The Marktpl. houses an **outdoor market** (Tu and Sa 7am-noon).

SIGHTS AND ENTERTAINMENT Feldkirch's Gothic **Dom,** the St. Nikolaus Kirche, forms one edge of the *Altstadt.* Mentioned in print as early as 1287, the edifice received a facelift in 1478 after a series of devastating fires and now boasts beautiful stained-glass windows and an elaborately vaulted ceiling. A *pietà,* crafted in 1521 by Wolf Huber (a master of the Danube School), graces the altar on the right. Frescoes of Feldkirch history and the coats of arms of local potentates adorn the 15th-century **Rathaus,** originally a granary, on Schmiedg. On nearby Schloßberg. stands the **Palais Liechtenstein,** completed in 1697. The palace once supported the royal seat of the Prince of Liechtenstein, but now houses the city archives and the town library. Its third-floor **art gallery** hosts frequent exhibitions, often free. At the edges of the *Altstadt,* three towers remain of the original city wall: the **Katzenturm,** the shrimpy **Pulverturm,** and the **Wasserturm.** Just outside the *Altstadt* lies the **Kapuzinerkloster** (Capuchin monastery), built in 1605. For a fantastic view of the *Altstadt,* hike up either the castle staircase or Burgg. to **Schattenburg,** Feldkirch's most impressive structure. From the early 1200s until 1390, the castle was the seat of the Count of Montfort. The town purchased the castle in 1825 to save it from demolition and converted it into the **Feldkirch Heimatmuseum,** Burgg. 1 (tel. 719 82). *(Open Tu-Su 9am-noon and 1-5pm. 25AS, youth 15AS, child 5AS.)* Make yourself at home in the museum's impressive medieval furnished rooms. Not really.

Feldkirch's annual **Schubertiade** (June 17-29 in 1998) honors one of its most famous residents. World class musicians, including Dietrich Fischer-Dieskau and members of the Vienna Philharmonic, perform works by and inspired by Schubert in Feldkirch's concert halls and manor houses, while painters, sculptors, and performance artists exhibit throughout the city. (Tickets (05576) 720 91; fax (05576) 754 50, or write to Schubertiade GmbH, Postfach 100, Schweizerstr. 1, A-6845 Hohenerns. Tickets 200-1400AS.) During the second weekend of July (9-11 in 1999), Feldkirch's annual **wine festival** intoxicates all those who venture to Marktpl. The circus comes to town toward the end of the month, when the annual **Festival of Traveling Entertainers** sweeps jugglers, mimes, and clowns into every cobblestone path. If that's not enough, you can go **hot-air ballooning** with G. Schabau (tel. 511 21; fax 524 25; 1½-2hr. flights 3800AS.) December brings the annual **Christmas bazaar,** with crafts, candy canes, and crèches for sale throughout Advent.

■ Bregenz

Bregenz, the capital city of Vorarlberg, spreads along the eastern coast of the **Bodensee** (Lake Constance). Separating three countries by only a few kilometers, the lake serves as an international conduit for (frequently Speedo-clad) Swiss, German, and Austrian tourists in search of Alpine and marine getaways. The Romans set up a thriving bath and spa center here. Later, Gallus and Columban, Irish missionaries, lifted their heads from their medieval beach blankets, observed the vast shimmering lake ringed by mountains, and dubbed the locale "Bregenz" (Golden Bowl), which is why it is called Bregenz. They set up camp on the hill above the lake, where modern tourists hike to soak up some medieval culture along with the sun's rays.

ORIENTATION AND PRACTICAL INFORMATION

Trains: Bahnhofstr. (tel. 675 50; call 1717 for information). **Trains to Bludenz** (40min., 5am-9:43pm, 150AS), to **St. Gallen** (1hr., 6:23am-9:22pm, 252AS) and to **Zurich,** (2½hr., 6:23am-9:22am, 594AS), to **Innsbruck,** (2¾hr., 5am-9:43pm, 560AS) **Vienna** (8hr., 5am-9:43pm, 640AS), and **Munich** (80min., 9:21am-7:21pm, 868AS). The station has **lockers, luggage storage** (30AS), **bike rental** (with ticket 90-160AS per day; otherwise 150-200AS per day), an **ATM,** and **public showers.**
Buses: BundesBuses leave from the train station.
Public Transportation: 4 bus lines run throughout the city. 13AS, day pass 25AS.
Taxis: tel. 17 18.
Car Rental: Hertz, Immler Schneeweiss, Am Brand 2 (tel. 449 95), at the intersection of Deuringstr. and Belruptstr. **Avis-ARBÖ,** Rheinstr. 86 (tel. 781 00).
Parking: Free parking by the Festspielhaus. **Hypobank parking garage** is in the city center, and there are metered parking spaces on most streets (5AS per 30min.).
Tourist Office: Bahnhofstr. 14 (tel. 005 44 95 90; email tourismus@bregenz.vol.at). From the train station, head left along Bahnhofstr. The brand new office makes hotel reservations (30AS) and dispenses *Privatzimmer* lists, hiking and city maps, and concert info. English spoken. Open M-Sa 9am-6pm, July-Aug. M-Sa 9am-7pm and Su 4-7pm. On the 5th floor you'll find a **regional information office** (tel. 42 52 50; fax 42 52 55; http://vorarlberg-tourism.at; open M-F 8am-5pm.) There is also a **free accommodations board** with a courtesy phone in the train station.
Consulate: U.K., Bundesstr. 110 (tel. 78 586), in neighboring Lauterach.
Post Office: Seestr. 5 (tel. 490 22; fax 457 57), across the street from the harbor. Open M-F 7am-7pm (cashier's desk closes at 6pm), Sa 8am-2pm (cashier closes at noon). **Postal Code:** A-6900.
Telephone Code: 05574.

ACCOMMODATIONS AND CAMPING

Bregenz caters to the wealthy, but backpackers can find a bed. When the *Festspiele* comes to town, prices soar and reservations are painfully necessary. A new **Jugendherberge (HI),** Mehreranerstr. 3-5 (tel. 428 67; fax 428 67 88; email oejhv-stmk@oejhv.or.at), will open its doors in June 1999. Its four- to six-bed dorms are projected to cost 185AS (with bath). Double rooms will also be available.

Pension Sonne, Kaiserstr. 8 (tel./fax 425 72; email gidiem@computerhaus.at; http://www.vol.at/PensionSonne). From the station, left on Bahnhofstr. then right on Kaiserstr. Quiet rooms and an English-speaking staff in the heart of the *Fußgängerzone*. Singles 350-440AS; doubles 640-800AS; triples 840-1050AS. From July 16th-Aug. add 90AS. Some rooms with private bath. Breakfast included.
Boss Erich und Eugenie, Pfänderweg. 27 (tel. 426 97). From the train station, follow Seestr. along the water, past the post office, and turn right on Schillerstr. Make the 1st left on Belrupstr., then go uphill on Pfänderweg. Impossibly clean doubles are kept *in Ordnung* by a vigorous hostess. Uncommonly beautiful balcony views and homemade jam for your (included) breakfast. 500AS.
Seecamping, Bodong. 7 (tel. 718 95; fax 718 96). Bus #2 (dir: Achsiedlung Weidach): "Viktoria." Or, take a left from the train station onto Strandweg and walk along the lake. Beautiful lakeside location and sparkling bathrooms. Currency exchange and grocery on premises. 60AS; tent, car, or caravan 60AS, children 30AS. Showers included. Guest tax 17AS. Open May 15-Sept. 15.
Camping Lamm, Mehrauerstr. 50-51 (tel. 717 01; fax 71 74 54), is closer to town but not nearly as nice. Follow Mehrauerstr. 20min. from the parking lot in front of the *Festspielehaus* (behind the train station). 45AS; tents 35AS; car or caravan 35AS; guest tax 17AS.

FOOD

Ikaros, Deuringstr. 5 (tel. 529 54), in the *Fußgängerzone*. A little taste of the Mediterranean on the Bodensee. Fish nets and wine bottles line the walls of this classy little café. Baklava (25AS), Greek salads (74AS), melitsones (42AS), and a thorough selection of olives. Open M-F 10am-midnight, Sa 9am-4pm.

VORARLBERG

Zum Goldenen Hirschen, Kirchstr. 8 (tel. 428 15). Look for the old wooden building with the small stained-glass windows and a flying gold reindeer over the door. Dark wooden furniture and a half-timbered interior. Delicious Austrian fare, including vegetarian *Krautspätzle* (85AS) and some non-native dishes like *chili con carne* (85AS). Open 10am-midnight. AmEx, MC, Visa.

SPAR Café Restaurant (tel. 422 91, ext. 15) on the 1st floor of the GWL building at Kaiserstr. and Römerstr. If Austrian food makes you daydream about fresh vegetables, the self-serve salad and fruit/dessert bars (10AS per 100g) are a godsend. Cafeteria-style entrees 56-98AS. Open M-F 8:30am-5:30pm, Sa 8:30am-3pm.

Farmer's Markets fill up Kornmarktstr. every Tuesday and Friday from 7am-noon.

SIGHTS AND ENTERTAINMENT

Bregenz's medieval residents snatched up some prime real estate on the hill overlooking the Bodensee. To reach the center of the historic town, the *Oberstadt*, or "high city," walk uphill on Maurachg. from the *Fußgängerzone* to St. Martinspl. The **Martinsturm,** originally built in 1362, looks stonily down on the *Oberstadt* and boasts Europe's largest onion dome. It's big. The second and third floors of the tower house the **Voralberg Militärmuseum.** *(Open May-Sept. Tu-Su 9am-6pm. 10AS, children 7AS.)* Although you can see all of the museum in 10 minutes (20 if you can read the German descriptions), you may want to spend more time on the third floor with its exhilarating view of the Bodensee and beyond. Next to the tower is the **Martinskirche,** filled with frescoes dating back to the early 14th century. Particularly noteworthy are the depictions of St. Christopher, the Holy Symbol of Grief, and the 18th-century Stations of the Cross. Across Ehregutapl. (with the fountain) is **Deuring Schloßchen,** a 17th-century castle that now houses a non-budget hotel.

The walk up to the **St. Gallus Pfarrkirche,** at the top of Kirchstr., provides a sweeping view of the *Oberstadt* and some exercise. The white-stucco sanctuary of the 11th-century church now glows under lavish gold ornamentation and a detailed painted ceiling that dates from 1738. The shepherdess in the altar-painting has the face of Empress Maria Theresa, who donated 1500 guilders to the church in 1740. The imposing **Herz-Jesu Kirche** looms one block from the youth hostel. Built in 1907 and recently renovated in neo-Gothic style, the huge sanctuary's brick, wood, and sea-green materials are a tasteful backdrop for the lovely Expressionist stained-glass windows. The **Voralberg Landesmuseum,** Kornmarktpl. 1, examines pre-tourist Bregenz. *(Open Tu-Su 9am-noon and 2-5pm. Ring the bell if the door's locked. 20AS, students 10AS.)* The museum's collection spans thousands of years, with carefully explained exhibits on the city's inhabitants from the Stone Age to the 18th century.

Bregenz's main attraction is not its gray medieval past but rather the Bodensee and its surrounding mountains. All along the waterfront, carefully groomed paths and strategically placed ice-cream stands surround fantastic playgrounds and mini-golf courses. **Boat rental** is available near the train station from 10am to 10pm in summer. *(Paddle- and rowboats are yours for 130AS.)* Away from the city center and past the train station lies the **Strandbad** (tel. 442 42), a huge swimming pool, sauna, and sunbathing area. *(Open in fair weather mid-May to mid-Sept. Tu-F 9am-noon, Sa 9am-7pm, Su 10am-6pm. 35AS, students 28AS, seniors 28AS, children 11AS.)* Ferries run to the **Blumeninsel Mainau** (Mainau Flower Isle; tel. (07531) 30 30), which features a Baroque castle, an indoor tropical palm house, a new butterfly house, and gardens rife with orchids, tulips, dahlias, and 1100 kinds of roses. *(Admission to all sights 116AS. Ferries depart Bregenz May-Sept. 9:20, 10:20, and 11am; return from Mainau 2:40, 4, and 4:20pm. Round-trip 286AS; special family packages available.)* The **Drei-Länder-Rundfahrt** (tel. 428 68) runs along the Swiss, German, and Austrian waterfronts. Ten different boat trips leave from the harbor, each with different lengths, prices, and gimmicks. Most cost roughly 140AS and stop in Constance on the German side. *(Eurailpass discounts. Children's discount. Bring your passport on all boat rides.)* The **Pfänderbahn** cable car (tel. 42 16 00; fax 42 16 04) near the hostel sways up the **Pfänder mountain** (the tallest peak around the Bodensee) for a panorama spanning from the Black Forest to Switzerland. *(Every 30min. Dec.-Oct. 9am-7pm. Ascent 88AS, descent 63AS, round-trip 125AS. Discounts for seniors*

(Sidebar, rotated) VORARLBERG

and children under 19.) At the top of the cable-car ride, wander with native animals in the **Alpen wild park.** *(Free.)* Watch **bird flight shows** from May to September at 11am and 2:30pm (45AS, children 24AS). Hiking down is a durned good idea (45min.-2hr.).

The concrete monstrosity on the edge of the lake is not a ski ramp gone awry but rather the world's largest **floating stage** and the centerpiece for the annual **Bregenzer Festspiele.** Every year from mid-July to mid-August, the Vienna Symphony Orchestra and other opera, theater, and chamber music groups come to town, bringing some 180,000 tourists with them. The main event is a performance on the floating stage, drawing capacity crowds of 6800. In 1999, the floating opera will be Verdi's *Masked Ball,* premiering on July 21st. The *Festspielhaus* opera will be Martinn's *Greek Passion,* premiering on July 20th. Tickets go on sale in October. (300-1550AS. Students under 26 100AS. Weekday performances rarely sell out more than a few days before the show. Standing room tickets available.) For more info, write to Postfach 311, A-6901 Bregenz, call 407 223, fax 407 400, or email ticket@bregenzer-festspiele.com. For late-night entertainment, check out **Uwe's Bier-Bar,** Kirchstr. 25, a popular jukebox bar with a mixed crowd. *(18 and older; open 7pm-1am.)* Or visit **CUBA,** a crowded dance club in the Kinz Keller off Kirchstr. Thursday is salsa and meringue, Friday is hip-hop and R&B, Saturday is house. *(Open Th-M 10pm-4am; 45AS cover after 11pm.)* There are many popular student hangouts on and around Kirchstr.

THE ARLBERG

Looming halfway between the Bodensee and Innsbruck, the jagged peaks of the Arlberg mountains make for some of the best skiing in the Alps. In summer, streams pour down each steep mountainside in continual waterfalls, creating gorgeous **hiking** prospects. Most lifts operate in summer for high-altitude hikes, but **skiing** remains the area's main draw. With hundreds of miles of ski runs ranging in altitude from 1000 to 3000m, the Arlberg offers unparalleled terrain from December through April. Dauntingly long cross-country trails (up to 42km) link various villages throughout the valleys. All resorts have ski schools in German and English for children, beginners, and proficient skiers. In fact, the world's first ski instructor still lives in Oberlech. The comprehensive **Arlberg Ski Pass** gives access to some of Austria's most lusted-after slopes, including the famed **Valluga** summit. The pass is valid for over 88 mountain railways and ski lifts in St. Anton, St. Jakob, St. Christoph, Lech, Zürs, Klösterle, and Stuben, amounting to more than 192km of prime snow-draped terrain. Locally, the Galzigbahn lift tends to attract the longest morning lines because of its central location just outside St. Anton's *Fußgängerzone,* while the Rendl ski area remains largely pristine. You must purchase passes at the Galzig, Vallugagrat, Vallugipfel, Gampen, and Kapall cable car stations from 8am to 4:30pm on the day prior to use. (1 day 470AS, 2 day 900AS, 1 week 2630AS, 2 week 4270AS. 10% senior discount, 40% discount for children under 15; 10% discount Apr. 21-Nov.)

On the eastern side of the Arlberg tunnel, in the province of Tirol, you'll find the hub of the region, **St. Anton,** and its distinctly less cosmopolitan cousin, **St. Jakob.** The western Arlberg is home to the classy resorts **Lech, Zürs,** and **St. Christoph.** In high season, book rooms six to eight weeks in advance; in off-season, two weeks is sufficient. **Buses** link the Arlberg towns together, and trains connect St. Anton to the rest of Austria. Bus #4235 runs from Landeck to St. Anton every hour; #4248 runs from St. Anton to St. Christoph, Zürs, and Lech five times per day and returns 4 times per day. For more info on the region, contact the **Arlberg Tourist Office** (tel. (05583) 216 10; fax 31 55; email info-lech@lechtourismus.vol.at; http://www.lech.at).

▓ St. Anton am Arlberg

Don't be fooled by the pious name, the bucolic hillside farms, or the cherubic school-children. As soon as the first winter snowflake arrives, St. Anton (non-tourist pop. 2300) awakens with a vengeance as an international playground brimming with play-boys, partygoers, and plenty of physical activity (including skiing, skating, and snow-shoeing). To escape the tabloid reporters in St. Moritz, many members of the Euro jet-set (including Prince Edward of England) winter here. St. Anton loves its flock of trav-eling socialites; establishments accept all major credit cards, and salespeople have a healthy knowledge of English. The occasional *Lederhosen*-clad marching band, color-ful festival, or early evening cattle drive through the *Fußgängerzone* round out the Tirolean experience. Be warned that this posh ski town doesn't emerge from spring hibernation until mid-July. If you visit in May or June, you may feel like you're at Dis-neyland after hours—the city has all the tourist machinery in place but no one to run it. Nonetheless, summer in St. Anton offers beautiful, isolated hiking trails and quiet, affordable accommodations.

ORIENTATION AND PRACTICAL INFORMATION St. Anton lies along several major rail and bus routes. Even the **Orient Express** stops here. More than 40 **trains** come and go daily, with destinations including **Innsbruck** (1½hr., 14 per day, 6:14am-6:05pm, 144AS), **Munich** (4hr., 6:14am-6pm, 478AS), and **Zurich** (2½hr., 5 per day, 5:45am-3:58pm, 434AS). The St. Anton **train station** (tel. 240 23 85) will **store lug-gage** for 30AS. During the high seasons (late June to Sept. and Dec.-Apr.) **buses** run 2-5 times per day between St. Anton and the neighboring Arlberg villages, including **Lech** (24AS) and **St. Christoph** (10AS). Year-round buses run frequently to **Landeck** (6am-7pm, 46AS). A *Tageskarte* allows unlimited bus travel between the towns (80AS). The bus station is across from the tourist office, under Sport Pangratz.

Though St. Anton has few street signs, there's really only one main road, which runs the length of the *Fußgängerzone*. From the train station, walk down the hill to the right (or straight ahead if you're coming from the tunnel beneath the platform). Within seconds you'll find yourself on the main drag, the *Fußgängerzone* to the left. To reach the **tourist office** (tel. 226 90; fax 25 32; email st.anton@netway.at; http://www.stantonamarlberg.com), turn right on the main road as you come out of the sta-tion. The tourist office is off a small square on the left just before the railroad crossing. The office is as chic as the town—leather chairs, polished wood reception stands, free maps, and brochures in multiple languages. (Open July to mid-Sept. M-F 8am-noon and 2-6pm, Sa-Su 10am-noon; May to early June and mid-Sept. to Dec. M-F 8am-noon and 2-6pm; Dec.-Apr. M-F 8am-6pm, Sa 9am-noon and 1-7pm, Su 10am-noon and 3-6pm.) You can **exchange currency** (at exorbitant rates) at any of the 24-hour ATM machines around town or at the three local banks, all in the *Fußgängerzone*. (Banking hours M-F 8am-noon and 2-4:30pm.) **Biking** in the Arlberg is arduous but rewarding. The folks at **Intersport Adler** (tel. 34 00; fax 31 06) in the pedestrian zone will be glad to rent you a bike and dispense maps and trail advice. (Full day rental 280AS, morning 150AS, afternoon 180AS, evening 150AS. Prices 20-30AS lower with guest card. Open M-F 9am-noon and 2-6pm, Sa 9am-noon.) **Taxis** await at tel. 37 30, 32 32, or at the late-night taxi stand to the left of the railroad crossing (10pm-7am). Call 25 65 for 24-hour **ski conditions;** for **weather reports,** 226 90. To **report acci-dents,** call 23 52. For the **police,** call 22 37. In an **emergency,** call 144. To find the **post office** (tel. 33 80; fax 35 30), turn left on the main road from the station and walk towards the end of the *Fußgängerzone*, then right across from the Hotel Schwarzer Adler. (Open summer M-F 8:30am-noon and 2-6pm; winter M-F 8:30am-7pm, Sa 9-11am.) The **postal code** is A-6580. St. Anton's **telephone code** is 05446.

ACCOMMODATIONS AND FOOD In the summer, affordable accommodations are relatively easy to find. During the ski season, however, prices generally double. If you book far enough in advance (about 2 months), you *may* find relatively cheap hous-ing. One useful resource is the **24-hour electronic accommodation board** outside the tourist office, which lists all *Pensionen*, hotels, and prices, and has a free tele-phone to call for reservations. **Pension Pepi Eiter** (tel./fax 25 50) sits to the right on the hill behind the train station. Turn right on the main road when you exit the sta-tion and continue past the tourist office, across the railroad tracks, and uphill. Take the fourth right on your way up, a drastic 135 degree turn up another hill. Pepi Eiter provides luscious beds, hearty repasts, light pine rooms, and a chocolate on your pillow. (Singles 220AS; doubles 400AS. Winter: singles 440AS; doubles 800AS. Add 20AS in summer and 50AS in winter for stays shorter than 3 nights. 2 apartments available for 850AS in summer, 1700-2300AS in winter. All rooms with TV. Breakfast and parking included.) **Pension Elisabeth** (tel. 24 96; fax 292 54) is one of the town's least expensive three-star B&Bs. Follow the directions to Pension Pepi Eiter; Pension Elizabeth is up the stairs to the right before you make the sharp turn uphill. The friendly young owner speaks fluent English. (240-260AS per person. Winter: 550AS. Bath, TV, radio, breakfast, and parking included.) To find **Haus Klöpfer** (tel./fax 28 00), start at the train station, turn left down the narrow, paved path in front of the station, then left up the larger road. Continue across the railroad tracks and follow the road as it curves right up the hill. Pension Klöpfer is on the left at #419, with small but pleasant rooms that have space for skis. (Singles 250AS; winter 500-700AS, depending on ski conditions. Doubles 500AS; 1000-1400AS. Private bathrooms, breakfast, **laundry,** and parking included.)

The *Fußgängerzone* is riddled with pricey, mediocre restaurants. A good choice is **SportCafé Schneider** (tel. 25 48), with no apparent sports theme, but a fine selection of soups and sandwiches for 35 to 55AS and ice cream desserts for 35 to 65AS. (Open 9am-midnight.) To combat St. Anton's generally high prices, the local supermarkets may be your best bet. The **Nah und Frisch Supermarket** (tel. 35 81) beckons from the *Fußgängerzone*. (Open summer M-F 7am-noon and 2-6pm, Sa 7am-noon; winter M-Sa 7am-noon and 2-6:30pm.) The local **Spar Markt** lies farther down the main road, just past the *Fußgängerzone*. (Open M-F 7am-noon and 2-6pm, Sa 7am-12:30pm.)

SIGHTS AND ENTERTAINMENT St. Anton in the summer is a quiet haven for mountain hikers and sport-lovers. On summer Sundays, the local **hikers** hit the **Wanderwege** with walking sticks and full Tirolean hiking costume—join them for some spectacular mountain views and beautiful hikes along rushing streams. For starters, try the **Mühltobelweg,** a shady trail that runs up the mountain alongside a thundering stream, complete with a misty 6m waterfall. To reach the trail head, go uphill toward Pension Pepi Eiter but turn right at the red Museum Café sign and follow the signs to the café. The trail starts along the right side of the mini-golf course. (1hr. round-trip, including several stops for open-mouthed gawking at the scenery.) Once a week, the tourist office sponsors wildflower hikes. The office has lists of hikes and a trail map. Crack cyclists might try for the **Arlberg Mountainbike Trophy,** bestowed every August upon the winner of a treacherous 20.5km race with steep climbs and dangerously rapid downhill sections. Entry in the tourney is 400AS, 100AS for kids. (Call 226 90 for information.) Otherwise, 60km of marked mountain bike paths await you, including the popular Ferwall Valley and Moostal trails. Swimming in St. Anton's **outdoor pool,** with a 36m twisty red slide, is also fun. *(60AS, children 15AS; open June-Sept. 9am-7pm.)* So are golf, tennis, fishing, and concerts. *(Free for families with guest cards.)*

In the winter (to reiterate), there is skiing. St. Anton's resorts boast a list of clientele that reads like the December special issue of *People* magazine. European royalty and Hollywood stars stay incognito in bulky ski-wear and extra-terrestrial goggles. Prince Edward, JFK Jr., Clint Eastwood, Charles Schulz, LaToya Jackson, and Paul Anka have all graced the slopes at St. Anton. Paul Anka? To follow in their ski tracks may be

The Arlberg Channel

St. Anton's economy (like its full name) depends on that pretty old hunk of rock, the Arlberg. Understandably, the town really likes its pet peak. A lot. How much? The town has set up a TV station that provides nothing but live footage of the mountain—hour after hour of trees, rocks, more rocks, and snow. All Arlberg, all the time. Showing up-to-the-minute weather, the channel is ostensibly a service for skiers, but anyone in town can tell you the real reason for it: St. Anton is simply paying high-tech homage to its provider. Twenty-four-hour surveillance replaces burnt offerings—and, anyway, you never know when the mountain might pack up and leave if no one kept an eye on it.

costly, but if you stay in St. Anton and ski for more than three days, you become eligible for a minor reduction in price (about 100AS off your Arlberg Ski Pass). If Demi Moore has crowded you out of the lift line, you might want to turn to St. Anton's winter spectator sports. In December, the town offers the professional **Isospeed tennis tournament,** which features moderately famous European players, like Goran Ivanisevic, Henri Leconte, and Javier Sanchez. In January, the **Kandahar Ski Race** on the World Cup circuit attracts the sport's best. (It fluctuates between men's and women's skiing on alternate years; 1999 brings the women's competition.) Or watch the **Synchro Ski World Cup,** where two skiers tackle the mountain simultaneously and are judged not only on speed but also on how closely they mirror each other's form with Germanic precision. Weird. Most exciting of all, St. Anton is gearing up for the Alpine Skiing World Championships in 2001. All races will finish at a single newly built stadium. Make plans early if you want to attend.

■ Near St. Anton: Lech

In 1300 the call went out: "There's gold in them thar hills," and the settlers came, leading their cattle from the Valais region of western Switzerland to Lech. As others found, however, the real gold here is powdery and white. The ski resort industry saw a seminal event here when some lost Tirolean daredevil skiers happened upon the Swiss dairymen in their little valley between the Rüflikopf (2362m), Karhorn (2416m), and Braunarspitze (2648m) peaks. Smiling contentedly at the mountain slopes, they took a quick swig of schnapps, checked their bindings, and immediately shooshed to the nearest bank. They mortgaged all they had to bring the sport of skiing (and its wealthy practitioners) to the valley. The skiing was so good that people couldn't head up the hill quickly enough; 1939 saw the first T-bar lift. Lech is farther up the mountain than its neighbor St. Anton—above the tree line, in fact. The snow-streaked mountains in all directions are an immediate temptation to start some serious **hiking,** while 1200 square meters of outdoor, heated swimming pool waters called the **Waldbad** invite you to go swimming (just down the road from Zug). Lech offers free access to all cable cars, local buses, child care, and swimming facilities to visitors with Lech guest cards.

Guest beds outnumber permanent Lech residents five to one, but when the snow-flakes fall the beds fill up and the prices rise. Luckily, there is a **youth hostel** in Lech, kept discreetly at a distance. From the bus stop, head down the main road into town, and continue along this road. Take the last fork downhill before leaving Lech, and cross back over the river. Continue for about 15 minutes, curving toward Lech at the tiny white chapel, and then head uphill around *Haus Tristeller.* **Jugendheim Stubenbach (HI)** (tel. 24 19; fax 24 194) is at the top of that hill, decorated by a large mural of a prophet right in the middle of a revelation. Lovely mountain views come for a bargain price. (180AS per person, stays of 2 nights or more 160AS. Winter: 300AS, 280AS. Breakfast included. Closed Oct., May, and June.) To get to **Haus Brunelle** (tel. 29 76), follow the main road downhill past the church and over the river. Haus Brunelle will be on your right at #220. (Singles 190-220AS. Winter: 330-350AS. Open late June to early Sept. and Dec.-Apr. Breakfast included.) **Pizza Charly** (tel. 23 39) will serve you food. Down the main road past the church and just after the bridge, it's underneath the cables of the *Schloßkopfbahn* (where they hang tablecloths in the summer). Pizza (90-205AS) and pasta (90-175AS) are served by the river. (Open July to late Apr. 11am-2pm and 4pm-midnight. Take-out available.) **S'Caserol Bistro** (tel. 37 41) lies beyond the church on the right beneath the Volksbank sign and serves crispy baguettes and pasta with vegetarian options for 95-150AS. (Open only during high seasons; 11am-1pm.)

During the off-season (May-July and Oct.-Dec.), Lech is almost inaccessible by public transportation, with only a few buses each day from nearby Langen. In the high skiing and hiking seasons (Dec.-Apr. and June-Sept.), several **buses** run daily to **St. Anton, Zürs, Langen,** and **Bludenz.** (44AS one-way, day pass 80AS; from St. Anton, the beautifully scenic ride takes 30min., and buses run from 8:12am-6pm. The last return bus is at 6:37pm.) **Taxis** respond to phone calls at 25 01 or 25 02. The **tourist office** (tel. 21 610; fax 31 55; email lech-info@lech.at; http://www.lech.at), is just down the road from the bus stop on the right. Hiking maps and English guidebooks are 60AS together. Guided hikes available. The **24-hour electronic accommodations board** in the foyer has a free phone to make reservations, and there's a **travel agency** in the office. There are **lockers** downstairs for 10AS. (Open late June to mid-Sept. M-Sa 8am-1pm and 2-6pm, Su 9am-noon and 3-5pm; mid-Sept. to Nov. M-F 9am-noon and 2-5pm, Sa 9am-noon; Dec.-Apr. M-Sa 9am-6pm, Su 9am-noon and 3-5pm; May to late June M-F 9am-noon and 2-5pm.) Nearby banks are generally open 8:30am to noon and 2 to 4pm. **Raiffeisenbank,** opposite the church and next to the post office, has a **24-hour ATM. Free parking** is available in the Esso garage under the church. For **weather reports,** dial 18 in Lech. To **report accidents,** dial 144. For the **police,** dial 22 03; for the **Red Cross,** call 20 32. Walk past the church and down the hill to the **post office** (tel. 22 40; fax 22 50). (Open M-F 8am-noon and 2-6pm; exchange closes at 5pm.) The **postal code** is A-6764, and the **telephone code** is 05583.

VORARLBERG

SWITZERLAND

US$1 = 1.49 Swiss francs (SFr)	1SFr = US$0.67
CDN$1 = 0.98SFr	1SFr = CDN$1.02
UK£1 = 2.42SFr	1SFr = UK£0.41
IR£1 = 2.10SFr	1SFr = IR£0.48
AUS$1 = 0.89SFr	1SFr = AUS$1.13
NZ$1 = 0.75SFr	1SFr = NZ$1.33
SAR1 = 0.24SFr	1SFr = SAR4.22
1AS = 0.12SFr	1SFr = 9.43AS
1DM = 0.83SFr	1SFr = DM1.20
1kč = 0.05SFr	1SFr = 21.69kč

Country code: 41
International Dialing Prefix: 00

Switzerland (*die Schweiz, la Suisse, la Svizzera, Confederatio Helvetica*) is a land of mountains. A mini-Switzerland was conceived in 1291; it grew slowly, accumulating canton after canton until it reached its present state of 23 cantons and 3 sub-cantons. Mere treaties formed for survival united linguistically and culturally distinct areas. High German is the country's official language, but some two-thirds of the 7.2 million Swiss speak Swiss-German (*Schwyzerdütsch*), one-fifth French, one-tenth Italian, and 1% Romansh (a Latinate relic). The vast majority speak more than two languages; a growing immigrant population accounts for the remaining 5%. Switzerland holds stubbornly to its complex identity, uniting inhabitants through a sturdy democratic tradition. Swiss politics generally have an old-fashioned, "small town" feel: about 3000 local communes retain a great deal of power, and national referenda routinely settle major policy disputes.

Official neutrality since 1815 has spared this snowy paradise from the devastation suffered by the rest of Europe. Neutrality has also nurtured the growth of trade routes and ultimately big money in the staid banking centers of Geneva and Zurich. Most Swiss are down to earth and enjoy the pleasures of hiking, skiing, and good food—all specialties of the extensive, experienced Swiss tourist industry.

The country's varied population conducts its affairs against a universal backdrop of unparalleled natural beauty. Hikers, skiers, bikers, and paragliders from everywhere journey to Switzerland's ice-capped peaks. Mountains cover 58% of the country's 41,293 sq. km and extend into four other countries. Surprisingly, the Swiss have put 77% of country's area to productive use (46% meadowland, 25% forest, 6% arable land). Victorian scholar John Ruskin dubbed the Alps that comprise the remaining 23% of area "the great cathedrals of the earth." You're welcome to worship here if you can spare the cash.

■ History and Politics

> In Italy for thirty years under the Borgias they had warfare, terror, murder, bloodshed—they produced Michelangelo, Leonardo da Vinci, and the Renaissance. In Switzerland they had brotherly love, 500 years of democracy, and peace. What did that produce? The cuckoo clock.
>
> —Orson Welles, *The Third Man*

EARLY YEARS (TO 500 CE)

Before 8000 BCE, Switzerland was too cold for regular habitation. When it got warmer, Mesolithic hunter-gatherers moved into the area and settled down. After two thousand years, Indo-European farmers arrived. Tools changed from stone to

SWITZERLAND

Swiss Rail Lines

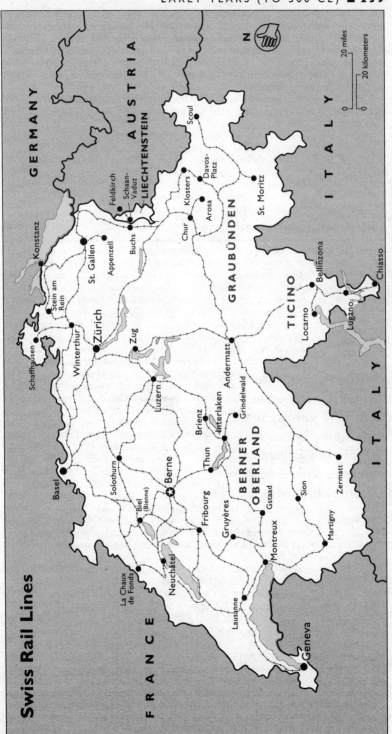

bronze and from bronze to iron, and by 750 BCE, Switzerland became an important center of **Celtic** culture. The artistic and warlike **Helvetians,** the most prominent Swiss-Celtic tribe, gained notoriety for their largely unsuccessful attempts to invade Roman Italy in 222 BCE and again as allies of Carthage between 218 and 203 BCE (when they aided Hannibal's famous elephant-assisted crossing of the Alps). Their attempts to advance into Gaul in 58 BCE were halted by Julius Caesar, who crushed then colonized the Helvetians. Romanized between 47 BCE and 15 CE, they survived as a settled, peaceful, urban civilization for the next two centuries. **Romansh,** more closely related to Latin than any other Romance language, is still spoken in former Roman territories.

Around 250, constant barbarian raids forced Switzerland to militarize, changing it from a peaceful farming province into an armed frontier. As Roman influence waned in the 5th century, the barbarians began to form permanent settlements. **Burgundians** settled the west, merging peacefully with the Romanized Celts and absorbing their culture and language. The less communicative **Allemanians** populated the center and northeast, eventually pushing the Burgundians west to the Sarine River, which remains the border between German and French Switzerland.

THE MIDDLE AGES (500-1517)

Roman influence declined over the next few centuries as local gentry began to struggle among themselves over land. Things turned feudal for a good long time, and certain landowners gained enormous dominion and influence (see **Tell-tale,** p. 262). After the break-up of the Carolingian empire in the 9th century, the feudal power of these **lords** grew even more. For a while, they were vassals of the Frankish king, but eventually they established themselves as part of the Burgundian dynasty. When the last Burgundian King died in 1032, his nephew, the King of Germania, incorporated Helvetica into his growing kingdom. Part of Switzerland thus enjoyed a stint in the **Holy Roman Empire,** during which Zurich and Solothurn prospered and Bern and Fribourg were founded. Meanwhile, the **Houses of Savoy, Habsburg,** and **Zähringen** fought over the territories left after the dissolution of Carolingian rule and the divisions wrought by the 12th-century **Investiture Conflict.** When Berthold V of Zähringen died in 1218 without an heir, the greedy Habsburgs immediately tried to overtake the Zähringen lands. Eventually defeated, the Habsburgs signed a letter of franchise in 1231 guaranteeing freedom to the inhabitants of Zähringen. Worried by constant regional conflict, the three forest cantons of Uri, Schwyz, and Unterwald signed a secret agreement in 1291 forming the *Ewige Bund* (Everlasting League), obligating the cantons to defend each other from outside attack. (Switzerland therefore celebrated its 700th anniversary in 1991.) After the **Battle of Morgarten** in 1315, in which the imperial Habsburg family tried to crush the confederation, Habsburg leaders agreed to a truce and granted the alliance official recognition.

> *Uri, Schwyz, and Unterwald signed a secret agreement in 1291 forming the Ewige Bund (Everlasting League), obligating the cantons to defend each other from outside attack.*

Over the next several centuries, the three-canton core of Switzerland expanded through merger and acquisition despite conflict between the League and the Habsburg Emperors. The increasing diversity of the population led to increasingly complicated problems, and in the middle of the 15th century, social tensions between the town and country residents threatened to erupt. Legend has it that conflict was averted due to the leadership of **Niklaus von Flüe** (a.k.a. Brüder Klaus), a mystical hermit-farmer, who convinced everyone to sign an oath of renewed brotherhood and association. Meanwhile, Swiss soldiers became terrifyingly efficient mercenaries, with clients including the pope and the northern Italian city-states. The **Swiss Guard** still defend the Vatican, resplendent in their 16th-century uniforms and armaments. The **Swabian War** with the Habsburgs of 1499-1500 brought virtual independence from the Holy Roman Empire, but the **Perpetual Peace** agreement of 1516, the result of Switzerland's inadequate defense of the pope against French attempts to reclaim Naples, made the Swiss mere functionaries in French armies, and thus prevented most autonomous action.

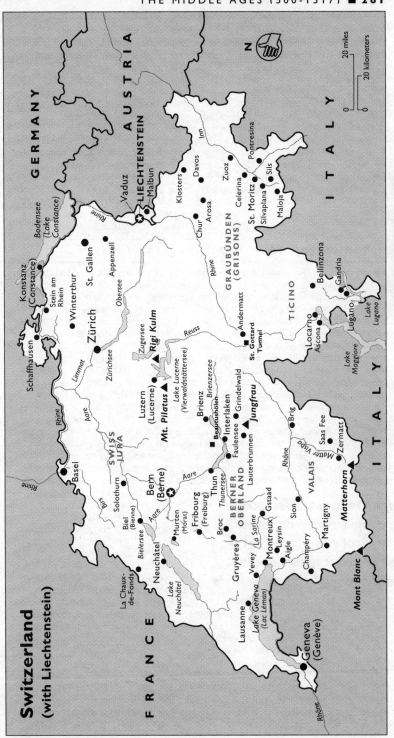

Switzerland
(with Liechtenstein)

Tell-tale

First found in a 15th-century ballad and probably the product of an older oral tradition, the tale of Wilhelm (William) Tell has appeared in wide and varied versions, culminating in Friedrich Schiller's drama *Wilhelm Tell* in 1804. The tale takes place sometime in the early 1300s, when Tell and his young son visited the town of Altdorf in his native canton of Uri. While in town, Tell refused to doff his hat to the hat of Gessler, the much-loathed Habsburg governor, which had been sycophantically affixed to a pole in the town square. Tell was arrested for his disobedience and made to shoot an apple off his son's head as punishment. As Tell prepared to shoot, Gessler found that Tell had two arrows in his quiver and asked why. Without a second's hesitation Tell replied that if the first arrow missed its mark, he would aim the second at Gessler's heart. Tell scored a bull's-eye, but because of his threat to Gessler, he was re-arrested and sent by boat to a prison on the opposite side of Lake Lucerne. As Tell and his captors traversed the lake, a violent storm seized the little boat and allowed Tell to overpower his guards. He returned safely, slew Gessler, and lived happily ever after. The Swiss herald the myth as befitting the country's tenacity in its struggle for freedom.

REFORMATION TO REVOLUTION (1517–1815)

The **Protestant Reformation** rocked the place to its foundations. As Lutheranism swept Northern Europe, radical theologian **Ulrich Zwingli** of Zurich spearheaded his own brand of reform that advocated a less literal reinterpretation of the symbols and gestures of Catholicism. In 1523, the city government of Zurich sanctioned Zwingli's proposed *Theses* and strengthened Zwingli's hold over the local government, banning the differently minded **Anabaptists** and imposing harsh disciplines on its inhabitants. **John Calvin,** a lawyer and priest born in France, preached a doctrine of predestination that implied a rigid moral framework. He soon took a theocratic grip of Geneva and instituted puritanical reforms, turning Geneva into a shining example of the ideal of protestant social control. In 1527, brawls erupted between Roman Catholic and Protestant cantons, culminating in the 1531 defeat of the Protestants at Kappel and Zwingli's death. The confederation finally took action, granting Protestants freedoms but prohibiting them from imposing their faith on others.

Despite religious differences, the confederation remained neutral during the **Thirty Years War,** escaping the devastation wrought on the rest of Central Europe. The 1648 **Peace of Westphalia** recognized the independence and neutrality of the 13 cantons. Independence and periodic inter-religious alignments did little to heal the Catholic-Protestant rift, however, and the next century saw the Catholics ally themselves with France and Spain to fight against the spread of Protestantism in Europe as the Protestants fostered hierarchies and social control, expanded banking and literacy, and hunted the witches they believed were plaguing Europe.

Despite religious differences, the confederation remained neutral during the Thirty Years War, escaping the devastation wrought on the rest of Central Europe.

Caught up in Revolutionary fervor and perhaps peeved at the Swiss Guard, who loyally defended King Louis XVI and the royal family until their death, French troops invaded Switzerland in 1798 and, by Napoleon's order, established the **Helvetic Republic.** In theory, the republic restructured relationships between the cantons and the federal government and granted citizens freedom of religion and equality before the law. Napoleon added six cantons, separated church and state, established internal free trade, and emancipated the peasantry. Napolean's reforms left social structures largely intact, however, and the landed aristocracy maintained control over the politics of the region. After Napoleon's defeat, the Congress of Vienna recognized **Swiss neutrality** and created a new conservative constitution, under which the old elite lost some of their previous monopoly on wealth and power. The constitution also added two cantons and returned Geneva, annexed into France by Napoleon, to Switzerland, bringing the total to 26—today's magic number.

THE NEUTRALITY THING (1815-1945)

A major period of economic growth began around 1815. While agriculture and tourism expanded, the industrial sector saw the most significant gains. Because a continental blockade excluded Britain from the European market during the Napoleonic Wars, the Swiss were forced to modernize and mechanize their own industry. Industrial growth brought relative material prosperity, but the era was not problem free. The Mediation Act disappeared with Napoleon, and the **Federal Pact** of 1815 that replaced Napoleon's decrees once again established Switzerland as a confederation of sovereign states united only for common defense—forming or executing united foreign policy was still impossible. Because of logistical barriers (each canton had its own laws, currency, postal service, weights, measures, and army), the confederation revoked the right to reside freely in any canton, and the inhabitants of one canton began to regard the inhabitants of other cantons as foreigners. Furthermore, civil liberties were almost non-existent and religious tensions re-emerged.

These religious differences led, in 1846, to the formation of a separatist defense league of Catholic cantons known as the **Sonderbund,** composed of Lucerne, Uri, Schwyz, Unterwalden, Zug, Fribourg, and Valais. In July 1847, the **Diet,** representing the other cantons, declared the Sonderbund incompatible with the Federal Pact and demanded its dissolution. In keeping with the fashion of the time, a civil war broke out. It only lasted 25 days. The federalist forces were victorious, and the country wrote a **new constitution** modeled after that of the United States in 1848 (modified in 1874). Finally balancing the age-old conflict between federal and cantonal power, the constitution guaranteed republican and democratic cantonal constitutions and set up an executive body for the first time. The central government established unified postal, currency, and railway systems and a free-trade zone among all the cantons. In that same year, a crisis arose over Neuchâtel, formerly the property of the King of Prussia. The citizens of Neuchâtel rebelled against the king and forced him to renounce his rights to the territory while allowing him to retain the title of Prince of Neuchâtel. The canton remained part of Switzerland.

Once turmoil had given way to stability, Switzerland cultivated its reputation for resolving international conflicts (or at least getting its name on anything diplomatic). The **Geneva Convention of 1864** established international laws for conduct during war. The **International Red Cross** set up its headquarters in Geneva. Free of the tangle of alliances that characterized Europe's turn-of-the-century balance of power, Switzerland remained neutral throughout the **Franco-Prussian war** and **World War I.** With the dawn of the 20th century, Swiss anxiety grew as German and Italian territories united to form nation-states. In an effort to prepare for possible conflict, Switzerland revised its constitution in 1874 to strengthen federal power over the military. The new constitution also revised labor laws to address rapidly advancing industrial mechanization. Throughout the first half of the century, power was increasingly turned over to the federal government—in 1912, the cantons yielded their control over civil law and, in 1942, penal law.

In 1920, Geneva welcomed the headquarters of the ill-fated **League of Nations,** becoming the place for international diplomacy. **World War II** found Switzerland surrounded by the Axis powers, but trade with both sides and a hard-hitting invasion-contingency plan kept the country neutral. While some Jews and other refugees from Nazi Germany found safe haven in Switzerland, the Swiss government, not eager to incur the wrath of the monster that surrounded it, generally impeded passage through its territory and assumed the hiding-tortoise position. Displeased, the Allies complicated Swiss diplomacy after the war. Switzerland has maintained strict neutrality to this day, and while the country hosts a branch of the **United Nations** and trains some army units for peacekeeping roles within it, it abstains from official participation in the organization.

Semper Paratus

Every household holds at least one Swiss Army knife. But as we open wine bottles, cut French bread, and spread pâté all with the same handy gadget, we rarely consider the oxymoronic nature of a Swiss Army. For a nation that has been neutral since its independence and the global icon of pacifism through the Cold War era, the concept, let alone the reality, is surprising. Behind the sweet-toothed, storybook facade stands one of the most heavily armed populations and most highly trained armies in the world. Mountains bristle with fortifications, pastures conceal airstrips, bridges are mined to self-destruct, and tanks and fighter jets lurk deep within the Alpine rock. Every Swiss male stores a gas mask, a repeating rifle, and a sealed, government-issued box of ammunition. He must participate in 17 weeks of military training and must return for an annual three-week refresher course until the age of 36—after that, and until retirement, the course lasts only two weeks. In 1986, a coalition of pacifists, socialists, and religious leaders dared to ask for what exactly the neutral nation was preparing. They brought the issue to a vote, and for the first time in history a European nation was presented with the option of abolishing its army. The referendum drew a passionate response: 35.6% of the population voted against the army, irked by the $1000 per capita spent annually on defense and the peculiar effects the army training has on the workforce: companies must overhire to compensate for the gaps left by men in training, but many employees work their way up the business ladder through army contacts (especially if they're in the officer corps) and use the refresher courses more as elite alumni meetings than as training. Despite the popular outcry, however, the measure failed, and for now Switzerland's charming landscape continues to hide not-so-charming military might. As the Swiss saying goes, "Switzerland does not have an army; it *is* an army."

CURRENT GOVERNMENT

Swiss government is based on a three-tiered system of communes, cantons, and confederation. Over 3000 **communes** (the smallest administrative unit of government) compose the 26 cantons. Each canton has its own constitution, legislature, executive office, and judiciary system. The cantons are in turn incorporated into the **Confederation** and its two-chamber legislature, the Federal Assembly. One chamber, the **National Council,** distributes its 200 seats based on population, the other, the **Council of States,** distributes equal seats to the cantons. Decisions of the Federal Assembly take effect only with a majority in both chambers.

The executive branch consists of a group of seven members—the **Federal Council**—elected to four-year terms by a joint meeting of both legislative chambers. No canton may have more than one representative in the Federal Council at a time. The Federal Council chooses the **president** from among its ranks. The president only holds office for one year. To maintain a system of checks and balances, the Federal Council provides the legislative branch with an annual account of its activities.

Politics play a role in Swiss daily life through **referenda** or **initiatives.** Citizens can bring a constitutional amendment to the fore by an initiative of at least 100,000 votes. A majority of citizens must approve any constitutional change by means of referendum before it can become law.

RECENT YEARS

Switzerland's policy of armed neutrality persists to the present: there is no standing army, but every adult male faces compulsory military service. And the desire for an army at all seems to be fading, as illustrated by a 1989 referendum proposing to disband the army (see **Semper Paratus,** above). Switzerland has become increasingly wealthy, liberal, successful, and service-oriented since WWII, and the country is still fiercely independent and wary of entanglements with the rest of Europe. After years of economic stagnation, Swiss citizens continue to feel strongly about the EU issue and a recent vote rejecting the treaty on a **European Economic Area** (EEA) boasted a voter turnout of almost 80%. The division between those who opt to resist change in order to retain *Sonderfall Schweig* **(the Swiss Way)** and those who envision growth and involvement with the EU reveals a split along linguistic lines: all six Francophone cantons lean towards integration, while the German-speaking cantons and Italian-speaking Ticino resist economic interdependence.

The world has recently begun to examine Switzerland's actual involvement with the Nazis during WWII, and accusations of complicity have spread world-wide. Switzerland's "blind account" policy, allowing Holocaust victims and Nazi leaders alike to deposit money, has created complex situations. In the summer of 1997, more names of bank accounts from the World War II era were released, even though several Swiss banks had in the past claimed they had released all that they could—a sticky P.R. situation, to say the least. A proposed constitutional amendment that would establish a humanitarian fund has pleased international Jewish organizations. It hasn't passed yet.

■ **Art and Architecture**

Art and architecture have long flourished in Switzerland, and the country's diversity, tolerance, and neutrality have allowed the development of some of Europe's most vibrant cultural centers. Even early on, there were artists. The Renaissance produced **Urs Graf,** a swashbuckling soldier-artist-poet excellently suited to court portraiture. Nineteenth-century painter **John Henry Füssli,** whose work featured horrifying images of demons and goblins, furthered the popularity of Romanticism in Switzerland. **Ferdinand Hodler,** an early Symbolist painter, worked with powerful images of Swiss landscapes and characters to convey metaphysical messages.

Switzerland's art scene was energized by an influx of talented refugees during the World Wars. A congregation of artistic personalities, combined with the increasing trend toward decadence in the early 1900s, produced the **Dada** explosion in Zurich in 1916, led by **Hans Arp, Richard Hülsenbeck, Janco, Tristan Tzara,** and **Hugo Ball.** Together they founded the "Cabaret Voltaire" and "Galerie Dada," short-lived centers of Dada activity. Marginal participants in the Zurich Dada scene later developed into artists in their own right. **Jean Tinguely** created kinetic, mechanized Dada fantasies that celebrated the beauty of motion. **Sophie Tauber-Arp** (wife of Hans Arp), a brilliant artist who died young, experimented with serial painting in an attempt to subvert Western compositional strategies. Twentieth-century artist **Paul Klee** was born near Bern but spent his childhood and early career in Germany, where he produced beautiful, ironic, and delicately mysterious works. He was a member of *der Blaue Reiter* school, a movement led by **Kandinsky,** and of the Bauhaus faculty. His paintings are somewhere near the beginning of abstraction, and call into question dominant modes of artistic expression. He returned to Switzerland just before World War II. The **Zurich School of Concrete Art,** a movement that occurred primarily between the wars, combined elements of Surrealism with ideas from Russian Constructivism in an attempt to work with objects and environments to explore interactions between humans and space. **Max Bill's** Mondrian-derived canvases, focusing on color relationships and the texture and form of the surface itself, are quintessential Concrete paintings. The school includes Paul Klee and **Meret Oppenheim,** a Surrealist famous for her *Fur Cup.* The philosophy guided sculptor **Alberto Giacometti** to play with spatial realities in creating his celebrated works in the 1930s. Later, Giacometti rejected the premise of Surrealism in order to concentrate on a deep representationalism, creating small, exaggerated, slender figures like *Man Pointing.* After sitting out the Second World War in London and spending time in Prague, Austrian Expressionist painter **Oskar Kokoschka** also moved to Switzerland in 1953, settling in Villeneuve. When Kokoschka died in 1980, his widow, Olda, found herself with an embarrassment of pictures and subsequently founded the Foundation Oskar Kokoschka in the Musée Jenisch in Vevey. In a sense, Switzerland was the primary space for liberal experimentation, a space that gave rise to the first subversive strains in

Western art, a space where the established categories for composition were called into question. That same subversive spirit led in 1976 to the genesis of New Wave music with the band **Lilliput** (née **Kleenex**), a quirky, jerky, and slightly obscure girl band exposed to the world through the British record label Rough Trade.

Off the canvas, **Robert Maillart** developed the slab technique for bridge design in 1900, and for the first years of the century produced elegant ferro-concrete bridges that were much more efficient and much less dense than any previous concrete bridge. The world-acclaimed architect **Le Corbusier** applied this ferro-concrete building technique to domestic and commercial building, inspired by the geometric shapes and rugged textures of his Swiss Jura home. Le Corbusier brought a new, animated spirit to contemporary architecture in Paris, Moscow, Stuttgart, Zurich, and Cambridge, Massachusetts based on an architecture in proportion to human stature.

■ Literature

Jean-Jacques Rousseau, born in Geneva in 1712 and best known for his *Social Contract* that inspired the French Revolution, always proudly recognized his Swiss background—despite the fact that he spent most of his time outside the country and that the Swiss burned his books. **Jacob Burckhardt** promoted a new history of culture and art from his Basel home in the late 19th century. An expert in Renaissance Italian art, his main works include *History of the Italian Renaissance* and *Cicerone: A Guide to the Enjoyment of Italian Art.* Writers of the same initials **J.J. Bodmer** and **J.J. Breitinger** advocated the supremacy of feeling and imaginative vision central to Romanticism. **Madame de Staël** (born Germaine Necker) was the primary force behind Romanticism's spread from Germany to France, as well as an important writer in her own right. As a result of her political intrigues and alleged rebuff of Napoleon's advances (she succeeded where Europe failed), de Staël was forced into a miserable exile in Coppet. **Benjamin Constant de Rebecque,** a native of Lausanne, one-time lover of Mme de Staël, and author of the novel *Adolphe,* joined **Léonard de Sismondi** of Geneva and Mme de Staël in contributing to the French Romantic movement. **Gottfried Keller** was a popular Swiss novelist and poet integral to the rising influence of Poetic Realism in late German Romanticism. He wrote the classic 19th-century German *Bildungsroman,* entitled *Der Grüne Heinrich.*

Conrad Ferdinand Meyer was another highly influential Swiss poet, whose writings feature strongly individualistic heroes and were some of the only German works to effectively unite Romanticism and Realism. **Hermann Hesse** moved to Switzerland in 1899 and became a Swiss citizen in 1924. He earned the Nobel Prize for literature in 1946 for his collected oeuvre, which dealt with the crisis of existence and the power of laughter. Another thinker concerned with the crisis of existence on a broad scale, **Carl Gustav Jung** wrote and set up a growing psychoanalytic practice in Zurich. He began as an acolyte of Freud but split off by 1915 when he wrote *Symbols of Transformation.* He invented the idea of the extroverted and introverted personalities, as well as the collective unconscious and its corollary, archetypes.

Twentieth-century Switzerland has produced two widely respected modern playwrights and a formerly obscure novelist who wrote with such tiny handwriting that he fit entire works on café bills. Critics laud **Max Frisch** for his Brechtian style and thoughtful treatment of Nazi Germany; his most widely known work is the play *Andorra.* **Friedrich Dürrenmatt** has written a number of excellent, cutting, funny plays, most notably *The Visit of the Old Lady* and *The Physicists.* Both Dürrenmatt and Frisch are critical of their home country. The novelist **Robert Walser** has been celebrated for his diffuse, existential works; they were largely ignored until his death in 1956 by an audience expecting clearly defined morals and themes. Posthumously, his novels, poetry, and plays are recognized for their fragile, shady, ironic, and melancholic language.

Switzerland also has a life in the literature of other nations. Henry James's Daisy Miller toured here; Mark Twain incorporated cuckoo clocks into his revenge fantasies and followed well-touristed paths with his own rough grace, chronicled in *A Tramp Abroad.* The ghosts of geniuses hover in the Alpine countryside surrounding Geneva: Gogol, Dostoyevsky, Hugo, Hemingway, and Fitzgerald.

■ Exiles and Emigrés

Voltaire arrived in Geneva in 1755; since then, a steady stream of intellectuals, artists, and soon-to-be-famous personalities has called Switzerland home. The notion of Switzerland as a neutral refuge among more quarrelsome nations has held appeal for many since the November 20, 1815 Treaty of Paris.

George Gordon, otherwise known as the opium-smoking Romantic **Lord Byron,** quit England in 1816 and fled to Switzerland. Here he met **Percy Shelley,** and the two composed some of their greatest works. Byron wrote "Sonnet on Chillon" while brooding on Lake Geneva; Shelley crafted "Hymn to Beauty" and "Mont Blanc" in the vale of Chamonix. During an especially wet summer in Switzerland, some ghost stories fell into **Mary Wollstonecraft Shelley's** hands; these stories, Switzerland's eternal mist, and the craggy Alps inspired the Gothic elements of *Frankenstein.*

Charles Dickens vacationed in the Lausanne area and wrote *Dombey and Son* on the shores of Lake Geneva. In the early 20th century, **T.S. Eliot** languished here while writing *The Wasteland.* **James Joyce** fled to Zurich during World War I and stayed to scribble the greater part of his modernist work *Ulysses* between 1915 and 1919; World War II drove him to Zurich once again, where he died in 1941.

Other great minds flocked from Germany, Austria, and Italy. **Johann Wolfgang von Goethe** caught his first distant view of Italy from the top of St. Gotthard Pass in the Swiss Alps, the clouded path that would serve as an allegory for the rest of his life. **Friedrich Schiller** wrote about the massive church bell in Schaffhausen before penning *Wilhelm Tell.* **Rossini** later turned the William Tell thing into an opera, whose overture is also known as the *Lone Ranger* theme song. While on holiday in the Engadin Valley, **Friedrich Nietzsche** went nuts, cooked up some historical and philosophical ramblings, and produced his mountaintop tome *Thus Spoke Zarathustra.* His complex personal relationship with **Richard Wagner** began here while Nietzsche held a professor's chair at Basel University. Wagner composed most of his major operas during his years in green, green Switzerland.

Zurich and Basel served as a wellspring for intellectual revolution in the sciences; smarty pants **Albert Einstein** studied there and by 1901 was a Swiss citizen. He moved to Bern to work in a patent office, where various applications inspired the foundation for the theory of relativity and the law of equality of matter and energy. He won the Nobel Prize for physics in 1924. **Karl Jaspers,** the German physician and psychologist of self-fulfillment and self-knowledge, has taught in Basel since 1948, and became a citizen in 1967.

The two German greats **Thomas Mann** and **Carl Zuckmayer** also found Switzerland a safe haven, Mann using one of the Swiss Alps as the setting for his novel *The Magic Mountain.* Switzerland's recent acquisitions include writers and scientists from the former Eastern bloc, notably Russian author **Alexander Solzhenitsyn** and Czech novelist **Milan Kundera.**

▓ Food and Drink

Little known to those individuals not among the ranks of chefs or culinary experts, Switzerland has one of the finest culinary traditions in all of Europe—the majority of famous French chefs were Swiss-educated. The reasons: Swiss neutrality and the endurance of traditional, hearty peasant cooking.

While most budget travelers may not be able to enjoy the *crème de la crème* of Swiss cuisine, trickle-down gastronomics operates in full force. Superseding all regional dishes and possible pretensions to four-star cuisine are Switzerland's culinary masterpieces: **cheese** and **chocolate.** While the words "Swiss cheese" may conjure images of lunch-boxed sandwiches filled with a hard, oily, holey cheese, Switzerland actually has innumerable varieties, each made from a particular type of milk. Cheese with holes is usually Emmentaler, from the eponymous northwest region, but nearly every canton and many towns have specialty cheeses. To name a few of the most well-known: *Gruyère* is a stronger and tastier version of *Emmentaler; Appenzeller* is a milder, hard cheese from the Appenzell region, sometimes made from sheep's milk instead of cow's milk; *tome* is a generic term for a soft, uncooked cheese similar to French *chèvre*. In the Italian regions, look for southern influences; cheese often resembles the *parmigiano* from Italy more than the cheeses of the north. As far as **chocolate** goes, Switzerland is home to two of the largest producers of chocolate: **Lindt** and **Suchard,** and each town has amazing concoctions at the local confectioner's shelves. With the invention of milk chocolate in 1875, Switzerland was positioned to **rule the world.** It's just biding its time.

The flavor of regional cooking bends with the contours of Switzerland's linguistic topography. The basic geography is simple and logical: Frenchified in the west, Italianish in the south, Swiss-German everywhere else. Each of these regions is represented, however, in the collective pool of "typical" Swiss dishes. A Swiss national menu might include the Zurich speciality, *Geschnetzeltes* (strips of veal stewed in a thick cream sauce), *Luzerner Chugelipastete* (pâté in a pastry shell), *Papet Vaudois* (leeks with sausage from the canton of Vaud), *Churer Fleischtorte* (meat pie originating from Chur), and Bernese salmon.

Three dishes in particular best represent Switzerland. **Rösti,** a patty of hash brown potatoes skilleted and occasionally flavored with bacon or cheese, is as prevalent in the German regions as **fondue** (from the French, *fondre*—to melt) is in the French. Usually a blend of Emmentaler and Gruyère cheeses, white wine, *kirsch,* and spices, fondue is eaten by dunking small cubes of white bread into a *caquelon* (a one-handled pot) kept hot by a small flame. The mother of all cheese dips originated as a way to use up stale bread and cheese shavings. **Raclette** is made by cutting a large cheese in half and heating it until it melts; the melted cheese is then scraped onto a baked potato and garnished with any number of other foodstuffs.

The Swiss are particularly good at baking and **confectionery.** To match each type of local cheese, there is usually a bread specific to the region or town. Ask for it by name (e.g., when in St. Gallen, ask for *St. Galler-brot*). Among the most tempting **cakes** are the *Baseler Leckerli* (a kind of gingerbread), *Schaffhauser Zungen, Zuger Kirschtorte,* Engadin nutcakes, the *bagnolet crème* of the Jura (eaten with raspberries and aniseed biscuits), soda rolls, *rissoles* (pear tarts), nougat and pralines of Geneva, and the *zabaglione* of Ticino. *Vermicelli* (not the Italian pasta but a dessert made of chestnut mousse) is popular all over Switzerland.

The Romans introduced **wine** to the region, but it was not until the 9th century that beer-drinking laity pried it away from the clergy—who used it, of course, for liturgical purposes. Sure. By the 19th century, production had grown so indiscriminately, and the results were so middling, that consum-

With the invention of milk chocolate in 1875, Switzerland was positioned to rule the world.

ers went back to drinking beer. But a wine statute in 1953 imposed rigorous quality controls, and since then Swiss wine has regained its reputation. Most wine is produced in the west and the Valais, about three-quarters of it white. The wine produced around Lake Zurich and in the Thurgau and Schaffhausen areas is predominantly *Blauburgunder,* with a small quantity of a *Riesling-Slyvaner* hybrid. Ticino specializes in reds made from the Merlot grape, and most restaurants offer a house wine as *nostrano* (one of ours). These wines are usually home-pressed blends, comparatively cheap, and delicious.

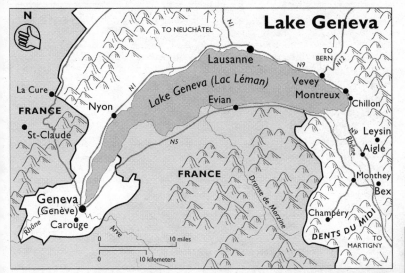

Lake Geneva (Lac Léman)

A reliable rule of economic geography states that incomes rise exponentially as you approach Lac Léman. Switzerland is not the first country that comes to mind when most budget travelers plan their low-to-the-ground itineraries—high-altitude prices are the general rule within Geneva, Lausanne, and Montreux. But the towns along the lake abound with at least three of Switzerland's cheapest commodities: quiet is just a short stroll along the tree-lined quay or up into the vine-laced hills, chocolate is a yummy pittance nearly everywhere, and the unforgettable views are, as always, free. The landscape of lakes lapping the shore and hills dotted by villas or festooned with the terraced garlands of ever-ripening grapes easily becomes familiar and seemingly settled—that is, until the haze clears and the rough-hewn mountain peaks become visible. And then the lake momentarily loses its cultivated prettiness and urbanity and takes on the energizing promise of unpeopled wilderness and wide lonely expanse.

🖐 HIGHLIGHTS OF LAKE GENEVA

- Geneva was home to John Calvin, Jean-Jacques Rousseau, and an outstanding collection of museums, including the International Red Cross, the Petit-Palais, and the Musée Barbier-Mueller.
- Lausanne's beautiful lakeside streets have drawn the likes of T.S. Eliot, Dickens, and Henry James, while their museums (including the fascinating Collection de l'Art Brut) draw tourists and art critics.
- Montreux draws the crowds to its famous jazz festival, but even off-season people come to see the Château de Chillon and the city's flower-lined quays.

GENEVA (GENÈVE, GENF)

"I detest Geneva," muttered Napoleon Bonaparte shortly before "liberating" the city in 1798, "they know English too well." They still do. Geneva is very much a cosmopolitan city: only one-third of the population are genuine *Genevois;* the other two-thirds are foreign-born internationals or transplants from other cantons. The large

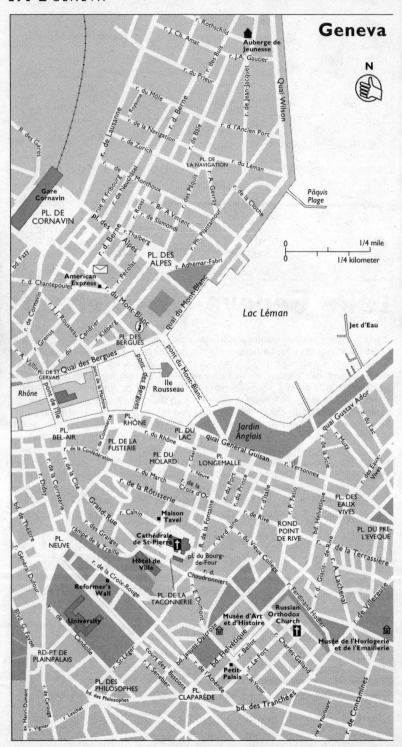

concentration of international banks and multinational organizations preserves the intricate mixture of the city's voices—quite a contrast to Switzerland's other, mostly homogeneous towns. Indeed, many say that all Geneva holds in common with the rest of Switzerland is its neutral foreign policy and the state religion, banking.

The French Emperor had more than linguistic contempt with which to contend. He knew all too well that Geneva's citizens have a long and belligerent tradition of doing battle to protect their political and religious independence. Medieval Geneva fended off constant attacks, protecting its strategic site on the outflow to Lac Léman. In 1536, however, Geneva openly welcomed a more insidious invader: the Protestant Reformation. The townspeople voted to convert *en masse* and invited an unknown 25-year-old, John Calvin, to their cathedral. His fiery sermons from Geneva's pulpit between 1536 and 1564 brought in waves of persecuted French and Italian refugees to the "Rome of Protestants." Geneva then waged a hard-won battle for freedom from the Catholic House of Savoy, whose Duke sought to crush both Protestantism and Genevan democracy (see **Soup's On,** below).

Unfortunately, that freedom did not spell tolerance. Calvin adopted the manner of the Catholic rule, renamed it the Protestant rule, and proceeded to burn those who didn't think he was running his new church correctly. The Reformists' ardent zeal continued for at least another century and a half, exemplified by the burning of Rousseau's books in a square just blocks from the house in which he was born. But Geneva's cosmopolitanism eventually won out, and the city became a gathering place for aesthetes and free thinkers. Voltaire lived and worked in the Geneva area for 23 years, and his compatriot Madame de Staël later held her salons in nearby Coppet. In the early 19th century, mountain-happy, heavy-tongued romantics Shelley and Byron found inspiration in the city's surroundings. Mary Wollstonecraft Shelley created *Frankenstein*'s monster here, and George Eliot set up house in Geneva, the city of her hero, Jean-Jacques Rousseau. One of Geneva's most famous political refugees was Lenin, who sat around from 1903 to 1905 and again in 1908 before being quietly shipped back to Moscow in a sealed train by Western leaders hoping to disrupt the turn-of-the-century Russian government.

Today's Geneva preserves and memorializes both extremes of its varied history. Street names alternate between rigid reformers and free-thinking artists and intellectuals. In many respects, the city lost its compact identity once its massive fortifications were scrapped to build up the lakefront. Now, it collects, adapts, and renews the various amorphous identities that flood its streets, protecting inhabitants with its tolerance rather than its military might. There are more McDonald's here than you'll find in the rest of Switzerland; there are more "traditional Swiss" restaurants in cubby-hole locations than McDonald's.

The city's unique atmosphere attracted refugee organizations as well as individuals. Under the inspiration of native Henri Dunant, the **International Committee of the Red Cross** established itself in Geneva in 1864, and nations from around the world signed the First Geneva Convention in the same year. In 1919, Geneva's selection as the site for the League of Nations confirmed the city's reputation as a neutral center

LAKE GENEVA

Soup's On

Before it became part of the Swiss Confederation, Geneva warded off almost constant attack. One of the most persistent invaders was the House of Savoy. Geneva battled the Savoys sporadically for over 200 years, but the city finally triumphed due to Swiss practicality. On the night of December 11, 1602, Savoyard soldiers attempted to scale the city walls. A lone housewife saw the attack and proceeded to dump a pot of boiling soup on the soldiers' heads, buying enough time to sound the city's alarm. Each year, the **Festival of the Escalade** (climbing) celebrates this event, as costumed citizens reenact the battle and children eat chocolate *marmites* (pots) filled with marzipan vegetables.

for both international organizations and arbitrations. Geneva still retains the European office of the **United Nations** (responsible for economic and humanitarian programs) and dozens of other international bodies ranging from the Center for European Nuclear Research to the World Council of Churches.

■ Getting to Geneva

Geneva's **Cointrin Airport** is a **Swissair** hub. To reach the city from the arrivals hall, go up a level and turn left to catch bus #10 to town (15min., every 6min., 2.20SFr; ticket dispenser requires exact change—large bills can be broken at the train ticket window down the escalator behind the bus stop) or take the train for a shorter trip to Cornavin Station (6min., every 10min., 4.80SFr). Geneva has two rail stations. **Gare Cornavin** is the primary station and departure point for all major Swiss and foreign cities. The second station, the tiny Gare des Eaux-Vives on the eastern edge of the city, connects to France's regional rail lines. By **car,** Geneva is more accessible from France than from the rest of Switzerland. To drive to Geneva from the west, take A40 or E62 east, which continues on to Lausanne and Montreux. From the south take N201 north. From the north, take E21 from France and E25/62 from within Switzerland. From the east, take A40 (E25) west. E62 is also the best way to reach Geneva from Lausanne or Montreux. Don't go crazy looking for the route numbers—they're not all that visible. You'll be better off just following the signs for Geneva posted on all of the auto routes. Hugely popular **ferries (CGN)** connect Geneva to Lausanne and Montreux. A round-trip ticket (16-25SFr; students receive half-off on regularly scheduled trips) includes the option of returning to Geneva by train, so sight-seeing itineraries need not depend on the infrequent boat services.

■ Orientation and Practical Information

Geneva began as a fortified city on a hill, and the historic *vieille ville*'s steep cobbled streets and quiet squares around John Calvin's Cathédrale de St-Pierre still occupy the heart of the urban landscape. Across the Rhône River to the north, billionaires' banks and five-star hotels gradually give way to lakeside parkland where rollerbladers weave their way through promenading couples and romping children. Farther north, another hill with higher-tech fortifications has become the center of Geneva's civic life, housing the headquarters of the United Nations, Red Cross, and World Trade Organization. South of the *vieille ville,* modern apartment buildings and urban sprawl house the hospital and Cité Universitaire. Farther south across the river lies the village of Carouge, home to an intense concentration of student bars and clubs (tram #12: "pl. du Marché"). Carouge gained a reputation for fun all the way back in Calvin's day, when those who wished to defy their leaders' ban on cafés gathered outside the city limits to drink the night into oblivion. Be sure to carry your passport with you at all times; the French border is never more than a few minutes away and regional buses frequently cross it, as does the local tram at Moillesular (#12 or 16). City buses provide swift Swiss service, with major hubs at the Gare Cornavin and pl. Bel Air (near the ponts de l'Ile); trips that stay within zone 10 (most of the city) officially cost 1.50SFr, but ticket purchasing is largely on the honor system and some schmucky backpackers try to get away with riding for free. Be warned, however: those caught without a ticket during checks face a 60SFr fine, and playing confused anglophone will probably not work well. Much of this small (pop. 200,000) and compact city can easily be walked in good weather.

TRANSPORTATION

Flights: Cointrin Airport (tel. 717 71 11, flight information tel. 799 31 11; fax 798 43 77) is a hub for **Swissair** (tel. (0848) 80 07 00). Several direct flights per day to New York, Paris, London, Amsterdam, and Rome. **Air France** (tel. 798 05 05) has 7 per day to Paris, and **British Airways** (tel. (0848) 40 10 10) has 7 per day to London. The **Taxi-Bus** (tel. 331 41 33) ferries you from your nearest bus stop to the train station early in the morning, when the local buses aren't running (8SFr).

Trains: Gare Cornavin, pl. Cornavin. To: **Lausanne** (40min., every 20min., 19.40SFr), **Bern** (1¾hr., every hr., 48SFr), **Zurich** (3hr., every hr., 74SFr), **Basel** (2¾hr., every hr., 67SFr), **Montreux** (1hr., every hr., 27SFr), **Interlaken** (3hr., every hr., 60SFr), **Paris** (3½hr., 6 per day, 80SFr plus reservation fee, under 26 20% off), and **Rome** (10hr., 1 per day, 122SFr, under 26 20% off). To book a seat on long-distance or international trains, take a number at reservation and information (open M-F 8:30am-7pm, Sa 9am-5:30pm) and settle down for a long wait. Train schedules at http://www.sbb.ch. **Gare des Eaux-Vives** (tel. 736 16 20), on av. de la Gare des Eaux-Vives, connects to France's regional rail lines through **Annecy** (1½hr., every hr., 14SFr) or **Chamonix** through St. Gervais (3¼hr., every hr., 24SFr). Beware: the ticket machine at the station does not return change.

Public Transportation: Geneva has an efficiently integrated bus and tram network. **Transport Publics Genevois** (tel. 308 34 34), next to the tourist office in Gare Cornavin, provides a free but intensely confusing map of the local bus routes called *Le Réseau.* Open 6:15am-8pm. 2.20SFr buys 1hr. of unlimited travel on any bus; 3 stops or less cost 1.50SFr. Your best bets are a full-day pass for 5SFr, six 1hr. trips for 12SFr, or 12 1hr. trips for 22SFr. Swisspass valid on all buses; Eurailpass not valid. Buy multi-fare and day tickets at the train station, others at automatic vendors at every stop. Stamp multi-use tickets before boarding or risk 60SFr fines. Buses run roughly 5:30am-midnight.

Taxis: Taxi-Phone (tel. 331 41 33). 6.30SFr plus 2.70SFr per km. Taxi from airport to city 25-30SFr., max. 4 passengers (15-20min.).

Car Rental: Avis, rue de Lausanne 44 (tel. 731 90 00). **Budget,** rue de Zurich 36 (tel. 900 24 00). **Europcar,** rue de Lausanne 37 (tel. 731 51 50; fax 738 17 80), is probably the cheapest: weekly unlimited-mileage rentals start at 104SFr per day. All have offices at Cointrin, but check for airport-supplements (around 11%).

Parking: On-street 0.60SFr per hr., 2hr. max. The garage (tel. 736 66 30) under Cornavin station (enter at pl. Cornavin), is 2SFr for 1hr., 6SFr for 2. **Garage Les Alpes,** rue Thalberg, has 350 spaces (2SFr per hr. weekdays, 1SFr per hr. nights and weekends). Strategically positioned digital boards on highways list several car-parks and the number of spaces free in each.

Bike Rental: Geneva is pedal-happy with well-marked bike paths and special traffic lights for spoked traffic. For routes, get *Itineraires cyclables* or *Tours de ville avec les vélos de location* from the tourist office. Behind the station, **Genève Route,** pl. Montbrillant 17 (tel. 740 13 43), has 28 free bikes available (sponsored by the Red Cross). A 50SFr deposit is required; 250SFr fine if bike is lost or stolen. Slightly nicer neon bikes go for 5SFr per day. Open 7:30am-9:30pm.

Hitchhiking: *Let's Go* does not recommend hitchhiking. Hitchers say, however, that Switzerland is one of the safer countries in Europe in which to hail a ride. Those headed to Germany or northern Switzerland take bus #4/44: "Jardin Botanique." Those headed to France take bus #4/44: "Palettes" then line D: "St. Julien." In summer, **Telstop** has a list of available rides in front of the CAR information booth.

TOURIST AND FINANCIAL SERVICES

Tourist Offices: Any town that can turn the random backflow of turned-off hydraulic pressure taps into an honest-to-God tourist attraction (the Jet d'Eau) knows how to market itself to visitors. Information offices (marked by a blue lower-case "i" sign) offer a deluge of information, but the free must-haves are: the city map, *Info Jeunes/Young People,* and *Genève pratique.* The **main office,** rue du Mont-Blanc 3 (tel. 909 70 00; fax 929 70 11; email info@geneve-tourisme.ch; http://www.geneve-tourisme.ch), lies just 1min. from the Mont-Blanc bus station and 5min. to the right of the train station. English-speaking staff books hotel rooms (5SFr fee), offers **walking tours,** and provides information on anything from local events to vegetarian and kosher restaurants. The office maintains a **free direct phone line** to Geneva hotels in Gare Cornavin. Open June 15-Sept. 15 M-F 8am-6pm, Sa-Su 9am-6pm; Sept. 16-June 14 M-Sa 9am-6pm. During the summer, head for the magic bus, Geneva's **Centre d'Accueil et de Renseignements** (CAR; tel. 731 46 47), parked during the summer at the top of rue du Mont Blanc after the pedestrian underpass beneath Gare Cornavin. The office answers all sorts of questions and posts a daily updated list of musical and theatrical performances. Open June 16-Sept. 6 daily

LAKE GENEVA

9:30am-11pm. As a last resort, call the **Anglo-phone** (tel. 157 50 14), a 24hr. hot-line (in English) that answers questions about any aspect of life in Switzerland. Be quick: 2.13SFr per min.

Budget Travel: SSR, rue Vignier 3 (tel. 329 97 34 or 329 97 33; http://www.ssr.ch), off av. Henri-Dunant near Plaine de Plainpalais by the Forget-Me-Not hotel. Very friendly service with special youth and student fares. Open M-F 9:15am-6pm, Sa 9am-noon. AmEx, MC, Visa.

Consulates: Australia, rue de Moillebeau 56-58 (tel. 918 29 00; fax 733 56 64). **Canada,** rue du Pré-de-Bichette 1 (tel. 919 92 00; fax 734 79 19). **New Zealand,** chemin du Petit-Saconnex 28a (tel. 734 95 30; fax 734 30 62). **South Africa,** rue de Rhône 65 (tel. 849 54 54; fax 849 54 32). **U.K.,** rue de Vermont 37-39 (tel. 918 24 00; fax 918 23 22). **U.S.,** rue de Pré-Bois 29 (tel. 798 16 05; recorded emergency information 798 16 15). Call each office to schedule appointments.

Currency Exchange: Throughout town. **Gare Cornavin** has good rates and no commission on traveler's checks, advances cash on credit cards (min. 200SFr), and arranges Western Union transfers. Open 6:45am-9:30pm; Western Union open 7am-9pm. **ATMs,** offering the best rates of all, dot Geneva.

American Express: rue du Mont-Blanc 7, P.O. Box 1032, CH-1211 Geneva 01 (tel. 731 76 00; fax 732 72 11). Mail held 2-3 months. All banking services; reasonable exchange rates. **ATM.** Hotel (30SFr) and train (20SFr) reservations and tickets for city tours and excursions. Open in summer M-F 8:30am-6pm, Sa 9am-noon; in winter M-F 8:30am-5:30pm, Sa 9am-noon.

LOCAL SERVICES

Luggage Storage: Gare Cornavin. 3-5SFr per day. Open 4:30am-12:45am.

Lost Property: rue des Glacis de Rive 7 (tel. 787 60 00). Open M-Th 8am-4:30pm, F 8am-4pm.

English-Language Bookstores: ELM (English Language and Media) Video and Books, rue Versonnex 5 (tel. 736 09 45; fax 786 14 29). A quality range of new books in English and a book-ordering service. Open M-F 9am-8pm, Sa 10am-7pm. AmEx, DC, MC, Visa. The adjoining video store (tel. 736 02 22) rents videos in English (from 5.50SFr). Open M-F 9am-8pm, Sa 10am-7pm. **Librairie des Amateurs,** Grand Rue 15 (tel. 732 80 97), in the *vieille ville.* Classy secondhand dealer has a roomful of English-language books in a strange mix of battered leather-bound classics and lurid late-70s romances and mysteries. Open M 2-6:30pm, Tu-F 10am-6:30pm, Sa 10am-5pm. **Book Worm,** rue Sismondi 5 (tel./fax 731 87 65; debrandt@mail.excite.com), near the train station off rue de Berne. Three long-haired chihuahuas keep watch over this genteel store (run by an American couple) of used books and classic English-language videos (4SFr for 2 days). Tea room serves pots of tea or coffee (3SFr), lunch (12:30-2pm, 8-13SFr including meat, soup, salad, drink...), and desserts (5.50SFr). Open Tu-Sa 10am-8pm, Su 10am-5pm. AmEx, MC, Visa. **Payot Libraire,** rue de Chantepoulet 5 (tel. 731 89 50; fax 738 48 03). Geneva's largest chain of bookstores, with an English-language section that includes a variety of new books. Open M noon-6:30pm, Tu-W 8:30am-6:30pm, Th 8:30am-8pm, F 8:30am-6:30pm, Sa 8:30am-5pm. AmEx, DC, MC, Visa.

Library: American Library, rue de Monthoux 3 (tel. 732 80 97), at Emmanuel Church. 20,000 titles. 1-month membership (25SFr) allows you to borrow books (6 max.) for 2 weeks with a 0.50SFr deposit and to rent from a small but eclectic collection of books on tape (2SFr). Open Tu and F 12:30-5pm, W 2-7pm, Th 2-5pm, Sa 10am-4pm, Su 11am-12:30pm.

Bi-Gay-Lesbian Organizations: Dialogai, rue de la Navigation 11-13 (tel. 906 40 40; fax 906 40 44; http://www.hivnet.ch/dialogai). From Gare Cornavin, turn left and walk 5min. down rue de Lausanne; turn right onto rue de la Navigation. Resource group with programs from support groups to outdoor activities. Publishes *Dialogai,* a guide to French-speaking Switzerland's gay scene. Mostly male; women are welcome. Phone-line and center open M, Tu, and F 3-6pm, W 3-10pm. **Gay International Group** (GIG; tel. 789 18 69; taped message 789 18 62). Group for international gay visitors or semi-permanents in Geneva, including Anglophones. Communal meals every 6 weeks. No permanent address, so call for upcoming meeting plans. **Centre Femmes Natalie Barney** (women only), av. Peschier 30,

CH-1211, Geneva 25 (tel. 789 26 00). Similar services to Dialogai, but smaller and lesbian-oriented. 24hr. answering machine; live phone answering W 6-8pm.

Travelers with Disabilities: CCIPH (Centre de Coordination et d'Information pour Personnes Handicapées), rte de Chêne 54 (tel. 736 38 10). The tourist office also provides a free comprehensive guide to the city for the disabled, called *Guide à l'Usage des Personnes Handicapées,* which lists accessibility of all the main hotels, sights, shops, and transport. Huge map included.

Laundromat: En 5 Sec SA, rue Cornavin 5 (tel. 73 23 25), just 2min. from Gare Cornavin. **Salon Lavoir St. Gervais,** rue Vallin 9 (tel. 731 26 46), off pl. St. Gervais. Wash 4SFr, dry 1SFr per 12min., detergent 1SFr. Open M-Sa 7:30am-9pm, Su 10am-9pm.

Public Showers: Point d'Eau, rue Chandieu 4 (tel. 77 34 22 40). Take bus #8: "Canonnière." Free hot showers and personal hygiene center for the ripe backpacker. Open Sa-Tu 10am-2pm, W-F 3-7pm.

EMERGENCIES AND COMMUNICATIONS

Emergencies: Police, rue Pecolat 5 (tel. 117), next to post office. **Fire,** tel. 118. **Ambulance,** tel. 144.

Rape Crisis Hotline: Viol-Secours (tel. 345 20 20). Open M 4-11pm, Tu 2-6pm, W and F 9am-noon, Th 2-9pm.

Late-Night Pharmacy: Every night a changing set of 4 pharmacies stays open late (9 or 11pm). Consult *Genève Agenda* for addresses and phone numbers or call 144 or 111 (7pm-8am). The pharmacy at the train station has the longest regular hours.

Medical Assistance: Hôpital Cantonal, rue Micheli-du-Crest 24 (tel. 372 33 11). Bus #1 or 5 or tram #12. Door #2 for emergency care, Door #3 for outpatients. Walk-in clinics dot the city; call the **Association des Médecins** (tel. 320 25 11) for further information.

Post Office: Poste Centrale, rue de Mont-Blanc 18, a block from Gare Cornavin in the stately Hôtel des Postes. Open M-F 7:30am-6pm, Sa 8-11am. Address *Poste Restante* to CH-1211, Genève 1 Mont-Blanc. **Postal Code:** CH-1211.

Internet Cafés: Café Video ROM, Galerie de la Gare (tel. 901 16 21). Surf for 5SFr per hr. Open M-Th 11am-8:30pm, F-Sa 11am-10pm, Su 1-8:30pm. **Point 6,** rue de Vieux-Billard 7a (tel. 800 26 00) rents spots at the screen for 10SFr per hr. Open Tu-Su 4pm-1am. **Funet Internet Café,** rue de Lausanne 44 (tel. 738 50 00; fax 738 50 21). Turn left on rue de Lausanne from Gare Cornavin and walk 5min. to find 7 PCs loaded with the latest netware. 15min. for 5SFr; 30min. 9SFr; 1hr. 15SFr. Open M-Sa 10am-noon and 2-10pm. MC, Visa. Internet access also available in increasing numbers of hostels as well as in the artists' colony (see **Artamis—Geneva's Guerrilla Artist Colony,** p. 280).

Telephone Code: 022.

■ Accommodations and Camping

Geneva is one of the most cosmopolitan cities in the world, and its five-star hotel system is geared more toward the international banker or diplomat than the friendly budget traveler. Luckily, the seasonal influx of university students and interns has created a second, far less visible network of decently-priced hostels, pensions, and university dorms moonlighting as summer hotels. The indispensable *Info Jeunes* lists about 50 options; we list the highlights below. The tourist office has responded to the demand with a brochure most imaginatively titled *Budget Hotels,* stretching definitions a bit to include rooms at 43-120SFr per person. Even for the shortest stays, reservations are a must. For longer stays, check *Tribune de Genève*'s weekly supplement of apartment classifieds or the tourist office's board. Employees of international organizations can contact the **Centre d'Accueil pour les Internationals de Genève,** rue de Varembé 9-11 (tel. 327 17 77; fax 327 17 27), for assistance.

Auberge de Jeunesse (HI), rue Rothschild 28-30 (tel. 732 62 60; fax 738 39 87). Walk 15min. left from the station down rue de Lausanne then right on rue Rothschild. Bus #1 (dir: Wilson) stops right in front of the hostel. With 365 beds distributed between two identical buildings, the 6-bunk bedrooms are less a hostel and more a hyper-efficient hiker-housing machine. Don't expect atmosphere; do expect a comfortable last-minute bunk and a ton of people to meet. Check-in lines can be verrry big. Get your hands on an arrival slip and fill it out before you get to the window to avoid losing your place and extending an already tedious wait. Amenities include a sizable lobby, restaurant (dinner 11.50SFr, dessert 1.80SFr), **kitchen** facilities, TV room with CNN, library, and snack bar. Singles 23SFr, non-members 28SFr; doubles 70SFr, 75SFr; triples with bath 85SFr, 120SFr. Breakfast, hall showers, sheets, and lockers included. **Laundry** 6SFr. Special facilities for disabled guests. Flexible 5-night max. stay. Reception in summer 6:30-10am and 4pm-midnight; in winter 6:30-10am and 5pm-midnight. Lockout in summer 10am-4pm, in winter 10am-5pm. Curfew midnight. MC, Visa.

Cité Universitaire, av. Miremont 46 (tel. 839 22 11; fax 839 22 23). Bus #3 (dir: Crêts-de-Champel) to the last stop. Find the bus at pl. de 22 Cantons on the far right as you exit the train station; buses stop in front of "Le Popeye" restaurant. Institutional college housing in a modern tower block with heaps of facilities: TV rooms, newspapers, restaurant, disco (all-night dancing Th and Sa, free to residents), ping-pong (paddles at the reception), tennis courts, **internet access** (7 computers, 5SFr per hr.), small grocery shop, and discount plane tickets. 4 dorms (July-Sept. only) 15SFr, including lockers; singles 36SFr; doubles 52SFr; studios with kitchenette and bathroom 65SFr. Hall showers included. Reception M-F 8am-noon and 2-10pm, Sa-Su 8am-noon and 6-10pm. Lockout 10am-6pm. Curfew 11pm for dorm residents only (sorry, kids). AmEx, MC, Visa.

Hôme St-Pierre, cours St-Pierre 4 (tel. 310 37 07; fax 310 17 27). Bus #5: "pl. Neuve." 15min. walk from the train station: cross the Rhône at pont du Mont-Blanc then go up rampe de la Treille and take the 3rd right. Mere seconds from the west entrance of the cathedral, this 150-year-old "home" for **women only** features comfy beds, large windows, an enormous spiral staircase, and a church-bell serenade every 15min. Ding dong. Ding dong. A large **kitchen,** dining room, and rooftop terrace with spectacular views create a convivial atmosphere. Dorms 22SFr; singles 40-45SFr; doubles 54-60SFr. Big breakfast (M-Sa) 5SFr. Showers and lockers included. Reception M-Sa 9am-noon and 4-8pm, Su 9am-noon. No lockout or curfew. Popular, so reserve ahead. AmEx, MC, Visa.

Forget-Me-Not, rue Vignier 8 (tel. 320 93 55; fax 781 46 45). Bus #4/44 or tram #12: "Plainpalais" then walk down av. Dunant and turn left on rue Vignier. Cement highrise on a busy street above a pool hall with a bizarre bohemian flair. Once the narrow cells of devout nuns, the tiny rooms now offer bright orange bed covers and sturdy desks to all. Though law students and UN interns stay on for months, backpackers join the ranks gathering in communal kitchens and lounges on each floor and on the wide rooftop terrace. **Kitchen, laundry,** TV/video room, night guard, phones, food and drink machines, 2 pianos, free luggage storage, study room, and a partridge in a pear tree. Dorms 25SFr; singles 50SFr; doubles 80SFr. Breakfast and showers included. Slightly more expensive "hotel" rooms, with carpeting, nicer sheets, and a fridge: singles 60SFr; doubles with shower 110SFr. No curfew. Reception M-F 9am-9pm, Sa 10am-4pm; call if you're arriving after 10pm.

Centre St-Boniface, av. du Mail 14 (tel. 322 26 00; fax 322 26 01). Bus #1 or 4/44 (dir: Voirets): "Cirque" or else tram #13, then continue down av. du Mail. To walk from the station (20min.), head right on blvd. Fazy, across pont de La Coulouvrenière and along av. du Mail. This Jesuit-run center has rooms just minutes from the *vieille ville*. Singles (mid-July to late Sept.) 39-45SFr; doubles (mid-July to late Sept.) 57-62SFr. Some have shower and balcony. Access to **kitchen,** TV room, and dining room included. No breakfast, but residents get 10% off at the restaurant next door, **La Pleine-Lune,** with a card from the reception. Reception M-F 9am-noon and 4-7pm. Reservations preferred.

Hotel Pension St-Victor, rue François-le-Fort 1 (tel. 346 17 18; fax 346 10 46; email stvictor@iprolink.ch; http://geneva.yop.ch/hotels/smp). Bus #1, 3, or 5: "pl. Claparède." An elegant building with a view of the Russian Church's gilded domes across an expanse of stately trees. Large, clean, rooms with healthy plants and dark wood furniture. Homemade jam and eggs fresh from the owner's farm for breakfast. Friendly Anglophone atmosphere. **Internet access** 1SFr per 5min. Singles from 65SFr; doubles from 98SFr; triples from 110SFr. Breakfast included. Reception M-F 7:30am-8pm, Sa-Su 8am-8pm. Reservations imperative. MC, Visa.

Hôtel de la Cloche, rue de la Cloche 6 (tel. 732 94 81; fax 738 16 12), off quai du Mont-Blanc across from the Noga Hilton. A genteel old hotel with high ceilings and richly ornate wallpaper. Converted from the mansion of the former manager of the casino across the street, the jewel of this 16-bed facility is the room with a balcony overlooking the Jet d'Eau—get that one if you can. Singles 55SFr; doubles 85SFr; triples 95SFr; quad 120SFr. Prices go down 5-10SFr. in winter. A few rooms have showers; hall showers 2SFr. Breakfast 2SFr. Reception 8am-midnight. Reserve 2-3 weeks in advance in summer. AmEx, MC, Visa.

Hôtel Beau-Site, pl. du Cirque 3 (tel. 328 10 08; fax 329 23 64). Bus #1 or 4/44: "Cirque." Or walk from the station: turn right on blvd. Fazy, cross the Rhône at pont de la Coulouvrenière, and follow blvd. Georges-Favon to pl. du Cirque (20min.) Slightly squeaky floors and battered doorways only add to the charm of this quirky hotel overlooking the cafés of pl. du Cirque. Paneled rooms with quilt-covered beds and semi-antique furniture—some even have marble fireplaces to accompany the ornamental plaster moldings. Singles 57SFr, with shower 63SFr, with bath 75SFr; doubles 79SFr, 83SFr, 102SFr; triples 94SFr, 98SFr, 120SFr; quads 104SFr, 108SFr. All rooms with sink and radio. 6 sinkless rooms, usually occupied by long-term guests, available for 45SFr each. Call ahead for availability. 10% student discount. Breakfast included; coffee and tea in lobby 10am-10pm. Reception 7am-11pm; call if you'll be arriving later. AmEx, MC, Visa.

Hôtel St-Gervais, rue des Corps-Saints 20 (tel./fax 732 45 72). From the train station, cross the street and walk right 3min. down rue de Cornavin to rue des Corps-Saints 1 block past Notre Dame church. The dark, low-ceilinged rooms provide some (but not much) refuge from the bright tartan carpeting that must have been laid down by deranged or color-blind Scots. Some of the very clean bonny bathrooms even have tartan ceilings to mesmerize droopy early morning eyes. Singles 62SFr; doubles 78SFr, with shower 98-105SFr; convert a double into a triple for 20SFr extra. Breakfast in the cozy café downstairs included. Reception 6:30am-midnight. Only 26 rooms, so reservations are preferred. AmEx, MC, Visa.

Camping Pointe-à-la-Bise, Chemin de la Bise, (tel. 752 12 96). Bus #9: "Rive" then bus E (north): "Bise" (about 7km). One person 12SFr, two for 17.50SFr. No tents provided. Reception 8am-noon and 2-8pm. Open Apr.-Oct. 31.

Camping d'Hermance, rue du Nord 44 (tel. 751 14 83). Take Bus E north, 14km out of town. One person 10SFr, two 17SFr. Open 9am-11pm. Consult *Info Jeunes* (at the tourist office) for additional locations.

■ Food

Although it's true that you can find anything from sushi to *paella* in Geneva, you'll generally need a banker's salary to foot the bill. For a picnic, shop at the ubiquitous supermarkets. Many supermarkets also have cafeterias with some of the best deals available, and *Info Jeunes* lists many university cafeterias that won't tax your wallet. Beware drink prices—a small Coke will often nearly double the cost of a meal.

Boulangeries and *pâtisseries* offer unparalleled opportunities for gourmet food at budget prices—6SFr goes a long way when you combine a fresh loaf of bread with an avocado and tomatoes from Migros or Co-op. *Pâtisseries* and pasta/pizza parlors permeate **place du Bourg-de-Four,** below Cathédrale de St-Pierre, as do some of the best cafés. There's also **Carouge** (tram #12: "pl. du Marché"), a suburb full of cheap eats.

Restaurant Manora, rue de Cornavin 4 (tel. 909 44 10), 3min. from the station on the right in the Placette Dept. Store. Huge affordable self-serve restaurant with a fresh, varied, high-quality selection. Salads (big bowl 4SFr), quiche (6.90SFr including salad), fruit tarts (3SFr), fresh fruit juice (3.90SFr), and entrees cooked on the spot (from 11SFr). Wheelchair accessible. Open M-Sa 7am-9pm, Su 9am-9pm.

Le Rozzel, Grand-Rue 18 (tel. 311 89 29). Bus #5 to pl. Neuve, then walk up the hill past the cathedral on rue Jean-Calvin to Grand-Rue. Breton-style *crêperie* with outdoor seating amidst cobblestones and inviting antique shops on the most elegant street in the *vieille ville*. Large dinner crepes 7-17SFr; dessert crepes 5-14SFr; cider 4.50SFr. Open 7:45am-8:30pm. AmEx, MC, Visa.

La Crise, rue de Chantepoulet 13 (tel. 738 02 64). From the station, go right on rue de Cornavin and turn left on rue de Chantepoulet. Eat among talkative regulars and watch the owner, Mme. LeParc, cook your food 0.5m away in this veggie-friendly restaurant hardly bigger than a kitchen. A small kitchen. Can't beat the prices or the portions: quiche and a plate full of veggies for a mere 6SFr; a hearty bowl of soup 3SFr; beer or wine 3SFr. Open M-F 6am-7:15pm, Sa 6am-3pm.

Auberge de Saviese, rue du Pâquis 20 (tel. 732 83 30; fax 784 36 23). Bus #1: Monthoux. From Gare Cornavin, turn left onto rue de Lausanne, then right on rue de Zurich, until you hit rue de Pâquis. *Genevois* load up on traditional Swiss specialties here. Rustic interior with wood-shingled roofs over the bar and entrance and flat, massive barrels for chandeliers. Share coffee (1.90SFr) with locals breakfasting behind newspapers (9-11am). In addition to a selection of 3 *plats du jour* (13-14SFr), the regular menu features an excellent *fondue au cognac* (19SFr), *raclette* with all the trimmings (28SFr), pasta (14-19SFr), and salads (4-17SFr). Open M-F 11:30am-11pm, Sa-Su 6-11pm. AmEx, DC, MC, Visa,

Sunset, rue St-Léger (tel. 320 15 13), off pl. des Philosophes. Is it the angel fish or the well-stocked bar that brings vegetarian students from the nearby university to this restaurant in droves? Polls suggest the angel fish. White and pink interior with sleek furniture evoke a Californian aesthetic. *Pita au champignons* (pita with mushrooms, 15SFr), inventive salads (13-17SFr), and gnocchi (15SFr). Open M-F 7:30am-7pm. AmEx, MC, Visa.

Mañana, rue Chaponnière 3 (tel. 732 21 31; fax 731 42 29). From pl. Cornavin, walk down rue du Mont-Blanc, then left onto rue Chaponnière. Hopping Tex-Mex joint with a guitarist strum strumming away in an atmospheric mix of stone arches, ceiling fans, and wooden tropical birds. Mexican entrees 18-20SFr. Vegetarian plates 15-22SFr; nachos 13SFr. Open noon-2pm and 6-11:30pm. AmEx, MC, Visa. Happy hour at the **Cactus Club** downstairs nightly 6-9pm cuts cocktail prices in half.

Les 5 Saveurs, rue du Prieuré 22 (tel. 731 78 70). Just off rue de Lausanne, 2 blocks from the *Auberge de Jeunesse*. A *very* health-conscious restaurant. Amid dire cancer warnings, stock up on super-good-for-you fresh veggies and luscious desserts (made, of course, with no sugar or processed flour) at the ever-changing noon-time buffet (400g for 12SFr), or enjoy the *plat du jour* (10-15SFr) in the beaded, kitcheny atmosphere. Open M-F noon-2pm and 6:30-9pm.

Navy Club, pl. du Bourg-de-Four 31 (tel. 310 33 98). Sail to this maritime mealplace and hook yourself some of the best *carpaccio de boeuf* you'll ever find, a little pricey at 20SFr but worth the treat. The *vieille ville* meets *The Love Boat*. Look for the titanic bell with a hand grenade ringer behind the bar. Pizza 11-18SFr; pasta 16-22SFr. Open in summer M-F 11am-2:30pm and 5:30pm-1am, Sa 6pm-2am; in winter M-F 11am-1am, Sa 6pm-2am: AmEx, MC, Visa.

Les Armures, rue du Puits-St-Pierre 1 (tel. 310 34 42; fax 818 71 13). One small step up in price, one giant leap up in atmosphere. Wear clean socks. Plaque announces that Clinton ate here, and for a small splurge you can too. Tucked behind a 5-star hotel, the terrace offers weary tourists a respite from a long day climbing the hills of the historic district. Good-sized fondue 21-24SFr; pizza 13-15SFr. Open M-F 8am-midnight, Sa-Su 11am-midnight. AmEx, MC, Visa.

EPA, pl. de Molard. The department store's restaurant serves sandwiches (4.50SFr.) and hot meals for 9 to 16SFr. Open Su-F 8:30am-6:45pm, Sa 8:30am-5pm.

MARKETS

Co-op, Migros, Grand Passage, and **Orient Express** branches speckle the city. On Sundays, the few options include Gare Cornavin's **Aperto** (open daily 6am-10pm) and scattered neighborhood groceries and bakeries. If you want to spare yourself the trek back to the station or a wild goose chase through empty streets for pain au chocolat, do your food shopping Saturday afternoon.

Co-op (tel. 310 77 11), corner of rue du Commerce and rue du Rhône. La Marmite on floor one has *Menüs* from 9.50SFr and salads for 2SFr per 100g. Open M 9am-6:45pm, Tu, W, and F 8:30am-6:45pm, Th 8:30am-8pm, Sa 8:30am-5pm. MC, Visa.

Migros, av. de Lausanne 18-20 (tel. 738 68 88), left from Gare Cornavin on the mezzanine level of Centre Commercial Les Cygnes. Also has reasonably priced (5-10SFr) cafeteria with salad bar. Open M-F 8am-7pm, Sa-Su 8am-6pm.

Marché des Eaux-Vives, bd. Helvétique, between cours de Rive and rue du Rhône. Huge, happy dairy, vegetable, and flower market. Open W and Sa 8am-1pm.

Public Market, rue de Coutance, leading down to the river just above the ponts de l'Ile. Fresh fruits and cheese. Open M-Sa 8am-6pm. Another produce market is located on Plaine de Plainpalais Tuesday and Friday mornings.

■ Sights

For centuries Geneva was tightly constrained by a belt of fortified walls and trenches. By the mid-19th- century when they were finally removed, the city's most interesting historical sites were already established in a dense, easily walkable space. The tourist office (which has thought of everything—and put it in a brochure) offers two-hour **walking tours** during the summer. *(June 14-Oct. 3 M-Sa. 10SFr.)* Qualified guides lead tours on all things *Genevois:* the Reformation, internationalism, the Red Cross, the *vieille ville,* even the city's museums. All tours start at 2:30pm; pick up the tourist office's leaflet for departure points and times. Recordings of the tours are available in winter, and a portable cassette player will walk you through 2000 years of Geneva's history for 10SFr plus a 50SFr deposit.

The *vieille ville*'s **Cathédrale de St-Pierre,** the belly button of the Protestant world, is as austerely pure as on the day that Calvin stripped the place of its popish baubles. *(Open June-Sept. M-F 9am-7pm, Su 11am-7pm; Oct. and Mar.-May M-Sa 10am-noon and 2-5pm, Su 11am-12:30pm and 1:30-5pm. Tower closes 30min. earlier and costs 3SFr July-Aug. Bell-ringing Sa 5pm and free organ recital Sa 6pm.)* From its altar, Calvin preached to full houses from 1536 to 1564. Diligent listeners recorded some 2300 of his sermons. Two plain rosette windows shed light onto lingering remnants of Catholicism from the amusingly demonic column capitals to the walnut misericords. The brightly painted **Maccabean Chapel,** restored in a flamboyant style, gives an idea of how the cathedral walls might have looked pre-Reformation. The 157-step **north tower** provides a commanding view of the old town's winding streets and flower-bedecked homes. The ruins of a Roman sanctuary, a 4th-century basilica, and a 6th-century church rest in an **archaeological site** below the cathedral. *(Open Tu-Sa 11am–5pm, Su 10am-5pm. 5SFr, students 3SFr.)*

Surrounding the cathedral are medieval townhouses and burger-scaled mansions. One minute from the west end sits **Maison Tavel,** Geneva's oldest civilian medieval building, a posh fortified urban palace. The 14th-century structure now houses a historical municipal museum (see **Museums, p. 281**). The **Old Arsenal** a few steps away struts a mural depicting the arrival of both Huguenot refugees and Julius Caesar. Five cannons stand guard on a nearby street corner opposite the **Hôtel de Ville** (town hall), whose component parts date from the 15th through 17th centuries. It was here that world leaders met on August 22, 1864 to sign the **Geneva Convention** governing conduct during war. That meeting was in the Alabama room, which gained its name from an 1872 settlement in which the British agreed to compensate America for sinking the Southern ship *Alabama* during the American Civil War.

Facing the Promenade des Bastions farther down, **Le Mur des Réformateurs** (Reformers' Wall) displays a sprawling collection of bas-relief narrative panels, a dizzying array of multilingual inscriptions, and the towering figures of the Reformers themselves. As the largest "elite 4" (Knox, Beze, Calvin, and Farel) jostle each other sternly for "leader of the Protestant pack" bragging rights, Cromwell and Rhode Island's Roger Williams trail behind. Beneath their lined faces, unreformed couples and sunbathers from the nearby wooded campus of **Geneva University** display sunnily short attention spans. Nearby, the glittering domes of the **Russian Orthodox Church,** rue Toepffer, next to the Musée d'Art et d'Histoire, preside over hauntingly lovely ikons, stained glass, and heavy incense-weighted air. Note that photography and short skirts or shorts are not allowed.

The **Grand-Rue** is crammed with medieval workshops and 18th-century mansions, often featuring hastily added third or fourth floors, the makeshift result of the real estate boom following the influx of French Huguenots after Louis XIV repealed the Edict of Nantes. Plaques commemorating famous residents abound, including one at number 40 marking the birthplace of philosopher **Jean-Jacques Rousseau.** Rousseau was exiled at the aforementioned Hôtel de Ville due to the radical nature of his writing, but The Man couldn't keep him down forever. In 1834, admirers finally persuaded the town council to erect a statue in his honor. The council, who want their homage to be too visible, placed the statue on a tiny island off the pont des Barques and surrounded it on three sides by poplar-tree walls and fenced-in swans so that only those on the lake (or those who eat at the lakefront's conveniently located restaurant) can see it. The much more visible **Jet d'Eau,** down quai Gustave-Ador, spews a spectacular plume of water 140m into the air. The sight is a self-consciously invented tourist spectacle. It was inspired by a faulty piping jet, which used to be located downstream on the Rhône and inadvertently gurgled water each evening when craftsmen turned off hydraulic pressure taps that pressurized their workshops. At any given time from March to October, the world's highest fountain keeps about seven tons of water aloft. The **floral clock,** in the nearby **Jardin Anglais,** pays homage to Geneva's watch industry with over 6,500 plants and has the world's largest second hand (2.5m). The clock is probably Geneva's most overrated attraction and was once the city's most hazardous. Almost a meter had to be cut away from the clock because tourists, intent on taking the perfect photo, continually backed into unfortunate encounters with oncoming traffic. The rose-lined quays lead to two fun-parks. Fun. On the north shore, **Pâquis Plage,** at quai du Mont-Blanc, is laid-back and popular with the *Genevois. (1SFr; open 9am-8pm.)* Farther from the city center on the south shore, **Genève Plage** offers a giant waterslide, an Olympic-sized pool, volleyball and basketball tournaments, and topless sunbathing. *(6SFr.)* The source of these waters, the Rhône, was consecrated by the pope during a particularly bad outbreak of the bubonic plague as a "burial" ground for plague victims. As you frolic in the lake, be reverent or revolted accordingly.

Ferry tours leave from quai du Mont-Blanc and offer an easier-on-the-feet way to see Geneva. **Swiss Boat** (tel. 732 47 47) and **Mouettes Genevoises** (tel. 732 29 44; fax 738 79 88) provide shorter winter cruises narrated in English *(35min. 8SFr, 1hr. 13SFr, 2hr. 20SFr; fair weather only).* Call ahead for reservations and departure times. **CGN** (tel. 732 39 16) has been sending cruises to lakeside towns, including Lausanne, Montreux, and the stupendous Château de Chillon, for the past 125 years. *(Round-trip 47-57SFr, Eurailpass and Swisspass valid.)* Pick up the brochure *Les Heures Bleues* from the tourist office for details.

Artamis—Geneva's Guerrilla Artist Colony

What do you do when you're a young artist in Geneva and have no place to work? If there's 300 others like you, you shut down the tourist industry until the city gives you a place of your own. That's what happened in the summer of 1996 when a group of artists staged a sit-in demonstration at place du Bourg-de-Four just below the Cathédrale de St-Pierre. They ripped up pavement, built bonfires, and confused the hell out of tourists for six days until the city capitulated and granted them a no-rent lease for an abandoned industrial park on the left bank, now called Artamis (tel. 320 39 30; http://www.artamis.org). You'll find it at 12 rue de Strand, on the #2 and 10 bus lines ("Palladium"). Rising from the wreckage of an old factory, this ten building complex houses a vibrant mix of art workshops, theaters, and fund-raising facilities as well as some of the best deals in town. There's an **internet café** (5SFr per hr.), a movie theater (2SFr), and bars. Electronic music enthusiasts should stop by the Database building, which houses a recording studio where many of the top house and jungle DJs in the area come to experiment and exchange ideas. Some of their efforts are put on internet stream radio at http://www.basic.ch. All facilities and the main phone line (with information on performances and events) are open 4pm-2am.

Spectacular views of Lac Léman with Mont-Blanc in the background can be found in the series of garden-parks farther up on the *rive droite*. The **Museum of the History of Science** (see p. 282) lives in one and the **World Trade Organization** (WTO) lies in another farther north. Opposite the WTO, the basilica-shaped greenhouses of the **Jardin Botanique** (see p. 282) grow a collection of rare plants whose aromas waft across rue de Lausanne. For even better vistas, climb the hill above these parks to Geneva's international city, where embassies and multilateral organizations abound. The best of these (from a tourist's point of view, of course) is the **International Red Cross**, which contains its own remarkable museum (see p. 281). In the Red Cross's shadow stands the European headquarters of the United Nations, housed in the building that used to shelter the now defunct League of Nations. The guided tour of the **United Nations**, on av. de la Paix, is quite dull, despite some art (typical title: "Peace: There is Room for All") donated by all the countries of the world. *(Open July-Aug. 9am-6pm; Apr.-June and Sept.-Oct. 10am-noon and 2-4pm; Nov.-Mar. M-F 10am-noon and 2-4pm. 8.50SFr, seniors and students 6.50SFr, children 4SFr, children under 6 free. For information, contact the Visitors' Service (tel. 907 45 60; fax 907 00 32), which also conducts 1hr. tours in any of 15 languages when a sizable group requests them.)* The constant traffic of international diplomats (often in handsome non-Western dress) provides more excitement than anything the tour guides have to say. There's also a not-so-subtle display of Cold War one-up-manship: the **armillary sphere** depicting the heavens and donated by the U.S. stands next to a monument dedicated to the **"conquest of space"** donated by the USSR. Don't miss the lovely view of the lake and France's Mont Blanc.

■ Museums

Geneva is home to many exceptional museums, usually housed in splendid surroundings, whether architectural or natural. Fortunately, a good number of them are free; unfortunately, the most interesting aren't.

International Red Cross and Red Crescent Museum, av. de la Paix 17 (tel. 734 52 48; fax 734 57 23). Bus #8, F, V or Z: "Appia" or "Ariana." Check your ironic detachment at the door lest it be ripped forcibly from you during this powerful tour, *Let's Go*'s surprise pick as best museum in Geneva. Built into a hillside and towering over the nearby UN on several levels, the Red Cross tour employs images, not rhetoric, to drive home its emotional narrative of historic humanitarianism. The stark, unadorned glass and steel building houses a maze of provocative graphics and audiovisual displays. Dostoyevsky's keynote words: "Each of us is responsible to all others for everything," resonate much more immediately and directly after a visit here. 7 million POW records, including de Gaulle's, from World War I. Displays in English, French, and German. Open Su-M and W-Sa 10am-5pm. 10SFr, students and seniors 5SFr, under 12 free. Self-guided audio tours 5SFr.

Petit-Palais, terrasse St-Victor 2 (tel. 346 14 33; fax 346 53 15), off bd. Helvétique. Bus #17: "Petit Palais" or #1, 3, or 5: "Claparède." If you visit just one art museum in Geneva, this should be the one. A beautiful mansion contains paintings, sculptures, and drawings by Picasso, Renoir, Gauguin, Cézanne, and Chagall. Theme exhibitions: the influence of primitive art on modern aesthetes, love, and the nude female form, daily life in the modern world, radiant meditations on nature. Open M-F 10am-6pm, Sa-Su 10am-5pm. 10SFr, students and seniors 5SFr. Visa.

Musée Barbier-Mueller, rue Jean-Calvin 10 (tel. 312 02 70; fax 312 01 90), off Grand Rue in the *vieille ville*. 3 floors of what the ethnocentric once called primitive art, encompassing time periods as distant as early European and regions as far-flung as southern Africa. Recent exhibits include a display of West African masks and the Picasso paintings they influenced. Exhibits change frequently; check with tourist office or email musee@barbier.mueller.ch for information on 1999 exhibitions. Open 11am-5pm. 5SFr, children 3SFr.

Musée d'Art et d'Histoire, rue Charles-Galland 2 (tel./fax 418 26 00). Bus #3, 5, 6, or 8: "Athenée." Low quantity but high quality collection of art and artifacts ranging from neolithic tools and an open Egyptian sarcophagus with an unwrapped mummy to Renaissance and contemporary art. Be sure to see Konrad Witz's 1444

Jesus and the Apostles Fishing on Lake Geneva (not the Sea of Galilee), one of the 1st Christian paintings drawn in a recognizably European landscape. Open Tu-Su 10am-5pm. Museum free; temporary exhibit rates vary.

Musée d'Art Moderne et Contemporaine, rue des Vieux-Grenadiers 10 (tel. 320 61 22; fax 781 56 81). Where, oh where, has the avant-garde art of the 1970s and 80s gone? Right here, in a sprawling collection spanning 4 warehouse floors. Huge diversity of works, from Minimalist paintings to bulbous sculptures and landscape photographs. Open 11am-6pm. 9SFr, students 6SFr.

Musée d'Histoire des Sciences, Villa Bartholoni, rue de Lausanne 128 (tel. 731 69 85; fax 741 13 08), in the park at La Perle de Lac. Bus #4/44: "Sécheron." This elegant *palazzo* houses esoteric scientific gear. Downstairs starts sensibly enough with sundials, astrolabes, globes, and a telescope or two, but upstairs gets odder and bloodier with amputation saws, trepanning kits, a wax model of a syphilis patient's erupting facial sores, skull drills, and the gruesomely crude tools of early gynecology and obstetrics. Exhibits in French. Open Su-M and W-Sa 1-5pm.

Musée d'Ethnographie, bd. Carl-Vogt 65-67 (tel. 418 45 50; fax 418 45 51; email jerome.ducor@ville-ge.ch; http://www.ville-ge.ch/musinfo/ethg/index.htm). Bus #1 or 4: "Bains." A pleasantly cluttered permanent collection of cultural artifacts and very compelling and challenging temporary exhibitions. Houses concentrations of Asian and Oceania-based art, including the menacing armor of Japanese samurai, Australian aboriginal paintings, and Edo culture sculptures. Open Tu-Su 10am-5pm. 5SFr, students 3SFr, children free.

Institut et Musée Voltaire, rue des Délices 25 (tel. 344 71 33). Bus #6 or 26: "Prairie" or #7, 11, or 27 (dir: Lignon): "Délices." To be perfectly candid, this 18th-century mansion (Voltaire's home from 1755-1760) is mostly interesting to the Voltaire specialist: its collection consists mainly of printed matter, manuscripts, and iconographical documents rather than visuals. Particularly diverting are Huber's cartoons of the *philosophe,* Frederick of Prussia's sycophantic letters, and Voltaire's cantankerous replies to Rousseau. Some paintings and sculptures (including works by Houdon.) Exhibits in French. Open M-F 2-5pm. Free.

Musée de l'Horlogerie (Museum of Watches and Enameling), rue de Malagnou 15 (tel. 418 64 70; fax 418 64 71). Bus #1, 6, or 8: "Museum." In this jewel of a museum, ear competes with eye for the visitor's attention and pleasure. Stroll to the subtle rhythms of hundreds of still-functioning antique horological masterpieces, a complex beat punctuated every few minutes by chimes, bells, cuckoos, or clockwork musical interludes. Fingernail-sized wonders, free-standing giants, and 80s swatches compete to be the first to ring before the hour and confuse wristbewatched tourists. Open Su-M and W-Sa noon-5pm, Su 10am-5pm. Free.

Musée Ariana, av. de la Paix 10 (tel. 418 54 50; fax 418 54 51). Bus #8 or 18: "Appia" or U-2: "Ariana." This mind-numbingly complete collection of ceramics is surpassed by the building in which it is housed: a late 19th-century monumental medley of colored marble that combines neo-Baroque and neo-Classical elements filtered through a bizarre combination of Italian palatial architecture and a Romanesque vocabulary. The result is either proleptic postmodern or tackier than tacky or maybe both. Open Su-M and W-Sa 10am-5pm. Free.

Musée d'Histoire Naturelle, rue de Malagnou 1 (tel. 418 63 00; fax 418 63 01). Bus #6 (dir: Malagnon): "Museum." Huge rambling exhibits of beasties stuffed with excelsior looking on lifelessly through glass eyes. There's a dodo and the front half of an elephant emerging disturbingly from a painted corner. 4th floor geological displays includes a psychedelic roomful of highly luminescent minerals. Open Tu-Su 9:30am-5pm. Free.

Maison Tavel, rue du Puits-St-Pierre 6 (tel. 310 29 00), next to the Hôtel de Ville. This house stores everything that the city couldn't bear to throw away: the 1799 guillotine from pl. Neuve, a collection of medieval front doors, and a vast zinc and copper model of 1850 Geneva that took 18 years to build. An anemic multilingual guidebook available at the entrance. Open Tu-Sa noon-5pm, Su 10am-5pm. Free.

Jardin Botanique, chemin de l'Impératrice 1 (tel. 752 69 69). Bus #4 or 18: "Jardin Botanique." Panting joggers and playful kids stream past flamingos, deer, peacocks, and the occasional greenhouse. A great place to spend a lazy Sunday afternoon. Open Apr.-Sept. 8am-7:30pm; Oct.-Mar. 9:30am-5pm. Free.

Château de Penthes (Museum of the Swiss Abroad), chemin de l'Impératrice 18 (tel. 734 90 21; fax 734 47 40). Bus V or Z: "Penthes." A small chateau cloaked in ivy and girdled by hydrangeas featuring a small collection focusing mainly on the world-famous, flamboyantly dressed, highly obedient Swiss Guard. Stroll the surrounding parks—Lac Léman will never look quite so languid. Guides in French, English, and German. Open Tu-Su 10am-noon and 2-6pm. 5SFr, students 1.50SFr.

Jean Tua Car and Cycle Museum, rue des Bains 28-30 (tel. 321 36 37; fax 321 83 84). Bus #1, by rue des Grenadiers. Fun collection of 70 cars as well as motorcycles and bicycles, all dating before 1939. Open W-Su 2-6pm. 8SFr.

■ Entertainment and Nightlife

Genève Agenda is available at the tourist office and lists events ranging from major festivals to daily movie listings (be warned—a movie runs about 15.50SFr). Summer days bring festivals, free open-air concerts, and **free organ music** in Cathédrale de St-Pierre. In July and August, the **Cinelac** turns Genève Plage into an open-air cinema that screens mostly American films. Check the listings in *Genève Agenda* for indoor cinemas (films marked "v.o." are in their original language with French and sometimes German subtitles while "st. ang." means that the film has English subtitles.) There's also the biggest celebration of **American Independence Day** outside the U.S. on July 4 and the **Fêtes de Genève** in early August filled with international music and artistic celebration culminating in a spectacular fireworks display. **La Bâtie Festival,** a performing arts festival traditionally held late August to early September, draws Swiss music-lovers down from the hills for a two-week orgy of cabaret, theater, and concerts by experimental rock and folk acts. Many events are free; students pay half-price for the others (regular prices 10-32SFr). For information, call 738 55 77 or email batie@world.com.ch. **Free jazz concerts** take place in July and August at the Théâtre de Verdure in Parc de la Grange. Most parks offer similar free concerts; check at the tourist office for information and tickets. **Nyon,** a few minutes by train from Geneva on Lac Léman, holds a rock festival at the end of July (30-35SFr per day). The best party in Geneva is **L'Escalade,** commemorating the dramatic repulsion of invading Savoyard troops (see **Soup's On,** p. 271). The revelry lasts a full weekend and takes place in early December.

Budget travelers should think about limiting their shopping in Geneva to the windows, especially on the upscale rue Basses and rue du Rhône. The *vieille ville* contains scads of galleries and antique shops to explore. Those looking for Swiss souvenirs like Swiss Army knives and watches should head to the department stores or buy them at home. **La Placette** in pl. Cornavin is particularly good for the cheap and chintzy. (Open M-W and F 8:30am-6:45pm, Th 8:30am-8pm, Sa 8am-5pm.) Exquisite Swiss chocolate is sold in any supermarket, but the specialty store *par excellence* is **Chocolats Micheli,** rue Micheli-du-Crest 1 (tel. 329 90 06), which makes 40 different exciting chocolates. It smells really really good. (Open Tu-F 7am-6:30pm, Sa 8am-5pm.) Bargain hunters head to Plainpalais to browse at the huge **flea market.** (Open W and Sa 8am-6pm.) Smaller markets grace pl. de la Madeleine (M-Sa 8am-7pm) and pl. du Molard (M-Sa all day). A **book market** fills the Esplanade de la Madeleine (M-Sa 8am-7pm). More ephemeral wares bloom at the **flower market,** usually hidden amid the sprawling outdoor cafés in pl. du Molard (M-Sa).

Late Night Workouts

Geneva can be an expensive place to party for locals as for tourists, especially now that unemployment is running around 10%. Groups of twenty-somethings have lately taken to moving into vacant buildings where they live communally as squatters. To raise money for electricity and basic expenses, they run **squat bars,** selling some of the cheapest drinks in Geneva. Essentially roving parties, squat bars attract the artsy set and electronic music, jungle, and house fans. They also attract the notice of local authorities after neighbors complain of noise, so most squat bars move around a lot, meaning that in order to find them you have to be in the know. To find the latest, make friends with a native or bartender, or else look for posters on the left bank.

Summer nightlife centers around the lakeside quays and the many cafés, where the city drinks, converses, flirts, and spies. Two popular areas brimming with cafés are **Place du Bourg-de-Four,** below Cathédrale de St-Pierre, and the village of **Carouge** (tram #12: "pl. du Marché"), both of which attract student types. As anywhere, listen to the word on the street to find out what's happening at night.

La Clémence, pl. du Bourg-de-Four 20 (tel. 312 24 92). Generations of students have eaten at this famous, chic bar, named after the big bell atop the Cathédrale de St-Pierre. Tables overflow into the square come nightfall, and waves of murmured small talk and sometimes forced laughter echo through otherwise quiet cobblestone streets. Plenty of ash-trays to go around. Come for breakfast (croissant 1.20SFr, coffee 2.70SFr) or beer (4-8SFr). Open M-F 7am-1am, Sa-Su 7am-2am.

Demi-Lune Café, rue Etienne Dumot 3 (tel. 312 12 90), just up the street from pl. du Bourg-de-Four. Munch *tapas*-style food (6SFr) or hamburgers (9SFr) or just get sloshed (beer 3-5SFr) while listening to John Coltrane in this low-key, funky little café-bar in the *vieille ville*. One of many cheap and fun restaurant-bars in the area, popular with a twenty-something crowd.

Au Chat Noir, rue Vautier 13, Carouge (tel. 343 49 98). Tram #12: "pl. du Marché," just off the square. The upside-down car hanging from the ceiling is a puzzle, but the sensuously curved old bar and dark red curtains set the mood in this popular venue for jazz, funk, rock, salsa, and sax-moaning blues. Changing live concerts every night (showtime 9 or 10pm, with a 10-15SFr cover.) Beers go for 5SFr, sangria 10-12SFr. Open M-Th 6pm-4am, F 6pm-5am, Sa 9pm-5am, Su 9pm-4am.

Call My Agency/RDV, route de St. Julien 7 (tel. 300 05 10), down Ancienne Rue and past the pl. du Rondeau, or take tram #13 to "Carouges" and walk 5min. away from the square. Look for a warehouse with a bright 2nd floor RDV sign, take the elevator past wall murals to the 5th floor. This mixed gay/straight dance club is the real thing, not a copy of the real thing, not some imaginary thing. DJs spin house on 2 floors with an open terrace (June-Aug.) Change out of your grungy white t-shirt and be friendly with the bouncer to get in; claims of being a private club are mostly designed to keep out aggressive drunks. Beer 8SFr. Best hours F-Sa 2-5am.

Casting Café, rue de la Servette 6 (tel. 733 73 00; fax 733 73 13), 2min. behind the station or bus #3, 9, or 10: "Lyon." This theme restaurant/café/bar is one of the city's most popular joints. Neon lights, blaring music, and cigarette smoke attract college students to the Wild West, gas station, and Hollywood bars. The waitstaff dresses up to play the roles of the characters in the latest American movies showing next door at the Cinéma des Grottes. DJs spin until closing. Karaoke occasionally available. There will be a change of ownership in 1999, so things may be different. Open M-F 11am-2am, Sa-Su 2pm-2am. AmEx, MC, Visa.

Flanagan's, rue du Cheval-Blanc 4 (tel. 310 13 14), off Grand Rue in the *vieille ville*. Friendly bartenders pull a good beer in this Irish cellar bar. Hangout for Anglophiles of all nationalities. Chat merrily in the mother tongue amid dusty, liquor-inspired memorabilia. Pint o' Guinness 7SFr. Happy hours Su-M and W-Sa 5-7pm, all day Tu; live, non-Irish contemporary music Th-Sa 10am-2am. Open 4pm-2am.

Post Café, rue de Berne 7 (tel. 732 96 63; http://ww.postcafe.ch), just off rue de Mont-Blanc. Billing itself as an "international meeting point," this popular food and drink joint attracts a range of Anglophones from older International School kids to young businessmen and twentysomething expat Americans. Inexpensive-ish drinks (7SFr for a Guinness), sandwiches (5-7SFr), and friendly atmosphere amid festooned beer-label garlands and several flashing TVs. Happy hour 5-8pm. Open M-F 6:30am-2am, Sa 10am-2am, Su 4pm-2am. AmEx, MC, Visa.

Lord Nelson, pl. du Molard 9 (tel. 311 11 00). Pseudo-English pub that attracts the young and very young to its outdoor tables. Downstairs find uncensored music videos and a 1950s Americana decor. Beer 3.50SFr. Open M-Th 7pm-1am, F-Sa 1pm-2am, Su 2pm-midnight.

Petit Palace, tour de Boel 6 (tel. 311 00 33). A fantastic discotheque-cabaret for the adventurous. Turn left from the Lord Nelson doors, then left again onto rue de Marché, left once more just before the movie theater at pl. Trois Perdrix. Knock and the bouncer slides back a panel before opening the door to an Emerald City of live DJ techno, psychedelic lighting, transparent stairs with a waterfall beneath them, and a cage of dancers of both sexes who strip in the wee hours. Su-Th 11:30pm to 3am and beyond.

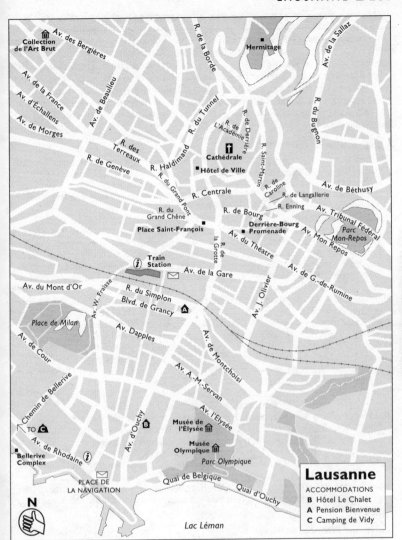

Lausanne

ACCOMMODATIONS

B Hôtel Le Chalet
A Pension Bienvenue
C Camping de Vidy

N

■ Lausanne

Two thousand years ago Romans came to the little town of Lausanne on the shores of Lac Léman and found it so enticing that they stayed until the collapse of their empire. Hundreds of years ago, a different sort of *roman* found the city a welcome nest with the arrival of Dickens and Thackery. T.S. Eliot managed to create the apotheosis of high Modernist pessimism here, writing *The Wasteland* near the placid Ouchy shoreline and the medieval labyrinth of the *vieille ville*. Today natural beauty and cultural history continue to pull in the outside world, and Lausanne's unique museums, vibrant nightlife, varied festivals, and magnificent parks make it well worth a stay.

ORIENTATION AND PRACTICAL INFORMATION

Lausanne was built on three steep hills that now connect to each other via vaulted bridge roads over valleys below, which makes two-dimensional maps confusing. The train station rests halfway up to the *vielle ville* from the lakefront. The Métro Ouchy and bus lines #1, 3, and 5 serve the station. Most buses are routed to pl. St. François, a vital reference point in the center of the city. Though the town is compact, the staggering steepness of uphill climbs often makes public transportation useful. Particularly useful is Lausanne's small underground metro, which runs from the lakefront into the heart of downtown.

Transportation

Trains: pl. de la Gare 9 (tel. 157 22 22; 1.22SFr per min.) To: **Montreux** (20min., every 30min., 8.40SFr); **Geneva** (40min., every 20min., 19.40SFr); **Basel** (2½hr., every hr., 57SFr); **Zurich** (2½hr., every hr., 62SFr); **Rome** (11hr., 2 per day, 73SFr); **Barcelona** (12hr., 2 per day, 95SFr); and **Paris** (4hr., 4 per day, 76SFr, 13SFr reservation required). Open 7am-9pm.

Public Transportation: The 5-stop **Métro Ouchy,** which runs from the *vieille ville* to the Ouchy waterfront, is useful for climbing the city's steep streets. The **Métro Ouest** runs from the center of town west to the University of Lausanne and the Federal Institute of Technology M-Sa 5:30am-12:15am, Su 6:15am-12:15am. Buses cross the city and run roughly 6am-midnight (check bus stops for specific lines). 3-stop ticket 1.30SFr; 1hr. pass 2.20SFr; 24hr. pass 6.50SFr. Métro free with Swisspass or Museum Passport, but not with Eurailpass.

Ferries: CGN, av. de Rhodanie 17 (tel. 614 04 44; fax 617 04 45). To: **Montreux** (1½hr., 6 per day, last ferry 6:05pm, 18SFr one-way, 31SFr round-trip); **Geneva** (3½hr., 4 per day, last ferry 5:15pm, 30SFr one-way, 47SFr round-trip); **Evian** (last boat 12:15am, 14SFr, 24SFr round-trip.) Purchase tickets at dock. Eurail and Swisspass valid. June-Sept. 8am-7:30pm; Oct.-May 8:30am-12:30pm and 1:30-5:15pm.

Taxis: Available at rue Madeline 1 (tel. 331 41 33), pl. St. François, and in front of the station. For late night or early morning service, call the **taxibus** (tel. 312 20 00) or the **taxiphone** (tel. (0800) 80 18 02).

Car Rental: Avis, av. de la Gare 50 (tel. 320 66 81; fax 320 05 76). **Hertz,** pl. du Tunnel 17 (tel. 312 53 11). **Europcar,** av. Rochonnet 2 (tel. 323 91 52).

Parking: Parking Simplon-Gare, rue du Simplon 2 (tel. 617 67 44), behind the station, has spots for 2SFr per hr. during the day, 0.50SFr per hr. at night, and 22SFr per day. On city streets, white zones indicate unlimited parking, red zones allow 15hr. parking, blue zones 1½hr. To park on the street, pick up a parking disc from the tourist office. Dial up the present time and the maximum stay time, and leave the disc prominently displayed on the dashboard.

Bike Rental: (tel. (0512) 24 21 62), at the baggage check in the station. Rentals 25SFr per day, 19SFr per half-day. Return bikes at another station for an additional 6SFr. Open 6:40am-7:40pm.

Tourist and Financial Services

Tourist Office: Branch office (tel. 617 73 73; email information@lausanne-tourisme.ch; http://www.lausanne.tourisme.ch) in the main hall of the train station. Open Apr.-Sept. 9am-8pm; Oct.-Mar. 9am-7pm. Similar office in the Metro Ouchy station (or bus #2: "Place de la Navigation"). Pick up the *Plan Officiel* (a map and public transportation guide) and *Welcome to Lausanne* (booklet listing cheap hotels and private rooms) for free. The staff sells museum passports (see p. 289) and makes hotel reservations for 4-6SFr. Wheelchair accessible. Open Apr.-Sept. M-F 8am-7pm, Sa 9am-6pm, Su 9am-1pm and 2-6pm; Oct.-Mar. M-F 8am-6pm, Sa 9am-1pm and 2-6pm.

Budget Travel: SSR Voyages, blvd. de Grancy 20 (tel. 617 56 27; fax 616 50 77; http://www.ssr.ch/ssr), 2 streets downhill from the station past the overpass. Books student tickets and organizes group travel. Open M-F 9:15am-6pm, Sa 9am-noon.

Currency Exchange: At the station (tel. 312 38 24). Good rates. No commission on traveler's checks. Western Union transfers 7am-7pm. Cash advances with AmEx, DC, MC, Visa. Open Nov.-Mar. 6:20am-7:30pm; Apr.-Oct. 6:20am-8:30pm.

LAKE GENEVA

American Express: av. Mon Répos 14 (tel. 310 19 00; fax 310 19 19), across from parking garage. Cashes traveler's checks, sells airline tickets, and holds mail for 2 months. Travel services open M-F 8:30am-5:30pm; financial office open 8:30am-12:45pm and 2-5:30pm.

Luggage Storage: At the train station. Lockers 3SFr and 5SFr per day. Open 24hr.

Lost Property: pl. Chauderon 7 (tel. 319 60 58). Open M-F 8am-noon and 1:45-5:45pm, Sa 8am-11:45pm.

Local Services, Emergencies, and Communication

Bookstore: Payot Libraire, pl. Pépinet 4 (tel. 341 31 31; fax 341 33 45). Large Anglophone section with contemporary and classic fiction, some nonfiction, and plenty of *Let's Go.* Open M 1-6:30pm, Tu-F 8:30am-6:30pm, Sa 8am-5pm.

Library: Cantonal and University Palais de Rumine, pl. de la Riponne 6 (tel. 316 78 80; http://www.unil.ch/BCU). Open for borrowing M-F 10am-6pm, Sa 9am-noon. Reading room open M-F 8am-10pm, Sa 8am-5pm. Borrowing card free with ID.

Laundromat: Quick Wash, bd. de Grancy 44, 2 streets behind the train station toward the lake. Wash and dry around 10SFr. Open M and W-Sa 8:30am-8:30pm, Tu noon-8:30pm, Su 9am-8:30pm. Last wash 1hr. before closing.

Emergency: Police, tel. 117. **Fire,** tel. 118. **Ambulance,** tel. 144.

24-Hour Pharmacy: Dial 111 to find out which pharmacy is open all night; they rotate weekly. **24-hr. medical service,** at the hospital (tel. 314 11 11).

Post Office: Centre Postal, av. de la Gare 43bis (tel. 344 35 14), on the right as you exit the station. Address *Poste Restante* to: 1000 Lausanne 1 dépôt. Open M-F 7:30am-noon and 1:30-6:30pm, Sa 8-11am. Express mail M-F 6:30-7:30am, noon-1:30pm, and 6:30-10pm, Sa 6:30-8am and 11am-8pm, Su 5pm-10pm. To dispatch your postcard from the site where in 1783-1793 Edward Gibbon wrote his *Decline and Fall of the Roman Empire,* visit **Poste St. Françoise,** 15 pl. St-François (tel. 344 38 31). Open M-F 7:30am-6:30pm, Sa 8-11am. **Postal Code:** CH-1002.

Telephone Code: 021.

ACCOMMODATIONS AND CAMPING

As the home of the world's oldest hotel school, Lausanne has a well-deserved reputation for service-industry excellence. The city offers a huge range of accommodations, from *fin-de-siècle* palaces to lakeside tent plots. Budget accommodations rarely fill completely, but in the summer you may need to pick up the tourist office's list of cheap hotels, private boarding houses, and family *pensions* due to innumerable festivals, conferences, and congresses. The owners of these establishments generally prefer stays of at least three nights and often as long as a month. Since Lausanne is a university town, many hoteliers and private citizens cater to those on a student budget. Travelers looking for apartments to rent can turn to the local paper *24 Heures,* which carries regular listings, or to the notice boards of big department stores.

Jeunotel, Chemin du Bois-de-vaux 36 (tel. 626 02 22; fax 626 02 26). Bus #2 (dir: Bourdonnette): "Bois-de-Vaux." Cross the street and follow the signs. The hotel is down a long concrete driveway on your right just past the Musée romain de Lausanne-Vidy. Huge sleek complex near the Roman ruins. Spartan concrete walls and harried staff but plenty of amenities and no curfew. Comfy beds and good showers compensate for lack of character. Dorms 24-36SFr; singles 50SFr, with shower 73SFr; doubles 72SFr, 88SFr; triples 81SFr; quads 108SFr. Monthly rates available. Wheelchair accessible. Reservations wise in the summer. MC, Visa.

Hotel "Le Chalet," av. d'Ouchy 49 (tel. 616 52 06). Métro Ouchy: "Jordils" or bus #2 (dir: Bourdonnette): "Jordils." Built in 1877, this comfy chalet has been run by the same charming matron since 1940. She still answers the door and sits guests down for a pleasant conversation. Mixing with guests are occasional *literati* hoping to commune with the spirit of longterm guest August Rindberg in the evergreen garden. 9 rooms with balcony or terrace. Singles 48-62SFr; doubles 87SFr. Hall showers. Breakfast 8SFr. Reception noon-10:30pm.

Pension Bienvenue, rue du Simplon 2 (tel. 616 29 80), 5min. from the train station. Turn right along av. de la Gare, right on av. d'Ouchy, right after the bridge.

Women only. Marred only by its proximity to a major rail line, this 25-room *pension* offers several communal TV rooms, **laundry, kitchen,** a piano, and free breakfast. Hall showers and bathrooms only. Singles 40SFr; doubles 70SFr. Reception 9-11:30am and 5-7:30pm. Try to reserve the night before.

Hotel Excelsior, chemin du Closelet 6 (tel. 616 84 51; fax 616 84 58), 5min. from the train station. Turn right along av. de la Gare, right on av. d'Ouchy, and left after the bridge on Closelet. Run-down hotel offers cheap rooms when hostels are full. Poorly lit, not all that clean hall bathrooms, but spacious rooms and lots of TV's. Singles 50SFr, 80SFr with shower; doubles 80SFr, 100SFr. 10SFr discount after 2 nights. Reception M-Sa 8am-10pm, Su 8am-noon. AmEx, MC, Visa.

Camping: Camping de Vidy, chemin du Camping 3 (tel. 624 20 31; fax 624 41 60; http://www.campinglausannevidy.ch). Bus #2 (dir: Bourdonnette): "Bois-de-Vaux." Cross the street and go down chemin du Bois-de-Vaux past Jeunotel and under overpass. The office is straight ahead across rte. de Vidy. More RV and camper van drivers than backpackers but plenty of space for tents. Well-tended fields separated by paved, rose-lined paths. Within earshot of the lake. Restaurant (8am-noon, 4-8pm), supermarket, playground, and swimming pool (2SFr). Reception 8am-12:30pm and 5-8pm. 6.50SFr, students 6SFr; tents 7-11SFr; 1- to 2-person bungalow 54SFr; 3- to 4-person bungalow 86SFr. City tax 1.20SFr per tent, 1.40SFr per vehicle. Showers included. Wheelchair accessible.

FOOD

No visit to Lausanne is complete without a taste of the famous perch of Lac Léman, available at every restaurant but more expensive (isn't everything?) closer to the waterfront. Restaurants, cafés, and bars cluster around pl. St.-François and the *vieille ville*; *boulangeries* sell cheap sandwiches on every street. Surprisingly fresh fare and crusty bread awaits at Metro stations. Numerous groceries, frequent markets, and an abundance of parks make for affordable and pleasant picnics.

Au Couscous, rue Enning 2 (tel. 311 86 87), at the top of rue de Bourg. Walk upstairs—a hanging carpet marks the door to the restaurant proper. Inside, a North African theme prevails with hinged menus, red tablecloths, mosaic-tiled floor, and sequined pillows. Extensive, veggie-friendly menu (14-24SFr). Couscous (surprise) is the real specialty (21-29SFr). Lunch specials (14.50SFr) served 11:30am-2:30pm weekdays. It reopens for dinner Su-Th 6pm-1am, F-Sa 6pm-2am. AmEx, DC.

Manora, pl. St-François 17 (tel. 320 92 93), Beneath Zürich Bank sign. Fill up a tray with a dizzying array. Salads, sandwiches, pastries, fruits, vegetables, and main-course-things. *Plats du jour* run 7-15SFr—one of the best deals in town. Open M-Sa 7am-10:30pm, Su 9am-10:30pm. Hot food 11am-10pm.

Crêperie d'Ouchy, pl. du Port 7 (tel. 616 26 07), 30 seconds to the left of Metro Ouchy. In 1816, Lord Byron wrote *The Prisoner of Chillon* at the Hotel D'Angleterre next door; 183 years later its patrons seem far too trapped by stuffy 3 piece suits to enjoy the lakeside crepes this place serves. Relaxed atmosphere clashes nicely with the neighbors; look over at white tuxedos and say, "Put on your sneakers and be a kid." Crepes 4-17SFr. Try the seasonal specialty garnishes, like fresh fruit and ice cream in the summer. Open spring 11am-11pm; summer 9am-midnight; fall 11am-8pm; winter 11am-7pm. Wheelchair accessible.

Le Barbare, Escaliers du Marché 27 (tel. 312 21 32), at the top of wood steps leading up to Cathedral from Pl. de la Palud. Stop by the little place for lunch or a mid-afternoon treat after climbing the Cathedral Tower. Exposed medieval ceiling timbers add ambience to taste. Sandwiches 4.50SFr, omelettes 7-9SFr. Might wanna try the *Chocolate Maison Viennois avec Chantilly,* a devastatingly rich hot chocolate drink. Open M-Th 8:30am-11:30pm, F-Sa 8:30am-midnight.

Crêperie "La Chandeleur," rue Mercerie 9 (tel. 312 84 19), just below the cathedral. Lace-veiled windows and light pine furniture. Crepes prepared to your tastes, whether traditional (with butter, sugar, or honey 4-8SFr), sugar-deprived (with ice cream 6-10SFr), or gourmet (*flambées* with your choice of liqueur 8-11SFr). Open Tu-Th 11am-10pm, F-Sa 11am-11:30pm. DC, MC, Visa.

Markets

Migros, 2 av. de Rhodanie (tel. 613 26 60), 30 seconds right of Metro Ouchy or bus #2: Pl. du Navigation. A rare grocery store **open Sundays** and late evenings. M-Sa 9am-9:45pm, Su 8am-9:45pm.

Co-op, rue du Petit Chêne. From the train station, head toward the town center. Bring your own bag or pay 0.10SFr for one the size of an envelope. Open M-F 8am-7pm, Sa 8am-5pm.

Produce markets, at Ouchy Su 8am-8pm Apr. to mid-Oct.; on rue de Bourg behind the Eglise St.-François W and Sa mornings; on blvd. de Grancy M and Th mornings; and on rue du Petit-Chêne off pl. St.-François F mornings.

SIGHTS

The medieval town center is known as the *vieille ville,* but the true old city is on the waterfront where digs have unearthed 2000-year-old remains of the *Vicus de Lousonna.* You can stroll through it and see the foundations of a temple, the remains of a basilica, a forum, a few villas, and the traces of a complete Gallo-Roman colony. (Bus #2: "Bois-de-Vaux," follow signs). Vidy gradually decayed as Rome waned, and the town's inhabitants moved up to the more easily defended hills of the *cité.* The population grew and built up the town, making it the largest in Switzerland by the time the Gothic **cathédrale** was consecrated in 1275 under Holy Roman Emperor Rudolph and Pope Gregory X. *(Cathedral open July to mid-Sept. 7am-7pm; mid-Sept. to June 7am-5pm. Free guided tours July-Sept. at 10:30, 11:15am, 3, and 3:45pm. Tower open 8:30-11:30am and 1:30-5:30pm. 2SFr, children 1SFr.)* Bus #16: "Cathédrale" or a series of medieval covered stairs take you to the hilltop, where the cathedral's huge wooden doors open up into the hushed, vaulted space illuminated by flashes of stained glass. Climb the 200-step **tower** for a spectacular view of the city, lake, and mountains beyond. Lausanne is one of the last towns in Switzerland to retain a night watchman who cries the hour from 10pm to 2am. Below the cathedral, the Renaissance **Hôtel de Ville** with bronze dragon roof serves as a meeting point for guided **tours** of the town. *(Tours M-Sa 10am and 3pm. 10SFr, students free, English available.)* Also in the square, at no. 23, an ornamental clock depicts the history of the canton on the hour. *(9am to 7pm.)*

Historical Lausanne competes with the splendid Ouchy waterfront as the city's major attraction. Ouchy's main promenades, the **quai de Belgique** and **place de la Navigation,** are both excellent spots to exercise those calf-muscles. The local word is that Lausanne's women have the best-looking legs in Switzerland, the hard-won prize of a life spent hiking the city's hills. Some of us wonder if Swiss men are half so buff.

You can see more of Ouchy's inhabitants at the **Bellerive Complex** (bus #2: "Bellerive"), a beach park where locals set their children loose on spotless, activity-filled lawns while both genders go topless and take in some sun. *(Open mid-May to Aug. daily from 9:30am until dark or rain. 4.50SFr, students and seniors 3SFr, under 17 2SFr. 0.50SFr discount after 5pm.)* The Bellerive Beach is just one of the many natural oases in Lausanne. At the **Vallée de la Jeunesse** rosegarden, an unassuming path of wildflowers bends to reveal a spectacular display of 1000 bushes arranged in a terraced semi-circle around a fountain to the tune of thousands of birds. More exotic birds trill from the aviaries of the downtown **Parc du Mon-Repos.** Centering around a small chateau where Voltaire wrote from 1755 to 1757 and where the original Olympic museum was housed, the park includes venerable trees, an orangery, and a small stone temple. The region's propensity to bloom is channeled at the **Derrière-Bourg Promenade,** where flowers depict a narrative of events from the canton's history. Those more inclined to stroll can explore gorgeous shore-line trails between Ouchy and Lutry, a picturesque medieval village 4km away; tired feet can ride back to the *quai* on bus #9.

MUSEUMS

In a region of the world filled with tremendous traditional museums reverent of the canvas, Lausanne offers some stand-outs. From the psychotic art of the **Collection de l'Art Brut** to the photographic archives of the **Elysée** (which recently displayed the

LAKE GENEVA

work of Richard Gere, mediocre actor but tremendous friend of the Dalai Lama) to the stunning video collections of the **Olympic Museum,** the city's exhibits are all about quirkiness. For multiday visits, consider the **museum passports** available at the tourist office that entitle visitors to free museum entry, unlimited use of bus and Metro, and a film at the **Cinémathèque Suisse,** allée E. Ansemet 3 (tel. 331 01 00). A 3-day pass is 26SFr, or 20SFr for students and seniors.

Collection de l'Art Brut, av. Bergières 11 (tel. 647 54 35; fax 648 55 21). Bus #2 or 3: "Jomini." An utterly unique gallery filled with disturbing and beautiful sculptures, drawings, and paintings by artists on the fringe—institutionalized schizophrenics, grindingly poor and uneducated peasants, and convicted criminals. Nearly as fascinating as the works are the biographies of their tortured creators, often accompanied by strange, intense photographs and displayed in English and French. From a prison cell wall painstakingly carved with a broken spoon to intricate junk and sea-shell masks, this collection of obsessions started by radical primitivist Jean Dubuffet ranks with the cathedral as the best Lausanne has to offer. Open Tu-Su 11am-1pm and 2-6pm. 6SFr, students and seniors 4SFr.

Musée Olympique, quai d'Ouchy 1 (tel. 621 65 11; fax 621 65 12; http://www.museum.olympic.org). Take bus #2 or Métro: "Ouchy." High-tech temple to modern Olympians with a smaller exhibit dedicated to the ancient games. Extensive video collection allows visitors to relive any requested highlight since the games were first filmed. Bilingual English/French displays of medals, mementos, and equipment arranged around central spiral ramp swarming with kids. Wheelchair accessible via av. de l'Elysée. Open May-Sept. M-W and F-Su 10am-7pm, Th 10am-8pm; Oct.-Apr. Tu-W and F-Su 10am-6pm, Th 10am-8pm. 14SFr, students and seniors 9SFr, ages 10-18 7SFr, families 34SFr max. MC, Visa.

Musée Romain de Lausanne-Vidy, chemin du Bois-de-Vaux 24 (tel. 652 10 84; fax 625 11 35), next door to Jeunotel. Bus #1 and 4: "Maladière," or 2: "Bois-de-Vaux." Signs point the way. Centers around excavation site of a Roman house whose wall murals still display bright colors after all these years. Wade knee-deep through local school children to examine 2 floors of carvings, tools, pots, and coins from the Vicus de Lousonna archaeological site down the street. Open Tu-W and F-Su 11am-6pm, Th 11am-8pm. Wheelchair accessible. 4SFr, students free.

Musée de l'Elysée, av. de l'Elysée 18 (tel. 617 48 21; fax 617 07 83; email dgirardin@ping.ch or waewing@swissonline.ch). Take bus #2: "Croix-d'Ouchy" and go left on av. de l'Elysée. The 18th-century mansion houses a stunning collection and photography archive. From the 1820 prints to the most contemporary artistic endeavors in film, the series of changing collections within the white-washed galleries prove engaging. The basement's resonant tile and hushed atmosphere make the images even more haunting. Open Tu-W and F-Su 10am-6pm, Th 10am-9pm. Archives open Th by appointment. 5SFr, students 2.50SFr.

Hermitage, rte. du Signal 2 (tel. 320 50 01; general info tel. 312 50 13; fax 320 50 71), north of the *vieille ville.* Bus #16: "Hermitage" stops infrequently out front. Magnificent house given over to temporary exhibitions that vary from single artists and special themes to individual public and private collections. Call ahead for a schedule, since the museum closes between shows. Open Tu-W and F-Su 10am-6pm, Th 10am-10pm. 13SFr, students 5SFr, under 19 and seniors free. Tours in English Th 6:30pm, Su 3pm. AmEx, MC, Visa.

Botanical Garden of Lausanne, av. de Cour 14bis (tel. 616 24 09; fax 616 46 65). A lovely terraced garden in one section of pl. de Milan-Montriond Park, down the road from the bus #1 stop "Beauregard." The observation spot a short hike up the large hill next to the gardens steals the show. After a lushly shaded trek up winding paths, visitors are greeted by a stunning view of the lake. A sign names each peak visible across the water and the date on which they were first conquered by climbers. Gardens open May-Sept. 10am-noon and 1:30-6:30pm; Mar.-Apr. and Oct. 10am-noon and 1:30-5:30pm.

ENTERTAINMENT AND NIGHTLIFE

For every exhibit in Lausanne's museums, there are several performances already in progress on stage and screen: the **Béjart Ballet, Lausanne Chamber Orchestra, Cinémathèque Suisse, Municipal Theatre, Opera House,** and **Theatre of Vidy** reflect Lausanne's thriving cultural life. The tourist office publishes *Momento,* a monthly update and schedule of the most significant events, and posters on the streets and in *tabacs* should clue you in on everything else. For information, reservations, and tickets, call Billetel (tel. 617 18 50). During the first two weeks of July, the **Festival de la Cité** brings the *vieille ville* to life with many free theater and dance events. Swiss craftwork fills the **Marché des Artisans** in pl. de la Palud from 10am to 7pm on the first Friday of every month from March to December. As for nightlife, you can't heave a brick in the pl. St.-François without putting it through the window of a café/bar or hitting the bouncer of a night-club. (He will hit back.) *Lausannois* party-goers inhabit the bars until 1am (2am on weekends) and dance at the clubs till 4 in the morning. The seriously hardcore then head over to the bar in the train station, which opens at 5am.

The Mad, rte. de Geneve 23 (tel. 312 29 19, info 312 11 22), left as you exit Lausanne-Flon Metro stop then 3min. down rte. de Geneve. 5-floor warehouse discotheque splashed with bright colors and the slogan "Mad But Not Mad" crawling up its corner. Pulse-pounding, platform-stomping, fog-spewing, weird-clothes-wearing dance parties surround a 3rd-floor chill-out room with ambient music and relaxing lighting. Worldclass DJs spin trance W, house Th, and progressive stuff F-Sa. Gay night Su. Beer 7.50SFr, mixed drinks 14SFr. Open W-Su 11pm-5am. 20SFr cover F-Sa before midnight, 25SFr after midnight, but if you can get a regular "member" in line to give you an invitation, you get in free.

Bleu Lézard, rue Enning 10/Lausanne 1003 (tel. 321 38 30). Art kids crowd this bistro, but somehow it's not too pretentious. Decor by local artists; paintings go for about 500SFr. Beer 3-6.50SFr, mixed drinks 8-12 SFr. Vegetarian dishes 17SFr. Live music of all kinds Tu downstairs at "La Cave." Open M-Th 6am-1am, F 6am-2am, Sa 9am-2am, Su 9:30am-1am. Hot food M-Sa 11:30am-2pm and 6:30-10:30pm, Su 10am-5pm and 6:30-10:30pm.

Au Lapin Vert, ruelle du Lapin Vert (tel. 312 13 17), off rue de l'Académie behind the cathedral. An ancient, subtly lit pub blasting English-language rock at mellow students and young professionals. Beer 3.50SF, mixed drinks 10SFr. Open Su-Th 8pm-1am, F-Sa 8pm-2am.

D! Club, Ruelle de Grand Point. Left! out of Lausanne-Flon Metro stop, walk! under Rue de Grand Point bridge, turn! left; it's at far end of parking lot under support wall. Lausanne's other hot discotheque. 10SFr cover. Open Th 11:30pm-4am, F-Sa 11:30pm-5am, Su 10pm-2am.

Dolce Vita, rue César Roux 30 (tel. 323 09 43). From pont Bessières, head up rue Caroline past the large crossroads. A funky and pungent room with frequent live shows of rap, indie, world music, and blistering acid jazz. Beer 4-5SFr. Happy hours W-Th and Su 10pm-midnight (beer 2SFr). Open Su and W 10pm-2am, F-Sa 10pm-4am; in summer also Th 10pm-3am. Weekend cover 5-25SFr depending on the act.

Ouchy White Horse Pub, av d'Ouchy 66 (tel. 616 75 75). A quiet evening by the lake. The equestrian theme gives way to lush carpets and dark wood, which work strangely with bright plaster molding and neon-filled jars. Beer on tap 5-7SFr per pint. *Tapas* 4.50-8SFr. Hamburger, fries, and coke 13SFr. Open Su-Th 7am-1am, F-Sa 7am-2am. Kitchen closes at 12:30am. AmEx, DC, MC, Visa.

■ Montreux

Although it's terribly gauche to drop names, Montreux can't seem to avoid it. Byron, Coward, Hemingway, Kundera, and Nabokov are a few bandied about on street signs and in tourist-office publications. Locals describe their home as somewhat staid; outsiders who pop in for the **Montreux Jazz Festival** in early July find a clutter of artsy people and events. Miles Davis wuz here. So were Freddie Mercury and Igor Stravin-

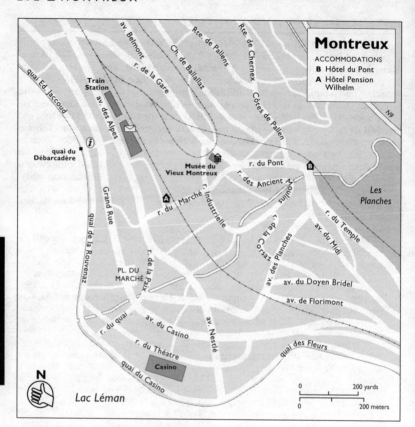

Montreux

ACCOMMODATIONS
B Hôtel du Pont
A Hôtel Pension
 Wilhelm

Les Planches

Lac Léman

0   200 yards
0   200 meters

sky. Once *le jazz* has come and gone, Montreux quietly hosts smaller music festivals throughout the year. Writers of earlier generations (most famously Lord Byron) were repeatedly inspired by Montreux's magnificent **Château de Chillon,** a macabre medieval fortress that alone makes the city worth visiting.

ORIENTATION AND PRACTICAL INFORMATION

Montreux and its surroundings rise rapidly from the eastern shores of Lake Geneva to the edge of the Alps at Les-Roches-de-Naye Jardin. Luckily for those backpackers who are running out of steam, the train station is within easy walking distance of most city sights. Hiking up rue du Marché will bring you to the *vieille ville,* of interest for the views as much as for the architecture.

Trains: (tel. 963 45 15) on av. des Alpes. To: **Geneva** (1hr., every hr., 5:35am-11:35pm, 27SFr); **Lausanne** (20min., every 30min., 5:35am-11:52pm, 8.40SFr); **Bern** (1½hr., every hr., 5:35am-10:35pm, 37SFr). Direct trains also go to **Martigny, Aigle, Sion,** and **Brig** and (literally) through the mountains to **Gstaad.**
Public Transportation: Buy tickets at the back of each bus. A map divides the area into several zones; your fare will depend on the number of zones you cross to reach your destination. 1 zone 1.70SFr, juniors 1.20SFr; 2 zones 2.40SFr, 1.60SFr; 3 zones 3SFr, 2SFr; 4 zones 3.60SFr, 2.40SFr. Swisspass valid. The tourist office offers a 5.50SFr daypass Apr.-Oct. Special late-night buses run during the Jazz Festival.
Boats: CGN, quai du Débarcadère (tel. 963 46 55), next to the tourist office. To: **Lausanne** (1½hr., 7 per day, 18SFr); **Geneva** (5hr., 4 per day, 35SFr); **Vevey**

(25min., 6 per day, 7SFr). Even shorter rides to Villeneuve and Château de Chillon. Buy tickets at the quay, the tourist office, or on board. Eurail and Swisspass valid.

Bike Rental: At the baggage check in the train station. 25SFr per day, 19SFr per half-day; mountain bikes 31SFr per day, 27SFr per half-day. 6SFr charge to return bikes to other stations (including Martigny, Aigle, and Sion) by prior arrangement. Open 5:40am-9:30pm. AmEx, MC, Visa.

Tourist Office: pl. du Débarcadère (tel. 962 84 84 or 963 81 13; fax 963 78 95; email tourism@montreux.ch; http://www.montreux.ch). Descend the stairs opposite the station and head left on Grand Rue. The office is set back on the right. Somewhat harried staff shares the office with desks for festival tickets and bus and train information. Free hotel reservation service within Montreux. Neither the free photocopied map nor the 1SFr map has all of Montreux's street names. Instead, grab the excellent free map from **Union de Banques Suisses**, av. de Casino 26. Tourist office open June-Aug. 9am-7pm; Sept.-May 9am-noon and 1:30-6pm.

Budget Travel: SSR Voyages, av. des Alpes 25 (tel. 961 23 00; fax 961 23 06). Open M-F 9:15am-12:30pm and 1:30-6:30pm, Sa 9:30am-12:30pm.

Currency Exchange: Good rates and no commission at the station. Western Union transfers and credit card advances. Open 5:50am-9:45pm. Banks in Montreux are generally open M-F 8:30am-12:30pm and 1:30-4:30pm.

Luggage Storage: At the station. Lockers 3-5SFr. Luggage watch 5SFr per bag. Open Nov.-May daily 5:40am-8:45pm, June-Oct. 5:50am-9:45pm.

Bookstore: Payot Libraire, av. du Casino 42 (tel. 963 06 07). Open M 10:30am-12:30pm and 1:30-6:30pm, Tu-F 8:30am-12:30pm and 1:30-6:30pm, Sa 9am-5pm. AmEx, DC, MC, Visa.

Laundromat: Salon-Lavoir, rue Industrielle 30. Open M-F 7am-9pm, Sa 7am-8pm. About 5SFr for one load. Also at the **hostel** (5SFr).

Jazz Hotline: tel. 983 82 82.

Late-Night Pharmacy: tel. 962 77 00.

Emergencies: Police, tel. 117. **Fire,** tel. 118. **Ambulance,** tel. 144. **Hospital,** tel. 966 66 66.

Post Office: Main Office, av. des Alpes 70. Left as you exit the station. A surfeit of employees to keep things running smoothly. Address *Poste Restante* to: CH-1820 Montreux 1. Open M-F 7:30am-6pm, Sa 8-11am. **Postal Code:** CH-1820.

Telephone Code: 021.

Sonnet

Eternal Spirit of the chainless Mind
Brightest in dungeons, Liberty! thou art;
For there thy habitation is the heart—
The heart which love of thee alone can bind;
And when thy sons to fetters are consigned—
To fetters, and the damp vault's dayless gloom,
Their country conquers with their martyrdom
And Freedom's fare finds whys on every wind.
Chillon! Thy prison is a holy place
And thy sad floor an altar—for't was trod,
Until his very steps have left a trace
Worn, as if thy cold pavement were a sod,
By Bonivard! —May none those marks efface!
For they appeal from tyranny to God.

—**Lord Byron,** excerpt from "The Prisoner of Chillon" (based on a true story)

ACCOMMODATIONS AND CAMPING

Cheap rooms are scarce in Montreux and almost non-existent during the jazz festival. Hotels and hostels are often fully booked by May. Revelers frequently stash their bags in the train station lockers and crash on the lakefront, but the police will move lakeside sleepers out at 7am. When Montreux seems packed, ask the tourist office for the list *Pensions et Petits Hôtels* or its copy of studio apartments available during the fes-

(Side tab:) LAKE GENEVA

tival. If you still can't find a room, try nearby Vevey's hostel. Otherwise, take bus #1 to "Villeneuve," 5km away, where there are a handful of budget hotels, or consider commuting from Lausanne or Martigny.

Auberge de Jeunesse Montreux (HI), passage de l'Auberge 8 (tel. 963 49 34; fax 969 27 29). Bus #1 on Grand Rue (dir: Villeneuve): "Territet." Up the street, the 1st right (rue du Bocherex), and down the stairs (passage de l'Auberge). Or walk 20min. along the lake past the Montreux Tennis Club. Thoroughly modernized and social hostel 5 seconds from the lakefront (and also, unfortunately, from noisy train tracks). 112 beds in rooms of 4, 6, or 8 beds. Call weeks in advance Apr.-Oct., when school groups, jazz fans, and tourists pack the hostel, some reserving space 6 months ahead. Singles 27SFr 1st night, then 24.50SFr; doubles 72.80SFr, 67SFr. Non-members add 5SFr per night. Breakfast and linens included. Dinner 11SFr. Lockers 2SFr deposit. **Laundry** 8SFr, including detergent. TV room. Free (non-affiliated) parking nearby. Reception Apr.-Sept. 7-10am and 4-11pm; Oct.-Mar. 7:30-9:30am and 5-10pm. Lockout 10am-5pm. Checkout 9:30am. Curfew midnight, but groups and families can request a key with a passport deposit. Wheelchair accessible. AmEx, DC, MC, Visa.

Hôtel Pension Wilhelm, rue du Marché 13-15 (tel. 963 14 31; fax 963 32 85). From the station, walk left 3min. up av. des Alpes and left on rue du Marché, uphill and past the police station. 4 generations of Wilhelms have operated this 60-bed hotel for over 100 years. Relentlessly pastel color scheme. All rooms have sinks. Singles (available during off-season only) 55SFr; doubles 120SFr. Breakfast included. Reception 7am-midnight. Closed Oct.-Feb.

Hôtel du Pont, rue du Pont 12 (tel./fax 963 22 49), at the top of the *vieille ville.* From the station, turn left 800m from the station on av. des Alpes (3min.) then right up rue du Marché. Continue uphill until it becomes rue du Pont; the hotel is on the left. Large rooms with comfortably clashing furniture next to a waterfall. All rooms have bathrooms and TVs. The café downstairs is part of this family-run establishment. Singles 60SFr; doubles 110-120SFr; triples 140-150SFr. Breakfast included. Evening meals 13.80SFr. Reception M-Sa 7am-midnight, Su 8:30am-midnight. AmEx, MC, Visa.

Camping: Les Horizons Bleues (tel. 960 15 47). Take bus #1: "Villeneuve." From the bus stop, follow the lake to the left (5min.). Supreme lakeside site. 7SFr per person; 4.50-11SFr per tent; municipal tax 1SFr. Free showers. 10% discount in winter. Cold in winter. Reception 8am-10pm.

FOOD

Montreux is very, very pricey. If you must dine lakeside, pack a picnic. The tourist office publishes a catalog listing establishments by cuisine, but it omits price ranges.

Restaurants

Babette's, Grand Rue 60 (tel. 963 77 96; fax 961 15 10), down the stairs from the station to the left. An order-out *pâtisserie* in front gives way to a plush, velvet-cushioned restaurant. Crepes of all types for lunch (10-14SFr) and dessert (6-9SFr). Sandwiches to go at the outside counter 5-13SFr. Open 7am-7pm.

La Locanda, av. du Casino 44 (tel. 963 29 33). A hidden little restaurant filled with bearded regulars. Large pizzas 12-19SFr; healthy portions of pasta from 11SFr; *gnocchi* 14.50-16SFr. Open M-Sa 11am-2pm and 6pm-midnight. AmEx, MC, Visa.

Caveau des Vignerons, rue Industrielle 30bis (tel. 963 25 70), at the corner of rue du Marché. Swiss dishes served in a whitewashed candlelit cave. Cook your own steak of horse meat at the table (with salad and potatoes 27-31SFr). Cheese fondue 20SFr; *assiette du jour* 14SFr. Open M-F 7am-midnight, Sa 3pm-midnight. Closed late July to mid-Aug. AmEx, MC, Visa.

The White Horse, 28 Grand Rue (tel. 963 15 92), opposite the covered market. A sign on the door declares this an "authentic" English pub. It's not, but whatever it really is, the food is good and the atmosphere friendly, from the francophone staff to the fuzzy white dog who snores at customers' feet. Sandwiches 4.50-7SFr; salads 6-8SFr; spaghetti, fish and chips, or chicken nuggets 12.50SFr. Beer 5.50SFr per pint. Pinball, darts, foosball, and arcade games in back. Open M-Sa 11am-1am (flexible), Su 3pm-midnight. Kitchen closes at 11pm.

Restaurant Le Palais "Hoggar," quai du Casino 14 (tel. 963 12 71). Blue-tiled decor and authentic Middle Eastern cuisine are an ideal backdrop for people-watching. Chicken curry 22SFr. Twenty different ice creams. Open Apr.-Nov. daily 11am-10:30pm. AmEx, DC, Visa.

Markets

Marché de Montreux, place du Marché. Covered outdoor market of fresh fruits, vegetables, meats, cheeses, breads, and pastries along both quai de la Rouvenaz and quai Jaccoud. Every Friday 7am-3pm. Also look for the **flea market** at this site.

Migros, av. du Casino. Restaurant next door. Open M 9am-7pm, Tu-Th 8am-7pm, F 8am-9pm, Sa 7:30am-5pm.

Co-op, Grand Rue 80. Open M-F 8am-12:15pm and 2-6:30pm, Sa 8am-5pm.

SIGHTS

The Montreux-Vevey **museum passport** (15SFr), available at the tourist office, covers entry to 10 museums. The museums are of wildly varying interest. The atmospheric **Château de Chillon** (tel. 966 89 10; fax 966 89 12), is the main draw. *(Open July-Aug. 9am-6:15pm; Apr.-June and Sept. 9am-5:45pm; Oct. 10am-4:45pm; Nov.-Feb. 10am-noon and 1:30-4pm; Mar. 10am-noon and 1:30-4:45pm. 6.50SFr, students 5.50SFr, ages 6-16 3SFr.)* Built on an island, Chillon is a perfect 13th-century fortress with all the comforts of home: prison cells, a torture chamber, an armory, and enough loopholes to fend off attackers who get past the moat. The eerie chateau inspired narratives by Rousseau, Victor Hugo, and Alexandre Dumas, as well as Lord Byron's *The Prisoner of Chillon*, which tells the tale of a priest manacled to a pillar for four years. The souvenir shop sells copies, and you can see where Byron scratched his name into a dungeon pillar. A brochure leads you through a tour of 28 chilly and chilling rooms. A lot less interesting than the castle, the **Musée du Vieux-Montreux,** rue de la Gare 40 (tel. 963 13 53), on the outskirts of the *vieille ville,* describes the history of Montreux from Roman times through its "colonization" by the resort industry in the late 19th-century. *(Open Apr.-Oct. 10am-noon and 2-5pm. 6SFr, students and seniors 4SFr.)*

When the weather isn't too hazy, **Rochers-de-Naye** (2045m) offers views as far as Mont Blanc and the Matterhorn. An expensive **cog railway** chugs up Montreux's stately Alps, and you can purchase tickets at the station or the tourist office. *(Round-trip 50SFr, one-way 30.80SFr; with Swisspass 31.50SFr, 15.80SFr; with Eurailpass 28.30SFr, 15.40SFr. Tourist office ticket counter open Apr.-Oct. M-F 9am-noon and 1:30-5:30pm.)* To shave a few francs off the price, take the train to Caux (11.80SFr) and walk up from there. The round-trip back to Montreux, following the ridge, takes seven hours.

THE MUSIC FESTIVALS

The **Montreux Jazz Festival,** a world-famous magnet for exceptional musical talent and one of the biggest parties in Europe, pushes everything aside for 15 days starting the first Friday in July. The 1999 lineup will be made public at Christmas 1998; the 1998 headliners included Bob Dylan, B.B. King, Herbie Hancock, Santana, Björk, Beck, and (God help us) the Phil Collins Big Band. Demand has sent ticket prices rocketing into the stratosphere: individual tickets range from 49 to 129SFr; a festival pass sells for 1300SFr. Standing room tickets range from 26 to 68SFr. Write to the tourist office well in advance for information and tickets. The **booking desk** (tel. 623 45 67; http://www.grolier.fr/festival/montreux) is open Monday-Friday 9am to noon and 1:30 to 6pm off-season and non-stop during the festival. From mid-March the **jazz hotline** in Montreux is active (tel. 963 82 82), run by the **Jazz Boutique** ticket sellers at Grand Rue 100. The **postal address** for ticket orders is Grand Rue 100, CP1325, CH-1820 Montreux. You can also get tickets from **Société de Banque Suisse** "ticket corners" in major Swiss cities; from the **Swiss National Tourist offices,** 608 Fifth Ave., New York, NY 10020 (212-757-5944); or from **Swiss Court,** London W1V 8EE (tel. (0171) 287 81 37). Most

The Passing of a Giant

On July 8, 1991, at the Montreux Jazz Festival, the great jazz trumpeter Miles Davis played his last live performance. An historic concert, the performance marked the first time Davis had returned to the musical style with which he began his career. Davis contributed much to jazz, including the "fusion" of jazz and rock and the invention, with Gil Evans, of "cool" jazz. In their pioneering collaboration, Davis and Evans broke away from the frenetic scale structure of be-bop improvization. Davis's smooth, modal improvisations, heard on such albums as *Kind of Blue* and over the rich orchestral settings of the Gil Evans Orchestra on *Sketches of Spain,* influenced a whole generation of artists, including John Coltrane and Bill Evans. Although other artists expanded and developed modal jazz, Davis moved on and never looked back, abandoning some of his most-loved works for over 20 years until Quincy Jones stepped in. Jones had long wanted to do a concert with Davis and revive Davis' earlier material. When Davis finally agreed, the two performed together at Montreux with the Gil Evans Orchestra (then under the direction of Evans's son, Miles) and the Charles Grundtz Concert Jazz Orchestra, playing songs that hadn't been performed live for a generation. Jones has said that he had never seen Davis as pleased and as connected with the audience in any other concert. Several weeks later, Davis fell ill. He died of pneumonia on September 28, 1991.

events sell out before July, some do so as early as January. If you can find a room but no tickets, come anyway for the **Jazz Off,** 500 hours of free, open-air concerts by new bands and established musicians.

From late August to early October, the **Montreux-Vevey Classical Music Festival** takes over with operas, symphonies, and classical recitals performed by musicians from Moscow to Memphis. Tickets to concerts in Montreux and neighboring Vevey, Martigny, St. Maurice, and Chillon range from 15 to 180SFr. Contact the Office of the Classical Music Festival at rue du Théâtre 5, 1st Floor, Case Postale 162, CH-1820 Montreux 2 (tel. 963 54 50; fax 963 25 06; email fmmvinfo@montreux.ch, http://www.montreux.ch).

NIGHTLIFE

Montreux caters to all tastes and personalities. Its vibrant nightlife centers around the polished atmosphere of the bar- and club-lined quays.

Casino de Montreux, rue du Théâtre 9 (tel. 962 83 83). From av. du Casino, turn on rue Igor Stravinsky toward the lake. The original casino, inaugurated in 1881, helped launch the careers of Stravinsky and great conductor Ernest Ansermet. It burned to the ground in 1971 during a Frank Zappa concert (an event later immortalized by the Deep Purple song "Smoke on Water") and the rebuilt hunk o' concrete has little of its predecessor's charm. 200 sultry slot machines and video poker things (5pm-3am; 21 and over); *boule,* a roulette variant (8:30pm-1am). Dance club downstairs on weekends. Open M-Sa 10pm-4am.

Rock Café, rue de l'Auberge 5 (tel. 963 88 88; fax 961 26 27), just up the stairs from the youth hostel. Its name and guitar-art may aspire to imitate the Hard Rock, but this neighborhood bar can't escape its more down-to-earth, "grungy" style. Loud music, young crowd, billiard room, video games, darts, and pinball. Beer 6SFr per pint; choose among bottles from 8 countries. Open Su-Th 4pm-midnight, F-Sa 4pm-2am. AmEx, DC, Visa.

Duke's Jazz Bar, Grand Rue 97 (tel. 962 50 70), 50m down Grand Rue toward Vevey past the Auditorium Stravinski. Enter through the posh Royal Plaza Inter-Continental Hotel. As one of the venues of the Montreux Jazz Festival, this high-class establishment bursts at the seams for 2½ weeks in July. After performing, artists often arrive to hang out with the crowd. Celebrate with 295SFr champagne or stick to the impressive 6-7.50SFr range of beers. Open Su-Th 3pm-2am, F-Sa noon-4am, during Jazz Festival until 6am. Happy hour 6-10pm.

■ Near Montreux

■ Vevey

Vevey's heyday as a resort town peaked in the 19th century, when hordes of upper-class English made it a virtual colony of the Queen's empire (as described in *Daisy Miller,* composed in Vevey by Henry James). The upside to its decline in 20th century is that Vevey has avoided the five-star stratification of nearby Montreux. Charlie Chaplin fled here from McCarthyism in 1953 (1 year after producing "Limelight") and Jean-Jacques Rousseau, Victor Hugo, Fyodor Dostoevsky, Henry James, le Corbusier, and Graham Greene have all worked within its borders. As you follow the tourist office's walking tour through all the famous "guess who slept here" spots, you'll see why handsome, serene Vevey drew so many great minds to its shores.

ORIENTATION AND PRACTICAL INFORMATION There are three ways to reach Vevey from Montreux: bus #1 to "Vevey" (20min., every 10min., 2.40SFr); train (5min., every 30min., 2.80SFr); and cruise (25min., 5 per day, 7SFr). The **tourist office** is at Grand-Place 29 (tel. 922 20 20; fax 922 20 24; email veveytourism@vevey.ch; http://www.veveytourism.ch). To get there from the station, cross pl. de la Gare, go past av. de la Gare, and turn left on av. Paul Cérésole. At the end of the road, cut across the parking lot toward the columned arcade; the office is inside. (Open June 15-Sept. 15 8:30am-7pm; Sept. 16-June 14 M-F 8:30am-noon and 1:30-6pm, Sa 8:30am-noon.) **Lockers** (3-5SFr) and **bike rental** (city bike 25SFr per day and 19SFr per half-day; mountain bike 31SFr, 24SFr) wait at the station. In an **emergency,** call 117. The **post office** is across pl. de la Gare (open M-F 7:30am-6pm, Sa 8-11am) and has a 24-hr. **ATM.** The **postal code** is CH-1800; the **telephone code** is 021.

ACCOMMODATIONS AND FOOD Overlooking the bustle of Grand Place just off the waterfront, the **Riviera Lodge,** pl. du Marché 5 (tel. 923 80 40; fax 923 80 41), presents an attractive alternative to its noisier sister in Montreux. Sixty bright, shiny rooms (renovated in 1997) offer comfortable beds and lavish facilities. The entrance foyer has lockers and an activities/dining room. On the fifth floor, the reception desk shares space with a terrace, a spotless **kitchen, laundry,** several common rooms, and the engaging manager, François. (4-, 6-, or 8-bed dorms 20SFr; doubles 70SFr. Breakfast 7SFr. Sheets 5SFr. Reception 7:30-10am and 4:30-6:30pm. Call if arriving later.) Many family homes also house travelers; one possibility is **Pension Bürgle,** rue Louis Meyer 16 (tel./fax 921 40 23), just off Grand-Place. Dark hallways contrast with the cheerful kitchen, where small kiddie Bürgles try to stay out from under the feet of various older Bürgles preparing meals. (39SFr. Payment for 1st night required for reservations. Breakfast included. Dinner 12SFr.)

For cheap, fresh food, check out the **produce and flea market** at the Grand-Place (pl. du Marché) Tuesday and Saturday mornings from 8:30am to noon. The rest of the week, do-it-yourself fare can be had at **Migros** (open M 9am-6:30pm, Tu-W 8am-6:30pm, Th 8am-8pm, F 8am-6:30pm, Sa 7:30am-5pm) and **Coop** (same hours), across av. Paul Cérésole off Grand-Place. Café-restaurants line Grand-Place, but food is cheaper away from the lakefront. Next to the train station entrance stands an **Aperto convenience store.** (Open 6am-9:30pm.) Standard café-restaurants line the Grand-Place offering *Menüs* for around 12-15SFr. Cross the square from the station to the post office and follow the underpass (passage St. Antoine) across the tracks for a more interesting experience. At the top of the stairs, in Vevey's industrial area, signs hang for **Les Temps Modernes,** rue des Deux Gares 6 (tel. 922 34 39). A factory turned café, record store, and dance studio, it has become a cultural junction for local artists. Live jazz and contemporary rock (Th-Sa) jolt the central stage area. (Salads 5-14SFr. *Plats du jour* 13-16SFr. Drinks 1SFr more during performances. Open Tu-Th 11am-midnight, F 11am-2am, Sa 5pm-2am.)

LAKE GENEVA

SIGHTS AND ENTERTAINMENT   The big story in 1999 will be the **Fête des Vign-erons** (Festival of the Wine-growers), a five-times-a-century Bacchanal from July 19 to August 15. Nearly half a million people are expected to imbibe copiously while watching 15 open-air performances, four parades with traditional costumes, 4500 local actors, two orchestras, and the last solar eclipse of the millenium (August 11). It ends in mid-August with a huge party and carnival in honor of Bacchus, Roman god of wine. Make reservations now! (You can contact them at http://www.fetedesvign-erons.ch.) Also in July and August, an **open-air cinema** at pl. Scanaven brings classical and current flicks to Vevey (13SFr). The **International Comedy Film Festival,** dedi-cated to former resident Charlie Chaplin, features official competitions during the day and more accessible screenings at night (13SFr). It usually comes to town during the summer months but has been pushed back to October in 1999 in order to avoid con-flicting with the *Fête des Vignerons* and the **International Festival of Music,** hosted jointly by Vevey and Montreux every year. The music festival lasts from August to September and attracts several renowned international orchestras as well as noted soloists for a series of concerts and master classes. Venues lie in both cities, but the **Theatre of Vevey,** rue de Théâtre 4 (tel. 923 60 55), provides information and han-dles reservations and ticket sales for Vevey. On years when the *Fête des Vignerons* is not being held, the **Folklore Market** (in pl. du Marché; open mid-July to Aug. Sa 9am-noon) allows you to sample all the local wine you can hold for only 5SFr. The **Wine-train** winds its way through 8km of villages and vineyards in Lavaux. *(Every hr. from Vevey station, round-trip up to 9.60SFr, Swisspass and Eurailpass valid.)* The tourist office has a list of tasting venues; a map with directions to Chexbres and Puidox (the two wine centers); and a guide to six hiking tours of the region.

   One of these hikes is more of a stroll that takes you past interesting museums along the quay on your way to the neighboring town of Tour-de-Peilz. For an excellent deal, pick up a Montreux-Vevey Museum Passport. *(15SFr; 10SFr if you stay overnight in Vevey.)* It grants free entrance to 10 museums in the cities, including the **Musée Jenisch,** av. de la Gare 2 (tel. 921 29 50; fax 921 62 92). *(Open Tu-Su Mar.-Oct. 10:30am-noon and 2-5:30pm; Nov.-Feb. 2-5:30pm. 10SFr, students 4SFr. Guided tours 14SFr.)* A collection of engravings and etchings by masters like Dürer, Rembrandt, Toulouse-Lautrec, and Corot graces the 1st floor, outshining the more contemporary Swiss artists upstairs. Near the tourist office, signs point to the **Swiss Camera Museum,** ruelle des Anciens-Fossés 6 (tel. 925 21 40; fax 921 64 58). *(Open Tu-Su Apr.-Oct. 11am-5:30pm; Nov.-Mar. 2-5:30pm. 5SFr, students 4SFr, children free. Guided tours 3SFr.)* There are three floors of his-toric photographic equipment from daguerreotypes to early spy cameras, one hidden in a walking cane handle. The fourth floor houses temporary photographic exhibi-tions. From the museum, you can turn left onto rue du Lac and stroll through the fountains and boutiques of Vevey's *vieille ville* or head straight for the quay. A few minutes either way will bring you to the **Alimentarium/Food Museum** (tel. 924 41 11), on the corner of rue du Léman and quai Perdonnet. *(Open Tu-Su Apr.-Oct. 10am-5pm; Nov.-Mar. 10am-noon and 2-5pm. 6SFr, students and seniors 4SFr, school groups free.)* Learn the story of food from its production in the sun to its processing in the human body. Food processing machinery, Nestlé commercials, and large, human-sized ham-ster wheels break up some of the more passive displays. Farther along the path, the **Swiss Museum of Games** (tel. 944 40 50; fax 944 10 79) sets up a small shrine for devotees to the twin ideals of skill and chance with its display of ancient chess pieces, cardboard Cold War games, and Nintendo. *(Open Tu-Su 2-6pm. 6SFr, students 3SFr, under 17 free. Guided tours an additional 2.50SFr.)* Be enticed by lucid psychological analyses of game phenomena and the chance to play a bit yourself.

■ Gstaad and Saanen

Lying at the juncture of four alpine valleys, Gstaad and its much less glamorous sister, Saanen, are at the heart of skiing country. Saanen has goats; Gstaad has glitzy five-star hotels and designer boutiques. Saanen has a lot of tractors; Gstaad has a lot of low-set lipstick-red convertibles. As Gstaad moves into the most rarefied realms of 20th-cen-tury tourism, Saanen lingers behind, hardly even registering when the late railroad finally connected it to the outside world.

Gstaad has a very friendly, well-organized **tourist office** (tel. 748 81 81, for room reservations and package deals, tel. 748 81 84; fax 748 81 83; email tvsl@gstaad.ch; http://www.gstaad.ch). It's just past the railway bridge on the main road to the right of the station. (Open July-Aug. M-F 8:30am-6:30pm, Sa 9am-6pm, Su 2-6pm; Sept.-June M-F 8:30am-noon and 2-6pm, Sa 9am-noon.) Saanen's main street also has a tourist office. (Open M-F, same hours.) By **train,** get to Gstaad from **Montreux** (1½hr., every hr., 8:30am-4:30pm, 19.40SFr, round-trip 34SFr) or **Interlaken** (2hr., every hr., 8:44am-4:50pm, 21SFr, change trains at Zweisimmen). **Buses** run to **Les Diablerets** (1hr., 8:27am-3:27pm, 11.40SFr). For **taxis** try 744 80 80. The train station in Gstaad has 3-5SFr **lockers** plus **bike rental** (25SFr per day, 19SFr per half-day; mountain bikes 31SFr, 24SFr per half-day), **currency exchange,** and a **ski rack.** Gstaad's **post office** is next to the train station. (Open M-F 7:45am-noon and 2-6pm, Sa 7:45-11am.) In an **emergency,** call 117. The **postal code** is CH-3780, and the **telephone code** is 033.

Gstaad proper has few hotels with fewer than three stars, but the tourist office publishes a list of budget options, usually quite far from town. The **Jugendherberge** (tel. 744 13 43) in Saanen is definitely the preferable alternative. From Gstaad station, take the train (5-7min., every hr., 2.40SFr) or post bus (10min., every hr., 2.40SFr). From Saanen's station turn right on the main street and follow the "youth hostel" signs (10min.). This slightly chilly rural hostel has an exceptionally warm welcome and lots of amenities: billiards, **bike rental and repair,** a TV room, a playground, a library (with English books), and foosball. The hostel offers six- and eight-bed dorms (25.40SFr), doubles (33.40SFr), triples, and quads with balconies for couples and families. (Children ages 2-6 are half price; children under 2 are free. Prices decrease after first night. Breakfast, sheets, and showers are included. Three-course dinner 11SFr. Reception 7:30-9am and 5-10pm. Curfew 11pm. Closed Nov. and May. Phone ahead in winter.) **Camping Bellerive** (tel. 744 63 30) rests between Gstaad and Saanen. Arrive any time. (6.40SFr, children 3.20SFr. Winter: 7.50SFr, 2.20SFr. Tent 5.30SFr. Shower 1SFr. Check-in 9-10am and 6-7pm.) Saanen has a **summer-only camping site** (tel. 744 61 91; fax 744 60 42) on the edge of town at the end of Campingstr. Arrive any time. (6.40SFr; tent 5.30SFr; caravan 8.50SFr. Showers 0.50SFr per min. Check-in 6-7pm. MC, Visa.)

Back in Gstaad, budget diners should take ruthless advantage of the **Co-op,** left on the main street from the train station. (Open M-Th 7:30am-6:30pm, F 8am-noon and 1:30-8pm, Sa 7:30am-4pm. Restaurant open M-Th 8am-6:30pm, F 8am-10pm, Sa 8am-4pm, Su 9am-5pm.) In front of the train station, the **Hotel Bernerhof café** (tel. 748 88 44) serves up a reasonably priced *menu du midi* (15-17SFr) and a healthy selection of vegetarian dishes (15-18SFr), along with views of the mountains. For a change of atmosphere, slide into soft leather chairs and have a burger and fries with a beer (14-18SFr) at **Richi's Pub** (tel. 744 57 87), just after the church on the main street to the right of the station. (Open noon-12:30am.)

These towns may be absurdly different, but they both share a superlative sports scene. **White-water rafting** starts at 80SFr for four to five hours in Gstaad (Eurotrek: tel. (01) 462 02 03) and 99SFr for three hours in Saanen (Swissraft: tel. 744 50 80). In July and August, Swissraft also goes **canyoning** (80SFr for approx. 3hr.). You can try **ballooning** with either CAST Balloonfahrten (tel. 744 62 59; 390-500SFr for 2hr.) or Hans Büker (tel. (026) 924 54 85; fax 924 76 42; 485SFr for 1½-2hr.). If you prefer the ocean blue to the wild blue yonder, **paragliding** (tel. 744 30 03; email parasport@spectraweb.ch; http://www.beo.ch/gstaad/paragliding) is an option at 130SFr for four to six hours. To see the countryside with at least your horses' feet planted firmly on the ground, try **horse-trekking** (tel. 744 24 60; 22SFr per lesson) or riding in a **horse-drawn cart** (tel. 744 24 60; 30min. ride 40SFr per person in a group of at least 5). Rounding out your options are 150km of hard-core **mountain-bike trails;** the tourist office publishes a helpful map and guide describing distances and difficulty. Within the city, covered tennis courts, saunas, and pools wait on every corner. For the **indoor public pool** (tel. 744 44 16), turn right on the main road out of the station and right after the river. (Open M 2-9pm, Tu and Th 10am-9pm, W and F 10am-10pm, Sa-Su 10am-7pm. 9SFr, with visitor's card 8SFr.) In July, the annual **Swiss**

Gstaar-Struck

Celebrities were first drawn to Gstaad in the 40s and 50s by the quality of its international schools. Prince Ranier of Morocco spent his boyhood at the city's Le Rosey school; he later returned to show off the town to his wife, Grace Kelly—and to show her off to the town. In fine Fitzgeraldian fashion, Gstaad filled with affluent British and Americans, who established an informal literary and artistic clique. Audrey Hepburn made frequent visits, and Elizabeth Taylor relaxed here with her two-time husband Robert Burton (maybe dreams of Taylor's Swiss chateau convinced Burton to try again). Not far down the hill, American economist John Kenneth Galbraith spent peaceful and prolific winters in the third floor of a chateau. Bill Buckley, Galbraith's political archrival, did the same, and the two engaged in good-natured competition to fill Gstaad's bookstore with more of their respective books. Just something to ponder while dodging screaming *Schulkinder* at the Saanen *Jugendherberge*.

Open Tennis Tournament (tel. (01) 22 25 60 60; fax 748 83 50; http://www.gstaad.ch/swiss.open) attracts players who opt to skip Wimbledon, and 40,000 spectators who make the same decision. (Tickets 40-100SFr; passes 380-430SFr.)

Once inspired to challenge the mountains, try a rugged panoramic hike up the **Giferspitz horseshoe.** Turn right on the main road from Gstaad station, left on the main road just before the river, and take the second big road on the right over the river (with signs to "Bissen"; the turn is 1km from Gstaad). Follow the yellow *Wanderweg* signs for Wasserngrat and power up the steep hill flank to the top cable car station (1936m). The very fit and adventurous continue up to the **Lauenehorn** (2477m) and, after a rocky scramble, farther to the **Giferspitz** (2541m), Gstaad's tallest peak. The path circles down to Bissen again, but a bus eases the descent (1800m ascent; perfect weather only; allow one full day). The tourist office sells hiking maps.

In winter, Gstaad turns to **skiing.** With 250km of runs and 69 lifts, the town generally has something open. Crack skiers will find little to challenge them, but middling ones will be very happy. The **Top Card ski pass** (tel. 748 82 82; fax 748 82 60; email ski.gstaad@gstaad.ch; http://www.skigstaad.ch) is 50SFr for one day on all sectors; more limited passes are slightly cheaper. A week of skiing will run about 263SFr, depending on your age. For the dedicated, a **season ski pass** (890SFr) from the Gstaad region gives allows skiing in Oberengadin/St. Moritz, Kitzbühel/Tirol, Adelboden-Lenk, Alpes Vaudoises, Ordino-Arcalis, and Pal Arinsal (Andorra). Consult the tourist office for details on **heliskiing, snowboarding, curling,** and **skating.** There are three **snow-boarding parks** in the region and a **glacier** for year-round skiing.

■ Leysin

Rumor has it that some of Leysin's residents are Swiss. In this laid-back town where people show up to work in sweats and flannels, the locals aren't so local. A clutch of American and Japanese colleges and international schools render the village Anglophone friendly without the usual coincident and overwhelming tourist industry. Leysin offers long views of the mountain-girded Rhône Valley and the distant shores of Lac Léman, but the town is far removed from the frenzy engulfing those areas. In the surrounding mountains, sports enthusiasts will find an abundance of skiing, snowboarding, climbing, mountain biking, paragliding, canyoning, and hiking. The town's well-developed indoor facilities add swimming, ice skating, tennis, and squash.

The only way to reach Leysin by transport is the **cog railway** from Aigle. The railway leisurely chugs passengers to the top of the steep climb (30min., every hr. 6am-10pm; Swisspass valid). There are four stops: Leysin-Village (7.80SFr), Versmont, Feydey (9SFr), and Grand-Hôtel (9.60SFr). Aigle lies on the high-speed train line from **Lausanne** (30min., 2 per hr., 5:24am-8:24pm, 12.20SFr) and **Montreux** (10min., 2 per hr., 5:24am-8:24pm, 4.80SFr). The staff of the **tourist office** (tel. 494 29 21 or 494 22 44; fax 494 16 16; email tourism@leysin.ch; http://www.leysin.ch) waits behind sleek metal and glass counters at the New Sporting Club just down from pl. du

Marché. (Open M-F 8am-9pm, Sa-Su 9am-9pm.) There is a **24-hour ATM** at the Banque Cantonal Vaudous just below Hefti Sports. For a **taxi,** call 493 22 93. **Bike rental** from station at usual rates, from **Hefti Sports** (mountain) 35SFr per day. **Pharmacie Leysin** (emergency tel. 493 45 00) sells medicines next to the Hefti Sports on pl. du Marché. (Open M-F 8:30-noon and 2-6:30pm; Sa 9am-12:30pm and 2-5pm.) For an **ambulance,** call 144. For the **police,** call 493 45 41. In an **emergency,** dial 117. In a **fire,** call 118. There are two **post offices,** one next to the Feydey station (tel. 494 14 06) and one down the hill in Leysin-Village on rue du Village (tel. 494 12 05). (Both open M-F 8-11:30am and 2:30-6pm, Sa 8:30-11am.) The Feydey office serves as the town's post bus station. The **postal code** is CH-1854, and the **telephone code** is 025.

The two sports centers in the village offer amenities at not-so-friendly rates. The pools and **Turkish bath,** however, in the **Place Large** (New Sporting Club; tel. 494 29 21; email o.t.leysin@pingnet.ch; http://www.leysin.ch), are only 5SFr and 3SFr with a **Leysin holiday card.** You receive the card (valid for 10-50% discounts at any of Leysin's sports centers, slopes, cable cars, and ski lifts) after your first night's stay at any hotel. The New Sporting Club also has squash and tennis courts and a (brand new) climbing wall—as well as guides and lessons for all three. (Open 9am-9pm; pools have slightly shorter hours.) Downhill near the campsite, the **Crettex-Jaquet** (Centre des Sports; tel. 494 24 42; fax 494 13 55) offers **ice skating.** (Open 8am-10pm; 6.50SFr, students 4.50SFr.) Skiers can rent equipment from **Hefti Sports** (tel. 494 16 77; fax 494 26 61), two minutes from the New Sporting Club on pl. du Marché (open M-F 8:30am-noon and 2-6:30pm, Sa 8:30am-noon and 2-5pm, Su 10am-noon and 2-5pm), then head off into the unknown reaches of the skies and slopes (skis or snowboard plus boots 43SFr). One-day ski passes average 38SFr, children 23SFr; weekly passes 212SFr, 128SFr. The holiday card also grants discounts on these passes and the cable car that bobs up to the nearby summit of Berneuse (June-Oct. and mid-Dec. to mid-Apr.; 13.50SFr, round-trip 18SFr; Visa, MC, AmEx). Another car rises to Mayen beneath the craggy **Tour d'Aï** (2331m; same dates and prices). At the end of January, the pros appear for the **European Snowboarding Championships** held in Leysin every year (Jan. 12-17, 1999), a week that shatters the general calm and expands the pocket of activity (usually centered around the American College) into the lower terraces of the town. For **paragliding,** call **M.E. Pantillon** (tel. (077) 38 26 02). They offer tandem flight with professional paragliders, weekends only.

Just 50m from the start of skiing and biking trails, the **Hiking Sheep Guesthouse,** Villa La Joux (tel./fax 494 35 35; portable (79) 416 37 82; email hikingsheep@leysin.net; http://www.leysin.net/hikingsheep), perches high over the valley below. Avoid the grueling hike up from the village by taking the cog train (or hourly bus during the high season) all the way to "Grand Hotel." Shining wooden bunks, a convivial dining room, breathtaking balconies, and pristine **kitchen** facilities await. Friendly owner Gérard supplies satellite TV, log fires, summer BBQs, game and meditation rooms, **internet access,** and **laundry** (10SFr). (June 15-Dec. 15 dorms 26SFr, doubles 33SFr; Dec. 16-June 14 dorms 30SFr, doubles 35SFr; for children subtract about 1SFr. Buffet breakfast 8SFr, English breakfast 10SFr. Sheets included. Checkout 10:30am. No curfew. MC, Visa.)

Down the road to the right is **Club Vagabond,** rte des Quatre Chalets (tel. 494 13 21; fax 494 13 22; email club-vagabond@bluewih.ch), well past its glory days as a hippie heaven for *la vie bohème* but still revered by under-30 English speakers for its live music, Sunday BBQ (in summer at 6pm; bring your own meat; 5SFr for bread and salad buffet), and occasional art exhibits. The floors have new carpeting, the walls fresh paint, and the bunk beds firm mattresses. Leather armchairs and an English library look out across Leysin's slopes. The discotheque in the cellar, "The Ice Cave," has, like Gloria Gaynor, survived with 70s style intact, and the late-night bar serves beer (5SFr). As "the home of mountain sports," Club Vagabond even offers its own rock climbing and mountain biking packages. (Dorms 21SFr; doubles 25SFr. Breakfast 6SFr. Sheets and towels 6SFr. Reception Tu-Su 8am-5pm; after hours head to the bar, open till 3am.) **Hotel de la Paix** (tel./fax 494 13 75), on av. Rollier, is opposite the "Versmont" train stop. Narrow hallways choking on oriental carpeting connect old-fashioned rooms with fading prints of *belle epoque* Leysin. In the garden, red-and-white-striped deck chairs swallow up the older clients. (44-64SFr per person. Breakfast included. Lunch or dinner 25SFr, both 37SFr. Reception 8am-8pm. AmEx, MC, Visa.) **Camping Semiramis** (tel. 494 11 48; fax 494 20 29) is a large grassy field at the foot of hill near evergreen forest. From Leysin-Village station, walk left on rue de Village then right on rte du Suchet past the post office. (5.80-6.20SFr, children 3.55SFr; tents 4SFr. Free showers. AmEx, DC, MC, Visa.)

A **Co-op** supermarket is just off the big bend in rue Favez, below pl. du Marché and the New Sporting Club. (Open M-F 8am-noon and 2-6:30pm, Sa 8am-noon and 2pm-5pm.) A stroll uphill to the Feydey district and **La Grotta** (tel. 494 15 32) promises the added attraction of the owner's gold-club member Swatch collection—a dazzling expo of all the editions since 1983, including special music alarm, beeper, and ski-pass versions. Slightly cheaper food awaits at **La Nonna Restaurant Pizzeria** (tel. 494 21 94), above the New Sporting Club. Eat on a rooftop terrace. (*Menüs* 16-20SFr, pasta 13-18SFr, 19 exotic pizzas (many vegetarian) 16-20SFr. Open M-F 7:30am-11:30pm, Sa-Su 8am-11:30pm.) Several mountain restaurants offer real charm and non-canned local atmosphere at the price of hiking up challenging slopes. **L'Horizon** (tel. 494 15005) is a local fave. A level 15-minute walk from the hostel past cow pastures gets you an excellent fondue (18-19SFr) in a mountain lodge atmosphere. Try the local valley delicacy, *Williamine*, a pear schnapps. (Open 10:30am until the last customer leaves; closed Su night and M.)

■ Les Diablerets

One of the few Swiss towns that can claim two high seasons, Les Diablerets' little devils frolic year-long among creaky chalets and glacial slopes. There may be only five lifts open on Diablerets' glacier in July and August, but the snow is 100% guaranteed. Come winter, the town stresses substance over the snootier stylings of local rivals Gstaad, Crans-Montana, and Verbier. The results: a younger, more sports-driven crowd. Snowboarders will appreciate the respect they receive, and hikers can putter about peacefully on the surprisingly varied terrain.

Only two public transport services connect Les Diablerets to the rest of Switzerland. The hourly **train** down to **Aigle** (1hr., 6:27am-9:27am, 9.60SFr), and the **post bus** over the mountains to **Gstaad** (11.40SFr) via the Col du Pillon, which leaves about 5 times per day depending on the season. In summer, buses are the only way to reach the Diablerets glacier cable cars. The first bus leaves at 9:39am and the last returns at 4:40pm, so plan accordingly or get ready for a 45-minute walk. The helpful and all-knowing **tourist office,** rue de la Gare (tel. 492 33 58; fax 492 23 48), in a chalet to the right of the train station, publishes a devilishly impressive range of literature. It keeps a list of activities and events like the **Adventura Sports Weekend** (25 sports over 2 days, June 21-22), the giant **Rösti Festival** at Isenau (July 14-Aug. 10), the **Crossing-roads Country Music Festival** (early Aug.), and the **International Alpine Film Festival** in late September. (Tourist office open M-F 8am-noon and 2-6pm, Sa-Su 9am-noon and 2-6pm; closed weekend afternoons during low seasons.) For **taxis,** call (079) 205 05 55. The **pharmacy** (tel. 492 32 83; fax 492 26 25) is just before the bend in rue de la Gare. (Open M-F 8am-12:30pm and 3-6:30pm, Sa 8am-12:30pm and 3-6pm, Su 10am-noon and 5-6pm.) **In an emergency,** call 492 32 83. For an **ambulance,** call 494 37 27. For the **police,** call 492 24 88. Turn right out of the train station for the **post office.** (Open M-F 8am-noon and 2:30-6pm, Sa 7:45-10:45am.) The **postal code** is CH-1865, and the **telephone code** is 024.

The cheapest accommodations are unfortunately on the outskirts of town. **Les Diabletins,** rte du Pillon (tel. 492 36 33; fax 492 23 55), is a big modern block popular with young snowboarding groups. From the station, turn right, bend around the hairpin at the pharmacy, and turn right along rte du Pillon at the top of the hill. Avoid the ensuing 20 minute uphill walk by calling from the station; the hostel will send a minibus. Two- to four-bed rooms are in good shape (all have private sinks and most have balconies) in spite of the thousands of school groups that tramp through the halls and shared showers. This large establishment features four dining halls, several lounges, and a bar and disco—all segregated by age and noise-tolerance levels. (Jan. and Apr.-Christmas 31SFr, youth under 18 26SFr; Christmas-New Year's and mid-Feb. to mid-Mar. 44SFr, youth 37SFr; Mar.-Apr. 40SFr, youth 34SFr. Price drops 3SFr after 4 nights. Breakfast included. Dinner 15SFr. Reception 8am-8pm. Reserve ahead in winter. AmEx, DC, MC, Visa.) Left from the station and down the road toward Vers l'Eglise, slightly older and hipper snowboarders call **Hotel Mon Abri** (tel. 492 34 81; fax 492 34 82) home away from the slopes. The hotel's nightlife centers around the B'bar and its satellite bar the Bar'B, which features two headless Barbies stapled above it. (Main disco 10pm-4am.) Activities from pinball to *petanque* offer the chance to blow off steam. (Doubles 35SFr. Showers and breakfast included. Reception 5-7pm. Closed May. MC, Visa.) Take the train one stop, wander uphill past the post office and church, turn right over the river to get to **Camping La Murée** (tel. 492 21 99), an attractive, flat site next to the river. (6.50SFr; tents 9SFr. Free hot showers.)

Hikers, bikers, and snowboarders load up packed lunches from supermarkets. Right from the station along rue de la Gare, **Pam Super Discount** stocks the cheapest stuff. (Open M 7:30am-noon, Tu-F 7:30am-noon and 2-6:30pm, Sa 7:30am-noon and 2-5pm.) The **Co-op** is on rue de la Gare, left of the station. (Open M-F 8am-12:15pm and 2:15-6:30pm, Sa 8am-12:30pm and 2-5pm.) **Le Muguet** (tel. 492 26 42), opposite the tourist office, puts the glacier center stage. Try a cheese and bacon *galette* (8SFr) or a dessert crepe (5-10SFr) with *cidre* (2.50SFr). Cross the channel for their sandwiches (7SFr) and the all-important pot of tea. (Open 6:30am-7pm.) Just around the big bend by the pharmacy, **Pizzeria Locanda Livia** (tel. 492 32 80) serves 22 kinds of pizza (13-19.50SFr, 4SFr less for miniature version), including a four-cheeser with gruyère called *rêve des souris* (mouse's dream). (Open Th-Tu 11:30am-6:30pm.)

The **summer skiing cable car** leaves from the **Col du Pillon** above the village (day pass 49SFr, children 30SFr). For multiple day excursions you must buy a pass for the whole Diablerets-Villars region (6 days 193SFr, students 164SFr, children 116SFr) and provide a photo. The slightly more expensive **Alpes Vaudoises pass** entitles its holder to all forms of transport (cable cars, trains, and post buses) as well as access to the Gstaad Super Ski Region and Lenk/Adelboden (6 days 233SFr, students 203SFr, children 140SFr). There are special deals for groups, families, and seniors. Through the **Swiss Village Club,** many hotels offer special three-day/four-night weekend or six-day/seven-night weekly deals that include half-board ski passes, a fondue evening, tobogganing, curling, skating, even babysitting services. The tourist office can offer suggestions, but you must book directly with the hotel. You can rent skis, boards, and boots (25SFr) at the top of the glacier, but in winter you must acquire your equipment before ascending. **Jacky Sports** (tel. 492 32 18; fax 492 11 64; http://www.swissrentasport.ch), near the tourist office, rents equipment in the Swiss Rent-a-Sport system. (Skis or snowboard 28SFr per day; 6 days 105SFr. Boots 15SFr, 52SFr. Open daily 8:30am-6:30pm in high-season; closes 12:30-2pm in low-season. AmEx, DC, MC, Visa.) The **ski/snowboard school** (tel. 492 20 02; fax 492 23 48), in the Maison du Tourisme, offers lessons (6 days 125SFr, children 117SFr). If no one's there, the tourist office can help you contact the ski instructor of your choice via cell phone. Everyone's got 'em these days.

Jacky Sports rents **mountain bikes** for 35SFr per day (6 days 125SFr). A circuit, also possible on foot, leaves the village from the tourist office. Head around the hairpin turn at the junction with the Col du Pillon road and climb upwards to La Ville and its long view of the Diablerets glacier spilling over the edge high above the village. Turn right along the valley wall to Métraille and La Crua, and begin a long descent to the crag-cradled Lac Retaud and Col du Pillon before free-wheeling back to Les Diablerets. (Full day, only with good weather.) If the hike above doesn't tempt, head deeper into the mountains by turning right across the river at the pharmacy, then right again so that you are facing the **Sommet des Diablerets** (3209m) and the glacier. The valley sides close in as you continue the level riverside walk, which deposits you on the stage of a rugged 200m-high amphitheater at **Creux de Champ** (1hr., 1320m, 160m ascent., very easy). The path starts to climb steeply up the sides to the refuge de Pierredar at 2278m (3hr. above Les Diablerets, 1110m ascent). The agile can then push on up the scrambly new track (ladders) to **Scex Rouge** (2971m), the cable car terminus on the glacier, which affords an unforgettable alpine view (full day hike, high summer and perfect weather only; guide recommended). For a more relaxing trek, take the guided **tour of mountainside medicinal plants** given Thursdays by a local druggist (meet at 8:30am at tourist office; 26SFr; children with parents free).

Once-in-a-lifetime thrills have their outlets too. **Mountain Evasion** (tel./fax 492 12 32) is anything but; they organize **canyoning** (70-160SFr), **ice canyoning** (65SFr), **glacier bivouacs** (140SFr), **rappelling** (60SFr), and guided **hiking** and **mountain biking** (40-120SFr). (Office at the Parc des Sports across the river. Open daily Dec.-Oct. 5:30-6:30pm. MC.) Left from the train station and past the post office along rue de la Gare, **Centre ParAdventure** (tel. 492 23 82; fax 492 26 28; email cevic@bluewin.ch) offers **paragliding** (60-150SFr), more **canyoning** (80SFr), and the all-new **mudbike** that lacks pedals and a motor but features giant wheels. (Open 9-9:30am and 5:30-6:30pm or call (079) 435 25 82 anytime). Snowboarders may be happy to know that the **New Devil School of Snowboarding** (tel. (079) 212 24 72) has entered its bid for the town's corniest name pun. A one-hour initiation into snowboardry costs 50SFr, while a more comprehensive day-long course costs 200SFr.

LAKE GENEVA

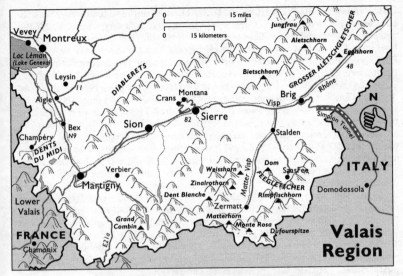

Valais (Wallis)

The territory bounded by Canton Valais sits snugly in the catchment of the Rhône valley, mainly in the deep, wide glacier cleft shaved by the river. In the west, Martigny and Sion are French-speaking; upriver in Brig, Swiss-German dominates. On the right bank rise the southern slopes of the Berner Oberland peaks; on the left bank along the Italian border jut the Valais Alps and their mighty Matterhorn. Switzerland stereotypes the Wallisers as dour folk with independent minds. But in Valais, there's a vibrant and riotous community life still untouched by the tourism that has engulfed the high mountain villages.

■ Martigny

Strategically located at the foot of the Grand St. Bernard Pass, Martigny was founded by Roman Emperor Claudius during the first century CE to control traffic between Switzerland and Italy. Recent archaeological digs have unearthed impressive ruins from that era, which go hand in hand with the medieval castle that towers over the city. Also of note is a 20th-century addition, the **Fondation Gianadda,** a leading center for modern art and classical music. While other towns adopt bears and cows as mascots, Martigny has mournful St. Bernards, their slack postures mirroring the valley's trees, beaten into tilted poses by the winds.

ORIENTATION AND PRACTICAL INFORMATION
Frequent **trains** run west to **Lausanne** (1hr., every 30min., 21SFr); **Montreux** (30min., every 30min., 13.20SFr); and **Aigle** (9SFr); and east to **Sion** (15min., every 30min., 8.40SFr). Two tiny private lines leave for **Orsières**, where you can change for **Aosta** in Italy via the **St. Bernard Pass** (30SFr); and for **Châtelard** where you can change for **Chamonix** in France (1¾hr., every hr., 28SFr). Martigny's **tourist office,** pl. Centrale 9 (tel. 721 22 20; fax 721 22 24), is straight down av. de la Gare at the far corner of pl. Centrale. (Open July-Aug. M-F 9am-6pm, Sa 9am-noon and 2-6pm, Su 10am-noon and 4-6pm; Sept.-June M-F 9am-noon and 1:30-6pm, Sa 9am-noon.) A **24-hour ATM** thrives at post office. The **train station** (tel. 723 33 30; open M-Sa 5:45am-8:45pm, Su 6:15am-8:45pm) provides all of the usual services: **currency exchange, lockers** (3-5SFr), **luggage storage** (5SFr), **bike rental** (22SFr per day), and a **rail information** office (open M-F 8am-noon and 1:30-6pm, Sa 9am-noon and 2-4pm). **Internet access** at **Le Coin Internet** at the Casino, (tel. 722 13 93; http://www.cybercasino.ch) halfway between station and pl. Centrale on rue de la Gare runs 20SFr per hour. (Open M-F 6:30am-midnight, Sa 7am-midnight, Su 9am-11pm). The **hospital** (tel. 721 97 21) has a switchboard that lets you in on the late-night doctor and pharmacy. **Pharmacie Centrale** (emergency tel. 722 20 32) is part of Migros supercenter at pl. du Manoir 5. For an **ambulance,** call 722 01 76. For the **police,** call 117. The large **post office,** av. de la Gare 32 (tel. 722 26 72), sits between the train station and the tourist office and has a public **fax** awaiting your next P.R. coup. (Open M-F 7:30am-noon and 1:30-6:30pm, Sa 7:30-11am.) The **postal code** is CH-1920, and the **telephone code** is 027.

ACCOMMODATIONS AND FOOD
Since travelers in Martigny are mainly business types, budget pickings are slim. Commuting from the recently built **Auberge de Jeunesse** in **Sion** (see p. 308) is an excellent idea, especially if you have a railpass. Otherwise, try **Le Ranch El Capio** (tel. 723 27 83), on Autoroute N9 (Sion-Simplon), 30 minutes' walk from the train station. From the station, turn left and walk to Rue Simplar, left again and walk to Aoste-Chamonin Autoroute overpass, left up the highway, then right, toward Sion, and continue until you see signs to the left. The ranch rents horses (23SFr per hour, 80SFr per day), and has four- to six-bed rooms for 20SFr per person and singles for 30SFr. (Breakfast 6SFr.) Giddy-up, Herr Kuhboy. Closer to the train station, the **Hôtel du Stand,** av. du Grand-St-Bernard 41 (tel. 722 15 06; fax 722 95 06), straight past the tourist office near the Fondation Gianadda. This unassuming family hotel comes highly recommended by Swiss regulars. The rooms are lined with stucco, wood paneling, and carpet; all come with their own desk and full bath. The restaurant downstairs has a *plat du jour* (16SFr) and three-course *Menüs* (22SFr). (Singles 65SFr; doubles 94SFr; triples 120SFr. Breakfast, shower, and parking included. Reception 7am-midnight. **Sauna** 5SFr. The hotel hosts many groups; reserve ahead July-Sept. MC. Visa.) **Camping Les Neuvilles,** rue du Levant 68 (tel. 722 45 44), packs its shaded plot with motor homes. From the station, head straight on av. de la Gare, take the second left on av. des Neuvilles, and turn right onto rue du Levant after the soccer field. The site's three-star amenities include playgrounds, a store, **laundry** machines, a **sauna,** a solarium, giant chess sets, and names for every "street." (5.80SFr, tents 7.50SFr, 4-person bungalow 85SFr; Sept.-June 4.80SFr, 65SFr, 60SFr. Shower included. Reception 8am-noon and 1:30-10pm. July-Aug.)

Cafés crowd Martigny's tree-lined pl. Centrale, some with *Menüs* in the 15-20SFr range. For cheaper fare, **Lords' Sandwiches,** av. du Grand-St-Bernard 15 (tel. 723 35 98), serves 36 sorts of sandwiches (4-11SFr), including a bacon burger with fries and the Zeus, an overflowing roast beef sandwich. (Open M-F 7am-midnight, Sa 8am-2am, Su 3-10:30pm.) **Le Rustique,** av. de la Gare 44 (tel. 722 88 33), has fashionably rustic mats around a terrace, behind which you can enjoy crispy savory crepes (9-13SFr) and sweet ones, too (5-10SFr). Wash them down with a mug of cider (3.50SFr). (Open 11:30am-10:30pm.) For straightforward Italian food, locals recommend **Pizzeria au Grotto,** rue du Rhône 3 (tel. 722 02 46), just off pl. Centrale on the left as you walk toward the station. It offers pizzas for 11-18SFr and pasta entrees for 13-30SFr. (Open 8:30am-midnight. MC, Visa.) The immense **Migros** supermarket at pl. du Manoir 5, just off pl. Centrale, has 18 different boutiques and moving sidewalks. (Open M-Th 7:30am-6:30pm; F 7:30am-8pm; Sa 8am-5pm.) Down rue de la Poste, a **Co-op** is (not surprisingly) open with the same services. (Open M-Th 8:15am-6:30pm; F 8:15am-8pm; Sa 8am-5pm.) Stroll down av. de la Gare on Thursday mornings to buy goods both edible and wearable at the **public market.** (Open 7:30am-noon.)

SIGHTS AND FESTIVALS The tourist office runs 1½-hour **guided foot tours** of Martigny at 10am and 2pm in July and August. (12SFr, students 5SFr, family ticket 25SFr; includes admission to the Fondation Gianadda.) The center's **permanent collection** includes works by Cézanne, Van Gogh, Ensor, Van Dongen, and Picasso; scheduled 1999 shows so far include a Hans Erni retrospective (through Feb 28) and *Turner et les Alpes* (March 5-June 6). Martigny's most engaging attraction is the **Fondation Pierre Gianadda,** rue du Forum 59 (tel. 722 39 78; fax 722 52 85; http://www.gianadda.ch). *(Foundation hours vary; call ahead. 12SFr, students 5SFr, family ticket 25SFr. Tickets include admission to the Gallo-Roman and Automobile Museums, the temporary exhibitions, and the Sculpture Gardens. Free guided tours W at 8pm or by prior arrangement. Wheelchair accessible.)* Local engineer Léonard Gianadda discovered the vestiges of a Gallo-Roman temple here in 1976 and, when his brother died in a plane crash two months later, set up a foundation to preserve his beloved brother's memory. Around and above the ancient temple he constructed an oddly shaped cultural center to bear his brother's name—think landing pod meets local branch library. More eclectic randomness awaits inside. The first floor **Gallo-Roman Museum** showcases classical works like the Octoduran bronzes discovered in Martigny, while the central courtyard below hosts blockbuster international traveling exhibitions. *(Open 10am-6pm.)* There are enough well-known lenders like the Centre Pompidou mixed in with mysterious "private collections" to impress upon viewers the once-in-a-lifetime nature of these assemblages. Descend the stairs to the **Automobile Museum** to scan more than 50 vintage cars—Bugattis, gleaming early Peugots, and a Rolls Royce Silver Ghost—built between 1897 and 1939, most in working condition and all unique. The surrounding garden successfully blends unearthed Roman remains with modern sculptures, including some by **Brancusi, Miró,** and **Rodin.** The foundation regularly hosts quality classical music concerts, many in conjunction with the **Festival Tibor Varga** and the **Montreux-Vevey Classical Music Festival.**

A self-guided archeological tour around the Fondation Pierre Gianaddu can be fun. 50m away, signs lead to the remains of a temple to the **sun god Mithra** dating from the 3rd century CE (now under some apartment complex). Past the railroad tracks, remnants of a Roman road point toward Britannia and, through the pass, Roma. Nearby, the grassy 4th-century **Amphithéâtre Romain,** re-opened in 1991 after two decades of excavation work, is the spectacular setting for the final contest of the Valais **cow fighting** season at the start of October. Moo. **Le Château de la Bâtiaz,** the ruins of a 13th-century castle that once belonged to the bishops of Sion, crouches on a hill overlooking Martigny. *(Open mid-July to mid-Aug. 10am-6pm. Free.)* From the station, head along av. de la Gare, and turn right at pl. Centrale along rue Marc-Morand. Climb the massive stone tower extending over an outcropping of bare rock for a bird's-eye perspective of the flat Rhône floodplain. Now an apartment building, the 17th-century **Grand Maison,** rue Marc Morand 7, near pl. Centrale, was once a hostel-stop for 18th- and 19th-century literati on their grand tours. Rousseau (1754), Goethe (1779), Stendhal (1800), Byron (1816), and Michelet (1830) all rested their weary heads here. Equally elegant, **Maison Supersaxo,** rue des Alpes 1, behind the tourist office, is Martigny's oldest building (1440). Within its walls, Valais bigwig Georges Supersaxo plotted his attack on the Château Bâtiaz. His 1518 siege ended in a ruinous fire, leaving only an old woman and her three goats in residence.

Each year in the beginning of October the town hosts the **Foire du Valais,** the regional trade fair of the Valais canton, in the blue and yellow CERM convention center. *(Oct. 1-10 10am-9pm. 8SFr, children 4SFr.)* Local businesses and farmers offer their best, from shoes to marble sculptures. The final Sunday brings all-day cow fighting; the knock-'em-all-down finale decides the reigning queen of all Valaisian cows. The event is a must-see if you are in southern Switzerland. Moo again. The **Foire du Lard** (Bacon Fair) has overtaken the pl. Centrale every first Monday in December since the Middle Ages. Traditionally, Valais mountain folk descended on Martigny to stock up on pork products for the winter, but now the festival has expanded to a large open-air market—although the theme is still "pig." Martigny also sponsors film, theater, and music festivals throughout the year, notably the **International Folklore Festival** every two years. The city is also an important venue for the annual **Tibor Varga Classical Music Season,** which brings big-league European orchestras and performers like Alfred Brendel and Vladmir Ashkenazy to town every July and August. Tickets are available through the Fondation Gianadda (20-80SFr; for more info, see http://www.nouvelliste.ch/varga/tvarga.htm).

■ Sion

Schizophrenic Sion is a noisy, heavy industrial tangle of towering blocks (including a major Swatch factory) bordering the Rhône, and a quiet, churchy old town cowering beneath two rocky bluffs topped with castle ruins. Sion's three castles sharpen the flat valley skyline and provide focal points for many local landscape painters. Sion has proven itself as forward-looking as it is adept in canned culture. The city lost its bid for the 1972 Winter Olympics to Sapporo and just recently for the 2002 Games to Salt Lake City, Utah. Nevertheless, it has enthusiastically announced its application for the 2006 Winter Games. Red and white flags flutter in the valley winds and the tourist shops are already glutted with pre-Olympic paraphernalia. Never say die.

PRACTICAL INFORMATION As a conspicuous addition to its Olympic candidacy profile, Sion now boasts an aspiring international **airport** (tel. 322 24 80; fax 322 29 68) just outside the town. At the moment, it's only a regional hub with daily flights to Zurich, charter flights of glacier aviation, and an Aviation School. **Trains** pass every 30 minutes in each direction along the Rhône Valley, going west (4:51am-10:47pm) to **Martigny** (15min., 8.40SFr), **Aigle** (25min., 16.60SFr), **Montreux** (50min., 21SFr), and **Lausanne** (1¼hr., 27SFr); and east (5:22am-12:52am) to **Sierre** (10min., 5.40SFr) and **Brig** (30min., 16.60SFr), where you connect to **Zermatt** (48SFr) and **Saas Fee** (28SFr). The **train station** (tel. 157 22 22; open 6am-8:45pm) provides **currency exchange** (open 6am-8:30pm), **lockers** (3-5SFr), **luggage storage** (3-5SFr for 24hr.; open 6am-8:45pm), **bike rental** (25SFr per day, mountain 31SFr per day; 19SFr per half-day, mountain 24SFr), and a **rail information** office (open M-F 8:30am-noon and 1:30-6:30pm, Sa 8am-12:30pm and 1:45-5pm). Just outside, Switzerland's largest **post bus station** congests the square with a blur of yellow buses, going near and far (mostly near). To get to the **tourist office,** pl. de la Planta (tel. 322 85 86; fax 322 18 82), from the train station, walk directly up av. de la Gare, and turn right on rue de Lausanne. The office provides free room reservations, a Billetel desk (tel. 322 85 93) for tickets to any event from Sion to Geneva, and two-hour guided tours. (July-Aug. Tu and Th 2pm, additional group tours on request; 8SFr, children and students 5SFr. Open July 15-Aug. 15 M-F 8am-6pm, Sa 10am-4pm; Aug. 16-July 14 M-F 8:30am-noon and 2-5:30pm, Sa 9am-noon.) Across pl. de la Gare to the right, **American Express** resides within **Valais Incoming,** in Lathion Voyages la Gare 4, av. de Tourbillon 3, P.O. Box 579, CH-1951 (tel. 329 24 23; fax 329 24 29; open M-F 8am-noon and 1:30-6pm, Sa 8am-noon). For a **taxi,** call 322 32 32. For the **police,** call 117. In a **fire,** call 118. For an **ambulance,** call 144. **Pharmacie Berger** (tel. 22 42 35), on av. du Midi just off av. de la Gare, is one of several modern apothecaries (open M 1:30-6:30pm, Tu-F 8am-noon and 1:30-6:30pm, Sa 9am-noon and 1:30-5pm) and for a 10SFr fee will provide **emergency after-hour services.** The **post office,** pl. de la Gare, is left of the train station. (Open M-F 8:30am-noon and 2-5:30pm, Sa 9am-noon and 2-6pm). The **postal code** is CH-1950, and the **telephone code** is 027.

ACCOMMODATIONS Built in 1991, the **Auberge de Jeunesse (HI),** av. de l'Industrie 2 (tel. 323 74 70; fax 323 74 38), maintains clean bathrooms, skinny semicircular balconies, and lockers in every room. Leaving the train station, walk left and descend the ramp to rue de la Blancherie; continue left underneath the train tracks. Look for crazy colorful artwork. The reception desk overlooks a high-ceilinged dining room that in turn leads onto a patio with table tennis. Although it's big, the hostel can often be fully booked by marauding school groups in July and August. The next closest HI hostel is in Montreux (ack!), so call ahead. (4-bed dorms 25.80SFr first night, then 23.30SFr; 2-bed dorms 32.80SFr, 30.30SFr. Breakfast included. Dinner 11SFr if you reserve it. **Kitchen** facilities 2SFr. Reception 7:30-9:30am and 5-10pm. Curfew 10:30pm; keys on request. Lockout 9:30am-5pm.) Staying anywhere else will give you a painful sting. The cheapest hotel rooms are at the smartly renovated **Hôtel Elite,** av. du Midi 6 (tel. 322 03 27; fax 322 23 61), on the edge of the *vieille ville* and surrounded by stores and cafés. From the station, head up av. de la Gare and turn right. Pristine rooms with TV, phone, private bathroom, and extravagant mountain views. (Singles 70SFr; doubles 120SFr. Breakfast included. Reception 6:30am-midnight. AmEx, MC, Visa.) Enterprising (or desperate) travelers seeking a cheap bed can try some of the villages outside Sion. The tourist office's booklet *Sion* gives details. (In **Pont-de-la-Morge** singles run 35-40SFr, doubles 68-80SFr; in **Saint-Léonard** 50-70SFr, 70-90SFr.) Post buses run to both towns. **Camping Les Iles,** rte d'Aproz (tel. 346 43 47; fax 346 68 47), is a riverside five-star site. Take a very short bus ride past the aerodome to Aprox. (6.80SFr; tents 9SFr. Low-season: 5.40SFr; 6.50SFr. Open Jan.-Oct.)

FOOD AND WINE The stone streets of the *vieille ville* are flanked by cafés and restaurants, most with white-washed terraces where patrons sip glasses of *Valais Fendant* or *Johannisberg-Tavillon,* the leading labels in town. Consult the tourist office for organized **wine-tasting excursions** and a list of local cellars. A long-distance path through the vineyards, *le chemin du vignoble,* passes close to Sion and through tasting territory. Always ring before you arrive at a *cave,* and try to rustle up a group if you want the proprietor to be more welcoming and forthcoming. One *centre de dégustation* is the **Varone vineyard,** av. Grand-Champsec 30 (tel. 203 56 83), just across the river. (Open M 2-6:30pm, Tu-F 10am-noon and 2-6:30pm, Sa 10am-noon and 2-5pm.) Picnics for hiking await immediate assembly at **Co-op City,** pl. du Midi, right off av. de la Gare along av. du Midi. (Open M 10:30-6:30pm, Tu-Th 7:30am-6:30pm, F 7:30am-8:30pm, Sa 7:30am-5pm.) Not bigger or better or noticeably different (same hours even), the **Migros Centre** has 19 different stores as well as a supermarket and restaurant (main courses 8-15SFr) on av. de France one block left from the station. **Manora,** at the corner of av. du Midi and rue de la Dent-Blanche, on the ground floor of the Placette department store and supermarket, leads the pack of the self-serve restaurants (entrees 7-13SFr) and has a kiosk devoted to fresh vegetarian entrees. (Open M-Th 8am-7pm, F 8am-7:30pm, Sa-Su 8am-6pm.) Huddle amid dark old wood in the **Restaurant la Bergère,** av. de la Gare 30 (tel. 322 14 81), which specializes in pizza and pasta (10-17SFr) and sandwiches (5-7SFr). (Open M-F 6am-1am, Sa 10:30am-1am, Su 5pm-1am. Closed Su in July and Aug. Amex, DC, MC, Visa.)

SIGHTS It's an age-old problem: how to keep the peace between a bossy bishop, a grumpy chapter, and a fractious town. Sion's solution was to build the bishop's house, the now-towering **Château de Tourbillon,** on one hill; the chapter's seat, the **Château de Valère,** on another; and the municipal powerhouse, the **Château de la Majorie,** downtown. (A laser beams around this power triangle Th-Sa nightfall-1am.) The first two castles stare each other down from across the hilltops and offer panoramas of the entire Valais valley, the Rhône, the Alps, and the city itself. From the station, proceed up av. de la Gare opposite and turn right on rue de Lausanne, left on rue du Grand-Pont, then right up the narrow rue des Châteaux just past the bright orange town hall. To the left on the way up is the Château de la Majorie et du Vidomnat, home to the **Musée des Beaux-Arts** (Fine Arts Museum), pl. de la Majorie 15-19 (tel. 606 4700). *(Open Tu-Su 10am-noon and 2-6pm. 5SFr, students 2.50SFr.)* Devotees of Valais art will be thrilled, but even the uninitiated will enjoy the 8-piece metal sculp-

VALAIS

ture suspended from the ceiling of the stark Jesuit chapel open only during temporary exhibits—from the right viewpoint, the sculpture resolves into a seamless crystal circle. See becastled landscapes and dour-looking Valais matrons galore. Up the Château de Valère's hill, the shabby but intriguing **Basilique du Château de Valère** boasts the oldest working organ in the world (c. 1390-1430) and presents its annual festival of ancient organ music in July and August every Saturday at 4pm. *(20SFr, students 10SFr; call the tourist office or 322 85 86 for details.)* The Château also houses the **Cantonal Museum of History and Ethnology** (tel. 606 47 10). *(Open Tu-Su 10am-noon and 2-6pm. Cathedral free. Museum 5SFr, students 2.50SFr.)* The more challenging lefthand hill projects higher with the imposing ruins of the **Château de Tourbillon.** *(Open Tu-Su 10am-6pm. Free.)* Once the summer residence of the bishop, it is now the seasonal nest of mice and the odd sparrow. Although the castle is endowed with typical ruin fare of crumbling walls and ambiguous architecture, the payoff for the grueling hike is definitely the view.

Sion's most amusing museum is the **Natural History Museum,** 42 av. de la Gare (tel. 606 47 30), up the road from pl. de la Planta and the tourist office. *(Open Tu-Su 2-6pm. 3SFr, students 1.5SFr, children up to 6 yrs. free.)* There are stuffed armadilloes, 3 sets of Siamese goats (2 stuffed, one skeleton), the contorted body of a mountain deer pulled from a glacier in 1920 after centuries on ice, and the scrappy last bear in the Valais dramatically hunted down in 1830 by a pair of local brothers.

The *vieille ville*, with its medieval churches and colorfully painted buildings, hosts yearly music festivals. The open-air **Jazz Festival** takes over the streets at 11pm on Friday the last weekend of June. *(20SFr, festival passes 150SFr; tickets available at tourist office or at the gate.)* Most summer evenings bring **free concerts** of classical music at the **Academie de Musique** (tel. 322 66 52). From July to September there are also major orchestral events during the **Tibor Varga Festival** (tel. 323 43 17; fax 326 46 62; email festivalvargasion@vtx.ch; http://www.nouvelliste.ch/varga/tvarga.htm; tickets 20-80SFr, available through Billetel).

■ Brig (Brigue)

A junction town at the base of the Simplon, Furka, and Grimsel passes, Brig grew up as a place to change your horses and trade your wares. Even now the town is mainly a place to go through rather than to. Nonetheless, Brig burgeons with slender-spired churches, narrow houses, and slate-gray squares. Along the Rhône Valley, trains go to **Sierre** (30min., every 30min., 12.20SFr); **Sion** (40min., every 30min., 16.60SFr); **Lausanne** (2hr., every hr., 43SFr); and **Geneva** (2¾hr., every hr., 55SFr). Through the Lötschberg tunnel, trains head to **Bern** (1¾hr., every hr., 46SFr) and **Interlaken** (1½hr., every hr., 39SFr). The Simplon tunnel trains lead to **Domodossola** in Italy (30min., every hr., 12.20SFr) and **Locarno** (2½hr., every hr., 48SFr, change at Domodossola). A mass of bus lines spread their tentacles through the surrounding hillsides from Bahnhofpl. The most important one leaves every hour for **Saas Fee** (1¼hr., 17.40SFr) from just left of the station exit. The hyper-helpful, cyber-friendly office in the station library helps bewildered travelers sort all of this out. (Open M-F 8am-6:30pm, Sa 8am-4:30pm.) If you insist on exploring, get information at the **tourist office** (tel. 923 19 01; fax 924 31 44), up the yellow stairs on the first floor of the train station. They have piles of hotel info but tend to clam up if you ask them about anything outside of Brig. (Open mid-June to mid-Oct. M-F 8:30am-noon and 1:30-6pm, Sa 8:30am-noon and 2-5:30pm; mid-Oct. to mid-June M-F 8:30am-noon and 1:30-6pm, Sa 8:30am-noon.) The station has **currency exchange** (tel. 922 24 24; open M-Sa 6:15am-7:30pm, Su 8-11:30am and 2-6pm), **lockers** (3-5SFr), **luggage storage** (open 7am-7pm), and a free phone line to all hotels. A **Migros** stands on Belalpstr., on your left as you leave the station. (Open M-F 8:15am-6:30pm, Sa 7:45am-4pm.) The **post office** is directly opposite the train station, Bahnhofstr. 1 (tel. 923 66 56; open M-F 7:30am-noon and 1:30-6:15pm, Sa 7:30-11am). The **postal code** is CH-3900, and the **telephone code** is 027.

■ Zermatt and the Matterhorn

A trick of the valley blocks out the great Alpine summits ringing Zermatt, allowing the Matterhorn (4478m) to rise alone above the town. Instantly recognizable and stamped on everything from scarves to pencils by Zermatt's merchants of kitsch, the peak still causes an intake of breath whenever one looks up. At dawn it blazes bright orange; some days—some weeks—it is swathed in clouds, completely hidden from view. Zermatt itself is mostly a missable mix of tourists (as opposed to our readership, all suave travelers and rock jocks, to be sure). The main road, Bahnhofstraße, is often populated by hikers with knee-pants and walking sticks, snowboarders crucified on neon boards slung across their shoulders, and skiers with their snow struts and unnatural tans. You can escape it all with a short hike or cable car ride to lonely Alpine meadows and splintered icefalls—feasts for the eye are the real reason to visit.

ORIENTATION AND PRACTICAL INFORMATION

To preserve the Alpine air from exhaust fumes, Zermatt has outlawed cars and buses; locals in toylike electric buggies alternately dodge and target pedestrians. The road head at Täsch has a covered **parking lot** for 6SFr per day; you can leave your car in an uncovered lot for 3-5SFr per day. The only way to Zermatt is by the hourly **BVZ (Brig-Visp-Zermatt) rail** line; Eurorailpass isn't valid. The main street, Bahnhofstraße, runs in front of the station and houses many of the town's hotels and restaurants.

Trains: Bahnhofpl. (tel. 967 22 07). The only way into or out of Zermatt is the hourly **BVZ** (Brig-Visp-Zermatt) rail line. Join at **Brig** (1½hr., 37SFr, round-trip 63SFr); **Visp** (if coming from Lausanne or Sion; 34SFr, round-trip 58SFr); **Stalden-Saas** (if coming from Saas Fee; 1hr., 30SFr, round-trip 51SFr); or **Täsch** (every 20min., 7.20SFr). The station has a free direct phone line to all of Zermatt's hotels, as well as **lockers** (2-8SFr) and **hotel taxis** waiting to round up guests after each train arrives. Trains leave Zermatt every hour from 6am to 9:10pm.

Currency Exchange: Zermatt Tours, next to the tourist office. No commission. Open M-Sa 8:30am-noon and 2-6pm, Su 9am-noon and 3-6pm. **Banks** are open M-F 8:30am-noon and 2:30-6pm.

Bike and Ski Rental: Roc Sport (tel. 967 39 27) on Kirchstr. (left at the church) or its outlet **Sulen Sport** on Hoffmattstr. Mountain bikes 35SFr per day. 10% discount on bikes and skis for youth hostelers. Open M-Sa 8-10am and 4-6pm. AmEx, DC, MC, Visa. **Slalom Sport** (tel. 966 23 66) on Kirchstr. Open M-Sa 8am-noon and 2-7pm, Su 8am-noon and 4-6:30pm. Also try **Bayard Sports** (tel. 966 49 60; fax 966 49 55) directly across from the station.

Tourist Office: Bahnhofpl. (tel. 967 01 81; fax 967 01 85; email zermatt@wallis.ch; http://www.zermatt.ch), in the station complex. All the hard facts you could possibly need on Zermatt are contained in the chunky free booklet *Prato Borni* and the glossy *Zermatt*. Both appear in summer and winter editions. Panorama plans with suggested hikes 1.60SFr. To navigate on a hike, however, you will need a real map, available here or at kiosks and bookstores along Bahnhofstr. Hiking trail map 24.60SFr. Open mid-June to mid-Oct. M-Sa 8:30am-6pm, Su 9:30am-noon and 4-6pm; mid-Oct. to mid-June M-Sa 8:30am-noon and 1:30-7pm.

Mountaineering (*Bergführerbüro;* tel. 966 24 66; fax 966 24 64; email skischule.zermatt@spectraweb.ch) and **Ski School Office** (*Skischulbüro;* tel. 967 24 66), both on Bahnhofstr. From the train station, turn right on Bahnhofstr. and walk 5min. past the post office. Posts detailed weather forecasts every morning for the next 4 days and coordinates guided private and group climbing expeditions. In summer, groups go daily up to the Breithorn (120SFr), Pollux (230SFr), and Castor (240SFr). The Matterhorn is 670SFr but requires technical experience and at least a week's prior training. Prices do not include equipment, hut accommodations, or lifts to the departure points. Whatever you do, get insured (30SFr) or be prepared to risk a 4-figure helicopter rescue bill from **Air Zermatt** (tel. 967 34 87; fax 967 40 04). Open July-Sept. M-F 8:30am-noon and 4-7pm, Sa 4-7pm, Su 10am-noon and 4-7pm. Ski/snowboard lessons for one or two people 180SFr for 3 hours (9am-noon). Open Dec.-Apr. 5-7pm.

English-Language Library: In the English Church behind the post office. Small collection of battered novels loaned on the honor system. Be honorable!

Weather Conditions: Call 162 or check the window of the *Bergführerbüro*. **Winter Avalanche Information,** tel. 187.

Emergencies: Police, tel. 117. **Fire,** tel. 118. **Ambulance,** tel. 67 12 12. **24hr. Alpine Rescue,** tel. 967 20 00.

Pharmacy: Pharmacie Internationale Zermatt (tel. 966 27 27; fax 966 27 25), Bahnhofstr. to right of station. High season hours M-Sa 8am-12:30pm and 2-7pm; Su 10am-noon. Provides 24hr. service for 10SFr surcharge (call ahead)

Post Office: Bahnhofstr., in Arcade Mont-Cervin 5min. to the right of the station. Open M-F 8am-noon and 1:30-6pm, Sat 8:30-11am. **24hr ATM** at post office as usual. **Postal Code:** CH-3920.

Internet Access: At **Matterhorn Hostel** for 10SFr per hr.; Hotel Post (tel. 967 19 32), Bahnhofstr. right of Station, for 6SFr per 15 min. and 18SFr per hr.

Telephone Code: 027.

ACCOMMODATIONS

Climbers, hikers, and snowboarders buoy up the demand for budget beds in Zermatt. A healthy supply generally provides adequate accommodations, but finding a dorm bed on the spot can be a squeeze July through August, Christmas and New Year's, and mid-February through mid-March. Many hotels in winter and all chalets in summer only accept bookings for a week at a time. In desperation, some campers are tempted to park their bods illegally in the wide-open spaces above town—this practice can incur fines between 50 and 100SFr.

Hotel Bahnhof (tel. 967 24 06; fax 967 72 16), on Bahnhofstr. 1min. from the station—turn left and pass the *Gornergratbahn*. Recently renovated rooms offer hotel housing at hostel rates with no hike from the station. Best budget deal in town. 4-bed rooms with private showers 40SFr; dorms 26-28SFr; singles 40-50SFr; doubles 71-79SFr. **Laundry** 2SFr. No breakfast, but **kitchen** and large dining room in the basement. Lockers for all. Open mid-Dec. to mid-Oct.

Matterhorn Hostel (tel. 968 1915; email matterhorn.hostel@smile.ch), a 12min. walk from station. Turn right along Bahnhofstr., left at the church, and take first right after the river onto Schluhmattstr. Hostel is 150-200m walk up the street. Brand-spankin-new independent hostel decorates its dorms with graffiti art and lets you decide on options. Basic dorm bed 24SFr in summer, 29SFr in winter. Breakfast 6SFr. Dinner 12.50SFr *Menü* in winter or à la carte choices (4.50-10SFr) in summer. Sheets 3.50SFr. **Internet** access 10SFr per hr. Coin-operated **laundry** 59SFr. Downstairs bar serves half-liters of beer for 4.30SFr. TV room, games, free showers, no curfew. AmEx, MC, Visa.

Jugendherberge (HI), Winkelmatten (tel. 967 23 20; fax 967 53 06), is a 15min. hike from the station, the last part up a steep hill. Turn right along Bahnhofstr. and left at the church. Cross the river, take the second street to the right (at the Jugendherberge sign), and select the left fork in front of Hotel Rhodania. The hostel's on the mountain side of town, so that you get a full frontal view of the Matterhorn from your bedroom window (which makes up for the slight overcrowding). Take your shoes off before entering this fully loaded hostel experience, where you get all the goodies...for a higher price. Stunning unobstructed views of the Matterhorn from bedroom windows, tasty dinner and typical breakfast fare, friendly staff, giant outdoor chess set, ping pong, and foosball await. Dorms 40SFr first night, then 37.50SFr; one double 108SFr, 96SFr. Breakfast, sleepsack, showers, and dinner (kosher and vegetarian available) included. **Laundry** 8SFr per load. Closed May and late Oct. to mid-Dec. AmEx, DC, MC, Visa.

Hotel Garni Tannenhof (tel. 967 31 88; fax 967 12 64). From the station, turn right on Bahnhofstr., walk 300m, turn left at Bayard Sports and then take the first right onto a path. Rustic furniture, thick rugs, and a generous breakfast buffet (7-10am); every room comes with a radio and telephone. Singles 45-50SFr; with private shower 58-70SFr; doubles 90-100SFr, 110-120SFr; triples 105-120SFr. Reception

7am-7pm. Reserve at least 1 month in advance in winter, 2-3 weeks in summer. Closed Oct.-Dec. 15. AmEx, DC, Visa.

Hotel Weisshorn, Bahnhofstr. (tel. 967 11 12; fax 967 38 39). From the train station, turn right along Bahnhofstr. The hotel is 30m past the church. Low, paneled ceilings and winding staircases draw guests into this hotel. The beds bulge with cushy comforters although the carpeting is not as soft. Singles 46-54SFr, with private shower, TV, and phone 62-75SFr; doubles 82-100SFr, 110-132SFr; triples 108-138SFr. Breakfast included. Reception 7am-10pm. Reservations necessary in winter high season, up to two months in advance. MC, Visa.

Hotel Cima Garni (tel. 967 23 37; fax 967 55 39), 250m from the station, straight down Getwingstr. This charming bed and breakfast blends a standard Swiss exterior (red shutters on brown building) with a remarkably modern interior of subdued grays and very shiny pine paneling—you can almost smell the polish. Oriental rugs line the stairs to the 25 rooms, all in a spotless state of Swiss comfort and almost all with balcony. Comfort, however, comes at a price. Singles 37-70SFr, with shower 50-100SFr; doubles 74-140SFr, 100-200SFr. Breakfast included. Visa.

Camping Alphubel (tel. 967 36 35), in Täsch. What with Zermatt car-free and all, caravanners and motorists can park their vehicles and stay here. 5.50SFr; tent 5SFr; car 4SFr; caravan 6SFr. Showers. Open May to mid-Oct.

Camping Matterhorn Zermatt, Bahnhofstr. (tel. 967 39 21), 5min. to the left of the train station. Perhaps Zermatt's only unscenic spot. The spotty, grass-covered area looks onto train tracks. Showers included. 8SFr. Reception May-Sept. 8:30-10am and 5:15-7pm.

Mountain Huts: The tourist office has a list of private huts in the Zermatt area. For 23SFr a night, they offer a good deal for bona fide climbers, but others will find them too high for a proper night's sleep. **Schönbiel** (tel. 967 13 54; 2694m), **Rothorn** (tel. 967 20 43; 3198m), the crowded **Gandegg** (tel. 967 21 96; 3029m), **Hörnli** (tel. 967 27 69; 3260m), and **Monte Rosa** (tel. 967 21 15; 2795m; crampons and guide advised) are all open July-Sept. and accessible to walkers if there's no snow. All are about full day's hike from Zermatt.

FOOD AND NIGHTLIFE

Rather than charge the usual inflated Alpine prices, a surprising number of the cafés along Bahnhofstr. leave both your wallet and your stomach pretty full. Several supermarkets provide picnic supplies for day hikes.

Restaurants and Bars

The Pipe Surfer's Cantina, (tel. 213 3807; http://www.webyourworld.com), right on Bahnhofstr. from station, then left at church on to Kirchstr. Overlooking the cemetery, this après-snowboarding joint offers "surf munchies with a Mexican twist" for those tired of fondue and pizza. Sombreros and surfboards look on as a college crowd consumes nachos (14SFr), burritos (17SFr), sandwiches (10-12SFr), and beer (3.50SFr). Free shot with coupon from Jugendherberge. Open summer 11am-1am, winter 3pm-2am.

Walliser Kanne, Bahnhofstr. (tel. 966 46 10), next to the post office. A great place to people-watch, this sedate establishment offers slightly upscale Swiss fare including such dishes as *Käsespatzl* (four tiny dumplings, 16.50SFr); *Käseschnitte mit Schinken and Tomate* (toasted cheese with ham and tomato, 16SFr), and fresh strawberries in whipped cream (9SFr), as well as the usual pizza and pasta (15-22SFr). Open 10am-midnight. AmEx, DC, MC, Visa.

The North Wall Bar (tel. 967 28 63). Head over the river on Kirchstr. and take the second right en route to the youth hostel. No frills, 100%-English-speaking climbers' haunt where skiing and mountaineering videos play every evening alongside the less dynamic (but still potentially dangerous) dart games. This is the place to scrounge a job in Zermatt. The kitchen will serve you anything you like, as long as it's pizza (10SFr, plus 1SFr for fancy topping like mussels, corn, broccoli, or egg). At 4.50SFr for 0.50L, the beer is probably the cheapest in town. Open mid-June to Sept. and mid-Dec. to Apr. 6:30pm-midnight.

Café du Pont, Bahnhofstr. (tel. 967 43 43), 7min. from the station at Bahnhofstr. and next to Hotel Weisshorn. Zermatt's oldest restaurant maintains its romantic atmosphere with subdued lighting and soothing music. Browse through the large menus, burnt into slabs of wood hanging from the wall in many languages, as you listen to the river. Then try to decide between Swiss dishes like *raclette* (7SFr), *Rösti* (14SFr), and *fondue du Pont* (22SFr). Sandwiches 6.50SFr. Open June-Oct. and Dec.-Apr. 9am-midnight; food served 11am-3pm and 5-10pm.

Swiss Rock Café, Bahnhofstr. (tel. 967 68 80). The entrance to this sleek piano-bar contains a metal staircase wrapped around a giant bubbling neon blue test-tube. Inside, the trendy frenzy continues while waitresses serve never-ending bratwurst with baked potatoes (15SFr), corn on the cob (5SFr), *enchiladas* (18SFr), and beer at 5.20SFr for 0.5L. 2-for-1 drinks 6-7pm. Live music 9pm 7 days a week. Open 10:30am-12:30am. Closed mid-Oct. to Nov.

Grampi's Pub, Bahnhofstr. (tel. 967 77 88). Central bar welcomes serious drinkers by day and thumps with pop dance music by night. Draft beer 3.50SFr for 0.25L; bottled beer 4.50-7SFr; long drinks 10SFr. DJ 8:30pm-2am. Open 9am-2am.

Markets

Co-op Center, across from the station. Open M-Sa 8:15am-12:15pm and 1:45-6:30pm, Su 4-6:30pm.

Migros, Hofmattstr., down from Bahnhofstr. between the station and the church. Open M-Sa 8:30am-12:15pm and 2-6:30pm, Su 4-6:30pm.

SKIING, SPORTS, AND ENTERTAINMENT

Seventy-three lifts, 14,200m of combined elevation, and 245km of prepared runs make Zermatt one of the world's best-equipped ski centers. Where it really outshines its rivals, however, is in its ski-mountaineering and high-level ski-touring potential. The town also has more **summer ski trails** than any other Alpine ski resort—36 sq. km of year-round runs between 2900 and 3900m. In the summer, the **ski school** (tel. 967 24 66) offers group classes for skiing and snowboarding (either activity: 1 day 60SFr, 6 days 130SFr). **Ski and boot rental** is standard throughout the area—43SFr for one day, 157SFr for six—but youth hostel residents secure an additional 10% discount at **Roc Sport** (see p. 311). Sports stores flood Zermatt, and finding a reliable dealer is not a problem. Note that most shops are open daily 8am to noon and 2 to 7pm and that renting equipment the evening before will maximize your time on the slopes. Zermatt's **ski passes** operate on a regional system. You can buy passes for any combination of days and regions (Matterhorn complex, Gornergrat complex, and Sunnegga complex). For example, the Matterhorn region costs 58SFr for one day, 240SFr for six days; all three regions combined cost 60SFr, 292SFr. The Klein Matterhorn/Trockener Steg sub-region is open in summer only, and you cannot use passes to ascend after 1pm (1 day 58SFr, 6 days 204SFr, 3 days within a 6-day period 150SFr).

Zermatt is at least three hours from any worthwhile indoor attraction; when it rains you will wish you had scheduled your trip to North Dakota instead. The posher hotels have **swimming pools,** with **Hotel Christiania** (tel. 967 19 07) offering the biggest. Follow the right bank of the river past the Rothorn/Sunnegga cable railway station. (10SFr, children 6SFr. Open M, W, and F-Sa 8am-8pm, Tu 2-8pm, Th 8am-10pm.) For an additional 10SFr, you can work up a sweat in the sauna or go off to another hotel to find a massage. Less literally sensual pursuits await at the **Cinema Vernissage** (tel. 967 66 36), at the Centre Culturel on Hofmattstr., which has two or three screenings nightly Monday to Saturday of nearly new releases, usually in English (15SFr, hostelers 13SFr; AmEx, DC, MC, Visa). Another rainy day refuge is the **Alpine Museum** (tel. 967 41 00), near the post office. Here, the courage of those adventurers who first conquered regional peaks with absurd equipment by modern standards is proven by homages to their not-so-fortunate comrades: broken ropes, mangled shoes, and bashed-in lanterns found with corpses sometimes months after tragic falls. (Open June-Sept. 10am-noon and 4-6pm; Dec.-May M-F and Su 4:30-6:30pm. Closed Nov-Oct. 4SFr, children 1SFr. Guide in English 1SFr.) Special attention is given to the first ascent of the Matterhorn, over half of whose expedition were killed on July 14, 1865, on their way back down. A haunting photograph is all that remains of one victim of that fall, **Lord Alfred Douglas** (love of Oscar Wilde's life), whose mortal remains were never found. Slightly more fortunate victims of the Matterhorn are buried in the cemetery, next to the church with picks and ropes defiantly carved into their graves.

The town celebrates with festivities throughout August. During the **Alpine Folklore Parade,** locals take a break from their mountain chores mid-month and dust off their alphorns and frilly costumes. The Roman Catholic church sporadically hosts **classical music concerts** (20-25SFr) throughout the month, and at the end of August, thighs burn through the **Matterhornlauf,** a fun-run that climbs 1001m from Zermatt to the Schwarzsee at the foot of the Matterhorn.

OUTDOORS AROUND ZERMATT

Outstanding walks into the world of glaciers and high mountains spread from Zermatt in every direction. Although these paths are well-made and well-marked, a proper non-panoramic map is essential for safety and adds to your appreciation of the mountains. Lifts and railways to the south and east are also valuable hiking tools; they can save you difficult climbs and precious energy. Swisspasses will win you a 25% discount on many of these lifts, but Eurailpasses are generally not valid. Prudent walkers should come prepared (see **Health,** p. 16). Zermatt is particularly prone to sudden electrical storms, and you may need to dive for cover. The *Bergführerbüro* posts a conservative pictoral weather forecast in its window on Bahnhofstr. To rent hiking boots, try **Skihaus Matterhorn,** Bahnhofstr. (tel. 967 29 56), **Glacier Sport,** Bahnhofstr. (tel. 967 21 67) or **Burgena Sport,** Bahnhofstr. (tel 967 27 94) next to Grampi's bar. One-day rentals are 14SFr; seven days 52SFr; 14 days 80SFr. All these stores are open daily 8am to noon and 2 to 7pm.

West and Northwest

West of Zermatt, the mountains are savage, spiky pinnacles. The **Zinalrothorn** (4221m), **Ober Gabelhorn** (4063m), and **Dent Blanche** (4357m) are some of the toughest climbs around. An easier, though long, walk to **Zmutt** (1936m, 1hr.) and the **Schönbielhütte** (2694m, 4hr.), leads along the base of these magnificent peaks and offers the most dramatic encounter with the Matterhorn's north face. The path is wide, clear, and well marked, and the views get exponentially better as you rise. From Zermatt, follow Bahnhofstr. past the church and to the river. Walk 100m past the bank and then follow the sign to the right. A steady gradient pulls you up through Arolla pines to the weathered chalets of the minuscule hamlet of Zmutt. The path then continues through the meadows above a small reservoir, granting views of the Hörnli ridge and the Matterhorn. As you go on, the Matterhorn's north wall, which drops 200m with an average gradient well over 45°, comes breathtakingly into view. The hike becomes more difficult as it ascends by lakes and waterfalls at the outlet of the rock-strewn Zmuttgletscher and follows the lateral ridge to the **Schönbielhütte,** an ideal spot for lunchtime carbo-loading of pasta or *Rösti* at the obligatory restaurant while you examine the icefalls rising from three sides. On the return journey, the valley frames the **Rimpfischhorn** (4199m) and **Strahlhorn** (4190m). The full-day hike is 25km, with 1050m of gentle, beautiful elevation.

Southwest

No visit to Zermatt is emotionally complete without struggling up to the **Hörnlihütte,** the base camp for the normal route up the Matterhorn and a good platform for watching brightly colored dots claw their way upward along the ridge. A legend in the history and literature of the Matterhorn, the 1600m ascent is for the fit and well-booted only; a cable car to the Schwarzsee saves you 900m of elevation (18.50SFr; round-trip 29.50SFr). Leave Zermatt along the left bank of the Matter Vispa, as for the Zmutt/Schönbielhütte hike. A mile or so from Zermatt, after a few minutes of climbing, a wide track marked *"Zum See, Schwarzsee und Hörnlihütte"* heads down left across the river. Follow the three-hour path as it zigzags steeply up to the tiny lake, the **Schwarzsee** (2552m), admiring the monstrous Gorner gorges on the left. A group of climbers caught in a snowstorm built the chapel on the lake in an act of piety when their prayers to Mary were answered and the clouds miraculously lifted. The path becomes rockier and wilder as it joins the true northeast ridge of the Matterhorn, climbing gently at first but ending in a merciless, exposed *arête* (sharp ridge) by the buildings at Hörnli. Rest at the finish and know that casual hikers *cannot* continue above the hut. More than 500 people have died in the mile above this point, as a sobering walk around Zermatt's cemeteries will prove. A guide, perfect physical condition, a 4am start, and extensive rock-climbing experience (at least PD+) are essential for proceeding. To descend a different way, bear right at the Schwarzsee to the Furgg cable car terminus and follow the path down to the beck. The path traverses a steep cliff but is stable underfoot and has even closer views of the gorges carved by the Gornergletscher.

South

South from Zermatt the Matterhorn changes its clothes again, this time parading the pyramidal west face. This direction is the way to wilderness—steep icefalls peel off the **Breithorn** (4164m), and below the icefalls are the glacier-scoured, sun-bleached boulder fields. The highest **cable car** in Europe alights on the **Klein Matterhorn,** 6km from the Matterhorn. (Operates high-season 7am-6pm; 56SFr.) A track leads out from the tunnel below the viewing platform to **Gobba di Rollin** (3899m), following the T-bar all the way, but the hike requires good weather, caution, and a tortoise pace due to the altitude. From the Trockner Steg cable-car station (2939m), however, you can walk back to Zermatt: leave the complex on the Monte Rosa side away from the Matterhorn and follow the path to the left along the gully in front of you (2½hr.).

Southeast and East

Southeast from Zermatt are the **Monte Rosa** (4634m) and the **Liskamm** (4527m), squat blocks that are the second and third highest mountains in Switzerland, respectively. **Leonardo da Vinci,** incidentally, thought the Monte Rosa was the highest mountain on Earth. Among its unlikely conquerors have been **Pope Pius XI,** who pioneered a new route to the Grenzsattel in 1889, and a youthful **Winston Churchill,** who climbed the monster in 1894. From the southeast, framed by woods and reflected in lakes, the Matterhorn takes on its best-known angle, reproduced on everything from tea towels to cookie tins. A rack railway winds up to the best viewpoint, the **Gornergrat** (3090m; 37SFr, round-trip 63SFr) by way of **Riffelalp** (2211m; 16.60SFr, round-trip 32SFr). Other stops include **Riffelberg** (2582m; 26SFr, round-trip 45SF) and **Rotenboden** (2815m; 32SFr, round-trip 55SFr). The train departs opposite Zermatt's main station (7am-7pm). The train's main path from Zermatt follows the right bank of the river upstream, stopping at all the stations. The round-trip hike to Gornergrat demands a great deal of stamina; grabbing a lift for part of the ascent will preserve your strength for clambering around the top or taking a more interesting path down. From the top, tracks lead down to the wide, flat Gornergletscher and along the ridge toward the **Stockhorn** (3532m). A cable car also runs to this point (12SFr each way). Each destination provides a closer encounter with the ice but loses a fraction of the panorama that makes the Gornergrat so special. You can also descend after the Riffelalp station by following the contour around to the Grüensee, facing the snout of the Findelngletscher, then crossing the river and returning to Zermatt by way of the **Moosjesee** and the **Leisee,** two small pools that provide a beautiful foreground to the majestic Matterhorn.

Northeast and Northwest

Compared to the well-trodden highways south of Zermatt, the hikes to the north are unsung. Rockier and steeper, these difficult paths lead to proper summits rather than huts or viewpoints. A **northeast hike** starts from the Zermatt station. Head down to the river beside the Gornergratbahn, cross it, turn left, then hop on the Sunnegga-Rothorn railway and lift as far as **Blauherd** (2560m; 24SFr, round-trip 32.40SFr). A wide path gently circles the Unterrothorn's right flank to a mountain pass at 2981m. Take the blistering series of zigzags on the right (some offering fixed handrails) up to the **Oberrothorn** (3415m), a satisfying rocky fang. A **northwest hike** begins midway between the church and post office and opposite Hotel de la Poste on Bahnhofstr. The path initially climbs steeply up toward **Alterhaupt** (1961m) and **Trift** (2337m) but then levels off. The little-known glacier cirque beneath the icefalls of the **Ober Gabelhorn** and **Zinalrothorn** provides a turn-around point, but supermen and women will bear right up the **Metterhorn** (3406m), accessible to agile walkers and a popular endurance-training hike for those about to try the Matterhorn.

■ Saas Fee

Nicknamed "the pearl of the Alps," Saas Fee (1800m) occupies one of Switzerland's most glorious sites. Situated in a hanging valley above the Saastal, the city snuggles among 13 grand 4000m peaks, including the **Dom** (4545m). The ice of the Fee-gletscher comes so low that you can visit the primordial giant on a 30-minute evening stroll. To protect all this Alpine glory, the entire resort town is closed to cars, giving electrically powered mini-vans and trucks free run of the rambling streets. As the cha-let roofs of the village crowd in toward each other, brightly clad tourists shuttle from souvenir store to sun terrace in search of instant memories. There really aren't nearly as many souvenir stores here as in Zermatt. (Actually, the city is pretty much 100% hotels.) Others go farther (and higher) afield. As in Zermatt, the abundance of red knee-highs and sleek neon suits set against the low serenading hum of electric motors proves that Saas Fee's main draw is the outdoor scene. Town officials prohibit dis-turbing "the fairy-like charm of Saas Fee" after 10pm (noisemakers fined 200SFr), but most guests are so exhausted from skiing, climbing, or hiking that few are likely to have energy for late-night carousing.

The **tourist office** (tel. 958 18 58; direct reservations 958 18 68; fax 958 18 60; email to@saas-fee.ch; http://www.saas-fee.ch), across from the bus station, is small and usually packed. The staff dispenses seasonal information, hiking advice, guides, and reasonably useful town maps with more hotels than street names. The room res-ervation service may cost as much as 10SFr; try the free phone board outside for DIY arrangements. Long-term visitors should pick up the list of available chalets. (Open high-season (July to mid-Sept. and mid-Dec. to mid-Apr.) M-F 8:30am-noon and 2-6:30pm, Sa 8am-7pm; Su 9am-noon and 3-6pm; low-season (mid-Sept. to mid-Dec and mid-Apr. to June) M-Sa 8:30am-noon and 2-6pm; Su 10am-noon and 4-6pm.) A **post bus** runs every hour to **Brig** (1¼hr., 17.40SFr, round-trip 33SFr); **Visp** (1hr., 13.20SFr), which connects to Lausanne, Sion, and the Valais; **Stalden Saas** (35min., 10.40SFr), which connects to Zermatt for another 30SFr; and **Saas Grund** (10min., 2.80SFr). The first bus is 5:35am, the last at 7:35pm for all destinations. You should reserve a place on all buses starting at Saas Fee at least two hours before departure. Call 957 19 45 or drop by the bus station. (Open M-Sa 7:25am-12:35pm and 1:15-6.35pm; Su 7:25-10:25am and 2:15-5.35pm.) Drivers can **park** at the lower end of the village with a guest card from their hotel (1 day 13SFr, in summer 11SFr; with guest card after 2nd day 9SFr, 7.50SFr). **Vallesin Apotheke** (tel. 957 26 18), sits on the main street down the road to your right as you leave the tourist office. (Open M-F 8:30am-noon and 2-6:30pm, Sa 8:30am-noon and 2-5pm.) In an after-hours emergency, call the pharmacist at 957 44 17 or (079) 417 67 18. In an **emergency,** call 117. **Internet access** is at **Hotel Dom** (tel. 957 51 01, fax 957 23 00, email Hotel.Dom@saas-fee.ch, http://ww.saas-fee.ch/dom) on the main drag. 10SFr per half-hr.; 18SFr per hr. The bus depot has small **lockers** (2SFr) and houses the **post office** with its public fax. 24-hour **ATM** at post office as always. (Open M-F 8:35am-noon and 2-6pm, Sa 8:35-11am.) The **postal code** is CH-3906. The **telephone code** is 027.

While spine-tingling mountain exploits are Saas Fee's main draw, the town also demands a different brand of courage—this resort is definitely not for the financially faint of heart. The town's unofficial mascot, the merry marmot, may not be quite so chipper when he receives his hotel bill. To complicate housing further, from early May to mid-June lifts, restaurants and hotels shut down for maintenance, renovations, and vacations for townspeople—keep this fact in mind when planning your visit.

The budget minded willing to sacrifice comfort can find a bargain in the basement of **Hotel Garni Imseng** (tel. 958 12 58, fax 958 12 55). From the station, head down main street, left of the tourist office, then turn left and pass the church. Next to the three-star hotel's bakery museum, seven rows of bunks are stacked three high like filing cabinets, with no space between rows. The payoff is waking to the smell of fresh bread and the price, as long as you don't add frills. (20SFr, sheets 3.50SFr, buffet breakfast 15SFr.) Across the street, **Hotel Garni Feehof** (tel. 957 23 08; fax 957 23 09) doubles the price but lifts quality of life exponentially. Warm, wooden, and wonderful, nearly all the creaky pine rooms have balconies and the beds are deliciously soft. (Singles 39-57SFr in summer, 45-99SFr in winter, with breakfast and shower. In winter, reserve 2 weeks in advance.) One of the town's better values is **Pension Garni Mascotte** and its two sister chalets, **Alba** and **Albana** (tel. 957 27 24; fax 957 12 16). With your back to the station, head down the road opposite you just left of the tourist office. At the main street, turn right and continue up the hill for 200m; Mascotte is on the left. (Alba dorms 27-30SFr. Albana 5-bed dorms 28-32SF; 4-bed dorms 30-35SFr; 2-bed dorms 38-45SFr. Albana's rooms have shower and toilet. Smarter rooms in Mascotte 45-55SFr. Breakfast included. Add 10SFr for half-pension. **Laundry** facilities, ski storage, and TV lounge. Open mid-Dec. to Apr. and July-Sept.) Right behind Hotel Feehof Garni, **Hotel Berghof** (tel. 957 24 84; fax 957 46 72) has expensive dorms in the basement. The clean, clinical 48-bed dorm provides fresh insight into Swiss order. Store your bags in the new, unforgettably pink lockers. (Dorms 35-40SFr. Breakfast included. Bring your own sheets. Closed in May.) If you're not burdened by luggage of the unwieldy, matched variety, a spunky alternative to staying in Saas Fee proper is a night in a **mountain hut.** From July to September, the **Mischabelhütte** (3329m; tel. 957 11 17; 26SFr), **Hoh-saas** (3098m; tel. 957 17 13; 22SFr), and **Weissmieshütte** (2726m; tel. 957 25 54; 25SFr) above Saas Grund are all accessible. All three huts serve breakfast and dinner to compensate for the tough hike up. The Saas Fee tourist office has further details.

Three supermarkets compete for hungry shoppers in small Saas Fee, and all three have the same hours (M-F 8:30am-12:15pm and 2:15-6:30pm, Sa 8:30am-12:15pm and 2:15-7pm). Nearest the tourist office and Pension Mascotte is the **Supermarkt,** right next to the pharmacy on the main street. A small **Konsum Center** stands next to the ski school across from the Alpine guide picture board. The pick of the lot, though, is the super-duper new **Migros,** just down the hill from the church. Saas Fee manages to support a few restaurants as well. **Spaghetteria da Rasso** (tel. 957 15 26), two minutes to the left of the pharmacy under the flower-strewn Hotel Britania, has 14 variations on spaghetti (13-20SFr; double portion with 4 different sauces 24SFr). Pizza (15-19SFr), salads (6-9SFr), and garlic bread (3.50SFr) also make an appearance. The shady terrace, grotesque wooden face, and occasional accordionists attract quite a crowd. (Open July-Aug. 10am-11:30pm; Oct.-Nov. F-Su 10am-11:30pm; Dec.-Apr. W-M 10am-11:30pm and Tu 5pm-11:30pm; closed May-June; AmEx, MC, Visa.) Up the main street just before Pension Garni Mascotte, **Rotisserie du Sport** at the Sport Hotel (tel. 957 20 44, fax 957 11 88) offers self-grill meals like chicken breasts with fries and salad (18SFr) and a variety of vegetarian dishes (15-23SFr). (Open 9am-11pm, closed Tu in low season.)

Once properly nourished, visitors turn their attention to the mountains. A **cable car** to Felskinn (3000m) and a discreet **underground funicular,** the "Metro Alpin," to Mittelallanin (3500m) enable summer **skiers** to enjoy 20km of runs and a stupendous Alpine view. (Round-trip to Mittelallanin 56SFr, to Felskinn 30SFr.) In winter, an immense network of lifts opens to the delight of impatient skiers everywhere (day ski passes 56SFr, children 32SFr; 6 days 260SFr, 150SFr; 13 days 465SFr, 265SFr). For those as-of-yet disinclined toward inclines, the **Ski School** (tel. 957 23 48; fax 957 23 66) offers a week of group skiing or snowboarding lessons. (Skiing 165SFr, snowboarding 152SFr; 15SFr reductions available in late Jan. Open M-Sa 9:30-11:30am and 3-6pm.) Renting equipment is fairly simple due to the impressive number of sports stores in the village—trust us, in Saas Fee, if it doesn't sell stuffed marmots, it rents skis. Stores in the **Swiss Rentasport System** (look for the black and red logo) offer good rates (skis or snowboard and boots 43SFr per day, 6 days 157SFr). The *über*-organized can call ahead of time and have equipment set aside for their arrival; call or fax the main Swiss Rentasport outlet in town, **Anthamatten Sport Mode** (tel. 958 19 18; fax 957 42 10).

In summer, Saas Fee is among the three or four best places to enjoy **Alpinism.** The **Alpine Guide's office** (tel. 957 44 64) by the church has a selection of climbs to 4000m summits like the Allalinhorn for both amateurs and experts. (Open Mon.-Sat. 9:30am-noon and 3-6pm.) Day tours can run anywhere from 130 to 370SFr per person. If the office is closed, you can choose and contact a guide from the display on the side of the building—note that questionable ties, but not mustaches, are standard uniform for the job. Regular **hikers** have 280km of marked trails from which to choose, but the whole mountain-town thing tends to create rather steep paths. A lovely half-day walk begins with a cable-car ride to **Plattjen** (2570m). The cable-car runs from the end of Saas Fee's main street (roundtrip 22SFr, children 11SFr). From the cable-car stop and its picture-perfect views of the Dom and Lezspitze, a path leads to the right and zigzags left after five minutes. From the top it descends for a quarter of an hour and then heads left around the cirque, spiralling slowly down below the Feegletscher. The view opens up to the other high peaks as you drop down to the Gletschersee (1910m) at the glacier snout, and the path then gently follows the left bank of the outlet stream back to Saas Fee. For a hard, steep, brutal, blunt walk, hike up to the **Mischabelhütte** (3329m), which has the single best panorama of the Saas Fee cirque accessible to walkers. Coming from the pharmacy along the main street, turn right after the church and take the right fork 100m farther on. Check for snow cover before you leave, however—the last part of the hike is rocky and highly unpleasant with any hint of ice (1550m ascent, full-day, June-Sept. only). A **Saas Valley Hiking Pass** (149SFr, family rate 299SFr) provides access for a week to all cable cars and post buses in the valley and entrance to the ice pavilion at Mittelallanin, the **Bielen Recreation Center,** and the Saas and Bakery museums. The pass is available at the tourist office or any cable car station. Note that most lifts close May to early June and mid-October to mid-December and that bad weather renders much of Saas Fee inaccessible. On those rainy days, you can amuse yourself at the Bielen Recreation Center (tel. 957 24 75), next to the bus station. The complex has an expensive but excellent **swimming pool** and **jacuzzi.** (Open June 14-Sept. 7 10am-8pm; June 15-July 13 and Sept. 8-Oct. 1:30-8pm. 14SFr, with guest card 12SFr; children 8SFr, 7SFr.)

V A L A I S

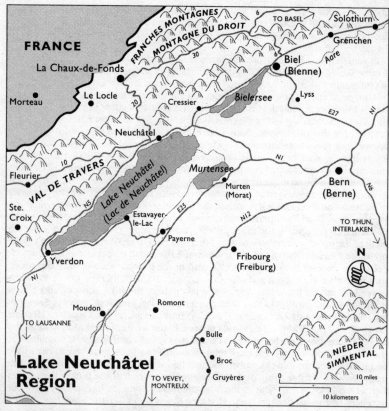

Lake Neuchâtel Region

The lake Neuchâtel region is characterized by relatively warm temperatures, vineyards producing red and white wines, and rolling hills and low mountains from the Jura mountain chain. The French of Neuchâtel French-speakers is supposed to be the purest accent in all of Switzerland.

HIGHLIGHTS OF LAKE NEUCHÂTEL

- Neuchâtel has butter-yellow stone buildings and a rough, crenellated, 12th-century castle overlooking its cliffs.
- Gruyères has an elaborately staged cheese industry as well as the grotesquely fascinating International Center for Fantastic Art.
- Basel has a lively university quarter, excellent modern, futuristic, and antique art museums, and a Gothic Protestant cathedral.

◼ Neuchâtel

Alexandre Dumas likened Neuchâtel to a city carved out of a block of butter. Although he was no doubt referring to the unique yellow stone that makes up a large part of the city's architecture, Dumas could easily be mistaken as an overly appreciative fan of the calorie-laden treats in the local *pâtisseries*. *Neuchâteloise* cuisine

WE GIVE YOU THE WORLD...AT A DISCOUNT

LET'S GO®

TRAVEL

LET'S GO Travel Gear

World Journey

Equipped with Eagle Creek Comfort Zone Carry System which includes Hydrofil nylon knit on backpanel and lumbar pads. Parallel internal frame. Easy packing panel load design with internal cinch straps. Lockable zippers. Detachable daypack. Converts into suitcase. 26x15x9", 5100 cu. in., 6 lbs. 12 oz. Black, Evergreen, or Blue. $30 discount with railpass. $225.00

Continental Journey

Carry-on size pack with internal frame suspension. Comfort Zone padded shoulder straps and hip belt. Leather hand grip. Easy packing panel load design with internal cinch straps. Lockable zippers. Detachable daypack. Converts into suitcase. 21x15x9", 3900 cu. in., 4 lbs. 5 oz. Black, Evergreen, or Blue. $20 discount with railpass. $175.00

Security Items

Undercover Neckpouch Ripstop nylon with a soft Cambrelle back. Three pockets. 5 1/2" x 8 1/2". Lifetime guarantee. Black or Tan. **$10.50**

Undercover Waistpouch Ripstop nylon with a soft Cambrelle back. Two pockets. 12" x 5" with adjustable waistband. Lifetime guarantee. Black or Tan. **$10.50**

Travel Lock Great for locking up your World or Continental Journey. Two-dial combination lock. **$5.25**

Hostelling Essentials

Hostelling International Membership

Cardholders receive priority, discounts, and reservation privileges at most domestic and international hostels.

Youth (under 18)	**free**
Adult (ages 18-55)	**$25.00**
Senior (over 55)	**$15.00**

European Hostelling Guide

Offers essential information concerning over 2500 European hostels. **$10.95**

Sleepsack

Required at many hostels. Washable polyester/cotton. Durable and compact. **$14.95**

International ID Cards 1999

Provide discounts on airfares, tourist attractions and more. Includes basic accident and medical insurance. **$20.00**

International Student ID Card (ISIC)
International Teacher ID Card (ITIC)
International Youth ID Card (GO25)

1-800-5LETSGO
http://www.hsa.net/travel

— Prices are in US dollars and subject to change.—

Euarailpass Unlimited travel in and among all 17 countries: **Austria, Belgium, Denmark, Finland, France, Germany, Greece, Holland, Hungary, Italy, Luxembourg, Norway, Portugal, Republic of Ireland, Spain, Sweden, and Switzerland.**

	15 days	21 days	1 month	2 months	3 months	10 days	15 days
First Class	*consecutive days*					*in two months*	
1 Passenger	$554	$718	$890	$1260	$1558	$654	$862
2 or More Passengers	$470	$610	$756	$1072	$1324	$556	$732
Youthpass (Second Class)							
Passengers under 26	$388	$499	$623	$882	$1089	$458	$599

Europass Travel in the five Europass countries: **France, Germany, Italy, Spain, and Switzerland.** Up to two of the four associate regions (Austria and Hungary; Benelux (Belgium, Netherlands, and Luxembourg); Greece; Portugal) may be added.

	5 days	6 days	8 days	10 days	15 days	first	second
First Class	*in two months*					*associate country*	
1 Passenger	$348	$368	$448	$528	$728	+$60	+$40
2 to 5 Passengers traveling together	$296	$314	$382	$450	$620	+$52	+$34
Youthpass (Second Class)							
Passengers under 26	$233	$253	$313	$363	$513	+$45	+$33

Pass Protection For an additional $10, insure any railpass against theft or loss.

Discounts *with the purchase of a railpass*
- $30 off a World Journey backpack
- $20 off a Continental Journey backpack
- Any *Let's Go* Guide for 1/2 Price
- Free 2-3 Week Domestic Shipping

Call about Eurostar–the Channel Tunnel Train–and other country-specific passes.

Airfares
& Special Promotions

Call for information on and availability of standard airline tickets, student, teacher, and youth discounted airfares, as well as other special promotions.

Publications & More

Let's Go Travel Guides—
The Bible of the Budget Traveler

USA • India and Nepal • Southeast Asia............22.99
Australia • Eastern Europe • Europe...................21.99
Britain & Ireland • Central America • France • Germany • Israel & Egypt • Italy • Mexico • Spain & Portugal...19.99
Alaska & The Pacific Northwest • Austria & Switzerland • California & Hawaii • Ecuador & The Galapagos Islands • Greece • Ireland.....18.99
South Africa • Turkey..17.99
New York City • New Zealand • London • Paris • Rome • Washington D.C. 15.99

Let's Go Map Guides
Know your destination inside and out! Great to accompany your Eurailpass.

Amsterdam, Berlin, Boston, Chicago, Florence, London, Los Angeles, Madrid, New Orleans, New York, Paris, Rome, San Francisco, Washington D.C. **8.95**

Michelin Maps

Czech/Slovak Republics • Europe • France • Germany • Germany/Austria /Benelux • Great Britain & Ireland • Greece • Italy • Poland • Scandinavia & Finland • Spain & Portugal **10.95**

LET'S GO® Order Form

Last Name*	First Name*	Home and Day Phone Number* (very important)

Street* (Sorry, we cannot ship to Post Office Boxes)

City*	State*	Zip Code*

Citizenship‡§□ (Country)	School/College§	Date of Birth‡§	Date of Travel*

Qty	Description	Color	Unit Price	Total Price

Shipping and Handling

			Total Purchase Price	
2-3 Week Domestic Shipping			Shipping and Handling	+
Merchandise value under $30	$4			
Merchandise value $30-$100	$6		MA Residents add 5% sales tax on gear and books	+
Merchandise value over $100	$8			
2-3 Day Domestic Shipping			**TOTAL**	
Merchandise value under $30	$14			
Merchandise value $30-$100	$16			
Merchandise value over $100	$18			
Overnight Domestic Shipping			☐ Mastercard ☐ Visa	
Merchandise value under $30	$24		Cardholder name:	
Merchandise value $30-$100	$26		Card number:	
Merchandise value over $100	$28		Expiration date:	
All International Shipping	$30			

When ordering an International ID Card, please include:
1. Proof of birthdate (copy of passport, birth certificate, or driver's license).
2. One picture (1.5" x 2") signed on the reverse side.
3. (ISIC/ITIC only) Proof of current student/teacher status (letter from registrar or administrator, proof of tuition, or copy of student/faculty ID card. FULL-TIME only).

* Required for all orders
‡ Required in addition for each Hostelling Membership
§ Required in addition for each International ID Card
□ Required in addition for each railpass

Prices are in US dollars and subject to change.

Make check or money order payable to:
Let's Go Travel
17 Holyoke Street
Cambridge, MA 02138
(617) 495-9649

1-800-5LETSGO

Hours: Mon.-Fri., 10am-6pm ET

(take in a rock show)

and use **AT&T Direct**^{SM} Service
to tell everyone about it.

It's all within **AT&T** your reach.

Exploring lost cultures? You better have an

AT&T Direct[SM] Service wallet guide.

It's a list of access numbers you need to call home fast and clear from

around the world, using an AT&T Calling Card or credit card.

What an amazing planet we live on.

For a list of **AT&T Access Numbers,**
take the attached wallet guide.

For your calling convenience tear off and take with you!

AT&T

AT&T Direct℠ Service

WALLET GUIDE

Inside you'll find simple instructions on how to use AT&T Direct Service to place calling card or collect calls from outside the U.S.

All you need are the AT&T Access Numbers when you travel outside the U.S., because you can access us quickly and easily from virtually anywhere in the world. And if you need any further help, there's always an AT&T English-speaking Operator available to assist you.

www.att.com/traveler

Calling From Specially Marked Telephones

Throughout the world, there are specially marked phones that connect you to AT&T Direct℠ Service. Simply look for the AT&T logo. In the following countries, access to AT&T Direct Service is *only* available from these phones: Ethiopia, Mongolia, Nigeria, Seychelles Islands.

Public phones in Europe displaying the red 3C symbol also give you quick and easy access to AT&T Direct Service. Just lift the handset and dial ✳60 (in France dial M60) and you'll be connected to AT&T.

Pay phones in the United Kingdom displaying the New World symbol provide easy access to AT&T. Simply lift the handset and press the pre-programmed button marked AT&T.

Customer Care

If you have any questions, call 800 331-1140, Ext. 707.

When outside the U.S., dial the AT&T Access Number for the country *you are in* and ask the AT&T Operator for Customer Care.

108-25   © AT&T 6/98

Printed in the U.S.A. on recycled paper.

To Call the U.S. and Other Countries Using Your AT&T Calling Card* or credit card∞, Follow These Steps:

1. Make sure you have an outside line. (From a hotel room, follow the hotel's instructions to get an outside line, as if you were placing a local call.)

2. If you want to call a country other than the U.S., make sure the country *you are in* is highlighted in blue on the chart like this: ▢

3. Enter the AT&T Access Number listed in the chart for the country *you are in.*

4. When prompted, enter the telephone number you are calling as follows:
   • For calls to the U.S., dial the Area Code (no need to dial 1 before the Area Code) + 7-digit number.
   • For calls to other countries,† enter 01 + the Country Code, City Code, and Local Number.

5. After the tone, enter your AT&T Calling Card* or credit card number (not the international number). If you need help or wish to call the U.S. collect, hold for an AT&T Operator.

 * You may also use your AT&T Corporate Card, AT&T Universal Card, or most U.S. local phone company cards.
 † The cost of calls to countries other than the U.S. consists of basic connection rates plus an additional charge based on the country you are calling.
 ∞ Credit card billing subject to availability.

AT&T

Special Features

Just dial the AT&T Access Number for the country *you are in* and follow the instructions listed below.

● To call U.S. 800 numbers: Enter the 800 number you are calling. (Note: Based upon the 800 number dialed, calls may be toll-free or AT&T Direct℠ Service charges may apply for the duration of the call; some numbers may be restricted.)

● To set up conference calls: Dial AT&T TeleConference Services at 800 232-1234. (Note: One conferee must be in the U.S.)

● To access language interpreters: Dial AT&T Language Line® Services at 408 648-5871.

● To record and deliver messages: Dial #123 if you get a busy signal or no answer, or dial AT&T True Messages® Service at 800 562-6275.

Here's a time-saving tip for placing additional calls: When you finish your conversation, or if there is a busy signal or no answer, don't hang up – press # and wait for the voice prompt or an AT&T Operator.

AT&T Access Numbers

AT&T Access Numbers (Refer to footnotes before dialing.) From the countries highlighted in blue below, like this ▢, you can make calls to virtually any location in the world; and from *all* the countries listed, you can make calls to the U.S.

Country	Number
Albania ●	00-800-0010
American Samoa	633 2-USA
Angola	0199
Anguilla✛	1-800-872-2881
Antigua✛	1-800-872-2881
(Public Card Phones)	#1
Argentina	0-800-54-288
Armenia ◆▲	8◆10111
Aruba	800-8000
Australia	1-800-881-011
Austria ○	022-903-011
Bahamas	1-800-872-2881
Bahrain	800-001
Bahrain✛	800-000
Barbados✛	1-800-872-2881
Belarus ✕, ━	8◆800101
Belgium ●	0-800-100-10
Belize ▲	811
(From Hotels Only)	555
Benin	102
Bermuda✛	1-800-872-2881
Bolivia	0-800-1112
Bosnia ▲	00-800-0010
British V.I.✛	1-800-872-2881
Brazil	000-8010
Brunei ●	800-1111
Bulgaria ▲, ●	00-800-0010
Cambodia:✱	1-800-881-001
Canada	1 800 CALL ATT
Cape Verde Islands	112
Cayman Islands✛	1-800-872-2881
Chile	800-360-311 or 800-800-288
China, PRC▲ (Easter Island)	800-800-311
China, PRC▲	10811
Colombia	980-11-0010
Cook Island	09-111
Costa Rica	0-800-0-114-114
Croatia ●	99-385-0111
Cyprus ●	080-90010
Czech Rep. ▲	00-42-000-101
Denmark ●	8001-0010
Dominica✛	1-800-872-2881
Dom. Rep.✕, ▢	1-800-872-2881
Ecuador ▲	999-119
Egypt● (Cairo)	510-0200
(Outside Cairo)	02-510-0200
El Salvador ○	800-1785
Estonia	8-00-8001001
Fiji	004-890-1001
Finland ●	9800-100-10
France ●	0800 99 00 11
French Antilles	0800 99 0011
French Guiana	0800 99 0011
Gabon ●	00◆001
Gambia ●	00111
Georgia ▲	8◆0288
Germany ●	0130-0010
Ghana	0191
Gibraltar	8800
Greece ●	00-800-1311
Grenada✛	1-800-872-2881
Guadeloupe✛,✱ (Marie Galante)	0800 99 00 11
Guam	1 800 CALL ATT
Guantanamo Bay↑ (Cuba)	935
Guatemala ○,✱	99-99-190
Guyana ✱	165
Haiti	183
Honduras	800-0-123
Hong Kong	800-96-1111
Hungary ●	00◆800-01111
Iceland	800 9001
India ✕,▶	000-117
Indonesia✱	001-801-10
Ireland ✓	1-800-550-000
Israel	1-800-94-94-949
Italy ●	172-1011
Ivory Coast▲	00-111-11
Jamaica ○	1-800-872-2881
Jamaica □	872
Japan KDD●	005-39-111
Japan IDC●,▲	0066-55-111
Kazakhstan ●	8◆800121-4321
Korea→	550-HOME or 550-2USA
Kuwait	800-288
Latvia (Riga)	7007007
(Outside Riga)	8◆27007007
Lebanon ○ (Beirut)	426-801
(Outside Beirut)	01-426-801
Liechtenstein ●	0-800-89-0011
Lithuania ✕, ━ (Canal Zone)	8◆196
Luxembourg ●	0-800-0111
Macau	0800-111
Macedonia, F.Y.R. of ●,○ (Asuncion City)	99-800-4288
Malaysia ○	1800-80-0011
Malta	0800-890-110
Marshall Isl.	1 800 CALL ATT
Mauritius	73120
Mexico▽¹	01-800-288-2872
Micronesia	288
Monaco ●	800-90-288
Montserrat ✛	1-800-872-2881
Morocco	002-11-0011
Netherlands ●	0800-022-9111
Netherlands Antilles ⊕	001-800-872-2881
New Zealand ●	000-911
Nicaragua	174
Norway ●	800-190-11
Pakistan ▲	00-800-01001
Palau	02288
Panama	109
Papua New Guinea	0507-12880
Paraguay ▲	008-11-800
Peru ●	0-800-50000
Philippines ●	105-11
Poland ●	0◆0-800-111-1111
Portugal ▲	05017-1-288
Qatar	0800-011-77
Reunion Isl.	0800 99 0011
Romania ●	01-800-4288
Romania↑	01-801-0151
Russia ●,▲ (Moscow)	755-5042
(Outside Moscow)	8-095-755-5042
Russia ●,▲ (St. Petersburg)	325-5042
(Outside St. Petersburg)	8-812-325-5042
St. Kitts/Nevis & St. Lucia ✛	1-800-872-2881
St. Pierre & Miquelon	
St. Vincent △	1-800-872-2881
Saipan ▲	1 800 CALL ATT
San Marino ●	172-1011
Saudi Arabia ◇	1-800-10
Senegal	3072
Sierra Leone	1100
Singapore ■	800-0111-111
Slovakia	00-42-100-101
Solomon Isl.	0811
So. Africa	0-800-99-0123
Spain	900-99-00-11
Sri Lanka ■	430-430
Sudan	800-001
Suriname △	156
Sweden	020-795-611
Switzerland ●	0-800-890011
Syria ●	0-801
Taiwan	0080-10288-0
Thailand ✕	001-999-111-11
Trinidad/Tob.	1-800-872-2881
Turkey ●	00-800-12277
Turks & Caicos ✛	01-800-872-2881
Uganda	800-001
Ukraine ▲	8◆100-11
U.A. Emirates ●	800-121
U.K.▲, ✦	0500-89-0011 or 0800-89-0011
U.S. ▼	1 800 CALL ATT
Uruguay	000-410
Uzbekistan ●	8◆641-7440010
Venezuela	800-11-120
Vietnam	1-201-0288
Yemen	00 800 101
Zambia	00-899
Zimbabwe ▲	110-98990

● Public phones require coin or card deposit. 2 Press red button. ✕ Additional charges apply when calling outside of Moscow. ◇ AT&T Direct® calls cannot be placed to this country from outside the U.S. ✱ Available from pay phones. Phnom Penh and Siem Reap only. ✦ Not available from public phones. ⊕ From St. Maarten or phones at Bobby's Marina, use 1-800-872-2881.

◆ From this country, AT&T Direct® calls terminate in designated countries only. → From U.S. Military Bases only. ▼ Not yet available from all areas. ✱ Select hotels. May not be available from every phone/public phone. †Collect calling from public phones. ▶ Available from phones with international calling capabilities or from most public phones. ✓ From Northern Ireland use U.K. access code.

★ Collect calling only. ○ Public phones require local coin payment through the call duration. ◆ Await second dial tone. ▽ When calling from public phones, use phones marked "Ladatel." Hf call does not complete, use 001-800-462-4240. △ Available from phones only. ● Public phones and select hotels. ⟨ When calling from public phones use phones marked Lenso.

□ Calling Card calls available from select hotels. ━ Use phones allowing international access. ✦ Including Puerto Rico and the U.S. Virgin Islands. ▼ AT&T Direct® Service only from telephone calling centers in Hanoi and post offices in Da Nang, Ho Chi Minh City and Quang Ninh. ✧ If call does not complete, use 0800-013-0011.

boasts distinctive quality, especially in its fondue, sausages, and the fresh fish from the lake and nearby rivers. The town also possesses pockets of remarkably intact medieval beauty, a vibrant café scene, and an extraordinary array of water-sports.

ORIENTATION AND PRACTICAL INFORMATION Neuchâtel sits atop a tube-shaped lake near the French border and the rugged Jura mountains. The city centers on pl. Pury, a major square and the hub of every bus line. **Trains** connect Neuchâtel to **Basel** (1¾hr., every hr., 6am-10pm, 35SFr); **Bern** (40min., every hr., 5:09am-12:14am, 16.60SFr); **Interlaken** (2hr., every hr., 5:38am-11:14pm, 39SFr); **Geneva** (1½hr., every hr., 5:54am-11pm, 41SFr); and **Fribourg** (1hr. via Ins, every hr., 5:09am-10:14pm, 18.20SFr). A series of stairs leads down to the shore from the station, and bus #6 goes to pl. Pury, the central **bus stop. Ferries** provide service to **Murten** (15SFr) and **Biel** (22SFr), **free** with Eurail or Swisspass. **Bike rental** is at the train station baggage check (10SFr per day). From pl. Pury, face the lake and walk two blocks to the left to find the **tourist office,** Hôtel des Postes (tel. 889 68 90; fax 889 62 96; email neuchatel@tourisme.ch; http://www.etatne.ch), which is in the same building as the main **post office.** (Tourist office open July-Aug. M-Sa 9am-7pm, Su 4-7pm; Sept.-June M-F 9am-noon and 1:30-5:30pm, Sa 9am-noon. **Post office** open M-F 7:30am-6:30pm, Sa 8-11am.) City maps are free, and the deluge of brochures will fit the needs of everyone. A useful regional biking guide is 22SFr. Also offered is *La Route du Vignoble Neuchâteloise,* a list of all local vineyards. The train station houses a tourist office geared toward rail travel. For the **police,** call 725 10 17; for the **hospital,** 722 91 11. The **postal code** is CH-2001. The **telephone code** is 032.

ACCOMMODATIONS AND FOOD The **Oasis Neuchâtel,** rue de Suchiez 35 (tel. 731 31 90; fax 730 37 09), is a long way from the center of town but, as the only hostel around, it works overtime to please its guests. From the station, take bus #6: "pl. Pury," then bus #1 (dir: Cormondrèche): "Vauséyon." Head uphill and follow the pedestrian signs up a flight of stairs. Turn right and the hostel will be up the road and to your left marked by yellow happy faces. Perched on a hilltop with a fine view from its many terraces, this quirky house offers 38 beds, table tennis, darts, a BBQ, and a friendly multilingual atmosphere (4- to 6-bed dorms 22.50SFr 1st night, then 20SFr; doubles 51SFr, 46SFr; 2- to 4-person garden teepee in summer 20SFr per person, 17.50SFr. Breakfast, shower, and sheets included. 20SFr key deposit. Free on your birthday! Reception 8-10am and 5-9pm. No curfew. Reservations recommended for July and Aug.) If Oasis is full, check the *Hôtel Restaurant* guide for cheap options in nearby towns. The closest **campground** is in Columbier: **Paradise Plage** (tel. 841 24 46), on the lakefront, boasts a four-star rating. (10SFr; single tent 14.50SFr; double tent 20SFr. July-Aug. 15 add 2SFr. Open Mar.-Oct.)

Neuchâtel may live off tourists in July and August, but the rest of the year it's a university town, which means good, cheap food. The student hang-out **Crêperie Chez Bach et Buck,** av. du Premier-Mars 22 (tel. 725 63 53), counters its laid-back atmosphere with an intensely detailed list of choices. Sugar crepes with fruit or ice cream are 2.70-6.80SFr. Salty crepes with meat or cheese cost 2.50-9.50SFr. (Open M-Th 11:30am-2pm and 5:30-10pm, F 11:30am-2pm and 5:30-11:30pm, Sa 11:30am-11:30pm, Su 5-10pm.) Locals crowd the cobblestone terrace of **A.R. Knecht Boulangerie, Pâtisserie,** pl. des Halles (tel. 725 13 21), munching croissants stuffed with spiced ham (1.70SFr), lacy fruit tarts (3.10SFr), and the house specialty *pain noix* (3.10SFr). Eaters are serenaded by enthusiastic street musicians. Past the *Halles des Maisons* at rue Moulins 37, the unassuming bistro **Chauffage Compris** (tel. 721 43 96) serves up a well-endowed *plat du jour* consisting of meat or fish, vegetables, and some form of starch. (Open M-Th 6am-1am, F-Sa 6am-2am, Su 2-11pm.) This café is the main source of income for the **Centre d'Art Neuchâtel** (CAN; tel. 724 01 60; http://www.can.ch/can), an experimental art center always and ever on the brink of financial collapse. In the town center, **Migros,** rue de l'Hôpital 12, has groceries. (Open M 1:15-6:30pm, Tu-W 8am-6:30pm, Th 8am-10pm, F 7:30am-6:30pm, Sa 7:30am-5pm.) A **Co-op** hangs out downhill and across the main road from the hostel.

LAKE NEUCHÂTEL

SIGHTS AND ENTERTAINMENT Neuchâtel's like the Rubik's cube: physically small but culturally huge. You can traverse the town in minutes unless maybe it's the last weekend in September and the three-day **wine festival** is going on, in which case it may take hours to wade through throngs of drunks enjoying parades, jazz concerts, and wine feasts. The heart of town is the *vieille ville,* which is dominated by a cobblestone marketplace (pl. des Halles), home of the **thrice-weekly market** (M, Th, and Sa 6:30am-noon). A steep flight of stairs leads to both the **Eglise Collégiale** (which is a church) and the **chateau** (which gives the town its name). *(Church open 8am-6pm; guided tours next-to-last Friday of the month; free concerts the last Friday; free.)* Begun in the 12th-century, the church took so long to complete that architectural styles changed from Romanesque to Gothic. The golden stars and blue skies of the vaulted ceiling arch harmoniously over stained-glass windows and faded wall murals re-installed after all the iconoclastic Reformation fervor died down. The gaudy **Cenotaph,** a sculptural composition of the successive counts of Neuchâtel 1372 onwards, was covered during to the Reformation to prevent destruction and is covered again today for restoration scheduled for completion in mid-1999. Next door, the 12th-century chateau served as the seat of the Count of Neuchâtel during the Middle Ages. Today the bureaucrats of the cantonal government sit behind the striped shutters and flower boxes. The interior can be seen only on dull but free **guided tours** (in English) which meet in the courtyard. *(Tours Apr.-Sept. M-F every hr. on the hr. 10am-noon and 2-4pm, Sa 10-11am and 2-3pm, Su 2-4pm.)* Look for splotches of red on the old outside walls, remnants of a disastrous fire in 1415 that literally baked the yellow stone. A small cloister garden connects the chateau to the **Tour des Prisons** on rue Jehanne-de-Hochberg and is well worth the 0.50SFr entry fee. *(Open Apr.-Sept.)* The town used the two wooden dungeons inside until 1848, but their unfortunate residents could not enjoy the magnificent view that tourists now climb up to see.

To explore the city museums, head toward the **Tour de Piesse,** which marks rue de Château, and turn right onto rue de l'Hôpital. *(Open Tu-Su 10am-5pm. 6SFr, students 3SFr, free W.)* Brown and white signs let you know when to turn left onto rue des Terreaux. At the top of the street, the museum displays Switzerland's animals, stuffed and mounted in surprisingly entertaining dioramas of their natural environment. This means everything from swans by a lake to bats in an attic to rats in garbage cans. Along rue de l'Hôpital, elegant gates and two exotic sphinxes invite a stroll into place du Peyrou. The clean lines and crunchy gravel walks of the formal garden lead up to the Hôtel du Peyrou, the home of Jean-Jacques Rousseau's friend and publisher, Pierre-Alexandre du Peyrou. Behind the mansion, the small **Archaeological Museum,** av. du Peyrou 7 (tel. (038) 33 69 10; fax (038) 39 62 86), is the home base of a passionate, expanding local investigation into the region's remote past. *(Open Tu-Su 2-5pm. Free.)* The museum houses some of the results of these continuing activities: pottery shards give way to increasingly recognizable artifacts, including an entire 7th-century grave (rocks, soil, and skeleton) and handsome marble busts from the Roman era. Toward the lake, the **Musée d'Art et d'Histoire,** esplanade Léopold-Robert 1 (tel. 717 79 20; fax 717 79 29), houses a dizzyingly comprehensive and eclectic collection of paintings, coins, weapons, and textiles to tell the history of Neuchâtel. *(Open Tu-Su 10am-5pm. 7SFr, students 4SFr, under 17 and Th free.)* The uncanny 18th-century automatons are a special sideshow; two barefoot boys in velvet coats scribble away while a lady plays the harpsichord. Performances are on the first Sunday of each month at 2, 3, and 4pm. Upstairs, the Art Nouveau decorations of the apocalyptic cupola include oil paintings, stained glass, and sculpted angels that literally fly out of the walls—making the jumbled collection of paintings arranged three high into the categories "Nature Living, Nature Dying" and "Civilization for Better and Worse," something of an anti-climax. If the museums haven't sated you, get an overview of the entire city with a **guided tour.** *(Th at 9:30am from the Tour de Piesse. 8SFr, children 3SFr.)*

Less traditional sightseeing options also abound. Take a bust to the **Fromagerie Les Martel cheese factory** in nearby Les Ponts-de-Martel for a free tour and sample tasting for a nominal fee (tel. 937 16 66; fax 937 14 19). *(Tours at 8am, noon, 5pm, and 7pm. Call or sign up at the tourist office.)* **Wine tasting** at vineyards is just 10 minutes away in Cressiers. On Saturdays show up at quai Louis Perrior on the lakefront between 10am and 7pm for free **waterskiing** with the Ski Nautique Club (tel. 725 82 45). Or sample chocolates at the **Wodey-Suchard chocolate factory,** rue du Seyon 5. *(Open M 11am-6:30pm, Tu-F 7am-6:30pm, Sa 7am-5pm).*

The university makes the nightlife predictably lively; the city is famous among regional club-goers for its techno DJs. Across the street from Crêperie Bach et Buck, the **Casino de la Rotonde,** fbg. du Lac 14 (tel. 724 48 48), boasts three simultaneous dance clubs specializing in jungle. *(Beers 3-5SFr. Admission from 10SFr, depending on event. Open M-Sa 10pm-4am.)* During the day, an arm of the Casino, **Arts Café,** serves gourmet pizzas from 12SFr. *(Open M-W 8am-9pm, Th-Sa 8am-midnight.)* Just behind the casino stands the **Bar Au 21** (tel. 725 81 98). Drink beers (2.50-4.50SFr) or long drinks (6-8SFr) on comfy couches under Pink Floyd posters or play pinball and foosball. At the popular **Shakespeare Pub,** rue des Terreaux 7, across from the Musée d'Histoire, medieval timbers and stone walls loom over a three-story pit lit by a combo of disco lights and British street lamps. *(Open Tu-Su 9pm-4am. Men pay 13SFr to get in with one drink voucher on weekends.)* Dance music tends toward Prince. (Beer 4-6.50SFr., long drinks 8.50-13.50SFr. Prices go up after 11pm). Food is served all night at the **Garbo** bar-discoteque, rue de Chavannes 5 and 7 (tel. 724 31 81; http://www.garbo.ch). *(Open 9pm-6am.)* Walk in past the large retro robot sculpture to karaoke *(Tu-Th)* and blistering techno *(F-Sa)*. Consume beer (7SFr), burgers (7-8SFr), and/or pizza (7-12SFr) all night long.

■ Near Neuchâtel: Cressiers

Just 10 minutes away from Neuchâtel by train but a world away in lifestyle, the sleepy medieval winemaking hamlet of Cressier presents a perfect opportunity for a day trip. Built around a tiny chateau that today houses the local government, the medieval village packs no less than seven **caves** (wine cellars) where one can participate in *la dégustation,* sampling wines poured by sunburnt hands that tend the grapes. To enter one of these rich and musty barrel-stacked cellars, ring the doorbell and ask: *"Deguster du vin, s'il vous plaît?"* Choose from *chasselas, pinot noir,* or *l'oeil-de-perdrix,* or leave it to the expert *("Votre choix"),* and you'll be poured a glass of Cressier wine, straight out of the vineyard's barrels. Many *caves* line the one and only main street. Of note is the particularly traditional and congenial *cave* of **Jean-Paul Ruedin,** rte. de Troub 4 (tel. (032) 757 11 51; fax 757 06 05). Jean-Paul is the 14th Ruedin son to operate the family vineyards, here since Jacques Ruedin first planted the grapes in 1614. Despite recent awards for their sparkling Chasselas and strong, pure Pinot Noir, the Ruedin cave presents a laid-back, congenial atmosphere as hosted by Mme. Ruedin. Jean-Paul's now-retired grandfather may just stop by and join you for a glass.

Though sampling is encouraged, it is considered impolite not to buy afterwards. As local restaurants are a bit pricey, however, this can be turned to your advantage. The cheapest bottles start around 9SFr, to which 4SFr can add a fresh baguette, cheese, and chocolate from the **Co-op** next to the church on rue Gustave Jeanneret. (Open M-Tu and Th-F 7:45am-12:15 pm and 1:30-4pm.) Take your bounty with you on a 10 minute stroll up into the vineyards for panoramic lunch time views of the valley by following the yellow *tourisme pédestre* signs off rue de Chateau. A set of shaded paths leads through verdant moss-covered trees into a land of great picnic spots.

Those willing to splurge can enjoy farm fresh regional delicacies at **La Croix Blanche,** rue de Neuchâtel 12 (tel. (032) 757 11 66; fax 757 32 15), serving local trout (15SFr) and large fondue (18.50SFr). Upstairs, the restaurants hotel offers spacious singles for 70SFr or doubles for 90SFr, shower and breakfast included. Hotel guests also get special lunch and dinner of regional delicacies and "surprises of the owner" for 15SFr. Reception hours vary; arrangements can be made at the café. (Open Tu-Th 11am-3pm and 6-10pm. AmEx, MC, Visa.) A few doors down, the **Hôtel de la Couronne,** rue de Neuchâtel 2 (tel. (032) 847 14 58; fax 847 32 01) serves a wide range of fresh fishies (19-34SFr). Upstairs, the attic rooms feature half-timbered walls. (Singles 40SFr, with shower 60SFr; doubles 60SFr, 90SFr. Reception at the bar. Restaurant open Tu-Th 8am-11:30pm, F 8am-12:30am, Sa 9am-12:30am, Su 9am-11:30pm.) **Trains** run every hour to Cressier from **Neuchâtel** (3.60SFr), the first train at 6:32am, the last at 11:58pm.

■ La Chaux-de-Fonds

Sprawling, lakeless, and largely free of medieval charm, La Chaux-de-Fonds seems an unlikely attraction amid the more scenic villes in the mountains of French Switzerland. But the city, birthplace of the architect Le Corbusier and auto magnate Louis Chevrolet, manages magnetism through time, terrain, and techno. A major historic watchmaking center, the town showcases a museum exploring "man and time," which may be the best horological gallery in Switzerland. Dubbed Europe's highest city thanks to its 1000m altitude, La Chaux-de-Fonds is a comfortable home base for skiers and mountain bikers wanting to explore thrilling mountain trails. The city's surging night scene has locals from Neuchâtel eagerly making the 40-minute (9.60SFr) train ride Thursday through Saturday to dance and drink the night into oblivion.

The **tourist office,** Espacité 1 (tel. 919 68 95; fax 919 62 97; email montagnes@tourisme.etatne.ch; http://www.etatne.ch), occupies the ground floor of an oddly incongruous gleaming silver and red tower. From the station, walk straight one block, then turn on av. Léopold-Robert. Ride the elevator (free) to the 14th floor for a panoramic view of the area after picking up a 2SFr city map and free info on sporting type stuff. (Open Sept.-June 9am-12:15pm and 1:30-5:30pm, Sa 9am-12:15pm and 1:30-5pm; July-Aug. M-F 9am-6:30pm, Sa 9am-12:15pm and 1:30-5pm.) **Skiers** can take regional rail to **Tête de Ran** (1422m), in **Les Hauts-Geneveys** (tel. 853 11 51), for downhill or cross-country (lift tickets run 15SFr per day), or a bus to **La-Vue-Des-Alpes** (tel. 853 30 18), which offers both night-skiing and ski lessons. (Buses run 3-4 times W and Sa-Su, 9:10am-5:30pm.) In summer, **bikers and hikers** will enjoy miles of well-marked trails that lace the region. (Bikes at the station, but ask the tourist office for trail maps and bike rental information.) The **telephone code** is 032.

The dim but spotless and roomy **Auberge de Jeunesse,** rue du Doubs 34 (tel. (032) 968 43 15; fax 968 25 18), sits at the corner of rue du Stand behind a wrought-iron gate; take bus #4 (dir. L'Hôpital): "Stavay-Mollondin," walk back a block, then go right on rue du Stand. Dark, wide hallways resemble the subdued streets of the neighborhood outside. (23-50SFr 1st night, then 20.50SFr; doubles 30SFr, 27.50SFr. Non-members add 5SFr. Breakfast and sheets included. **Laundry** 6SFr (no dryers). Reception 7:30-9am and 5-10pm. Wheelchair accessible. AmEx, DC, MC, Visa.)

The **Musée International d'Horlogie,** rue des Musées 29 (tel. (032) 967 68 61; fax 967 68 89), not content merely to display examples of the Swiss watch industry, chronicles humanity's quest to measure the great continuum, from Stonehenge to the atomic clock. (Open June-Sept. Tu-Su 10am-5pm; Oct.-May 10am-noon and 2-5pm. 8SFr, students 4SFr; free Su 10am-noon.) The vast and the minuscule unite. Dardi's astrarium and Ducommun's planetarium illustrate the rigidly timed dance of the planets in the Ptolemian and Copernican systems. Here underground, sleek cylindrical and spherical display cases rise from the floors and hang from the ceiling like space-age stalagmites and stalactites. Dominating one corner of the museum's park outside, the **carillon,** an artistic conglomeration of steel pipes and colored slats, measures time to the hundredth of a second and emits acoustically precise musical ditties in synch with carefully orchestrated panel movements every 15 minutes. Next door, the **Musée des Beaux-Arts,** rue des Musées 33 (tel. (032) 913 04 44; fax 913 61 93), looks like it was trying to get to Miami's South Beach and got very, very lost. The not-so-great 19th- and 20th-century works, Swiss derivatives of French schools, aren't really worth the effort. But there are two pockets of dense excellence: a room full of Le Corbusier paintings wild with color and chaos that contrast startlingly with the functional and minimalist straight lines of his architectural style, and an roomful of recently bequeathed paintings, including works by Delocroix, Van Gogh, Gauguin, Renoir, and Courbet. (Open Tu-Su 10am-noon and 2-5pm. 6SFr, students 3SFr.) To

Man and Machine

Born Charles Edouard Jeanneret-Gris in 1887, **Le Corbusier,** architect, city planner, and painter, has a monumental presence in 20th century art. This son of a La-Chaux-de-Fonds watchmaker rebelled against the monumental tendencies of 19th-century nationalism and historicism, seeking pure, precise forms motivated by function rather than cultural reference. He therefore designed in glass and reinforced concrete, a revolutionary choice of material that was to be repeated by countless others throughout the 20th-century. He was also infatuated with iconic machines of modernity, like the automobile and the airplane, and believed that houses and cities should be designed and organized like a machine, with regard to economy of structure and efficient use. As he said in his seminal work *Toward a New Architecture,* "the house is a machine for living."

reach both museums, turn right as you exit the station on rue Jacquet-Droz and follow *musées* signs. Bus #3 (dir: Les Foulets): "Polyexpo" deposits you in front of the **Musée Paysan et Artisanal** (Museum of Farming and Crafts; tel. (032) 926 71 89). This authentic 16th-century farmhouse reconstructs the home, workshop, and general lifestyle of the medieval peasant family. It suggestively illustrates how the confinement of long Jura winters gave rise to the region's watchmaking obsession. (Open May-Oct. Sa-Th 2-5pm; Nov.-Apr. W and Sa-Su 2-5pm. 3SFr, students 2SFr.)

Cheap food is most easily found in megachains like the **Co-op Super Centre** on rue du Modulor off av. Léopold-Robert (open M 1-6:30pm, Tu-W and F 8am-6:30pm, Th 8am-8pm, Sa 8am-5pm) or the **Migros** restaurant's 6-10SFr *plats du jour,* two blocks right of the station on rue Daniel-Jean Richard (M 1-6:30pm, Tu-W and F 11am-6:30pm, Th 11am-8pm, Sa 11am-5pm). **La Pinte Neuchâteloise,** rue du Grenier 8 (tel. (032) 913 38 64), just past the fountain, offers authentic Swiss *Rösti* (8SFr) and excellent fondue (17SFr). A huge basket of fresh, chewy bread accompanies dinner at **Le P'tit Paris,** rue du Progrès 4 (tel. (032) 928 65 33), a student-crowded café with vaulted ceilings and live jazz and blues in the musty **Paris Cave** in back. (Succulent shrimp scampi 10SFr, beer 2.60SFr. 10SFr cover after 11. Open M-Th 8am-midnight, F-Sa 8am-2am.) The **Bikini Test,** La Joux-Perret 3 (tel. (032) 968 06 66), is a 20-minute stroll under the stars from the hostel. Converted from a late medieval barn, the discoteque sports murals of monsters and musicians cavorting on a lunar landscape. Inside, Terminator-esque robot gargoyles made from car parts glare down on the 2nd story loft as the DJ mixes salsa with techno. Kids dance and drink away (beer 3-5SFr) while smoke of various persuasions drifts by. Downstairs, the chillout room shows shark movies and Monty Python clips. From the hostel, walk downhill two blocks to rue de la Serre, then turn left. The street becomes rue du College. Head for the music. For a closer nightspot, try the popular **Dublins,** 42 rue Docteur Coutery (tel. (032) 914 11 18). Walk three blocks left from the hostel, then left and downhill. On weekend nights, hundreds of 16- to 20-year-old students turn out for 2.50SFr beers, spilling out into the cobblestones beyond the doors of the pub.

■ Solothurn

Snugly sandwiched between the Jura Mountains and the Aare River, Solothurn gained fame in the late Middle Ages for its rich and ruthless army of mercenaries. Looming gates, towers, and a huge arsenal museum testify to the vicious past, but today's residents are much friendlier. Bursting with cultural and natural attractions, the city hosts major festivals of film, literature, and classical music each year. Solothurn is also a good base for launching explorations into the nearby Jura mountains.

ORIENTATION AND PRACTICAL INFORMATION Trains leave Solothurn for **Basel** (1hr., every 30min., 5:41am-11:14pm, 24SFr), **Neuchâtel** (40min., every 30min., 5:38am-11:21pm, 17.40SFr), and **Bern** (40min., every 15min., 5:21am-11:54pm, 13SFr). For hiking tips, a map, or free room reservations, head to the **tourist office,**

Hauptg. 69 (tel. 626 46 46; fax 626 46 47; email info@stadt-solothurn.ch, http://www.stadt-solothurn.ch). From the train station, walk through the underpass toward the *Zentrum* and follow Hauptbahnhofstr. across Kreuzackerbrücke up Kroneng. The office is left of the cathedral. (Open M-F 8:30am-noon and 1:30-6pm, Sa 9am-noon.) **Exchange currency** or **rent bikes** (22SFr per day) at the **train station**. (Both open 6am-10pm.) For **taxis**, call 622 66 66 or 622 22 22. **Lockers** and **luggage storage** (3-5SFr) are at the station, as is an **Aperto grocery**. (Open 6am-10pm.) For the **police**, call 117; in a **fire**, 118; for the **hospital**, 627 31 21. The **post office** (tel. 625 29 29) is past the hostel on Postpl., a left off Kreuzackerbrücke and onto Landhausquai. (Open M-F 7:30am-6pm, Sa 8-11am.) The **postal code** is CH-4500. The **telephone code** is 032.

ACCOMMODATIONS AND FOOD Overlooking the Aare river on the edge of the *Altstadt*, the organic exterior of the **Jugendherberge "Am Land" (HI)**, Landhausquai 23 (tel. 623 17 06; fax 623 16 39), conceals a modern glass and steel frame. From the train station, walk over Kreuzackerbrücke and take the first left onto Landhausquai. A wrought-iron staircase connects four white-walled, wood-floored stories. Picture windows overlooking the river and chrome track lighting keep the place well lit day and night. Enjoy the amenities: pool table, roof terrace, music room, and conference room. There's an Art Deco dining room. (Dorms 24.50SFr, with shower 35.50SFr. Additional nights 22SFr, 33SFr. Breakfast included. Dinner 11SFr. Reception 7:30-10am and 3:30-10:30pm.) The **Hotel Kreuz**, Kreuzg. 4 (tel. 622 20 20; fax 621 52 32), offers more privacy but less sparkly newness. (Spartan singles 48SFr; doubles 87SFr. Prices drop for multiple nights. Breakfast and showers included.)

Cafés and restaurants line the streets of the *Altstadt*. The **Taverna Amphorea**, Hauptg. 51 (tel. 623 67 63), is unbeatable with large portions of vegetarian-friendly Greek and Middle Eastern specialties under 20SFr. (Open Tu and Th 11am-11:30pm, W 9am-11:30pm, F 11am-12:30am, Sa 9am-12:30am.) The **Sandwich House**, Stalden 9 (tel./fax 623 33 78) offers an astounding array of stuff to put between two halves of a fresh roll, made to order for 3.50-12SFr. (Open M 11:30am-6:30pm, Tu-W and F 8:30am-6:30pm, Th 8:30am-9pm, Sa 10:30am-5pm.) Stock up on foodstuffs at the **Manora** grocery store and restaurant on Gurzelng. (open M-W and F 9am-6:30pm, Th 8:30am-9pm, Sa 8am-5pm), or try the **farmer's market** at Marktpl. (W and Sa 8am-noon). **Co-op** and **Migros** are outside old city walls near the post office. (Both open M-W and F 8am-6:30pm, Th 8am-9pm, Sa 7:30am-5pm.)

SIGHTS AND ENTERTAINMENT Solothurn's well-preserved Baroque architecture is enough to justify a visit. Several excellent museums augment the visual menu. On the fringes of town, the **Kunstmuseum**, Werkhofstr. 30 (tel. 622 23 07), houses an extensive collection of post-1850 Swiss stuff and a work or two by Cézanne, Picasso, Matisse, Degas, Renoir, Klimt, and Van Gogh as well as a lovely medieval "Virgin with Strawberries." *(Open Tu-W and F-Sa 2-5pm, Th 2-9pm, Su 10am-noon and 2-5pm. Free.)* In the heart of the old town, the **Museum Altes Zeughaus**, Zeughauspl. 1 (tel. 623 35 28), holds one of Europe's largest collections of weapons and armor, from huge artillery pieces to rows of battle axes to 400 suits salvaged from Solothurn's famous mercenary army. *(Open May-Oct. Tu-Su 10am-noon and 2-5pm; Nov.-Apr. Tu-F 2-5pm, Sa-Su 10am-noon and 2-5pm. 6SFr, students 4SFr.)* The orgy of death devices is housed in an enormous 1609 arsenal staffed by little old lady volunteers. The **Naturmuseum**, Klosterpl. 2, (tel. 622 70 21) within the town walls to your right as you cross Kreuzackerbrücke, lets kids poke and prod animals and minerals; no vegetables. *(Open Tu-W and F-Sa 2-5pm, Th 2-9pm, Su 10am-noon and 2-5pm. Free.)* Take bus #4: "St. Niklaus" walk 10 minutes up Riedholzstr. and take the Solothurn-Niederbipp train: "Feldbrunnen," to see the stately **Schloß Waldegg**, a castle surrounded by wheat fields and tree-lined walks. Aristocratic life is preserved in the castle's tribute to the French embassy, the **Ambassadorial Museum**. *(Open Apr.-Oct. Tu-W and F 2-5pm, Th 2-7pm, Sa-Su 10am-noon and 2-5pm; Nov.-Mar. Sa-Su 10am-noon and 2-5pm. Wheelchair accessible. Parking available. 6SFr, students 4SFr.)* Don't miss the ruler-perfect formal French gardens.

Solothurn is a major center of **festivals**. In 1999, the **Swiss Film Festival** will bring lovers of celluloid to the city from January 26-31. In February, **Chesslete**, a procession with bizarre masks and festivities intended to drive away winter, marks the beginning of topsy-turvy Carnival. Citizens re-name their town "Honolulu," since the tropical city is exactly on the other side of the world. Swiss writers gather to read, drink, and sit on panels during the annual **literature festival** May 14-16 in 1999. When the jazz festival winds down in nearby Montreux, fans of classical music and opera find their party just beginning with the arrival of the **Classic: Open Air Fest** (July 9-18 in 1999.)

The Jura mountains gaze over Solothurn, and their many trails encourage fans of Mother Nature to get up close and personal. Marked **hiking and biking trails** lead through the Jura to nearby Altreu (2hr.), where the oldest and best-known stork colony in Switzerland rests and poops. The trek to the Weissenstein Alpine center is more challenging and rewarding (2hr., trail head at the corner of Wengisteinstr. and Verenawegstr.; follow the yellow signs to Weissenstein). Take the chairlift down from Weissenstein and hop on a train (4.20SFr) in Oberdorf to return. **Boat tours** leave Solothurn for Biel and from there to Murten or Neuchâtel. (25SFr one-way, 43SFr round-trip, free with Swiss pass.) In the winter, **skiing** dominates the athletico-scene. Weissenstein (1280m) has 7km of cross-country trails and two chairlifts for downhill skiing on two small slopes best suited to beginners.

Nightlife in sleepy Solothurn does not exist outside of the Thursday-Saturday window. A (maybe less than) critical mass of hipsters can find each other on weekends for live music at the **Creep Club,** Dammstr. 59 (tel. 621 20 60; http://www.solnet.ch/creep). For funky dance music there's **Kofmehl Fabrik,** Gibelinstr. (tel. 623 50 60), on the outskirts of town. Just off the railroad tracks, this old metal factory is now decked out in trippy graffiti. Kofmehl holds occasional movie nights. **Löwen,** Löweng. 15 (tel. 62 25 055), serves up good beer, cheap Italian food (pasta and pizza for under 15SFr), and a mix of world music (funk, jazz, reggae). In the old town, **The Cinema Palace,** Hauptg. 57 (tel. 622 25 15), shows recently released, subtitled American films (13-15SFr).

▨ Biel (Bienne)

In 1765, Rousseau spent what he called the happiest moments of his life in Biel. Little of the small fortified town has remained the same through the tumultuous years that followed the philosopher's sojourn. In 1798 Biel was overrun by Napoleon's armies; today one third of the city's residents still speak French. The arrival of the watch-making industry in the late 19th century meant a population explosion, and the town grew from 6400 in 1864 to the current 50,000. The industrial parks for Rolex and Omega now overpower the vestiges of the *Altstadt* Rousseau loved. Meanwhile, the nearby lake and mountain terrain have made Biel attractive to a new strain of visitor, and things have changed to accommodate the wilderness-lover types.

Trains run to Biel from **Solothurn** (20min., every hr., 5:424am-11:58pm, 8.40SFr); from **Bern** (30min., every 30min., 5:18am-12:04am, 10.40SFr.); and from **Neuchâtel** (20min., every 30min., 5:38am-11:42pm, 9.60SFr). The Biel **tourist office** (tel. 322 75 75; fax 323 77 57) is just outside the **train station** at Bahnhofpl. (Open May-Oct. M-F 8am-12:30pm and 1:30-6pm). The train station **exchanges currency** (M-F 6am-8pm, Sa-Su 6am-7pm), **rents bikes** (22SFr, half-day 17SFr; mountain bike 30SFr, 24SFr), rents **lockers** and **stores luggage** (3-5SFr; open 5am-12:30am). You can call a **taxi** at 32 21 11 11. For the **police,** call 344 51 11; for the **hospital,** 324 24 24. The **post office** (tel. 321 18 40) is just left of the train station. The **telephone code** is 032.

The two best **hikes** pass through magnificent gorges: the walk to Twannbach-schlucht leads to open mountaintop fields ripe for picnics, and the jaunt to Tauben-loch threads through a rugged canyon and its canopy forest. To get to **Twannbachschlucht,** take bus #11 from the train station to "Maggligenbahn/FuniMa-colin," then take the rail car from Biel to Maggligen (every 30min; 4.20SFr, Swisspass and Swiss Card valid.) From this vantage point, signs point to Twannberg, which leads to Twannbachschlucht. The trail follows a ridge perched above Lake Biel and passes through dense forest and flower-filled meadows. The journey from Biel to the lakeside town of **Twann** at the bottom of the gorge lasts about three hours. Return to Biel by train or by lake ferry (6SFr, Eurailpass not valid), or move on to Neuchâtel. **Taubenloch** is a less ambitious hike, though perhaps more rewarding. Bus #1, 2, and 3 run to "Taubenloch" where you can enter the canyon through the Zum Wilden Mann Restaurant's garden (2SFr suggested donation). The trail hugs the edges of 30m drops of sheer rock walls carved eons ago by the rushing rapids beneath you. Cool, semi-subterranean breezes move through water-sculpted caves, tunnels, and sheets of mist. Waterfalls plunge past mossy cliffs, illuminated by the sunlit green canopy above. Many hikers turn back at the water treatment plant (35-40min.), but hungrier souls who press on just a few minutes will find the **Eau de Berge du Taubenloch restaurant** at Frinvillier 2535 (tel./fax 358 11 32). Fill up on a delicious three-course *Menü* for under 14SFr while the owner's baby goats and friendly dog romp around your feet. (Open May-Sept. M-Sa 9am-11pm, Su 9am-7pm; Oct.-Apr. closed M). The well-marked walk back from Frinvillier to Biel takes about an hour. Many vineyards line the lake, ripe for a walking tour (1-4hr., map at tourist office) or bike ride.

A **boat tour** of the lake provides a more leisurely introduction to the city. There's sun to be had at the *Strandbaden*. To reach the harbor and beach from the train station, take a left onto Veresiusstr. then a left onto quai du Bas. Walk straight and follow the signs. Boat tours range from 12SFr (Biel-Twann, 25min.) to 46SFr (Biel-Murten with a change at Neuchâtel, 4hr.) round-trip. In early July, an **open-air cinema** called "Yellow Movie Nights" runs recent releases and classic films in **Schloßpark Nidau.** Tickets (15SFr, 25SFr for two) can be purchased at the tourist office or through Hello Yellow (tel. 157 18 18; http://www.post.ch).

Since few budget accommodations bless Biel, consider making it a daytrip from Solothurn, Neuchâtel, or Bern. **The Hostel,** Solothurnerstr. 137 (tel. 341 29 65; email hostelbiel@access.ch), is lodge-style with a pony field next door. Run by a commune-style management, it features 45 sheeted beds, no lockout, no curfew, free breakfast, access to a **kitchen,** and **bike rental.** (Dorm singles 23SFr, doubles 60SFr. Reception 8am-10pm.) Take bus 3N or 3S: "Renferstr." and walk 1 block away from town down Solothurnerstr. For picnic supplies, there is always **Migros,** Freierstr. 3 (open M-F 7:30am-6:30pm, Sa 7:30am-1pm), or the **Co-op,** Rechbergerstr. 1 (open M-F 8am-12:30pm and 2-6:30pm, Sa 7:30am-4pm).

■ Fribourg (Freiburg)

Founded on the banks of the Sarine by the Zaehringen dynasty in 1157, Fribourg displays peculiarities common to many cities built by 12th-century German dukes—it's established on a site with very sharp cliffs, it's protected by natural formations, and it's laid-out in a rectangle dominated by a major commercial street with the fortress and public buildings off to the side. Backpackers are drawn here by the siren call of lake and mountain. Fribourg was an isolated bastion of Catholicism during the Reformation, and that means French-speakers and a lot of well-preserved medieval religious art. Religious foundations sit on every corner, and even the local brew, Cardinal beer, celebrates the career development of a 19th-century bishop. The city also has a remarkable interest in modern art, as evidenced by its museums and many art-oriented festivals. Meanwhile, Fribourg bridges the main Swiss linguistic divide: 30% of the population firmly count themselves *Freiburger*; the remaining 70% *Fribourgeois*.

ORIENTATION AND PRACTICAL INFORMATION Fribourg sits on the main train line between Zurich and Geneva. Connections leave nearly every 30 minutes to **Bern** (25min., 5:14am-12:16am, 10.40SFr) and **Lausanne** (45min., 5:15am-11:47pm, 21SFr). Other connections include **Neuchâtel** (1hr., 1 per hr., 4:45am-9:49pm, 18.20SFr); **Interlaken** (1½hr., 1 per hr., 6:36am-10:48pm, 32SFr); and **Basel** (1¾hr., 1 per hr., 6:13am-10:48pm, 43SFr). For a **taxi,** call (079) 219 46 10. Fribourg's friendly **tourist office,** av. de la Gare 1 (tel. 321 31 75; fax 322 35 27; email Office.Tour-

LAKE NEUCHÂTEL

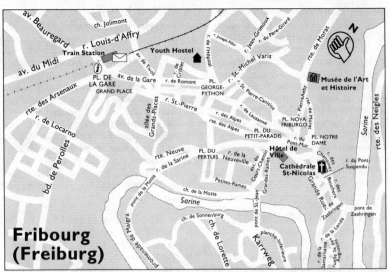

Fribourg (Freiburg)

isme@fribourg.ch; http://www.FribourgTourism.ch), is 100m to the right of the station door. (Open M-F 9am-12:30pm and 1:30-6pm, Sa 9am-12:30pm and 1:30-4pm. Closed Sa afternoons Oct.-Apr.) You can make hotel reservations through the tourist office (3SFr fee). **Currency exchange** waits at the train station (open 6am-8:30pm) or at one of the many banks lining rue du Romont. **GMT buses** for Bulle and the Schwarzsee (13.20SFr each) leave from the station. **Lockers** (3-5SFr), **luggage watch** (open M-Sa 6am-8:55pm, Su 7am-8:55pm; 5SFr per item), and **bike rental** (19SFr per day, ID deposit) available at the station. Call 117 for the **police** and 426 73 16 for **medical assistance**. **Internet access** is available for 10SFr per hr. at the **Scottish Bar**, rte. de Jura 67 (tel. 466 82 02; http://scottish.mcnet.ch). Take bus #3: "Veuille." (Open M-F 7:45am-6:30pm, Sa 7:45am-5pm.) The **post office**, av. de Tivoli, is the skyscraper left of the station. The **postal code** is CH-1700; the **telephone code** is 026.

ACCOMMODATIONS AND FOOD   The **Auberge de Jeunesse** stands at rue de l'Hôpital 2 (tel. 323 19 16; fax 323 19 40). Hang a left out the train station and walk past the overpass, across av. de Tivoli, past the post office, onto the narrow rue du Criblet, left at the playground, and up the path to the hostel. With long, quiet corridors, piped-in music, and white, low-slung arched ceiling, this place has a converted hospital feel, as though a WWI Hemingway hero should be "recovering" with a pretty nurse behind one of the identical doors. (Dorms 23SFr 1st night, then 20.50SFr. Nonmembers add 5SFr. Breakfast, sheets, and showers included. Lunch 11SFr. Lockers, **laundry, kitchen,** and ping pong tables available. Reception 7:30-9:30am and 5-10pm. Curfew 10pm; key deposit 20SFr. Open Feb.-Nov. Reservations recommended.) **Hotel du Musée,** rue Pierre Aeby 11 (tel./fax 322 32 09), above a Chinese restaurant, is one block from the cathedral. Large, well-furnished rooms have plush carpets. (Singles 40SFr, with shower 50SFr; doubles 80-90SFr, 90-100SFr. Breakfast 5SFr. AmEx, MC, Visa. Reserve 2-3 days ahead.) From the station, campers can catch a GFM bus: "Marly," where **Camping La Follaz** (tel. 436 24 95) offers lakeside plots and showers. (Reception 9am-10pm. 4SFr. Open Apr.-Sept.)

Small cafés selling quasi-Italian or German Swiss wares line rue de Romont and rue de Lausanne. For great, cheap food and a laid-back student atmosphere, head to **Café Populaire,** rue St. Michel 3 (tel. 323 23 09), near pl. Georges Python. Outside, twentysomethings lounge over coffee and beer (3.50-6SFr) while inside a short-order chef at the **O'Neils** counter serves up huge juicy burgers for 5-8SFr. Patrons at the long wooden tables can enjoy the vegetarian or meat *plat du jour* (10-12SFr) or partake of the only bagels available this side of Zurich. (Open M-Th 7am-11:30pm, F-Sa 7am-1am; O'Neils opens at 11am.) **Bindella Ristorante Bar,** rue de Lausanne 38 (tel. 322 49 05), cooks inventive, high-quality pasta from 11SFr and pizza dishes in a low-lit Mediterranean interior (leather sofas). Come hear live jazz on the last Thursday of every month at 8:30pm. (Cover 8SFr. Open M-Sa 9am-11:30pm.) Better deals and unusual food lie hidden deeper in the city. Workers and locals pack the bar and restaurant of **Les Tanneurs,** pl. du Petit-St.-Jean (tel. 322 34 17), filling its outdoor tables on the pleasant old town square. Plates are piled high with steak and fries (15SFr), and the beer is cheap (2.60SFr). A **produce market** stands in pl. Georges Python between rue de Romont and rue de Lausanne on Wednesdays 7am-noon or in pl. Hôtel de Ville on Saturdays 7am-noon. The virtually inseparable supermarket twins, **Co-op** and **Migros,** share the same street (6a and 2 rue St-Pierre) and the same hours (M-F 8am-6:30pm, Sa 8am-5pm). There is a **supermarket** in the basement of La Placette Shopping Mall (the 1st building on rue de Romont) and a **Manora** self-service restaurant on the 6th floor with meat, fruit, salad, and dessert kiosks that produce a fine meal for 8-15SFr. (Open M-F 8:30am-6:30pm, Sa 8am-5pm.)

SIGHTS AND ENTERTAINMENT

A walking tour provides a taste of Fribourg's many churches, monasteries, and convents. From the station, head down rue de Romont, past pl. Georges Python, and along rue de Lausanne and its open-air shopping galleries. Rue de Lausanne empties into pl. Nova-Friburgo, a busy intersection with a fine view of the **Hôtel de Ville** and its whimsical clock tower. Renaissance automatons regularly chime in the hours. A fountain of St. George dominates the courtyard below, and gives unexpected showers to visitors and the commemorative **Morat Linden Tree** in heavy winds.

From pl. Nova-Friburgo, rue Pierre Aeby leads to the **Musée d'Art et d'Histoire,** rue de Morat 12 (tel. (037) 22 85 71; fax (037) 23 16 72). *(Open Tu-W and F-Su 10am-5pm, Th 10am-5pm and 8-10pm. Free; special exhibits 8SFr, students 5SFr.)* Run-of-the-mill 18th-century portraiture shares space with the truly macabre products of local monks. The medieval statuary recovered from the cities' fountains and the porch of Cathédrale St-Nicolas stare silently as modern artist Jean Tinguely's noisy chains and motored cogs power huge sculptures bristling with metal and bone. From the museum, rte. de Morat leads to the impressive **Eglise des Cordeliers,** part of a Franciscan monastery. *(Open Apr.-Sept. 7:30am-7pm; Oct.-Mar. 7:30am-6pm.)* Inside, walls rise to a beautifully scrolled ceiling, and an intricate altar lies in star-topped, arched darkness. Farther down the road is the **Basilique de Notre-Dame,** whose dim, incenseladen atmosphere contrasts sharply with the stark lines of the Franciscan church. Across pl. Notre-Dame rises the bell tower of the **Cathédrale St-Nicolas,** the focal point of Fribourg. *(Cathedral open M-F 6:15am-7pm, Sa 7:45am-7pm, Su 9am-9:30pm. Free. Tower open June-Aug. M-Sa 10am-12:15pm and 2-5pm. 3SFr, students 2SFr.)* The 76m, 368-step tower offers dizzying views of the town; the art inside induces speechlessness.

A few blocks downhill along rue du Pont-Suspendu, right on rue de Zaehringen, left on rue Stalden, left on rue de la Lende brings you to the ruelle des Augustins and its highlight, the 13th-century **Eglise des Augustins** (Augustinian Monastery). A huge wooden altarpiece and many statues and paintings dedicated to Mary and her Sacred Heart adorn the interior. Just off pl. du Petit-St-Jean is an odd little **Musée Suisse de la Marionette,** rue Derrière-les-Jardins (tel. 322 85 13), housing hundreds of puppets from everywhere in the world. *(Open Sa-Su 2-5pm; 5SFr, students 3SFr.)* A nearby arched stone bridge, the **pont du Milieu,** lets you put town in perspective with panoramic vistas. Planche-Supérieur leads up the hillside, depositing climbers next to the postage-stamp-sized **Chapelle de St. Jost,** built by the Capuchin convent, **Montorge,** across the street. Farther uphill, the **Chapelle de Lorette** overlooks the gorge. The tiny chapel houses a magnificently illuminated statue of the Virgin Mary.

Fribourg's university, music conservatory, art groups, and civic institutions come together to host a number of festivals throughout the year, including a **Carnival,** an **International Film Festival** (March 8-14, 1999), an **International Guitar Festival** (mid-March), an **International Jazz Festival** (mid-July), and the **Bellvard Bollwerk**

International festival of modern art performances (late June to early July). There's also an **open-air cinema** from mid-July to mid-August.

At night, most *Fribourgeois* sleep. **Café des Grand Places,** 12 Grand Places (tel. 322 26 58), plays live funk, blues, salsa, industrial hardcore, and karaoke, depending on the night. *(Open M-Tu 11am-11:30pm, W 11am-1:30am, Th 11am-2am, F 11am-3am, Sa-Su 5pm-3am. Music starts at 9pm. AmEx, MC, Visa.)* The restaurant upstairs has *Menüs* at 13.50SFr and 15.50SFr. Its terrace overlooks the intriguing Jean Tinguely fountain on Grand Places. On the right from the station, **Rock Café,** blvd. de Pérolles 1 (tel. 322 24 14; fax 322 24 24), has mid-air motorbikes and fenders on the wall, resembling the Hard Rock Café without offending too much.

■ Near Fribourg

■ Gruyères

Tiny Gruyères carries a weighty reputation for its cheese. Unfortunately, everyone there knows it. The local tourist industry goes to absurd extremes (strategically placed milk cows, locals in medieval garb photogenically sewing lace on the streets of the *vieille ville,* and suspiciously artificial-smelling smoke permeating rooms of a castle where the hearths have clearly been bare and unlit for years), but the schlocky kitsch can't obscure the underlying beauty of the area. A splendid château filled with striking contemporary art and the milky calm of working cheese dairies make this eccentric town well worth a daytrip. **GFM buses** run between **Fribourg, Bulle,** and Gruyères regularly (40min., 15.80SFr.). **Trains** pass through Gruyères every hour in each direction, but the last train from Gruyères to Bulle leaves at 8:17pm and the last bus from Bulle to Fribourg departs at 9:35pm.

The **Cheese Dairy,** near the train station at Pringy, can deal with all urgent queries. (Open 8am-7pm. Tours in English. Free.) They churn 35kg wheels of cheese for visitors at 12:30 and 3pm. A multilingual presentation details the particulars of production as visitors watch cheesemakers in action from an observation booth, reminiscent of instructional surgery sessions. A lovely slide show set to swelling, heroic music lets you watch the progress of curds into cheese and explains how "the best milk cows get to know the finest bulls in the world." Samples for sale in the gift shop.

The obligatory cheese-history lesson under your belt, you can lay siege to the steep hill. Steep. The **tourist office** (tel. (026) 921 10 30; fax 921 38 50) lies at the top of the stairs leading to the *vieille ville* from the **parking lot.** (Tourist office open mid-May to Oct. M-Su 8am-noon and 1:30-5pm; Oct. to mid-May M-F 8am-noon and 1:30-5pm.)

As the *Dent-de-Broc* mountains loom in the background, you can clamber over town walls and past some of the best ramparts in the region. Cow bells echo cacophonously in the valley below, and one beautiful vista follows another as the geranium-lined main street leads you to the **Château de Gruyères** (tel. (026) 921 21 02; fax 921 38 02). Nineteen counts lived lawlessly from the 11th to 16th centuries in its walls until the last Gruyère was exiled in 1554 and the castle reverted to the Crown. Only the dungeons remain of the original feudal castle; the living quarters burned to the ground in 1493 and were rebuilt as the first Renaissance castle on the Northern Alps. They now house the **International Center of Fantastic Art,** a museum that roams freely between the erotic, the demonic, and the grotesque. (Open June-Sept. 9am-6pm, Mar.-May and Oct. 9am-noon and 1-5pm; Nov.-Feb. 9am-noon and 1-4:30pm. 5SFr, students 3SFr, essential English guide 0.50SFr.) Upstairs the museum gets normal with a presentation of historical tapestries and **Franz Lizst's** pianoforte (yup, he lived here too.) After the castle, a meal of Gruyère's cheese fondue can prove a budget buster (25-45SFr), but the region's other specialty, *la double-crème de la Gruyère avec fraises* (strawberries in clotted cream), is deliciously affordable at around 5-8SFr.

LAKE NEUCHÂTEL

■ Murten

Murten is a place where most people speak German, despite the linguistic flexibility of most of the region. The 12% French-speaking minority insists on calling the town "Morat." Stubborn lot. Murten/Morat, surrounded by its medieval *Ringmauer/ramparts,* overlooks the pale blue Murtensee/Lac de Morat and, despite orthographic schizophrenia, proves to be a surprisingly unified town. The high altitude town has a bloody history: Charles the Bold, Duke of Burgundy, was defeated in 1476 by an army of the old Swiss Confederacy in what came to be known as the Battle of Murten; Napoleon defeated a similar contingency in 1798, the ostensible reason for the existence of the minority of French-speakers.

Largely free from the crass commercialism that infects other nearby villages, Murten is an excellent daytrip. The **train station** (tel. 670 26 46) shares its tiny square with the **post office** and sends trains to **Fribourg** (26min., 1 per hr., 8:40am-12:27am, 9.60SFr); **Neuchâtel** (30min. via Ins, 1 per hr., 5:47am-10:25pm, 10.40SFr); and **Bern** (50min. via Lyss, 1 per hr., 5:47am-10:25pm, 18.20SFr). The station also **changes currency** and **rents bikes** (25SFr per day). In addition, **ferries** leave regularly for **Neuchâtel** (90min., every 2hr., 9:20am-6:35pm, 15SFr), as well as for **tours of the lake** (13SFr). For more information concerning special tours and evening cruises, call LNM (tel. (032) 725 40 12; fax 724 79 61). There is a **Co-op** grocery store halfway up Bahnhofstr. with a cafeteria upstairs (9.50-10.50SFr). The **postal code** is CH-3280.

As Bahnhofstr. curves uphill, it leads to the crowd of swaying lindens that mark the town's entrance. Following the road past the impressive château (rather, *Schloß*) and to the right brings you to the main street, Hauptstr., and its arcades, crowded with the odd jumble of vendors' wares and cafés full of people slurpin' coffee. A climb up onto the **ramparts** (you'll find stairs behind the church on Franz Kirchg.) affords backyard views of the red-clay-tiled roofs below and the lake beyond. On the other side of the ivy-covered walls is the Staatgraben—a set of garden allotments rife with roses, pink honeysuckle, and skyscraper cities of multicolored lupins.

The Staatgraben path descends the ramparts and ends at the linden tree park. Follow Lausannestr. in the opposite direction and obey the signs to reach the town's old mill, now the **Murten Historisches Museum** (tel. 670 31 00). (Open May-Sept. Tu-Su 10am-noon and 2-5pm; Oct.-Dec. and Mar.-Apr. Tu-Su 2-5pm; Jan.-Feb. Sa-Su 2-5pm. 4SFr, students 2SFr.) The water wheel still churns outside, and inside you'll find leather fire buckets, bottles of Murten's famously strong and famously psychedelic absinthe ("Poison Vert"), relics from the Battle of Murten, even the cannonball used to kill an American circus elephant that went wild in the city streets in 1866.

Death, the Maiden, and a Linden Tree

Once upon a time (June 22, 1476) in a land far, far away (Fribourg), there lived an old man named Nicholas who declared that he would give his daughter Beatrice's hand to the man who proved himself most valiant on the battlefield. As the knights went off to battle Charles the Bold in Murten, Beatrice waved a linden branch at Rudolphe, her childhood love. Determined to win her hand, Rudolphe proved himself the bravest knight on the battlefield—at the cost of a mortal wound. Undaunted, he ran back to Fribourg, waving a linden branch and shouting "Victory!" When he finally reached Beatrice's balcony in pl. Hôtel de Ville, he collapsed. Beatrice ran to her love, who could say only "Homeland! Love! To Heaven!" before dying in her arms. The town planted the linden branch as a relic of the victory in the square. In 1984, a traffic accident uprooted the tree, but the town salvaged a shoot and replanted it in the tree's original spot, where it flourishes today. In memory of the battle and of Rudolphe's plight, runners from Morat and Fribourg race between the two cities every October.

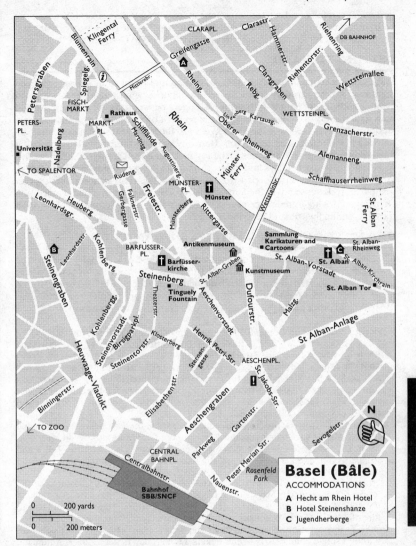

Basel (Bâle) ACCOMMODATIONS

A Hecht am Rhein Hotel
B Hotel Steinenschanze
C Jugendherberge

■ Basel (Bâle)

Perched on the Rhine near France and Germany, Basel is home to a large medieval quarter as well as one of the oldest universities in Switzerland—a school whose graduates include Erasmus of Rotterdam, Bernoulli, and Nietzsche. The kids keep Basel young, and the biggest party of them all, Basel's *Fasnacht*, allegedly rivals Mardi Gras; residents have a mad carnival until the onset of Lent. There's also an industrial side—Switzerland's second largest city is home to pharmaceutical giants Roche, Sandoz, and Ciba-Geigy.

Basel has world-class museums and river walks, and as you wander the streets you may just find sculptures by the likes of Arp, Picasso, Rodin, and Tinguely. The *Münster* presides over the *Altstadt* in a towering conglomeration of red sandstone, stained glass, and sprouting spires. Farther along the river, the elegant St. Alban district houses 30 carefully orchestrated museums in its hilly, winding streets. You can see art from Roman times to the 20th century in one stroll, as the green waters of the serpentine Rhine drift slowly through the city on their way to Germany.

GETTING TO BASEL

The **Euroairport** (tel. 325 25 11) serves continental Europe; all trans-continental flights are routed through Zurich. There are flights several times per day to both Geneva and Zurich. Shuttle buses run passengers between the airport and the SBB train station every 20 to 30 minutes from 5am until 11:45pm. The city has three **train stations:** the French SNCF station is next door to the Swiss SBB station in Centralbahnpl. near the *Altstadt,* and trains from Germany arrive at the DB station, across the Rhine down Riehenstr. City trams to the town center depart from the SBB every five to 10 minutes on weekdays and every 15 minutes on weekends. **Buses** to Swiss, French, and German cities depart from their respective train stations. Don't forget that passport. Basel stands at the international crossroads of Switzerland, France, and Germany. If **driving** from France, take A35, E25, or E60; from Germany, E35 or A5. If traveling within Switzerland, take Rte. 2 north.

ORIENTATION AND PRACTICAL INFORMATION

Basel sits in the northwest corner of Switzerland, so close to France that the *Tour de France* annually bikes through the city. The *Gross-Basel* portion of town, where most sights are located, lies on the left bank of the Rhine on two hills separated by the Birsig valley. *Klein-Basel* lies on the right bank. Be sure to pick up a city map (0.50SFr) and other useful publications at either of the two tourist offices.

Trains: SNCF station (tel. 156 10 56), on Centralbahnpl. **SBB station** (tel. 157 22 22; 1.19SFr per min.), on Centralbahnpl. **DB station** (tel. 690 11 97), across the Rhine down Riehenstr. To: **Zurich** (1hr., every 15-30min., 5:20am-midnight, 30SFr) **Geneva** (3hr., every hr., 6:22am-9:53pm, 67SFr) **Lausanne** (2½hr., every hr., 5:22am-9:22pm, 57SFr) **Bern** (1hr., every hr., 5:49am-midnight, 34SFr) **Salzburg** (7hr., 2 per day, 124SFr); **Vienna** (10hr., 2 per day, 126SFr); **Paris** (5-6hr., 7 per day, 5:53am-12:28am, 70SFr). Make international connections at the French (SNCF) or German (DB) stations.

Ferries: 4 cable ferries, the **Vogel Gryff** at Klingental; the **Leu** below the cathedral terrace (Mar. to Oct. 9am-noon and 1-7pm except F morning), the **Wild Maa** at St. Alban (Apr.-Sept. M-F 7am-7pm, Sa-Su 10am-7pm; Mar. and Oct.-Nov. 7-8am and 11:30am-6pm, Sa-Su 10am-6pm) and the **Veli** at St. Johann will help you cross the golden Rhine. 1.20SFr. In summer, boats run 9am-7pm; in winter 11am-5pm. Rhine cruises depart from the *Schiffstation* (tel. 639 95 00; fax 639 95 06) next to the tourist office. 4 per day May-Oct. 13. Enjoy "Dixie Night" or "Pasta Pasta" on one of the special Rhine cruises (ferries leave at 7:30 or 10pm, 16 SFr). Round-trip to Rheinfelden 42SFr, to Waldhaus 16SFr. Tickets available 30min. before departure.

Public Transportation: Trams and buses run daily 5:45am-11:45pm. Most sights are within a single zone (#10). 1-zone tickets 2.60SFr, day ticket 7.40SFr. Automatic vendors at all stops sell tram tickets. Maps at the tourist office or the train station.

Taxis: In front of the train station, or call **MiniCab 33er,** tel. 271 11 11, **Taxi AG,** tel. 633 33 33, or **Taxi Central,** tel. 271 22 22.

Parking: Jelmoli, Rebg. 20; **Aeschen,** Aeschengraben 7; **Bahnhof SBB,** Güterstr. 2.50SFr per hr.

Bike Rental: At train stations. 25SFr per day; mountain bikes 31SFr. Open M-Sa 7am-8:30pm.

Hiking: near Basel: 1200km of yellow *Wanderweg* marked trails crisscross the Basel countryside. Take Bus #70 to "Reigoldswil" to take the **Gondelbahn** to the Jura mountain peak "Wasserfallen" (937m) and hike through the woods nearby. (Wasserfallen-Waldenburg 2½-3hr.; Wasserfallen-Jägerwegli 1½-2hr.). Call 941 18 81 for information on hiking near Reigoldswil/Wasserfallen.

Basel Tourismus: Schifflände 5 (tel. 268 68 68; fax 268 68 70; email office@basel-tourismus.ch). From the SBB station, tram #1: "Schifflände." The office is on the river, near Mittlerebrücke. Lists of hotels, restaurants, museums, cultural events, and tours and excursions in Basel and the surrounding area. A **bus tour** of the city leaves from the SBB station. (May-Oct. at 10am. 20SFr.) Open M-F 8:30am-6pm, Sa 10am-4pm. The **branch office** (tel. 271 36 84; fax 272 93 42; email hotel@messe-basel.ch) at the SBB station also makes hotel reservations (10SFr). Open M-F 8:30am-7pm, Sa 8:30am-12:30pm and 1:30-6pm, Su 10am-4pm.

Currency Exchange: At any bank or the SBB station bureau (open 6am-9pm).

American Express: Reise Müller, Steinenvorstadt 33, CH-4002 (tel. 281 33 80). Tram #1: "Barfüsserpl."; the office is 1 block from the square. Checks cashed, mail held. Open M-F 9am-6:30pm, Sa 10am-4pm.

Luggage Storage: At all stations. 3-7SFr. Open 5:30am-12:15am.

Bookstores: Buchhandlung Biden und Tanner, Bankenpl., Aeschenvorstadt 2 (tel./ fax 206 99 99), is Basel's travel and map bookshop. Open M-W and F 8:15am-6:30pm, Th 8:15am-8pm, Sa 8:15am-5pm. **Jäggi Bücher,** Freiestr. 32 (tel. 261 52 00; fax 261 52 05), carries English-language paperbacks. Open M-W and F 9am-6:30pm, Th 9am-8pm, Sa 9am-5pm.

Bi-Gay-Lesbian Organizations: Arcados (gay center), Rheing. 69 (tel. 681 31 32; fax 681 66 56), at Clarapl. has oodles of information on bars, restaurants and hangouts. Open Tu-F 2-7pm, Sa 11am-5pm. **Schlez** (gay and lesbian center), Gärtnerstr. 55, Wiesenpl. Case postale 640, CH-4010 (tel. 631 55 88). Ask for the "Schwules Basel" brochure at the Tourist Office for a listing of groups, bars, discos, and shops.

Emergencies: Police, tel. 117. **Medical,** tel. 144. **Hospital,** tel. 265 15 15.

Hotlines: Helping Hand, tel. 143. **Rape Crisis Line,** tel. 261 89 89. **Assistance For Young Women Travelling Alone** (tel. 271 37 23). Open M-F 8am-1:30pm and 2-7:30pm, Sa 8am-1pm.

Post Office: Rüdeng 1. Tram #1 or 8: "Marktpl." Open M-F 7:30am-6pm, Sa 8am-12:30pm. **Emergency Post:** To your right as you exit the station. Open M-F 6-7:30am and 6:30-10pm, Sa 6-8am and 11am-8pm, Su 9am-noon and 3-10pm. Only accepts packages, EMS, and priority mail. **Postal Codes:** CH-4000 to CH-4051.

Internet Café: Cyberzone, Gerberg. 43 (tel. 262 08 88) offers email services as well as MS Office/Word for 0.25SFr per min., 12SFr per hr. Open M-Th 11am-11pm, F-Sa 10am-2pm, Su 1-7pm.

Telephone Code: 061.

ACCOMMODATIONS AND CAMPING

Basel is a vibrant town with an atmospheric *Altstadt,* superb museums, and a raucous nightlife—don't miss it because you didn't call ahead. There is but one overpacked hostel and very few hotels remotely approaching budget status. Just one phone call— you have time. Stop reading this sentence and make a reservation. Now. Trust us.

Jugendherberge (HI), St. Alban-Kirchrain 10 (tel. 272 05 72; fax 272 08 33). Tram #2 "Kunstmuseum" and 5min. down St. Albangraben, passing St. Albanchurch. Or walk 10-15min. from the SBB station down Aeschengraben to St. Alban Anlage. At the tower, follow the signs down the hill. Near a calm stretch of the river, this curious old building is a mecca for sky-scraper-weary travelers, near a brook and warbling thrushes. Very peaceful and within 2min. of 5 museums. The efficient institutional set-up has lockers for every bunk and wheelchair access. Dorms 26.80SFr the 1st night, then 24.30SFr; singles 56.70SFr; doubles 37.80SFr, 35.30SFr. Breakfast, showers, and sheets included. Dinner 11SFr. **Laundry** 8SFr. Reception 7-10am and 2pm-midnight. Check-out 7-10am. Curfew midnight. Reservations recommended. MC, Visa.

Hotel-Pension Steinenschanze, Steinengraben 69 (tel. 272 53 53; fax 272 45 73). From the SBB station, turn left on Centralbahnstr. and continue toward Heuwage-Viadukt. Three-star advantages abound: rooms with phone, radio, TV, private bathrooms, and balconies over the hotel garden or the street. Breakfast of unlimited bread, juice, *müesli,* yogurt, and espresso included. Singles 105-160SFr, under 25 with ISIC 55SFr; doubles with shower 150-240SFr, 100SFr. 3-night max. stay for students. Daytime luggage storage. 24hr. reception. AmEx, DC, MC, Visa.

Hecht am Rhein, Rheing. 8 (tel. 691 22 20; fax 681 07 88). Cross Mittlerebrücke next to the tourist office and turn right onto Rheing. The patched carpets and the general decor change from room to room. Lone women may not feel comfortable in the neighborhood. Single 70SFr, with river view 80SFr; doubles 120SFr, 130SFr. Breakfast and hall showers included. AmEx, DC, MC, Visa.

Camping: Camp Waldhort, Heideweg 16 (tel. 711 64 29), in Reinach. Tram #11: "Landhof." Backtrack 200m toward Basel, cross the main street, and follow the signs. Beautiful location far from Basel but in a residential area. Reception 8am-12:15pm and 2:30-10pm. 7SFr; tents 4-6SFr. Open Mar.-Oct.

FOOD

With all the students about, relatively cheap eateries are numerous, even in the heart of the city. Barfüsserpl. and Marktpl. are especially full of restaurants.

⊛**Hirscheneck,** Lindenberg 23 (tel. 692 73 33). Cross Wettsteinbrücke and go left. An unabashedly left-of-center restaurant-bar where dreadlocks, piercings, and the hammer and sickle prevail. Occasional live shows for the kids. Features at least 2 vegetarian and organically grown dishes every day. *Menü* 15SFr. Open M 5pm-midnight, Tu-Th 9am-midnight, F 9am-1am, Sa 2pm-1am, Su 10am-midnight.

Zum Schnabel, Trillengässlein 2 (tel. 261 49 09). Marktpl.; walk one block on Hutg. to Spalenberg., then left onto Schnabelg. In this corner terrace, Italian-speaking servers present well-prepared German dishes. 12.80SFr buys bratwurst with caramelized onions, *Rösti,* and a salad. Pasta 14-22SFr. Open M-Su 8am-midnight. AmEx, DC, MC, Visa.

Topas Kosher Restaurant, Leimenstr. 24 (tel. 206 95 00), next to the Basel Synagogue and down the street from the Marcel Hess (self-proclaimed "kosher sausage king") deli. Entrees 13-28SFr. Open Su-Tu and Th 11:30am-2pm and 6:30-9pm, F 11:30am-2pm. Friday dinner and Saturday lunch by reservation only.

Café XL, Steinenvorstadt 27 (tel 281 10 88) boasts a creative variety of crepes (try "Boris Becker" with Nutella filling, 5.50SFr, or "Crêpe Bombay" with chicken curry, 8.50SFr) and salads. Fruit *Punsches* to tempt eye and wallet (hot green punch, mandarin with Curacao blue 8.50SFr).

Markets

Migros, Steinenvorstadt; Clarapl. 17. Open M-W and F 8am-6:30pm, Th 8am-8pm, Sa 8am-5pm. At Bahnhof SBB. Open M-F 6am-10pm, Sa-Su 7:30am-10pm.

Co-op, on Centralbahnpl. Schifflände; Steinenvorstadt. Open M-F 6am-10pm, Sa-S 7:30am-10pm.

Public market, on Marktpl. Fresh fruits, vegetables, and baked goods are offered every weekday morning. Open until 6:30pm on M, W, and F.

SIGHTS

The **Münster,** Basel's medieval pride, stands on the site of an ancient Celtic town and a Roman fort, a fact catalogued by the archaeological excavation in the crypt beneath the apse. *(Open in summer M-F 10am-5pm, Sa 10am-noon and 2-4pm, from July 1 also Sa noon-5pm, Su 1-5pm; in winter M-Sa 11am-4pm, Su 2-4pm. Free.)* The red sandstone facade features hundreds of figures in various acts of piety ranging from trumpet-playing to dragon-slaying. Behind the altar, gilt Latin inscriptions memorialize the life of **Erasmus,** the renowned scholar and staunch Catholic who remained loyal to his faith

---

Lizard Lunacy

In 1529, Basel's residents enthusiastically joined the Reformation and threw out the bishop, but they kept his *crozier* (staff) as the town's emblem. The staff shares this honor with the basilisk (Basel-isk), a creature part bat, part dragon, and part rooster, which spawned what may have been the world's first and only public trial and execution of a chicken. In 1474, a hen allegedly laid an egg on a dung heap under a full moon, an action sure to hatch the horrible creature. The bird was tried, found guilty, and beheaded, and the egg was ceremonially burnt.

even after his beloved Basel joined the Reformation. When he died, the city set aside dogma to give him a proper Catholic burial in its Protestant cathedral. **Bernoulli,** the mathematician who discovered the math behind the spiral and laws concerning flight, also rests in the cloister. (Bernoulli's Principle explains why a piece of paper rises when you blow on its edge.) The **tower** boasts the city's best view of the Rhine, *Klein Basel,* and Black Forest tower. *(Tower closes 30min. before the church. 2SFr. Due to recent suicides, you can't go up alone.)* For a contrasting aesthetic, walk toward Barfüsserpl. onto Theaterpl., where the **Jean Tinguely Fountain** freezes a moment of modern chaos as iron sculptures parodying human foibles maniacally spew water.

Petersgraben leads to the University and Peterspl. The park forms a *de facto* quadrangle and bicycle parking lot for the university and is ideal for picnicking, napping, or reading Kant. Bargain-hunters flock here every Saturday morning for the **flea market,** which starts at 9am and goes until early afternoon.

Basel's friendly easy-to-use pedestrian tourist signs point the way back to Freiestr., the main shopping avenue, and to Marktpl. The very red **Rathaus,** erected in the early 1500s to celebrate Basel's entry into the Confederation, brightens Marktpl. with a blinding facade adorned with gold and green statues. In an attempt to gain influence in state affairs, Basel's then-powerful guilds locked the government inside the *Rathaus* in 1691. While the politicians starved inside, the guilds partied outdoors, feasting on ale and sweets in an uprising later dubbed the "Cookie Rebellion." Tread softly on the **Mittlere Rheinbrücke,** for it is more than 750 years old. Built in 1225, the Middle Rhine Bridge connects Greater Basel to Little Basel. St. Ursula's pilgrimage of girls to the Holy Land during the Children's Crusade passed through the **Elftausendjungfern-Gässlein** (Lane of 11,000 Virgins). The medieval practice of gaining indulgences by walking this lane is now defunct, but people still stagger through after overindulging at nearby clubs. A colorful Gothic fountain spices up the nearby **Fischmarket,** while a more refined, pastel-and-eggshell theme dominates the St. Alban district, home of many established Basel families. By the hostel, on a calm stretch of the Rhine, **St. Alban-Tor** is one of the old city wall's three remaining towers.

The **Zoologischer Garten,** Binningerstr. 40 (tel. 295 35 35; fax 281 00 05), one of the best zoos in Europe, is 10 minutes down Steinenvorstadt from the *Altstadt. (Open daily May-Aug. 8am-6:30pm; Sept.-Oct. and Mar.-Apr. 8am-6pm; Nov.-Feb. 8am-5:30pm. 11SFr, students 9SFr.)* The zoo is famous for successfully breeding several endangered species, and the gardens are as much of an attraction as the animals. Restaurants, picnic areas, and ice cream vendors abound.

MUSEUMS

Basel's 30 museums may seem overwhelming, but they warrant more than a casual glance. The **Kunstmuseum** is deservedly the most famous, but many esoteric galleries are also fascinating. Subjects range from medieval medicine to mechanized mannequins. Pick up the comprehensive museum guide at the tourist office, or visit Basel's website, http://www.unibas.ch/museum. A **Swiss Museum Pass,** valid for one month (all over Switzerland at participating museums) costs students 25SFr.

⊛Kunstmuseum (Museum of Fine Arts), St. Alban-Graben 16 (tel. 271 08 28; fax 271 08 45). Tram #2. In 1661, the culturally minded city started the 1st independent public gallery. There's a collection of 13th-, 14th-, and 15th-century stuff from Mathias, Witz, and the Holbeins, and a collection of 19th- and 20th-century works from Matisse, Van Gogh, Dalí, Miró, Klee, Arp, Chagall, and Kandinsky. The collection of Picassos was acquired when the city government granted the cash-strapped museum money to buy 2 through a resoundingly affirmative electoral referendum. The man himself, touched by the move, donated 4 more. Open Tu-Su 10am-5pm, W 10am-9pm. 7SFr, students 5SFr. Free Su. Special rates for exhibitions.

⊛Museum für Gegenwartskunst (Museum of Contemporary Art), St. Alban-Rheinweg 60 (tel. 272 81 83; fax 271 05 36), by the youth hostel. Clever art from the 1960s onward; made accessible. Excellent English and German guide. See a collection of recent and important pieces by Beuys, Judd, Peyton, Fritsch, and Carsten Höllen (who stays until 1999). Video art from Gary Hill, Bill Viola, and Matthew Barney. Open Tu-Su 11am-5pm. 7SFr, students 5SFr.

Museum Jean Tinguely, Grenzacherstr. 210, (tel 681 93 20; fax 681 93 21). Tram #2 or 15 to "Wettsteinpl." and bus #31: "Museum Tinguely." Everything rattles and shakes in this intriguing homage to metal and movement. The alarming "le Ballet des Pauvres" is a fury of twisting skeletal figures. Open W and Sa 2-5:30pm, Su 10am-5:30pm. 6SFr, students 3SFr.

Fondation Beyeler, Baselstr. 101, Riehen (tel. 645 97 00). Tram #6: "Riehendorf." This sprawling villa designed by Renzo Piana on the undulating lawns of Berover Park houses one of Europe's finest private collections of art. From Monet, Cézanne, van Gogh, and Seurat to Kiefer, Klee, Pollock, and Warhol. Open 11am-7pm, W 11am-8pm. 9SFr.

Antikenmuseum (Museum of Ancient Art), St. Alban-Graben 5 (tel. 271 22 02; fax 272 18 61), near the Kunstmuseum. Houses a treasure trove of antiquities in 2 elegant, Neoclassical mansions. Greek and Roman works predominate, but the gorgeous Egyptian and Etruscan works are worth your while. Open Tu-Su 10am-5pm. 5SFr, students 3SFr. First Su of the month is free.

Museum der Kulturen Basel (Museum of Ethnology) and **Naturhistorisches Museum** (Natural History Museum), Augusting. 2 (tel. 266 55 00; fax 266 56 05), off Munsterpl. The Museum of Ethnology's mansion topped by Neoclassical friezes contains an excellent collection of non-Western art. A dizzying variety from the South Seas, South America, and Central/Western Africa. The Natural History Museum in the same building has engaging exhibits of woolly mammoths and inventive displays pitting model animals against their own skeletal mirror images. Open Mar.-Aug. Tu and Th-Su 10am-5pm, W 10am-9pm; Sept.-Apr. Tu and Th-Su 10am-5pm. 6SFr, students 4SFr.

Barfüsserkirche (Historical Museum), Steinenberg 4 (tel. 271 05 05; fax 271 05 42), on Barfüsserpl. Collection includes stained glass windows emblazoned with cantonal coats-of-arms and the oldest *crozier* city banner. The interior is an old church with pink stone columns and huge windows veiled in transparent linen. The downstairs rooms contain original medieval and Renaissance furniture. Open M and W-Su 10am-5pm. 5SFr, students 3SFr, free on the 1st of the month.

Papiermühle (Paper Mill), St. Alban-Tal 37 (tel. 272 96 52; fax 272 09 93), a quick float down the river from the hostel. Everything there is to know about paper. A restored medieval mill with a noisy water wheel continues to mash rags so that visitors can make their own. Sprawling exhibits upstairs on the history of paper, writing, and printing. Try writing with a quill or typesetting a souvenir. Open Tu-Su 2-5pm. 9SFr, students 6SFr. Family ticket (min. 2 adults, 1 schoolchild) 22SFr.

Sammlung Karikaturen and Cartoons (Cartoon and Caricature Collection), St. Alban-Vorstadt 28 (tel. 271 13 36; fax 271 12 71). The carefully mounted cartoons in German amuse visitors from everywhere. Funny stuff from the 20th-century from *Peanuts* and *Calvin and Hobbes* to the work of Gerhard Glück. Open W and Sa 2-5:30pm, Su 10am-5:30pm. 6SFr, students 3SFr.

Jüdisches Museum der Schweiz (Jewish Museum of Switzerland), Kornhausg. 8 (tel. 261 95 14). Bus #37: "Lyss." Small, well-done exhibits on the law, the Jewish year, and Jewish life. Open M and W 2-5pm, Su 11am-5pm. Free.

Puppenmuseum Basel, Steinenvorstadt 1 (tel. 225 95 95; fax 225 95 96) Barfüsserpl. Right in your line of sight as you step off a tram in Barfüsserpl. Four floors of toys. Check out the teddy bear in a bubble bath and intricate Louis XIV mini-furniture. Open M-W and F-Su 11am-5pm, Th 11am-8pm. 7SFr, students 5SFr.

ENTERTAINMENT AND NIGHTLIFE

In a year-round party town, the carnival, or **Fasnacht,** still manages to distinguish itself as fun fun fun. The festivities commence the Monday before Lent (February 22 in 1999) with the *Morgestraich,* a not-to-be-missed-four-in-the-morning parade over 600 years in the running. Fife and drum music plays to revelers in brilliant masks lampooning the year's local and regional scandals. The goal is to scare away winter. It rarely succeeds. During the rest of the year, Basel still has a lot to offer from an accomplished ballet to several theaters. Music is especially popular here; one rewarding event is the free weekly **organ recital** at St. Leonard's Church, Friday at 6:15pm. Call *Au Concert* (tel. 272 11 76) for details. The best sources of information are tourist office pamphlets, which have lists in English of concerts, plays, gallery exhibits, fairs, and other happenings for a three-month period.

A university town through and through, Basel's varied nightlife is a change of pace from the surrounding bucolic history stuff. Start bar-hopping at **Barfüsserplatz,** where students sit at outdoor tables and drink wine on the steps of the Barfüsserkirche. The two most popular local beers are **Warwick** and **Cardinal.** When the bars close, kids in black often head for after-hours clubs. Most places have a 21 and older policy, but the crowds get younger on weekends.

Atlantis, Klosterburg 13. Big. Hot. Smoky. Loud. Raucous. A large bar that sways to reggae, jazz, and funk. Bands play every night the Italian soccer team does not. Cover 5-7SFr. Open Su-Th 10am-midnight, F-Sa 10am-1am.

Brauerei Fischerstube, Rheing. 45 (tel. 692 66 35). Cross Mittlerebrücke and take the 1st right. This old-school *Biergarten* is also Basel's only brewery, crafting 4 of the best beers in town. The delectably sharp *Hell Spezial* goes well with the homemade pretzels. *Bier* 2.40SFr-5.70SFr. Open M-Th 10-midnight, F-Sa 10pm-1am, Su 5pm-midnight. MC, Visa.

Pickwick Pub, Steinenvorstadt 13 (tel. 281 86 87), near Barfüsserpl. This English-style pub, draped in football memorabilia, hosts students and adults alike. Bartenders are happy to go the extra mile, even if it means shot for shot. Open M-W 11am-midnight, Th 11am-1am, F-Sa 11am-3am, Su 3pm-midnight. Beers from 3.80SFr.

Caveau Mövenpick Wine Pub, Grünpfahlg. 4 (tel. 261 22 12), by the post office. A sophisticated change from the bar scene. Fine regional wine selection, particularly Alsatian. Steep prices. 4.40-10SFr. Open M-Sa 11am-midnight.

Fifty-fifty, Leonardsburg 1 (tel. 261 33 22). 50s Americana on the walls; wine, beer, and "energy drinks" for under 5SFr on the menu. Beers 3.80SFr 'til 10:30pm, after 10:30pm, 5SFr. "Gourmet" burgers 14-19SFr; buffalo wings with blue cheese dip (30 pieces) 35SFr. Open W-Th 6:30pm-1:30am, F-Sa 6:30pm-3:30am.

Babalabar, Gerbeg. 74 (tel. 261 48 49), next to Fifty-fifty. Dark, modern dance club for the beautiful people. Techno nights meet disco mirrors; samba rhythms from the Latin-crazy DJ. Cover Su-Th 5SFr, F-Sa 10SFr. Open in summer Su-Th 10pm-2am, F-Sa 10pm-3am; in winter Su-Th 9pm-1:30am, F-Sa 8pm-3am.

Elle et Lui, Rebg. 39 (tel. 691 54 79). A chic, coiffed gay and lesbian bar catering to all ages and tastes. Open Su-Th 4pm-midnight, F-Sa 4pm-1am.

Dupf, Rebg. 43 (tel. 692 00 11), right next to **Elle et Lui,** is a trendy teenage gay haunt that welcomes a mixed crowd, too. Beers from 3.80SFr. It sponsors a "Travestaile" (a very popular song contest featuring locals as well as random passers-by) in November. Open daily 4pm-whenever.

Willi's Café, Gerbgässlein 2 (tel. 261 98 30) has the cheapest beer in town. American paraphernalia, Swiss furniture, and cosmopolitan customers spell schizophrenia. Beers from 3.50SFr. Open Tu-F 4:30pm-midnight, Sa 8:30pm-2am.

■ Near Basel: Augusta Raurica

The twin towns of **Augst** and **Raurica** will take you farther back than medieval Basel. Founded in 43 BCE, **Augusta Raurica,** the oldest Roman colony on the Rhine, grew into an opulent trading center by the 2nd century CE. After destruction at the hands of the Alemanni in the late 3rd century, the Romans built an adjacent fortress. Ongoing excavations continue to uncover temples, baths, and workshops. If time is short, skip the smallish **Roman Museum** (tel. 816 22 22; fax 816 22 61) for a ramble through the fields to the **Roman Farm Animal Park,** where bullying pigs and selfish donkeys will invite you to smoke tobacco. (Sites and museum open Mar.-Oct. M 1-5pm, Tu-Su 10am-5pm; Nov.-Feb. Tu-Su 10am-noon and 1:30-5pm. Museum 5SFr, students 3SFr; parks free.) You can also stomp through sewers Ninja-turtle style at the cold, dark, damp, and spooky **Roman cellars** and **sewers** dating from 43 BCE.

To get to the ruins from Basel, take the hourly regional **train** (dir: Laufenberg) three stops to Kaiseraugst (4.80SFr). A **ferry** (tel. 639 95 06) runs from Schifflände, by the Basel tourist office, to Kaiseraugst (1½hr., 4 per day, June-Sept. Tu-Su, 16SFr, round-trip 29SFr). Follow the signs.

Lodging is hard to come by in Augusta Raurica, so if you really want to spend the night try **Camping Kaiseraugst** (tel. 811 10 66). Exit the train station on the far end and follow signs. The grounds sit pretty on the Rhine about 20 minutes away from Roman ruins. (6SFr per person; tents 3-5SFr; electricity 2.20SFr, shower deposit 20SFr. Free swimming pool. Reception 8am-10pm. Open Apr.-Sept. Beware of the hedgehogs.) Bring a full picnic to the temples or the amphitheater; the only nearby restaurant with reasonable prices is **Ristorante Römerhof Pizzeria** (tel. 811 17 67), just past the museum, with pizzas for 12 to 17SFr. (Open M-Sa 11am-2:30pm and 6pm-midnight, Su 11am-midnight. AmEx, DC, MC, Visa.)

Zurich (Zürich) Region

Switzerland has one bank for every 1200 people, and half of those banks are in Zurich. The battalions of briefcase-toting, Bally-shoed, Armani-suited executives charging daily through the world's fourth-largest stock exchange and largest gold exchange help pump enough money into the economy to keep the upper-crust boutiques and expense account restaurants thriving. There is, however, more to Zurich than money. The city was once the focal point of the Reformation in German Switzerland, led by the anti-Catholic firebrand Ulrich Zwingli. This Protestant asceticism succumbed to the avant-garde spirit of 1916, a year in which artistic and philosophical radicalism shook the town's staid institutions. During this time, living at Universitätstr. 38, James Joyce toiled away to produce *Ulysses,* the quintessential modernist novel, deriving inspiration from the Limmatquai and Bahnhofstr., whose "gray way" is now home to the city's popular temporary collection of plastic cows. Nearby at Spiegelg. 14, Russian exile Vladimir Lenin bided his time, read Marx, and watched over this capitalist center, dreaming of revolution and trying to ignore all the brouhaha next door as a group of raucous young artists calling themselves the Dadaists founded the seminal proto-performance art collective, the Cabaret Voltaire. A walk through the *Altstadt* will reveal the upside-downness of Dadaism in the very cobblestoned paths that, in their tortuous climb through the maze of the old city, are delightful to get lost in.

👀 HIGHLIGHTS OF ZURICH REGION

- Zurich's Bahnhofstraße is famous for its many powerful banks, boutiques, and streams of people.
- Its main cathedral, the Gothic Grossmünster, boasts gorgeous stained-glass windows by Marc Chagall.
- Dada was invented in Zurich; you can visit former Dada cabarets around town.
- Zurich's many excellent museums include the *Kunsthaus,* the *Museum Rietberg,* and the *Völkerkundemuseum.*
- Lucerne's lovely *Altstadt* is set on a lake and is in easy distance of the Glacier Garden's lunar landscapes.

■ Getting to Zurich

Because PTT buses cannot go into Zurich proper, the easiest way into the city is by plane, train, or car. **Kloten Airport** (tel. 816 25 00) is the largest hub for Swissair (tel. 157 10 60 for general flight information) and a layover for many international flights. Zurich has daily connections to Frankfurt, Paris, London, and New York. **Trains** leave every 10 to 20 minutes from the airport for the *Hauptbahnhof* in the city center (train operates 5:37am-12:20am; 6SFr; Eurailpass and Swisspass valid). Zurich is a city of trains. The *Hauptbahnhof* faces the legendary Bahnhofstr. on one side and the Limmat River on the other. Zurich has connections to all major European and Swiss cities. **By car,** A1 connects Bern, Austria and southern Switzerland to Zurich. From Basel, A2 connects directly to Zurich. From Geneva, take A1 to Lausanne, A9 to Vevy, and A12 to Zurich.

■ Orientation and Practical Information

Zurich sits smack in the middle of northern Switzerland, not far from the German border and surrounded by numerous Swiss playgrounds: the resort lake Bodensee to the north, the ski resorts in the Engadin Valley to the east, and the hiking bases in the Berner Oberland to the south and west. Zurich lies among the lowest land in Switzerland, quite distant from the mountains and skiers that have made the nation famous. Although the suburbs sprawl for miles, most of the activity within Zurich is confined

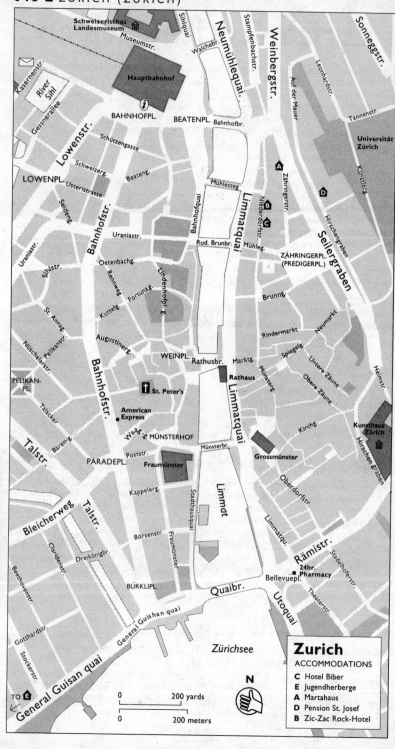

Schweizerisches
Landesmuseum
Museumstr.
Sihlquai
Neumühlequai
Stampfenbachstr.
Walchebr.
Weinbergstr.
Sonneggstr.
Kasernenstr.
River
Sihl
Gessnerallee
Hauptbahnhof
BAHNHOFPL.
BEATENPL.
Bahnhofbr.
Bahnhofstr.
Auf der Mauer
Leonhardstr.
Universität
Zürich
Tannenstr.
Schützengasse
LOWENPL.
Lowenstr.
Schweizerg.
Beareng.
Usteristrasse
Seideng.
Uraniastr.
Mühlesteg
Bahnhofquai
Limmatquai
Zähringerstr.
Niederdorfstr.
A
B
C
Künstlerg.
D
Hirschengraben
Seilergraben
Uraniastr.
Sihlstr.
Oetenbachg.
Rennweg
Fortunag.
Lindenhofstr.
Rud. Brunbr.
Mühleg.
ZÄHRINGERPL.
(PREDIGERPL.)
St. Anng.
Pelikanstr.
Nüschelerstr.
Kuttelg.
Augustinerg.
Brunng.
Rindermarkt
Neumarkt
PELIKAN-
PL.
Bahnhofstr.
Talacker
Bäreng.
WEINPL.
Rathusbr.
Marktg.
Rathaus
Münsterg.
Spiegelg.
Untere Zäune
Obere Zäune
Heimstr.
St. Peter's
American
Express
Waag.
MÜNSTERHOF
Limmatquai
Kirchg.
Kunsthaus
Zürich
Talstr.
PARADEPL.
Fraumünster
Poststr.
Münsterbr.
Grossmünster
Oberdorfstr.
Hirschengraben
Bleicherweg
Talstr.
Kappelerg.
Börsenstr.
Fraumünster
Stadthausquai
Limmat
Limmatqu.
Rämistr.
Claridenstr.
Dreikönigbr.
Beethovenstr.
BÜRKLIPL.
Quaibr.
Bellevuepl.
24hr.
Pharmacy
Stadelhoferstr.
Theaterstr.
Gotthardstr.
Stockerstr.
TO E
General Guisan quai
General Guishan quai
Uroquai
Zürichsee
N

0   200 yards

0   200 meters

Zurich
ACCOMMODATIONS
C Hotel Biber
E Jugendherberge
A Martahaus
D Pension St. Josef
B Zic-Zac Rock-Hotel

to a relatively small, walkable area. The **Limmat River** splits the city down the middle on its way to the Zürichsee. Grand bridges, offering elegant views of the stately old buildings that line the river, bind the two sectors together. The university presides from the hillside of the lively far bank that, like Paris's Left Bank, pulses with crowded bars, hip restaurants, and a student's quarter, all loud and lively into the wee hours of the night. By contrast, Zurich's real Left Bank is rather conservative and very expensive. Bahnhofstrasse, at the head of the Limmat, overflows with bankers and well-coiffed shoppers by day and falls dead quiet when the shops and banks close around six. Sprawling across the Limmat, the *Altstadt* is surrounded by pedestrian zones. The **Sihl River** edges the other side of the city, joining the Limmat around the train station. The *Altstadt*'s **Limmatquai,** which develops into the Uto-Quai and Seefeldquai, across the bridge from the *Hauptbahnhof,* is a favorite strolling destination for many residents and tourists.

The **Zürich Night Card,** available at the main tourist office, entitles the holder to discounts and bonuses on Zurich's nightlife offerings, as well as free passage on public transport for three consecutive evenings after 5pm (20SFr).

TRANSPORTATION

Trains: Bahnhofpl. To: **Winterthur** (20min., every 15min., 4am-11:51pm, 10.60SFr); **Lugano** (3hr., 1-2 per hr., 6:33am-10pm, 59SFr); **Lucerne** (1hr., 1-2 per hr., 6am-12:15am, 19.40SFr); **Geneva** (3hr., every hr., 6:04am-9:06pm, 74SFr); **Basel** (1hr., 2-4 per hr., 4:46am-12:03am, 30SFr); and **Bern** (1¼hr., 1-2 per hr., 4:46am-12:03am, 42SFr).

Public Transportation: Trams criss-cross the city, originating at the Hauptbahnhof. Long rides (more than 5 stops, valid for 1hr.) cost 3.60SFr (press the blue button on automatic ticket machines), and short rides (1hr. or less) cost 2.10SFr (yellow button)—the city is small enough to avoid long rides for the most part. Buy a 24hr. *Tageskarte,* valid on trams, buses, and ferries if you plan to ride several times (7.20SFr). Purchase a ticket before boarding and validate it by inserting it into the ticket machine. Stern, merciless policeman won't hesitate to fine you (50SFr and up) if you try to ride for free. *Tageskarten* are available at the tourist office, hotels, hostels, the automatic ticket machines, or the **Ticketeria** under the train station in Shop-Ville (open M-Sa 6:30am-7pm, Su 7:30am-7pm). The ticketeria also offers 3- and 7-cards. All public buses, trams, and trolleys run 5:30am-midnight. Nightbuses run from the center of the city to outlying areas F-Sa at 1,1:30, and 2am.

Ferries: Boats on the **Zürichsee** leave from Bürklipl. and range from a 90min. jaunt between isolated villages (every 30min., 11am-6:30pm, 5.40SFr, no getting off) to a "grand tour" (4-5hr., every hr., 9:30am-5:30pm, 20SFr). Ferries also leave from the top of the Bahnhofstr. harbor daily every 30min, 10am-9pm (3.60SFr). The Zürichsee authorities offer theme tours ranging from sunset and nightboats with Swiss music to summer serenade and oldies cruises (under 22SFr). There's even a chance for a jump-suited night with the "Swiss Elvises" Wednesday at 8pm during July on the Zürichsee (22SFr). For more information, call 482 10 91. On the **Limmat River,** boats run daily Apr.-Oct. (1hr., 6.80SFr). Eurailpass valid; reduced fare for *Tageskarte.*

Taxis: Hail a cab or call **Taxi 2000 Zürich** (tel. 444 44 44), **Zürich Taxi** (tel. 222 22 22), or **Taxi for the disabled** (tel. 272 42 42). 6SFr plus 3SFr per km.

Car Rental: Hertz (tel. 814 05 11), at the airport; Morgartenstr. 5 (tel. 242 84 84); Hardturmstr. 319 (tel. 272 50 50) runs 98SFr per day. **Avis** (tel. 241 70 70), at the airport, is much more expensive at 202SFr per day. **Europcar** (tel. 813 20 44; fax 813 49 00), at the airport; Josefstr. 53 (tel. 271 56 56); and Lindenstr. 33 (tel. 383 17 47). The train station tourist office also arranges car rental.

Parking: Metropolitan Zurich has many public parking garages; the Zurich police advise parking in the suburbs and taking a tram or train from there. **Universität Irchel** (tel. 634 11 11), near the large park on Winterthurstr. 181, and **Engi-Märt,** Seestr. 25 (tel. 202 11 42), are both suburban lots. City parking costs 2SFr for the 1st hr. and 2SFr for each subsequent 30min.; "Blue-Zone" 24hr. parking 10SFr; 0.50SFr per hr. in the suburbs. In the city, try the garages at the major department stores: **Jelmoli,** Steinmühlepl. (tel. 220 49 34), **Migros Limmatplatz,** Limmatstr.

152 (tel. 277 21 11), and **Globus** (tel. 221 33 11) at Löwenstr. (open M-F 7am-7:30pm, Th 7am-10pm, Sa 7am-5pm; 1hr. 2SFr, 2hr. 5SFr).

Bike Rental: At the baggage counter *(Gepäckexpedition Fly-Gepäck)* in the station. 19SFr per day; mountain bike 25SFr; 6SFr surcharge if you leave it at another station. Open daily 6:45am-7:45pm. **Free bike loans** at Globus (tel. (079) 336 36 10); Enge (tel. (079) 336 36 12); Oerlikon (tel. 336 36 13); Altstetten (tel. 336 36 14); and Hauptbahnhof (tel. 323 48 58). Passport and 20SFr deposit.

Hitchhiking: Hitchers to Basel, Geneva, Paris, or Bonn take streetcar #4: "Werdhölzli" from the station or take bus #33 to Pfingstweidstr. under the bridge. Those bound for Lucerne, Italy, and Austria take streetcar #9 or 14: "Bahnhof Wiedikon" and walk 1 block down Schimmelstr. to Silhölzli. For Munich, they often take streetcar #14 or 7:"Milchbuck" and walk to Schaffhauserstr. toward St. Gallen and St. Margarethen or take the S1/S8 train to Wiedikon and hitch at Seebahnstr. Hitchhiking is illegal on the freeway.

TOURIST AND FINANCIAL SERVICES

Tourist Offices: Main office in the station at Bahnhofpl. 15 (tel. 211 40 00; fax 215 40 44; email zhtourismus@access.ch; http://www.zurichtourism.ch; hotel reservation service tel. 215 40 40). Exit the station to Bahnhofpl. and walk left behind the taxi stand along the building. The über-friendly and multilingual staff stands ready to help with anything from biking directions to nightlife. Concert, movie, and bar information in German and English and copies of *Zürich News* and *Zürich Next*, which print restaurant and hotel listings. Decipher the German *ZüriTip*, a free entertainment newspaper, for tips on nightlife and alternative culture. Walking tours (see below). The special reservation desk finds rooms after 10:30am. Open Apr.-Oct. M-F 8:30am-9:30pm, Sa-Su 8:30am-8:30pm; Nov.-Mar. M-F 8:30am-7:30pm, Sa-Su 8:30am-6:30pm. For bikers and backpackers in Switzerland, the **Touring Club des Schweiz** (TCS), Alfred-Escher-Str. 38 (tel. 286 86 66), offers maps and travel info.

Tours: The tourist office leads frequent, expensive tours: the "Stroll through the Old Town" (2hr., 18SFr, May-Oct. M-F 2:30pm, Sa-Su 10am and 2:30pm); a standard tour of major sites (2hr., 29SFr, Apr.-Oct. 10am, noon, and 2pm; Nov.-Mar. 10am and 2pm); and the same tour plus a cable car and boat ride (2½hr., 39SFr, May-Oct. 9:30am).

Budget Travel: SSR, Ankerstr. 112 (tel. 297 11 11). Open M 12:30-pm, Tu-F 10am-6pm. Branch office at Bäckerstr. 40 (tel. 241 12 08). Arranges student package tours, provides STA travel help, issues ISIC cards, and helps with most travel questions. Open M 12:30-6:30pm, Tu-F 10am-6:30pm, Sa 10am-1pm. **Globe-Trotter Travel Service AG,** Rennweg 35 (tel. 213 80 80; fax 213 80 88), specializes in overseas travel. Caters to individual travelers, particularly campers (no package tours), and arranges European transport and accommodations. Student discounts, STA tickets, and ISIC cards available. Open M-F 9am-6pm, Sa 9am-2pm.

Consulates: U.K., Minervastr. 117, 8032 Zürich (tel. 383 65 60; fax 383 65 61), near Kreuzpl. Open M-F 9am-noon. **U.S.,** Dufourstr. 101 (tel. 422 25 66). Visas available only at the embassy in Bern. Open M-F 10am-1pm. **Australian, Canadian, Irish,** and **South African** citizens should contact their embassies in Bern. **New Zealand's** consulate is in Geneva.

Currency Exchange: At the main train station. Cash advances with DC, MC, Visa, and a photo ID. Open 6:30am-10:45pm. **Credit Suisse,** Bahnhofstr. 53, charges 2.50SFr commission. Open M-F 9am-6pm, Th 9am-7pm, Sa 9am-4pm. **Swiss Bank,** Bahnhofstr. 45 and 70, also charges 2.50SFr, but its ATMs take both MC and Visa. Other branches at Paradepl. and Bellevupl. (open M-F 9am-5:30pm). **ATMs** are all over the city, but most only take MC.

American Express: Uraniastr. 14, CH-8023 (tel. 228 77 77; fax 228 77 00). Mail held. Travel services. Checks cashed and exchanged, but limited banking services. ATM. Open M-F 8:30am-6pm, Sa 9am-1pm. Traveler's check toll-free **emergency line** (tel. 0800/55 01 00).

LOCAL SERVICES

Luggage Storage: At the station. Lockers 4SFr and 8SFr per day. Luggage watch 5SFr at the *Gepäck* counter. Open 6am-10:50pm.

Bookstores: Librairie Payot, Bahnhofstr. 9, has a large selection of original-language English and French literature. Also has travel books, including *Let's Go.* Open M noon-6:30pm, Tu-F 9am-6:30pm, Sa 9am-4pm. **Travel Bookshop** and **Travel Maps,** Rindermarkt 20 (tel. 252 38 83), have...travel books and travel maps. Open M 1-6:30pm, Tu-F 9am-6:30pm, Sa 9am-4pm. **Buchhandlung zum Rennwegtor,** Oetenbachg. 11 (etl. 221 39 19), in the *Altstadt,* has a fine selection of English books and biographies. Open M-F 9am-8pm, Sa 9am-4pm.

Libraries: Zentralbibliothek, Predigerpl. (tel. 261 72 72). Open M-F 8am-8pm, Sa 8am-5pm. **Pestalozzi Library,** Zähringerstr. 17 (tel. 261 78 11), has foreign magazines and newspapers. Open June-Sept. M-F 10am-7pm, Sa 10am-2pm; Oct.-May M-F 10am-7pm, Sa 10am-4pm. Reading room open M-F 9am-8pm, Sa 9am-5pm.

Bi-Gay-Lesbian Organizations: Homosexuelle Arbeitsgruppe Zürich (HAZ), Sihlquai 67, P.O. Box 7088, CH-8023 (tel. 271 22 50), offers a library, meetings, and the free newsletter *InfoSchwüll* (open Tu-F 7:30-11pm, Su noon-2pm and 6-11pm). **Frauenzentrum Zürich,** Matteng. 27 (tel. 272 85 03), provides information for lesbians. Ask the tourist office for **Zürich Gay Guide,** listing groups, discos, saunas, bars, and restaurants.

Laundromat: Self-Service Wachari, Weinbergstr. 37 (tel. 242 99 14). Wash and dry 5kg for 10.20SFr. Open M-Sa 7am-10pm, Su 10:30am-10pm. Other branches at Müllerstr. 55; Matteng. 29; Badenstr. 655; and Birmendorferstr. 221.

Public Showers and Toilets: At the train station. Toilets 1.50SFr. Showers 10SFr. Open daily 6am-midnight.

24-Hour Pharmacy: Theaterstr. 14 (tel. 252 56 00), on Bellevuepl.

EMERGENCIES AND COMMUNICATIONS

Emergencies: Police: tel. 117. **Fire:** tel. 118. **Ambulance:** tel. 144; English spoken. **Medical Emergency:** tel. 261 61 00. **Rape Crisis Line:** tel. 291 46 46. **First Aid:** tel. 361 61 61.

Internet Access: Internet Café, Uraniastr. 3 (tel. 210 33 11; fax 210 33 13; email info@cafe.ch), in the Urania Parkhaus. Access to World Wide Web and email 0.25SFr per min. Open M 10am-6pm, Tu-Th 10am-midnight, F-Sa 10am-2am, Su 10am-11pm. **Cybergate,** at STARS (opposite the Bahnhofpl. tourist office), combines a snappy American atmosphere with a taco-munching, Swiss, cyberjunkie crowd. 20min. 5SFr, 1hr. 15SFr. Open daily 11:30am-11pm. Restaurant open 11am-midnight. AmEx, DC, MC, Visa.

Post Office: Main office, Kasernenstr. 95/97 (tel. 296 21 11). Tram #13, 14, or 31: "Kaserne." Open M-F 7:30am-8pm, Sa 8am-4pm. Additional emergency services and *Poste Restante* M-F 6:30-7:30am and 8-10:30pm, Sa 6:30-8am and 4-8pm, Su 11am-10:30pm. Address *Poste Restante* to: Sihlpost, Kasernenstr., Postlagernde Briefe, CH-8021 Zürich. **Branches** throughout the city. **Postal code:** CH-8021. **Telephone Code:** 01.

■ Accommodations and Camping

There are a few budget accommodations in Zurich, and these bargain basement way stations often emulate the ritzy hotels that made Switzerland famous. They're not quite five-star, but they are clean, comfortable, and easily in reach of Zurich's extensive public transportation system. Reserve at least a day in advance, especially during the summer.

Jugendherberge Zürich (HI), Mutschellenstr. 114 (tel. 482 35 44; fax 480 17 27). Trains S-1 or S-8: "Bahnhof Wollishofen" (Eurailpass and Swisspass valid). Take tram #7 (dir: Wollishofen): "Morgantal" and walk 5min. back toward Zurich along Mutschellenstr. Huge, orderly, and impeccably clean, the hostel's pink stucco structure looms well outside the city center as a haven for globetrotters. The kiosk, lounge, and dining room are perhaps the largest and most comfortable in Switzerland. Tune in to CNN or watch one of the free nightly laser disc movies. 29SFr, non-members 34SFr. Subsequent nights 26.50SFr, non-members 31.50SFr. Doubles with bath 88SFr, non-members 98SFr. All-you–can-eat dinner 11SFr. Showers, sheets, breakfast, blow-dryers, and wake-up calls included. Lockers available, but bring your own padlock. 24hr. reception. Check-out 6-10am. No lockout. MC, Visa.

The City Backpacker-Hotel Biber, Niederdorfstr. 5 (tel. 251 90 15; fax 251 90 24). Take tram #3, 4, 6, 7, or 10: "Central" and walk through Niederdorfstr. until you reach the Spaghetti Factory. The hotel is down the street on the right. In the heart of the *Altstadt,* Biber boasts a (party-happy) rooftop deck as well as a prime location for tantalizing bar-hopping possibilities on the boisterous street. Rosenhof courtyard just behind Hotel Biber rolls with laughter and clinking glasses all night and hosts a small market on weekends. The busy *Bibers* (beavers) who staff the hotel are incredibly friendly and helpful. Pick up a copy of the very useful *Swiss Backpacker News* to supplement your itinerary. 4- to 6-bed dorms 29SFr; singles 65SFr; doubles 88SFr. In winter: dorms 27SFr; doubles 88 SFr. **Kitchen** access and showers included. Lockers available. Sheets 3SFr. **Laundry** 9SFr. **Internet** 2SFr per 10min. Reception 8am-noon and 3-10pm.

Justinus heim Zürich, Freudenbergstr. 146 (tel. 361 38 06; fax 362 29 82). Take tram #9 or 10: "Seilbahn Rigiblick" then take the hillside tram (by the Migros) uphill to the end. Perched on a hill overlooking Zurich, the student-run hotel features freshly painted rooms with huge windows providing a spectacular view. Singles 35SFr, with shower 50-60SFr; doubles 80-100SFr; triples 120-140SFr. Breakfast included. Reception 8am-9pm.

Zic-Zac Rock-Hotel, Marktg. 7 (tel. 261 21 81; fax 261 21 75; email rockhotel.ch@bluewin.ch). A night in "Pink Floyd" or "Led Zeppelin?" It's possible only at Zic-Zac. Funky furniture, trendy lighting, and rock 'n' roll superstar names set each room apart from each other room (trust us, "Bryan Adams" is *very* different from "The Rolling Stones"). All rooms have TV and phone. Singles 65SFr, with shower 85SFr; doubles 110SFr, 150SFr; studio 150SFr; triples 150SFr, 160SFr; quads with shower 240SFr. Breakfast included. Reception 24hr.

Martahaus, Zähringerstr. 36 (tel. 251 45 50; fax 251 45 40). Left out of the station, cross Balinkofbrücke, and take the 2nd (sharp) right after Limmatquai at the Seilgraben sign. Simple but comfortable with a pleasant dining room, lounge, and prime river location near nightlife. Private balconies on every floor. Dorms have partitions and curtains. Apr.-Oct. dorms 34SFr; singles 68SFr; doubles 96-100SFr; triples 120SFr. Nov.-Mar. dorms 33SFr; singles 62SFr; doubles 94SFr; triples 111SFr. Shower and breakfast included. Locker deposit 5SFr. Airport shuttle after 6:20am every hr. 20SFr. Reception 24hr. AmEx, DC, MC, Visa.

Studenthaus, Rötelstr. 100 (tel. 361 23 13; contact Heidi Aubert). Take tram #11: "Bucheggpl." and walk downhill 5min. on Rötelstr. Student housing turns into a backpacker haven in summer. Youthful feel with leafy potted plants, well-equipped VCR/gameroom, and a beautiful view of Zurich and the lake from the rooftop terrace. Singles 45SFr; doubles 60SFr. **Kitchen** available. **Laundry** 3SFr. Call ahead. Open July 15-Oct. 15.

Pension St. Josef, Hirschergraben 64/68 (tel. 251 27 57; fax 251 28 08). Left out of the train station, cross Bahnhofbrücke, trot up the steps at the Seilgraben sign, then head right a few hundred meters to the *Pension* (10min.). One of the most comfortable places to stay in Zurich. A 100-year-old, green-shuttered exterior encloses elegant, wood-paneled, gracefully silent rooms and a small 24hr. chapel. Cabel TV/VCR lounge. Singles 70SFr; doubles 105SFr; triples 140SF; quads 210SFr. Huge breakfast included. Reception M-S 7:30am-7pm, Su 7:30am-2pm.

Aparthotel, Karlstr. 5 (tel. 422 11 75; fax 383 65 80). Tram #2 or 4 (dir: Tiefenbrunner Bahnhof): "Fröhlichstr." This family-run hotel is a 3min. walk from the beach (though somewhat farther from Zurich, alas). The jazzy black-and-white exterior gives way to flowery rooms with ladybug chocolates on the pillows, each with cable TV. Jacuzzi/sauna. Singles 68-78SFr; doubles 98-128SFr. No smoking. Showers included. Breakfast 12SFr, but **Konditorei Kirch** across Seefeldstr. has freshly baked goods for less (open M-F 6:30am-6:30pm). Reception 8am-8pm. Check-in noon-9pm.

Foyer Hottingen, Hottingenstr. 31 (tel. 261 93 15; fax 261 93 19). Take tram #3 (dir: Kluspl.): "Hottingerpl." Surrounded by plants and biblical flourishes, the guardian nuns tend to admit **women only** in the large dorms (men can stay in 3- and 4-bed rooms). 5 languages spoken at the front desk. Sleek, modern facilities draw many women traveling solo. Dorms 25SFr, with partitions 30SFr; singles 55SFr; doubles 85SFr; triples 105SFr; quads 120SFr. Breakfast and **kitchen** access (with deposit) included. Reception 6am-midnight. Curfew midnight.

Hotel Splendid, Roseng. 5 (tel. 252 58 50; fax 262 61 40). Small hotel atop a very popular, loud, brash piano bar. Newly renovated rooms are small and sparsely furnished. Convenient for Niederdorfstr. bar-hopping or hanging out downstairs and listening to lounge music. Singles 56SFr; doubles 93SFr. Breakfast 10SFr. Showers included. Reception 5:30am-2am. Check-out 11am. AmEx, DC, MC, Visa.

Camping Seebucht, Seestr. 559 (tel. 482 16 12; fax 482 16 60). Take tram #7: "Wollishofen" and walk downhill toward the lakeside and right on Seestr. (5min.), or take bus #161 or 165: "Stadt Grenze" from Bürgklipl. at the lake end of Bahnhofstr. Far away, but scenic lakeside location makes up for it. Shop, terrace, and café on premises. Tents and caravans available. 8.50SFr per person; 12SFr per tent. Showers 2SFr. Reception 7:30am-noon and 3-10pm. Open May to late Sept.

■ Food

Zurich boasts over 1300 restaurants, covering every imaginable ethnic, dietary, and religious preference, but few are meant for budget travelers. The cheapest meals in Zurich are at *Würstli* stands, which sell sausage and bread for 3 to 4SFr, or at fruit and vegetable stands. For hearty appetites, Zurich prides itself on its *Geschnetzeltes mit Rösti*, slivered veal in cream sauce with hash-brown potatoes. Check out the *Swiss Backpacker News* (available at the tourist office and Hotel Biber) for more info on budget meals in Zurich. (See also **Food and Drink Sampling**, p. 352.)

RESTAURANTS

Mensa der Universität Zürich, Rämistr. 71 (tel. 632 62 11; fax 632 10 71). Streetcar #6: "ETH Zentrum" from Bahnhofpl. or take the red Polybahn uphill from Central Station. Exquisite cafeteria food in a posh, pastel room with plants and colonnades in Cafeteria Lichthof. Look at the bulletin boards in the university buildings for info on rides, apartments, rooms for rent, and events. Hot dishes 7.50SFr with ISIC card, salad buffet 6SFr. Open July 15-Oct. 21 M-F 11am-2pm; Oct. 22-July 14 M-F and alternate Sa 11am-2:30pm and 5-7:30pm. Mensa B open M-F 6:30am-7:30pm. **Mensa Polyterrasse** is just down the street at #101. 8.50SFr with ISIC. Open M-Sa 11:15am-1:30pm and 5:30-7:15pm. Self-service cafeteria open Oct. 22-July 14 M-F and alternate Sa 11am-2:30pm, July 15-Oct. 21 M-F 7am-5:30pm. Closed during winter vacations.

Zeughauskeller, Bahnhofstr. 28a (tel. 211 26 90), near Paradepl. This *Biergarten* features 17th-century knights from the Burgundy wars staring hungrily down from the walls. Serves Swiss specialties like fondue, *Rösti*, sausage, and *Bratwurst* (5-30SFr) from multilingual menus on long wooden tables. Outdoor seating affords prime people-watching. Open M-Sa 11:30am-10pm.

Restaurant Raclette-Stube, Zähringerstr. 16 (tel. 251 41 30), near Central Library. Swiss fondues are at their richest, largest, and cheapest in this tiny, candle-lit restaurant on the *Altstadt* outskirts. *Rösti* "side-dishes" are meals in themselves. All-you-can-eat fondue or *Raclette* 28.50SFr. Open 6-10:30pm. AmEx, MC, Visa.

Ban Song Thai Restaurant, Kirchg. 6 (tel. 252 33 31), near the Grossmünster. This tiny place in the *Altstadt* bursts with flavor. Specialties include fish, coconut *currigo,* and *pad thai.* Lunch buffet from 15SFr; all-you-can-eat 24.50SFr. Open M and Sa 6:30-11:30pm, Tu-F 11:30am-3pm and 6:30-11:30pm.

Rheinfelder Bierhalle, Niederdorfstr. 76 (tel. 251 54 64), in the *Altstadt.* At the narrow end of the food pyramid—the Rheinfelders liberally wield the meat cleaver and also serve up *Rösti* in all its variations. A local crowd enjoys the food and the self-proclaimed "cheapest beer in town" (from 2SFr). Simple Bürli 1.20SFr, bread 0.20SFr. Good for people- and party-watching. Entrees 11-30SFr. *Menüs* 15-28SFr. Open 9am-midnight.

Hiltl, Sihlstr. 28 (tel. 227 70 00; fax 227 70 07). Trade carrot sticks with the vegetarian elite at this swank restaurant, whose exterior is carpeted with grass that staid cows (models, of course) munch. Huge, scrumptious salad buffet (supposedly the best in Zurich, 3.80SFr per 100g) and fresh pastas are among the highlights. Entrees 14-25SFr. Open M-Sa 7am-11pm, Su 11am-11pm.

Gleich, Seefeldstr. 9 (tel. 251 32 03). Take tram #4 (dir: Tiefenbrunnen): "Opernhaus." Not enough green in Zurich? *Mais si!* This completely vegetarian restaurant and bakery may be the oasis you need. Although the interior is rather dark, the bright orange terrace glows cheerily beneath orange canopies. Try the delicious Gleich specialty, carmelized *Apfelpfannkuchen* (12.50SFr), or the fresh juices (3-4.50SFr). Salads ("create your own") 4.50-6.40SFr. Entrees 10-14SFr. *Menus* 14-19SFr. Open M-F 6am-9pm, Sa 7:30am-4pm.

Schalom Café Restaurant, Lavaterstr. 33 (tel. 201 14 76). Tram #5, 6, or 7: "Enge" on General Willis; then turn right on Lavaterstr. Don't let the tight security deter you—asking for some picture ID is a precaution (avoidable by calling ahead) due to slight religious tensions, not a cue to leave. Kosher delights from falafel (9.50SFr) to salmon (21SFr). Most items 10-30SFr. Open M-Th 11am-2:30pm and 6-10pm, F 11am-2:30pm.

Tres Kilos, Dufourstr. 175 (tel. 422 02 33), at Fröhlichstr. Mexican dishes (from 24.50SFr) served outside beneath a leafy trellis and inside on tables with sombrero-shaped ashtrays. Avocado salad (12.50SFr), beers including Corona (from 4SFr), and free chips and salsa set the mood. The *chile con carne* (26.50SFr) gets rave reviews. Open M-F 11:45am-2pm and 6pm-12:30am, Sa-Su 6pm-12:30am. AmEx, DC, MC, Visa.

Spaghetti Factory, Niederdorfstr. 5 (tel. 251 94 00). Come to this chain restaurant only when howling with late night hunger. Cheap food abounds, with (surprise) spaghetti from 12.50SFr and salads from 9.50SFr. Open 11am-2am. MC, Visa.

Bodega Española, Münsterg. 15 (tel. 251 23 10). Catalan delights abound in this atmospheric Spanish restaurant founded in 1892. Traditional dishes from 15.50SFr, mouth-watering salads 8.50SFr. Open 10am-midnight.

CAFÉS

Sprüngli Confiserie Café, Paradepl. (tel. 224 47 11; fax 224 47 35). A Zurich landmark, founded by one of the original Lindt chocolate makers who sold his shares to his brother. A chocolate heaven, the *Confiserie-Konditorei* lays out exquisite confections and concocts delicious sundaes (2-8SFr) with homemade ice cream and sherbet. You can smell emanations of chocolate as soon as you hit Paradepl. Lunch *Menüs* 19.50-24.50SFr. Confectionery open M-F 7:30am-8pm, Sa 8am-4pm. Café open M-F 7:30am-6:30pm, Sa 7:30am-5pm.

Zahringer Café, Zahringerpl. 11 (tel. 252 05 00), across the square from the library. Sip coffee, frappes, or other caffeinated beverages with a hip young crowd. Opens early on weekends so late-night revelers can top off the night with requisite grease (*Rösti* topped with a fried egg 13SFr). Open M 6pm-midnight, Tu-F 8am-midnight, Sa-Su 5am-midnight.

Gran-Café, Limmatquai 66 (tel. 252 31 19). Great views abound at this people-watching place *par excellence.* Enjoy delicious, dairy-fresh ice cream (from 4SFr) while watching the sun set over the Zürichsee, or decipher the intriguing *Kaffee Lexikon* (Dictionary of Coffee). Entrees from 9SFr, *Menüs* from 11.80SFr. Open M-F 6am-midnight, Sa-Su 7:30am-midnight.

Infinito Espresso Bar, Sihlstr. 20. Chic, angular bar with a coffee selection broader than broad: Espresso from 3SFr, beers from 6SFr, sandwiches and snacks 4-9SFr. Open M and W-F 7am-9pm, Sa 8:30am-5:30pm.

Café Odeon, Limmatquai 2, Bellevuepl. Frequented by a famous gay and mixed crowd, Odeon provides a popular place to chatter, chat, and grab an espresso. Open Su-Th 7am-2am, F-Sa 7am-4am.

MARKETS AND BAKERIES

Two bakery chains that you can find throughout Zurich, **Kleiner** and **Buchmann,** offer freshly baked bread, sweets (whole apricot pies around 9SFr), and *Kuchen*

(*Bürli* rolls 0.50SFr, *Chäsechüechli* (cheesecake) 2SFr) for reasonable prices (open M-F 6:30am-6:30pm). The 24-hour vending machine in the Shop-Ville beneath the train station has pasta, juice, and other staples, but you may feel uncomfortable heading over there alone at night.

Farmer's Market, at Burklipl. Fruit, flowers, and veggies. Tu and F 7am-noon.

Co-op Super Center. The Co-op to end all Co-ops straddles the Limmat River next to the train station. Watch for free promotional treats. Open M-F 7am-8pm, Sa 7am-4pm. **Branch** at Albisstr. 54, next to the tram stop near the hostel. Open M-F 8am-12:30pm and 1:30-6:30pm, Sa 7:30am-4pm. Another **branch** at Bahnhof Enge. Open M-F 7:30am-6:30pm, Sa 8am-4pm.

Migros, Mutschellenstr. 189, near the hostel (open M-F 8am-6:30pm, Sa 8am-4pm with adjoining café); under the train station in Shop-Ville (open M-F 7am-8pm, Sa-Su 8am-8pm); and at Bahnhof Enge (open M-F 7am-6:30pm, Sa 7:30am-12:15pm).

■ Sights

It's virtually inconceivable to start your tour of Zurich anywhere except the stately neon **Bahnhofstraße,** just outside of the *Bahnhof* at the head of the Zürichsee. Shaded by the trees along this causeway of capitalism, shoppers peer into the windows of Cartier, Rolex, Chanel, and Armani. One square meter of the street will run you 250,000SFr; start saving up for that lemonade stand. To avoid the I'll-just-charge-it urge, cross the Zürichsee and you'll find yourself in one of the many more affordable side streets in the *Altstadt,* where antique, curiosity, and second-hand shops dominate. **Spiegelgasse** is Zurich's oddly bureaucratic memory lane. Commemorative plaques honor the greats Wladimir Illitsch Uljanow (aka "Lenin") at #14 and German author Georg Büchner at #12. The "Cabaret Voltaire" (former haunt of Hans Arp, Tristan Tzara, and Hugo Ball) at #3 is now a funky bar called "Castel Dada." Halfway down Bahnhofstr. lies **Paradeplatz,** the town center, under which Zurich's banks reputedly keep their gold reserves. At the Zürichsee end, **Bürkliplatz** hosts a colorful Saturday **market** *(May-Oct. 7:30am-3:30pm),* with vendors hawking everything from vinyl records to elephantine cowbells to Swiss Smurfs. Across Quaibrücke from Bürkliplatz, locals stroll and rollerblade along the tree-lined Uto-Quai, emptying bags of stale bread for the Zürichsee swans and their June cygnets.

Two giant cathedrals stonily face off in the *Altstadt.* To the east loom the diademed twin towers of the **Grossmünster,** built by Charlemagne on the site of a spirited deer chase. *(Church open Mar. 15-Oct. 9am-6pm; Nov.-Mar. 14 10am-4pm.)* The blood-red and cobalt-blue stained-glass windows designed in 1932 by **Augusto Giacometti** (not to be confused with his uncle Alberto) brighten this otherwise forbidding church. Zwingli spearheaded the Swiss Reformation from its pulpit. A splendid copper-colored organ with golden angels riding fluted pipes graces the nave of the church. Venture downstairs to the 12th-century crypt to see Charlemagne's statue and seven-foot sword. The **Kreuzgang** (cloisters) lies to the left of the main entrance. *(Open M-Sa 9am-4:30pm.)* Across the river rises the steeple of the 13th-century **Fraumünster,** founded in the 9th century by the daughters of the local sovereign. The church holds one transept window by Giacometti and a magnificent series of stained-glass scenes by **Marc Chagall.** Asked to design the windows in 1970 despite his Jewish ancestry, Chagall created these five gorgeous Old and New Testament-inspired panels. From left to right, they are the Window of the Prophets, Jacob's Window, the Window of Christ, the Window of Zion, and the Window of Law. The crazily expressionist win-

ZURICH REGION

Mad Cow

Plastic, clay, and paper cows have sprouted on the sidewalks, elevators, balconies, and walls of Zurich in a fit of obsession dedicated to the bovine. No one seems to be able to explain the phenomenon, other than a government-organized attempt to enliven the city and make tourists happy. *Let's Go* feels very happy, and can only hope that the temporary insanity will last beyond this summer. Moo.

dows pool green, blue, yellow and orange light to an intense, jagged effect. Around the Fraumünster on Fraumünsterstr., a mural decorates the Gothic archway in the courtyard. On the right, angels embrace the three decapitated patron saints of Zurich, who clutch their impossibly placid heads in their hands. On a more pedestrian note, the nearby **St. Peter's Church** has the largest clock face in Europe; the second hand reaches nearly 12 feet. Just down Thermeng. from St. Peter's, the recently excavated Roman baths of the original, first-century customs post Turricum lie underneath the iron stairway. Up the steps at the intersection of Strehlg., Rennweg, and Glockeng. is the park **Lindenhof**, the original site of Turricum and the birthplace of Zurich. Play some giant chess under the trees, then see the Zurich that inspired Nietzsche, Joyce, and Lenin.

Directly opposite Lindenhof, the **University of Zurich** presides over the city. The school was the first in Europe to admit women, and home, albeit briefly, to Einstein and the inventors of the electron microscope. Trams #6, 9, and 10: "ETH" uphill from the university run to the **graves of James Joyce** and **Elias Canetti** in the Fluntern Cemetery. (Open May-Aug. 7am-8pm; Mar.-Apr. and Sept.-Oct. 7am-7pm; Nov.-Feb. 8am-5pm. Free.) The **Zürich Zoo**, Zürichbergstr. 221 (tel. 252 71 00), lies next door, packing over 2000 species of animals. (Open Mar.-Oct. 8am-6pm; Nov.-Feb. 8am-5pm. 14SFr, students 7SFr.) Take tram #5 or 6: "Zoo."

Botanical buffs will want to sniff out Zurich's many gardens and parks. The University's **Botanical Garden,** Zollikerstr. 107 (tel. 385 44 11), houses such oddities as the blue Himalayan poppy and a huge aquarium filled with carnivorous plants. (Open Mar.-Sept. M-F 7am-7pm, Sa-Su 8am-6pm; Oct.-Feb. M-F 8am-6pm, Sa-Su 8am-5pm.) Take tram #2 or 4: "Höschg." Even the horticulturally challenged will enjoy strolling through clumps of myrtle and lavander, lounging on the surrounding grassy hills, and watching lily-leaves bob up and down. Escape from the city on tram #3 to "Hubertus," where you can forage through the jungle courtesy of the **Stadtgärtnerei,** Sackzeig 25-27 (tel. 492 14 23). (Open 9-11:30am and 1:30-4:30pm. Free.) This greenhouse worthy of Dr. Livingston shelters hundreds of varieties of tropical and sub-tropical plants, including an eye-catching display of foggy-smelling orchids. The lush, perfect-for-a-picnic **Rieterpark**, overlooking the city, creates a romantic backdrop for the **Museum Rietberg.** Take tram #7: "Museum Rietburg."

Uetliberg, also known as the "top of Zurich," is the king of picnic spots, with a view of Zurich's urban sprawl on one side and a view of pristine countryside on the other. The flat walk from Uetliberg to Felsenegg is a peaceful escape from the city's bustle. From Zurich's Hauptbahnhof, take the train to "Uetliberg" (15min., every 30min., discount with *Tageskarte*), then follow the yellow signs to Felsenegg (1½hr.). A cable car runs from Felsenegg to Adliswil, where a train returns to Zurich. (Buy tickets at any train or cable car station or at most hotels. Free with Eurailpass.)

■ Museums

Zurich has channelled much of its banking wealth into its universities and museums, fostering very smart people and outstanding collections. The larger institutions hold the core of the city's artistic and historical wealth, but many of the smaller museums are equally spectacular. The specialized schools of the university, scattered throughout the city, open the doors of their museum collections to the public.

Kunsthaus Zürich, Heimpl. 1 (tel. 251 67 65), at Rämistr. Take tram #3, 5, 8, or 9: "Kunsthaus." One of Switzerland's most extensive collections of 15th- and 20th-century art. Consider using a map; an inadvertent jump from Dalí to medieval devotionals can be disturbing (or exciting). Cézanne and Picasso hold their own in the sprawling rooms of modern art. Works by Klee, Chagall, and the Dada artists, as well as an entire loft devoted to Alberto Giacometti and his intriguing spindly sculptures. Contemporary design within the museum itself using everything from cardboard boxes to wires makes for an extraordinary experience. Open Tu-Th 10am-9pm, F-Su 10am-5pm. 4SFr, students and disabled 3SFr. Su free. Added charge for special exhibits.

Da, Da, Da

The silent walls of the *Altstadt*'s Spiegelg. 3 witnessed one of Zurich's most rebellious movements. The infamous years between the world wars offered no lull for the city's citizens, as a group of pissed young artists spilled their creativity into the craziest forms of art, yielding *Dadaism*, an art which refused to be art, and a style whose guiding principle was confusion and paradox humor. Dada's aim is to provoke a rude awakening from standardized thought and bourgeois preconceptions. Dada is said to have derived its name alternately from the French word for "hobby-horse," which Hugo Ball selected by sticking a penknife into a German-French dictionary, or from the refrain of two Romanian founders of the movement, who used to mutter "Da, da" ("yes, yes" in Romanian). Distinguished painter/sculptor Alberto Giacometti, in a sojourn in Zurich, entered the demonstration—it is said that one day, he opened the door of Cabaret Voltaire, stepped out, shouted, "Viva Dada!" at the top of his lungs, and disappeared as promenadeurs on the Limmatquai stopped in their tracks. It is likely that, the next morning, Giacometti woke up in his own sick. Lenin reputedly enjoyed Cabaret Voltaire. Today's Cabaret Voltaire is preserved (no formaldehyde, thanks) in the entrails of the disco/bar Castel Dada (see **Entertainment and Nightlife**, p. 353). If you decide to visit Dadaland, however, *Let's Go* does not recommend waking up in your own sick.

E.G. Bührle Collection, Zollikerstr. 172 (tel. 422 00 86; fax 422 03 47). Tram #2 or 4 (dir: Tiefenbrunnen): "Wildbachstr." From Seefeldstr. turn left on Münchaldenstr., walk uphill, and turn right on Zollikerstr. Bührle's mansion overlooking the Zürichsee holds a prestigious collection of French Impressionists such as Seurat, Manet, Van Gogh, Toulouse-Lautrec, and Cézanne, Dutch Masters like Ruysdael and Rembrandt, along with medieval figures and a Grecian urn or two. Small and accessible, this museum may hold Zurich's finest collection of artwork. Open Tu and F 2-5pm, W 5-8pm. 9SFr, students 3SFr.

Museum Rietberg, Gablerstr. 15 (tel. 202 45 28; fax 202 52 01). Tram #7: "Museum Rietberg." An exquisite collection of Asian, African, and other non-European art housed in 2 mansions set in the Rieter Park. **Park-Villa Rieter** features internationally acclaimed exhibits of Chinese, Japanese, and Indian works. Open Tu-Sa 1-5pm, Su 10am-5pm. **Villa Wesendonck** stores most of the permanent collection, including exquisite gold figurines from Tibet, a multi-armed Shiva from India, and a somewhat terrifying collection of African masks. Open Tu-Su 10am-5pm. 5SFr, students 3SFr. Main exhibitions and collections, including a great collection of Indian paintings showing love-making and feast-devouring in exquisite, gold-tinted detail, 5SFr, students and seniors 3SFr. Special exhibits 12SFR, 6SFr.

Museum für Gestaltung (Museum of Design), Ausstellungsstr. 60 (tel. 446 22 11; fax 446 22 33). Tram #4 or 13: "Museum für Gestaltung." Outstanding photography, film, and design exhibits. Past endeavors include shows on steam-shovel art, 100 years of Swiss commercials, Beat Generation, and giant corn. Open Tu and Th-Fr 10am-6pm, W 10am-9pm, Sa-Su 10am-5pm. Special collections by appointment. 7SFr, students 4SFr; gallery only 5SFr, 3SFr.

Museum Bellerive, Höschg. 3 (tel. 383 43 76; fax 383 44 68). Take tram #4 (dir: Tiefenbrunnen): "Höschg." and walk right on Höschg. Located opposite the gorgeous Zurich Ballet House, this museum specializes in constantly changing "out-of-the-ordinary" exhibits. No X-Files displays, but the truth is out there. Past exhibits include "Travel in Silk," "Lingerie," and ceramic, pottery, and multimedia works by ateliers. Open June 13 to Sept. 13 Tu and Th-Su 11am-7pm, W 11am-9pm. 6SFr, students 3SFr.

Völkerkundemuseum, Pelikanstr. 40 (tel. 634 90 11). Tram #2 or 9: "Sihlstr." Snugly ensconced in "Park zur Katz," this small museum features music and religious artifacts from non-European cultures. From Lapplander shoes to antlers to totem poles to a candle-lit Tibetan sanctuary, the museum houses a varied collection. Past

ZURICH REGION

exhibits include a comparison of African and contemporary Züricher tattoos. Open Mar.-Sept. M-F 7am-7pm, Sa-Su 7am-6pm; Oct.-Feb. M-F 8am-6pm, Sa-Su 8am-5pm.

Schweizerisches Landesmuseum, Museumstr. 2 (tel. 218 65 11; fax 211 29 49). Housed in a castle behind the *Hauptbahnhof,* the Swiss National Museum may be old news for field-tripping Swiss schoolkids, but visitors gawk happily at exhibits dating from prehistory to the present. Skip the rather generic 1st floor of medieval artifacts to inspect the intricately wood-panelled, gnome-like rooms from Wiggan castle. A mechanized, 16th-century, gold astrological globe, the weapons used by Ulrich Zwingli in the Battle of Kappel in which he died (1531), and a tiny bejeweled clock, complete with a golden skeleton morbidly pointing to the hour all await. Open Tu-Su 10:30am-5pm. Free. Special exhibit prices vary (about 8SFr).

Paleontology Museum and the **Zoological Museum,** Karl-Schmid-Str. 4 (tel. 634 38 38; fax 634 20 71). Tram #6, 9, or 10: "ETH." Home to a mammoth, a moose and an elephant-sized armadillo, as well as a menagerie of mandibled day-glo bugs (also happily inert), these museums could cast the next Spielberg movie. The museums take a hands-on approach, with interactive computer exhibits and microscope viewing stations. Open Tu-F 9am-5pm, Sa-Su 10am-4pm. Free.

Museum of Classical Archaeology, Rämistr. 73 (tel. 257 28 20). Tram #6, 9, or 19: "ETH." A tiny museum on the 1st floor of the archeological lecture halls with an extensive collection of Greek vases and coins—use the microscope to peruse both sides—and Mesopotamian and Egyptian artifacts. Temporary exhibits in the basement next to statue storage. Open Tu-F 1-6pm, Sa-Su 11am-5pm. Free.

Mühlerama Museum, Seefeldstr. 231 (tel. 422 76 60). Tram #2 or 4: "Wildbachstr." Originally a brewery, this fully-operational mill has been processing grain since 1913. Grind wheat on an exercise bike or see the flour fly and the wooden parts spin as the miller takes you through the art of making *Brot* (bread). Mainly for kiddie food-lovers. Open Tu-Sa 2-5pm, Su 1:30-6pm. 7SFr, students 5SFr.

Zinnfiguren Museum, Obere Zäune 19 (tel. 262 57 20), captures a Swiss facet of European history on 2D tin figures as flat soldiers march through Russia and Egypt. A charmingly dinky museum. Open M, W, and Sa 2-4pm, Su 11am-3pm.

FOOD AND DRINK SAMPLING MUSEUMS

Zurich's many food and beverage industries offer visitors a behind-the-scenes look and a taste of the action. The **Lindt and Sprüngli Chocolate Factory,** Seestr. 204 (tel. 716 22 33), welcomes visitors to its **chocolate museum** with an open box of Lindt chocolate and a movie about wonky chocolate machines. The chocolate spree ends as visitors leave with free boxes of—what else?—souvenir Lindt chocolate. (Open W-F 10am-noon and 1-4pm. All exhibits in German. Free.) To reach the factory, take the train S-1 or S-8: "Kilchberg" from the Hauptbahnhof (5.40SFr) or take bus #165: "Kilchberg." From the stop, take a right out of the station, a left down the first street, and an immediate right for a three-minute walk straight to the factory. The **Johann Jacobs Museum: Collection on the Cultural History of Coffee,** Seefeldquai 17 (tel. 388 61 51), commemorates that foundation of modern civilization and kernel of all that is good and right and wholesome in the world, the coffee bean. The museum houses black-box display cases into which visitors peer to see historical and modern coffee pots. The place is caffeinated down to the stair-rug patterned with the infamous bean. At the end of the exhibits, enjoy a cuppa joe in the villa's drawing room. (Open F-Sa 2-5pm, Su 10-5pm. All exhibits in German; summaries in English. Free.) Take tram #2 or 4: "Feldeggstr." and walk two minutes down Feldeggstr. The museum is on the right at the end of the street.

■ Entertainment and Nightlife

Bathing areas line the shores of the Zürichsee. **Strandbad Mythenquai** (tel. 201 00 00) lies along the Western shore. Take tram #7: "Brunaustr." and follow the signs (open M-F 9am-8pm, Sa-Su 9am-7:30pm; 5SFr). Many movie theaters offer **English films** with German and French subtitles (marked E/d/f). For information, check the huge posters that decorate the streets, the cinemas at Bellevuepl. or Hirschenpl., or

Zürich News and *ZüriTip*. Films generally run 11SFr. After July 18, the open-air cinema at Zürichhorn (tram #4 or 2: "Frölichstr.") attracts huge crowds to its lakefront. To ensure a seat, arrive at least an hour before the 9pm showing (15SFr) or reserve a seat at the open-air ticket counter at the Bellevue tram station. Niederdorfstr. rocks as the epicenter of Zurich's nightlife. Due to the high number of strip clubs, however, women may not want to walk alone in this area at night. On Friday and Saturday nights during the summer, Hirschenpl. on Niderhofstr. hosts sword-swallowers and other daredevil street performers from around the world. Other hot spots include Münsterg. and Limmatquai, both lined with cafés and bars that overflow with people well into the wee hours of the morning. Beer in Zurich tends to be extremely expensive (from 6SFr). **Kaufleuter,** the most posh and popular bar in Zurich charges a 20SFr cover before you even hit the bar. Tourists and locals whose wallets have passed out before they've downed their first beer often buy alcohol at Migros or along Niederhofstr. and head to the benches and fountain of Rosenhofpl.

Casa Bar, Münsterg. 30 (tel. 262 20 02), a tiny, crowded pub with 1st-rate live jazz. Drink prices hasten poverty (beer from 9.50SFr). No cover. Open daily 7pm-2am.

Oepfelchammer, Rindermarkt 12 (351 23 36). A popular Swiss wine bar (3-5SFr per glass) with low wooden ceilings and crossbeams, all covered with initials and messages from 200 years of merry-making. Those who climb through the rafters and drink a free glass of wine through the beams get to engrave their names on the furniture. It's harder than it looks. Open Tu-Sa 11am-midnight.

Luv, Dufourstr. 43 (tel. 262 40 07), entrance around the corner on Kreuzstr. Take tram #2 or 4: "Kreuzstr." Groove on down to Luv for some musical "psychic entanglement." With its bizarre music (watch for Tuesday SciFi jazz night or Wednesday Laundry Day) and dance floor, Luv attracts all types, from spike-heeled to spike-headed. Beer starts at 6SFr. Tu and Su 5SFr, F-Sa 13SFr. Open Su-Th 8pm-2am, F-Sa 9pm-4am. Concerts at 9:30pm.

Bar Odeon, Limmatquai 2 (tel. 251 55 20), Bellevuepl. Thornton Wilder and Vladimir Lenin used to get sloshed in this posh, atmospheric, artsy joint. Great street-side seating. Beers from 6SFr. Open 7am-2am, F-Sa 7am-4am.

Oliver Twist, Rindermarkt 6 (tel. 252 47 10). Please, sir, could I have some more…Anglophiles? English-speaking crowd enjoys Guinness (7SFr per pint) and British beers in this pukka English pub with an Irish twist. Celebrates St. Patrick's Day and South African and Australian National Days. Open M-F 11:30am-midnight, Sa 3pm-midnight, Su 4pm-midnight.

Castel DADA, Münsterg. 26 (tel. 266 10 10), next to Casa Bar. At the former site of the "Cabaret Voltaire," this lively bar and disco keeps the inner chamber intact. Beers from 6.50SFr. Open Su-Th 6pm-2am, F-Sa 8pm-2am. Disco open until 4am.

Limmatbar, Limmatquai 82 (tel. 261 65 30). Tiny, candle-lit, and cozy bar attracts weekend crowds of locals. Beers from 8.30SFr, cocktails 16SFr. No cover. Open Su-Th 9pm-2am, F-Sa 9pm-4am.

Cinecittà Bar Club, Stadthausquai 13 (tel. 211 57 52). Sleek, young, black-leather-clad Swiss clamor to enter this male-dominated bar on the Limmat banks. Wacky theme nights include Pizza Disco, AmaZone, and Gay Happening on Sunday. Fight with all of Zurich's teenagers to get in. F-Sa 8SFR; obligatory coat check. Open M 9pm-4am, Tu-Th 6-9pm, F-Sa 9pm-5am.

Rockfabrik, Niederdorfstr. 13 (tel. 251 42 52). Serves cheap beer under a tip-tilted "Welcome to Partyland" neon sign. Beers from 5SFr, martinis 8SFr. Open Su-Th noon-2:30am, F-Sa noon-4:30am.

Emilio's Bagpiper Bar, Zähringerstr. 11 (tel. 252 05 00). A gay bar (the 1st in Zurich) serving good drinks, snacks, and occasional male strip shows. (Nice pipes!) Extremely crowded on weekends. Beers 4.30SFr. Open daily 3pm-midnight.

■ Near Zurich: Einsiedeln

An hour by train from Zwingli's Protestant pulpit in Zurich, the tiny town of Einsiedeln attracts pilgrims from all over Europe to its spectacular cathedral and legendary Black Madonna. A surprising blend of enlightened Catholicism, regional pride, and rabid capitalism, this happy Alpine valley is home to one of the biggest Baroque buildings in Switzerland, and, just centimeters away, hordes of souvenir booths hawking plastic holy water bottles and giant rosaries.

ORIENTATION AND PRACTICAL INFORMATION Trains leave **Zurich** for **Wädenswil** every 20 minutes, connecting to Einsiedeln 15 minutes later. Einsiedeln's **tourist office,** Hauptstr. 85 (tel. 418 44 88; fax 418 44 80), distributes hiking maps and cathedral brochures in German. Turn left at the station and walk down the main street for about seven minutes. (Open M-F 9am-noon and 2-5:30pm, Sa 9am-noon and 2-4pm.) Change **currency** at **Raiffeisbank,** Hauptstr. 19. (Open M-F 8am-noon and 1:30-5:30pm.) The **ATM** outside accepts MC. **Credit Suisse** (tel. 418 91 11), just behind the tourist office, provides 24-hour ATM service and accepts MC and Visa. (Open M-F 8am-noon and 1:30-5pm; W 8am-noon and 1:30-6pm. 2.50SFr charge for currency change.) Check your email at Einsiedeln's **Internet Bar** (tel. 422 14 50) just off Hauptstr. (2SFr per 10min., 12SFr for 1hr. Open M-W 11am-1:30pm and 4:30-10pm, F 4:30-10pm, Sa 4-10pm, Su 4-8pm.) The **post office** is in the train station. (Open M-F 7:30am-noon and 1:30-6pm, Sa 7:45-11am.) The **postal code** is CH-8840. The **telephone code** is 055.

ACCOMMODATIONS AND FOOD You won't need more than half a day to see all of Einsiedeln, but rooms abound for sleepy pilgrims deciding to stay the night. The only truly budget accommodation is **Schweizer Jugend und Bildungs Zentrum** (SJBZ; tel. 412 91 74), about 15 minutes from town. Facing town from the cathedral entrance, turn right and follow the road heading to Ybrig. After about seven minutes, make a left just past the cemetery at the purple SJBZ sign. The hostel is a few meters beyond the Lincoln Restaurant sign. Rooms open onto beautiful lake and valley views marred only by the unfortunate 60s architecture. Reservations are advisable from June to August, when swarms of school groups descend upon the hostel. (Singles 26SFr with breakfast, 39SFr with two meals, 59SFr with three. Reduction of 2SFr after 3 nights. Reception 8am-6:30pm. Checkout 10am.) Across from the cathedral, **Hotel Sonne** (tel. 412 28 21; fax 412 41 45) offers cozy, rustic rooms with forest murals, pine beams, radios, and phones. (Singles 45SFr; doubles 70SFr. Breakfast included. Reception open 8:30am-10pm. AmEx, MC, Visa.) The **Hotel Rot-Hut** (tel. 412 22 41; fax 412 71 37), also across from the cathedral, provides a snug and affordable resting place for the night. (Singles 65SFr; doubles 100SFr. Breakfast included.) Down the street from the tourist office on Hauptstr., **Restaurant Glocke** (tel. 412 24 83) blares perky Swiss music onto the street, luring tourists into its cheery, bratwurst-happy interior. (Schnitzel and salad 12.50SFr. Open Tu 5-11pm, W-Sa 11am-11pm, Su 11am-4pm.) To the left of the cathedral, **Restaurant Juanito** (tel. 412 27 41) offers spicy Mexican food at bargain prices set to funk music, a fave with young Einsiedelners. (Starters 4-7SFr. Entrees 12-19SFr. Open Tu-W and F-Sa 6pm-midnight, Su all day; May-Aug. 10am-3pm and 6pm-midnight.) For a glass of relaxing Haldengut beer, **Doc Holliday's Pub 'n' Dancing** (tel. 412 14 41) just off Hauptstr. provides a vibrant, youthful atmosphere. (Open daily 4pm-midnight.) If baked goods are your desire, the **Goldapfel**, 1 Kronenstr., has been browning pastries and gingerbreads (including the local Einsiedler Schafböcke) for the past 120 years. (Open daily 1:30-5pm.) **Migros** looms huge and shining behind the station, offering reasonably priced groceries and its usual, simple fare at the restaurant. (Open M-Th 8am-6:30pm, F 8am-10pm, Sa 8am-4pm.)

SIGHTS AND ENTERTAINMENT To find the **Klosterkirche** (cathedral), take a right onto the small lane in front of the train station and a left on Hauptstr. Go straight for a while and you'll end up there. Consecrated in 1735, the cathedral's Milanese exterior with twin lemon-shaped domes dominate the surrounding hills. The Asam brothers dreamed up the interior, its ornate Baroque ceiling overflowing with plump, blushing cherubs floating by an overwhelming pastel background of lavender, green, and gold. Priests welcome pilgrims with services in the Madonna chapel. Don't forget to bring coins if you feel inspired to light a candle for meditation (1SFr). The three-foot **Black Madonna,** resplendent in Royal Spanish attire and set against a glowing backdrop of golden clouds, is the cathedral's centerpiece. Years of smoky candlelight and underground storage during the French Invasion darkened the figure. An Austrian craftsman once restored her natural color, but locals, refusing to accept the change in hue, had her painted black again.

Einsiedeln's other attractions include a **monastery** with horse stables and a renowned **library** (tours Su at 4pm); a **panorama** of Jesus' crucifixion (3.50SFr); and the **largest crèche in the world,** with 450 carved kings, angels, and camels on display at the **Diorama Bethlehem,** all within five minutes of the Klosterpl. Einsiedeln's position amid lush hills beside the Sihlsee and its 100km of well-marked trails attract **horseback riders** and **hikers.** The 3km (30min.) walk along the **Kreuzweg** offers a spectacular view of the village. For more information on trails, riding, and Sihlsee windsurfing, contact the tourist office. For guided outdoor adventures, talk to Röbi Kälin (tel. 412 87 22).

■ Winterthur

Once the country home of eastern Switzerland's wealthy industrialists, Winterthur (VIN-ter-tur) continues to profit from the cultural endowment of philanthropy. Overshadowed in all things commercial by its omnipotent neighbor, Zurich, Winterthur fights anonymity with a brave artistic barrage of 15 museums, a few private galleries, several castles, and a lively street scene, as performers strum, yodel, and swallow fire to attract audiences in the *Altstadt* along hustly bustly Marktgasse.

ORIENTATION AND PRACTICAL INFORMATION Trains run twice per hour every hour to **Zurich** (20SFr round-trip) and connect there to **Basel** and **Geneva;** trains leave every hour for **St. Gallen** (18.20SFr). **Parking** is available at **Parkhaus Theater am Stadtgarten** and **Parkhaus Winterthur,** both off Museumstr., and **Parkhaus SSB** at the station for 0.50SFr per hour. Winterthur's **tourist office** (tel. 212 00 88; fax 212 00 72) inside the train station overflows with pamphlets packed with excursion ideas and info on museums. The office's hotel reservation service costs 3SFr. (Open M-F 9am-6pm, Sa 9am-4pm.) **Currency exchange** (open daily 5:35am-9:30pm), **bicycle rental** (25SFr per day; open M-Sa 6:40am-7:50pm, Su 8:10am-12:30pm), and **luggage storage** (5SFr, same hours as bike rental) are at the **train station.** The **post office** steadfastly awaits your correspondence across from the train station. (Open M-F 7:30am-6:30pm, Sa 7:30-11am.) The **postal code** is CH-8401. The **telephone code** is 052.

ACCOMMODATIONS AND FOOD If you've ever wanted to try living in a 13th-century castle, **Jugendherberge Hegi (HI),** Hegifeldstr. 125 (tel. 242 38 40; fax 242 58 30), inside the **Schloß Hegi,** gives you that chance. To reach the castle, take the postal bus: "Schlossacker." You can also take the train or bus # 1: "Oberwinterthur Bahnhof," exit the station left, turn left on Hegifeldstr., go through the underpass, then walk 10 minutes down Hegifeldstr. Surrounded by marvelous meadows, hedges, and fruit trees and serenaded by clucking hens and turkeys, the hostel offers no-frills, 13th-century living. (Dorms 16SFr. No breakfast. Kitchen facilities. Reception 7-10am and 5-10pm. Checkout 7-10am. Lockout M and F 10am-5pm, Tu-Th and Sa-Su 10am-2pm. Curfew 11pm. Open Mar.-Oct.)

The **Cafe-Restaurant Urban,** Seenerstr. 191 (tel. 230 07 95), a happy vegetarian hangout, provides an abundance of healthy options. Another local fave, **Pizzeria Pulcinella,** behind Stadtkirche St. Laurentius on Metzg., serves up pizzas (13-19SFr) and Italian specialties, none of which top 28SFr. (Open M-F 11:15am-1:45pm and 5:45-11:30pm, Sa-Su 5:45-10:30pm.) Fruit and vegetable **markets** invade the streets of the *Altstadt* on Tuesdays and Fridays. The **Manor** supermarket and café, across from the tourist office, is crammed with prepackaged goodness. (Open M-W and F 8am-

6:30pm, Th 8am-9pm, Sa 7:30am-4pm.) The **Hegimart** supermarket sits across from the Schloß Hegi. (Open M-F 7:15am-12:15pm and 2:30-6:30pm, Sa 8am-4pm.)

SIGHTS AND ENTERTAINMENT The **Oskar Reinhart Collection**, Winterthur's best collection of art, is preserved in the **Museum am Römerholz**, Haldenstr. 95 (tel. 213 41 21). The two most famous paintings, Manet's Au Café and Van Gogh's L'Hôpital à Arles, are on display along other exquisite works by Poussin, Greco, Goya, Renoir, and Cézanne. Winterthur's **Kunstmuseum**, Museumstr. 52 (tel. 267 51 62), holds an extensive collection of 16th- to 20th-century Swiss and French works, including pieces by Maillol, Bonnard, Léger, and van Gogh, as well as German works from the 19th and 20th centuries by Klee, Hesse, and Rabinowitch. In the summer, temporary exhibits of 20th-century art energize the collection. *(Open Tu 10am-8pm, W-Su 10am-5pm. 10SFr, students 7SFr.)* The museum is five minutes up Marktg. from the station, or left from the Museum am Stadtgarten and through the Stadtpark. Closer to the town proper and to the right of the train station, the **Museum am Stadtgarten**, Stadthausstr. 6 (tel. 267 51 72), balances broad international holdings with works by more obscure 18th- to 20th-century Swiss, Austrian, and German artists. *(Open Tu 10am-8pm, W-Su 10am-5pm. 10SFr, students 7SFr.)* At the **Uhrenmuseum Kellenberger und Museum Jakob Briner**, Marktg. 20 (tel. 267 51 26), the miniatures of the Dutch "little masters" and timepieces from every corner of the globe glimmer in the town hall. *(Open Tu-Sa 2-5pm, Su 10am-noon and 2-5pm; free.)*

The **Technorama der Schweiz** (Swiss Technology Museum), Technoramastr. 1 (tel. 243 05 05), serviced by Marktg. bus #5 (dir: Technorama), is an absorbing experience even for the most technophobic. *(Open Tu-Su and public holidays 10am-5pm. 15SFr, students 10SFr.)* The center lets its visitors perform hands-on experiments on everything from textile production to mechanical music. Visitors also experience giant bubble production, flying bikes, and a Lilliputian train that chugs around the museum's park. Surf the internet exhibit or land a jumbo jet on the flight simulator. The **Fotomuseum**, 44 Grüzenstr. (tel. 233 60 86), is one of the most well-respected museums of photography in Europe and is the only institution of its kind in the German part of Switzerland. *(Open Tu-F noon-6pm; Sa-Su 11am-5pm. 7SFr, students 5SFr.)* Visitors into bones and stones trek to the **Naturwissenschaftliche Sammlungen** (Museum of Natural Science), Museumstr. 52 (tel. 267 51 66), in the Kunstmuseum. *(Open Tu-Su 10am-5pm. Free.)* Geological models explain the creation of the Alps and classify the region's flora and fauna.

Winterthur's environs boast two remarkably well-preserved medieval castles. The **Mörsburg** (tel. 337 13 96), former home of the Kyburg family dynasty beginning in the 13th century, now holds 17th- to 19th-century fine art and furniture. *(Open Mar.-Oct. Tu-Su 10am-noon and 1:30-5pm; Nov.-Feb. Su 10am-noon and 1:30-5pm. Free.)* Take bus #1: "Wallrüti," then follow the yellow signs for a 40-minute hike through forest, fields, and farms. This fortress on a hill is a favorite spot for weekend family hikes and school bike tours. The **Schloß Hegi**, Hegifeldstr. 125 (tel. 242 38 40), overlooks the grassy meadows of Oberwinterthur. *(Open Mar.-Oct. Tu-Th and Sa 2-5pm, Su 10am-noon. Free.)* The original heirs to this 15th-century castle still maintain the creaky staircases, 800-year-old tower, working cannon, and iridescent stained glass. Take the train (Eurailpass valid) to Oberwinterthur or bus #1: "Oberwinterthur." While at the Hegi, give gliding a go at the **Gliding Club** (tel. 337 23 93), not five minutes away from the Schloß. *(Open 4-10pm F-Su.)* You can soar the skies with an able glider pilot for a mere 33SFr. The **Stadtkirche St. Laurentius,** off Marktg., was built in 1180 and renovated in the late-Gothic style between 1501 and 1515 and now blazes with Alberto Giacometti's stained-glass windows and Paul Zehnder's 1925 murals of green-haired Jesuses against glowing heavens. *(Open daily 10am-4pm.)* The church acquired its 1766 organ from the Salem Cloister in 1809.

Vierwaldstätter See

Zinggentorstr.

D

Hofkirche St. Leodegar und Mauritius

Denkmalstr.

Denkmalpl.

Zurichstr.

Stiftsstr.

Löwenstr.

TO LION OF LUCERNE AND MUSEUMPL.

C

Alpenstr.

Töpferstr.

Nationalquai

Schweizerhofquai

Seehofstr.

Dachliturm

Museggstr.

Hertensteinstr.

SCHWANEN-PLATZ

Grendelstr.

Gerberg.

KAPELL PLATZ

FALKEN-PLATZ

Brambergstr.

Allenwindenturm

Pulverturm

Grabenstr.

Weggisg.

Mariahilfg.

Schirmerturm

Zeitturm

Schützenstr.

Wachtturm

Luegislandturm

Männliturm

Nölliturm

Rebhalde

Museggmauer / Museggwall

Diebold Schilling-Str.

Cysatstr.

Löwengraben

Museggstr.

Auf Musegg

Brüggli

St. Karli-Quai

Reuss

Mühlemattstr.

Geissmattstr.

Luegetenstr.

Geissmattstr.

St. Karlistr.

Militarstr.

N2

Sonnenberg's Tunnel

Gütschstr.

Baselstr.

Bruchstr.

Gerliswilstr.

Pfistergasse

Schützenmattstr.

Natur-Museum

Zähringerstr.

KORNMARKT

HIRSCHEN-PLATZ

Rösslig.

Kornmarkt

WEINMARKT

Kramg.

MÜHLENPL.

Reussbr.

Spreuerbrücke

Reusssteg

Kapellg.

Furreng.

Rathausquai

Rathaus Steg

Picasso Museum

Kapellbrücke

Seebr.

BAHNHOFPL

Hauptbahnhof

Zentralstr.

Rob-Zündstr.

Inseliquai

Frohburgstr.

E

Floraweg

Seidenhofstr.

Morgartenstr.

Theaterstr.

Pilatusstr.

Frankenstr.

Hirschmattstr.

Blumenweg

Winkel-riedstr.

Bahnhofstr.

Münzg.

Franziskaner-kirche

PILATUS PLATZ

Bürgerstr.

Rütlig.

Hirschengraben

Klosterstr.

Pilatusstr.

A

ZURICH REGION

Lucerne
ACCOMMODATIONS

E Backpackers
A Hotel Alpha
C Jugendherberge
D Privat Pension Panorama
B Tourist Hotel

Lucerne (Luzern)

Although this northern gateway to the Swiss Alps bristles with antique towers, turrets, and ramparts, Lucerne's natural fortifications—the queenly peaks of Mt. Pilatus—tower over puny human efforts. Pilatus rises 2132m in a tumult of craggy rocks, snow, and ice. The Reuss River flows into the placid Vierwaldstättersee (Lake Lucerne), which separates Pilatus from Rigi Kulm, a gentler peak (1800m) dotted by meadows, villages, and grazing cattle. These are the mountains that inspired the likes of Twain, Wagner, and Goethe. Although the landscape is hard to beat, the city holds its own with a nice little *Altstadt*, a fine set of museums that covers everything from Picasso to glaciation, and some eerie painted wooden bridges.

ORIENTATION AND PRACTICAL INFORMATION

From Zurich, take A4 south to A14 in order to enter the town on Baselstr. (1hr., traffic permitting). The mammoth train station owns the junction of the Reuss River and the Vierwaldstättersee. Most of Lucerne's museums line the quays that hem the river and the lake, but they're not confined to any specific area or neighborhood. Numerous bridges connect both sides of the town. The largest one, Seebrücke, is also closest to the center of town activity.

Trains: Bahnhofpl. (tel. 157 22 22). To: **Basel** (1¼hr., 2 per hr., 5:03am-11:34pm, 30SFr); **Bern** (1¼hr., 1-2 per hr., 5:31am-11:34pm, 31SFr); **Geneva** (3¼hr., 1 per hr., 5:03am-9:56pm, 65SFr); **Interlaken** (2hr., 1 per hr., 6:30am-8:24pm, 25SFr); **Lausanne** (2½hr., 1 per hr., 5:03am-9:56pm, 55SFr); **Lugano** (2¾hr., 1 per hr., 55SFr); **Zurich** (1hr., 1 per hr., 5:01am-11:10pm, 19.40 SFr) and Zurich **airport** (1¼hr., 1 per hr., 5:27am-10:10pm, 24SFr).

Public Transportation: VBL buses depart from in front of the station and provide extensive coverage. A ho(s)tel stamp on your city guide guarantees 3 days of travel for only 8SFr. 1 zone 1.50SFr, 2 zones (to the youth hostel) 2SFr, 3 zones 2.50SFr. *Tageskarte* 10SFr, 2-day pass 15SFr. Swisspass valid.

Taxis: Cabs congregate in front of the train station, at Schwanpl., at Pilatuspl., and in front of the Municipal Theater. Summon at 211 11 11, 310 10 10, or 250 50 50.

Car Rental: Epper, Horwerstr. 81 (tel. 310 14 33). Compact car 88SFr per day for up to 200km of driving; 0.25SFr per additional km. 20SFr insurance. **Europcar,** Luzernerstr. 17 (tel. 440 81 91) has small VWs for 118 SFr; 27SFr insurance. **Hertz,** Luzernerstr. 44 (tel. 420 02 77; fax 429 88 03), rents Renaults for 72SFr per day.

Parking: Lucerne has 10 parking garages, including **Bahnhof-Parking,** Bahnhofpl. 2, under the train station, and **City Parking,** Zürichstr. 35 (tel. 410 11 51). Parking garages run 25-50SFr per day. Free parking at the **Transport Museum.**

Bike Rental: At the train station. 22SFr per day. Open 7am-7:45pm. Also at the **Backpackers** hostel.

Tourist Office: Frankenstr. 1 (tel. 410 71 71; fax 410 73 34). Follow the "i" signs behind the McDonald's to the left of the station to grab your copy of the free city guide (with an unwieldy map). Large selection of maps (free-1SFr) and a hotel reservation service (5SFr refundable deposit). **Guided walking tours** of major monuments (mid-Apr. to Oct. M-Sa at 9:45am and 2pm; Nov. 4-Apr. 13 W and Sa 9:45am; 15SFr including a free drink). Ask about the Visitor's Card, which, in conjunction with a hotel or hostel stamp, gives discounts at museums, bars, car rental agencies, and more. Open Apr.-Oct. M-F 8:30am-6pm, Sa 9am-5pm, Su 9am-1pm; Nov.-Mar. M-F 8:30am-noon and 2-6pm, Sa 9am-1pm.

Budget Travel: SSR Reisen, Grabenstr. 8 (tel. 410 86 56). ISIC cards, student travel deals, and discount flights. Open M-W and F 10am-6pm, Th 10am-8pm.

Currency Exchange: At the station. Open M-F 7:30am-8:30pm, Sa-Su 7:30am-7:30pm. One reliable place is **Migros bank,** Seidenhofstr. 6, off Bahnhofstr. Open M-W and F 9am-5:15pm, Th 9am-6:30pm, Sa 8:15am-noon.

American Express: Schweizerhofquai 4, P.O. Box 2067, CH-6002 (tel. 410 00 77). Offers all services including **ATMs** even for non-members. Mail held and checks cashed for member. Travel services open M-F 8:30am-6pm, Sa 8:30am-noon. Money exchange open M-F 8:30am-5pm, Sa 8:30am-noon.

Luggage Storage: At the station. **Luggage watch** for 5SFr per item. Open 6am-9pm. **Lockers** 3-8SFr.

Bookstores: Buchhandlung Josef Stocker, Weinmarkt 8 (tel. 410 49 47). English paperbacks, travel books, and maps. Open M 1:30-6:30pm, Tu-W and F 9am-6:30pm, Th 9am-9pm, Sa 8am-4pm. MC, Visa.

Bi-Gay-Lesbian Organizations: Schwullesbisches Zentrum Uferlos, Geissentein-ring 14. (tel. 360 30 14) hosts a number of activities, bars, café nights, social events, including the smaller group **Why Not,** Postfach 2304, CH-6002 Luzern, which offers Wednesday discussion groups for young gays at 8 and 11:30pm. **Homosexuelle Arbeitsgruppen Luzern** (HALO), (tel. 360 1460; fax 260 9216) Postfach 3112, CH-6002 Luzern, PC-Konto 60-5227-2, publishes a monthly calendar of events available at the tourist office.

Laundromat: Jet Wasch, Bruchstr. 28 (tel. 240 01 51). Full laundry service. Wash and dry 16SFr; wash, dry, and fold 19SFr. Soap included. English-speaking staff. Open May-Oct. M-F 8:30am-12:30pm and 2:30-6:30pm, Sa 9am-1pm; Oct.-Feb. M-F 8:30am-12:30pm, Sa 9am-1pm.

Emergency: Police, tel. 117. **Fire,** tel. 118. **Ambulance,** tel. 144. **Medical Emergency,** tel. 111. For the **24hr. pharmacy** on duty, call 248 81 17.

Internet Café: Parterre, Mythenstr. 7 (tel. 210 40 93) off Neustadtstr. near Bundespl. 4SFr for 15min., 15SFr for 1hr.

Post Office: Main branch near the station on the corner of Bahnhofstr. and Bahnhofpl. Address *Poste Restante* to: Hauptpost; CH-6000 Luzern 1. Open M-F 7:30am-6:30pm, Sa 8-11am. **Emergency** post at Luzern 2, behind the main station. **Postal Code:** CH-6000.

Telephone Code: 041.

ACCOMMODATIONS AND CAMPING

Relatively inexpensive beds are available in limited numbers in Lucerne, so call ahead in order to ensure a roof over your head.

Backpackers, Alpenquai 42 (tel. 360 04 20; fax 360 04 42), 15min. from the station. Facing the lake, turn right, walk along Inseli-Quai, and then cross the concrete bridge to Alpenquai. It's on the right at the end of Alpenquai. Brand-new and lovingly decorated, this hostel boasts balconied rooms with lake or mountain views, plus a comfy dining room with fresh flowers and hundreds of travel books and magazines. Gorgeous lakeside location with a beach just over the little bridge. A bomb-shelter and "survival" kits (8SFr) of pasta, sauce, and wine await in case of Armageddon. 2-bed dorms 26.50SFr; 4-bed dorms 21.50SFr. Breakfast 6SFr. **Kitchen** facilities. Sheets 2SFr. **Bike rental** 7SFr per day. Tickets sold for Rigi Kulm and Mt. Pilatus. Reception 7:30-11am and 4-11pm. No lockout.

Jugendherberge (HI), Sedelstr. 12 (tel. 420 88 00; fax 420 56 16). Bus #18: "Jugendherberge." After 7:30pm you must take bus #1: "Schlossberg" and walk 15min. down Friednetalstr. A contemporary, white-concrete building with a beautiful valley view you'll have to share with up to 11 fellow travelers. Dorms 30.50SFr 1st night, then 28SFr; doubles 37.50SFr, 35SFr, with shower 43.50SFr, 41SFr. Breakfast buffet, lockers, sheets, and shower included. Dinner 11SFr. **Laundry** 10SFr. Reception 7-10am and 2pm-midnight. Lockout 10am-2pm, but the lounge is always open. Call ahead in summer. AmEx, DC, MC, Visa.

Tourist Hotel Luzern, St. Karliquai 12 (tel. 410 24 74; fax 410 84 14). From the station, go underground, take the elevator or the steps to the *Altstadt,* turn left along the river to the 2nd wooden bridge, cross it, and make a left onto St. Karliquai. Train station pick-up for 3 or more people. Pleasant, peppermint-stick rooms are fresher than the bathrooms. Huge windows onto the river. 4-bed dorms 36SFr, students 33SFr; 11-bed dorms 31SFr, students 28SFr; doubles 98-108SFr; triples 123-135SFr; quads 156-172SFr. In winter, rooms 10-15SFr less per person. Add 10SFr per person for private shower. Breakfast included. Free luggage storage. **Laundry** 10SFr. Free scooter for city travel. Reception 7am-10:30pm. AmEx, MC, Visa.

Privatpension Panorama, Kapuzinerweg 9 (tel. 420 67 01; fax 420 67 30; email panorama@swissonline.ch). Bus #7 or 5 (dir: Wesemlin): "Kapuzinerweg" drops you up the street. For 8SFr, the owner will pick you up at the station. Clean, homey, comfortable, and on a hill with unbeatable sunset views of Pilatus or the *Altstadt*. Singles 45SFr; doubles 70-90SFr; triples 120SFr; quads 140SFr. Apartment for 2 people 100-120 SFr. Breakfast, **kitchen** facilities, and limited parking included. Ring the bell or yell for reception. AmEx, MC, Visa.

Hotel Alpha (tel. 240 42 80; fax 240 91 31), at the corner of Pilatusstr. and Zähringerstr. 24. From the station, walk 10min. left down Pilatusstr. This sprawling *Pension* is in a residential area, removed from the *Altstadt*. The rooms are airy, comfy, spick and span. Singles 60SFr; doubles 92SFr, with shower 120SFr; triples with shower 123SFr; quads with shower 156SFr. Prices 2-3SFr cheaper in winter. Breakfast included. Reception 7am-9:30pm. AmEx, MC, Visa.

Camping: Camping Lido, Lidostr. 8 (tel. 370 21 46; fax 370 21 45). 30min. from the station on the Lido beach. Cross the Seebrücke and turn right along the quay, or take bus #2 (dir: Würzenbach): "Verkehrshaus." Mini-golf, tennis, and swimming nearby. 6.50SFr; tent 3SFr; car 5SFr. Showers 0.50SFr per 3min. Reception 8am-6pm. Open Mar. 15-Oct.

Camping Horw (tel. 340 3558). Bus #20 (dir: Horw): "Horw Rank." Quiet campsite by a lake. 11SFr per person; 5.80SFr per tent. Showers included.

FOOD

Lucerne's gastronomics are overwhelmingly Swiss. Saturday morning markets along the river purvey inexpensive picnic goods, but the restaurants in supermarkets and department stores offer the cheapest meals in town. The restaurant upstairs in **EPA**, at Rösslig. and Mühlenpl., has 8-13.50SFr menus of healthy, cheap food. (Open M-W 8am-6:30pm, Th-F 8am-9pm, Sa 8am-4pm.) **Hotel Drei Könige,** Bruchstr. 35 (tel. 240 88 33; fax 240 88 52), serves heated kosher food for 45SFr per meal. (Open 11:30am-1:30pm and 6-9pm. Call ahead.)

Krone, Rösslig. 15 (tel. 419 44 90; fax 419 44 00). Create your own sandwich or try the kebabs (8.90SFr), chop suey (8.90SFr), burgers, or ice cream. Vegetarian sandwiches for 7.50SFr. Daily specials include an 11SFr *Menü*. Kitchen open 10am-9pm; bar open 'til midnight. AmEx, MC, Visa.

Café Emilio, Grendelstr. 10. In the *Altstadt* off Schwanenpl., this elegant caffeinated den boasts surprisingly good deals. Locals munch yogurt and *muesli* while tourists head for the 2 mini-pizza and salad combo (8.80SFr) or the tortellini (10.20SFr). Open M, W, and F 6:30am-8pm, Th 6:30am-10pm, Sa 7am-6pm, Su 9am-6pm.

Kam Tong Chinese Take Away, Inseliquai 8, is a dim, red-papered eatery with cheap Asian fare. Vegetable fried rice 9SFr. Open M-W 9am-6:30pm, Th-F 9am-9pm, Sa 9am-4pm.

La Paninoteca da Mario, Haldenstr. 9 (tel./fax 410 90 70), a few blocks before the casino. Pasta and pizza for 5-15SFr; after 10pm, 12SFr pizzas discounted to 7.50 SFr.

Ciao Pep, Murbacherstr. 4 (tel. 228 90 50; fax 228 90 59), is a stylish garden restaurant off Pilatusstr. Play giant chess while munching on *ciabattas* (8-9SFr) or pasta (from 12SFr). Open 7am-12:30am.

Pourquoi Pas, Nationalquai (in front of the Musikpavillon). This place caters to a sun-loving crowd, providing delectable crepes for just 6.50SFr. Chew on a 'shroom crepe while listening to jazz and rock from the nearby free concerts on the Nationalquai. 10% discount for City Backpacker hostelers. Open M-F 11:45am-1:30pm, and 5-8pm, Sa-Su 1pm-whenever.

Markets

Migros, Hertensteinstr. 44, and Kasernepl. Open M-W and F 8am-6:30pm, Th 8am-10pm, Sa 8am-4pm, Su 9am-6pm.

Reformhaus Müller, Wienmarkt 1. Sells tofu, lentils, and organic, whole-grain bread. Open M 1:30-6:30pm, Tu-F 8:15am-noon and 1:30-6:30pm, Sa 8am-4pm.

Co-op, Kasernepl. Open M-W and F 8am-6:30pm, Th 8am-9pm, Sa 8am-4pm.

SIGHTS AND ENTERTAINMENT

The *Altstadt* is famous for its frescoed houses and oriel windows, especially those on the buildings in Hirschenpl. If you can wade through the camera-eager tourists, you might be able to traverse the 660-year-old **Kapellbrücke,** a wooden, roofed bridge originally part of Lucerne's fortification. It was accidentally set on fire by a barge in 1993, but appalled citizens quickly restored it. Confront your mortality as you cross the covered **Spreuerbrücke,** adorned with Kaspar Meglinger's eerie *Totentanz* (Dance of Death) paintings. On the hills above the river, the **ramparts of the medieval city** *(Musegg Mauern)* still dominate the city skyline. The Schirmer, Zeit, and Männli towers are accessible by a narrow set of stairs. The **clock tower,** with a view of the valleys surrounding Lucerne, provides another excellent opportunity for panoptic pleasure. *(Open 8am-7pm.)* To find it, walk along St. Karliquai, make a right uphill, and follow the brown castle signs.

The city mascot, the dying **Lion of Lucerne** (carved out of a cliff on Denkmalstr. by Lukas Ahorn) casts pained eyes over a reflecting pool. World traveler Mark Twain described the lion as "the saddest and most moving piece of rock in the world." The 9m monument honors the Swiss Guard who defended Marie Antoinette to the death at the Tuileries in 1798. Next door is the **Glacier Garden,** with its lunar landscape of smooth rocks curved and pot-holed into odd almost-sculptures. *(Open Apr.-Oct.15 9am-6pm; Mar. and Oct. 16-Nov. 15 9am-5pm; Nov. 16-Feb. Tu-Su 10:30am-4:30pm. 8SFr, with visitors card 6.50SFr, students 6SFr.)* Admission includes the **Glacier Garden Museum** with models of glaciation and reconstructed pictures of prehistoric humans. Roam among the wooly mammoths and the *Spiegellabyrinte* (mirror maze)—be careful not to lose yourself (or your mind, or your mind). Wexstr. leads to the **Hofkirche St. Leodegan und Mauritius,** at the end of Schweizerhofquai. An 8th-century Romansque basilica, the church was refurbished in the 14th-century in Gothic style and filled with crowds of sad-eyed, gilted wooden saint statues.

A cruise on the **Vierwaldstättersee** (see **Near Lucerne,** p. 362) takes visitors past the beautiful countryside and deposits them in one of the many tiny villages that dot the lake. Glass-blowing demonstrations lie in wait at **Hergiswil,** while a short but scenic hike lurks at **Bürgenstock,** ex-U.S. president Jimmy Carter's top choice in Swiss resorts. Says Jimmy: "Yes." For an easier walk along the lake, alight at **Weggis.** To return to Lucerne, just jump back on board. The length of the journey determines the fare. Consult the Lucerne tourist office for specifics on each town.

From mid-August to mid-September, Lucerne will host its **International Festival of Music.** The festival celebrates sometimes provocative classical, folk, and contemporary music. It draws a highly talented crowd of artists—past years have seen the likes of Daniel Barenboim, Martha Argerich, Charles Dutoit, and Anne Sofie Mutter perform. For tickets or further info, contact: Internationale Musikfestwochen Luzern; Postfach/Hirschmattstr. 13; CH-6002 Luzern (tel. 210 35 62; fax 210 77 84; tickets 20-220SFr). On June 28, Lucerne celebrates its **anniversary** with fireworks and parties throughout the *Altstadt.* The **Nationalquai** is the scene for free summertime **Pavillon Musik** concerts, featuring brass and jazz bands playing Hollywood tunes, Gershwin, Duke Ellington, and even a little Andrew Lloyd Weber every other night from June to August. Every summer, elite crews from all over the world snake their way to Lucerne for the **National and International Rowing Regattas** on the Rotsee by the hostel. *(10SFr entry fee.)* Usually held on back-to-back weekends, the 1999 *Internationale Ruderregatta* will take place on the July 3-4 and 9-11. On Saturdays from 8am to noon, catch the **flea market** (May-Oct.) along Burgerstr. and Reussteg.

MUSEUMS

Lucerne, sometimes called the "washing machine" of Switzerland due to frequent precipitation, has more than ample entertainment ready for rainy days. If you plan to visit several museums, but a 25SFr **museum pass,** good for one month and available at most museums and the tourist office.

Picasso Museum, Am Rhyn Haus, Furreng. 21 (tel. 410 35 33), presents a slice of the great artist's life through photographs taken by close friend David Duncan. Though the lithograph collection of Picasso's later work is less interesting, Duncan's photographs of Picasso painting, kicking up his heels, and chomping on fish are unforgettable. Open Apr.-Oct. 10am-6pm; Nov.-Mar. 11am-1pm and 2-4pm. 6SFr, with guest card 5SFr, students 3SFr.

Richard Wagner Museum, Wagnerweg. 27. (tel 360 23 70) Bus #6 or 8: "Wartegg.," or turn right from the station and walk 25min. along the lake. Wagner's secluded former lakeside home now houses original letters, scores, and instruments as well as a collection of historic instruments from around the globe. Wagner's years in Lucerne, often known as the "Tribschen years" (1866-1872), were marked by an enormous creative output, as well as private happinesses—it was here that he wed Cosima von Bülow. Open mid-Mar. to Nov. Tu-Su 10am-noon and 2-5pm.

Verkehrshaus der Schweiz (Transport Museum), Lidostr. 5 (tel. 370 44 44; fax 370 61 68), near Camping Lido, is the Disney World of transportation. If you can drive, fly, steer, float, or roll it, it's here. Climb into big-rigs and jet planes or go for a ride in virtual reality. Planetarium and 4 IMAX shows every day. Open Apr. 4-Oct. 9am-6pm; Nov.-Mar. 10am-5pm. 18SFr, students 16SFr. Imax 14SFr. Both 28SFr, students 24SFr; discounts with Eurailpass or guestcard.

Natur-Museum, Kasernenpl. 6 (tel. 228 54 11). Hands-on exhibits, including live animals, distinguish this 1987 "European Museum of the Year." Special exhibits include all sorts of insectoids, from the household cockroach to butterflies. 1999 promises new exhibits on *Märchen-Tiere* (animals from fairy tales), lichen, and "Birds of the World." All exhibits in German; English summaries available. Open Tu-Sa 10am-noon and 2-5pm, Su 10am-5pm. 5SFr, students and possessors of the local guest card 4SFr. Add 1SFr for special exhibits.

NIGHTLIFE

Lucerne's nightlife is a delocalized mass with a center of gravity in the *Altstadt*. On the river, **Mr. Pickwick's Pub,** Rathausquai 6 (tel. 410 59 27), has a heavily tourist-fueled Anglophile feel and plenty of dark beers (from 4.50SFr). (Open M-Sa 11am-midnight, Su 4pm-12:30am.) Up the river, **Hexenkessel,** Haldenstr. 21 (tel. 410 92 44 or 410 92 64), goes for that mock-pagan look. Replete with broomsticks, it boils Lucerne's twentysomethings in a two-story cauldron of loud music and spinning DJs. Saturday night is "Heaven's Gate," while the odd Thursday brings live music. (Obligatory beer 7SFr; no cover. Open 9pm-2:30am.) Down the street lies the bright yellow **Kursaal,** Haldenstr. 6, with its ritzy casino offering poker, blackjack, and low-stakes gambling to the masses. **Cucaracha,** Pilatusstr. 15 (tel. 210 55 77), has a daily happy hour (5-7:30pm) and offers free Tex Mex snacks with your drink (Corona costs 7.50SFr). (Open 5pm-midnight.) **Uferlos Bar,** Geissenringstr. 14 (tel. 360 3014 or 360 1460) is a popular gay and lesbian hangout. For a mellow night by the waves, dance, eat, or thrill to Swiss folklore from May to September on **Night Boats** (tel. 319 49 78), which leave at 8:45pm from piers 5 and 6. (40SFr, with Eurailpass 33SFr. Ride, the night's entertainment, and 1 drink 50SFr, with Eurailpass 43SFr.)

■ Near Lucerne: Engelberg and the Vierwaldstättersee

Lucerne's position in the heart of Switzerland makes it a daytrip departure point *par excellence.* Boats from the train station cruise the Vierwaldstättersee; get a list of destinations from the tourist office (day pass for unlimited boat travel 41SFr, free with Eurailpass or Swisspass). The hour-long train ride (14.20SFr) to **Engelberg** is well suited for outdoors people and sightseers alike. Ride the world's first revolving cable car (tel. 639 50 50; email titlis@titlis.ch) to the top of **Mount Titlis** (3020m), the highest outlook in central Switzerland. The panoramic ride gives magnificent views of the crevasses below and peaks above. An illuminated ice grotto, observation deck, and schlocky restaurants conclude the trip. (Departs from Engelberg at 8:30am-5:15pm every 30 seconds. 73SFr, with Eurailpass 58.40SFr, with Swisspass 54.80SFr, with Engelberg guest card 20% discount. Guided tours from Lucerne including round-trip rail and Titlis fares 85SFr, same discounts.) The mirror-like glacier lake, **Trübsee,** awaits your ogling halfway up Mt. Titlis (round-trip 30SFr, same discounts).

Engelberg also attracts **hikers** to its many trails, including an exceptional route from Engelberg to Herrenrüti along the valley floor next to the cliffs of Titlis (2hr. round-trip, easy terrain). Ask the tourist office for maps of other hikes and guided jaunts. The weak-kneed may prefer a hike to the local **Benedictine Monastery.** Over 850 years old, the monastery boasts some impressive Biblical wood inlay, not to mention Switzerland's largest organ. The biggest trip is just looking at the place from a distance against the irregular, snow-topped mountain gorges. Tours at 10am and 4pm Monday through Saturday are free, but donations are appreciated. Enter through the door marked "Kloster." As always, when winter rolls around, the skiers roll in. (Daypass M-F 47SFr, Sa-Su and holidays 54SFr. 10% off with guest card.)

The little village of Engelberg is no great shakes, but if you wanna stay stop over at the **Jugendherberge Berghaus (HI),** Dorfstr. 80 (tel. (041) 637 12 92), just a 10-minute walk out of town. Turn left off Bahnhofstr. onto Dorfstr., and keep walking. This place is built along the standard Swiss chalet model, with wooden beams and lots of natural insulation. (Dorms 25.50SFr 1st night, then 23SFr; doubles 31.50SFr, 29SFr. Non-members add 5SFr. Breakfast and sheets included. Key available on request. Reception 8-11am and 5-10:30pm. Curfew 10:30pm, key deposit 20SFr.)

Engelberg's **tourist office,** Klosterstr. 3 (tel. 637 37 37; fax 637 41 56), is a left on Bahnhofstr. from the train station, a right onto Dorfstr., and another right onto Klosterstr. It hosts daily activities like hikes on the Brunni trail, or across Gross-Titlis glacier (both Tu 9am, each 15SFr, with guest card 10SFr). (Open June 23-Oct. 19 M-Sa 8am-6:30pm, Su 8am-noon and 2-7pm; Oct. 20-Dec. 15 M-F 8am-12:15pm and 2-6:30pm, Sa 8am-6:30pm; Dec. 16-Apr. 13 M-Sa 8am-6:30pm, Su 9am-6pm; Apr. 14-June 21 M-F 8am-12:15pm and 2-6pm, Sa 8am-6:30pm).

▓ Mount Pilatus and the Rigi Kulm

We could not speak. We could hardly breathe. We could only gaze in drunken ecstasy and drink it in.

—Mark Twain

Soaring 2132m into the sky, the peak of Mt. Pilatus provides views that stretch all the way to Italy. Legend has it the devil threw St. Pilatus up here during the Ascension, but *Let's Go* does not recommend the Evil One as a safe means of transportation—cable cars tend to be much more reliable. Catch a boat to Alpnachstad and ascend by the **steepest cogwheel train in the world** (48° gradient). For the well-rounded experience, tourist-watch and capitalize on those Kodak moments, then descend by cable car to Kriens and take the **bus** to Lucerne (round-trip 77SFr, with Eurailpass 40SFr, half-price with Swiss Half-Fare Card). From July to September 15, the **Pilatus railway** (tel. (041) 329 11 11) offers special half-price evening fares after 4:30pm from Alpnach and Krienz between July and September. If it's cloudy, don't waste your money—visibility is next to nothing. Banned until the 17th century due to fear of Pilate's angry ghost, climbing the thing is now legal. From Alpnachstad, Pilatus is five hours away. Meeting the cable car at one of its two stops on the way up the mountain shortens the hike. The descent to Kriens takes about four and a half hours. For a **weather report** in German, call 162.

Across the sea from Pilatus soars the **Rigi Kulm.** Sunrise on the summit is a Lucerne must; sunsets get pretty good reviews, too (see Mark Twain's 1879 travelogue *A Tramp Abroad*). Staying at **Massenlager Rigi Kulm** (tel. (041) 855 03 03) on the summit makes early morning viewing possible. Part of Hotel Rigi Kulm, this dormitory has 28 simple bunks (25SFr). Reception is open 8am-10pm, sometimes even later. Trips to Rigi begin with a ferry ride to Vitznau and a cogwheel railroad ride on the mountain railway to the top. Return the same way, or hike down to **Rigi Kaltbad** (1hr.), take a cable car to **Weggis,** and return to Lucerne by boat (round-trip 82SFr, with Eurailpass 42SFr, with Swiss Half-Fare Card 39SFr).

ZURICH REGION

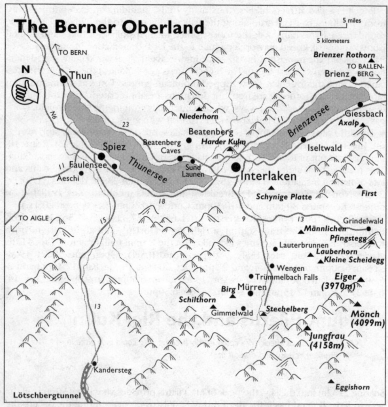

The Berner Oberland

If you made a list of things the Swiss are fiercely proud of, the Bernese Oberland would be at the top of that list. Pristine and wild, the savage beauty of the Swiss Alps best lends itself to discovery through scenic hikes around the twin lakes, the *Thunersee* and *Brientersee*. When World War II threatened to engulf the country, the Swiss army resolved to defend this area, *le réduit*, to the last. A young, international, and rowdy crowd migrates here every summer to get a fill of crisp Alpine air and clear, starry nights. Opportunities for paragliding, mountaineering, and whitewater rafting are virtually unparalleled and bewitch not only rubber-boned physical types, but also romantics, and fans of (almost any work of) 19th-century English literature.

The only form of budget travel in the Bernese Oberland is your own two feet. Minimize transportation costs by using a town or village as a hub from which to explore. The Thun-Interlaken-Brienz rail link is a standard Swiss railway, but the various cable cars to the snowy peaks and the Berner Oberland Bahn (the string of mountain trains that link Interlaken to the valleys) charge high-altitude fares. Eurailpass sometimes ekes out a 25% discount, and even the magic Swisspass, valid on trains to Grindelwald, Wengen, Lauterbrunnen, and Mürren, loses its power here—it barely scrapes together a 25% reduction to the higher peaks. Certain towns, notably Mürren and Wengen, are closed to cars. Of dubious value is the 15-day **Bernese Oberland Regional Pass** (200Fr; with Swisspass or Half-Fare card 160SFr; Eurailpass not valid.) The Pass gives a 50% discount on regional transport for 10 days; the remaining days

Bern

ACCOMMODATIONS
A Pension Marthaus
B Hotel National
D Hotel Goldener Schlüssel
E Hotel Landhaus
C Jugendherberge

Lauberg-str.
Rosengarten
Aargauerstalden
Muristalden
Klösterlistutz
Bärengraben (bear pits)
Untertorbrücke
Nydegg-Kirche
Nydegg-brücke
Grosser Muristalden
Aare
Schänzlistr.
Altenbergstr.
Langmauerweg
Postgasshalde
Gerberng.
Postg.
Gerechtigkeitsg.
Junkerng.
Rathaus
Münster (cathedral)
MÜNSTER-PLATZ
Herreng.
Schifflaube
Englische Anlagen (English Garden)
Kollerweg
Grybenhübeliweg
Jungfraustr.
Dufourstr.
N
1/4 mile
1/4 kilometer
Rabbental-str.
Brunngasshalde
Einstein Haus
Münsterg.
Casinoplatz
Aarstr.
Marienstr.
Thunstr.
Kornhausbr.
Kornhauspl.
Brunng.
Clock Tower
Hotelg.
Theaterplatz
Münzgraben
Kirchenfeldbr.
Kunsthalle
HELVETIA-PLATZ
Postal Museum and Alpine Museum
Helvetiastr.
Historical Museum
Bernastr.
Aare
Nägelig.
Schüttestr.
WAISENHAUS-PLATZ
Zeughausg.
Amthausg.
Kocherg.
terrasse
Parliament
Funicular train
Dalmazibrücke
Dalmaziquai
Kunstmuseum
Speicherg.
Marktg.
BÄREN-PLATZ
BUNDES-PLATZ
Aare
Aarstr.
Lorrainebrücke
Aarbergerg.
Neueng.
Spitalg.
Heiliggeistkirche
Schauplatzg.
Bundesg.
Bundes-Marzili B
Marzilistr.
Brückenstr.
Reithalle
Genferg.
Bollwerk
Hauptbahnhof
BAHNHOF-PLATZ
Bubenbergpl.
Aarstr.
FALKEN-PLATZ
Universität
Hochschulstr.
Stadtbach. Graben
Sulgeneckstr.
Länggass. Sidlerstr.
Schanzenstr.
Monbijoustrasse
Monbijoustr.
Kapellenstr.
Schwarztorstr.

are free. A seven-day variation is available for 160SFr, offering 50% off for four days and the remaining days free. Both are available at train stations or any tourist office. Train service usually ends at midnight. Boat service ends around 7pm in summer and 5pm in the spring and fall, and winter hours are extremely limited.

🐻 HIGHLIGHTS OF BERNER OBERLAND

- In honor of the fact that Bern's mascot is the bear, the city maintains a bear pit in the center of town near both the Nydegg church and a 13th-century fortress.
- Bern has many excellent museums including the *Kunstmuseum,* which holds the world's largest collection of Klee paintings, and the *Albert Einstein Haus.*
- The Thunersee is home to Thun, Spiez, and Interlaken. The latter is overtour-isted but provides good access to the famous Jungfrau mountain.
- Grindelwald is a good base for visiting the Eiger mountain, with its multiple gla-ciers, excellent hiking, and year-round skiing.

■ Bern (Berne)

The Duke of Zaehringen founded Bern in 1191, naming it for his mascot, the bear, and the city has been Switzerland's capital ever since 1848. Don't expect fast tracks, power politics, or men in black—Bern prefers to focus on the lighter things in life. Some old wag once claimed that "Venice is built on water, Bern on wine." While the the Bernese seem a little too sober to merit proverb-status, they do appreciate the grape, local Toblerone chocolate, and their ubiquitous flower gardens. Situated in a bend of the winding Aare River, Bern's giant bridges span lush, green banks. Cobble-stone streets of the medieval *Altstadt* twist past bright fountains, 15th-century arcades, and lots of chocolate shops. Rebuilt in 1405 after a devastating fire, Bern's sandstone and mahogany buildings lend the city a compactness and unity dominated mainly by a fat *Bundeshaus* and the stately spire of the Gothic *Münster.*

GETTING TO BERN

The **Bern-Belp Airport** (tel. 960 21 11 for general info; Air Engadina tel. 960 21 21; Crossair tel. 960 12 11) is 20 minutes from central Bern and is served by Swissair, Crossair, and Air Engadina. Direct flights go daily to Basel, Amsterdam, London, Lugano, Brussels, Munich, Paris, Rome, and Vienna. Fifty minutes before each flight, an airport bus that guarantees you'll make your flight runs from the station (10min., 14SFr). Bern's main **train station,** in front of the tourist office, is a stressful tangle of essential services and extraneous shops. Check-in, information, buses, luggage watch, bike rental, and a pharmacy are upstairs; tickets, lockers, police, showers, toi-lets, and currency exchange are downstairs. If **driving** from Basel or the north, take A2 south to A1. From Lucerne or the east, take 10 west. From Geneva or Lausanne, take E62 east to E27/A12 north. From Thun or the southeast, take A6 north.

ORIENTATION AND PRACTICAL INFORMATION

Bern occupies a diplomatic location, tangential to the French- and German-speaking areas of the country. Most of medieval Bern lies in front of the train station and nes-tled along the Aare River. **Warning:** Like many cities, Bern has a nocturnal drug com-munity that occasionally settles in the area around the Parliament park and terraces.

Transportation
  Trains: Bahnhofpl. For rail info, call 157 22 22 (6am-10pm). The **rail information office** is open M-F 8am-7pm, Sa 8am-5pm. To: **Geneva** (2hr., every 30min., 6am-11:24pm, 48SFr); **Lucerne** (1½hr., 23 per day, 5:27am-11:14pm, 31SFr); **Inter-laken** (1hr., every hr., 7:22am-11:26pm, 24SFr); **Zurich** (1½hr., every hr., 6:10am-11:50pm, 42SFr); **Lausanne** (1¼hr., every 30min., 5:57am-11:24pm, 30SFr); **Basel** (1¼hr., every 30min., 4:50am-11:50pm, 34SFr); **Paris** (4½hr., 3 per day, 6:45am-

11:56pm, 76SFr); **Prague** (12½hr., 1 per day, 8:14am-11:50pm, 163SFr); and **Munich** (5¾hr., 1 per day, 6:10am-11:53pm, 115SFr).

Public Transportation: SVB (tel. 321 86 41; fax 321 86 86). A visitor's card from the ticket offices downstairs in the station or at the Jurahaus office, Bubenbergpl. 5 (tel. 321 86 31), entitles the holder to unlimited travel on all SVB routes and a 10% discount on city tours. 24hr. pass 6SFr; 48hr. 9SFr; 72hr. 12SFr. Automatic vendors dispense daypasses (7.50SFr) and one-way tickets (1-6 stops 1.50SFr; 7 or more stops 2.40SFr; Swisspass valid). Buses run 5:45am-11:45pm. **Nightbuses** (nicknamed the "Moonliners") leave the train station from 12:45-1:25am F-Sa nights (some stop before 1:25am), covering major bus and tram lines (5-12SFr; depending on distance). Both SVB offices in the train station distribute maps and timetables. Open M-W and F 6:30am-7:30pm, Th 6:30am-9:30pm, Sa 6:30am-6:30pm.

Taxis: Bären-Taxi (tel. 371 11 11) or **NovaTaxi** (tel. (0800) 87 98 79). Stands at Bahnhofpl., Bollwerk, and Casinopl.

Parking: Bahnhof (tel. 311 22 52), entrance at Schanzenbrücke or Stadtbachstr. **Parking Casino,** Kocherg. (tel. 311 77 76). **City West,** Belpstr. (tel. 381 93 04), costs 3.20SFr per hr., 28SFr for a day, 12SFr for 2nd and 3rd day.

Car Rental: Avis AG, Wabernstr. 41 (tel. 372 13 13). **Hertz AG,** Kasinopl. (tel. 318 21 60). **Europcar,** Laupenstr. 22 (tel. 381 75 55).

Bike Rental: Blubike, Casinopl. (tel. 311 22 34) rents bikes for free. Just hand them a 20SFr deposit plus ID. Reserve ahead. Open M-W and F 8am-6:30pm. Weekend bikes available. Otherwise, try **Fly-Gepäck** (tel. (0500) 12 20 34 61) at the station. 25SFr per day, 100SFr per week; mountain bikes 31SFr, 124SF; children's bikes 16SFr, 64SFr. Reservations recommended. Open 6:10am-11pm.

Tourist and Financial Services

Tourist Office: Bern Tourismus (tel. 328 12 12; fax 312 12 33; email info@berne-tourism.ch; http://www.bernetourism.ch), on the street level of the station. Distributes maps and *Bern Aktuell,* a 2-week guide to events in the city. Room reservations 3SFr. The 24hr. electronic board outside the office has a free phone line to hotels, computerized receipts, and directions in German, French, and English. **City tours** available by bus, on foot, or by raft. Most tours cost 12-22SFr and run daily in summer. Contact the tourist office for more details.

Budget Travel: SSR, Rathausg. 64 (tel. 312 07 24). Bus #12: "Rathaus." Sells BIJ tickets, ISIC cards, Europass, *usw.* Open M-W and F 9:30am-6pm, Th 9:30am-8pm, Sa 10am-1pm. **Wasteels,** Spitalg. 4 (tel. 311 93 93; fax 311 90 10), has BIJ and plane tickets, and changes currency. Open M 2-6:15pm, Tu-W and F 9am-12:15pm and 2-6:15pm, Th 9am-12:15pm and 2-7pm, Sa 9am-noon.

Embassies: Australia, Alpenstr. 29 (tel. 351 01 43). Open M-Th 10am-12:30pm and 1:30-3pm, F 10am-12:30pm. To get to the Canadian, U.K., Irish, and Australian embassies, take tram #3 (dir: Saali): "Thunpl." **Canada,** Kirchenfeldstr. 88 (tel. 352 63 81). Open M-F 8am-noon and 1-4:30pm. **Ireland,** Kirchenfeldstr. 68 (tel. 352 14 42). Open M-F 9:15am-12:30pm and 2-5:30pm. **South Africa,** Jungfraustr. 1 (tel. 352 20 11). Open 8am-12:30pm and 1:30-5:15pm. **U.K.,** Thunstr. 50 (tel. 352 50 21). Open M-F 8:30am-12:30pm and 1:45-5:15pm. **U.S.,** Jubiläumsstr. 93 (tel. 357 70 11). Bus #19 (dir: Elfenau): "Ka-We-De." Open M-F 8:30am-5:30pm.

Currency Exchange: Downstairs in the station. No commission on traveler's checks. Credit card advances on DC, MC, and Visa, as well as Western Union transfers. Open June to mid-Oct. 6:15am-9:45pm; mid-Oct. to May 6:15am-8:45pm. **ATMs** at **Credit Suisse** and **Swiss Bank Corp.** Banks are generally open M-W and F 8am-4:30pm, Th 8am-6pm.

Local Services

Luggage Storage: Downstairs in the train station. 24hr. Lockers 4-8SFr. **Luggage watch** at the Fly-Gepäck counter upstairs 5SFr. Open 6:10am-11pm.

Lost Property: Downstairs in the station. Open M-F 8am-noon and 2-6pm.

Bookstore: Stauffacher, Neueng. 25 (tel. 311 24 11). From Bubenbergpl., turn left on Genferg. to Neueng. 6 floors of books, including lots of English and French. Open M-W and F 9am-6:30pm, Th 9am-9pm, Sa 8am-4pm. **Branch** at the train station. Open 9am-10pm.

BERNER OBERLAND

Libraries: Municipal and University Library, Münsterg. 61 (tel. 320 32 11), stacks books for the central library of the University of Bern and the city's public library. Lending library open M-F 10am-6pm, Sa 10am-noon. Reading room open M-F 8am-9pm, Sa 8am-noon. **Swiss National Library,** Hallwylstr. 15 (tel. 332 89 11). Lending library and catalog room open M-Tu and Th-F 9am-6pm, W 9am-8pm, Sa 9am-2pm. Reading room open M-Tu and Th-F 9am-6pm, W 9am-8pm, Sa 9am-4pm.

Bi-Gay-Lesbian Organizations: Homosexuelle Arbeitsgruppe die Schweiz-HACH (Gay Association of Switzerland), c/o Anderland, Mühlepl. 11, CH-3011. The headquarters of Switzerland's largest gay organizations. **Homosexuelle Arbeitsgruppe Bern** (HAB), Mühlepl. 11, Case Postale 312, CH-3000 Bern 13 (tel. 311 63 53). in Marzilibad, along the Aare. Hosts informal get-togethers every Wednesday at 7pm with coffee, drinks and library access. **Schlub** (Gay Students Organization), c/o Studentinnenschaft, Lercheweg 32, CH-3000 Bern 9 (tel. 381 18 05).

Laundromat: Jet Wash, Dammweg 43 (tel. 372 50 45). Bus #20: "Lorraine." Wash 8.2kg for 5SFr, 4.6kg 4SFr; dryers 3SFr. Open M-Sa 7am-9pm, Su 9am-6pm.

Public Showers at the train station. Toilets 1-1.50SFr; showers 10SFr. Open 6am-midnight.

Information: General info tel. 111.

Pharmacy: In the station. Open 6:30am-8pm. **Bären Apotheke,** at the clock tower. Open M 1:45-6:30pm, Tu-W and F 7:45am-6:30pm, Th 7:45am-9pm, Sa 7:45am-4pm. AmEx, DC, MC, Visa. For the **24hr. pharmacy on duty,** call 311 22 11.

Emergencies and Communication

Emergencies: Police, tel. 117. **Ambulance,** tel. 144. **Doctor,** tel. 311 22 11. **Rape Crisis Hotline,** tel. 332 14 14.

Internet Café: Basement of JäggiBücher, Spitalg. 47-51 (tel. 320 20 20) in Loeb dept. store. Free for 20min. Open M-W and F 9am-6:30pm, Th 9am-9pm, Sa 8am-5pm.

Post Office: Schanzenpost 1, next to the train station. Address *Poste Restante* to Schanzenpost 3000, Bern 1. Open M-F 7:30am-6:30pm, Sa 7:30-11am. Express counter M-F 6-7:30am and 6:30-10:30pm, Sa 6-7:30am and 11am-6pm, Su 10am-noon and 4-10pm. **Postal codes:** CH-3000 to CH-3030.

Telephone Code: 031.

ACCOMMODATIONS AND CAMPING

Bern's shortage of inexpensive hotels thwarts budget travelers. Even outside the city itself, cheap accommodations are rare. Consider staying in Fribourg (30min. by train).

Jugendherberge (HI), Weiherg. 4 (tel. 311 63 16; fax 312 52 40). From the station cross over the tram lines and go down Christoffelg. Take the road by the Park Café down to Weiherg., following the signs. The hostel is on the warm green banks of the Aare. The majority of the 186 beds are in noisy 8-bed rooms. You can buy candy and city excursion tickets at the office. Dorms 19.25SFr; overflow mattresses on the floor 15.25SFr. Nonmembers add 5SFr. Breakfast 6SFr. Lunch or dinner 11SFr. **Laundry** 6SFr. 30SFr key deposit. 3-night max. Reception June-Sept. 7-9:30am and 3pm-midnight; Oct.-May 7-9:30am and 5pm-midnight. Check-out 7-9am. Lockout June-Sept. 9:30am-3pm, Oct.-May 9:30am-5pm, but the dining room/lounge stays open. Curfew midnight. Closed 2 weeks in Jan. MC, Visa.

Landhaus Hotel, Altenbergstr. 4/6 (tel. 331 41 66; fax 332 69 04; email landhaus@spectravels.ch.) Take bus #12 (dir: Schlosshalde): "Bärengraben," and walk down to the Aare on the left. This newly renovated hotel has dorms with refreshing views of the Aare, and is within walking distance of the bear-pits and the rose gardens. Dorms 30SFr; doubles 110SFr-120SFr, with shower 140-160SFr. Duvet for bedding 5SFr. Breakfast 7SFr. **Kitchen** access. Restaurant open 11am-11pm. **Laundry** 4-6SFr. **Internet access.**

Pension Marthahaus, Wyttenbachstr. 22a (tel. 332 41 35; fax 333 33 86). Bus #20: "Gewerbeschule," then the 1st right. Or walk from the station: turn left onto Bollwerk, cross Lorrainebrücke on the right, bear right onto Victorian, then take the 1st left onto Wyttenbachstr. Matronly hostess maintains a comfortable *Pension* in a quiet suburb. Its 1-star status offers a few small luxuries, including privacy amid fluffy white blankets, a shiny sink for every room, and sitting rooms. Singles 60SFr, with shower 90SFr; doubles 95SFr, 120SFr; triples 120SFr, 150SFr. Prices drop 5-10SFr in winter. Group rate is 35SFr per person. Breakfast included. **Laundry** 8SFr. Limited parking available. Reception 7am-9pm, but a porter accommodates late-comers. Reservations recommended. MC, Visa.

Hotel National, Hirschengraben 24 (tel. 381 19 88; fax 381 68 78). From the station, cross over the bus stops/tramlines to Bubenberg. on the right. Hirschengraben is the 2nd road downhill. English-speaking staff and beautiful rooms with oriental rugs. The restaurant downstairs has a 15SFr *Menü*. Singles 60-75SFr, with shower 85-110SFr; doubles 100-120SFr, 120-150SFr; 3- to 5-person family room 170-260SFr. Breakfast included. Reception 7am-10pm, but the night porter opens the doors for latecomers. Reservations recommended in summer. AmEx, DC, MC, Visa.

Camping: Camping Eichholz, Strandweg 49 (tel. 961 26 02). Take tram #9: "Wab-ern," backtrack 50m, and take the 1st right. Verdant riverside location across from the zoo, within earshot of snuffling wild boars, drooling bison, and bounding mountain goats. There's a restaurant on-site. 6.90SFr, students 5.50SFr, children 3SFr; tents 5-8.50SFr; 2-bed rooms 15SFr. Showers 1SFr. Electricity 3SFr. **Laundry** 5SFr. Reserve ahead. Open May-Sept.

FOOD

The **Bärenplatz** is a lively square overflowing with cafés and restaurants, most with *Menüs* and lighter fare in the 9-17SFr range. Try one of Bern's hearty specialties: *Gschnätzltes* (fried veal, beef, or pork), *suurchabis* (a sauerkraut), or *Gschurelti* (steamed potatoes). The sweet-toothed will enjoy an airy meringue or the world-renowned **Toblerone chocolate** (yup, this is where it comes from).

Manora, Bubenbergpl. 5A (tel. 311 37 55), over the tramlines from the station. As usual, this self-service chain tends to be overheated and crowded but serves big platefuls that are indisputably nutritious and cheap. Salad bar 5-10SFr; pasta 8-10SFr; veggie burger plate 9SFr. Open M-Sa 7am-10:45pm, Su 9am-10:45pm. Hot food served until 10:30pm.

Zähringerhof, Hallerstr. 19 (tel. 301 08 60), at Gesellschaftstr., slightly uphill from Bern University. This neighborhood joint cooks up great Italian dishes, with pizza and pasta from 11.50SFr. A green wall of bushes and hanging vines shield the out-door terrace from street dust and noises. Open 8:30am-11pm.

Café des Pyrenées, Kornhauspl. 17 (tel. 311 30 63). Named after a novel by Swiss author Daniel Himmerberg, this buzzing little bistro-café complete with a super-small sidewalk terrace is a haven for journalists, office-goers, and busy types. Inven-tive sandwiches (calamari 6.50SFr) meet conservative spaghettis (9.50-12SFr). Veg-etarian possibilities abound. The spirits list is extravagant, with 6 types of Spanish brandy. Open M-F 9am-12:30am, Sa 8am-5pm.

Cave 49, Gerechtigkeitsg. 49 (tel. 312 55 12), is a spicy, dimly lit Mediterranean eat-ery tucked away in one of *Altstadt*'s cellars. Enjoy *tortellini alla panno con parmesan* (14.50SFr) or a meaty paprika *chorizo* (5.50SFr) while relishing the war-like Corsair decor. Beers from 2.70SFr.

Café Bubenbeg Vegi, Bubenbergpl. 8 (tel. 311 75 76), across the tram lines from the Berner Kantonalbank. A lemon-yellow interior enhances the health-food ambience of this completely vegetarian restaurant. Organic ingredients are used. Many Indian dishes (18-24SFr) and an Indian buffet on Wednesdays (30SFr, 6pm.) Open Aug.-June 8:30am-10:30pm; July M-Sa 8:30am-10:30pm.

Pizza Camarque, Kramg. 42 (tel. 311 70 51). Red geraniums on the terrace give way to a dining room that sports blood-red brick and rippled plaster walls—an appro-priately oven-like setting for a pizzeria. While staring, try some pizza (11.50-13SFr), pasta (10.80-20SFr), or beer (4SFr). Open M 9am-11:30pm, Tu-Th 9am-1am, F-Sa 9am-2am, Su 11am-midnight.

Markets

Migros, Marktg. 40; Bubenbergpl. Open M 9am-6:30pm, Tu-W and F 8am-6:30pm, Th 8am-9pm, Sa 7am-4pm.

Co-op, Spitalg. 1, Waisenhauspl. Open M-F 8am-6:30pm, Th 8am-9pm, Sa 8am-4pm. AmEx, DC, MC, Visa.

BERNER OBERLAND

Reformhaus M. Siegrist, Marktg.-Passage, is a popular health food market. Open M 2-6:30pm, Tu-F 8am-12:15pm and 1:30-6:30pm, Sa 7:45am-1pm.

Fruit and vegetable markets sprawl fresh produce daily over Bärenpl. (May-Oct. 8am-6pm) and every Tu and Sa over Bundepl. (all year). The crazy **onion market** on the 4th M of Nov. is probably Bern's single best known festival.

SIGHTS

Church and state combat for control of the Bernese skyline; the Alps come in a close third. The massive **Bundeshaus** (tel. 322 85 22) dominates the Aare river and hides its politicians in the **Parlamentsgebäude.** (45min. tour every hr. 9-11am and 2-4pm when Parliament is not in session; free.) From the state house, Kockerg. and Herreng. lead to the 15th-century Protestant **Münster.** (Open Easter-Oct. Tu-Sa 10am-5pm, Su 11am-5pm; Nov.-Easter Tu-F 10am-noon and 2-4pm, Sa 10am-noon and 2-5pm, Su 11am-2pm. Tower closes 30min. before the church. 3SFr.) The imagination of the late-Gothic period runs riot in the stern, Calvin-influenced portal sculpture of the Last Judgment, where the naked damned shuffle off unhappily to Hell on God's left. For a fantastic view of the Aare and beyond, climb the the Münster's spire—it's the highest in all of Switzerland. Cobblestoned Münsterg. runs parallel to Kramg. before reaching the 13th-century **Zytglogge** (clock tower). (Tours of the interior May-Oct. daily at 5:15pm; min. 3 people. 6SFr.) Join the crowd four minutes before the hour to watch bears dance, jesters drum, and a squeaky rooster announce the hour. The similarly gaudy fountains were the whimsical notion of Hans Gieng, who loyally carved them on Bernese themes between 1539 and 1546. Even Bern's brown bears turn up in gummy-bear red.

The slender fingerlike copper spire of the **Nydegg Kirche** rises from the intersection of Kramg. and Gerechtigkeitsg. The church stands on the remains of the Nydegg imperial fortress that was destroyed in the mid-13th century. Farther down the street and across the Bärengrabenbrücke lie the **Bärengraben** (bear pits). (Open Apr.-Sept. daily 8am-6pm; Oct.-Mar. 9am-4pm. 3SFr to feed the bears.) The pitted cages date back to the 15th century; imagine generations and generations of caged bears sullenly enduring tossed carrots and screaming kiddies. Juicy screaming kiddies. On Easter, newborn cubs are displayed for the first time in public. The path snaking up the hill to the left leads to the **Rosengarten;** sit among the blooms and admire one of the best views of Bern's Altstadt.

The **Botanical Gardens** of the University of Bern, Altenbergrain Bus # 20 "Generberschule" (tel./fax 631 49 11), sprawl down the river at Lorrainebrücke. (Park open Mar.-Sept. M-F 7am-6pm, Sa-Su 8am-5pm. Greenhouse open 8-11:30am and 2-5pm. Free.) Exotic plants from Asia, Africa, and the Americas thrive cheek to leaf with native Alpine greenery. A walk south along the Aare (or bus #19: "Tierpark") leads to the **Dählhölzli Städtischer Tierpark** (Zoo), Tierparkweg 1 (tel. 357 15 15; fax 357 15 10). (Open daily in summer 8am-6pm; in winter 9am-4:30pm. 7SFr, students 5SFr,

---

Bären Brain

No kidding—Bern's citizens have got bears on the brain. The city's ursine mascot pervades even the most godforsaken alleyways in the form of statuettes, fountains, flags, stained-glass windows and matchbox covers. The Bärengraben, whose name is unpleasantly close to the German word for "bear graves," are the pits in the center of the city where live bears are kept behind bars like some sort of strange totem or Roman genus of the city. Legend has it that Duke Berchtold V of Zähriagen, founder of Bern, wanted to name the city after the first animal he caught when hunting on the site of the planned construction. The animal was a you know what, and Bern (etymologically derived from Bären) was born. The Bärengraben themselves weren't built until the Bernese victory at the Battle of Nouana in 1513, when they dragged home a live bear as part of the war booty. A hut was erected for the beast in what is now Bärenplatz (Bear Square!) and his descendants have been Bern's collective pets ever since.

children 3SFr. Parking available.) The heated vivarium barely contains its reptilian, amphibian and insect life. *Achtung,* piranhas. In a towering forest of cedar and pine, the **24-hour Tierpark** gives you the chance to animal-watch at night, too. The zoo relegates its less crowd-pleasing inhabitants—bison, boars, and jowly vultures—to out-of-the-way riverfront pens. Farther down the river is the entrance to the **Stadtgärtnerei Elfenau** (tel. 352 07 13), a nature reserve that was once an 18th-century country estate. *(Open M-Sa 8am-5pm, Su 8am-5:30pm; in winter same times except Su 8am-4:30pm. Free.)* The English-style landscaping offers belvederes, greenhouses, and concerts in the orangery.

MUSEUMS

Several of Bern's museums sit in a compact ring around **Helvetiaplatz** across Kirchenfeldbrücke (tram #3 or 5). A **day ticket** (*Tageskarte;* 7SFr, students 5SFr) grants admission to the Historical Museum, Natural History Museum, Swiss Alpine Museum, Kunsthalle, PTT Museum, and the Rifle Museum. Other tiny museums lurk throughout the *Altstadt.*

Kunstmuseum, Hodlerstr. 8-12 (tel. 311 09 44; fax 311 72 63), near Lorrainebrücke. This mostly modern Swiss collection sprawls over 3 floors and a couple of buildings, top-heavy with the world's largest Paul Klee collection. 2500 works, from his school exercise-books to his largest canvases, along with some works by his chums Kandinsky and Feininger, culminate in 2 solid rooms of Klee's beautiful and witty art. Upstairs holds a smattering of the century's big names: Braque, Picasso, Giacometti, Ernst Kirchner, Pollock, and some Dada works by Hans Arp. Ernst Barlach, Max Pechstein, Erich Heckel and other Swiss Impressionists are relegated to the basement. The museum also holds a chic café and screens art films. Open Tu 10am-9pm, W-Su 10am-5pm. 6SFr, students and seniors 4SFr.

Bernisches Historische Museum, Helvetiapl. 5 (tel. 351 18 11; fax 351 06 63), in the downtown museum district. So big you won't know where to begin. Luckily, multilingual explanatory notes await in almost every room in the museum's 7 jam-packed levels. Nicolaus Manuel's witty and macabre *Dance of Death* and a bizarre exhibit called "Changes in Daily Life" are some of the highlights. The belvedere offers a relatively close-up view of the climbers on the Münsterspire looking back at you. Open Tu-Su 10am-5pm. 5SFr, students 3SFr, free for those under 17 and school groups. Additional charge for special exhibitions. Free on Saturday.

Museum of Natural History, Bernastr. 15 (tel. 350 71 11), off Helvetiapl. Most people come to see Barry, the now-stuffed St. Bernard who saved over 40 people in his lifetime. Some of the other hyper-realistic dioramas, however, get a bit more intense—hyenas feed on zebra corpses, weasels carry stolen eggs from a henhouse away in their mouths, and more dynamic cousins of the *Bärengraben* bears dispute a recently downed moose. Open M 2-5pm, Tu-F 9am-5pm, Sa-Su 10am-5pm. 5SFr, students 2.50SFr, free on Su.

Swiss Alpine Museum, Helvetiapl. 4 (tel. 351 04 34; fax 351 07 51). Vast, spellbindingly intricate models of Switzerland's most popular mountains and a history of Swiss cartography. The 2nd floor exhibit on mountain life may be more interesting—check out the devil masks used to protect against threats from the other world. Open mid-May to mid-Oct. M 2-5pm, Tu-Su 10am-5pm; mid-Oct. to mid-May M 2-5pm, Tu-Su 10am-noon and 2-5pm. 5SFr, students and seniors 3SFr.

Museum of Communication, Helvetiastr. 16 (tel. 357 55 55), explores the history of the post and telecommunication, including exhibits of decades old postage stamps. Open Tu-Su 10am-5pm. 5SFr, students 3SFr.

Albert Einstein's House, Kramg. 49 (tel. 312 00 91; fax 312 00 41). This small apartment where the theory of general relativity was born in 1905 is now filled with photos, a few of Einstein's letters, resonating brain waves, and not much else. The museum emphasizes that Albert loved Bern and Bern loves Albert. Open Feb.-Nov. Tu-F 10am-5pm, Sa 10am-4pm. 3SFr, students and children 2SFr.

ENTERTAINMENT AND NIGHTLIFE

Artsy Bern has symphonies, concerts, and theater performances galore. Productions at the **Stadttheater** (tel. 311 07 77) range from operas to ballets. That's a pretty wide range. The summer season runs July to August 17th. Tickets are 6-115SFr, and students receive a 50% discount. For more info, contact Theaterkasse, Kornhauspl. 18, CH-3000 Bern 7. (Open M-F 10am-6:30pm, Sa 10am-6pm, Su 10am-12:30pm.) The **Berner Altstadtsommer** picks up the slack with free dance and music concerts, ranging from tango to jazz to funk to choral, in the squares of the *Altstadt*. Bern's **Symphony Orchestra** plays in the fall and winter at the Konservatorium für Musik at Kramg. 36. For tickets, call 311 62 21. July's **Gurten Festival** has attracted such luminaries as Bob Dylan, Elvis Costello, Björk, and Sinead O'Connor. For ticket info, contact the Bern Tourist Office (tel. 311 66 11), check http://www.gurtenfestival.ch, or write to Gurten Festival, Billett-Versand, Postfach, 3000 Bern 13. Tickets are about 55SFr per day. Jazz lovers arrive in early May for the **International Jazz Festival.** For tickets, go to the ticket counter at any Bankverein Swiss Bank branch. Other festivals include the Berner Easter egg market in late March and the notorious onion market (Zwiebelmarkt) on the fouth Monday in November. The orangery at the Stadgärtnerei Elfnau (tram #19: "Efnau") has free Sunday concerts in summer.

Bars and late-night cafés line Bärenpl., but venture farther into the *Altstadt* for a Bern tradition: the **Klötzlikeller Weine Stube,** Gerechtigkeitsg. 62 (tel. 311 74 56). Bern's oldest wine cellar resides in a brick-roofed cavern that resonates with loud talk and slurred choruses of German drinking songs (wines 3.40-5.20 SFr per glass). January and February bring the house specialty, *Treberwurst* (sausage cooked in wine liqueur). (Open Tu-Sa 4pm-12:30am.) **Art Café,** Gurteng. 3 (tel. 311 42 64), is a café by day and a smoky bar by night. The black and white walls and changing decor—the walls have seen James Bond posters, 18 post-Warhol Donald Ducks, and larger-than-life Batman in recent times—creates a warped Disney feel. (Beers from 3.50 SFr.)

A seedier but more interesting scene takes place under the gargoyles and graffiti of the Lorrainebrücke, a bridge by Booverkstr. Sous le Pont is the den of alternative culture, with a laid back, international feel fed by an undercurrent of smoke and sound from Ella Fitzgerald. The **Reitschule,** Bern Neubrückstr. 8 (tel 302 83 72), caters to a patchwork crowd of students and loafers. (Beers from 3SFr; 5SFr Menü; open M and Sa 5pm-12:30am, Tu-F 11am2:30am.) **Dachstock,** on the floor above, is an electronic music disco with a turnover of talented DJs. (Open M-Th 7am-12:30pm, F-Sa 7am-7pm and 8pm-2:30am, Su 6pm-12:30am.) **Lirum Larum,** Kramg. 19a (tel. 312 24 42), is hard to miss—just look for a huge phosphorescent aluminum tree in the windows of Kramg. This electronic music bar is named after a nonsensical Dütsch byword, and tries to live up to a topsy-turvy sense of style. (Beer from 3.50SFr. Open 7pm-12:30am.) **Different Bar,** Gerechtgkeitsg. 50 (tel. 311 91 01), is ultra-hip and one of Bern's few gay bars. It's lots of fun. (Open W 6pm-12:30am, Th-Sa 6pm-3:30am.)

Born in Bern

The Theory of Relativity was born in Bern in the hyperactive brain of Albert Einstein, resident of Kramgasse 49. Einstein left Germany for Switzerland and became a citizen in 1901. A poor, shabbily dressed, unemployed 23-year-old (no good bum) the future relativity-ist became a private tutor then a patent clerk. Einstein would complete his office work in a few hours and spend the rest of the day furiously scribbling equations other human beings could not begin to understand. He shuffled around in his green slippers carrying a market bag and being smart and underappreciated. Finally, the "miraculous year" of 1905 hit, and his theory was published. He left in 1909, always wishing but never able to return to that "happy time in Bern."

THE THUNERSEE

Two jade-green lakes framed by steep wooded mountainsides and the distant snowy summits of the Jungfrau sandwich the town of Interlaken. The westerly **Thunersee** is more settled and the mountains less stark than around its twin, the **Brienzersee,** but its northwestern shores are strewn with castles. Though the Thunersee lacks sky-piercing alpine panoramas like its sister lakes, its gentle, dewy slopes offer a certain relief from rocks and breath-shortening altitudes.

The Thunersee's three significant towns, **Thun, Spiez,** and **Interlaken,** all lie on the main rail line from Bern to Interlaken to Lucerne. **Boats** putter to the smaller villages between the Thun and Interlaken West railway stations (every hr., June-Sept. 8am-8pm; special evening cruises available; from June-Dec. Eurailpass, Swisspass, and Berner Oberland pass valid). The whole trip from Thun to Interlaken takes two hours. A ferry day-pass plus train and bus travel along the regional lines costs 32SFr in June and September, 42SFr in July and August. Point-to-point tickets may be cheaper depending on how much ground you wish to cover in one day. For current information, consult the BLS shipping company (tel. 334 52 11; http://www.thunersee.ch).

▨ Thun

Creatively named the "Gateway to the Berner Oberland," the bustling city of Thun lies on the banks of the Aare river and the *Thunersee.* The city's name is derived from the Celtic "dunum," or hill settlement (kind of an understatement). The town's oldest fortifications date back to the 12th century, and the first settlements to 100BCE. Surrounded by castles of every imaginable size and most colors, Thun is a city that seems to be permanently on holiday. Take it from Johannes Brahms: "Relaxing in Thun is delightful, and one day will not be enough."

Thun's main street is the tree-lined boulevard Bälliz. The oldest squares and the castle (all hung with red-and-white flags) lie on Aare's north bank. Thun's **tourist office,** Seestr. 2 (tel. 222 23 40; fax 222 83 23), is outside and to the left of the station. (Open July-Aug. M-F 9am-7pm, Sa 9am-noon and 1-4pm; Sept.-June M-F 9am-noon and 1-6pm, Sa 9am-noon.) **Trains** leave every hour for **Interlaken East** (14SFr) and **Interlaken West** (13SFr) and every half-hour for **Spiez** (6SFr) and **Bern** (11.40SFr). There is a rail **information desk.** (tel. 222 95 86; open Mar. to mid-Oct. M-F 8am-7:40pm, Sa 8am-5pm; mid-Oct. to Feb. 8am-6:30pm) The **boat landing** (tel. 223 53 80) is just to the right of the station. Boats depart for **Interlaken West** (15.60SFr), **Spiez** (7.80SFr), **Faulensee** (8.60SFr), **Hilterfingen** (4.40SFr), and **Oberhofen** (5SFr). The train station has a **currency exchange** (open daily 5:50am-8:30pm), **bike rental** (25SFr per day; open M-Sa 7am-7:50pm, Su 8:20am-noon and 2-7:50pm), and **lockers** (3-5SFr). **Taxis** are usually waiting outside the train station, or call 222 22 22 or 222 78 26. **Park** at the Parkhaus Aarestr. on Aarestr. (tel. 222 78 26; 1.30-2SFr per hr., 10.50SFr for 8hr.). The **post office** is at Bälliz 60, opposite Mühlebrücke. (Open M-F 7:30am-6pm, Sa 7:30-11am.) The **postal code** is CH-3600. The **telephone code** is 033.

Accommodations in Thun are not cheap. Your best bet is probably **Hotel Metzgern,** Untere Hauptg. 2 (tel. 222 21 41; fax 222 21 82), which (conveniently enough) is in the Rathauspl. Carpeted hallways lead to sunny rooms, attractively furnished and equipped with sinks. (Singles 55SFr 1st night, then 50SFr; doubles 110SFr, 100SFr; triples 165SFr, 150SFr. Breakfast included. Reception Tu-Th 8am-11:30pm; F-Sa 8am-12:30am. MC, Visa.) Other options lie farther away from town, toward Gwatt. Take the bus toward Interlaken to "Schadausdal," then take the first right. **Gasthof Rössli Dürrenast,** Frutigenstr. 73 (tel. 336 80 60; fax 335 28 66) offers six recently renovated doubles. Four have private showers and bathrooms (108SFr); the other two share hallway facilities (94SFr). Single travelers can use the rooms for 59SFr, with shower 66SFr, three-bed rooms 42SFr per person, and groups of three pay 120SFr, with shower 141SFr. (Breakfast included. Reception 8am-11:30pm. Reservations recommended, especially in summer. MC, Visa.) Campers should schlepp down to

Camping Bettlereiche (tel. 336 40 67). Take bus #1: "Bettlereiche" or turn right from the station and walk 45 minutes. The place is somewhat crowded with schoolkids, but it's green and near the water. (July-Aug. 6.20SFr; Apr.-June and Sept.-Oct. 4.60 SFr. Showers 0.60SFr. Reception 9am-11:30am and 2-8pm.)

Unlike hotel rooms, food in Thun is surprisingly cheap. Affordable restaurants line Bahnhofstr., and both **Migros** and **Co-op** have markets and restaurants on Allmend-str. straddling the Kuhbrücke. (Both open M-W and F 8am-6:30pm, Th 8am-9pm, Sa 7am-4pm.) At the **open-air market** in the *Altstadt* (across the river from the train station), vendors hawk souvenirs, clothes, and fresh produce. (Open Sa 8am-9pm.) A **food market** takes over Bälliz on the island all day on Wednesdays. On the second floor of the *Aare-Zentrum* building is **Le Pavillon** (tel. 222 70 23), a self-service restaurant featuring spicy, Asian specialties as well as Swiss staples. (*Menüs* 10-14SFr; chicken fried rice 5SFr, spaghetti 5SFr. Open M, W, and F 7:45am-6:30pm, Th 7:45am-9pm, Sa 7:30am-4pm.) For delectable pastries and sandwiches in a comfy corner tea room, try **Confiserie Steinmann,** Bälliz 37 (tel. 222 20 47). Enjoy tarts for 2.40SFr or a mouth-watering *Thuner Leckerli* made from an 18th-century recipe involving honey, lemon rind, and nuts. (6SFr for 5 pieces. Open M 1-6:30pm, Tu-F 6:45am-6:30pm, Sa 6:45am-4pm.)

To get to the **Schloß Thun** (tel. 223 20 01) from the station, bear left down Bahnhofstr. and go over two bridges, right on Obere Hauptg., left up the stone steps, and left again at the top. (Castle open June-Sept. 9am-6pm; Apr.-May and Oct. 10am-5pm. 5SFr, students 2SFr, children 1SFr.) Inside the castle, the **Turm Zähringer** houses an historical museum whose upper floors juxtapose a collection of vicious weaponry with a selection of antiquated musical instruments. The tower was the site of a gruesome fratricide in 1322, when Eberhard of Kyburg unsportingly defenestrated his brother Hartmann. The Romanesque square tower with four corner turrets looks especially imposing with the Alps as a backdrop. Downstairs in the *Rittersaal* (Knight's Hall) the castle hosts summer classical music concerts the last two weeks of June (call 223 35 30 or contact the tourist office; tickets 30-50SFr). Turning left on Hauptg. at the bottom of the Risgässli steps or taking bus #6: "Thunerhof" leads to the **Kunstmuseum,** Hofstettenstr. 14 (tel. 225 84 20; fax 225 82 63). (Open Tu and Th-Su 10am-5pm, W 10am-9pm. 3SFr, students 2SFr, children free.) Housed in Thun's hoary administration building, the museum is a tribute to Swiss contemporary artists. That means Paul Klee, Werner Ritti, Arnold Bügger, and pop artist Samuel Buri. Not bad.

The popular local walk up **Heilingenschwendi,** the hillside above Thun on the lake's north shore, provides a view of the distant Jungfrau mountains. Past the casino and the village of Seematten (where the lake proper starts), turn left, cross the river, and head up through the wooded ridge (1152m). Continue farther to the **Dreiländeregg** and **Niesenbänkli** for a panoramic view (3hr.). From the village of Schwendi near the top, you can head back to Oberhofen, keeping the castle on the right (600m ascent, half-day). At Oberhofen, the 13th-century **Schloß Oberhofen** (tel. 243 12 35; fax 243 35 61) attracts visitors with its wild and riotous gardens. (Open May to mid-Oct. daily 10am-noon and 2-5pm. 5SFr, children 1SFr. Garden open May-Oct. 9:30am-6pm. 1SFr.) The owner, an enterprising American lawyer, bought the castle in 1926. He left the exterior intact, but transformed the interior into a crazy museum of furniture from the 12th to 19th centuries. Medieval, Baroque, Renaissance, Louis XVI, and Napoleon III styles all brush shoulders. Bern museum veterans may recognize pieces of the History Museum's Islamic collection in the lavishly languid decor of the Turkish smoking room. Ferries and buses run back to Thun, but you can also continue down the road to the **Schloß Hünegg** (tel. 243 19 82), on a cliff above the boat landing at **Hilterfingen** (10min.). (Open mid-May to mid-Oct. M-Sa 2-5pm, Su 10am-noon and 2-5pm. 8SFr, students 7SFr.) The most elaborate of the Thunersee castles, its Victorian rooms are excitingly gaudy. The castle grounds, known as the **Hünegg Park,** are the dim and leafy home of deer, rabbits, and lots of wild birds.

The very pink **Schloß Schadau,** Seestr. 45 (tel. 223 14 32), in the Walter Hansen Schadaupark, was built in the style of the Loire castles. (Open Tu-Su May-July and Sept.-Nov. 10am-5pm. 4SFr, students 3SFr, under 17 free.) This Victorian folly in a tree-lined, lakefront garden hosts frequent temporary exhibitions. Stick around for the yearly **Ausschiesset,** where young cadets shoot it out in the *Altstadt* on the last Monday and Tuesday in September. The *Fulehung* (a bogeyman) chases the cadets afterwards in a friendly game in the Market. A **William Tell Shoot** honors the cadet who takes the best aim at a model of Gessler. The *Altstadt* rollicks with merry music during the **Festival of Barrel Organs and Ballad Singers** every July.

■ Spiez

Quiet and rural, Spiez fills its tiny harbor with bobbing boats and surveys the **Thunersee** from its gentle hills. **Trains** leave every 30 minutes and connect the town with **Bern** (30min., 15.80SFr), **Thun** (10min., 6SFr), and **Interlaken West** (20min., 8.40SFr). **Boats** float to **Thun** (17.80SFr) and **Interlaken** (10.60SFr). Spiez's **tourist office** (tel. 654 20 20; fax 654 21 92), left as you exit the train station, sells hiking maps and helps find inexpensive rooms for 3SFr. (Open July-Aug. M-F 8am-7pm; Sa 9am-noon and 2-4pm; May-June and Sept. M-F 8am-noon and 2-6pm, Sa 9am-noon and 2-4pm; Nov.-Apr. M-F 8am-noon and 2-5pm.) The **post office** is to the left of the station. (Open M-F 7:30am-noon and 1:45-6pm, Sa 8:30-11am.) The **postal code** is CH-3700, and the **telephone code** is 033.

 Budget accommodations are almost non-existent in Spiez itself. **Hotel Krone,** Oberlandstr. 28 (tel. 654 41 31; fax 654 94 31), has smallish, plain, very clean rooms, some with great views. It's also got an amiable Alsatian named Rocky. (Singles 45SFr; doubles 90SFr. Breakfast and hall showers included. Reception Tu-Th 8am-11:30pm, F-Sa 8am-12:30am, Su 9am-noon. Open May-Mar. AmEx, MC, Visa.) Better options exist in surrounding villages. A bus to "Rössli" or a 20-minute hike to Spiezwiler leads to **Hotel Rössli** (tel. 654 34 34; fax 654 56 35), on Frutigenstr., above the village. The hotel offers dorms for 20SFr, breakfast included. The cellar bunks and showers have a definite meat-locker temperature, so bring your own sleepsack or your toes may develop serious chilblains. The upstairs attic rooms cost more but are much cleaner (and warmer!). A bowling alley is available for rainy day entertainment. (Singles 58SFr; doubles 102SFr. Off-season: 54SFr; 90SFr. Breakfast included. Reception M-Tu and Th 7:30am-11:30pm, F-Sa 7:30am-12:30am. AmEx, DC, MC, Visa.) **Camping** awaits at **Panorama Rossern** (tel. 654 43 77 or 223 36 15; fax 223 36 65), on Aeschi. To find the campsite, catch the bus to Mustermattli (2SFr), and then follow the signs. (5.50SFr; showers 1SFr; tents 7-8SFr. Open May-Sept.) The **Migros** market and restaurant is across the train station parking lot to the right. (Open M-Th 8am-6:30pm, F 8am-9pm, Sa 7:30am-4pm.) Seestr. leads to Oberlandstr. and its banks and **Co-op.** (Open M-Th 7:30am-12:15pm and 1:30-6:30pm, F 7:30am-12:15pm and 1:30-9pm, Sa 7:30am-4pm.)

 Spiez's castle, the **Schloß Spiez** (tel. 654 15 06; next to the dock), was a medieval fortress that became a residence for Oberlander bigwigs like the Bubenbergs and Erlachs. (Open July-Aug. M 2-6pm, Tu-Su 10am-6pm; Apr.-June and Sept.-Oct. M 2-5pm, Tu-Su 10am-5pm. 4SFr, students 3SFr.) A stone tower with unconventional spiral shutters leads to a quiet grassy courtyard, a 10th-century churchyard, and a rose garden. Inside the fortress is an historical museum with enormous bear skins hanging at a mantelpiece and almost Mediterranean views of the lake. Around the corner, the **Wine-Making Museum,** Spiezbergstr. 48, has rustically decorated rooms, a caskmaker's workshop, and a pressing shed. (Open May-Oct. W and Sa-Su 2-5pm. Guided tours available. Free.) The mountain piercing the sky is the **Niesenberg** (2363m). Hikes on the mountain, while not for beginners, are certainly accessible. Pick up hiking maps at tourist offices in Interlaken, Thun, or Spiez. Hiking all the way up or down the mountain is prohibited, but a **funicular** chugs to the top, and the **Lötschberg train** from Spiez (every hr., 7.20SFr round-trip) connects with the funicular at Mülenen. (May-Oct.; 8am-5:30pm; 23SFr, 38SFr round-trip, 14SFr one-way to Schwandegg.) The funicular's builders pushed the frontiers of human achievement by building steps alongside the track, which thereby became the **longest flight of steps in the**

world. Unfortunately, only the company's maintenance teams are allowed to walk on them (all 11,674 of them). There used to be an annual race for thunder-thighed locals called the **Niesen Steps Race**, but it was discontinued for safety reasons. Hiking routes head down from the summit to **Mülenen** (3hr.) and **Wimmis** (3½hr.). For more scenic bliss, hike to Schwandegg (1¼hr.) and take the train again through the woods to Mülenen. To spend a night in an unspoiled, friendly *Berggästehaus,* visit the **mountain guest-house** (tel. 676 11 13) on the summit. The hotel has seven guest rooms with 15 beds, a roomy dining area, and a large terrace and wine cellar hewn into the rock-face. (38SFr per person. Breakfast 14SFr. The "Sunset-Sunrise" package offers dinner, breakfast, and round-trip transportation for 110SFr, children 58SFr.)

■ Beatenberg and the Caves

Beatenberg consists of sunny chalets stretched over 7km of mountainside. Perched 600m above the Thunersee, it is chock full of hiking trails. Bus #21 from Interlaken to Thun stops in the village, where the **tourist office** waits (tel. (033) 841 18 18; fax 841 18 08; open M-F 8am-noon and 2-6pm, Sa 9am-noon; July-Sept. also Sa 3-6pm).

The superb **Güggisgrat ridge** rewards a short climb with crazy views (2hr.). Yellow signs from town center point up (as in almost straight up) the Niederhom (1950m; 830m ascent; 2½hr.). Ten kilometers of airy ridgeway then lead northwest to the Gemmenalphorn (2061m) at an easy gradient (3hr.). Dozens of paths loop back to civilization; the tourist office's topographical map helps to untangle them. **Funiculars** climb the Niederhorn. (8:30am-6pm in summer, 8:30am-4:30pm Dec. 19-Mar. 12, 20SFr, 30SFr round-trip; with guest card, Eurail or Swisspass 15SFr, 22.60SFr. Closed 2 weeks in Nov. and Apr.). Routes start at the eastern (Interlaken) end of the village. The **restaurant** (tel. (033) 841 11 10) at the top has **dorm beds** with woolen comforters (30SFr; breakfast included), as well as 12-bed dorm rooms 100m from the main house (25SFr). (Singles 45SFr. Reception 8am-6pm.)

Down from Beatenberg village, **Beatushöhlen** (St. Beatus' Caves) riddle the hillside. You can spelunk through 100m of glistening stalactites, waterfalls, and grottoes. At the entrance a wax St. Beatus (the Irish hermit and dragon-slayer) stares down some (also wax) cavemen; at the exit, a sarcastic little dragon bids you *"Auf Wiedersehen."* Even on hot summer days, the cave stays a cool 8 to 10 degrees Celcius. One-hour tours leave every hour from the entrance. To get there, walk 15 minutes uphill from the Sundlauenen Schiffstation, which is a 30-minute boat ride from Interlaken (every hr., 7:34am-6:34pm), or take bus #21 (8.20SFr round-trip from Interlaken). You can also walk from Interlaken (2hr.) or Beatenberg (1hr. on a steep path downhill through woods and farmland). Admission includes entry to the **Caving Museum** (tel. (033) 841 16 43), five minutes downhill. (Caves open Apr.-Oct. 10:30am-5pm. Museum Apr.-Oct. Tu-Su noon-5pm. 14SFr, students 12SFr, children 6SFr.) That's "cave" used as a verb. This tiny room chronicles the discovery and mapping of Swiss grottoes, with lots of stuff about bats.

THE BRIENZERSEE

The more rugged of the sister lakes, the Brienzersee lies still, clear, and cold beneath sharply jutting cliffs, waterfalls, and dense forests. Lake cruises depart from Interlaken's *Ostbahnhof.* (June-Sept. every hr. 9:40am-6:05pm; Apr.-May and Oct. 3 per day, 5 Su. Eurail and Swisspass valid.) Brienz, at the eastern end of the lake, is the Brienzersee's only sizable town. The south shoreline has mostly escaped human attention (apart from the hamlet of Iseltwald), and makes for good walks.

■ Brienz and the Rothorn

Occupying the thin strip of level land between brilliant tourmaline water and deep green hillside, Brienz overflows with Alpine flowers, wooden figurine shops, and intricately carved houses with wood-scalloped walls. The station, dock, and Rothorn rack railway terminus occupy the center of town, flanked on Hauptstr. by the post office, banks, and a supermarket. At the west end of town is Brienz-Dorf wharf; at the eastern end lie the hostel and 2 campsites. Brienz is 20 minutes by **train** (6:10am-9:53pm, 10.60SFr) or 1¼ hours by **boat** (1 per hr., 8:20am-5:32pm, 12.40SFr) from Interlaken, and makes an ideal daytrip.

The campy **Ballenberg Swiss Open-Air Museum,** on the outskirts of town along Lauenenstr. (tel. 951 11 23; fax 951 18 21), is a 50-hectare country park displaying traditional rural dwellings, big-belled cows, happy muddy pigs, and Swiss artisans toiling away. (Open mid-Apr. to Oct. 10am-5pm. 12SFr; with visitor's card 10.80SFr; students 10SFr.) Free hot bread samples (which make you wanna buy more bread) come straight from the oven of the old-timey baker's house. The park is about an hour's walk from the Brienz train station, but a **bus** (every hr., 7:56am-7:02pm, round-trip 5.60SFr) connects the two, and the local train from Brienz to **Meiringen** and **Lucerne** halts in Brienzwiler opposite the museum at stop #5 (every 2hr.). The **Wood-Carving Museum** (tel. 951 17 51) on Schleeg. is 15 minutes down the main road and to the right. (Open M-Th 8-11:30am and 2-5pm. F 8-11:30am and 2-4pm. Free.) The **Violin-Making School** (tel. 951 18 61) is just around the corner on Oberdorfstr. (Open M-F 8-11am and 2-5pm. Sept.-June W 2-4pm. Free.) Home to 10 students ages 15 to 30, the school houses a collection of antique instruments and a showroom of gleaming, finished violins (approx. 5000SFr a pop). Many local wood-carvers also let you watch them work; contact the tourist office for a list. Open-air plays are performed every summer in Ballenberg's **Open Air Theater** (tel. 952 15 15). Inquire about tickets at the museum (tickets 38-48SFr).

Brienz's **tourist office,** Hauptstr. 143 (tel. 952 80 80; fax 952 80 88), across and left from the train station, suggests trails for hikers of all levels. Ask about *Privatzimmern,* guided hikes, tours of wood-carving schools, "carve your own cow" fests, and other fab happenings. (Open July-Aug. M-F 8am-6:30pm; Sa 9am-noon and 4-6pm; Sept.-June M-F 8am-noon and 2-6pm, Sa 8am-noon.) The **train station** rents **bicycles** (25SFr per day, 19SFr per half-day), **exchanges currency,** and offers **lockers** (2SFr). (All open 6am-10pm.) The **post office** (tel. 951 25 05) is next door. (Open M-F 7:45am-6pm, Sa 8:30-11am.) The **postal code** is CH-3855. The **telephone code** is 033.

For lodgings, cross the tracks at the station, face the lake, and walk left on the shore path (15min.) to find the **Brienz Jugendherberge (HI),** Strandweg 10 (tel. 951 11 52; fax 951 22 60). The lakeside hostel also **rents bicycles** (12SFr per day) to mountain-hungry guests. (Dorms 23SFr 1st night, then 20.50SFr; doubles 28SFr, 25.50SFr. Guest tax 2.10SFr. Breakfast included. Dinner 11SFr. **Kitchen** facilities. Reception 8-10am and 5-10pm. Open May-Oct.) The cheapest hotel in town is **Hotel Sternen am See,** Hauptstr. 92 (tel. 951 35 45), left from the station, with a winning lakeside terrace. (Singles 50-60SFr; doubles 90SFr, with shower 130SFr; triples 120SFr, 160SFr; quads with shower 200SFr. Breakfast included. Reception 8am-8pm. MC, Visa.) Continue past the hostel to hit two waterfront campgrounds. **Camping Seegärtli** (tel. 951 13 51) offers free lake-swimming and fresh bread at 8am. (7SFr; tents 5-7SFr; cars 3SFr. Reception 8am-8:30pm; open Apr.-Oct.) **Camping Aaregg** (tel. 951 18 43; fax 951 43 24) is somewhat more organized and has an on-site restaurant. (9.20SFr; tents 13SFr. Reception 8am-noon and 2-9pm; open Apr.-Oct.) A **Co-op** sits on Hauptg. across from the station. (Open M-Th 7:45am-6:30pm, F 7:45am-8pm, Sa 7:45am-4pm. MC, Visa.) **Restaurant Adler,** Hauptstr. 131 (tel. 951 41 00), has a terrace with a spectacular view of the Brienzersee and the Axalphorn. (Fondue special from 18SFr. Veggie dishes from 13SFr. Spanish *paellas* 17-19SFr. Oberland specialties 14-16SFr. Open June-Oct. 7:30am-11:30pm; Nov.-May Tu-Su 8am-11:30pm.) **Steinbock Restaurant** (tel. 951 40 55), farther along Hauptstr., has outside tables and a warm, dark, low-ceilinged wooden interior. (Swiss-style macaroni with apple sauce 16SFr. Veggie dishes 12-17SFr. Open 8am-11pm. AmEx, DC, MC, Visa.)

For even more Switzerland-exposure, you can ascend the **Rothorn** (2350m) for an outstanding view of the Brienzersee and the Berner Oberland mountain chain, well beyond the familiar Eiger, Mönch, and Jungfrau. From June to October, the **Brienz**

Rothorn Bahn (tel. 951 44 00) huffs and puffs its way up every hour (last ascent 4pm, last descent 4:55pm). Over 100 years old, this small open train is the only steam rail line left in Switzerland. The one-hour trip is pricey (41SFr, round-trip 64SFr; with regional pass 20SFr, 32SFr; with Swisspass 31SFr, 48SFr) but guarantees buttercup-filled pastures and sightings of nimble mountain-cows. A trip to **Planalp** in a hanging valley at 1341m leaves you three hours from the top (26SFr). The view on the way down is breathtaking. Either follow the railway, turning left below Planalp through Baalen and Schwanden (3½hr.), or leave the summit to the east toward the lake and turn right at the Eiseesaltel, continuing down to Hofstetten, Schwanden, and Brienz (4hr.). After a long day of hiking, you can spend the night on Rothorn's peak at the **Berggasthaus** (tel. 951 12 21; fax 951 12 51; dorms 32SFr; singles 65SFr; doubles 130SFr; hall showers; breakfast included; reception 7:30am-10pm). To restock some of those calories, visit the **farmer's market** that comes to Fischerbrunnenpl. on mornings of the first Saturday in summer months.

■ The South Shore

Boat service gives easy access to the wild, romantic south shore of the lovely Brien-zersee. Float 10 minutes from Brienz or one hour from Interlaken to **Giessbach Falls,** and climb along its 14 frothy cascades. You can walk up the hill in 15 minutes (turn left at the docks) or take the **cable car.** (Open May to mid-Oct. 3SFr, round-trip 5.50SFr; students and Regional Pass holders 2.50SFr, 3SFr.) The path criss-crosses and passes behind the falls—a deafening, dampening, exhilerating experience. Trails (1½hr., easy terrain) stretch around the lake from the falls to **Iseltwald,** a small village whose only tourist attraction is professional fishing.

To reach Brienz's relatively short peak, the **Axalphorn** (2321m), you can take a bus from Brienz station to **Axalp** (8:20am-4:40pm, 8.40SFr) and head up either the east or west ridge (800m, half-day). Get a map (check the tourist office at Brienz) and some navigational skills, since both paths are indistinct in places.

■ Meiringen and Reichenbach Falls

Few places are as steeped in fable as Meiringen. The little town, about 10 minutes from Brienz by **train** (4.20SFr) and 30 minutes from Interlaken, is home to many a figment of fertile imaginations: the monster worm of the *Aareschlucht* once lurked in its rocky chasms, the fork-tongued **Tatzelwürmli** inhabits the neighborhood gorge, and master detective **Sherlock Holmes** "died" at the nearby falls. The **Gorge of the Aare** (the nearby gorge) is 200m deep and only 1m wide at some points. Direct sunlight hardly ever reaches the bottom. (Open 9am-5pm. 6SFr, students and guest-card holders 5SFr.) To get there, follow signs from Meiringen's main street. In July and August, the gorge shines under the buzzing filaments of floodlights from 9 to 11pm.

Only slightly less spectacular, the **Reichenbach Falls** hurl their glacier water into the Aare River at Meiringen. Sherlock Holmes and Professor Moriarty tumbled together into the falls on May 4, 1891, apparently ending the greatest struggle between good and evil in the history of the detective novel. To reach the falls, walk down Meiringen's main street and turn right over the river to Reichenbach. From there, take the **funicular** (open mid-May to Sept. 8:15am-5:45pm; 4.60SFr, 6.70SFr round-trip, 5SFr with regional pass) or walk up. Continue onward and you will soon reach the deserted, high-alpine pastures of the Rosenlaui valley, the icefall of the Rosenlaui glacier, and the shapely Wellhorn peak (600m ascent, half-day). The **Sherlock Holmes Museum** (tel. 971 42 21) in the old Anglican church is a polished chestnut-wood representation of the imaginary 221B Baker Street. (Open May-Sept. Tu-Su 1:30-6pm; Oct.-Apr. by appointment only. 3.80SFr, 2.80SFr with guest card.) The **Rosenlaui glacier** offers a spectacular view of the unique glacial gorge-formations of the Hasli valley. (Open Apr.-Nov. 9am-5pm; July-Aug. 8am-6pm and floodlit 9-11pm. 6SFr, children 3.50SFr.) Meiringen hosts **Musikfestwoche** from mid-June to mid-July,

10 days chock full of classical music concerts. Youth orchestras from around the world perform. Tickets are sold at the church on Kirchstr. (left off Bahnhofstr.)

The **tourist office**, Bahnhofstr. 22 (tel. 972 50 50) gives info on local legends as well as good advice on where to eat and sleep. (Open July-Aug. M-F 8am-6pm, Sa 8am-noon and 2-4pm; Sept. M-F 8am-noon and 2-6pm, Sa 8am-noon and 2-4pm; Oct.-June 8am-noon and 2-6pm, Sa 8am-noon.) The fun and friendly **Simon's Herberge,** Alpbachstr. 17 (tel. 971 17 15), is a 10-minute walk toward the gorge. Surrounded by a not-so-nice bus parking lot but in the vicinity of the gorgeous Halisberg mountains, Simon's is a good place to rest your pack. (Dorms 28SFr 1st night, then 26SFr. Doubles 30SFr. Breakfast, sheets, and shower included. Lunch 11SFr.)

Eat something at the **Co-op,** Bahnhofstr. 37, opposite the Holmes Museum. (Open M-Th 8am-6:30pm, F 8am-8pm, Sa 8am-4pm.) The **Lüthi Bakery** next to the tourist office offers a tantalizing variety of confectionary *Haslikuchen,* meringues, and dragon-shaped *Taztelwürmli* candy, complete with bloody strawberry-candy teeth (3-9.20SFr).

■ Interlaken

In 1130, two ruthlessly literal-minded Augustinian monks named the land between the Thunersee and the Brienzersee "Interlaken." Most of its visitors, however, come not for the lakes but for the giant mountains to the south: the Eiger, Mönch, and Jungfrau. Although the sight of the Jungfrau rising 4158m above the gardens lining Höheweg is entrancing, Interlaken is a way-station for the villages to the south and not really much of a destination in itself. Unfortunately, this doesn't stop the hordes of English- and Japanese-speaking tourists who have virtually eliminated Swiss-German from menus and street signs. Each year, swarms of thrill-seekers descend on the town in search of canyoning, rafting, and bungee-jumping. Without the painted wooden cows and distant mountains, tourists might forget they were in Switzerland.

One of the eeriest and most fascinating sights in the Berner Oberland is the face in the **Harder Mountain,** called the **Harder Mann.** No human hand sculpted him, but there he is, looking out over Interlaken with his brooding gaze. On a clear day he is easy to see, a pale triangular face resting against a pillow of trees on one side and a wedge of naked rock on the other. His black moustache has a certain despondent droop, and his deep-socketed eyes have a melancholic, hunted look. To see him, stand on Höhenmatte across from the casino and look up through the buildings. There are many legends about the Harder Mann, most of them dark: a monk, guilty of murder or rape, fled to the mountains and was turned to stone, his face left behind for all eternity. For the children of Interlaken, there is a happier story: every year the Harder Mann comes down from the mountains to fight off winter. On January 2, they celebrate this fight with wooden Harder Mann masks and a large carnival. Hikers can hike this landmark, but they should not leave the marked paths. Deaths occur every summer when people attempt to climb roped-off areas.

Loch Meiringen?

Meiringen's mythic Gorge of Aare, a narrow mountainside chasm so deep that light barely penetrates its recesses, is said to harbor the fearsome Tatzelwürmli, a Nibelungian worm of monstrous, scaly proportions. Recently, a foreign photographer from Berlin named Balkin visited Meiringen and "accidentally" snapped photos of what he claimed was the Tatzelwürmli in its natural habitat. Resembling a very fat snake, the *Wurm* was brown with liver spots on its skin, and possessed a legendarily forked tongue. Balkin published his film in the *Berlin Illustrated Newspaper,* unleashing a torrent of speculation about the the snake-like inhabitant of Meiringen's rocky slopes. Although serious investigations have mostly died out at this point, the town still remembers its specter of a dragon with the perversely conceived Tatzelwürmli candy, shaped like the beast down to the marzipan tongue, cream belly, and bloody strawberry-candy teeth. Now you, too, can symbolically ward off dragon scourges by eating the poor beast in sugary effigy.

ORIENTATION AND PRACTICAL INFORMATION

Interlaken lies south on A6, west on A8, and north on Route 11, and the city has 2 train stations. The **Westbahnhof** stands in the center of town bordering the Thunersee, near most shops and hotels; trains from Bern, Basel, and other western towns stop here first. The **Ostbahnhof**, on the Brienzersee, is 10 minutes from the town center by foot or bus (2.20SFr), but quite near the youth hostel. Both stations have hotel prices posted and direct free phones for reservations.

Trains: The **Westbahnhof** (tel. 826 47 50) and **Ostbahnhof** (tel. 822 27 92) have trains to: **Bern** (5:32am-10:37pm, 24SFr), **Basel** (5:32am-10:37pm, 54SFr), **Zurich** (5:32am-10:37pm, 60SFr), **Geneva** (5:32am-9:43pm, 60SFr), **Lucerne** (5:32am-8:45pm, 25SFr), and **Lugano** (7:23am-6:12pm, 69SFr), among others. Trains to the mountains leave every 30min. from the Ostbahnhof to: **Wengen** (6:35am-11:32pm, 11.40SFr), **Grindelwald** (6:24am-11:32pm, 9SFr), **Mürren** (28.20SFr, change at Lauterbrunnen), **Lauterbrunnen** (6:35am-11:32pm, 6SFr), **Kleine Scheidegg** (34.60SFr), and the **Jungfraujoch** (158.20SFr round-trip; see **The Jungfraujoch**, p. 388). Swisspass valid for Wengen, Grindelwald, and Mürren, 25% discount at higher stops. Eurailpass 25% discount on mountain trains. Computers on the platforms at both stations spew information in English, German, and French. **Jungfraubahnen,** the steel arteries of the Jungfrau regions circulation system, connect the mountain towns. Head office Harderstr. 14 (tel. 828 71 11; fax 828 72 64).

Taxis: **City Taxi** (tel. 823 33 33). **Bödeli Taxi** (tel. 0800 801 802). **Interlaken Ost** (tel. 822 80 80).

Parking: Lots at the train stations, behind the casino, and on Centralstr.

Bike Rental: At either **train station,** 25SFr per day, mountain bikes 30SFr. Open 5am-10pm. At **Zumbrunn Velo,** Postg. 4 (tel. 822 22 35), 8SFr per day, mountain bikes 18SFr. Open Tu-Sa 8am-noon and 1:30-6:30pm. At **Intersport Oberland,** Postg. 16 (tel. 822 06 61; fax 822 73 07) 20SFr per day, mountain bikes 30SFr. Open M-Sa 8am-6pm.

Tourist Office: Höheweg 37 (tel. 822 21 21), in the **Hotel Metropole.** From the Westbahnhof, turn left on Bahnhofpl. and right on Bahnhofstr., which becomes Höheweg. From the Ostbahnhof, turn right as you exit the station. Free maps and schedules, tickets to the Jungfraujoch, and a TV link to all cable cars and railway stations. Open July-Aug. M-F 8am-noon and 1:30-6:30pm, Sa 8am-noon and 1:30-5pm, Su 5-7pm; Sept.-June M-F 8am-noon and 2-6pm, Sa 8am-noon.

Currency Exchange: Good rates at the **train station** (although you might do 1% better in town). No commission on traveler's checks. Credit card advances and Western Union transfers. Open daily 8am-noon and 2-6pm. **Credit Suisse** and **Swiss Bank** near the Westbahnhof have **ATMs,** as do both train stations.

Bookstore: Buchhandlweg Haupt, Höheweg 11 (tel. 822 35 16). English-language books, German and French dictionaries, and travel books. Open M-F 8:30am-6:30pm, Sa 8:30am-4pm.

Library: Marktpl. 4 (tel. 822 02 12). German, French, and English books. Open July-Aug. M, W, F, and Su 4-6pm, Tu and Th 9-11am and 3-7pm. Sept.-June M-Tu and Th-F 4-6pm, W 9-11am and 3-7pm, Sa 10am-noon.

Laundromat: Self-Service Wash & Dry, Beatenbergstr. 5. Cross the bridge next to the Westbahnhof and make a right on the far side of the Aare. Service 12SFr per load; self serve 6SFr. Open 24hr. **Spot On,** Hauptstr. 16, opposite Balmer's. Ritzily priced laundry 20SFr. Open 8am-8pm.

Snow and Weather Info: For the Jungfrau, call 855 10 22.

Late-Night Pharmacy: Call 111. **Grosse Apotheke,** Bahnhofstr. 5A (tel. 822 72 62), is open M-F 7:30am-6:30pm, Sa 7:30am-5pm. AmEx, MC, Visa.

Emergencies: Police, tel. 117. **Hospital,** tel. 826 26 26. **Doctor,** tel. 823 23 23.

Internet Access: Buddy's, Höheweg 33 (see p. 384). **Backpackers' Villa Sonnenhof,** Alpenstr. 16 (tel. 826 71 71; fax 826 71 72). 4SFr for 20min. Open 7:30-11am and 4-9pm. **Open Air Bar Belvedere,** opposite Höhenmatte, next to the casino. 2SFr for 5min. 24SFr for 1hr.

Post Office: Marktg. 1 (tel. 224 89 50). From the Westbahnhof go left on Bahnhofpl. Open May-Sept. M-F 7:45am-6:15pm, Sa 8:30am-11am; Oct.-Apr. M-Sa 7:45am-noon and 1:30-6:15pm, Sa 8:30-11am. **Postal Code:** CH-3800. **Telephone Code:** 033.

ACCOMMODATIONS AND CAMPING

Hotels in the mountains are going through a lean patch, and Interlaken is seriously over-bedded. Finding a place to sleep is easy. The tourist office has a list of self-catering chalets for rent, but in high-season these accommodations are often unavailable.

Hostels and Hotels

Ⓜ**Balmer's Herberge,** Hauptstr. 23-25 (tel. 822 19 61; fax 823 32 61), in the nearby village of Matten. Bus #5: "Hotel Sonne" (2.20SFr) and then backtrack 1min., or walk 15-20min. from either station. From June to Aug., Balmer's runs a shuttle bus from both stations approx. every hr. Sign in, drop off your pack, and return at 5pm when beds are assigned (no reservations). When you see Americans in Interlaken, it's not hard to guess where they're staying. Balmer's is the country's oldest private hostel (since 1945) and a legend on the international hostelers' circuit. During U.S. college vacations, it takes on a frat-party, summer-camp atmosphere. "Uncle Erich" provides a mama-load of services for his guests, including **mountain bike rental** (30SFr per day), nightly movies, TV with CNN and MTV, a book exchange, **email facilities** (5SFr for 15min.), a **kitchen** (1SFr per 20min.), **laundry** (8SFr per load), a mini-department store (open 7:30am-9pm), safety deposit boxes (2SFr for the entire stay), and tons of information. A **club-room** with **jukebox** and a **game-recreation room** entertain Balmer's guests into the wee hours of morning. Participate with caution—wake-up music starts at 7:30am to get half-conscious guests out by 9:30am. The staff makes a big effort to get guests out on the trails and slopes. In winter, there are **free sleds** and a 20% discount on ski and snowboard rental. Many of those in the dorms or Balmer's **tent** (a huge white circus tent with no insulation) value comradeship above comfort. Dorms and tent 17-19SFr; singles 40SFr; doubles 56SFr; triples 72SFr; quads 96SFr. If beds are full, crash on a mattress (13SFr). Showers 1SFr per 5min. of hot water. Breakfast included. No one gets turned away, but it's best to show up early. Reception in summer 6:30am-noon and 4:30-11pm; in winter 6:30-9am and 4:30-11pm. AmEx, MC, Visa with a 5% surcharge.

Backpackers Villa Sonnenhof, Alpenstr. 16 (tel. 826 71 71; fax 826 71 72) at the corner of Höhenmatte. This new shiny villa offers warm beds with million-dollar views of the Jungfrau and Silberhorn. 27SFr, 30SFr to face the Jungfrau; doubles 33SFr, 43SFr with shower. Breakfast, lockers, and **kitchen** (nice kitchen, too) included. Reception 7:30-11am and 4-9pm. No curfew. AmEx, DC, MC, Visa.

Jugendherberge Bönigen (HI), Aareweg 21 (tel. 822 43 53; fax 823 20 58). Bus #1 (dir: Bönigen): "Lütschinenbrücke" (3 stops). Catering to a more international crowd, this *Jugi* is the ying to Balmer's yang. The lake laps at the doorstep while garden gnomes squint in the garden. It's pretty far from town, though. Try to snag a 6-bed dorm instead of the noisy 25-bed behemoths on the top floor. No lockout. 6- and 25-bed dorms 25.30SFr 1st night, then 22.80SFr; 4-bed dorms 29.30SFr, 26.80SFr; doubles 76.60SFr. Breakfast, showers, sheets included. Lockers 20SFr deposit. Dinner 11SFr. **Kitchen-use** 1SFr for 20min. **Laundry** 8SFr. **Bike rental** 12SFr. Reception 6-10am and 2pm-midnight. Reserve at least 2 days in advance June-Aug. Open mid-Feb. to Jan. 10th.

Funny Farm, next to Hotel Hatterhof, around the corner from Balmer's. This laid-back, den of grunge knows no law. Come and go as you like. Psychedelic, hypnotic spirals painted neon all over. Swimming pool, dude. Dorms 25SFr, or sleep in the "ghetto" (read: no bathrooms) for 20SFr. Breakfast included and served until noon.

Heidi's Garni-Hotel Beyeler, Bernastr. 37 (tel./fax 822 90 30). From the Westbahnhof, turn right, then bear left on Bernastr. (behind the Migros), and walk straight for about 3min. A friendly, family-run hotel in a rambling old house decorated with sleds, bells, old photographs, and carousel horses. Wood-beamed TV room with CNN and lots of information on things to do. Some of the comfy, home-quilted rooms with bath have balconies, views, and flowery Swiss furniture. Dorms 25SFr; doubles 60-75SFr; triples 93SFr; quads 100-

124SFr. More expensive modern doubles (80-90SFr) across the street in an apartment with kitchen, phone, balcony, and TV room. Free lollipops. MC, Visa.

Happy Inn Lodge, Rosenstr. 17 (tel. 822 32 25; fax 822 32 68). Turn left as you exit the Westbahnhof, make a right on Bahnhofstr., go past the post office, and then make a right onto Rosenstr. Look for the yellow happy face. Hostel-type dorms with exceptionally fluffy pillows and quads and doubles with a less institutional feel. Thin walls do little to block out the occasional live bands playing downstairs at the restaurant/bar, **Brasserie 17.** 6-bed dorms 19SFr, with breakfast 26SFr; doubles 70SFr, 82SFr; quads 108SFr, 136SFr. Hall showers and sheets included. Reception M-Sa 6:30am-12:30am, Su 3pm-12:30am. AmEx, MC, Visa.

Camping

Camping Sackgut (tel. (079) 656 89 58) is closest to town, just across the river from the Ostbahnhof. Head toward town, but take a right across the 1st bridge and another right on the other side. 7.60SFr; tent 6.50-14.50SFr. Reception 9-11am and 4-7pm. Open May-Oct.

Camping Jungfrablick (tel. 822 44 14; fax 822 16 19). Bus #5 from the Westbahnhof, 5min. past Balmer's on Gsteigstr. Peaceful location with splendid views. 12SFr; off-season 7SFr. Open May-Sept.

Manor Farm (tel. 822 22 64; fax 823 29 91) on the Thunersee. 10.70SFr; tents 4-8SFr, including showers. Open all year.

Alpenblick (tel. 822 77 57) in Unterseen. 7.10SFr, tents 9-16SFr. Open all year.

Hobby (tel. 822 96 52; fax 822 96 57) has a spectacular view. 8SFr, tents not available. Open Mar.-Sept.

Lazy Rancho (tel. 822 87 16, fax 823 19 20) is equipped with a swimming pool, grocery store, bowling alley, and horseys for riding. Showers 0.50SFr. Open Mar.-Oct.

Camping Jungfrau (tel. 822 57 30) is a happy place with kitchen, tennis, golf, bowling, and a dance room. 8.10SFr, tents upon request. Open Mar.-Oct.

FOOD

Interlaken's restaurants, unlike its accommodations, are as expensive as the rest of Switzerland. Along Höheweg, restaurants are exorbitant and overwhelmingly touristy. Head across the river to old Interlaken (from Höheweg turn onto Marktg. and cross the bridge) for cheaper meals, a better atmosphere, and menus that are actually in German. Generally, the Balmer's crowd eats at Balmer's (fondue, bratwurst, and burgers all under 10SFr), and the hostel crowd eats at the *Jugendherberge* (11SFr).

Pizpaz, Bahnhofstr. 1 (tel. 822 25 33), is a buzzing, central Italian restaurant with pinkish outdoor tables. "Farinaceous dishes" (presumably pasta) 9.50-17.50SFr, pizza 11-17.50SFr, shrimp and gorganzola risotto 18SFr. Open July-Aug. 11am-midnight; Sept.-June Tu-Su 11am-midnight. AmEx, MC, Visa.

Matahari, General Guisanstr. 31 (tel. 823 80 01; fax 823 80 02), off Bahnhofstr. behind the Migros. Thai parasols decorate this spicy haunt, which concocts Indonesian *Rijstafel* on a banana leaf for 20SFr. Fresh-from-the-wok, all-you-can-eat specialties 24SFr. Asian specialties (often veggie-happy) from 12SFr. *Menüs* 12SFr. Open W-Su 11am-2:30pm and 5:30pm-midnight. AmEx, DC, MC, Visa.

Runft Tea Room and Restaurant, Bahnhofpl. 51 (tel. 823 83 83), next to the Migros, opposite Westbahnhof. Swiss dishes 7-24SFr. Indian specialties 11-18.50SFr. Open 6am-2:30am.

Café Restaurant Spatz, Spielmatte 49 (tel. 822 97 22), 5min. from Höheweg. Turn onto Marktg. and cross the 1st bridge. This café serves up the cheapest fondue in town (13.50SFr); a platter of chicken, potatoes, and veggies (11SFr); and *Apfelstrüdel* with whipped cream (4.50SFr) on a terrace overlooking the river. Open M-Sa 8:30am-11pm.

Confiserie Schuh (tel. 822 94 41; fax 822 94 27). An Interlaken landmark, around since the 19th century. Traditional chocolate boots (from 1.60SFr) and strawberry tarts (3.90SFr) sell like mad in the summer. Open Tu-Su 8am-10:30pm.

Mr. Hong's Chinese Take-Out, Marktg. 48 (tel. 823 55 44). For evenings too beautiful to eat inside, friendly Mr. Hong cooks up a huge variety of stir-fries to go. Chomp on mixed veggies (10SFr), sweet and sour chicken (13SFr), or shrimp fried rice (13SFr). Open Apr.-Oct. 11:45am-10pm; Nov.-Mar. 11:45am-2pm and 5-9pm.

Markets

Migros, across from the Westbahnhof, also houses a restaurant with giant prancing cows on the ceiling. Open M-Th 7:30am-6:30pm, F 7:30am-9pm, Sa 7:30am-4pm. Restaurant also open Su 9am-5pm.

Co-op, Bahnhofstr. 35 (tel. 826 44 80), on the right after you cross into Unterseen. Market open M-Th 7:30am-6:30pm, F 7:30am-9pm, Sa 7:30am-4pm. Restaurant open M-Th 8am-6:30pm, F 8am-9:30pm, Sa 8am-4:30pm, Su 9am-5pm.

OUTDOORS NEAR INTERLAKEN

Interlaken is the base for many outdoor excursions, boasting such adrenaline-stimulating, muscle-building, heart-attack-producing activities as bungee jumping, parachuting, glacier climbing, canyoning, kayaking, and paragliding. Guests at Balmer's can sign up near the reception desk for activities run by **Adventure World,** Kirchg. 18 (tel. 826 77 11; fax 826 77 15), Interlaken's main "adventure coordinator." Thrill-seekers flock to a host of daredevil pursuits. On the water, there's **river rafting** (half-day 85SFr) and **canyoning,** a sport where wet-suited, harnessed future stunt doubles rappel and swim down a waterfall (half-day 85-150SFr). On land, struggle up and rappel down the alps on your **rock-climbing** adventure (half-day 75SFr). In the air, enjoy the graceful beauty of **tandem paragliding** (half-day 140-200SFr, depending on altitude) or experience the free-fall rush of **bungee jumping** from the Schilthorn, the highest jump from a funicular. (100m 100SFr; 180m 229SFr). Adventure World also offers combination packages (155-333SFr).

Interlaken's *Flugschule* **Ikarus** (tel. 822 04 28) offers intensive and expensive classes in **parachuting** and **paragliding,** as well as a one-day program of **tandem paragliding** (from 100SFr; 1 week 890SFr). Contact Claudia or Hanspeter Michel, Brunng. 68, CH-3800 Matten (tel. 822 04 28). **Alpin Raft,** another Interlaken-based group, also offers **rafting** (50-83SFr), **canyoning** (75-112SFr), **kayaking** (35SFr), **horseback riding** (75SFr for 2hr.), and **hang-gliding** (155SFr). Contact Heinz Looshi, Postfach CH-3800, Matten (tel. 823 41 00; fax 823 41 01).

Minutes from Interlaken on the Brienzersee, Alpin Raft's **sea-kayaking** provides a strenuous day in the sun and on the water (54-70SFr). For those who want to get really cold and wet, **Alpine Guides** Joyce and Hano Tschabold, Bergführer, CH-3852 Ringgenberg (tel. 22 05 69), offer **glacier climbing** (June-Oct., 125SFr), one-day **rock-climbing courses** (95SFr), and one-day **glacier walks** (110SFr) daily in summer. Interlaken's winter activities include skiing, snowboarding, ice canyoning, snow rafting, and glacier skiing. Contact **Verkehrsverein Interlaken,** Höheweg 37 (tel. 822 21 21; fax 822 52 21), or Adventure World for information. **Paragliding Interlaken,** P.O. Box 451 CH-3800 Interlaken (tel. 823 82 33; fax 823 82 34) offers the opportunity to discover why birds sing (tandem flights 120-230SFr). They also do **rafting** (85SFr), **canyoning** (85SFr), and **bungee jumping** (129-259SFr). There's also **Tandem Hang-Gliding** (tel. 823 48 48) with a guy named Greg Haas. For 155SFr, you fly around and see lakes, alps, glaciers, and stuff.

With all these activities, the situation is very fluid; companies tend to come and go as individual guides and instructors move into and out of Interlaken. Shop around, and watch the fine print for insurance coverage and travel costs to the starting point.

HIKES FROM INTERLAKEN

Interlaken is in a deep valley, so picture-perfect views require that you sweat. A gentle lakeside path rings the Brienzersee, and the south shore provides a scenic walk or bike ride from Böningen or the youth hostel garden. The half-day climb up the **Harderkulm** (1322m) brings you touchably close to the white wall of the Jungfrau,

Eiger, and Mönch peaks, towering 3700m above Interlaken's rooftops. The hike zig-zags through dense, dull woods, but the view from the top is extraordinary. From the Ostbahnhof, head toward town and take the first road bridge right across the river. On the other side, the path has yellow signs (destination: Harderkulm) that later give way to white-red-white *Bergweg* flashes on the rocks. A house in a clearing stands halfway from Interlaken West; from here, turn left and left again across the river on Bahnhofstr., later called Scheidg. After seven minutes the path intersects with Beaten-bergstr. at the edge of town and then rises at the junction across the road. Bus #21: "Beatenberg" also stops at the trailhead (2 per hr. from both stations). The path is not very difficult, but rain can make it gloopy (750m ascent, 2hr. up, 1½hr. down). A **restaurant** at the top serves spaghetti for 11.50SFr and *Rösti* with fried eggs for 11.80SFr, but try to carry liquids to protect your bank balance. To facilitate your ascent, a **cable car** climbs up from the start of the Interlaken Ost path (roughly May-Oct.; 12.80SFr, 20SFr round-trip; 25% discount with Eurailpass and Swisspass). After the ascent, the path extends across the ridge's crest where the views improve, the gradient lessens, and you start to lose the accursed trees. Paths on the right dive down to Ringgenberg and Niederried, where buses run back to Interlaken.

A grueling hike for a hot, clear day is the climb up **Schynige Platte** (2070m). Although the path is very long and very steep, the panoramic view is one of the best in the Jungfrau region. Take bus #5 south of Interlaken (or any of the mountain trains from Interlaken Ost) to the village of Wilderswil across the river; the path heads up (and up and up) from the back of the churchyard (1500m of ascent, full day, steep in places). In May and early June check for snow before heading out. From roughly June to mid-October, a train leaves from Wilderswil (31.80SFr, 53.60SFr round-trip; 25% discount with Eurail and Swisspass). If you are considering taking the railway up and walking down, bear in mind that the descent is out of sight of the Jungfrau *massif* and that walking off Schynige Platte northwards to Zweilütschinen, while possible, is extremely steep and only for the experienced. You can come back down to Wilderswil pretty safely. One option is to take the railway up to Breitlauenen (half-way up, 9.60SFr), at which point the path is free of forest and the views are incredible. Check out the **garden** up top, which boasts rare flowers (Edelweiss, Edelweiss) and obese bumblebees. (Open mid-June to Sept. 15 8:45am-6pm. 3SFr, 2SFr with guest card.)

NIGHTLIFE

Interlaken's nightlife heats up during high season but never quite gets red-hot. **Balmer's** (see p. 381) is like a freakin' frat, in part because the beer there is cheap (3.50SFr; bar open 9pm-1am). Many revelers head to **Buddy's,** Höheweg 33, a small, crowded English pub where the beer is also cheap (3-5SFr) but the **email** ain't (6SFr for 15min.; bar open daily 10am-12:30am). The drunken herds then migrate to Interlaken's oldest disco, **Johnny's Dancing Club,** Höheweg 92, downstairs in the Hotel Carlton. (Drinks from 6SFr. Open Tu-Su 9:30pm-3am.) For smoky blues try **Brasserie,** Rosenstr. 17 (tel. 822 32 25), where live bands play Thursdays. Beers aren't bad there, either (from 3SFr). (Open M-Sa 8:30am-12:30am, Su 3pm-12:30am.)

If you want to see the whole "Swiss" thing, there's the **Swiss Folklore Show** (tel. 827 61 00) at the casino for 16SFr. (Shows at 8:30pm M and W-Sa July-Aug., sporadically May-Oct.) At 6:30pm the theater serves fondue and ice cream for an additional 39.50SFr. The other apex of Interlaken's cultural life is the summer production of Friedrich Schiller's **Wilhelm Tell** (in German; English synopsis 2SFr). Two-hundred fifty local men with bushy beards and heavy rouge and lasses with flowing locks ham up the tale of the Swiss escape from the thumbscrew of Austrian rule. The showmanship is great—20 horses gallop by in every scene, and a vaudeville-like stage around the corner from Balmer's allows the cast to make real bonfires. A cunning distraction leaves you pondering whether they actually shoot the apple off the boy's head, however. (Shows late June to mid-July Th 8pm; mid-July to early Sept. Th and Sa 8pm.) Tickets (12-32SFr) are available at Tellbüro, Bahnhofstr. 5A (tel. (036) 822 37 22; open May-Sept. M-F 8:30-11:30am and 2-5pm; Oct.-Apr. Tu 8-11am and 2-5pm), or at the theater on the night of the show. Children under 6 are not admitted.

THE JUNGFRAU REGION

A few miles south of Interlaken, the hitherto middling mountains rear up and become hulking white monsters. Welcome to the Jungfrau, home to Europe's largest glacier and many of its steepest crags and highest waterfalls. The Jungfrau region's list of firsts reflects its irresistible appeal to sportsmen: the first Alpine mountaineering, the first skiing, and the first part of Switzerland opened to tourists. In summer, the Jungfrau region's hundreds of kilometers of hiking blast the senses with spectacular mountain views, wildflower meadows, roaring waterfalls, and pristine forests. The three most famous peaks in the Oberland are the **Jungfrau,** the **Eiger,** and the **Mönch.** In English, that's the Maiden, the Ogre, and Monk. Natives say that the monk protects the maiden by standing between her and the ogre. Actually, the Jungfrau is 4158m high, so she'd probably kick the Eiger's puny little 3970m butt.

Staying in a half-hidden town's wooden chalet may be the highlight of your tour— simple homemade breakfasts and Swiss hospitality are perfect companions as you wander at the beauty of the Alps. The slower and cheaper mode of transportation is your own two legs. Hiking makes your budget go farther and this is the place to do it.

■ Grindelwald

The town of Grindelwald, beneath the north face of the **Eiger,** is a cold weather Shangri-La for skiers and climbers. The lush green valley ringed with blue glaciers glinting in the sun is Switzerland distilled to its purest and most stunning. Although it only has two streets of any size, Grindelwald is the most developed part of the Oberland's valleys. The Berner-Oberlander-Bahn runs from **Interlaken's** Ostbahnhof (9SFr; sit in the rear half of the train). Trains to **Kleine Scheidegg** (26SFr, 45SFr round-trip; Eurailpass and Swisspass 25% discount) and the **Jungfraujoch** (round-trip 142SFr, with "Good Morning" ticket 103SFr; Eurailpass and Swisspass 25% discount) start from the station. There is also a bus from Balmer's (round-trip 15SFr).

The **tourist office** (*Verkehrsbüro;* tel. 854 12 12; fax 854 12 10), located in the Sport-Zentrum in the middle of town, provides hiking maps (9.50SFr), chairlift information, and a list of free guided excursions. Turn right from the train station, ignoring the "i" sign that points down the hill. The office finds a limited number of rooms in private homes (25-50SFr; usually 3-night min. stay). (Open July-Aug. M-F 8am-7pm, Sa 8am-5pm, Su 9-11am and 3-5pm; Sept.-June M-F 8am-noon and 2-6pm, Sa 8am-noon and 2-5pm.) Do **laundry** at **Wash 4 Dry** (tel. 853 11 68) opposite Hotel Adler on Haupstr., where you'll pay 3SFr for washing; 1SFr for 10 minutes of drying. There is a **post office** opposite the station. (Open M-F 8am-noon and 1:45-6pm, Sa 8-11am.) The **postal code** is CH-3818, and the **telephone code** is 036.

Grindelwald's hotel prices push most budget travelers into dorms. The **Jugendherberge (HI)** (tel. 853 10 09; fax 853 50 29) is a ranking contender for the title of World's Best Youth Hostel. And for Heavyweight Champion of the World, too. To get there, head left from the station (5-7min.) then cut uphill to the right (8min.) by the minuscule brown sign, past two big parking lots, turn left at the fork by the blue SJH sign. The living rooms with fireplaces and dorms still smell of freshly cut pine. The surprisingly private dorms have state-of-the-art bar code locks and balconies facing the Eiger. (Dorms 29.50SFr 1st night, then 27SFr. Double or quad with sink 34.50SFr, 32SFr; double with shower 45SFr, 42.50SFr. Non-members add 5SFr. Breakfast included. Giant dinner 11SFr. Huge, free lockers and proper bed linen (not sleeping sacks) included. **Laundry** 3SFr. Reception M-Sa 6:30-9:30am and 3-11pm, Su 6:30-9:30am and 5-11pm. No lockout.) Its rival is the bright blue **Mountain Hostel** (tel. 853 39 00; fax 853 47 30) at the Grund station next to the river. Turn right out of the train station, then right downhill just after the bus station. At Hotel Glacier, bear right, and head past the station. Renovated in 1996, the hostel has gleaming four- and six-bed dorms and a plush reception area with TVs, ping-pong, and pool. (Dorms 29-34SFr; doubles 78-88SFr. Buffet breakfast included. Outside cooking facilities 0.50SFr.

Laundry 12SFr.) One hour from town (see below) but a step from the Upper Glacier, **Hotel Wetterhorn** (tel. 853 12 18) has snug, quilted dorm-beds (42SFr, doubles 105SFr; breakfast included). The rooms have a view of the Upper Glacier and the trails that lead to it. The Grosse Scheidegg bus (5.40SFr) stops at the door. *Zimmer frei* (room for rent) notices are also posted on the information board at the bus station, though most rooms require a one-week minimum stay. A stay at the warm and friendly **Lehmann's Herberge** (tel. 853 31 41) will do you good. To get there, follow the main street past the tourist office and look on the right. Enjoy the comfort of Verena and Fritz Lehmann's home as well as their homemade, hearty breakfasts for 54SFr. (After 1st night 40SFr. Bath and breakfast included. Doubles 54SFr.) **Gletscherdorf** (tel. 853 14 29; fax 853 31 29) is the nearest of all Grindelwald's **campgrounds.** From the station, take a right, then the first right downhill after the tourist office, then the third left. The small grounds have clean facilities and a phenomenal view of the mountains. (9SFr; tents 4-9SFr; reception M-Sa 8-10am and 5:30-7:30pm, Su 5-8pm.) **Camping Eigernordwand** (tel. 853 42 27) is across the river and to the left of the Grund station. (9.50SFr; tents 7-8SFr.)

Frugal gourmets shop at the **Co-op** across from the tourist office. (Open M-F 8am-6:30pm, Sa 8am-4pm.) A **Migros** is farther along the main street away from the station. (Open M-Th 8am-noon and 1:30-6:30pm, F 8am-noon and 1:30-9pm, Sa 8am-5pm.) For huge plates of *Rösti*, omelettes, salads, and fresh-baked desserts, hit the **Tea Room Riggenburg** (tel. 853 10 59) on the main street past the tourist office away from the station. Drink a huge hot cocoa (3SFr) on the heated terrace as sparrows dive-bomb for crumbs. Main courses run 12 to 16SFr, cakes 2SFr, and more extravagant frozen desserts are 9 to 20SFr. (Open Tu-Sa 8am-10pm, Su 10am-9pm.) **Gepsi Bar** (tel. 853 21 21) is just past the tourist office on the left. Watch cows go crazy in this upbeat bar/restaurant where the kids yodel like berserkers. Swiss music night is Wednesday, and Gepsi Toast happens every happenin' Tuesday (for 7SFr). Entrees start at 12SFr, beer at 4SFr. Grindelwald plate goes for 18SFr. Bar open 5pm-1am. **Ye Olde Spotted Cat** is on Hauptstr. (tel. 853 12 34). Winston Churchill and Field-Marshall Montgomery visited the place (see the wall). Scratch a few wooden cats' heads while sipping beer (3.50SFr). (Open summer 11am-12:30am; winter 3pm-2:30am.)

Outdoor Activities near Grindelwald

Only Zermatt could challenge Grindelwald's claim as Switzerland's premier hiking hotspot. The town has nearly everything: easy valley walks, high-altitude level walks, accessible glaciers, and peaks to challenge top climbers. The terrain varies in every direction, and a network of railways, cable cars, and buses makes the most exciting areas accessible without hours of uphill toil. Ride **Europe's longest chairlift** (tel. 854 80 80) to the top of the **Männlichen,** which separates Grindelwald and the Lautenbrunnen Valley. (8am-4pm, 28SFr, round-trip 45SFr; 25% discount with Swisspass; 50% with Eurailpass.) The summit affords a glorious vista of the Eiger, Mönch, and Jungfrau. Other transport links north and east are buses to **Bussalp** (1807m; 8 per day, 15SFr, half-price with Swisspass) and to **Grosse Scheidegg** (1926m; 8 per day, 8:20am-5pm 15.80SFr, round-trip 31SFr, same discounts). Budget combinations for non-circular hikes are possible. In the south and west, the **Männlichen** (2230m) separates the Grindelwald and Lauterbrunnen valleys. Grindelwald's **First Mountain** affords idyllic scenery complete with meddling marmots (why you yellow-bellied...), icebergs, lakes, rare flowers, and excellent access to the Faulhorn and Schwarzhorn peaks. First Mountain provides tons of hiking, unlike the less accessible Jungfrau and Schilthorn. You can take the First Bahn there (tel. 833 50 50; 1st departure 8:30am, last 3:45pm in winter, 4:30pm in summer). The **Kleine Scheidegg railway** (tel. 828 71 11) costs 26SFr, round-trip 43SFr, and the tiny **Pfingstegg cable car** on the path to the Lower Glacier costs 9.20SFr, round-trip 14SFr (1st departure 10:55am, last 5:45pm). Show your railpass at all trains and lifts. Past the tourist office from the station stands the joint **Bergführerbüro** (Mountain Guides Office) and **Ski School** (tel. 853 52 00; fax 853 12 22). The office sells maps for hiking and coordinates rugged activities like glacier walks, ice climbing, and mountaineering. (Open June-Oct. M-Sa 9am-noon and 3-6pm, Su 4-6pm. 1-day activities about 100-400SFr. Reserve ahead for multi-day expeditions.)

A classic level mountaintop walk is from **Männlichen** to **Kleine Scheidegg** (1hr.), a hike that provides stunning panoramas and a close-up view of the Eiger. Every September, a marathon beginning in Interlaken finishes on the Kleine Scheidegg ridge, 2061m above the starting line. Descending from either end to Grindelwald-Grund station takes three to four hours at a gentle pace through trees and forests. Another satisfying hike is from **First** to **Schynige Platte** (1 day) past high hidden alpine valleys and the lovely Bachalpsee (2265m), up to the Faulhorn peak (2680m). (Path generally closed Oct. to mid-June because of snow.) A compact version of the First-Schynige Platte hike involves taking the cable car to First, hiking up the Faulhorn (the path crosses large and slippery snowbanks), descending to Bussalp, and catching the bus back to Grindelwald. This cheater version captures the long views and marmot glens of the longer walk but is cheaper and more manageable. You can even walk down from First or Grosse Scheidigg back to Grindelwald, a two- to three-hour downhill stroll through fields and pastures. A new hiking route follows the **Eiger Trail** (4hr. 50min. up and down) from the Eiger Glacier Station (70SFr from Grindelwald) to the Jungfraujoch. It affords spectacular views of the North Wall, ice fields, rock formations and waterfalls. (Guided tour every Tu and W June-Oct; tel. 853 52 00.)

For those who aren't satisfied with just a day's easy hike, the **Schwarzwaldalp** (2928m) offers a simple, challenging alternative to the smaller Faulhorn. From Grosse Scheidegg or First, go up through the high valley of Chrinnenboden. The finish is steep and treacherous when covered in snow, but the peep from the top covers a dozen 4000m peaks. Allow three to four hours for the ascent; buses and cable cars quicken the descent. (Last descent 5pm; 19.40SFr; 25% off with Swiss/Eurailpass.) **Mountaineers** should contact the Mountain Guides Office for excursions, but should note that even the first train to Jungfraujoch is too late for the high peaks, requiring an overnight stay at the Mönchsjochhütte. Guides lead big climbs most summer days. For two people the Eiger is 890SFr, Mönch 560SFr, and Jungfrau 900SFr. They also give skills training for a day, weekend, or week. Always reserve three days in advance.

Many mountaintops have places to spend the night, and nothing is more beautiful than waking up to a still dawn over the mountains. At Kleine Scheidegg (2061m), dorm beds go for 32 to 35SFr at **Grindelwaldblick** (tel. 855 13 74) and 28 to 50SFr at **Bahnhofbuffet** (tel. 855 11 51). At Männlichen (tel. 853 10 68; 2227m), a bunk is 35SFr, and on the Faulhorn (tel. 853 27 13; 2681m), dorms are 33SFr. **Berggasthaus First** (tel. 853 12 84) at the cable car terminus has a blue 'n' yellow **Touristenlager** (tourist camp) for 40SFr including breakfast; dinner is 22SFr.

After a long hike, cool off with some **glaciers.** Tasty. Take Grindelwald's main street right from the station past the church, turn right just after Mounty's (yellow sign: "Hotel Wetterhorn"), then follow signs from Hotel Wetterhorn (1½hr. ascent, easy grade). Paths go up both sides of the **Upper Glacier** via Restaurant Milchbach or the Schreckhomhütte; both are tricky, exposed, and linked with terrifying ladders. You can visit the ice-blue **Glaciergorge** (*Gletscherschult*) while you're there—plod through the frozen tunnel to check out ice sculptures (5SFr). (Open mid-May to mid-Oct 9am-6pm.) The **Lower Glacier,** though less spectacular, is much more approachable. Turn right just after the church, cross the river, and zigzag up to Pfingstegg. On the way, there's a detour to **Glacier Gorge.** At Pfingstegg (1392m), turn right to the glacier and follow the edge as far up as you please (1½-3hr. up, 45min.-2hr. down).

Winter **skiing** is phenomenal. Ski passes are 105SFr for two days, 254SFr for a week, and 400SFr for two weeks (ages 16-20 80SFr, 204SFr, 320SFr; under 16 50SFr, 127SFr, 200SFr). Eagle-eyed rental companies watch one another's prices, so there isn't much to be gained by shopping around. For 10SFr you can rent a **sled** from a ski rental store and rocket down the mountain. For winter hikes, some mountain paths get cleared. All year, **Adventure World** (tel. 826 77 11) coordinates high adrenaline activities: **paragliding** (120-200SFr), **rock-climbing** (75SFr), **canyoning** (85SFr), and **rafting** (85SFr). Write to Adventure World, 3800 Interlaken.

BERNER OBERLAND

■ The Jungfraujoch

The area's most arresting ascent is up the **Jungfraujoch**, a head-spinning, breath-shortening, 3454m adventure on Europe's highest railway. Chiseled into solid rock, the track tunnels right through the Eiger and Mönch mountains. Its construction was one of the greatest engineering feats of all time, taking 16 years and a work force of 300 men. The line was to have gone even higher to the Jungfrau summit itself (4158m), but by 1912, the project was so over budget that the final 700m were left to the gods and the hard-core mountaineers. Thanks to the rarefied air's lack of pollution, the top now shelters Europe's highest manned meteorology station and the **Sphinx Laboratory** for the study of cosmic radiation. Half a million visitors per year explore the **Ice Palace** (free), a super-smooth maze cut into the ice replete with sculptures. Beware skidding children and blindness due to flash photography. Beware the gargantuan ice sumo wrestler. Siberian huskies pull lazy mountaineers across the snow on sleds for 10SFr. Budget sportsmen opt for free "snow-hurtling," i.e., sledding down bunny-level slopes on garbage bags (bring your own bag). Gaze down the 24km **Aletschgletscher**, Europe's longest, and, at 900m, thickest glacier. If the weather is perfect, try the 30-minute, snowy trek to the **Mönchsjoch** climbing hut.

Trains start at Interlaken's Ostbahnhof and travel to Grindelwald and Lauterbrunnen, continuing to **Kleine Scheidegg** and finally to the peak itself. The entire trip costs an insane sum, depending on where you alight, but the earliest trains from Interlaken's Ostbahnhof, the Lauterbrunnen, and Grindelwald can cost as little as 91SFr. All tickets are round-trip, and there is no way down from the top except by train (Eurail 25% off, Swisspass 30% off). You can get a "Good-Morning" ticket on the *Bahn* if you depart between 6:24-7:30am and leave the top by noon. (From Interlaken W 163SFr, good-morning ticket 124SFr; Interlaken E 158.20SFr, 119.20SFr; Lauterbrunnen 140.80SFr, 101.80SFr; Grindelwald 142SFr, 103SFr; Wengen 130SFr, 91SFr; Kleine Scheidegg 97SFr, 58SFr; Murren 158SFr, 119.80SFr.) Call 855 10 22 for a **weather forecast** or use the cable TV broadcast live from the Jungfraujoch and other mile-high spots (in all tourist offices and big hotels). Bring winter clothing and food—it can be 10°C (50°F) on a July day, and in winter alcohol thermometers crack and car antifreeze freezes. Beware of overwhelming crowds. They will rip you apart.

■ Wengen

Tiny Wengen occupies the only ledge on the cliff-curtained *Lauterbrunnental.* The village offers raw grandeur and craggy waterfalls along with gentle, local slopes for hiking and skiing. Wengen is accessible on hourly trains from **Interlaken** (6:27am-11:27pm; 11.40SFr) and **Lauterbrunnen** (6:05am-11:05pm, 5.40SFr) to **Kleine Scheidegg** (7:57am-7pm, 20SFr) and the **Jungfraujoch** (9am-6:10pm, 130SFr, morning ticket 91SFr). Leave cars in the Lauterbrunnen parking garage (9SFr per day).

To reach the **tourist office** (tel. 855 14 14; fax 855 30 60), turn right from the station, then immediately left. The office issues hiking details and finds you a tennis partner. (Open mid-June to mid-Sept and mid-Dec. to Easter M-F 8am-noon and 2-6pm, Sa 8:30-11:30am and 4-6pm, Su 4-6pm; mid-Oct. to mid-Dec. and Apr. to mid-June M-F 8am-noon and 2-6pm, Sa 8:30-11:30am.) At the **train station** you can **exchange currency**, book hotel rooms, and watch the cable car TV channel. The **pharmacy** (tel. 855 12 46), left out of the station, is two minutes past the tourist office. (Open M-F 8am-noon and 2-6:30pm, Sa 8am-noon and 2-5pm.) A public **laundry** hides under the Hotel Silberhorn between the station and the tourist office (5SFr for wash 'n' dry; open 7am-9:30pm). For a **doctor**, call 856 28 28; for the **hospital**, 826 26 26. The **post office** is next to the tourist office. (Open M-F 8am-noon and 1:45-6pm, Sa 8-11am.) The **postal code** is CH-3823. The **telephone code** is 033.

Ski passes for the Wengen-Kleine-Scheidegg-Männlichen area start at 52SFr for one day, 95SFr for two; for longer periods, purchase a Jungfrau regional pass. (Ages 6-16 50% discount, ages 16-20 20%.) Ski rentals are 28SFr per day, 105SFr for 6 days. Boots are 15SFr, 52SFr. The **Swiss Ski School** (tel./fax 855 20 22), by the Co-op one minute right of the station, is the cheaper of the town's two schools. (Open late-Dec. to early Apr. Su-F 8:30am-noon, 1-2:30pm, and 3:30-6pm, Sa 9-11am and 4:30-6:30pm.) For **snow information** for Jungfraujoch, call 855 10 22. For a **weather report,** call 157 45 06. As you watch golf carts schlepping lazy tourists around, you may find it hard to believe that Wengen attracts the athletically intense to its slopes and trails twice a year. Every January, Wengen hosts the (skiing) World Cup's longest and most dangerous downhill race, the **Laubehorn.** Hotels generally won't allow you to book rooms until about a week in advance so that they can guarantee all the racers and support crews a place to sleep. The downhill course starts 2315m above Kleine Scheidegg, curls around Wegenalp, and ends at Ziel (1287m) at the eastern end of the village, a drop of nearly 3500 feet in two-and-a-half minutes. In early September, Wengen marks the 30km point to the **Jungfrau marathon.** Beginning in Interlaken, hundreds of runners huff and puff their way to Kleine Scheidegg, a tortuous 1424m ascent.

The funkiest place to eat, sleep, drink, and sit around is **Hot Chili Peppers** (tel. 855 50 20), smack dab in the center of town. Turn left from the station and head past the tourist office. The hybrid decor of this Tex-Mex-eatery-turned-hostel is decidedly freaky. The newly renovated dorms are 24-26SFr; a small breakfast is 5SFr and a hot breakfast is 12.50SFr. Jalapeño keys complement day-glo comforters. Smart, freshly painted singles are 38 to 48SFr and doubles are 76 to 96SFr, including breakfast and **kitchen** access. (Sheets 5SFr. Reception 8am-2am.) And the food? Beers cost 3.50SFr; Sangria 3.50SFr; *chili con carne* in a bread bowl 12SFr; a house sandwich 9.50SFr; chips 'n' salsa 5SFr. (Restaurant open 8am-2am.) Much closer to what you might expect out of Wengen, **Eddy's Hostel** (tel. 855 16 34; fax 855 39 50) has three-story bunks and 20 beds to a room. (Dorms 26SFr. In winter 30SFr, including hall shower. Breakfast buffet 15SFr. Reception 7am-10pm.) **Eddy's Corner** has beer (4.50SFr a pint) and main courses like bratwurst and spaghetti (from 7.50SFr). Jam on your accordion at the free-for-all folklore evenings on Fridays.

Wengen is expensive. Opposite the station, the **Co-op** is cooperatively central (open M-F 8am-12:15pm and 1:30-6:30pm, Sa 8am-6pm), while fancier fodder awaits at the **Victoria Lauberhorn** just past the tourist office. Wolf down some hot apple and ice cream crepes (11SFr). Pasta, *raclette,* and other vegetarian options range from 9 to 20SFr. (Open 10am-11pm.)

Hikes from Wengen

Wengen snoozes beneath the steep flanks of the **Lauberhorn** (2472m, 4hr., only the last stretch is steep) and **Männlichen** (2343m, 3hr., you're confronted with a small, stony path up top) peaks. The ultimate view of the Eiger Norwand and a superb panorama make the climb worthwhile. Since hiking down the sharp gradients is less tiring than hiking up, make use of the **Männlichen cable car** (20SFr, round-trip 33SFr; 25% off with Swisspass, closed in Nov. and May) and the railway to Kleine Scheidegg (same rates). You can buy a combination ticket lifting you up to Kleine Scheidegg and down from Männlichen, which turns the excursion into a half-day outing (39.60SFr, with Swisspass 30SFr). For mountaintop sleeping, see **Grindelwald,** (p. 385). For a perfect view of the Lauterbrunnen valley, turn right out of the station under the tracks to the Ziel chair lift. The easy walk skirts the valley wall and drops into the secluded cove above the Trümmelbach Falls (2hr. round-trip). Descend steeply into the valley base and walk 30 minutes to reach Lauterbrunnen, where a 5.40SFr train ride returns you to Wengen (half day through spectacular landscapes).

■ Lauterbrunnen Valley

The "many springs" that give Lauterbrunnen its name are really 72 waterfalls that plummet down the sheer walls of the narrow, glacier-cut valley. Stark but beautiful Lauterbrunnen is home to Switzerland's highest waterfall, the Staubbach (280m), inspiration for Goethe's poem "Song of the Spirit over the Waterfall" that Franz Schubert set to music. Some of Mendelssohn's "Songs without Words" were composed in Lauterbrunnen. The small **Lauterbrunnen tourist office** (tel. 855 19 55; fax 855 36

04) is 200m to the left of the train station on the main street. (Open M-F 8am-noon and 2-6pm; July-Aug. also Sa 9am-noon and 3-7pm and Su 9am-3pm.) **Trains** connect every 30 minutes with **Interlaken East** (6SFr), **Wengen** (5.40SFr), **Kleine Scheidegg** (25.40SFr), **Jungfraujoch** (round-trip 140.80SFr, good morning 101.80SFr), and **Mürren** (9SFr). The station has **lockers** (2SFr) and **currency exchange.** The **post office** is between the train station and the tourist office. (Open M-F 7:45-11:45am and 1:45-6pm, Sa 7:45-11am.) The **postal code** is 3822. The **telephone code** is 033.

Lauterbrunnen has a wide range of shops and services and an array of cheap, basic beds. Near the post office, there's a small **Co-op.** (Open M-F 8am-noon and 2-6:30pm, Sa 8am-noon and 1:30-5pm.) **Matratzenlager Stocki** (tel. 855 17 54), a farmhouse-hostel, offers a full **kitchen** stacked with spices and a mellow atmosphere. Leave the train station's rear exit, descend the steps, cross the river, turn right, and walk 200m. The sign on the house to the right will read *"Massenlager."* (12SFr. Reception 10am-6pm. Open Jan.-Oct. Reserve ahead.) **Valley Hostel** (tel. 855 2008) is on the left off the main street, downhill, past the Co-op on the right. The brand-new (opened in Dec. 1997) family-run hostel makes for a perfect sojourn in the valley. The beds (with fuzzy, cow-patterned sheets) have a view of the glistening Staubbach Falls (especially good view when the Falls are lit up at night), and Alfred and Martha are the friendliest of hosts. (Dorms 20SFr include showers, sheets, **kitchen** access; double room (only one) 22SFr. Breakfast 5SFr. **Laundry** 4SFr. You can request a fondue (in advance) for 15SFr. Reception 6:15am-10pm.) **Chalet im Rohr** (tel./fax 855 21 82), on the main street near the church, has 40 beds in comfortably lived-in rooms with balconies and thousand-dollar views. (Dorms 26SFr 1st 2 nights, then 24SFr. **Kitchen** facilities 0.50SFr. Parking available.) Lauterbrunnen also has two souped-up campsites with cheap eats. **Camping Jungfrau** (tel. 856 20 10; fax 856 20 20), up the main street from the station toward the large Staubachfall, provides cheap beds, kitchens, showers, lounges, and a mini-department store. (8-10SFr; tents 6-15SFr; dorms 18SFr. Restaurant *Menüs* 10-14.50SFr. **Laundry** 5SFr. Reception in summer 7am-9pm; winter 8am-noon and 2:30-6:30pm. AmEx, DC, MC, Visa.) **Camping Schützenbach** (tel. 855 12 68; fax 855 12 75) is on the way toward Trümmelbach from the station (15min.; follow the signs). Take a left on the main road and a left over the river by the church. (6SFr; tents 11SFr; dorms 16-19SFr; doubles with sink 46-56SFr; 4-bed "tourist rooms" in barracks-like huts 18-20SFr per person. Shower 0.50SFr. **Kitchen** facilities 1SFr. **Laundry** 5SFr. Reception 7am-noon and 2-7pm. Fully-equipped grocery store.)

Since it's at the bottom of a trough, Lauterbrunnen's **hikes** are either very steep or very flat. An easy 40-minute hike or a quick postal bus ride from the main street (every hr., 3.20SFr) are the fabulous **Trümmelbach Falls,** 10 glacier-bed chutes that gush up to 20,000 liters of water per second and generate mighty winds and a roaring din. The Trümmelbach Falls are the only drains of the glacial waste of the Eiger, Mönch, and Jungfrau glaciers. The deafening noise caused by the turbid gush of water upon rock gave the falls its name "Trümmelbach," which means "like the beating of a drum." Explore tunnels, footbridges, and an **underground funicular.** (10SFr with Jungfrau region visitor's card 9Sfr. (Open July-Aug. 8:30am-6pm; Apr.-June and Sept.-Nov. 9am-5pm.) The best flat walk is a **waterfall** tour. From the western side, follow the main road past the church. In succession the Staubbachfall, Spissbachfall, Agertenbachfall, and Mümenbachfall crash from overhead, leaving dark cones on the rock where the wind has blown the spray. Crossing the river by the Stechelberg power station (5-7km) brings you face to face with the Staldenbachfall and Matten-bachfall. The return leg, with gorgeous views of the Lauthorn, passes the Trümmel-bachfälle and the Hasenbachfall. (3hr. with virtually no climbing; the best walk in the area during a prolonged wet spell.) Follow the signs along the river to **Stechelberg,** a scattered, three-horse town with the **Breithorn campground** (tel. 855 12 25), near the Trümmelbach Falls (8-10SFr. Showers 1SFr. Reception 24hr. **Grocery** store with freh baked goods at your service.) Nearby is also the **Schilthorn Bahn cable car** leading to **Gimmelwald** (7.20SFr), **Mürren** (14SFr), **Birg** (33.20SFr), and the **Schilthorn** (48SFr). The first two free are with Swisspass, with Eurailpass 25% off all four destinations. Since Gimmelwald and Mürren are carless by fiat, leave your car at the parking lot near the cable car (day 5SFr, week 21SFr, month 30SFr) or back at Lauterbrunnen.

Imboden Bike Adventures (tel. 855 21 14), on the main street, rents out mountain bikes at 20-30SFr per day and bursts with suggestions about where to go with them. A favorite is the **Mürren Loop,** where you take your bike for free on the funicular to Grütschalp (6.60SFr), pedal along to Mürren and Gimmelwald, and free-wheel it down to Stechelberg and Lauterbrunnen. Imboden lets you leave the bike at Central Sport in Wengen opposite the tourist office or the sports center in Mürren for no extra charge. (Open Tu-Su 9am-noon and 2-9pm.) Stechelberg's other campsite, **Camping Rütti** (tel. 855 28 85), near the Schilthorn Bahn parking lot, commands views of at least three waterfalls, as well as the misty Lauthorn in the distance. (6-10SFr, including showers. Electricity 2SFr. Reception 8am-noon and 4-7pm.)

Cheap eats are at hand at **Restaurant Oberland** (tel. 855 12 41; fax 85 54 52 41), diagonally to the Valley Hostel. For a mere 10SFr, chow on *spaghetti Napoli, chili con carne*, or try the *Fondue Chinoise* (25SFr). (Open 7am-11pm. AmEx, MC, Visa.)

Lauterbrunnen: Songs of the Waterfall

From its most famous visitor, J.W. Goethe, who immortalized the valley's Staubbach Falls in his "Gesang der Geisten über den Wassern," to lesser-known but fiercely-loved painters, the Lauterbrunnen Valley has inspired poet and artist alike with its silvery cascades. The last verse of Goethe's poem, possibly the most famous lines in German verse, were set to music by Schubert when he visited the falls. Lord Byron was inspired to write *Manfred* here. Among the many other renowned people who have paid tribute to the Staubbach and Trümmelbachfälle are Caspar Wolf, Albrecht von Haller, Alexandre Calame, Conrad Escher von der Linter, Kaiser Wilhelm, and Napoleon I's wife, Marie Louise von Habsburg, while her husband plotted his comeback in Elba.

■ Mürren and the Schilthorn

The cogwheel train from Lauterbrunnen (1st 6:40am, last 9pm, 9SFr), the cable car from Stechelberg (14SFr) or Gimmelwald (7.20SFr), or a brisk hike from Gimmelwald will take you to **Mürren,** a car-free skiing and sport resort. A noticeably large British population dominates Mürren, as they have ever since George Bernard Shaw came for Fabian fresh air and Field Marshal Montgomery for mushrooms. More of a paved cow path than a main street, "downtown" Mürren features spectacular gnome gardens, gingerbread houses with chamois antlers on the walls, and lovely pastoral and mountain views. The all-knowing **tourist office** (tel. 856 86 86; fax 856 86 96) in the sports center is five minutes from the train station, off the right fork. Ask about *Privatzimmer,* hiking trails, and skiing prices. Check the bulletin board at the train station for dorms (30-35SFr), or get the list of cheap sleeps in Mürren. You can also rent **mountain bikes** for 20-40SFr, as well as buy **Adventure World** packages. (Open July-Aug. M-F 9am-noon and 1-6:30pm, Sa 1-6:30pm, Su 1-5:30pm; Sept.-June M-F 9am-noon and 2-5pm.) The **pharmacy** is on the left fork near the Co-op (open M-Sa 8am-noon and 2-6pm). For **medical assistance,** call 855 17 10. For the **police,** call 856 80 81. For the **Alpine rescue service,** call 855 45 55. The **post office** is on the station side of the main street. (Open M-F 8am-noon and 2:30-5:30pm, Sa 8-10:15am.) **Lockers** are at the station (2SFr). The **postal code** is CH-3825, and the **telephone code** is 033.

To rest your weary bones after a long day of hiking, seek shelter at the central **Chalet Fontana** (tel. 855 26 86). Its seven lovely, distinctive rooms are run by an enthusiastic English woman who opens the reception whenever she's in—the best time to catch her is in the morning. (35-45SFr per person; breakfast included. Oct. 30SFr per person; no breakfast. Reservations recommended.) **Hotel Belmont** (tel. 855 35 35; fax 855 35 31) is right next to the train station and has bunk beds in warm rooms with quilted tapestry on the walls. (39SFr; doubles 90SFr, with shower 130SFr. Breakfast included. AmEx, MC, Visa.) There is a **Co-op** (tel. 855 13 18) on the town's main walkway (open M-F 8am-noon and 1:45-6:30pm, Sa 8am-noon and 1:45-4pm), but eating out in Mürren is unexpectedly cheap. You can get *raclette* for as little as 11SFr at Hotel Alpina. Next door to the Co-op is **Restaurant Stägerstübli** (tel. 855 13 16), a family joint with a tiny wooden interior featuring many portraits of men smoking pipes. The creamy, rich *raclette* (14SFr) melts in your mouth. Entrees are 5.50 to 12.50SFr. Cheese fondue is 19.50SFr, Rösti 12.50SFr. (Open Su-M and W-Th 9am-11:30pm, F-Sa 9am-12:30am.) **Singapore Snacks & Drinks** (tel. 856 01 10), off the left fork from the train station, is a steaming spicy Asian restaurant that cooks pan-fried noodles and other soy-sauce nourishments for cheap. (Won ton noodles 11.50SFr, vegetable fried rice 12.50SFr.)

The 2970m **Schilthorn,** made famous by the Alpine exploits of James Bond in *On Her Majesty's Secret Service* (the worst James Bond movie ever, incidentally), is a short (albeit expensive) cable car trip from Mürren (34SFr, round-trip 57SFr; morning ticket 43SFr round-trip). It's as close to snow-blindness as you'd want to get. The four-hour ascent, one of the rockiest and snowiest around, requires sturdy hiking boots. At its apex spins the immoderately priced **Piz Gloria Restaurant.** Daily *Menüs* run 19 to 29SFr. High-altitude restaurants charge snooty prices. A James Bond breakfast costs a shocking 22.50SFr, and it won't make you suave, either. Warm up (summer or winter) with *Glühwein* (mulled wine; 7SFr), or take in the astounding 360° Alpine panorama from the Schilthorn station's deck. The staff at the Mürren stop courteously remind you that there is very little to do at the top when it's cloudy. At the Schilthorn cable car stops (Birg, Mürren, Gimmelwald), beautiful rocky paths lace the mountains. In snowy early summer, consider the one-way trip down to **Birg** (17.40SFr). Check with the tourist office for maps before embarking on any of these trips, however, and get a weather forecast via the live TV link at the cable car station. From the train station take either road to the other end of the village (10min.). Mürren pioneered two graceful ways of enjoying the mountains. In 1910 the first Alpine balloon crossing was made from the village, a fact now celebrated annually in mid-August with an **international ballooning week** that fills the skies with big colorful bulbs. The other sport, **skiing,** took off with even more panache. Mürren was the stage for the first major slalom (1922), the first ski school (1930), and the first World Championship for downhill slalom (1931). **Ski passes** for the Mürren-Schilthorn area are 50SFr for one day and 254SFr for a regional week pass; ages 6-16 receive a 50% reduction, ages 16-20 20%. The **ski school** (tel. 855 12 47) has a comprehensive spread of classes for downhill, slalom, and snowboarding. Six half-days of group lessons cost 130SFr. The calf-killing **Inferno Run** seeks volunteers every January (usually for 3 days from the 20th) for the **Inferno** downhill ski; the Inferno Triathlon takes place in August; the Mürren Schilthorn stretch comes last.

■ Gimmelwald

A tiny speck on the massive valley wall, Gimmelwald is accessible only by foot or the Schilthorn cable car (6.80SFr) from Stechelberg or Mürren. The nearby Schilthorn claims the title of "Magic Mountain," climbed by Hans Castorp in the famous novel by Thomas Mann. Gimmelwald is along its slopes. In a village with probably more cows than people, Gimmelwald provides that repose you were longing for in a crazy city and a crazy world. Most visitors walk 30 minutes down from Mürren, take the left fork after the post office, and follow the yellow signs. Gimmelwald has a **post office** (open M-F 8:30-10:15am and 4-5pm, Sa 8:30-10:15am), and its **postal code** is CH-3826. The **telephone code** is 033.

Accommodations in Gimmelwald are definitely back to basics. Some local barns offer haystacks for a ridiculous 19SFr (including breakfast). Continue past Pension Gimmelwald, on the right, and you'll find more civilized bungalows that are nicer, cheaper, and equipped with real beds. Next door to the cable car station awaits the crunchy **Mountain Hostel** (tel. 855 17 04). Run by a laid-back couple, Petra and Walter, the hostel exudes friendliness. There's a communal **kitchen** and life's essentials—bread (2SFr), milk (2SFr), and chocolate (2SFr). You can reserve a bed, but only after 9:30am on the day you plan to arrive. Come early, as beds fill very fast. (Dorms 15SFr. Showers 1SFr for 3min. of hot water. Sheets included. Reception 8:30-11am and 5:30-10:30pm.) You can sign up for rooms on the sheets when the reception is closed—drop the pack, take a hike, and be back for the 5:30pm check-in. **Pension Gimmelwald** (tel./fax 855 17 30) has tiny loft-bed dorms for 25SFr (Singles 45SFr. Breakfast included. Access to TV room and restaurant—tourist menu 12SFr; *raclette* 8SFr. Reception 8am-midnight.) At **Hotel Mittaghorn** (tel. 855 16 58), up the hill toward Mürren, you can sample some *Glühwein* (mulled wine) or Heidi cocoa (spiked with peppermint *schnapps*) made by the owner, Walter. Often seen sporting Edelweiss suspenders, Walter cooks a three-course dinner for his guests for only 15SFr. (Dorms 25SFr; doubles 60-70SFr; triples 85SFr; quads 105SFr. Add 3SFr for a 1-night stay. Order meals in advance. Open May-Nov.) Be forewarned that Gimmelwald lacks a market, so stock up on food at the **Co-op** in Lauterbrunnen or Mürren.

The descent to Stechelberg—down the hill by the Mountain Hostel, over the river, and through the woods—gives a great long view of the sheer rock slabs lining the Lauterbrunnen valley. It's a grand approach to the **Trümmelbach Falls** (1½hr.), with a return facilitated by the cable car. The hikes from Gimmelwald radiate in other directions. Five minutes after the river crossing on the Stechelberg path, you can fork right and climb along the flank of the unsettled Lauterbrunnen valley head. At the top lies the tiny Oberhornsee (2065m; 7hr.—a day's hike—bring some eats), a lilliputian lake fringed by gargantuan glaciers. The climb up the oft-snowcapped Schilthorn (2970m), zigzagging straight up the hill, is for *Übermenschen* only (1600m ascent). Lauterbrunnen-lovers who don't intend to leave anytime soon should buy *Exploring the Lauterbrunnen Valley,* a thick pamphlet bursting with detailed trail info (7SFr; available at Hotel Mittaghorn). To hike to the waterfall **Sprutz** take a left from Hotel Mittaghorn (30min.); to hike to **Gimmelwald-Kilchbalm** (1¼hr.), take a left from Gimmelwald's firehouse in the village center. Both are easy.

Ticino Region

Olivone

Torrente Alte ▲

N2

Ticino

Verzasca

TO SAN
BERNADINO PASS

N13

Bellinzona

VALLE MÀGGIA

Marmontana ▲

Locarno

Ascona

Magadino

N2

Cannobio

340

Gandria

Menàggio

Lugano

*Lake Maggiore
(Lago Maggiore)*

*Lake Lugano
(Lago di Lugano)*

*Lake Como
(Lago di Como)*

Verbania

ITALY

Stresa Laveno

33

TO
MILAN

N

*Lago di
Varese*

Ispra

0 ——— 10 miles
0 ——— 10 kilometers

Italian Switzerland (Ticino)

The Swiss won Ticino from Italy in 1512 and never gave it back. Ever since, the Italian-speaking canton of Ticino (Tessin, in German and French) has been renowned for its refreshing mix of Swiss efficiency and Italian *dolce vita*. The white and charred-wood chalets of the Graubünden and Berner Oberland fade away, replaced by jasmine-laced villas painted the bright colors of Italian *gelato*. Come here for lush, almost Mediterranean vegetation, emerald-green lakes, and shaded castles. Pastel church facades lead to ancient sanctuaries where faith, not tourism, is still the main draw. Varieties of the **Ticino Card,** available at most tourist offices, provide unlimited travel on all area cable cars and funiculars for any seven days (100SFr) and discounts on regional museum entrances (2SFr).

🌐 HIGHLIGHTS OF TICINO

- Italian-speaking Locarno's Mediterranean climate, Italian cooking, frescoes by Ciseri and Raphael, and the renowned Locarno Film Festival make it one of the happiest and happeningest places to visit in all of Switzerland.
- Bellinzona, Ticino's capital, is a city of castles, towers, and Blues Festivals.
- Lugano is a peachy lakeside resort town with pleasant architecture and an excellent modern art museum featuring Klee, Degas, and Renoir.

▓ Lugano

Lugano, Switzerland's third-largest banking center, hides from German Switzerland in the crevassed bay between San Salvatore and Monte Brè. Warmed by a Mediterranean climate, Lugano's shady streets are lined with tiles, climbing vines, and blood-red wildflowers. Old men gather under palm trees to argue over outdoor chess played with waist-high chess pieces. Younger Swiss on vacation flock to either of the two extraordinary youth hostels in town, both built from luxury villas with swimming pools and magnificent gardens. By day, crowds throng the markets of linked piazzas in the main city, while bars, cafés, and the annual Blues Fest keep the streets full at night.

GETTING TO LUGANO

The small **Lugano-Agno Airport** services Crossair flights from Basel, Bern, Geneva, London, Nice, Rome, and Zurich. Trains go to the Lugano train station from Agno Airport (every 20min., 4.20SFr). From **Geneva** in the west, trains run to Lugano through **Domodossola, Italy.** (52SFr, Swisspass valid. You must change trains in Locarno; see times from Locarno below.) From **Chur** and **St. Moritz** in the east, postal buses go to **Bellinzona** (8:15am-12:25pm), where you can catch a train to Lugano (3½hr., 3 per day, 60SFr plus 5SFr reservation fee, Swisspass valid). For info, call 807 85 20. To reach Lugano **by car,** take Rte. N2/E35 (or just follow the signs).

ORIENTATION AND PRACTICAL INFORMATION

Cobblestone *piazze* dot Lugano's large pedestrian zone, bounded by the ridge on which the train station sits, Corso Pestalozzi, and the Fiume Cassorate. The arcaded **Piazza della Riforma** is the town's center. Northwest of this lies the **Piazza Cioccaro,** home to the **cable car** that carries passengers from the waterfront to the train station (0.80SFr, Swisspass valid). The town boasts an extensive public transportation system. Buses run from the neighboring towns into the center and criss-cross the city (0.90-1.70SFr per ride, 24hr. "Carta Giorno" 4.40SFr, Swisspass valid). If you can navigate the winding roads (and have the calf muscles), the super-steep uphill journey from town to the station should take only 15 minutes.

Trains: P. della Stazione (tel. 157 22 22). To: **Locarno** (via Bellinzona, 1hr., every 30min., 5:57am-12:09am, 15.80SFr); **Basel** (4½hr., every hr., 5:37am-11:07pm, 77SFr); **Zurich** (3hr., every hr., 5:57am-8:41pm, 59SFr); and **Milan** (1½hr., every hr., 6:15am-10:02pm, 14SFr).

Public Transportation: Buses run from the neighboring town to the center of Lugano and also traverse the city. Schedules and automatic ticket machines at each stop (0.90-1.70SFr per ride, 24hr. "Carta Giorno" 4.40SFr, Swisspass valid).

Taxis: Associazone Concessionari Taxi (tel. 922 88 33 or 922 02 22).

Car Rental: Avis, 8 via C. Maraini (tel. 922 62 56). **Budget,** 14 via C. Maraini (tel. 964 17 19). **Hertz,** 13 via San Gottardo (tel. 923 46 75).

Parking: Several parking garages, but little long-term parking *("Autosilo").* **Comunale Balestra,** on via Pioda, offers hourly rate (1SFr), daily ticket (10hr., 15SFr),

Lugano
ACCOMMODATIONS

A Casa della Giovane
B Hotel Garni Zurigo
C Hotel Montarina
D Hotel Pestalozzi
E Ostello della Gioventù
F Pensione Selva

0   200 yards

0   200 meters

N

and a half-day ticket (5hr., 10SFr). Open 7am-7pm. **Autosilo Central Park** has hourly rates (1SFr, 12hr. max.). Open 7am-7pm. For information regarding parking, call 800 71 76. City parking meters scattered about are 1SFr per hr.

Bike Rental: At the baggage check in the train station (32SFr per day for a mountain bike, 6SFr to return bike to another station). Open 5:20am-8:45pm.

Tourist Office: (tel. 921 46 64; fax 922 76 53; email ltoinfo@lto.ch) in the Palazzo Civico, Riva Albertolli, at the corner of P. Rezzonico. From the station, cross the footbridge labeled "Centro," and proceed down via Cattedrale straight through P. Cioccaro as it turns into via Pessina. Take a left on via dei Pesci, a left on Riva via Vela, which becomes Riva Giocondo Albertolli. The office is just past the fountain on the left, across the street from the ferry launch. Pick up free maps or make hotel reservations (4SFr). The tourist office also offers a free guided city walk Apr.-Oct. at 9:45am on Mondays, starting at Chiesa degli Angioli. Open Apr.-Oct. M-F 9am-6:30pm, Sa 9am-12:30pm and 1:30-5pm, Su 10am-noon and 2-4pm; Nov.-Mar. M-F 9am-12:30pm and 1:30-5pm.

Consulates: U.K., 19 via Motta (tel. 923 86 06; open M-F 10am-noon).

Currency Exchange: Decent rates in the train station. Open M-Sa 7:10am-7:45pm, Su 8am-7:45pm.

American Express: In **VIP Travels,** 10 via al Forte, P.O. Box 3530, CH-6901 (tel. 923 85 45; fax 922 02 66). Mail held, but traveler's checks cannot be cashed. Open M-F 8:30am-noon and 2-6pm, Sa 9am-noon.

Luggage Storage: Lockers at the train station. Open 24hr. 3-5SFr.

Lost Property: Held at tourist office.

Bookstore: Melisa, 4 via Vegezzi, across from post office (tel. 923 83 41), stocks a relatively broad mix of English-language books downstairs. Open M-F 8am-noon and 1:30-6:30pm, Sa 8am-noon and 1:30-5pm. AmEx, MC, Visa.

Library: Biblioteca Cantonale, 6 viale Cattaner (tel. 911 53 56; fax 911 53 59). From tourist office turn left and walk along waterfront; library is just before Fiume Cassarante canal. Open M-F 9am-7pm, Sa 9am-noon and 2-5pm; July-Aug. closed on Sa.

Medical Services: tel. 111.

Emergencies: Police, tel. 117. **Ambulance,** tel. 144. **Fire,** tel. 118.

Internet Access: City Disc (tel. 924 14 00; http://www.citydisc.ch), 1 block up via P. Pen from piazza Dante. 4SFr for 20min., 10SFr per hr. Open M-F 9am-6:30pm, Sa 8am-5pm.

Post Office: via della Posta, 2 blocks up from the lake near via al Forte. Open M-F 7:30am-6:30pm, Sa 8-11am. Telephones, telegraphs, and faxes at the Via Magatti entrance to the PTT building. Open M-F 7:30am-8pm, Sa 9am-7pm, Su 9:30am-12:30pm and 2:30-7pm. **Postal Code:** CH-6900.

Telephone Code: 091.

ACCOMMODATIONS

Though Lugano's lakesides are lined with five-star hotels and restaurants, surprising bargains can be found even in the center of town.

Hotel Montarina, 1 via Montarina (tel. 966 72 72; fax 966 12 13), just behind the train station. Walk 200m to the right from the station, cross the tracks, and walk 1min. uphill. Converted from a former luxury villa, this newly renovated independent hostel draws young families and students with its huge swimming pool, natural caverns, lush jasmine grounds, volleyball, ping-pong, chandeliered reading room, and terrace with a view. One drawback: large, echoing dorm rooms may necessitate earplugs. The adventure company ASBEST is located in the adjoining Hotel Continental. Dorms 20SFr; singles 45-65SFr; doubles 80-120SFr. **Laundry** (4SFr). Good cheap coffee (1SFr). Buffet breakfast 15SFr. Sheets 4SFr. Reception 9am-8:30pm. Open Mar.-Dec.

Ostello della Gioventù (HI), Lugano-Savosa, 13 via Cantonale (tel. 966 27 28; fax 968 23 63). Note: there are 2 vias Cantonale, one in downtown Lugano and one in Savosa, where the hostel is. Take bus #5 (from the left of the station, go down the 2nd ramp, cross the street, and uphill 100m) to "Crocifisso" (6th stop), then backtrack a bit and turn left up via Cantonale. Converted from a luxury villa, this sprawling hostel retains lush secluded gardens, a pool with a waterslide, and a decidedly elegant atmosphere. 110 beds. Dorms 17SFr; singles 32SFr, with kitchenette 42SFr; doubles 46SFr, 60SFr. Price drops after 3 nights. Apartments available for families (7-day min. stay; 80-120SFr per day). Breakfast 7SFr. 1SFr for **kitchen** use (after 7:30pm only). Sheets 2SFr. Reception 7am-noon and 3-10pm. No lockout. Reserve ahead. Open mid-Mar. to Oct.

Casa della Giovane, 34 corso Elvezia (tel. 911 66 46; fax 911 66 40), 3 blocks from the hospital and across the street from Basilica Sacro Cuore. Take bus #9 (leaves opposite train station) to "Corso Elvezia." For **women only.** Crayola-colored furniture fills bright, immaculate rooms. Beautiful rooftop terrace with views of lake and mountains allows some serious tanning. Candle-lit sanctuaries are downstairs from the TV room. Dorms 20SFr. In summer: doubles with bathrooms with breakfast and 1 meal 35SFr, with all 3 meals 40SFr. Breakfast 4.50SFr. Lunch or dinner 12SFr. **Laundry** 3SFr. Reception 7am-10pm. Under age 18, curfew 9:30pm; ages 18 and up M-Th 11:15pm, F-Su 2am. Make reservations during the school year.

Hotel Pestalozzi, 9 P. Indipendenza (tel. 921 46 46; fax 922 20 45), on the main *piazza* away from the waterfront, 2 blocks up from the casino. Live it up for a night staying in this upscale version of a budget hotel. Small singles with Turkish rugs, a sink, wood-tile flooring, and bright flower-spattered wallpaper. Singles 58-95SFr; doubles 96-150SFr; triples 135-230SFr. Breakfast included. Lunch or dinner at hotel restaurant 16SFr. 24hr. reception. Reserve ahead. Visa.

Pensione Selva, 36 via Tesserete (tel. 923 60 17; fax 923 60 09). Bus #9: "Sassa." Walk 20min. from the station, then along via Gottardo for 250m and turn right on via Tesserete. Comfy rooms spruced up by paintings. Outdoor pool and grapevine-draped lattice. Singles 49-75SFr; doubles 108-134SFr.

Hotel Garni Zurigo, 13 corso Pestalozzi (tel. 923 43 43; fax 923 92 68), down the street from the Pestalozzi, across from the AmEx office. All rooms have radio, TV, telephone, and Raskolnikovian yellow walls. Singles 60SFr, with shower 85-95SFr; doubles with shower 90SFr, with bath 130-140SFr; triples with shower 160SFr. Breakfast and parking included. 24hr. reception. Closed in Dec. AmEx, MC, Visa.

Camping: There are 5 campsites, all in **Agno.** Take the Ferrovia-Lugano-Ponte-Tresa (FLP) train to Agno (4.20SFr). From the train, turn left, then left again on Via Molinazzo for **La Palma** (tel. 605 25 61; fax 604 54 38) or **Eurocampo** (tel. 605 21 14; fax 605 31 87). 7.50SFr; tents 4-15SFr. All sites have showers. Open Apr.-Oct.

FOOD

As the central city in the Ticino, Lugano knows the way to visitors' hearts. Serving up plates of *penne* and *gnocchi* and freshly spun pizzas, Lugano's many outdoor restaurants and cafés pay homage to the canton's Italian heritage. Lugano's specialty is (very visibly) sausage. For some quick *al fresco* shopping and eating, **via Pessina** livens up at midday with outdoor sandwich and fruit shops. **Salumeria,** 12 via Pessina, is one of the better tasty and quick outdoor sandwich and fruit shops along via Pessina.

La Tinèra, 2 via dei Gorini (tel. 923 52 19), behind Banque Suisse in P. della Riforma. Tucked away in a tiny alley off a quiet cobblestone road, this low-lit underground restaurant is full of Ticinese ambience. You can't go wrong with the daily specials (10-15SFr). The *pollo alla compagnola* (13.50SFr) is particularly scrumptious. Open M-Sa 11am-3pm and 5:30-10pm. AmEx, MC, Visa.

Pestalozzi, 9 P. Indipendenza (tel. 921 46 46), in the hotel. Simple, non-alcoholic restaurant offers 10 veggie dishes (from 10.50SFr), including tofu burgers. *Lasagne bolognese* and mixed salad 8.50SFr. Open 11am-9:30pm. MC, Visa.

Ristorante Cantinone, P. Cioccaro (tel. 923 10 68; fax 646 70 87). Friendly pizzeria serves lunch and dinner crowds pasta and pizza (10.50-18SFr) at outdoor tables. Tuscan pizza with apples and nuts (14SFr). Large salads from 12SFr. Open 9am-midnight. AmEx, MC, Visa.

Ristorante Sayonara, 10 via Soave (tel. 922 01 70; fax 922 07 56), in P. Cloccaro across from Cantinone. You can't miss the fluorescent orange chairs or the ferns spilling out into the square. A huge lunchtime crowd comes for homemade pasta (12-18SFr) and pizza (from 11.50SFr). Open 8am-midnight. AmEx, MC, Visa.

Ristorante Inova, 3rd floor of Placette Department Store in Piazza Dante. Budget eaters can't beat these self-serve goodies no matter what town they're in: salad bar (4-10SFr), grand pasta bar (7-10SFr per plate), and other warm entrees-of-the-day (8-13SFr). Open M-F 8:45am-6:30pm, Sa 8am-5pm.

Markets

Migros, 15 via Pretoria, 2 blocks left of post office from p. Dante, in the center of town, offers freshly made pasta and delicious Italian *ciabatta*. **Branch** around the corner from the hostel. Open M-F 8am-6:30pm, Sa 7:30am-5pm. The snack shop **DiGustibus** on the ground floor of Migros saves the near-penniless with huge slices of tomato, eggplant, and zucchini pizza (3.90SFr), and ice-cream (1.40SFr).

Public Market, P. della Riforma. Displays the seafood and produce of the region and yummy veggie sandwiches (4SFr). Open Tu and F 8am-noon.

Reformhaus Centro Dietetico Müller in the Quartiere Maghetti (next to Chiesa San Rocco). Health food. Open M-F 8am-6:30pm, Sa 8am-5pm.

SIGHTS AND ENTERTAINMENT

The leafy frescoes of the 16th-century **Cattedrale San Lorenzo,** just below the train station, gleam through centuries of dust and the scars of teenage lovers' initials. In the vaults, brilliant red, yellow, and blue-black suns burst with snake-like rays, evoking hell more than heaven. Downhill and through the town center in the piazza Maghetti, the 14th-century **Chiesa San Rocco** houses an ornate Madonna altarpiece and gruesome Discopli frescoes of apostles being flayed alive, shot through with arrows, or stabbed. The national monument **Basilica Sacro Cuore,** on corso Elevezia across from the Casa della Giovane, features Swiss hikers walking alongside the disciples in an altarpiece. The most spectacular fresco may be Bernardio Luini's gargantuan **Crucifixion,** in the **Chiesa Santa Maria degli Angiuli** on the waterfront near the tourist office, which is dense with action and fade-resistant colors.

Lugano once had a world-class museum—the **Thyssen-Bornemisza Gallery,** in Villa Favorita, Castagnola (tel. 962 17 41). Nearly all the paintings have been uprooted and sent to Madrid (see **Art for Art's Sake,** p. 399), but out of sheer stubbornness the gallery is still open with lackluster modern art on display. *(Open Apr. 4-Nov. 3 F-Su 10am-5pm. 10SFr, students 6SFr.)* The **Museo Cantonale d'Arte,** 10 Via Canova (tel. 910 47 80), features a more interesting collection of 19th- and 20th-century works, including Swiss artists such as Vela, Ciseri, and Franzoni, and foreign artists like Klee, Nicholson, Morandi, Degas, and Renoir. *(Open Tu 2-5pm, W-Su 10am-5pm. Special exhibits 12SFr, students 5SFr; permanent collection 7SFr, students 5SFr.)* Beware: the superstar foreign artists exhibit is sometimes closed for temporary exhibits on modern art. The **Museo d'Arte Moderna,** Villa Malpensata, 5 riva Caccia (tel. 944 43 70), has a decent collection of European and American 20th-century art, as well as yearly retrospectives and special exhibitions. *(Open only for special exhibitions. Contact the tourist office for information.)* The Brignoni family heirlooms at the **Museo delle Culture Extraeuropee,** 324 Via Cortivo (tel. 971 73 53), on the footpath to Gandria in the Villa Heleneum, include a jumble of masks, statues, and various non-European stuff. *(Open Mar. 5-Oct. 31 Tu-Su 10am-5pm. 5SFr, students 3SFr.)*

Lugano's waterfront parks are ideal places for a few hours' introspection. The **Belvedere,** a zonking sculpture garden with emphasis on modernist metalwork on quai riva Caccia, stretches along the lakeside promenade in the direction of Paradiso. The lakefront gets pretty exciting in summer. At the end of June, the **Tour de Suisse** comes to a dramatic finish in Lugano. From the end of June to early August, **Cinema al Lago** shows international films on the beach. A huge screen is installed at water level on the lake, with 1000 seats available for viewers. In early July, Lugano's **Jazz Festival** heats up at no charge. Previous performers include Miles Davis and Bobby McFerrin. The looser **Blues to Bop Festival** celebrates R&B, blues, and gospel at the end of August, hosting international singers as well as local amateurs. The festive season wraps up with the **Wine Harvest Festival** in late September and early October, boozing away those faded summer memories.

Art for Art's Sake? Whatever.

The **Thyssen-Bornemisza Gallery,** in Villa Favorita, once housed one of the most outstanding private collections in Europe, until the owner (a fantastically rich old Baron) and his young Spanish wife (a former beauty queen) started looking around for a permanent home for all of those Rembrandts, Dürers, Van Goghs, and Kandinskys. In the international bidding war that ensued, the collection first moved into the hands of the Spanish government for a while to up the ante. When Spain became attached to the paintings, the Baron talked them into building a museum and paying him a cool US$350 million for the stash. Spain wins, Switzerland loses, end of story. The Villa is still maintained by the very piqued Swiss and open to the public with some leftovers and pleasure-dome architecture. Learn a lesson in Swiss tact by asking the guides—with the best look of open innocence you can muster—where all of the paintings have gone.

Though the tops of the Ticinese mountains are littered with tourists, the dizzying views stretch into Italy. The tourist office and hostel both have topographic maps and trail guides (the tourist office sells them; the hostel lends them). The bay's guard towers, **Monte Brè** (933m) and **Monté San Salvatore** (912m), are especially tempting hikes. With a 13th-century church teetering on craggy cliffs that extend to the water, San Salvatore is easily the more striking of the pair. The trail head is just past the funicular station at Paradiso (about 20min. from the tourist office, to the right along the shore). Carona, a small village halfway up the mountain, has an Olympic-sized **pool** with high dive (10SFr, children 6SFr). Continue down to Morcote, on the shore, and you can catch a ferry back to Lugano (14SFr, Swisspass valid). The walk from the summit takes about three and a half hours. Both mountains have **funiculars** (12SFr, 18SFr round-trip, children under 16 6SFr, 8SFr). For more info contact the San Salvatore Funicular office (tel. 985 28 28) or the Monte Brè office (tel. 971 31 71). More rugged hikers should ask at Hotel Montarina for info on hiking **Monte Boglio.**

The arcades of the town *piazze* fill at night with trains of people taking a *passaggio,* or a stroll around the city center in their best duds to see and be seen. The outdoor cafés of P. della Riforma are especially lively. Poker and some siren-like slot machines will swallow your cash at **Casinò Kursaal di Lugano** (tel. 923 32 24), near the tourist office. *(Casino open 9pm-2am for game tables, noon-midnight for slots.)* The **Pave Pub,** riva Albertolli 1 (tel. 922 07 70), is a self-proclaimed *museo de birra* (beer museum), offering 50 different beers and an English pub atmosphere with a great lakeside view of the fountains. *(Beers start at 4-5SFr. Open 11am-1am.)* The Latin American **Mango Club,** 8 P. Dante (tel. 922 94 38), mixes salsa and techno for a sweaty good time. *(Open from 11pm until last person leaves.)*

Travelers feeling the uncontrollable urge to throw themselves off cliffs should seek relief with the **ASBEST Adventure Company,** via Basilea 28, CH-6900 Lugano (tel. 966 11 14; fax 966 12 13; http://www.tourism.ticino.ch/text/asbest.html). Based in the Hotel Continental, the ebullient ASBEST Alpine guides offer dozens of spinning, splashing, diving, and snow-shoeing expeditions. In the winter, **snowshoe** and **ski** (full-day 85SFr) or **paraglide** over icy crags (150SFr). **Canyoning** (85SFr) and **river-diving** are nice in Ticino because the water isn't as cold as the numbing mountain Alpine glacier streams. Or choose from **rock-climbing** (85SFr), **mountain biking** (25SFr to rent; a guide for groups of up to 8 people costs 150SFr), and the insane **Rapjump,** a kind of spinning bungee that's a bit slower (85SFr). AmEx, MC, Visa.

■ Near Lugano: Gandria

Advertised as a "small fishing village" and a former smuggling port for pirates, Gandria now relegates its poles and pirates to shop windows, although nooks in the cliff wall make you want to break out the shovels. A sandy walk from Lugano along the lakeshore (1hr.), through overgrown vegetation just above the lapping waters, leads to the almost absurdly sweet village. **Boats** also travel from **Lugano** (every 30min., 8:30am-10pm, 10SFr, round-trip 16.60SFr, Swisspass valid). Gandria's winding streets escape the ravages of modern design—city ordinances forbid construction and prohibit cars—but not modern tourists. When there's not much to do, a slow afternoon of eating ice cream while looking over the lake is always pleasant. Naughty pirates head to **Chiesa Parrochiale San Vigilio** for confession, lured by a huge gold crown over the altar. The church is a cool spot to beat the heat and view some lovely sculpture and architecture. From the boat landing, walk up the stairs, turn left, stroll about 100m, turn right at the "Commestibili" sign and walk up more stairs to the church door. A short boat ride from Gandria's town center to **Gandria-Cantine** (boat stop "Museo delle Dogane") leads to the **Swiss Customs Museum,** cantine di Gandria (tel. 910 48 11). (Open 1:30-5:30pm. Free. Exhibits in Italian and German, with some introductory notes in English and French.) The museum glorifies Swiss border guards through an array of contraband ranging from **cocaine-filled condoms** and passport forgeries to fake Levi's jeans. False-bottomed shoes, cars with secret compartments, historic uniforms, and a sublimely absurd mechanically animated display case showing Barbie and Ken dolls catching a smuggler round out the exhibit. The 140-year-old building that houses the museum served as a barracks for frontier guards until just after World War II, after men complained that their isolation from women was preventing them from finding wives. Guards were also transferred to the post for disciplinary reasons. If you need a place to rest after an exhausting day of lounging by the lake, stroll over to **Hotel Miralago** (tel. (091) 971 43 61; fax 971 41 13), at the boat landing. The hotel offers tropical rooms with Tarzan jungle scenes, floral everything, and a leafy lakeside breakfast terrace. 5 rooms hold 2-4 people each. Open Mar. 1-Nov. 30. (38SFr per person. Breakfast included. Reception 8am-10pm.)

■ Locarno

On the shores of **Lago Maggiore,** Locarno basks in warm near-Mediterranean breezes and bright Italian sun. Luxuriant palm trees replace the starkly rugged Alps. More serene even than its Italian cousin to the south, Locarno offers balmy evenings and *al fresco* lounging to its visitors from film festival spectators to pilgrims journeying to the striking Madonna del Sasso church high above the city. For much of the inter-war era, hopes for peace were symbolized by "the Spirit of Locarno"—a futile attempt in 1925 by England, France, and Italy to appease Germany after World War I. History records that Locarno was chosen over other Swiss cities because the mistress of one of the representatives insisted that the conference be held on the Maggiore. Perhaps the *bella donna* needed some work on her tan. Sun-worshippers flock to pay homage to the UV deities in this relatively unspoiled resort town that gets over 2200 hours of sunlight per year—the most in all of Switzerland. James Joyce loitered around Mag-

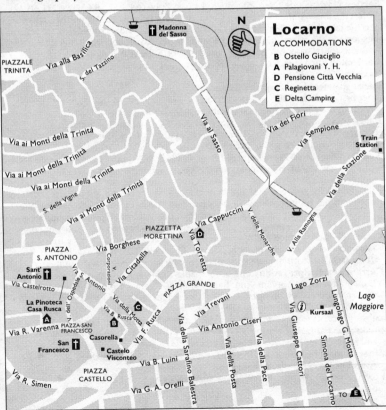

giore's waters in 1917, waiting for Ezra Pound to return a critique of *Ulysses*. Nestled in the Ticinese foothills, Locarno is also an excellent starting point for mountain hikes along the pristine **Verzasca** and **Maggia** valleys, or for regional skiing.

ORIENTATION AND PRACTICAL INFORMATION

By car, Locarno is accessible from motorway N2, which extends from Basel to Chiasso (exit: Bellinzona-Süd). **Piazza Grande,** home of the International Film Festival, anchors Locarno, with the town's cultural and commercial life gravitating around its century-old Lombardian arcades. Just above P. Grande, **Città Vecchia** in the old town is blessed with 16th- and 17th-century architecture, as well as extravagantly economical accommodations. **Via Ramogna** connects the Piazza to the train station and ferries groups of gawking tourists to the Madonna del Sasso via the funicular. **Via Rusca,** extending from the other side of the Piazza, winds up at the Castello Visconti. South of the Piazza lies the residential district, in a traditional grid plan. The vacation homes of many Swiss are here.

Trains: P. Stazione (tel. 157 22 22). To: **Bellinzona** (20min., 5:30am-1:09am, every 30min., 6.60SFr), connecting every hour north to **Lucerne** (2¾hr., 54SFr) and **Zurich** (3hr., 57SFr) and south (7:54am-7:20pm) to **Lugano** (15.80SFr) and **Milan** (2½hr., 22SFr). For **Zermatt** (85SFr), **Montreux** (69SFr), or **Geneva** (5½hr., 84SFr), change trains in **Domodossola,** Italy.

Buses: Buses depart from the train station or from the lakeside of Piazza Grande to Locarno and to nearby towns such as Ascona (#31) and Minusio. Buses also run regularly through the **San Bernadino Pass** to Eastern Switzerland.

Ferries: Navigazione Lago Maggiore, 1 Largo Zorzi (tel. 751 18 65; fax 751 30 24), presents tours of the entire lake, all the way into Italy. A full day on the Swiss side of the lake costs 10SFr. Trips to Ascona (20min., 9 per day, round-trip 10SFr) and especially the Island of Brissago (40min., 9 per day, round-trip 19SFr), an island famous for its gardens and cigars, are well worth the visit.

Car rental: Europcar, 5a Viaggi Verbano (tel. 791 43 24).

Taxi: tel. 743 11 33.

Parking: Metered public parking found on via della Posta and major streets (1.60SFr per hr.). Also, the 24hr. parking garage, **Autosilo Largo SA** (tel. 751 96 13), awaits beneath the *Kursaal,* and is accessible by via Cattori.

Bike Rental: At the train station. 21SFr per day, 84SF per week; mountain bike 29SFr per day. Open 5:45am-9pm. To return a bike to another station 6SFr. At youth hostel, 20 mountain bikes available for 12SFr per day, 8SFr per half-day.

Tourist office: Largo Zorzi (tel. 751 03 33; fax 751 90 70, email locarno@ticino.com; http://www.lagomaggiore.com), on P. Grande. From the main exit of the train station, walk diagonally to the right, and cross via della Stazione; continue through the pedestrian walkway (via alla Ramogna). As you come out, cross Largo Zorzi to your left; the tourist office is in the same building as the *Kursaal* (casino). Hotel reservations for 5SFr deposit, deducted from the hotel room price. The office also organizes **bus excursions** around Lago Maggiore and beyond. City tours in English leave the tourist office mid-Mar. to mid-Oct. Tu at 9:45am. Pick up a free map of Locarno and browse the many brochures. Open mid-Mar. to mid-Oct M-F 8.30am-7pm, Sa-Su 10am-4pm; mid-Oct to mid-Mar. M-F 9am-12:30pm and 2-6pm.

Currency exchange: Try any one of the banks lining P. Grande, or at the train station. Station open 5:45am-9pm; banks open M-F 9am-4.15pm. Western Union at station open M-Sa 8am-6pm. **ATMs** (which accept MC and Visa) are at station and post office.

Luggage Storage: At the train station. 5SFr. Open 5:45am-9pm. **Lockers** 3SFr.

Bookstore: Fantasia Cartoleria Libreria, 32 P. Grande. English books, travel books, and maps (open M-F 8am-6:30pm, Sa 8am-5pm).

Emergencies: Police, 117. **Fire,** 118. **Road rescue,** 163. **Weather,** 162. **Medical Assistance,** 111. **Ambulance,** 144.

Post Office: pl. Grande. Open M-F 7:30am-6:30pm, Sa 8-11am. **Postal Code:** CH-6600.

Telephone Code: 091.

ACCOMMODATIONS

A display board outside the train station offers free phone calls to most of the city's hotels and pensions. Reserve everywhere a week in advance during high-season; during the film festival, book a year ahead.

Palagiovani Youth Hostel (HI), 18 via Varenna (tel. 756 15 00; fax 756 15 01). From station, turn left, follow via alla Romogna to P. Grande, cross the square and turn right on via B. Rusca to P.S. Francisco, take via Varenna to hostel (HI signs point the way from via B. Rusca on). This former convent and girl's home was converted into a 122-bed hostel in 1997. High hedges and floral bushes conceal a thoroughly renovated complex with its own pop music radio station upstairs (Radio Ticino, 90.7FM and 100.5FM). New pine bunks in rooms of two to six beds, most with balconies, sinks, lockers. Several rooms have **kitchenettes** at no extra charge. 30-32SFr (non-members add 5SFr), with private bath 37-42SFr, sheets and buffet breakfast (7-9:30am) included. Lunch and dinner 11SFr each. **Laundry** 6SFr (with soap). Towels 1.50SFr. Mountain **bikes** 12SFr per day. Reception 7-10am and 3-11pm. Reserve at least one month in advance during high season.

Pensione Città Vecchia, 13 via Toretta (tel./fax 751 45 54). From P. Grande, turn right on via Toretta (*not* vigola Toretta; look for a brown sign with the *pensione*s on it) and continue to the top. A gorgeous 300-year-old fresco clashes charmingly with freshly painted walls and a brand-new, bright pink facade. Coed rooms, bathrooms and showers make life more interesting. With a great price and a location to match, it's no small wonder that it's always full. 22SFr per person; monkish singles 33SFr. Sheets 4.50SFr. Small breakfast 4.50SFr. Reception 8am-9pm. Check-in 1-6pm; call ahead if arriving between 6-9pm. Reserve ahead. Open Mar.-Oct.

Reginetta, 8 via della Motta (tel./fax 752 35 53; email reginetta.locarno@bluewin.ch). Walk along the arcades to the end of P. Grande, and make a right onto via della Motta. Ruined by fire while the owner was vacationing in Australia in March '97, the restored hostel offers shiny new everything: pine furniture, soft blue carpet, and gleaming white walls. The friendly owner offers good advice on local sights; check the board for events of interest. 39SFr per person, 45SFr with breakfast. Showers included. Reception 8am-9pm. Open Mar.-Oct. AmEx, MC, Visa.

Ostello Giaciglio, 7 via Rusca (tel. 751 30 64; fax 752 38 37). Walk to the end of the P. Grande, make a right onto via della Motta, and take the left fork in the road onto via Rusca. Sunshiny, black-and-white-checked dorms for 4, 6, or 8 people. 30SFr per person. **Kitchen** facilities available, along with a sauna (20SFr) and **tanning salon** (10SFr) in case a cloud invades Locarno's air space. Book rooms early since rowdy high-school groups take over July-Aug...you can book up to a year in advance. If the hostel is full, cross the street to **Hotel Garni Sempione** to find the hostel's supervisor. AmEx, MC, Visa.

Delta Camping, 7 via Respini (tel. 751 60 81; fax 751 22 43). A 20min. walk along the lakeside from the tourist office brings you to campstyles of the rich and famous; a reservation fee of 100SFr, which is not deducted from the bill, is recommended for July and August. Offers a rock beach nearby and an enticing view of the lake. No dogs allowed. 24SFr, kids 2-14 7SFr. Site 70-80SFr; lake site 30-40SFr. Reception open 8am-noon and 2-9pm. Open Mar. 1-Oct. 31.

Rivabella (tel. (091) 745 22 13; fax 745 66 38), in nearby **Tenero,** is much more affordable and is accessible by boat (free boat to Locarno leaves 5 times a day, 8:40am-7:05pm, July-Aug.) or a 45min. walk along the water in the opposite direction of Delta Camping. 11SFr; tents 20SFr.

FOOD

Panini and pasta reign supreme in Locarno, as Gruyère gives way to Gorgonzola. While the majority of restaurants lean toward the expensive side, many offer pasta and pizza in the 10-20SFr range.

Compagna da Ernesto, P. del Corporazioni (tel. 751 12 08). Specializes in pizza (10-16SFr) and fresh pasta (12-18SFr), with wine racks, red and white picnic tablecloths, courteous Italian waiters, and a gurgling fountain in front of the outdoor seating. Open 7am-midnight. AmEx, MC, Visa.

Inova, 1 via della Stazione (tel. 743 76 76), left as you exit the station. Huge self-serve restaurant. Wooden food bars bring affordable meals to your fingertips: fruit bar (4-7SFr), salad bar (4-11SFr), grand pasta buffet (9.60SFr), sandwiches 2.90-7.50SFr. Also a tantalizing host of desserts. Open M-F 7:30am-10pm, Sat. 8am-10pm.

Contrada, 26 P. Grande (tel. 751 48 15), offers outdoor dining ideal for people-watching. Pizzas and pasta (10.50-16SFr). Ask for the list of specials (14SFr). Open 8am-midnight. AmEx, MC, Visa.

Gelatina Primavera, 4 via all'Ospedale (tel. 31 77 36), across from the Chiesa San Francesco. Feel like those 2200 hours of sun are hitting you all at once? Grab a store-made ice cream cone (2.30-5.50SFr) and cool off. Sandwiches from 5.50SFr and brick oven pizza from 11SFr. Open W-M 8am-midnight, Sa-Su 10am-midnight.

Markets abound; try **Aperto,** at the station (open 6am-10pm), the **Co-op,** 28 P. Grande (open M-F 8am-6.30pm; Sa 8am-5pm), and **Migros,** P. Grande (open M-W and F 9am-6.30pm. Th 9am-9pm, Sa 8am-5pm).

SIGHTS AND ENTERTAINMENT

For centuries, visitors have journeyed to Locarno solely to see the church of **Madonna del Sasso** (Madonna of the Rock) founded over 500 years ago when a Franciscan monk had a vision telling him to build a church high above the city. Religious pilgrims may prefer the original access route up 20 minutes of steep stairs (the via al Sasso), but tourists can ride up the **funicular** that leaves every 15 minutes from a small station just left of the McDonald's. *(6SFr roundtrip, 4.50SFr with Swiss pass.)* On the way into the complex, visitors pass by a sequence of life-size wooden statues in niches depicting scenes from Christ's passion, including a Pietà, a Pentecost, and a 1650 Last Supper. The **sanctuary** itself envelopes the visitor with an intense display of gilded carvings, frescoes, and statuary; the ceiling is oddly low, rendering details of the fresco easier to see but also changing the emotional impact of the religious space—instead of feeling compelled to gape at the heavens, one feels semi-claustrophobic. *(Grounds open daily 7am-10pm, Nov.-Feb. 7am-9pm. Museum open Apr.-Oct. M-F 2-5pm, Su 10am-noon and 2-5pm. 2.50SFr, students 1.50SFr.)* The museum next door houses an unusual collection of ancient relic holders and pilgrims souvenirs, but its highlight is definitely the second floor collection of disaster paintings—near drownings, fires, attempted murders, battle scenes, carriage and train accidents, and lightening strikes—all commissioned by survivors of the events thanking the Madonna for answering their prayers and intervening to save their lives. English language guides, available free at the entrance, add a great deal to the experience.

Closer to sea level the cavernous **Chiesa Sant' Antonio** presides over the outskirts of the *città vecchia.* Built between 1668 and 1674 it features vaulted ceilings and an immense and colorful fresco depicting Christ being taken off the cross. The monastery and church that founded the Madonna del Sasso, the **Chiesa San Francesco,** rests much more modestly within the city. From P. Grande, turn right on Via B. Rusca and left on Via S. Francesca. Founded by the Franciscans shortly after the death of St. Francis of Assisi in the 13th century, the church displays a melange of architectural styles and all-but-faded frescoes beneath a now-sagging roof. Built from stones scavenged from a demolished castle, its exterior contains incongruous inscriptions from the material's original incarnation. Similarly, a vanished cemetery once surrounded the building of which the only remnant is a curious skull-and-crossbones from the Orelli family monument, now used as an entrance stone in the courtyard in front of the church. Uphill 2 blocks, the cavernous **Chiesa San Antonio,** presides over the outskirts of the **Città Vecchia.** Built between 1668 and 1674, it features vaulted ceilings, expanses of richly colored marble, and a large fresco depicting an unusually muscular Christ being taken off the cross as Moses and Kind David look on. Above, frescoed angels achieve an illusory three-dimensionality by having their backgrounds cut away. Downhill from Chiesa San Francesco along via Ripacanova, the **Castello**

Visconteo gazes on Locarno. After learning about the spirit of Locarno in the room where the pact was signed, wander through dungeons and up towers where soldiers poured boiling oil on attackers in the truly pacific spirit of the Middle Ages. The medieval castle, constructed between the 13th and 15th centuries, now houses the **Museo Civico e Archeologico** (tel. 756 31 80), which exhibits Roman glassware, pottery, and coins. (Open Apr.-Oct. Tu-Su 10am-5pm. 5SFr, students 3SFr.) Each room's function in medieval times is explained.

As the sun sets and the temperature drops, gamble at the **Kursaal** (casino) next to the tourist office, more a video arcade than a casino. (Open Su-Th. noon-2am, F-Sa noon-4am. Must be over 19. Proper attire required: no shorts, no T-shirts.) Catch recent American and Italian movies for 10SFr at the **Cinema Rex** on via Bossi next to the Co-op, just off P. Grande, or nurse a long drink at one of the numerous cafés along P. Grande. The **Record Rock Café,** via Trevani 3 (tel. 751 4433), a Hard Rock look-a-like, pumps out American and English rock from the 1950s to today. (Open July-Aug. Tu-Su 5pm-1am; Sept.-June Tu-Su 4pm-1am. Cover 10SFr.) The sign over the bar reads "All you need is love," but you'll still need 10SFr for the cover, and an additional 6SFr for any beer. Live bands play from September to June.

Locarno is the ideal starting/stopping/break point for outdoor enthusiasts. To escape the city, head out on Postal Bus 630-55 to **Sonogo** (1hr., 15.80SFr, Swisspass valid) and bask amid the extraordinarily rugged peaks at the end of **Val Verzasca** (Verzasca valley). From the bus stop, make your first left and follow the yellow signs to Lavertezzo. Pass through cool, shady glens and rocky riverbeds as you follow the Verzasca river through the pristine valley. Peaks rise on either side as you walk (primarily downhill) by deserted villages and cascading waterfall. Close to **Lavertezzo,** the river eases its rapid, crashing pace and offers the soul-cleansing cold of its refreshing pools to hikers, thermally overloaded or otherwise. Pick your swimming hole carefully, however, as currents can be fast and it's colder than you think. Climb the **Ponte dei Salti,** a vaulted stone bridge built at the end of the Middle Ages, and gaze into the clear green ponds. The walk from Sonogroto Lavertezzo takes about three and a half hours, but you can rest anytime by meeting the postal bus at stops along the valley. The trail is marked by yellow signs with direction and town names and also by painted red stripes sandwiched by two white stripes.

The Locarno Film Festival

For 11 days every August everything else stops for the **International Film Festival,** one of the six most important movie premiere events in the world. Unlike Cannes, no invitations are required and over 150,000 big screen enthusiasts descend upon the resort for the spectacle—book your room six months to a year ahead to stand a chance. The famous centerpiece of the festival is a giant 26m by 14m outdoor screen set up in Piazza Grande for big name premieres by the likes of Jean Luc Goddard, Woody Allen, Stanley Kubrick, Spike Lee, and Bernardo Bertolucci. Smaller screens throughout the city highlight young filmmakers and groundbreaking experimentation. (Festival information International Film Festival, via della Posta 6, CH-6601 Locarno; tel. 751 02 32, fax 751 74 65; email pardo@tinet.ch; http://www.pardo.ch.)

■ Near Locarno: Ascona

"Supposing you would like to make this region visible and open it up for an enthusiastic traveler who has never spent a day in Ascona," writes Jacob Flach in **The First Step into Wonderland,** "the easiest way to explain would certainly be: Here lies a piece of the Mediterranean Sea embedded in rough mountains, a sun-bathed, blooming Cape of the Côte d'Azure, a mile of the Riviera beach sprinkled with azaleas and carnations, and a good dose of the blue sky!" Sharing Flach's delight for this lovely resort village on the shores of Lake Maggiore, waves of quirky people have colonized **Monte Verità,** the mountain above the town, since 1869: anarchists, communists, nudists, vegetarian-agrarians, proto-feminists, mystics, religious dancers, and artists.

ORIENTATION AND PRACTICAL INFORMATION Reach Ascona via a 15-minute city bus ride from Locarno (#31, every 15min., 2.40SFr). Several **tourist offices** flourish in this small resort, but the one closest to the bus stop is just downhill; the larger main office (where English is more likely to be spoken) is in the Casa Serodine, just behind the Chiesa S.S. Pietro e. Paolo (tel. 791 00 90; fax 792 10 08; email ascona@etlm.ch; http://www.ascona.ch). **Guided tours** of Ascona leave the main office from March to November on Tuesdays at 10am (30min., 5SFr). The office also **exchanges currency** at standard rates. (Open Mar. 20-Oct. 20 M-F 9am-6:30pm, Sa 10am-5pm; Oct. 21-Mar. 19 M-F 9am-12:30pm and 2-6pm). **Parking** in Ascona shouldn't be too difficult, although cars cannot enter the center of town. Try the **Autosilo** at the corner of Via Papio and via Buonamno. **Bike rental** at **Noleggio,** via Circonvallazione 14 (tel. 791 33 24), costs 15-20SFr per day. (Open M-Sa 8:30am-noon and 2:30-6:15pm, Su 8:45-11:45am.) The **post office** is at the corner just uphill from the bus stop at the intersection of via Papio, via Borge, and via Locarno. (Open M-F 7:30am-noon and 1:45-6pm, Sa 8-11am); an **ATM** at the post office offers 24hr. banking. The **postal code** is CH-6612. The **telephone code** is 091.

ACCOMMODATIONS AND FOOD A village of only 4500 inhabitants, Ascona with its neighboring twin, Losone, boasts over 3000 hotel beds. Unfortunately, hardly any fall into a budget price range. If the youth hostel in Locarno doesn't appeal, try the rooms above the **Ristorante Verbano** (tel. 791 12 74) on via Borgo near the museum (45SFr per person, breakfast included), or ask the tourist office for a list of **camere private** (private rooms; 24-65SFr per person). Grab a bite to eat at **Otello** on via Papio 8 (tel. 791 33 07), just downhill from the bus stop. Their specialty is crepes (from 6.50SFr), but they also have expensive Chinese and cheap Italian food. During the jazz festival and on other random occasions, you can hear New Orleans jazz in the bandstand on the terrace in back. (Open Su-Th 7am-midnight, F-Sa 7am-1am. MC, Visa.) **Ristorante La Torre,** Piazzo Motta 61 (tel. 791 54 55), offers prime lakeside people-watching as well as pizza and pasta starting at 11SFr and sandwiches from 6SFr. (Open Mar.-Oct. daily 9am-1am; Jan.-Feb. M-F 8am-6:30pm; Sa 8am-5pm. AmEx, Visa.) And you can't miss the **Co-op**'s orange sign from the bus stop. (Open M-F 8am-12:30pm and 2-6:30pm, Sa 8am-5pm.)

SIGHTS AND ENTERTAINMENT The extremely sympathetic **Museo Casa Anatta** (tel. 791 03 27) immortalizes the dashed dreams of Utopia in documents and photographs (unfortunately without English labeling). Take bus #33 from the post office up the winding hillside road or walk 15 to 20 minutes up the stairway (scallinata della Ruga) from the town center. (Open Apr.-June and Sept.-Oct. Tu-Su 2:30-6pm; July-Aug. 3-7pm. 6SFr, students 4SFr.) One block downhill from the bus stop, the **Collegio Pontifico Papio** has a magnificent 16th-century court and arcade decorated with balconies and the coat of arms of many a departed collegiate administrator. Presiding over the still-operating private Superior school (1399), the church of **Santa Maria della Misericordia** next door spruces up its dim, incense-laden interior with frescoes by Seregnesi and Antonio da Tradate (1455-1526) as well as an incongruously brand-new organ. Backtracking half a block toward the bus station and turning left on via Collegio, then turning right, one arrives at the **Chiesa S.S. Pietro e. Paolo** in the heart of the pedestrian sector. Although the basilica and three enclosed naves date from the 16th century, the beautiful frescoes inside are a century older. Just across the street, the rich stucco of the **Casa Serodine** marks the neighborhood of the old studios of a colony of painters and sculptors who settled in Ascona during the Renaissance. Walking farther downhill to the waterfront and turning left, one passes the sole remaining ivy-covered tower of the 13th-century **Castello del Ghiriglion,** 26 Piazza Motto, now reborn as a hotel and expensive restaurant. Further along the waterfront, just past the Eden Roc hotel, the **Museo Epper,** 14 via Albarelle (tel. 791 19 42), presents temporary exhibitions of 20th-century art. *(Open Apr.-June and Sept.-Oct. Tu-F 10am-noon and 3-6pm, Su 3-6pm; July-Aug. Tu-F 10am-noon and 8-10pm, Sa-Su 8-10pm. Free.)* From the waterfront, turn right on via Borgo to reach Ascona's **Museo**

Comunale d'Arte Moderna, 34 via Borgo (tel. 791 67 57), whose extensive permanent collection includes Klee, Utrillo, Amiet, and Jawlensky, as well as a collection of caricatures done both in color and black-and-white. *(Open Mar.-Dec. Tu-Sa 10am-noon and 3-5pm, Su 10am-noon. 5SFr, students and seniors 3SFr.)* Private galleries line the winding streets, promoting such artists as Niki de St. Phalle, Chagall, and Braque. Just prior to reaching the museum, you'll pass the beginning of the Scalinata della Ruga staircase leading to Monte Verità.

In late June and early July, Ascona sets up the bandstands and claps its hands to the beat of the **New Orleans Music Festival.** Musicians play jazz, gospel, soul, blues, and even zydeco on the waterfront and in local cafés. The festival takes place in late June; entrance is 5SFr per night, 30SFr for the whole festival. If you like festivals, also consider stopping by for the **international horse jumping competition** at the end of July, an **international music festival** (late Aug. to mid-Oct.), and an **international puppet festival** (early to mid-Sept.). Locarno's discotheque crowd flocks to Ascona's subterranean dance club, **Cincilla,** via Moscia 6, located beneath mysterious arcades beside Lago Maggiore. *(Open W-Th and Su 11pm-3am, F-Sa 11pm-4am.)* The club is a little heavy on the zebra motif.

■ Bellinzona

Dominated by three hilltop medieval strongholds, the capitol of Ticino is trying to throw off its image as a primarily administrative crossroads town linking the lakeside resorts of Lugano and Locarno. Extensive restorations (and, more controversially, radical renovations) of its ancient architecture along with a century's investment in Corbusier-like modern and glass buildings among the churches and castles give this windy city a unique atmosphere.

ORIENTATION AND PRACTICAL INFORMATION Bellinzona's tourist office, 2 Via Camminata (tel. 825 21 31; fax 825 38 17), adjacent to the city hall, makes free hotel reservations. From the train station, walk left 10 minutes along Viale Stazione, past P. Collegiata, and along Via Nosetto, until you hit a big blue "i" sign at P. Nosetto. (Open Apr.-Oct. M-F 8am-6:30pm, Sa 9am-5pm; Nov.-Mar. M-F 8am-noon and 1:30-6:30pm, Sa 8-11am.) The easiest way to Bellinzona is by **train.** There are direct connections to Basel (4hr., every hr., 6:06am-11:35pm, 70SFr), Lugano (30min., 3 per hr., 5:07am-1:49pm, 10.40SFr), Locarno (20min., 2 per hr., 5:38am-12:35am, 6.60SFr), Lucerne (2¼hr., 8am-10:20pm, 50SFr), Zurich (2½hr., every hr., 6:26am-8:36pm, 54SFr), Milan (2hr., every hr., 5:07am-1:20am, 23SFr), and Rome (7hr., 3 per day, 5:07am-12:35am, 65SFr). Trains to and from Geneva require a change in Italian Domodossola (5½hr., 10 per day, 87SFr). Call 157 22 22 for train information. Post **buses** leave from the station for Chur and San Bernadino (2½hr., 5 per day, 6am-4:20pm, 50SFr) and points in eastern Switzerland. **Motorists** arrive from the north on N2/E35 or N13/E43; from Lugano or the south, on N2/E35 north; from Locarno or the west, on Rte. 13 east. The train station has currency exchange, luggage storage (5SFr at baggage check), lockers (3SFr), and bike rental (22SFr per day at baggage check; open 6am-9pm). Public parking is available at the train station or in the Colletivo at P. del Sole (1SFr per hr.; open 8am-7pm). The ultra-new **post office** on Viale Stazione is a block left from the station. (Open M-F 6:30am-noon and 1-7pm, Sa 8-11am.) The **postal code** is CH-6500. The **telephone code** is 091.

ACCOMMODATIONS AND FOOD Bellinzona has yet to build a youth hostel, even though any one of those castles would be perfect for one (hint, hint). To reach **Hotel Moderno Garni,** 17b Viale Stazione (tel./fax 825 13 76), go left from the station, turn right on Via Claudio Pelladini, and take another immediate right on Via Cancelliere Molo. All rooms come with dark carpeting, a sink, and two framed art prints; half also have balconies. (Singles 55SFr; doubles 90SFr; triples 120SFr; quads 160SFr. Shower and breakfast included. Reception in the hotel café 6:30am-midnight. MC, Visa.) If the Moderno Garni is full, fall back on the less charming **Hotel San Giovanni,** 7 via San

Giovanni (tel./fax 825 19 19). From the station, go left on Viale Stazione and right down Scalinata Dionigi Resinelli; continue straight for 100m. (Singles 60SFr; doubles 90SFr. Breakfast included. Parking available. Reception 6:15am-midnight. MC, Visa.) Stark metal bedframes rest on linoleum floors, but there are big, breezy rooms and a popular restaurant downstairs. Postal bus #2: "Arbedo Posta Vecchia" leads to **Camping Bosco de Molinazzo** (tel. 829 11 18; fax 829 23 55) and to sleeping fitfully under the stars. (5-6SFr, children half-price; tent 5.20SFr; car 16SFr. Open Apr. 3-Oct. 6).

Aromas from the restaurant in Castelgrande waft over the campgrounds, but, alas, the five-star eatery is for dukes and duchesses only. Those who are nobles in spirit but peasants in pocket head to **Ristorante Inova,** Viale Stazione 5, in the Inovazione. Sometimes you can even find salmon. (Entrees 10-13SFr, salads 5-10SFr. Open M-F 8:30am-6:30pm, Sa 8:30am-9pm, Su 8am-5pm.) Or fill your stomach with cappuccino (3SFr), *panini* (5SFr), choco-bugs (2SFr), and huge pizza slices (7SFr) at **Peverelli Panetteria Tea Room Pasticceria** in P. Collegiata off Viale Stazione. (Open M-F 7am-7pm, Sa 7am-6pm.) **Migros** is in P. del Sole, across from the Castelgrande entrance. (Open M-F 7am-6:30pm, Sa 7:30am-5pm.) **Bio Casa,** next to the tourist office, stocks organic fruits and veggies, tofu burgers, and vitamins. (Open M-F 8:30am-6:30pm, Sa 8am-5pm. MC, Visa.) The huge **outdoor market** along Via Stazione lays out everything from typical fruits and breads to incense and rugs. (Open Sa 8am-noon.)

SIGHTS AND ENTERTAINMENT

Looming 50m above the center of town, the oft-renovated **Castelgrande** occupies a site inhabited since the neolithic period (5500-5000 BCE) and fortified from the 4th century CE on. *(Open in summer Tu-Su 10am-12:30pm and 1:30-5:30pm; in winter Tu-Su 9am-noon and 2-5pm. 4SFr, students 2SFr.)* Construction on the current fortress began in the 13th century with major enlargements in 1473-86. The *bianca* (white) and *nera* (black) towers, rising 27 and 28m high, date from the 13th and 14th centuries. The town extensively transformed the castle from 1984-91 in an effort to make it more hospitable to tourists, adding an elevator, an expensive courtyard restaurant, and a (dare we say anachronistic) concrete and TV-laden **museum** (tel. 825 81 45) in the interior with hundreds of brightly painted, allegorical tablets rescued from the decaying 14th-century wooden ceiling of a medieval Bellinzona inn. The Castelgrande is accessible by the free elevator near P. del Sole or by the winding paths up the hill from P. Collegieta and P. Nosetto. Another 90m above Castelgrande, on an opposing hill, the smaller **Castello di Montebello** offers visitors working drawbridges, ramparts, dungeons, and views as far as Lake Maggiore on a clear day. *(Open in summer Tu-Su 9am-noon and 2-6pm; in winter Tu-Su 9am-noon and 2-5pm. Museum 2SFr, students 1SFr.)* The tower and former residential quarters now house an **archaeological and civic museum** containing vases, jewelry, and ceramics, as well as the usual ancient bric-a-brac of ceremonial and military arms. The castle can be reached on foot from Piazza Collegiata up the slippery mossy steps of Via Motta or by bus from Viale Stazione. Worth a look but not the walk, the **Castello di Sasso Corbaro** (230m above city level), the smallest of Bellinzona's three castles, surveys the Ticinese mountains. The Duke of Milan had the place slapped together in six months after the battle of Giornico. Available at the castles and the tourist office, a **"3 Castelli" ticket** grants entry to all three castle museums. *(8SFr, students 4SFr.)*

A fire charred the interior of the beloved 15th-century **Chiesa Santa Maria della Grazie** (now being restored), but the nearby **Chiesa di San Biagio** flaunts a gigantic 16th-century painting of St. Christopher and a flock of saints on its columned interior. From the train station, walk 15 minutes to the left or take bus #4: "Cimiterio"; cross under the railroad tracks, turn left up the stairs, turn left again, and follow tracks 50m. The **Ticino River,** all the way down to Lago di Maggiore, is perfect for idle strollers out for mountain air and scenery. For a 45-minute hike with grand views of Sasso Corbaro and the valley, first take a short postal bus ride to Monti di Ravecchia. The trail begins at the hospital parking lot and follows an ancient mule path, leading to now-deserted Prada, an ancient trading post possibly dating to pre-Roman times.

The annual **Blues Festival** draws crowds from throughout Switzerland in late June (June 24-26 in 1999). Previous performers include Luther Allison and Joe Louis

Walker. Free concerts occur in the piazzas. Contact the tourist office for more information. Near Bellinzona, **Alcatraz** (tel. 859 31 34), the biggest dance club in Ticino, draws skanky partiers from the nearby countryside. Take the train to nearby Riazzino, but hurry, Cinderella—the club closes at 3am, but the last train runs at midnight. Taxis are available but rates are exorbitant.

■ Near Bellinzona: San Bernardino Pass

A short bus ride from Bellinzona, the San Bernardino Pass (1626m) leads into the heart of the Alps, tunneling through rock, twisting around horn-honking curves, and crossing deep river gorges. San Bernardino village is practically bite-sized, a tiny collection of lichen-roofed houses and minuscule churches. Though slightly marred by ugly modern ski chalets, the surrounding hills and craggy peaks give immediate rise to hiking daydreams. Several hikes lead up to the village of **Ospizio** and the **San Bernardino Pass** (2065m). The easiest route is along the road past the Capanna Genziana for 1½ hours. The trails through the taiga and Alpine trees are only sporadically marked by white and red paint marks or posts, so bring a map. The shores of the pure Alpine **Lago Moesola**, a congregation point for cyclists and hikers, await, as do commanding views of the valley. A small restaurant marks Ospizio, where you can refuel and exchange stories with other hikers. A postal bus travels on to **Thusis** (22SFr); from there, catch a train to **Chur** (12.20SFr). Or keep on truckin'—the valley seems to go on forever.

The San Bernardino **tourist office** (tel. (091) 832 12 14; fax 832 11 55) has maps and information on hiking and skiing. (Open M-F 8:30am-noon and 2-5pm, Sa-Su 10am-3pm.) From the bus stop, walk straight 10m, take the first left, and walk straight on this road (there are no street names) for 200m. The tourist office is on the left. **Ristorante Pizzeria Postiglione** (tel. 832 13 47), at the bus stop, cooks lotsa pizzas. (11-15SFr. Open Tu-Su 8am-midnight. MC, Visa.) Or stock up on trail mix at the **Satellite Denner**. Go right from the bus stop—in the opposite direction from the tourist office—and the Satellite supermarket is 100m away on your left. (Open M-F 8:30am-noon and 3-6:30pm, Sa 8:30am-noon and 2-5:30pm.) Bushed after a long climb from Bellinzona? The Alpine hut **Capanna Genziana** (tel. (091) 832 12 04) has Spartan rooms with bunk beds. To reach the hut, continue past Denner over a small stream, bear left, then bear right at the next intersection and follow the signs to the San Bernardino Pass. The hut is on your right. (Dorms 27SFr, half-pension 37SFr.)

Map: **Graubünden (Grisons)**

Labels on map: TO ZURICH, Rhein, AUSTRIA, Landquart, *Madrisahorn*, Klosters-Dorf, *Gotschnagrat*, Klosters-Platz, N13, Chur, *Weisshorn*, Arosa, *Piz Linard*, Davos-Dorf, Davos-Platz, *Jakobshorn*, Zernez, *Piz Sesvenna*, N3, SWISS NATIONAL PARK, Zuoz, S-chanf, *Piz Platta*, Celerina, Inn River, St. Moritz, Pontresina, ITALY, Adda, Silvaplana, *Diavolezza*, N, Sils (Segl), Maloja, 0 10 miles, 0 10 kilometers, Chiavenna, Tirano

Graubünden (Grisons)

The largest, least populous, and most Alpine of the Swiss cantons, Graubünden's remote valleys and snow-clad peaks are bound to bring out the wild-hearted, lusting-for-life yodeler in everyone. Deep, rugged gorges, forests of larch and fir, and eddying rivers imbue the region with a wildness seldom found in ultra-civilized Switzerland. The area is also a microcosm of Swiss cultural heterogeneity—from valley to valley the language slips easily from German to Romansh to Italian, with a wide range of dialects in between. Though only 1-2% of the country (and 26% percent of the canton) converses in the ancient Romansh tongue, it is a fiercely preserved subject in schools and books—especially hymnals—and is recognized as an official language. *Schwyzer-Dütsch* (Swiss-German) is just a dialect of German.

Once a summer visiting spot, the region was changed forever by the St. Moritz hotel pioneer Johannes Badrutt in 1864. The innkeeper made four British summer visitors an offer they couldn't refuse: if they came in winter and didn't like it, he would pay their travel costs. If they liked it, he'd let them stay as long as they wanted, *for free*. Alas, that was the last of cheap housing in Graubünden. The prime ski venues and Graubünden's hotels provide luxuries that unfortunately cost dearly.

Travel around the Graubünden is made easier with the **Graubünden Regional Pass,** which allows 5 days of unlimited travel in a 15-day period and a 50% discount on the other days (163SFr, children under 16 66.50SFr), or three days of unlimited travel in a seven-day period and a 50% discount on the other days (100SFr, children

50SFr). The Regional Pass is issued only in Switzerland from May through October. The ubiquitous **Swisspass** is valid as well. Visitors should plan excursions carefully in this part of the country, especially in ski season (Dec.-Apr.), when reservations are absolutely required, and in July and August. In May and early June, virtually everything shuts down as locals take vacations.

■ Chur

Chur is the capital of Graubünden and, at 5000 years old, probably Switzerland's oldest settlement. A quixotic combination of Romanesque cathedrals and alternative lifestyles, Graubünden's biggest city is a happening, artsy place to hang out. The city is also an important transportation hub, shuttling visitors to nearby Austria and Liechtenstein, and farther south to the Italian canton Ticino.

From the Ticino, **postal buses** run between Chur and **Bellinzona** (2½hr., 5 per day, 50SFr plus 5SFr reservation fee). Chur connects to the rest of Switzerland by rail through **Zurich** (1½hr., every 30min., 6:04am-10:16pm, 37SFr), and direct trains also link Chur with **Basel** (2½hr., every hr., 6:16am-10:16pm, 59SFr), **Disentis** (for the **Furka-Oberalp line**; 2½hr., every hr., 5:25am-9:57pm, 25SFr), **Arosa** (1hr., every hr., 5:28am-8:50pm, 11.40SFr), **St. Gallen** (1½hr., every hr., 6:22am-9:16pm, 32SFr), and **St. Moritz** (2hr., every hr., 6:42am-8:52pm, 39SFr). The **train station** provides **currency exchange** (open 5:40am-9:15pm), **luggage storage** (5SFr), **bike rental** (25SFr at baggage check; open 5:40am-9:15pm), and **lockers** (2SFr). Chur's **tourist office**, Grabenstr. 5 (tel. 252 18 18; fax 252 90 76), finds rooms in Chur for free. From the train station, walk to the left and up Bahnhofstr.; at the second intersection (Postpl.), turn left on Grabenstr. (Open M 1:30-6pm, Tu-F 8:30am-noon and 1:30-6pm, Sa 9am-noon.) Graubünden's **regional tourist office**, Alexanderstr. 24 (tel. 254 24 24; fax 254 24 00), is located in Chur and brims with brochures for every city in the canton. From the station, go down Bahnhofstr. and turn left on Alexanderstr. (Open M-F 8am-noon and 1:30-5:30pm.) **English books** await at **F. Schuler**, Gäuggelistr 11 (tel. 252 11 60; open M 1-6:30pm, Tu-Th 8:30am-6:30pm, F 8:30am-9pm, Sa 8:30am-4pm.) **Laundry** can be done at **Maltesen's Wash Self-Service**, Malteserg. 1. Wash and dry from 9SFr. (Open M-Sa 9am-midnight, Su noon-midnight.) In an **emergency**, dial 117. There's a **pharmacy** at Quaderstr. 16 off Bahnhofstr. (Open M-F 8am-12:15pm and 1:15-6:30pm, Sa 8-11am.) Chur's **postal code** is CH-7000. Its **telephone code** is 081.

On the outskirts of the old town, high-altitude **Hotel Rosenhügel**, Malixerstr. 32 (tel./fax 252 23 88) offers warm beds and city sunset views (that is, if you manage to fathom the puzzling set of stairs). From the train station (15min.) head right, and take Engadinstr. to the river. Cross the bridge to the inclined Malixerstr. and the hotel is five minutes away, to your right. (Singles 45-50SFr; doubles 90SFr, with shower 100SFr. Breakfast included. Parking included. Reception 8am-midnight. AmEx, DC, MC, Visa.) **Hotel Schweizerhaus**, Kasernenstr. 10 (tel. 252 10 96; fax 252 27 31) is off Weischdörfli, at the foot of Malixerstr. Spare, barrack-like *Touristsenlager* dorms cost 25SFr. (Singles with shower 55SFr; doubles 80SFr. Breakfast and shower included. Sheets 5SFr. Reception 7am-midnight.) **Camp Auchur**, Felsensustr. 61 is a green and grassy campsite on the Rhine. Take bus #2 to "Obere Au" past the sports complex; it's on the left, on the gravel path. (6SFr, tents 6-12SFr. Electricity 3.30SFr. Showers

0.50SFr. Equipped with kiosks and a restaurant.) **The Co-op Center** market is at the corner of Alexanderstr. and Quadenstr. off Bahnhofstr. (Open M-Th 8am-6:30pm, F 8am-9pm, Sa 8am-5pm.) Hit the alternative scene at **Shoanna Grill,** Untereg. 5 (tel. 252 73 22), packed with twenty-somethings, painted sheets, world music, and alternative beats. Heaven? No. (Kebabs 8SFr. Falafel with veggies 7SFr. Beer from 3.50SFr. Open M-F 11:45am-2pm and 5pm-midnight, Sa 11:45am-midnight, Su 11:45am-10pm.) **Restaurant Falken,** St. Martinspl. 9, near the St. Martin's Church, has organic dishes featuring cheese, tofu, and salad. *Menüs* run 16SFr. Veggie *Menüs* 15SFr. (Open M-Sa 9am-midnight.) **Restaurante Controverse,** Steinbruchstr. 2 (tel. 252 99 44), to the left of the tourist office, tries very hard to defy the norm. An Art Nouveau decor combines Louis XIV drapes with black coffee tables and neon lights. Lots of lip-smacking good food, often vegetarian. (Spaghetti 10-20SFr. Oriental noodles 10.50SFr.) If you can make out the upside-down menus, you can tell that the wines are 4-8SFr. (Open M-Sa 11am-2pm and 5pm-midnight, Su 6-11pm.) Dig the art scene at **Street Café,** Grabenstr. 47 (tel. 253 79 17). Scary, modern-art Mona Lisas with Marlboro lights and Elgin marble lookalikes in a red-draped setting are witness to a young, beer-happy crowd. (Beers from 3.50SFr.) The **Street Castle** upstairs is a *Ritterstil* (knight-style) chamber where wine flows from the decanter and cask (from 4SFr; cover F-Sa in winter; open 9am-midnight.)

Chur's sights are all within walking distance of the town's center. The highlight, a 12th-century Romanesque **cathedral** at the top of the old town, boasts eight altarpieces in addition to the **Hochaltar,** a flamboyant 15th-century masterpiece of gold and wood. Paradisiacal flora adorn the nave ceiling while gruesome, infernal beasts gnaw on wide-eyed sinners on the columns. The crypts, where the Capuchin martyr St. Fidelis is buried, also house the **Dom-Museum** (tel. 252 92 50), replete with relics. (Open Tu-Sa 10am-noon and 2-4pm.) The **Martinskirche** downhill counters the cathedral's grandiose flair with understated simplicity: the church's sole decorations are three stained-glass windows by Augusto Giacometti (not to be confused with his sculptor-relative Alberto). The eerie panels depict the birth of an oddly beefy Christ. Clad in blood-red instead of her usual blue, Mary stares with wide, alien eyes beside her thoroughly befuddled husband. Chur's **Bündner Kunstmuseum,** Bahnhofstr. 35 (tel. 257 28 68), at the corner of Bahnhofstr. and Grabenstr., blazes with the glowing works of the three Giacomettis: Giovanni, Alberto, and Augusto. Take a break from the color-crazed family with works by Curo Amiet, Seagantini, Ernst Kirchner, Not Vital (not vital? rather obscure, actually), Kurt Sigrist, and Corsin Fontana. Swiss artists Angellick Kauffman and Ferdinand Hodler occupy the ground floor. (Open Tu-W and F-Su 10am-noon and 2-5pm, Th 10am-noon and 2-8pm. 10SFr, students 7SFr.)

If ever you desired to gather random info on Graubünden, the **Retic Museum,** Quaderstr. 15 (tel. 257 28 88), gives you that chance. A fine collection of tapestries, coins, and archaeological trivia documents the origin of "Rhaetia" and its development into the current Swiss canton with changing exhibits. (Open Tu-Su 10am-noon and 2-5pm. 5SFr, students 2SFr, seniors and groups 3SFr.)

■ Arosa

Blessed with a salutary air (that to non-Swiss is slightly below freezing), Arosa is a tiny city spread out along a main street that curves from the Obersee to the Untersee. Once a simple farming village, Arosa was transformed by a certain Mr. Herwig's "discovery" of the area's stimulating climate in 1888. Arosa has undergone several reincarnations since then—it's now a skier's and hiker's mecca thanks to the fringe of craggy peaks at the end of the Alpine valley. Arosa's mountain peaks barely dip under 2000m, and the tallest, the **Weisshorn,** towers 2653m above sea level. The 25km of cross-country ski trails, ice rinks, indoor tennis courts, and swimming pools are perfect winter treats. Best of all, Arosa is a little less glitzy and glamorous than its sister resorts in the Engadin Valley.

ORIENTATION AND PRACTICAL INFORMATION A **free bus** (every 30min. in summer, every 7min. in winter) shuttles visitors from the newsstand to the tourist office two stops away at "Kursaal." (Open Dec. 7-Apr. 13 M-F 9am-6pm, Sa 9am-5:30pm, Su 10am-noon and 4-5:30pm; Apr. 14-Dec. 6 M-F 8am-noon and 2-6pm, Sa 8am-1pm; June 29-Aug. 17 also open Sa 2-4pm.) Arosa is accessible by **train** only by way of a scenic route from **Chur** (1hr., every hr., 11.40SFr). **Parking** is free in summer at the **Parking Garage Obersee,** 2SFr per hour in winter. Beware—a strict traffic ban has been imposed from midnight to 6am every night. Climb on board the **free public bus,** which stops at the Hörnli and Prätschli ski lifts, the Untersee, the train station, and everywhere in between. Arosa's pink **tourist office** (tel. 378 70 20; fax 378 70 21), on Poststr. in front of the moving-eyeball fountain, arranges ski lessons and hiking trips and makes free hotel reservations. Head right from the station and then take the first right onto Poststr. The **train station** provides **currency exchange** (M-Sa 5:30am-8:05pm, Su 6:30am-8:05pm), **lockers** (2SFr), and **bike rental** (25SFr, mountain bikes 30SFr). In an **emergency,** dial 117. The **post office** is in Arosa's main square, to the right of the train station. (Open M-F 7:45am-noon and 1:45-6:30pm, Sa 8-11am.) The **postal code** is CH-7050, and the **telephone code** is 081.

ACCOMMODATIONS AND FOOD Arosa's hotels tend to demand high prices for "Bliss at 1800 Meters," but there are a number of budget options. Arriving in town without reservations is a bad idea. Reserve well in advance for prime ski-season vacation spots. The **Jugendherberge (HI),** Seewaldstr. (tel./fax 377 13 97), has a friendly, multilingual staff. Walk right from the station, take the first right onto Poststr., go past the tourist office, and bear left down the hill (you'll see a sign). Each dorm has a balcony overlooking either the lovely Untersee or the rugged Engadin slopes. Be sure to stock up on 0.50SFr coins for the shower. (Dorms 24SFr; doubles 58SFr; triples 87SFr; quads 116SFr. High-season (Dec. 26-Jan. 10, Feb. to mid-Mar., and Easter week): 36SFr; 92SFr; 138SFr; 184SFr. Sheets and hearty breakfast included. Bag lunch 7.50SFr; dinner 12SFr. Reception 7-10am and 5-10pm. No lockout. Curfew 10pm; key available. Open mid-June to mid-Oct. and mid-Dec. to mid-Apr.) Hidden up in the woods, **Pension Suveran** (tel. 377 19 69; fax 377 19 75) is the quiet, homey, wood-paneled chalet that you came to Switzerland to find. To the right of the Co-op, head up the small walkway to the left. At the top, turn right and follow the sign up the gravel path. (Singles 47SFr; doubles 84SFr. Winter: 53SFr; 106SFr. Add 5SFr in winter for stays of less than 3 nights. Breakfast included. Closed in Nov. Reserve in winter.) **Hotel Garni Haus Am Wald** (tel./fax 377 31 38), behind the train station and 150m to the left of the Weisshornbahn, offers tiny double-doored rooms and a small café downstairs. Call ahead to verify that they're accepting guests. (Singles 45-55SFr; doubles 90-104SFr. Winter: 70-80SFr; 120-180SFr. Breakfast included. Reception 8am-8pm.) **Hotel Bellaval** (tel. 378 84 84; fax 378 84 48), next to the Weisserhornbahn station, offers back-to-basics dorms and not much else for 30SFr. An additional 13SFr turns that into a dorm-and-hiking pass, which means free use of the Weiserhornbahn. **Kitchen** access, hall showers. **Camping Arosa** (tel. 377 17 45; fax 377 30 05), downhill from the hostel, is open year-round in a brook-filled valley and offers showers (0.50SFr) and cooking facilities. (7.30-8.30SFr, children 4-4.50SFr; tents 4.50SFr. Check-in 5-5:30pm.)

   With a broad, glassed-in or terraced view of mountains, try **Orelli's Restaurant,** Poststr. (tel. 377 12 08), after the post office and before the tourist office. Hikers young and old chomp happily in this panoramic family restaurant decorated with Mickey Mouse and stained glass. Thriftmeisters can eat soup and four slices of bread for only 4.50SFr. A special vegetarian *Menü* (9.50-14SFr), salad buffet (7-14SFr), and warm entrees (7.50-16SFr) round out your options. (Open 7:30am-9pm. Closed May and Nov. MC, Visa.) **Café/Restaurant Oasis** (tel. 377 22 20), diagonally across the street from Orelli's, has an outdoor deck just over Poststr., good for people-watching and mountain-gazing. Entrees include spaghetti *bolognese* for 11SFr, or chicken *cordon bleu* with fries for 15SFr. (Open 8:30am-11pm.) For saccharine treats, **Café-Confiserie Kaiser** (tel. 377 34 54; fax 377 42

44), on Poststr. around the bend from Orelli's, concocts confections and other nice things (meringues 7SFr). The *Menüs* aren't too bad either: spaghetti with tomato sauce is 11SFr; *Spätzle Gemüse gratin* 14SFr. Get groceries at the **Co-op,** before the tourist office on Poststr. (open M-F 8am-12:30pm and 2-6:30pm, Sa 8am-4pm), or **Denner Superdiscount** in the main square (open M-W and F 8:30am-12:15pm and 2:30-6:30pm, Sa 8:30am-12:15pm and 1:15-5pm).

SKIING, HIKING, AND ENTERTAINMENT Fourteen **ski lifts and cableways** hoist skiers to the 70km network of slopes in the Arosa-Tschuggen ski area. Ticket offices in Arosa seem to love making passes (day passes, morning passes, afternoon passes, 1½-day passes, "choose-your-day" passes, etc.). The town offers **passes** for all 14 lifts and cableways. *(49SFr per day, 249SFr for 1 week, and 377SFr for 2. All accept AmEx, DC, MC, Visa.)* The smaller Tschuggen-sector day pass is 30SFr. Children under 15 ski for half-price; young people 16-19 and seniors get a 15% discount.

When the snow melts, spring brings golf courses, baby rabbits, and flower-covered **hiking** paths, with over 200km. An **Alpine guide** leads seven- and nine-hour hikes at beginning, intermediate, and advanced levels for only 10SFr. *(Late June to mid-Oct. Tu-Th. Contact the tourist office for details.)* For a mellow hike below treeline, start at the hill right of the Co-op and cruise along the ridge overlooking the Obersee to the small town of Maran, where you can catch a bus back to Arosa (1hr.). The **Weisserhornbahn cable-car** departs behind the train station and whisks travelers to the top of the Weisserhorn. *(Every 20min. 24SFr, round-trip 30SFr; 30% off with Swisspass.)* From the 2653m summit, you can gaze upon all of the Engadin, even back to San Bernardino. Several splendid trails (usually 2-2½hr.) lead down to Arosa. For more snow-capped peaks than you can shake a walking stick at, follow the yellow signs down along the ridge to the **Hörnli-Express.** *(1½hr. 24SFr, round-trip 30SFr; 30% off with Swisspass.)*

For the more sedentary, the **fish** of the Obersee and local rivers bite friskily. *(Permits at the tourist office; day 25SFr, week 65SFr, 2 weeks 100SFr, month 125SFr.)* The Untersee's **free beach** welcomes swimmers and sunbathers. The **International Jazz Festival** happens in late July with free admission to various local venues. The festival features New Orleans jazz played by American, Swiss, Australian, and English bands. Previous performers include Tuba Fats and Jambalaya. The **Humorfestival** revs up in mid-December with artists from all over Switzerland, Austria, and Germany putting up comedy shows, pantomimes, and skits. Tickets for morning and evening shows (30SFr) are available at the tourist office. The **Ski and Country** festival in mid-March features special country vocalists along with discounted ski passes.

■ Samnaun

In the snowy corner of Switzerland that greets Austria on one side, and Germany and Liechtenstein on the other, Samnaun is the best ski resort this side of the Alps. Made famous by the local fairy tale "Murmina and Murmin" (2 marmots who go in search of a wild herb to cure their ailing parents), the dimpled hillside makes for easy hiking in summer and divine skiing in winter.

ORIENTATION AND PRACTICAL INFORMATION To get to Samnaun, take the bus from **Swol** (1hr., 6 per day, 7:35am-8:05pm, 18.20SFr) or **Martina** (45min., 6 per day, 8:15am-7:50pm, 9SFr). Swol in turn is connected to **Samedan** (1¼hr., every hr., 7:52am-8:34pm, 23SFr), **St. Moritz** (1½hr., every hr., 7:52am-8:34pm, 12.50SFr), and **Chur** (4-5hr., every hr., 7:52am-6:52pm, 64.20SFr). Free **buses** shuttle you to Samnaun's five villages every hour (8:19am-9pm). The **tourist office** (tel. 868 58 58; fax 868 56 52; email info@samnaun.ch), right next to the bus stop, has loads of brochures about the area. (Open Dec.-May and June-Sept. M-F 8am-6:30pm, Sa 9am-noon and 1-5pm; Dec.-May also Sa 8am-5:30pm and Su 8-10am and 2:30-5:30pm; Oct.-Nov. M-F 9am-6pm).

ACCOMMODATIONS AND FOOD Samnaun, a town of 740 inhabitants, has 2200 guest beds. A little ambitious there, guys? The ski season draws a comparable crowd, eager to hit those purdy slopes, a crowd that comes largely from nearby Austria, Germany, and Liechtenstein. Winter reservations are a fine idea. **Hotel Alpina** (tel. 868 51 22; fax 868 57 23), on the main drag opposite the shopping center, provides warm rooms and lovely views of the slopes for 30SFr. (Breakfast and sheets included. Open Dec.-Mar. and June-Oct.) In nearby Ravaisch, **Ganni Pro** (tel. 868 53 33; fax 868 57 23) is accessible via the free bus. A three-minute walk uphill from the station, this place provides high comfort at low prices. (Summer singles 35-40SFr; doubles 70-80SFr. Add 20SFr in winter high-season. Breakfast, private bath, TV, radio, plush towels, and whatnot included. Open Dec.-May and July-Oct. MC, Visa.)

Pizzeria Camona (tel. 861 83 83), to the right of the main shopping center, serves sizzling oven-fresh pizzas (7-20SFr) and wines (from 4.80SFr). Try the *al funghi* (14SFr) topped with mushrooms, tomato, mozzarella, and oregano. (Open 7am-midnight.) **Restaurant des Alpes** (tel. 868 52 73), behind the parking lot in the *Dorfzentrum*, conjures up veggie dishes (11-14.50SFr), *raclette* (15SFr), and fondue (15SFr). (Open 7am-11pm.)

HIKING AND OUTDOOR ACTIVITIES Starting from the Samnaun-Compatsch, many trails branch off into Switzerland's last claim to the Alps before Austria takes over. If you head to Zanderstal (2hr.), the hike takes you over the Austrian border, so bring your passport. Guided hikes are available for nature-lovers, wildlife-watchers, and just plain people who like good things. Contact the tourist office, which can also take you **canyoning** (4hr., F at 9am, 99SFr; bring sturdy gear). Winter skiing is real durned nice. **Skipasses** run 48SFr per day, 92.50 2-day, 271.50 per week. Children and seniors get 15-20% off.

▓ Davos

Davos challenges St. Moritz's title as the ski and spa capital of Graubünden. Settled in 1289 by the Wallisers, Davos emerged as a health resort in the 19th century and quickly became a finely tuned ski center. Now, while most ski resorts feel as remote as their host mountains, Alpine Davos maintains a cosmopolitan atmosphere and a pleasing blend of town and country.

ORIENTATION AND PRACTICAL INFORMATION Davos is easily accessible from the rest of Switzerland by **train** through **Chur** via **Landquart** (1½hr., every hr., 4:59am-9:06pm, 26SFr) or **Klosters** (8.40SFr) on the Rhätischebahn lines. The town is divided into two areas, **Davos-Dorf** and **Davos-Platz**, each with its own train station and linked by the long **Promenade**. Davos-Dorf is closer to most hotels and the Bergbahn, while Davos-Platz holds the tourist office and the main post office. An intra-city **bus** (2SFr, with Swisspass 1SFr) runs between the two train stations and stops near major hotels and the hostel on the Davosersee. Drivers to Davos can find many **parking lots** along the Promenade and Talstr. but should be aware that the Promenade traffic is one-way west (parking generally 1SFr per hr.; free at Kongresszentrum). Rent **bikes** at the Davos-Dorf station (23SFr per day) or the hostel (see below). The high-tech **main tourist office**, Promenade 67 (tel. 415 21 21; fax 415 21 00; email davos@davos.ch; http://www.davos.ch), in Davos-Platz, plans skiing and hiking packages and helps find rooms. Walk up the hill to the right of the Davos-Platz train station and then right along the Promenade for five minutes. The tourist office is on the left. A smaller **branch** office, across from the Davos-Dorf train station, also offers information and calls hotels. (Both offices open M-F 8:30am-6pm, Sa 8:30am-4pm.) The train stations **exchange currency** and **store luggage** (5SFr; both open M-Sa 5:45am-8:10pm, Su 6:50am-8:10pm), as well as rent **lockers** (2SFr). There is **internet access** at **Rampa**, Promenade 123 (25SFr per hr.; open M-F 8am-noon and 1:30-6:30pm, Sa 8am-4pm; AmEx, MC, Visa). Call 111 for a **late-night pharmacy.** The main **post office** is in Davos-Platz at Promenade 43. (Open M-F 7:45am-6pm, Sa 8:30am-11pm.) The **postal code** is CH-7270. The **telephone code** is 081.

GRAUBÜNDEN

ACCOMMODATIONS AND FOOD Wherever you stay, ask for the Davos **visitor's card,** which grants unlimited travel on the city's buses and reduced tickets for plays, concerts, ice rinks, swimming pools, and golf courses. The **Jugendherberge Höhwald (HI)** (tel. 416 14 84; fax 416 50 55) in Davos-Wolfgang has seen its share of ski seasons. Take bus #6 or 11 (dir: Davos-Wolfgang): "Hochgebirgsklinik," backtrack 100m, and turn left; or head right from the Davos-Dorf train station and walk 30 minutes along the Davosersee. The old house sits directly on the Davosersee and has a large front porch and swimming dock. The gorgeous bamboo and green wood dining room looks far too elegant for a hostel—but don't worry! Eight to 14 sardine-like beds in each dorm room reassure with the sweet smell of roommates. (Dorms 22.70SFr 1st night, then 20.20SFr; doubles 53SFr, 48SFr. In winter there are no multi-day discounts and tax is 0.40SFr extra. Family rooms available. Breakfast (8-9am), sheets, and showers included. Dinner at 6:30pm. **Kitchen.** Bag lunch or dinner 11SFr. **Bike rental** 12SFr per day. Reception 8-9:30am and 5-9pm. No lockout. No curfew. Quiet time from 10:30pm. Closed Apr. 22-June 7 and Oct. 24-Dec. 13.) Spic-'n'-span lodgings beckon from **Hotel Edelweiss,** Rosswiedstr. 9 (tel. 416 10 33; fax 416 11 30), in Davos-Dorf. Head left on Bahnhofstrassedorf, turn right on Mühlestr., turn left on Dorfstr. (which quickly becomes Promenade), walk 10 minutes, then turn right on Bohbahnstr. and left on Rossweidstr. This huge old house pampers skiers and hikers with a big-screen TV, a heart-filled dining room, and pretty, wallpapered bedrooms. (Basic singles 38-57SFr; doubles 80-97SFr (depending on time of year). Breakfast included. Dinner 17SFr. Reception 7am-10pm. AmEx, MC, Visa. Closed mid-Apr. to mid-June.) The **Sportzentrum Davos,** Talstr. 41 (tel. 415 36 36; fax 415 36 37), just opened a large, spotless, locker-roomish dormitory with shocking color schemes (brown, chartreuse, blue, and orange) and airy balconies overlooking the tracks. (Dorms 42SFr; doubles 100SFr. Breakfast included. Guests skate free at the ice rink. Reception 7:30-9:30am, noon-1pm, and 6-7pm. If no one's at the desk, check in at the restaurant downstairs.) **Camping Färich** (tel. 416 10 43) in Davos-Dorf is a four-star facility relatively close to the ski lifts and attractions of the town. Take bus #1 (dir: Pischa): "Stilli." (5-7SFr, children half-price; tents 6SFr. Open May 18-Sept. 29.)

Haven't had your *Rösti* fix for the day yet? Shame on you. Visit **Röstizzeria,** Promenade 128 (tel. 416 33 23), and satisfy your craving for 14.50SFr and up in a dining room decorated with carved wood and Japanese fans. There's also pizza from 11SFr. (Open 6-11pm; AmEx, MC, Visa.) The bright, flowery, locally beloved **Café-Konditorei Weber,** Promenade 148 (tel. 410 11 22), in Davos-Dorf, offers colorful and friendly service to match. Choose from the daily *Menü,* which includes at least one vegetarian dish (14-18SFr), or order à la carte (from 11SFr). (Open daily 6:30am-7pm.) Grab a Bud and a bar stool—American style—at **Café Carlo's,** Promenade 58 (tel. 413 17 22), in Davos-Platz across from the tourist office. The café offers a daily *Menü* (9.50-16.50SFr), salad (6-14SFr), sandwiches (10-14SFr), and pasta (13-18SFr) under the gaze of a 3-D Mona Lisa in the corner. (Open 8am-midnight. AmEx, MC, Visa.) For a local hole in the wall, try **Restaurant Helvetia,** Talstr. 12 (tel. 413 56 44), a 10-minute walk out of the train station and to the right. Adorned with sports memorabilia and oddities (look for the New Hampshire "Davos" vanity plate), the restaurant serves up spaghetti (9.50SFr), *Kalbsbratwurst* with *Rösti* (14SFr), and burgers (7SFr).

Luge Much?

Before the advent of spandex uni-suits and titanium, flying down mountains was a very simple affair. As early as 1883, the natives of Arosa increasingly found their rustic sleds missing and the hills outside the town sprinkled with very bored and very insane recovering English invalids. These dashing chaps officially brought the sport of tobogganing to Switzerland in 1883 when they started the Davos Tobogganing Club and inaugurated the famed Cresta Run. Among the many innovations tested on the Arosa hills were iron runners and the head-first plunge technique. A quote from *The Bystander* in 1905 perhaps summed it up best: "Tobogganing itself is absurd. It glories in being absurd."

(Open M-F 10am-1:30pm and 5pm-midnight, Sa 5pm-midnight.) For hiking snacks, stop by **Migros** on the Promenade in both Davos-Dorf (open M-F 8:30am-12:30pm and 1:30-6:30pm, Sa 8am-4pm) and Davos-Platz (open M-F 8:30am-6:30pm, Sa 8am-4pm). An enormous brand-new **Co-op** is across from the train station. (Open M-F 8am-6:30pm, Sa 8am-5pm; restaurant open M-Sa 8am-8pm, Su 10am-8pm.)

SIGHTS AND ENTERTAINMENT Davos provides direct access to three mountains—the **Parsenn, Schatzalp,** and **Jakobshorn**—and five **skiing areas,** covering every degree of difficulty. *(Jakobshorn ascent 23SFr, descent 23SFr, round-trip 27SFr. Schatzalp 10SFr, 8SFr, 12SFr.)* **Day** passes start at 25SFr for the Schatzalp and go all the way to 49SFr for the Jakobshorn. **Regional ski passes** are available for the Davos-Klosters area, including unlimited travel on most transport facilities. *(2 days 115SFr, 1 week 265SFr.)* Comprehensive information and maps are available at the tourist office. In addition to downhill runs, Davos boasts 75km of **cross-country trails** throughout the valley, including a flood-lit trail at night and a trail on which dogs are allowed. **The Swiss Ski School of Davos,** Promenade 157 (tel. 416 24 54; fax 416 59 51 for information and booking), offers lessons, starting at 30SFr for a half-day downhill lesson and at 55SFr for a half-day snowboard lesson. Europe's largest natural **ice rink** (tel. 415 36 00; 22,000 sq. meters) reserves space for figure skating, ice dancing, hockey, speed skating, and curling. *(5SFr; skate rental at the rink.)*

Davos doesn't wilt when the snow melts. In the summer the town offers indoor/outdoor **swimming pools** with **sauna** and solarium. *(6.50SFr, students 4.50SFr.)* You can swim, fish, sail, and windsurf in and on the **Davosersee**. The police station (tel. 414 33 11) handles **fishing permits.** *(Day 73SFr, week 211SFr, month 447SFr.)* Davos's snowless slopes uncover a web of over 450km of **hiking** trails. The exquisite mountains engulfing the area provide views deep into the Dolomites and all along the valley. One possible day hike begins at the top of Jakobshorn (2590m) and traverses a ridge over Jatzhorn (2682m) to Tällifurgga (2568m). Or meander down the velvety green ski slopes to the village of Sertig Dörfli. The difficult hike from the summit to Sertig Dörfli takes three hours, and the easy walk from there, down the Sertigal valley, to Davos-Platz is another two and a half hours. The last Saturday in July brings the **Swiss Alpine Marathon,** a grueling 72km mountain race.

A hike (or funicular ride) up to the Schatzalp reveals the **Alpine Garden** with 800 different species of plants. *(Open mid-May to Sept. 9am-5pm. 3SFr. Guided tours in German every Monday at 2pm—other languages by arrangement.)* Exercise your eyes at the **Davos Kirchner Museum** (tel. 413 22 02), the frosted glass structure across from the grand Hotel Belvedere on the Promenade, which houses an extensive collection of **Ernst Ludwig Kirchner's** artwork. *(Museum open July 15-Sept. Tu-Su 10am-noon. 7SFr, students 4SFr. Exhibitions open Tu-Su 10am-noon and 2-6pm. 9SFr, 6SFr.)* This avatar of early 20th-century German Expressionism lived in Davos for nearly 20 years before his death, and is buried in the Davos cemetery. Davos's **Heimatmuseum** (tel. 416 17 82), on Museumstr. behind the train station in Davos-Dorf, displays a collection of centuries-old furniture and crafts of the Graubünden region. (Open June to mid-Oct. and Jan. to mid-Apr. W, F, and Su 4-6pm, or by appointment.)

■ Klosters

Across the Gotschna and Parsenn mountains lies Davos's sister ski resort, Klosters. Though a smaller, more subdued town, Klosters doesn't suffer in Davos' shadow. The charming and surprisingly mellow town draws just as many skiers and, as a four-star resort, its share of royals. But while Davos makes an extra effort to be a city, Klosters keeps a low profile—even its upper-crust hotels look like unassuming Swiss chalets. Aromas from five-star restaurants mingle with the sweet smell of hay from barns just down the road. Mercedes roll down the street next to tractors.

Like Davos, Klosters is divided into **Klosters-Platz** and **Klosters-Dorf,** connected by a 20-minute walk, a 5-minute bus ride, or a 3-minute train ride. There are **tourist offices** in both Platz and Dorf, but the **main tourist office** is in Klosters-Platz (tel. 410

20 20; fax 410 20 10; email info@klosters.ch; http://www.klosters.ch). From the train station, walk to the right, make a right at the Co-op, and cross the street to the building with the "i." The friendly staff can help locate lodgings, suggest hikes, and **exchange currency.** They also plan ski packages with the ski school and offer the **Klosters guest card** (also available at hotels), valid for bargain tickets to events and reduced admission to local facilities. (Open May-Nov. M-F 8:30am-noon and 2:30-6pm, Sa 8am-noon and 2:30-5pm; Dec.-April M-F 8am-noon and 2-6pm, Sa 8:30am-noon and 2-6pm, Su 9:30am-noon and 2:30-6:30pm.) **Trains** arrive in Klosters-Platz and Klosters-Dorf, from **Chur** through Landquart (1hr., every hr., 5:21am-9:29pm, 18.20SFr) and **St. Moritz** (2hr., every hr., 5:38am-9:27pm, 32SFr). The local **bus** runs between Dorf and Platz and the major ski lifts (1-6 stops 1SFr, 7-10 2SFr, more than 10 3SFr; free with guest card). **Parking** is free in summer; in winter, get a public parking card (8 days 20SFr, 16 days 40SFr, 1 month 80SFr) from the tourist office or the local **police** (tel. 422 35 33). The Klosters-Platz **train station** provides **currency exchange** (open 6am-8:30pm), **lockers** (2SFr), and **luggage storage** (open 6am-8:30pm; 3SFr) and **rents scooters** (18SFr per day, 12 SFr per half-day). Rent **bikes** at standardized prices at all over town (info tel. 410 20 20), including **Madrissa Sport** (tel. 422 28 65) on Haus Bahnhofpl. (38SFr per day; 130SFr for 6 days). A **pharmacy,** the Helios Apotheke, is across from the main tourist office. (Open M-F 7:45am-noon and 2-6:30pm; Sa 7:45-noon and 2-4pm; call 111 for late-night pharmacy.) The **post office** is right from the station. (Open M-F 7:30am-noon and 1:45-6:15pm; Sa 8:30-11am). The **postal code** is CH-7250. The **telephone code** is 081.

Like everything else in Klosters, the **Jugendherberge Soldanella (HI),** Talstr. 73 (tel. 422 13 16; fax 422 52 09), is quietly elegant, laid back, and unassuming. Head right from the Klosters-Platz train station, bear left at the rotary, turn right on Talstr., and hike 10 min. uphill. Run by a friendly and knowledgeable family, this massive renovated chalet with wood paneling, a comfortable reading room, and a flagstone terrace treats guests to a view of the Madrisa and distant glaciers. (Dorms 25.50SFr hihgseason, 23SFr low-season; doubles 36.50SFr, 34SFr. Family rooms available. Add 1.90SFr tax per day in summer; in winter 2.20SFr. Sheets, shower, and breakfast included. Dinner 11.50SFr. Reception 7-9:30am and 5-10pm. No lockout, no curfew. Quiet time from 10pm. Closed May to mid-June and Nov. to mid-Dec. AmEx, MC, Visa.) **Gasthaus Casanna,** Landstr. 171 (tel. 422 12 29; fax 422 62 78), offers pink-flowered comforters that clash with the brown carpeting and lamps, and a smoky restaurant that serves diverse fondues (20-30SFr). (Singles 45SFr; doubles 60SFr. Winter: 60SFr, 120SFr. Breakfast included.) Better yet, choose from the list of **private rooms** starting at 15SFr (list at the tourist office).

Pretend you aren't a budget backpacker for a few hours at **Chesa Grischuna,** Bahnhofstr. 12 (tel. 422 22 22; fax 422 22 25), to the right of the Klosters-Platz train station. They serve some pricey meat dishes, but if you stick to the cheeses and salads, you can still leave sated and financially solvent: cheese plate 8SFr, salads 9-16SFr, soups and sandwiches 9-12SFr, vegetarian plate 18.50SFr. Make reservations during winter—even the celebrities who come here have to phone in advance. (Open 7am-11pm, or until the last person leaves; hot meals served 11:30am-9:30pm. Closed June to mid-July and mid-Oct. to mid-Dec. AmEx, MC, Visa.) **À Porta,** Bahnhofstr. 22 (tel. 422 14 96), at Landstr., is a 70-year-old, family-run restaurant and bakery closed for renovation but promising to reopen in 1999 that serves fresh pizzas (from 12SFr) and *Rösti* with ham and onions (14.50SFr). **Tasty bakery** serves sugary treats and fresh bread. (Open 7:30am-10:30pm; Nov. and May-June closed M-Tu Bakery open 10:30am-6:30pm.) If all this non-budget food will require several nights on lovely park-bench accommodations, visit the **Co-op,** halfway to the train station, for sustenance. Get cheap groceries, or chow down at the restaurant upstairs on *spaghetti Napoli* for 8SFr. (Open M-F 8am-12:30pm and 2-6:30pm, Sa 8am-4pm. Retaurant open M-Sa 9am-8pm, Su 10am-8pm.)

One words sums up entertainment in Klosters: plastics. Er… **skiing.** Klosters has some of the best skiing in Switzerland, with 315km of trails stretching from the city into the neighboring Davos mountains. **Ski passes** for the Klosters-Davos region run

113SFr for two days and 288SFr for one week (includes public transportation). For the Klosters area, a Grotschna-Parsenn-Strela/Schatzalp-Madrisa one-day ticket goes for 52SFr, one week 246SFr. The **ski school** in Klosters, conveniently located in the tourist office, offers ski and snowboard lessons for children and adults. (Class instruction from 50-60SFr per day; call 410 20 28 the day before to book private lessons.) All this skiing combines with 40km of **cross-country trails, an ice rink,** and **sled runs** to make Klosters a winter *Wunderland.* From early July to early October, the **mountain cable car** to the **Madrisa** provides a means to explore the peaks all the way into Austria. (Ascent 15SFr, descent 10SFr, round-trip 18SFr.)

Klosters offers plenty of bang for your shoe leather, even for the less ambitious. In the summer, the tourist office has an extensive list of **hiking** suggestions, with exact directions, elevation levels, anticipated times, and a trail map. To start, the **Gotschna-bahn** cable car whisks you up to Gotschnagrat (2285m) for incredible views of the Silvrettagletscher, Klosters, and the quintessentially Swiss valley embracing the village. Take a leisurely three-hour walk down to Klosters, crossing the ski runs just below the striking, jagged peak (Casanna Alp). Drop below treeline and follow the signs to Serneuser Schwendi and Klosters. Got vertigo? Stay closer to the luscious green valley floor and make a large loop, going from the Klosters Protestant church up-valley on Monbielstr. to Monbiel. Loop again around toward the left and follow the signs to Pt. 487 and Monbieler Wald. The trail ends at the Alpenrösli restaurant, from where you can grab Talstr. back to the hostel. The **Klosters Adventure Program** offers guided hikes and mountain tours, canyonning, horseback riding, river rafting, glacier walks, canoeing, mountain-bike tours, paragliding, and more every weekday mid-June to mid-October. Most events are free or discounted for Adventure hotel guests; the Adventure hotels include Jugendherberge Soldanella (see below). (Guided hikes 15SFr with guest card, free for Adventure hotel guests. River rafting 100SFr, 80SFr. Horse-drawn sled rental 40-100SFr. Mountain bike tours 15SFr, free.)

ENGADIN VALLEY

Swiss downhill-skiing connoisseurs often rate the Engadin Valley behind the Jungfrau and Matterhorn regions—still a glowing compliment, since Switzerland's skiing outranks almost everything anywhere else. But not so fast—hiking here rocks, too. The trails lead you away from the valley's resort facade and into the Swiss wilderness. Whether you're out for a stream-side stroll or scaling ancient glaciers, the Engadin delivers beauty and adventure. Most local tourist offices provide excellent hiking tips and maps. Sitting proudly at the center of Upper Engadin, glam St. Moritz is the hub of the Valley. Either St. Moritz, Pontresina, or Maloja, the only three villages with youth hostels, make good bases for daytripping to the other villages in the valley.

The regional culinary specialties please many a visiting tummy. *Capuns,* ham and potato wrapped in leaves run from 9 to 18SFr. Famous throughout Switzerland (and deservedly so) is the **Engadin torte,** a variation on the simple nutcake found only in a lone Pontresina bakery (see p. 427). Candied almonds and raisins top multiple layers of cream and nut puree. Yum.

Three hundred and fifty kilometers of **ski trails** and 60 **ski lifts** lace the lower Graubünden, and thousands of ski bunnies gather here each year. Unlike Zermatt and the Jungfrau regions, where Japanese and American tourists abound, the Engadin valley attracts mostly German and Swiss visitors to its trails, making it not as kitschy but also not as convenient, since English info is often difficult to get in smaller towns. Ski rental is standard throughout the region (downhill 35-45SFr per day, cross-country 25SFr). Novices should head for **Zuoz** or **Corviglia,** experts for **Diavolezza, Corvatsch, Piz Nair,** or **Piz Lagalb** (for more information, call (081) 833 88 88 or fax 833 76 68). Anyone hoping to catch a glimpse of Hollywood should head for **St. Moritz.** Passes covering transport and T-bars for the entire area run 48SFr per day (available in St. Moritz only), 286SFr per week, 442SFr for two weeks, and 900SFr for the season (all lifts and access to indoor swimming pools). Cross-country fanatics should glide to

Pontresina, where hundreds train for the cruel and unusual **Engadin Ski Marathon,** stretching from Maloja to Zuoz. The race takes place every year on the second Sunday in March (call (081) 842 65 73 or fax 842 65 25 for application/registration; entry fee 70SFr). **Ski schools** in just about every village offer private lessons.

■ Maloja

Maloja is the St. Moritz that couldn't. In 1880 Belgium's Count Camille de Renesse decided to turn this tiny village at the source of the Inn and Rhine rivers into a health resort that would rival the nearby resort superstar. He purchased nearly the entire village and sank his family's fortune into building a palatial casino, luxury hotel, and a medieval-style stone castle for his private residence. Alas, the rich and famous did not share his vision and remained in St. Moritz, and the bankrupt count left Maloja in 1896, never to return. He died in Nice in 1904. The unfortunate count's loss is the contemporary backpacker's gain. Maloja rests atop a gorgeous precipice separating the Engadia and Bregaglia Valley, centerpiece of a splendid outdoors paradise unspoiled by St. Moritz-style yuppification.

Postal buses run between Maloja and **St. Moritz** (40min., every 30min. 7am-7pm, 9SFr), leaving the **post office** (open M-F 8am-noon and 2-6pm, Sa 8-11am). The **tourist office** (tel. 824 31 38; fax 824 36 37; email maloja@bluewih.chi; http://www.maloja.ch) sits just beyond the youth hostel 300m to the right of the bus station. The English-speaking staff provides info about hikes and local lore (open M-F 8:30am-noon and 2-6pm). The **postal code** is CH-7516 and the **telephone code** is 081.

Maloja's Jugendherberge (HI) (tel. 824 32 58; fax 824 35 71) offers some of the cheapest dorm beds in Switzerland, though accommodations are a little cut rate (mattresses lined up side by side in loft spaces instead of individual bunks). Walk 200m to the right from the post office to reach twin darkwood former farmhouses, now converted into somewhat chilly lodges. (Dorms 15SFr. Non-members add 5SFr. City tax 1.85SFr. Breakfast (for groups only) 7SFr. Sheets and showers included. **Kitchen** facilities 2.50SFr. **Laundry** 10SFr. Reception 8-9am and 5-7pm. No lockout. No curfew. Quiet time 10pm. Open year-round but call ahead during the low season. Note: prices are due to be revised in Dec. 1998.) **Camping TCS** (tel. 824 31 81) offers a lovely lakeside site with a swimming beach and windsurfing 20 minutes from the town center. Walk right from the bus stop, turn left on the small street after Hotel Schweizenhaus, and take the right fork after the candy-cane church. The camp also **rents mountain bikes** (35SFr per day) and has a cheap restaurant selling *bursas* (5.85SFr) and lasagna (8SFr) while reception is open. (4.40-5.20SFr, children half-price; tents 4.20-5.30SFr. Guest tax 2SFr. Free showers. Reception 8am-10pm. Open June-Sept.)

The **Alimentari** across from the post office peddles groceries (open M-F 8am-noon and 2-6pm, Sa 8am-noon and 2-5pm). The restaurant at the **Schweizhaus** (tel. 824 34 55), the luxury hotel built by Count de Renesse, serves yummy *cupons* (17.50SFr) and grills up tasty *Zigeunerspiess* (beef, bacon, sausage kebabs; 16.50SFr), but may deliver slothful service to those who don't order a 50SFr bottle of wine with their meal. (Open 8am-9pm. MC.)

On most mornings and late afternoons, the **Malojaschlange** (literally "Maloja snake"), a stream of confused clouds, creeps over the pass and, unable to adjust to the altitude change, takes the form of an enormous twisted tube falling toward St. Moritz. During most of the day, though, artist Giovanni Giacometti found he could not remember "a sun so bright and clear as shines upon the plateau of Maloja." This brightness ensnared Italian Expressionist painter Giovanni Segantini, who spent the last 15 years of his life in Maloja and was buried in the village's idyllic mountain cemetery in 1899. Private pictures, sketches, documents, and personal memorabilia are on display in the artist's refurbished studio, **Atelier Segantini** (open July 5-Oct. 10, Tu-Su 3-5pm, 2SFr). The **Belvedere Tower,** a 15-minute walk from the post office, was the only part of Count de Renesse's dream castle to be constructed. (Open 8am-5pm. Free.) Abandoned with the rest of the castle's foundation walls when the count left, it now houses various exhibits on the Engadia and Bregadia Valleys. The observation tower provides a phenomenal panoramic view extending across the border into Italy. Here the *Malojaschlange* ruffles your hair as it blows over the valley floor. Fauna, flora, and *Gletschermühlen* (massive glaciated potholes, some 4.6m wide and 5.5m deep) in the protected nature reserve surround the tower. The tiny reflective pools at the bottom of the *Gletschermühlen* resemble enchanted wishing wells.

Hiking in this region is glorious. A challenging guided walk (in German) of the **Septimer Pass** to **Juf,** the highest village in Europe that is inhabited year-round, takes place every other Tuesday at 6:45am (rise and shine!), starting from the PTT station (June 25-Sept.; 50SFr). A guided **historical tour** leaves the Maloja tourist office for the heart of the **Bregaglia Valley** (June 20-Oct. 3 Th 8am; 12SFr). In the opposite direction, a seven-hour trek over the hills to the northeast will take you through **Grevasalvas,** the village where *Heidi* was filmed, all the way to **Signal,** where you will find Heidi's hut. From there, a cable car departs for **St. Moritz.** The hike to Grevasalvas begins to the left of Aparthotel Interhomeutoring; follow the signs to Signal Cable Car. To cut this journey down to Heidi size, you can take the postal bus from Maloja (dir: St. Moritz): "Plaun da Lej" and begin there.

One final, lovely hike is a bit more complicated and requires a map from the tourist office. On the Italian frontier, 22km down the valley from Maloja, lies **Soglio,** a matchbox Swiss-Italian village with narrow, crooked streets. Soglio lies on the legendary **Panorama Highway,** a footpath that begins at **Casaccia,** just south of Maloja. The natives call the trail "the beauty of the Graubünden" with good reason. The gorgeous route follows the Bregaglia valley downstream, meandering past waterfalls, bright Alpine blossoms, and deserted Roman ruins. Views of the needlepoint peaks towering overhead alternate with tree-covered patches on the trail. You can reach Casaccia by foot (the path starts 200m to the right of the post office, across from the youth hostel) or catch the **postal bus** (every 30min., 3.60SFr). The bus goes on to Soglio (1hr., 11.40SFr; change in Promontogno). If you decide to sojourn in Soglio, the **Mürias Hotel** (tel. 822 15 00), run by the Cadisch family, offers bed, shower, and breakfast for 55-60SFr but only has 10 beds. Another option is the **Stüa Granda** (tel./fax 822 19 88), which offers 20 beds with breakfast for 60-78SFr.

■ St. Moritz

In St. Moritz are the hangers-on of the rich... the jewel thieves, the professional backgammon players and general layabouts, as well as the high-class ladies of doubtful virtue (if such a thing still exists)...
—Peter Viertel

St. Moritz (1856m) is one of the most famous ski resorts in the world. Chic, elegant, and exclusive, it caters to the filthy rich whom Robin Leach used to crow about. This "Resort at the Top of the World" will convert almost anyone into a window-shopper, tamed by the likes of Armani, Calvin Klein, and Prada. St. Moritz hosted the Olympic Games in 1928 and again in 1948, and nowadays the town offers every winter sport imaginable from world-class skiing and bobsledding to golf, polo, greyhound racing, cricket on the frozen lake, and *Skikjöring*—a sport similar to water skiing in which the water is replaced by snow and the motorboat is replaced by a galloping horse.

ORIENTATION AND PRACTICAL INFORMATION Trains run every hour to **Chur** (2hr., 39SFr), **Celerina** (5min., 2.40SFr), **Pontresina** (15min., 4.20SFr), and **Zuoz** (30min., 8.40SFr). Yellow **postal buses** (*not* the local blue buses) cover almost all the same routes as the trains. They're also your only access from the southwest tip of the Upper Engadin Valley, since St. Moritz is the railway terminus. Buses run twice every hour to **Silvaplana** (15min., 3.60SFr), **Sils** (20min., 6SFr), and **Maloja** (40min., 9SFr), departing from the left of the train station. The resort's huge **tourist office** (*Kurverein*), Via Maistra 12 (tel. 837 33 33; fax 837 33 77; email kvv@stmoritz.ch; http://

www.stmoritz.ch), beats in the heart of town. From the train station, cross the street, climb Truoch Serlas, and take Via Serlas to the left past the post office. As you pass the Badrutt's Palace Hotel on your left, make a right up the Réduit Passage. Emerge from the shopping arcade onto Via Maistra; the tourist office is on the right. The office provides free hotel reservations (tel. 837 33 99; fax 837 33 66), skiing info, and advice on hiking in the smaller towns of the Engadin Valley. (Open July to mid-Sept. and mid-Dec. to mid-Apr. M-Sa 9am-6pm; May-June and Nov. M-F 8am-noon and 2-6pm.) From the Matterhorn to the Engadin Valley, the legendary **Glacier Express** covers the 270km to **Zermatt** in a leisurely eight-hour chug (9, 9:30, and 10am, 142SFr, Swisspass valid), affording ample time to take in the magnificent Alpine landscapes while crossing 291 bridges and going through 91 tunnels. If you can't sit still for that long, the **Bernina Express** makes the excursion to **Tirano, Italy** (2½hr., every hr., 27SFr, Swisspass valid). It's the only Swiss train that crosses the Alps without entering a single tunnel. The **train station** provides **currency exchange** and Western Union services (open daily 7am-9:10pm), **luggage storage** (5SFr; open daily 7:50am-6:40pm), **bike rental** (22SFr per day; open daily 8am-6:30pm), and **lockers** (2SFr). Bikes can also be rented at the youth hostel for 12SFr per day. In an **emergency,** call 111. The **post office** (open M-F 7:45am-noon and 1:45-6:15pm, Sa 8-11am) is located on Via Serlas and has a 24-hour **ATM.** There is **internet access** at Bobby's Pub, Via del Bagn 52 (tel. 834 42 83 or 833 47 67; email info@bobbys-pub.ch; http://www.bobbys-pub.ch), for 12SFr per hour. (Open M-Sa 7:30am-1:30am, Su 2pm-1:30am.) One of many **pharmacies** is Galerie Apotheke, next to the Giardino Cafe and Bobby's Pub on Via del Bagn. (Open M-F 8am-noon and 2-6:30pm, Sa 8am-noon.) The **postal code** is CH-7500. The **telephone code** is 081.

ACCOMMODATIONS AND FOOD You can rest your ski-weary bones at **Jugendherberge Stille (HI),** Via Surpunt 60 (tel. 833 39 69; fax 833 80 46). Follow the signs around the lake to the left of the station (30min.), or take the postal bus (dir: Maloja): "Hotel Sonne" (2.40SFr) and then go left on Via Surpunt for 10 minutes. Bigger and better than your average hostel with wall-to-wall carpeting, small dorms (max. 4 per room), strong hot private showers, a new pool table (2SFr), cheap **mountain bike rental** (12SFr), and a tasty budget-saving **dinner** built into the package. (Dorms 41.50SFr 1st night, then 39SFr; doubles 108SFr, 103SFr, with shower 130SFr, 125SFr. Non-members add 5SFr. Sheets, showers, lockers, breakfast, and dinner included—show up before 7:15pm for dinner. **Laundry** 4SFr. Reception 7-10am and 4-10pm. No lockout. Curfew midnight; keys available. Quiet hours start at 10pm. AmEx, MC, Visa.) You might opt instead to take the "See" exit at the train station and drop all your belongings at **Hotel Bellaval,** Via Grevas 55 (tel. 833 32 45; fax 833 04 06). This two-star hotel has 43 relatively inexpensive beds, a lakeside garden, and a restaurant that serves omelettes (11-12SFr), pasta (12-14SFr), and daily *Menüs* starting at 12SFr. (Singles 60-78SFr; doubles 116-148Fr. Restaurant open 11:30am-2pm and 6-9:30pm. Huge, delicious breakfast included. Reception 7:30am-10pm. Closed Oct.-Dec. and Easter-May. AmEx, MC, Visa.) For camping, catch the postal bus to **St. Moritz-Bad Signal** (tel. 833 40 90). From the stop, walk along the foot path across the street to the right (away from the lake) for 10 minutes. (4.20-6SFr, children half-price; tent 5-6SFr. Open May 19-Sept. 27.) It's near the Olympic ski jump and has showers.

Living the four-star lifestyle of St. Moritz is expensive. Unfortunately, *looking* as though you're living it is almost as pricey. An outdoor lunch at the **Giardino Café,** Via dal Bagn 54 (tel. 837 07 07), on the flower- and gnome-ridden terrace of the Hotel Schweizerhof, is a prime spot for glitterati-gazing. Try the salad buffet (7-9SFr), daily special (16-18.50SFr), or something grilled (12-21SFr; open 10am-6pm if it's not raining). The red-checked **Restaurant Engadinia,** P. da Scoula (tel. 833 32 65), serves up classic Swiss favorites including bratwurst with fries (16SFr), fondue for two (25SFr per person), or the more Italian spaghetti *bolognese* (16.50SFr; open M-Sa 8:30am-11pm). It never hurts to forage for groceries at the **Co-op Center,** one square up from the tourist office or at Via dal Bagn 20, en route to the youth hostel. (Open M-F 8am-12:15pm and 2-6:30pm, Sa 8am-12:15pm and 2-5pm.) If you're here in late January, try the culinary delights of the annual week-long **St. Moritz Gourmet Festival.**

SIGHTS AND ENTERTAINMENT The **Engadiner Museum,** Via dal Bagn 39 (tel. 833 43 33; fax 833 50 07), down from the tourist office, gives tourists a sneak-peek at the unbelievably intricate carved wood interior of those unassuming white houses. *(Open June-Oct. M-F 9:30am-noon and 2-5pm, Su 10am-noon; Dec.-Apr. M-F 10am-noon and 2-5pm, Su 10am-noon. 5SFr, students 4SFr, children 2.50SFr.)* The house, built in 1905 by an obsessed collector, features tiny gnomish doorways, beautiful and unpronounceable *Chuchichästli*s (cupboards), and a 17th-century four-poster sick-bed displaying the macabre culture of death during the Plague Era: the dying occupant stared all day at a skeleton on the ceiling along with an inscription translating to "As you are, I would like to be" (i.e., still alive). Supposedly the original owner's friend, who preceded him into Plague death, gave him the bed with inscription. One street up from the Engadiner Museum sits the domed tower of the **Segantini Museum,** Via Somplaz 30 (tel. 833 44 54), dedicated to the Italian Expressionist painter. *(Open June-Oct. Tu-Sa 9am-12:30pm and 2:30-5pm, Su 10:30am-12:30pm and 2:30-4:30pm; Dec.-Apr. Tu-Sa 10am-12:30pm and 3-5pm, Su 3-5pm. 7SFr, students 5SFr, children 2SFr. Joint pass for Engadiner and Segantini museums 10SFr, students 8SFr. Museum is under renovation, but scheduled to reopen June 12, 1999.)* Housed in a stone basilica, the museum features some of Segantini's well-known wall-sized, speckly Alpine landscapes with floating wood nymphs. The **Mili Weber House,** Via Dim Lej 35 (tel. 833 33 09, 833 31 86, or 833 53 55), features a huge collection of Alpine paintings by Mili, a tiny red-headed legend in St. Moritz. *(Call for an appointment.)* The leaning tower at the top of the village is all that is left of the 13th-century **St. Mauritius Church,** pulled down in 1890.

A roundabout **day hike** from St. Moritz to Pontresina takes you past the rail station and towering glaciers, and through narrow Alpine valleys. From St. Moritz-Bad, at the junction of Via Mezdi and Via Tegiatscha, walk to the **Hahnensee,** an Alpine lake. From there, follow the signs to Fuorcla-Surlej. The trail then snakes along to the Ova da Roseg and the Roseg valley downstream to **Pontresina** (6hr. total). To scout out the slopes on foot before the ski season begins, ride from St. Moritz up to **Corviglia** (14SFr, round-trip 21SFr; under 17 7SFr, 10.50SFr) and pick your line down (about 2hr.). From the top of Corviglia another lift glides up to **Piz Nair** (3075m). *(14SFr, round-trip 21SFr; under 17 7SFr, 10.50SFr.)* After admiring the rooftop view of the Engadin, you can hike down to Survetta Lake (2580m). Picnics at **Suvretta Lake,** underneath the majestic **Piz Julier** (3380m), are a must. Follow the Ova da Suvretta back down to the Signalbahn or St. Moritz. *(3hr.)*

You've probably heard about St. Moritz's **skiing.** *(Call 837 33 99 for ski packages; week packages start at 550SFr.)* Surprisingly, a larger number of guests travel to St. Moritz in the summer than in the winter. **Windsurfing** is one draw (tel. 833 44 49). *(2hr. rental 30-40SFr, private lessons 50SFr per hr. 10 lessons 240SFr.)* **River rafting** is certainly another (with Eurotrek (tel. (01) 462 02 03), half-day 80SFr, day 140SFr; with Swissraft (tel. (081) 911 52 50), half-day 60SFr, day 143SFr). **Horseback riding** (tel. 833 57 33; 45SFr per hr., 80SFr for 2hr.), **llama trekking** (tel. (079) 411 26 44; 4hr., 70SFr, children 55SFr), and **skeet shooting** (tel. 833 54 88; 15SFr) also bring people.

■ Silvaplana

At the foot of the Julier mountain pass, Silvaplana (1815m) is situated amid the magnificent Upper Engadin lake country, and (surprise) the town's main attraction is its **See** (lake). Silvaplana's beaches beckon sun-worshipers, campers, sailors, and hikers eager to soak their aching feet. The "Gorge" of Switzerland, the See hosts a bevy of wet-suited windsurfers, and from afar the lake appears to be populated by gargantuan freshwater sharks with neon fins. Silvaplana's hyperactive winds also frolic with kites, the fancy loop-de-looping variety, christened at the town's annual **kite festival** in September. Rent **sailboards** (tel. 828 92 29) next to the campground. (1hr. 20-25SFr, with wet-suit 25-30SFr; 2hr. 30-40SFr, 40-50SFr; 1 day 50-60SFr, 70-80SFr. Group lessons start at 50SFr per hr. Longer lessons advised for novices: 9hr. 240SFr, 18hr. 380SFr. Open June 15-Sept. 15 daily 9am-7pm.) While the lake is free for all to enjoy, windsurfing, sailing, and fishing fees reflect the lake's prime location and southern

GRAUBÜNDEN

winds. Go **fish** after buying a day ticket (28SFr), weekend ticket (66SFr), or monthly permit (132SFr) at the tourist office. In August, Silvaplana hosts the **Nitro-Cup** (International Slalom Windsurfing Competition), and in July the **Swiss National Sailing and Windsurfing Championships** come to town.

Unfortunately, due to rising temperatures, the Corvatsch glacier is no longer large enough for summer skiing. Not to worry; snow is guaranteed in the winter. A **cable car** (tel. 838 73 73; fax 838 73 10) ascends from **Surlej** (on the other side of the lake) high up into the **Piz Corvatsch** peak region (up 23SFr, down 16SFr, 32SFr round-trip; children under 17 up 12SFr, down 8SFr, round-trip 16SFr). The intermediate station of **Murtèl** (up 18SFr, down 13SFr, round-trip 25SFr; children under 17 up 9SFr, down 7SFr, round-trip 13SFr) is the center of an extended and varied ski region with links to Sils' Furtschellas runs and the downhill run past the Hahnensee Lake to St. Moritz (day pass 54SFr, children 42SFr; half-day 45SFr, 34SFr; with Graubünden pass and Swiss Card 50% off, with Swisspass 25%). From the Corvatsch cable car station, yodel your way up the rest of the glacier to **Piz Corvatsch** (3451m) and you'll see the entire glacier and the striking surrounding peaks. Resist the urge to jump into what appears to be a large bowl of Ben and Jerry's glacial vanilla. The trip up takes one to one-and-a-half hours; the trip down is approximately 20 minutes of hiking and 10 minutes of world-class glissading. The **Wanderbillet** takes you from Surlej up to Corvatsch and then halfway down to Murtèl (27SFr, children 16 and under 14SFr). For a hike below the glaciers, walk from the mid-station to Fuorcla Surlej (2755m) and down to Pontresina, crossing the mountain range along the Roseg valley (about 4hr.). For flatlandlubbers, Silvaplana's **Sportszentrum Mulets** (tel. 828 93 62) offers tennis (18SFr per hr.), volleyball (2hr. 20SFr), and soccer (2hr. 60SFr). In winter, soccer gives way to ice-skating, hockey, and that esoteric and bizarre European pasttime, curling.

Silvaplana is a mere one-hour hike or 10-minute bus ride from **St. Moritz** (every 30min. 7am-8pm, 3.60SFr). The **tourist office** (tel. 838 60 00; fax 838 60 90; email silvaplana@bluewin.ch; http://www.silvaplana.ch) at the corner of Via Maistra and Via dal Farrer can help plan hikes, arrange wind-surfing lessons, or reserve a room. Walk two blocks left from the **post office.** (Open M-F 8:30am-6pm, Sa 9am-noon and 4-6pm, Su (winter only) 4-6pm.) The **postal code** is CH-7513. The **phone code** is 081.

This village of 870 residents offers several very expensive hotels. Stay instead at the youth hostel in **St. Moritz** (see p. 422) or **Maloja** (see p. 420) or sleep on the beach at **Camping Silvaplana** (tel. 828 84 92). (7.60SFr; tent 5-7SFr; open mid-May to mid-Oct.) Grab food at the **Volg supermarket,** to the left of the tourist office. (Open M-F 8am-noon and 2-6:30pm, Sa 8am-noon and 2-4pm.) **Chesa Corvatsch Mexican Bar-Restaurant** (tel. 828 83 85), one block past the tourist office from the post office, offers a much-needed break from pizza and fondue in the form of tacos, burritos, and tostadas (19.50-32SFr for full entrees, knocked down to 11.50-13.50SFr during the high-season "tortilla festival," margarita's for 12-14SFr; open 4:30pm-midnight).

■ Sils (Segl)

More than a century ago, **Friedrich Nietzsche** praised Sils as "the loveliest corner of the Earth," adding, "It is good to live here, in this bracing cold air, where in a wonderful way nature is simultaneously both wildly 'festive' and mysterious—in fact, I like Sils-Maria more than any other place." Fortunately, the village praised by Nietzsche (as well as Adorno, Thomas Mann, Boris Pastoraki, and Marcel Proust, to name a few) has largely escaped the ravages of subsequent ski and tourist industry colonization, in part thanks to a traffic ban (a parking garage waits at the edge of town). The town is divided into two areas: **Sils Baselgia,** a small cluster of homes near the **Silsersee,** and **Sils Maria,** the town center. After a morning hike, stop by the **Nietzsche House** (half-way between the post office and the tourist office along Sils' main road), where the philosopher spent his summers in 1881 and from 1883-1888 before his final mental breakdown. Exhibitions include his workroom, preserved in its original Spartan decor, photographs, letters, notebooks, and two death masks: the genuine one and another his sister Elisabeth Foerster-Nietzsche had sculpted because she thought the real one was not "impressive" enough. There is also, incongruously, a small exhibit on Anne Frank—perhaps a subtle refutation of the Third Reich's later use and abuse of Nietzsche's writings? (Open Tu-Su 3-6pm. 4SFr, students 2SFr.)

Sils' side valleys, untamed and teeming with flora and fauna, are accessible only by foot and horse. The path of choice through **Val Fex** to **Curtins** begins just in front of the tourist office and winds its way beneath glaciers and 3000m peaks. If the hiker in you is dormant, **horse-driven omnibuses** make the round trip in 2 hours (19SFr). Grab your team in front of Hotel Maria, just to the right of the post office. Those who wish to commune with nature on a higher level may ascend the **Furtschellas cable car** (tel. 826 54 46) for a fascinating view of the entire Upper Engadin Valley (ascent 12SFr, descent 10SFr, round-trip 18SFr). The Furtschellas cable car is a 10-minute walk to the right of the post office (the opposite direction from the tourist office). From the summit, hike north over rocky hills and through green fields to **Murtèl,** where you can catch the cable car back to **Surlej** (12SFr). For a mellow afternoon beneath snowy peaks and along breezy shores, walk along the Silsersee to **Maloja** (2hr.) and return by boat (4 per day, 11:30am-5:50pm, 12SFr, round-trip 18SFr). From December to April, Furtschellas and its 14 downhill runs offer **skiing** the way it's meant to be—without waiting (day pass 47SFr, children 34SFr; half-day 39SFr, 29SFr). For private or group skiing lessons, contact the tourist office.

It is a short **bus** ride from **St. Moritz** (a **postal bus** leaves every 30min. 7am-8:30pm; 6SFr). The **tourist office** (tel. 838 50 50; fax 838 50 59; email sils@compunet.ch), down the street to the left from the post office, provides maps for hiking and skiing and can call hotels for vacancies. (Open M-F 8:30am-noon and 2-6pm, Sa 9am-noon and 4-6pm; Apr.-June and Oct.-Dec. closed Sa.) The Sils Maria **post office** stands just at the "Sils/Segl Maria" bus stop (open M-F 8am-noon and 2-6pm, Sa 8-11am). The **postal code** is CH-7514, and the **telephone code** is 081.

The town's studied tranquility doesn't come cheaply. Sils' housing choices are limited, with few hotels in the budget range. **Pension Schulze** (tel. 826 52 13), up the street behind the tourist office, houses you in large rooms with jungle wallpaper, 70s decor, and delicious scents wafting in from the downstairs bakery/café. (Singles 60SFr, with shower 70SFr; doubles 120SFr, 140SFr. Breakfast included. Reception 7:30am-noon and 2-6:30pm.) The bakery specializes in huge chocolate **marzipan balls** (3.50SFr), supposedly akin to the legendary larch-needle-wrapped food that little friendly goblins floated to Sils during a bad flood and famine. Eat the fairy-tale delights and survive happily ever after. To carbo-load for hikes, dash to **Volg,** just left of the post office. (Open M-F 8am-noon and 2-6:30pm, Sa 8am-noon and 2-4pm.)

▨ Celerina

Celerina possesses all the merits of the more famous Engadin towns—skiing, hiking, biking, and fonduing—yet resides just outside the resort veneer created by the likes of St. Moritz, attracting a more laid-back and down-to-earth crowd. The proudest moments in Celerina's history came when St. Moritz hosted the Winter Olympics in 1928 and 1948. Visitors can see the remains of the games in the **Bob-run** and **Cresta-run,** both of which came to a dramatic, revelry-filled finish in Celerina. Each run is re-built every year around the end of November by 14 specialized laborers from the village of **Naturns, Italy.** They use 5000 cubic meters of snow and 4000 liters of water to make a mush that's like cement. The exclusive band of crazed thrill seekers, better known as the **St. Moritz Tobogganing Club** (tel. 833 46 09; fax 833 46 10), presides over the runs and offers non-members a chance to ride on most mornings for a stiff fee. (210SFr for one run, one photo, one drink, and one certificate.) The **Cresta Run** (tel. 833 31 17) is a modified, head-first toboggan ride down the icy course (first 5 rides with lessons 450SFr, subsequent rides 44SFr). For the more moderate (or budget-conscious) sledder, Celerina now offers a family-friendly track on Muottas Muragl descending from 2400m to 1745m (sled rental 12SFr; daily cable car card 36SFr, under 16 28SFr). Besides these runs, Celerina offers…well…hmmm…hiking and skiing away from the large crowds. The **Celerina gondola** and **Marguns chairlift** bring you to the midst of 80km of hiking trails in the summer. (Celerina-Marguns 17SFr; round-trip 26SFr; Marguns-Corviglia 8SFr, 12SFr.) In winter, it's all snow, baby (tel. 833 80 15; daily ticket 50SFr, half-day 42SFr, children 35SFr). A moderate hike from Marguns (the top of the Gondola), the Chna Saluvan sits just below the mighty peak of the same name. Traverse the valley, head down to Alp Clavadatsch, and back to Celerina—the hike will take you from the rocky Alpine ski area down through the green, open fields rising above Celerina (total time 4hr.). Easy day hikes can be found in the well-marked trails of the **Staz forest** below town. Cross the bridge past the church below town to find the trailheads (pick up a free map at the tourist office).

The closest town north of **St. Moritz**, Celerina is easily accessible **by foot** (45min.), **train** (2.40SFr), or **postal bus** (2.80SFr). For additional suggestions, contact the friendly **tourist office** (tel. 830 00 11; fax 830 00 19) in the middle of town. From the Cresta Run train station, turn right; from the bus stop, turn left. The staff is a solid resource for hiking and skiing info, but hotel bookings are not their forte. (Open M-F 8:30am-noon and 2-6pm, Sa 10am-noon and 4-6pm.) Unfortunately, super-cheap housing has been run out of town by valley competition. The brand-new **Inn Lodge** (tel. 834 47 95; fax 834 47 96) imitates a youth hostel with bright dorm rooms of four to eight red bunks, blue carpet, and yellow lockers, but hasn't quite got the hostel price scheme down (beds 35-38SFr; sheets and shower included; breakfast 6SFr; dinner 14SFr). From the tourist office, walk two minutes down the road to St. Moritz; the Inn is on your right. The friendly family at the **Hotel Garni Trais Fluors** (tel. 833 88 85; fax 832 10 01) can put you up in spacious, clean, 300-year-old rooms with old-fashioned floral wallpaper and wood cabinets. The place feels like home but smells much better—sweets and breads abound in the in-house bakery. (Singles 48-63SFr; doubles 92-116SFr, with shower 110-154SFr. Breakfast included. Closed May and Nov.)

Across from the tourist office is a **Volg** supermarket. (Open M-F 8am-noon and 2-6:30pm, Sa 8am-noon and 2-4pm.) If Volg isn't going to cut it, head for the elegant pueblo-style interior of **Restaurant La Cuort** (tel. 837 01 01), in Hotel Chesa Rosatsch and right on the river. Eat under the restaurant's huge skylight or outside by the river. (Salad buffet 7.70SFr, lasagna 13.50SFr, *Capuns* 18SFr. Open noon-10pm.) The **Church of San Gian** proudly stands on a knoll just outside of town. (Open M 2-4pm, W 4-5:30pm, F 10:30am-noon; free guided tour W 4-4:40pm.) In the center of the valley, the crumbling spire and ancient graveyard add a sense of history to the modern ski lifts and hotels. From anywhere in town, follow the yellow church signs to the Church of San Gian, 10 minutes from the town center. Occupying its own tiny tree-filled knoll, the church hides beautiful ancient frescoes from the 1320s beneath its crumbling spire. The **postal code** is CH-7505. The **telephone code** is 081.

■ Pontresina

Pontresina lies in one of the highest wind-sheltered valleys of the Upper Engadin, along a mountainside terrace facing southwest. Surrounded by candy-bright Alpine meadows and fragrant woods, the town is a popular starting and stopping point for outdoorsy people. Rather than the credit cards and love-you-dahlings of St. Moritz, ice axes and crampons abound. This rugged *Burg* is internationally acclaimed thanks to the skiers' paradise of **Diavolezza,** the only glacier in the Engadin Valley that still offers summer skiing on its eternal snow. (All the other glaciers have melted due to rising temperatures and are no longer large enough for summer skiing.)

ORIENTATION AND PRACTICAL INFORMATION **Postal buses** connect Pontresina to the villages of the Upper Engadin Valley all the way to **Maloja**. Trains run to Pontresina from **St. Moritz** (10min., every 30min., 4.20SFr) and **Chur** through **Samedan** (2hr., every hr., 39SFr). Pontresina's **tourist office** (tel. 838 83 00; fax 838 83 10; email pontresina@compunet.ch; http://www.pontresina.com), in the center of town, plans free excursions (see below), gives hiking advice, and finds hotel vacancies. From the train station, head right and follow Via de la Stazium to its end. (Open mid-Apr. to mid-Oct. M-F 8:30am-noon and 2-6pm, Sa 8:30am-noon and 3-6pm, Su 4-6pm; mid-Oct. to mid-Dec. and mid-Apr. to mid-June M-F 8:30am-noon and 2-6pm, Sa 8:30am-noon; late Dec. to mid-Apr. M-F 8:30am-noon and 4-6pm.) The train station provides **currency exchange** (daily 6:40am-7pm), **luggage storage** (5SFr), **lockers** (2SFr), and **bike rental** (22SFr at baggage check; open daily 6:40am-7pm). The **postal code** is CH-7504. The **telephone code** is 081.

ACCOMMODATIONS AND FOOD The **Jugendherberge Tolais (HI)** (tel. 842 72 23; fax 842 70 31), in the modern, salmon-pink building directly across from the train station, is quite convenient for early-morning ski ventures and connections throughout the Engadin Valley. The hostel boasts a full-fledged restaurant, ping pong, swings, a soccer field, and friendly service that blows St. Moritz away. (Dorms 30.50SFr 1st night, then 28SFr; doubles 130SFr, 125SFr; quads 200SFr, 190SFr. Breakfast, lockers, and sheets included. Lunch 11SFr. Dinner at 6:30pm 11SFr; mandatory July-Aug. and Feb.-Mar. 15. **Laundry** 5SFr. Reception 7:30-9:30am, 4-6:30pm, and 7:30-9pm. No lockout. Quiet time from 10pm. Open June 16-Oct. 20 and Dec. 15-Apr. 7. AmEx, MC, Visa.) **Hotel-Pension Hauser,** Cruscheda 165 (tel. 842 63 26; fax 842 65 41), is another option. Head left from the tourist office uphill along Cruscheda. You'll feel right at home in this residential neighborhood, and once you've slept in the inviting beds you might never want to get up and hit the slopes—well, maybe only to escape the 70s color scheme in each balconied room. (Singles 55-65SFr, with shower 65-75SFr; doubles 110-130SFr, with bath 130-180SFr. Parking and buffet breakfast included. Reception 7:30am-midnight. Open mid-Dec. to mid-Apr. and mid-June to mid-Oct.) Right in the heart of town, **Pension Valtellina** (tel. 842 64 06) features a boisterous Italian staff, pink bathrooms, and traditional rooms with warm down blankets. (Singles 48-56SFr; doubles 94-106SFr. Breakfast included. Closed June.) The tourist office also has an extensive list of **private rooms** starting at 25SFr per person. Beautiful **Camping Plauns** (tel. 842 62 85) offers all the amenities a tent-dweller could hope for, from showers to clotheslines. From the train station, walk 3km towards the Bernina Pass to Morteratsch; the trail is clearly marked. (7.50SFr; tents 9SFr plus 3SFr tax. Open June to mid-Oct.)

Pontresina's dining choices are more limited. If the alluring perfume of chlorine triggers your appetite, try **Bistro im Hallenbad,** in the swimming complex across from the tourist office and 50m up the hill. The restaurant offers a hearty daily *Menü* (19SFr), salads (9SFr), big sandwiches (including vegetarian options; 5SFr), hot dogs (4.50SFr), and a daily vegetarian dish. They also have a chlorine-free outdoor patio. (Open M 2pm-midnight, Tu-F 9am-midnight, Sa 10am-midnight, Su 10am-7pm.) The **Co-op** resides at the corner of Via Maistra and Via da Mulin. (Open M-F 8am-12:15pm and 2-6:30pm, Sa 8am-5pm.) Try an *Engadiner Torte* (a local delicacy made from candied almonds, raisins, layers of cream and nut puree, and crunchy crust; 4.50SFr) at **Puntschella Cafe-Restaurant** (tel. 838 80 30), across the street from the Co-op (open in summer 7am-10pm, in winter 7am-9pm).

SIGHTS AND ENTERTAINMENT If the idea of perpetual snow sounds exciting to you, then you might want to ski on it. The Diavolezza **summer ski lift** (tel. 842 64 19) operates in June and July from 8:30am to noon. *(Day pass 33SFr, children 16 and under 25SFr. Winter: 44SFr, half-day 36SFr; children 31SFr, 26SFr.)* When the ski lift closes, trade your ski boots for **hiking** boots and explore the nearby valleys and vales. The tourist office has extensive hiking maps (ranging from 2.50SFr for a simple panoramic to 14-17SFr for the topographic variety) and suggestions. One nearby hike takes you along a green ridge, just below the mighty 3157m **Piz Muragl.** From Pontresina, walk or take the postal bus: "Punt Muragl." From there a **funicular** whisks hikers away to **Mouttas Muragl** (2456m). *(Every 30min. 8am-11pm. 16SFr, round-trip 25SFr; children 8SFr, 12.50SFr.)* Follow the signs to **Alp Languard** (2330m; 2½hr.), hike down to Pontresina (1hr.), or take the lift back. *(13SFr, round-trip 19SFr; children 6.50SFr, 9.50SFr; open 8:30am-5:30pm.)* To see global warming in action, hike to the receding **Morteratsch Glacier.** From the station, walk toward town on Via de la Stazium and hang a right at the trail sign just before the second bridge. Walk for two hours along the valley floor through pine groves and tall grassy meadows. Or you can take the train (every hr., 3.60SFr) to Morteratsch. From the train station, bear right and follow the signs to the glacier. *(30min.)* Signs mark the glacier's recession since the turn of the century along the gushing river created by the melting waters. Though disappearing, the glacier is still a massive wall of ice and snow, seemingly arrested in motion as it crawls through the rugged valley. **The Mountaineering School Pontresina** (tel. 838 83 33) offers daily guided hikes over the Diavolezza and Pers glaciers and down through the Morteratsch glacier and valley. No technical equipment or experience necessary, but a raincoat, warm clothes, and rubber-soled hiking boots are a must. *(20SFr, children 7-16 10SFr; 4hr.)* The school also leads easier hikes daily through regional valleys. *(30SFr.)* If you're tired of physical exertion, **horse-drawn carriages** and winter **sleighs** offer (at least) four legs and a good time. Call 842 60 57 for booking. *(Carriages hold 2-4 people. For the hour trip between Pontresina and Rosengletscher: 14SFr one-way, 24SFr round-trip; children 7SFr, 12SFr.)*

Guests of Pontresina—that's you—are entitled to a number of **free sports, tours,** and **excursions,** including free trout fishing in Lej Nair and Lej Pitschen, free botanical excursions, and free excursions to experience an unforgettable sunrise on Piz Lagalb. In a well-preserved 17th-century farmhouse, the **Museum Alpin,** Chesa Delnon (tel. 842 72 73), up the street from the tourist office on your left, presents life in the Engadin as it used to be: void of wimpy polypropylene and high-tech hikers and full of hundreds of birds and flowers now kaput. *(Open mid-June to mid-Oct. M-Sa 4-6pm. 5SFr, children 1SFr.)* Photos of bearded, pipe-smoking, wool-clad mountaineering men with picks and ropes adorn the walls of the mountaineering room, while 60 varieties of recorded bird calls arranged by species twitter forth at the touch of a button in the adjoining aviary room, also home to 133 stuffed representatives of Engadine fowl. Don't miss the trippy blend of music and picture in the slide-show thriller *Mountain Experience* from 4:30 to 5:15pm.

At the highest point of the village, the typically Romanesque exterior of the **church of Santa Maria** masks some opulent insides. A number of well-preserved frescoes, including the **Mary Magdalene cycle** (1495), exhibit a strong Byzantine influence that rippled forth from the capture of Constantinople in 1204 AD, beginning the second golden Byzantine Age.

■ The Swiss National Park

Switzerland's only national park is flanked by **Zernez** (the official park town) and **S-chanf.** Wildflowers scarce elsewhere, like the bearberry, edelweiss, and the yellow alpine poppy, abound; **ibex, red deer,** and **chamois** roam free; and fluorescent butterflies flit about in this naturalist's nirvana. The park spearheads many re-introduction programs for such nearly extinct animals as the much underrated bearded vulture and, as a result, forbids fires, dogs, biking, straying from the well-marked trails, or picking mushrooms. Zernez is accessible by rail from **St. Moritz** (1hr., every hr., 15.80SFr) or **Chur** (2¾hr., every hr., 46SFr, change at Samedan). **Zernez's tourist office** (tel. (081) 856 13 00; fax 856 11 55) has information about the park, as do the **National Park House** (tel. (081) 856 13 78; fax 856 17 40) and any surrounding tourist offices, including Zuoz's. The house displays the park's highlights and relevant scientific information and is a good starting point for hikes. Walk past the bus stop in front of the train station and make a left, then walk past the **Co-op** (open M-F 8am-noon and 2-6:30pm, Sa 8am-noon and 2-4pm) and turn right at the intersection. The building is 200m on the right. (Open June-Oct. Tu 8:30am-10pm, Su-M and W-Sa 8:30am-6pm. 4SFr, students 3SFr. Park admission free.) The Zuoz tourist office organizes **guided hikes** (15SFr) during the summer high season. Tuesdays at 8am, a guide goes to Margunet where the bearded vultures are. Wednesdays at 7am, a hike leaves from S-chanf for a four-hour trek through the Trupchun Valley section of the park, which boasts of the highest concentration of wild deer in all of Europe.

Only one road penetrates the park. **PTT buses** depart from the train station and take hikers and strollers to the nine stops within the park. This road provides access to the park's limited hiking potential; flora, fauna, and footpaths are all within easy reach. To see the quest to save the endangered bearded vulture, take the bus to stop #7 and climb through **Val dal Botsch** to **Margunet** (2328m), where the birds are being re-introduced. These giant birds with 2½m wingspans often return and congregate at the park release zone from June to August to steal the food set out for the newest birds to be re-introduced; park rangers can show the way. If the vultures don't grab you, the views certainly will. Hike back down over the **Stabelchod pass** (1958m) to stops #8 or 9 (round-trip 3hr.).

If you feel a bus ride would interfere with your enjoyment of your natural surroundings, hike directly from the Park House to the Chamana Cluozza, an Alpine hut and one of the few places to sleep in the park proper. From the Park House, head to the right, and cross the covered bridge 200m to the right. Signs to Cluozza will soon appear. The trail starts out as a weedy access road but soon becomes soft and pine-needle-cushioned, leading up the foothills facing Zernez, ultimately to 2329m. A 15-minute detour to **Bellavista,** near the summit, yields spectacular views of the mountain, the valley, and Zernez. From Bellavista, signs again lead the way to Cluozza through the Alpine forest and out onto the rocky ridge traversing Val Cluozza. The **Blockhaus Cluozza** (tel. (081) 856 12 35) lies 100m up from the river on the other side of the valley. Recharge with pasta from 11SFr. (Accessible by foot only. 3hr. from Zernez, 2½hr. back. Dorms 25SFr. Breakfast included. Open June to mid-Oct.) You can rest here before scaling **Spi Murter** (2545m), a majestic peak presiding over the valley. Exit the park down **Plan dals Poms** to bus stop #3 (3½hr.).

Shelter outside the park in Zernez is expensive, but camping is cheap and pleasant at riverside **Camping Cul** (tel. 856 14 62). Take a right out of the train station and follow the tent signs for five minutes, passing behind the lumber yard. (6.50SFr; tents 4SFr; cars 2.50SFr. Guest tax 0.90SFr. Open May-Oct. 15.) Across the park from Zernez, S-chanf can also serve as base camp for hiking in the park or Engadin Valley skiing. Downhill from the S-chanf train station and left from the church lies **Gasthaus Sternen,** Via Maistra (tel. (081) 854 12 63). Though dwarfed by the vibrant Parc-Hotel Aurora next door, the *Gasthaus* allows sufficient beauty sleep for the next day's hike. (45SFr per person, with shower 55SFr. Add 10SFr in winter. Breakfast included.) **S-chanf's tourist office** (tel. (081) 854 13 48) in the Banca Raiffeisen can offer more information about lodgings. (Open M-Tu and F 8:30-11am and 4-5:30pm, W 8:30-11am, Th 8:30-11am and 4-6:30pm.)

■ Zuoz

Burnt to the ground by residents in 1499 to keep it from the Austrians, Zuoz rebuilt itself in the early 16th century and is today the best preserved medieval village in the Upper Engadin. Ibexes, pinwheels, and flowers float on the whitewashed walls of village houses, and a big carved bear defends the fountains from bloodthirsty Imperial Habsburg troops. In town you can also catch the sounds of Switzerland's leftover Latinate dialect, Romansch. Zuoz is not for the thrill-seeker, but the town has a few ancient customs that may baffle the accidental tourist. On March 1, the **Chalandamarz** engulfs all of Engadin as young boys wander from house to house, ring huge bells, and sing songs to drive off evil spirits and welcome the spring. Originally a pagan fertility rite, the more peculiar **San Gian's Day** commemorates John the Baptist on July 24, when village boys spritz girls with water from Zuoz's many fountains. The defenseless Swiss maidens then flee to their houses and pour huge buckets of water over the boys' heads. Perhaps there's some Italian blood in this region yet.

The **tourist office** (tel. 854 15 10; fax 854 33 34; zuoz@compunet.ch), on Via Maistra, provides keys for the church and tower and suggests hikes in the area. From the station walk up La Passarella, directly across from and perpendicular to the station. At the top of the pedestrian walkway, turn right on the main street, and the tourist office will be past the main square on your right. (Open July-Aug. and Dec.-Apr. M-

F 9am-noon and 2-6pm, Sa 9-11am; May-June and Oct.-Nov. M-F 9am-noon and 3-5pm.) Zuoz is a short **train** ride from **St. Moritz** (30min., every hr., 6:53am-9:26pm, 10SFr) on the way to the Swiss National Park. The **train station** provides **luggage storage** (5SFr), **bike rental** (22SFr), and **currency exchange.** For a **late-night pharmacy,** call 111. The **postal code** is CH-7524. The **telephone code** is 081.

The 400-year-old **Chesa Walther** (tel. 854 13 64), before the tourist office, offers rooms that look decorated by the Swiss Family Robinson after the whole island thing. Zebra, cougar, and other critter skins adorn the ivy-tangled walls, competing for space with gold-fringed mirrors and antique Graubünden stoves. (Dorms 35SFr. Partial **kitchen** facilities 5SFr.) **Restaurant Chesa Albanas,** also before the tourist office, offers seven vegetarian entrees (not counting pasta) for 12-15.50SFr, pasta (12-15SFr), chicken curry with rice (15SFr), or a bratwurst for just 4SFr. (Open M-Sa 8:30am-midnight, Su 10am-midnight.) Raw materials for a meal await at the **Co-op** opposite the station (open M-F 8am-12:15pm and 2-6:30pm, Sa 8am-12:15pm and 2-5pm) or at the **Volg** supermarket next to the tourist office (open M-F 8am-noon and 2-6:30pm, Sa 8am-noon and 2-4pm).

The small **Church San Luzius** on Via Maistra has sweet-smelling pine pews and hymnals in Romansh. Next door is the **prison tower,** filled with spiky, blood-curdling, gut-wrenching implements of torture and chilling dungeon cells that you can climb into (ask the tourist office for the key). The *graffito* carvings in Zuoz are eye-catching in their detail—look up at **Crusch Alva** in the main square. The town also woos **bikers** with 37km of marked trails, and **hikers** can use the Inn River as a starting point for many delightful jaunts. The path to **Punt Muragl** (4hr.) follows the river along the Engadin's green valley floor. To put a bit of altitude into your walk, follow the trail from Zuoz to **Madulain** (2hr.) along the ridge overlooking the valley floor. The trail crosses others leading to alpine huts, including the Chamana d'Es-cha (a full day's hike away), and to the terraced farms of the other valley villages. To find the trail, start uphill from Zuoz's main square and head 300m up Somvih street. For a more rugged afternoon, follow the **Ova d'Arpiglia** to a crashing 20m waterfall. From the other side of the train tracks and the highway at the Resgia Parking lot past the Restaurant Dorta, signs lead the way to **Sagl d'Arpiglia** along a magnificent rock-strewn gorge. That's the view of the falls from below—now climb the **"Stairway to Heaven."** Tickling the skies, this steep, green meadow to the right of the falls burgeons with purple wildflowers and prehistoric-looking leaves and fronds. At the top of the stairway, chase butterflies to you heart's content and hum your favorite Zeppelin riff in the valley's swath of green. Signs point the way from this perfect picnic-haven back to Zuoz (round-trip 1½hr.).

Buna Saira!

Switzerland's oft-forgotten fourth national language, Romansh, is spoken only in the province of Graubünden, where it is an official cantonal language along with German and Italian. Up until about 1850, it was the most spoken language in the canton. By 1880, Romansh speakers dropped to 39.8% of the population, a percentage that kept dropping, then leveled out as the primary language for 23.6% of the residents in Graubünden. In some villages like S-chanf, Romansh speakers are in the majority, and even in large towns like Chur they form a quarter of the population. All Romansh speakers (except toddlers) are fully bilingual. Romansh is taught in the schools, and its speakers support five Romansh newspapers and 13-14 hours of TV broadcast time in Romansh. The language is fully supported by the Swiss government, but its survival is threatened by the fact that its speakers are divided by at least four major dialects that arose from the mountain isolation of many high-altitude villages. Romansh didn't become a written language until the 16th-century, when people began publishing catechisms and tracts on preserving Romansh identity (already!). Now, Romansh has a small literature of its own and translations of everything from the Bible to Asterix comics. Maybe when you're traveling through Switzerland, you'll overhear someone calling out, "Bun di!" (hello), "grazia" (thank you), or even "Tge bel che ti es!" (how beautiful you are!).

THE BODENSEE

The third largest lake in Europe, the Bodensee forms a graceful border at the conjunction of Austria, Switzerland, and Germany. Ancient castles, manicured islands, and lots of suntanning opportunities draw residents of all three countries (and then some) to the lake throughout the summer to at least partially relieve pent-up *Mittelmeerlust*.

■ Constance (Konstanz)

Spanning the Rhine's juncture with the Bodensee is the elegant university city of Konstanz. Though technically in Germany, the city extends into Switzerland, which spared it the bombing that leveled many German cities of similar size in WWII. This German/Swiss mix, the residues of Austrian rule, and the city's large student population create an open, international feel. Locals and students crowd the old resort beaches on the edge of town, and the *Altstadt*'s narrow streets wind around beautifully painted Baroque and Renaissance facades crowned with a tangle of ancient tiles, stork nests, and TV antennae. Along the river promenades, gabled and turreted 19th-century houses gleam in sunlight reflected off the water. Be aware that Constance's currency is the Deutschmark, the phones are on the German system, and border controls are in effect—you will need to show your passport to walk into Constance from the Swiss hostel, and border guards occasionally search bags.

ORIENTATION AND PRACTICAL INFORMATION Trains connect Constance every hour to **Stein am Rhein** (30min., 9SFr) and **Schaffhausen** (1hr., 15SFr). Travelers looking for ride-sharing options can contact the small but spunky **Mitfahrzentrale**, Münzg. 22 (tel. 214 44; open M-F 9:30am-1pm and 2-6pm, Sa 9:30am-2pm), or the university **ride board.** You can buy tickets for the Meersburg-Constance **ferry** from any machine or on board. The tourist office sells a two-day pass for DM34. Ships depart about once every hour from behind the Constance train station to all ports on the Bodensee. One ferry stops at various points in Germany (June to late Sept. daily). For more information and schedules independent of the tourist office, contact the **Weiße Bodenseeflotte** counter (tel. 28 13 89), in the harbor behind the train station. (Open Su-F 7:40am-6:10pm, Sa 7:40am-8:15pm. Trips on the lake half-price with Eurailpass.) **Giess Personenschiffahrt** sends boats every hour from behind the train station to the **Freizeitbad** and the **Freibad Horn** (45min., June-Aug. 10:30am-5:30pm, May and Sept. Su 10:30-5:30pm, 2.50-3SFr). **City buses** in Constance cost DM2.40 per ride. **Paddleboat** and **rowboat** rentals are available at **Am Gondelhafen** (tel. 218 81) for about DM14 per hour from 9am to dusk. The **tourist office** (tel. 13 30 30; fax 13 30 60; email info@touristinfomation.stadt.konstanz.de), in the arcade to the right of the train station, provides an excellent walking map (DM0.50) and lots of area information. The office will find rooms for a three-night minimum stay in private homes (DM5). The free, self-guided walking tour brochure includes a map, suggested routes, and a brief explanation of the many sites. (Open May-Sept. M-F 9am-6:30pm, Sa 9am-1pm; Oct. and Apr. M-F 9am-12:30pm and 2-6pm, Sa 9am-1pm; Nov.-Mar. M-F 9am-noon and 2-6pm.) Wash your rank and stanky clothing at **Waschsalon und Mehr,** Hofhalde 3 (tel. 160 27; wash DM7, dry DM5 per 10min.; open M-F 10am-7pm, Sa 10am-4pm). For the **police,** call 110. The **post office,** 78421 Konstanz, is across the street from the train station at Bahnhofpl. 2 (open M-F 8:30am-6pm, Sa 8:30am-noon). Check your **email** at **Schauzer & Schauzer Internet Café,** Pfaueng. 11 near the Schnetztor. The **postal code** is D-78462. The **German telephone code** is 0049, and the city's **telephone code** is 07531.

ACCOMMODATIONS AND FOOD Far and away the nicer of Constance's two youth hostels is the clean, comfortable **Jugendherberge Kreuzlingen (HI),** Promenadenstr. 7 (tel. (071) 688 26 63; fax 688 47 61; use the Swiss access code), resting in an old manor house on the water in Kreuzlingen, Switzerland (but actually the closer hostel to downtown Constance). From the Constance Bahnhof, cross the tracks on the left and walk 20 minutes on the trail that hugs the water. From the park path—shortly after the caged sheep—take a right into the castle-like villa grounds, walk a bit, and then take a soft right onto a tree-lined path that leads straight to the hotel. (Dorms 21.20SFr 1st night, then 18.70SFr. Mar.-Apr. and Oct.-Nov.: 18.70SFr, 16.20SFr. Breakfast and sheets included. Dinner 11SFr. **Kayak rental** 10SFr per 2hr.; **mountain bike rental** 12.50SFr per day. Reception 8-9am and 5-9pm. Closed Dec.-Feb.) **Jugendherberge Otto-Moericke-Turm (HI),** Zur Allmannshöhe 18 (tel. 322 60; fax 311 63), considerably less luxurious, is probably the world's only hostel housed in a former water tower. Take bus #4: "Jugendherberge." (DM21.50, over 26 DM26.50. Members only. Breakfast included. Sheets DM5.50. Reception Apr.-Oct. 3-10pm; Nov.-Mar. 5-10pm. Curfew 10pm. Open Mar.-Oct. Call ahead.) **Jugendwohnheim Don Bosco,** Salesianerweg 5 (tel. 622 52; fax 606 88), is an excellent alternative to the hostels. From the station, take bus #1: "Salzberg" then walk two minutes, following the main road around the corner, and turn at the yellow Bosco sign into the gargantuan yellow Bosco house. The building is the Swiss youth hostel's version of Pinocchio's sin city: a huge game room with foosball, chess, pinball, board games, and screaming school groups. A TV in the dayroom crackles with 39 channels, including MTV. (Curfew 12:30am; key available. 4- to 8-bed dorms DM26. Sheets DM5. Call ahead.) **Campingplatz Konstanz-Bruderhofer,** Fohrenbühlweg 50 (tel. 330 57), offers a cheaper alternative. Take bus #1: "Staad"; the campground is along the water. Definitely make reservations. (DM6; tent DM5-8. Open April 15-Sept.)

Compared to the rest of Switzerland, German Constance has refreshingly low prices. The **University Mensa** dishes out Constance's cheapest food—lunches, including dessert and a view of the lake, cost DM8-9. Take bus #9, 9a, or 9b: "Universität." The cafeteria on floor K6 has lighter fare, such as sandwiches and desserts, with no ID required. (DM2-5. Open M-Th 7:45am-6:30pm, F 7:45am-5pm; Aug. M-F 11am-2pm.) The area around Rheing., the oldest part of Constance and now the center of a vibrant alternative scene, overflows with health-food stores, left-wing graffiti, student cafés, and bars. **Sedir,** Hofhaldestr. 11, serves big bowls of vegetarian noodles for DM9.50, and other non-meat dishes from DM12. The photographs on the wall take you to Turkey, the music to vintage 1970 America. (Open M-F 11am-2pm and 6pm-midnight, Sa-Su 6pm-2am.) A **Tengelmann grocery store,** at the corner of Münzg. and Brotlaube, sells the raw materials for a good meal. (Open M-F 8:30am-8pm, Sa 8am-4pm.)

SIGHTS AND ENTERTAINMENT

Konstanz's **Münster,** built over the course of 600 years, features a soaring Gothic spire, 17th-century vaulting, and a display of ancient religious objects. *(Open daily 10am-5pm. Free.)* Elaborate frescoes on the 14th-century **Rathaus** depict Constance's history. **Seestraße,** near the yacht harbor on the lake, and **Rheinsteig,** along the Rhine, are lovely water promenades. The tree-filled **Stadtgarten** next to Constance's main harbor provides an unbroken view down the length of the Bodensee, while a voluptuous revolving statue of "Imperia" guards the Gondelhafen harbor.

Constance boasts a number of grass and pebble **public beaches;** all are free and open from May to September. **Strandbad Horn,** the largest and most crowded, sports a section for nude sunbathing. In inclement weather, thwarted sunbathers head next door to **Freizeitbad Jakob,** Wilhelm-von-Scholz-Weg 2 (tel. 661 63), an ultra-modern indoor-outdoor pool complex with thermal baths and *faux*-summer sun lamps. *(Both open daily 9am-9pm. DM8, students DM5.)* To reach both complexes, walk 30 minutes along the waterfront from the train station, or take bus #5. **Strandbad Konstanz-Litzelstetten** and **Strandbad Konstanz-Wallhausen** can both be reached via bus #4. Twentysomethings frolic at the beach by the university. Take bus #5 to "Egg" and walk past the playing fields, or take a 10-minute walk through the fields from the Konstanz youth hostel.

■ Near Constance: Mainau

The rich and magnificently manicured garden covering the German **island of Mainau** is the result of the horticultural prowess of generations of Baden princes and the Swedish royal family. A lush arboretum, greenhouses, and **huge animals made of flowers** surround the pink Baroque palace built by the Knights of the Teutonic Order, who lived here from the 13th to the 18th century. Now, thousands of happy little tourists scamper across the foot bridge from Constance to pose with the blooming elephants and watch the 30 different varieties of butterflies fluttering about the tropical-climate greenhouse. Truly amazing are the dozens of fully grown palm trees planted around the palace, able to survive year-round due to the lake's moderating effect on the climate and the magic green fingers of the island's massive gardening army. To reach the island, take a romantic boat trip from behind the Constance train station (one-way DM5.40, round-trip DM9). Bus #4: "Mainau" also runs to the island. (Park open 7am-8pm. DM17, students DM9, seniors DM13.50, children DM5.50. After 6pm and from Nov. to mid-Mar. DM9, students and children free.) For more info on concerts, performances, and tours call (49 07531) 30 30 or fax 30 32 48.

■ Lindau im Bodensee

When geological forces violently crunched their way through southern Germany millenia ago, Mother Nature obviously intended for Lindau to be a resort. Connected to the lake shore by a narrow causeway, the pseudo-island that is **Lindau im Bodensee, Germany,** sits cupped in the aquamarine waters of an oddly warm Alpine valley. The central part of town around **Maximilianstraße** features captivating half-timbered houses, and the view of the Alps is almost the same as the one you see on good chocolates. The **Städtische Kunstsammlung** (town art museum) is located in **Cavazzen-Haus,** an ornate Baroque mansion. (Open Apr.-Oct. Tu-Su 10am-noon and 2-5pm. DM4, students DM1.) The harbor is framed by a rather imposing 19th-century **Bavarian Lion** and the **New Lighthouse,** the latter offering an illuminating overview of the neighborhood. (Open daily 10am-7pm. DM2, students DM1.) The **Rathaus,** halfway along Maximilianstr., is a fruity blend of frescoes. A walk down the less touristed equivalent of Maximilianstr.—**In der Grube** (In the Pit)—will lead you to the **Diebstahl Turm** (robbery tower). Covered with ivy and newly renovated, the color-speckled, tin-roofed turret looks more like Rapunzel's tower than a former prison. For those over 21 and possessing a coat and tie or a formal dress, the **casino** on the island (one of 4 in Bavaria), has roulette and sundry other games of chance. The bet ceiling is DM12,000. Hey there, big spender. (Open 3pm-2am. Admission DM5 and a passport—and please, daaahling, no jeans.)

The **tourist office,** Ludwigstr. 68 (tel. 26 00 30; fax 26 00 26), across from the station, finds rooms for a DM5 fee. (Open M-Sa 9am-1pm and 2-7pm.) **Tours** leave from the office at 10am (Tu and F in German, M in English; DM5, students and overnight guests DM3). **Ferries** link Lindau with Constance, stopping at **Meersburg, Mainau,** and **Friedrichshafen** (3hr., 5-7 per day, one-way DM18.40, under 24 DM11.20). Crazy kids can rent **boats** (tel. 55 14) 50m to the left of the casino, right next to the bridge. (Open mid.-Mar. to mid.-Sept. daily 9am-9pm. Rowboats DM10-18; paddleboats DM12-15 per hr. for up to 5 people; motorboats DM45.) One-hour excursions (tel. 781 94) on a small boat leave from the dock behind the casino at 11:30am, 1, 2:30, and 6pm (DM12, children DM6). **Rent bikes** at the train station (tel. 212 61) for DM15. (Open M-F 9am-noon and 2:30-6pm, Sa 9:30am-noon.) The **post office,** 88101 Lindau im Bodensee (tel. 277 70), is 50m right of the train station. (Open M-F 8am-6pm, Sa 8:30am-noon.) The **telephone code** is 08382.

The spectacular **Jugendherberge,** Herbergsweg 11 (tel. 967 10), lies across the Seebrücke off Bregenzerstr. Walk (20min.) or take bus #1 or 2: "Anheggerstr.," then transfer to bus #3 and get off at "Jugendherberge." Sleekly modern interior has a staff that is just as hip. The only downside of this place is their policy for single travelers—they don't hold beds for same-day arrivals. Call ahead. (Under 27 and families with

GRAUBÜNDEN

small children only. Dorms DM29. Breakfast, sheets, and tax included. Reception 7am-midnight. Curfew midnight.) You could eat off the floor in the fine rooms at **Gästehaus Holdereggen,** Näherweg 4 (tel. 65 74). Follow the railroad tracks across the causeway to the mainland (after the bridge, the path continues to the left of the tracks); turn right onto Holdereggeng. and left onto Jungfernburgstr. Näherweg is on the left (20min.). (Singles DM38; doubles DM70. Add DM3 extra per person for one-night stands. Showers DM2.) **Campingplatz Lindau-Zech,** Frauenhoferstr. 20 (tel. 722 36), 3km south of the island on the mainland, is within spitting range of the Austrian border and a beach. From the station, take bus #1 or 2: "Anheggerstr.," then bus #3 (dir: Zech) to finish the journey. (DM9.50; tent DM4. *Kurtaxe* DM1.50. Showers included. Open May-Oct.)

Lindau has three beaches. (All open June to mid-Aug. and weekends year-round daily 10am-8pm; other times 10:30am-7:30pm. Last entrance 1hr. before closing.) **Römerbad** is the smallest and most familial, located left of the harbor on the island (DM4, students DM3). To reach the quieter **Lindenhofbad,** take bus #1 or 2: "Anheggerstr." and then bus #4: "Alwind" (DM4, students DM3). Lindau's biggest beach is **Eichwald,** about a 30-minute walk to the right facing the harbor along Uferweg. Alternatively, take bus #1 or 2: "Anheggerstr.," then bus #3: "Karmelbuckel" (DM5, students DM3). Sit down for Greek at **Taverna Pita Gyros,** Paradiespl. 16 (tel. 237 02), which offers big platters (DM6-19) on the sidewalk or inside. (Open daily 10am-9pm.) There is a **Plus grocery store** in the basement of the department store at the conjunction of In der Grub and Cramerg. (Open M-F 8:30am-6:30pm, Sa 8am-1pm.)

■ St. Gallen

St. Gallen may well be the tourist's dream come true. At St. Gallen, you can feed your Dark Ages cobblestone fetish and your urge for sweaty student-fueled nightlife, all in the same town. This small medieval city beats to the pulse of the 20th century. From the alternative culture of the *Altstadt* to the venerable grandeur of the *Stiftsbibliothek,* a Baroque library named a World Heritage Treasure by UNESCO, St. Gallen hits all the angles that travelers look for in a city. Its proximity to the Bodensee, Zurich, Germany, Austria, and smaller mountain villages makes it a regional hotspot.

ORIENTATION AND PRACTICAL INFORMATION

Trains: To: **Zurich** (1hr., 5:09am-10:41pm, 26SFr); **Geneva** (4½hr., 5:09am-8:43pm, 87SFr); **Bern** (2½hr., 5:09am-10:43pm, 59SFr); **Lugano** (4hr., 74SFr); and **Munich** (3hr., 69SFr, under 26 49SFr).

Buses: Convenient buses cross the hills and valleys of the St. Gallen region. Single fare 2SFr, children 1SFr, *Tageskarte* (day card) 7.20SFr, 12 rides 20SFr. Buy tickets at each stop; multi-fares and *Tageskarten* available at large kiosks or the **VBSG Transit Authority** across from the train station.

Taxis: Sprenger AG, Rohrschacherstr. 281 (tel. 222 23 33).

Car Rental: Herold Autovermietung AG, Molkenstr. 7 (tel. 228 64 28; fax 228 64 25). 72SFr per day, 3 days 151SFr. **Budget Rent-A-Car** or **Europacar/Interrent,** City Garage AG, St. Leonhardstr. 35 (tel. 222 11 14; fax 222 01 57). 118SFr per day, F-M package for 201SFr.

Parking: Neumarkt Parking Garage (tel. 222 11 14). Conveniently located near the Neumarkt Supermarket on St. Leonhardstr. 5am-9pm 2SFr per hr.; 9pm-5am 1SFr per hr. Open M-Sa 5am-12:30am. **Rathaus Parking Garage** (tel. 223 60 00). 7am-10pm 1.80SFr per hr.; 10pm-7am 0.50SFr per hr. Open 24hr. Or park in one of the city's **blue zones** for 5.50SFr per day M-F, free Sa-Su.

Tourist Office: Bahnhofpl. 1a (tel. 227 37 37; fax 227 37 67). From the train station, cross straight through the bus stop and pass the fountain on the left; the tourist office is on the right. The English-speaking staff makes free hotel reservations within St. Gallen. Maps, brochures, and a **city tour** are also available. (Tour June 12-Sept. 28 M, W, and F 2:30pm. 15SFr, museum admissions and snack included.) Office open M-F 9am-noon and 1-6pm, Sa 9am-noon.

Currency Exchange: Union Bank of Switzerland, Bahnhofpl., is convenient. Open M-W and F 8:30am-4:30pm, Th 8:30am-6:30pm.

Luggage Storage: At the train station. Lockers 3-5SFr. Luggage watch 5SFr. Open M-F 7:30am-7:45pm, Sa-Su 7:30am-noon and 2-6:45pm.

Laundromat: Quick Wash, Rohrschacherstr. 59 (tel. 245 31 73). Soap 0.80-2.50SFr, wash 6-8SFr, dry 1.80-3.80SFr. Open M-Sa 8am-10pm.

Internet Access: Media Lounge, 10 Katerineng. (tel. 244 30 90). Your back to the bus stop at Marktpl., cross at the lights into Katerineng. Blue-carpeted lounge offers surprisingly cheap access to your neglected email account. 2SFr minimum; after 10min. 1SFr for 5min., 12SFr for 1hr. Open M-F 9am-9pm, Sa 9am-5pm.

Post Office: St. Leonhardstr. 7, across the street and to the right of the train station exit. Open M-F 7:30am-6:30pm, Sa 7:30-11am. **Postal Code:** CH-9000.

Telephone Code: 071.

ACCOMMODATIONS

Jugendherberge St. Gallen (HI), Jüchstr. 25 (tel. 245 47 77; fax 245 49 83). From the train station, take the *Trogenerbahn* (Orange Train) from the smaller Appenzeller/Trogener station to the right. From Marktpl. take the orange train (dir: Speicher-Trogen): "Schülerhaus," walk uphill on the right, make a left across the train tracks at the sign, and walk downhill 2min. Perched on a hill overlooking St. Gallen, the hostel is filled with bright murals, posters, and friendly potted plants. Breakfast room, terrace, barbecue pit, grassy lawn, juke box, library, billiard and disco room, English-speaking staff, and board games. Fall asleep to the tuneful clanking of Swiss cowbells. Dorms 23SFr 1st night, then 20.50SFr; singles 57SFr; 54.50SFr; doubles 64SFr, 59SFr. Non-members add 5SFr. Breakfast, shower, and sheets included. Parking available. Reception M-Sa 7-10am and 5-10:30pm, Su 6-10:30pm. Check-out 9am (9:30am in winter). Lockout 10am-5pm, but lounge is open. Closed Dec. 15-Mar. 7.

Hotel Elite, Metzgerg. 9-11 (tel. 222 12 36; fax 222 21 77). Simple and snug rooms with chocolates on the pillows. Convenient location near the Marktpl., bus station, and *Altstadt*. Singles 60-90SFr; doubles 90-140SFr. Breakfast included.

Hotel Weisses Kreuz, Engelg. 9 (tel. 223 28 43; fax 223 28 43), 1 block from Hotel Elite and atop a lively bar run by a trendy, cheerful staff. Shabby stairs lead up through storage spaces to plain, tired rooms, but the beds are cozy and the location's great for digging into the *Altstadt*'s nightlife. Singles 40SFr; doubles 80SFr. Breakfast and hall showers included. Reception 6:30am-2pm and 5pm-midnight.

FOOD

Restaurants

Christina's, Weberg. 9 (tel. 238 808). A sleek, indigo-tinted Swedish bar/café/restaurant. Exotic vegetarian specialties. Bring your sunglasses and prepare to ooze sophistication. Sunday smorgasbord brunch 10am-noon. Veggie dishes from 17SFr. Fish and meat dishes from 19SFr. Open Tu-Th 9:30am-11:30pm, F-Sa 9:30am-12:30am, Su 10am-11:30pm. AmEx, MC, Visa.

Pizzeria Testarossa, Metzgerg. 20 (tel. 222 03 30), in the center of the *Altstadt*. This romantic roof-top garden has the cosy Swiss feel as well as the intimacy of a small Italian restaurant. Delicious vegetarian pizzas from 13SFr as well as numerous "make-your-own-pizza" options. Open daily 10am-midnight. AmEx, MC, Visa.

Restaurant Spitalkeller, Spitalg. 10 (tel. 222 50 91). From Marktpl., head down Marktg., left on Spitalg. Unidentifiable plastic fruit hangs from this smoky, wooden-raftered joint. Hearty Alpine food for mountain folks taking a break from the wilderness. Appenzeller macaroni with sausage or Ticino *Rösti* (with tomatoes and cheese) 12.50SFr. Daily *Menüs* from 10SFr. Open Tu-Sa 8am-midnight.

Markets

Migros, St. Leonhardstr., 2 blocks up from the train station. Open M-W and F 8am-6:30pm, Th 8am-9pm, Sa 7:30am-5pm. Buffet-equipped restaurant open M-W and F 6:30am-6:30pm, Th 6:30am-9pm, Sa 6:30am-5pm.

Reformhaus Müller, Spiserg. 13, sells organically grown goodies and health foods. Open M-F 8am-6:30pm, Sa 8:30am-5pm.

Public market, on Marktpl. Fresh produce, bread, and meat daily 7am-7pm.

SIGHTS

Anyone who loves books will gasp at the sight of St. Gallen's main attraction, the **Stiftsbibliotek** (abbey library; tel. 227 34 15) and the abbey that houses it. *(Open Apr.-Nov. M-Sa 9am-noon and 1:30-5pm, Su 10am-noon and 1:30-4pm.; Dec.-Mar. M-Sa 9am-noon and 1:30-4pm.)* Dazed visitors shuffle across the shiny parquet floors in huge gray slippers that the library provides to protect the floors. The library maintains a collection of 140,000 volumes and 2000 manuscripts, 500 of which date back to the 13th century. Although the appearance of the resident death-blackened mummy might indicate otherwise, the *Stiftsbibliotek* is a living, lending library serving scholars the globe over. Umberto Eco was seen sniffing around here to get inspiration for *The Name of the Rose.* The **Kathedrale St. Gallen** (tel. 227 33 88), a part of the abbey founded in the 8th century and renovated in the mid-18th, is technically Neoclassical and Baroque but exudes a gothic spookiness. The bright abbey courtyard is a great place for a picnic or a sunbath. Nearby, the **Evangelical Church of St. Lawrence,** founded in the 9th century, sports castle-like organ pipes, Easter-egg wall patterns, and a geometric, blue ceiling. *(Open M-F 9:30-11:30am and 2-4pm.)* Across the train tracks to the left and uphill (a bit of a walk from the center of town), at the **Peter and Paul Wildpark** (tel. 222 67 92) on Rosenberg in Romontum, ibex, saved from near extinction through the efforts of the park, roam the grounds freely. *(Open 24hr. Free.)* Explore the campus of the **St. Gallen University** by taking bus #5 (dir: Rotmonten): "Hochschule." The huge park donated to the city of St. Gallen in 1963 provides a magnificent view of the city and the Bodensee.

MUSEUMS

St. Gallen's aptly named Museumstraße holds four museums. One ticket grants admission to all four.

Kunstmuseum, Museumstr. 32 (tel. 245 22 44). juxtaposes the modern art of Jonathan Lasker and Sengantinit on the top floor with works by more traditional 19th- and 20th-century artists like Monet and Giacometti. **Natural History Museum** is in the same building, housing examples of almost everything Mother Nature has birthed in the last four billion years, arranged in thoughtful, philosophical exhibits. Both open Tu-Sa 10am-noon and 2-5pm, Su 10am-5pm. 6SFr, students 2SFr.

Historical Museum, Museumstr. 50 (tel. 244 78 32). The local half of the museum displays linen processing, ancient kitchens, a random barber shop, and spiky weapons a tad more formidable than the modern Swiss army knife. The **Ethnology Collection** (tel. 244 88 02) brims with exquisite artifacts and art from Lappland to Southern Africa. The star of the collection is the 12th-century wooden statue of the Bodhisattva Kuan-yin. Open Tu-Sa 10am-noon and 2-5pm, Su 10am-5pm. 6SFr, students 2SFr.

Kirchofer House Museum, Museumstr. 27 (tel. 244 75 21). Modest art collection but an impressive array of coins, Russian imperial silver, and the Appenzeller cave bear skeletons, all in the house of one of St. Gallen's first families. A rare painting depicts 3 sets of 18th-century St. Gallen twins. Call for a viewing of the museum. Open Tu-Sa 10am-noon and 2-5pm. 6SFr, students 2SFr.

ENTERTAINMENT AND NIGHTLIFE

St. Gallen's (oxymoronically) young *Altstadt* resonates with techno beats and the heavy clink of beer mugs. Cafés and bars in Marktpl. are popular but money-hungry. Head instead for the streets radiating out from Marktpl., which are packed with cheaper, hole-in-the-wall bars and their tattooed, chained, and bejewelled clientele.

St. Gallen's celebration of music and general debauchery takes over the fields surrounding the town at the end of June. The **Open Air St. Gallen Music Festival** (tel. 222 21 21; box office address Open Air St. Gallen Festival Boutique, Bahnhofstr. 6, CH-9000, St. Gallen, Switzerland) features over 20 live bands. Past headliners have included the Beastie Boys, Garbage, the Red Hot Chili Peppers, Cypress Hill, the legendary B.B. King, and the Godfather of Soul, James Brown. You must buy a ticket for all three days. Tickets run a steep 139SFr, but housing is included if you bring a tent and camp out (showers and toilets available). Or stay in St. Gallen and take the free shuttle bus from the train station to the concert grounds. The **Stadttheater**, Museumstr. 24 (tel. 242 06 06), located in a fancy Art Nouveau building, hosts over 200 concerts and dramatic works by renowned artists and musicians annually (Sept.-June). There are several **movie theaters** at Marktpl. (movie info tel. 122).

Filou, Schwertg. (tel. 222 35 96). Smoky bar pumps 80s rock for a twenty-something crowd. Beer-guzzlers overflow into the camp-like picnic tables outside. Good luck finding space to dance on the weekend. Open M-Sa 5pm-midnight.

Goliathstübli, Goliathstr. 27 (tel. 222 35 96). A dark, local joint with red velvet walls, a crooked wooden bar, and a diverse crowd. Open Su-F 8pm-1am.

Ozon, Goliathg. 28 (tel. 244 81 24). Non-stop chrome and mirrors lend the illusion of size to this compact club. If the flashing lights and smoke don't blind you, the prices will (beer from 9SFr). DJ spins different wax each night (Thursday techno). Cover usually 10SFr. Open Su and Tu-Th 10pm-2am, F-Sa 10pm-3am.

Club Negresco, Katharineng. 6 (tel. 245 70 92). The hip teenage St. Gallender's favorite place to be on a Saturday night. A snazzy, mixed crowd graces the palm-fringed interior of this cool bar. Cover 3.80SFr. Open Tu-Sa 5pm-whenever.

Dancing, Brühlg. 18 (tel. 226 09 00). Dance-floor action is projected onto a field of screens. Local bands, karaoke, and other theme nights (foxtrot, anyone?). Monday is taxi-drivers' night. Are you talkin' to me? Su-W no cover, Th-Sa 7-17SFr. Open July-Aug. Th-Tu 10pm-5:30am; Sept.-June 9pm to whenever.

Birreria, Brühlg. 45 (tel. 223 25 33). Over 700 types of beer let you take a barley trip around the globe without moving your lazy gut. Take them away or drink them at the bar. Open M 11am-midnight, Tu-Th 9am-midnight, F-Sa 9am-1:30am.

■ Near St. Gallen: Appenzell

Cheese, chocolate, and Edelweiss...can you get any more Swiss than that? Appenzell does its best to prove that you can't. The tiny foot-of-the-Alpstein village, renowned for its *Appenzeller Käse* (cheese), boasts of those and many other Swissy things, like panoramic views, hospitality, and political conservatism. In an interesting feat of Swiss political obfuscation, women weren't allowed to vote until 1991. The **Rathaus,** which houses the museum, town hall, cantonal library, and tourist office, is itself remarkable, especially the **Großratssaal,** with intricately carved wood-paneled walls and 16th-century frescoes. The *Rathaus,* built in 1563, escaped Baroque encrustation of its heavy wooden beams and parquet flooring. The stately **Pfarrkirche St. Mauritius,** with Rococo stained-glass windows and a magnificent chandelier in gold and glass, stands next door on Hauptg. (Open daily 9am-7pm.)

ORIENTATION AND PRACTICAL INFORMATION Buses connect Appenzell to the smaller towns of the canton, and the rattling **Appenzellerbahn** chugs to St. Gallen every hour (1hr., 10.20SFr). **Parking lots** are across from the Co-op and along the Sitter river across the bridge from the St. Mauritius Church. The Appenzell **tourist office,** Hauptg. 4 (tel. 788 96 41; fax 788 96 49), is next to the Rathaus. (Open June-Oct. M-F 9am-noon and 2-6pm, Sa 9am-noon and 2-4pm; Nov.-May M-F 9am-noon and 2-5pm, Sa 9am-noon.) From the train station, walk down Bahnhofstr., bearing right as the road curves and intersects Hauptg. The tourist office is to the left of the church. They make hotel reservations, book cable car excursions (round-trip 32-38SFr), provide detailed hiking maps, and give specific dates for all of Appenzell's intriguing festivals, like the early October **Viehschau** (cattle show) or the pulse-pounding **goat show** the next day. You'll have to wait 'til November for the **sheep show.** There are different activities arranged by the tourist office every day: Wednesdays at 10am, a free tour of the Appenzeller Alpenbitter factory, the factory responsible for production of the region's unique and delicious alcoholic drink, departs from Weissbadstr. 27; Thursdays at 2pm there's a course in woodcarving where, for 20SFr, you can make your own butter dish. For these and other tourist sponsored events, register the day before by 5pm. Appenzell's **telephone code** is 071. The **postal code** is 9050.

ACCOMMODATIONS AND FOOD Particularly picturesque lodgings await at **Haus Lydia,** Eggerstrandenstr. 53 (tel. 787 42 33). A staff member will pick you up at the train station if you call ahead. Otherwise, walk 20 minutes from the station on Bahnhofstr. and turn right on Gringelstr., left on Weissbadstr., right on Gaiserstr., and right onto Eggerstrandenstr. Run by a friendly, English-speaking family, the house offers large rooms with great pastoral views and a kitchen for guest use. When the weather's good, the sons of the owners provide Swiss musical entertainment. (Singles 40-42SFr; doubles 62-72SFr. Breakfast included. Reservations required.) The **Gasthaus Hof** (tel. 787 22 10; fax 787 58 83), near the center of the Altstadt, is a bustling family-run restaurant with guest-rooms upstairs. (Dorms 80SFr; doubles with TV 130SFr. Showers in hall. Breakfast included. Check-in 11am. Restaurant open 8am-11pm.) Many hiking trails are dotted with **Gasthöfe** (guest houses), gorgeous old farmhouses and restaurants for the road-weary. One of the nicest farmhouses is **Berggasthaus Seealpsee** (tel. 799 11 40, winter tel. 799 14 40; fax 799 18 20), with sweet-smelling wood rooms and a pristine location on the edge of the peaceful waters of the Seealpsee. Take the Appenzellerbahn to Wasserauen and follow the yellow "Wanderweg" signs from the left of the station as you exit from the rear. Hike about 45 minutes. (Dorms 22SFr; doubles 80SFr. Children 17SFr. Breakfast included.) **Gasthof Freudenberg** (tel. 787 12 40) provides gorgeous, oh-so-Swiss painted beds and wardrobes and Appenzell's best panoramic view of the Alpstein from its hilltop locale. Call ahead and someone will pick you up from the train station. Otherwise, exit rear from the train station, look for the signpost "Freudenberg," walk about 12 minutes still following the signs, eventually taking the gravel footpath uphill. (Singles 58SFr; doubles 98SFr. Breakfast included. Reception and restaurant open Dec.-Oct. 7:30am-midnight.) The **restaurant** downstairs offers huge portions, and all prices are under 31SFr (even the steak). For more Swiss specialties—with a cheesy twist—try some of the Appenzeller specialties at **Restaurant Traube,** Marktg. 7 (tel. 787 14 07). The candle-lit restaurant has Chäsdörfli, an Appenzeller specialty of cheese, potatoes, and noodles. (Soups 3.50-7.50SFr; Appenzeller specialties 13-18.50SFr. Open Mar.-Jan. Tu-Su 8:30am-midnight.) For groceries, try the **Co-op,** Marktg. 14. Walk along Rathauspl. to Marktg. on the left, and look for the orange sign behind Marktpl. (Open M and Th 8am-12:15pm and 1:30-6:30pm, Tu-F 8am-12:15pm and 1:30-8pm, Sa 8am-4pm.)

SIGHTS AND ENTERTAINMENT Smack in the heart of the Alpstein, Appenzell is ideal for **hiking** without the temperature extremes of Zermatt or the Ticino region. The area has an extensive network of marked trails connecting the small towns of the canton to the larger urban areas of St. Gallen and Winterthur. Ask at the tourist office for Wandervorschläge: Appenzellerland, which has a detailed map with all rest areas marked. For an easy walk through the green pastures whose grass eventually becomes the renowned Appenzeller cheese, walk along the Sitter River to Weissbad by exiting the tourist office, turning left on Hauptg., and follow the signs to Weissbad at the river (about 1hr.). You can take the Appenzellerbahn back (Eurailpass valid). For phenomenal views above the treeline, take the train to Jakobsbad, then a cable car to the top of **Mt. Kronberg** (1663m; round-trip 21SFr, with Eurailpass 14SFr). Follow the trail through remote villages all the way back to Appenzell (about 3hr.).

Tucked inside the **Rathaus** and the adjoining Haus Buherre Hanisefs, the **Museum Appenzell,** Hauptg. 4 (tel. 787 9631), holds a six-floor collection of Swiss crafts, costumes, and culture. Mannequins stand frozen mercilessly in the acts of cheese- and lace-making. (Open Apr.-Oct. daily 10am-noon and 2-5pm; Nov.-Mar. Tu-Su 2-4pm. 5SFr, students 3SFr.) On Wednesday mornings, visit

Herr Fässler, an eager, friendly Swiss farmer and cheesemaker in Grosshütter who loves talking about cheese—for free! Contact the tourist office for details. (Mid-June to mid-Sept.)

■ Schaffhausen

Surrounded by Germany on three sides, Schaffhausen understandably retains a rather Teutonic language and look. *Oriel* (bay) windows, gilded shopkeepers' signs, and fountains fill the pedestrian Marktpl. and *Altstadt*. The U.S. (in dire need of a geography lesson) mistakenly bombed much of Schaffhausen during WWII, but preservation-minded citizens have painstakingly rebuilt each structure in the same fashion as the original.

Schaffhausen's **Munot Fortress,** built in the 1500s to protect the citizens, stands tall and valiant above the city. Since no one ever attacked, the fortress proved rather unnecessary, and the citizens apparently used the time spared from military operations to kick back—the local *Falkenbier* is reputedly the best in the canton, and a mug or two of the frothy ferment will put you in an excellent mood to enjoy the ambience and architecture.

ORIENTATION AND PRACTICAL INFORMATION Schaffhausen is accessible by train, bus, and boat. A **Tageskarte** (26SFr) allows one day of unlimited travel on Bodensee area railways, waterways, and roadways, including those belonging to Schaffhausen, Stein am Rhein, Constance, and St. Gallen. **Trains** arrive every hour from **Zurich** (6:15am-12:45am; 15.80SFr), **St. Gallen** (26SFr), and **Winterthur** (19.20SFr). PTT **buses** connect Schaffhausen to the smaller towns in St. Gallerland (2SFr). Numerous **ferries** traverse the Bodensee, departing from Schaffhausen to **Stein am Rhein** (3 per day, 25SFr) and **Constance** (3 per day, 26SFr). **Parking** is available in the parking garage off of Rheinstr., in the lots near the cathedral, off Moeratz, and behind the train station. The local **tourist office** (tel. 625 51 41; fax 625 51 43) looks out onto the lively Fronwagpl. at the head of Vordenstr., to the right. From the train station, head down Schwertstr., the narrow street to the right, and walk until you reach the main square and fountain. The office has maps, hotel listings, and hiking information, and gives city tours in German, French, or English. (Open Apr.-Sept. M-F 10am-noon and 2-5pm, Sa 10am-noon; Oct.-Mar. M-F 2-5pm. Tours Apr.-Oct. M, W, and F 2:15pm; 1½hr. 10SFr, children 5SFr.) The train station **exchanges currency** (M-Sa 7am-7pm, Su 9am-5pm), **rents bikes** (25SFr per day with photo ID; 6SFr extra to return bike at another station), and **stores luggage** (3SFr; open M-F 6am-7:30pm; Sa-Su 8am-7:30pm). The **postal code** is CH-8200. The **telephone code** is 053.

ACCOMMODATIONS AND FOOD Schaffhausen's **Jugendherberge (HI),** Randenstr. 65 (tel. 625 88 00; fax 624 59 54; email schaffhausen@youthhostel.ch), is in the newer—i.e., early 19th-century—section of town. Take bus #3 or #6 (dir: Hallbaden). Once a villa, the building that now houses the huge hostel is surrounded by shady birch paths and pine-filled glades. Hermann Hesse was frequently a guest of the former villa's owner, and his novel Rosshalde is partially set in the house. (Dorms 21.50SFr 1st night, then 19SFr; singles 27SFr, 24.50SFr; doubles 54SFr, 49SFr. Members only. Breakfast, sheets, and showers included. **Kitchen**-use 2SFr. Reception 7-9am and 5:30-10pm. Check-out 9am. Curfew midnight; keys available.) A public **swimming pool** just down Randenstr. (2 min. to the left) completes the luxury. (Open M-F 8am-9pm, Sa 8am-6pm, Su 9am-5pm. Adults 5SFr, ages 16-18 4SFr, under 16 3SFr.) **Camping Rheinwiesen** (tel. 659 33 00) stands at the edge of the Rhine, 3km from Schaffhausen. Take the bus to "Langswiesen" or the train to Kreuzlingen, then two stops to the office. (6SFr; tents 15SFr. Sept.-June 4SFr; 8SFr.)

The Fronwagpl. comes alive during the day with outdoor cafés, restaurants, and live entertainment ranging from mimes to fire-breathers. **Restaurant Falken,** Vorstadt 5 (tel. 625 32 21; fax 624 92 53; email rtm@bluewin.ch), has been a Schaffhausen landmark for ages. The first brewery (founded in 1799) and oldest restaurant (1899) in Schaffhausen, Falken is still home to many beer-drinking traditions and clubs, and provides an ambitious extravaganza of beer and fine cuisine. Create your own *Rösti* for 8SFr and up. The owner of **Restaurant Tiergarten** (tel. 625 32 38), across from the Allerheiligen Monastery, adds atmospheric spice by serving a different national cuisine each year and decorating to extremes. Past influences include the Caribbean, Greece, Mexico, and Australia. Find out where he's off to next, or dig into one of the seasonal specialties, such as longhorn sheep in winter. Bratwurst and *Rösti* for 14.50SFr are among the permanent Swiss classics. (Open daily 9am-11pm.) If you're not in the mood to sit around, grab some take-out at **Chinatown,** 36 Vorstadt (tel. 624 46 77), a snappy restaurant ideal for those itching to picnic out in the sun. (Dishes 14.50SFr and under. Open daily 11am-3pm.) Schaffhausen's modern **Migros,** Vorstadt 39, puts up a good medieval front, staking a spot in the Gothic alleys that define Schaffhausen. (Open M-W and F 8:15am-6:30pm, Th 8:15am-8pm, Sa 7:30am-4pm.) Consider stocking up on fresh produce at the **farmer's market** at Johannkirche. (Tu and Sa 7am-noon.)

SIGHTS AND ENTERTAINMENT At the corner of Vorstadt and Löwengässchen in the Altstadt, the gilded oriel windows on the medieval **Goldener Ochsen** shine in the sun. Throughout the Altstadt, colorful frescoes and fountains and intricate clocks and carvings transport the casual stroller into an age of knights, heraldry, and Teutonic bravery. On the other side of town, the 16th-century **Munot Fortress** chills and thrills with its stone splendor, cavernous ground floors, dimly lit interiors, and narrow, winding staircases. *(Open daily May-Sept. 8am-8pm; Oct.-Apr. 9am-5pm.)* Medieval skylights cast yellow circles on the cool, dark interior, conjuring visions of townsfolk huddling around fires to the sound of thudding catapults. On the outskirts of the Altstadt, the **Münsterkirche** is an oddly charming combination of medieval architecture and 20th-century furnishings, with its simple wooden pews set against Cubist stained-glass windows. The Reformation stripped the 11th-century church of ornamentation, leaving the interior cool and white. The adjoining monastery, **Kloster Allerheiligen,** is a labyrinth of porticoes and courtyards and houses a music school, museum, and the enormous **Schiller Bell,** inspiration for Schiller's famous poem. The poet, however, never actually saw the bell—his chum Goethe described it to him. The monastery also shelters well-tended herb gardens still used for medicinal purposes (or so they claim). The **Museum zu Allerheiligen** holds the **Natural History Museum** (tel. 633 07 77; fax 633 07 88) and the **Kunstverein Schaffhausen.** *(Open Tu-Su 10am-noon and 2-5pm. Free.)* This huge museum complex houses stuffed boars, modern Schaffhausener art, and antler-bedecked monastic dining halls. The highlight is the onyx, a bedazzling hunk of gold jewels and a priceless cameo styled in the first century CE in Augustan Rome.

■ Near Schaffhausen: Rheinfalls

A short bus ride from the Schaffhausen train station to **Neuhausen** (bus #1 or 9: "Rheinfalls") leads to the **Rheinfalls,** a waterfall so huge that Goethe thought it was the source of the ocean. A path leads along the river's edge, and a bridge offers a closer look at the massive column of water (1SFr). **Rhein Travel,** Schlauchbootfahrten, 8455 Rüdlingen (tel. (01) 867 06 38), has information about **river rafting.** Boats float downstream with guide **Werner Mändli** (tel. 672 48 11), departing approximately every 45 minutes from Schloß Laufen. (June-Aug. 11am-6pm; May-Sept. 11am-5pm; 5.50SFr, children 3SFr.)

The rushing river lulls backpackers to sleep at **Jugendherberge Dachsen (HI)** (tel. 659 61 52; fax 659 60 39). Take the train: "Schloß Laufen am Rheinfall," two stops from Schaffhausen, and then walk up the stairs to the castle and follow the signs for the hostel. Simple rooms recall the castle's 15th-century origins and offer splendid views of the Rhine. The hostel fills up quickly; reserve in advance. (Dorms 22SFr 1st night, then 19.50SFr; triples 72SFr, 64.50SFr; quads 96SFr, 86SFr. Members only.

Breakfast included for dorms. Kitchen facilities 2SFr. Reception 7-10am and 5-9pm.) The **Bannerstube** (tel. 659 67 67) in the castle serves a number of reasonably priced dishes, including delectable salads and the acclaimed *Fürtopf à discretion* (Fondue Chinoise), and has a fantastic view of the falls. Also unique to the Schloß Laufen "restaurants am Rheinfall" are special menus to honor Mother's Day, Easter, National Day, and other happy holidays. (Soups 6-8SFr. Pasta from 14SFr. Children's menu available. Open daily Mar.-Dec. 11:30am-2pm and 6:30-9:30pm.)

■ Stein am Rhein

Stein am Rhein is a Swiss hamlet steeped in tradition and stuffed with oddities ranging from the stately *Rathaus* to the meticulously crafted recreations of past life at the Museum Lindwurm. A port of call for the brightly colored ferries that cruise the lake, Stein am Rhein has nimbly converted its vantage point on the Rhine into an unobtrusive tourist industry. Cobblestone streets, old fountains, and intricate medieval façades render the town old-fashionedly picturesque, attracting the nature-lover as well as the *Kultur*-o-phile.

ORIENTATION AND PRACTICAL INFORMATION Trains connect Stein am Rhein to **Schaffhausen** (6.60SFr), **St. Gallen** (23SFr), **Winterthur** (11.40SFr), and **Constance** (9SFr). **Buses** connect the city to the string of small towns in the area and to Germany. **Boats** depart three times each day (once on Sunday) for **Schaffhausen** (1¼hr., 13.80SFr), **Constance** (2½hr., 16.60SFr), and other Bodensee towns. **Parking** is available along Hemihoferstr., off Untertor (lot open 10am-6pm). The Altstadt lies down Bahnhofstr. and across the bridge from the train station. Stein am Rhein's **tourist office**, Oberstr. 9 (tel. 741 28 35; fax 741 51 46), lies on the other side of the Rathaus. The staff can recommend hotels, provide maps, and give cruise information. (Open M-F 9-11am and 2-5pm.) The train station has **currency exchange** and **bike rental** (25SFr a day, half-day 19SFr; open M-F 6:15am-7:35pm, Sa 6:15am-6:35pm, Su 7:15am-7:35pm). The **post office** is at the train station. (Open M-F 7:30am-noon and 2-8pm, Sa 8-11am.) The **postal code** is CH-8260. The **telephone code** is 052.

ACCOMMODATIONS AND FOOD The suburban **Jugendherberge (HI)** stands at Hemihoferstr. 87 (tel. 741 12 55; fax 741 51 40). From the train station, take the bus: "Singen" to Standbad, cross the street, and walk along the gravel path to the end. You'll see the flags in front of the hostel across the street. A friendly, English-speaking staff maintains this clean and colorful hostel. Many rooms have a view of the Rhine (aka Rhein). (Dorms 21.50SFr 1st night, then 19SFr; doubles 27SFr, 24.50SFr. Non-members add 5SFr. Breakfast, sheets, and showers included. Reception 7:30-9am and 5:30-10pm. Curfew 10:30pm; keys available. Open Mar.-Oct.) Picnickers fill up their baskets at the **Co-op** at the corner of Rathauspl. and Schwarzhorng. (Open M-F 8:15am-12:15pm and 2-6:30pm, Sa 7:30am-4pm.) Rathausplatz's many outdoor restaurants and cafés provide great people-watching venues. **The Spaghetteria,** Schifflände (tel. 741 22 36), sits directly on the Rhine and serves cheap but tasty Italian fare, with pasta dishes from 11SFr and beers at 4.20SFr for 0.5L. The restaurant houses the **world's longest piece of spaghetti** at 188.8m. (Open Mar. 15-Oct. daily 9am-midnight. Free beer with lunch if you show your Let's Go.) **Restaurant Roten Ochsen**, Rathauspl. 9 (tel. 741 23 28), cooks up Swiss dishes (9-29SFr) and tosses a mean salad (11-17SFr) beneath a grapevine ceiling fresco. (Open Tu-Th and Su 9:30am-11:30pm, F-Sa 9:30am-12:30am.) The many inviting Café-Konditerei that pave the Steiner streets are designed to tempt purse and palate. **Café "Zur Hoffnung"** is chock full of Steiner Scherben. (Open Tu-Sa 8am-6pm, Su 9am-6pm.)

SIGHTS AND ENTERTAINMENT Stein am Rhein first came into prominence in the 12th century with the establishment of the **Kloster St. George** (tel. 741 21 24), a Benedictine monastery. *(Open Mar.-Oct. Tu-Su 10am-5pm. 3SFr, students 1.50SFr.)* Perhaps the best preserved in the German-speaking world, the monks' rooms have remained unaltered since the 16th-century. To the right of the monastery, the stately

Rathaus surveys Stein am Rhein's main thoroughfare. The third floor holds a to-die-for collection of high fashion his-and-her armor, Roman coins from 112 BCE, and magnificent stained-glass windows presented to the town in friendship by neighboring cantons. Call for a viewing (tel. 741 54 25). On Untertor, the **Wohnmuseum Lindwurm,** Understadt 18 (tel. 741 25 12; fax 741 45 82), reconstructs domestic life as it was in the 19th century. Despite the scary stuffed cat and St. Bernard dog run, this painstakingly crafted museum welcomes visitors with authentic period kitchens, nurseries, and barns with live chickens. For some gorgeously lazy river-gazing, chug along the banks of the Rhine on the **Lilliput-Bahn** (tel. 741 37 39) on Schifflände, just past the Spaghetteria. *(Open daily July-Aug. 1:15-5pm; Sept.-June Sa 1:15-5pm, Su 10:30am-5pm. 4 SFr; children 2.50SFr.)*

The town's most dramatic event is the open-air play **"No e Wili,"** performed irregularly between June 11th and August 15th (call ahead for exact dates). It's a tale of power, greed, and betrayal acted entirely by amateurs. (Contact Museum Lindwurm or call 183 within the town for information. Tickets 20SFr-35SFr; children half price.)

Liechtenstein

Liechtenstein's minute size (160 sq. km, about the same as Manhattan) and population (31,000 people) render it a fave among sadistic geography teachers. Famous chiefly for its wines, royal family, and postage stamps, the principality itself is more of a tourist attraction than any individual sight it contains. Brochures entreat visitors to "go *to* Liechtenstein, not through it," but most travelers pause only long enough to buy the official *"Hurra! Ich bin da"* (hurray, I'm here!) postage stamp or hastily record the visit in a passport.

The only German-speaking monarchy in the world, Liechtenstein is one of the last vestiges of the Holy Roman Empire. It has been an independent country since 1719. Its last standing army was an 80-man force that patrolled the Italian border without firing a shot. That was 1868. German is the official language, but the inhabitants also speak an Alemannic dialect, English, and French. The flatter areas of this green kingdom provide great **biking,** and an efficient and cheap **postal bus** system links all 11 villages (short trips 2.40SFr; Swisspass valid). A one-week bus ticket (10SFr, students 5SFr) covers all (and we mean *all*) of Liechtenstein and includes buses to Swiss and Austrian border towns. If you plan to stay more than three days (a sojourn that may tax the imagination), it's a great buy. To enter the principality, catch a postal bus from **Sargans** or **Buchs** in Switzerland or **Feldkirch** in Austria (3.60SFr). For the **police,** call 117. In a **fire,** call 118. In a **medical emergency,** dial 144. The principality has used the Swiss franc as its currency since 1924 and has adopted the Swiss postal and telephone systems. The **postal code** is FL-9490, and the **telephone code** is 075. Liechtenstein uses the Swiss **country code** (041) and **international dialing prefix** (00).

■ Vaduz

The hamlet of Vaduz is Liechtenstein's capital and tourist center. It's not a budget-friendly place. Tour buses deposit loads directly in front of the dozens of souvenir shops on the main streets under the swollen eyes of restauranteurs and their greedy bellies bulging from inflated menu prices. Liechtenstein's **national tourist office,** Städtle 37 (tel. 392 11 11 or 232 14 43; fax 392 16 18; email touristinfo@lie-net.li), one block up the hill from the Vaduz postal bus stop, will stamp your passport with Liechtenstein's bi-colored seal (2SFr). It also locates rooms free of charge, makes hotel reservations (2SFr), and distributes free maps and advice on hiking, cycling, and skiing in the area. (Open June-Oct. M-F 8am-noon and 1:30-5:30pm, Sa 9am-noon and 1-4pm, Su 10am-noon and 1-4pm; Nov.-May M-F 8am-noon and 1:30-5:30pm. English spoken.) If the tourist office is closed

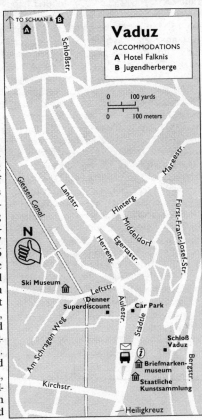

Vaduz

ACCOMMODATIONS
A Hotel Falknis
B Jugendherberge

and you are in desperate need of a passport stamp, head to the postage museum across the street. For **currency exchange** at acceptable rates, go to Switzerland. No kidding. **Bicyclists** can rent trusty steeds (20SFr per day) at **Mellinger AG,** Kirchstr. 10 (tel. 232 16 06) or at **Rad-Zenterttermann,** Feldkirchstr. 74 (tel. 233 35 36). It helps to call ahead. The tourist office sells bike maps for 2.50SFr. **Swimmers** bathe at **Mühlehölz,** Schaanerstr. 60, just down the street from the youth hostel. The complex boasts two high dives and a wading pool. Walk down the hostel's driveway and then continue straight ahead on the path directly opposite. (Open June-Aug. 9am-8pm. 4.50SFr, children 2SFr. Lock deposit 10SFr.) The main **post office** (tel. 232 21 55) is near the tourist office and has an amazing selection of...postage stamps. (Open M-F 7:45am-6pm, Sa 8-11am.)

Liechtenstein's lone **Jugendherberge (HI),** Untere Rütig. 6 (tel. 232 50 22; fax 232 58 56), is in **Schaan,** one town over from Vaduz. From the Vaduz bus stand, take the bus (dir: Schaan): "Mühleholz" walk toward the intersection with the traffic lights, and turn down Marianumstr. Walk four to five minutes and follow the signs to this spotless pink hostel, set on the edge of a farm. An arcade junkie's paradise, with foosball, pinball, air hockey, video games, and ping-pong tables. (Dorms 26.30SFr; doubles 64.60SFr; family quads 113.20SFr. Showers and breakfast included. Dinner 12SFr. Leave your bags in the basement lockers for a 2SFr deposit anytime. **Laundry** 8SFr. Members only. Reception M-Sa 7-9:30am and 5-10pm, Su 7-9:30am and 6-10pm. Lockout 9:30am-5pm. Curfew 10pm. Open Mar.-Nov. 15.) Walk 10 minutes back up the road toward Vaduz or take the bus (dir: Schaan): "Falknis" to reach **Hotel Falknis,** Landstr. 92 (tel. 232 63 77), another happy budget option. (Singles 50SFr; doubles 100SFr. Breakfast and showers included. Reception 7:30am-10pm. Closed Dec. 24-Jan. 15.) Eating out cheaply in Liechtenstein is extremely hard. Groceries are available at **Denner Superdiscount,** Aulestr. 20, across from the tour bus parking lot. (Open M-F 8:30am-1pm and 1:30-6:30pm, Sa 8am-4pm.) In the same shopping complex, **Azzuro Pizza** (tel. 232 48 18) has (surprise) pizzas (6-12.50SFr) and kebabs (8SFr) for take-out. (Open M-F 8am-8pm, Sa 8am-5pm, Su 10am-5pm.)

Above the town sits the 12th-century **Schloß Vaduz,** regal home to Hans-Adam II, Prince of Liechtenstein. Although the interior of the ruler's residence is off-limits to the bourgeois masses, you can hike up to the castle for a closer look and a phenomenal view of the whole country. (The numerous "Castle this way: No visit" signs, seemingly designed to tease tourists, are only meant to stop the commoners from knocking on the royal front door and inviting themselves inside. Only rich politicians, students with very good university final exams, and retirees, are asked to visit the Prince...usually on New Year's Day.) Along with *Seine Durchlaucht* (His Highness), the castle allegedly houses an excellent art collection, primarily Dutch and Flemish, gathered by the royal family over the last 400 years. Much of the art makes its way to the **Staatliche Kunstsammlung,** Städtle 37, next to the tourist office. (Open daily Apr.-Oct. 10am-noon and 1:30-5:30pm; Nov.-Mar. 10am-noon and 1:30-5pm. 5SFr, students 3SFr, children 2.50SFr.) Reproductions of the Prince's art almost inevitably end up on postage stamps and thus in the one-room **Briefmarkenmuseum** (Stamp Museum) on the other side of the tourist office. (Open daily Apr.-Oct. 10am-noon and 1:30-5:30pm; Nov.-Mar. 10am-noon and 1:30-5pm. Free.) Nearly one-fourth of the country's income comes from its stamps. It is also a major manufacturer of false teeth and dental appliances. Groups of 10 or more can arrange to visit the **Hofkellerei des Regierenden Fürsten von Liechtenstein** (Wine Cellars of the Ruling Prince of Liechtenstein) and taste wines from the Prince's private vineyards. For the necessary reservations, call 232 10 18 or fax 233 11 45. (20SFr per person.) Smaller groups (up to 3) can try knocking on the door of the wine cellars. If the cellar has an open bottle, they'll often let you try some.

■ Upper Liechtenstein

It seems impossible that a country so small could have regions, but the cluster of villages in the upper country do have a character of their own. The "upper" in Upper Liechtenstein does not refer to a northern position but to the elevation. High above the sleepy town of Vaduz, one is surrounded by clouds, cows, and gorgeous views of the **Rhine Valley.** Buses run to all these towns from Vaduz in under 40 minutes, and the trips are well worth the price even if you're only spending one day in the country.

The Walsers, a group of Swiss immigrants forced to flee Valais due to overpopulation, religious intolerance, and natural disaster, founded **Triesenberg,** the principal town, in the 13th century. The **Walser Heimatmuseum** chronicles the Walsers' religious customs, hut construction, cattle trade, and crafts. The ground floor houses wooden sculptures by folk artist Rudolf Schädler, as well as traditional local noodle-shaped candles. (Open Tu-F 1:30-5:30pm, Sa 1:30-5pm, Su 2-5pm; Sept.-May closed Su. 2SFr, children 1SFr.) The **tourist office** (tel. 262 19 26; fax 262 19 22) is in the same building as the museum and has the same hours. **Pension Alpenblick,** Neudorf 383 (tel. 262 35 77), offers beds in spacious rooms 10 minutes (downhill) from the tourist office. Walk down the main road, take the second right, follow the street as it loops back. (Singles 40SFr; doubles 70SFr; triples 105SFr. After 3 nights: 35SFr, 60SFr, 90SFr. Breakfast included. Shower 3SFr. Check-in 11am-10pm.) Liechtenstein's two **campgrounds,** peaceful almost to a fault, are easily accessible by postal bus. **Camping Bendern** (tel. 373 12 11) is on the #50/51 bus line (dir: Schellenberg): "Bendern" and walk past the village church. (6SFr; tents 3-5SFr; showers 1SFr.) **Camping Mittag-spitze** (tel. 392 26 86) is between Triesen and Balzers on the road to Sargans. Gorgeous sites at the mountain's foot rest near a cold Alpine brook. (Reception 8am-noon and 2-10pm. 8.50SF; tent 5SFr. Shower and pool included. Open year-round.)

On the other side of the mountain, **Malbun,** dubbed "the undiscovered St. Moritz," offers secluded and affordable ski slopes and has served as a training ground for many an Olympian. Two chairlifts, four T-bars, and two ski schools, service you and not too many other people. (Daypass 33SFr; 6-day pass 136SFr, off-season 129SFr.) **Malbun A.G.** (tel. 263 97 70 or 262 19 15) offers one-day classes (50SFr), three-day classes (120SFr), and even private snowboard lessons (1 day 200SFr). The **Fun Factory** (tel./fax 263 26 36) across the street rents snowboards. The Valüna valley, 2km from Malbun, offers four-track, lit cross-country trails. The superb chalet duo of **Hotel Alpen** and **Hotel Galina** (tel. 263 11 81; fax 263 96 46) provides the best accommodation options in Malbun. Family-run, with wood paneling and a heated swimming pool, these hotels are perfect for *après*-ski unwinding. (Reception in Hotel Alpen for both. Singles 40-65SFr, with shower 70-100SFr; doubles 80-130SFr, 140-200SFr. Breakfast and pool included. Open mid-May to Oct. and Dec. 15-Apr. 15.) Malbun's got a **tourist office** (tel. 263 65 77). (Open May-Oct. and Dec.-Apr. M-F 9am-noon and 1:30-5pm, Sa 9am-noon and 1-4pm.)

As two-thirds of the country is undeveloped mountains, **hiking** in Upper Liechtenstein is damn nice. The upper country has 150km of trails, clearly marked with yellow *Wanderweg* signs. The tourist offices in Vaduz, Triesenberg, and Malbun offer a free booklet of short hike suggestions; detailed maps cost 15.50SFr at any bookstore or the tourist offices. The top pick is the round-trip hike from Gnalp to Masescha (roughly 3hr.). Others include the **Pfälzer-Hütte** (2108m, 4-5hr. through Augustenberg to Bettlerjoecht), **Schönberg** (2104m, 4-5hr.), and **Galinakopf** (2198m, 6-7hr.). **Alpine guides** offer group and individual climbing courses in Liechtenstein as well as in neighboring Austria and Switzerland. Contact Michael Bargetze, pat. Bergführer, Lavidina 755, FL-9497 Triesenberg (tel. 268 10 05). A guided tour isn't always necessary; easier hikes start from the Triesenberg church (postal bus: "Philosophenweg") and run from **Masescha** and back (2-3hr.) or the *Waldlehrpfad* through Vitapancour from Triesenberg (1hr.). The **Liechtenstein Alpine Association** offers free guided

---

A Mooving Tail

Every year in an early October, hundreds of Liechtensteinians await the migration of the cows (the **Alpabfahrt**) from the higher, grassier Alpine meadows back into the valley's villages. The fattest and best-looking are displayed at the **Prämiermarkt** where the "best cow of the season" is adorned with ribbons, bells, flowers and a one-legged **Mälchschdual** or milking stool. A 19th-century legend tells the story of **Ludmila,** a skinny, sickly beast destined for the butcher's chop. The cow prayed mutely to the eponymous Ludmila, **patroness of the ruminants,** for aid. Her pleas were answered when, wandering alone one day across grassy alpine slopes, she happened upon **Alchemilla** or **Mutterkraut,** a grass whose magical powers enabled the cow to give forth foaming, frothy milk. Ludmila ate so much that she didn't stop giving milk for days. On her **Alpabfahrt,** the cow was beribboned and made belle of the valley. Sadly, she died soon after reaching the lowlands in triumph. Ludmila's legend was memorialized in Lichtensteinian hearts when it was filmed by the local Baroness von Falz Fein after she had a love affair with the man (Paul Gallico) who transcribed the oral legend of Ludmila, and became captivated by the story.

---

full- and half-day hikes every Thursday in summer. The Saturday newspaper publishes routes and contact numbers, and the tourist office also has information. If hiking seems too pedestrian, try **paragliding** with **Hang Loose AG Fly and Fun World,** Grabenweg 10, Vaduz (tel. 230 07 07; fax 230 07 06; 150SFr for a passenger flight).

Gateway Cities

■ Prague (Praha)

According to legend, Princess Libuše stood on Vyšehrad above the Vltava and declared, "I see a city whose glory will touch the stars; it shall be called Praha (threshold)." Medieval kings, benefactors, and architects fulfilled the prophecy, building soaring cathedrals and lavish palaces that gave notice of Prague's status as the capital of the Holy Roman Empire. But the city's character differed sharply from the holy splendor of Rome and Constantinople: legends of demons, occult forces, and mazes of shady alleys lent this "city of dreams" a dark side that inspired Franz Kafka's tales of paranoia. Only in this century has the spell been broken, as the fall of the Iron Curtain brought hordes of Euro-trotting foreigners to the once-isolated capital. Tourists and entrepreneurs have long since explored and exploited every nook and cranny of the city. On the other hand, these same visitors give Prague a festive air that few places in the world can match.

ORIENTATION AND PRACTICAL INFORMATION

Sprawling over a bend in the Vltava, Prague is a gigantic mess of suburbs and curvy streets. **Staré Město** (Old Town) sits on the southernmost bend of the river; across the Vltava sits the **Hradčany** castle with **Malá Strana** at its south base. Southeast of the Old Town spreads **Nové Město** (New Town), and farther east across **Wilsonova** lie the **Žižkov** and **Vinohrady** districts. **Holešovice** in the north has an international train terminal; **Smíchov,** the southwest end, is the student-dorm suburb. All train and bus terminals are on or near the Metro system. **Metro B: "nám. Republiky"** is the closest stop to the principal tourist offices and accommodations agencies. *Tabak* stands and bookstores vend indexed *plán města* (maps). The English-language weekly *The Prague Post* provides news and tips for visitors.

> Prague is in the process of reforming its telephone system. Businesses often receive no more than three weeks' notice before their numbers change. The eight-digit numbers in these listings are least likely to be obsolete by the time you read this—but then again, nothing is certain.

Transportation Services

Flights: Ruzyně Airport (tel. 20 11 11 11), 20km northwest of city center. Bus #119 from Dejvická or the **airport bus** (tel. 20 11 42 96) from nám. Republicky (90kč) or Dejvická (60kč). Taxis to the airport are exorbitant. Many major carriers fly into Prague, including **ČSA** (Czech National Airlines; tel. 20 10 43 10).

Trains: info tel. 24 22 42 00, international fares tel. 24 61 52 49. Prague has 4 terminals. **Praha Hlavní Nádraží** (tel. 24 61 72 50; Metro C: "Hlavní Nádraží") is the biggest, but most international trains run out of **Holešovice** (tel. 24 61 72 65; Metro C: "Nádraží Holešovice"). To: **Vienna** (5hr., 4 per day, 735kč, Wasteels 521kč); **Berlin** (5hr., 5 per day, 1574kč, Wasteels 1346kč); **Budapest** (8hr., 6 per day, 1279kč, Wasteels 1040kč); **Bratislava** (5hr., 9 per day, 426kč); and **Warsaw** (10hr., 3 per day, 937kč, Wasteels 651kč). Domestic trains go from **Masarykovo** (tel. 24 61 72 60; Metro B: "nám. Republiky") on the corner of Hybernská and Havličkova, or from **Smíchov** (tel. 24 61 72 55; Metro B: "Smíchovské Nádraží"), opposite Vyšehrad. **B.I.J. Wasteels** (tel. 24 61 74 54; fax 24 22 18 72), at Hlavní Nádraží, on the 2nd floor, to the right of the stairs, sells cheap international tickets to those under 26 and books couchettes. Open in summer M-F 7:30am-8pm, Sa 8-11:30am and 12:30-3pm; winter M-F 8:30am-6pm. Wasteels tickets also available at **Czech Railways Travel Agency** (tel. 80 08 05; fax 80 69 48) at Holešovice. Open daily 7-11:25am, noon-5:40pm, 6:20-9:45pm, 10:35pm-2am, and 3:15-6:35am.

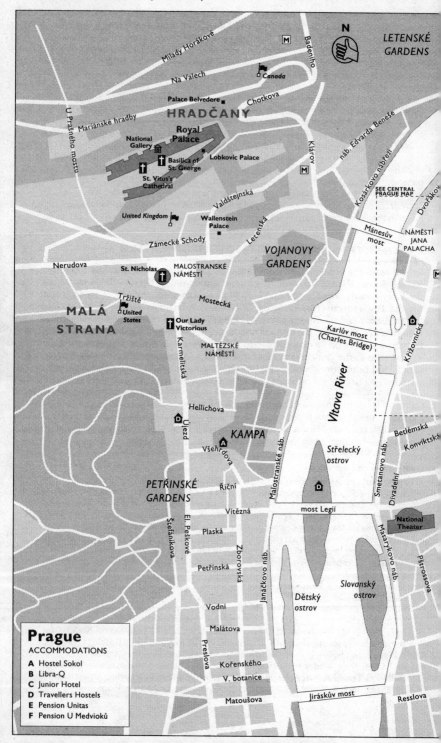

Prague
ACCOMMODATIONS

A Hostel Sokol
B Libra-Q
C Junior Hotel
D Travellers Hostels
E Pension Unitas
F Pension U Medvíků

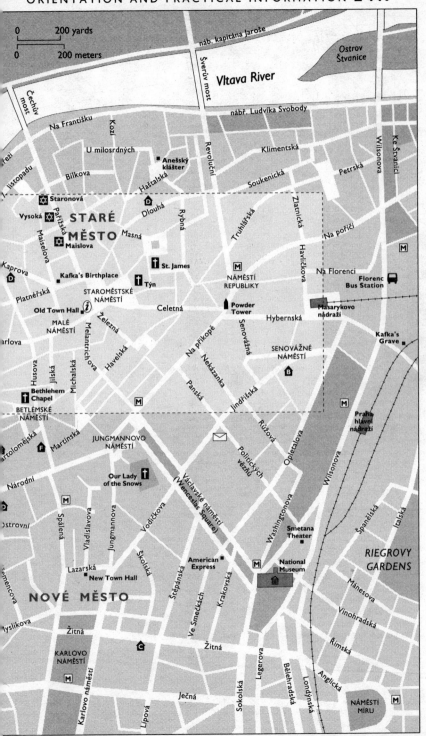

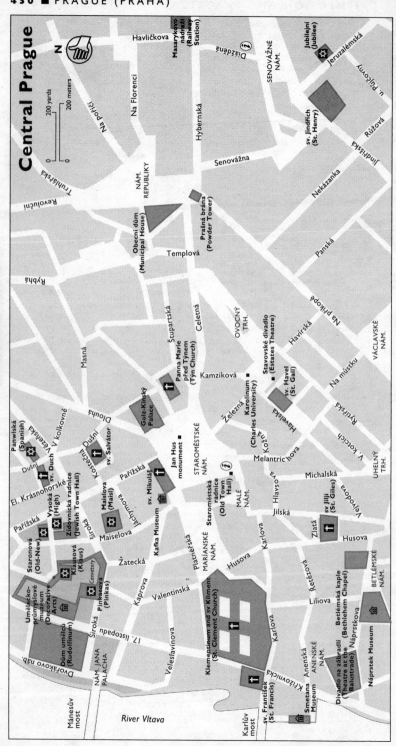

Central Prague

N

200 yards

200 meters

Havlíčkova

Masarykovo nádraží (Railway Station)

Jubilejní (Jubilee)

Jeruzalémská

Dlážděná

SENOVÁŽNÉ NÁM.

Na Florenci

Hybernská

u. Pujčovny

Na Poříčí

sv. Jindřich (St. Henry)

Růžová

Jindřišská

Senovážná

Revoluční

Truhlářská

NÁM. REPUBLIKY

Nekázanka

Panská

Obecní dům (Municipal House)

Prašná brána (Powder Tower)

Templová

Rybná

Celetná

Masná

Štupartská

OVOCNÝ TRH.

Na příkopě

VÁCLAVSKÉ NÁM.

Havířská

Panna Marie před Týnem (Týn Church)

Stavovské divadlo (Estates Theatre)

Dlouhá

Kamzíková

sv. Havel (St. Gall)

Na můstku

Golz-Kinský Palace

Železná

Karolinum (Charles University)

Havelská

Panvská (Spanish)

Vězeňská

V kolkovně

Kožná

Rytířská

UHELNÝ TRH.

sv. Duch

sv. Salvátor

Melantrichova

Jan Hus monument

STAROMĚSTSKÉ NÁM.

Michalská

V. koželích

Dušní

Kostečná

Maislova (Maisel)

Pařížská

sv. Mikuláš

Hlavso

Jilská

sv. Jiljí (St. Giles)

El. Krásnohorské

Vysoká (High)

Staroměstská radnice (Old Town Hall)

Karlova

Zlatá

Husova

Pařížská

Židovnická radnice (Jewish Town Hall)

Jáchymova

Kafka Museum

MALÉ NÁM.

Vlašská

BETLÉMSKÉ NÁM.

Staronová (Old-New)

Šíroká

Maiselova

Platnéřská

MARIÁNSKÉ NÁM.

Husova

Liliova

Klausová (Klaus)

Žatecká

Řetězová

Betlémská kaple (Bethlehem Chapel)

Umělecko-průmyslové muzeum (Decorative Arts)

Cemetery

Pinkasová (Pinkas)

Kaprova

Valentinská

Husova

Karlova

Náprstek Museum

Dům umělců (Rudolfinum)

Šíroká

17. listopadu

Klementinum and sv. Klimenti (St. Clement Church)

Anenská ANENSKÉ NÁM.

NÁM. JANA PALACHA

Dvořákovo náb.

Veleslavínova

Křížovnická

Divadlo na zábradlí (Theatre at the Balustrade)

Mánesův most

sv. František (St. Francis)

Smetana Museum

Karlův most

Náprstkova

River Vltava

Buses: **ČSAD** has several *autobusové nádraží* (bus stations). The biggest is **Florenc,** Křižíkova 4 (tel. 24 21 49 90; info 24 21 10 60; Metro B or C: "Florenc"). Staff speaks little English, and the tricky timetables require some study (symbol meanings aren't posted in English). Look for the bus stop number of your destination. Get tickets in advance. To: **Vienna** (8½hr., 6 per week, 400kč) and **Berlin** (6hr., 1 per day, 820kč). 10% discount for students. The **Tourbus** office upstairs (tel. 24 21 02 21) has Eurolines and airport bus tickets. Open M-F 8am-8pm, Sa-Su 9am-8pm.

Ferries: **PPS,** Rašínovo Nábřeží (tel. 29 38 03; fax 24 91 38 62), between the Jiráskův and Palackého bridges. Various river trips daily; 2hr. Vltava cruise 200kč.

Taxis: Cab drivers are sketch; before getting in, check that the meter is set to zero, and ask the driver to start it by saying *"Zapněte taximetr."* For longer trips, agree on a price before starting. Always ask for a receipt *("Prosím, dejte mi paragon")* with distance traveled, price paid, and the driver's signature. If the driver doesn't write the receipt or reset the meter, you aren't obligated to pay. Prague has instituted set rates: 17kč per km with a 25kč flat rate for getting into the taxi. You're likelier to get ripped off if you hail a taxi on the street, so stick to public transport or call. **Taxi Praha** (tel. 24 91 66 66) and **AAA** (tel. 24 32 24 32) run 24hr.

Hitchhiking: Hitching in the area has become increasingly dangerous and isn't recommended. Those going east take tram #1, 9, or 16 to the last stop. To points **south,** they walk from Metro C: "Pražskeho povstání" to 5. května (highway D1). To the **north,** they take a bus to "Kobyliské nám.," then bus #175 up Horňátecká. To **Munich,** hitchers take tram# 4 or 9 to Plzeňská at Kukulova/Bucharova.

Public Transportation: The **metro, tram,** and **bus** services are pretty good and share the same ticket system. Buy tickets from newsstands, *tabák,* machines in stations, or **DP** (*Dopravní Podnik;* transport authority) kiosks. Punch tickets upon 1st use. A 12kč ticket is valid for 1hr. anywhere in the city with unlimited bus, tram, and metro connections, as long as you keep heading in the same direction. An 8kč ticket is good for 30min. or 4 stops on the metro. Large bags are 6kč each, as are bikes and prams without babies in them (*with* babies free, so don't forget the baby). If a plainclothes DP inspector issues you a 200kč spot fine, make sure you see a badge and get a receipt. **Night trams** #51-58 and **buses** run all night after the metro quits; look for dark blue signs at bus stops. **DP offices** by the Jungmannovo nám. exit of Můstek station (tel. 24 22 51 35; open daily 7am-9pm) or by the Palackého nám. exit of Karlovo nám. station (tel. 29 46 82; open M-F 7am-6pm) sell **tourist passes** (24hr. 50kč, 3 days 130kč, 1 week 190kč).

Tourist and Financial Services

Tourist Offices: An "i" sign indicates a tourist agency that books rooms, arranges tours, and sells maps and guidebooks. Be wary: these private firms didn't appear in a burst of benevolence. **Prague Information Service** (*Pražská Informační Služba),* Staromwstske nám. 1 (tel. 24 48 25 62, English information tel. 54 44 44), happily sells maps (40-49kč), arranges tours, and books musical extravaganzas. Open M-F 9am-7pm, Sa-Su 9am-6pm. **Čedok,** Na příkopě 18 (tel. 24 19 71 11), has a formidable institutional memory from 40 years of socialist monopoly but isn't yet fully user-friendly. Open M-F 8:30am-6pm, Sa 9am-1pm.

Budget Travel: CKM, Jindřišská 28 (tel. 24 23 02 18; fax 26 86 23; email ckmprg@mbox.vol.cz). Metro A or B: "Můstek." Sells budget air tickets for students and those under 26 and the discount cards to qualify for them (ISIC, GO25, and Euro26 180kč). Also books rooms in Prague (from 350kč). Open M-Sa 9:30am-1pm, M-Th also 1:30-6pm, F also 1:30-4pm.

Passport Office: Foreigner police, Olšanská 2 (tel. 683 17 39). Metro A: Flora. Turn right onto Jičínská so that the cemetery is on your right, and turn right onto Olšanská, or take tram #9 (dir: Spojavací): "Olšanská." Visa extensions involve a 90kč stamp and up to a 2hr. wait. Little English spoken. Open M-Tu and Th 7:30-11:45am and 12:30-2:30pm, W 7:30-11:30am and 12:30-5pm, F 7:30am-noon.

Embassies: Travelers from **Australia** and **New Zealand** have honorary consuls (tel. 24 31 00 71 and 25 41 98, respectively) but should contact the British embassy in an emergency. **Canada,** Mickiewiczova 6 (tel. 24 31 11 08). Metro A: "Hradčanská." Open M-F 8am-noon and 2-4pm. **Hungary,** Badeního 1 (tel. 36 50 41). Metro A: "Hradčanská." Open M-W and F 9am-noon. **Ireland,** Tržiště 13 (tel. 53

09 02). Metro A: "Malostranská". Open M-F 9:30am-12:30pm and 2:30-4:30pm. **Poland,** Valdštejnská 8 (tel. 57 32 06 78). Metro A: "Malostranská." Open M-F 7am-noon. **Russia,** Pod Kaštany 1 (tel. 38 19 45). Metro A: "Hradčanská." Open M, W, and F 9am-1pm. **Slovakia,** Pod Hradbani 1 (tel. 32 05 21). Metro A: "Dejvická." Open M-F 8:30am-noon. **South Africa,** Ruská 65 (tel. 67 31 11 14). Metro A: "Flora." Open M-F 9am-noon. **U.K.,** Thunovská 14 (tel. 57 32 03 55). Metro A: "Malostranská." Open M-F 9am-noon. **U.S.,** Tržiště 15 (tel. 57 32 06 63, emergency after hours tel. 53 12 00). Metro A: "Malostranská." From Malostranské nám., head down Karmelitská and right on Tržiště. Open M-F 8am-1pm and 2-4:30pm.

Currency Exchange: The best rates are for AmEx and Thomas Cook traveler's checks, cashed commission-free at the appropriate office. Exchange counters are everywhere, and rates vary wildly. **Chequepoints** mushroom around the city center, and may be the only places open when you need to change cash, but they can take off a 10% commission. **Komerční Banka,** Na příkopě 33, buys notes and checks for 2% commission. Open M-F 8am-5pm. **ATMs** are all over the place.

American Express: Václavské nám. 56 (tel. 22 80 02 51; fax 22 21 11 31). Metro A or C: "Muzeum." Mail held. MC and Visa cash advances (3% commission). **ATM.** Open July-Sept. M-F 9am-6pm, Sa 9am-2pm; Oct.-Apr. M-F 9am-5pm, Sa 9am-noon. Another office near the Karlův most at Mostecká 12. Open daily 9:30am-7:30pm.

Local Services

Luggage Storage: Lockers in all **train and bus stations** take 2 5kč coins. If these are full, or if you need to store your pack for longer than 24hr., use the left luggage offices in the basement of **Hlavní nádraží** (15kč per day for 1st 15kg) and halfway up the stairs at **Florenc** (10kč per day up to 15kg; open daily 5am-11pm). Watch your bags as you set your locker code.

English-Language Bookstore: The Globe Bookstore, Janovského 14 (tel. 66 71 26 10). Metro C: "Vltavská." Many used books, a big noticeboard, and a coffeehouse. A legendary (pick-up) center of Anglophone Prague. Open daily 10am-midnight.

Gay Information: SOHO (tel. 24 22 03 27), the Association of Organizations of Homosexual Citizens in the Czech Republic.

Laundromat: Laundry Kings, Dejvická 16 (tel. 312 37 43), 1 block from Metro A: "Hradčanská." Cross the tram *and* railroad tracks then turn left onto Dejvická. Wash 60kč. Dry 15kč per 8min. Soap 10-20kč. Beer 11kč (ah, Prague). Dirty backpackers come here to spin-wash their duds and pick each other up. Bulletin board for apartment seeking, English teaching, and friend locating. Open M-F 6am-10pm, Sa-Su 8am-10pm.

24-Hour Pharmacies: At Konĕvova 210 (tel. 644 18 95) and Štefánikova 6 (tel. 24 51 11 12). You may have to ask for behind-the-counter items like: *kontrcepční prostředky* **(contraceptives),** *náplast* **(bandages),** or *dámské vložky* **(tampons).**

Emergency and Communications

Emergencies: Na Homolce (hospital for foreigners), Roentgenova 2 (tel. 52 92 21 46, after hours tel. 57 21 11 11). Open M-F 8am-4pm. **American Medical Center** (tel. 80 77 56). **Canadian Medical Centre** (tel. 316 55 19).

Internet Access: Terminal Bar, Soukenická 6 (tel. 21 87 11 15; http://www.terminal.cz). Metro B: "nám. Republiký." A multimedia cafe with style. 100kč per hr., half-price for members. Only 8 computers; be prepared to wait. Open daily noon-1am. **Internet Cafe,** Národní třída 25 (tel. 21 08 52 84; email internetcafe@highland.cz; http://www.internetcafe.cz). Metro B: "Národní třída." 11 PCs (2kč per min.) and virtually no wait. Open M-F 9am-10pm, Sa-Su 2-10pm.

Telephones: Everywhere, especially at the post office. Phone cards are 150kč for 50 units at kiosks, the post office, and some exchange places: don't get ripped off.

Post Office: Main office, Jindřišská 14, 110 00 Praha 1. Metro A or B: "Můstek." *Poste Restante* at window 17. For stamps, window 16; letters and parcels under 2kg, windows 12-14. Open daily 7am-8pm. Parcels over 2kg can be mailed only at **Celní stanice** (customs office), Plzeňská 139. Tram #4, 7, or 9 from Metro B: "Anděl" to "Klamovka." Open M-F 7am-3pm, W 'til 6pm. **Postal Code:** 110 00.

Telephone Code: 02.

ACCOMMODATIONS AND CAMPING

While hotel prices rise, the hostel market is glutted. Prices have stabilized around 250-350kč per night. The smaller hostels are homey but often full. The Strahov complex and other student dorms bear the brunt of the summer's backpacking crowds. A few bare-bones hotels are still cheap, and a growing numbers of residents are renting rooms. Sleeping on Prague's streets is too dangerous to consider. Don't do it.

Hostels

In the Strahov neighborhood west of the river next to the Olympic stadium, an enormous cluster of dorms/hostels opens up in June-August. These rooms may be the best bet for those arriving in the middle of the night without a reservation, but many prefer the smaller, more personable hostels. Unfortunately, too many no-shows have forced many places to refuse reservations. To snag a bed, call the night before you arrive or around check-out at 10am. Staffs generally speak good English.

◉Penzion v podzámčí, V podzámčí 27 (tel. 472 27 59). From Metro C: Budějovická, take bus #192 to the 3rd stop—ask for "Nad Rybníky." Eva & co. run the homiest hostel in Prague. **Kitchen,** satellite TV, umbrellas for borrowing, and killer cat. About 40 beds; 2- to 4-person dorms 240kč per person. **Laundry** 100kč per 5kg.

◉Hostel Boathouse, V náklích 1a (tel. 402 10 76). From the train station, Karlovo nám., Staro Město, or the Charles Bridge, take tram #3 or 17 south (dir: Sídliště Modřany): "Černý Kůň," then follow the yellow signs to the Vltava. Vera the owner says, "This isn't a hostel. It's a crazy house." An energetic twentysomething crowd happily agrees. There's games, TV, comfy beds, and a communal **kitchen.** 70 beds; 3- to 5-bed dorms 250kč (300kč for 1 night). Big breakfast 50kč, dinner 70kč. **Laundry** 100kč per load. 50kč key deposit. Call ahead.

Domov Mládeže, Dykova 20 (tel. 25 06 88; fax 25 14 29). From Metro A: "nám. Jiřího z Poděbrad," follow Nitranská and go left on Dykova. 80 beds in the peaceful, tree-lined Vinohrady district. Clean rooms and a terrace where you can drink sundowners. 2- to 7-person dorms 350kč per person (lone double 400kč). Breakfast included. If they're full, try one of their sister hostels: **Amadeus,** Slavojova 108/8. From Metro C: "Vyšehrad," descend the bridge to Čiklova, then turn left onto Slavojova. **Máchova,** Máchova 11. From Metro A: "Náměstí Míru," walk down Ruská, then turn right onto Máchova. **Košická,** Košická 12. Same as to Máchova, but continue on Ruská; turn right on Moskevská, then right again on Košická. All use the same reservation number as Domov Mládeže.

Libra-Q, Senovážné nám. 21 (tel. 24 23 17 54; fax 24 22 15 79). Metro B: "nám. Republiky." From nám. Republiky, walk down Hybernská to Senovážná, which brings you to Senovážné nám. Tidy, spartan rooms whose main attraction is the great location near Staré Město. 8-bed dorms 310kč per person; triples and quads 330kč per person.

Hotels and Pensions

With so many tourists in Prague, hotels are upgrading service and appearance, and budget hotels are now scarce. Beware: hotels may try to bill you for a more expensive room than the one you stayed in. The good, cheap ones require reservations up to a month ahead, but as with hostels, many places no longer accept reservations. Call, then confirm by fax. Be sure to cancel if you aren't going to keep your reservation.

B&B U Oty, Radlická 188 (tel./fax 57 21 53 23). From Metro B: "Radlická," up the slope 400m. Ota is an affable Anglophone who strives to take the kinks out of your stay in Prague. **Kitchen** facilities and free **laundry** service after 3 nights. Singles 500kč; doubles 770kč; triples 950kč; quads 1250kč. Additional 100kč per person if staying only 1 night.

Pension Unitas/Cloister Inn, Bartolomějská 9 (tel. 232 77 00; fax 232 77 09; email cloister@cloister-inn.cz; http://www.cloister-inn.cz), in Staré Město. Metro B: "Národní." Cross Narodní and head down Na Perštýně away from Tesco's, then turn left on Bartolomějská. An old monastery where Beethoven once performed, later transformed into a Communist jail. Now it has funky artwork and very soft beds. Singles US$65-90; doubles US$85-105; triples US$100-125.

Camping

Tourist offices sell a guide to campsites near the city (15kč). For a tranquil setting, try **Císařská Louka,** on a peninsula on the Vltava. Metro B: "Smíchovské nádraží", then tram #12 (dir: Hlubočepy): "Lihovar." Walk toward the river and onto the shaded path. **Caravan Park** (tel. 54 09 25; fax 54 33 05), near the ferry, has 2- (480kč) and 4-bed (720kč) bungalows. **Sokol Troja,** Trojská 171 (tel./fax 688 11 77), is Prague's largest campground. From Metro C: "Nádraží Holešovice," take bus #112: "Kazanka," the 4th stop. 100kč per person; 80-160kč per tent. Dorm, bungalow, and flat accommodations at 165kč, 175kč, and 150kč per person respectively. If it's full, at least 4 nearly identical places are on the same road.

FOOD

The general rule is that the nearer you are to the tourist throngs on Staroměstské nám., Karlův most, and Václavské nám., the more you'll spend. Check your bill carefully—restaurants charge for everything the waiter brings, including ketchup and bread. In Czech lunch spots, *hotová jídla* (prepared meals) are cheapest. Vegetarian eateries are opening up, but in many restaurants veggie options are limited to fried cheese. Outlying Metro stops become marketplaces in summer. Look for the daily **vegetable market** at the intersection of Havelská and Melantrichova in the Old Town. For a real bargain, go to the basement in the **Krone department store,** on Wenceslas Square at the intersection with Jindřišská (open M-F 8am-7pm, Sa 8am-6pm, Su 10am-6pm).

Restaurants

⊕Universal, V jirchářích 6. From Metro B: "Národní Třída," turn left onto Spálená, right on Myslíkova, then right on Křemencova; it's on the left-hand corner. The biggest and freshest salads (87-125kč) in Prague. Stoplights and acid jazz make the fondue (140kč) taste that much better. Open daily noon-11pm.

Lotos, Platnéřská 13. Metro A: "Staroměstská." Turn left down Valentinská, then right on Platnéřská. Vegetarian restaurant that deserves applause for its innovative and organic food (bean goulash 49kč). Wheat-yeast *Pilsner* 22kč for 0.5L. Open M-Sa 11am-10pm.

Velryba (The Whale), Opatovická 24 (tel. 241 23 91). Metro B: "Národní tř," then go left on Spálená, take an immediate right onto Ostrovní, then walk left down Opatovická. Locals, American expats, hipsters, and the accidental tourist enjoy cheap Czech dishes (33-89kč) and adventurous vegetarian platters. Open daily 11am-2am.

Góvinda Vegetarian Club, Soukenická 27, upstairs at the back of the building. Metro B: "nám. Republiky." Delicious vegetarian stews; a plate with the works is 75kč. Menu changes daily. Open M-Sa 11am-5pm.

Restaurace U Pravdů, Žitná 15. Metro B: "Karlovo nám." A deservedly popular Czech lunch spot, with a shady beer garden. Fish dishes 59-83kč, soya "meat" 41kč, pork 80-99kč, potato *knedlíky* 15kč. Big glass of *Staropramen* beer 13kč, *Radegast* 17kč. Open M-F 10am-11pm, Sa-Su 11am-11pm.

Malostranská Hospoda, Karmelitská 25, just by Malostranské nám. Metro A: "Malostranská." Chairs spill out onto the street from the pub's vaulted interior. Good *guláš* (68kč) and even better sauerkraut (7kč). Draft *Staropramen* 15kč per 0.5L. English menu. Open daily 10am-midnight.

Bar bar, Všehrdova 17. Metro A: "Malostranská." Follow the tram tracks from the metro station down Letenská, through Malostranské nám., and down Karmelitská. Turn left on Všehrdova after passing the museum. Salads (54-89kč) and pancakes (18-92kč). Good vibe, good music, and 40 varieties of good whiskey (from 41kč). Open M-F 11am-midnight, Sa-Su noon-midnight.

Bohemia Bagel, Újezd 16. Metro A: "Malostranská," and take tram #12 or 22: "Újezd." Fast on the heels of Budapest's New York Bagels, this is a 2nd place in Eastern Europe for bagelophiles to get their fixes. All the usual flavors and more. Bagel with exceptional cream cheese 35kč. Open M-F 7am-2am, Sa-Su 9am-2am.

Klub Architektů, Betlémské nám. 169 (tel. 24 40 12 14). Walk through the gates and descend to the right. A 12th-century cellar thrust into the 20th century with sleek table settings and copper pulley lamps. Veggie options 60-70kč. Meat dishes around 100kč. Chinese cabbage soup 20kč. Open daily 11am-midnight.

Cafés

When Prague journalists are bored, they churn out another "Whatever happened to café life?" feature. Ignore their pessimism as you gaze soulfully into your coffee at one of the places listed below.

🏅**Umalého Glena,** Karmelitská 23. Metro A: "Malostranská." Their motto: "Eat, Drink, Drink Some More." Light menu has 70kč veggie plates and delicious stuffed pita breads 70-95kč. Great margaritas (50kč). Basement bar has nightly jazz or blues at 9pm. Cover 50-70kč. Open daily 7:30am-2am.

Cafe Gulu Gulu, Betlémské nám. 8 (tel. 90 01 25 81). From Metro A: "Staroměstká," turn left on Křižovnická toward the Charles Bridge. Turn left again onto windy Karlova, then right onto Husova. A chill hangout for Prague's hippest twentysomethings. Fun-loving, from the Miro-esque wall characters to the frequent impromptu musical jams and blaring ska. By 11pm, people are hanging out of windowsills to get a place to sit. *Eggenberg* 25kč. Great food 20-45kč. Open daily 10am-1am.

Andy's Cafe, V Kolkovně 3. Metro A: "Staroměstská." Walk down Dlouhá; when it becomes Kozí, turn left on V Kolkovně. Stay late enough drinking beer (25kč) and soup (20kč) to skip the night buses and catch the morning metro. Open M-F 10am-6am, Sa-Su noon-6am.

SIGHTS

Orient yourself before tackling the city's many scattered sights. Central Prague is structured by three streets that form a leaning "T." The long stem of the T is the boulevard **Václavské nám.** (Wenceslas Sq.). The **Národní Muzeum** sits at the bottom of the T. The busy, pedestrian **Na příkopě** forms the right arm, leading to **nám. Republiky.** On the left, **28. řijna** becomes **Národní** after a block, leading to the **Národní Divadlo** on the river. From the tip of the T-end of Václavské nám. opposite the museum, **Na Můstku** turns into **Melantrichova** after one block and leads to **Staroměstské nám.,** northwest of Václavské nám. There are two prominent **St. Nicholas churches**—in Malá Strana near the castle and in Staroměstské nám.—and two **Powder Towers**—one in the castle and another in nám. Republiky. Strollers will find that Prague has plenty of green space along Malá Strana's **Petřínské Sady.** Miles of pathways traverse the Kinsky, Strahov, Lobkowic, Schönborn, and Seminář **gardens,** but most are badly eroded. Many try the promenade on the banks of the Vltava south of **most Legií** along Nové Město's **Masarykoro nábřeží.** On hot or humid days, the river is known to give off quite a stench. Gorgeous greenery lies southeast of Staré Město in **Vinohrady.** This quarter's hills also offer great views of the town.

VÁCLAVSKÉ NÁMĚSTÍ (WENCESLAS SQUARE)

Not so much a square as a broad boulevard, **Václavské nám.** owes its name to the equestrian statue of the Czech ruler and saint **Václav** (Wenceslas), in front of the National Museum. Václav has presided over a century of turmoil and triumph, witnessing no fewer than five revolutions from his pedestal since 1912. The new Czechoslovak state was proclaimed here in 1918, and in 1969, Jan Palach set himself on fire in protest against the 1968 Soviet invasion. Václavské nam. sweeps down from the National Museum past department stores, overpriced discos, posh hotels, sausage stands, and trashy casinos. The **Radio Prague Building,** behind the National Museum, was the scene of a tense battle during Prague Spring between Soviet tanks and Prague citizens trying to protect the radio studios by human barricade. North of the Václav statue, the Art Nouveau style, expressed in everything from lampposts to windowsills, dominates the square. The premier example is the 1903 **Hotel Europa.**

From the north end of Václavské nám., turn left onto 28. rijna and take a quick detour to Jungmannovo nám. and **Panna Marie Sněžná** (Church of Our Lady of the Snows). The Gothic walls are highest of any church in Prague, but the rest of the structure is still unfinished. Enter **Františkánská zahrada** through the arch at the intersection of Jungmannova and Národní. *(Open daily Apr. 15-Sept. 14 7am-10pm; Sept. 15-Oct. 14 7am-8pm; Oct. 15-Apr. 14 8am-7pm. Free.)* No one knows how the Franciscans who tend the rose gardens have managed to maintain such a bastion of serenity in Prague's commercial district, perhaps because most friars are too busy talking to the birds to answer questions. Under the arcades halfway down Národní stands a **memorial** honoring the hundreds of Prague's citizens beaten by the police on November 17, 1989. Václav Havel's Civic Forum movement was based at the **Lanterna Magika** (Magic Lantern) theater, Národní 4, during the tense days now known as the **Velvet Revolution.**

STAROMĚSTSKÉ NÁMĚSTÍ (OLD TOWN SQUARE)
A labyrinth of narrow roads and Old World alleys leads to **Staroměstské nám.**, Staré Město's thriving heart since 965. **Jan Hus,** the Czech Republic's most famous martyred theologian, sweeps across the scene in bronze. No fewer than eight magnificent towers surround the square. The building with a bit blown off is the **Staroměstská radnice** (Old Town Hall), partially demolished by the Nazis in the final week of World War II. *(Open for tours in summer daily 9am-5:30pm; 30kč, students 15kč.)* **Crosses** on the ground mark the spot where 27 Protestant leaders were executed on June 21, 1621 for staging a rebellion against the Catholic Habsburgs. Crowds gather on the hour to watch the wonderful **astronomical clock** *(orloj)* chime with its procession of apostles, a skeleton, and a thwarted Turk. Across from the *radnice*, the spires of **Matka Boží před Týnem** (Týn Church) rise above a huddled mass of medieval homes. Famous astronomer **Tycho Brahe** is buried inside. The flowery **Goltz-Kinský palác** on the left is the finest of Prague's Rococo buildings and the official birthplace of Soviet Communism in the Czech Republic: on February 21, 1948, Klement Gottwald declared communism victorious from its balcony. **Sv. Mikuláš** (Church of St. Nicholas) sits just across Staroměstské nám. *(Open Tu-F 10am-5pm, closes early in summer for daily concerts.)* Between Sv. Mikuláš and Maiselova, a plaque marks **Franz Kafka's** former home.

JOSEFOV
Prague's historic Jewish neighborhood, Josefov, is located north of Staromětstské nám. along Maiselova and several side streets. In 1180, Prague's citizens complied with a pope's decree to isolate Jews by surrounding the area with a 3½m wall, which stood until 1848. The closed city bred disease but also stories, many focusing on **Rabbi Loew ben Bezalel** (1512-1609) and his legendary *golem*, a creature made from mud that came to life to protect Prague's Jews. Hitler's decision to create a "museum of an extinct race" resulted in the preservation of the old cemetery and five synagogues despite the destruction of Prague's Jewish community in the Holocaust. *(Open Su-F 9am-5:30pm; closed on Jewish holidays; museums and synagogues 450kč, students 330kč.)* **Starý židovský hřbitov** (Old Jewish Cemetery) lies at the 90-degree bend in U Starého hřbitova. Between the 14th and 18th centuries, 12 layers of 20,000 graves were laid. The 700-year-old **Staronová synagóga** (Old-New Synagogue) is Europe's oldest operating synagogue. The Hebrew clock in the exterior of the neighboring **Židovská radnice** (Jewish Town Hall) runs counterclockwise. Walking down Maiselova and turning right on Široka takes you to the **Pinkasova synagóga,** whose walls list the names of victims of Nazi persecution.

KARLŮV MOST (CHARLES BRIDGE)
Head out of Staroměstské nám. on Jilská, and go right onto Karlova. Wandering left down Liliová leads to **Betlémské nám.**, where the **Betlémské kaple** (Bethlehem Chapel) stands. The present building is a reconstruction of the medieval chapel made famous by Jan Hus, the great Czech religious reformer. Turning back onto Karlova and left toward the river will lead to **Karlův most,** mobbed with tourists and people trying to sell them things. At the center of the bridge is the statue of legendary hero **Jan Nepomucký** (John of Nepomuk), confessor to Queen Žofie. Brave Jan was tossed over the side of the Charles for faithfully guarding his queen's extra-marital confidences from a suspicious King Václav IV. The right-hand rail, where Jan was supposedly ejected, is now marked with a cross and five stars between the fifth and sixth statues. It is said that if you make a wish with a finger on each star you will return to Prague. Climb the Gothic **defense tower** on the

Malá Strana side of the bridge or the tower on the Old Town side for a superb view of the city. *(Both towers open daily 10am-6:30pm. 35kč, students 20kč.)* The stairs on the left side of the bridge (as you face the castle district) lead to **Hroznová,** where a crumbling mural honors John Lennon and the 60s peace movement.

MALÁ STRANA (LESSER SIDE)

MALÁ STRANA (LESSER SIDE) The seedy hangout of criminals and counter-revolutionaries for nearly a century, the cobblestone streets of Malá Strana have, in the strange sway of Prague fashion, become the most prized real estate on either side of the Vltava. From Karlův most, continue straight up Mostecká and turn right into **Malostranské nám.** Dominating the square is the magnificent Baroque **Chrám sv. Mikuláše** (Church of St. Nicholas) with its remarkable high dome. Classical concerts (many of which are frankly not worth the price of admission) take place nightly. *(Church open daily 9am-4:30pm; 30kč, students 15kč. Concert tickets an absurd 390kč, students 290kč.)* Nearby on Karmelitská rises the more modest **Panna Maria Vítězna** (Church of Our Lady Victorious). The famous polished-wax statue of the **Infant Jesus of Prague** resides within. *(Open in summer daily 7am-9pm; off-season 8am-8pm; English mass Su noon.)* A simple wooden gate just down the street at Letenská 10 opens onto **Valdštejnská zahrada** (Wallenstein Garden), one of Prague's best-kept secrets. This tranquil 17th-century Baroque garden is enclosed by old buildings that glow golden on sunny afternoons.

PRAŽSKÝ HRAD (PRAGUE CASTLE)

PRAŽSKÝ HRAD (PRAGUE CASTLE) Founded 1000 years ago, Pražský Hrad has always been the seat of the Bohemian government. Give the castle a full day—just don't make it Monday. From Metro A: "Hradčanská," cross the tram tracks and turn left onto Tychonova, which delivers you to the glorious and newly renovated **Královský Letohrádek** (Royal Summer Palace) and the serene and shady 1534 **Královská zahrada** (Royal Garden). The **castle entrance** lies at the other end of the garden and across the **Prašný most** (Powder Bridge). Before entering, you'll pass the **Šternberský palác,** home of the National Gallery's European art collection, featuring Goya, Rubens, and Rembrandt. *(Gallery open Tu-Su 10am-6pm. 45kč, students 25kč.)*

Inside the castle walls stands Pražský Hrad's centerpiece, the colossal **Katedrála sv. Víta** (St. Vitus's Cathedral), which may look Gothic but was actually finished in 1929—600 years after it was begun. The cathedral's stained-glass windows were created by some of the most gifted Czech artists, including Alphonse Mucha. To the right of the high altar stands the **tomb of sv. Jan Nepomucký,** 3m of solid, glistening silver, weighing two tons. Look for an angel holding a silvered tongue.

Emperor Karel IV's tomb is in the **Royal Crypt** below the church along with a handful of other Czech kings and all four of Karel's wives, who are tactfully buried in the same grave to his left. Back up the stairs in the main church, the walls of **Svatováclavská kaple** (St. Wenceslas's Chapel) are lined with precious stones and a painting cycle depicting this saint's legend. Try the 287 steps of the Cathedral Tower, which lead to the best view of the entire city. *(All sights open daily summer 9am-5pm; Sept.-Mar. 9am-4pm. Ticket office across from St. Vitus's Cathedral, inside the castle walls. Ticket valid for 3 days; 100kč, students 50kč.)*

The **Starý královský palác** (Old Royal Palace), to the right of the cathedral behind the Old Provost's House and the statue of St. George, houses the lengthy expanse of the **Vladislav Hall,** where jousting competitions once took place; upstairs is the **Chancellery of Bohemia,** the site of the second Defenestration of Prague. On May 23, 1618, angry Protestants flung two Habsburg officials (and their secretary) through the windows and into a steaming dungheap that broke their fall, signaling the start of the extraordinarily bloody Thirty Years' War in Europe.

Directly behind the cathedral stand the **convent** and **basilika sv. Jiří** (St. George). The convent is home to the **National Gallery of Bohemian Art,** with stuff from the Gothic to the Baroque. *(Open Tu-Su 10am-6pm. 50kč, students and seniors 15kč. 1st F of each month free.)* The palace street Jiřská begins to the right of the basilica. Halfway down, the tiny **Zlatá ulička** (Golden Lane) heads off to the left. Alchemists once worked here, later Kafka lived at #22, and today there is a small forest of cramped souvenir shops for tourists to squeeze in and out of. Back on Jiřská, the **Lobkovický Palác** contains a replica of Bohemia's coronation jewels and a history of the Czech lands. *(Open Tu-Su 10am-6pm. 40kč, students 20kč.)* After passing between the two armed sentries on your way out of the castle, peer over the battlements on the right for a fine cityscape, then descend the **Staré Zámecké Schody** (Old Castle Steps) into the Malá Strana.

OUTER PRAGUE The **Petřínské sady,** the largest gardens in central Prague, are topped by a model of the Eiffel Tower and the wacky castle **Bludiště.** *(Castle open Tu-Su 10am-7pm.)* Take a cable car from just above the intersection of Vítězná and Újezd for spectacular views. *(8kč; look for lanová dráha signs.)*

The former haunt of Prague's 19th-century romantics, **Vyšehrad** is clothed in nationalistic myths and the legends of a once-powerful Czech empire. It is here that Princess Libuše foresaw Prague and embarked on her search for the first king of Bohemia. The 20th century has passed the castle by, and Vyšehrad's elevated pathways now escape the flood of tourists in the city center. Quiet walkways lead between crumbling stone walls to a magnificent **church,** a black Romanesque rotunda, and one of the Czech Republic's most celebrated sites, **Vyšehrad Cemetery,** where Dvořák and other national heroes are laid to rest. To reach the complex, take Metro C: "Vyšehrad." *(Complex open 24hr.)*

ENTERTAINMENT

For a list of current concerts and performances, consult *The Prague Post, Threshold,* or *Do města-Downtown* (the latter two are free and distributed at most cafés and restaurants). Most shows begin at 7pm; unsold tickets are sometimes available 30 minutes before showtime. **Národní Divadlo** (National Theater), Národní třída 2/4 (tel. 24 91 34 37), is perhaps Prague's most famous theater. (Box office open M-F 10am-6pm, Sa-Su 10am-12:30pm and 3-6pm, and 30min. before performances.) Equally impressive is **Stavovské Divadlo** (Estates Theater), Ovocný trh 1 (tel. 24 21 50 01), where Mozart's *Don Giovanni* premiered (same box office as National Theater, or show up 30min. before a performance). Most of Prague's theaters shut down in July and return in August with attractions for tourists. Around mid-May to early June, the **Prague Spring Festival** draws musicians from around the world. Tickets (300-2000kč) may sell out a year in advance; try **Bohemia Ticket International,** Salvátorská 6 (tel. 24 22 78 32), next to Čedok. *(Open M-F 9am-6pm, Sa 9am-4pm, Su 10am-3pm.)*

The most authentic way to enjoy Prague at night is through an alcoholic fog; the venues below should satisfy the need for a *pivo* and a sweaty dance floor. Gay bars distribute the linguistically confused *Amigo* (15kč), a guide to gay life in the Czech Republic and Slovakia.

⊚Kozička (The Little Goat), Kozí 1 (tel./fax 231 08 52). Metro A: "Staroměstské nám." This giant cellar bar is always packed, and you'll know why after your 1st super-cheap 0.5L *Krušovice* (20kč). Twentysomething crowd comes early and stays all night. Open M-F noon-4am, Sa-Su 4pm-4am.

Cafe Marquis de Sade, a.k.a. **Cafe Babylon,** Templová 8. Metro B: "nám. Republiky." Relax on the red velvet couches with a beer (25kč), while the band strikes up old pops or mellow jazz for a packed house. Open M-F noon-2am, Sa-Su 3pm-2am.

Újezd, Újezd 18. Metro B: "Národní třída." A mid-20s crowd smokes the night away at this mecca of mellowness—a giant mushroom chandelier hangs above the bar. DJ or live acid jazz 3 times a week. Open nightly 6pm-3am.

Roxy, Dlouhá 33. Metro B: "nám. Republiky." Walk up Revoluční toward the river and turn left on Dlouhá. Experimental DJs, theme nights, and endless dancing. Open Tu-Su from 8pm.

U Staré Paní, Michalská 9. Metro A or B: "Můstek," then walk down na Můstku at the end of Václavské nám through its name change to Melantrichova. Turn left on Havelská and right on Michalská. "At the Old Lady's" showcases some of the finest jazz vocalists in Prague in a classy upstairs venue. Shows nightly 9pm-midnight. Cover 90kč; with ISIC or GO25 45kč, plus 10% off drinks. Open daily 7pm-4am.

U Střelce, Karoliny Světlé 12. Metro B: "Národní Třída," then walk down Národní toward the river, and turn right on Karoliny Světlé; the club is under the archway on the right. Gay club pulls a diverse crowd with F and Sa night cabarets, when fabulous female impersonators take the stage. Cover 100kč. Open nightly 6pm-4am.

■ Karlštejn and Kutná Hora

The Bohemian hills around Prague contain 14 castles, some built as early as the 13th century. A train ride southwest from Praha-Smíchov (45min., 12kč) brings you to **Karlštejn** (tel. (0311) 846 17), a walled and turreted fortress built by Karel IV to house his crown jewels and holy relics. The **Chapel of the Holy Cross** is decorated with more than 2000 inlaid precious stones and 128 apocalyptic paintings by medieval artist Master Theodorik. (Open Tu-Su 9am-5pm. Admission with English guide 150kč, less for students, with Czech guide, or with no guide.) Ask at the Prague tourist office if they have finished restoring the chapel before setting out.

An hour and a half east of Prague is the former mining town of **Kutná Hora** (Mining Hill). A 13th-century abbot sprinkled soil from Golgotha on the cemetery, which made the rich and superstitious keen to be buried there. In a fit of whimsy, the monk in charge began designing flowers out of pelvi and crania. He never finished, but the artist František Rint completed the project in 1870 with flying butt-bones, femur crosses, and a grotesque chandelier made from every bone in the human body. (Open daily Apr.-Sept. 8am-noon and 1-6pm; Oct. 9am-noon and 1-5pm; Nov.-Mar. 9am-noon and 1-4pm. 30kč, students 15kč.) The *kostnice* (ossuary) is 2km from the bus station: take a local bus to "Sedlec Tabák" and follow the signs. **Buses** arrive regularly from Prague's Florenc station (1½hr.) and from station 2 at Metro A: "Želivského" (1¾hr.).

From Palackého nám., follow 28. října to Havlíčkovo nám. in the old part of the city. Originally a storehouse for Kutná Hora's stash, the imposing **Vlašský Dvůr** (Italian Court) got its name after Václav IV invited the finest Italian architects to refurbish the palace. (Open daily 9am-6pm. Tours every 15min. 20kč, students 10kč. Infrequent English tours 50kč, students 25kč.) Pass the ancient **St. James Church** and follow Barborská, which becomes a statue-lined promenade and ends at the beautiful Gothic **St. Barbara's Cathedral.** (Open Tu-Su 9am-5pm. 20kč, students 10kč.) **Buses** arrive from Prague's Florenc station (6 per day M-F, 1 per day Sa-Su, 1½hr., 44kč) and station 2 at Metro A: "Želivského" (9 per day M-F, 2 per day Sa-Su, 1¾hr., 44kč).

■ České Budějovice

No amount of beer can help you correctly pronounce České Budějovice (CHESS-kay BOOD-yay-yov-ee-tzeh). Luckily for pint-guzzlers, the town was known as Budweis in the 19th century, when it inspired the name of the popular but pale North American *Budweiser,* which bares little relation to the malty local *Budvar.* But the town has been blessed with more than good beer: mill streams, the Malše, and the Vltava wrap around an amalgam of Gothic, Renaissance, and Baroque houses scattered along medieval alleys and 18th-century streets. The city also serves as a launchpad to South Bohemia's castles and natural wonders.

Surrounded by Renaissance and Baroque buildings, cobbled **nám. Otakara II** is the largest square in the Czech Republic. Near the square's northeast corner, **Černá věž** (Black Tower) looms over the town. Beware: the treacherous stairs, rising 72m, are difficult even for the sober. (10kč. Open Tu-Su July-Aug. 10am-7pm; Sept.-Nov. 9am-5pm; Mar.-June 10am-6pm.) The tower once served as a belfry for the neighboring 13th-century **Chrám sv. Mikuláše** (Church of St. Nicholas; open daily 7am-6pm). The city's most famous attraction, the **Budweiser Brewery,** Karoliny Světlé 4, offers tours of the factory for groups of six or more; arrange them at the tourist office. To reach the brewery, take bus #2 or 4 from the center of town. České Budějovice also sports a super-hip **second-hand shopping** scene. Shops with large "Second Hand" signs pop up everywhere, but are particularly abundant along Riegrova, off nám. Otakara II.

GATEWAY CITIES

This Bud's for EU

Many Yankees, having tasted the malty goodness of a Budvar brew, return home to find it conspicuously unavailable. That Budvar was the Czech Republic's largest exporter of beer in 1995 makes its absence from American store shelves even stranger. Where's the Budvar? The answer lies in a tale of trademarks and town names. České Budějovice (Budweis in German) had been brewing its own style of lager for centuries when the Anheuser-Busch brewery in St. Louis came out with its Budweiser-style beer in 1876. Not until the 1890s, however, did the Budějovice Pivovar (Brewery) begin producing a beer labeled "Budweiser." International trademark conflicts ensued, and in 1911 the companies signed a non-competition agreement: Budvar got markets in Europe and Anheuser-Busch took North America. But the story continues…

A few years ago, Anheuser-Busch tried to end the confusion by buying a controlling interest in the makers of Budvar. The Czech government replied "nyeh." In response, the following year Anheuser-Busch didn't order its normal one-third of the Czech hop crop. Anheuser-Busch is now suing for trademark infringement in Finland, while Budvar is petitioning the EU to make the moniker "Budweiser" a designation as exclusive as that of "Champagne," meaning that any brand sold in the EU under that name would have to come from the Budweiser region. As long as the battle continues on European fronts, there is little chance that a Budvar in America will be anything but an illegal alien.

The **train** station welcomes travelers from **Brno** (4½hr., 126kč) and **Prague** (2½hr., 92kč). To reach the gigantic nám. Otakara II from the station, take a right out of the main entrance onto Nádražní and turn left at the pedestrian Lannova tř., which becomes Kanovnická. The **tourist office,** nám. Otakara II 2 (tel./fax (038) 594 80), books private rooms. (Around 350kč. Open May-Sept. M-F 8am-6pm, Sa 8am-3pm, Su 8am-1pm; Oct.-Apr. closes 1hr. earlier.) The University of South Bohemia **dorms** (tel. (038) 777 44 00) on Studenstská open to travelers in July and August. Take tram #1 from the bus station five stops to "U parku," then head back down Husova, and turn right (doubles 300kč).

■ Český Krumlov

Winding medieval streets, scenic promenades, and the looming presence of Bohemia's second-largest castle might have earned Český Krumlov its coveted UNESCO-protected status. Of course, the town's wonderful location on the banks of the Vltava also makes it ideal for bicycling, canoeing, and kayaking. Looming high above town, the **castle's** stone courtyard is open to the public for free, and two tours cover the lavish interior, which includes frescoes, a Baroque theater, and crypt galleries. (Open Apr. and Oct. Tu-Su 9am-noon and 1-3pm; May-June and Sept. Tu-Su 9am-noon and 1-4pm; July-Aug. Tu-Su 9am-noon and 1-5pm. Tours in English 70kč, students 30kč.) Housed in an immense Renaissance building, the **Egon Schiele International Cultural Center,** Široká 70-72, displays hours of browsing material, including works by Picasso and other 20th-century artists. (Open daily 10am-6pm. 120kč, students 80kč.) The **city museum,** Horní 152, features bizarre folk instruments, bone sculptures, and log barges. (Open May-Sept. daily 10am-12:30pm and 1-5pm. 30kč, students 5kč.) The **Five-Petal Rose Festival,** Krumlov's medieval fair, happens the third weekend in June and provides a great excuse to dress up in tights and joust with the locals.

Sixteen kilometers southwest of České Budějovice, the town is best reached by frequent **buses** (35min., 10 per day, fewer on weekends, 20kč). The **tourist office,** nám. Svornosti 1 (tel. (0337) 71 11 83), in the town hall, books rooms in pensions starting at 550kč and cheaper private rooms. (Open daily 9am-6pm.) Overlooking the castle tower, **Vegetarian Restaurant,** Parkán 105 (tel. (0337) 71 25 08), serves up heaping portions of tasty veggie dishes (50-60kč; open daily 11am-8:30pm). The **Cikanská jízba** (Gypsy bar), Dlouhá 31 (tel. (0337) 55 85), serves traditional gypsy fare to a faithful crowd of American expats and locals. The spicy goulash (57kč) should not be missed (main dishes around 60kč; open M-Th 2-11pm, F-Sa 3pm-1am).

■ Bratislava

After 80 years of playing second fiddle to starlet Prague, Bratislava, a burgeoning city nestled between Vienna and Budapest on the Danube, has been thrust into a new role as the capital of Slovakia. The Baroque and Renaissance (and pedestrianized) city center is home to infinite cafes, talented street musicians, chic boutiques, and surprisingly stylish Bratislavans and expats. Lightly touristed in comparison with Vienna and Prague, this city of half a million merits a visit.

ORIENTATION AND PRACTICAL INFORMATION

Bratislava lies on the banks of the Danube, a proverbial stone's throw from the Austrian and Hungarian borders. Avoid getting off at the **Nové Mesto** train station, which is much farther from the center than **Hlavná stanica** (the main station). To get downtown from Hlavná stanica, take tram #1 to "Poštová" at **nám. SNP,** the administrative center. Uršulínska leads to the tourist office. From the bus station, take bus #107 to **nám. J. Štúra** by the river. Walk up Mostova, cross Hviezdoslavovo nám. onto Rybárska brána, then turn right at Hlavné nám. onto Kostolná—the tourist office is across Primaciálne nám.

Trains: Bratislava Hlavná stanica (info tel. 204 44 84), north of town center. Go up Štefánikova, right onto Šancová, and left up the road that runs past the waiting buses. International tickets at counters 9-16. **Wasteels** office at front of station offers discounts to those under 26. Open M-F 8:30am-4pm. To: **Berlin** (11hr., 2837Sk, Wasteels 2127Sk), **Budapest** (3hr., 447Sk, Wasteels 335Sk), **Prague** (5hr., 243Sk), and **Vienna** (1hr., 239Sk). **Lockers** 5Sk.

Buses: Mlynské nivy 31 (tel. 542 22 22), east of Old Town. To: **Budapest** (5hr., 350Sk), **Prague** (4½hr., 260Sk), and **Vienna** (1½hr., 340Sk). Check ticket for bus number (*č. aut);* several different buses may depart simultaneously. **Lockers** 5Sk.

Public Transportation: All daytime trips on **trams** and **buses** require a 7Sk ticket available at kiosks and orange automats found at most stops. Night buses have black and orange numbers in the 500s and cost 14Sk. Most trams pass by nám. SNP; most buses stop at the north base of Nový Most (bridge).

Hitchhiking: Those hitching to **Vienna** or to **Hungary** (via Győr) cross the SNP bridge and walk down Viedenská cesta. Those headed to Prague take bus #104: "Patronka." Hitching is legal and common, but not recommended.

Tourist Offices: Bratislavská Informačná Služba (BIS), Klobučnícka 2 (tel. 533 37 15 or 533 43 70; fax 533 27 08; email bis@isnet.sk; http://www.isnet.sk/bis). Sells maps (28Sk), gives city tours, and books rooms. Open M-F 8am-7pm, Sa-Su 8:30am-1:30pm. **Branches** in train station and at airport open daily 8am-6pm.

Embassies: Canada, Kolárska 4 (tel. 36 12 77). Open M and W 3-5pm. **South Africa,** Jančova 8 (tel. 531 15 82). Open M-F 9am-noon. In emergencies, **Irish** citizens and **Commonwealth** nationals should contact the embassy of the **U.K.,** Panská 16 (tel. 531 96 32; fax 531 00 02). **U.S.,** Hviezdoslavovo nám. 4 (tel. 533 08 61 or 533 33 38; after hours emergency tel. 09 01 70 36 66). Open M-F 8am-4:30pm (visas M-F 8-11:30am).

Currency Exchange: Všeobecná Úverová Banka (VÚB), Gorkého 9 (tel. 515 79 76), cashes traveler's checks (2% commission) and handles MC and Visa cash advances. Open M-W and F 8am-5pm, Th 8am-noon. An outdoor machine at Mostová 6 changes US$, DM, and UK£ into Sk for a 3% commission.

American Express: No office in Bratislava, but **Wings Travel Agency,** Františkánske nám. 3, Bratislava 81101 (tel. 533 55 36), cashes (2% commission) and sells (1% commission) traveler's checks and holds mail. Open M-F 10am-6pm, Sa 9am-noon.

24-Hour Pharmacy: At the corner of Gorkého and Lavrinská (tel 36 37 31).

Post Office: Main office at nám. SNP 35. *Poste Restante* at counter 6. Open M-F 7am-8pm, Sa 7am-6pm, Su 9am-2pm. **Postal Code:** 81000 Bratislava 1.

Telephone Code: 7.

ACCOMMODATIONS AND CAMPING

In July and August, dorms open up for backpackers on their way to Vienna. Cheap rooms and beds are hard to find before early July, so book early and/or call ahead. **BIS** (see above) has addresses for private rooms (singles from 400Sk; doubles 600Sk).

Pension Gremium, Gorkého 11 (tel. 32 18 18; fax 533 06 53). From nám. SNP, turn left on Michalská. Left on Panská, right on Rybárska Brána, then left on Gorkého. Fluffy beds in the heart of Old Town; popular cafe downstairs. Only one single (890Sk) and 4 doubles (1290Sk), so call ahead. Breakfast included.

Youth Hostel Bernolak, Bernolákova 1 (tel. 39 77 23). From the train station, bus #22, 23, or 210 or tram #3: "Vazovova"; from the bus station, #37 or trolley #210: "Račianské Mýto." Friendliest hostel in town with the best English. Spacious singles 480Sk; doubles 580Sk; triples 660Sk; all with bath. 10% discount for those with a Euro26, ISIC, or HI card. Open July-Aug.

Youth Hostel, Wilsonova 6 (tel. 39 77 35). On the street parallel to Bernolákova (see YH Bernolak above). Rooms remarkable only for being cheap. Dorms 180Sk. 30% discount with Euro26, HI, or ISIC. Checkout 9am. Open July-Aug.

Camping: Autocamping Zlaté Piesky, Senecká cesta 2 (tel. 25 73 73), in suburban Trnávka by the lakeside. Tram #2 or 4 or bus #118 to the last stop and cross the footbridge. 100Sk per person, 90Sk per tent. Bungalows 650-900Sk.

FOOD

Bratislava's restaurants serve the region's spicy meat mixtures with West Slovakia's celebrated **Modra** wine. Find **markets** at Žilinská 5, near the train station, and outside Tesco's (open M-Sa 6am-4pm), and a **late-night deli** at Špitalská 45. For groceries, head to **Tesco's Potraviny,** Kamenné nám. 1 (open M-W 8am-7pm, Th 8am-8pm, F 8am-9pm, Sa 8am-5pm, Su 9am-5pm).

Prašná Bašta, Zámočnícka 11, off Michalská. Sheep cheese *halušky* (55Sk), fine onion soup (22Sk), and generous glasses of wine (10-16Sk). Dark alcoves full of funky sculptures inside, a leafy terrace outside. Open daily 11am-11pm.

Cafe London, Panská 17, in the British Council's courtyard. Serves up Anglophile nostalgia to expats and burger-and-sheep's-cheese-saturated travelers. Tuna salad, grilled cheese, and roast beef sandwiches 49-98Sk. Open M-F 9am-9pm.

Vegetarían Jedáleň, Laurinská 8. From nám. SNP, walk away from the castle and turn right. Young Slovak herbivores graze at this purely vegetarian lunch spot. Menu changes daily (50-100Sk). Open M-F 11am-3pm.

SIGHTS AND ENTERTAINMENT

From **nám. SNP,** which commemorates the bloody Slovak National Uprising against the fascist Slovak state, walk left down Uršulínska to **Primaciálné nám.** The Neoclassical **Primaciálny Palác** (Primate's Palace) dates from 1781; Napoleon and Austrian Emperor Franz I signed the Peace of Pressburg here in 1805. *(Open Tu-Su 10am-5pm; 25Sk.)* The **Múzeum Histórie Mesta** (Town History Museum) is in the **Stará Radnica** (Old Town Hall), accessible from Primaciálné nám. *(Open Tu-Su 10am-5pm; 25Sk, students 10Sk.)* Inside, past a wonderful 1:500 model of Bratislava, galleries display exhibits on the city's history. Stará Radnica fronts onto **Hlavné nám.,** the domain of tourists during the day and loud teenagers at night.

Bratislavaburg

The only thing more incomprehensible than a Slovak menu is a Bratislava menu at one of the city's ubiquitous burger stands. A cheeseburger costs less than a *hamburger so syrom* (hamburger with cheese) because, as the stand owner will explain with humiliating logic, a cheeseburger is made of cheese. A *pressburger* consists of bologna on a bun, and hamburgers are actually ham. Everything comes boiled (except the cheese) on a roll with cabbage, onions, and sauce.

From Hlavné nám., walk left down Rybárska Brána until **Hviezdoslavovo nám.**, dominated at its eastern end by the 1886 **Slovenské Národné Divadlo** (Slovak National Theater). A left along the Dunaj leads to the **Slovenské Národné Múzeum** (Slovak National Museum), Vajanského nábr. 2, which houses local archaeological finds, including casts of Neanderthal skeletons. *(Open Tu-Su 9am-5pm; 20Sk.)* Also on the river, the **Slovak National Gallery,** Rázusovo nábr. 2, displays Slovak Gothic and Baroque art. *(Open Tu-Su 10am-6pm; 25Sk, students 5Sk.)* The SNP suspension bridge spans the Dunaj, its reins held by a giant flying saucer. *(10Sk.)* From Rázusovo nábr., go right on the next-to-last street before the bridge to reach the fairly unspectacular **Dóm sv. Martina** (St. Martin's Cathedral), where the kings of Hungary were crowned for three centuries. Across the highway from the cathedral (use the pedestrian overpass), the road zooms over what used to be **Schlossberg,** the old Jewish quarter. The **Múzeum Židovskej Kultúry** (Museum of Jewish Culture), Židovská 17, preserves valuable fragments of a vanished population. *(Open Su-F 11am-5pm; 35Sk.)* From the cathedral, go down Kapitulská, right onto Prepoštská, and left onto Michalská, a busy pedestrian street guarded by the **Michalská Brána** at the north end. *(Open W-M 10am-5pm, last entrance 4:30; 25Sk.)* Trot up to the top.

From the banks of the Danube to the center's historic squares, the four-towered **Bratislavský hrad** (castle) is a visible landmark. Of strategic importance for more than a millennium, the castle's heyday was in the 18th century, when Maria Theresa held court here. The castle was burned down in 1811 and bombed during World War II, so what the visitor sees today is largely Communist-era restoration. There's also a **Historické Múzeum.** *(Open Tu-Sa 9am-5pm; 30Sk.)*

For concert and theater schedules, pick up a copy of *Kám v Bratislave* at BIS. It's not in English, but the info is easy to decipher. Unfortunately, the Filharmonia and many theaters take their vacations in July and August. **Slovenská Filharmonia** plays regularly at Palackého ul. 2, which fronts onto Mostová; the box office (tel. 533 33 51) is around the corner on Medená. *(Tickets 800-1000Sk; open M-F 1-5pm.)* **Národné Divadlo** (National Theater) tickets are sold at the box office at Laurinská 20. *(Around 50Sk; open M-F noon-6pm).*

Bratislava's sleekest twentysomethings gather at the **Alligator Club,** Laurinská 7, to hear live rock and blues bands. *(Nightly at 7pm; Gambrinus 27Sk; open M-F 10am-midnight, Sa noon-midnight, Su noon-10pm.)* **Dubliner,** Sedlarská 6, Bratislava's *ersatz* Irish pub, has sewing machines for tables, a leaky roof, and a tremendously lively atmosphere as it fills up after dinner. *(Open M-Sa 10am-1am, Su 11am-midnight.)* Konnect at **Klub Internet,** Vajanského nábr. 2. *(Open M-F 9am-9pm, Sa-Su noon-9pm.)*

▓ Munich (München)

Only 120km from Salzburg, Munich's sensual air of merriment—most obvious during the wild *Fasching* and the legendary *Oktoberfest*—make for a very attractive sidetrip. The modern city emerges from a powerful and troubled history: the Bavarian Golden Age of the 18th and 19th centuries, characterized by the wildly extravagant castles of Ludwig II, ended abruptly with Germany's defeat in World War I, and World War II shattered the city, leaving less than 3% of its center intact. But Munich has proved resilient—today, it shines unabashedly with Western German postwar economic glory. World-class museums, handsome parks and architecture, a rambunctious arts scene, and an urbane population combine to create a city of crazy vitality.

ORIENTATION AND PRACTICAL INFORMATION

A map of Munich's center looks like a skewed circle quartered by one horizontal and one vertical line. The circle is the main traffic **Ring,** within which lies the lion's share of Munich's sights. The east-west and north-south thoroughfares cross at Munich's epicenter, the **Marienplatz** (home to the **Neues Rathaus**), and meet the traffic Ring at **Karlsplatz** in the west, **Isartorplatz** in the east, **Odeonsplatz** in the north, and **Sendlinger Tor** (Sendlinger Gate) in the south. The **Hauptbahnhof** is just beyond

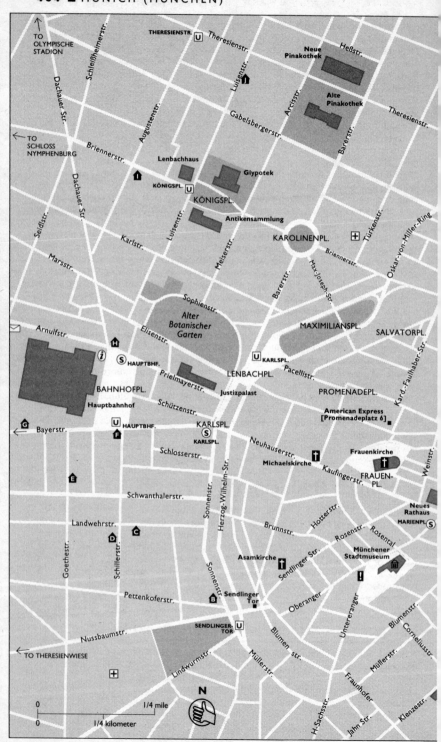

TO OLYMPISCHE STADION

TO SCHLOSS NYMPHENBURG

THERESIENSTR. U Theresienstr.

Schleißheimerstr.

Dachauer Str.

Augustenstr.

Briennerstr.

Neue Pinakothek

Heßstr.

Arcistr.

Alte Pinakothek

Theresienstr.

Gabelsbergerstr.

Barerstr.

Lenbachhaus

Glypotek

KÖNIGSPL. U

KÖNIGSPL.

Antikensammlung

KAROLINENPL.

Türkenstr.

Luisenstr.

Karlstr.

Meiserstr.

Briennerstr.

Barerstr.

Max-Joseph-Str.

Oskar-von-Miller-Ring

Marsstr.

Seidlstr.

Dachauer Str.

Sophienstr.

Alter Botanischer Garten

MAXIMILIANSPL.

SALVATORPL.

Kard.-Faulhaber-Str.

Arnulfstr.

H
S HAUPTBHF.

BAHNHOFPL.

Hauptbahnhof

Elisenstr.

Prielmayerstr.

Schützenstr.

Justizpalast

U KARLSPL.

LENBACHPL.

Pacellistr.

PROMENADEPL.

American Express
[Promenadeplatz 6]

Bayerstr.

G

U HAUPTBHF.
F

KARLSPL.
S
KARLSPL.

Schlosserstr.

E

Schwanthalerstr.

Landwehrstr.

Goethestr.

Schillerstr.

D

C

Sonnenstr.

Herzog-Wilhelm-Str.

Neuhauserstr.

Michaelskirche

Kaufingerstr.

Frauenkirche

FRAUEN-PL.

Weinstr.

Neues Rathaus

MARIENPL. S

Brunnstr.

Hotterstr.

Rosenstr.

Rosental

Asamkirche

Sendlinger Str.

Münchener Stadtmuseum

Pettenkoferstr.

B Sendlinger Tor

Oberanger

Unteranger

Blumenstr.

Corneliusstr.

Nussbaumstr.

SENDLINGER-TOR U

Lindwurmstr.

Müllerstr.

Blumen str.

Müllerstr.

Fraunhofer

H.-Sachsstr.

Jahn Str.

Klenzestr.

TO THERESIENWIESE

N

0   1/4 mile
0   1/4 kilometer

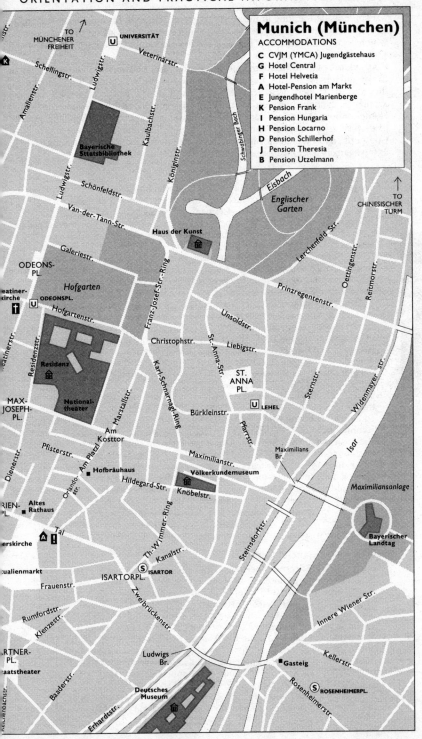

Munich (München)

ACCOMMODATIONS

- **C** CVJM (YMCA) Jugendgästehaus
- **G** Hotel Central
- **F** Hotel Helvetia
- **A** Hotel-Pension am Markt
- **E** Jungendhotel Marienberge
- **K** Pension Frank
- **I** Pension Hungaria
- **H** Pension Locarno
- **D** Pension Schillerhof
- **J** Pension Theresia
- **B** Pension Utzelmann

TO
MÜNCHENER
FREIHEIT

UNIVERSITÄT

Veterinärstr.

Schellingstr.

Ludwigstr.

Amalienstr.

Kaulbachstr.

Königinstr.

Schwabinger Bach

Bayerische Staatsbibliothek

Schönfeldstr.

Ludwigstr.

Eisbach

Englischer Garten

TO
CHINESISCHER
TURM

Van-der-Tann-Str.

Haus der Kunst

Galeriestr.

Lerchenfeld Str.

Oettingenstr.

Reitmorstr.

ODEONS-PL.

Theatiner-kirche

ODEONSPL.

Hofgarten

Prinzregentenstr.

Hofgartenstr.

Franz-Josef-Str.-Ring

Unsöldstr.

Christophstr.

Liebigstr.

Sternstr.

Residenzstr.

Residenz

ST. ANNA PL.

St-Anna-Str.

Karl-Scharnagl-Ring

Widenmayer str.

Isar

MAX-JOSEPH-PL.

National-theater

Marstallstr.

Bürkleinstr.

LEHEL

Pfarrstr.

Am Kosttor

Pfisterstr.

Dienerstr.

Maximilianstr.

Maximilians Br.

Maximiliansanlage

Orlando-str.

Am Platzl

Hofbräuhaus

Völkerkundemuseum

Hildegard-Str.

Knöbelstr.

RIEN-PL.

Altes Rathaus

Steinsdorfstr.

Bayerischer Landtag

erskirche

Tal

Th.-Wimmer-Ring

Kanalstr.

ualienmarkt

Frauenstr.

ISARTORPL.

ISARTOR

Zweibrückenstr.

Rumfordstr.

Klenzestr.

Innere Wiener Str.

Kellerstr.

RTNER-PL.

aatstheater

Baaderstr.

Ludwigs Br.

Gasteig

ROSENHEIMERPL.

Rosenheimerstr.

Deutsches Museum

Erhardstr.

Karlspl. outside the Ring in the west. To get to Marienpl. from the train station, go straight on Schützenstr. to Karlspl., then continue through Karlstor to Neuhauserstr., which becomes Kaufingerstr. before it reaches Marienpl. (15-20min.). Or take S-Bahn #1-8 two stops from the main train station to "Marienpl."

At Odeonspl., the **Residenz** palace sprawls, and **Ludwigstraße** stretches north to the university district. **Leopoldstraße,** Ludwigstr.'s continuation, reaches farther into the student area, **Schwabing** ("Schwabylon"). To the west is the **Olympiazentrum;** even farther west sits the posh **Nymphenburg,** built around the **Schloß Nymphenburg** (Nymphenburg palace). Southwest of Marienpl., **Sendlingerstraße** leads past shops to the Sendlinger Tor. From there, Lindwurmstr. proceeds to Goethepl., from which Mozartstr. leads to **Theresienwiese,** site of the annual beer extravaganza—*Oktoberfest.*

Transportation

Flights: For flight info, call 97 52 13 13. **Flughafen München** is accessible from the train station by S-Bahn #8, which runs daily every 20min. 3:35am-12:35am (DM14 or 8 strips; Eurail, InterRail, and German railpasses valid).

Trains: Munich is the transportation hub of southern Germany. The **Hauptbahnhof** (tel. 22 33 12 56) has connections throughout Europe several times per day to **Vienna** (4-5hr.), **Amsterdam** (9hr.), **Berlin** (7½hr.), **Frankfurt** (3½hr.), **Hamburg** (6hr.), **Paris** (10hr.), and **Prague** (6-8½hr.). Call 194 19 for schedules, fare information, and reservations (6am-10:30pm); you can also get a **destination booklet** *(Städteverbindungen)* from the Reisezentrum info counters.

Public Transportation: The **MVV** system runs M-F 5am-12:30am, Sa-Su until 2:30am. Eurail, InterRail, and German railpasses are valid on any S-Bahn (commuter rail) but *not* on the U-Bahn (subway), *Straßenbahn,* or buses. Single ride tickets (with transfers) are DM3.50 within the *Innenraum* (city center). A *Streifenkarte* (11-strip ticket) costs DM15. Use 2 strips per person. Single-day tickets give 1 person unlimited travel (city center DM8.50). The **Innenraum 3-day pass** (DM21) is available at the *Hauptbahnhof* MVV office behind tracks 31 and 32. Stamp your ticket in the boxes marked with an "E" *before you go to the platform* (or on board a bus). If you cheat, the fine is DM60.

Bike Rental: Radius Bikes (tel. 59 61 13), in the rear of the *Hauptbahnhof* near tracks 30-31. 2hr. DM10; full-day DM30. DM100 deposit. 10% student or Eurail discount. Offers **biking tours** (DM12-19). Open daily Apr. to early Oct. 10am-6pm.

Hitchhiking: Those offering rides post info in the **Mensa** (cafeteria) on Leopoldstr. 13. Otherwise, hitchers try *Autobahn* on-ramps. Hitchers heading to E11 **"Salzburg-Vienna-Italy"** take U-Bahn #1 or 2 to "Karl-Preis-Pl." For E11 in the other direction ("Stuttgart/France"), they take streetcar #17 "Amalienburgstr." Those aiming for the E6 interchange north to **Berlin** take U-Bahn #6 to "Studentenstadt" and walk 500m to the Frankfurter Ring. A safer bet is **McShare Treffpunkt Zentrale,** Klenzestr. 57b and Lämmerstr. 4 (tel. 59 45 61), which matches drivers with passengers (Berlin DM54; open daily 8am-8pm). **Frauenmitfahrzentrale,** Klenzestr. 57b, is for **women only.** Take U-Bahn #1 or 2 to "Fraunhoferstr.," up Fraunhoferstr. away from the river and turn right. Open M-F 8am-8pm.

Tourist and Financial Services

Tourist Offices: Fremdenverkehrsamt (tel. 23 33 02 56 or 23 33 02 57; fax 23 33 02 33; http://www.munich-tourist.de), on the main train station's east side. Books rooms (free with a 10-15% deposit) and sells accommodations lists (DM1) and excellent city maps (DM0.50). *München Infopool* (DM1) is aimed at young tourists. Open M-Sa 9am-10pm, Su 10am-6pm. A **branch office** (tel. 233 03 00), at the airport in the *Zentralgebäude,* provides general info, but no room bookings. Open M-Sa 8:30am-10pm, Su 1-9pm. **EurAide in English** (tel. 59 38 89; fax 550 39 65; http://www.cube.net/kmu/euraide.html), along Track 11 (room 3) of the *Hauptbahnhof,* is good for transportation needs. Room reservations DM7. Open from June-*Oktoberfest* daily 7:45am-noon and 1-6pm; Oct.-Apr. M-F 7:45am-noon and 1-4pm, Sa 7:45am-noon; May daily 7:45am-noon and 1-4:30pm.

Tours: Mike's Bike Tours (tel. 651 42 75). 4hr. tours 1-2 times daily Mar.-Oct. from the *Altes Rathaus* (6hr. tours daily June-Aug.); DM31-45. **Munich Walks** (tel.

(0177) 227 59 01). 2½hr. guided tours in English provide an historical overview (1-2 times daily) or emphasize Nazi history (1-3 times weekly Apr.-Oct.). DM10-15.

Budget Travel: Council Travel, Adalbertstr. 32 (tel. 39 50 22; fax 39 70 04), near the university, sells ISICs. Open M-F 10am-1pm and 2-6:30pm.

Consulates: Australians contact the consulate in Bonn (tel. (0228) 81 030). **Canada,** Tal 29 (tel. 219 95 70). Open M-Th 9am-noon and 2-5pm, F 9am-noon and 2-3:30pm. **Ireland,** Mauerkircherstr. 1a (tel. 98 57 23). Open M-F 9am-noon and 1-4pm. **New Zealanders** head to the consulate in Bonn tel. (0228) 22 80 70). **South Africa,** Sendlinger-Tor-Pl. 5 (tel. 231 16 30). Open M-F 9am-noon. **U.K.,** Bürklein-str. 10 (tel. 21 10 90), 4th fl. Consular section open M-F 8:45-11:30am and 1-3:15pm. **U.S.,** Königinstr. 5 (tel. 288 80). No longer handles visas; for info, call (0190) 27 07 89 for a recording, (0190) 91 50 00 M-F 7am-8pm for an official. Open M-F 8-11am.

Currency Exchange: American Express is cheapest; otherwise pick up a copy of EurAide's free publication *Inside Track* and take it to the **Reise Bank** (tel. 55 10 80), at the main station, in front of the main entrance on Bahnhofpl., for a 50% discount on commission (regularly DM3-10) if cashing US$50 or more in U.S. traveler's checks (open daily 6am-11pm). Also at track 11 (open M-Sa 7:30am-7:15pm, Su 9:30am-12:30pm and 1-4:45pm).

American Express: Promenadepl. 6 (tel. 29 09 00; 24hr. hotline (0130) 85 31 00; fax 29 09 01 18), in the Hotel Bayerischer Hof. Holds mail, cashes traveler's checks, no fee. Open M-F 9am-5:30pm, Sa 9:30am-12:30pm.

Local Services

Luggage Storage: At the **train station;** staffed storage room *(Gepäckaufbewahrung)* open daily 6am-11pm. DM4 per piece per day. Lockers DM2-4 per 24hr.

Bookstore: Anglia English Bookshop, Schellingstr. 3 (tel. 28 36 42). Reams of books in a gloriously chaotic atmosphere. Open M-F 9am-6:30pm, Sa 10am-2pm.

Gay and Lesbian Organizations: Gay services info tel. 260 30 56. Lesbian info tel. 725 42 72 (open F 6-10pm), or **Lesbentraum LeTra** (tel. 725 42 72; open Th 7-10pm).

Laundromat: The **City SB-Waschcenter,** Paul-Heyse-Str. 21, near the station; wash and soap DM6. Open daily 7am-11pm. **Münz Waschsalon,** Amalienstr. 61, near the university. Wash DM6.20. Open M-F 8am-6:30pm, Sa 8am-1pm.

Emergency: Police, tel. 110. **Ambulance,** tel. 192 22. **Emergency medical service,** tel. 55 17 71. **Fire,** tel. 112. **Poison Control,** tel. 192 40.

Crisis Lines: Rape Crisis, Frauennotruf München, Güllstr. 3 (tel. 76 37 37). **AIDS Hotline,** tel. 520 73 87 or 520 74 12 (open M-Th 8am-3pm, F 8am-noon) or 194 11 (open M-Sa 7-10pm).

Pharmacy: Bahnhof Apotheke, Bahnhofpl. 2 (tel. 59 41 19 or 59 81 19), outside the station. Open M-F 8am-6:30pm, Sa 8am-2pm. 24hr. service rotates—call 59 44 75 for info in German, or get a schedule at the tourist office or EurAide.

Medical Assistance: Klinikum Rechts d.Isar, across the river on Ismaningerstr. (U-Bahn #4 or 5 "Max-Weber-Pl."). U.K. and U.S. consulates carry lists of English-speaking doctors.

Post Office: Post/Telegrafenamt, Arnulfstr. 32., 80074 München (tel. 54 54 23 36). *Poste Restante* and money exchange. Go out of the train station and turn left onto Arnulfstr.; the post office is on your right. Open M-F 8am-8pm, Sa 8am-noon.

Internet Access: Internet-Café (see **Food,** p. 469), or at **Hotel Kurpfalz.**

Telephone Code: 089.

ACCOMMODATIONS AND CAMPING

Munich accommodations fall into one of three categories: seedy, expensive, or booked. Reserve in advance in summer and during *Oktoberfest,* when all three often apply. Sleeping in the *Englischer Garten* or train station is unsafe and illegal. HI hostels are not supposed to accept solo travelers over 26, although families may book rooms.

Hostels and Camping

Jugendlager Kapuzinerhölzl ("The Tent"), In den Kirschen 30 (tel. 141 43 00). Streetcar #17 (dir. Amalienburgstr.):"Botanischer Garten," go straight on Franz-Schrank-Str., then turn left. Sleep with 400 others on a foam pad under a circus tent with ping pong and its own beer garden. **Kitchen** and **laundry** facilities (DM4). DM13. Breakfast included. Actual "beds" DM17. Lockers provided; bring a lock or rent 1 for DM2. Reception 24hr. Reservations for groups over 15. Open mid-June to early-Sept.

4 you münchen (ökologisches Jugendgästehaus), Hirtenstr. 18 (tel. 552 16 60; fax 55 21 66 66), 200m from the *Hauptbahnhof*. Beautiful and ecological, with facilities for the handicapped. Dorms DM24-29; singles DM54; doubles DM76; over 27 15% surcharge. Breakfast DM7.50. Sheets DM5. Key deposit DM20. In adjoining hotel, singles DM79; doubles DM110. Breakfast included. Reception 7am-1:30pm, 3-7pm, and 7:30-10pm.

Jugendherberge München (HI), Wendl-Dietrich-Str. 20 (tel. 13 11 56). U-Bahn #1: "Rotkreuzpl." then cross Rotkreuzpl. toward the Kaufhof store. This hostel is well-located. Dorms DM23-25.50. Breakfast and sheets included. Mandatory key deposit DM20. Safes with DM50 deposit. Check-in at 11am, but lines start before 9am. Reception 24hr. Reservations only accepted a week in advance; if you get 1, arrive by 6pm or call first.

Jump In, Hochstr. 51 (tel. 48 95 34 37), S-Bahn #1-8: "Rosenheimerpl."; take the Gasteig. Exit. Small and delightfully informal. Accessible location; spartan rooms. DM29-35; doubles DM78. **Kitchen.** Reception 10am-1pm and 5-10pm. No curfew.

Jugendhotel Marienberge, Goethestr. 9 (tel. 55 58 05), less than a block from the train station, staffed by merry nuns. **Women under 26** only. **Kitchen** and **laundry** facilities (wash/dry DM2 each). Dorms DM30; singles DM40; doubles DM70. Breakfast included. Reception 8am-midnight. Curfew midnight.

Camping: Campingplatz Thalkirchen, Zentralländstr. 49 (tel. 723 17 07; fax 724 31 77). U-Bahn #1 or 2: "Sendlinger Tor," then #3: "Thalkirchen," and change to bus #57. **Laundry** facilities and a restaurant (meals DM3-8). Showers DM2. DM7.90 per person; tent DM5.50-7. Curfew 11pm.

Hotels and Pensions

When the city is full, finding clean singles under DM55-65 and doubles under DM80-100 in a safe area is nearly impossible. Reserving weeks ahead is particularly important during *Oktoberfest*. The tourist office and EurAide find rooms for a DM5-6 fee.

Hotel Helvetia, Schillerstr. 6 (tel. 590 68 50; fax 59 06 85 70), to the right as you exit the station. Recently renovated. Singles DM53-62; doubles DM68-115; triples DM99-120. Breakfast included. Hostel-like dorms DM19-24. Breakfast DM7. Sheets DM4. **Laundry** service DM8.50. *Oktoberfest* prices 10-15% higher. Reception 24hr.

Pension Frank, Schellingstr. 24 (tel. 28 14 51; fax 280 09 10). U-Bahn #3 or 6: "Universität." Fabulous location for café and bookstore aficionados. Dorms DM35; singles DM55-65; doubles DM78-85; during *Oktoberfest* add DM5. Breakfast included. Reception 7:30am-10pm.

Hotel Kurpfalz, Schwanthalerstr. 121 (tel. 540 98 60; fax 54 09 88 11; email hotel-kurpfalz@munich-online.de). Exit the station onto Bayerstr., turn right down Bayerstr., and veer left onto Holzapfelstr. Free **Internet access.** Singles DM89; doubles DM129, with extra cot DM165. Breakfast included. Reception 24hr.

FOOD

Munich's gastronomic center is the vibrant **Viktualienmarkt,** two minutes south of Marienpl., with a rainbow of bread, fruit, meat, pastry, cheese, wine, vegetable, and sandwich shops. (Generally open M-F 9am-6:30pm, Sa 9am-2pm.) Otherwise, look for cheap meals in the **university district** off Ludwigstr. **Tengelmann,** Schützenstr. 7, near the train station, satisfies grocery needs quickly and conveniently. (Open M-W and F 8:30am-6:30pm, Th 8:30am-8:30pm, Sa 9am-2pm.) You can also eat at several university cafeterias, all of which serve at least one vegetarian dish. The **Ludwig Maximilian University,** Leopoldstr. 13 (behind the large pink building; U-Bahn #3 or 6) serves food (Dec.-July M-Th 9am-4:30pm, F 9am-3pm; Aug.-Nov. M-Th 9am-3:45pm, F 9am-3pm). The **Technical University,** Arcisstr. 17, to the left of the Pinothek museum, also sells grub (M-Th 8:30am-4:15pm, F 8:30am-2:30pm; student ID required).

Türkenhof, Türkenstr. 78. Smoky and buzzing from noon till night. Creative dishes (*Schnitzel,* omelettes, soups) DM7-14. Vegetarian-friendly. Open Su-Th 11am-1am, F-Sa 11am-3am.

Schelling Salon, Schellingstr. 54. Bavarian *Knödel* and billiard balls since 1872; Lenin, Rilke, and Strauss used to drop in. Breakfast DM5-9; *Wurst* DM6-7. Restaurant and billiards museum open M and Th-Su 6:30am-1pm.

buxs, Frauenstr. 9, on the Viktualienmarkt. Vegetarian café/restaurant with salads (DM3 per 100g) and tasty pastas. Open M-F 11am-8:30pm, Sa 11am-3:30pm.

Internet-Café, Nymphenburgerstr. 145 (http://www.icafe.spacenet.de). U-Bahn #1: "Rotkreuzpl." Unlimited free **Internet access** with an order of pasta (DM9.50), pizza (DM7.50-10), or beer (DM4.90 for 0.5L). Open daily 11am-4am.

SIGHTS

The **Marienplatz** serves as an interchange for major S-Bahn and U-Bahn lines as well as the social nexus of the city. On the square, the onion-domed towers of the 15th-century **Frauenkirche** have long been one of Munich's notable landmarks. *(Towers open Apr.-Oct. M-Sa 10am-5pm. DM4, students DM2.)* At the neo-Gothic **Neues Rathaus** (new city hall), the **Glockenspiel** marks the hour at 11am, noon, 5, and 9pm with jousting knights and dancing barrel-makers. *(Tower open M-F 9am-7pm, Sa 9am-7pm, Su 10am-7pm. DM2.50.)* According to legend, the barrel-makers coaxed citizens out of their homes by singing and dancing to convince them that the latest attack of the black plague had passed. At 9pm, a mechanical watchman marches out and a Guardian Angel escorts the *Münchner Kindl* ("Munich Child," the city's symbol) to bed.

The 11th-century **Peterskirche** is at Rindermarkt and Peterspl.; 302 steps scale the saintly tower, christened *Alter Peter* (Old Peter) by locals. *(Tower open M-Sa 9am-7pm, Su 10am-7pm. DM2.50, students DM1.50.)* Nearby, Ludwig II of Bavaria rests in a crypt of the 16th-century Jesuit **Michaelskirche,** on Neuhauserstr. *(Crypt DM2, students DM1.)* A Bavarian Rococo masterpiece, the **Asamkirche,** Sendlingerstr. 32, is named after brothers Cosmas and Egid, who vowed to build it if they survived a shipwreck. The magnificent **Residenz,** Max-Joseph-Pl. 3, boasts richly decorated rooms built with the wealth of the Wittelsbach dynasty, Bavaria's ruling family from the 12th to the early 20th century. *(Open Tu-Su 10am-4:30pm; last admission 4pm. DM6, students with ID and seniors DM4.)* The grounds now house several museums, and the **Schatzkammer** (treasury) contains jeweled baubles, crowns, swords, and ivory from as early as the 10th century. To reach the *Residenz,* take U-Bahn #3, 4, 5, or 6 to "Odeonspl."

Ludwig I's summer residence, **Schloß Nymphenburg,** is worth the trip northwest of town; take streetcar #17 (dir: Amalienburgstr.): "Schloß Nymphenburg." *(Open Tu-Su Apr.-Sept. 9am-noon and 1-5pm; Oct.-Mar. 10am-12:30pm and 1:30-4pm. Main palace DM6, students and seniors DM4; entire complex DM8, students DM5. Grounds free.)* A Baroque wonder set in a winsome park, the palace hides treasures like a two-story granite marble hall seasoned with stucco, frescoes, and a Chinese lacquer cabinet. Check out Ludwig's "Gallery of Beauties"—whenever a woman caught his fancy, he would have her portrait painted. Next door is the immense **Botanischer Garten,** where greenhouses shelter rare and exotic flora. *(Open daily 9am-8pm; greenhouses 9-11:45am and 1-7:30pm. DM4, students DM2.)* Abutting the city center is the **Englischer Garten,** one of Europe's oldest landscaped parks.

MUSEUMS Munich is a supreme museum city. Take a break from Monet et al. at the **Deutsches Museum,** on the *Museumsinsel* (Museum Island) in the Isar River (S-Bahn #1-8: "Isartor"), one of the world's largest, most exciting museums of science and technology. *(Open daily 9am-5pm. DM10, students DM4.)* Particularly interesting are the mining exhibit, which winds through a labyrinth of recreated subterranean tunnels,

GATEWAY CITIES

the planetarium (DM3), and the daily electrical show. The **Neue Pinakothek,** Barer-str. 29, exhibits the work of 18th- to 20th-century masters such as Van Gogh and Klimt, while the **Alte Pinakothek,** next door, displays Giotto, da Vinci, Raphael, Rembrandt, Dürer, and Rubens, among others. *(Both open Tu and Th 10am-8pm, W and F-Su 10am-5pm. DM7, students DM4.)* **Lenbachhaus,** Luisenstr. 33, houses Munich city-scapes, along with works by Kandinsky, Klee, and other members of the Blaue Reiter school, which forged the modernist abstract aesthetic. *(Open Tu-Su 10am-6pm. DM8, students DM4.)* Between them, **Glyptohek,** Königspl. 3, and **Antikensammlung,** Königspl. 1, hold Munich's finest collection of ancient art. *(Glyptohek open Tu-Su 10am-5pm, Th until 8pm. Antikensammlung open Tu-Su 10am-5pm, W 'til 8pm. Joint admission DM10, students DM5.)* **Staatsgalerie moderner Kunst,** Prinzregentenstr. 1, in the **Haus der Kunst,** has an excellent 20th-century collection that includes Klee, Picasso, and Dalí. *(Open Tu-Su 10am-5pm, Th until 8pm. DM6, students DM3.50.)* The Haus der Kunst was built by Nazis and opened with the famous exhibit on "degenerate art." The **ZAM: Zentrum für Außergewöhnliche Museen** (Center for Unusual Museums), Westenriederstr. 41, includes favorites like the Corkscrew Museum, Museum of Easter Bunnies, and the Chamberpot Museum. *(Open daily 10am-6pm. DM8, students DM5.)* If you're looking for the kinky rather than the quirky, try the **Museum für erotische Kunst** (Museum of Erotic Art), Odeonspl. 8. *(U-Bahn #3-6: "Odeonspl." or bus #53. Open Tu-Su 11am-7pm. DM8, students DM6.)*

ENTERTAINMENT

Munich's streets erupt with bawdy beer halls, rowdy discos, and cafés every night. Pick up *Munich Found* (DM4), *in münchen* (free), or the hip and hefty *Prinz* (DM5) at any newsstand to find out *was ist los* (what's up.)

BEER To most visitors, Munich means beer. The six great city labels are Augustiner, Hacker-Pschorr, Hofbräu, Löwenbräu, Paulaner-Thomasbräu, and Spaten-Franzins-kaner; each brand supplies its own beer halls. Beer is served by the Maß (about a liter; DM8-11). The biggest keg party in the world, Munich's **Oktoberfest** (Sept. 18-Oct. 3 in 1999) features speeches, a parade of horse-drawn beer wagons, and the mayor tapping the first ceremonial barrel. The Hofbräu tent is the rowdiest (for more info on the Oktoberfest see http://www.munich-tourist.de). Most Müncheners claim that **Augustiner Keller,** Arnulfstr. 52 (S-Bahn #1-8: "Hackerbrücke"), is the finest beer garden in town, with lush grounds and 100-year-old chestnut trees. (Maß DM11. Open daily 10am-1am; beer garden open 10:30am-midnight. Food (DM10-28) served until 10pm.) The world-famous **Hofbräuhaus,** Am Platzl 9, two blocks from Marienpl., has been tapping barrels for commoners since 1897 and now seems reserved for drunken tourists; 15,000-30,000L of beer are sold each day (Maß DM10.40; sausages and sauerkraut DM10; open daily 9:30am-midnight). The largest beer garden in Europe, **Hirschgarten,** Hirschgartenallee 1 (U-Bahn #1: "Rotkreuzpl.," then streetcar #12: "Romanpl."), is boisterous and verdant (Maß DM8.60; open daily 11am-11pm; restaurant open Nov.-Feb. Tu-Su).

THEATER, MUSIC, AND NIGHTLIFE Stages sprinkled throughout the city span styles and tastes from dramatic classics at the **Residenztheater** and **Volkstheater** to comic opera at the **Staatstheater am Gärtnerplatz** to experimental works at the **Theater im Marstall** in Nymphenburg. The tourist office's Monatsprogramm (DM2.50) lists schedules for all of Munich's stages. Standing tickets sell for about DM10. Munich's **Opera Festival** (in July) is held in the **Bayerische Staatsoper** (tel. 21 85 19 20), accompanied by a concert series in the Nymphenburg and Schleissheim palaces. (Regular season standing-room and student tickets DM6-20. Box office open M-F 10am-6pm, Sa 10am-1pm.) **Gasteig Kulturzentrum,** Rosenheimerstr. 5 (tel. 48 09 80, box office tel. 54 89 89), hosts diverse musical performances on the former site of the Bürgerbräukeller, where Adolf Hitler launched his abortive Beer Hall Putsch. (Box office in the Glashalle open M-F 10:30am-2pm and 3-6pm, Sa 10:30am-2pm, and 1hr. before curtain.) The **Muffathalle,** Zellerstr. 4 (tel. 45 87 50 00), in Haidhausen, a former power plant, still generates energy with techno, hip-hop, jazz, and dance performances (DM30; M-Sa until 4am, Su until 1am).

Munich's nightlife is a curious mix of Bavarian *Gemütlichkeit* (smugness) and trendsters, so dress well. **Münchener Freiheit** is the most famous and touristy bar/café district. More low-key is the southwestern section of **Schwabing**, directly behind the university on Amalienstr. The center of Munich's homosexual scene lies within the "Golden Triangle," defined by Sendlinger Tor, the Viktualienmarkt/Gärtnerpl. area, and Isartor. Mingle with an English-speaking crowd at **Günther Murphy's**, Nikolaistr. 9a (Guinness DM6; open M-F 5pm-1am, Sa 2pm-3am, Su noon-1am). Things get rolling late at **Nachtcafe**, Maximilianspl. 5, with live jazz, funk, soul, and blues until the wee hours (beer DM8 for 0.3L). Dance clubs include the huge complex **Kunstpark Ost**, Grafingerstr. 6 (hours, cover, and themes vary—call 49 00 29 28 for info and tickets) and **Nachtwerk and Club**, Landesbergerstr. 185, twin clubs spinning mainstream dance tunes for sweaty crowds (beer DM6; cover DM10; open daily 10pm-4am). **Backstage**, Helmholzstr. 18, has a wide range of music and funky theme nights (open W-Th until 3am, F-Sa until 5am). **Club Morizz**, Klenzestr. 43, reminiscent of *Casablanca* scenes, is frequented by gay men and a few lesbians (open Su-Th 7pm-2am, F-Sa 7pm-3am).

■ The German Danube: Passau

Napoleon once said, "I have not seen a city as beautiful as Passau in all of Germany." Sitting on two peninsulas forged by the confluence of the Danube, Inn, and Ilz Rivers, other people sometimes call Passau the "Bavarian Venice." Draw your own conclusions. A heavily fortified medieval castle, a musty Gothic *Rathaus*, and a row of residential palaces of erstwhile bishops bear witness to the fact that this Dreiflüssestadt (3-river city) was once an administrative, commercial, and ecclesiastical power. The city's bombastic architecture reaches its apex in the lovely **Stephansdom** (St. Stephen's Cathedral). Hundreds of cherubs are sprawled across the ceiling, and the world's largest **church organ** looms above the choir. (Open M-Sa 8-11am and 12:30-6pm. Free. **Organ concerts** May-Oct. M-Sa noon DM4, students DM2; Th 7:30pm DM10, DM5.) The **Domschatz** (cathedral treasury), within the **Residenz** behind the cathedral, houses an extravagant collection of gold and tapestries. (Open May-Oct. M-F 10am-4pm. DM2.) Nearby is the gilded **St. Michael**, built by the Jesuits. (Open Apr.-Oct. Tu-Su 9am-5pm; Nov.-Jan. and Mar. 10am-4pm. DM3, students DM1.50.) The 13th-century **Rathaus** is less opulent but stunning. (Open May 16-Sept. daily 10am-5pm; Easter-May 15 10am-4pm; Oct. M-F 10am-4pm. DM2, students DM1.)

The **tourist office**, Rathauspl. 3 (tel. (0851) 95 59 80), has free maps and reserves rooms for a DM5 fee. (Open Apr.-Oct. M-F 8:30am-6pm, Sa-Su 10am-2pm; Nov.-Mar. M-Th 8:30am-5pm, F 8:30am-4pm.) The **train station** (tel. (0851) 194 19), west of downtown on Bahnhofstr., serves **Vienna** (3¼hr.), **Regensburg** (1-2hr.), **Nuremburg** (2hr.), and **Munich** (2hr.). Ferries chug along the Danube to **Linz**, Austria from May to October daily at 9am (5hr.). The **Jugendherberge (HI)**, Veste Oberhaus 125 (tel. (0851) 413 51; fax 437 09), is a long walk for decent facilities. (Dorms DM16.50. Breakfast included. Sheets DM5.50. Reception 7-11:30am and 4-11:30pm; new arrivals after 6pm only. Curfew 11:30pm.) The **Mensa**, Innstr. 29, offers cafeteria meals for DM2.40-4.50; any student ID will do. From Ludwigspl., follow Nikolastr. and turn right. (Open July-Aug. M-Th 8am-3:30pm, F 8am-3pm; Sept.-June M-Th 8am-4pm, F 8am-3pm.) **Ratskeller**, Rathauspl. 2, a bustling restaurant in the back of the *Rathaus* overlooking the Danube, serves salads (DM4) and daily "local cuisine" specials (DM8-17; open daily 10am-11pm).

■ Budapest

At once a cosmopolitan European capital and the stronghold of Magyar nationalism, Budapest awakened from its Communist cocoon with the same pride that rebuilt the city from the rubble of World War II and endured the Soviet invasion of 1956.

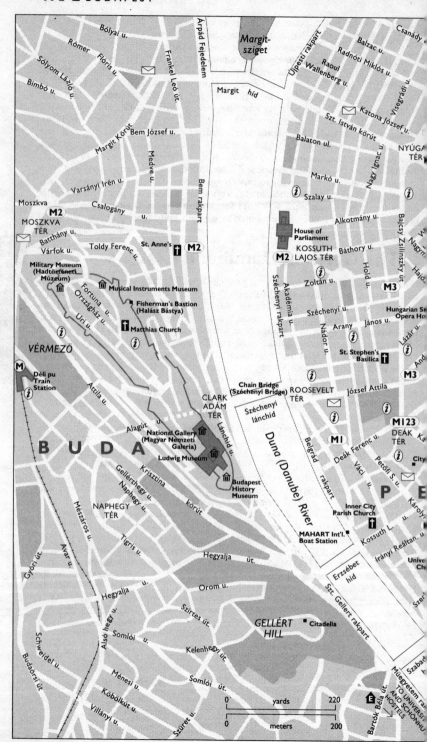

Bólyai u.

Árpád Fejedelem

Margit-
sziget

Csanády

Rómer

Florís u.

Balzac u.

Radnóti Miklós u.

Sólyom László u.

Frankel Leó út.

Margit híd

Raoul
Wallenberg u.

NYÚGA
TÉR

Bimbó u.

Bem József u.

Katona József u.

Medve u.

Szt. István körút

Margit Körút

Balaton ul.

Nagy Ignac u.

Varsányi Irén u.

Bem rakpart

Markó u.

Bácsy Zsilinszky út.

Csalogány

u.

Markó u.

Alkotmány u.

Moszkva

Szalay u.

Nagy

MOSZKVA
TÉR

M2

House of
Parliament

Hold u.

Batthány u.

KOSSUTH
LAJOS TÉR

Báthory u.

M3

Várfok u.

Toldy Ferenc u.

St. Anne's

M2

M2

Zoltán u.

Military Museum
(Hadtörténeti
Múzeum)

Musical Instruments Museum

Akadémia u.

Széchenyi rakpart

Hungarian S
Opera Ho

Fortuna
Országház u.

Fisherman's Bastion
(Halász Bástya)

Széchenyi u.

Arany

János u.

Uri u.

Matthias Church

Nádor u.

St. Stephen's
Basilica

M3

VÉRMEZŐ

Lázár u.

And

Chain Bridge
(Széchenyi Bridge)

ROOSEVELT
TÉR

József Attila u.

M

Déli pu
Train
Station

Attila u.

CLARK
ADÁM
TÉR

Széchenyi
lánchíd

M123

DEÁK
TÉR

B U D A

Alagút

National Gallery
(Magyar Nemzeti
Galeria)

Lánchíd u.

Duna (Danube) River

Belgrád rakpart

M1

Deák Ferenc u.

City

Krisztina

Ludwig Museum

Váci u.

Petőfi S. u.

Károly

Gellérhegy u.

Naphegy u.

Budapest
History
Museum

Inner City
Parish Church

NAPHEGY
TÉR

körút

Kossuth L.

Mészáros u.

Tigris u.

Hegyalja út.

MAHART Int'l.
Boat Station

Irányi Reáltan. u.

Unive
Ch

Avar u.

Orom u.

Erzsébet
híd

Győri út.

Hegyalja

Szirtes út.

Szt. Gellért rakpart

Szer

Schweidel u.

Alsó hegy u.

Somlói u.

Kelenhegy út.

GELLÉRT
HILL

Citadella

Budaörsi út.

Ménesi u.

Somlói út.

Szabad

Köbölkút u.

Muegyetem ra
AND SCHONHU
TO UNIVERS
AND HOSTELS

Villányi út.

Szüret u.

Barók Béla út.

0   yards   220

E

0   meters   200

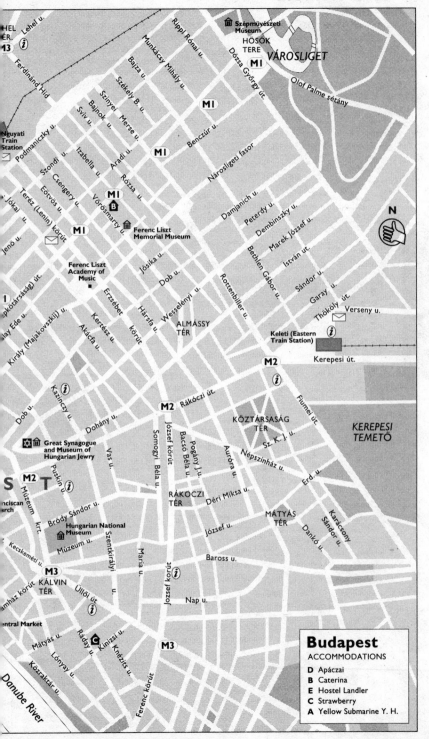

Budapest

ACCOMMODATIONS

D Apáczai
B Caterina
E Hostel Landler
C Strawberry
A Yellow Submarine Y. H.

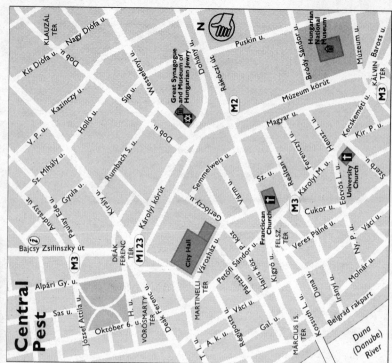

Central Pest

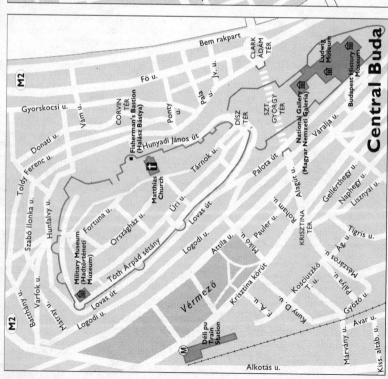

Central Buda

Endowed with an architectural majesty befitting the Habsburg Empire's number two city, Budapest is graceful and multifaceted. Today, the city maintains its charm and vibrant spirit—although neon lights and hordes of tourists have added a new twist to the Budapest rhapsody, the main theme is still, below it all, expertly played by unspoiled Magyar strings.

ORIENTATION AND PRACTICAL INFORMATION

Previously two cities, Buda and Pest (PESHT), separated by the **Duna** (Danube), modern Budapest straddles the river in north-central Hungary 250km downstream from Vienna. On the west bank, **Buda** inspires countless artists with its hilltop citadel, trees, and cobblestone **Castle District,** while on the east side **Pest** pulses as the heart of the modern city. Three bridges bind the two halves together: **Széchenyi lánchíd,** slender, white **Erzsébet híd,** and green **Szabadság híd.**

Moszkva tér (Moscow Sq.), just down the north slope of the Castle District, is where virtually all trams and buses start or end their routes. One metro stop away in the direction of Örs vezér tere, **Batthyány tér** lies opposite the Parliament building on the west bank; this is the starting node of the **HÉV commuter railway.** Budapest's three metro lines converge at **Deák tér,** at the core of Pest's loosely concentric ring boulevards, next to the main international bus terminal at **Erzsébet tér.**

Many street names occur more than once in town; always check the district as well as the type of street. Moreover, streets arbitrarily change names from one block to the next. Because many have shed their Communist labels, an up-to-date **map** is essential. To check if your map of Budapest is useful, look at the avenue leading from Pest toward the City Park (Városliget) in the east: the name should be Andrássy út. The **American Express** and **Tourinform** offices have reliable and free tourist maps, while *Belváros Idegenforgalmi Térképe* is available at any metro stop (199Ft).

Transportation Services

Flights: Ferihegy Airport (tel. 267 43 33, info tel. 357 71 55, reservations tel. 357 91 23). Volánbusz (every 30min., 5:30am-9pm) takes 30min. to terminal 1 and 40min. to terminal 2 (500Ft) from Erzsébet tér. The **airport minibus** (tel. 296 85 55) will pick you up anywhere in the city, or take you anywhere from the airport (1200Ft). Call for pick-up 24hr. in advance. Youth and stand-by discounts available at the **Malév office** (see **Budget Travel,** below).

Trains: For domestic info, call 461 54 00, international 461 55 00. The word for train station is *pályaudvar,* often abbreviated "pu." Those under 26 get a 33% discount on international tickets. Show your ISIC and tell the clerk *"diák"* (DEE-ak; student). The 3 main stations—**Keleti pu., Nyugati pu.,** and **Déli pu.**—are also metro stops. Each has schedules for the others. To: **Vienna** (3hr., 6800Ft, reservation 620Ft), **Belgrade** (8hr., 7500Ft), **Berlin** (13hr., 20,400Ft, reservation 2500Ft), and **Prague** (6hr., 11,000Ft, reservation 1600Ft). The **Orient Express** arrives daily from Paris and continues on to Istanbul. **Luggage storage** at Keleti pu. (80Ft).

Buses: Info tel. 117 29 66. **Volánbusz main station,** V, Erzsébet tér (tel. 317 25 62). M1, 2, or 3: "Deák tér." Buses to the Czech Republic, Slovakia, Poland, Romania, Turkey, and Ukraine depart from the **Népstadion** terminal on Hungária körút 48/52, as do most domestic buses to eastern Hungary. M2: "Népstadion." Buses to the **Danube Bend** leave from the **Árpád híd** station. To: **Berlin** (14½hr., 15,400Ft), **Bratislava** (4hr., 1970Ft), **Prague** (8½hr., 5100Ft), and **Vienna** (3½hr., 4390Ft).

Public Transportation: The **Metro** (M) is rapid and punctual. There are 3 lines—M1 is yellow, M2 is red, and M3 is blue. "M" indicates a stop, but you won't always find the sign on the street; look for stairs leading down. Most public transportation stops about 11:30pm. The subway, buses, and trams all use the same blue **tickets** that are sold in Metro stations, *Trafik* shops, and by some sidewalk vendors. A single-trip ticket costs 70Ft; punch it in the orange boxes at the gate of the Metro or on board buses and trams (10-trip *tíz jegy* 630Ft; 1-day pass 560Ft; 3-day pass 1120Ft). The **HÉV commuter rail** runs between Batthyány tér in Buda and Szentendre, 40min. north on the Danube Bend, every 15min.

Hydrofoils: MAHART International Boat Station, VI, Belgrád rakpart (tel. 318 19 53; fax 318 77 40), on the Duna near Erzsébet híd, has information and tickets. Open M-F 8am-4pm. Or try **IBUSZ,** VII, Dob u. (tel. 322 16 56; fax 322 72 64). M2: "Astoria." Open M-F 8am-4pm. Arrive at the docks 1hr. before departure for customs and passport control. Eurailpass holders receive a 50% discount. To **Vienna** (6½hr., 12,700Ft, students 10,000Ft).

Taxis: Budataxi, tel. 233 33 33. 100Ft base fare plus 80Ft per km. **Főtaxi,** tel. 222 22 22. These companies are generally much cheaper than taxis hailed in the street. Always make sure the driver starts his meter, and ask about rates before getting in.

Tourist and Financial Services

Tourist Offices: All tourist offices have *Budapest Kártya,* which buys 3 days of public transportation use, entrance to all museums, and other discounts (2900Ft). **Tourinform,** V, Sütő u. 2 (tel. 317 98 00; fax 317 95 78), off Deák tér just behind McDonald's. M1, 2, or 3: "Deák tér." Busy and multilingual. Open M-F 9am-7pm, Sa-Su 9am-4pm. Accommodations bookings available at **IBUSZ** and **Budapest Tourist** (offices in train stations and tourist centers). The 24hr. IBUSZ central office is at V, Ferenciek tér 10 (tel. 337 09 39; fax 318 49 83).

Budget Travel: Express, V, Szabadság tér 16 (tel. 131 77 77). Some reduced international air and rail fares for the under-26 crowd (reductions also available at train stations). ISIC for 700Ft. Open M-F 8am-6pm, Sa 8am-noon. Amazing discounts for those under 26 available at the **Malév office,** V, Dorottya u. 2 (tel. 235 38 04; fax 266 27 84), on Vörösmarty tér. Open M-F 7:30am-5pm.

Embassies: Australia, XII, Királyhágó tér 8/9 (tel. 201 88 99). M2: "Déli pu.", then bus 21: "Királyhágó tér." Open M-F 9am-noon. **Canada,** XII, Budakeszi út 32 (tel. 275 12 00). Take bus #158 to the last stop. **New Zealanders** should contact the British embassy. **U.K.,** V, Harmincad u. 6 (tel. 266 28 88), off the corner of Vörösmarty tér. M1: "Vörösmarty tér." Open M-F 9:30am-noon and 2:30-4pm. **U.S.,** V, Szabadság tér 12 (tel. 267 44 00). M2: "Kossuth Lajos;" walk down Akademia and turn left on Zoltán. Open M and W 8:30-11am, Tu, Th-F 8:30-10:30am.

Currency Exchange: The bureaus with longer hours generally have less favorable rates. **GWK Tours** (tel. 322 90 11), in the Keleti station. Good rates and convenient for rail travelers. Open daily 6am-9pm. **Magyar Külkereskedelmi Bank,** V, Váci u. 38 (tel. 269 09 22). 2 blocks north of the Metro, at the basilica's entrance. Perhaps the most comprehensive exchange place in town, with very good rates and outdoor **ATMs.** Open M-Th 8am-2pm, F 8am-1pm. **Budapest Bank,** V, Váci utca 1-3. Cash advances on credit cards, Western Union services, cash traveler's checks in US$ (3.5% commission), and possibly the best exchange rates in town. Open M-F 8:30am-5pm, Sa 9am-2pm.

American Express: V, Deák Ferenc u. 10 (tel. 235 43 30; fax 267 20 28). M1: "Vörösmarty tér," next to Hotel Kempinski. Sells traveler's checks and cashes checks in US$ for variable commission. Cash advances only in forints. Mail held free for cardholders. AmEx **ATM.** Office open June-Sept. M-F 9am-6:30pm, Sa 9am-2pm; Oct.-May M-F 9am-5:30pm, Sa 9am-1pm. **Currency exchange** open daily 9am-6:30pm.

Local Services

English Bookstore: Bestsellers KFT, V, Október 6 u. 11, near Arany János u. M: "Deák tér"or M1: "Vörösmarty tér." Open M-F 9am-6:30pm, Sa 10am-6pm.

Gay and Lesbian Organizations: Cruise Victory Co., II Váci u., 9 (tel./fax 267 38 05). Eponymous free brochure with gay listings. Open M-F 9am-5pm.

Laundromats: Irisz Szalon, V, Városház u. 3-5 (tel. 317 20 92). M3: "Ferenciek tere." Wash: 5kg 700Ft. Dry: 270Ft per 15min. Pay the cashier before you start. Open M-F 7am-7pm, Sa 7am-1pm. Many hostels let you use their machines for a fee.

Emergency and Communications

Emergencies: Ambulance, tel. 104. **Fire,** tel. 105.

Police: tel. 107. For tourist police, call 343 00 34 and ask for "K.E.O."

24-Hour Pharmacies: II, Frankel L. út 22 (tel. 212 44 06); III, Szterdrei út 2/A (tel. 388 65 28); IV, Pozsonyi u. 19 (tel. 389 40 79); VII, Rékóczi út 39 (tel. 314 36 95); At night, call the number on the door, or ring the bell to summon the manager.

GATEWAY CITIES

Medical Assistance: Falck Személyi Olvosi Szolgálat KFT, II, Kapy út 40/B (tel. 200 01 00 or 275 15 35). English spoken. Open 24hr. First aid is free for foreigners.

Post Office: *Poste Restante* Open M-F 8am-8pm, Sa 8am-2pm. at V, Városház u. 18 (tel. 318 48 11). Open 24hr. Sending mail via American Express may be better. **Postal Code:** 1052.

Telephones: V, Petőfi Sándor u. 17. English-speaking staff. Fax service. **Internet access** (500Ft per hr.). Open M-F 8am-8pm, Sa-Su 8am-2pm. Also try the post office. Many public phones use **phone cards,** available at newsstands, post offices, and Metro stations. 50-unit card 800Ft, 120-unit card 1600Ft. **Card phones** are better than coin phones for **international calls,** but both will probably cut you off. **Telephone Code:** 1.

ACCOMMODATIONS AND CAMPING

Travelers arriving in Keleti station enter a feeding frenzy of hostel solicitors. Don't be drawn in by promises of free drinks or special discounts, and keep in mind that the best options are not always represented at Keleti. The newly formed **Hungarian Youth Hostel Association** has consolidated a number of Budapest hostels and has a booth at Keleti. Make sure that the room is easily accessible by public transportation, preferably by Metro. Ask to be shown on a map where the lodging is located and see the room before you hand over any cash.

Hostels

Open year-round

Backpack Guesthouse, XI, Takács Menyhért u. 33 (tel. 209 84 06; tel./fax 385 89 46). From Keleti pu. or the city center, take bus #1, 7, or 7A (black numbers dir: Buda): "Tétényi u.," after the rail bridge. Go back under the bridge, turn left, and follow the street parallel to the train tracks for 3 blocks. Look for the most colorful house on the block. Carpeted rooms, clean bathrooms, and humor in every niche. 1100-1400Ft; doubles 1700Ft. Showers, private locker, and use of **kitchen,** TV, and VCR. **Internet access.**

Station Guest House, XIV, Mexikói út 36/B (tel. 221 88 64; email station@free-mail.c3.hu). From Keleti, take bus #7: "Hungária Körút," go under an overpass, then right on Mexikói út for 2 blocks. Close to the train station with clean rooms, eclectic decor, and a friendly Doberman. **Kitchen.** Live music W and Su nights. Dorms 1400-2000Ft. **Laundry** 300Ft per 4kg.

Yellow Submarine Youth Hostel, VI, Teréz Körút 56 (tel./fax 331 98 96). Across the street from Nyugati pu. *Gulyás* party once a week. Dorms 1600-2000Ft; nice doubles 2600Ft. 10% off with HI card. **Kitchen, laundry,** and individual lockers.

Summer Hostels

Almost all dorms of the **Technical University** (Műegyetem) become youth hostels in July and August; they are conveniently located in district XI, around Móricz Zsigmond Körtér. From M3: "Kálvin tér," ride tram #47 or 49 across the river to "M. Zsigmond."

Strawberry Youth Hostels, IX, Ráday u. 43-45 (tel. 218 47 66), and Kinizsi u. 2/6 (tel. 217 30 33). M3: Kálvin tér. Two converted university dorms within a block of one another in Pest, off Kálvin tér. Spacious rooms with refrigerators and sinks. Disco on the premises. Doubles 2600Ft; triples and quads 2300Ft per person. 10% off with HI card. **Laundry** 300Ft. Check-out 10am.

Martos, XI, Stoczek u. 5/7 (tel. 463 37 76; tel./fax 463 36 50; email reception@hotel.martos.bme.hu), near the Technical University. From Keleti pu. take red bus #7 to Moric Zsigmond Körtér and trek back 300m toward the river on Kainthy F. u. Take a left on Egri Tózset and another left onto Stoczek u. Free use of **washers** and **kitchens. Internet access** available. Singles 2000Ft; doubles 3000Ft. Comfy 6-person apartment 10,000Ft. Reception 24hr. No curfew. Check-out 9am.

Universitas, XI, Irinyi József u. 9-11 (tel. 463 38 25 or 463 38 26). 1st stop after crossing the river on tram #4 or 6. In-room fridges and communal bathrooms. Satellite TV, active nightlife in the disco and bar on weekends. Doubles 5200Ft. **Laundry** 200Ft. HI members 10% off. Fine cafeteria with 540Ft *menü.* Check-out 9am.

GATEWAY CITIES

Guest Houses

Guest houses and rooms for rent in private homes include a personal touch for about the same as an anonymous hostel bed. Proprietors carry cellular telephones so they can always be reached for reservations. In stations, bypass the pushier hostel representatives and look for the quieter ones hanging around in the background.

Caterina, V, Andrássy út 47, III. 48 (tel. 291 95 38, cellular tel. 06 20 34 63 98). M1 or tram #4 or 6:"Oktogon." A century-old building only a few min. from downtown Pest. 2 guest bathrooms. Dorms 1200Ft; doubles 4400Ft. TV in all rooms. Owners speak only some English.

Weisses Haus, III, Erdőalja u. 11 (cellular tel. 06 20 34 36 31; tel./fax 387 82 36). Bus #137 from Flórián tér: "Iskola." On a hillside in residential Óbuda. Panoramic view across the Danube. Doubles 4400Ft. Breakfast included.

"Townhouser's" International Guesthouse, XVI, Attila u. 123 (cellular tel. 06 30 44 23 31; tel./fax 405 25 96). M2: "Örs Vezér tere," then 5 stops on bus #31 to Diófa u. A quiet residential area 30min. from downtown in east Pest. Doubles 4400-5200Ft; triples 5400Ft. 3 apartments at Vaci u. 44—smack dab in the middle of the downtown area—are also available (6800-11,000Ft per night). Béla transports guests to and from the travler station.

Camping

Római Camping, III, Szentendrei út 189 (tel. 368 62 60; fax 250 04 26). M2: "Batthyány tér," then take the HÉV commuter rail: "Római fürdő," and walk 100m toward the river. Tip-top security with grocery, swimming pool, and huge park on the site. Communal showers. 1700Ft per tent, 10% off with HI card. Bungalows 1050-1600Ft per person. Open Apr. to mid-Oct.

Zugligeti "Niche" Camping, XII, Zugligeti út 101 (tel./fax 200 83 46). Take bus #158 from Moszkva tér to last stop. Closest camping to central Budapest. Beautiful camping site, partially forested. Restaurant and buffet. Communal showers. 700Ft per person; 450Ft per tent; 650Ft per car; 400Ft for electricity. English-speaking reception.

FOOD

Most restaurants in Budapest will fit your budget, though the food at family eateries may be cheaper and yummier. An average meal runs 700-900Ft, a 10% tip is usual, plus another 10% for live music. Seek out a *kifőzde* or *vendéglő* for a taste of Hungarian life. Cafeterias lurk under **Önkiszolgáló Étterem** signs (vegetarian meals 180Ft, meat meals 300-400Ft). Travelers may also rely on markets and tiny 24-hour stores labeled *Non-Stop* for staples. The king of them all is the **Central Market,** V, Kőzraktár tér u. 1 (M3: "Kálvin tér"). Two great markets can be found near central Pest. **Hold utcai piac,** V, Hold u. 13, is just off Szabadság tér (open M 6:30am-5pm, Tu-F 6:30am-6pm, Sa 6:30am-2pm). **Vámház vásárcsarnok,** IX, Vámház krt. 1/3 is at Fövám tér (open M 6am-5pm, Tu-F 6am-6pm, Sa 6am-2pm).

Gandhi, V, Vigyázó Ferenc u. 4. Take a right at the northern end of Roosevelt tér. Outstanding vegetarian restaurant. New menu every day, herb teas, organic wines, and wheat beers. Main dishes 560-780Ft. Open daily noon-10:30pm.

Korona Passage, V, Kecskeméti u. 14. M3: "Kálvin tér," in the Mercure Korona Hotel. Giant Hungarian crepes served with a large variety of toppings (350-510Ft) make filling meals in and of themselves. Open daily 10am-10pm.

Fatâl Restaurant, V, Váci u. 67. One of the most popular restaurants in Budapest. Large, hearty, and delicious Hungarian meals in pleasant, rustic surroundings. Main dishes from 900Ft. Open daily 11am-11pm.

New York Bagels (The Sequel), VI, Bajcsy-Zsilinszky út 21. M3: "Arany János u." Assorted bagels baked hourly, freshly made spreads, sandwiches, salads, and cookies. Bagel sandwich specials 300-500Ft. Open M-F 7am-10pm, Sa-Su 9am-10pm.

Cafés

These dim and smoky establishments were the haunts of Budapest's literary, intellectual, and cultural elite, echoing the café culture in Vienna and Prague. Excellent, strong coffee and ornate pastries are cheap, even in the most genteel places.

Café New York, VII, Erzsébet krt. 9-11. M2: "Blaha Lujza tér." Resplendent with velvet, gold, and marble, this is 1 of the most beautiful cafés in Budapest. Cappuccino 250Ft. Ice cream and coffee delights 400-900Ft. Open daily 9am-midnight.

Művész Kávéház, VI, Andrássy út 29, diagonally across the street from the State Opera House. M1: "Opera." Golden Age wood panelling and gilded ceilings. One of Budapest's most elegant. Cappuccino 170Ft. Open daily 9am-midnight.

Ruszwurm, I, Szentháromság u. 7, just off the square on Várhegy in the Castle District. Confecting since 1826 and strewn with period furniture. Stop by to relax after the majesty of Mátyás Cathedral down the street. You won't be hurried. Ice cream 50Ft per scoop. Cakes 80-280Ft. Open daily 10am-7pm.

Litia Literatura & Tea, I, Hess András tér 4 (tel. 175 69 87), in the Fortuna Passage. Choose from an immense selection of teas in this airy gardenhouse café in a quiet courtyard. Adjoining artsy bookstore. Coffee 80Ft. Open daily 10am-6pm.

SIGHTS

BUDA The **Castle District** rests 100m above the Duna, atop the 2km mound called **Várhegy** (Castle Hill). Find a path up the hill, or cross the **Széchenyi lánchíd** (Széchenyi Chain Bridge) from Pest and ride the *sikló* (cable car) to the top. *(Operates daily 7:30am-10pm. Closed 2nd and 4th M of each month. 250Ft.)* Built in the 13th century, the hilltop castle was leveled in sieges by Mongols then by Ottoman Turks. Christian Habsburg forces razed the rebuilt castle while ousting the Turks after a local 145-year occupation. A reconstruction was completed just in time to be destroyed by the Germans in 1945. Determined Hungarians pasted the castle together once more, only to face the new Soviet menace—bullet holes in the palace facade recall the tanks of 1956. The current **Budavári palota** (Royal Palace) houses several notable museums. During recent reconstruction, excavations revealed artifacts from the earliest castle here; they are now displayed in Wing E in the **Budapesti Történeti.** *(Budapest History Museum. Open Mar.-May 15 M and W-Su 10am-6pm; May 16-Sept. 15 daily 10am-6pm; Sept. 16-Oct. M and W-Su 10am-8pm; Nov.-Feb. M and W-Su 10am-4pm. 100Ft, students 50Ft, W free.)* Wing A contains the **Kortárs Művészeti Múzeum** (Museum of Contemporary Art) and the **Ludwig Museum,** a collection of international modern art. *(Open Tu-Su 10am-6pm. 100Ft, students 50Ft.)* Wings B-D hold the **Magyar Nemzeti Galéria** (Hungarian National Gallery), a vast horde of the best Hungarian painting and sculpture. *(Open Tu-Su 10am-6pm. All wings 150Ft, students 50Ft. W free. English tour 200Ft.)*

From the castle, stroll down Színház u. and Tárnok u. to **Szentháromság tér** (Trinity Sq.), site of the Disney-esque **Fisherman's Bastion.** This arcaded stone wall supports a squat, fairy-tale tower, but you'll have to pay for the view across the Danube *(100Ft, free on M)*. Behind the tower stands the delicate, neo-Gothic **Mátyás templom** (Matthias Church); it served as a mosque for 145 years after the Turks seized Buda. These days, high mass is celebrated Sundays at 7, 8:30, 10am, noon, and 8:30pm with orchestra and choir. On occasional summer Fridays at 8pm, **organ concerts** reverberate inside. *(Open daily 7am-7pm.)* Intricate door-knockers and balconies adorn the Castle District's other historic buildings; ramble through **Úri u.** (Gentlemen's Str.) among Baroque houses, or **Táncsics Mihály u.** in the old Jewish quarter. There's a tremendous view of Buda from the Castle District's west walls.

The **Szabadság Szobor** (Liberation Monument) crowns neighboring **Gellért-hegy,** just south of the castle. This 30m bronze woman honors Soviet soldiers who died while liberating Hungary from the Nazis. The **Citadella,** adjacent to the Liberation Monument, was built as a symbol of Habsburg power after the 1848 Revolution; climb the hill to it from Hotel Gellért (bus #27 also drives up). The hill itself is named for the 11th-century bishop sent by the Pope to help King Stephen convert the Magyars. Unconvinced Magyars hurled poor St. Gellért to his death from atop the hill.

North of the castle, the **Margit híd** spans the Danube and connects to the **Margitsziget** (Margaret Island). Off-limits to private cars, the island offers capacious thermal baths, luxurious garden pathways, and numerous shaded terraces. According to legend, the *sziget* is named after King Béla IV's daughter; he vowed to rear young Margit as a nun if the nation survived the Mongol invasion of 1241. The Mongols decimated Hungary but did not destroy it, and Margaret was confined to the island convent. Take bus #26 from "Szt. István krt." to the island.

The **Szoborpark Múzeum** (Statue Park Museum), XXII, on the corner of Balatoni út and Szabadkai út, is a collection of the statues removed from Budapest's parks and squares after the collapse of Communist rule. Take the yellow long-distance bus from Kosztelányi tér toward Érd. *(Open 10am-dusk. 100Ft, students 50Ft.)*

PEST Across the Danube lies Pest, the capital's throbbing commercial and administrative center. The old **Belváros** (Inner City), rooted in the pedestrian zone of Váci u. and Vörösmarty tér, is a tourist haven. On the riverbank, a string of modern luxury hotels leads up to the magnificent neo-Gothic **Ovszágház** (Parliament) in Kossuth tér. *(Tours available in English W-Su 10am. 750Ft, students 350Ft. Purchase tickets at gate #10 at the Parliament. Reservations recommended; call 268 49 04.)* Nearby, at Kossuth tér 12 in the former Hungarian Supreme Court, the **Néprajzi múzeum** (Museum of Ethnography) hosts an outstanding exhibit of pre-World War I Hungarian folk culture. *(Open Tu-Su Mar.-Nov. 10am-5:45pm; Dec.-Feb. 10am-4pm. 200Ft, students 100Ft. Tu free.)*

Sz. István Bazilika (St. Stephen's Basilica), two blocks north of Deák tér, is by far the city's largest church, with room for 8500 worshippers. Climb 302 spiraling steps to the Panorama tower for a 360-degree view of the city. *(Tower open Apr.-Oct. daily 10am-6:30pm. 200Ft, students 100Ft.)* St. Stephen's holy **right hand,** one of Hungary's most revered religious relics, is displayed in the **Basilica museum.** *(Basilica open M-Sa 9am-5pm, Su 1-5pm. 120Ft, students 60Ft. Museum open Apr.-Sept. M-Sa 9am-4:30pm, Su 1-4:30pm; Oct.-Mar. M-Sa 10am-4pm, Su 1-4pm.)* At the corner of Dohány u. and Wesselényi u., the **Zsinagóga** (Synagogue) is the largest active temple in Europe and the second-largest in the world. *(Open M-Sa 10am-2:30pm, Su 10am-1:30pm. 400Ft, students 200Ft.)* Next door, the **Jewish Museum** juxtaposes magnificent exhibits dating back to the Middle Ages with haunting documentation of the Holocaust. *(Open Apr.-Oct. M-F 10am-3pm, Su 10am-1pm.)*

To the east of the basilica, **Andrássy út,** Hungary's grandest boulevard, extends from the edge of Belváros in downtown Pest to **Hősök tere** (Heroes' Sq) some 2km away. The **Magyar Állami Operaház** (Hungarian State Opera House), VI, Andrássy út 22 (M1: "Opera"), is laden with sculptures and paintings in the ornate Empire style of the 1880s. If you can't actually see an opera, at least take a tour. *(Daily at 3 and 4pm. 700Ft, students 300Ft.)* The **Millenniumi emlékmű** (Millennium Monument), commemorating the nation's most prominent leaders and national heroes from 896 to 1896, dominates Hősök tere. The **Szépművészeti Múzeum** (Museum of Fine Arts) on the square maintains a splendid collection; highlights include an entire room devoted to El Greco and an exhaustive display of Renaissance works. *(Open Tu-Su 10am-6pm; Jan.-Mar. 15 until 4pm. 200Ft, students 100Ft. Tours for up to 5 people 1500Ft.)*

The ruins of the north Budapest garrison town of **Aquincum** crumble in the outer regions of the third district. To reach the area, take M2: "Batthyány tér," then the HÉV to "Aquincum;" the site is about 100m south of the HÉV stop. Here are the most impressive vestiges of the Roman occupation that spanned the first four centuries AD. The **museum** on the grounds contains a model of the ancient city, musical instruments, and other household items. *(Open Apr.-Oct. daily 10am-6pm. 300Ft, students 60Ft.)*

ENTERTAINMENT

Budapest hosts cultural events year-round. Pick up a copy of the English-language monthly *Programme in Hungary, Budapest Panorama,* or *Pestiest,* all available free at tourist offices; they contain daily listings of all concerts, operas, and theater performances in the city. The "Style" section of the weekly English-language *Budapest Sun* is another excellent source for schedules of entertainment happenings.

The **Central Theater Booking Office,** VI, Andrassy út 18 (tel. 312 00 00), next to the Opera House, and the branch at Moszkva tér 3 (tel. 212 56 78; both open M-Th 9am-6pm, F until 5pm), sell commission-free tickets to almost every performance in the city. An extravaganza at the gilded, neo-Renaissance **State Opera House,** VI, Andrássy út 22 (tel. 332 81 97; M1: Opera), costs only US$8-10; the box office (tel. 353 01 70), on the left side of the building, sells unclaimed tickets at even better prices 30 minutes before showtime (open Tu-Sa 11am-1:45pm and 2:30-7pm, Su 10am-1pm and 4-7pm). The **Philharmonic Orchestra** is also world-renowned; concerts thunder through town almost every evening September to June. The ticket office (tel. 317 62 22) is located at Vörösmarty tér 1. (Open M-F 10am-6pm, Sa-Su 10am-2pm. Tickets 1000-1500Ft; less on the day of performance.)

In late summer, the Philharmonic and Opera take sabbaticals, but summer theaters and concert halls pick up the slack. The **Margitsziget Theater,** XIII, Margitsziget (tel. 340 41 96), features opera and Hungarian-music concerts on its open-air stage. Take tram #4 or 6 to "Margitsziget." Folk-dancers stomp across the stage at the **Buda Park Theater,** XI, Kosztolányi Dezső tér (tel. 366 99 16); ticket office at Vörösmarty tér 1 (open M-F 11am-6pm; tickets 200-300Ft).

To soak away weeks of city grime, crowded trains, and yammering camera-clickers, sink into a **thermal bath,** an essential Budapest experience. The post-bath massages vary from a quick three-minute slap to a royal half-hour indulgence. Some baths are meeting spots, though not exclusively, for Budapest's gay community.

Gellért, XI, Kelenhegyi út 4-6 (tel. 466 61 66). Bus #7 or tram #47 or 49 to Hotel Gellért, at the base of Gellért-hegy. Venerable indoor thermal baths, segregated by sex, where you may soak nude if you like, plus a co-ed (and clothed) indoor pool surrounded by statues. Outside awaits a rooftop sundeck and a wave pool. Also a huge range of inexpensive *à la carte* options, from mudpacks to pedicures. Thermal bath 600Ft, with pool privileges 1200Ft. 15min. massage 550Ft. Open May-Sept. M-F 6am-6pm, Sa-Su 6am-4pm; Oct.-Apr. M-F 6am-6pm, Sa-Su 6am-2pm. Pools open daily until 7pm except weekends Oct.-Apr., when they close at 5pm.

Király, I, Fő u. 84 (tel. 202 36 88). M2: "Batthány tér." Bathe in the splendor of Turkish cupolas and domes. Thermal bath 400Ft. Massage 550Ft per 15min. Men only M, W, and F 6:30am-6pm. Women only Tu and Th 6:30am-6pm, Sa 6:30am-noon.

NIGHTLIFE

An unenforced drinking age and cheap drinks draw old and young alike to Budapest's clubs and bars. As clubs become more and more sophisticated, the cover prices are rising—a night of techno may soon cost the same as an opera ticket. To find out what's going on and when, pick up a copy of *Budapest Week* (96Ft).

Old Man's Pub, VII, Akácfa u. 13. M2: "Blaha Lujza tér." Live blues and jazz in a classy and upscale environment. Kitchen serves pizza, spaghetti, and salads. Occasional free samples of beer. Open M-Sa 3pm-dawn.

Fat Mo's Speakeasy, V, Nyári Pal u. 11. M3: "Kálvin tér." Pricey food, but hip bands and a large selection of tap beer (12 varieties, 250-540Ft for 0.5L). Su-Tu live music, Th-Sa DJ after 11:30pm. Open M-F noon-3am, Sa-Su 6pm-3am.

Piaf, VI, Nagymező u. 25. Popular after-hours place and the final destination of any decent pub crawl in Budapest. Guests are admitted after knocking on a rather inconspicuous, though large, door and meeting the approval of the person behind the peephole. Open 4pm-4am. Cover 500Ft—good for a drink.

Angel Bar, VII, Szövetség u. 33. A giant, 3-level, mostly gay disco, café and bar. Lowest floor plays loud, eardrum-shattering music; bring your earmuffs. Only Sa is exclusively gay. Back room. Cover 400Ft. Open daily 1pm-sunrise.

■ Danube Bend (Dunakanyar)

North of Budapest, the Danube sweeps south in a dramatic arc known as the Danube Bend *(Dunakanyar)* as it flows east from Vienna along the Slovak border. Within 45km of Budapest, the region offers a variety of daytrips and overnights from the capital. Ruins of first-century Roman settlements cover the countryside, and medieval palaces and fortresses overlook the river in **Esztergom.** An artist colony thrives today amid the museums and churches of **Szentendre.**

Szentendre By far the most touristy of the Danube Bend cities, Szentendre's proximity to Budapest, narrow cobblestone streets, and wealth of art galleries keep the visitors coming. On Szentendre's **Templomdomb** (Church Hill), above Fő tér, sits the 13th-century Roman Catholic **parish church.** Facing it, the **Czóbel Museum** exhibits works of Hungary's foremost Impressionist, Béla Czóbel. (Open Mar. 15-Oct. Tu-Su 10am-4pm; off-season F-Su 10am-4pm. 90Ft, students 50Ft.) To the north across Alkotmány u., the Baroque **Szerb Ortodox Templom** (Serbian Orthodox Church) displays Serbian religious art (open W-Su 10am-4pm; 60Ft). Szentendre's most impressive museum, **Kovács Margit Múzeum,** Vastagh György u. 1, exhibits brilliant ceramic sculptures and tiles by the 20th-century Hungarian artist Margit Kovács. (Open Mar. 17-Oct. Tu-Su 10am-6pm; Nov.-Mar. 14 Tu-Su 10am-4pm. 250Ft, students 150Ft.) The HÉV, train, and bus station is south of the Old Town; to get to **Fő tér,** use the underpass, and head up Kossuth u. The HÉV **commuter rail** leaves for Budapest's Batthyány tér (45min., every 20min., 190Ft). Hourly **buses** run from Budapest's Árpád bridge station to Szentendre (30min., 146Ft), many continuing on to **Visegrád** (45min. farther) and **Esztergom** (1½hr. from Szentendre). The **MAHART boat pier** is a 10-minute walk north of Fő tér (3 per day to Budapest, 520Ft; May 17-Aug. only). The helpful staff of **Tourinform,** Dumsta Jenő u. 22 (tel. (26) 31 79 65 or 31 79 66), provides brochures and 50Ft maps (open M-F 10am-5pm, Sa-Su 10am-2pm).

Esztergom If you can't find the Esztergom **cathedral,** you're either too close or in the wrong town; take a step back and look up. Hungary's largest church, consecrated in 1856, is chiefly responsible for the town's nickname "The Hungarian Rome." On a smaller scale, the red marble **Bakócz Chapel** on the south side of the cathedral is a masterwork of Renaissance Tuscan stone-carving. Climb to the 71.5m-high **cupola** for a view of Slovakia (50Ft), or descend into the solemn **crypt** to honor the remains of Hungary's archbishops. (Open daily 9am-5pm.) The **cathedral treasury** (Kincstár), on the north side of the main altar, protects Hungary's most extensive ecclesiastical collection. The jewel-studded cross labeled #78, in the case facing the entrance to the main collection, is the **Coronation Cross,** on which Hungary's rulers pledged their oaths from the 13th century until 1916. (Open daily 9am-4:30pm. 130Ft, students 65Ft.) Beside the cathedral stands the restored 12th-century **Esztergom Palace.** (Open in summer Tu-Su 9am-4:30pm; off-season Tu-Su 10am-3:30pm. 80Ft, students 20Ft, free with ISIC.) For an extra 10Ft, you can ascend to the roof to survey the kingdom. At the foot of the hill, **Keresztény Múzeum** (Christian Museum), Berenyi Zsigmond u. 2, houses an exceptional set of Renaissance religious artwork. (Open Tu-Su 10am-6pm. 100Ft, students 50Ft.)

Trains connect to Budapest (1½hr., 312Ft). Catch **buses** a few blocks south of Rákóczi tér on Simor János u. to Budapest (1½hr., 326Ft) and Szentendre (1hr., 237Ft). **MAHART boats** depart from the pier (tel. (33) 31 35 31) at the end of Gőzhajó u., on Primas Sziget island in the south, for Visegrád (1½hr., 450Ft) and Szentendre (3½hr., 915Ft) on the way to Budapest (5hr., 1270Ft). Twice a day on weekends, a **hydrofoil** leaves from the same pier and scoots directly to Budapest (1hr.) and Visegrád (40min.).

Appendix

▓ Climate

The climate in the **mountainous areas** of Austria and Switzerland (northern and western Austria and central and northeastern Switzerland) is chilly and wet throughout the year. Temperatures depend largely on altitude; as a rule, they decrease an average of 1.7°C (3°F) each additional 300m of elevation. Unless you're on a mountain, the countries don't normally get brutally cold, even in the dead of winter. Summer temperatures can reach 38°C (100°F) for brief periods, although summer evenings are usually cool. Warm sweaters are the rule September to May; add a thick coat, hat, and gloves in winter. Snow cover lasts from late December to March in the valleys, from November to May at about 1800m, and stays year-round above 2500m. Switzerland's **lake areas,** in the temperate swath of plain that extends across from Lake Constance in the northeast through Zurich and Bern down to Geneva, are very rainy all year. Summertime brings very frequent rains in both countries, making rain gear an extremely useful addition to your luggage. Switzerland's Italian-speaking canton of **Ticino** lies in a fairly low plateau and boasts a pseudo-tropical clime. The following chart gives the average high and low temperatures in degrees centigrade (Celsius) and the average yearly rainfall in centimeters during four months of the year.

| Temp.(C)/ | January | | April | | July | | October | |
Rain(cm)	Temp.	Rain	Temp.	Rain	Temp.	Rain	Temp.	Rain
Basel	4/-3	5.3	16/4	6.4	26/13	8.0	15/6	5.2
Bern	2/-4	19.0	14/4	12.0	22/13	11.0	13/5	6.0
Budapest	1/-4	3.7	17/7	4.5	28/16	5.6	16/7	5.7
Geneva	4/-2	6.3	15/5	5.1	25/15	6.4	14/7	7.2
Graz	1/-5	2.5	15/5	5.0	25/14	12.5	14/6	7.5
Innsbruck	1/-7	5.4	16/4	5.2	25/13	13.4	15/5	6.7
Linz	1/-4	3.9	12/5	4.5	24/14	8.4	14/5	5.6
Lucerne	2/-3	7.4	14/4	7.6	25/14	13.6	14/6	7.7
Lugano	6/-2	6.3	17/7	14.8	27/16	18.5	16/8	17.3
Munich	-4/2	4.8	2/11	7.1	12/22	12.7	4/12	6.0
Prague	0/-5	1.8	12/3	2.7	23/13	6.8	12/5	3.3
Salzburg	2/-5	6.5	12/3	8.5	23/13	19.5	14/4	8.0
Vienna	1/-4	3.9	15/6	4.5	25/15	8.4	14/7	5.6
Zermatt	-7/-11	20.2	-2/-6	16.6	8/3	30.2	2/-3	18.3
Zurich	2/-3	7.4	15/4	7.6	25/14	13.6	14/6	7.7

To convert from °C to °F, multiply by 1.8 and add 32. For an approximation, double the Celsius and add 25. To convert from °F to °C, subtract 32 and multiply by 0.55.

°C	-5	0	5	10	15	20	25	30	35	40
°F	23	32	41	50	59	68	77	86	95	104

▓ Holidays and Festivals

The *International Herald-Tribune* lists national holidays in each daily edition. If you plan your itinerary around these dates, you can encounter the festivals that entice you and circumvent the crowds visiting the ones that don't. This information is also valuable when determining when to arrive where—many services shut down on holidays and could leave you strapped for food and money in the event of an ill-timed arrival. Note also that in Austria, the first Saturday of every month is *Langer Samstag* (long Saturday); most stores stay open until 5pm. In small towns, stores are often closed

APPENDIX

from noon Saturday until 8am Monday—important to remember when stocking up on food for weekends. Check the individual town listings for information on the festivals below.

Date	Festival	Region
AUSTRIA		
January 6	Epiphany	National
January	Hahnenkamm World Cup Ski Races	Kitzbühel
February 1-16	Fasching (Carnival)	Regional
April 17-24	Easter Festival	Salzburg
May 1	Labor Day	National
Mid-May to Mid-June	Wiener Festwochen	Vienna
May 11	Ascension Day	National
May 22	Whit Monday	National
June 2	Corpus Christi Day	National
June 6-7	Procession of Samson	Tamsweg
End of July	Salzburg Festival	Salzburg
Late July to Mid-August	Music Festival	Bregenz
Late July to Late August	Salzburg Music Festival	Salzburg
August 1	Folklore fair	Villach
August 3-4	Fröhlichgasse	Graz
August 14	Eve of the First Feast of the Assumption	Wörther See
August 15	Feast of the Assumption	National
October 26	Flag Day	National
November 1	All Saints' Day	National
November 11	St. Martin's Day	Regional
November 29	Kathreinsonntag	Regional
December 8	Feast of the Immaculate Conception	National
SWITZERLAND		
January 6	Epiphany	National
March 1-3	Fasnacht (Carnival)	Basel
April 22-29	European Watch, Clock, and Jewelry Fair	Basel
May	International Jazz Festival	Bern
May 1	Labor Day	Regional
May 11	Ascension	National
May 22	Whit Monday	National
June	International June Festival: classical music, theater, art	Zurich
June 2	Corpus Christi	Regional
June 15-20	International 20th-century Art Festival	Basel
July 2-17	International Jazz Festival	Montreux
August 1	Swiss National Day	National
August 24-27	Folklore Festival	Fribourg

September 12-13	Knabenschiessen	Zurich
October 22-November 6	Autumn Fair	Basel
November 21	Traditional Onion Market	Bern
December 11-12	Escalade (Historic Festival)	Geneva

■ Telephone Codes

Basel	061
Bern	031
Bregenz	05574
Budapest	1
Geneva	022
Graz	0316

Interlaken	036
Innsbruck	0512
Lausanne	021
Liechtenstein	075
Linz	0732
Lucerne	041

Lugano	091
Munich	089
Prague	02
Salzburg	0662
Vienna	01
Zurich	01

Country Codes

Australia	61
Austria	43
Canada	1
Czech Republic	42

Germany	49
Hungary	36
Ireland	353
New Zealand	64

South Africa	27
Switzerland	41
U.K.	44
U.S.	1

■ Time Zones

Switzerland, Austria, Munich, Prague, and Budapest all use Central European time (abbreviated MEZ in German). Add six hours to Eastern Standard Time and one hour to Greenwich Mean Time. Subtract nine hours from Eastern Australia Time and 11 hours from New Zealand Time. Austria and Switzerland use the 24-hour clock for all official purposes: 8pm equals 20.00.

■ Measurements

The metric system is the rule in Austria and Switzerland. Conversions are provided below for our American readers. Unconventional local units for measuring wine or beer are explained in the text when necessary.

1 inch = 25 millimeter (mm)	1mm = 0.04 inch (in.)
1 foot = 0.30 meter (m)	1m = 3.33 foot (ft.)
1 yard = 0.91m	1m = 1.1 yard (yd.)
1 mile = 1.61kilometer (km)	1km = 0.62 mile (mi.)
1 ounce = 25 gram (g)	1g = 0.04 ounce (oz.)
1 pound = 0.45 kilogram (kg)	1kg = 2.22 pound (lb.)
1 quart = 0.94 liter (L)	1 liter = 1.06 quart (qt.)

Comparative Values of Measurement

1 foot	= 12 inches
1 yard	= 3 feet
1 mile	= 5280 feet
1 pound	= 16 ounces (weight)
1 cup	= 8 ounces (volume)
1 pint	= 2 cups
1 quart	= 2 pints
1 gallon	= 4 quarts

Note that gallons in the U.S. are not identical to those across the Atlantic; one U.S. gallon equals 0.83 Imperial gallons.

Electrical Current

Most European outlets are 220 volts, which will melt 110-volt North American appliances. If you absolutely cannot live without your hair-dryer or lava lamp, bring an adaptor and a converter. See **Packing,** p. 30, for more information.

■ Distance

	Vienna	Salzburg	Innsbruck	Graz	Linz
Vienna		295	481	195	181
Salzburg	295		180	264	130
Innsbruck	481	180		432	316
Graz	195	264	432		227
Linz	181	130	316	227	

	Bern	Geneva	Zurich	Lugano	Interlaken
Bern		171	125	279	57
Geneva	171		292	446	230
Zurich	125	292		221	177
Lugano	279	446	221		221
Interlaken	57	230	177	221	

■ Language

German is a difficult language for many English speakers to learn, what with three genders, four cases, and five ways of saying "the." Fortunately, most younger Austrian and Swiss urbanites speak at least a smattering of English—usually much more—thanks to the establishment of English as a requirement for high school diplomas. Outside of cities and among older residents, however, the English proficiency becomes sketchier and you may have to rely on phrasebooks or an impromptu translation by the local tourist office for help. It's somewhat rude to assume that all Austrians or Swiss are comfortable speaking English, especially in isolated Alpine villages. Try prefacing your questions with a preliminary *"Sprechen Sie Englisch?"* or *"Parlez-vous anglais?"* or *"Parla inglese?"* in the appropriate regions.

Have no fears about attempting a bit of German, French, or Italian. People will generally appreciate your effort to acknowledge their culture, and feel more inclined to help you once you've made the gesture of attempting to communicate in their language. If you're unsure in a foreign vocabulary, it's best to err on the side of formality.

For example, it never hurts to use phrases like *Herr* (Mr.) or *Frau* (Mrs.) or the French equivalents of *Monsieur* (Mr.) or *Madame* (Mrs.). *Fräulein,* on the other hand, is a loaded word and should be avoided by shakier German speakers, since it sometimes carries class connotations. When in doubt, use the formal pronoun (*Sie* in German, *vous* in French) with the plural form of the verb. People will let you know when it's time to *tutoyer* or *duzen*— to switch to more familiar language.

Pronunciation

Once you learn a few rules of **German** pronunciation, you should be able to sound out even the longest compound noun. Consonants are the same as in English, with the exception of C (pronounced K); F (pronounced V); J (pronounced Y); K (always pronounced, even before N); P (always pronounced, even before F); QU (pronounced KV); S (pronounced Z at the beginning of a word); V (pronounced F); W (pronounced V); Z (pronounced TS). The ß, or *ess-tsett,* is simply a double S. Pronounce SCH as SH. Vowels are as follows: A as in "father"; E as the A in "hay" or the indistinct vowel sound in "uh"; I as the ee in "creep"; O as in "oh"; U as in "fondue"; Y as the oo in "boot"; AU as in "sauerkraut"; EU as the oi in "boil." With EI and IE, pronounce the last letter as a long English vowel—*heisse* is HY-ssuh; *viele* is FEEL-uh.

French pronunciation is more difficult, as many of the letters in a word are silent. Do not pronounce any final consonants except L, F, or C; an E on the end of the word, however, means that you should pronounce the final consonant sound, e.g., *muet* is mew-AY but *muette* is mew-ET. This rule also applies to plural nouns—don't pronounce the final S. J is like the S in "pleasure." R is rolled—listen to Swiss people around you and have fun trying to imitate. C sounds like a K before A, O, and U; like an S before E and I. A ç always sounds like an S. Vowels are short and precise: A as the O in "mom"; E as in "help" (é becomes the a in "hay"); I as the ee in "creep"; O as in "oh." UI sounds like the word "whee." U is a short, clipped oo sound; hold your lips as if you were about to say "ooh," but say ee instead. OU is a straight OO sound. With very few exceptions, all syllables receive equal emphasis in French.

■ Phrasebook

No.	German	French	No.	German	French
		NUMBERS			
0	null	zéro	17	siebzehn	dix-sept
1	eins	un	18	achtzehn	dix-huit
2	zwei or zwoh	deux	19	neunzehn	dix-neuf
3	drei	trois	20	zwanzig	vingt
4	vier	quatre	21	einund-zwanzig	vingt et un
5	fünf	cinq	30	dreißig	trente
6	sechs	six	40	vierzig	quarante
7	sieben	sept	50	fünfzig	cinquante
8	acht	huit	60	sechzig	soixante
9	neun	neuf	70	siebzig	soixante-dix
10	zehn	dix	80	achtzig	quatre-vingt
11	elf	onze	90	neunzig	quatre-vingt-dix
12	zwölf	douze	100	(ein)hundert	cent
13	dreizehn	treize	101	hunderteins	cent-et-un

14	vierzehn	quatorze	200	zweihundert	deux-cent
15	fünfzehn	quinze	1000	(ein)tausend	mille
16	sechzehn	seize	2000	zweitausend	deux-mille

English	German	Pronunc.	French	Pronunc.
		PHRASES		
Hello	Hallo!	hah-LOH	Bonjour!	boh-zhoor
Thank you	danke	DAHN-kuh	merci	MEHRR-see
please	bitte	BIT-tuh	s'il vous plaît	see voo PLAY?
I want	Ich will	ikhh vill	je veux	zhuh vuh
I need	Ich brauche	ikhh BROW-kuh	j'ai besoin de	zhay buh-ZWAE de
Why?	Warum?	vah-ROOM?	Pourquoi?	poor-KWAH?
Good morning	Guten Morgen	goo-ten MOR-gen	Bon matin	bohn mah-TAH
Goodbye	Auf Widersehen/ Tchuß	owf VEE-der-zay-n	Au revoir	oh reh-VWAR
I would like	Ich möchte	ikhh MUHKHH-tuh	je voudrais	zhuh voo-DRAY
How much does it cost?	Wieviel kostet es?	VEE-feel kos-tet es?	Combien ça coûte?	cohm-bee-eng sah koot?
Do you speak English?	Sprechen Sie Englisch?	SHPREKHH-en zee ehn-GLEESH	Parlez-vous ang-lais?	PARR-lay voo ahn-GLAY
Excuse me	Entschuldigung	ehnt-SHOOL-dee-gung	Pardon	parrr-don
Sorry	Es tut mir leid	es toot meer LIDE	Je suis désolé	zhuh swee deh-soh-LAY
Where is...	Wo ist...	voe ISST?	Où est...	oooh ay...
When is...	Wann ist...	vann isst?	Quand est...	kahnt ay...
Check, please.	Zahlen, bitte	TSAH-len BIT-tuh	L'addition, s'il vous plaît	lah-di-seeONG, see voo play
friend	Freund	froynd	ami	ah-MEE
Go away/leave me alone	Lasse mich in Ruhe.	lass mikhh in ROO-uh.	Laissez-moi tran-quille.	lay-say mwah trang-KEEL
I don't under-stand	Ich verstehe nicht.	ikhh fair-STAY-uh neekhht	Je ne comprends pas	zhuh neh kom-prang PAH
Please speak slowly	Bitte Sprechen Sie langsam.	BIT-tuh SHPREKHH-en zee LAHNG-sam	Parlez lentement, s'il vous plaît.	parr-LAY lahn-teh-MAH, see voo PLAY
Could you please write it down?	Schreiben Sie es bitte auf?	SHRIY-ben zee ess BIT-tuh owf?	Ecrivez-le, s'il vous plaît?	AY-kree-vay luh, see voo PLAY
good	gut	goot	bon	bohhhn
because	weil	vile	parce que	PARR-suh keh
a strike	ein Streik	ayn STRIKE	le grève	leh grehf
Could you help me?	Können Sie mir bitte helfen?	Keuh-nen zee meer BIT-tuh HELL-fen?	Pourriez-vous m'aider?	Poo-rree-ay voo may-DAY?
Go away, cretin!	Geh weg, Kretin!	gay veg, KRAY-teen	Va t'en, cretin!	vah TAEHN, crray-TEHN
May I buy you a drink?	Darf ich Sie einen Trink kaufen?	darrf ikhh zee ayn-en TRREENK kow-fen?	Est-ce que je peux vous offrir un bois-son?	ess kuh zhuh peh vooz off-REER ung bwah-SOHN?
I love you, I swear.	Ich liebe dich, ich schwöre es.	ikhh LEE-buh dikhh, ikhh, SHVUH-ruh ess.	Je t'aime, je te le jure.	zhuh TEM, zhuh teh leh ZHOOR.

| I'm drunk. | Ich bin besoffen. | ikhh been buh-SOFF-fen | Je suis saoul. | zhuh swee SAH-OOL |
| Certainly! | Natürlich! | nah-TOOR-likhh | Bien sûr! | BEE-ehn SOOR |

TIME

At what time	Um wieviel Uhr…?	oom VEE-feel oohr…?	A quelle heure…?	ah kell err…?
What time is it?	Wie spät ist es?	vee SPAYT ist ess?	Quelle heure est-il?	kell er ay-teel?
What's the date?	Der wievielte ist heute?	dayr vee-FEEL-tuh ist hoy-tuh?	Quelle est la date?	kell ay lah daht?
June 1st	ersten Juni	AYR-sten YOO-nee	le premier juin	luh preh-MEE-AY zhoo-weh
quarter past seven	viertel acht	FEER-tell ackt	sept heures et quart	set err ay kar
half past seven	halb acht	halp ackt	sept heures et demi	set err ay deh-mee
quarter to eight	viertel vor acht	dry-FEER-tell ahkt	huit heures moins le quart	weet err mwaeh luh kar
morning	Morgen	MOR-ghen	matin	ma-TEH
noon	Mittag	MIT-ahk	midi	mee-dee
afternoon	Nachmittag	NACK-mit-ahk	après-midi	ah-PRAY-mee-dee
evening	Abend	AH-bent	le soir	luh swahr
night	Nacht	nahkt	la nuit	lah nwee
midnight	Mitternacht	MIT-er-nahkt	minuit	min-WEE
day	Tag	tahk	jour	zhoor
week	Woche	VOH-kuh	semaine	suh-MEN
month	Monat	MON-aht	mois	mwah
year	Jahr	yahr	an	ahn
now	jetzt	yetst	maintenant	mehnt-noh
yesterday	gestern	GUEST-urn	hier	ee-ayr
today	heute	HOY-tuh	aujourd'hui	oh-zhord-WEE
tomorrow	morgen	MOR-gen	demain	duh-meh

DIRECTIONS

direction	die Richtung	dee RIK-toong	la direction	lah dee-rek-see-yon
left	links	linx	à gauche	ah gohsh
right	rechts	rekts	à droite	ah dwaht
straight ahead	geradeaus	ger-AHD-uh-ows	tout droit	too dwaht
here	hier	eer	ici	ee-see
there	da	dah	là-bas	lah-bah
far	fern	fayrn	loin	loo-wahn
near	nah	nah	près	pray

HEALTH

hospital	das Krankenhaus	das KRANK-en-hows	l'hôpital	loh-pee-TAHL
pharmacy	die Apotheke	dee a-POH-ta-kuh	la pharmacie	lah farm-ah-SEE
sick	krank	krahnk	malade	mah-LAHD
tampon	Tampon	tampon	tampon	tah-pohh
doctor	der Arzt	dayr artst	le médecin	luh mayd-SEH
police	die Polizei	dee poh-lee-TSY	la police	lah POH-lees
Help!	Hilfe!	HILL-fuh!	Au secours!	oh suh-KOOR!
Caution!	Achtung!/Vorsicht!	ack-TOONG!/for-SICKT!	Avertissement!	ah-VAYR-tees-moh!

Danger!	Gefahr!	geh-FAHR!	Danger!	dahn-ZHAY!
Fire!	Feuer!	FOY-ehr!	Feu!	Fuh!
Stop!	Halt!	Halt!	Arrêt!	ah-RAY!
Ouch!	Autsch!	OWCH!	Aïe!	AH-EE!
consulate	das Konsulat	das KON-soo-laht	le consulat	luh coh-soo-lah
English (language)	Englisch	AYN-glish	Anglais	an-GLAY
German (language)	Deutsch	doytsh	Allemand	ah-luh-moh
French (language)	Französisch	frahn-TSER-zish	Français	frahn-SAY
How are you?	Wie geht's?	vee GAYTS?	Comment allez-vous?	kohm-mahn tah-lay voo?
Fine, thanks.	Ganz gut, danke.	gahnts GOOT, dahn-kuh	Bien, merci.	byehn, mer-SEE
Yes	Ja	ya	Oui	wee
No	Nein	nine	Non	noh
Sir	Herr	hayr	Monsieur	mi-syer
Madam	Frau	frow	Madame	muh-dahm
I don't speak...	Ich spreche kein...	ick shprek-uh kine	Je ne parle pas...	zhu ne parl pah
How do you say...in...	Wie sagt man...auf...?	vee zakt mahn...owf...?	Comment dit-on ...en...?	koh-MOHN deet ohn...ehn...?
What did you say?	Wie, bitte?	vee, BIT-uh?	Qu'avez-vous dit?	KAH-vay voo dee?
Non-smoking	Nichtraucher	nikt-RAU-ker	Non-fumeur	noh-foom-ER
Smoking	Raucher	RAU-ker	Fumeur	foom-ER

RESERVATIONS

Phone greeting	Servus!	sayr-VOOS!	Allo	ah-loh
Do you speak English?	Sprechen Sie Englisch?	SHPRECK-en zee AYN-glish?	Parlez-vous anglais?	PAR-lay-voo ahn-GLAY?
Do you have a room (single, double) free...	Haben Sie ein Zimmer (Einzelzimmer, Doppelzimmer) frei...	HAH-ben zee iyn TSIM-er (IYN-tsel-tsim-er, DOP-el-tsim-er) fry...	Avez-vous une chambre (simple, pour deux) libre?	AH-vay-voo oon shahm-bruh (sehm-pluh, poor doo) lee-bruh?
for tonight?	für heute abend?	fer HOY-tuh AH-bent?	pour ce soir?	poor suh swahr?
for tomorrow?	für morgen?	fer MORG-en?	pour demain?	poor duh-MEH?
for a day/for two days?	für einen Tag/ zwei Tage?	fer IYN-en tak/tsvy TAK-uh?	pour un jour? pour deux jours?	poor uh zhoor? poor doo zhoor?
from the fourth of July...	vom vierten Juli...	fum FEER-ten YU-lee...	de la quatrième juillet...	duh lah kat-ree-em zhwee-ay...
until the sixth of July?	bis zum sechsten Juli?	bis tsoom SEK-sten YU-lee?	à la sixième juillet?	ah la see-zee-em zhwee-ay?
with bathroom/ shower?	mit W.C./Dusche?	mit vay-tsay/ DOO-shuh?	avec toilettes/ une douche?	ah-VEK TWAH-let/ oon doosh?
with breakfast?	mit Frühstuck?	mit FROO-shtook?	avec le petit déjeuner?	ah-VEK luh puh-TEE day-zhoon-AY?
How much does it cost?	Wieviel kostet es?	VEE-feel KOST-et es?	Combien?	kohm-bwehn?
What's your name?	Wie heißen Sie?	vee HIGH-sehn zee?	Comment appellez-vous?	kohm-mehn tah-play voo?
My name is...	Ich heiße...	ikh HY-suh	Je m'appelle	zhuh mah-PEL

I'm coming immediately.	Ich komme gleich.	ikh KOM-uh glyk	Je viens tout de suite.	zhuh vee-YEN toot sweet
I'm coming at eight in the morning/ evening.	Ich komme um acht Uhr am Morgen/Abend.	ick KOM-uh oom akt oor am MORG-en/AH-bent	Je viens à huit heures du matin/ du soir.	zhuh vee-YEN ah wheet err doo mah-TEHN/ doo swahr
No, we're booked/full.	Nein, es ist alles besetzt/voll.	nyn, es ist ALL-us be-SETZT/fol	Non, c'est complet.	noh, say COHM-play
We don't take reservations by phone.	Wir machen keine Vorbestellungen/ Reservierungen am Telephon.	veer MAK-en KYN-uh for-BEST-el-oong-en/ ray-sayr-FEER-oong-en am TAY-lay-fone	Nous ne pouvons pas reserver une chambre au téléphone.	noo ne poo-voh pah ray-sayr-vay oon shahm-bruh oh tay-lay-fohn
You have to arrive before two o'clock.	Sie müssen vor zwei Uhr ankommen.	zee MOOS-en for tsvy oor an-kom-en	Vous devez arriver avant que deux heures.	voo duh-VAY AH-reev-ay ah-VAHN kuh duhz err

ACCOMMODATIONS

toilet	die Toilette/ das WC	twah-LET-uh/ vay-tsay	les toilettes	twah-let
shower	die Dusche	DOOSH-uh	une douche	doosh
key	der Schlüssel	SHLOOS-uhl	une clé	klay
house	das Haus	hows	une maison	may-zon
youth hostel	Jugendherberge	YOONG-ent-hayr-bayr-guh	Auberge de jeunesse	oh-bayrzh duh zhoon-ess
campground	der Campingplatz	comp-eeng-PLATZ	un terrain de camping	tayr-ehduh cahmp-eenk
guest-house	die Pension	PEHN-zee-ohn	une maison d'hôtes	may-zon doht
hotel	das Hotel	HO-tel	un hôtel	oh-tel
inn	das Gästehaus	gehs-teh-hows	une auberge	oh-bayrzh
private apartment	das Privatzimmer	PREE-vaht-tsim-er	appartement privé	ah-pahr-tuh-mohn pree-VAY
bed	das Bett	bet	un lit	lee
single	das Einzelzimmer	IYN-tsel-tsim-er	une chambre pour une personne	shahm-bruh poor oon payr-sun
double	das Doppelzimmer	DOP-el-tsim-er	une chambre pour deux personnes	shahm-bruh poor doo payr-sun

TRAVEL

travel ticket	die Fahrkarte	dee FAHR-kar-tuh	un billet	uh bee-yay
reservation	die Reservierung	dee RAY-sayr-VEER-oong	une réservation	oon ray-sayr-vah-see-yon
one-way	einfache Fahrt	IYN-fak-uh fahrt	billet simple	bee-yay sehm-pluh
round-trip	Hin- und Rück-fahrt	hin-oont-ROOK-fahrt	aller-retour	al-lay-ruh-toor
arrival	die Ankunft	dee AHNK-unft	l'arrivée	lah-ree-VAY
departure	die Abfahrt	dee AHB-fahrt	le départ	luh DAY-pahr
schedule	der Fahrplan	dayr FAHR-plahn	les horaires	layz or-are
baggage	das Gepäck	dahs guh-PEK	les bagages	lay bah-gazh
airplane	das Flugzeug	dahs FLOOK-zoyk	un avion	uhn ah-vyon
airport	der Flughafen	dayr FLOOK-hah-fen	un aéroport	uhn air-o-por
customs	der Zoll	dayr tsol	la douane	lah doo-wahn
train	der Zug	dayr tsuk	le train	luh treh

train station	der Bahnhof	dayr BAHN-hof	la gare	lah gahr
main train station	der Hauptbahnhof	dayr HOWPT-bahn-hof	la gare centrale	lah gahr sahn-tral
(train) track	das Gleis	dahs glys	les rails	lay rehl
train platform	der Bahnsteig	dayr BAHN-styk	le quai	luh kay
express train	der Eilzug	dayr IYL-tsuk	un train exprès/direct	uh trehn ex-pray/deer-ekt
railway	die Bahn	dee bahn	le chemin de fer	luh shuh-meh duh fuh
subway	die U-Bahn	dee OO-bahn	le métro	luh may-troh
subway stop	die Haltestelle	dee hahl-tuh-shtel-uh	un arrêt de métro	uhn ah-RAY duh may-troh
tram, trolley	die Straßenbahn	dee SHTRAHS-en-bahn	le tramway	luh trahm-vay
urban railway	die S-Bahn	dee ESS-bahn		
ferry	die Fähre	dee FEH-ruh	le passage	luh pahs-ahj
bus	der Bus	dayr boos	l'autobus	loh-toh-boos
bus station	der Busbahnhof	dayr BOOS-bahn-hof	la gare routière	lah gahr roo-tee-yare
bus stop	die Bushaltestelle	dee BOOS-halt-uh-shtel-uh	l'arrêt d'autobus	lah-RAY doh-toh-boos
car	das Auto	dahs OW-toh	la voiture	lah vwah-tyoor
no stopping	Halten verboten	hahl-ten fer-BOHT-en	interdit d'arrêter	ehn-tayr-dee dah-ret-ay
parking	parken	PARK-en	parking	pahr-KEENG
no parking	parken verboten	PARK-en fer-BOHT-en	interdit de stationner	ehn-tayr-dee duh stah-shun-ay
parking spot	Parkplatz	PARK-plahtz	place de stationnement	plahs duh stah-shun-uh-moh
short-term parking	Kurzfristzone	kurz-FRIST-tsohn	une stalle	oon stahl
speed limit	Geschwindigkeitsbegrenzung	guh-SHVIND-ik-kyts-bug-RAYN-tsoonk	limite de vitesse	lee-MEET duh vee-tess
do not enter	Eintritt verbotten	IYN-trit fer-BOHT-en	passage interdit	pah-sahj ehn-tayr-dee
expressway/highway	die Autobahn	dee OW-toh-bahn	l'autoroute	loh-toh-root
federal highway	die Bundesstraße	dee BOON-duhs-stras-uh	l'autoroute	loh-toh-root
one-way street	die Einbahnstraße	dee IYN-bahn-strahs-uh	rue à sens unique	roo ah sahn zoon-eek
dead-end street	die Sackgasse	dee ZAHK-gahs-uh	une impasse/cul de sac	oon ehm-pahs/cool duh sahk
old part of town	die Altstadt	dee AHLT-shtaht	la vieille ville	lah vee-ay vill
bicycle	das Fahrrad	dahs FAR-ahd	la bicyclette	lah bee-see-klet
moped	das Moped	dahs MOH-ped	la mobylette	lah moh-bee-let
motorcycle	das Motorrad	dahs MOH-toh-rahd	la moto	lah moh-toh

FOOD AND DRINK

meat	der Fleisch	flysh	la viande	vee-ahnd
bacon	der Speck	shpeck	le bacon/le lard	bay-koh/lahr
beans	die Bohnen	BOHN-en	les haricots	ahr-ee-koh
beer	das Bier	BEE-ehrr	la bière	bee-ayr
beer hall	die Bierstube	BEE-ehr-shtoob-uh		

bread	das Brot	broht	le pain	peh
cheese	der Käse/ Käsekrainer	KEZ-uh/ KEZ-uh-krayn-er	le fromage	froh-mazh
chicken	das Huhn/Hendl	hoon/hen-duhl	le poulet	pool-ay
chocolate	die Schokolade	shock-oh-LAH-deh	le chocolat	shoh-kuh-lah
coffee	der Kaffee	KAH-fay	le café	kah-fay
coffee and cream	Kaffee mit Sahne	KAH-fay mit SAH-nuh	le café au lait/ café crème	kah-fay oh lay/ kah-fay krem
duck	die Ente	EN-tuh	le canard	kuh-nahr
egg	das Ei	IY	un oeuf	uhf
french fries	die pommes frites	pum freet	les pommes frites	pum freet
fruit juice	der Fruchtsaft	FROOKT-zahft	le jus de fruit	zhoo duh fwee
fruits	das Obst	ohbst	les fruits	fwee
ham	der Schinken	SHINK-en	le jambon	zhahm-boh
hors-d'oeuvres	gemischte Vorspeise	guh-MISH-tuh FOR-spy-zuh	les hors-d'oeuvres	ohr doov-ruh
milk	die Milch	meelk	le lait	lay
mushrooms	die Champignons	shahm-pin-yon	les champignons	shahm-peen-yoh
onions	die Zwiebeln	TSVEE-beln	les oignons	oh-nyoh
pasta	die Teigwaren	TYK-var-en	les pâtes	paht
pepper	der Paprika	PAH-preek-a	le poivre	pwah-vruh
potato	die Kartoffeln/ Erdäpfel	kar-TOF-eln/ ary-DEP-fel	les pommes de terre	pum duh tayr
roll	das Brötchen/ die Semmel	BROHT-shen/ SEM-el	un petit pain	puh-tee peh
sausage	die Wurst	vurst	le saucisse	soh-sees
tea	der Tee	tay	le thé	tay
tomatoes	die Tomaten	toh-MAH-ten	les tomates	toh-maht
vegetables	das Gemüse	guh-mew-zuh	les légumes	lay-goom
water	das Wasser	VASS-er	l'eau	(l)oh
wine	der Wein	viyn	le vin	veh
wine hall	die Weinstube	VIYN-stoob-uh	la cave	kahv

DINING

diabetic	der Diabetiker	DEE-ah-BET-ik-er	un(e) diabétique	dee-ah-bayt-eek
vegetarian	der Vegetarier	vayj-ay-tah-reer	un(e) végétarien(ne)	vay-zhay-tah-ree-yeh/yen
I'm hungry.	Ich habe Hunger.	ick HAH-buh HOONG-er	J'ai faim.	zhay feh
I'm thirsty.	Ich habe Durst.	ick HAH-buh DOO-uhst	J'ai soif.	zhay swahf
meal	das Essen	ESS-en	le repas	ruh-pah
dessert	der Nachtisch	NAHK-tish	le dessert	deh-sayr
lounge, café	die Kneipe	Kuh-NY-puh	le café	ca-fay
pastry shop	die Konditorei	kon-di-TOHR-eye	la pâtisserie	pah-tees-ayr-ee
restaurant	die Gaststätte	GAHST-stet-uh	un restaurant	ray-stayr-ahn
Waiter!	Kellner! (Herr Ober!)	KELL-ner (herr OH-ber)	Monsieur!	miss-yer
Waitress!	Kellnerin!	KELL-ner-in	Madame!	muh-dahm
bill, check	die Rechnung	REK-noong	l'addition	(l)ah-dees-yoh
Check, please	Zahlen, bitte	TSAH-len BIT-uh	L'addition, s'il vous plaît	lah-dees-yoh sih voo play

breakfast	das Frühstück	froo-shtewk	le petit déjeuner	puh-tee day-zhoon-ay
lunch	das Mittagessen	MIT-ak-ess-en	le déjeuner	day-zhoon-ay
dinner	das Mittagessen	MIT-ak-ess-en	le dîner	dee-nay
supper	das Abendessen	AH-bent-ess-en	le souper	soop-ay

THE POST OFFICE

post office	die Post	pohst	la poste/ le bureau de poste	pohst/byoor-oh duh pohst
main post office	der Haupt- postamt	HOWPT- pohst-ahmt	le bureau de poste principal	byoor-oh duh pohst preen-see- pahl
address	die Adresse	ah-DRES-uh	l'adresse	(l)uh-dres
express	der Eilbote	IYL-boht-uh	exprès	ex-press
air mail	die Luftpost	LOOFT-pohst	par avion	pahr ah-vyon
letter	der Brief	breef	la lettre	let-truh
parcel	das Paket	PAH-ket	le paquet	pah-kay
postcard	die Postkarte	POHST-kar-tuh	la carte postale	kart poh-stahl
Poste Restante	Postlagernde Briefe	POHST-lah- gayrn-duh BREEF-uh	Poste Restante	pohst ruh-stahnt
stamp	die Briefmarke	BREEF-mark-uh	le timbre	tehn-bruh
telegram	das Telegramm	tay-lay-GRAHM	le télégramme	tay-lay-grahm
telephone	das Telefon	tay-lay-FOHN	le téléphone	tay-lay-fohn
telephone number	die Telefon- nummer	tay-lay-fohn- NOOM-er	le numero de téléphone	nu-mayr-oh duh tay-lay-foh
to exchange	wechseln	VEK-sayln	échanger de l'argent	ay-shahn-zhay duh lahr-zhahn
money	das Geld	gelt	l'argent	(l)ahr-zhahn

Index

Researcher-Writers

Judith Batalion   *Vienna, Lower Austria, Carinthia*
Stylish researcher Judy "Roo-shooter" Batalion romped through eastern Austria, collecting copious details on every art museum and falafel joint in sight. We were wowed when she interviewed feminist activists and prominent politicians; we were awed when she mailed home installment after installment of her *Bathroom Guide to the World*, Chapter One: Austria (*Jugendstil* commodes? Biedermeier porcelain? Royal thrones?). She is a blue-blood sleuth of new towns, new restaurants, and new ways of saying "yummy." She always saved us the best news clippings. Don't let the bed bugs bite!

Daniel Engber   *Salzburg, Tyrol, and Western Austria*
Star researcher Dan "The Hand" Engber is perhaps the keenest intellect of our time. He pored over ferry schedules, analysed skiing logistics, and drew copious illustrations of the Growth of a Beer Belly. With one hand he warded off crazy tourists and the crazy tourist industry of Salzburg; with the other he found the best *Knödeln* and penned excellent, witty copy. He kept us in stitches. We were grateful for his uncanny ability to find the right word, his unerring judgment, and his happy sense of taste. Thanks for the trip, Dan. All that was missing was the moustache. Memphis Blues: Ready for Test Flight!

Charles Savage   *Geneva, Neuchâtel, and Italian Switzerland*
Charlie "Charlie" Savage did not grow a moustache. Ever in the grip of existential crisis (and we know it's only because he was moustacheless), he sought something in the rugged mountains we can only begin to name with the word "himself." We loved the clarity, style, and rigor of his copy (not to mention the ibex pictures, sonnets, and Swiss chocolate he sent home). He tamed craggy Switzerland with his pen. A stealthy adventurer, he frequently found himself staring down sunrise full to the gills with wine, listening to stories told by old Swiss men. The old Swiss men had moustaches.

Sharmila Surianarain   *Zurich, Bern, and Liechtenstein*
Sharmila "Lucky Sharms" Surianarain moved with grace and ease through the beautiful Alps. Her eye pressed to the ground, she found and reported every wondrous detail. Sharmi got the fully autographed story of Ludmila the cow from a Liechtensteinian baron, admired the bear pits in Bern, and dished us the dirt on every youth hostel and tourist facility in northern Switzerland. Perhaps the bravest member of the team, she is renowned for her paragliding skill. Takin' the world by storm!

Andras Forgacs   *Budapest*
Melissa Gibson   *Prague, Bratislava*
Winnie Li   *Bodensee*
Dáša Pejchar   *Munich*

Acknowledgments

Thanks to Nic Rapold, Andrew Nieland, Tom Moore, Alex Leichtman, Allison Arwady, and Karen Paik for lending a helping hand in times of need. Alex Speier's sharp eye caught all our italicized periods and helped keep us sane and the book on track even in times of crisis. Dan Visel and his productionists fixed everything, a lot, and then some. Doug Muller and Erica Silverstein, es war ein tolles Teutonisches Roo. Many thanks and mad props to Derek McKee and his fellow cartographers, who tweaked and re-fonted our maps late into the night. Thanks go out also to our trusty intern, David Washburn, the letter ß, and to the many typists and proofers who made this book possible. **A&S**

First of all thanks to Justin for late nights, loud music, and a creative editorial eye. The *New York Times* was never half so fun. Thanks many times over to Alex for being such a sweet, sweet ME, especially when the unexpected imploded. Nic, thanks for furry teacups and all those extra hands. Dan, thanks for fixing the layout of my wack book and ocean-swimming. Derek and Matt, thanks for all the cable cars. Doug, thanks for all the peanuts. Karen, thanks for late nights, early mornings, and all the crazy stuff that happened in between. Thanks to everyone in Zwirnhaus for shelter, food, and the Guinness. Finally, thanks to me mum and dad, as always. **CS**

Thanks to the office kids who sat through longs nights of aching eyes and fingers. Thanks to Christina for patience and smarts and kicking the knowledge; to Alex for being Alex and dang if he don't have a lot of energy. Thanks to them pesky Germans who put up with the smell; thanks to the third floor coffee and midnight snacks, which really means thanks to the people who put it all together and kept things running. Thanks for fonts and working computers production people; thanks for giving them up with wit and funny jokes. Books are harder than they'll lead you to believe, but worth the effort and full of smiles. Finally, thanks to Dr. Pepper for being such a fine beverage. **JR**

Editor	Christina Svendsen
Associate Editor	Justin Rice
Managing Editor	Alexander Z. Speier
Publishing Director	Caroline R. Sherman
Publishing Director	Anna C. Portnoy
Production Manager	Dan Visel
Associate Production Manager	Maryanthe Malliaris
Cartography Manager	Derek McKee
Design Manager	Bentsion Harder
Editorial Manager	M. Allison Arwady
Editorial Manager	Lisa M. Nosal
Financial Manager	Monica Eileen Eav
Personnel Manager	Nicolas R. Rapold
Publicity Manager	Alexander Z. Speier
New Media Manager	Måns O. Larsson
Map Editors	Matthew R. Daniels, Dan Luskin
Production Associate	Heath Ritchie
Office Coordinators	Jodie Kirschner, Eliza Harrington, Tom Moore
Director of Advertising Sales	Gene Plotkin
Associate Sales Executives	Colleen Gaard, Mateo Jaramillo, Alexandra Price
President	Catherine J. Turco
General Manager	Richard Olken
Assistant General Manager	Anne E. Chisholm

Thanks to Our Readers...

Mano Aaron, CA; Jean-Marc Abela, CAN; George Adams, NH; Bob & Susan Adams, GA; Deborah Adeyanju, NY; Rita Alexander, MI; Shani Amory-Claxton, NY; Kate Anderson, AUS; Lindsey Anderson, ENG; Viki Anderson, NY; Ray Andrews, JPN; Robin J. Andrus, NJ; L. Asurmendi, CA; Anthony Atkinson, ENG; Deborah Bacek, GA; Jeffrey Bagdade, MI; Mark Baker, UK; Mary Baker, TN; Jeff Barkoff, PA; Regina Barsanti, NY; Ethan Beeler, MA; Damao Bell, CA; Rya Ben-Shir, IL; Susan Bennerstrom, WA; Marla Benton, CAN; Matthew Berenson, OR; Walter Bergstrom, OR; Caryl Bird, ENG; Charlotte Blanc, NY; Jeremy Boley, EL SAL; Oliver Bradley, GER; A.Braurstein, CO; Philip R. Brazil, WA; Henrik Brockdorff, DMK; Tony Bronco, NJ; Eileen Brouillard, SC; Mary Brown, ENG; Tom Brown, CA; Elizabeth Buckius, CO; Sue Buckley, UK; Christine Burer, SWITZ; Norman Butler, MO; Brett Carroll, WA; Susan Caswell, ISR; Carlos Cersosimo, ITA; Barbara Crary Chase, WA; Stella Cherry Carbost, SCOT; Oi Ling Cheung, HK; Simon Chinn, ENG; Charles Cho, AUS; Carolyn R. Christie, AUS; Emma Church, ENG; Kelley Coblentz, IN; Cathy Cohan, PA; Phyllis Cole, TX; Karina Collins, SWITZ; Michael Cox, CA; Mike Craig, MD; Rene Crusto, LA; Claudine D'Anjou, CAN; Lizz Daniels, CAN; Simon Davies, SCOT; Samantha Davis, AUS; Leah Davis, TX; Stephanie Dickman, MN; Philipp Dittrich,GER; Tim Donovan, NH; Reed Drew, OR; Wendy Duncan, SCOT; Melissa Dunlap, VA; P.A. Emery, UK; GCL Emery, SAF; Louise Evans, AUS; Christine Farr, AUS; David Fattel, NJ; Vivian Feen, MD; David Ferraro, SPN; Sue Ferrick, CO; Philip Fielden, UK; Nancy Fintel, FL; Jody Finver, FL; D. Ross Fisher, CAN; Abigail Flack, IL; Elizabeth Foster, NY; Bonnie Fritz, CAN; J. Fuson, OR; Michael K. Gasuad, NV; Raad German, TX; Mark Gilbert, NY; Betsy Gilliland, CA; Ana Goshko, NY; Patrick Goyenneche, CAN; David Greene, NY; Jennifer Griffin, ENG; Janet & Jeremy Griffith, ENG; Nanci Guartofierro, NY; Denise Guillemette, MA; Ilona Haayer, HON; Joseph Habboushe, PA; John Haddon, CA; Ladislav Hanka, MI; Michael Hanke, CA; Avital Harari, TX; Channing Hardy, KY; Patrick Harris, CA; Denise Hasher, PA; Jackie Hattori, UK; Guthrie Hebenstreit, ROM; Therase Hill, AUS; Denise Hines, NJ; Cheryl Horne, ENG; Julie Howell, IL; Naomi Hsu, NJ; Mark Hudgkinson, ENG; Brenda Humphrey, NC; Kelly Hunt, NY; Daman Irby, AUT; Bill Irwin, NY; Andrea B. Jackson, NY; John Jacobsen, FL; Pat Johanson, MD; Russell Jones, FL; J. Jones, AUS; Sharon Jones, MI; Craig Jones, CA; Wayne Jones, ENG; Jamie Kagan, NY; Mirko Kaiser, GER; Scott Kauffman, NY; John Keanie, NIRE; Barbara Keary, FL; Jamie Kehoe, AUS; Alistair Kernick, SAF; Daihi Kielle, SWITZ; John Knutsen, CA; Rebecca Koepke, NY; Jeannine Kolb, ME; Elze Kollen, NETH; Lorne Korman, SWITZ; Robin Kortright, CAN; Isel Krinsky, CAN; George Landers, ENG; Jodie Lanthois, AUS; Roger Latzgo, PA; A. Lavery, AZ; Joan Lea, ENG; Lorraine Lee, NY; Phoebe Leed, MA; Tammy Leeper, CA; Paul Lejeune, ENG; Yee-Leng Leong, CA; Sam Levene, CAN; Robin Levin, PA; Christianna Lewis, PA; Ernesto Licata, ITA; Wolfgang Lischtansky, AUT; Michelle Little, CAN; Dee Littrell, CA; Maria Lobosco, UK; Netii Ross, ITA; Didier Look, CAN; Alice Lorenzotti, MA; David Love, PA; Briege Mac Donagh, IRE; Brooke Madigan, NY; Helen Maltby, FL; Shyama Marchesi, ITA; Domenico Maria, ITA; Natasha Markovic, AUS; Edward Marshall, ECU; Rachel Marshall, TX; Kate Maynard, UK; Agnes McCann, IRE; Susan McGowan, NY; Brandi McGunigal, CAN; Neville McLean, NZ; Marty McLendon, MS; Matthew Melko, OH; Barry Mendelson, CA; Eric Middendorf, OH; Nancy Mike, AZ; Coren Milbury, NH; Margaret Mill, NY; David H. Miller, TX; Ralph Miller, NV; Susan Miller, CO; Larry Moeller, MI; Richard Moore, ENG; Anne & Andrea Mosher, MA; J. L. Mourne, TX; Athanassios Moustakas, GER; Laurel Naversen, ENG; Suzanne Neil, IA; Deborah Nickles, PA; Pieter & Agnes Noels, BEL; Werner Norr, GER; Ruth J. Nye, ENG; Heidi O'Brien, WA; Sherry O'Cain, SC; Aibhan O'Connor, IRE; Kevin O'Connor, CA; Margaret O'Rielly, IRE; Daniel O'Rourke, CA; Krissy Oechslin, OH; Johan Oelofse, SAF; Quinn Okamoto, CA; Juan Ramon Olaizola, SPN; Laura Onorato, NM; Bill Orkin, IL; K. Owusu-Agyenang, UK; Anne Paananen, SWD; Jenine Padget, AUS; Frank Pado, TX; G. Pajkich, Washington, DC; J. Parker, CA; Marian Parnat, AUS; Sandra Swift Parrino, NY; Iris Patten, NY; M. Pavini, CT; David Pawielski, MN; Jenny Pawson, ENG; Colin Peak, AUS; Marius Penderis, ENG; Jo-an Peters, AZ; Barbara Phillips, NY; Romain Picard, Washington, DC; Pati Pike, ENG; Mark Pollock, SWITZ; Minnie Adele Potter, FL; Martin Potter, ENG; Claudia Praetel, ENG; Bill Press, Washington, DC; David Prince, NC; Andrea Pronko, OH; C. Robert Pryor, OH; Phu Quy, VTNM; Adrian Rainbow, ENG; John Raven, AUS; Lynn Reddringer, VA; John Rennie, NZ; Ruth B.Robinson, FL; John & Adelaida Romagnoli, CA; Eva Romano, FRA; Mark A. Roscoe, NETH; Yolanda & Jason Ross, CAN; Sharee Rowe, ENG; W. Suzanne Rowell, NY; Vic Roych, AZ; John Russell, ENG; Jennifer Ruth, OK; William Sabino, NJ; Hideki Saito, JPN; Frank Schaer, HUN; Jeff Schultz, WI; Floretta Seeland-Connally, IL; Colette Shoulders, FRA; Shireen Sills, ITA; Virginia Simon, AUS; Beth Simon, NY; Gary Simpson, AUS; Barbara & Allen Sisarsky, GA; Alon Siton, ISR; Kathy Skeie, CA; Robyn Skillecorn, AUS; Erik & Kathy Skon, MN; Stine Skorpen, NOR; Philip Smart, CAN; Colin Smit, ENG; Kenneth Smith, DE; Caleb Smith, CA; Geoffrey Smith, TX; John Snyder, NC; Kathrin Speidel, GER; Lani Steele, PHIL; Julie Stelbracht, TN; Margaret Stires, TN; Donald Stumpf, NY; Samuel Suffern, TN; Michael Swerdlow, ENG; Brian Talley, TX; Serene-Marie Terrell, NY; B. Larry Thilson, CAN; J. Pelham Thomas, NC; Wright Thompson, ITA; Christine Timm, NY; Melinda Tong, HK; M. Tritica, AUS; Melanie Tritz, CAN; Mark Trop, FL; Chris Troxel, AZ; Rozana Tsiknaki, GRC; Lois Turner, NZ; Nicole Virgil, IL; Blondie Vucich, CO; Wendy Wan, SAF; Carrie & Simon Wedgwood, ENG; Frederick Weibgen, NJ; Richard Weil, MN; Alan Weissberg, OH; Ryan Wells, OH; Jill Wester, GER; Clinton White, AL; Gael White, CAN; Melanie Whitfield, SCOT; Bryn Williams, CAN; Amanda Williams, CAN; Wendy Willis, CAN; Sasha Wilson, NY; Kendra Wilson, CA; Olivia Wiseman, ENG; Gerry Wood, CAN; Kelly Wooten, ENG; Robert Worsley, ENG; C.A.Wright, ENG; Caroline Wright, ENG; Mary H. Yuhasz, CO; Margaret Zimmerman, WA.

★Let's Go 1999 Reader Questionnaire★

Please fill this out and return it to **Let's Go, St. Martin's Press,** 175 Fifth Ave., New York, NY 10010-7848. All respondents will receive a free subscription to *The Yellowjacket*, the Let's Go Newsletter. You can find a more extensive version of this survey on the web at http://www.letsgo.com.

Name: _____

Address: _____

City: _____ **State:** _____ **Zip/Postal Code:** _____

Email: _____ **Which book(s) did you use?** _____

How old are you? under 19   19-24   25-34   35-44   45-54   55 or over

Are you (circle one)   in high school   in college   in graduate school   employed   retired   between jobs

Have you used Let's Go before? yes no **Would you use it again?** yes no

How did you first hear about Let's Go? friend   store clerk   television   bookstore display   advertisement/promotion   review   other

Why did you choose Let's Go (circle up to two)? reputation budget focus   price   writing style   annual updating   other: _____

Which other guides have you used, if any? Fodor's   Footprint Handbooks   Frommer's $-a-day   Lonely Planet   Moon Guides   Rick Steve's   Rough Guides   UpClose   other: _____

Which guide do you prefer? _____

Please rank each of the following parts of Let's Go 1 to 5 (1=needs improvement, 5=perfect). packaging/cover   practical information   accommodations   food   cultural introduction   sights   practical introduction ("Essentials")   directions   entertainment   gay/lesbian information   maps   other: _____

How would you like to see the books improved? (continue on separate page, if necessary) _____
_____

How long was your trip?   one week   two weeks   three weeks   one month   two months or more

Which countries did you visit? _____

What was your average daily budget, not including flights? _____

Have you traveled extensively before? yes no

Do you buy a separate map when you visit a foreign city? yes no

Have you used a Let's Go Map Guide? yes no

If you have, would you recommend them to others? yes no

Have you visited Let's Go's website? yes no

What would you like to see included on Let's Go's website? _____
_____

What percentage of your trip planning did you do on the Web? _____

Would you use a Let's Go: recreational (e.g. skiing) guide gay/lesbian guide   adventure/trekking guide   phrasebook   general travel information guide

Which of the following destinations do you hope to visit in the next three to five years (circle one)? Canada Argentina Perú Kenya Middle East   Caribbean   Scandinavia   other: _____

Where did you buy your guidebook?   Internet   independent bookstore   chain bookstore   college bookstore   travel store   other: _____